ASANTE IN THE NINETEENTH CENTURY

AFRICAN STUDIES SERIES

The African Studies Series is a collection of monographs and general studies which reflect the interdisciplinary interests of the African Studies Centre at Cambridge. Volumes to date have combined historical, anthropological, economic, political and other perspectives. Each contribution has assumed that such broad approaches can contribute much to our understanding of Africa, and that this may in turn be of advantage to specific disciplines.

BOOKS IN THIS SERIES

ASANTE IN
THE NINETEENTH CENTURY

The structure and evolution of a political order

IVOR WILKS
Professor of History, Northwestern University

CAMBRIDGE UNIVERSITY PRESS

Published by the Syndics of the Cambridge University Press
Bentley House, 200 Euston Road, London NW1 2DB
American Branch: 32 East 57th Street, New York, N.Y. 10022
© Cambridge University Press 1975

Library of Congress Catalogue Card Number: 74-77834

ISBN: 0 521 20463 1

First published 1975

Printed in the United States of America by Vail-Ballou Press Inc., Binghamton, N.Y.

To my father, G. W. Wilks (1900–56),
who taught me a love of history
and initiated me
into its ways and byways

Contents

Tables, Figures and Maps

TABLES

viii

FIGURES

MAPS

Plates

The plates appear between pages 206 and 207.

Plates

Preface

This book has grown out of a series of lectures first delivered for the Department of History in the University of Ghana in 1962–3. Over the eleven years which have since passed, I have been fortunate in having the support of a number of institutions of learning each of which enabled me, whatever my other responsibilities, to devote a considerable part of my time and energies to the expansion of those lectures into the present work: the University of Ghana until 1966, the University of Manchester from 1966 to 1967, Northwestern University from 1967 to 1968, the University of Cambridge and Churchill College from 1968 to 1970, and Northwestern University again from 1971. It will be readily apparent to the reader, however, that this book is still not intended as a comprehensive history of the Asante nation in the nineteenth century. Indeed, in view of the quite extraordinary range and complexity of the source materials available to the student of the Asante past, it may well be many years before any definitive account of the period can – or should – be attempted. This work is offered, none the less, in the belief that there is a time when the historian must be prepared to risk being wrong in the effort to develop a synthesis of the materials in terms of which new issues may be posed – though not necessarily resolved even to the satisfaction of the author himself. Despite the many attempts I have made to clarify the matter of the evolution of the two principal Asante councils, for example, I remain convinced that the account offered here is still inadequate. Similarly, I realize that further analysis of the organization of the Asante *nkwankwaa* – the so-called 'youngmen' – is essential to the better understanding of the turbulent late nineteenth century period. I can only express the hope that, whatever the virtues and defects of this book, it will help stimulate the further research which is so necessary if the nature of the highly complex society which was (and is) Asante is to be the more fully understood.

This study falls into four distinct but closely related parts. Chapters

1–3 synthesize the extant evidence on the spatial structure and demography of nineteenth century Asante, relating such factors as communications and relative population size to government. Chapters 4–8 offer an account of the central government's conduct of provincial and foreign affairs, and present the contrast between Asante's role as a coastal power on the one hand and as a savannah power on the other. In Chapters 9–11 a description is given of the structure of the ruling dynasty, of the two legislative councils, and of the major executive agencies. Finally, in Chapters 12–15 an analysis of the main thrusts of Asante policy is attempted, with reference to the conflict in the first three quarters of the century between the imperial ('war') and mercantile ('peace') interests, and to the challenge offered to the preeminence of the mercantilists after 1874 by a rising middle class actuated by a belief in *laissez-faire* principles.

Three consequences of the approach essayed here may be commented upon briefly, that the reader may be forewarned (and the author forearmed). First, it will be found that the materials are not arranged chronologically, and many of the chapters range over the whole of the nineteenth century. While I do not feel that this feature stands in need of justification, I do offer an apology for a certain amount of repetition which thereby became unavoidable. Secondly, throughout this study I have been concerned less with those aspects of Asante society which are unique to it, and more with those aspects which it has in common with other complex societies whether on the African continent or elsewhere. Accordingly, I have felt no hesitation in applying such terms as 'bureaucratization', 'mercantilism', 'modernization' and the like to those aspects of the Asante experience which invite comparison with similarly identified phenomena in other societies. To critics on this score I reiterate my belief that only thus can the Asante past be viewed within the wider perspectives of human endeavour and its place within comparative history ultimately be assured. The alternative, always to stress the unique and unrelated and to reject the use of concepts developed in geographically and temporally different contexts, can lead the scholar towards the morasses of a nationalistic or 'tribal' mystique and an underlying historical solipsism. And thirdly, throughout this book I have consistently viewed Asante history from the centre: from the perspectives of those in the capital involved in the business of central government. It should not be inferred that I am insensitive to the urgent need for local studies in Asante, but only that I assign a certain logical priority to the investigation of national institutions over regional and district ones. Greater Asante comprised many different societies – ethnically, culturally and linguistically distinct, and economically disparate – and each deserves attention in its own right. But all were part of the one political order, and it is that order which is the central concern of this study. It will follow that although the majority of Asante lived and worked in a village environment, rural history is not among the themes pursued here. I wish to register my view, however, that it is among the most important of the topics awaiting investigation. The exploitation of the resources of the Asante forests by hunters, snail-collectors, and kola and later rubber traders, and the slow but steady encroachment of the farmers upon the forests – clearing and cultivating new land and establishing new villages protected by their shrines from the malevolent spirits of the adjacent untamed lands: these are part of a saga which regrettably remains as yet unchronicled.

In a work tending to be overburdened with references to sources not readily available to the reader, I have attempted to observe certain rules. Thus citations have been given to the more accessible British Parliamentary Papers, rather than to the Original Correspondence or Confidential Print in the Public Record Office, whenever material in the two latter series is also available in the former. For the same reason references have been made to the second and revised edition of Reindorf's *History of the Gold Coast and Asante* rather than to the very rare first edition of 1895. Again, I have usually refrained from citing oral interviews whenever the information does no more than support extant documentary sources. I would not wish this procedure, however, to obscure the extent of my debt over the years to the many Asantes who have patiently initiated me into the intricacies of their society and its past. Without their co-operation, the understanding and interpretation of the documents would often have been impossible. I have been particularly grateful to the late Asantehene, Nana Sir Osei Agyeman Prempeh II, and to the present Asantehene, Nana Opoku Ware II, for the support they have given to my enquiries, and I owe a major debt to Joseph Agyeman-Duah who has frequently worked with me since 1958. Without his tutorship, and the generosity with which he has given of both his time and knowledge, this book could not have been written.

I owe very special thanks to my close associate Phyllis Ferguson. Without her intellectual stimulation, and encouragement during a number of crises of confidence, this book would never have been completed. Without the care and attention with which she read and criticized each chapter, this book would have been fraught with many undetected errors of fact and faults of logic. In the earlier stages of my work I enjoyed the close collaboration of Edmund Collins, and in the later stages that of Thomas McCaskie. Both generously shared with me both their ideas and materials, and I am much indebted to them.

Preface

Among those whose assistance was invaluable in overcoming the many practical obstacles to the completion of this work, I must express my thanks to Eva Thorpe and Michael Culhane for their patience in typing, and to Donna Weaver and Eva Thorpe for undertaking the preparation of the extensive working index without which the writer (long before the reader) would have been helplessly stranded in a confusion of fact. My mother, Lilian Wilks, and Susan Fyvel McCaskie, assisted greatly in bringing much raw data under control; and to Polly Hill I am grateful not only for her encouragement – as a seasoned author – but also for generously making available her charming house in Cambridge within which the writing of this book reached a point of no return. The preparation of the final index presented problems of daunting complexity. My colleagues Charles ('Places') Berberich and Robert ('People') Hamilton selflessly sacrificed a glorious summer upon that altar and my gratitude to them is profound. Phyllis Ferguson gave essential additional support at a stage when the end, seemingly near, proved yet so far. Donna Weaver and Thomas Lewin first tested the index, and thereby enabled at least some of its problems to be anticipated. Thomas Lewin, with assistance of Phyllis Lewin, also generously assumed the burden of reading the page proofs.

My gratitude also goes to those many scholars who have so willingly and readily allowed me access to, and have discussed with me, their materials: not only again to Phyllis Ferguson, Edmund Collins and Thomas McCaskie, but also to René Baesjou, Robert Hamilton, Paul Jenkins, Raymond Kea, Norman Klein, Marion Johnson and Thomas Lewin. I have also benefited greatly from access to the translations of sources made by Graham Irwin, Paul Jenkins, Marie van Landewijk, Nehemia Levtzion, and the late J. T. Furley (whose papers are deposited in the Balme Library at the University of Ghana). Of the many librarians and archivists upon whose assistance I have depended, it will perhaps not be invidious on my part if I acknowledge my special thanks to Hans Panofsky and Daniel Britz of the Africana Library at Northwestern University. While it would also be impossible to name the many other colleagues and friends who have read and commented upon parts of this work, or from whom I have benefited in conversation or in other ways, I would like to express my particular gratitude to al-Ḥājj 'Uthmān b. Ishaq Boyo, Francis Agbodeka, Agnes Aidoo, Kwame Arhin, Ronald Atkinson, Charles Berberich, Adu Boahen, William Boatin, Kwame Daaku, Albert van Dantzig, John Fynn, Peter Gibbons, Bruce Haight, Richard Horowitz, Alex Kyerematen, William Longwell, Paul Ozanne, Isaac Tufuoh, and finally, but only so because he has a very special place in this list, Thomas Hodgkin. The length of even so incomplete a roll-call testifies to the extent to which I have been dependent upon that community of scholars concerned with Asante and Ghana studies – though I must, as a matter of etiquette, hasten to absolve them from any responsibility for my errors and shortcomings. And finally, I must express my gratitude to the editors of the Cambridge University Press who have proved so patient and helpful in coping with my many derelictions of duty as an author.

Although the research upon which this book was based was not financed by any one major grant, I am grateful to the Institute of African Studies in the University of Ghana, to the Program of African Studies at Northwestern University, and to the American Philosophical Society, for awards which enabled me to undertake specific enquiries in Asante. I wish also to thank the Managers of the Smuts Memorial Fund of the University of Cambridge, and the Department of History of Northwestern University, for grants towards the preparation of the typescript and plates, and to the Northwestern University Program of African Studies again for the provision of numerous support facilities.

Evanston   IVOR WILKS
September 1974

CHAPTER 1

Spatial aspects of government: the network of communications

The great-roads of Asante

In the early nineteenth century the Asante capital of Kumase had, so the British Consul Dupuis observed, 'free and unobstructed communication with all the leading provinces, by roads or paths, which by way of distinction are collectively called great roads'.[1] These were, in the Twi language of the Asante, the *akwan-tempɔn*, from *ɛkwan-pɔn*, 'great-road', and *ten*, 'straight'.[2] The southern roads linked the capital with the series of coastal ports between the Volta and Komoé Rivers, and so with the maritime highways to Europe and the Americas. The northern roads led to such towns as Bonduku, Daboya and Yendi on the frontiers of Greater Asante, where they articulated with major trans-continental caravan trails leading to the Mediterranean shores via the great entrepôts of the Western and Central Sudan: Timbuktu and Jenne, Kano and Katsina. But, as Huydecoper remarked, 'no Asante is familiar with these places because the King's highways do not run there'.[3] The system of great-roads was maintained by the central government, and was to be distinguished from the many smaller and localized networks of roads the responsibility for which rested with the district authorities.

Each of the great-roads bore a name, for example, that of a ruler in whose reign it had been constructed, or of a province to which it led.[4] That to the northeast, to Salaga, was known as Maniampon-tempɔn, 'Maniampon's great-road', after the early Mamponhene of that name.[5] In 1817 Bowdich listed 'nine great paths leading from Coomassie': the Dwaben, the Akyem or Accra, the Assin, the Wassa or

1 Dupuis, 1824, p. xxvii.
2 They appear also to have been referred to as *akwan-tɛmpɔn*, see for example, Christaller, 1881, p. 48, probably from *ntɛm-pɔn*, 'great speed'.
3 General State Archives, The Hague, KvG 349: W. Huydecoper, Journal of a Visit to Kumase, entry for 18 August 1816.
4 Dupuis, 1824, p. xxvii.
5 Arhin, 1970a, p. 1. For Maniampon, see Agyeman-Duah, 1960, p. 22, and Wilks, 1960, pp. 26–7. The major road to Anomabo and Cape Coast, however, could be referred to simply as *Tempɔn Kwan*, with the sense of '*The* Great-road'.

Elmina, the Sehwi, the Gyaman or Bonduku, the Nsoko or Banda, the Gbuipe or Daboya, and the Salaga or Yendi.[6] Three years later Dupuis was led to believe that there were, strictly, only eight great-roads, namely, 'four great maritime causeways' through Aowin, Wassa, Assin and Akyem, and 'four inland roads', the Bonduku, Banda, Gbuipe and Salaga.[7] It will be seen below that the two authorities are in fact in close agreement, Dupuis choosing, however, not to include among the great-roads that to Dwaben.

In this study, for purposes of identification eight great-roads will be numbered consecutively and clockwise, with the north-western way to Bonduku as Route I. Fortunately it is possible to follow in detail the courses of most of the great-roads from the succession of 'appointed halting-places' [8] which lay along them, many of which survive as present-day villages and towns. The establishment of such halting-places was considered an essential aspect of road building: as a minute by Asantehene Kwaku Dua I dated 1837 shows, they were important not only for the accommodation and provisioning of travellers, but also as centres of local authority to which reference could be made when cases of banditry were reported on the roads.[9] As such, they might enjoy special protection in time of war.[10] The recognized halting-places were, in principle, equidistant the one from the other, and were separated by a conventional measure of one journey: in Twi, *kwansin*, literally 'part of the road'.[11] Each journey or *kwansin* was further divided into 'watches' or 'hours': in Twi, *kwansimma*, 'the little *kwansin*'. A *kwansin* apparently consisted of seven *nkwansimma;* that is, a journey comprised seven travelling 'hours'.[12] In practice, however, the halting-places were not equally spaced along the roads, since their precise location was determined by such factors as the adequacy of water supplies, or the nature of the local terrain. It follows then that the *kwansin* cannot be expressed as a standard distance in miles.

Many halting-places developed into sizeable towns, where large parties of travellers could obtain overnight lodgings and adequate

6 Bowdich, 1819, pp. 162; 482–3.
7 Dupuis, 1824, pp. xxvii–xxviii.
8 Christaller, 1881, p. 273.
9 General State Archives, The Hague, KvG 772: letter from Huydecoper dd. Kumase, 13 September 1837.
10 See, for example, Huydecoper's Journal, entry for 28 April 1816: 'the Asante made a point of not burning it [Afontu, near Elmina] because they make use of it as a resting place'.
11 Christaller, 1881, p. 273: *ɛkwansin*, 'the extent, length or distance of a way or road, from one appointed halting-place to another'.
12 See, e.g. General State Archives, The Hague, KvG 384: Daendels to Director General of Trade and Colonies, Report IV dd. 6 December 1816. In modern Twi *kwansin* is used to mean 'mile'. It was seemingly the traditional 'little *kwansin*' which approximated to that distance.

supplies of foodstuffs from the local retail market. Other places, in contrast, might consist of only a few sheds, with diminutive plantations unable to supply the requirements of more than a few visitors. At Dunkwa on Route VI, for example, the Asante commander of an Anglo-Asante party proceeding northwards to Kumase in 1820 found it necessary to issue instructions that sufficient provisions should be obtained for the next four days' journeys through the eastern edges of the Konkom Forest; and in fact virtually no food was found at the three successive halting-places of Manso, Abandu and Akomfode, each of which consisted of only a few bamboo-framed sheds for the most part already occupied. It should be added, however, that the party was over four hundred strong, while the whole area of the Konkom Forest had been devastated in the campaigns of the previous two decades.[13] By the mid-nineteenth century references occur to slaves who accompanied large parties of Asante travellers, and who belonged 'to the commissariat department, and carry provisions for two or three days'.[14]

Data on the great-roads system of Asante, including the more important branch roads, are compiled below on the basis of the available nineteenth century sources. Approximate distances are computed from the 1:250,000 sheets of the Ghana Ordnance Survey maps, and no allowances are made for the winding of the roads. It was Bowdich's view that on journeys in general, $33\frac{1}{3}\%$ of the distance covered was accounted for by the sinuous character of the roads; and Dupuis estimated the figure at 25% in forest country, 20% in savannah.[15] All distances given, therefore, should probably be increased by between one-fifth and one-third in order to obtain the actual mileages covered by travellers. Unless there is evidence to the contrary, the assumption is made that halting-places retain their nineteenth century locations.

The four northern great-roads

Route I linked Kumase with the important Dyula trading town of Bonduku in the north-western province of Gyaman. Bowdich placed Bonduku eleven journeys distant from the capital, and listed the ten intermediate halting-places: Bare (mile 14) or Pasoro (mile 12); Biemso (mile 22); Nsuta (mile 38); Duayaw Nkwanta (mile 52); Odumase (mile 74); Nsuatre (mile 86); Berekum (mile 96); Nyame (mile 114);

---

[13] Dupuis, 1824, pp. 22, 29. Hutton, 1821, pp. 166–7; 170. Of Manso, Hutton observed that it was then 'merely a resting-place for the Ashantee traders and other travellers'. Of Foso, an alternative halting-place in the forest, Bowdich, 1819, pp. 21–2, commented that 'it presented but a few sheds, in one of which we observed the Ashantee traders to deposit yams and plantains to subsist them on their return'.

[14] Trotter and Allen, 1848, II, 183.

[15] Bowdich, 1819, pp. 162; 200. Dupuis, 1824, pp. xix, xx.

'Kirribeeo' (unidentified); Kyekyewere (unidentified); and Bonduku (mile 144).[16] This road was followed by Abū Bakr al-Ṣiddīq of Tim-buktu, and his captors, in the first decade of the century; unfortunately only three of the halting-places are named in his autobiography – Kyekyewere, Nyame, and possibly Nsuatre ('Ansiri').[17] Dupuis gave no detailed itinerary of the route, but several of the halting-places are marked on his map: Bare ('Boary'), Nsuta, Berekum ('Brequoma'), Nyame ('Yammy'), and 'Ketaby'.[18] Beyond Bonduku the great-road continued northwestwards through Nassian to the Asante frontier on the Komoé River: a further seven journeys. There it linked with the road to the Watara capital of Kong, five journeys beyond.[19] Another road, *Route I(a)*, passed from Bonduku northwards to Buna, and there joined others that converged on that town from the north.[20]

An important branch of Route I, *Route I(b)*, led to the province of Sehwi ('Shouy', 'Sauee'), eight journeys from Kumase, and to that of Bonzina ('Boinzan', 'Moinsan'), a further seven journeys. Neither Bowdich nor Dupuis listed the halting-places, but it appears to have branched off Route I at Nsuta (mile 38) and to have passed through 'Wom', that is, Kukuom (mile 80) and 'Sannasee' (unidentified) to Bonzina (mile 120).[21] A different path which led from Kumase to the more southerly districts of Sehwi was not regarded as a great-road.[22]

Route II linked Kumase with Banda, capital of the northerly province of the same name. The road passed through Nsoko, which Bowdich located at eleven journeys from the capital: Tafo (mile 3); Offinso (mile 15); Abofo (mile 32); Nkenkaso (mile 48); Akumadan (mile 56); Tanoso (mile 61); Kuntunso (mile 67); Takyiman (mile 71); Wankyi (mile 90); Ewisa (mile 95); and Nsoko (mile 110). Bowdich maintained that it was a further four journeys to Banda, but inspec-tion of the itinerary shows that he had inserted in error two halting-places which were on different roads: Bima (mile 121) was in fact the only stage between Nsoko and Banda (mile 145).[23] In an obscure passage Dupuis appears to indicate that the great-road continued northwards from Banda to the Black Volta ('River Aswada', i.e.,

16 Bowdich, 1819, pp. 169, 482.
17 Renouard, 1836, p. 111.
18 Dupuis, 1824, p. xxviii, and map facing p. 265. On p. lvii Dupuis refers to the 'Ketaby' of his map, the 'Kirribeeo' of Bowdich, as 'the large Moslem town Kherabi'. Enquiries in the locality failed to reveal the identity of this town, unless by metathesis the reference is to the village of Kabri.
19 Bowdich, 1819, pp. 169, 181–2. Dupuis, 1824, p. xxviii.
20 Renouard, 1836, p. 111. See also Dupuis, 1824, p. xxviii, whose 'Enkasy' probably refers to the Kulango state of Buna since the 'Enkasy' capital, 'Soke Aila', is presumably Sukalia, one of the principal wards of Buna town.
21 Bowdich, 1819, p. 169. Dupuis, 1824, p. xxviii.
22 Dupuis, 1824, p. xxix.
23 Bowdich, 1819, pp. 170, 483.

4

Arabic *aswad*, 'black'), and thence to the 'mountains of Sarga': presumably the Sala-Konkori hills in west-central Gonja.[24] It is also apparent from Bowdich's itinerary that a branch road, *Route II(a)*, ran westwards from Nsoko (mile 110) through Namasa (mile 117) and presumably joined Route I at Bonduku.

Route III linked Kumase with the central Gonja provinces of Gbuipe and Daboya. A full itinerary is given in an Arabic route-book compiled by Imām Muḥammad al-Ghamba' ('the Gambaga') in 1820.[25] It corresponds closely with routes given by Bowdich from Kumase to Sekyedumase and from Nkoransa to Daboya.[26] Gbuipe was accounted sixteen journeys from the capital: Adwumakase Kese (mile 8); Boaman (mile 17); Tetrem (mile 24); Kyekycwere (mile 32); Anyinasu (mile 41); Sekyedumase (mile 46); Donkoro Nkwanta (mile 57); Nkoransa (mile 68); Boaben (mile 78); Kyirehi (mile 92); Kintampo (mile 104); Kaka (mile 116); Dawadawa (mile 130); and two non-appointed stops in what was described as the 'desert' (*saḥra*) of Gbuipe before reaching Gbuipe town (mile 164). From Gbuipe it would seem that two roads ran to Daboya (mile 222), the one in three journeys through 'Minsiru' and 'Moronko' near the White Volta (both unidentified), and the other – perhaps the wet season way – in four journeys through 'the town of the king's son' (unidentified); Lakantere (mile 196); and Chutadi (mile 206).[27] Dupuis commented that Routes III and IV were 'sometimes called the old roads, from their antiquity and pre-eminence'.[28] Certainly part of the importance of Route III was that it was continuous with a road leading to Jenne, the great trading centre near the Niger, and thence to Timbuktu and beyond. Imām Muḥammad detailed the course of the route northwards from Daboya through Yagaba on the Kulpawn River; Kanjarga; Boromo; Safane; and Nouna to Jenne. Between Daboya and Jenne, a horizontal distance of some 420 miles, he listed thirty-eight halting-places.

Route IV linked Kumase with Salaga, in the eastern Gonja province of Kpembe, and with the Dagomba capital of Yendi. There was some difference of opinion about the number of journeys separating Salaga from Kumase: the Tatar traveller Wargee stated fourteen, Dupuis and Huydecoper fifteen, and Bowdich sixteen or seventeen.[29] In fact,

24 Dupuis, 1824, pp. xxviii and liii. Dupuis' map, facing p. 265, showed a route through 'Binkab', 'Garabo', and 'Chounie' to 'Ain al Esha' in the hills. None of the places has been identified.
25 Arabic texts printed in Dupuis, 1824, pp. cxxxi–cxxxii, and see p. cxxix, note, for authorship. See also Dupuis, p. xxxvi and map facing p. 265.
26 Bowdich, 1819, pp. 171, 483 (paths 9 and 11).
27 *Ibid.* p. 171. Dupuis, 1824, p. cxxxi.
28 Dupuis, 1824, p. xxviii.
29 For Wargee, see Wilks, 1967b, p. 189. Dupuis, 1824, pp. cxxvii, cxxx. Huydecoper's Journal, entry for 15 July 1816. Bowdich, 1819, pp. 172, 483.

as Bowdich observed, there were a number of alternative paths that might be taken: [30] all converged near Mampon (mile 34), but the traveller might choose between faster, or slower but less arduous, ways through the rugged hill country south of that town. Bowdich gave two versions of the route, the one derived from an Arabic source.[31] Dupuis reproduced the Arabic texts of route-books in possession of Muḥammad Kamaghatay of Kumase, and of a Katsina visitor there.[32] On the sixteen journeys' route, the halting-places were Antoa (mile 8) or Asokore Mampon (mile 5); Domakwai (mile 16) or Effiduase (mile 17); Mampon Akurofonso (mile 22); Nsuta (mile 30); Mampon (mile 34); Dinkyin (mile 42); Adidwan (mile 49); Adwira (mile 59); Amantin (mile 75); Akukua (mile 81) or Patura (mile 91); Atebubu (mile 99); Nyomoase (mile 111); Pran (mile 119); 'Sakinim' (unidentified, but in the marshes of the 'Buru', i.e., the Pru River); Yeji (mile 143); and Salaga (mile 167). It was possible to shorten the travel time by two journeys by proceeding from Kumase to Adwumakase Wadie (mile 10); Gyamase (mile 22); and Mampon on the third day (mile 30 by this road).[33] Half a century later the same route was still in use, though travel time had been reduced to twelve days. Sa'īd Koko, a Salaga trader,[34] detailed the stages as:

Kumase to Tikrom	8 hours	(8 miles)
Tikrom to Effiduase	8 hours	(9 miles)
Effiduase to Nsuta	6 hours	(13 miles)
Nsuta to Dinkyin	8 hours	(12 miles)
Dinkyin to Adidwan	8 hours	(7 miles)
Adidwan to Adwira	8 hours	(10 miles)
Adwira to Amantin	9 hours	(16 miles)
Amantin to Patura	8 hours	(16 miles)
Patura to Atebubu	2 hours	(8 miles)
Atebubu to Pran	10 hours	(20 miles)
Pran to Yeji	12 hours	(24 miles)
Yeji to Salaga	14 hours	(24 miles)

Beyond Salaga the great-road continued to Yendi, according to most sources in a further seven journeys,[35] or in twenty-two days from Kumase according to Dupuis' informant.[36] The halting-places are listed in an Arabic route-book as 'Bokoki' (unidentified); Gyafo (mile 189); Deroa (Bentripe, mile 203); Nienseli (mile 213); Kpabia (mile

30 Bowdich, 1819, p. 485.
31 *Ibid.* pp. 483, 486.
32 Dupuis, 1824, pp. cxxvii–cxxix; cxxxiv.
33 This shorter way was used, for example, by R. La T. Lonsdale in 1881, see *Further Correspondence regarding Affairs of the Gold Coast*, C. 3386, 1882, p. 67.
34 *Ibid.* p. 16: notes taken by Kirby at Accra, dd. 14 October 1881.
35 Bowdich, 1819, p. 177. Barth, 1859, III, 645. Wargee gave the lower figure of five days, see Wilks, 1967b, p. 189.
36 Dupuis, 1824, p. xc.

227); 'Laja' (unidentified); [37] and Yendi (mile 250).[38] From both Salaga
and Yendi roads ran to Zabzugu, where they combined to form a major
caravan route to the Central Sudan: that passing Bafilo, Zugu and
Nikki to Birnin Yauri and the greater markets of Hausaland.[39] Another important road ran northwards from Yendi through Sakpiegu
to Sansanne Mango, whence one branch passed through Kupela,
Mane, and Hombori to Timbuktu,[40] and another through Manduri
and Birnin Kebbi into north-western Hausaland.[41]

An important branch of Route IV, *Route IV(a)*, led to the 'ferry at
Odanty', that is, to Kete Krakye. According to Bowdich, the road ran
from Atebubu (mile 99) through Kokofu (mile 108); 'Guia' (unidentified); Wiase (mile 120); Basa (mile 140); 'Tariso' (unidentified), to
Kete Krakye (mile 166).[42] Dupuis added that this was the preferred
route between Kumase and the Dahomean capital of Abomey.[43]

The four southern great-roads

Route V linked Kumase with Accra in the southeast. The itinerary
given by Bowdich, in fifteen journeys, is incomplete, but the course of
the road can be reconstructed with reasonable accuracy.[44] It ran
through Asiempon (mile 12); Asoboi (mile 22); 'Assuennie' (unidentified); an unnamed halting-place; Ntronan (mile 62); Amonum (mile
74); Akuopon (mile 82); 'Abirriwantoo' (unidentified, but in the
Atwiredu hills); an unnamed halting-place; Adadientem (mile 88);
Kukurantumi (mile 104); an unnamed halting-place; Adawso (mile
126); Aburi (mile 134); and Accra (mile 156). Several minor southerly
branches of Route V led to various other coastal towns: Ningo, Prampram and Ada to the east of Accra, and Senya Bereku and Winneba to
the west.[45] An alternative route between Kumase and Kukurantumi,
the exact course of which is unclear, was longer by two or three
journeys.[46] Neither route seems to have proven popular with travellers,

37 But 'Laja' is undoubtedly a misreading of the Arabic for 'Lakha', that is, the
Daka River a branch of which runs between Kpabia and Yendi.
38 *Ibid.* pp. cxxxiii–cxxxiv.
39 Arabic route-books, in Dupuis, 1824, pp. cxxiv–cxxvi (Salaga to Mecca via
Katsina); Walckenaer, 1821, pp. 453–6 and Bowdich, 1819, pp. 490–2 (Gonja to
Mecca via Yendi – 'Balago' – and Kano); Dupuis, 1824, p. cxxx (Yendi to Birnin
Yauri).
40 See Wargee, in Wilks, 1967b, p. 189.
41 Arabic routes in Dupuis, 1824, pp. cxxviii–cxxix and cxxxiii–cxxxiv. For the
roads system focussed on Yendi, see Ferguson, 1973, pp. 230–3 and 349–50.
42 Dupuis, 1824, pp. xxviii and xl. Bowdich, 1819, p. 483. 'Guia' is presumably
Dwae, but should then be east of Wiase.
43 Dupuis, 1824, pp. xxviii–xxix; xl.
44 Bowdich, 1819, pp. 163, 483.
45 Dupuis, 1824, p. xxix.
46 Bowdich, 1819, pp. 163, 483.

who for most of the nineteenth century preferred to follow a cross-country road branching off from Route VI (see below).[47]

A major branch of Route V, *Route V(a)*, led to the province of Kwawu and apparently to a crossing of the Volta at Edzebeni ('Jiabee') a little north of its confluence with the Afram.[48] Presumably little used by the traders who were the principal informants of both Bowdich and Dupuis, neither writer obtained a detailed itinerary. Bowdich, however, reported that it was 'entered immediately on leaving Coomassie': probably at or near Asoboi (mile 22). Thence it passed 'Oseemadoo' (unidentified); Obogo (mile 38); Dampon (mile 44); and a series of unidentified halting-places, 'Assebanasoo', 'Minidasoo', and 'Assoona' to 'Wantomo'. Since the last town was situated near the source of the Pra River, yet eight journeys from Kumase, it must be assumed to have been to the north of the Kwawu hills.[49] From 'Wantomo' the presumption is that the road led through Kwawu Tafo to a crossing of the Afram, and thence to Edzebeni. A continuation passed southwards from Edzebeni through the Volta gorge to Akwamu, whence one 'extremely hazardous' route led into Dahomey, and another, bandit-infested in the earlier nineteenth century, along the Lower Volta to Anlo and beyond.[50]

A minor road, located between Routes IV and V, led from Kumase via Pakuso and 'Boomfeea', that is, Bonwire, to Dwaben (mile 18), Asokore (mile 23), and 'Mohoo', Kumawu (mile 30).[51] For convenience, this will be designated *Route V(b)*, since, certainly by the later nineteenth century, a way existed that linked Asokore with Kwawu Tafo on Route V (a), via Agogo (mile 50) and Abene (mile 75).[52] The first section of this minor road, however, was identical with that of Route IV as far as Asokore Mampon (mile 5).

Route VI led southwards from Kumase to Anomabo and adjacent towns on the central Gold Coast. Because of the heaviness of the traffic along it, there appears to have been considerable choice in the selection of halting-places. In the earlier nineteenth century Anomabo was generally accounted eleven journeys from the capital, and a favoured sequence of halts was Eduabin (mile 10); Amoafo (mile 18); Kwisa (mile 32); Akrofuom (mile 42); Ansa (mile 48); Kyekyewere (mile 60) or Praso (mile 62); Akomfode (mile 72); Foso (mile 82); Manso (mile 98); Dunkwa (mile 112); and Anomabo (mile 126).[53]

47 See, e.g. Riis, 1840, p. 238.
48 Bowdich, 1819, p. 163.
49 *Ibid.* p. 482. Dupuis, 1824, p. xxviii.
50 Dupuis, 1824, pp. xxxi–xxxii, xxviii.
51 Bowdich, 1819, pp. 482, 163.
52 Ramseyer and Kühne, 1875, pp. 31–53.
53 See, e.g. Huydecoper's Journal, entries for 28 April to 22 May 1816. Bowdich, 1819, pp. 14–31. Hutton, 1821, pp. 139–206. Dupuis, 1824, pp. 1–68.

From near Foso an important branch, *Route VI(a)*, led eastwards to Nsaba (mile 122), and thence southwards through Swedru (mile 132) to Winneba on the coast (mile 147).[54] From Dunkwa a lesser road ran to Mouri, likewise on the coast.[55]

Two detailed itineraries for the early 1840s are interesting for their reporting of actual travel times between somewhat different sequences of halting-places.[56] Mileages are computed from modern maps. Although the average length of a day's journey approximates to the notional seven travelling 'hours' (see p. 2), it will be apparent that the deviation in the sample is high.

Anonymous Journey	Time	Miles	Pel Journey	Time	Miles
Anomabo–Nyankomase	8 hr 37 m.	18			
Nyankomase–Manso	4 hr 28 m.	10	Nyankomase–Manso	7 hr	10
Manso–Foso	5 hr 43 m.	16	Manso–Foso	7 hr 30 m.	16
Foso–Pra River	6 hr 44 m.	19	Foso–Dansame	8 hr	16
Pra River–Apegya	3 hr 3 m.	5	Dansame–Asaman	8 hr 30 m.	13
Apegya–Akwansirem	9 hr 0 m.	18	Asaman–Moase	9 hr	15
Akwansirem–Kwisa	2 hr 41 m.	8	Moase–Ankase	10 hr	12
Kwisa–Amoafo	5 hr 30 m.	14	Ankase–Eduabin	6 hr 30 m.	14
Amoafo–Kaase	6 hr 40 m.	14	Eduabin–Kaase	4 hr	8
Kaase–Kumase	2 hr 2 m.	4	Kaase–Kumase	—	4

In 1862 the merchant R. J. Ghartey (later Ghartey IV of Winneba) published an interesting gazetteer of the towns and villages on the road: *Guide, for Strangers Travelling to Coomassie, the Capital City of Ashantee*.[57] By that period the journeys had been reduced to nine, and Ghartey recommended as halting places, proceeding northwards, 'Worratchell' (a little south of Nyankomase), Manso, Foso, Pra River, Akrofuom, Fomena, Amoafo, Kaase, and thence Kumase.

Route VII linked Kumase with Elmina to the south. The itinerary given by Bowdich, apparently in ten journeys, is clearly incomplete; indeed, he himself noted that the crossing of the Pra River occurred on the tenth day and that because of the westerly curvature of the road it was always accounted slower than Route VI.[58] The statement of the Asantehene Osei Bonsu may therefore be accepted, that it was thirteen

---

54 Bowdich, 1819, p. 167.
55 Dupuis, 1824, p. xxvii.
56 Anonymous itinerary in *Report from the Select Committee on the West Coast of Africa*, C.551–II, House of Commons, 5 August 1842, Part II, p. 42. Pel, n.d., pp. 1–6. See also T. B. Freeman, 1843, pp. 13–45, 97–122. National Archives of Ghana, Accra, ADM. 1/2/4, Despatches to Secretary of State, Book 3: Governor Winniet's Diary of a Journey to Kumase, entries for 28 September to 9 October 1848.
57 Reprinted in Boyle, 1874, Appendix.
58 Bowdich, 1819, pp. 168, 482.

journeys from his capital to Elmina.[59] Determination of the course of the road, however, is complicated by the fact that a major reconstruction and realignment of it was started on 2 December 1816.[60] It appears to have run from Kumase to Eduabin (mile 10, and also on Route VI); Asanso (mile 16) or Bekwae (mile 18); Asikaso (mile 26); 'Agyankremu' or 'Yankeren' (unidentified); Betinase (mile 54); Nsodweso (the old capital of the Twifo, abandoned *ca.* 1825); Mbem (mile 64); Bepowkoko (mile 72); Kaireku (mile 88); 'Prassie' (unidentified, but on the Pra River); Dumama (mile 106); 'Dadiasoo' (unidentified); and Elmina (mile 134).[61] Various lesser branches ran to adjacent coastal towns such as Komenda and Shama.[62] A major branch, *Route VII(a)*, led to the coastal towns to both east and west of Cape Three Points, from Takoradi to Axim. Its course is unknown in detail, but it probably left Route VII at Kaireku and passed through an unidentified Wassa town of 'Assankary' to Mpoho near the littoral (mile 140).[63]

Route VIII linked the capital with the southwestern provinces. Bowdich was clearly wrong in regarding it as a branch of Route VII, though both passed through Wassa territory.[64] The first section of the road was that described by Bowdich as leading from Kumase to Dako (mile 7); Trebuom (mile 13); and Manso Nkwanta (mile 26). From Manso Nkwanta a branch led to the old Denkyira capital of Abankesieso, abandoned *ca.* 1825 but near the present Abuakwa (mile 40).[65] The main road, however, continued in a southwesterly direction from Manso Nkwanta to Saraha (mile 62).[66] 'Two grand branches' of the route there diverged, one to the west and one to the east of the Tano River.[67] *Route VIII(a)* ran through Asankrangwa (mile 86) and Samreboi (mile 102)[68] and thence across the Tano to Dadieso and Aboisso (mile 152), the commercial centre for Kwankyeabo, capital of

59 General State Archives, The Hague, KvG 350: Asantehene to Daendels, dd. Kumase, 29 November 1816. See also the Asantehene's statement that the Wassa road (Route VII) to the coast was two journeys longer than the Assin road (Route VI), in Bowdich, 1819, p. 147.

60 Huydecoper's Journal, entry for 2 December 1816.

61 Bowdich, 1819, p. 482. Dupuis, 1824, map facing p. 265. Huydecoper's Journal, entries for 22 April to 18 May 1817. For an early attempt to chart this route, see Map 2 by A. Petermann, in *Petermann's Mittheilungen*, vol. 20, 1874.

62 Dupuis, 1824, p. xxvii.

63 *Ibid.* p. xxvii and map facing p. 265. For 'Assankary' see also Bowdich, 1819, p. 217. Note also M. Allen, 1874, p. 40: from Axim 'a native road leads almost directly to Coomassie, and this facility of communication with the interior of the country is the chief advantage possessed by Axim'.

64 Bowdich, 1819, p. 168.

65 *Ibid.* p. 482.

66 Dupuis, 1824, map facing p. 265: 'Sasara'.

67 Bowdich, 1819, p. 168.

68 Dupuis, 1824, map facing p. 265: 'Isankory' and 'Sakofoy'.

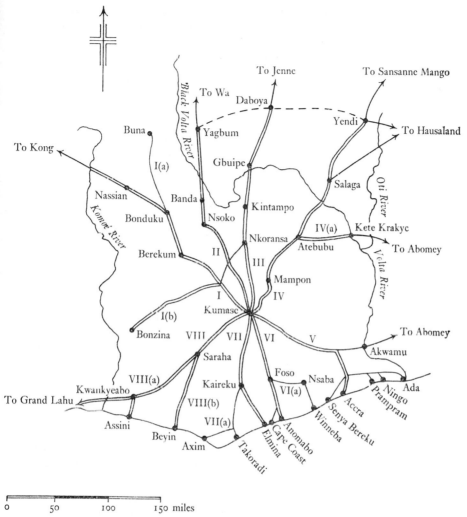

i The great-roads of Asante in the early nineteenth century

Sanwi,[69] and to the series of ports between Assini at the mouth of the Bia River, and Grand Lahu at that of the Bandama.[70] Route *VIII(b)* ran from Saraha to Beyin on the coast (mile 150). No details of its course in the early nineteenth century have been found. An itinerary survives, however, from a later period. The journey from Kumase to

[69] Anon., 1850, p. 36.
[70] Bowdich, 1819, p. 168. Dupuis, 1824, p. xxvii. Much of the difficulty in following the course of this road arises from the confusion in the sources between the 'Assinee' River, i.e. the Tano, and the 'Seenee', i.e. the Ankobra, see, e.g. Bowdich, 1819, pp. 168–70.

11

Beyin was reckoned to take twelve or thirteen days,[71] and ran from the capital through Bawdiase ('Bordiassie') and Manso Nkwanta to Asaman near the Offin River, and thence to Saraha ('Sawora'), Akyekyere ('Tittjijerrie', mile 88) and Amape (mile 102).[72]

The great-roads system of Asante, as it existed in the early nineteenth century, is shown in Map i. Although reconstruction of various routes was to engage the attention of government in later years, there is little evidence of further major highways being built. Some of the great-roads, however, did fall into disuse. In particular, the growth of the British interest in the southern provinces of Asante, and the emergence of the Protectorate and later Colony of the Gold Coast, deprived the government in Kumase of control over sections of the four southern great-roads. The uneasy relations which frequently prevailed between the Asante and British administrations were not generally conducive to the maintenance of good communications between Kumase and the Gold Coast towns. In the 1860s, for example, the British induced the Wassa to close Route VIII(a) to Kwankyeabo, a town whence the Asante obtained many of their military supplies. It thus became necessary to consign goods from Kwankyeabo by a road which passed northwards through Ebilassekro, to join Route I(b) probably near Bonzina;[73] the journey took between thirty and thirty-five days, or about double the time by the direct route.[74] In the circumstances, probably in 1868, the Asante government opened a new route through the still loyal provinces of Sehwi and Aowin in order to maintain access to both Kwankyeabo and Beyin.[75]

The attitude of the British administrators on the Gold Coast was, in itself, scarcely an enlightened one on the matter of communications. Even as late as 1870 the Colonial Office in London was informed of eight reasons why good roads should not be kept up. 'It was not necessarily through lack of money', it was observed, 'that nothing was being done about roads, but it would simply be useless to clean roads that would be overgrown in a year.'[76] Route VI to Anomabo, in fact, alone remained more or less continuously open throughout the century: it was the principal channel for diplomatic exchanges between Kumase and Cape Coast, seat of the British administration until 1876. The

71 General State Archives, The Hague, KvG 1099: Beyin Journal, entry for 4 September 1869.
72 *Ibid.* KvG 1101: Register of outgoing letter, Beyin, Report for 1869.
73 PRO, CO. 879/37, African (West) 435: enclosure in Lang to Colonial Office, dd. 17 November 1892.
74 KvG 1099, Beyin Journal, entry for 4 September 1869.
75 KvG 1101, Beyin, Report for 1869; KvG 1099, Beyin Journal, entry for 7 December 1869.
76 See Dickson, 1969, pp. 218–9 for the full text of the dispatch.

modern motor road follows the old great-road for virtually the whole of its course. Route V to Accra and the southeast, by contrast, appears largely to have fallen into disuse by the 1870s, though sections of it remained of local importance and were incorporated into the later network of motor roads.[77] The southern sections of Route VII lost their importance after the Dutch ceded their post at Elmina to the British in 1872, and although the Asante government made strenuous efforts, as noted above, to keep open Route VIII to the southwest, by 1879 the British were able to report with satisfaction the closure of 'the old road to the coast to Krinjabo and Assinee, by which Ashanti once received large quantities of warlike stores'.[78] The four northern great-roads, by contrast, appear to have remained operative through-out the century. Thus, for example, Austin Freeman followed Route I on his journey from Kumase to Bonduku in 1888–9;[79] in 1882 Lonsdale used Route II to Nsoko, and from there proceeded to Bonduku;[80] in 1884 Kirby followed Route III to Kintampo;[81] and in 1881 Lonsdale passed by Route IV to Salaga and Yendi.[82] Indeed, taking Bonduku, Banda, Daboya and Yendi as notional termini of the four northern trunk roads, it is noteworthy that over two-thirds of the system survive as all-season motor roads.

The great-roads system of Asante as such ceased to exist at the end of the century, when the French and Germans occupied the westernmost and easternmost parts of Greater Asante, and the British apportioned the remainder between three distinct administrative units: the Colony of the Gold Coast, the Crown Colony of Asante and the Protectorate of the Northern Territories. Nevertheless, even cursory inspection of a map of present day Ghana reveals the extent to which Kumase was able to recover much of its nineteenth century importance: it is once more the point at which numerous roads converge, many of which follow more or less closely the course of earlier great-roads. The development of the communications network in this century has been investigated in detail by Gould, who failed, however, adequately to consider its nineteenth century antecedents.[83] But the high degree of correspondence between the nineteenth and twentieth

[77] PRO, CO. 96/116: despatch by Gouldsbury, dd. 13 November 1875.

[78] PRO, CO. 96/126: despatch by Governor Ussher, dd. 24 July 1879.

[79] R. A. Freeman, 1898, pp. 133–69.

[80] *Further Correspondence regarding the Affairs of the Gold Coast*, C. 3687, 1883, pp. 117–18.

[81] *Further Correspondence respecting the Affairs of the Gold Coast*, C. 4477, 1885, pp. 93–5.

[82] *Further Correspondence regarding the Affairs of the Gold Coast*, C. 3386, 1882, pp. 67–75.

[83] Gould, 1960, *passim*.

century networks suggests, perhaps, that the former approached optimal design in relation to the geo-political configuration of the territory comprising the old Greater Asante – the modern Ghana.

The topology of the great-roads

The great-roads system of Asante, as it had evolved by the early nineteenth century, possessed a clearly defined topological structure. First,
the network was organized with reference to one central node:
Kumase. Secondly, the network was of radial design, each of the eight
trunk roads converging upon Kumase and thus linking to it a number
of satellite places. Thirdly, a number of satellite places not lying upon
trunk roads were nevertheless integrated into the network by a series of
branch roads. But in addition to the trunk roads and their branches,
which have been described above, a few arc roads of importance
existed. Thus an 'inner circular road' linked Routes I, II and III. It
appears to have run from Bekyem (Route I, mile 44) through Takyi-
mantia to Akumadan (Route II, mile 56), and thence through Boinso
to Nkoransa (Route III, mile 68).[84] Similarly an 'outer circular road'
apparently linked at least three of the northern great-roads. Running
from Zabzugu ('Jabdhughu') to Yendi ('Balaghu') on Route IV (mile
250), it continued thence through Tampion ('Tanbi') and Vogo
('Bughu', 'Boo') to the Volta at 'Burughu', that is, Daboya on Route III
(mile 222). From there the road perhaps extended to the Gonja capital
of Yagbum, to link with the northern section in Route II.[85] This
traverse of the Asante hinterland was followed, in the late eighteenth
century, by the Fezzan trader Sharīf Imhammad, some account of
whose travels has survived.[86] It was also presumably the route by
which Asante officials transferred the detained Tatar, Wargee, from
Banda on Route II via Daboya on Route III to Salaga on Route
IV.[87] Such arc roads were, however, probably not part of the great-
roads system as such, but represented surviving portions of roads existing prior to the development of that system. Thus the outer ring road
had probably been pioneered, in the seventeenth century or earlier, by
Muslim traders and pilgrims as a way between such early Dyula
centres as Kong, Boron and Koro in the west, and Hausaland and

---

84 Bowdich, 1819, p. 483. It will be noted that the first section of what Bowdich calls
   the 'Boopee', i.e. Gbuipe, path in fact follows Route I through Biemso ('Bumsoo').
85 See Bowdich, 1819, pp. 177, 483, 491; and Dupuis, 1824, p. xxviii.
86 Reported by Lucas, in *Proceedings of the Association for Promoting the Discovery
   of the Interior Parts of Africa*, 1791, pp. 329–32 and map facing p. 311.
87 Wilks, 1967b, p. 188. A direct route from Salaga to Bonduku, given by Barth,
   1859, III, 646, appears to have been an irregular one, and since the daily journeys
   averaged 30 miles, his source must be considered suspect.

Bornu in the east.[88] Other older roads had apparently fallen into more or less total disuse as the government in Kumase had progressively engrossed trade, such as that which had led from Axim on the coast through Aowin to the northern savannah lands.[89]

In a simple topological model of a radial system with eight trunks, roads converge on the central node at angles of 45°, assuming the homogeneity of the environment: that is, that no variable factors exist such as to produce an asymmetry of the trunks about the nodal place. Table 1 shows the extent of divergence from the model of the actual distribution of the Asante trunk roads, where for purposes of computation Bonduku, Banda, Daboya, Yendi, Accra, Anomabo, Elmina and Kwankyeabo have been taken as their notional termini. Identification of the variables which determined the actual course of the great-roads is clearly impossible without reference to the historical factors treated briefly in the next section. Nevertheless, no satisfactory analysis of the system is attainable solely by reference to such factors. Examination of Table 1 suggests that explanations different in kind are required to account for the existence of roads which diverge sharply from each other (characterized by high positive discrepancy values), and of those which diverge little (with high negative values). Thus the region between Routes IV and V included the vast but thinly populated Afram Plains, and that between Routes VIII and I, the extensive and equally thinly populated forests of Ahafo and Sehwi.[90] The absence of great-roads through these regions seems, therefore, to need no special explanation, and indeed, as Map 1 shows, branch roads did exist to link with the main network such important towns as, for example, Kwawu Tafo, Kete Krakye and Bonzina. By contrast, the smallness of the regions between Routes VI and VII, and Routes I and II, does appear to call for explanation: the termini of Routes VI and VII, Anomabo and Elmina, were less than twenty miles apart, and of Routes I and II, Bonduku and Banda, only some thirty.

Table 1   *The great-roads: angles of convergence*

Roads	Angles of convergence		
	Model	Actual	Discrepancy
IV–V	45	101	+56
VIII–I	45	88	+43
VII–VIII	45	59	+14
II–III	45	31	−14
V–VI	45	30	−15
III–IV	45	26	−19
I–II	45	16	−29
VI–VII	45	9	−36
TOTALS:	360	360	0

88 Wilks, 1968, pp. 175–6.
89 General State Archives, The Hague, WIC 114: Elmina Journals, entry for 19 January 1752.
90 Large areas within these regions remain virtually unpopulated to the present, see, e.g. Hilton, 1960, pp. 30, 33, 35.

The problem arises from the fact that the great-roads system of Asante was designed to achieve two different ends: to promote the flow of trade, and to facilitate the maintenance of political control. The principles of optimum location for highway networks have been analysed with reference to commodity flow patterns by Beckmann, who argues that the extent of a network (that is, the total length of the roads) will optimally be determined so as to minimize the total expense of the network measured in terms of construction and upkeep costs, while maximizing the benefits to users of the network in terms of reduced transportation costs.[91] The formulae offered by Beckmann for the computation of optimal network design will not be considered here, since although data on road construction and maintenance in nineteenth century Asante are available, these are inadequate for purposes of quantification. It may be noted, however, that Dupuis observed that road-building might be 'a severe tax upon the industry of the nation';[92] and that, while much of the labour employed on the roads was probably unpaid, certainly when in 1816 major reconstructions of Routes VI and VII were initiated by government, substantial disbursements from the Treasury had to be made to those appointed overseers of different sections of the work.[93] Road maintenance costs, moreover, were heavy, particularly if account is taken of the considerable expenditure on the *nkwansrafo* or highway-police. In general, then, it would seem unlikely that the construction and maintenance costs of a great-road were sufficiently low to have justified, in terms of reduced transportation costs, the existence of such contiguous routes as I and II, or VI and VII. Their existence must, in other words, be explained in other than economic terms.

Table 2 shows in diagrammatic form the 'political profiles' of Routes VI and VII. It will be observed that the great-roads, while spatially proximate, are not politically coextensive: that is, they pass through quite different sequences of provinces and terminate, the one at Anomabo whence it was customary to pass by canoe or along the shore to the English headquarters in Cape Coast, and the other at Elmina, headquarters of the Dutch. An interesting illustration of the role of politics in communications, having reference to these two routes, is provided by the events of 1810, when a state of general unrest among the Fante and sections of the Assin had made Route VI unsafe

91 Beckmann, 1967, *passim*, and especially p. 107 for a network of the Asante type. See also Haggett and Chorley, 1969, ch. III, part 1.
92 Dupuis, 1824, p. xxx.
93 See, e.g. Huydecoper's Journal, entries for 2 December 1816 and 24 April 1817. Also General State Archives, The Hague, KvG 349: Huydecoper to Daendels, dd. Kumase, 9 December 1816. On 2 December 1816, for example, 13½ oz of gold were disbursed from the Treasury to 'different Village Chiefs for the cutting of the great-road'.

to Asante messengers. Accordingly, in May, the Asantehene decided temporarily to redirect his correspondence with the British along Route VII and via Elmina. The British immediately lodged an official protest with the Asantehene, and asked that, until Route VI could be reopened, all couriers should be sent by Route V to the English lodge at Accra, whence they would be transported to Cape Coast by boat: even though, as it was noted, 'this prevents our hearing from the King so speedily as we could wish'. The Asantehene replied, diplomatically, 'that he did not mean to give offence by sending . . . through the medium of the Dutch'.[94]

Table 2 *Routes VI and VII: political profiles*

Route VI	Route VII
Metropolitan Asante	Metropolitan Asante
Assin Apemanim	Denkyira
Assin Attendansu	Twifo
Fante	Wassa Fiase
English H.Q., Cape Coast	Dutch H.Q., Elmina

While in fact each of the great roads possessed a distinctive political profile, it is in the existence of such spatially proximate routes as VI and VII that the general principle is the most clearly exemplified: that the topology of the great-roads system of Asante was determined by political as well as economic factors. Indeed, recognition of the dual function of the great-roads was implicit in the Asante attitude toward disorder on them. When those who used the roads in a political capacity – the government's messengers and envoys – were harmed, the matter was regarded as indicative of rebellion. 'An Injury done to any of them is considered to affect the Honour of those they Represent or are sent from', it was observed in 1767, 'but the Murder of such Persons is regarded always as a Challenge or a mark of Defiance.'[95] The Asantehene, commented his ambassador to the British in 1820, 'always considers messengers sacred either in peace or war',[96] and the traveller, whether within Greater Asante or beyond, was well-advised to obtain some form of official sponsorship for his journey:

no heathen can be perfectly secure in his person and property beyond the precincts of his sovereign's jurisdiction, excepting, however, the character of ambassador, whose person should be held inviolate, that of king's merchant or trader which is equally sacred, hunters of elephants in the king's name, and on his account; and lastly, men of rank, or others whose influence or interest at court is powerful enough to gain for them a travelling protection by the use of the king's name or recommendation to other sovereigns and princes. These, and only such characters, are passports for the subjects of Ashantee, by which they may travel in security. . . Hence the favour of

94 PRO, T. 70/35: letter from De Veer, dd. Elmina, 7 May 1810; and White *et al.* to Council, dd. Cape Coast, 27 July and 7 November 1810.
95 PRO, T. 70/31: Petrie to Council, dd. Cape Coast, 9 October 1767.
96 Hutton, 1821, p. 311.

using the king's name is great, and the king of Ashantee never confers it except upon those whom he has confidence in, as men of ability and prudence.[97]

Conquest, incorporation, and the great-roads

Any detailed account of the history of Asante in the eighteenth century is beyond the scope of this study. Some brief review of the development of the great-roads system in that century will, however, be offered, since its evolution was closely related to the process of the political incorporation of conquered territories into Greater Asante. The early phases of Asante expansion were of necessity predominantly military in character, for few rulers, confronted by the new phenomenon of Asante imperialism, were able to view the matter *sub specie aeternitatis,* in the manner of one early nineteenth century British observer:

With a number of little independent hordes, civilization is impossible. They must have a common interest before there can be peace; and be directed by one will, before there can be order. When mankind are prevented from daily quarrelling and fighting they first begin to improve; and all this, we are afraid, is only to be accomplished, in the first instance, by some great conqueror. We sympathize, therefore, with the victories of the King of Ashantee – and feel ourselves, for the first time, in love with military glory.[98]

The campaigns which destroyed the independent power of Asante's neighbours to north, south, east and west occurred for the most part in the half-century 1700–50. The more important expeditions can be dated with reasonable accuracy, the archives of the European trading companies on the Gold Coast being especially useful for the thrusts southwards, and the local chronicles in Arabic (notably those of Gonja provenance) for those northwards.[99] The major lines of Asante expansion, as indicated in such sources, are shown on Map ii.

In 1820 Dupuis found himself impressed by the number of the territories which, as he observed, 'have successively been engulphed in the vortex which has since spread under its modern name of Ashantee, into that great political association of kingdoms, that have fallen under the sword of the ruling dynasty, and are now only to be distinguished as provinces dependent on the court of Coomassy'.[100] But in

97 Dupuis, 1824, pp. cviii–cix.
98 *Edinburgh Review,* LXIV, October 1819, 398–9: anonymous review of Bowdich, 1819.
99 For the European sources see e.g., Daaku, 1970; Fynn, 1971. An edition of the Gonja Arabic chronicles, including the important mid-eighteenth century *Tadhkira li 'l-Muta'akhirīn,* 'An Account for Posterity', is in course of preparation by Wilks and Levtzion.
100 Dupuis, 1824, p. xxvii.

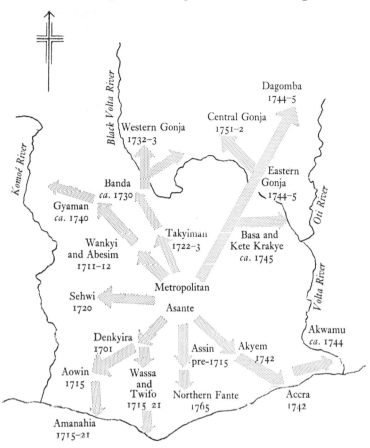

ii Major campaigns of Asante expansion in the eighteenth century

so far as Dupuis' comment suggests the equation of military conquest with political incorporation, it ignores the quite different phasing of the two processes. Whereas the wars of expansion accomplished to a greater or lesser extent the destruction of pre-existing centres of organized political, military and economic power, nevertheless in many cases long periods of disorder and near anarchy followed before the conquered peoples were – if ever – pacified and brought under a civilian administration. After the overthrow of the Denkyira kingdom in 1701, for example, a considerable number of the defeated chiefs and their followers did indeed transfer their allegiance to Asante and, through a redefinition of their authority and responsibilities, were

politically incorporated into the Kumase division; others, however, retired into the forests and maintained constant guerrilla operations
against the victors, harassing traders passing to the coast and, in 1707,
carrying out a massacre of Asante gold-miners at Manso Nkwanta.[101]

In the northern hinterland of Asante the open nature of the terrain
was not conducive to sustained resistance to the aggrandizing power.
Moreover, by virtue of its ability to regulate the movement of armaments from the coast northwards, Asante was able to maintain a
superiority in weaponry over its northern neighbours. An agent in the
Sultan of Fezzan's slave trade, who had travelled in Gonja and
Dagomba in the 1770s or 1780s, commented on the absence of firearms
in the countries he had visited: 'the Kings in the neighbourhood of the
coast, persuaded that if these powerful instruments of war should reach
the possession of the populous inland States, their own independence
would be lost, have strictly prohibited, and by the wisdom of their
measures, have effectually prevented this dangerous merchandize from
passing beyond the limit of their dominions'.[102] Of Asante in particular, the trader added, 'there is no communication between this coast
(which we may suppose to be the Gold Coast) and the country of
Gonjah: for that the King of Assentai, who possesses the space between, prohibits his Inland Neighbours from passing through his
country'.[103] The pacification of the northern countries through their
absorption into Greater Asante was therefore a comparatively rapid
process. The various stages of conquest and political incorporation are
well illustrated by the case of the eastern Gonja chiefdom of Kpembe.
It is possible that this district was overrun during the campaigns of
1732/3, though it is more likely that these were directed rather against
central and western Gonja.[104] Certainly, however, Kpembe must have
been occupied – if not before – by 1744–5, during the major invasion
of the northeast.[105] An obituary notice of the Asantehene Opoku Ware,
who master-minded these campaigns until his death in 1750, testified
to the harsh and capricious nature of the early Asante overlordship:

In that year Opoku, king of the Asante, died, may Allah curse him and place
his soul in hell. It was he who injured the people of Gonja, oppressing them
and robbing them of their property at will. He ruled violently, as a tyrant,
delighting in his authority. People of all the horizons feared him greatly.[106]

---

101 General State Archives, The Hague, WIC 100: Nuyts' Journal, entries for 31 July,
    16 August, and 30 October 1706, and 10 February and 16 April 1707.
102 Sharīf Imhammad, as reported by Lucas, in *Proceedings*, 1791, p. 267.
103 *Ibid.* pp. 331–2.
104 *Tadhkira li 'l-Muta'akhirīn*, entry for 1145 AH.
105 *Ibid.* entry for 1157 AH. Rømer, 1760, pp. 218–21, reported eyewitness accounts
    of the expedition from Osu messengers in Asante.
106 *Tadhkira*, entry for 1163 AH.

In 1751 Kpembe was reoccupied by another Asante force under Safo Katanka of Mampon, apparently as a result of the civil disorders there which followed the death of Kpembewura Morukpe. Meeting with opposition, the Asante commander arrested the new Kpembewura Nakpo and two of his kinsmen and sent them under escort though whether to Mampon or Kumase is not clear. 'Conditions were imposed upon him', reported the Gonja chronicler of these events, after which Nakpo was permitted to return to Kpembe in the company of Asante representatives.[107] By a fortunate chance some independent account has survived of the nature of the conditions. The nineteenth century Gã historian Reindorf misdescribed Nakpo as 'King of Yane', that is, Dagomba, by an understandable confusion with the Dagomba Na Gariba who was later arrested in similar circumstances (see below). But Reindorf's use of the Arabic form of Nakpo – 'Nakawa' or 'Nakaw' as in the eighteenth century Gonja chronicles – suggests that he had access, direct or indirect, to a surviving copy of that contract between the Asantehene and the Kpembewura which he briefly described: 'Nakawa's life was spared, but he was made to write a contract in Arabic to the effect that he and his successors should remain vassals to the kings of Asante and pay a tribute of 1,000 slaves yearly to the king, this document was signed by Nakawa and all his generals'.[108] The contract is to be seen as marking the acceptance by the local Kpembe authorities of a legally defined position within Greater Asante: intermittent military control was replaced by a regular civilian administration. Although Route IV to the northeast was described by Dupuis as one of the older roads, and had the name of a late seventeenth century Mamponhene attached to it, it may be supposed that it was after the incorporation of Kpembe into Greater Asante that it acquired great-road status.

The sequence of events in eastern Gonja appears not atypical of the evolution of Asante's relations with others of its northern neighbours, such as Dagomba and Gyaman. The first invasion of Dagomba occurred in 1744–45. Although strategically well-conceived, in terms of both tactics and logistics the Asante commanders were ill-prepared: militarily the operation proved at best an indifferent success.[109] The Dagomba nevertheless subsequently sued for peace, and acknowl-

---

[107] *Tadhkira*, entry for 1164 ĀH.

[108] Reindorf, 2nd ed., n.d., pp. 132–3.

[109] The account of the invasion in Rømer, 1760, pp. 218–21, does not refer to Dagomba by name, but an entry in the *Tadhkira* for Dhū al-Hijja 1157 (January 1745) refers to Opoku Ware's entry into the 'town of Ghughu', that is, Dagomba, compare Gonja *Gwong*, Twi *Anwa*. Kyerematen, 1966, reports Asante traditions that the invasion was occasioned by the Dagomba having allowed Takyiman refugees to settle in their territory.

edged some sort of Asante overlordship.[110] The regularization of their relations with the imperial power, however, appears not to have been accomplished until the reign of the Asantehene Osei Kwadwo (1764–77), when, civil disorders having occurred there, a force under Kwaaten Pete – later Adontenhene of Kumase – was sent to effect a reoccupation and to arrest the Ya Na 'Abdallāh Gariba.[111] 'In his days', wrote the author of the *Ta'rīkh Daghabāwī*, 'the soldiers of Asante came and seized him. His sons ransomed him for a thousand slaves. This became a tribute between Dagomba and Asante'.[112] The reoccupation was probably carried out in 1772, when it was reported that a 'Donkor' district had been overthrown.[113] The regularization of the tributes was one aspect of the settlement that followed, but under its terms the Asante probably agreed to undertake a reorganization of the Dagomba fighting forces: a corps of gunmen was created, the Kambonse – literally 'the Asante' – and the controlled importation of firearms was permitted.[114]

The invasion of Gyaman occurred shortly before that of Dagomba, probably in 1740. Its ruler, Abo Kofi, was slain.[115] A section of the defeated, under the leadership of Kofi Sono, found refuge in the Watara state of Kong and, fearing to return to their homeland, remained there for almost a decade. In 1748 or 1749, however, an understanding with the Asantehene Opoku Ware was achieved; Kofi Sono returned to Gyaman and was recognized as successor to Abo Kofi. In 1749 he was actively campaigning to establish his authority within Gyaman, and to overthrow such local chiefs as Demba Korokon of the Senufo of Jamala, who had sprung into prominence during the interregnum.[116] In 1751 he met with envoys of the new Asantehene Kusi Obodom, and a full peace settlement was drawn up in the presence of messengers from the Dutch at Elmina.[117]

110 Bowdich, 1819, p. 235.
111 Various accounts, differing in detail, exist of this episode from both Asante and Dagomba tradition, see, e.g. Fuller, 1921, pp. 34–5; Tamakloe, 1931, ch. IV; Institute of African Studies, University of Ghana, Tait MSS: MS/A, pp. 17 ff., and MS/B, pp. 42 ff. For a recent discussion of the matter, see Ferguson, 1973, pp. 219–26.
112 Institute of African Studies, Arabic Collection, IASAR/241: 'History of the Dagomba', compiled in its present form by Imām Khālid of Yendi, probably *ca.* 1930.
113 General State Archives, The Hague, WIC 976: letters from Shama, dd. November 1772.
114 National Archives of Ghana, Accra, ADM. 11/824: A. W. Davies, 'History and Organization of the Kambonse in Dagomba', 1948, *passim.* See also Tait, 1955, pp. 194–5.
115 *Tadhkira,* entry for 1162 AH.
116 *Ibid.* entries for 1162 and 1163 AH. Gyaman traditions, reported by Tauxier, 1921, especially pp. 91, note, and 92.
117 General State Archives, The Hague, WIC 490: despatch from Van Voorst, dd. Elmina, 17 November 1751.

It is unfortunate that no complete versions of such settlements or contracts as those of 1751 in the cases of Kpembe and Gyaman, and *ca.* 1772 in that of Dagomba, survive: for these were the legal mandates for the ongoing incorporation of the respective territories into Greater Asante. That such mandates existed, however, was no guarantee that movements of resistance to central government would not from time to time arise as the machinery of incorporation – which will be examined later – began to be activated. Thus extensive uprisings occurred in Gyaman and western Gonja early in the reign of Osei Kwadwo, and again early in that of Osei Bonsu: the former originated as a protest against taxation or tribute,[118] and the latter in a movement seemingly to restore to the throne the ex-Asantehene Osei Kwame.[119] But of whatever nature, such rebellions were comparatively infrequent in the northern provinces of Asante. The advantages of association in the Asante common market area outweighed, by and large, the disadvantages in the loss of full sovereignty. No major conflict is reported, for instance, between the rulers of Dagomba and the central government in a period of over a century after 1772. In the territories south of Kumase, by contrast, the situation remained a highly unstable one throughout the eighteenth, and into the nineteenth, century. There the broken and thickly forested nature of the terrain was particularly well suited to the maintenance of prolonged opposition to Asante attempts to develop a system of regular civilian administration.

By 1707 Amankwatia, Bantamahene of Kumase, had succeeded in destroying most of the Denkyira partisan groups which had been operating in the forests of the southwest,[120] but efforts to open a great-road to Elmina and the western coast were frustrated by a shifting alliance of the Aowin, Wassa and Twifo. In a series of campaigns between 1715 and 1721 the armies of Asante overran these territories. The Aowin were the first to submit: in 1715 a number of their chiefs formally acknowledged, through a payment of 600 oz of gold, the Asantehene's overlordship.[121] The Twifo, who had assisted the Asante against the Aowin, fell next, and probably in 1721 the Wassa ruler Ntsiful was driven from his country and took refuge in Ahanta, behind Takoradi.[122] By 1727–8 it seemed that the Wassa might submit, and Ntsiful was offered the land of the defeated Twifo chief Bafo

118 See, e.g. Dupuis, 1824, p. 241.
119 *Ibid.* p. 245.
120 General State Archives, The Hague, WIC 100: Nuyts' Journal, letter from Landman, dd. Axim, 11 April 1707; WIC 99: letter from Landman, dd. Axim, 30 April 1707.
121 *Ibid.* KvG 82: letter from Butler, dd. Axim, 24 January 1715.
122 PRO, T. 70/4: Braithwaite and Cruickshank to Committee, dd. Cape Coast, 30 June 1729.

Kyei on the condition that a road to the coast should be kept open through it.[123] It was in fact at this seemingly propitious time that the Asante, as Rømer noted, 'built a road to Elmine, Cap Cors [Cape Coast], and the forts situated west of Elmine'.[124] This was the first of the great-roads to the coast, Route VII passing through the old Twifo capital of Nsodweso. Its importance was acknowledged in 1729, in a comment on 'the country of Cuifferoe [Twifo] which is the key of Ashantee and the path by which their trade is brought to the water-side'.[125] In the 1730s, however, Ntsiful led the Wassa into an anti-Asante coalition with the Fante and Akyem, the history of which has been treated in several recent studies.[126] The new road became extremely hazardous, and in 1744 it was temporarily closed down.[127]

In 1742 Asante armies invaded the countries of the Akyem, and occupied in strength Accra and the coastal towns to its east. Almost 20,000 Asante troops, under the Akyempemhene of Kumase Owusu Afriyie, were reported to have encamped near Accra.[128] The Gã and Adangme peoples of the southeastern plains, militarily too weak to resist the invasion, offered their submission: by the terms of the settlement between the Accra ruler Tete Ahene Akwa and representatives of the Asantehene, the Gã accepted Asante overrule but obtained exemption from paying tribute.[129] The major task confronting the government in Kumase, then, was to accomplish the pacification of the Akyem and to open a great-road to Accra and the eastern coast. Apparently arriving at an understanding with two members of the Akyem royal houses who had been captured in the invasion, Broni of Akyem Kotoku and Asare of Akyem Abuakwa, Opoku Ware proposed placing them in authority in their respective countries with guarantees of Asante protection and of an exemption from tribute, in return for their undertaking to allow, as it was reported, 'free passage for his men and traders through the Akim [Akyem] countries to Accra, as that was more accessible to him than Elmine'.[130] In the event, the Akyem Kotoku accepted the proposals, but not the Akyem Abuakwa. As a result the attempt to open a direct road – the later Route V – through the Akyem forests to Accra had to be abandoned at this

123 General State Archives, The Hague, KvG 94: Elmina Journal, entry for 16 September 1727.
124 Rømer, 1760, p. 167.
125 PRO T. 70/4: Braithwaite and Cruickshank to Committee, dd. 30 June 1729. For 'Cuifferoe' see Wilks, 1958b, p. 216.
126 See Priestley, 1961; Fynn, 1965; Tenkorang, 1968; and Daaku, 1970, ch. VII.
127 Rømer, 1760, pp. 222–3. General State Archives, The Hague, WIC 490: despatch from Van Voorst, dd. Elmina, 17 November 1751.
128 Rømer, 1760, pp. 181–5. The campaigns are reported in detail in the journals of the Dutch and Danish factors in Accra in 1742.
129 Reindorf, 2nd ed., n.d., pp. 167–9.
130 Rømer, 1760, pp. 187–9. See also Reindorf, 2nd ed., n.d., pp. 81–2.

time.[131] 'Then', observed Rømer, 'the Assiantees thought of making a road to the sea coast via Crepe, or east of Rio Volta to Fredensborg, the English fort at Prampram, and the Dutch lodge of Pomz', that is, Route V(a) running through Kwawu territory into Akwamu – already in process of incorporation into Greater Asante [132] – and thence to the mouth of the Volta and along the coast through the Danish, English and Dutch lodges at Ningo, Prampram and Kpone.[133] The road was opened in 1749 after satisfactory arrangements for its operation had been agreed with the Akwamu.[134] By the following year large parties, or 'passages', of traders were already making use of it to proceed to Accra. The Dutch factor there received constant reports of their progress from the Akwamu: for example,

that in a country named Kwawu, five or six days walk into the interior from Akwamu, a large party of Asante have arrived, so numerous that they had fears about getting them across the river. But the Asante must first cross this before they enter Akwamu . . . It is a great passage of traders who are coming down, and they are accompanied by an escort of soldiers to protect them against the Akyem or Krepi [i.e., Ewe], should they be attacked by them.[135]

A full history of the great roads of Asante remains to be written. But it will be apparent that the development of the system was a critical aspect of the incorporative process. Indeed, opposition to the central government's road building programme was one of the principal features of the syndrome of resistance to its imperial expansion, just as the closure of existing roads became one of the earliest indications of rebellion. Certainly a number of the great-roads must have originated in the military ways cut during the eighteenth century wars of expansion, as comparison of Maps i and ii will suggest. The creation of the great-roads system, however, involved much more than the construction of actual highways: for example, numerous agreements had to be negotiated with local chiefs through whose lands the roads were routed, the chains of appointed halting-places had to be established, and control posts manned by the highway-police had to be set up at strategic points along each road.

---

131 State Archives, Copenhagen, West Indian and Guinea Company, miscellaneous documents from Guinea, Sekretprotokoller 1755–62: despatch dd. Christiansborg, 5 March 1755.
132 See Wilks, 1958a, pp. 135–40.
133 Rømer, 1760, pp. 222–3.
134 General State Archives, The Hague, KvG 110: letter from Brunner, dd. Accra, 18 September 1749.
135 For details of the organization of the route, and the continuing danger from Akyem, Krobo and Ewe raiders, see *ibid.* KvG 111: letters from Brunner dd. Accra, 10 April, 6 September and 18 December 1750.

Much of the source material for the history of Asante in the eighteenth century derives from those with commercial interests, whether the European merchants on the Gold Coast or the Muslim merchants of the towns of the northern hinterland. Such writers almost invariably, and quite naturally, conceived of the roads as essentially channels for the flow of trade.[136] But they were, as noted above, also channels for the flow of authority: that is, not only instruments for the maximization of economic benefits (trade and production), but also instruments for the maximization of political control (government). The matter of the roads figured prominently in the prolonged negotiations of the 1750s, when both the Dutch and the English merchants on the coast, with the support of the Fante, took an initiative in attempting to persuade the Wassa, Twifo, Denkyira and Akyem Abuakwa to accept a peace settlement with the Asante government.[137] Largely because each feared that the others might enter into unilateral arrangements with that government, representatives of the four territories held a series of meetings in 1753, and finally agreed to go to Kumase and 'to swear to the peace and open the paths'.[138] The Asantehene Kusi Obodom responded by intimating his willingness 'to sheath the sword', that is, to consider replacing military by civilian control, but demanded a pacification fee of 2,000 oz of gold from the supplicants: apparently 800 oz from the Wassa and 400 oz each from the Twifo, Denkyira and Akyem Abuakwa.[139] The sum handed over, both sides agreed to accept representatives of the Dutch as observers at the negotiations. The Asante government then announced its terms for settlement. First, the Wassa, Twifo, Denkyira and Akyem were to cease all hostilities against those southerly districts which were in process of incorporation into Greater Asante and were therefore, so it was claimed, 'living at peace with one another' – including Akwamu, Assin, Kwawu, Sehwi, Akyem

---

136 But see the interesting observations in Rømer, 1760, pp. 200–1, that when the road to Elmina was opened, Opoku Ware recruited into his service four Dutchmen to open a distillery in Kumase, and also created a new weaving industry by importing woollen and silken fabrics which were unravelled and the thread introduced into the local cotton cloths: presumably a reference to the origin of the *kente* industry.

137 See Fynn, 1965, pp. 26–8; Tenkorang, 1968, pp. 6–9.

138 PRO, T. 70/30: Melvil to Committee, dd. Cape Coast, 5 and 11 November 1753. See also Fynn, 1965, p. 27.

139 PRO, T. 70/30: Melvil to Committee, dd. 30 October 1754. General State Archives, The Hague, WIC 114: Despatch from Ulsen, dd. Elmina, 20 November 1758, enclosing the report of the missions of Dwumo and Andafo to Kumase, September 1754 to November 1758. The 2,000 oz of gold was distributed between the Asantehene and Asantehemaa, various Kumase functionaries including Bantamahene and the treasurer, and the Bekwae chiefs whose territories were proximate to those of the Wassa and others.

Kotoku and Aowin. Secondly, no opposition should be offered to the opening of the great-roads to the coast: Asante travellers should be allowed to obtain provisions on their journeys, and in the event of their incurring unpaid debts or committing actionable offences, the local authorities must refer such cases to Kumase. Thirdly, in the interests of maintaining a rule of law in the countries through which the roads ran, all criminals and outlaws should be sought out and arrested. And fourthly, the right to tribute would be waived.[140]

For reasons not of immediate concern here, the negotiations broke down. In consequence, the Asante government was obliged to plan a systematic military reoccupation of the recalcitrant territories. In 1764, faced with the threatened invasion, dissension occurred within the coalition:

The Warsaws, Dinkerahs, Akims and Tufferoes, who have been in league these many years to prevent the Ashantees from cutting them off separately have at last quarrel'd among themselves. Ousabody [Owusu Bore], King of Dinkirah, was suspected by his allies abovementioned of carrying on a Correspondence privately with the Ashantees and of having formed a Design of abandoning his own country in order to assist the Ashantees in destroying the other Nations in Alliance with them . . . The Ashantees now give out that they will join the Dinkerahs and then attack the Warsaws, Akims and Tufferoes, in which case they will in all probability become their Masters and consequently force a trade to the Waterside.[141]

By April 1765 it was reported that the Wassa, Twifo and Denkyira forces had left their countries and had assembled to the northeast of Cape Coast to meet the invading armies,[142] but in June the two former abandoned their ally.[143] The Asante thus met with little resistance in the reoccupation of Akyem Abuakwa. Amidst constant speculation that the government would then turn its arms against the southwest, the Fante entered into a new coalition with the Wassa and Twifo: 'To guard against the danger arising from the passage being now clear for the Ashantees to the Waterside by the Conquest of the Akims, the Fantees have entered into an Alliance, offensive and defensive, with the Warsaws and Tufferoes . . .' [144] But the policy of the Asante government at the time was first and foremost to secure the pacification of the Akyem Abuakwa. In the mid-1750s, in the course of the negotia-

---

140 Report of the missions of Dwumo and Andafo, General State Archives, The Hague, WIC 114.
141 PRO, T. 70/31: Mutter to Committee, dd. Cape Coast, 21 January 1765.
142 *Ibid.* Mutter to Committee, dd. Cape Coast, 25 April 1765.
143 *Ibid.* Mutter to Committee, dd. Cape Coast, 20 July 1765, who stated that the Wassa and Twifo retired to Hemang ('Ahiman') northwest of Cape Coast, according to report by permission of the Asantehene.
144 *Ibid.* Hippisley to Committee, dd. Cape Coast, 20 March 1766.

tions to which the Akyem Abuakwa were party, a direct road through their territory to Accra had been opened.[145] It remained hazardous, however, and probably fell into disuse with the failure of the negotiators to reach agreement. In 1766, in the aftermath of the military reoccupation, the government renewed its efforts to obtain agreed terms for the incorporation of the Akyem Abuakwa into Greater Asante, and the great-road to Accra – Route V – was finally opened in that year. 'Before I left Accra', reported the Africa Company Governor Petrie,

messengers from the King of Ashantee came down there on pretence of receiving pay of Arrears due to him for Ground Rent, but in Reality to receive the Subjection, or at least to make peace with, the residue of the Akim Nation, and the several other States inhabiting the Country between Accra and Ashantee, and thereby to open a communication with the Europeans by a more direct and a much shorter Road than that hitherto used by the Ashantees [i.e. Route V(a)] on account of the late power and opposition of their Enemies the Akims.[146]

Yet although the government had attained a limited objective in the south, Akyem resistance was by no means ended. In 1767 it was recorded,

The Residue of the Akim Nation made an attempt to escape from the Dominion of Ashantee, and take Sanctuary on the other side the River Volta, with Ashampoe, King of Popoe. The Shantees, soon after receiving advice of their Design, appeared in two Bodies, on each side of them; the one to hinder their escape by the route they had taken, and the other to Windward to prevent their junction with the Warsaws.

Thus out-manoeuvred, it was added, 'the wretched Akims . . . resolved to have recourse to the Clemency of the Conquerors, which the principal Men amongst them are now gone up to make trial of'.[147] Only six years later Obiri Koran led the Akyem Abuakwa into another revolt, and the central government was again obliged to despatch troops there to restore order.[148] Other risings, as will be seen below, were to follow.

The case of the Akyem Abuakwa was not unique. The fact of the matter was, that Asante was able to maintain its authority over the countries in its northern hinterland – Dagomba, Gyaman, Gonja and the others – with relative facility: each had independent links with the markets of the Western and Central Sudan and, by incorporation into

---

145 General State Archives, The Hague, KvG 115: letter from Woortman, dd. Apam, 20 July 1754; KvG 116: letter from Woortman dd. Apam, 3 June 1755. State Archives, Copenhagen, miscellaneous archives from Guinea, letterbook 1065: despatch from Jessen *et al.*, dd. Christiansborg, 16 August 1757.

146 PRO, T. 70/31: Petrie to Committee, dd. 13 September 1766.

147 *Ibid.* Petrie to Committee, dd. 20 August 1767.

148 *Ibid.* Mill to Committee, dd. 30 January 1773.

Greater Asante, might assume a profitable role in its import-export trade. Most of the communities along the coast between the Volta and Komoé Rivers, by virtue of their association with the trading forts and lodges of the European companies, might similarly benefit from the access to the markets of Greater Asante which came with incorporation into it. But for the several powerful and populous countries that lay across the hinterland of the Gold Coast, including most notably the Wassa, Twifo, Denkyira and Akyem Abuakwa, the advantages of incorporation into the imperial system were not so apparent. Themselves important centres of the extractive industry in gold, and in that way quite unlike the countries either of the northern hinterland or the southern littoral, political absorption into Greater Asante appeared so much more the likely to entail economic exploitation. Such control as the Asante government was able to achieve over these countries was obtained, therefore, at the expense of the continual and sometimes almost continuous application of the instruments of coercion. As one contemporary observer noted, in a plea to the Asantehene Osei Kwadwo for peace, 'that most Countries were destined for the possession of the Natives, and that Invaders, beside the constant fatigue of Body and Mind to keep possession were in the end generally drove out.' [149] In the nineteenth century political opinion in Asante became divided as to the desirability and indeed wisdom of attempting to retain control of territories so resistant to incorporation; and in circumstances that will be described later, the advocates of the novel view – that administrative control of certain of the southern provinces should be relinquished to the British who would thereby assume responsibility for keeping open the southern sections of the relevant great-roads – gained a majority for their policy.

Of the period of the earlier eighteenth century, Rømer had remarked that it took fourteen days to travel from Accra to the Akyem frontier, and a further eight or ten days to reach the main Aykem towns. Kumase presumably lay considerably over a month away. 'When our Accras travel inland', he added, 'to Akyem or Asante, they stay by the edges of small freshwater streams; for they were unable to penetrate through the bush, and one may well contemplate how many miles could be saved if only there were proper roads in Africa.' [150] It has been seen that in the later part of that century the Asante encountered much difficulty in opening roads, the more especially in the coastal hinterland. But that they did finally succeed in creating the great-roads system must, whatever its imperfections, be accounted a major achievement of both planning and execution.

149 *Ibid.* Hippisley to Committee, dd. 13 July 1766.
150 Rømer, 1760, ch. iv.

It will be taken as self-evident that if a given territory is within the field of control of a central government, then adequate channels must exist for the flow of information from the territory to the government and for the flow of instructions from the government to the territory. It will be postulated that the degree of political control exercised by the central government over the territory will be positively correlated with the rapidity with which information and instructions, that is, 'messages', can be transmitted between the two. The interval of time between the despatch of information from a territory to central government, and the receipt by that territory of the relevant instructions from government, will be referred to as 'message-delay'. There will, then, be an inverse relationship between message-delay and efficacy of control. Minimization of message-delay – the subject of this section – is therefore a necessary condition of effective government. But its sufficient conditions will include other such factors as the quality of the information reaching the central government, and the aptness of the decisions reached by it: components in the analysis which will be held constant for the present purpose, but treated in later sections.

A feature of the great-roads system of Asante, as seen above, was that outlying places were thought of as lying a fixed number of journeys from the capital: in the early nineteenth century, for example, Bonduku eleven, Gbuipe sixteen, Accra fifteen, Elmina thirteen. It was the opinion of Bowdich that an average journey in the forest region was equivalent to about 15 British miles, five of which were to be accounted for by the winding of the road. Dupuis gave the slightly higher figure of 16 miles, twelve of which were on the straight.[151] For savannah country, both Bowdich and Dupuis estimated the average journey at 20 miles, the former calculating the direct distance at $13\frac{1}{3}$ miles, the latter at 16.[152] Hutton argued that a traveller might in general expect to accomplish 14 miles on the straight 'without any extraordinary exertion'.[153]

That these estimates are reasonably accurate is shown from an examination of the actual (direct) mileages between appointed halting-places on the eight great-roads. Using the data presented on pp. 3–12, it is observable that while some journeys, where the terrain was particularly rugged, were ones of under three miles, others in open dry grassland were as high as 24 miles. The data are compiled in Figure 1,[154] which shows the percentage frequencies of all journeys in the ranges

151 Bowdich, 1819, p. 162; Dupuis, 1824, p. xix.
152 Bowdich, 1819, p. 200; Dupuis, 1824, p. xx.
153 Hutton, 1821, pp. 401–2.
154 It should be noted that there are factors producing distortions in the data: for example, the first journeys out of Kumase tended to be artificially low since it was common for both traders and couriers to depart from the capital late in

under 3 miles, 4–7 miles, 8–11 miles, etc. The tendency to constancy in the length of a journey, shown in both forest and savannah regions, reflects the attempts of those concerned with the development of the great-roads evenly to distribute the halting-places along the routes in so far as the nature of the terrain, and similar environmental factors, permitted. For the forest, the (arithmetical) mean distance of a journey was about 10½ miles, and for the savannah about 13⅓.

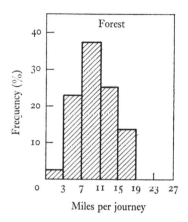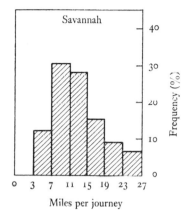

Fig. 1   Distances travelled per day, forest and savannah country

It was clearly the case in nineteenth century Asante that, in travelling between two distant places, the conventional number of journeys was usually exceeded. Days of travel were interspersed with days of rest of one sort or another: there were, for example, various 'bad days' (Twi, *dabone*) in the month, on which no journey was undertaken.[155] Large parties in general made less rapid progress than small: days, for instance, had to be set aside for securing provisions where supplies *en route* were likely to prove inadequate.[156] Traders in particular tended to travel slowly, especially when the carriers were heavily loaded. At the end of the century, for example, Ferguson noted that while 'an ordinary traveller' might cover 14 miles a day, 'the caravans travel slowly, indeed very slowly at times, not more than 8 or 10 miles being accomplished in the day'.[157] This had reference to the savannahs, and even slower progress might be made in forest country,

the day after having completed various formalities considered necessary: in the case of the couriers, final briefing by one of the king's officials.

[155] See, e.g. Hutton, 1821, p. 166: 'This being a fetish-day with our Ashantee guide, and it being unusual for the Ashantees to travel on those days, he declared he could not proceed until tomorrow.' The day was Friday, 11 February 1820: *Fiadafɔfie* in the Asante calendar.

[156] See, e.g. Bowdich, 1819, p. 17. Hutton, 1821, pp. 166–7.

[157] PRO, C. 879/38, African (West) 448: Ferguson's report dd. 1892, p. 58.

especially during the wet season: Dupuis for example met a small party of traders near the coast at Mouri (Route VI, branch), which had left Kumase twenty-one days earlier.[158] The problem was one of particular concern to the Asante governments since, certainly until the beginning of the nineteenth century, they were heavily dependent upon traders for information about the state of affairs in outlying provinces.

In 1816 Huydecoper showed clearly how the government relied for its intelligence about the policies of the Dutch in Elmina upon the traders who did business there. 'Merchants', commented the Asantehene, 'bring nothing but bad news and ill reports'; [159] and Huydecoper himself observed that 'all the time the Elminas are sending via the merchants messages to the King asking him for troops and stating that the [Dutch] General is hostile to the Asante but friendly to the Wassaw'.[160] In more general terms Dupuis noted that traders, on leaving Kumase, would be sworn not to divulge information about the situation there, but on returning would be required to give a full account of what they had observed. 'The oath draught', he pointed out,

is administered in all cases where the monarch's interests are concerned, and it was usual to compel the traders to take it during the Gaman war, that they might divulge nothing prejudicial to their sovereign, during their sojournment at the settlements. On their return to Coomassy, the oath was repeated under another obligation, viz. that they should report faithfully every political circumstance which came within the compass of their knowledge, binding themselves by the usual covenant of invocations and imprecations.[161]

An actual case of the administration of the Asantehene's oath in such circumstances was described by Huydecoper, when the penalty for transgression was death, commutable to a fine of 120 peredwans, or 270 oz of gold.[162]

The reliance upon traders for information, and conversely for the transmission of instructions from the central government to the local authorities, was clearly incompatible with efficient administrative control: message-delay was unduly high. There is evidence to show that this problem was one of considerable concern to the Asantehene Osei Bonsu in the second decade of the century. 'He who goes out on legitimate business', he exclaimed to Huydecoper, 'ought not to remain out long.' [163] A series of edicts was passed ensuring that com-

158 Dupuis, 1824, p. 5.
159 Huydecoper's Journal, entry for 5 September 1816.
160 *Ibid.* entry for 6 April 1817.
161 Dupuis, 1824, p. 211, note.
162 Huydecoper's Journal, entry for 29 November 1816.
163 *Ibid.* entry for 18 June 1816.

munications were increasingly carried by 'special messengers' or 'couriers', and establishing rules for their conduct in transit. Thus in 1816 Huydecoper found that despatches to Elmina given to ivory traders had been stopped: all such had to be sent by what he called 'express post' or 'express messengers'.[104] Similarly, a year later, it appeared that Asante resident commissioners in outlying areas had been instructed to refuse passage to traders who were carrying letters: 'the King', commented the commissioner at Dunkwa, 'expects that especial messengers will be engaged here [Cape Coast] to proceed with all letters to the capital'.[165] An edict of mid-1817 dealt with the provisioning of such messengers: 'All persons sent on the King's business shall no longer seize provisions in any country, whether tributary or otherwise, in his name; but requiring food, shall offer a fair price for the first they meet with, if this is refused, they shall then demand one meal, and one meal only, in the King's name, and proceed.' The penalty for infraction of the regulation was fixed at 110 peredwans, or almost 250 oz of gold.[166] It may, too, have been in this same period that regulations were made to ensure that messengers used only the great-roads, a matter to which Henty referred later in the century:

It appears that it is altogether opposed to Ashanti laws for any messenger to go to the king except along the high road. This custom, no doubt, had its origin with the object of preventing insurgents or suspected chiefs who had omitted to answer a summons of the king from averring that they had sent a messenger by some by-path, but that he must have been murdered on the way. No such casualty could occur on the main road, where villages are frequent, and where the passage of a messenger could be traced. Day by day, consequently, the custom or law became established that messengers bearing a letter to the king should travel only by the high or royal road.[167]

The British quite failed to share the Asantehene's enthusiasm for the reform of communications, and protested: 'the expense of employing messengers here on every occasion would be material, which is quite unnecessary, as opportunities almost daily occur for forwarding letters by the different traders going from hence'.[168]

Osei Bonsu's concern with the speed of communications was apparent also in his programme for the modernization of the great-roads. It has been noted that work was started on the reconstruction of Routes VI and VII late in 1816.[169] The project had been enthusiastically en-

---

[164] *Ibid.* entry for 11 August, 1816; see also under 19, 22, and 24 June 1816.
[165] Bowdich, 1819, p. 79.
[166] *Ibid.* pp. 255–6. See also Hutton, 1821, p. 204, for a supposed case of infraction.
[167] Henty, 1874, p. 166.
[168] Bowdich, 1819, p. 79.
[169] General State Archives, The Hague, KvG 349: Elmina Journal, 16 December 1816, reporting information from Adu Gyawu, son of the Bantamahene Amankwatia and later himself to hold that office.

dorsed by the Dutch Governor-General Daendels in a letter to the Asantehene:

You and your great men shall drive in comfortable coaches drawn by six horses along the roads which you, Sir, will have made, and which will convey you in the most comfortable manner from one part of your Kingdom to another, or you shall ride on beautiful horses like the Moors and Arabs . . . Your Generals will have the opportunity to exercise themselves in the arts of war, to which the new laid roads, on the making of maps of both your own country and that of your neighbours, will contribute so much, and you Sir shall thereby extend your boundaries as far as you shall wish . . .[170]

The roads were to be straightened, cut to a standard width of 30–40 feet, and all roots dug up to prevent regeneration.[171] Work on Route VI appears soon to have been discontinued, possibly as a result of worsening relations between Asante and the English, though in 1820 Osei Bonsu spoke of restarting it.[172] That on Route VII by contrast went ahead rapidly, and in April 1817 Huydecoper was able to travel along part of it. Of some advanced sections he noted, 'the highway is fairly good, despite the roots and tree-stumps that still remain'.[173] Other sections, however, had clearly overtaxed local resources. Between Eduabin (mile 10) and Asanso (mile 16), for example, Huydecoper noted that,

the highway has been partly cut through, though the stumps and roots are growing again fast. On the way we noticed three small and wretched villages, all of which had accepted gold and promised to prepare for the highway by cutting down trees and rooting out stumps, but the task has clearly been beyond them. The inhabitants consist mostly of old women.[174]

Two years later work had commenced on the reconstruction of Route I to Gyaman; for this, however, the Asantehene had decided to employ troops as a pioneer labour force.[175]

The renovated Route VII to Elmina appears to have been consid-

170 *Ibid.* KvG 349: draft letter from Daendels to Osei Bonsu dd. Elmina, 19 June 1816. Daendels proposed to have coaches built, and to train horses which the Asantehene would procure from the north, see KvG 349: Daendels to Huydecoper, dd. Elmina, 29 May 1816.
171 KvG 349: Huydecoper to Daendels, dd. Kumase, 22 June and 9 December 1816. It was anticipated that 5,000–6,000 men would work on Route VII.
172 Dupuis, 1824, p. xxx, note. The war party in the Asante government appears in general to have regarded the construction of major highways to the coast as a potential military hazard, see, e.g. Huydecoper's Journal, entry for 15 October 1816. Brun noted, however, that in various places large trees were left standing near the roadside, that might be felled in the event of invasion, see Gros, n.d., pp. 160–1; in this practice is to be found the origin, perhaps, of the famed Asante stockades, for which see, e.g. Biss, 1901, pp. 186–7; 222.
173 Huydecoper's Journal, entry for 25 April 1817.
174 *Ibid.* entry for 24 April 1817.
175 Dupuis, 1824, p. xxviii.

34

ered, by 1820, the fastest route to the coast by one day, or one day and two 'watches' (*nkwansimma*).[176] It was anticipated that the new road to Gyaman would shorten the time between Kumase and Bonduku by two journeys.[177] Such savings, however, resulted less from major reorientations of the routes,[178] as from the construction of well-defined roads that did not become, as Dupuis described it, 'shut up, from time to time, by fallen timber, swamps, and barriers of matted vegetation, cemented together by uncommon rains, tornados, or the sudden rush of torrents from the hills'.[179] Improved road maintenance was obviously an important concern to a government so involved in problems of communications, so that, as Dupuis added, 'sometimes it occurs that the most frequented tracks are reported by the last traveller to have become impassable, in which case it is usual for the government to employ men to remove the obstructions, or to cut a new opening in the parts adjacent, as may be effected most expeditiously'.[180] In fact, not surprisingly the organization for the maintenance of the roads, the *akwanmofo*, was one of the oldest of all the Asantehene's administrative agencies. According to Reindorf, it was Kusi Obodom (1750–64) who first 'ordered inspectors to be appointed for cleaning the roads and paths of the kingdom of nuisances'. His successor, Osei Kwadwo, created the office of *akwanmofohene*, 'chief inspector of the nuisances and path cleaners'. First to be appointed to it was Adabo, a son of Kusi Obodom who had been castrated for having intercourse with one of his father's wives.[181] He is perhaps to be identified with the 'old Assianthee Lieutenant Adiobing' who was in the Accra region in 1775–6 and was described as having been sent there 'in order to inspect the road' and as having been 'entrusted in the country's affairs with opening the roads from Assianthee'.[182] The badges of office of the *akwanmofo* were a gold sword and gold and silver whips. The

176 *Ibid.* p. xxxviii.
177 *Ibid.* p. xxviii.
178 Indeed, without adequate maps it is questionable whether such major reorientations could be achieved except by chance; the new Gyaman road, for example, following a more westerly course than its predecessor, could only have *added* to the total mileage.
179 Dupuis, 1824, p. xxix.
180 *Idem.* See also, for example, Bowdich, 1819, p. 29: 'the path had been cleared by the king's order'; and Winniet's Diary, 1848, concluding remarks: 'When assured of my intention to visit him, he [the Asantehene] sent orders for the cleaning of the Road from Kumasi to the Prah – a distance of about 100 m. that I might travel with greater ease.'
181 Reindorf, 2nd ed., n.d., pp. 131–2. In Reindorf, 1895, pp. 138–9, the official was described as 'chief surveyor of the nuisance and paths clearers'.
182 National Archives, Copenhagen, Guinea Company 1765–78: Fredensborg accounts book, entry for 31 December 1775, and Christiansborg accounts book, entry for 20 November 1776. I am indebted to R. Kea for drawing my attention to these references.

inspectors and their subordinates were authorized to make payments to those they employed in clearing the roads, and to fine those committing a nuisance; and the standard penalty was fixed at one *domafa* or about one-twentieth of an ounce of gold. The revenue which accrued was known as *nsumen*, 'sweeping money', and Reindorf reported that it might amount to as much as 3,000 peredwans, or 6,750 oz of gold, annually. One third of the money went to the Asantehene, and two-thirds to the *akwanmofo* and the Kontihene of Kumase under whose authority they had seemingly been placed.[183]

The improvement of communications: successes and failures

The results of Osei Bonsu's bid to improve communications, by the expansion of the messenger corps and the reconstruction of roads, are difficult to assess. In Yendi members of the special corps of messengers were reckoned able to cut the journey between that town and Salaga from the seven days taken by traders to four and sometimes three.[184] Certainly by 1816 and 1817 the special messengers were being formally instructed as part of their brief, and put on oath, to accomplish the journey to Cape Coast in nine days and to Elmina in nine or ten.[185] It is clear, however, that the messengers seldom did arrive at Cape Coast or Elmina in nine or ten days. Hutton indeed specifically commented that those despatched to Cape Coast 'consider it expeditious travelling if they perform the journey in twelve days': [186] that is, one day longer than the conventional time. Examination of a number of actual journeys in the period suggests that there was in fact considerable seasonal variation: in the dry season couriers travelled between Kumase and Cape Coast in twelve days or fewer,[187] and to Elmina in thirteen days or fewer,[188] but in the wet season the former journey might frequently take sixteen days or more,[189] and the latter upwards of seventeen or eighteen.[190] It was, however, as a result of a cultural

---

183 Reindorf, 2nd ed., n.d., p. 131.
184 Phyllis Ferguson, field-notes: interview with Imām al-Ḥājj 'Abdallāh, dd. Yendi, 29 January 1970.
185 Huydecoper's Journal, entry for 22 June 1816. Bowdich, 1819, p. 66.
186 Hutton, 1821, p. 489.
187 See, e.g. PRO, T. 70/41, letters from Smith to Hutchison dd. Cape Coast, 2 November 1817, and Hutchison to Smith dd. Kumase, 16 November 1817: letter written 2 November, despatch date unknown, received Kumase 15 November. *Ibid.* letters from Hutchison to Smith dd. Kumase, 29 December 1817, and Williams to Hutchison dd. Cape Coast, 9 January 1818: letter written 29 December, despatch date unknown, received Cape Coast on or before 9 January.
188 See, e.g. Huydecoper's Journal, 26 May 1816, and KvG 349, 7 June 1816: letter written Kumase 26 May, despatch date unknown, received Elmina 7 June.
189 See, e.g. Bowdich, 1819, p. 133: letter dd. Cape Coast, 25 August 1817, despatch date unknown, received Kumase 11 September.
190 See, e.g. KvG 349, 12 June 1816, and Huydecoper's Journal, 29 June 1816: letter despatched from Elmina 12 June, received Kumase 29 June. Huydecoper's

rather than climatic factor that couriers were often unable to arrive at their destination in the conventional number of days. In 1820 the Imām of Kumase maintained that less than half the days in the year were considered by the Asante as ideal for transacting business: council meetings would not be held on 'bad' days, for example, nor troop movements carried out.[191] 'I was told', observed Bowdich, 'that our month of September contained fewer bad days than any other, and was besides deemed auspicious to travelling . . . I have known Ashantees thirty days coming with dispatches from Cape Coast Castle to Coomassie, in August; and in September, to have arrived in twelve.'[192]

For the early nineteenth century there is one interesting limiting case of travel between Kumase and Cape Coast: in 1820 Hutton accomplished the whole journey in only six days, by leaving behind his carriers, by travelling by torchlight into the night, and by sleeping in the forest.[193] 'Master pass all men in the country for travel', declared those carriers who finally caught up with him at Dunkwa; 'no black man or white man before ever travel from Coomassie to Paintrey [Dunkwa] in five days'; and Asante travellers subsequently confirmed that no one had been known to accomplish the complete march to Cape Coast in six days.[194] It is clear, however, that most users of the great-roads, whether couriers or traders, had a marked antipathy toward travelling at night or sleeping in the forest, and indeed commonly endeavoured to arrive at an appointed halting-place by early afternoon, so avoiding moving in the hottest part of the day while allowing ample time to secure provisions and prepare accommodation well before nightfall. The seven 'watches' or *nkwansimma* which constituted one journey seem to have approximated closely to hours, and typically, the actual travelling time in a day might be from 7 to 11 a.m. and from 12 to 3 p.m.[195] The attempts by government in the early nineteenth century to reduce message-delay might seem, then, to have met with only limited success, in that improvements in the quality of the great-roads were not matched by any corresponding cultural adjustment by those who used them.

Osei Bonsu's policies in the field of communications were reactivated

Journal, 22–5 June 1816 and KvG 349, 11 July 1816: letter despatched from Kumase 25 June, received Elmina 11 July.

[191] Dupuis, 1824, p. 213, note.

[192] Bowdich, 1819, p. 266. For the *adaduanan* calendar of the Akan, see Rattray, 1923, pp. 114–15; Meyerowitz, 1951, ch. IX; and unpublished work by J. B. Danquah, '*Adaduanan*', n.d. but *ca.* 1960.

[193] Hutton, 1821, ch. XI.

[194] *Ibid.* pp. 299 and 402.

[195] This general observation is based on various marches described in the earlier nineteenth century literature. But see Dupuis, 1824, p. 54: 'we generally travelled as long as the day-light lasted, excepting the two or three last stages'. It will be appreciated, however, that at these latitudes nightfall occurs between 6 and 7 p.m.

by his successor once removed, the Asantehene Kwaku Dua I (1834–67), whose attitude toward the newer European modes of transportation is on record: 'The rapidity with which travelling is performed by rail-roads and steam-packets, very much interested and astonished him.' [196] In the years 1836–8 another major reconstruction of Route VII was in progress.[197] By 1839 the traveller on Route VI would notice in Assin the existence of permanent camps of road labourers: 'here and there a few huts occupied by Ashantis, whom the King sends to take care of the path'.[198] Most important, however, was the work started on the construction of bridges. Larger rivers were, of course, either forded in the dry season or crossed by canoe or line-and-raft ferries.[199] In the early nineteenth century smaller rivers were either waded, or were bridged by an unhewn tree: in both cases a rope handrail was usually stretched across the river to assist the traveller.[200] But in 1841 the large Anglo-Asante party conveying a four-wheeled carriage to Kumase found that the Asantehene Kwaku Dua had ordered proper bridges to be thrown across the streams in the metropolitan area. 'They are constructed', observed Freeman,

in the following manner: some stout, forked sticks or posts are driven in the centre of the stream, at convenient distances, across which are placed some strong beams, fastened to the posts with withes, from the numerous climbing-plants on every hand. On these bearers are placed long stout poles, which are covered with earth from four to six inches thick; and this completes the bridge.[201]

This was on a section of Route VI that became known, presumably from its superior character, as 'the king's road'.[202] By the middle of the nineteenth century it had become common to travel between Kumase and Cape Coast in as little as eight journeys, with perhaps one or two rest-days. Freeman twice accomplished this, in 1839 and 1841, as did for example Wharton in 1846.[203] In 1848 Governor Winniet made the northbound passage in comfort in eleven journeys and one rest-day, and the southbound in ten journeys flat.[204] A letter despatched from

196 T. B. Freeman, 1843, p. 132.
197 General State Archives, The Hague, KvG 518: report by Bartels dd. Elmina, April 1836; KvG 362: Elmina Journal, entry for 26 August 1837; KvG 772: letter from Huydecoper dd. Kumase, 13 September 1837; Archives of the Ministry of the Colonies, 1814–49: letter from Verveer *et al.*, dd. Elmina, 5 August 1838.
198 Freeman, 1843, p. 18.
199 See, e.g. Huydecoper's Journal, entry for 11 May 1816. Bowdich, 1819, p. 164.
200 See, e.g. Huydecoper's Journal, entry for 14 May 1816.
201 Freeman, 1843, p. 118.
202 Boyle, 1874, p. 290.
203 Freeman, 1843, pp. 62–7, 178–81. Moister, 1875, pp. 98–103.
204 Winniet's Diary, entries for 28 September to 9 October, and 26 October to 4 November 1848.

Kumase on 19 November 1841 was delivered at Praso (mile 62) early on the morning of the 22nd: thus halving the conventional travel time over this section of the route.[205] It is quite clear from an examination of these various itineraries that it was in fact in the metropolitan regions of Asante that the better travelling times were achieved. Nor apparently were the improvements confined to the most important routes. In 1869 for example it was possible for the missionary Ramseyer, travelling to Kumase from the east, to observe, 'as we approached Ashantee proper, we were struck by the increasing fertility and richness of the well-watered country. In the vicinity of every important place the roads were good, and sometimes for miles together, suitable for traffic.' [206]

Nevertheless, such improvements to the roads system notwithstanding, it remains true that in the half-century between 1820 and 1870 no real revolution in communications was achieved. In 1871 it was still accepted that 'a messenger cannot possibly travel [from Elmina] to Coomassie and back in three weeks',[207] and in 1872 twenty days was the regular time fixed for the couriers to travel from Kumase to Cape Coast and back.[208] Examination of the actual progress of the special messengers in this period shows that delays occurred for a number of apparently quite avoidable reasons. Indeed, it is arguable that the government of Asantehene Kofi Kakari (1867–74), dominated by the war interest, showed less concern with problems of communications than had its predecessors. Thus a party of messengers under Kotirko received for transmission to Cape Coast a number of letters written by the Asantehene, by the English agent Plange, and by Ramseyer and Bonnat, dated between 29 August and 5 September 1872. Kotirko, however, remained in Kumase for the celebration of the Akwasidae on 8 September and did not leave until the 9th, arriving in Cape Coast probably ten days later.[209] The next couriers for Cape Coast, under Owusu Koko Kuma, left Kumase on 24 September, carrying urgent despatches from the Asantehene to the British Governor. This party failed to arrive in Cape Coast until 13 October, and did not depart until 28 October. 'Your Majesty's envoys', commented the English Acting Administrator Salmon, 'were longer on the road than they should have been.' Elsewhere he noted, 'I cannot discover any cause for the

205 Freeman, 1843, p. 106.
206 Ramseyer and Kühne, 1875, p. 45.
207 Dutch Foreign Ministry, papers on the withdrawal from Guinea, Afstand IV, BZ/B79: report of a meeting at Elmina dd. 20 May 1871.
208 House of Commons, Return 266, *Gold Coast*, Part 1, 30 June 1873: p. 153, letter Plange to Governor dd. Kumase, 2 September 1872; p. 150, letter Asantehene to Governor, dd. Kumase, 24 September 1872.
209 *Ibid.* pp. 149–57: Hennessy to Kimberley, dd. Sierra Leone, 11 October 1872, enclosing various letters from Kumase.

delay, except the fact that they are here in the double capacity of traders and envoys'.[210] Whatever the reason for the departure on this occasion from the practice established in Osei Bonsu's reign, of not permitting traders to carry important mails, the government suffered a major diplomatic set-back as a result: runners despatched secretly by the agent Plange, carrying information of Asante intentions, arrived in Cape Coast more than a week before the official couriers.[211]

A courier entrusted with a verbal message had to be carefully in-structed in its contents until word-perfect.[212] A concern for accuracy of transmission, even if at the expense of speed, appears therefore to have led the Asante government to reject the introduction of a relay system such as that which operated in the neighbouring state of Dahomey.[213] In the nineteenth century, however, the Asantehenes came increasingly to conduct their correspondence in writing: in Dutch to Elmina, in English to Cape Coast, and in Arabic to the provincial rulers and imāms of the northern hinterland. By the 1810s the courier with his despatch box – sometimes 'a little Moroccan trunk' – had already become a familiar sight.[214] As the use of the written form in-creased, so the disadvantages in the introduction of a relay system diminished. Yet the government failed to innovate – and so for that matter did the local British authorities on the Gold Coast who, after 1831, had assumed responsibility for parts of the great-roads network. In 1862 R. J. Ghartey stated the case for action:

The only way to get the quickest communication is to set up posts or runners, for the purpose of conveying letters, and Messages at intervals, from the protectorate boundary to the coast, the intervening distance not exceeding 10 or 12 miles, from the station of one post to another, in the transposal of letters, and Messages, 'prevention is better than cure,' and shortest, the dis-tance quickest the reception, and oh! should this be put to practice forthwith, letters and Messages will reach to the coast on the second day, instead of three or four days journey from Prahsu [Route VI, mile 62], and it will bear some resemblance of a telegraph to us.[215]

But while the Asante government continued willing to initiate im-provements in the channels of communication, that is, the roads, it

---

210 *Ibid.* pp. 160–4: Hennessy to Kimberley, dd. Sierra Leone, 28 October 1872, en-closing various letter from Kumase and Cape Coast; also pp. 167–8: Hennessy to Kimberley, dd. Sierra Leone, 7 November 1872, enclosing letters from Cape Coast.
211 *Idem.* See also Ramseyer and Kühne, 1875, p. 184.
212 Compare, PRO, T. 70/31: Hippisley to Committee, dd. Cape Coast, 13 July 1766 – 'By frequent talking with my Messenger I have made him Master of the same sentiments, and as he is an intelligent Man I dare say will repeat them pretty justly.'
213 Herskovits, 1967, II, 34.
214 Bowdich, 1819, pp. 82; 94. Dupuis, 1824, Introduction, p. xx.
215 Ghartey, in Boyle, 1874, p. 398.

seems to have displayed an all but total inactivity in the matter of modernizing the agencies of communication – the corps of messengers. The one exception to this observation would seem to be the employment, in the reign of Kwaku Dua I, of mounted couriers at least in the metropolitan districts. Thus in 1841 Freeman noted the arrival at Kaase (Route VI, mile 4) of a party of messengers from the Asantehene, the chief of which 'rode on a strong Ashanti pony, with an Arabic or Moorish saddle and bridle'.[216] Clearly, however, the incidence of the tsetse-fly in the forest effectively ruled out the extensive use of the horse to speed communications.

It will be shown subsequently that from the reign of Mensa Bonsu onwards, the Asante government began to explore the possibilities of utilizing European capital and skills to create a railroad system in Asante. In the event, however, the next major revolution in communications in the region was to occur with the introduction by the British of the telegraph. Without it their gradual subjugation of Asante in the last quarter of the nineteenth century would unquestionably have been not only much slower but also more costly and sanguinary. The British administrators, who took over in the northern hinterland from their Asante predecessors at the turn of the century, immediately appreciated the extraordinary problems created by the absence of a telegraph service there: 'it is difficult to realise', observed Commissioner Watherston, 'what it means to have to deal with urgent matters when it takes 16 days for a message to come and 16 days for it to return'.[217] But the Asante themselves had had no difficulty in appreciating the critical importance, for purposes of political control, of the telegraph. Although the technical aspects of the invention were to elude them for some time, they fully recognized its 'magical' property of reducing message-delay to almost negligible dimensions. 'The Ashantis', wrote Ellis with reference to the British expedition of 1874,

thought that the telegraph-posts and wires, placed at the side of the Prah road, were some sort of fetish used by us to ensure success, and to counteract their hostile effect they raised an imitation of the telegraph, with sticks and string, north of the river Prah. Even now [1881] they deny that our success was owing to our superior prowess and weapons, but insist that it was solely due to our having employed some fetish more powerful than any they could invoke to their aid.[218]

In 1900 the Asante soldiers, though still lacking a telegraphic system of their own, were at least able to remove many miles of the British

216 T. B. Freeman, 1843, p. 122.
217 Watherston, 1908, p. 355.
218 Ellis, 1881, p. 76. Stanley, 1874, p. 165. Wolseley, 1903, II, 331.

wires – and found the material eminently suited to the manufacture of ramrods! [219] But it was not to be until 1903, seven years after British military occupation of Asante, that the first locomotive was to steam into Kumase.

[219] Biss, 1901, pp. 59–60.

CHAPTER 2

Spatial aspects of government: the structure of empire

Greater Asante and its regions

It will be apparent that there will be a certain critical value of message-delay such that below it effective political control is at least possible, but above it, impossible. One of the important factors determining the location in space of the frontiers of authority of a government will be, then, message-delay. In this section the attempt will be made to determine empirically the territorial extent of the Asante state, and to relate this to the condition of communications within it. Since Greater Asante [1] was at its fullest extent in the early nineteenth century, it is this period which will be of central concern. And since, as it has been argued, no changes in the modes of communication occurred throughout most of the nineteenth century (until, that is, the introduction of the telegraph), it will be assumed that the conventional measures of distance between the capital and outlying places, as enumerated above, reflect with sufficient accuracy the actual travelling times: that minimum message-delay, for example, between Kumase and Salaga (sixteen journeys) remained throughout the century of the order of thirty-two days, or between Kumase and Accra (fifteen journeys), thirty days.

One of the earliest references to the extent of Asante in the aftermath of the wars of expansion was that by the English trader and administrator Hippisley in 1764, who remarked, 'The Asiantes are the most numerous, powerful and wealthy people we know of in Guinea. How far they extend inland we have not been able to discover, but the breadth of their country is almost equal to that of the whole Gold Coast'.[2] Half a century later Huydecoper, then in Kumase, attempted to define its inland extent. 'Cong', he noted with reference to the northwestern Gonja division of that name, 'is 60 to 80 hours distant from here, and belongs to the King. The King's domains stretch for

---

1 This term was introduced in a paper by Arhin, 1967a, which presents a somewhat different analysis of the structure of Asante from that offered here.
2 Hippisley, 1764, p. 52.

iii   Bowdich's map of Greater Asante, early nineteenth century

about 400 hours. His villages are at least ten thousand in number, mostly acquired by war. This total of villages does not include those belonging to the King on the Accra and Appolonia sides.'[3] In 1817 Daendels estimated the size of Asante from Denkyira in the west to Akwamu in the east as 120–50 hours, and its northwards spread to Salaga and Bonduku ('the town of Gyaman') as about the same.[4] In such figures the 'hour' is presumably to be interpreted as the *kwan-simma*, that is, one-seventh of a day's journey.

The earliest attempt to delineate the frontiers of Greater Asante with accuracy was that by Bowdich, whose map published in 1819 showed what he described as the 'boundary of Ashantee authority' (Map iii).[5] Bowdich's method clearly was to question those familiar with the great-roads as to where each left Asante territory. Thus, for example, of the crossing of the Komoé at eighteen journeys on Route I, he remarked, 'I could not find any Ashantee who had travelled beyond

3   Huydecoper's Journal, entry for 18 August 1816. The figure of 400 hours is clearly intended as an estimate of distance round the perimeter, and seems to be based upon the treatment of the mean distance from Kumase to Kong – 70 hours – as a radius.
4   General State Archives, The Hague, KvG 350: Elmina Journal, entry for 22 January 1817.
5   Bowdich, 1819, frontispiece.

44

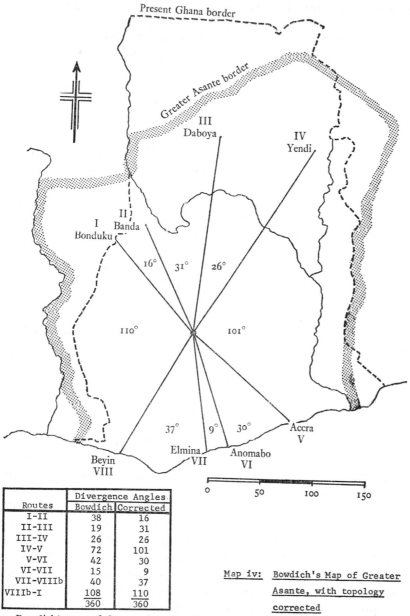

Routes	Divergence Angles	
	Bowdich	Corrected
I-II	38	16
II-III	19	31
III-IV	26	26
IV-V	72	101
V-VI	42	30
VI-VII	15	9
VII-VIIIb	40	37
VIIIb-I	108	110
	360	360

Map iv: Bowdich's Map of Greater Asante, with topology corrected

iv Bowdich's map of Greater Asante, with the topography corrected

this river, which is the northern limit of their authority'.[6] Map iv shows Greater Asante as depicted by Bowdich, but with the topography corrected by reference to the true angles of convergence of the eight

6 *Ibid.* pp. 181–2.

great-roads. The quality of Bowdich's information was such that for several decades observers were unable to improve upon it. In 1853, for example, Cruickshank – for all his eighteen years' residence on the Gold Coast – was content to remark of the territories between Assini and the Volta, that the rulers of Asante had, 'at one time or other, within the last hundred years, exercised dominion over, and received tribute from, all these countries, besides others extending inland to Kong'.[7] Indeed, the next systematic attempt to describe the extent of Greater Asante appears to have been that in the 1870s by Christaller, who by virtue of his close association with the intinerant preachers of the Gold Coast Christian community, may be regarded as having had a reasonably informed view of the matter.[8]

Christaller distinguished three categories into which the component parts of Greater Asante could be classified: first, that of 'the confederate provinces, which constitute Asante proper'; second, that of 'the subject provinces' defined as 'having Asante law and Asante rights'; and third, that of the 'tributary countries'.[9] Earlier nineteenth century writers had been not unaware of such distinctions, but had failed to state them so clearly. Thus, in 1819 for example, Robertson, trader and briefly Acting Vice-consul for Asante, had contrasted such provinces as Denkyira, 'annexed to Ashantee Proper . . . under its immediate government', with others such as Amanahia, which merely paid tribute 'as an acknowledgement of dependency' and in recognition of the Asantehene's 'right of sovereignty'.[10] Dupuis likewise distinguished between the class of 'tributaries' and that of 'subjects', or, in other terms, between 'tributary rank' and 'annexation . . . to Ashantee as a province'.[11] Here, in order to avoid at this stage subscription to any particular view of the nature of the relationships between Kumase and its dependent territories, a threefold distinction will be made between metropolitan region, inner provinces, and outer provinces. In the use of the qualifiers 'metropolitan', 'inner' and 'outer', only political distance is necessarily implied: that is, the inner provinces will be the more closely, and the outer provinces the less closely, associated with the metropolitan region. The extent to which political distance is correlated with spatial distance will remain a matter for empirical determination – though there is clearly a presumption that the inner provinces will be located between the metropolitan region and the outer provinces. Together, the metropolitan region and the inner and

7 Cruickshank, 1853, I, 44–5.
8 Christaller, 1875, pp. xii–xiv. See also Christaller, 1881, pp. 644–9, which included additional data but was less reliable: the author's views having been to some extent adjusted to the prevailing British misconceptions of the structure of Asante.
9 Christaller, 1875, pp. xii–xiv.
10 G. A. Robertson, 1819, pp. 77, 104–5 and 125.
11 Dupuis, 1824, pp. 233, 263–4, xxxix.

outer provinces will be regarded as comprising Greater Asante. To the three categories should be added a fourth: that of the adjunct territories which, while beyond the political frontiers of Greater Asante, were nevertheless in some sense within the imperial ambit.

The structure of the metropolitan region

There is a reasonable measure of agreement in nineteenth century accounts of the structure of the metropolitan region of Asante. In 1817 Bowdich obtained estimates of its manpower resources, which he listed under the various component districts, namely, Kumase itself; the five major *aman* or polities of Dwaben, Mampon, Nsuta, Kokofu and Bekwae; and the lesser districts and towns of Eduabin, Effiduase, Denyase, Kuntanase, Gyamase and Amoafo.[12] The missionary T. B. Freeman, who visited Kumase on a number of occasions during the reign of Kwaku Dua I, included Adanse, Kwawu and Nkoransa within the metropolitan region, of which he remarked:

Asantee proper, is divided into provinces or districts, as follows: –
1st Coomassie, and its dependent towns and villages, and the smaller districts on the frontier, such as Adansee on the southern frontier and Quawoo, on the borders of Eastern Akim. 2nd. The larger provinces, governed by subordinate Kings, or great Chiefs, namely Juabin, Baquay, Cucoofoo, Mampon and Quaransah.[13]

In 1875 Christaller listed the constituent territories of 'Asante proper' by geographical rather than political units: Atwoma, with the capital Kumase; Sekyere, with the two capitals of Dwaben and Mampon; Kokofu, with the capital of the same name; Amansie, capital Bekwae; Kwabre, capital Mamponten; Nsuta, capital Nsuta; and Adanse, capital Fomena.[14] In 1881 Christaller produced a more exhaustive list in which he named not only many of the smaller towns and districts – Kumawu, Agona, Asumegya, Eduabin, Amoafo, Manso, Gyamase and so forth – but also included within 'Asante proper' a number of more distant places: the Ahafo region in the west, and Berekum and apparently Domaa Ahenkro in the northwest.[15]

It will be appreciated that the concept of 'Asante proper', as used by such writers as Freeman and Christaller, was a complex one. Within it was included not only the home country inhabited by the Asante in the pre-imperial period, but also those acquired territories the incorporation of which into the Asante system was far advanced. It will follow, then, that a certain indeterminacy may exist as to just which

12 Bowdich, 1819, p. 316.
13 *The Western Echo*, I, no. 12, 17 March 1886, p. 8.
14 Christaller, 1875, pp. xii–xiii.
15 Christaller, 1881, pp. 644–5.

territories were to be accounted within the metropolitan region. While Freeman had included Kwawu and Nkoransa within it, Christaller had by contrast classified both as 'subject provinces', into which category, in 1875, he had also placed Ahafo. Nevertheless, the metropolitan region did possess a distinct identity within Greater Asante, and its boundary was a bureaucratically maintained one: that is, officials of the central government – the *nkwansrafo* or highway-police [16] – were stationed at the various points where the great-roads crossed it. The function of the *nkwansrafo* as agents of general political control was remarked on by many writers. 'It is the practice', commented Dupuis in 1824, 'to arrest all strangers upon the confines, and conduct them to court, where the *palaver* is discussed . . .' [17] Half a century later Bonnat observed,

The great roads which lead there [to Kumase] are guarded by the Nquam-Sarafs or wardens, who question the stranger when he presents himself, and send one of their number to inform the king of the stranger's arrival and of the purpose of his journey. Meanwhile another warden leads the traveller to the nearest village, where he awaits the royal authorization allowing him to continue his journey to the capital.[18]

Rattray, citing evidence likewise relevant to the later nineteenth century, showed that the *nkwansrafo* were also responsible for the collection of tolls (*akwanne*): 'The King of Ashanti had all the roads guarded and all traders were detained until inquiries had been made about them, when they were allowed to pass, on payment of 3s. to 4s. worth of gold-dust'.[19] Evasion of the control posts – often for purposes of smuggling or otherwise subverting the trade regulations – was an actionable offence. Around 1840, for example, when Fante traders were permitted to operate within the metropolitan region but not beyond, it was reported that a number 'sometimes penetrate beyond the interior boundary of Ashantee proper, and press onwards towards the open plains of the far interior, where they are generally arrested by order of the viceroy-chiefs of Ashantee, and sent back as prisoners to Coomassie'.[20]

It is possible to identify a number of the places on the metropolitan boundary at which control posts were maintained. The great-road IV to Salaga and Yendi passed out of the metropolitan region at Adwira (mile 59), the town of the Adontenhene of Mampon, of which Lonsdale remarked in 1881: 'Stationed at this town are three of the Coomassie or

16 Twi ɛkwan, 'road', and sra, 'to guard'. But note also sra, 'to reconnoitre', hence in a miltary sense, nkwansrafo, 'scouts'.
17 Dupuis, 1824, p. cix.
18 Gros, 1884, p. 178.
19 Rattray, 1929, p. 111.
20 T. B. Freeman, in *The Western Echo*, I, no. 10, 24 February 1886, p. 8.

King's officials, as there appears to be at all border towns of Ashanti. It is the duty of these men to keep a careful watch on the border, and an eye on the Ashantis living on it; to report all things to the King.' [21] On Route V(b) the *nkwansrafo* were stationed at Asokore (mile 23), which Ramseyer and Kühne, in 1869, described as 'a custom-house station of Ashantee proper, where it is necessary, for all travellers from the interior, to obtain official permission before proceeding further'.[22] On Route VI the control post was at Kwisa (mile 32). Huydecoper was detained there for several days in 1816, awaiting orders 'from the King about how we are to proceed'.[23] In 1839 Freeman was likewise halted there, and obliged to stay in the nearby Adanse capital of Fomena for some six weeks until those he described as the 'King's path-keepers' in Kwisa had obtained permission from Kumase for him to continue his journey.[24] The Adansehene, who clearly cooperated closely with the *nkwansrafo* at Kwisa, was himself referred to in the 1870s as 'the custom-house officer'.[25] But the *nkwansrafo* were directly responsible to the central government, and not to the local authority. Thus in 1862 Ghartey wrote of Kwisa, 'this is the first town of Ashantee proper . . . here resides the Officers of His Majesty who take guard of this main road toward the coast'.[26] Kwisa had in fact become a post of particular importance after the conclusion of the Anglo-Asante treaty of 1831, when it served as the principal point of entry for Fante traders wishing to do business in the metropolitan region.[27] It is some measure of the importance it retained, that in 1862 between five and six hundred armed patrolmen were reported as attached to the control post, being responsible for policing the great-road as far south as Apegya (mile 58).[28] During the British invasion of Asante in 1874 the commander of the scouts, Lord Gifford, mistook the *nkwansrafo* for combat troops, and was greatly puzzled when they refused to fight without first obtaining the Asantehene's permission. 'A dialogue', it was reported,

of the Homeric fashion had been exchanged between Lord Gifford's scouts and the 'Captain's guard' stationed here to protect traders. The Ashantees met our scouts fearlessly, lifting the butt-ends of their guns, and asked what

21 *Further Correspondence*, C. 3386, p. 68. See also Rattray, 1929, pp. 110–11, who reported the existence of another post on Route IV at Atebubu (mile 99), which, it must be assumed, was in some way responsible for traffic on Route IV(a) which branched off at this point.

22 Ramseyer and Kühne, 1875, p. 51.

23 Huydecoper's Journal, entries for 15–17 May 1816.

24 T. B. Freeman, 1843, pp. 18, 37.

25 Ramseyer and Kühne, 1875, p. 297.

26 See Boyle, 1874, pp. 406–7.

27 Freeman, in *The Western Echo*, I, no. 10, 24 February 1886, p. 8.

28 Ghartey, in Boyle, 1874, p. 407.

they wanted. 'To fight!' replied Lord Gifford. 'Impossible!' exclaimed the enemy, 'we have no palaver with white men!' 'Are you going to fight or not?' asked Lord Gifford. 'My king has sent me here for that purpose. What has your king sent you for?' 'Not to fight white men. We must go and ask him.' 'Be quick then,' our scout master answered, 'for I shall attack you in the morning.' [29]

Identification of the location of the metropolitan boundary control posts on the other great-roads is more conjectural, and further investigation is necessary. That on Route VIII was apparently located near Domi-Keniago (mile 45), where, according to the traditions of that stool, local groups were commissioned as *nkwansrafo* in the eighteenth century – 'to be resident Bodyguard-Chiefs of the Asantehene at the Ashanti/Denkyira border'.[30] On the great-roads to Accra via the Akyem countries – Route V and its alternate – Bowdich named 'Feea', at three journeys from Kumase, as a 'frontier town', and 'Obirribee', at four journeys, as the first Akyem town.[31] On Route V(a) he described Obogo (mile 38) as the 'frontier Quaoo town',[32] and on Route VII 'Abatea' (reached on the fourth day and clearly occupying a position in the Adanse Hills similar to that of Kwisa some eight miles to the east) as 'the frontier town of Dankara'.[33] The implication is that the control posts were located at or near these places, and in the case of Obogo some confirmation is to be found: the Obogohene customarily held an appointment from Asantehene as Mponnuahene, boundary chief.[34] No firm evidence is available, unfortunately, on the position of the control posts on Routes II and III: the probability is, however, that these were located – at least in the later nineteenth century – at Akumadan (mile 56) and Sekyedumase (mile 46) respectively.[35] Reference to Map v (p. 62) will show the general configuration of the metropolitan region as reconstructed from the distribution of the *nkwansrafo* posts.

Although a number of control posts like that at Kwisa were continuously in operation from at least the early nineteenth century onwards, suggesting an absence of boundary changes in such areas, it should not be assumed that the situation was everywhere so stable. Nkoransa, for example, must be regarded on balance as having for most of the nineteenth century the status of an inner province, yet in the 1840

29 Boyle, 1874, p. 285.
30 Institute of African Studies, University of Ghana, IASAS/150: Domi-Keniago stool history, recorded by J. Agyeman-Duah, 24 February 1965.
31 Bowdich, 1819, pp. 163, 482.
32 *Ibid.* p. 482, and see also p. 163.
33 *Ibid.* p. 482.
34 IASAS/55: Obogo stool history, recorded by J. Agyeman-Duah, 5 February 1963.
35 This observation is based solely upon conversations with informants at Akumadan, a number of whom agreed in suggesting these locations.

period its incorporation into the metropolitan system had seemed sufficiently advanced for Freeman to regard it as within that region. It was, however, to both west and east of Kumase, where the new districts of Ahafo and Asante-Akyem were being created, that the situation was the most fluid. The Ahafo district, lying across Route I(b) and on either side of the Tano River, was overrun by Asante forces early in the eighteenth century. Osei Tutu subdued, so Dupuis recorded, 'a great extent of country beyond the Tando [Tano] river',[36] and in so far as the evidence suggests that its thinly populated forests may earlier have been claimed by the Aowin, the occupation perhaps occurred after that people's submission to Asante in 1715. Systematic colonization of Ahafo became the policy of successive Asante governments, and ultimately twenty-eight stools were created there, each of which was made the responsibility of one or other of the senior Kumase functionaries.[37] It has been seen that whereas in 1875 Christaller had classed Ahafo as an inner ('subject') province, in 1881 he had included not only it, but also the Berekum and (Domaa) Ahenkro districts immediately to its north, as within 'Asante proper'. The Ahafo question has in fact continued to be an acute political one to the present time, as sections of the colonists have attempted, with varying success, to unify the twenty-eight stools into a distinct Ahafo polity.[38] To the east, in the country traversed by Routes V and V(b) and lying between the Anum and the Pra Rivers, the situation was in some respects similar. There lands belonging to the Akyem Kotoku and Akyem Abuakwa had been finally alienated from them in the early nineteenth century, and were in process of incorporation into the metropolitan region as the Asante-Akyem district. The southernmost area including Banka, Amentia and Muronaim was awarded to the Kokofu for colonization, reputedly by the Asantehene Kwaku Dua I who ordered the building of those towns. An area around Odumase had been colonized by the Dwaben, probably somewhat earlier. Finally other villages were placed under such places as Obogo, Bompata and Agogo, all directly responsible to Kumase.[39]

36 Dupuis, 1824, p. 230.
37 National Archives of Ghana, Kumase, File D.104: Report on Ahafo lands, by F. Fuller, dd. Sunyani, 11 September 1934.
38 The British colonial administrators recognized Ahafo as a paramountcy under Kukuomhene after 1896, but in 1935 it was included within the new Asante 'Confederacy'. In 1958 the Nkrumah government removed Ahafo into the Brong-Ahafo Region, but in 1966 the military government abolished the paramountcy and effected a return to the pre-1896 position. For a useful account of the changes, see A. F. Robertson, 1973, *passim*. See also Tordoff, 1959, *passim*; 1965, pp. 88–90, 162–4, 409–10.
39 National Archives of Ghana, Kumase, File D.46: Governor Nathan to Akyem Kotokuhene, dd. Accra, 23 January 1902, with Précis of Akyem Claims to

Spatial aspects of government: the structure of empire

From the inception of the Asante nation it appears to have been the policy of its rulers to encourage immigration into, and settlement within, the metropolitan region, thereby ensuring the dynamic density of its population *vis-à-vis* that of surrounding territories as measured by the availability of surplus manpower for military, administrative and other purposes. But though the population originally grew, agricultural technology remained by and large unchanged, with a result that acute food shortages from time to time occurred as, for example, when a considerable part of the rural population had to be mobilized for military service. In the early nineteenth century Bowdich was led to comment: 'the extent and order of the Ashantee plantations surprised us, yet I do not think they were adequate to the population: in a military government they were not likely to be so'.[40] Hence he observed further, the policy of the government was to make use of unfree subjects 'to create plantations in the more remote and stubborn tracts; from which their labour was first to produce a proportionate supply to the household of their Chief, and afterwards an existence for themselves'.[41] By the colonization of the newly created extensions of the metropolitan region, such as Ahafo and Asante-Akyem, new land was brought into cultivation, and production organized to meet the requirements of the metropolitan markets.

Inner and outer provinces

The metropolitan region of Asante constituted a recognizable geopolitical unit, the boundaries of which were administratively maintained through the agency of the *nkwansrafo*. Assuming the provinces to have similar structural characteristics, identification of the inner ones should in principle be possible by the determination of the course of the boundary which separated them from the outer ones; and of the outer ones, by the determination of the course of the frontier of Greater Asante. In practice, considerable problems present themselves. In the early nineteenth century Robertson had observed that 'the extent of the Empire of Ashantee is great, though imperfectly known to Europeans'. He correctly saw, however, that the area of doubt was a result not simply of ignorance, but of a fundamental indeterminacy in the system of political control exercised over the outlying provinces:

even to the Ashantee government it [the frontier] must be ill-defined: for where there are no archives, or records of any kind, and the communications

Asante-Akyem. NAG, Accra, ADM. 11/3: Davidson-Houston to Chief Commissioner, dd. Kwisa, 7 January 1903 and dd. Kumase, 1 April 1903.
40 Bowdich, 1819, p. 325. Compare Dupuis, 1824, p. 164.
41 Bowdich, 1821b, p. 18.

are merely made by those who levy the tribute of the different states not immediately under its dominion, no certainty can be attained from them, of either geography or population.[42]

Robertson – many of whose observations were made on the basis of conversations with a prominent Asante trader, Adu Gyese – offered some further analysis of the indeterminacy by reference to the Akan view of the nature of political allegiance:

. . . they have no territorial boundaries which are accurately defined; they claim that as a part of their states, where people who have sought their protection, reside: but as this protection is frequently changed by the inhabitants of villages placing themselves under the protection of others, when they have reason to conceive that they are oppressed, such limits are very imperfect and varying.[43]

One of the variables in the situation has already been isolated: that is, the failure of the central government to formulate terms of incorporation fully acceptable to the peoples of the belt of states lying across the hinterland of the Gold Coast. A second variable was a function more of external factors. Although the military strength of Asante made it virtually immune to invasion from outside (until the British finally achieved this in the late nineteenth century), nevertheless foreign powers made attempts from time to time to subvert the authority of the central government in the provinces, and to encourage in them secessionist movements. In the 1760s the principal threat had been presented by the rulers of Dahomey and their overlords the *alafins* of Oyo, who had supported a revolt which had spread through the easterly territories of Akyem, Kwawu and Bron.[44] In the first three decades of the nineteenth century it was the British who sought systematically to foster secessionist sentiment throughout the southern provinces of Asante, and it will be seen later that their efforts met with qualified success when the Anglo-Asante treaty of 1831 was ratified. In the last three decades of the century the British were to launch a similar but more ambitious operation within the Asante northern provinces.

Despite the changing status of various provinces, it is possible nevertheless to determine with reasonable accuracy the extent of Greater

---

[42] G. A. Robertson, 1819, p. 177.

[43] *Ibid.* pp. 124–5. For Adu Gyese ('Adoo Ghessé') see, for example, pp. 89, 122–3, 181. He was probably the Gyese who was a revenue collector; who was in disgrace in 1817, see Huydecoper's Journal, entry for 8 January 1817; and who incurred the Asantehene's displeasure again in 1821 when he was recalled from Elmina, see General State Archives, The Hague, KvG 351: Elmina Journal, entries for 16, 17 and 18 February 1821.

[44] PRO, CO. 388/52: Mutter to Committee, dd. Cape Coast, 27 May 1764. Dupuis, 1824, pp. 237–9.

Asante at certain fixed points in time. Thus both Bowdich and Dupuis showed a high measure of agreement about its composition in the second decade of the nineteenth century, though neither was able to distinguish methodically between inner and outer provinces. Bowdich referred to twenty-one 'tributaries' which regularly provided the central government with troops, but on his map of Greater Asante (Map iii) showed, in all, twenty-six provinces.[45] Dupuis made reference to the forty-seven 'tribes and nations' which, so the Kumase Muslims informed him, constituted Greater Asante: the figure included the districts of the metropolitan region and twenty-nine provinces, whether tributary or otherwise.[46] Of the twenty-six provinces named by Bowdich, and twenty-nine by Dupuis, twenty-two are clearly identical: the septentrional provinces of Banda, Bron ('Booroom'), Gonja ('Nta'), Gyaman, Nkoransa, Nsoko and Takyiman; the meridional provinces of Accra, Adangme, Ahanta, Akuapem, Akwamu, Akyem, Amanahia, Aowin, Assin, Denkyira, Fante, Twifo and Wassa; the east-central province of Kwawu; and the west-central province of Sehwi. To these Bowdich added Dagomba, which Dupuis incorrectly had maintained was 'no part of the empire'; [47] 'Gamba', that is, Mamprussi, which was no more than an adjunct territory; 'Moinsan', that, is, Bonzina, which had been subjugated reportedly during the reign of Osei Kwadwo;[48] and 'Guasoo', apparently the country of the Adele and Ntribu to the west of Kete Krakye. Dupuis' list was extended by the inclusion of Sekyedumase, Adwira and 'Akeya', all parts rather of the metropolitan region; of Gbuipe, a part of Gonja; of 'Yobati' and 'Baboso' lying either side of the Pru river south of its confluence with the Volta; and of 'Toosequa', lying north of Sehwi and perhaps identical with Bonzina.

While the boundary between inner and outer provinces cannot be determined with great accuracy, sufficient evidence is extant to show that, like that of the metropolitan region, it was an administratively maintained one. On Route II a control post was located, certainly in the early nineteenth century, at Banda (mile 145), where the Tatar Wargee remarked that 'he was stopped by an Ashantee chief, who

45 Bowdich, 1819, p. 317, and map facing title-page.
46 Dupuis, 1824, p. 236, and see pp. xxvi–xxvii for the principal list, and pp. 224–35 and xxxix for additions.
47 *Ibid.* p. xxxix.
48 Bowdich, 1819, p. 237. I am indebted to Dr. P. A. Roberts, of Newnham College, Cambridge, for information on Bonzina obtained in an interview with Nana Yao Ntaadu III and elders, 21 September 1969. Although by the later nineteenth century Bonzina had been incorporated into Sehwi Wiawso as its Kronti division, it was itself an Aowin state, and earlier in the century the Asantehene Kwaku Dua I had been obliged to intervene to prevent the Bonzina and Sehwi fighting each other.

told him he would not allow him to advance until he had sent to consult the king'.[49] On Route III a later nineteenth century source indicated that a control post was operative at Dawadawa (mile 130), where the Asantehene was reported to levy transit tolls on the cara vans.[50] On Route IV Dupuis named 'Yansala' and 'Coobcya' as 'north-east frontier towns':[51] since the Dagomba-Gonja border ran between Nienseli (mile 213) and Kpabia (mile 227), it seems clear that his informants regarded the great-road as entering the outer provinces at that point. On Route IV(a) an *nkwansrafo* station was located at Ahenkro (mile 175), of which Lonsdale commented in 1882:

This is a town established by the Ashantis during the period of their dominion, and here were stationed certain of the King's officials whose duty it was to prevent or control the passage of arms and ammunition. Nothing from the coast of this nature was permitted to pass beyond this town unless the Ashantis permitted it.[52]

The existence of a similar station was reported as early as 1786 at Mamfe, through which the great-road to Accra then ran. There, it was observed, 'an officer of the King of Asante is stationed, who holds the post of collector of the tolls which the black slave traders are obliged to pay. He is located at this place because all the roads leading to the sea-coast from Asante and Akyem meet here.'[53] Finally, on Route V(a), Edzebeni (mile 130) was described in the later nineteenth century as the 'frontier post . . . beyond which no strangers are allowed to pass',[54] and on Route VI Bowdich noted the presence of a customs post, where traders were taxed, near Ansa (mile 48).[55] The inner provinces, then, constituted a recognizable unit within Greater Asante in so far as a boundary was maintained between them and both metropolitan region and outer provinces. The real area of indeterminacy in the system related, therefore, to the peripheral territories; for the central government appears not to have attempted to establish control posts at those points on the frontier where the great-roads linked with ongoing routes, whether maritime or land ones, and in so far as the outer border was in any way policed, it was presumably a responsibility of the local authorities in each area.

49 *The Royal Gold Coast Gazette,* 31 December 1822 and 7 January 1823. See also Wilks, 1967b, p. 188.
50 Kling, cited in Johnson, 1965, p. 34.
51 Dupuis, 1824, p. xxxix.
52 *Further Correspondence,* C. 3386, 1882, p. 79.
53 Isert, 1788, p. 276. Mamfe lay about 8 miles east of Adawso (Route V, mile 126).
54 *Further Papers relating to the Ashantee Invasion,* no. 1, C. 890, 1874: memoir by De Ruvignes, dd. 28 May 1873, references to 'Durbin' or 'Dwebin'. According to Wallis, 1953, p. 23, Edzebeni was founded only about 1850, but its importance is reflected in its control over sixteen villages.
55 Bowdich, 1819, p. 320.

In the southwest the frontier of Greater Asante was located along the lower Tano ('Assinee') River by Bowdich,[56] and at Cape Lahu by Dupuis.[57] Robertson's cartographical skills unfortunately failed to match those of either Bowdich or Dupuis: he identified Nsoko (Route II, mile 110) with Segu on the Middle Niger, and in consequence regarded Asante territory as extending north of that river! Nevertheless, much of the evidence which Robertson recorded but misinterpreted was sound. Thus Robertson, in agreement with Dupuis, reported the 'prevalent opinion, that Cape Lahoo pays tribute to Ashantee, and is, in fact, part of that empire', and added the interesting detail that at the time of the Asante invasion of Fante country in 1807, troops were moving through the Cape Lahu district to join the main army.[58] It was Robertson's further opinion that districts even to the west of Cape Lahu – Fresco, Cape Palmas, and Cape Mount – were tributary to Asante.[59] Despite, however, the amount of circumstantial detail supplied by Robertson, it is better to err on the side of caution by regarding any country to the West of Cape Lahu as at most an adjunct territory. In the northwest Bowdich's reference to the frontier on the Komoé River between Bonduku and Kong provides a fixed point in that quarter corresponding to that of Cape Lahu on the coast.[60] Between these two points the frontier appears to have followed for much of its course the Komoé River, to include within Greater Asante the country of the Ndenye. In 1819 Robertson referred to 'Abocro', that is, Abengourou some fifty miles west of Bonzina – Route I(b), mile 120 – as having been 'partially destroyed by order of the King of Ashantee'.[61] Abengourou and the other Ndenye towns were in fact generally acknowledged to be provinces of Asante throughout most of the nineteenth century; as late as 1894 the Asantehene Agyeman Prempe sent troops there to aid the Ndenyehene Kwasi Dehye in his struggle with the French, and subsequently received the provincial ruler in Kumase.[62]

To the east similar problems are involved in the identification of the Asante frontier. Robertson was clearly in error in maintaining that the whole coastal region between the Volta River and Lagos was

56 *Ibid.* map facing title-page.
57 Dupuis, 1824, p. xli.
58 G. A. Robertson, 1819, pp. 88–9, 178.
59 *Ibid.* pp. 29–30, 65–6, 77, 177–8. See also Reindorf, 2nd ed., n.d., p. 132: 'the terror of [Asantehene Osei] Kwadwo was felt beyond Cape Palmas'.
60 Bowdich, 1819, p. 182.
61 Robertson, 1819, pp. 109–10.
62 For a useful account of the provincial status of the Ndenye, see Forlacroix, 1969, *passim.* See also Perrot, 1970, pp. 1672–3. Relations between Kumase and the Ndenye were mediated by the Sehwi Wiawsohene.

'subject and tributary to Ashantee', though he himself qualified the observation by adding that the local chiefs 'in most cases, exercise absolute authority over the inhabitants without controul'.[63] Bowdich, on the other hand, was equally clearly in error in excluding from Asante the trans-Volta region of 'Kerrapay', that is, the Ewe country, with its southernmost component, Anlo ('Agwoona').[64] The matter of the Asante presence east of the Volta has been discussed recently by Kea and Johnson. Anlo, long associated with Asante by virtue of its close links with the old province of Akwamu, appears to have accepted a closer relationship in 1792, when envoys from there visited Kumase.[65] Certainly by 1811 the central government could require military assistance from the Anlo.[66] M'Leod, whose evidence related to the early years of the century, remarked that 'Little Popoe, being a frontier town of Creppee, is protected by the king of Ashantee'.[67] Kea has shown how old-standing rivalries between Anlo and Little Popo – or Anecho, some seventy miles east of the mouth of the Volta – diminished with the growth of Asante influence in the area.[68]

To the north of Little Popo, the town of Nuatja was regarded by Robertson as tributary to Dahomey,[69] while the Agu district some thirty miles to its west was within Greater Asante: it is probably the 'Nagho' referred to by Dupuis as 'a capital town now subject to the dominion of Ashantee',[70] and the 'Aja, a mountain in Krepi' mentioned as late as the 1870s as the administrative responsibility of the Nsumankwaahene of Kumase.[71] The means by which the Akwamu province extended and maintained Asante authority in the Agu region have been documented by Kea.[72] Continuing north from Agu, Atakpame appears to have existed for much of the nineteenth century in a sort of neutral zone between Asante and Dahomey,[73] though this did

63 G. A. Robertson, 1819, p. 231 and see also pp. 236–7.
64 Bowdich, 1819, map facing title-page; Bowdich, 1821c, p. 62. It would seem that Bowdich's ambitious plan for a British mission to Dagomba via the Volta, see 1819, pp. 453–8, was incompatible with his acknowledging that Asante authority extended east of that river.
65 Kea, 1969, pp. 45–6.
66 *Ibid.* p. 51.
67 M'Leod, 1820, p. 140.
68 Kea, 1969, pp. 46–7.
69 G. A. Robertson, 1819, pp. 236–7.
70 Dupuis, 1824, p. xl, who referred to a road through Akwamu to the ferry at Nagho. Agu comprised nineteen 'towns', see Biørn, 1788, p. 224, and the ferry may have been at Nyive on the Akwamu-Agu road, a town the final incorporation of which into Greater Asante is probably to be dated to 1792, see Kea, 1969, p. 34.
71 Ramseyer and Kühne, 1875, p. 163.
72 Kea, 1969, pp. 34–5. See also Debrunner, 1965, pp. 15–19.
73 The British having established their claims to Asante, and the French to Dahomey, it will be appreciated that it was the existence of the neutral corridor between Asante and Dahomey that permitted the Germans to create the small Colony of Togo.

not protect it from attack by the one when the influence of the other over it disturbed the balance of power.[74] Dupuis' reference to a 'Toubary' or 'Tonbory', a town 'serving as a frontier on the Dahoman side',[75] may have been to Atakpame. The effective frontier of Greater Asante must, however, have passed close to its west, and included a cluster of small provinces – among them Buem, Pae, Akposso, Akebu, Adele, and Adjuti – over which the government maintained control largely through the agency of a group of Kwawu colonists there, the Dokoman.[76] Further north still, Robertson described Chamba, or 'Dunco',[77] as the northeastern district of Ashantee proper': [78] the Chamba are a Konkomba people incorporated into Dagomba at the time of Ya Na Andani Sigili in the early eighteenth century,[79] and in view of the subsequent inclusion of Dagomba within Greater Asante, Robertson's information may be accepted. On the other hand, a late nineteenth century report, that the Kotokoli country east of that of the Chamba had been 'under the sway' of Asante should be taken as at most indicative of the relationship of adjunct territory.[80] Bowdich's reference to 'Gamba', that is, Gambaga in Mamprussi, as being 'the boundary of Ashantee authority' is probably also to be seen in the same light.[81] Yet, on the other hand, the indications of the extension of Asante's authority into the far north, beyond the Dagomba towns, are surprisingly persistent. In 1878 the Kpembewura asserted that until 1874 the Asante 'had controlled and ruled up to fourteen long days' journeys north of Salaga',[82] that is, presumably to Sansanne Mango in the northeast which was about that distance from Salaga by Route IV.[83] Indeed, in 1882 Lonsdale remarked quite specifically, that in former times 'Ashanti power made itself felt even beyond Dagomba as far as Sansane Mangho'.[84]

Finally, in the northwestern hinterland, the frontier of Greater Asante can again be broadly but not precisely determined. As Owusu

[74] Kea, 1969, p. 35.
[75] Dupuis, 1824, p. xxxix.
[76] Johnson, 1965, pp. 34–8; Kea, 1969, p. 57; Debrunner, 1965, pp. 14–15.
[77] That is, Twi ɔdɔnkɔ, plural nnɔnkɔfo, used to describe peoples of the northern hinterland not otherwise readily identifiable as, for example, Gonja ('Ntafo') or Dagomba ('Anwafo').
[78] G. A. Robertson, 1819, p. 269.
[79] See P. Ferguson, 1973, pp. 176–91, who shows just how far to the east the power of the Ya Nas of Yendi did extend in the eighteenth and nineteenth centuries.
[80] PRO, CO. 879/45, African (West) 506: report by G. E. Ferguson on his mission to the interior, 1894.
[81] Bowdich, 1819, pp. 179; 240; and frontispiece map.
[82] Beck, 1880–1, see Johnson, 1966a, *Salaga Papers*, I, SAL/9/1.
[83] See the Arabic route book in Dupuis, 1824, p. cxxxiv, for the fourteen stages between Salaga and Sansanne Mango. Wargee's report that it was ten journeys between the two, see Wilks, 1967b, p. 189, was clearly inaccurate.
[84] *Further Correspondence*, C. 3386, 1882, p. 66: Lonsdale's report on his mission to Kumase, Salaga and Yendi, 1881–2.

Ansa, son of Asantehene Osei Bonsu, remarked in 1873, 'he could give
. . . no idea of the area of the Ashantee country; but that Prince
Jabon [the Yagbumwura of Gonja], one of the greatest of the Ashantee
nobles, lives at a place 200 miles from Coomassie, and yet was within
the Ashantee territory'.[85] There is no doubt, in fact, that all the divisions of Gonja were regarded as within Greater Asante. The most
northerly, that of Kong, was referred to by Huydecoper in 1816,[86]
and by Cruickshank in 1853,[87] as on the frontier of Asante – though
both may have confused it with the better known state of the same
name some 180 miles further west. It will be seen below that in the
1840s Kwaku Dua despatched forces from Kumase to restore political
stability in western Gonja, where a struggle for power had developed
between Kong and the neighbouring division of Bole. Again, the central Gonja division of Daboya, lying to the east of Kong and Bole,
was referred to by Bowdich as being specifically a responsibility of the
Adontenhene of Kumase.[88] As in the northeast, however, there are
strong indications in the evidence that the power of Asante extended
beyond the districts which were clearly and unequivocally within the
empire. In the far northwest the Kulango state of Buna was well known
to have a close relationship with Asante. In 1892 Ferguson described
it as an 'Ashanti country' and four years later remarked that Asante
'was feared by the King of Bona, whose head priest was also chief
priest of Kumasi' [89] – an allusion to the fact that the Imāms of Asante
were educated in Buna. Fuller reported a tradition that news of the
death of an Asantehene was always communicated to Bunamansa and
vice versa,[90] and in the early 1880s the Asantehene Mensa Bonsu is
known to have solicited aid, apparently unsuccessfully, from the Buna
at the time of the dispute with Gyamanhene.[91] Taking a cautious view
of the matter, Buna will be classed with the adjunct territories.[92]
Again, in a mid-nineteenth century source reference is made to 'Bulega
. . . confederate with Kambonse'.[93] 'Kambonse' is the Mole-Dagbane
name for Asante, and it is possible that the reference is to Bolgatanga,

85 *Further Correspondence respecting the Ashantee Invasion*, Part II, 1874: Barrow
   to Colonial Office, dd. London, 18 September 1873.
86 Huydecoper's Journal, entry for 18 August 1816.
87 Cruickshank, 1853, I, 44–5.
88 Bowdich, 1819, p. 236, and see also p. 171.
89 PRO, Co. 879/38, African (West) 448: Ferguson to Griffith, dd. Accra, 19
   November 1892, p. 35. PRO, CO. 879/45, African (West) 506: Ferguson's report of
   1894.
90 Fuller, 1921, p. 1.
91 *Further Correspondence*, C. 3687, 1883, p. 120: report by Lonsdale on his mission
   to Asante and Gyaman, April to July 1882.
92 See further National Archives of Ghana, Tamale, ADM/1/126: Informal Diaries,
   Commissioner of the Southern Province, N.Ts., 23 June 1927, reporting rumours
   that Agyeman Prempe I was about to take over Buna!
93 Koelle, 1854, p. 6.

some 100 miles northeast of Daboya. 'Bulega' is presumably to be placed in the same category as Buna, Kotokoli and Mamprussi: among the territories, that is, aligned with Asante though not provinces of the empire.

Communications and the politics of empire

The evidence presented in the previous section is summarized in Table 3. The columns D (distance) show approximate mileages from Kumase, and the columns T (time) the corresponding number of days' journeys estimated on the basis of the conventional measures given above (pp. 3–12). It must be stressed that the figures are minimal ones: that is, that the mileages do not allow for the winding of the roads, nor the times for the days on which no travelling was done. It must also be pointed out, that although the Table is based mainly upon evidence from the early nineteenth century, when Asante was at its greatest extent territorially, nevertheless some data derived from earlier and later sources are used in the reconstruction. Although the measures of time and distances are necessarily approximate, the divergences from the actual are probably relatively constant throughout. Observable regularities in the data may be accepted, therefore, as significant.

Table 3   *Greater Asante: inner boundaries and outer frontier*

Route	Metropolitan boundary Location	D	T	Inner provincial boundary Location	D	T	Conjectural outer frontier Location	D	T
I	unknown	—	—	unknown	—	—	Komoé R.	250	18
I(b)	unknown	—	—	unknown	—	—	Komoé R.	190	19
II	Akumadan (?)	56	5	Banda	145	13	Kong	250 *	20
III	Sekyedumase (?)	46	6	Dawadawa	130	13	Daboya	222 *	18
IV	Adwira	59	6	Nienseli	213	20	Yendi	250 *	23
IV(a)	unknown	—	—	Ahenkro	175	17	Akposso (?)	245	22
V	'Feea'	—	3	Mamfe	130	13	Accra	156	15
V(a)	Obogo	38	4	Edzebeni	130	13	Little Popo	250	20
V(b)	Asokore	23	3	unknown	—	—	unknown	—	—
VI	Kwisa	32	3	Ansa	48	5	Anomabo	126	11
VII	'Abatea'	—	4	unknown	—	—	Elmina	134	13
VIII	Domi-Keniago	45	5	unknown	—	—	Cape Lahu	290	24

* Estimated to the provincial capital.

It will be seen, first, that the boundaries of the metropolitan region lay between three and five journeys from Kumase in the heavily forested and more southerly districts, and five or six journeys in the more open northerly districts. Secondly, the inner provincial boundaries in the north lay typically at about thirteen journeys from the capital. The anomalous position of the boundary on Route IV, at twenty journeys, reflected the central government's need to establish the highest possible measure of control over the important market town of Salaga (mile 167), while the anomalous position of the boundary on Route IV(a), at seventeen journeys, was more apparent than real: it reflected only the absence of a direct road thence to Kumase. Thirdly, in the south, the paucity of the data on the course of the inner boundary results from the confused nature of the situation there which was to lead to the government, after 1831, relinquishing control of a number of provinces to the British administration on the Gold Coast. But that in the early nineteenth century the control post on Route VI was only five journeys from Kumase, and six from the coast at Anomabo, presumably resulted from the lateness (1807) of the Asante occupation of the southern Fante country. The location in the late eighteenth century of the post on Route V at thirteen journeys from the capital, and only two or three from the coast, conversely reflected the earliness (1742) of the extension of its rule over Accra. Finally, it will be apparent from Table 3 that the frontier of Greater Asante, other than on the three shorter routes to the coast, lay characteristically at between about eighteen and twenty-four conventional journeys from Kumase. The data are presented in a more readily visual form in Map v.

On the assumption that central government officials travelling to and from the capital accomplished their journeys in the conventional number of days, the minimal value of message-delay between Kumase and the metropolitan regional boundary was from six to twelve days; between Kumase and the inner provincial boundary, typically about one month; and between Kumase and the frontier districts of Greater Asante other than to the south, of the order of five to seven weeks. The implication is that when the value of minimal message-delay exceeded these magnitudes, the exercise of political control ceased to be realistically attainable: and the outer provinces gave way to the adjunct territories and beyond those, foreign powers. The values for actual as opposed to minimal message-delay, however, have to be increased to allow for several variables: first, the number of days on which little or no distance was covered, a function of the incidence of 'bad days' in the month, the health of the traveller, and other such incalculable factors; secondly, the time taken for the central government to make decisions on the basis of incoming information from the provinces, and to convert these into orders for outward transmission; and thirdly, the additional time taken for the agents of government themselves to convey these orders to the local authorities in the out-

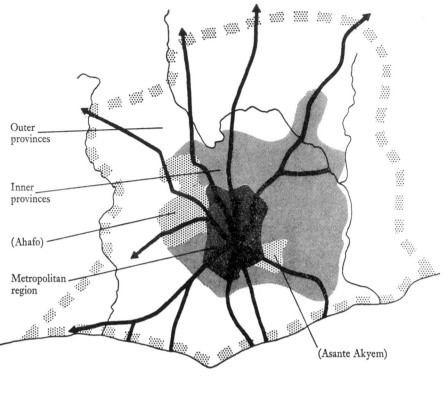

Outer provinces

Inner provinces

(Ahafo)

Metropolitan region

(Asante Akyem)

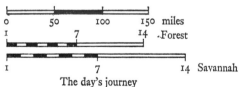

0   50   100   150 miles
1   7   14 .Forest

1   7   14 Savannah
The day's journey

v   Greater Asante: major geo-political regions

lying districts before commencing the return journey to the capital with new information about their reception. The nature of these second and third variables, that is, of the decision-making and executive processes, will be discussed in later chapters of this study.

Map v shows the morphology of Greater Asante as reconstructed with particular reference to the early nineteenth century. There is a *prima facie* assumption that political control could the more easily be exercised by the central government over the inner provinces than over the outer: that the inner provincial boundary may be regarded as delimiting those territories in principle capable of being the more fully incorporated by virtue of their relative nearness to Kumase, and

the outer frontier as delimiting those territories to be the less fully incorporated by virtue of their relative distance from Kumase. The
distinction clearly corresponds to the one acknowledged by many
nineteenth century writers, between the 'subject' provinces on the one
hand, and the 'tributary' provinces on the other. Two different *modes*
of political control are in question, yet the distinctive features of each
are singularly difficult to specify.[94] Christaller characterized a subject
province, in contrast to a tributary, as 'having Asante law and Asante
rights'.[95] More than half a century earlier Dupuis had made the same
point in reverse, identifying provinces belonging 'rather to the class
of tributaries, than subjects' by the fact of 'the people being left to
the government of their caboceers, and the jurisdiction of their own
laws'; [96] and it was with reference to such provinces that Robertson
similarly observed, 'it appears to be a maxim of the Ashantee government not to enquire generally into the domestic affairs of the provinces, if the exactions be regularly paid'.[97] Central government rule
over the tributary provinces may, then, be broadly characterized as
'indirect'. The system was interestingly described by Cruickshank in
the middle of the century, who drew attention to the cost in military
terms of any attempt radically to change the social, legal and cultural
systems of the more distant territories:

It is astonishing to mark the rise and progress of this bold and ambitious
nation. One hundred years had only elapsed since their greatest king, Sai
Tootoo, made Coomassie the capital, but in that short space of time they
had extended their conquests over numerous states. Nor was their ambition
content with conquest alone. The enterprise of the warrior was nobly
seconded by the policy of the statesman. Wise regulations were adopted, for
the purpose of maintaining them in a state of subjection . . . They had for
their sole object the maintenance of Ashantee superiority, without any
attempt to assimilate the conquered tribes with them, which they well knew
would have met with strong opposition, and rendered necessary the continual
presence of such a military force as must greatly have interfered with their
career of conquest. The native rulers continued to exercise their wonted
authority, and were only burdened with the payment of a tribute, which in
many cases was but a cheap requital for the superior protection which they
enjoyed.[98]

The 'indirect' mode of rule in the tributary provinces should not be
assumed necessarily to have been associated with a greatly diminished

[94] The reader is again referred to the interesting discussion of this topic by Arhin,
1967a, *passim*.
[95] Christaller, 1875, p. xiii.
[96] Dupuis, 1824, p. xxxix.
[97] Robertson, 1819, p. 231.
[98] Cruickshank, 1853, I, 58–9.

degree of central government control over them. At the end of the nineteenth century Kenney-Herbert gave, for example, some account of the character of Asante overrule in Dagomba:

It must be remembered that in the days of the Ashanti power Yendi was a vassal kingdom, and, moreover, the Ashantis were able to keep their vassal states in very real subjection. Any demand, however exorbitant, was cheerfully complied with, and all sorts of rules restricting those insignia of royalty, which most appeal to the native mind, were devised and strictly enforced, e.g. the number of sacred and war drums were limited, and the kings and chiefmen were not allowed to use palanquins, etc. When the annual tribute or any special fine was to be collected, a commissioner was despatched from Kumasi for this purpose. He was not accompanied by any powerful escort, but his slightest wish was readily obeyed, and opposition of any sort was never dreamt of.[99]

It was the case, too, that since message-delay was too high for lesser matters requiring decision by the central government to be in fact referred to it, resident commissioners were appointed from Kumase to the distant provinces. 'The management of these districts', commented Cruickshank, 'was confided to the king's chief captains, who each had his own particular department to attend to. These resided in Coomassie, and employed secondary agents to watch the conduct of the tributaries.' [100] The responsibilities of these commissioners will be discussed more fully in later chapters.

Tributes and taxes

It will be shown below that there were in Asante many politicians who subscribed to the view that the prosperity of the nation was vitally bound up with the maintenance of the flows of tribute from outlying provinces to the capital, and who supported therefore those programmes the most concerned with the preservation of the *status quo* in the tributary territories. The imperial outlook which was dominant in the eighteenth century was gradually to lose its appeal in the nineteenth. It was the case, however, that it was difficult for even a reforming Asantehene such as Osei Bonsu to conceptualize any geopolitical situation other than in terms of the tribute relationship:

Europe, or the 'land of white men,' he supposed to contain several tribes or families, of which the English was the most warlike, and powerful, of the day; and the Portuguese the most ancient, and formerly the mistress of all the other tribes. These several tribes, he imagined, inhabited a number of large islands

99 PRO, CO. 879/52, African (West) 549: Report on the Neutral Zone, by Captain A. H. C. Kenney-Herbert, dd. 24 June 1898.
100 Cruickshank, 1853, I, 59.

which were subordinate to the king of England (or the English island) who received annual tributes from the whole.[101]

The apparatus for the exaction of tribute in Asante was a highly complex one. On the basis of discussions with the Gyaasewahene (or Head of the Exchequer) in Kumase, Bowdich commented:

The tributes of the various nations they had subdued, were in some instances fixed, but more frequently indefinite, being proportioned to the exigencies of the year; indeed from various conversations with Apokoo [Gyaasewahene Opoku Frefre] and others, and my own observations during state palavers, it appeared that the necessities and the designs of the Ashantee government were the superior considerations, and the rule in levying tribute everywhere.[102]

A special exchequer court existed in Kumase, one of the major responsibilities of which was to hear pleas for the adjustment of tribute.[103] Each territory was assessed, so a late nineteenth century observer remarked, 'in proportion to the capability of their meeting the demand'.[104] But it was an aspiration of the tributaries, as a protection against inflated demands, to negotiate agreements by which the annual payments became fixed rather than exigent. As late as 1817 the Aowin and Amanahia provinces were described as 'at the mercy of the Ashantees, who extort gold from them frequently, though they have not yet fixed the tributes',[105] but in that year Aowin envoys arrived in the capital to attempt to obtain an agreed level of payment.[106] In the course of the nineteenth century many tributary provinces which had not already achieved this concession, did so. Provinces which lay within the gold-producing regions were required to give tribute in that metal. In the early nineteenth century Bonzina and Sehwi in the west were reported to pay the annual sums of 100 and 450 oz of gold respectively.[107] In the same period the tribute from the rich province of Gyaman was only partially fixed: it was reported at 225 oz annually, but in addition all 'large pieces of rock gold' found by its prospectors and miners had to be surrendered to government.[108] Much later in the century the Gyamanhene Agyeman was to claim that the annual value of the tribute was then running in excess of 18,000 oz yearly.[109] Pay-

101 Dupuis, 1824, p. 100.
102 Bowdich, 1819, p. 320.
103 Bowdich, 1819, p. 296.
104 *Further Correspondence*, C. 3386, 1882, p. 66: Lonsdale's report on his mission of October 1881 to February 1882.
105 Bowdich, 1819, p. 168.
106 *Ibid.* p. 244.
107 *Ibid.* p. 321.
108 *Idem.*
109 *Further Correspondence*, C. 3687, 1883, p. 127: Lonsdale's report on his mission of April to July 1882. Robertson, 1819, p. 181, referred to the Gyaman tribute being paid for a time in cotton, and Pitt, 1926, p. 74, in slaves and produce.

ment of tributes in gold appears to have been the more insisted upon as the value of slaves dipped sharply in the early nineteenth century following the withdrawal of the major European companies from the trade. The policy change, however, triggered off a series of tax revolts in those provinces affected by it. Wassa envoys, for example, appeared in Kumase in late 1817 to negotiate the matter,[110] but by 1820 the situation had deteriorated to a point at which the government had to despatch troops there. 'I am assured beyond a doubt', reported Robertson, 'that the Ashantee Government are much perplexed and cannot find means even by extortion to sustain their power. The difficulty of paying the annual Tribute in Gold or Ivory is so much greater than when it was paid in Slaves that almost every district is in a state of insurrection.' [111]

Most of the tributary provinces which lay outside the auriferous region made payments to the central government in people, sometimes supplemented with other commodities. In the early nineteenth century the major divisions of Gonja and Dagomba were reported to pay 500 slaves, 200 cows, 400 sheep, 400 cotton cloths and 200 cotton and silk cloths annually, and the minor divisions proportionately smaller quantities.[112] These figures, however, may again reflect the government's policy in the period of reducing that part of the tribute paid in slaves, in this case by increasing that in livestock and cloth. Later in the century the demand for unfree labour, whether to meet the requirements of the Asante farms or for re-export to the Gold Coast, stabilized at an unexpectedly high level, and the indications are that the northern provinces increasingly made payment in that medium. In 1882 Lonsdale noted that 'a part of the yearly tribute demanded from Dagomba was 1,500 slaves'; [113] twenty years later Ferguson gave the number as 'a thousand slaves and more a year'; [114] and in 1920 Cardinall, who spoke with a nephew of the last Asante commissioner there, gave the figure of 2,000.[115] In 1870 the Yendi tribute alone was reported as having been 500 slaves and 1,000 dollars (or the value of about 62 oz of gold).[116] Similarly, in 1878 Buss learned that the

110 Hutchison's diary, entry for 17 October 1817, in Bowdich, 1819, p. 392.
111 PRO, CO. 2/11: Robertson to Earl Bathurst, dd. Cape Coast, 27 November 1820.
112 Bowdich, 1819, pp. 320–1. A local Gonja manuscript probably of late nineteenth century composition referred to the Yagbumwura, or ruler of all Gonja, as paying tribute in 'slaves, goats and beef', see Institute of African Studies, Ghana, Arabic Collection, IASAR/254 (Hausa) and 255 (Arabic): account of relations between Yagbumwura Jakpa and Asantehene Osei Tutu.
113 *Further Correspondence*, C. 3386, 1882, p. 66: Lonsdale's report on his mission of October 1881 to February 1882.
114 PRO, CO. 879/38, African (West) 448, p. 56: Ferguson to Governor, dd. 9 December 1892.
115 Cardinall, 1920, p. 9.
116 Basel Mission Archives: Kromer's Report for the Third Quarter of 1870, dd. October 1870.

Kpembe division of Gonja had provided annually 'a quota of 1,000 slaves, cattle and money',[117] seemingly the sum agreed upon in the contract signed by Kpembewura Nakpo in or about 1751. At least one source, however, indicates that before 1874 the Kpembe tribute had been variously adjusted first to 600 men and a monetary payment, and later to only 'a small subsidy in money'.[118] A late nineteenth century observer commented, 'Gonga country was an Ashanti province before the 1874 expedition. An Ashanti chief visited Salaga yearly, in order to collect the tribute paid by the Gongas to the King of Ashanti. A certain portion of this tribute, which consisted of sheep and cattle, was collected in each district and sent into Salaga.' [119] Although, then, the tribute might thus be adjusted according to the prevailing political and economic circumstances, a figure of 1,000 men per division annually appears to have been the basic assessment for Gonja for the greater part of the century. In 1892, for example, when the Tuluwewura entered into a treaty of friendship and trade with the British, he is reported as observing that the Governor of the Gold Coast, by assuming the overrule, has 'rid me of paying a thousand slaves a year to the Ashanti monarch'.[120] The Daboya division was no exception to the rule.[121] Nor apparently was the Yagbumwura himself: a group of Gonja petitioners in Kumase in 1937 maintained that the Gonja ruler 'collected and despatched to the Otumfuor Asantehene 1,000 (one thousand) persons to progress the Administration of The Asantehene, to match and advance the Asanteman . . .' [122]

Such northern tributary powers as Gonja and Dagomba were expected to raise tributes in men presumably with facility, since they possessed an all but total military superiority over the farming peoples ('tribes without rulers') of the surrounding territories. 'Ashanti', writes J. A. Braimah,

posted resident court officials (*Etangpo,* plural; *tangpo,* singular) all over Gonja to collect slave tributes . . . Hundreds of slaves had to be paid annually by Gonja to Ashanti and this forced the Gonjas to wage war on the Grunshies and other tribes in the North for the required slaves . . . the Ashantis were always present in Gonja to collect them.[123]

117 Cited in Johnson, 1965, p. 39. See also *Further Correspondence,* C. 3386, 1882: Lonsdale's report of 1881–2, p. 66: stating that Gonja (in the context, Kpembe) paid 1,000 men annually as part of the tribute.
118 Glover, 1874.
119 PRO, CO. 879/52, African (West) 549, p. 125: Report on the Gonja and Dagomba countries, by C. H. Armitage, dd. Kpembe, 1 January 1898.
120 PRO, CO. 96/230: report by G. E. Ferguson, enclosed in Brandford Griffith to Ripon, dd. 10 January 1893.
121 Wilks, field-notes, interview with al-Ḥājj Karamoko Abū Bakr, of Kandinga, dd. 11 September 1968.
122 State Council Archives, Manhyia, Kumase: petition of various Gonja residents in Kumase to the Asantehene Sir Osei Agyeman Prempeh II, dd. 12 June 1937.
123 Braimah, 1970, p. 32. The Gonja incursions into the village communities of

In the 1860s the Dagomba were obliged, in circumstances described below, to make heavy payments to the government in Kumase. Ya Na 'Abdallāh (*ca.* 1864–76) despatched expeditions into the Bassari lands to the east and the Grunshi lands to the northwest. He strengthened his forces by recruiting into service Zabarima mercenaries: horsemen from the southern fringes of the Sahara.[124]

The numerous small districts within the outer provinces to the east of the Volta, a region likewise well outside the gold producing area, seem also to have paid their tributes in men. References to those from Adele, Akebu and Nchumuru are unfortunately not specific on this point,[125] but the many small Ewe chiefships further south are reported each to have sent to Kumase annually, two men.[126] By contrast with this very modest requirement, the tribute imposed upon the southern province of Akuapem in the early nineteenth century had been fixed at 1,000 men and 300 bags of snails, and the virtual impossibility of procuring the former if not the latter was one of the major causes of the revolt of the Akuapemhene Kwao Saforo Twie in 1811.[127] Another report suggests that subsequently the Akuapem tribute was renegotiated, and fixed at two large pewter plates, one hundred baskets of salt, three hundred men, and 660 dollars (or a little over 40 oz of gold).[128] Elsewhere the composition of the tribute was decided with reference to local specialities, or the lack thereof. Thus the small rural district of Bamboi, on the Black Volta in the northwest, paid only in sheep and fowls;[129] the southeastern coastal towns of Accra and Tema sent to Kumase lime prepared locally from shells;[130] and at least part of the Fante tribute was despatched in salt.[131] The Asante government regarded the British, Dutch and Danish establishments on the Gold Coast as falling essentially within the class of tributaries, a matter

Sisala, Numuna, Kasena, Builsa and others, were by no means always successful, see for example Northcott, 1899, pp. 16–17.

124 National Archives of Ghana, Accra, unaccessioned Arabic and Hausa MSS compiled by Malam Isḥāq of Wa *ca.* 1922 (and see also IASAR/22): *Al-Khabār Zabarima*. See also Tamakloe, 1931, pp. 37–8. For the Zabarima in Dagomba, see Holden, 1965, *passim.*

125 PRO, CO. 879/48, African (West) 529, p. 199: Ferguson's report of 1896 – 'chief Kojo of Tetepene [Dutukpeme] . . . paid tribute to Ashanti'. Cornevin, 1952, *passim.* Johnson, 1965, p. 38, citing David Asante, 1877.

126 Institute of African Studies, Ghana, IAS/EWE/V/3: Botoku tradition, recorded by E. Y. Aduamah, June 1963.

127 Samson, 1908, ch. III. But see Biørn, 1788, p. 204, for an earlier arrangement.

128 Basel Mission Archives: Maden's Quarterly Report, dd. 25 May 1853. (The dollar was valued at one-sixteenth of an ounce of gold, or at about 4*s* 6*d* taking the coast price of gold at £3 12*s* an ounce.)

129 National Archives of Ghana, Tamale, unaccessioned: Inquiry into the claims of the *omanhene* of Longero to paramountcy over the *koro* of Bamboi, etc., dd. Kintampo, 5 January 1933.

130 Reindorf, 2nd ed., n.d., p. 169.

131 *Ibid.* pp. 178–9.

made explicit in a statement by the Asantehene Kofi Kakari concerning the nature of the Dutch occupancy of Elmina. 'The fort of that place', he wrote, 'have from time immemorial paid annual tribute to my ancestors to the present time by right of arms. . . .'[132] Fixed by usage at 4 oz of gold per month for the major trading stations such as Elmina and Anomabo, and 2 oz for the lesser, payment of the tribute was usually taken in guns, gunpowder and other imported commodities.[133] And finally the Assini province, heavily involved in the French trade, was not surprisingly assessed accordingly: in December 1870, eighteen envoys from there arrived in Kumase with the tribute – 'several dozens of rum, liqueur, champagne, and some beautiful silk stuff'.[134]

It will be apparent that the tributaries mentioned were all located beyond the inner provincial boundary, with one exception: the Kpembe division of Gonja, which was treated as outer province with respect to tribute even though the disposition of the control posts was such as to include the Asante market town of Salaga, and therefore of necessity Kpembe, within the inner provincial region. In general, however, the inner provincial boundary may be regarded as having separated the tributary provinces from those having subject status: exemption from the payment of tribute being a distinguishing mark of the latter. Thus the inner and subject province of Nkoransa,[135] according to Bowdich, was 'generally excused, from fidelity . . .' from the payment of tribute.[136] The acceptance by the Akyem Kotoku of terms of incorporation that specifically referred to exemption from tribute (p. 24) clearly marked their acquisition of subject status.

A part, then, of what was involved in the subject province having, *pace* Christaller, 'Asante law and Asante rights', was seemingly its inclusion within the tax structure of the metropolitan region; that is, like the towns and districts of that region, the subject province became liable only to those taxes which could be levied by the councils in Kumase under accepted constitutional procedures, for example, *awunyadie* or death duty, *apeatoɔ* or war tax, *fotobɔ* or accession tax,[137] and other such sums for specific named purposes.[138] It may be that

[132] *Correspondence relative to the Cession . . . of the Dutch Settlements*, C. 670, 1872, p. 13: Kofi Kakari to Governor Ussher, dd. Kumase, 24 November 1870.
[133] See, e.g. Bowdich, 1819, pp. 58–9.
[134] Ramseyer and Kühne, 1875, p. 107.
[135] See, e.g. Christaller, 1875, p. xiii.
[136] Bowdich, 1819, p. 321.
[137] That is, a special tax to build up the Treasury on the accession of a new ruler, compare Busia, 1951, p. 81, *Yedi toɔ bɔ ɔhene fotoɔ*, 'we raise a levy for the chief's treasury'; and as such to be distinguished from the *adidieaseda*, fees paid to the Asantehene by a newly enstooled chief.
[138] For a somewhat different account of the tax and tribute structures, see Arhin, 1967b, *passim*.

Bowdich's observation that 'Akim, Assin, Warsaw, Aowin, etc. etc. were taxed indefinitely by crooms [towns]' [139] is to be taken as indicating that it was the central government's policy – whether successful or not is another issue – to manage those provinces as subject rather than tributary ones. Some account of the system of tax collection in the Adanse district of the metropolitan region was given by the missionary Freeman for the early 1840s. 'The slaves', it was reported,

are employed in cultivating the plantations of their masters, or in trading for them; and have such an allowance for their support, as their owners may deem sufficient. A caboceer, or principal chief, derives an indirect benefit from the slaves of his captains. Every captain or subordinate chief gives up, in the form of a tax, a certain portion of his income to his superior; and he, again, pays a tax to the king. While Mr. Freeman was detained at Fomunah, he frequently saw the captains of Korinchi [Adansehene Kwantwi] bring their respective quotas, amounting from one toku, value five-pence to four tokus; but by what rule those payments were regulated, he did not ascertain. [140]

But whatever the nature of the system of assessment at that time, there are indications that it became the policy of the central government to consolidate the various permissible levies into an annual head-tax payable by all married males. An account of the system as it operated over large parts of the metropolitan region (though not within the territories of the greater *amanhene*) in the later nineteenth century was given by the Asantehene Agyeman Prempe I. Three months before the annual Odwira ceremonies, tax officials from the capital visited every village and, with the assistance of the *odekuro* or headman, collected one-tenth of an ounce of gold (that is, *domma*) from every married man. The sum was divided three ways, three-sevenths going to the Treasury, three-sevenths to the local *odekuro*, and one-seventh to the tax officials as stipend. [141] While no detailed account has yet come to light of the methods of tax collection in the subject provinces, it would seem likely that the practice was much the same. In the nature of the case the burden of taxation in the inner provinces, as in the metropolitan region, was probably best apportioned village by village and town by town, with rights of appeal against the assessment to the courts in Kumase. For while outer provinces such as Dagomba and Gonja might always sponsor military expeditions beyond the frontiers of Greater Asante for revenue raising purposes, such opportunities were not readily available to the inner districts. 'During

139 Bowdich, 1819, p. 321.
140 Beecham, 1841, pp. 115–16.
141 Kumase Divisional Council Archives, Manhyia: letter from the Asantehene Nana Agyeman Prempe I to District Commissioner, Kumase, dd. 26 October 1927. Compare NAG Accra, ADM 12/3/6: Hodgson to Chamberlain, dd. Accra, 14 May 1896.

the Slave-trade', Robertson remarked, 'in *lenity* to their subjects, the chiefs of the provinces actually committed depredations on each others dominions to obtain the measure of payment, as the supreme government never interfered provided it shared in the spoil.' [142] Whether or not his observation was true of the eighteenth century, it is clear that in the nineteenth the government recognized a major commitment to the prevention of fighting between province and province in any part of its territories.

Acculturation and the processes of political incorporation

While political control over the tributary provinces rested upon a system of indirect rule, that over the subject provinces was seen, certainly by earlier nineteenth century writers, as amounting rather to 'annexation'. Thus Robertson referred to Denkyira as 'a province of Ashantee, which bounds Wassa on the north, and was formerly a part of its dominions, but was annexed to Ashantee Proper, about the year 1775, and has since remained under its immediate government'.[143] Similarly, after the collapse of the Gyaman rebellion in 1819, the central government's attempt to bring the area the more fully under its control was described by Dupuis as 'the annexation of that kingdom to Ashantee as a province, in lieu of the tributary rank it enjoyed before'.[144]

It is difficult to measure in terms of the acculturative process the results of closer association with (or 'annexation to') the metropolitan region, since, as Arhin has stressed, the populations of so many of the inner provinces in both north and south were, like the Asante themselves, essentially Akan in culture and language.[145] Yet the possibility must be allowed for, that at least some of these societies had acquired strongly Akan cultural traits precisely in consequence of their incorporation into the Asante polity. In the 1870s Christaller was well aware of the significant distinction still made between the *Akanfo* or 'pure' Twi-speaking peoples, and the Kwawu, Bron and others in the subject provinces who spoke *Apɔtɔkan*, 'impure Akan dialects'.[146] The matter was one which had engaged the attention in the 1840s of H. N. Riis, whose observations are of considerable interest. 'The boundaries of the empire of Asante', he commented,

and those of the language, spoken in the principal and more southern part of this kingdom, do not coincide . . . The term Asante originally marks only

142 G. A. Robertson, 1819, p. 192, and see also pp. 91–2.
143 *Ibid.* p. 125.
144 Dupuis, 1824, p. 264.
145 Arhin, 1967a, p. 81.
146 Christaller, 1875, p. xv; 1881, p. 644.

a smaller province, which is the centre and probably the germ of the present empire. It may be applied to the whole, if referred to as a political body. But speaking of the tribe as connected not by political unity but by the ties of ethnological consanguinity, comprising all those who have the same vernacular idiom, the natives themselves will never use the term Asante, but they will speak of the Oji – [that is, Twi] tribe and the Oji-language . . . The Oji-language then is spoken primarily in the original Asante, the heart of the present empire of Asante, and in its central and southern dependencies. As the inhabitants of these parts have so entirely got the ascendancy in political respect over their kindred tribes, and language always partakes in the prevailing influence, which the tribe by whom it is spoken has obtained, we may justly consider the idiom of Asante as the principal dialect of the Oji-language. Besides, the flourishing state of a nation always exerts an influence upon the development of its language. . .[147]

Whatever the nature of the acculturative process to which Riis drew attention, there were certainly obligations incurred by a subject province such that a sense of political if not cultural identification with the nation – the Asanteman – was built up. This was especially so in the military sphere. In most of the outer or tributary provinces, the local ruling hierarchies maintained their own military forces upon which would devolve the responsibility in the first instance for securing their own, and Greater Asante's, outer frontier. Such forces were referred to by Dupuis as 'auxiliary', in which category he listed those of Banda, Gyaman, and 'the upper provinces on the banks of the Aswada' – presumably the Gonja division along the Black Volta and the other countries to the north and east of the river.[148] The northern outer provinces were not, in other words, fully integrated into the national military structure. Bowdich commented that the troops of Dagomba and Gonja in particular were too much despised to be used,[149] but this seems to be in need of qualification in view of the fact that in the former, at least, Asante military advisers had assisted in forming and training a corps of gunmen – the Kambonse. The situation, presumably, was that the government recognized the advantages in leaving such frontier forces relatively autonomous and of not drawing upon them for services in other parts of its territories. By contrast, in the early nineteenth century the inner provinces, and those outer provinces enjoying unexposed positions on, for example, the seaboard, had no heavy local defence commitments. They possessed their own fighting forces 'independent of the actual armies of Ashantee', so Dupuis remarked,[150] but they were, in the words of Bowdich,

147 H. N. Riis, 1854, Introduction.
148 Dupuis, 1824, p. xxxix, note.
149 Bowdich, 1819, p. 317.
150 Dupuis, 1824, p. xxxix, note.

'contingencies at command': [151] that is, such provinces were obliged to mobilize their troops and place them at the disposal of the central government for service wherever required. Within this category, Bowdich and Dupuis named the inner or in some cases outer provinces of Akuapem, Akyem, Amanahia, Aowin, Assin, Bron, Denkyira, Kwawu, Nkoransa, Nsoko, Sehwi, Takyiman and Wassa. Thus the Denkyirahene Kwadwo Tsibu took his place in the armies that campaigned in Gyaman in 1818–19,[152] whilst the Nkoransahene Kwadwo Owusu Ansa fought at Katamanso, on the southeastern coastal plains, in 1826.[153]

Later in the nineteenth century it appears to have become the policy of government in Kumase progressively to integrate the fighting forces of the inner provinces into the national army, bringing them under a unified system of conscription and mobilization. Essentially, every district, assessed on the basis of its population, was assigned a quota of troops which it had to supply in the event of full mobilization – and proportionately less in the event of partial mobilization. In 1882 Lonsdale was quite specific that the system was in force not only within 'Ashanti Proper', the metropolitan region, but also within the provinces. 'The outlying Chiefs', he reported, 'of the Protectorate of Ashanti in the districts to the N.W., N., and N.E., would be called upon to furnish to the general strength, according to their supposed population . . .' [154] British intelligence was able to obtain a number of versions of the quotas; that for the early 1870s, obtained through Dawson, gave for example the assessment for Nkoransa as 6,000 men, for Kwawu also as 6,000, for Sehwi as 1,500, and for Abesim, the same: [155] all four provinces were listed by Christaller in the period as subject ones.[156] At the time, however, all the senior commands in the national army were apparently assigned to office-holders from the metropolitan region, with one exception: one of the five commanders of the *Benkum* or left-wing was the Nkoransahene.[157] It will be seen later that one of the fundamental causes of the unrest which spread throughout Asante in the 1870s and 1880s, during the reigns of Kofi Kakari and Mensa Bonsu, was a popular rejection of the system of military conscription. Yet it was precisely because induction procedures had become standardized over the metropolitan and inner pro-

[151] Bowdich, 1819, p. 317.
[152] Reindorf, 2nd ed., n.d., p. 165.
[153] Ricketts, 1831, p. 125. Reindorf, 1st ed., 1895, Appendix: Asante generals and captains at Katamanso.
[154] *Further Correspondence*, C. 3687, 1883, pp. 114–15: Lonsdale's report on his mission of April to July 1882.
[155] See Brackenbury, 1874, II, 362.
[156] Christaller, 1875, p. xiii.
[157] Brackenbury, 1874, II, 362–3.

vincial districts, that the issue was not one to divide the nation on regional lines.

To describe certain provinces as inner ones is to call attention to their spatially intermediate position between the metropolitan, and the outer provincial, regions. To describe those same provinces as 'subject' or 'annexed' ones was, for the nineteenth century writers, to call attention to their politically intermediate status between the fully incorporated districts characteristic of the metropolitan region, and those outlying districts the incorporation of which into the Asante state was greatly restricted by their distance from the seat of government. It must be emphasized again, however, that the imperial system was one not in a state of equilibrium. As Dupuis interestingly commented, 'powerful as the monarchy of Ashantee certainly is, collectively estimated, it may be considered as a fabric whose foundation is subject to periodical decay, and therefore requires unremitting attention . . .' [158]

The growth of the apparatus of central government – of the elaborate decision-making and administrative structures – will be treated in Chapters 10 and 11. But there were ways, other than through military service, by which the provincial authorities became involved in matters national rather than regional or local. To some extent, for instance, tax-farming devices were used, partly no doubt in order to relieve the agencies of central government of the burdens of collection, but also perhaps, as Arhin has argued, to give provincial rulers 'an opportunity, as in the case of Ashanti chiefs proper, to derive some material gain from the Ashanti expansion and so bind them closer to state interests'.[159] Thus the Akwamuhene assumed responsibility for the collection of tribute from many of the small Ewe chiefdoms east of the Volta,[160] and the tribute from Longero, on the southern loop of the Black Volta, was remitted to Kumase through the Nkoransahene.[161] A number of confused passages by Robertson – whose misunderstanding of his Asante informant led to the false identification of Bonduku (Route I, mile 144) as capital of Nsoko (Route II, mile 110) – may be read to indicate that Nsoko received the tribute ('the revenues of the northwestern provinces') possibly from Gyaman itself but more certainly from a number of districts which included the Mfantra ('Pantera') and Nkoran ('Koram') villages. The Nsoko authorities, he noted, 'receive the consular direction and transmit the revenues and tribute to Akoomassey as they are received by them from those states which are

158 Dupuis, 1824, pp. 236–7.
159 Arhin, 1967b, p. 289.
160 IAS/EWE/V/3: Botoku tradition, recorded by E. Y. Aduamah, June 1963.
161 National Archives of Ghana, Tamale: Inquiry dd. Kintampo, 5 January 1933.

under their controul'.[162] Again, Ethiaha ('Anithira'), lying near Kwankyeabo in the Sanwi district, was seat of an official responsible for the
collection of tributes from further west. Thus, Robertson observed,
the people of 'Piquininy-Bassam . . . are subject to the dominion of
Grand-Bassam, and pay a small sum annually, which the chief of the
latter place sends to Anithira, where a viceroy of the King of Ashantee
resides.' [163] But perhaps the most instructive case of provincial involvement in tribute collection was that of the northerly Fante district of
Esikuma-Breman, lying off Route VI to the east of Manso.

Esikuma had passed under Asante control after the southern campaigns of 1765. Until 1807, however, it could still be described as one
of the 'frontier states',[164] and as only having 'preserved connexions and
some shadow of allegiance to the sovereign of Ashantee'.[165] With the
Asante conquest of the southern Fante country in 1807, Esikuma lost
its frontier position, and its chief Kwasi Amankwa was given the responsibility of conveying the Fante tributes to Kumase. According to
Robertson, indeed, his duties were even more extensive. 'The king of
Wassa', he reported, 'levied the revenue of the Ahantan states, and
accounted to the king of Ashantee for the amount', for which purpose
'Coomeh, king of Wassa, comes twice a year to Asycama, the capital of
Braman, to adjust his affairs with the chief magistrate of that district,
who is empowered by the Ashantee government to receive the amount
which has been exacted from the frontier provinces'.[166] It may be that
the important role assigned to Esikuma in the administrative reorganization after 1807 [167] reflected the central government's decision to incorporate it, like the Assin provinces to its north, within the inner
provincial region. But certainty is impossible, for in June and August
1823 British-led forces twice occupied and sacked the town, Kwasi
Amankwa was forced to flee to Kumase, and the province passed out of
Asante control.[168]

The existence of differential systems of rights and obligations as between the chiefs of the metropolitan, and inner and outer provincial
regions, had political implications the significance of which will be a
recurrent consideration throughout this study. But the major institution which transcended these differences, and embodied the overriding
national purpose, was the annual Odwira ('Yam Custom'). 'They are
all compelled to attend', wrote Bowdich, 'even from the most remote

162 Robertson, 1819, pp. 181–3.
163 *Ibid.* pp. 93–4. Ethiaha was seat of one of the three 'royal' chiefs of Sanwi.
164 *Ibid.* pp. 150–3.
165 Dupuis, 1824, p. 253. See also Meredith, 1812, p. 134.
166 G. A. Robertson, 1819, pp. 122–3.
167 For the role of the Esikumahene Akom in the invasion of 1807, see PRO, T.
70/35: Torrane to Committee, dd. Cape Coast, 20 July 1807.
168 See, e.g. Reindorf, 2nd ed., n.d., pp. 178–9; Claridge, 1915, I, 342–3.

provinces',[169] though in fact such important outer provincial rulers as the Ya Na of Dagomba and the Yagbumwura of Gonja were permitted to send representatives rather than attend it in person.[170] In the mid-nineteenth century Cruickshank drew attention to certain functional aspects of the Odwira:

To check the spirit of revolt, which the absence of any adequate physical force would naturally encourage, there was an annual general muster of these [the chiefs] at the capitol, which had a tendency to inspire them with high ideas of the king's power, from the ostentatious displays which he was then in the habit of making. Advantage was also taken of this opportunity to arrange differences, to encourage obedience, to punish disaffection, and sometimes to remove an obnoxious opponent.[171]

In fact the council of the metropolitan and provincial chiefs comprised in terms of the constitution, the sovereign body in Asante: the Asantemanhyiamu or Assembly of the Asante Nation. The character of the Assembly will be discussed in Chapter 10. Nineteenth century observers tended often to stress its judicial rather than legislative functions. Thus Bowdich commented, 'If a chief or caboceer has offended, or if his fidelity be suspected, he is seldom accused or punished until the Yam Custom, which they attend frequently unconscious, and always uncertain of what may be laid to their charge.' [172] But it was seemingly not cases of a civil nature which were brought before the Asantemanhyiamu. The dispute between rival claimants to the Lepo skin in the Kpembe division of Gonja was for example transferred to Kumase in 1817 for hearing before the Asantehene's Kumase court,[173] and so was an adultery suit, in the same period, between the Akwamuhene Akoto and one Pobi Asawa of Accra.[174] It was rather cases under the law of treason – an offence which by the laws of Okomfo Anokye carried a mandatory death penalty – which were brought before the National Assembly: the practice being thus to give the accused chief the privilege of trial by his peers. An interesting case, probably heard before the Asantemanhyiamu in 1810, arose from the protest of the Akuapemhene Kwao Saforo Twie at the magnitude of the tribute that had been imposed upon him:

he saw that his country was being depopulated by the yearly taxation of men, so he ordered one of his horns to be blown: *Ashante Kotoko! Moye ohaw, Moye ohaw papa!* (meaning in English: Porcupine Ashantes, you are very

169 Bowdich, 1821a, p. 27.
170 Bowdich, 1819, p. 274.
171 Cruickshank, 1853, I, 59–60.
172 Bowdich, 1819, p. 274.
173 Hutchison's diary, entries for 20, 25 and 28 November 1817, in Bowdich, 1819, pp. 396, 401.
174 Reindorf, 2nd ed., n.d., p. 178.

troublesome!) This horn blowing was at once reported to Osei Tutu [i.e., Osei Bonsu, otherwise known as Osei Tutu Kwame] at Kumase, who swore that Safrotwe's head must be forfeited as a penalty for the blowing of the horn. When Safrotwe went to Kumase with the kings of Akim and Akwamu to attend the annual custom of their emperor (Osei Tutu), he was ordered to explain what words his horn said. Being afraid of losing his head, he mis-interpreted the horn in these words: Porcupine Ashantes, you are most social, you are very social! (rendered thus in the vernacular: *Ashante Kotoko, monim agoru, monim agoru papa!*) The king (Osei Tutu) being thus satisfied with the praise of his people and their kindness, loaded king Safrotwe with many valuable presents, including rich country clothes and sandals . . .[175]

While, then, the Odwira might be marred by trials of individual chiefs on treason charges, it was also the occasion on which loyalty was recognized, and rewarded. 'The King of Kumasi', noted Ferguson, 'distributed honours and court decorations to the various Kings of his kingdom.'[176] The services of the Nkoransahene Ata Fa (died 1885) were, for example, thus publicly acknowledged by Kofi Kakari:

While Kalkali was King of Ashanti his relations with the King of Nkoranza were very friendly, so much so that the former conferred upon the latter court decorations, consisting of gold sandals, state umbrella and accoutre-ments, articles which, according to the prescriptions of the customs of Ashanti were, when made of gold, hitherto beyond the rank of the King of Nkoranza, and which he was not privileged to use. This act of Kalkali naturally pro-duced a certain amount of sympathy between him and the King of Nkoranza. . .[177]

Similarly in 1888 the Asantehene Agyeman Prempe I afforded recog-nition to Ata Fa's successor once removed, Kwasi Poku, by presenting him with 'a gold sword and other decorations'.[178] Earlier in the cen-tury, after the participation of Nafana troops from Banda (Route II, mile 145) in the invasion of Fante country in 1807, the Bandahene Mgono Mulodwo had appeared on the honours' list, receiving from Osei Bonsu a palanquin, six ceremonial swords, and a drum.[179] Few districts, in fact, failed to be in receipt of such honours at one time or another: [180] the low-ranking chiefship of Bamboi, for example, on three occasions was presented with *asipim* chairs from Kumase,[181] and

175 Samson, 1908, ch. III.
176 PRO, CO. 879/45, African (West) 506, 1896, p. 253.
177 *Further Correspondence*, C. 7917, 1896, p. 135: Ferguson's memorandum on Ashanti and the Brong Tribes, dd. 9 November 1893.
178 *Ibid.* p. 136. For a recent discussion of Asante 'political art', see Bravmann, 1972, *passim.*
179 Institute of African Studies, Ghana, BA/1: Tradition of Banda, recorded by Kwabena Ameyaw, 20 November 1965, pp. 6–7.
180 See further, Johnson, 1965, p. 35.
181 National Archives of Ghana, Tamale: Inquiry dd. Kintampo, 5 January 1933, p. 5.

in 1929 the Yejihene (Route IV, mile 143) still displayed 'a rather fascinating gold medallion' awarded to him by the Asantehene Mensa Bonsu.[182] Nor was the conferment of honours restricted to Asante subjects. It was Mensa Bonsu, too, who chose officially to recognize the public services of the Sierra Leonean Dr Horton, and a text of the letter offering him admission to the order of *Prince of Asante* is extant:

Coomassie, June 18, 1879.
To Doctor J. A. B. Horton, M.D., Edin., F.R.G.S., Surgeon-Major of the Army Medical Department, etc., etc.
Sir, – His Majesty the King of Ashantee has heard with much pleasure the great interest you have always taken in the material advancement of his people and country, and the prompt assistance you rendered to the great Chief of Mampom, when written to about the Chief's sufferings, who had been laid up for such a long time. His Majesty the King has also been informed of your endeavours, extended over several years, towards the general improvement of your countrymen throughout the whole coast, and expresses a hope that you may yet continue to be of great service to them. His Majesty is informed that you are likely to leave the Gold Coast shortly, and not to return to it. He has therefore commissioned me to offer for your acceptance the *Title and Dignity of a Prince,* and trust that, wherever you may be stationed, you will continue to manifest great interest in Ashantee affairs. I can assure you that I congratulate you at this offer from the King; and, having known you for several years, and personally acquainted with your views, and endeavours for Ashantee, I consider it a fitting offer to you from my King, King Mensah of Ashantee. – I am, sir, faithfully yours,
J. Ossoo Ansah, Prince of Ashantee.[183]

An observer in the early 1880s remarked of what he called the 'Ashanti peerage system', that 'the Ashantees acknowledge the advantage of encouraging every virtue, the direction of which is to advance the interest of the country, by enlisting amongst the nobility any person who distinguishes himself in the patriotic display of every such virtue'.[184] Much earlier in the century Bowdich, who had participated in the Odwira of 1817, had seen it as 'instituted like the Panathenaea of Theseus, to unite such various nations by a common festival',[185] and from his observations of the state of the kingdom around 1840, Freeman had little doubt that a national consciousness was indeed emerging. 'Its despotism', he maintained, 'is so modified as to

182 National Archives of Ghana, Tamale, ADM/1/126, Informal Diaries, Commissioner, Southern Province of the Northern Territories: entry for 29 October 1929.
183 *The African Times,* XXIV, no. 266, 1 November 1883, p. 122.
184 *The Sierra Leone Reporter,* cited in *The African Times, idem.*
185 Bowdich, 1819, p. 256.

secure entire unity of action in all things, while it has a sufficient mingling of the aristocratic element, to enlist in its favour the sympathies of the great Chiefs, and through them, those of the subordinate Captains, and the masses of the people.' [186]

[186] *The Western Echo,* I, no. 12, 17 March 1886, p. 8.

CHAPTER 3

The politics of population:
the demography of metropolitan Asante

The military manpower statistics

Kumase, it has been seen, lay at the centre of a network of great-roads which, running to the metropolitan regional boundary in usually between three and six journeys, continued onwards to link the capital with the inner and outer provinces. The area of the metropolitan region approximated to 10,000 square miles, excluding the extensive Ahafo lands to the west: it comprised probably of the order of one-tenth of the total land area of Greater Asante at the apogee of its growth in the early nineteenth century. No reliable population statistics are available before the twentieth century. Such enumerations as were conducted by the Asante government in the nineteenth century, yielded only gross approximations, and were intended primarily to assist in military planning. 'The number of an army is ascertained or preserved in cowries or coins', noted Bowdich,[1] and it is likely that such returns were also used for general taxation purposes since the Gyaasewahene of Kumase, who was responsible for the returns, was also in charge of the Exchequer.

Little is known of the methods used by government in fixing the quotas of fighting men to be filled by the various districts in the event of mobilization. In view of the fundamental importance of agriculture in the Asante economy, however, the assessments had to be made at levels that did not denude the villages of too many men at any one time. By the 1870s British military intelligence had become anxious to obtain information on the quotas, and a number of incomplete and by no means identical lists were procured from various sources. Of those shown in Table 4, that for 1873 – 'the names of the states of the kingdom, with their supposed men of war' – was obtained in Kumase by the Fante Dawson,[2] and that for 1879 by Captain Hay at Fomena, while those for 1881(a) and (b) were given respectively by

1 Bowdich, 1819, p. 300.
2 Brackenbury, 1874, II, 362.

Table 4   *Metropolitan Asante: quotas of fighting men*

Metropolitan district	1873	1879	1881(a)	1881(b)
Kumase	5,000	6,000	5,000	5,000
Dwaben	2,000	—	—	—
Mampon	2,000	1,000	800	4,000
Bekwae	2,000	1,000	3,000	3,000
Kokofu	2,000	1,500	4,000	3,000
Nsuta	2,000	—	—	—
Adanse	3,000	—	—	—
Effiduase	1,000	—	—	—
Denyase	—	700	200	1,000
Amoafo	300	300	200	1,000
Kuntanase ('Inkwantansi')	—	200	150	700
Atwoma ('Archwa')	—	150	100	1,000
Asanso	200	—	—	—
Asumegya	100	60	60	1,000
Adankranya ('Allen Kereya')	20	—	—	—

Owusu Taseamandi, a son of the Asante heir-apparent Osei Kwadwo (died 1859), and by a messenger of the chief of Fante Nyankomase.[3] Although figures are lacking for a number of districts, and although the fourth list appears consistently to distort the size of the quotas for the smaller districts, there are nevertheless sufficient regularities in the lists for them to be regarded as bearing some significant relationship to the original records kept by the Gyaasewahene.

It was a corollary of the operation of a quota system, that central accounts of the casualties suffered on active service by the various contingents had to be kept. This, in fact, appears to have been the practice throughout the nineteenth century. Among the service units in the Asante army which invaded the Fante states in 1807 was 'an Arab medical staff' which was responsible for recording casualties: a clear reference to the Muslims attached to the Nsumankwaa or Court Physicians.[4] Later in the century more traditional procedures were in favour. 'The number of common soldiers who fall', it was reported, 'is denoted by small sticks fastened to a pole, and carried by one of the company.' On the return to the capital for review, it was then the procedure that 'every chief who passed before the king threw into a vase as many grains of corn as he had lost people'.[5] The indications are that casualties tended to be high, those dying from disease – especially smallpox – and even of starvation when the commissariat proved inadequate to its role, often outnumbering those killed in fighting.

3 *Affairs of the Gold Coast and threatened Ashanti Invasion*, C. 3064, 1881, p. 21: enclosure 12 in Brandford Griffith to Commodore Richards, dd. Cape Coast, 23 January 1881.
4 G. A. Robertson, 1819, p. 151.
5 Ramseyer and Kühne, 1875, pp. 136, 256.

The reoccupation of the British Protected Territory in 1872–3 involved total mobilization: 'we had often been told', observed Ramseyer and Kühne, 'that the whole Ashantee army had gone to the war'.[6] Under interrogation, a staff officer of the Bantamahene and commander-in-chief Amankwatia who had fallen into British hands, gave the strength of the forces assigned to the Benkum or left-wing as 8,000 men, to the Nifa or right-wing as 32,000, and to the Adonten or main body, 30,000.[7] Other estimates made by the British military authorities indicated the broad accuracy of the figures: it became generally accepted that the three Asante divisions under the commander-in-chief Amankwatia numbered upwards of 60,000 men, and that with the several smaller independent forces such as that in the west under the Gyaasewahene Adu Bofo, the total number of men in the field approximated to 80,000.[8] Reference to Table 4 will suggest that, even allowing for districts which were omitted from the quota lists, probably considerably less than half of the men under arms could have been drawn from the metropolitan region. It seems in fact that the majority of the 10,000 men under the Nkoransahene's command in the Nifa of the main army,[9] for example, were the forces of the Nkoransa province (quota, 6,000);[10] that troops from Kwawu province (quota 6,000)[11] comprised a large part perhaps of the 12,000 men under the Mamponhene likewise in the Nifa;[12] and within the army of the west a contingent of 3,000 or more men under Akyampon Yaw had been mobilized largely from Sehwi province (quota, 1,500)[13] and Kwankyeabo.[14] Ramseyer and Kühne witnessed the return of the armies to Kumase on 22 December 1873, four days after the commander-in-chief had sent a deputation to the Asantehene 'to announce to him the number of those who had fallen, and the names of the important chiefs'.[15] According to the two observers, two hundred and eighty chiefs died, and 'about half the army survived'.[16] Casualty figures are notoriously liable to distortion, but there are indications that these figures were not entirely unrealistic. J. H. Brew, for example, who was present at the battle near Fante Nyankomase (Route VI, mile 108) on 8 April 1873, com-

6 *Ibid.* p. 256.
7 Boyle, 1874, pp. 146–7.
8 See, e.g. *The African Times*, XII, no. 140, 28 February 1873, p. 97; no. 141, 29 March 1873, p. 110.
9 Boyle, 1874, p. 146.
10 Dawson's list, in Brackenbury, 1874, II, 362.
11 *Idem.*
12 Boyle, 1874, p. 146.
13 Dawson's list.
14 Ramseyer and Kühne, 1875, p. 213.
15 *Ibid.* p. 255.
16 *Ibid.* p. 256. See also Boyle, 1874, pp. 272–3, citing Kühne.

puted that of the total divisional strength of 38,500 men, the Asante losses, which included five senior commanders and about forty junior, totalled 900 killed and 3,000 wounded; and that at the second battle there on 14 April, the Asante lost another 1,500 men, with over twice that number wounded.[17] The assault force of 3,000 men, equipped with scaling ladders, which attempted to take Elmina Castle on 13 June, in two attacks reputedly suffered a further 1,000 casualties, dead or wounded.[18] Throughout the campaign the Dwabenhene Asafo Agyei was said to have lost, from all causes, three-quarters of the 12,000 men assigned to him.[19] The Bekwaehene Yaw Poku, as second-in-command in the Nifa, had 10,000 troops at his disposal,[20] of which, *pace* Dawson, some 2,000 may be supposed to have been drawn from his own district. At the review of the armies in the capital, when losses were reported district by district, those of Bekwae totalled 1,000,[21] or 50% – a figure that may provide the obvious explanation of why the Bekwae quota had been scaled down to 1,000 by 1879.[22]

The resettlement of captives

Military operations were, then, extremely costly in terms of man-power. It will be seen in Chapter 12 that for much of the nineteenth century the mercantilist or 'peace' party in the councils of the nation maintained a comfortable majority over the imperial or 'war' party; while in the 1870s and 1880s a strong popular movement of agitation against the system of military conscription arose. Despite the quite extraordinary – and universally acknowledged – fighting abilities of the Asante soldier, the society from which he came was not one with any strong commitment to the use of military means in the pursuit of its ends. Indeed, that this was so was in part consequent upon the insights into the economics of warfare which most Asante administrations came to possess. The necessity was recognized of what Dupuis called, 'recruiting the losses [the] armies had sustained': [23] that is, it was

17 *The African Times*, XII, no. 144, 30 June 1873, pp. 138–9: Brew to Editor, dd. Cape Coast, 20 May 1873.
18 *Ibid.* no. 145, 29 July 1873, pp. 160–1: pseudonymous letter, dd. Cape Coast, 23 June 1873. Compare also Rattray, 1929, p. 240, citing evidence of a participant in the battle of Abakrampa on 5 and 6 November 1873, that 1,000 men apparently under the Mamponhene's command, were lost there.
19 *The African Times*, XIII, no. 152, 26 February 1874, p. 16: evidence of a captured slave of Obogohene. For the method of assigning troops to a commander, see Reindorf, 2nd ed., n.d., p. 111.
20 Boyle, 1874, p. 146.
21 Ramseyer and Kühne, 1875, p. 255.
22 For an interesting contemporary discussion of the matter of casualties, see Henty, 1874, pp. 333–4.
23 Dupuis, 1824, p. 241.

policy to hold losses in war at a level at which the resultant decline in population was offset by controlled increase through immigration. Commonly, part of the population of an occupied territory – usually that of a rebellious province – was transferred and resettled in the metropolitan region or in other loyal provinces. After the campaigns of 1806–7, for example, which were occasioned in part by the revolt of Kwadwo Tsibu of Assin Attendansu, it was reported of his subjects that 'thousands [were] sent into slavery in the more northern provinces of the empire'.[24] Some of these were presumably among the Gyaman, Fante and Assin captives distributed between the numerous towns and villages around Lake Bosomtwe, whose number was probably over-estimated at 25,000 in 1820; some of them were free, others slave.[25] A number of Fante refugee families were brought into Kumase in October 1817, when the Council decided to resettle them at Breman, to build a new village.[26] In 1820 the Asantehene Osei Bonsu was considering the possibility of removing into the metropolitan region the entire population of Cape Coast. 'I will', he suggested, 'bring them all to Coomassy and send another tribe to live among the whites; I will not kill them, but will give them land, and a good governor to make them obedient. . .' [27] The design was not in this case carried out, but Dupuis maintained that, as a result of transplantations of populations, many states which had been of importance in the period before the rise of Asante, by the early nineteenth century 'barely enjoy their present oblivious rank and names as provinces of the Ashantee Empire'. Many other places, he added, 'are totally extinct, and their ancient glory is supplanted by the ingress of a foreign population . . .' [28]

One remarkable instance of transplantation, involving not a hostile but a friendly population, occurred in 1871, at the conclusion of Adu Bofo's campaigns east of the Volta. Preparing to return with his armies for a triumphal entry into Kumase, the Asante commander induced the people of two Ewe districts which had remained loyal – Tonkor some six miles east of Edzenbeni (Route V(a), mile 130), and Wusuta some fifteen miles further north – to precede him there. Bonnat witnessed the reception of an advance force in Kumase on 3 July, and noted the presence of

two thousand individuals, men, women, children and old people. These were the inhabitants of two villages Tougo and Ossoutrou, situated in the country of Crepe. They had allied themselves against their country, and to the

24 *Ibid.* pp. 38–9.
25 *Ibid.* pp. xxx–xxxi and note, reporting the evidence of two of the lakesiders.
26 Hutchison's diary, entry for 21 October 1819, in Bowdich, 1819, pp. 392–3.
27 Dupuis, 1824, p. lxiv, note.
28 *Ibid.* pp. xlviii–xlix.

Achantis, to whom they had rendered great services. The chiefs of the victorious army took them away with them, on the pretence of greeting the king who, they said, wanted to thank them and to give them valuable presents. The important persons of the two villages had at first refused; then the promises and inducements of the Achanti changed to threats . . .[29]

Bonnat commented that the Tonkor and Wusuta were treated little better than the prisoners-of-war; [30] several hundreds of them had died on the road although the Asantehene had had food sent out to them.[31] But whatever the facts of the matter, the Ewe were refused permission to return home. Ramseyer and Kühne reported that four hundred of them left Kumase in April or May 1872, and 'were sent northward, under an Ashantee colonel, whither and for what purpose no one knew'.[32] Subsequently it was said that Kofi Kakari received supplies of gunpowder on credit from the Sanwi ruler, Amandufo of Kwankye-abo; and that he offered the Wusuta in return to Amondufo who rejected any exchange in that form by insisting on payment in gold.[33] The Wusuta today maintain that their kinsfolk were resettled at 'Kontsiabu', that is, Kwankyeabo, but describe it as an Asante gold-mining village: it is perhaps not to be identified with the Sanwi town but with the village of the same name about two miles south of Manso Nkwanta. On their arrival in Kumase, so their own remembrance of the matter has it, the Wusuta

reported themselves to the Asantihene, Karikari at Kumasi. Nana Karikari was happy to see his soldiers back home after 3 years stay in the Ewe country and said he would reward the chief of Wusuta with royal objects made of gold. The Wusuta chief should therefore remain at Kumasi while three hundred of his men should go and fetch gold from an Ashanti village called Kontsiabu. This was good news for our people for their chief would become the first of the Ewe chiefs whose royal objects would be adorned with gold. This was also an occasion for our men to see the 'gold rivers' of Ashanti. Everyone was happy to go to Kontsiabu. They left Kumasi by night and after crossing a large river they entered Kontsiabu. Then immediately our people were allocated to the inhabitants of Kontsiabu. The Ashanti intention was now clear. Our men had been sold into slavery.[34]

29 Gros, 1884, pp. 227–8.
30 See also Ramseyer and Kühne, 1875, pp. 26–7.
31 *Ibid.* p. 130. Gros, 1884, p. 228.
32 Ramseyer and Kühne, 1875, pp. 168–9.
33 *Ibid.* pp. 183–4.
34 Institute of African Studies, Ghana, Volta Basin Research Project, 9, Traditions from the Afram Plains, recorded by E. Y. Aduamah, January 1964, p. 5: interview with Togbi Amedui Bami of Nframa. See also EWE/V/2, pp. 4, 6, and 16, and EWE/V/5, pp. 8–9: Tonkor and Wusuta Tradition, recorded by E. Y. Aduamah, June and July 1963.

After living for some three decades in Asante, many of the Ewe nevertheless chose to return to their homelands in the early years of this century. But others had already become sufficiently absorbed into Asante society to decide to remain there, as instanced by Poku in 1969: 'those descended from forced immigrants may even form their own independent lineages. In one village I know all those descended from Ewe captives brought in 1869–70 have formed a pseudo-lineage taking their Ewe origin as the criterion of membership, though they do not know two words of Ewe between them.' [35] In fact, the adoption of Asante social and cultural values by those of diverse origins was not only permitted but, seemingly, enjoined. Communities of unfree background merged, within a generation or two, into the class of free Asante commoners,[36] and their acquired status was fully protected in Asante law. *Obi nkyerɛ obi ase* – one does not disclose another's origins – was described by Rattray as 'a legal maxim of tremendous import in Ashanti',[37] and Reindorf referred to the Asante 'national law', that

whoever dares tell his son: these people were from such and such a place, conquered and translocated to this or that town, was sure to pay for it with his life. Neither were such people themselves allowed to say where they had been transported from. Considering these captives as real citizens, any rank or honour was conferred freely on them according to merit, but not otherwise.[38]

Bowdich, earlier, had noted that traditions of origin were in general 'very cautiously adverted to, the government politically undermining every monument which perpetuates their intrusion, or records the distinct origins of their subjects'.[39] The offence of disclosing another's origins is called in Asante, *asekyerɛ*, a word sometimes graphically translated as 'pedigreeing'. Sheep had to be slaughtered upon commission of the offence.[40]

Two aspects of the Asante approach to warfare have, then, to be taken into account: the level of mobilization had to be determined so that, first, the withdrawal of labour from the villages was not such as seriously to disrupt agricultural production, and second, that anticipated losses on campaign were commensurate with projected figures

35 Poku, 1969, p. 37.
36 See, e.g. Bowdich, 1821b, pp. 16–17: 'the identifying of those diminished importations of slaves . . . with the lowest class of the free population'. See also Rattray, 1929, pp. 35, note; 42. For a recent discussion of the matter, see Klein, 1969, *passim*.
37 Rattray, 1929, pp. 40, 82.
38 Reindorf, 1895, p. 51.
39 Bowdich, 1819, pp. 228–9.
40 Kumase Divisional Council Archives, Manhyia: Kumasihene's Tribunal, Civil Record Book 3, Osei Kwame v. Yaw Buampon, commencing 29 November 1927.

for the intake of immigrants – whether voluntary or otherwise – for resettlement. The quota system was designed to achieve these ends, by limiting the number of men who could at any one time be put at risk by mobilization for military purposes. It is, however, unfortunately impossible to determine the relationship between total population, and that part of the adult male population liable for conscription, other than within wide margins of error.

The gross population figures

In 1817 Bowdich was able to obtain estimates of the total number of 'men able to bear arms'. His figures, by metropolitan district, are shown in Table 5.[41] Believing that an estimate of total population in

Table 5 *Metropolitan Asante: men able to bear arms*

Metropolitan district	Men able to bear arms
Kumase	60,000
Dwaben	35,000
Mampon	15,000
Nsuta	15,000
Kokofu	15,000
Bekwae	12,000
Eduabin	12,000
Effiduase	10,000
Denyase	8,000
Kuntanase	8,000
Gyamase	8,000
Amoafo	6,000
Total	204,000

the metropolitan region might be obtained by the use of a multiplier of five, Bowdich accordingly assessed this at approximately one million.[42] His computations are of considerable interest. In an attempted reconstruction of the age-structure of the male population, based partly upon his 'impressions' of Asante society, he established four categories between which he distributed it in the proportions shown in Table 6. His conclusions may not have been entirely unrealistic. For purposes of comparison the age-structure in 1948 of the male population of the 'Native State' of Asante, which corresponded very closely to the old metropolitan region, is also shown.[43] It will be apparent that the two sets of data, for 1817 and 1948, are compatible, and there seems

41 Bowdich, 1819, p. 316.
42 For a discussion of such multipliers, see Hollingsworth, 1969, pp. 227–32.
43 *Census of Population, 1948: Report and Tables,* Accra, 1950: table 10.

Table 6 *Metropolitan Asante: male population by age group*

1817			1948		
Category of males	Number	% of total	Age-group of males	Number	% of total
Children	101,000	28	0–16	185,279	45
Youths	50,000	14			
Able-bodied men	204,000	56	16–45	177,948	43
Incapacitated by age or accident	7,000	2	45 and over	51,959	12
Totals	362,000	100	Totals	415,186	100

no obvious reason to reject Bowdich's schema. On the other hand, his estimate of the ratio of male to female in the population was clearly grossly in error. On the basis of his observation that members of the 'higher orders' in society had many wives, of the 'lower order of free-man' generally one, and of the slave group seldom any, Bowdich con-cluded that the proportion of women to men was somewhat under two to one: and therefore rounded off the total population at about one million.[44] There are, however, no indications in the censuses of popu-lation taken in this century of any significant disbalance in the sex-ratio. In fact, although Bowdich himself noted the high frequency of marriage between older men and younger women,[45] he had failed to appreciate that in such circumstances polygamy remains possible even when male and female populations are numerically equal. Hence, if the basic reliability of Bowdich's data on numbers of men able to bear arms is accepted, his calculation of the total population of the metropolitan region must nevertheless be reduced from the figure of one million to one of around 725,000. But although the information may have been obtained from the Gyaasewahene – who became, so Bowdich remarked, 'very communicative of Ashantee politics' [46] – the totals are clearly no more than very rough approximations, while a number of districts, most notably Adanse, are unlisted. In 1839 the missionary Freeman estimated independently the population of 'all of Ashanti' as between 700,000 and 800,000 – figures which, since they presumably referred to the metropolitan region, are in close agreement with the adjusted one based upon Bowdich.[47]

In 1863 *The African Times* published population figures for the metropolitan region of Asante which were of a kind comparable with those obtained by Bowdich almost half a century earlier: they were,

44 Bowdich, 1819, p. 317.
45 *Ibid.* p. 302.
46 *Ibid.* p. 92.
47 Methodist Mission Archives, London: Freeman to General Secretaries, dd. Cape Coast, 9 May 1839.

that is, for men 'able to carry arms'.[48] Unfortunately, these were listed only for the more important districts. In Table 7 the two sets of figures are collated for these districts, and the percentage change indicated.

Table 7 *Metropolitan Asante: men able to*
bear arms, 1817 and 1863

District	1817	1863	% change
Kumase	60,000	50,000	−16⅔
Dwaben	35,000	15,000	−57
Bekwae	12,000	20,000	+66⅔
Kokofu	15,000	10,000	−33⅓
Mampon	15,000	12,000	−20
Nsuta	15,000	10,000	−33⅓
Totals	152,000	117,000	−23

On a projection from the revised estimate for 1817, assuming that the decline in population was standard throughout society, and that the age- and sex-structure did not change significantly, the total population of the metropolitan region around 1863 may be computed at about 558,250. The total male population of the Kumase district alone was given in *The African Times* as 120,000. Although the district was unquestionably the most populous one, the figure seems too high. Again, a projection from the 1817 data, using 16⅓% as the relevant rate of decline, suggests that the total should have been more like 90,000.

In order to obtain some perspective in the matter, in Table 8 the estimates for 1817 and 1863 are shown in series with figures available (in each case for the administrative areas the most nearly equivalent to the nineteenth century metropolitan region) from the Gold Coast and Ghana counts and censuses conducted in this century. The figure for 1960 is that for the Asante ('Ashanti') Region as it then existed.[49] That for 1948 is for the Kumase, Bekwae and Mampon administrative districts.[50] Those for 1931 and 1921 are for the then Eastern Province of Asante.[51] Finally, those for 1911 and 1901 are calculated from the total returns for Asante [52] by giving the eastern and western provinces the same weights as they had in 1921, that is, 2.6:1. It is of interest to note, in passing, that the traditional methods of accounting in nineteenth century Asante (see pp. 80 and 81 were used by the British administrators in some areas as late as 1921.[53] 'I understand', wrote

48 *The African Times*, 23 August 1863, cited in XII, no. 147, 29 September 1873, p. 183.
49 *1960 Population Census of Ghana*, Accra, 1962, I, xxiii.
50 *1948 Census of Population*, p. 42.
51 *Appendices Containing Comparative Returns and General Statistics of the 1931 Census*, Accra, 1932, p. 159.
52 *Ibid.* p. 1.
53 *1948 Census of Population*, p. 7.

Brandford Griffith to the chiefs in 1900, in preparation for the Census of the the following year,

that the way you count your people is to divide each town or village into companies, which are again sub-divided into families. The heads of families are then directed to drop into a calabash, or similar article provided for the purpose, a grain of corn or a cowrie, according to the number of their people – and that these calabashes are then collected and the contents counted . . . when the numbering takes place different articles are to be used for each sex – that is to say, Indian corn for males and cowries or kernels for females.[54]

Table 8 *Metropolitan Asante: population figures, 1817–1960*

Year	Population
1817	725,000
1863	558,000
1901	250,000
1911	208,000
1921	292,444
1931	393,810
1948	636,935
1960	1,109,130

The population trend indicated by the data in Table 8 is shown in Figure 2. It will be observed that the putative decline between 1817 and 1863, of rather less than an average of 0.5% per annum, apparently continued over the next forty-eight years at a much increased rate of about 1.3% per annum, until the trend was reversed between 1911 and 1921. The significance of the graph, however, is most difficult to assess. In the first place, no explanation is apparent for a decline in population between 1817 and 1863. The period was, for the most part, one of peace and material advancement, and no unusually virulent and widespread outbreaks of plagues or the like are known to have occurred during it. On the other hand, the data in Table 7 should not be too lightly rejected. It is germane to note that the district showing the highest loss, namely Dwaben, was the one which, in circumstances to be outlined below, was occupied by central government forces after heavy fighting in 1831; most of its people sought refuge in the British Protected Territory, and although many subsequently returned to Asante,[55] the Dwaben district was never to regain the pre-eminence it had enjoyed in the earlier part of the century.[56] Conversely, the only district showing a gain, Bekwae, was the one geographically situated the most favourably to gain advantage from the boom in Asante trade with the British Protected Territory which occurred under the administrations of Kwaku Dua I and Governor Maclean respectively: by the 1870s and 1880s Bekwae was probably the most powerful of all the metropolitan districts. It may well be, then, that the figures for 1817 and 1863 reflect a genuine trend, although it is also arguable that, perhaps as a result of a per-

54 Letter dd. 22 December 1890, cited in full in De Graft-Johnson, 1969, p. 3.
55 T. B. Freeman, 1843, pp. 156–8, who stated that although many of the refugees returned to Dwaben in 1840, about 1,000 chose to remain in the Protectorate.
56 See, e.g. Dupuis, 1824, p. xxx.

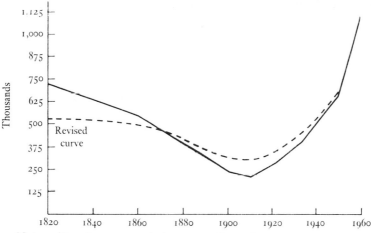

Fig. 2   Metropolitan Asante: population curve 1820–1960

sisting exaggeration in the revised estimate for 1817, the decline would have been considerably less than that indicated in Table 8.

There is, by contrast, no difficulty in accepting a very considerable decline in the population of the metropolitan region in the period 1863 to 1911. The years were ones of military campaigns against the British and against secessionist districts and provinces, of civil war, and of the British occupation and final Anglo-Asante war of 1900. Quite apart from losses incurred in the fighting, whole populations are known to have abandoned their towns and villages and to have sought refuge outside the metropolitan region. The total number of Dwabens who moved into British Protected Territory in 1875, after the second occupation of their country, is uncertain, but the New Dwaben state which they created in the Gold Coast Colony had a population of 26,526 by 1931. In 1891, in a letter to the Asantehene, the British Governor could comment,

. . . a part of Koranza, and also a part of Mampon, together with Dadiassi, Kokofu, and Inquanta, all powerful tribes, have crossed from Ashanti and sought refuge in the British Protectorate, and the countries they have left are being rapidly overrun by bush and forest, farming and trade operations having ceased in them whereby much food and profit are lost. Adansi also, independent until it entered into unwise conflict with Becquah, is without population. The country is fast becoming forest.[57]

Some figures are extant which indicate the magnitude of the population displacement in the last quarter of the nineteenth century. The

[57] *Further Correspondence*, C. 7917, 1896, pp. 48–9: Brandford Griffith to Asantehene, dd. Accra, 11 March 1891.

91

Adanse had in fact quitted their lands in the course of the hostilities of 1886, and between 13 and 15 June of that year, 12,411 of them were reported to have crossed the Pra River into the Protectorate.[58] In 1888 a mass exodus of Kokofu and Dadiase occurred, and three years later 16,862 Kokofu and 3,920 Dadiase were resident in the Western Akyem district of the Protectorate alone.[59] When Brandon Kirby had travelled through Asante in 1884 he had found many districts in a state of general malaise. Of Kokofu he had noted that 'all that now remains of one of the strongest provinces of the Ashanti Nation is the ruins of a very fine town (Kokofoo) and a starving population of about 50 people'. On entering Mampon he was impressed by 'its utter state of ruin and wretchedness', while Nsuta town he found 'mostly in ruins and very scantily populated'.[60] Although many of the refugees did subsequently return to their hometowns, a net loss through emigration undoubtedly occurred in the period. It is apparent, too, that an increasing mortality-rate resulted not only from losses in fighting, but also from the increasing incidence of disease in such conditions of instability: in 1884, for example, Brandon Kirby noted that the Bekwae villages 'have suffered most severely from small-pox' and that in Nsuta 'small-pox was raging very severely'.[61] It is also likely that in such circumstances the birth-rate began to fall, and, in part perhaps the intangible result of foreign conquest,[62] continued to do so until the second decade of the twentieth century.

In 1948 the Census Commissioner argued that the decline in population between 1901 and 1911 was apparent only, resulting from overstatement in 1901 and understatement in 1911. On this assumption, Szereszewski has suggested revised estimates of the Asante population for the period 1891 to 1911 which would assume continuous growth.[63] In the light of the evidence for the nineteenth century, however, these revisions are open to doubt: the view that it is more 'normal' for a population to increase rather than decrease is to be questioned. It may nevertheless be reasonable to accept the view that the counts of both 1901 and 1911 tended to understate population. As the compilers of the 1911 Census Report remarked of those

58 *Further Correspondence*, C. 4906, 1886, p. 63: Brandford Griffith to Earl Granville, dd. Accra, 21 June 1886.
59 *Further Correspondence*, C. 7917, 1896: Brandford Griffith to Knutsford, dd. Accra, 19 May 1891, and enclosure, Hull's Report on his Visit to Western Akim, dd. 28 January 1891.
60 *Further Correspondence*, C. 4477, 1885, pp. 91–3: Report by Brandon Kirby, dd. 15 April 1884.
61 *Idem.*
62 See, e.g. Hollingsworth, 1969, pp. 251, 307–11, 330.
63 *1948 Census of Population*, pp. 10–11. Szereszewski, 1965, p. 126. For further consideration of the matter, see De Graft-Johnson, 1969, *passim*.

counted in Asante, 'the main underlying feeling [was] one of nervousness of the Census being taken as a basis for a possible future taxation'.[64] The average annual rate of decline was therefore probably considerably less than the figure of 1.3% indicated from Table 8. The revised curve plotted on Figure 2 does no more than smooth out that based on Table 8, in light of the reservations which have been expressed about the quality of the data. If the curve is tentatively accepted, as the best possible approximation obtainable in the absence of further evidence, then in effect the population of metropolitan Asante is being estimated at somewhat over a half-million in the earlier nineteenth century, declining throughout the remainder of the century and only to be halted, perhaps at around 350,000, in the second decade of the twentieth century.

The hierarchy of settlements

It would seem that in the nineteenth century the Asante conceptualized the distribution of population within the metropolitan region in terms of an hierarchical order of settlements, in four tiers. The first tier was uniquely occupied by Kumase – the seat of government, the largest urban centre in the region, and the point of convergence of the eight great-roads. In 1817 Bowdich estimated the 'average resident population' of the town as from 12,000 to 15,000.[65] Three years later Hutton gave it as 15,000, and elsewhere as 15–20,000.[66] Freeman, after his visit to the capital in 1839, was of the opinion that the population was then somewhat larger than in Bowdich's time,[67] and estimated it at 30,000.[68] In 1848 Winniet gave a lower figure of 25,000.[69] In view of the high degree of consensus, the population of Kumase may be accepted as numbering most probably between 15,000 and 25,000 in the first half of the nineteenth century. As Bowdich pointed out, however, the capital was surrounded by many small settlements which were essentially part of the urban complex:

. . . the higher class could not support their numerous followers, or the lower their large families, in the city, and therefore employed them in plantations, (in which small crooms [villages] were situated,) generally within two or three miles of the capital, where their labourers not only feed themselves, but supply the wants of the chief, his family, and more immediate suite. The

64 *Gold Coast Colony, Census of Population 1911*, Accra, n.d., p. 5.
65 Bowdich, 1819, p. 324.
66 Hutton, 1821, pp. 32, 329.
67 Beecham, 1841, pp. 131–2.
68 Methodist Mission Archives, London: Freeman to General Secretaries, dd. Cape Coast, 9 May 1839.
69 Winniet's Diary, entry for 9 October 1848.

middling orders station their slaves for the same purpose, and also to collect fruits and vegetables for sale, and when their children became numerous, a part are generally sent to be supported by these slaves in the bush.[70]

The people of these auxiliary settlements returned to their town houses for the celebrations of the Adaes – occurring twice in every forty-two days; [71] for funerals and the like; and on such occasions as the public reception of important visitors. In 1816 Huydecoper estimated the number of people in town at the time of his reception as about 50 or 60,000.[72] More conservatively (perhaps), Bowdich thought the expanded population to be 'much greater' than 30,000 – 'from the extended masses of crowd . . . observed on festivals, when the plantations of the environs are almost wholly deserted'.[73] Freeman, at his reception in 1839, reported those present to be in excess of 40,000 people, including many women.[74] It is apparent that of the *total* population of the Kumase district (which by the application of the revised curve of Figure 2 to the data of Table 5 and 6 may be estimated at around 155,000 for the early part of the century),[75] perhaps of the order of one-third was concentrated in and around the capital. Indeed, Bowdich had specifically remarked, on approaching Kumase, that 'the plantations became more frequent and extensive, and numerous paths branching off from that we travelled, shewed that the country was thickly inhabited, and the intercourse of the various parts direct and necessary for an interchange of manufacture and produce: the crooms hitherto had appeared insulated'.[76] Once a year at the time of Odwira, moreover, the population of Kumase would become swollen still further by the enormous influx of people not only from other districts within the metropolitan region, but also from inner and outer provinces. The city then became one, so the Asante insisted to Bowdich, of over 100,000 people.[77] Certainly when Governor Winniet visited there shortly after the close of the Odwira of 1848, he remarked that it was 'swelled by strangers called in by the King or detained after the close of the recent Yam Custom on account of my visit, from the usual amount of about 25 thousand to upwards of 80 thousand'.[78]

Constituting the second tier of settlements were the towns of the

[70] Bowdich, 1819, pp. 323–4.
[71] For an early description of which, see *ibid.* pp. 280–2.
[72] Huydecoper's Journal, entries for 22 and 26 May 1816.
[73] Bowdich, 1819, p. 323. Compare Dupuis, 1824, p. 67.
[74] T. B. Freeman, 1843, p. 48.
[75] Dupuis, 1824, p. xxx, may thus not have been grossly in error in regarding the population of Kumase – presumably meaning the district and not the town – as somewhat over 200,000.
[76] Bowdich, 1819, p. 29.
[77] *Ibid.* p. 323.
[78] Winniet's Diary, entry for 9 October 1848.

akan aman nnum, perhaps best translated as 'the five polities (*aman*) of first rank (*kan*)'. The five towns usually placed in this category were Bekwae, Dwaben, Kokofu, Mampon and Nsuta, all lying from eighteen to thirty-four miles from the capital.[79] Different views were possible, however, about specifically which towns were to be included within the five, and the number was to some extent a notional one. T. B. Freeman, for example, named what he described as five 'larger provinces': Bekwae, Dwaben, Kokofu, Mampon – but substituted for Nsuta the inner province of Nkoransa.[80] Ramseyer and Kühne classified the *amanhene* or rulers of Bekwae, Dwaben and Mampon as 'the three dukes of the kingdom', but relegated those of Kokofu and Nsuta to the category of 'chiefs of provinces'.[81] Again, Rattray commented that Asumegya had been 'formerly one of the great Amanto' but had 'unhappily sunk into a position of minor importance',[82] and reference to Table 4 will show that he was most certainly correct on at least the second point.

Data on the sizes of the towns belonging – or perhaps aspiring – to inclusion within the second order of settlements are unfortunately few. In 1820 Dupuis was informed that the population of Dwaben – obviously of the district – was 70,000 [83] (though by the application again of the revised population curve to the materials of Tables 5 and 6, this is calculable at the considerably higher figure of about 100,000). In 1842 Freeman visited Dwaben town, still in a state of decay after the hostilities of 1831, and estimated its size from the extent of the ruins as having been about half that of Kumase. 'The population', he surmised, 'including that of the surrounding crooms, may have been from ten to fifteen thousand'.[84] In 1846 the population of Kokofu was estimated by Wharton, who visited there, as 5,000 [85] Winniet learned, in 1848 and probably from the Bekwaehene, that the population of Bekwae town was then about 5,000, and that it ranked next in size to Dwaben.[86] But it might seem that by 1848 Bekwae had already entered into that phase of growth to which reference has been made above, for the 1817 data (see Table 5) suggest that at that time Bekwae ranked only sixth in size. No comparable data exist for Mampon and Nsuta. But by 1881 the former had declined

---

[79] See, e.g. Christaller, 1875, p. xiii; and compare Bowdich, 1819, pp. 168, 172, 232, 256, 289; Bowdich, 1821a, p. 21; Brackenbury, 1874, II, 332–3, citing Kühne.
[80] *The Western Echo,* I, no. 12, 17 March 1886, p. 8.
[81] Ramseyer and Kühne, 1875, p. 308.
[82] Rattray, 1929, p. 131.
[83] Dupuis, 1824, p. xxx.
[84] Freeman, 1843, p. 158.
[85] Methodist Mission Archives, London: extracts from Wharton's Journal, in Wharton to General Secretaries, dd. Kumase, 31 May 1846.
[86] Winniet's Diary, entry for 27 October 1848.

in population to only about 1,800 people though it was noted that it retained 'the appearance of having formerly contained a very much larger population'.[87]

In the third tier of settlements were the *nkuro* (singular, *kuro*), the smaller towns; like the larger centres, however, each possessed its own subordinate villages. Notionally, perhaps, the *nkuro* were thought of as numbering sixty. 'I do not wish', stated the Asantehemaa or 'queen-mother' before Council late in 1873, 'for our successors to say my son [Kofi Kakari] was the cause of the disturbance of the sixty nkurow'.[88] Finally, the *nkuro* were in turn to be distinguished from the villages – the *nkuraa* (singular, *akuraa*) – which constituted the fourth tier of settlements, and in which the greater part of the population of Asante dwelt. 'His villages', remarked Huydecoper of the Asantehene, 'are at least ten thousand in number . . . This total does not include those belonging to the King on the Accra and Appolonia sides.' [89]

The northern Route IV and southern Route VI: demographic profiles

Features of the patterns of settlement in Asante in the nineteenth century may be illustrated with reference to the sections of Routes IV and VI running between the capital and the metropolitan boundary at the control posts at Adwira and Kwisa respectively. Table 9 lists each village and town lying along the two roads in 1881, with the number of dwellings and approximate population. For comparative purposes, the equivalent data for 1931 are shown.[90]

Some doubt might seem cast upon the figures for 1881 in that the totals suggest an average of about 2.6 persons per dwelling on both roads, whereas for 1931 the average was just over 9 for Route IV and just over 8 for Route VI. In fact, the discrepancy almost certainly reflects the introduction of urban-style large open-court houses – long popular in the capital [91] – into the outlying towns and villages, where they progressively replaced the single-roomed free standing huts.[92] Indeed, as early as 1820 a few of the smaller towns were already adopt-

87 *Further Correspondence*, C. 3386, 1882, pp. 67 and 88: Lonsdale's report on his mission of 1881–2.
88 Ramseyer and Kühne, 1875, p. 247.
89 Huydecoper's Journal, entry for 18 September 1816.
90 For the 1881 figures, see *Further Correspondence*, C. 3386, 1882, pp. 85–9: Lonsdale's report on his mission of 1881–2. For the 1931 figures, see *Appendices . . . 1931 Census*.
91 For descriptions of Kumase building styles, see, e.g. Bowdich, 1819, pp. 304–9; Winniet's Diary, entry for 9 October, 1848. See also chapter 10, below.
92 For the distinction see, e.g. Dupuis, 1824, pp. 48, 61.

Table 9   *Routes IV and VI: population changes, 1881 to 1931*

Route IV					Route VI				
	Dwellings		Population			Dwellings		Population	
Settlement	1881	1931	1881	1931	Settlement	1881	1931	1881	1931
Kumase					Kumase				
Buokurom	14	36	40	181	Kaase	18	—*	25	—*
Duase	33	89	60	400	Kankuase	3	—*	15	—*
Kenyase	100	105	460	427	Asago	4	7*	20	51*
Bosore	26	—*	40	—*	Odaso	7	5*	30	41*
Saman	6	—*	20	—*	Dedesua	9	16*	30	128*
Adwumakase	200	92	500	822	Eduabin	12	45	30	256
Wono	5	18	15	199	Adunku	8	32	38	124
Ntonso	90	81	300	786	Adwumam	25	42	50	163
Kona	150	78	450	433	Asumegya	10	76	70	529
(Tan)odumase	120	37	300	484	Dwabema	3	—*	30	—*
Agona	900	154	2000	1622	Amoafo	130	94	600	556
Gyamase	910	147	2000	1525	Edwenase	5	17*	20	50*
Tabre	20	35	60	294	Kwaman	30	36	60	209
Nintin	10	32	40	255	Sanfo	9	33	60	187
Bosofo	7	20	30	141	Adadwase	15	14	30	98
Mampon	600	216	1800	2476	Ankase	150	61	400	424
Kyeremfaso †	30	34	60	290	Detsieso	20	—*	50	—*
Bobin	4	8	15	78	Esiankwanta	13	24	30	90
Nkwanta	3	22	10	245	Kyeaboso	50	1	60	45
Dinkyin	10	—*	30	—*	Dompoase	230	139	500	874
Bosomkyekye	7	9	12	96	Fomena	250	225	500	2431
Adidwan	15	12	60	119	Kwisa	150	145	300	2188
Adwira	120	263	550	2688					
Totals	3380	1488	8852	13561	Totals	1151	1012	2948	8444

* No figures for 1931, but given for 1948 when available.

† Listed in 1881 as 'Entyem (i.e. Kyerem)-Mudiah.'

ing the urban style: Dupuis noted of Amoafo, for example, that one in twelve houses on the main street were built in it, and it is significant that in 1881 Amoafo, with 4.6 occupants per dwelling, was considerably above the average. Much more surprising, however, are the increases in population, over the half-century 1881 to 1931, of about 53% for the settlements on Route IV and of about 186% for those on Route VI. Of the towns and villages along Route IV, in 1881 Lonsdale remarked that most were in a prosperous state, with much new building in evidence; only Mampon manifested, in its many abandoned houses, signs of decay.[93] If in fact the phenomenal growth of Adwira – due to immigration of northern traders – is discounted, then the increase in the half-century was 29%. If the depressed state of affairs in Mampon in 1881 is also discounted, by allowing for an extra

[93] Lonsdale's report on his mission of 1881–2, *Further Correspondence*, C. 3386, 1882 p. 67.

1,000 inhabitants, then the increase in the half-century is reduced further to under 16%: a figure clearly more compatible with the population curve for the metropolitan region tentatively reconstructed above. It will be observed, moreover, that the growth of settlements along Route IV with populations of 300 and over in 1881 was, including Adwira, about 35% by 1931, but of those with lower populations in 1881, an extraordinary 368%. The implication seems to be that in the settled conditions that prevailed after 1900, many of the rural peoples abandoned their hamlets in the forest and settled in large compact villages along the roads.[94] By contrast with the complexity of the factors accounting for population change in the settlements along Route IV between 1881 and 1931, the explanation of the changes along Route VI in the same period is straightforward: every village and town between Kwisa and Kumase had been abandoned as the British expeditionary force moved northwards along the road in 1874, and many of them were put to fire. Fomena, for example, was occupied by the British but destroyed in an Asante counter-attack.[95] In 1881 it was still being rebuilt but had not, so Lonsdale observed, 'regained its former dimensions'.[96]

Earlier lists are extant, for 1816,[97] 1848,[98] and 1862,[99] of the settlements along Route VI. All virtually identical with that for 1881, it is clear that whatever the vicissitudes of the period, few places were abandoned other than temporarily, and few new settlements were created. When Winniet travelled the road in 1848 he estimated the average population of the settlements on it as 300, or the total population at 7,500: some two and a half times greater than that reported in 1881.[100] The history of the five larger settlements can in fact be reconstructed in some detail, and it shows a pattern of fairly regular development in the nineteenth century. In 1820 Dupuis gave the population of Amoafo – 'a croom of the first class' – as 7,000, but remarked that this included the many prisoners-of-war detained there after the

94 Compare the observation by Freeman on Fomena in 1839, that 'when he first went . . . he had not the slightest idea of the extent to which the neighbourhood was inhabited; and was afterwards surprised, in his perambulations around the town, to find many crooms or villages, containing a considerable population, situated in places where he had supposed there was nothing but a dense forest', Beecham, 1841, pp. 133–4.

95 Boyle, 1874, p. 337.

96 Lonsdale's report on his mission of 1881–2, *Further Correspondence*, C. 3386, 1882, p. 58.

97 Huydecoper's Journal, appendix.

98 Winniet's Diary, appendix.

99 Ghartey, in Boyle, 1874, pp. 406–9.

100 Winniet's Diary, appendix. Winniet's average figure of 300 should probably be increased somewhat, since it also covered the small villages between Kwisa and the Pra River, largely abandoned by the Assin in the first three decades of the nineteenth century, and never fully recolonized.

Gyaman campaign of 1818–19.[101] Hutton stated that the town proper was one of some 400 houses and 2,000 people.[102] Twelve years later Simmon counted only between seventy and eighty dwellings there:[103] indicating a resident population of perhaps upwards of 300. Winniet mentioned it only as 'the residence of a respectable Ashanti chief',[104] but by 1874 the British, before they razed it to the ground,[105] had found it 'a large town . . . capable of containing two or three thousand inhabitants'[106] (Plate I). Although the population had risen to only 600 in 1881, reference to Table 4 (p. 81) will show that the Amoafohene was still required to supply, from the town and villages, 300 fighting men to the Asante armies. Lying some six miles further south, Ankase was reported in 1820 to be 'a little croom . . . containing about seventy hovels'.[107] In 1832 its size was recorded as fifty-five to sixty huts,[108] and seven years later Freeman thought of it as a 'small town'.[109] By 1874 it had grown into a large, compactly built town that was thought to have a population as high as 3,000.[110] Abandoned in that year, its revival dated from its appointment as a market by the Asantehene in the later 1870s. Although still only some 400 people lived there in 1881, it had become a major centre where merchants from the Gold Coast transacted business with their opposite numbers from Kumase.[111]

The three remaining large towns on Route VI, Dompoase, Fomena and Kwisa, all lay within the local jurisdiction of Adanse. In 1874 the Adansehene was reported as stating, 'that he was king over eleven villages, the most northern of which were Adubiassie and Dompoassie; and that his kingdom extended as far as the Prah, all his villages lying either on the main road [Route VI] or to the west of it, and that he could produce 1000 armed men in war'.[112] Although not usually considered among the *akan aman nnum*, in the 1870 period Adanse could be regarded, on one account, as ranked sixth after Kokofu, Dwaben, Mampon, Bekwae and Nsuta.[113] Certainly the Adansehene's eleven

101 Dupuis, 1824, p. 61.
102 Hutton, 1821, p. 198.
103 General State Archives, The Hague, KvG 360: Simmon's Journal of a Mission to Asante, 1831–2, entry for 8 February 1832.
104 Winniet's Diary, entry for 7 October 1848.
105 Reade, 1874, p. 365.
106 Boyle, 1874, p. 327. Henty, n.d., p. 332. Henty, 1874, p. 391.
107 Dupuis, 1824, p. 60.
108 Simmon's Journal, General State Archives, The Hague, KvG 360, entry for 6 February 1832.
109 T. B. Freeman, 1843, p. 44.
110 Boyle, 1874, p. 316.
111 Lonsdale's report on his mission of 1881–2, *Further Correspondence*, C. 3386, 1882, pp. 58–9.
112 Brackenbury, 1874, II, 271.
113 *Ibid.* II, 332–3, citing Kühne.

'villages' were the *nkuro* and not the *nkuraa* within his territory. All probably lay within Adanse proper, and therefore in the metropolitan region of Asante, rather than in the former Assin lands which lay between the southern metropolitan boundary and the Pra River, over which the Adansehene also had jurisdiction. In 1817 Bowdich had noted of Dompoase, the most northerly of the Adanse towns on Route VI, that although much of it had been destroyed in a punitive action by the Asantehene against its late chief, it remained nevertheless 'the most industrious town on the path: cloths, beads and pottery were manufacturing in all directions, and the blacksmiths' forges were always at work'.[114] Three years later Hutton reported its population as being between 1,600 and 1,800 persons, living in 350 huts; and Dupuis, impressed by the flourishing state of its plantations, assigned to it 15,000 people – presumably a typographical error! [115] By 1832, however, the settlement had decreased to only some sixty or seventy houses; [116] it was, as Freeman observed, a 'little town'.[117] Although descriptions of it in 1874 ranged from 'large village' to 'important town',[118] there is no indication that its population had ever reached again its level of 1820.

Only two miles south of Dompoase lay Fomena, seat of the Adansehene. To Huydecoper in 1816 it appeared a 'village of no consequence',[119] though in the following year Bowdich remarked that it 'had been a very considerable town'.[120] In 1820 Dupuis found it only 'another little village, containing about a hundred and fifty inhabitants'. He was informed, moreover, that while once more populous, Fomena had always been a place of insignificance.[121] In 1832 the town consisted of only between sixty and seventy houses.[122] It is possible (although not the traditional account of the matter) that the Adansehene had only recently established his residence there when Freeman arrived in 1839 to find it 'a neat little town', much larger than Kwisa.[123] While details of the subsequent growth of Fomena have not been reconstructed, by 1874 it was clearly a place of some presence. 'As we entered the capital of Adansi', reported Stanley,

114 Bowdich, 1819, p. 28.
115 Hutton, 1821, p. 192. Dupuis, 1824, p. 57.
116 Simmon's Journal, entry for 6 February 1832.
117 T. B. Freeman, 1843, p. 43.
118 Dooner, 1874, p. 48. Stanley, 1874, p. 132.
119 Huydecoper's Journal, entry for 17 May 1816.
120 Bowdich, 1819, p. 27.
121 Dupuis, 1824, p. 54.
122 Simmon's Journal, entry for 7 January 1832.
123 Freeman, 1843, pp. 18, 22. For an account of the political reorganization of the Adanse division at the time of the Asantehene Osei Yaw, see Ayase Sub-State Council Office: petition to the Minister of Local Government from Nana Bosompem Buobai *et al.*, dd. Ayase, 8 February 1960.

we discovered that it was not by any means a despicable village. A broad avenue, flanked by family residences one story high, with very steep roofs, led through the town, and when we had arrived in the central part, where the king's house was located, we saw that another broad street ran at right angles from it . . . I should say there were quarters enough for a force of 5,000 white troops in Fomannah.[124]

Most southerly of the five towns, Kwisa was situated less than one mile from Fomena, and like it, appeared to Huydecoper in 1816 to be of no consequence [125] – even though the central government had already established a highway control post there by that time. In 1820 Dupuis noted there thirty 'hovels',[126] and Simmon, in 1832, forty to fifty 'huts'.[127] It achieved, however, a take-off as a result of the Anglo-Asante concord of 1831, when it was designated the principal trading station for the merchants of the Gold Coast and Kumase.[128] By 1848 its population numbered about 750,[129] and by 1874 had risen to not less than 1,500.[130]

Broadly, then, Fomena and Amoafo were centres of administration; Dompoase of industry and agriculture; and Kwisa and later Ankase of business. With the exception of Dompoase, all showed significant growth in the first three-quarters of the nineteenth century. Other towns on Route VI, however, had declined. Asumegya, with claims to have been once one of the leading towns of the region,[131] still impressed Dupuis in 1820 as being 'of some distinction', though it seems doubtful whether, even with its villages, he was correct in assigning it a population of 7–8,000.[132] Certainly Asumegya went virtually unnoticed by most later travellers, and by the decade 1870–80 supplied only between 60 and 100 men to the national army (see Table 4, page 81). In 1817 Eduabin was required by quota to mobilize 12,000 men for war (Table 5, page 87), a figure which must be understood as the total assessment of the Adontenhene of Kumase whose traditional seat it had been. The beginning of the decline of the town as such probably began in the second half of the eighteenth century, when the office had been reorganized and its occupant required to reside in the capital itself. In 1832 the town consisted of only between 80 and 100 houses,[133] and seven years later, Freeman commented that it was 'in

124 Stanley, 1874, pp. 165–6. Compare Henty, 1874, p. 358.
125 Huydecoper's Journal, entry for 17 May 1816.
126 Dupuis, 1824, p. 53.
127 Simmon's Journal, entry for 7 January 1832.
128 T. B. Freeman, in *The Western Echo*, I, no. 10, 24 February 1886, p. 8.
129 Winniet's Diary, entry for 6 October 1848.
130 Boyle, 1874, p. 298.
131 See, e.g. Rattray, 1929, p. 235.
132 Dupuis, 1824, p. 63.
133 Simmon's Journal, entry for 11 February 1832.

a very dilapidated state, many of the houses being tenantless, and tumbling down'.[134] In 1841, however, Freeman noted some improvement, and estimated its population at from 700 to 800.[135] Thereafter, like Asumegya, there is little information on the town. It will be noted that between its abandonment in 1874, and 1881, few people returned to it, which suggests that its decline to village size had antedated the British invasion.

Although places might thus, like Fomena, grow from villages into towns, or, like Eduabin, undergo the reverse process, the distinction between the various tiers of settlements remained nevertheless quite clear. The large towns constituting the second tier were exemplified by Dwaben, with its population of 10–15,000 in 1842, or by Bekwae, with 5,000 inhabitants in 1848 rising, on one estimate, to 15,000 by 1874.[136] The *nkuro* of the third tier, by contrast, ranged in size from a few hundred people on the one hand, to two or three thousand on the other. Reference to Table 9 (page 97) will show, however, that the *nkuro* were in turn clearly distinguishable from the *nkuraa:* thus on Routes IV and VI the *smallest* towns in 1881 were four or five times bigger than the *largest* villages.

Population and the patterns of power and authority

Every settlement within the metropolitan region was linked to every other, whether immediately or remotely, by relationships of political subordinacy or superordinacy. The capital, Kumase, was apical to the system in that all other settlements were in some way subordinate to it, but it alone (prior to 1896) was subordinate to none. The nature of these linkages was intricate, or, in other words, the political structure of the metropolitan region was complex. Thus many *nkuraa* or villages were subordinate to *nkuro* or towns; many *nkuro* were subordinate to *aman;* and all *aman* were subordinate to the capital. But some *nkuraa* were directly subordinate to *aman,* and some directly subordinate to the capital. Some *nkuro,* similarly, were directly subordinate to the capital. The complexity may be illustrated by reference to Mampon, to which the towns and villages along Route IV from Gyamase to Adwira were subordinate.

The ruler of the *oman,* the Mamponhene, was immediately subordinate to the Asantehene in Kumase, and held a traditional appointment as Nifahene, or commander of the right wing, of the Asante army. A number of villages – just under forty in the earlier part of the

134 T. B. Freeman, 1843, p. 44.
135 *Ibid.* p. 119.
136 Boyle, 1874, pp. 332–3.

present century [137] – were directly attached to Mampon. Each was managed by a functionary known not as *odekuraa,* but by the honorific *odekuro* (plural, *adekurofo*), literally 'holder of the town', and rendered, for example, by Bonnat in French as *magistrat.*[138] A very few *adekurofo* were directly accountable to the Mamponhene for the conduct of their village affairs; these, by custom, owed certain personal services to him, such as the *odekuro* of Nokwareasa southeast of Adwira, who supplied bathroom-attendants.[139] Administrative responsibility for most of the villages was, however, delegated by the Mamponhene to various of his functionaries who resided in Mampon town. Thus the *adekurofo* of eight villages, including Adidwan on Route IV, were answerable to the Kontihene of Mampon; those of ten villages, including Bosofo, Bobin and Dinkyin on Route IV, to the Akwamuhene of Mampon; those of eight villages, including Kyeremfaso and Bosomkyekye, to the Kyidomhene of Mampon; and those of nine villages, including Nintin and Nkwanta, to the Gyaasehene of Mampon.[140] Additionally, a number of towns were immediately subordinate to Mampon. The three most important, Adwira, Gyamase and Effiduase, all lay on Route IV – but the second on the alternative road between Kumase and Mampon referred to above (p. 6). The Adwirahene also held the post of Adontenhene to Mamponhene; the Gyamasehene that of Benkumhene to Mamponhene; and the Effiduasehene that of Nifahene to Mamponhene. But all three resided in their own towns and not in Mampon. All three possessed, furthermore, their own villages. Thus the *adekurofo* of some twelve villages were responsible for the administration of their affairs to the Adwirahene; those of seven villages, including Tabre on Route IV, to the Gyamasehene; and those of about thirteen villages, to the Effiduasehene.[141] By virtue of their possession of distinct local territorial jurisdictions, the relationship of such as the Adwirahene, Gyamasehene and Effiduasehene to Mamponhene is described as that of *abirempon* (singular, *birempon*), literally perhaps, 'big men'. By contrast, those functionaries who lacked comparable jurisdictions and resided in Mampon town, such as the Kontihene and Akwamuhene, were classed as *mpaninfo* (*singular, ɔpanin*), literally 'elders', of the Mamponhene.

It will be apparent with reference back to Table 9 (page 97), that a high correlation predictably existed between population, that is, resources of man- and woman-power, and political standing: that the Adwirahene, Gyamasehene and Effiduasehene were powerful because

---

[137] *Appendices . . . 1931 Census,* p. 173. Rattray, 1929, pp. 242–5.
[138] Gros, 1884, p. 189.
[139] Rattray, 1929, p. 242. Busia, 1951, p. 64.
[140] Rattray, 1929, pp. 242–5.
[141] *Idem.* See also Busia, 1951, pp. 61–3. *Appendices . . . 1931 Census,* p. 172.

each controlled a town and a number of villages, while the Mampon-hene was more powerful in that he controlled a town and many more villages. Predictably, too, a situation of tension existed between the *omanhene* and his *abirempon*. The political history of Mampon was in fact characterized by a series of conflicts between the Mamponhene and the *abirempon* of Gyamase and Effiduase. Thus, in or about 1780 the Gyamasehene and Effiduasehene are reported to have rebelled against Mamponhene Atakora Kwame, and to have driven him into exile.[142] Some years later the two towns again rebelled against his successor, Owusu Sekyere Panin, in circumstances which will be out-lined below, and he too was banished;[143] the Gyamasehene Bediako and Effiduasehene 'Babu' are said on this occasion to have been sup-ported by the Adwirahene Boadu Toto.[144] Yet again, in or about 1810, Gyamase and Effiduase rose against Owusu Sekyere's successor, Safo Yaw, and killed him.[145] In the two last rebellions at least, the *abirem-pon* appear to have acted with the support of the government in Kumase. In 1845 the Gyamasehene was again among those implicated in the assassination of Mamponhene Abonyawa Kwadwo. This time, however, the culprits were placed on trial by the Asantehene Kwaku Dua at the Odwira of 1846, and the Gyamasehene and other Mampon functionaries were executed.[146] And finally, in the contest for the suc-cession that followed the removal from office of the Asantehene Mensa Bonsu in 1883, the Mamponhene Yaw Boakye supported the unsuc-cessful candidate Kofi Kakari, and the Gyamasehene Brobe the suc-cessful one, Kwaku Dua Kuma. Since Gyamase town had by then outgrown Mampon itself in size, in the circumstances there was specu-lation that the Gyamasehene might usurp the Mampon stool. 'I think', reported Brandon Kirby on his visit there early in 1884, 'in a short time Chief Brobee of Jamanassie, one of the principal Chiefs of Mam-pong and by far stronger than the King [i.e. Mamponhene] in the number of his fighting men and adherents, will oust the King from the stool of Mampong and place himself upon it.'[147]

A situation in some ways comparable existed in the Kokofu district. There the Dadiasehene, who was Nifahene to Kokofuhene, enjoyed

142 Rattray, 1929, pp. 238–9.
143 *Ibid.* p. 239. Busia, 1951, p. 87.
144 Reindorf, 2nd ed., n.d., p. 134.
145 Rattray, 1929, p. 239.
146 *Ibid.* p. 240. Methodist Mission Archives, London: Wharton to General Secre-taries, dd. Kumase, 9 November 1846.
147 *Further Correspondence*, C. 4477, 1885, p. 93: report by Brandon Kirby, dd. 15 April 1884. It is worthy of note, that the Gyamasehene Brobe was first husband of an Asante royal. This was Ohene Afrewo, whose father, the Kumase Kyidom-hene Krapa, was a son of Asantehene Kwaku Dua I, and whose mother was Akua Afriyie, daughter of the Asantehemaa Afua Kobi, see below, Chapter 9.

birempon status and presided over a number of villages stretching as far away as the Anum River. Early in 1883 the Dadiasehene Amofa rebelled against Kokofuhene Osei Yaw and, gaining the support of many of the Kokofu *mpaninfo*, later in the year entered Kokofu town and took Osei Yaw prisoner, banishing him to an outlying village. 'Kokofoo as a kingdom', reported Brandon Kirby early in 1884, 'has ceased to exist.' [148] Although in fact Gyamasehene could not, traditionally, occupy the Mampon stool, nor the Dadiasehene that of Kokofu, such constitutional conventions were essentially based upon older configurations of power which did not necessarily correspond to the current reality. Had either the Gyamasehene or the Dadiasehene succeeded in their bids for the two senior stools, their positions – once recognized by government – would then have been legitimated through a recasting of the history ('traditions') of those stools. It follows, then, that the transformations within the system of subordinacy and superordinacy which have occurred over time cannot easily be reconstructed from the official and orally transmitted stool 'histories', for these tend to present as in a state of relative equilibrium a system that was in fact in one of considerable flux.

The history of the Mampon stool illustrates well the nature of the problem. Some early occupants of the stool belonged, apparently, to the Tana *abusua* or matri-clan.[149] During the reign of Opoku Ware (died 1750), the Tana fell into disfavour. The *abusua* was formally abolished and a claim to membership of it declared a capital offence. The stool was transferred into the Bretuo *abusua,* and the requirements of legitimacy satisfied by incorporating the founding ancestress of the Tana, so Rattray reported, into the Bretuo genealogies. The Tana, however, survived albeit as a proscribed organization, and in favourable political circumstances from time to time made bids for office. In June 1946, Tana affairs were discussed at several sessions of the Asante Confederacy Council. 'During the reign of my ancestor Katakyie (Nana Opoku Ware)', observed the Asantehene, 'the Tena Clan was abolished, if not entirely annihilated. . .' A number of the Mampon *abirempon* and *mpaninfo,* including the Adwirahene and the Effiduasehene, who had referred to the continuing existence of the Tana, were arrested and required to slaughter eight sheep – 'for having uncovered what had been covered by the Katakyie, Nana Poku Ware'.[150]

[148] *Ibid.* p. 82: Brandon Kirby to Governor, dd. Kumase, 4 February 1884.
[149] Rattray, 1929, pp. 235–6, who recorded local traditions at a time when the Asantehene was in exile, and official control over such matters therefore minimized.
[150] Asanteman Council Archives, Manhyia, Kumase: emergency sessions of the Ashanti Confederacy Council, 13, 17, 18 and 21 June 1946.

Lochman perspicuously remarked in 1912 (before social anthropologists spearheaded by Rattray had come to place a quite different construction on the matter), that the *mmusua* (singular, *abusua*) were 'original families . . . but not in the meaning of consanguinity, rather [they] may be described as an alliance offensive and defensive whose members have to support themselves in paying debts and defraying expenses of funeral customs, etc.'.[151] It is true that membership of an *abusua* was most commonly acquired by descent, and only secondarily by some form of adoption. It is true, moreover, that many stools, including those of the *amanhene* and their *abirempon,* were regarded as vested in lineages within specific *mmusua.* But whatever the importance of descent group theory to an understanding of the nature of the *abusua,* it is germane to the present enquiry to emphasize two aspects of its politico-legal standing. First, it became increasingly accepted that the occupant of a stool could belong to an *abusua* different from that of the stool itself; the best known case is that of the Dwabenhene Asafo Agyei, a non-Oyoko who held the Oyoko stool of that *oman* from 1858 or 1859 until 1875. And secondly, it is quite apparent that *mmusua* could be created, abolished, merged or divided, by governmental decree. Thus in 1946 the Asantehene notified surviving members of the Tana *abusua,*

that henceforth you shall be known as members of the Bretuo Clan i.e. you are merged into the Bretuo Clan of Mampong . . . I, as the successor of Katakyie, confirm the decision taken by him in respect of this clan and decree that there is no Tena Clan in Mampong or for that matter in the whole of Ashanti. All you who termed yourselves as Tena people are, as from today, classified as Bretuo people. . .[152]

The market in towns and villages

Transformations within the system of relations of political subordinacy and superordinacy could be generated by changes in the size of settlements relative to one another; that is, the situation in which the head of a larger town was the political inferior of the head of a smaller, was unlikely to be a stable one. It was a consequence of the intimate connection of power with population that towns and villages were regarded as scarce resources, and the demand for them exceeded supply. The transference of settlements by sale or pledging was thus a factor which vitally affected the distribution of power, to the disadvantage

151 *West African Lands Committee: Minutes of Evidence,* etc., Colonial Office, London, 1916: evidence of Rev. Lochman, Basel Mission, Nsaba, dd. 19 October 1912.
152 Emergency sessions of the Ashanti Confederacy Council, June 1946: Asanteman Council Archives, Manhyia, Kumase.

of the vendor who was usually obliged to sell or pledge because of debt. Transfers were effected by due process of law, as Ramseyer and Kühne noted of a transaction which was completed in 1871 by the Asantehene Kofi Kakari: 'Kari-Kari was just then engrossed with an important domestic transaction. He had elevated one of his wives above all the rest, and had made her a present of six villages, with six hundred inhabitants. More than a hundred ounces of gold dust were given away on the occasion, and the legal arrangements were very important.'[153] It is unclear whether the missionaries are to be understood as indicating that the price of each village was under 20 oz of gold, or whether that sum represented merely the *ntrama* paid on each transaction – that is, the fee which made the sale an outright one. If the former interpretation is taken, then certainly this particular transaction would seem not to have reflected true values, which had stood much higher even in the eighteenth century. Thus in the earlier part of that century a Mamponhene had, for example, sold the three villages of Safo, Nantan and Asoromaso – all in the vicinity of Ntonso (Route IV, mile 15) – to the Asantehene Opoku Ware for *mperedwanha*, that is, 100 peredwans or 225 oz of gold: they were used to strengthen the new Dadiesoaba stool of Kumase.[154] In the same period the Bekwaehene Asantifo reputedly purchased from Offinso the village of Agyeimpra (Route II, mile 17) for 60 peredwans, or 135 oz of gold.[155]

Although sale prices have not been systematically recorded and analysed, the market in towns and villages was clearly a lively one. Many such transactions were brought to the notice of Rattray in the 1920s: the factual accuracy of the accounts is less the issue than their indication of the sorts of transfers that might occur. One Asokorehene, who may previously have been an *obirempon* to the Mamponhene, sold to Kumase the town of Asokore (Route V(b), mile 23) and all of its villages, which then became the responsibility of the Anantahene.[156] An Offinsohene (Route II, mile 15) is said to have been obliged to sell to Bekwae some seven or eight villages, after having been heavily fined for rebellion probably in the reign of Asantehene Opoku Ware.[157] Again, seemingly in the time of the Asantehene Kusi Obodom, the Nsutahemaa or 'queen-mother' Abena Siabura transferred eight villages to Kumase in payment for assistance given her after the *coup d'état* in which the Nsutahene Oduro Kuma was assassinated.[158]

153 Ramseyer and Kühne, 1875, p. 124.
154 Emergency sessions of the Ashanti Confederacy Council, June 1946, Asanteman Council Archives, Manhyia, Kumase.
155 Rattray, 1929, p. 149.
156 *Ibid.* p. 245.
157 *Ibid.* p. 149 and note 3.
158 *Ibid.* p. 259.

When Nunu Akyamfo of Pekyi No. 1, a town belonging to the Akyeremadehene of Kumase, incurred a debt of 30 peredwans, he decided to put his lands and people up for sale; the Asantehene Osei Kwadwo purchased them, and granted them to the new Hiawu stool.[159] During the reign of either Osei Kwadwo or Osei Kwame, Apea Panin of Ahenkro (Route II, mile 13) sold to the Kumase Kyidomhene the village of Anyinasu: charging 30 peredwans for the land and 40 for the people.[160] The Asumegyahene Owusu Ansa is reported to have been fined when a central government messenger was molested in his territory, and to have surrendered three of his villages to the Asantehene Osei Bonsu in settlement.[161] In the same reign, and probably in the second decade of the nineteenth century, the town of Apa, belonging to Mampon, was bought by the Asantehemaa Adoma Akosua for 100 peredwans.[162] And to offer one final example, in circumstances that are not clear, the Bekwae town of Odumase (Route VII) and villages of Akotakyi (Route VII) and Kyeaboso (Route VI: 1881 population, 60), were transferred to Adanse by the Asantehene Kwaku Dua I; they were reclaimed only in 1886 when the secessionists held power in Adanse.[163]

The market in towns and villages was one that could be manipulated by central government for political ends, and the accumulation of capital in the hands of the Asantehene gave him virtual command of it. Through the operation of the system of death-duties – *awunyadie* – and more generally through selective application of the law of torts, debts were generated which could only be liquidated by the sale of real estate. Thus, for example, the seven or eight villages acquired from Offinso by Bekwae were all subsequently taken by Asantehene Opoku Ware in payment of *awunyadie*, and only in the reign of Osei Bonsu did a Bekwaehene become repossessed of three of them.[164]

The case of Edweso is instructive in this context. One of the more powerful components of the coalition which fought in the Denkyira wars at the turn of the seventeenth century, the Edweso established their principal town only some twelve miles east of Kumase on land

159 Kyerematen, 1966, pp. 306 ff.
160 National Archives of Ghana, Kumase, D. 728, Kwame Kudwo to Chief Commissioner, dd. Kumase, 27 June 1908. *Ibid.* statement by Kofi Sekyere, n.d., but 1908. In or about 1889 the Kyidomhene Kofi Adwene, having opposed the election of Agyeman Prempe, abdicated and was obliged to transfer the same village to Edweso. He refused to give up the land, it is said, but surrendered the people without reclaiming the 40 peredwans.
161 Rattray, 1929, p. 135 and note 3, who wrongly names Mensa Bonsu.
162 *Ibid.* p. 245.
163 *Further Correspondence*, C. 4906, 1886, pp. 39 and 41: Firminger to Governor, dd. Praso, 17 April 1886.
164 Rattray, 1929, p. 149.

reputedly purchased from the Akyiawkromhene for 30 peredwans. Subsequent Edwesohenes, however, failed to achieve or maintain full *aman* status, and although Agyeman Prempe I transferred to them a number of places, at the time of the British occupation only some thirty to forty villages served the town.[165] The Edweso saw the relative stagnation of their district as having been an outcome of central government designs: 'The Ejisuhene was dwindled by harassing, ransacking and devastating village after village under, and placing the inhabitants under heavy penalties which imposed upon the villagers the necessity of transferring their allegiance to those who could pay the fines for them.'[166]

The evidence suggests that all transfers of land and villages had not only to be approved by the Asantehene, but that he had a pre-emption on all sales: that is that any village or town coming on to the market was in some sense 'purchased' by him, and then resold or in some cases granted to the third party to the transaction. A case which appears to have followed standard procedure may be cited. The Asantehene imposed a fine upon one Aferi Awua of Breman, who was obliged to sell some of his land. He offered a parcel for 1½ peredwans to Kyerewa Mansa, paternal half-sister of the late Kwaku Dua I and sister of Akyampon Tia (Akyampon Kwasi) and Akyampon Yaw of the Boakye Yam Kuma stool. Kyerewa Mansa decided to buy only part of the land, and paid for it ¾ peredwan and a small *ntrama* fee. She settled forty persons on the land. She then went to the Asantehene Kofi Kakari to present the land and the subjects, on oath, 'through him' to her brother Akyampon Yaw. Akyampon Yaw 'thanked' his sister, again 'through' the Asantehene, with a sum of three peredwans – which Kofi Kakari deputed the Debosohene Ata Famfam to hand over to her.[167] Whatever interpretation is to be offered of the role of the Asantehene in the transactions, it would seem that in some way the land was surrendered to him, in order that he might then confirm Akyampon Yaw in ownership of it. It is in this sense, at least, that in 1942 members of the Confederacy Council assented to the view that 'in former times all land in Ashanti belonged to the Asantehene and ownership was vested in the Golden Stool; the land belongs to the Asantehene by right of conquest and he gave the land to the various chiefs'.[168] But whatever the

165 The Gold Coast Civil Service List, 1902, pp. 150–1; 1907, p. 407.
166 Kumase Divisional Council Archives, Manhyia: History of Edweso, by Edwesohene and twenty-nine councillors, *adekurofo*, etc., dd. Edweso, 27 June 1933. Unaccessioned document.
167 Kumase Divisional Council Archives, Manhyia: Kumasihene's Tribunal, Civil Record Book 4, Kwasi Kwaakye v. Yaw Mensa, commencing 25 June 1928.
168 Kumase Divisional Council Archives, Manhyia: notes on Warrington's report by the Asantehene and Councillors, dd. Kumase, 24 July 1942.

precise legal interpretation to be placed on the Asantehene's title, the fundamental relationship of politics to land cannot be in question. *Otumi nyinaa wo asase so,* it is always said: 'all power is in the land'.

The origins of the political order

Asante emerged as a distinct political entity only in the later seventeenth century. A detailed report on the hinterland of the Gold Coast compiled by the Dutch Director-General at Elmina in 1679 made reference, for example, to Adanse and Tafo, but not to Asante.[169] The earliest mention of Asante as such known to the writer is that in a Dutch letter of 1698. By that date, however, the kingdom was clearly already well-established, and thereafter references become frequent. The earlier decades of the seventeenth century appear to have been marked by a gradual northwards drift of Twi-speaking farming peoples out of the Adanse region: a series of relatively small-scale and politically uncoordinated migrations perhaps in part at least a result of land shortages brought about by the introduction, via the maritime trade with the Americas, of new food crops.[170] Around the middle of the century some sort of political direction was imparted to these movements by the growth in power – not unconnected with the increasing importation of firearms from the coast – of certain lineages especially associated with the Ekuono and Oyoko *mmusua*. In the 1660s and 1670s a struggle for control of the Kwaman area around the old trading town of Tafo – already known as an important gold mart in the sixteenth century[171] – involved the immigrant groups in a series of wars which are still vividly recounted in Asante tradition.[172] Following the death of the Oyoko leader Obiri Yeboa in the course of these struggles, Osei Tutu was chosen to succeed him: his knowledge of statecraft and war acquired during his stay in the two southern courts of Denkyira and Akwamu, then the dominant powers along the Gold Coast, presumably decided his selection.[173] Returning northwards from Akwamu with arms purchased on the coast, and with levies provided by the Akwamuhene Ansa Sasraku (died 1689), Osei Tutu defeated first the

---

169 General State Archives, The Hague, WIC verspreyde stukken, 848: report by Director-General Abrams, dd. Elmina, 23 November 1679.
170 Compare Bowdich's reference, 1819, pp. 228–9, from 'tradition, scanty in itself', to the 'emigration of numerous enterprising or discontented families'.
171 See, e.g., Brasio, 1952–6, II, 246–7; III, 110.
172 See, e.g. Rattray, 1929, pp. 169, 235, 256; Kyerematen, 1966, pp. 177 ff. 158 ff., 186, 189, 190–4. For recent discussions of the rise of Asante, see Daaku, 1966, *passim;* Fynn, 1966, *passim;* 1971, chapter II. See also Wilks, *Land, Labour, Capital, and the Forest Kingdom of Asante:* paper presented to the Seminar on the Evolution of Social Systems, Department of Anthropology, University College London, 1974.
173 For the Akwamu background, see Wilks, 1957, *passim,* and especially pp. 126–7.

Domaa of Suntreso, and then the Tafo, Kaase and Amakom, and so established his supremacy within the Kwaman region.

From that time – perhaps about 1680 – onwards, it becomes permissible to speak of the kingdom of Asante. Osei Tutu built his new capital, Kumase, only some two miles from Tafo, and received the allegiance of such of the conquered as chose to remain: they were incorporated within the new Asante military organization, the Amakom for example within the *adonten* or centre division of Kumase, and the Tafo within the *benkum* or left wing. Meanwhile the conquest and pacification of the districts around Kwaman were accomplished by those described by Bowdich as 'other leading men of the party',[174] that is, by those of the allied groups who were in process of establishing their own towns and villages in adjacent territory. 'The Ashantee government', commented Bowdich, earliest of the European writers to give any coherent account of these events, 'concentred the mass of its original force, and making the chiefs resident in Coomassie and the few large towns they built in its neighbourhood, with titular dignities, conciliated those whom they subdued by continuing them in their governments. . .'[175] Among the new towns founded at about the same time as Kumase were, according to Bowdich, Bekwae, Kokofu, Mampon and Nsuta.[176] Dwaben, he maintained, had been an 'aboriginal town',[177] – apparently known as Apeayinase before its absorption into Asante.[178] These, together with associated towns such as Edweso, and the conquered and incorporated settlements, comprised pre-imperial Asante – the 'metropolitan region' of this study; 'the Colony whose conquests established the Empire' following Bowdich; and 'the centre and . . . the germ of the present empire' following Riis.[179] Over the new state Osei Tutu became king: the first Asantehene, though not the first of his dynasty. By the turn of the century he begins to figure in the records of the European trading companies on the Gold Coast: as, for example, 'the great Asjante Caboceer Zaay' of the Dutch reports. In a succession of wars which culminated in two battles in 1701, the Asante destroyed the power of the Denkyira, whose rulers were exacting tribute from the new nation; and the Dutch hastened to send David van Nyendaal to Kumase. He was the first European ambassador to be accredited to the Asante court.[180]

---

174 Bowdich, 1819, p. 231.
175 *Ibid.* p. 233.
176 *Ibid.* p. 256.
177 *Ibid.* p. 232.
178 See Daaku, 1966, p. 13.
179 PRO, T. 70/41/95(b): Bowdich to J. Hope Smith. Riis, 1854, Introduction.
180 General State Archives, The Hague, KvG 233: instructions to van Nyendaal, dd. Elmina, 9 October 1701. See Fynn, 1971, pp. 156–9. See in general, Priestley and Wilks, 1960, p. 84.

The unity of the new state was symbolized in the institution of the *Sika Dwa,* the Golden Stool.[181] For obvious ideological reasons – that the Golden Stool could not have come from elsewhere and hence have stranger status – it was regarded as having been called down from the sky. For similar reasons, all older stools and other tokens of political authority were surrendered and, so it is claimed, buried in the bed of the old Bantama creek in Kumase.[182] 'It was', remarked the Asantehene in 1962, 'considered improper that any stool in the nation should be regarded as having preceded the Golden Stool.[183] But the unity of the new state was also given practical expression in the regulation requiring of all those recognizing the authority of the Golden Stool, 'frequent attendance' – as Bowdich described it – 'at festivals, politically instituted'.[184] Most important of these was the annual Odwira to which reference has already been made: the first celebration of it is believed to have been held immediately after the Denkyira wars, when the skull of the slain Denkyirahene Ntim Gyakari became the focus of certain cultic aspects of the festival. The historical significance of the Odwira, however, was interestingly analyzed by the Edwesohene and others in 1933:

This occasional meeting at Kumasi for the observance of the Odwira custom was the beginning of what was later to be subordination to the Kumasi Stool, and since that time Kumasi has ever continued to be the central meeting place of the Ashanti Chiefs. From the foregoing it would be seen that the meeting at Kumasi was decreed by Komfuo Anotchi [Okomfo Anokye] after the fall of Denkyira. This occasional meeting was turned to mean subjection.[185]

Subjection, nevertheless, even within the metropolitan region was a matter of degree. The rulers of the more populous districts, owning many towns and villages, were able to maintain what Bowdich called 'palatine privileges'.[186] They enjoyed, as Freeman observed,

more or less of a kind of feudal independence. This peculiar feature is seen most strikingly developed in Juabin [Dwaben], and least so in Cucoofoo [Kokofu], but it is clearly apparent in all . . . [They] have all their own private establishments or town houses in Coomassie, where they reside during those periods of the year when they have to attend the great customs or when obeying the special call of the sovereign. In their own provincial capitals, from which the districts derive their names, they assume almost

181 See, e.g. Rattray, 1923, ch. XXIII; Kyerematen, 1969, pp. 2–5; Hagan, 1968, *passim.*
182 Kyerematen, 1969, pp. 2–3.
183 *Daily Graphic* (of Ghana), 24 March 1962.
184 Bowdich, 1819, p. 233.
185 Kumase Divisional Council Archives, Manhyia: History of Edweso, dd. 27 June 1933.
186 Bowdich, 1819, p. 256.

regal state, and their towns are, as to the kinds of streets and houses, all on the model of the capital.[187]

Bonnat made much the same point when he commented, 'this country is divided into districts, each of which has its capital and a viceroy, with a court modelled on that of the sovereign'.[188] The first writer to give any clear account of the nature of the prerogatives exercised by the powerful *amanhene* of the metropolitan region was Bowdich. 'The governors of the four great Ashantee districts of Soota, Marmpon, Becqua, and Kokoofoo', he noted, 'possess distinct treasuries, levy tributes, administer justice, celebrate the great annual festival in their own capitals after they have assisted in that of Coomassie, and are alone permitted to wear the little silver circles like buckles, which distinguish the sandals of the king'.[189] But Bowdich was also aware of the ways in which the jurisdictions of these four *amanhene* were limited. 'They have', he observed, 'an independent treasury, though subject to the demands of the government, and a judicial power, with the reserve of an appeal to the King.' [190] To Bowdich, only the Dwabenhene appeared to enjoy so complete an autonomy as to be regarded as 'an independent ally' [191] – a view of which the Asantehene hastened to disabuse Consul Dupuis some three years later. 'I suggested', reported Dupuis,

that it would afford me pleasure to meet the king of Juabin . . . 'The king,' replied the monarch, with some appearance of jealous indignation, 'who is he? Am not I the king? Is there another king then besides me? Does the book [the 1817 treaty] say that too? If so, it spreads a shameful lie in the white country.' [192]

The Aman and the loss of a sub-imperial role

While Bekwae, Dwaben, Kokofu, Mampon and Nsuta were regarded by most observers as the five more powerful *aman* within the metropolitan region in the nineteenth century, there was seemingly no agreed opinion as to the order in which they were to be ranked. In 1817 Bowdich placed Dwaben second only to Kumase in power, but treated the other four as of coordinate rank.[193] Freeman regarded Dwaben as first of the *aman*, and Kokofu as fifth, listing the other three as Bekwae, Mampon and Nkoransa – the latter strictly an inner prov-

187 T. B. Freeman, in *The Western Echo,* I, no. 12, 17 March 1886, p. 8.
188 Gros, 1884, p. 188.
189 Bowdich, 1821a, p. 21.
190 Bowdich, 1819, p. 256.
191 *Ibid.* pp. 232, 245.
192 Dupuis, 1824, p. 138.
193 Bowdich, 1819, p. 256.

ince.[194] Writing in 1875, Ramseyer and Kühne placed Dwaben, Bekwae and Mampon in the first rank, Kokofu and Nsuta in the second, and Adanse in the third.[195] This was, however, probably Ramseyer's view, for a year earlier Kühne, independently, had given the rank-order as Kokofu, Dwaben, Mampon, Bekwae, Nsuta and Adanse.[196] The implication is that the situation was not one of equilibrium, but that major changes in the distribution of power were occurring. It has been shown above how the jurisdictions of the greater *amanhene* were open to challenge at the local level by such of their subordinates as the Dadiasehene in Kokofu or the Gyamasehene in Mampon. But it was also the case that their joint power might be challenged at a regional level: that is, that one or several lesser towns might bid for *aman* status. Certainly in the late nineteenth century, when Bekwae was much weakened by its losses in the numerous campaigns it had fought in the preceding two decades, and when much of Kokofu had become depopulated as a result of emigration, the Edweso and Offinso assumed increasingly prominent political roles within the nation and their rulers commenced expanding their jurisdictions to embrace the prerogatives of the greater *amanhene*. To the conservative constitutionalists (*amanyɔ-mmara pɛfo*) of Asante, such changes were unwelcome, and their disapprobation seems to have been reflected in a situation report, put together in 1891 by Thomas Odonkor and based upon information collected from Krobo compatriots long resident in Kumase:

... the Bekwais, owing to the frequent encounters in which of late years they have been engaged, have lost much of their power. Owing also in part to the coolness which has sprung up between them and the Kumasis, the Ofinsus and Ajinsus have come more prominently forward and, though still remaining loyal, have given themselves airs and slipped more or less from under the control of Kumasi, which place, now that the Kokofus are away, has not the power to reduce them to their former state of subjection.[197]

The position of the conservatives at the time was made quite clear: 'according to Ashanti tradition, the Kumasis, Kokofus, Bekwais, Mampons and Insutahs have always stood as the only powerful Ashanti tribes, and these have regarded the Koranzas, Inkwantas, Adansis, Dadiasies, Ofinsus and Afisus [*sic:* Edweso] as slaves'.[198]

It will be shown in a later chapter, that in the nineteenth century

194 *The Western Echo*, I, no. 12, 17 March 1886, p. 8.
195 Ramseyer and Kühne, 1875, p. 308.
196 Brackenbury, 1874, II, 333.
197 *Further Correspondence*, C. 7917, 1896, p. 64: H. M. Hull to Governor, dd. Kumase, 6 April 1891.
198 *Ibid.* p. 63.

the conservatives who advocated a rigidly constructed and rigidly interpreted constitution based upon a view of the confederative origins of the nation,[199] and including therefore guarantees of states' rights, were in the nature of the case the most strongly entrenched in the upper house, the Asantemanhyiamu. But it was in the lower house, the powerful but extra-constitutional Council of Kumase which was dominated by the mercantilist or 'peace' party for so much of the nineteenth century, that policies were seemingly evolved which were directed toward the erosion of the constitutional prerogatives of the *aman,* and to the promotion of Asante's emergence as a unified nation-state.

Conflicts of interest between the central government and certain of the leading *aman* had developed in the later eighteenth century, with respect to the question of authority over conquered provinces. Both Mampon and Dwaben had, for example, played important roles in the establishment of Asante hegemony in the northern savannah lands. The campaigns of Safo Katanka of Mampon against eastern and central Gonja in 1751, have been referred to above (p. 21), and within the next decade or so the Dwabenhene Kofi Akraase led expeditions against the Basa, Krakye and Nchumuru.[200] The Dwaben invasion of Nanumba, reported in the traditions of that polity as having been authorized by Opoku Ware and as having occurred in the reign of the Na Damba, may also have taken place in the same period.[201] As a result of the thrusts into the northern hinterlands, the Mampon came to regard as in some sense under their jurisdiction the succession of provinces and districts lying along Route IV: Atebubu, Pran, Yeji, Kpembe and Dagomba. Similarly the Dwaben claimed authority over the districts lying along Route IV(a) as far as the Volta at Kete Krakye, and over those north of the road including Nanumba (or Namonsi) the capital of which, Kukuo, lay only some fifty miles east of Kpembe.[202] Both Mampon and Dwaben apparently received from such districts, in the early period, miscellaneous tributes in grain, meat, fish, honey, yams, grindstones and the like.[203]

[199] Succinctly treated in Rattray, 1929, chapters IX and X.
[200] See, e.g., Institute of African Studies, University of Ghana: JEK/5, Basa traditions recorded by J. E. K. Kumah, 1966; IASAS/16, Juaben Stool History recorded by J. Agyeman-Duah, 1963. See also Rattray, 1929, p. 171. Kofi Akraase's successor, Akuamoa Panin ('Quamboa', 'Quama'), was already in office by 1767, see General State Archives, The Hague, KvG 301: list of presents sent to Asante, 1767; and was apparently dead before 1777, see Bowdich, 1819, p. 237.
[201] Institute of African Studies, Ghana: E. F. Tamakloe, MS 'History of the Kingdom of Nanun'. The invasion is probably that referred to by Reindorf, 2nd ed., n.d., p. 84, in a particularly confused passage.
[202] Reindorf, 2nd ed., n.d., p. 133.
[203] Rattray, 1929, p. 239, note 2. Institute of African Studies, University of Ghana: JEK/5, p. 3.

While the existence of such sub-imperial systems presumably could not be tolerated indefinitely by the central government, its active intervention was in any case necessitated when Mampon and Dwaben took recourse to arms in a dispute about their respective spheres of influence in the north. Traditional accounts of the conflict report that the Mampon inflicted a defeat on the Dwaben in Nanumba, as a result of which the Asantehene ordered the case to be brought before his court in Kumase. The consensus of the accounts is that these events occurred at the time of the Asantehene Osei Kwadwo, the Mamponhene Atakora Kwame, and the Dwabenhene Akuamoa Panin: which is indicative of a date in or about 1770.[204] The traditions are conflicting as to whether the judgement in the Kumase court favoured the Mamponhene or Dwabenhene. Certainly, however, relations between central government and the local government in Mampon began to worsen rapidly after Osei Kwame became Asantehene in 1777.

The Mamponhene Atakora Kwame, who had been principally instrumental in bringing Osei Kwame into power, was overthrown by Owusu Sekyere Panin, paternally a prince (*oheneba*) of the Golden Stool.[205] The new Mamponhene committed himself to policies inimical to Kumase and appears to have commenced creating a new power base in the Nchumuru country south of Salaga.[206] The council of the Asantehene, failing in an attempt to have Owusu Sekyere Panin assassinated at Yeji, authorized despatch of an army against him under command of the Ankasehene Yamoa Ponko.[207] Meanwhile Owusu Sekyere Panin was declared destooled by a faction in Mampon which had the support of the powerful *abirempon* of Gyamase, Effiduase and Adwira, and the Asantehene approved the choice of Safo Yaw as successor.[208] According to Reindorf, however, Safo Yaw was subsequently obliged to relinquish all claims to authority over the northern provinces: '. . . he was deprived of the provinces of Nta [Gonja] and Brong. Krupi was also taken from his jurisdiction and the inhabitants removed to Pami [Kpembe]. Osafo in memory of this downfall ordered different horns to be blown, showing how he had been deprived of everything he possessed, and would therefore be mute.'[209] Rattray re-

204 Reindorf, 2nd ed., n.d., p. 133. Kyerematen, 1966, pp. 302 ff. Rattray, 1929, pp. 172 and 238–9.
205 Both Rattray, 1929, fig. 68, and Busia, 1951, p. 87, give Owusu Sekyere Panin as a son of Osei Kwame. This, however, appears chronologically unlikely, and he was almost certainly a son of Osei Kwadwo.
206 Reindorf, 2nd ed., n.d., p. 134.
207 *Idem*. Busia, 1951, p. 87.
208 Rattray, 1929, p. 239. Reindorf, 2nd ed., n.d., p. 134. Reindorf refers to Safo Yaw as Safo Katanka II; according to Rattray, 1929, fig. 67 facing p. 254, Safo Yaw was Safo Katanka I's sister's daughter's son.
209 Reindorf, 2nd ed., n.d., p. 134.

116

ported from Mampon a somewhat fuller tradition, that it was after the Fante campaign of 1807 in which Safo Yaw fought, that the Asantehene Osei Bonsu brought charges of disloyalty against him, and used the occasion to transfer to the central government whatever authority Mampon had exercised over the northern provinces. Since Atakora Kwaku, successor to Safo Yaw, was already in office by 1816,[210] the transfer would have occurred between 1807 and that date. In fact, the legal process by which the change was effected can also be established. The Asantehemaa Konadu Yaadom had lent large sums of money to the Mampon stool, and successive Mamponhenes had been unable to repay the debt; the central government accordingly assumed all rights over the northern provinces in discharge of it.[211] Konadu Yaadom is known to have died in 1809.[212] The presumption is, that whatever the truth of the accusations of disloyalty levelled against Safo Yaw, it was the death of Konadu Yaadom which provided the opportunity for central government, within the framework of the law, to foreclose the debt and take over Mampon's northern interests. According to Rattray's informants, responsibility for the districts and provinces of Amantin, Atebubu, Pran, Yeji, Kpembe and Dagomba was transferred to six Kumase functionaries: the Nsumankwaahene, Bremanhene, Ankobeahene, Gyaasewahene, Nkonnwasoafohene, and Anantahene respectively.[213]

The sub-imperial role which had thus finally been relinquished by Mampon in or about 1809 was still retained by Dwaben in the early nineteenth century: such is the implication of Bowdich's several references to Dwaben, alone of all the *aman*, as possessing 'dependencies'.[214] It would seem, then, no coincidence that the next major conflict between central and local authorities was one which was to culminate in the curtailment, in turn, of that district's jurisdiction. As early as 1817 Bowdich had observed: 'it is clear that the King of Ashantee contemplates the reduction of the King of Dwabin from an independent ally to a tributary'.[215] Discord was generated initially over specific questions of legal jurisdiction. In 1817 the Dwabenhene and Dwabenhemaa brought a case before the Asantehene Osei Bonsu in which a Dwaben subject was accused of plotting to subvert their authority.

210 Huydecoper's Journal, entry for 19 August 1816.
211 Rattray, 1929, p. 239, note 2.
212 PRO, T. 70/984, Accra Diary, entry for 28 June 1809. See also Bowdich, 1819, pp. 240–1, 289.
213 Rattray, 1929, p. 239 and note 2. But for Anantahene read Adontenhene.
214 Bowdich, 1819, pp. 105, 126, 163.
215 *Ibid.* p. 245. Bowdich's description of the Dwabenhene as an 'independent ally' was politically motivated, and the text of the Anglo-Asante treaty of 1817 that was despatched to London was falsified. For the correct text, see Dupuis, 1824, pp. cxix–cxx, and see also his observations on the matter, pp. 138–9.

Osei Bonsu not only acquitted the defendant, but showed him clear marks of favour – although the same person had, a short time before, apparently urged the Dwabenhene Kwasi Boaten to refuse demands made upon his treasury by the Asantehene, on the grounds that there was no national emergency.[216] Between 1824 and 1830, during the reign of the Asantehene Osei Yaw, there occurred a number of what were in effect test-cases, seemingly designed to explore the strength of the Dwabenhene's jurisdiction relative to that of central government. The case of Asumi, who fled to Kumase after having surprised a wife of the Dwabenhene while bathing, was tried before Osei Yaw. Asumi was acquitted but, on his return to Dwaben, was seized and put to death by Kwasi Boaten.[217] A more complex issue arose following the death in 1826 of the Nsutahene Yaw Sekyere. Two factions contended for control of the vacant office. The one, headed by Owiredu Kwatia and Berifi, appealed to the Dwabenhene for support, while the other, headed by Mafo and Okwawe Dokono, appealed to the Asantehene. Osei Yaw summoned the Nsuta leaders and Kwasi Boaten to Kumase, giving guarantees of safety to all. Unexpectedly, however, Mafo produced evidence before court to show that Owiredu Kwatia and Berifi had robbed and murdered some eighty of the Asantehene's servants who had been travelling to Salaga via Nsuta. Finding them guilty, despite his guarantees of safety Osei Yaw ordered their execution and, by making Mafo the new Nsutahene, completed the discomfiture of the Dwabenhene.[218] Yet another case followed shortly afterwards, when a Dwaben court official, Kotieku alias Yaw Odabo, was accused of having raped three wives of the Dwabenhene. Kotieku fled to Kumase, and was arrested there. Kwasi Boaten was summoned to the capital for the trial, but refused to appear, insisting that the accused should be returned to Dwaben. Owusu Nkwantabisa, Adontenhene in Kumase, was sent as head of a delegation to escort Kwasi Boaten into Kumase, but its members were insulted, stoned, and driven out of Dwaben.[219] Since 1826, moreover, accusations had been made unofficially, though never tested in court, that the Dwabenhene had appropriated to his own use property of the central government which had fallen into his hands at the battle of Katamanso, when he had been instrumental in averting loss of the Golden Stool itself. 'Envious captains of the Asantes', so Reindorf reported it, 'added to this ill-will by putting unfavourable construction upon the conduct of Boaten during the battle. They even accused him of having re-

216 Bowdich, 1819, pp. 245–6.
217 Rattray, 1929, p. 173.
218 Reindorf, 2nd ed., n.d., pp. 276–7; Rattray, 1929, p. 261.
219 Reindorf, 2nd ed., n.d., pp. 277–80. Fuller, 1921, pp. 82–3.

tained some of the public treasury lost in the campaign, insinuating that as he had managed to secure the golden stool, the public treasury chest carried with it must likewise be in his possession'.[220]

The whole affair reached its climax in 1831, when Osei Yaw finally ordered a military occupation of Dwaben. 'Osai [Yaw] Akoto', reported Freeman, 'sent an army to advance upon Jabin, to bring the refractory Chief to obedience.' After heavy fighting, the town was taken, and Kwasi Boaten, the Dwabenhemaa Sewaa, and many of their subjects fled southwards into Akyem Abuakwa where they sought, and obtained, British protection.[221] In 1835 the new Asantehene Kwaku Dua, who had himself been raised in Dwaben (see Chapter 9), entered into a treaty of peace with the Dwaben government-in-exile,[222] but it was not until late 1837 that, with funds provided by central government, the first party of refugees – some 250 strong, and principally women and children – returned to Kumase for resettlement. Panicking, however, they left again,[223] and only in 1841, two years after the death of Kwasi Boaten, were the majority of his people induced to return to their homeland.[224]

The Aman and the issue of states' rights

The sequence of events between 1817 and 1841 had demonstrated the impotence of those who might stand upon a strict construction of the constitution in the face of the powerful alignment of forces within the nation committed to the development of a unified system of political and legal administration. For almost half a century after the collapse of Dwaben power, the proponents of states' rights – or, broadly, those opposed to the centralizing policies of the Council of Kumase – seem to have lacked both cohesiveness of purpose and a common base for action. It will be seen in Chapter 10 that under Kwaku Dua, who ruled increasingly by executive instrument until his death in 1867, the decision-making functions of the Asantemanhyiamu were much eroded. It was only in the 1870s and 1880s that the matter of states' rights became once again a major political issue, when within each of the *aman* and even in the provinces there emerged pro- and anti-Kumase parties. The 'left', as it were, held to the aim of trans-

220 Reindorf, 2nd ed., n.d., p. 276. Rattray, 1929, p. 172.
221 T. B. Freeman, 1843, pp. 156–7. A. Riis, 1840, pp. 92 ff. Reindorf, 2nd ed., n.d., pp. 280–4.
222 PRO, CO. 267/136, Treaty of Peace, dd. 16 November 1835.
223 *Report from the Select Committee on the West Coast of Africa*, Part II, House of Commons, 1842: Topp and Swanzy to Committee, dd. Cape Coast, 8 May 1838. A. Riis, 1840, pp. 229–30.
224 T. B. Freeman, 1843, p. 158.

forming Asante into a unified nation-state, while the 'right' supported local nationalisms and, in its more extreme manifestations, secessionist movements. Between the two was to be found a broad spectrum of conservative opinion, advocating a federal form of government but divided as to the precise degree of autonomy to be allowed the *aman* and provinces. Their basic position was admirably stated by the Fante lawyer Casely Hayford, who combined with his many other activities a sympathetic interest in Asante affairs: [225]

in Ashanti . . . there were the Manpons, the Juabins, the Kokofus, the Beckwas, the Adansis, and several other large and important communities, owning allegiance to the stool of Kumasi as the paramount stool of all Ashanti. Each of these important communities, when regarded with respect to the entire State, was a sort of *imperium in imperio* – in fact, several distinct native states federated together under the same laws, the same customs, the same faith and worship, the people speaking the same language, and all owning allegiance to a paramount king or president, who represented the sovereignty of the entire Union.[226]

Within the two decades 1875–95 the British government moved slowly towards the decision to incorporate Greater Asante within their larger imperial system, and its representatives on the Gold Coast found themselves embroiled in the major issue of Asante politics. They were faced with the choice of pursuing one of two incompatible policies. On the one hand, the thrust of British policy might be designed to strengthen the authority of the central government in Kumase, with the ultimate aim of appointing a Resident there who would oversee and influence its decisions. On the other hand, policy might be directed to undermining precisely that authority, by supporting the proponents of states' rights but more especially the extremists of the movement – the secessionists – and so ultimately assuming direct control over the various virtually autonomous local administrations in *aman* and provinces.

In 1891 the British Governor of the Gold Coast sent Acting Travelling Commissioner Hull to Kumase, where he met with the Asantehene Agyeman Prempe I and his Council (see Plate II). He invited them 'to place their country under British protection': and so to prevent it 'gradually falling into decay'. In a courteous reply, the Asantehene declined the offer:

The suggestion that Ashanti in its present state should come and enjoy the protection of Her Majesty the Queen and Empress of India, I may say this is

225 See, e.g. Casely Hayford, 1903, pp. 264–6. It is worthy of note that Casely Hayford's father (the later Reverend) Joseph De Graft Hayford of Anomabo, had been appointed resident ambassador in Kumase by Maclean in 1835, see Methodist Mission Archives, London: Freeman to Boyce, dd. 21 May 1874.
226 Casely Hayford, 1903, p. 19.

a matter of a very serious consideration and which I am happy to say we have arrived at this conclusion, that my kingdom of Ashanti will never commit itself to any such policy; Ashanti must remain independent as of old, at the same time to be friendly with all white men. I do not write this with a boastful spirit, but in the clear sense of its meaning. Ashanti is an independent kingdom and is always friendly with the white men; for the sake of trade we are to bind to each other, so it is our Ashanti proverb, that what the old men eat and left, it is what the children enjoyed. I thank Her Majesty's Government for the good wishes entertained for Ashanti; I appreciate to the fullest extent its kindness, and I wish that my power of language could suitably tell you how much and how deeply I appreciate those kindness of Her Majesty's Government towards me and my kingdom. Believe me, Governor, that I am happy to inform you, that the cause of Ashanti is progressing and that there is no reason for any Ashantiman to feel alarm at the prospects, or to believe for a single instant that our cause has been driving back by the events of the past hostilities.[227]

Disarming in tone, the refusal of the Asante government to accept the offer of protection nevertheless appears finally to have decided the British upon the more aggressive policy. In a memorandum to the London Colonial Office in 1894, Governor Griffith of the Gold Coast argued:

. . . I am of opinion that it will be false policy to continue to treat Ashanti as a compact state. We should recognise the fact that it is only composed of a bundle of states, kept together by no common interest, but which, by their internal wars and intrigues, menace the interests and security of the trade of the protected territories.[228]

The transactions of the embassy headed by Kwame Boaten and John Owusu Ansa, which was sent to London in 1895 to negotiate on behalf of the Asante government (but which was refused official recognition by the Colonial Office), will be fully discussed in Chapter 14. Its members arrived back on the Gold Coast only after a new British expeditionary force had already been launched on an invasion of Asante. On 17 January 1896 the force entered Kumase, the government having decided not to oppose its advance, but to negotiate a settlement with the British from a position of military weakness and of moral strength. The invaders' intention was, however, different. On 20 January, as Governor Hodgson was later to report it, 'the whole system of native administration was paralyzed by the removal as political prisoners of Prempeh and the principal members of his Court, as well as the Kings who were his chief and open supporters'.[229] The deportees were held

227 *Further Correspondence*, C. 7917, 1896, pp. 70–2; letter from Asantehene to Governor, dd. 7 May 1891. For the offer of protection see Tordoff, 1962, *passim*.
228 *Ibid*. pp. 224–7: Memorandum on Relations with Kumase, dd. 25 October 1894.
229 *Correspondence relating to the Ashanti War 1900*, C. 501, 1901: Hodgson to Colonial Office, dd. 29 January 1901.

first in Elmina, and were then transferred to Sierra Leone and finally to Seychelles (see Plate III).

In pursuance of the aim, *pace* Governor Maxwell, of 'the destruction of the central power of Kumasi',[230] separate treaties of submission were obtained from each of the *aman* and the larger towns: from Bekwae and Nsuta on 11 and 30 January 1896, and from Mampon, Dwaben, Kokofu, Agona, Kumawu, Offinso and Edweso on 10 February.[231] But the Mamponhene Kwame Apea Osokye, Offinsohene Kwadwo Apea and Edwesohene Kwasi Afrane Kuma, all known to be strong adherents to central government policies, were among those deported with the Asantehene. The Offinso and Edweso treaties were thus clearly signed under duress by the Offinsohemaa Ama Afraniwaa and the Edwesohemaa Yaa Asantewaa, while in the case of Mampon the former *omanhene* Owusu Sekyere (who had been removed from office in 1888) was reinstated by the British in time to oblige Maxwell with his signature. The Kokofu district was committed to protection by Kwabena (George) Asibe II,[232] whilst the acquiescence of the Dwabenhene Yaw Sapon, another strong supporter of the central authority, was procured by promises that Dwaben stools in British hands would be returned to him.[233] On 10 February 1896, Governor Maxwell addressed an assembly of chiefs in Kumase, virtually to inform them that the Asante nation had ceased to exist. 'I told them', he reported, 'that there is no desire to interfere with native administration further than is necessary to secure the due fulfilment of treaty conditions, that each country will be separate and independent, and that old feuds and hatreds must be forgotten.'[234] With the Asantemanhyiamu thus abolished, some attempt was made to secure the loyalty of the *amanhene* to the British by redistributing between them a number of Kumase towns and villages.[235]

In the capital itself the Council of Kumase was dissolved, and a 'Native Committee of Administration' was created to advise the new military administration. To it the British appointed three members: the Gyaasewahene Opoku Mensa, the Akankade counselor Kwaku Nantwi Kaakyera; and the Atwomahene Antwi Agyei (replaced on his death by Toasehene Kwame Afrifa). 'It may be expected', wrote Governor Maxwell of the Gold Coast, 'that the few remaining officials of the late King of Kumasi will continue to regulate their conduct by

230 Maxwell, 1896, p. 46.
231 PRO, Co. 879/113, Collection of Treaties with Native Chiefs: Part III, The Gold Coast.
232 Maxwell, 1896, p. 44.
233 PRO, African (West) 500: Chamberlain to Maxwell, dd. London, 12 December 1895. See also Rattray, 1929, p. 177.
234 Maxwell, 1896, p. 44.
235 See, e.g. Tordoff, 1965, pp. 328 ff.

the political idea which makes Kumasi supreme and all Kings of neighbouring tribes subordinate to it.' [236] In fact, there is little doubt that many Asante regarded the triumvirate as having essentially assumed the role and responsibilities of the exiled Asantehene and thus it was the three who were able, in conditions of the greatest secrecy, to undertake in 1898 the initial planning of new military operations against the British.[237] When war finally came in 1900, the nation was divided. The *amanhene* of Bekwae, Dwaben, Mampon and Nsuta failed to rise, not out of any satisfaction with the results of British overrule as such but rather because each evaluated the intervention of the British in the affairs of the nation in relationship principally to the states' rights issue. But in any case the war ended with the defeat of the Asante forces, as inevitably it had to in view of the extreme disparity in the military resources of the protagonists.

By the Ashanti Administration Ordinance of 1 January 1902, the metropolitan region was divided mainly between the newly created Central and Southern Provinces; and the remaining territories outside the metropolitan region, between the Western and Northern Provinces. The new provinces were purely administrative units; each district within them, Mampon, Dwaben, Offinso, Agona and so forth, was directly responsible to a Provincial Commissioner, and through him to the Chief Commissioner in Kumase and the Governor of the Gold Coast in Accra. The Asantemanhyiamu had been legislated out of existence. The Council of Kumase, by contrast, was to be revived as a committee, convened in mid-1905, to advise the Chief Commissioner on matters relating to Kumase itself. The arrangement was justified by Fuller, Chief Commissioner from 1905 to 1920, in the following terms:

The officious, unjust, and often cruel interference, in the past, of the Coomassie chiefs with the internal affairs of the outlying tribes having been the cause of perennial dissatisfaction, the obvious policy of the Administration was to break off all political connection between the two. The Coomassie chiefs were strictly forbidden to obtrude in matters that did not concern their proper territories. The resentment this caused among them was more than compensated for by the sense of relief and security experienced by the others.[238]

The decision of the Colonial Administration in the early 1930s to restore to the Asante a modicum of political unity, was one that was

[236] PRO, CO. 96/298: memorandum of an interview in Kumase, by Maxwell, 16 August 1897.
[237] *Correspondence relating to the Asshanti War 1900*, C. 501, 1901, pp. 110–15: Hodgson to Colonial Office, dd. Surbiton, 29 January 1901. See also Hodgson, 1901, especially chapter v.
[238] Fuller, 1921, pp. 216–17.

dependent upon a statement of the old nineteenth century conservative tradition. In order to avoid the re-emergence of a strong central power capable of confrontation with the Colonial Administration, the British naturally inclined to acceptance of the confederative theory of the origins of the nation and so to the advocacy of states' rights. And in order to obstruct the renewal of party political activity in Asante – and thereby to retain control of the direction of change – the British saw as a necessary precondition of a system of indirect rule the existence of a rigidly constructed constitution. Curiously, then, the conservative tradition in Asante was in fact brought to fruition – in terms of a written codification of the constitution – through the work of British political officers.[239] Guidelines were established by R. S. Rattray in the 1920s, who published his *Ashanti Law and Constitution* in 1929 – a work 'of paramount importance to the local Administration, engaged as it is in framing "Native Jurisdiction Ordinances", in schemes for the working of "Native Tribunals", and in plans for "Indirect Rule" '.[240] Three years later Chief Commissioner Newlands acknowledged, somewhat disingenuously, that the conflict between constitutionalists and others was by no means dormant:

The work of re-establishing the old Ashanti constitution and fitting each Omanhene, Ohene, etc., into his proper place in the hierarchy will be both complicated and laborious – not because any real doubt exists as to the true position of each of these stools, but because of the natural desire of each occupant of a stool to secure for himself, as the price of his support of the restoration of the Asantehene, some higher place, rank, or influence than his stool formerly occupied.[241]

Opposition to the introduction of Indirect Rule came principally from some of the greater *amanhene,* notably Mamponhene and Bekwaehene, and from many of the rulers of what in the nineteenth century had been inner provinces, for example, the Takyimanhene and Berekumhene: all of whom adhered to an essentially secessionist position.[242] An attempt to articulate opposition was made by the Friends of Ashanti Freedom Society, the sponsorship of which extended from the Edwesohene on the one hand to Wallace-Johnson, Sierra Leonean editor of *The West African Sentinel,* on the other.[243] Petitioning by

239 Compare Ferguson and Wilks, 1970, *passim.*
240 Rattray, 1929, p. v.
241 See Tordoff, 1965, p. 353.
242 See Tordoff, 1965, pp. 402–14.
243 As Tordoff points out, however, Wallace-Johnson had shifted his position by the time of the restoration, *ibid.* p. 343, note 2. See also Asanteman and Kumase State Council Archives, Manhyia, Kumase: Report on the Restoration of Ashanti Confederacy, compiled by T. A. Wallace-Johnson through the kind permission of Otumfuo Osei Agyeman Prempeh II, dd. Accra, 6 February 1935.

telegram the Secretary of State for the Colonies in London, the Society maintained that the 'Confederacy movement solely work Ashanti Political Officers' – that is, of the colonial administrators in Asante – and appealed for support to the League Against Imperialism and for National Independence on the broad ground that Indirect Rule would in effect increase rather than diminish the British Administration's control over the Asante masses.[244] Dismissing the Freedom Society, however, as 'a coterie of disgruntled Ashantis and bombastic strangers . . . whose energies have been directed towards political intrigue',[245] on 31 January 1935 the Administration brought the 'Ashanti Confederacy' into existence. Essentially, the Asantemanhyiamu was revived, and assigned limited decision-making powers; renamed the 'Ashanti Confederacy Council', it was convened as erratically and infrequently as its nineteenth century predecessor, being in regular session only eight times in the first eleven years of its existence. Osei Agyeman Prempeh II was recognized as Asantehene, an office virtually redefined, however, as that of President of the Ashanti Confederacy Council, and a Committee of Privileges was set up to continue the work of codifying Asante constitutional procedures: its work came as near to completion as it ever could when in 1942 a committee set up by the Confederacy Council recommended acceptance of its redrafted version of an earlier document drawn up by J. C. Warrington, *Notes on Ashanti Custom*.[246] The work of the Confederacy Council has been the subject of a number of studies [247] and will not be of concern here. The fact was that most major functions of central government exercised by the Asantemanhyiamu and the Council of Kumase in the nineteenth century had been taken over by the Colonial Civil Service. Most importantly, however, the councils which the British reconstituted, the Kumase 'Council of Chiefs' in 1905 and the Asante 'Confederacy Council' in 1935, were so comprised as to be responsive to no political ideology in Asante other than the conservative and constitutionalist one of which the new rulers of empire approved.

244 Tordoff, 1965, pp. 342–9. Wallace-Johnson, dd. Accra, 6 February 1933.
245 Tordoff, 1965, p. 345.
246 Asanteman Council Archives, Manhyia, Kumase: notes on Warrington's Report by the Asantehene and Councillors, dd. Kumase, 24 July 1942.
247 See, e.g. Busia, 1951, chapter VIII; Tordoff, 1965, chapter XV; Triulzi, 1972, *passim*.

CHAPTER 4

Kumase and the southern provinces: the politics of control

The southern provinces and the beginning of administrative reform

In the early nineteenth century, excluding certain distant territories east of the Volta and west of the Tano rivers, writers identified some sixteen southern and central provinces as forming part of Greater Asante: Accra, Adangme, Ahanta, Akuapem, Akwamu, Akyem, Amanahia, Aowin, Assin, Bonzina, Denkyira, Fante, Kwawu, Sehwi, Twifo and Wassa (see above, p. 54). In 1819 Bowdich was able to list the number of fighting men which several of these provinces were required to provide to the national army upon demand: Akyem, 4,000 (but earlier in the century, 16,000); Akuapem ('etc.'), 1,000; Assin, 8,000; Denkyira, 5,000; Sehwi, 4,000; and Wassa, 7,000.[1] Occupying an area of somewhat over 20,000 square miles, or about twice the size of the metropolitan region, no reliable estimates of the population of these provinces exist for the earlier nineteenth century. The opinion of T. B. Freeman, that the population of Fante, Akyem and Akuapem, with the seaboard districts, numbered between 800,000 and one million, must presumably be discounted.[2] Within the area of approximately 6,000 square miles over which the British claimed jurisdiction by 1846, Governor Winniett estimated the population at upwards of 275,000.[3] Augmented in 1850 to an area of some 8,000 square miles by the addition of districts previously regarded by the Danes as under their administration, Governor Hill estimated the population at 400,000 in 1851, but revised the figure to 300,000 in 1853.[4] After the invasion of Asante in 1874, the British incorporated into the Gold Coast Colony virtually all of the former southern dependencies of Asante. In 1883 Governor Rowe estimated its area as 18,784 square miles and its population, on the basis of figures for the number of men able to bear arms in each district, as 651,000.[5] In the first census of the

1 Bowdich, 1819, p. 317.
2 Beecham, 1841, p. 135.
3 See De Graft-Johnson, 1969, p. 1.
4 *Ibid.* p. 2.
5 *Idem.*

Gold Coast Colony, taken in 1891, 764,508 persons were enumerated within, broadly, the area of the old Asante dependencies, excluding Kwawu and the country of the 'Krepi' east of the Volta.[6] It was generally acknowledged, however, that the count was incomplete, and Szereszewski has suggested reasons for revising the figure to one of about 970,000.[7] Although the quality of the data is not such as to warrant a definitive approach to the topic, it would seem reasonable to suppose that the population of the southern dependencies of Asante in the earlier nineteenth century was of the order of somewhat over a half-million, and that the density of population was thus significantly lower than that of the metropolitan region.

The establishment of an Asante hegemony over the southern territories has been briefly discussed above (pp. 23–5). Although the final occupation of the coastal Fante districts was not to occur until 1807, by the middle of the eighteenth century the expansionist aims of the Asante generals – whether in the south or north – had been largely achieved, and the Asantehene Opoku Ware was faced with the problem of incorporating into an imperial system peoples with highly diverse forms of social, cultural, political and economic organization.[8] Broadly, so it will be argued, government had to be extended in *range,* to control areas far distant from the metropolitan region; in *scope,* to regulate spheres of activity previously untouched by central authority; and in *proficiency,* beyond the managerial resources of the hereditary aristocracy of the pre-imperial period. The development of a new apparatus of administration to effectuate the transition from policies of expansion to those of incorporation was not without attendant upheaval. In 1748 the Dutch traders on the Gold Coast reported that Opoku Ware was 'much embroiled with his chiefs'.[9] Dupuis, seemingly following the testimony of Muslim informants in Kumase, gave some account of the nature of the troubles. 'In this stage of politics', he recorded of the period immediately following the major campaigns of the 1740s,

Sai Apoko [Opoku Ware], in the latter part of his reign, enacted new codes of laws, adapted for the government of the various departments of the state; but some of these regulations being considered inimical to the interests of the chiefs, and as they represented it again, to the public welfare, a dangerous conspiracy was raised against the throne, in the very heart of the kingdom. The capital, moreover, took a share in these transactions, and the king was obliged to fly his palace, by night, and seek refuge at Juabin, where he

6 *Report on the Census of the Gold Coast Colony for the Year 1891*, London, n.d.
7 Szereszewski, 1965, pp. 126–7.
8 See, e.g. Dickson, 1969, Parts 1 and 2.
9 General State Archives, The Hague, WIC 490: Van Voorst to Amsterdam, dd. Elmina, 30 September 1748.

convened a sort of diet; but some of his enemies were already in arms, and he was compelled to the same alternative.[10]

Opoku Ware fought and defeated the rebels at Dinkyin (Route IV, mile 42), and granted them a conditional pardon. The programme of reform, however, was not pushed through: Opoku Ware died, reputedly while in council, in 1750.[11] The subsequent contest for the stool between the two candidates, Dako and Kusi Obodom, was resolved in favour of the latter.[12] Regarded by contemporary observers, and by most later writers, as a weak ruler, in a recent reappraisal of his reign Fynn has argued that by virtue of his preference for negotiation to military intervention, Kusi Obodom was able to retain at least token authority over many of the territories occupied by his predecessor.[13] 'He was', maintained Reindorf, 'the most humane of all the kings; forbade human sacrifices, and made peace among the chiefs' – by restoring fully to them the constitutional powers of which they had been deprived by Opoku Ware.[14] In internal politics Kusi Obodom was then, in the context of the mid-eighteenth century, conservative and constitutionalist in approach. As Dupuis reported it, after the death of Opoku Ware

a revocation of the obnoxious edicts took place, whereby an ample scope for ambition was again enjoyed by the chiefs of the army, whose object it was to preserve the old constitution, upon that basis which guaranteed to all the principal officers of state, and generals, or captains in the army, a proportionate share of influence in the city, a political preponderance in the councils of the nation, and a princely rank in the provinces.[15]

The question of Opoku Ware's abortive attempts at reform was still one of debate in Kumase seventy years later. 'Had it been practicable', recorded Dupuis,

to have given stability to the wise regulations of Sai Apoko, it is generally believed by the Moslems, that the empire of Ashantee, at this day, would have held a rank proportionate to several of the most powerful monarchies inland; and instead of exhibiting that unstable force of tribes and nations (forty-seven, as they say, in number), whose interests are, in some instances, necessarily the reverse of that of the court, from the oppression they daily groan under, (owing mainly to the arbitrary influence of the chiefs), it would have exhibited an irresistible union between every tribe, and every principality of the empire.[16]

10 Dupuis, 1824, p. 235.
11 *Idem.*
12 Priestley and Wilks, 1960, p. 93. Fynn, 1965, p. 25.
13 Fynn, 1965, *passim.*
14 Reindorf, 2nd ed., n.d., p. 130.
15 Dupuis, 1824, p. 235.
16 *Idem.*

The Muslim analysis of the failure of successive Asante governments to achieve a higher degree of national integration was not enlightening: '. . . this wisdom', observed the Imām of Kumase, 'they are not gifted with; the eternal decree is sealed upon the hearts of infidels; therefore are they suffered to wander in ignorance'.[17] But there seems little doubt that the Muslim scholars of early nineteenth century Kumase had taken a quite unduly sceptical account of the matter. Major political reforms had in fact been initiated in the later part of the eighteenth century.

Upon the death of Kusi Obodom in 1764, Osei Kwadwo came to the throne. He was, so the Dutch Director-General at Elmina commented, 'a courageous young man . . . who would surely follow in the footsteps of the former king Poku',[18] and the English Governor in Cape Coast noted of him, that he 'admired so much and revered the Memory of Apoeka'.[19] In his reign, and in that of his successor Osei Kwame, administrative agencies were developed to facilitate the political incorporation of the many dependencies; and civilian officials progressively took over responsibility from the military commanders. By the earlier nineteenth century something of the nature of the new infrastructure was becoming apparent to observers. In 1823, for example, a writer in the notoriously anti-Asante *Royal Gold Coast Gazette* could reluctantly concede of the Asante, that

taking the extent of the territory they claimed before the present war, it is suprising how they conducted their affairs, when everything is considered . . . Without archives, or even the advantage of books or writing, they appear to have managed every state so that the government were advised of their proceedings. The extensive connexions of their merchants, must have put those in power in possession of much valuable information . . . By those facilities they have aggrandised themselves at the expense of every people, without exception, to whom they could extend their military intrusion. The system of placing a caboceer, or chief, in every conquered town of consequence, has tended much to enrich the superior classes of society generally.[20]

Cruickshank, resident on the Gold Coast in the 1830s and 1840s, similarly subscribed to a reductivist view of the Asante state as essentially an instrument for the exploitation of the masses – of 'the superior preying upon the inferior classes' – but was able to give a somewhat fuller account of the system of imperial administration. 'It was no part of the Ashantee policy', he commented,

17 *Ibid.* pp. 235–6.
18 General State Archives, The Hague, WIC 115: Director-General Huydecoper to Assembly of Ten, dd. Elmina, 15 October 1764.
19 PRO, T. 70/31: Governor Hippisley to Committee of Merchants, dd. Cape Coast, 13 July 1766.
20 *The Royal Gold Coast Gazette*, 7 June 1823.

to alter the government of the conquered country. The chiefs of the different tribes remained in possession of what power the conqueror thought fit to leave them, with the style and rank of a captain of the king; and in that capacity they acted as so many lieutenants, governing the country in the king's name, at the same time that they continued to receive the allegiance and service of their own vassals and slaves.

But the king was not content to leave the government entirely in the hands of the native chiefs, who might possibly in the course of time rally the prostrate energies of the country, and combine to throw off his yoke. In consequence of this suspicion, which ever haunts the minds of usurpers, he appointed pro-consuls of the Ashantee race, men of trust and confidence, to reside with the fallen chiefs, to notify them of the royal will, to exercise a general superintendence over them, and especially to guard against and to spy out any conspiracies that might be formed to recover their independence.[21]

The 'pro-consuls' of Cruickshank's account are otherwise variously referred to in the European literature as consuls, magistrates, lieutenants, captains, residents, resident ambassadors, governors, and the like. In Twi they were apparently known as *amradofo*.[22] There seems little objection here to using those terms by which the British administration designated the colonial officials who came to assume the responsibilities and duties of their Asante predecessors: hence references will be standardized, as to District Commissioners, Provincial or Regional Commissioners, and, more generally, resident commissioners. Bowdich specifically associated the development of the new civil administration in the southern provinces with the reign of Osei Kwadwo. 'It was a law of Sai Codjo', he wrote, 'which granted to particular captains the honourable patent of receiving the pay of small forts, distinctly, each being responsible for his separate duties to his settlement.'[23] The growth of the provincial administration can, in fact, be reconstructed in some detail.

The provincial administration in the southeast

In 1838 Governor Maclean of Cape Coast, noting that Akyem and Akuapem had been 'to all intents and purposes provinces of that

21 Cruickshank, 1853, I, 340.
22 See, for example, National Archives, Copenhagen, Miscellaneous Archives from Guinea, Kongensten Letterbook: Flindt to Schiønning, dd. Kongensten, 30 November 1816. Flindt confessed to not knowing the word *amrado* (Danish, *marandeur*), but added that it seemed to mean 'important Asante'. The term appears in fact to have been borrowed from the Portuguese *amiral* (cf. English *admiral*), and adopted into Asante Twi via perhaps the Gã *amralo*. Subsequently the Asante were to use the term as translation of the English *governor*, see Ramseyer and Kühne, 1875, p. 266. The borrowing into Asante Twi, as a term for a new class of officials, was presumably reinforced by association with the Asante *mmara*, 'law'; the early connotation of *amradofo* was thus probably 'those responsible for the maintenance of law'.
23 Bowdich, 1819, p. 83.

Kingdom', namely Asante, added that they had been governed 'by resident Lieutenants of the King of Ashantee, paid taxes to their Sovereign, and joined him in all his wars'.[24] For reasons of politics rather than of ignorance, Maclean maintained that the arrangements dated only from 1807. It has been noted above, however, that in 1786 an Asante official was stationed at Mamfe in Akuapem, where he was responsible for the collection of tolls from traders, and in 1788, apparently of the Akuapem capital of Akuropon, Biørn remarked: 'here the King of Asante keeps a senior Lieutenant (minister or ambassador) for the protection of his subjects from affront'.[25]

In 1853 P. Keteku recorded, in Twi, Akuapem accounts of the circumstances of the transition in that province from Asante military to Asante civilian administration. After the Akuapem had been persuaded into revolt by the Akyem Abuakwa, he reported, an Asante army under command of Adusei, reinforced by Akwamu troops, invested the rebels in the Krobo hills. Unexpectedly, the Asantehene ordered the withdrawal of his forces, and despatched a commissioner, Odenkyem, to reside in Akuapem as his representative there. Reciprocally, the ruler of Akuapem sent a member of his house, Awuku, to Kumase with gifts, to express gratitude for the withdrawal of the army and to enter into a peace settlement. Thirty-two ounces of gold were despatched from Akuapem to Kumase in confirmation of the agreement.[26]

It is clear from contemporary sources that the revolt in question was that which broke out late in 1772, when Osei Kwadwo was Asantehene and Obiri Koran and Obuobi Atiemo ruled over the Akyem Abuakwa and Akuapem respectively.[27] Odenkyem ('the crocodile', and hence sometimes referred to in European sources as Caiman) had been active in the affairs of the southeastern provinces certainly as early as 1766, when he had conducted a mission to Accra.[28] His appointment by Osei Kwadwo to the Akuapem residency cannot be exactly dated, but by 1776 his authority was fully acknowledged there: in the middle of that year he arranged for Obuobi Atiemo to take an oath in the presence of the Danish authorities in Christiansborg, that he acknowledged Osei Kwadwo as his sovereign and protector, and that he would

24 PRO, CO. 267/150: Minute by Governor Maclean, dd. Cape Coast, 4 June 1838.

25 Biørn, 1788, p. 204.

26 Basel Mission Archives, Aus dem Nachlass Christallers, *Akuapem Adɔnsɛm*, by P. Keteku, 1853, Ic: *Asantefo ko a wɔne Akuapem ne Krɔbɔ koe*. See also *Native Reports in Twi*, 1913, p. 39.

27 National Archives, Copenhagen, Archives of the West Indian and Guinea Company, Sekretprotokoller, Kiøge to Council dd. Christiansborg, 21 December 1772; Kystdockumenter, minutes of Council, dd. Christiansborg, 12 January 1773. The identity of the Asante commander Adusei cannot be established with certainty, but he was probably either the Kumase Gyaasewahene Adusei Atwenewa or Akyempemhene Adusei Kra; both were sons of Opoku Ware.

28 General State Archives, The Hague, KvG 127: Elmina Journal, entry for 19 September 1766.

keep open through Akuapem territory the great-road from Kumase to the eastern coast.[29]

It was at much the same time that the formalized civilian administration was established in the important trade centres in Accra. By 1770, and perhaps earlier, three officers had been assigned duties there: Ankra at the English post, Kyerematen at the Danish, and Kra Kese, by inference, at the Dutch.[30] Of the three, Kra Kese was senior, and had earlier been stationed at Akwamu on the lower Volta, whence he had proceeded to Accra to collect rents from the forts.[31] Ankra – said by his descendants to have been from Kokofu [32] – had been a member of Kra Kese's staff in Accra in 1770, and in 1772 had acted as intermediary between Adusei, commander of the expeditionary force in the southern provinces, and the Gã.[33]

In 1776 Kyerematen died. The very considerable personal debts which he had incurred with the Danes were regarded by them as claimable against the office. The situation was such as to draw attention to the necessity of establishing effective codes of conduct for the new administrators. The *amradofo* from Accra were seemingly recalled to Kumase. Three officers were reposted to Accra in November 1776.[34] Ankra was among them, having been confirmed in his residency. The post held by Kyerematen was assigned to his brother, Nkansa; [35] and Kra Kese was replaced by Boakye Asofu – perhaps the 'Batty' or 'Butty' who had collected rents from the English in Accra in the 1750s.[36] It may be that the receipt, which is extant, for the first payments made to Boakye Asofu by the Dutch, attests to the stricter administrative procedures introduced after 1776:

I the undersigned herewith acknowledge receipt from the hands of Jacob van den Peuye, on the account of the Asante King Zaay Coma [Osei Kumaa, i.e. Osei Kwadwo], the *kostgeld* owing by the Honourable Company from 1 October, 1771, to the end of December, 1776, inclusive, amounting in all to 126 oz. of merchandize, at 2 oz. each month, received to satisfaction, for

29 National Archives, Copenhagen, Archives of the West Indian and Guinea Company, palaver book, entry for 8 June 1776.
30 *Ibid.* Christiansborg palaver book, entry by Frøelich *et al.* dd. 6 December 1770. *Ibid.* Kystdokumenter, minute by Frøelich *et al.*, Christiansborg, 31 March 1772.
31 General State Archives, The Hague, KvG 127: Elmina Journal, Wortman to Elmina, dd. Accra, 27 March 1766.
32 Wilks, field notes, interview with Chief Ankra of Dadebana, Accra, dd. 19 May 1957, who referred to his ancestor as Abonɔte Ankra.
33 PRO, T. 70/979: Accra Day Book, entry for 10 December 1772.
34 General State Archives, The Hague, KvG 144: Elmina Journal, letter from Van den Peuye, dd. Accra, 9 November 1776, entered 13 November.
35 National Archives, Copenhagen, Sekretprotokoller: Aarestrup *et al.* dd. Christiansborg, 15 November 1776.
36 PRO, T. 70/974: Accra Day Book, various entries between 1 November 1752 and 28 February 1759.

the collection of which I have been sent here by the abovementioned Asante King Zaay Coma. In the Honourable Company's fort Crèvecoeur at Accra, 11 December, 1776 . . .

(The mark of) Booyattje Asofou, envoy of the Asante King Zaay Coma.[37]

It seems to have been the case also, that the chain of command was strengthened by making the three District Commissioners ('Lieutenants') in Accra immediately responsible to the Provincial Commissioner ('great caboceer') in Akuapem. It was presumably to this arrangement that Robertson was to allude in the early nineteenth century:

Notwithstanding Accra has the privileges of a free port, and an oligarchical domestic government, it is subject to the Cabocier of Aquapiem, as viceroy of the king of Ashantee, who receives a trifling tribute annually on account of that sovereign. The European settlements also pay a ground rent to the superior government as an acknowledgment of their being subject to its power.[38]

In fact, Odenkyem and the three Accra commissioners appointed in 1776 were rapidly to become embroiled in the dispute which had broken out between the Dutch and Danish trading companies over commercial rights on that stretch of the Gold Coast between Accra and the Volta.[39] The subsequent proceedings were such as to put Osei Kwadwo's new administrative machine to a most severe test, and were to demonstrate the necessity of providing the commisioners with adequate guidelines to central government policy.

Odenkyem initially expressed his support for Danish claims to a trade monopoly on 'Rio Volta', and visited Ada to advise its ruler not to treat with the Dutch.[40] A month later, however, on 24 December 1776, word reached the Danes from Akuapem that Odenkyem had instructed Boakye Asofu to advise Obuobi Atiemo to support the Dutch rather than the Danes; that Odenkyem had also authorized Nkansa to inform the Danes to this effect; and that while Obuobi Atiemo had rejected a bribe from the Dutch of 60 oz of gold, Odenkyem had accepted 20 oz.[41] Early in 1777 an Asante trader, Abi, arrived in Accra, represented himself as a government official authorized to inquire into the dispute, and reported back to Kumase that both

[37] General State Archives, The Hague, KvG 145: entry for 7 March 1777.
[38] G. A. Robertson, 1819, pp. 221–2.
[39] For the background of the dispute, see Nørregård, 1966, chapter 16.
[40] General State Archives, The Hague, WIC 148: Differences with the Danes, Factor to Elmina, dd. Accra, 22 November 1776.
[41] National Archives, Copenhagen, Archives of the West Indian and Guinea Company, Aarestrup to Company, dd. Christiansborg, 27 December 1776. See also Royal Library, Copenhagen, Ny kongelig samling fol. 445, précis dd. 3 December 1779.

Odenkyem and Boakye Asofu had accepted bribes from the Dutch. In August a commission headed by a member of the Kumase *nseniefo* appeared in Accra, investigated the complaints, aquitted Odenkyem and Boakye Asofu of the charges, but, finding that Abi had misrepresented his status, ordered his arrest to stand trial in Kumase.[42] Finally, in late September, further messengers from Kumase arrived in Accra and met with the Dutch authorities. The Asantehene, they announced, had heard reports that he had both been asked to support the Dutch against the Danes, and the Danes against the Dutch; he would do neither, however, for his policy was to encourage both parties to cooperate so that his brokers could come freely and without hindrance to the coast to trade with merchants of the two nations.[43]

Although cleared of accusations of corruption, Boakye Asofu received orders to return to the capital early in October 1777. Claiming, however, that the Akuapem and Krobo were plotting to seize him on the return journey, he lingered in Accra until 30 November, when, having received news of the death of the Asantehene Osei Kwadwo, he decided suddenly that affairs in Kumase 'called him there in order to avert problems that might occur in his absence'! Odenkyem may also have been recalled to Kumase: certainly he was remembered as having resided in Akuapem for a short time only.[44]

The Asantehene Osei Kwame clearly accepted the policies of administrative innovation as conceived by his predecessor: there is no suggestion that any significant change in direction occurred. In Akuapem, Odenkyem's post was filled by one Kra Kwaaten (Koranten), a member of the Asantehene's *atumtufo* or personal bodyguard. He was presumably the 'powerful Asante at Akuapem' who enforced a trade embargo against the Danes in 1806.[45] He was recalled to Kumase when revolt broke out in Akuapem in 1811. Having married a woman from the Akuapem royal house, Kra Kwaaten took with him one of their three sons, Owusu Akyem. Trained in Kumase to follow his father in service in the *atumtufo,* he accompanied him to Katamanso in 1826.[46] There he was taken prisoner, but was ransomed by his maternal uncle, the then Akuapemhene Adow Dankwa.[47] He remained

---

42 General State Archives, The Hague, WIC 142: Gallé and Stadlander at Accra, journal entry for 11 August 1777.

43 *Ibid.* WIC 143: journal entry for 27 September 1777.

44 General State Archives, The Hague, WIC 143; Differences with the Danes, journal entries for 12 October and 30 November 1777. *Akuapem Adɔnsɛm,* by P. Keteku, 1853, Basel Mission Archives.

45 See Kea, 1970b, p. 39.

46 Reindorf, 1st ed., 1895, Appendix, listing Kra Kwaaten among those who fought in the 'Atufuo'.

47 Basel Mission Archives: Aus dem Nachlass Christallers, *Akuapem Amansɛm,* by E. Samson, 1880, p. 12. Samson, 1908, chapter IV.

domiciled in Akuapem for the rest of his life. The well-known David Asante, trained as a missionary in Basel from 1857 to 1862, was his son – and so grandson of Kra Kwaaten. It is of particular interest, therefore, that a short work in German, which includes an account of the last phases of Asante administration in Akuapem, is attributed to him. A more detailed description of the military reoccupation of the southeastern provinces between 1811 and 1816 will be given below. By 1816, however, when the Asante commander Amankwa Abinowa began withdrawing his forces, all resistance had collapsed and rebel chiefs had for the most part been superseded in office by loyal ones. In that year Danish sources report the reassumption of authority by civilian administrators from the military commanders.[48] 'When Amankwa went home', likewise reported David Asante, 'he left officers behind in Accra, Akuapem and Akyem, to superintend the activities of the newly-installed kings.' [49] The German text, while clearly reflecting the biases of a Christianized Akuapem writing in the period after the replacement of Asante overrule by British, is nevertheless interesting for its indication of the degree of political control that the central government in Kumase was able to exercise over outlying provinces:

The Asante treated the people very arrogantly; if an Asante saw in the hands of an Akuapem something that pleased him, he took it. Even the food of an Akuapem, which seemed good to him, even if it was hidden, and an Asante found it, he took it and ate it. If an Akuapem felled a palm tree, and an Asante came, he took the pot and the palm-wine together, and drank. If a minor case was made with the oath Osei (king's oath), the whole family was ruined. They say that the women of Akuropon began to play the dance known as *nkoruwa*, and when an Asante heard it, he had scarcely arrived back in Kumase when he informed Osei that they had a dance in Akuropon, the words of which were not suitable to the ears of the listeners. No sooner had the King heard of it, than he chose messengers who were to seize and bring to Kumase those who danced this dance, so that they could dance it to him. Had God in his goodness not sent Mankata [Sir Charles MacCarthy] from Europe, all the women of Akuropon would have been sent to Kumase. They were also forced, on command, to carry lime from Accra to Kumase, to whiten the house of Osei. Had God not been with those who took it, they would have been taken prisoner and made slaves.[50]

Reindorf's notes on the period between 1816 and 1824 confirm this picture of strong central control:

48 National Archives, Copenhagen, Guinea Journals: report by Flindt, dd. 30 October 1816.
49 Struck, 1923, p. 482.
50 *Idem*. I have followed the translation kindly placed at my disposal by Marion Johnson.

King Ado Dankwa [of Akuapem], who had promised General Amankwa to be punctual in paying the annual tribute to the King of Asante, at one time found it impossible to do so in money or in men; and he was to pawn his nephew to the Asante tax master, Owusu Afriyie, promising to redeem him as soon as possible. Adum was brought to Kumase . . .[51]

Owusu Afriyie, perhaps better known as Owusu Gyamadua, was presumably successor in the Akuapem residency to Kra Kwaaten. His appointment was indicative of the increasing importance attached to the provincial service. Owusu Afriyie was a son of the Asantehene Osei Kwadwo, and a grandson of the Akyempemhene Owusu Afriyie. The position of Nkarawahene was created for him by his father, and of Apagyahene by Asantehene Osei Kwame. He married the Asantehemaa Afua Sapon and was father, among others, of the future heir-apparent Osei Kwadwo and of the Asantehemaa Afua Kobi.[52] He died at Katamanso in 1826,[53] the last Asante resident commissioner for Akuapem.

Meanwhile, in Accra, the administrative structure created by Osei Kwadwo was also maintained by Osei Kwame and his successors. Following the recall to Kumase of Boakye Asofu in 1777, he was succeeded as commissioner for the 'Dutch' wards by Boakye Awua, and he in turn, upon his death in 1798, by Boakye Kusi ('Acoesie').[54] The commissioner for 'English' Accra under Osei Kwadwo, Ankra, retained his position for some years. He was still active in Accra affairs in 1782,[55] and in 1783 he proceeded thence to Krobo to enstool Aniano as successor to Krobo Saki.[56] He married into the Otublohum stool family in Accra, of which ward his son, Twumase Ankra, became in time head by matrifiliation.[57] The commissioner for 'Danish' Accra, Nkansa, likewise remained in office for some years. He was presumably the 'lieutenant Kantza' whose complaints about the quality and price of Danish merchandise was one of the causes of the central government's interdiction on the Danish trade in 1788–9. Nkansa was withdrawn to near Kumase, and then posted back to administrative headquarters in Akuapem pending settlement of the issue.[58] It is possible that he was the Nkansa who later, under Osei Bonsu, came to hold the office of Ankobeahene of Kumase. In the early 1790s a 'lieutenant Cantza the younger' was in charge of the protracted negotiations which followed

[51] Reindorf, 2nd ed., n.d., p. 308.
[52] Asante Collective Biography Project: Owusu Afriyie.
[53] Ricketts, 1831, p. 125.
[54] General State Archives, The Hague, KvG 183: journal entry for 25 October 1798.
[55] PRO, T. 70/978 and 980: Accra Day Books, entries for 12 August 1779 and 20 November 1782.
[56] PRO, T. 70/980: Accra Day Book, entry for 21 January 1783.
[57] For the importance of Otublohum, see Wilks, 1959, *passim*.
[58] Kea, 1970b, *passim*.

Danish requests for Asante military assistance in Anlo and Little Popo.[59] Whether the junior Nkansa succeeded the senior in office is unclear. By the last decade of the century, however, a second residency appears to have been established in 'Danish' Accra, reflecting its importance as headquarters of the Danish establishments of the Gold Coast. It was held by one 'Adumgoth', that is Adomako.[60]

Aspects of the work of the Accra commissioners, in the promulgation of central government legislation, have been described in a recent paper by Kea. 'Four important Assianthees', it was reported in the early nineteenth century,

namely Sacki Acomia, Atjampung, Banah and Bequaei, have in the Assianthee King's name proclaimed that all swearing by the King's name should be discontinued; that theft shall be punished with threats, restoration or compensation and nothing further, and also that all slaves who place themselves in fetish shall be immediately handed over, or the fetish priest will be punished as a thief.[61]

The enactments were publicized in the various wards of Accra and in the nearby towns of Teshi and Labadi. The four commissioners then prepared to travel to the more easterly districts, Ningo, Krobo, and the Volta towns between Malfi and Ada, in order to announce the decrees there and at the same time to confer upon various of the local chiefs – those of Krobo, Malfi and Ada – honours (see pp. 77–8): that is, gifts 'in token of the King of Asante's love for the three towns and because the King is persuaded that they are definitely pleased about the King's victory over the Fante [in 1807]'.[62] By 1808, then, the authority of the four commissioners for Accra had apparently been extended to encompass the Adangme towns and various of the riverain Ewe communities, even though there may have been other commissioners stationed in those districts – such as the 'Osay Bosa' who in 1802 had jurisdiction over Ningo,[63] or the 'powerful man on the Lower Volta' who came from Bantama, Kumase, and whose descendants form the small Kpono section in the town of Ada.[64] The Danes, however, apprehensive of the consequences of the consolidation of central government control over the Lower Volta, challenged the credentials of the four commissioners: none, it was claimed, had any authority east

[59] National Archives, Copenhagen, Guinea Journals, reports of Biørn, von Hager, and Hammer, 1791–4. See Fynn, 1971, pp. 131–2, 136.
[60] Kea, 1970b, pp. 37–8.
[61] National Archives, Copenhagen, Christiansborg letter-book: minute to the Council, dd. 19 November 1808, cited in Kea, 1970a, p. 43.
[62] *Idem*, cited in Kea, 1970a, p. 44.
[63] Kea, 1970a, p. 43.
[64] Wilks, field-notes: interview with J. D. Amenyah, Big Ada, dd. 2 October 1957.

of Accra, while 'Sacki Acomia' and 'Bequaei' were only *omløbere,* wanderers.[65] Such charges were clearly tendentious.

Banna and Bekoe were first and second commissioners for Osu, and perhaps immediate successors to Nkansa and Adomako respectively. Banna was first posted to Osu in September 1808. Described by the Danish Governor as the Asantehene's *told casseerer,* customs collector, his commission was reported to be 'to increase Danish trade and collect customs from the Asante merchants who go to Christiansborg and the underlying traders' houses' [66] He held the position for a comparatively short time, however, for by the beginning of 1811 one Kwame Adwuma ('Adjuma', 'Guma', etc.) was referred to as Danish *told forvalter,* customs administrator.[67] In 1808 Kwame Adwuma had been described as one of the Asantehene's senior counselors.[68] He was the father of the incumbent junior commissioner Bekoe.[69] Indeed, when Kwame Adwuma was slain in Akyem Abuakwa later in 1811, in company with other officials conveying revenues from the coast to Kumase, Bekoe was appointed to the more senior post.[70] In 1817, for example, Bowdich referred to him as 'Becqua, captain of Danish Accra'.[71]

Of the two other Asante officers involved in the promulgation of the enactments of 1808, Sakyi Akomea was a successor of Ankra in the commissionership for 'English' Accra. He was later promoted to the more important post of commissioner at Cape Coast, headquarters of the English African Company on the Gold Coast – a position he must have assumed by, if not before, 1817, when Asokwa Amankwa of the *asokwafo* of Kumase had become 'captain of English Accra'.[72] Similarly, Akyampon ('Atjampung') was commissioner for 'Dutch' Accra, and was therefore a successor to Boakye Asofu, Boakye Awua, and Boakye Kusi.[73] He, too, received promotion, to become commissioner at

65 Kea, 1970a, p. 45.
66 National Archives, Copenhagen, Christiansborg letter-books: minute to Council, dd. 17 September 1808, cited in Kea, 1970a, p. 43.
67 *Ibid.* minute dd. 12 January 1811, cited in Kea, 1970a, p. 43.
68 *Ibid.* Christiansborg Diaries and Accounts: entry for 19 February 1808, cited in Kea, 1970a, p. 46.
69 Bowdich, 1819, p. 241.
70 *Idem.* See also Reindorf, 2d ed., n.d., p. 153, who records that the party ambushed in Akyem Abuakwa consisted of ninety Asante traders under the command of Owusu Manhwere ('Mantshiri'). According to one report, Kwame Adwuma blew himself up with gunpowder to escape capture, see National Archives, Copenhagen, Miscellaneous Archives from Guinea, Christiansborg letter-book: letter to Council, dd. 12 January 1811.
71 Bowdich, 1819, p. 241.
72 *Ibid.* p. 83. PRO, T. 70/41: letter from Bowdich to Governor, dd. Kumase, 9 July 1817.
73 Akyampon was probably a son of one of the three Boakyes: in Asante the two

Elmina, headquarters of the Dutch. His place in Accra seems to have been filled temporarily by Kwadwo Abrantia, one of the Asantehene's revenue collectors.[74] In 1816 he was actively engaged in the attempt to restore normal trade relations in the Accra hinterland after the rebellions of the Akyem Abuakwa and Akuapem, but in December of that year he was recalled to Kumase.[75] He arrived in the capital on 14 March 1817, and was almost immediately reassigned to Elmina to strengthen the administration there.[76] He in turn was replaced as commissioner for 'Dutch' Accra by Owusu Bannahene. Like the Akuapem commissioner Owusu Afriyie, Owusu Bannahene was a son of Osei Kwadwo. Known originally as Owusu Nsemfo, he held a position as *okyeame* under Kusi Obodom but was appointed Adomasahene by his father. In the late 1770s he had been trading at Danish Christiansborg. As resident for 'Dutch' Accra, in October 1816 he was reported to be in daily communication with the Commandant of Crèvecoeur. By the end of that year he had left the town.[77] He deputized for the blind Kyidomhene Gyasi Tenten in the Gyaman campaigns in 1818–19, and on his return was given that office. He died at Katamanso in 1826.[78]

It is indicative of the status of the Asante functionaries, that it became the practice certainly of the Dutch to accord them a salute of seven guns whenever they visited the forts.[79] It is fortunate that the Accra historian Reindorf, many of whose informants would have remembered the Asante commissioners of the early nineteenth century, was able to give some account of their administration. Referring to 'the feelings of friendship and brotherhood which existed between Asantes and Akras', and to 'the existence of true respect, mutual self-interest and friendship',[80] Reindorf essayed an account of the situation at the time of the commissionership of Sakyi Akomea around 1810:

names are generationally counterposed; that is, grandfathers and sons are Boakye, and fathers and grandsons are Akyampon.

74 General State Archives, The Hague, KvG 501: letter from R. Roelosson to Director-General, dd. Accra, 22 October 1816.

75 General State Archives, The Hague, KvG 501: letter from Roelosson, dd. Accra, 17 December 1816.

76 *Ibid.* KvG 372: Minutes of the Great Council, Elmina, dd. 19 June 1817. Huydecoper's Journal, entries for 14 March and 3 April 1817.

77 General State Archives, The Hague, KvG 501: letters from Roelosson, dd. Accra, 22 October and 22 December 1816.

78 Asante Collective Biography Project: Owusu Bannahene. He was known to both Bowdich (1819, pp. 74, 109, 299) and Dupuis (1824, pp. 111, 155). He is to be distinguished from the Owusu Bannahene who was probably his grandson, and who was appointed by Osei Yaw to the same *okyeame* stool which the senior man had held early in his career.

79 General State Archives, The Hague, KvG 182: Elmina Journal, Factor to President, dd. Accra, 25 October 1798. Huydecoper's Journal, entry for 7 May 1817.

80 Reindorf, 2nd ed., n.d., pp. 152, 168.

All difficult cases, that occurred among the Akras, were settled by a special Commissioner from Kumase. Several of the principal chiefs, among the Akras, were befriended by the Asante kings, but they were never tributaries to them like the Fantes, Akyems, Akwamus, and Akuapems. The observance of Osei's oath, of which offenders were fined by the Asante residents in the country, was, however, prevalent.

Kwame Ata was accused of using terms of great disrespect to the King and, thereupon, Saki Akomia of Akra was commissioned by the chiefs of Akra to take him to Kumase to be judged by the king but, being found not guilty, he was sent back unpunished . . .[81]

At the time when Reindorf wrote, however, so favourable a view of the Asante administration was incompatible with the image which the British had formed of the system which they had supplanted. Reindorf accordingly presented another and contrasting account of the matter:

. . . the Asante chiefs and headmen, residing in the principal towns, exercised more power over the people than the King at Kumase. Everybody, merchants, mechanics, clerks, canoemen, the poor, the rich; in fact, high and low, were subjected to a system of cruel extortion on every possible occasion, and on pretences ludicrous and unheard of. People were deprived of their wives when they were handsome; if one had any words with an Asante, or inadvertently touched, or even alluded to an Asante, he was punished. In Fante as well as in Akra, several chiefs were made to pay enormous fines under various pretences . . . Most of the best kings and chiefs as well as the greater part of the population had been crushed or brought over to Asante as captives for life. Many populous and large towns lay in ruins, and poverty prevailed everywhere, but chiefly in the interior countries.[82]

To what extent such accounts were propagandist in intent – atrocity stories utilized to assist in legitimating the overrule of the British by defaming that of the Asante – need not be decided here. But while it had certainly become fashionable in coastal circles by the mid-nineteenth century to regard the former imperial administration in the south as 'a systematic course of oppression and spoliation practised by the king's officers',[83] this had not been the view of contemporary observers. Thus in 1816 Daendels, Marshal of France and Dutch Director-General of Elmina, had observed, 'Law and order is just as great in the Asante kingdom as with the Asiatic Eastern peoples. There thus exist no palavers between one town and another, and panyarring finds no place.' [84] Three years later Robertson, private trader of long standing on the west coast of Africa, remarked of Akuapem, 'Nothing is

81 *Ibid.* p. 169.
82 *Ibid.* p. 162.
83 Cruickshank, 1853, I, 341.
84 General State Archives, The Hague, KvG 384: despatch from Daendels to Board of Trade and Plantations, dd. Elmina, 6 December 1816.

wanted to render Agricultural pursuits profitable here, but security, which might easily be obtained, as the influence of the government of Ashantee extends to the shore',[85] and in the following year Dupuis, in Asante as His Britannic Majesty's Agent and Consul, was led to remark: 'The ponderous power of Ashantee, in lieu of contributing to the security of life and property, *alone guarantees both* to us, by its friendship, its *interests,* and the position it occupies in the rear of the maritime province.' [86] The view of such observers that the development of the central government's administrative control over the provinces was correlative with the extension of the rule of law, was not incompatible with the fact of the existence, in those provinces, of factions committed to the belief that the obligations incurred through incorporation within Greater Asante were not offset by the advantages to be gained from it. The protagonists of just such a position, indeed, led Akyem Abuakwa and Akuapem into rebellion in 1810–11.

The administration in the Akyem Abuakwa and Kwawu provinces

Both the Okyenhene – traditional ruler of Akyem Abuakwa – and the Akuapemhene had fought loyally in the Asante armies which had occupied the southern Fante country in 1807. Both, however, had apparently been alienated by their subsequent treatment: the Okyenhene, for example, was said to have been obliged to make a substantial payment to the Asantehene to recover the body of his brother who had died on the campaign.[87] The first indication of trouble appears to have been the failure of the Okyenhene, Ata Wusu Yiakosan, to visit Kumase for the Odwira of 1810.[88] The matter might well have been treated as one of no great urgency had not the government wished to send an army through Akyem Abuakwa – where hopefully the Okyenhene would strengthen it with further men – into the Accra area, there to eliminate the threat offered to that town by Obutu, Gomoa and Winneba armed bands who claimed that their families and property sent there for safety at the time of the 1807 campaign had been either sold or surrendered to the Asante.[89] Probably late in 1810 a commission was appointed in Kumase to inquire into the Akyem Abuakwa and Akuapem complaints. It was headed by a senior counselor, Boakye Yam, and by Odenkyem: the former may have been one of the Boakyes who had earlier held the 'Dutch' Accra

85 G. A. Robertson, 1819, p. 218.
86 Dupuis, 1824, p. lxi.
87 PRO, T. 70/35: Governor White to Committee, dd. Cape Coast, 25 March 1811. Meredith, 1812, p. 167. Bowdich, 1819, p. 241.
88 Reindorf, 2nd ed., n.d., p. 153.
89 *Ibid.* pp. 141–2; 152. Bowdich, 1819, p. 241.

commissionship, and the latter was certainly the official who had held that of Akuapem. Proceeding first to Dampon (Route V(a), mile 44), Boakye Yam and Odenkyem solicited the assistance of the Akyem Kotoku ruler Kwaakye Adeyefe in arranging for the commission to proceed into Akyem Abuakwa.[90] A gift of 4 oz of gold was despatched to the Okyenhene. Messengers arrived back from Ata Wusu Yiakosan, however, who stated that the Okyenhene would indeed fight, but against and not for the government.[91] Shortly after, and probably in February 1811, news reached the commissioners in Dampon that Ata Wusu Yiakosan had intercepted, and permitted the massacre of, a large Asante party carrying revenues and goods from the coast to Kumase. Among the slain was the leader of the group, Owusu Manhwere and the resident commissioner for Osu, Kwame Adwuma.[92]

Early in 1811, then, it had become apparent to the government that the normal processes of civil administration had broken down in the southeast. Boakye Yam and Odenkyem returned to Kumase, their commission unfulfilled. Meanwhile, news had reached the capital that the Akuapemhene Kwao Saforo Twie – whose dissatisfaction with the size of the tribune imposed upon him has been noted above (pp. 76–7) – had joined the rebellion. At that point, direction of the matter passed into the hands of the military commanders. The Atene Akotenhene of Kumase, Adusei Kra, marched south with a force reputedly of ten thousand men, but was repulsed by the rebels. A larger army, estimated at twenty or twenty-five thousand men, took the field under command of the Gyaasewahene Opoku Frefre – serving in his military capacity.[93] Both the Akyem Kotoku and the Accra remained loyal, and supplied the government with additional troops.[94] The details of the subsequent campaigns, which ended in the collapse of the rebel cause, are well-known and will not be recounted here,[95] but what is of considerable interest is the role played at the time of the revolt by the Asante provincial commissioner for Akyem Abuakwa, Tando. Writing in 1812, Meredith observed that the Okyenhene Ata Wusu Yiakosan, 'in conjunction with Tando, governed the Akim country, and was

90 Reindorf, 2nd ed., n.d., pp. 152–3.

91 PRO, T. 70/35: White to Committee, dd. Cape Coast, 25 March 1811.

92 Bowdich, 1819, p. 241. Reindorf, 2nd ed., n.d., p. 153. Owusu Manhwere is clearly the person described by Bowdich, 1819, p. 241, as 'one of the King's sons'. See also Cruickshank, 1853, I, 92–3.

93 Reindorf, 2nd ed., n.d., pp. 153–5. Bowdich, 1819, pp. 241–2. Meredith, 1812, pp. 166–8; 229–33. PRO, T. 70/35: White to Committee, dd. Cape Coast, 25 March and 23 May 1811.

94 Reindorf, 2nd ed., n.d., p. 153.

95 See, e.g. Claridge, 1915, I, 263–79. In 1820 Osei Bonsu himself gave the names of ten southern provinces which had become associated in the rebellion, see Hutton, 1821, pp. 342–3.

tributary to the king of Ashantee'. Meredith makes it clear, however, that Tando commanded sufficient support in Akyem Abuakwa to prevent the Okyenhene using his own territory as a base for rebel activity. Ata Wusu Yiakosan, he recorded, 'refused obedience to the king's orders, by not going against the Fantees: which produced a dispute between himself and Tando, who drove him out of Akim; and, being joined by a number of persons hostile to the Ashantee government, he became a respectable, an unsettled, and desperate warrior'.[96] Ata Wusu Yiakosan attempted, in fact, to establish a rebel base in Akuapem but, unable to hold it, moved westwards to link up with dissident Fante groups. He died of smallpox in October 1811.[97] Tando, by contrast, was recalled to Kumase and made to stand trial for maladministration – apparently a standard procedure in such situations. He was acquitted. 'He had been retired', reported Bowdich,

from his embassy to Akim, in consequence of a dispute with Attah, then the king of that country; for though Attah was adjudged to be in fault, after the palaver was talked at Coomassie, the Ashantee government thought it politic to displace Tando, though he had become disagreeable to the other, only for his vigilance and fidelity.[98]

Tando, however, was never posted back to the southeastern provinces. Instead, so it was reported, he enjoyed 'a long interval of the most luxurious life the capital could afford'.[99] He may perhaps have been appointed Asomfohene of Kumase, that is, head of the *afenasoafo* or 'swordbearers' who constituted the corps of official messengers, for the post appears to have been held in the relevant period by one Amoako Tando.[100] However that may be, in circumstances which will be detailed below, in 1816 Tando was placed in command of a mission to Wassa. The outcome was to prove disastrous to his career. An Accra who met him in Kumase in 1817, reduced to poverty, could recall how, by contrast, Tando would visit the coast as commissioner for Akyem Abuakwa 'in great pomp, never going the shortest distance, but in his taffeta hammock, covered with a gorgeous umbrella, and surrounded by flatterers, who even wiped the ground before he trod on it'.[101]

It will be apparent that the evidence, incomplete as it is, nevertheless indicates that the offices of the resident commissioners in the

96 Meredith, 1812, p. 169.
97 PRO, T. 70/35: White to Committee, dd. Cape Coast, 25 March, 23 May, and 13 October 1811.
98 Bowdich, 1819, p. 123.
99 *Idem.*
100 See Institute of African Studies, University of Ghana, IASAS/76: Asomfo Stool History, recorded by J. Agyeman-Duah, 25 May 1963.
101 Bowdich, 1819, p. 123.

southeastern provinces were established in the reign of the Asantehene Osei Kwadwo. It may be, however, that despite the frustration of Opoku Ware's earlier essays in administrative reform, he had been able to create commissionerships in some of the inner provinces, which survived to serve as a model for the latter Kwadwoan innovations. Thus from the province of Kwawu, lying north of Akyem Abuakwa and linked to Kumase by Route V(a), Perregaux recorded the tradition that Opoku Ware appointed 'Esen Kagya, the ambassador, and the sword-bearer Dongwa as commissioners of the country'. On the other hand, it may be that the tradition as transmitted to Perregaux was corrupt in associating the two with so early a reign, since Dongwa is probably the 'Degowar' or 'Degour' who in 1842 was described as 'a privileged servant of the king's' and in 1846 as 'one of the king's messengers'.[102] However that may be, the Kwawu posts remained occupied until 1874, when the province was incorporated into the Colony of the Gold Coast. At that time the last commissioner, Antwi Ankomia, and forty of his staff were massacred and their property seized. Only one member of the residency was spared, Kra Prem, apparently since he was by origin an Akyem Kotoku.[103] Among those to be executed was one Kwaaten (Koranten), whose position *vis-à-vis* Antwi Ankomia is unclear. Described as 'Asante representative in Kwawu', he was reported to have been one of the 'chief captains' of Kumase and to have had an excellent reputation as an arbitrator.[104]

The administration in the central southern provinces

Data on the origins of the Asante administration in the central provinces of the south – that is, those lying across or adjacent to Route VI to Anomabo – are somewhat less precise than those for the southeast. It is probable that the Asante government regarded itself as exercising some sort of authority within the northernmost parts of the Fante country by the later eighteenth century. As early as 1765 Osei Kwadwo, then newly enstooled, had sought and obtained Fante permission to establish a military base, for operations against both the Wassa to the west and the Akyem Abuakwa to the east, at Abora.[105]

102 Methodist Mission Archives, London: Brooking to Freeman, dd. Kumase 6 April 1842; Brooking to General Secretaries, dd. Kumase, 23 August 1842; and Wharton to General Secretaries, dd. 31 May 1846.
103 Perregaux, 1903, p. 448.
104 Basel Mission Archives: Asante to Basel, dd. 31 January 1878, and Date's report on the Kyebi Boarding School, dd. 9 February 1878. Kwaaten's son, Ofosuhene, was captured with his father, sold into slavery in Akyem, and later admitted to the Basel Mission school in Kyebi.
105 See, e.g. Priestley, 1961, pp. 41–4. Fynn, 1971, pp. 99–115.

Although the Fante authorities subsequently reversed their decision and became embroiled in an ineffective coalition with the Wassa, the northern Fante of Esikuma chose instead to recognize an Asante overlordship (above, p. 75). Through the Esikumahene the Asante government thus came to transact its business with the other Fante districts. Hence it was the Esikumahene Akom who, in 1806, sought Fante permission for Asante troops to enter their territory in pursuit of the Assin rebels Kwadwo Tsibu and Apute.[106] The politically powerful priests of the Mankessim shrine – Nanaanom Mpow – seemingly advised that the Asante request be acceded to,[107] but the Anantahene of Kumase Apea Dankwa, who commanded the army of the south, met resistance as he deployed his troops, and found many Fante among the prisoners he took. In the first half of 1807 the central government accordingly directed the military occupation of the whole of Fanteland, the Asantehene Osei Bonsu accompanying the armies in person.[108] The incorporation of the Fante districts into Greater Asante, however, remained to be accomplished. 'Upon the king's return to Coomassie at the close of 1807', reported Cruickshank,

the Fantees were relieved for a brief space of time from active warfare; but no treaty of peace having been concluded, they still continued to maintain a hostile attitude, boasting, indeed, that the Ashantees had been obliged to retreat from the country. The scarcity of provisions and the claims upon the king's attention among other of his refractory tributaries, no doubt compelled him to grant this respite, and even rendered it very desirable to be at peace with Fantee. His general at Accra, in the early part of 1809, communicated a wish to this effect to the [British] governor, requesting him to sound the Fantees upon the subject. These were encamped at this time in great numbers at Abrah [Abora]. They obstinately refused to listen to the king's advances, saying he had inflicted upon them all the injury he could, and that they would not be at peace with him.[109]

The government was forced to take action as Fante militants seized control of the countryside around the loyal towns of Elmina and Accra, and held the citizenry beleaguered. The government ordered military reoccupation of the Fante territory. Apea Dankwa was given command of the army to relieve Elmina, and Opoku Frefre of that to relieve Accra – though the second force had to be redeployed to suppress the revolt of the Okyenhene of Akyem Abuakwa and the Akuapemhene.[110] It was not until 1816 that the military commanders

106 Meredith, 1812, p. 134. PRO, T. 70/35: Torrane to Committee, dd. Cape Coast, 20 July 1807.
107 Cruickshank, 1853, II, 174.
108 See, e.g. Meredith, 1812, pp. 135–63.
109 Cruickshank, 1853, I, 86–7.
110 See Reindorf, 2nd ed., n.d., chapter XII.

could regard their work as relatively complete: the major rebel groups had been isolated and destroyed, and, as it was reported, 'the Fantee nation has been brought into such subjection that the impoverished residue desires nothing more than to preserve its life and liberty, to cultivate its lands, and to begin petty trading again'.[111] By early April, 1816, negotiations for a peace settlement were in fact already well advanced, and representatives from various of the Fante towns had met with government officials from Kumase and handed over 100 oz of gold as a token of their good faith. Reciprocal oaths of 'friendship' were exchanged.[112] It was in this period, according to Reindorf, that 'Asante residents were left in charge of the principal districts, whose duty it was to keep the Fantes in subjection and collect the king's tribute'.[113]

The old and important Fante town of Abora had been destroyed in the course of the campaigns of 1806 and 1807.[114] A successor town, Dunkwa or Abora-Dunkwa (Route VI, mile 112), was founded with the approval of the Asantehene by one Opentri ('Paintry'), who became recognized as its chief.[115] Son of an Asante father and Fante mother,[116] Opentri may have earlier acted as a headman of the Asante in Abora before its destruction.[117] However that may be, it was the town of Abora-Dunkwa which the government chose after 1816 as head-quarters of the new administration for Fanteland. Opentri was regarded as more or less in retirement,[118] and Kwame Butuakwa, as provincial commissioner, assumed the direction of affairs. The early career of Kwame Butuakwa, first in the Treasury in Kumase, and subsequently in the provincial service, is discussed below (pp. 424–5). He held the commissionership at Abora-Dunkwa for some six years, before returning to Kumase to fill a new counselor's position there. The period was one of rapidly deteriorating relations between the Asante government and the British authorities on the coast. In serving the interests of the former Kwame Butuakwa incurred the intense hostility of the latter. In 1817 the British made formal complaints to Osei Bonsu that Kwame Butuakwa was intercepting despatches at Dunkwa: he was, in fact, putting into effect the government's policy

111 General State Archives, The Hague, KvG 384: Daendels to Department of Trade and Colonies, dd. Elmina, 17 June 1816.
112 *Ibid.* KvG 658: Governor Dawson to Daendels, dd. Cape Coast, 10 June 1816. PRO, T. 70/36: Dawson to Committee, dd. Cape Coast, 27 March and 21 April 1816. Reindorf, 2nd ed., n.d., p. 159.
113 Reindorf, 2nd ed., n.d., p. 161. Compare Bowdich, 1819, p. 83.
114 Meredith, 1812, pp. 135–6.
115 Dupuis, 1824, pp. 13–14.
116 Hutton, 1821, p. 162.
117 Ricketts, 1831, p. 8.
118 Dupuis, 1824, pp. 14–15.

that only official messengers should carry official mails (above, p. 33).
In the same year Kwame Butuakwa became further embroiled with
the British over the matter of Samuel Brew: a Fante merchant who,
with the backing of the government in Kumase and the active collaboration of Muslim traders there,[119] was attempting to establish himself
in the disused Dutch lodge at Mouri, as a middleman in the trade in
slaves between Asante and Spanish merchantmen from the Americas.[120]
Again, in 1822, it was Kwame Butuakwa who took custody of a
Fante sergeant in British service, who had been arrested for speaking
abusively of the Asantehene. The Asantehene apparently wished to
have the prisoner released, but he was overruled by his councillors
who ordered the sergeant's execution by Kwame Butuakwa.[121] On 21–
2 February 1823, the British Governor Sir Charles MacCarthy – newly
arrived in Cape Coast from Sierra Leone – ordered troops to Abora-
Dunkwa to seize the Asante commissioner. They were ambushed en
route, and obliged to fall back on Anomabo with very heavy
losses.[122]

In the administration of Fante affairs Kwame Butuakwa was assisted
by a number of junior commissioners. Thus Reindorf listed the 'Asante
residents at Abora' in 1822 as Kwame Butuakwa, Amon Bata and
Apenten Nto. From their names Amon Bata may be presumed to have
belonged to the *batafo,* or state traders, of Kumase, and Apenten Nto
to the Apenten group in the Royal Household.[123] Another commissioner resided in Cape Coast: 'the Ashantee captain resident had been
stationed by the king at Cape Coast', remarked Dupuis, 'and was considered there as the organ of his government'.[124] The position was
held at least as early as April 1817, by Kwaku Sakyi,[125] who, in view
of the rareness of the name in Asante, was almost certainly the same
person as the Sakyi Akomea who had been commissioner in Accra a
decade earlier. He appears to have been from the Asante Akyem
town of Dampon, on Route V(a).[126] Late in 1817 Kwaku Sakyi was

119 Hutchison, in Bowdich, 1819, p. 413.
120 For Samuel Brew, see Priestley, 1969, chapter 11. For Kwame Butuakwa's involve-
ment in the affair, see PRO, T. 70/41: letters from Hutchison to Governor dd.
Kumase, 11 October, 7 and 21 November, and 20 December 1817, and letter from
Osei Bonsu to Governor dd. Kumase, 25 October 1817.
121 Reindorf, 2nd ed., n.d., pp. 171–2. See also PRO, CO. 267/56: letter from
Chisholm to MacCarthy dd. Cape Coast, 30 September 1822. *The Royal Gold
Coast Gazette,* 11 March 1823, p. 71.
122 See, e.g .Ricketts, 1831, p. 20; Reindorf, 2nd ed., n.d., p. 173. In a despatch to
London MacCarthy claimed a notable victory, see PRO, CO. 267/58: MacCarthy
to Earl Bathurst dd. Cape Coast, 7 April 1823.
123 Reindorf, 2nd ed., n.d., p. 172.
124 Dupuis, 1824, Introduction, p. xi.
125 Bowdich, 1819, p. 9.
126 Ibid, p. 482: 'Adumpong, the Government of the C. Coast Captain'.

the official chosen to negotiate with the Dutch in Elmina permission for Samuel Brew to occupy Mouri lodge: he requested that Brew be allowed to keep guns, gunpowder, gold and slaves of the Asantehene there. The Dutch agreed to all but the last item.[127] In late December, however, messengers from Kwaku Sakyi arrived in Kumase to report British opposition to the scheme, and the government sent instructions back to him, that he should continue to advocate the Fante merchant's case.[128] In the following year, 1818, when the Asantehene Osei Bonsu accompanied in person the armies engaged in suppressing the revolt in Gyaman, the situation in Cape Coast and the adjacent towns became highly unsettled, and Kwaku Sakyi found his authority challenged. 'While the king remained in his capital', remarked Dupuis,

> the maritime states were cautious of giving offence; but when the southern provinces were no longer overawed by the presence of the monarch on his throne, the natives of Cape Coast, encouraged, it must be admitted, by the gossips of the castle, thought proper to take a sudden umbrage at the resident, whom they looked upon as a spy or inspector over their actions.[129]

Despite Kwaku Sakyi's protestations to the Fante chiefs, reports were circulated of the defeat of the Asante armies in Gyaman, and even of the death of the Asantehene.[130] At the end of 1818, however, messengers from the government arrived on the coast to announce the successful conclusion of the campaigns, and to levy a special tax (*apeato*) towards the costs. The people of Cape Coast were assessed at 160 oz of gold, and those of Komenda a like sum. Both refused to meet the claims.[131] The Komenda, moreover, turned the messengers out of town, refusing to allow them even drinking water while permitting the youths to insult them and pelt them with stones.[132] In March 1819 further messengers from the government arrived at Cape Coast. Led by Kra Dehye, they carried 'the gold-hilted sword' as mark of their authority, and informed the Fante that further refusal to pay the tax could only lead to punitive action. The British Governor in Cape Coast, John Hope Smith, encouraged the townsfolk in their continued refusal to pay.[133] Reluctant to believe the report which

---

127 General State Archives, The Hague, KvG 350: Elmina Journal, entry for 28 November 1817.
128 PRO, T. 70/41: Hutchison to Governor, dd. Kumase, 30 December 1817.
129 Dupuis, 1824, Introduction, pp. xi–xii.
130 *Ibid.* Introduction, pp. xii; xiv. PRO, T. 70/1604: Governor Smith *et al.* to Committee, dd. Cape Coast, 3 October 1818.
131 PRO, T. 70/1605: Smith *et al.* to Committee, dd. Cape Coast, 11 January 1819.
132 PRO, T. 70/1606: Smith *et al.* to Committee, dd. Cape Coast, 22 March 1819. Hutton, 1821, pp. 48, 122. Dupuis, 1824, Introduction, p. xii.
133 Dupuis, 1824, Introduction, p. xv. Kra Dehye has not been identified but a person of the same name occupied the Gyakye counselorship in Kumase later in the century, see IASAS/127; Jachie Linguist Stool, recorded by J. Agyeman-Duah,

Kra Dehye presented to government on his return to Kumase, further messengers were sent to Cape Coast in June. Finally, in September 1819, a senior official travelled there carrying with him a copy of the Anglo-Asante Treaty of 1817, under the terms of which it was claimed that the British were obligated to support Asante authority in the province.[134] In the midst of the proceedings, Kwaku Sakyi died. That he was a young and athletic man encouraged speculation that he had been poisoned by the Cape Coast Chief Aggrey, a stipendiary of the British.[135]

In the circumstances, Kwaku Sakyi's post was not immediately filled. Instead, in January 1820, a travelling commissioner arrived from Kumase in Cape Coast, with a staff of some one thousand two hundred soldiers, carriers and servants (see p. 440).[136] This was Owusu Dome, from the Atene Akoten or torchbearers' organization in Kumase (Plate IV).[137] He was instructed to levy a fine of 1,600 oz of gold upon the people of Cape Coast for their refusal to pay the *apeato*, and the same sum upon the British Governor for his failure to observe the terms of the treaty of 1817. When, however, the government learned of the arrival in Cape Coast of Joseph Dupuis, with authority from London to renegotiate the Anglo-Asante treaty, Owusu Dome was instructed to suspend all demands, but to remain in Cape Coast as resident. In Kumase, in March 1820, the government reached agreement with Dupuis on the terms of a revised treaty. The consul returned to Cape Coast accompanied by members of an embassy instructed to proceed with him to London. The party comprised a treasurer, two counselors, a priest, two members of the *afenasoafo* or

September 1964. It was later believed that John Hope Smith 'became antagonist enemy to the Ashantee King' under the influence of his Fante wife, Fanny Smith, see NAG, Accra, ADM. 11/1483: 'The Ashantis' to Griffith, dd. Cape Coast, 15 December 1894.

134 Dupuis, 1824, Introduction, pp. xix–xx. Hutton, 1821, pp. 124–8.

135 Dupuis, 1824, Introduction, pp. xiii–xiv.

136 *Ibid.* Introduction, p. xxviii; pp. 184 and 185, note. Hutton, 1821, p. 128. Many loyal Fante from Abora and Mouri, and Assin, joined Owusu Dome's retinue.

137 Hutton, 1821, Plate facing p. 214. Owusu Dome was a son of the Asantehene Osei Kwame. Banished from Kumase in the early part of the reign of Osei Bonsu for 'unprecedented mad conduct', he was later restored to favour and given office, see National Archives, Copenhagen, miscellaneous archives from Guinea, Christiansborg Council Proceedings 1807–11: entry by Flindt, dd. 23 March 1811. Reindorf, 1895, Appendix, listed Owusu Dome as from the Atene. Dupuis stayed in his house in Kumase in 1820, and it is significant that he was accompanied there by torchbearers, and that his patron in the capital was the Atene Akotenhene Adu Kwame, see Dupuis, 1824, pp. 83, 105. Owusu Dome was taken prisoner in 1826 at Katamanso, see Ricketts, 1831, p. 125, but after his release became Kyidomhene of Kumase in succession to Owusu Bannahene (see above, p. 139. Owusu Dome died in Kumase on 2 August 1837, see Van Dantzig, 1966, p. 24, at the age of about fifty, see Dupuis, 1824, Introduction, p. xxviii. See further, Asante Collective Biography Project: Owusu Dome.

swordbearers, and one of the *nseniefo* or heralds.[138] Arriving in Cape Coast, the whole party was taken under protection by Owusu Dome, since the local British authorities in Cape Coast were accounted as hostile to Dupuis as they were to the Asante.[139] When finally Sir George Collier, commanding H.M.S. *Tartar,* arrived off Cape Coast, he refused categorically to permit the Asante ambassadors on board.[140] Dupuis therefore departed alone on 15 April 1820, having admonished Owusu Dome, so he reported, 'never [to] proceed to hostilities against the town, but wait until he heard from me'.[141] In the event, the London government declined to ratify the revised treaty. Owusu Dome remained in Cape Coast as the attitude of the British authorities became increasingly uncompromising. Finally, after the slaying of Opentri at Mouri in February 1821, Owusu Dome was ordered to withdraw his mission to Abora-Dunkwa.[142] Although for a brief period the Cape Coast commissionership was held by Adomako – presumably the same person who had earlier been junior commissioner in 'Danish' Accra – by 1821 the government had recognized that the British authorities on the Gold Coast were unprepared to cooperate with its accredited representatives. 'This monarch', remarked Dupuis of Osei Bonsu, 'having lost the original confidence he possessed, was not to be amused with vain negociations.' [143] In Kumase those urging upon the government the necessity for a new aggressive policy towards the British were acquiring a majority in the councils, and, in circumstances which well be detailed later, a trial of military strength became inevitable.

Comparatively little evidence survives of the structure of the Asante administration in the northernmost Fante districts and in the Assin provinces lying along Route VI. Dupuis referred to a certain 'Coinin Akim', who was responsible to the Bantamahene in Kumase, and who, 'besides his deputy viceroyalty of Assin, is also Caboceer over the desolate forests of Fantee'.[144] His seat was at Ansa (Route VI, mile 48), where there was also a central government customs post (see p. 55). Dupuis also referred to one 'Akassy' who resided at Kyekyewere (Route VI, mile 60), and who was a 'representative of Coinin Akim'.[145] It seems clear that both were Assins who had demonstrated their loyalty to Asante during the Assin rebellion of 1805–7, and who had subsequently been rewarded with territorial chiefdoms there. In 1820 the

138 Dupuis, 1824, p. 168.
139 *Ibid.* p. 185.
140 *Ibid.* pp. 188–90.
141 *Ibid.* p. 193.
142 *Ibid.* pp. 197 and 201, note.
143 *Ibid.* p. 199.
144 *Ibid.* pp. 42, 44–5.
145 *Ibid.* p. 45. See also Introduction, p. xxxiv, and p. 36. 'Akassy' joined the Owusu Dome mission to Cape Coast in 1820.

central government commissioner whose area of responsibility was co-extensive with that of 'Coinin Akim' was one Asamoa Kwadwo.[146] Described as 'the head captain over Assin and Fantee' (though clearly his jurisdiction did not overlap with that of his contemporary, Kwame Butuakwa, in the southern Fante districts), Asamoa Kwadwo appears later to have become Anantahene of Kumase in succession to Apea Dankwa.[147]

The administration in the southwest

A key position in the administration of the southwestern provinces was that of the commissioner for Elmina: not only one of the oldest and most loyal of the maritime provinces, but also the headquarters of the Dutch on the Gold Coast. In a letter of May, 1817 – over which the Kumase Muslims were required to make prayers – the Asantehene Osei Bonsu outlined the basis of relations with the Dutch:

He [Osei Tutu, *ca.* 1700] went to Dankara [Denkyira] and fought, and killed the people, then he said: give me the book [i.e. the rent-notes] you get from Elmina, so they did, and now Elmina belongs to him . . . When the King killed the Dankara caboceer and got two ounces from Elmina, the Dutch Governor said, this is a proper King, we shall not play with him, and made the book four ounces.[148]

The first resident commissioner to be stationed in Elmina was probably the Agyerakwa appointed to the post by Osei Kwadwo in 1765 shortly after his accession, and described as a brother of the Asantehene.[149] It is not until the early nineteenth century, however, that the record becomes sufficiently full for specific details of the responsibilities of the commissioners to be recoverable. On 18 May 1817, Kwadwo Abrantia, previously a revenue collector in Accra, arrived from Kumase to take up the post temporarily. He was accompanied by a junior

---

[146] See, e.g. Meredith, 1812, pp. 132–6. Dupuis, 1824, p. 166.
[147] Apea Dankwa died on campaign in 1816. His brother, Apea Nyanyo, was appointed acting Anantahene in the field, but was put on trial in Kumase in 1817 and subsequently committed suicide. Yet another Apea commanded the Ananta at Katamanso in 1826, but it appears that no one filled the substantive post until Asamoa Kwadwo was appointed to it; see, e.g., Bowdich, 1819, pp. 15, 129, 243; Huydecoper's Journal, *passim*; Reindorf, 2nd ed., n.d., p. 159; Reindorf, 1st ed., 1895, Appendix. Asamoa Kwadwo may have been the 'Assiamoa' who was involved in Accra affairs as early as 1776, see National Archives, Copenhagen, Archives of the West Indian and Guinea Company, Sekretprotokoller: minute by Aarestrup *et al.*, dd. Christiansborg, 15 November 1776.
[148] Osei Bonsu to Governor Smith, dd. Kumase, 26–8 May 1816, in Bowdich, 1819, pp. 66–72.
[149] General State Archives, The Hague, WIC 115: Director-General Huydecoper to the Assembly of the Ten, dd. Elmina, 27 June 1765.

officer, Kwame Dendo from the *asokwafo* of Kumase.[150] The Dutch Great Council in Elmina – anxious, unlike the British in the period, to work with the Asante administrators – hastened to offer Kwadwo Abrantia an allowance:

For the good of these establishments, to preserve a good relationship with the King of Asante, it was agreed to allow subsistence money to he who has been sent here to collect the stipends, who will reside in the town here as an intermediary between the King and us, and so, without charge to the King, to make him a dependant of the Netherlands' Government.[151]

Kwadwo Abrantia was recalled to Kumase within a few months, for in December 1817 a certain Akyampon appears to have been the central government's representative in Elmina.[152] He was presumably the Akyampon who had held the residency in 'Dutch' Accra in 1808. A different Akyampon so it would seem, Kwadwo Akyampon Bakki, assumed duties in Elmina on 17 January 1822: he arrived with a staff of forty.[153] In 1824, after the death of Governor Sir Charles MacCarthy on 21 January in the course of the abortive invasion of Asante, the British protested to the Dutch about the presence of an Asante 'resident' in Elmina, who, they argued, 'must naturally be hostile to our cause'. The Dutch refused to accede to the British request that Kwadwo Akyampon Bakki be surrendered to them. For a time, however, the commissioner ceased to frequent the Dutch fort,[154] and his government sent a small force to garrison the Elmina residency: it was headed by a certain 'Kunnoi, a captain of the King of Asante, a brave soldier'.[155] Kwadwo Akyampon Bakki was to remain in Elmina for many years more. In 1831 he was asked to return to Kumase to perform rites for members of his family who had died during his long absence. The Dutch, however, protested. 'The recall, or sending back of an ambassador such as Atjampon', argued the Dutch Commandant, 'would be regarded by any King as a rupture of the existing friendship', and furthermore: 'the Commandant must not fail to add that he considers Atjampon and his people as almost his children. Atjampon, from his long residence, has become a real part of the soil and

150 *Ibid.* KvG 350: Elmina Journal, entry for 18 May 1817. Huydecoper's Journal, entries for 3 and 22 April 1817.
151 *Ibid.* KvG 372: Minutes of the Great Council, dd. 19 June 1817.
152 Hutchison, in Bowdich, 1819, p. 404.
153 General State Archives, The Hague, KvG 351: Elmina Journal, entries for 17 and 18 January and 23 July 1822.
154 *Ibid.* KvG 663: Governor, Cape Coast Castle, to Director-General, Elmina, dd. 3 August 1824; KvG 351: Elmina Journal, entry for 13 April 1823. See also *Royal Gazette and Sierra Leone Advertiser*, VI, 331, 2 October 1824.
155 General State Archives, The Hague, KvG 352: Elmina Journal, entry for 17 February 1825.

Administration in the southwest

flag. . .'[156] On 18 February 1832, the order of recall was rescinded.[157] On 18 September of the same year, however, the Commandant of Elmina minuted in his journal: 'Asante Resident Atjampon
died this morning here, at a very old age.'[158] Messengers were despatched to Kumase for instructions, and on 20 December the Commandant noted further, 'Today the body of the deceased Asante
Resident Atjampon was carried away to Kumase in accordance with
the request of his King. Salute of 5 shots.'[159]

The structure of the Asante administration on the coast to the west
of Elmina remains little known. A commissioner for the Amanahia
province, however, was stationed at Beyin, terminus of Route VIII(a)
and site of the British fort Appolonia constructed between 1768 and
1770. The first commissioner appears to have assumed duties there
after Asante troops had 'forced a way to Appolonia' in 1780: that is,
had opened the great-road to Beyin.[160] The Asante commissioner, described as 'a principal man of that Country', was immediately invited
by the British to Cape Coast – 'to get some Valuable Information from
him . . . of the State of Affairs in the Inland Country'.[161] The post
was to remain an operative one until the later nineteenth century. In
1870, for example, it was held by one Ahuru Kwame. He presided
over some three hundred Asante there who served as both constabulary
and traders dealing not only with the merchant-houses but with the
ships in the roads. Although he enjoyed the close cooperation of the
pro-Asante local ruler, Amaki, Ahuru Kwame was unable to prevent
civil disorders in the province and late in 1871 he was recalled to
Kumase and a replacement posted to Beyin.[162] As late as 1881 one
Kete Kwabena was commissioner in Beyin, while the local chief –
then Awusi Akka – also had a messenger resident in Kumase.[163]

[156] *Ibid.* KvG 360: Elmina Journal, letter from Last to Asantehene, dd. 26 December
1831.
[157] *Ibid.* KvG 360: Simmon's Journal, entry for 18 February 1832.
[158] *Ibid.* KvG 360: Elmina Journal, entry for 18 September 1832.
[159] *Ibid.* KvG 360: Elmina Journal, entries for 27 September and 20 December 1832.
[160] See Tenkorang, 1968, p. 15.
[161] PRO, T. 70/32: Governor Roberts to Committee, dd. Cape Coast, 8 and 31
October 1780.
[162] *Gold Coast, Part 1,* C. 266, 1873: Asantehene Kofi Kakari to Acting Administrator
Salmon, dd. Kumase, 23 November 1871; Salmon to Kofi Kakari, dd. Cape Coast,
13 December 1871; Salmon to Governor Henessy, dd. Cape Coast, 18 August 1872;
report of Commissioners Dyer and Johnston to Administrator, dd. 13 August
1872, diary entries for 5 and 11 August 1872, and attached remarks. For useful
information on Asante relations with Amanahia in the period, see Dyer, 1876,
passim.
[163] Ellis, 1883, pp. 223–4. *Affairs of the Gold Coast and threatened Ashanti Invasion,*
C. 3064, 1881, p. 32: Firminger, District Commissioner, Axim, to Colonial
Secretary, dd. Axim, 26 January 1881.

The administration in the Wassa provinces

The regularization of the central government's administration in the western coastal provinces in the late eighteenth and early nineteenth centuries had always been conditional upon the pacification of the Wassa, through whose territory both Routes VII and VIII passed. The history of the earlier relations between Asante and the Wassa has been touched upon above (pp. 26–7): the inability by 1744 to keep open the great-road to Elmina may be taken as signalizing the failure of the first programme of pacification. An attempt to reoccupy Wassa territory in 1776 apparently proved unsuccessful.[164] Dupuis' account of an Asante military victory of major proportions must therefore presumably refer to the later campaigns of 1785–7: 'The province of Wassa fell . . . under the avenging sword of the king, who let loose the fury of his troops upon its northern confines, and bereaved several large districts of their whole population.'[165] In 1819 Robertson remarked of Wassa, that since *ca.* 1787,

it has been tributary to Asantee, and is, *bona fide,* nothing more than a vice-royalty of that empire, although the king can exercise his regal authority over his subjects without controul. Adoo Ghessey, an Ashantee man, assured me that the king of Wassa levied the revenue of the Ahantan states, and accounted to the king of Ashantee for the amount, which I believe to be a fact.[166]

Robertson's Asante informant, however, had taken a somewhat optimistic view of the matter, and the continuing attempts to arrive at acceptable terms for the incorporation of the Wassa into Greater Asante are reported in detail: they constitute an interesting case study of the central government's procedures and goals in this sphere of its activity.

The immediate effect of the military reoccupation of the 1780s was to break down the indigenous Wassa political structures, so that, as it could be observed some thirty years later, 'their power is weak and their Government of no repute, each chief being, as it were, a King to himself'.[167] One consequence of political fragmentation, indeed, was that the Wassa attitude during the upheavals of 1811–16 varied from district to district. At a meeting with Wassa chiefs summoned to Ku-

164 See Tenkorang, 1968, p. 14.
165 Dupuis, 1824, pp. 241–2. Dupuis reported that many Wassa were forcibly re-settled in the northeastern and east-central provinces of Bron and Kwawu, 'either to supply a deficiency of the population of those parts, or to secure their future allegiance'.
166 G. A. Robertson, 1819, pp. 122–3.
167 General State Archives, The Hague, KvG 384: Daendels to Department of Trade and Colonies, dd. Elmina, 17 June 1816.

mase, the Asantehemaa Adoma Akosua had announced that the Asante armies would not be used against the Wassa, and she had the chiefs swear that they would not assist the rebels.[168] While most of them remained in fact loyal,[169] reports reached the government that others had given assistance to the Fante dissidents.[170] In the aftermath, however, of the victories of the government forces in 1816, when it was remarked that the peoples of the southwestern districts 'now feel the ascendancy of the Asante so well, that they can be compelled to do any work',[171] the Wassa took an initiative in opening negotiations for the regularization of their position within Greater Asante. Using the examples of the more fully incorporated provinces of Denkyira and Assin on their northern borders as the model, the Wassa chiefs chose to use the Dutch as mediators. In a letter which Director-General Daendels addressed to the Asantehene Osei Bonsu in mid-1816, he observed:

King Eltifor and the Caboceers of Wassa have given their palaver into my hands, to pray you Sir to give them an enduring peace, and should there be a palaver between you and them, to settle it for them in such a manner that they acknowledge you as their Protector, and besides whatever they will pay you immediately in gold, to pay an annual contribution in gold, in return for which they will be allowed, just as you Sir now allow it in Dinkera [Denkyira], to carry on trade throughout the whole Asante Kingdom, while Asante caravans shall pass everywhere throughout Wassa, in order to trade on the coast.[172]

Daendels requested the Dutch agent then in Kumase, Huydecoper, to determine first what fine the government would impose on the Wassa for the transgressions of the agreement made with the Asantehemaa Adoma Akosua, and secondly, at what level the annual tribute would be fixed.[173]

The debate on the Wassa issue in Kumase found the Council divided between those who urged the military occupation of Wassa as a prelude to negotiations, and those who favoured immediate talks conducted with the Dutch as intermediaries. Both parties acknowledged the overriding importance, for the whole system of administration in the southwestern provinces, of securing free movement along Routes VII and VIII. After lengthy deliberations the Council decided against

168 *Ibid.* KvG 350: Osei Bonsu to Daendels, dd. Kumase, 29 November 1816.
169 *Ibid.* KvG 384: Daendels to Department of Trade and Colonies, dd. Sierra Leone roads, 28 December 1815 (reporting evidence of an English official from Cape Coast), and dd. Elmina, 23 March 1816.
170 *Ibid.* KvG 350: Osei Bonsu to Daendels, dd. Kumase, 29 November 1816.
171 *Ibid.* KvG 349: Daendels to Huydecoper, dd. Elmina, 24 May 1816.
172 *Ibid.* KvG 349: Daendels to Osei Bonsu, dd. Elmina, 19 June 1816.
173 *Ibid.* KvG 349: Daendels to Huydecoper, dd. Elmina, 23 June 1816.

military intervention, though the communiqué it issued kept open the possibility:

The General [Daendels] should himself deal with the matter as a mediator who wished to make the world good, and not as if it came from the King that peace should be made with him [the Wassa ruler], because it would not cause him an hour's trouble to plunder the Wassas and drive them out of the whole country: but that he had only taken this trouble out of respect for the King of Holland and for you [Daendels].[174]

At the same time the council decided to send officers to Wassa to negotiate the return of Asantes held prisoner there. The mission was entrusted to Tando, the former provincial commissioner for Akyem Abuakwa (see pp. 142–3). Discussions between Tando and the Wassa chiefs began in mid-July 1816, at the unidentified town of 'Abroadie'.[175] Meanwhile Daendels made known to the Wassa the terms of an agreement he had drawn up for their signature. Article 3 defined broadly the position of the Wassa within Greater Asante: '3. The King of Wassa, the Caboceers, and the whole Nation, receive the King of Asante as their Protector: they will not make war or peace without his permission.' The matter of the fine for acts of hostility committed against Asante troops was covered in Article 9: '9. The Wassas agree to pay into the hands of the Dutch Governor General, in one month, 200 Bendas [400 oz] of gold for the King of Asante as a compensation for what has passed.' The issue of tribute was dealt with in Article 15: '15. There shall be paid annually into the hands of the Governor General by the King, and the Caboceers of Wassa, for the King of Asante as Protector of the Wassa country, 200 Bendas of gold.' Articles 17 and 18 treated the question of the reconstruction of the greatroad through Wassa:

17. The King, Caboceers, and people of Wassa engage to begin and finish in three months, a good road from the utmost borders of their country on this side of Asante, to the Dutch territory on the side of Great Komenda, 30 feet wide, rounded and so made that the water will run off, that it may be passable in every season; following for that purpose the directions which shall be given to them by the Dutch Governor General. They engage to keep the road at all times in good order.

18. The Wassa people not complying with the 17th Article, 6,000 Asante shall make and complete the road through the Wassa country at the Wassa's expense.[176]

174 *Ibid.* KvG 349: Huydecoper to Daendels, dd. Kumase, 22 June 1816. Huydecoper's Journal, entries for 19 and 20 June 1816.
175 *Ibid.* KvG 349: Elmina Journal, entry for 24 July 1816.
176 *Ibid.* Archives of the Department of Foreign Affairs, B. 57, xli: draft articles of a 'Treaty and Settlement . . . between the magnificent King of Asante and the King and Caboceers of the Wassa country'.

The Wassa found the document, as Daendels commented: 'a bitter pill to swallow, and hesitated to sign the 24 articles I had drafted'.[177]

In Kumase the situation became increasingly tense as rumours circulated that the Dutch might intend using the reconstructed great road increasingly to intrude their presence into the metropolitan region. The conservative elements in the Council, led by the Asafohene Kwaakye Kofi, became more articulate in their opposition to the current policy, and expressed disquiet about the activities of the Tando mission.[178] The government, moreover, was in no position to reply to the critics: Tando was thought to have left Elmina on or about 24 July and his return to the capital was anxiously awaited. Finally, in early November, news reached the council that he was still in Denkyira. On 7 November messengers were despatched to him, to state: 'Tando's actions are not pleasing to the court at Kumase; and that he must remember that he will have to render an account of these actions later, which account had better be satisfactory'.[179] What in fact had happened was, that with the encouragement of Daendels Tando had taken over from him the negotiation of the Wassa settlement, and had been successful in inducing the Wassa chiefs to subscribe to a document drawn up formally at Elmina on 4 September:

We Herman Willem Daendels Governor General, in the name of His Majesty the King of the Netherlands on the Coast of Guinea hereby make known and certify that the Asante messenger and Caboceer Tando has addressed himself to us giving information that he has concluded an agreement with the Wassa King Eltifor and other Elders whereby they acknowledge the mighty King of Asante, his overlord, as their Protector; they sending immediately with Tando on his return, messengers to the King of Asante to hear from the King's own mouth, the conditions upon which he will accept them as his vassals; and what also they shall pay annually to him as their Protector, and the amount of gold which the Wassa shall lay at the feet of the King by way of penalty for all the evil deeds which they have so often perpetrated against the Asante and the Netherlands' coast-people. The ambassador Tando further gave information that he had here drunk oaths with the Wassa King and other Elders that from henceforth the traders and travellers passing to and fro, shall without distinction, be free from all palavers; they having drunk oaths together that no one either in person or in goods may be panyarred; that fugitive slaves shall be given back, and that a murderer shall be delivered up without any further palavers arising or 'customs' being paid therefore. That he, Tando, requested that the Kings and Elders of Elmina, and Great Komenda, should drink the same oaths, which has been done at the hands of Caboceer Tando in our presence this day, the 4th. inst., in the

177 *Ibid.* KvG 349: Daendels to Huydecoper, dd. Great Komenda, 24 July 1816.
178 Huydecoper's Journal, entries for 3 July and 15 October 1816.
179 KvG 349: Daendels to Huydecoper, dd. Great Komenda, 24 July 1816. Huydecoper's Journal, entries for 23 October and 7 November 1816.

Palaver Hall of the Chief Castle St. George D'Elmina. After the drinking of this oath one shot was fired from the General's Battery: and we have fixed the cost of this shot, 25 Bendas gold, to be paid into the hands of the King of Asante, by the person who breaks this oath. In affirmation of this solemnly made oath, we grant this document to the Kings of Asante, Wassa, Elmina, and Great Komenda, ratifying the same with our signature and the Great Seal of the King.[180]

Tando left Elmina the following day, 5 September, and was in Denkyira awaiting the Wassa envoys who were to accompany him to Kumase when the messengers from the Asantehene arrived to inform him of the government's displeasure.[181]

Tando finally arrived back in the capital, having waited no longer for the Wassa envoys, in mid-November.[182] A letter which Daendels sent to Huydecoper in Kumase contained an evaluation of Tando's capabilities clearly intended for the attention of the Asantehene:

He is a trusty servant of the King and has not made his purse in Wassa, for he has not been able to buy anything and has even left behind the guns that he had already bought, for want of gold. We have given him some presents and subsistence, but he is worthy of further reward from the King his Master, and of being in future always employed as the chief confidant of his King in weighty commissions, for he has intelligence, judgement and patience, three qualities so necessary in a negotiator.[183]

He seemed, then, to exemplify the most desirable characteristics of the new career officers: loyalty, honesty, and professional competence. The Council, however, took a quite different view of the matter. After deliberations that did not end until midnight on 19 November, Huydecoper was summoned before that body and informed that the Elmina Agreement of 4 September had been repudiated, but that the Articles of the settlement drawn up by Daendels in July would be ratified upon confirmation that the 400 oz of gold demanded as damages had been paid by the Wassa. The council regarded Tando's conduct of the whole affair as highly culpable, and he was charged with having subverted the government's policies. An official messenger, the Asantehene pointed out,

took to Elmina the letters containing the request that the General [Daendels] should settle the Wassa palaver, but Tando prevented the Wassa from going there; Tando claimed that he himself could set everything in order; the result was that the Wassa failed to appear before the General . . . Tando,

180 *Ibid.* KvG 349: Elmina Journal, text entered for 4 September 1816.
181 *Ibid.* KvG 349: entry for 6 September 1816. KvG 384: Daendels to Department of Trade and Colonies, dd. Elmina, 6 December 1816, Report II on relations with the English, Asante, Wassa, etc.
182 Huydecoper's Journal, entry for 14 November 1816.
183 KvG 349: Daendels to Huydecoper, dd. Elmina, 5 September 1816.

with a view to filling his own purse, took the whole matter upon himself, and said that it was the King's wish that he, Tando, should arrange everything; he claimed the Wassa did not want to go to Elmina; he also told them that it was he alone who could settle the palaver; only if they found he could not do so were they to place their case before the General; the result of all this is that nothing has been achieved.[184]

When Bowdich arrived in Kumase a few months later, he found Tando a beggar. Declaring 'that no man must dare to do good out of his own head, or perhaps he would find he did bad', the Asantehene had ordered that all of Tando's property should be confiscated.[185]

On 29 November 1816, Osei Bonsu despatched a letter to Daendels informing him of Tando's dismissal, and reiterating that the Wassa had to pay 190 peredwans – in fact considerably over 400 oz – in damages before any final settlement could be ratified.[186] Somewhat to the surprise of the Council, only five days later the Wassa envoys who were to have accompanied Tando back to the capital did in fact arrive there.[187] The party, however, consisted only of four young men, who carried as token of their earnestness no more than two cases of gin! At meetings of the Council on 5 and 6 December, members swore the Great Oath that if, as appeared to be the case, the Wassa were not seriously concerned to arrive at a settlement, then war was inevitable. The Wassa envoys left Kumase convinced that Tando had lulled them into a false sense of security.[188] Characteristically, Daendels assumed a bellicose attitude and probably did much to strengthen the war party in the council by the secret message that he sent to Asantehene: 'to send an army of 30,000 men through the Wassa country to kill the Wassa Caboceers and all who should aid them, and to destroy with the Wassa, the Fante living under their protection'.[189] Equally characteristically, Osei Bonsu – who 'never appealed to the sword while a path lay open for negociation' [190] – succeeded in restraining the war party. In mid-October 1817, a new mission arrived in Kumase from Wassa. 'It is thought', reported Hutchison from the capital, 'a fine to

184 Huydecoper's Journal, entry for 19 November 1816.
185 Bowdich, 1819, p. 123. Bowdich maintained that Tando had in fact persuaded the Wassa envoys to bring to Kumase the sum of the damages, and also to pay twenty-four slaves for every Asante killed or injured by their countrymen. The Dutch reports do not bear out this version.
186 KvG 350: Osei Bonsu to Daendels, dd. Kumase, 29 November 1816.
187 Huydecoper's Journal, entry for 4 December 1816.
188 *Ibid.* entries for 5 and 6 December 1816. KvG 349: Huydecoper to Daendels, dd. Kumase, 9 December 1816.
189 General State Archives, The Hague, Archives of the Department of Foreign Affairs, B. 57, xli: Daendels to Osei Bonsu, dd. Elmina, 10 January 1817, and Statement by J. H. Baarens, n.d.
190 Dupuis, 1824, pp. 225–6.

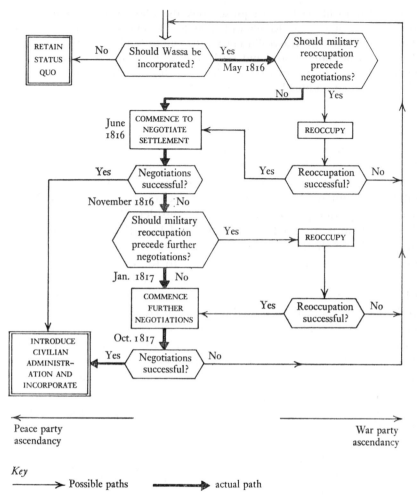

Fig. 3 Osei Bonsu's government: Wassa policy, 1816–17. Decision-logic

the King and future tribute may compromise the matter.' [191] Details of the settlement that was reached have not been found. It seems, however, that among the central government's terms were ones enjoining the replacement of Wassa chiefs with a record of hostility towards Asante by ones known to be cooperative.[192]

The underlying decision-logic of the situation facing the central government, with respect to its Wassa policy, is shown in Figure 3. It will be apparent that the conflict in council in 1816–17, between

[191] Hutchison, in Bowdich, 1819, p. 392.
[192] PRO, CO. 2/11: Robertson, Acting Consul for Asante, to Bathurst, dd. Cape Coast, 27 November 1820.

'hawkish' and 'dovish' elements, was one that resulted not from a lack of consensus about the goal, since no councillor seemingly argued for disengagement from Wassa affairs, but from a lack of agreement about the effective way of attaining the goal of incorporation. The Wassa case has been described in some detail since it exemplifies particularly well the nature of the problems facing central government in the evolution of policy towards its acquired territories: first, in the formulation of the goal (acknowledgment of sovereignty, compensation for past hostilities, determination of tribute, maintenance of roads, appointment of resident commissioners, and so forth), and second, in the selection of the path to that goal and in the ongoing evaluation of the effectiveness of that path (with especial reference to the complex equation between utilization of the costly coercive resources of the military machine and the cheaper negotiating resources of the agencies of the administration).

The apogee of the provincial administration in the south

By 1817 the Asante government might reasonably have been optimistic about the political situation in the southern provinces. The extensive rebellions that had swept across the coastal hinterlands in the first part of the decade had been suppressed, and the three who had been considered the principal architects of resistance had all been hunted down and slain: Kwadwo Kuma who had usurped the stool of Akyem Kotoku from the loyal Kwaakye Adeyefe and had assumed command of both Akyem Kotoku and Akyem Abuakwa rebel forces after the death of Ata Wusu Yiakosan; [193] the Akuapemhene Kwao Saforo Twie, who was killed and his body surrendered to the Asante by his close relative Adow Dankwa; [194] and Kofi Asante, the Akyem Abuakwa who had led the surviving rebel groups after Kwadwo Kuma's death in May 1816.[195] One army in the south, that commanded by the Kumase Nkonnwasoafohene Yaw Kokroko, arrived back in the capital on 14 March 1816. The other two, commanded by

[193] Kwadwo Kuma was killed, or according to one account, committed suicide, after capture by troops of Apea Nyanyo, see PRO, T. 70/36: Dawson *et al.* to Committee, dd. Cape Coast, June 1816. Bowdich, 1819, pp. 242; 244. Huydecoper's Journal, entry for 5 June, 1816. Reindorf, 2nd ed., n.d., pp. 152–61. Institute of African Studies, Ghana, KAG/7: Akim Oda (Kotoku) Tradition, recorded by Kwabena Ameyaw, 18 January 1966. Kwadwo Kuma, by virtue of his dual command of Kotoku and Abuakwa forces, is sometimes cross-listed as an Okyenhene, see e.g., Djang, 1936, p. 104.
[194] PRO, T. 70/36: Dawson *et al.* to Committee, dd. Cape Coast, 14 August 1816. Bowdich, 1819, p. 244. Reindorf, 2nd ed., n.d., pp. 160–1.
[195] Reindorf, 2nd ed., n.d., pp. 157; 161.

Amankwa Abinowa and Apea Nyanyo, entered Kumase on 3 March 1817.[196]

The recall of the armies initiated a period of intense activity by officials of the civil administration, who took over the exacting task of restoring public order in the districts formerly held by the rebels. Everywhere fines were imposed upon those who had given their support to the dissidents, and disloyal local chiefs were replaced by ones known to be favourably disposed towards the government. The Akuapem, for example, were required to pay in damages the value of four hundred slaves by one account,[197] and 2,000 rigsdallers (or about 125 oz of gold) by another.[198] Adow Dankwa, who had cooperated with the Asante armies, was confirmed as new Akuapemhene.[199] In the Akyem country, according to Bowdich, fines were apportioned town by town: 'the King and the Ashantee Government had proposed that every croom [*kuro*, 'town'] of Akim should pay 20 periguins [45 oz] of gold as an atonement for their late revolt. Ten periguins were advanced immediately by each, and the other moiety was excused until after the harvest'.[200] When the chief of the Akyem Kotoku town of Manso [201] resolutely refused to pay his part of the fine, 'the King's messengers', it was reported, 'appealed to his people with so much address, that they rose upon their caboceer, killed him, and sent his head to the King, with the 20 periguins required'.[202] The total amount paid by the Akyem Kotoku towns was said to have been 300 peredwans, or 675 oz of gold.[203] Amoako Panin, who had refused to support Kwadwo Kuma in rebellion, was made new Akyem Kotokuhene, and the former Akuapem resident Odenkyem was one of the two functionaries sent by the Asantehene to conduct the enstoolment.[204] In Akyem Abuakwa no successor to Kofi Asante was immediately chosen: the queen-mother Dokuwa, whose younger sister Yeboa Akua was among the Asantehene's wives, ruled the province presumably after having satisfied the government of her loyalty.[205] Probably late in 1816 the Aowin of the southwest, recognizing the trend of the times, sent envoys

196 Huydecoper's Journal, entries for 14 August 1816, and 3 March 1817.
197 KvG 501: Roelossen to Daendels, dd. Accra, 22 October 1816.
198 National Archives, Copenhagen, Archives of the West Indian and Guinea Company, Christiansborg Diaries: despatch from Richter, dd. Christiansborg, 2 August 1816. Reindorf, 2nd ed., n.d., p. 160.
199 Reindorf, 2nd ed., n.d., p. 160.
200 Bowdich, 1819, pp. 116–17.
201 Manso, 20 miles north of Nsaba, Route VI(a), mile 122.
202 Bowdich, 1819, p. 117.
203 Reindorf, 2nd ed., n.d., p. 160.
204 *Ibid.* pp. 158, 160.
205 *Ibid.* p. 156.

to Kumase to re-affirm their allegiance to the government, and to ask that the amount of the tribute be regularized.[206] The negotiation of the Wassa settlement, in 1816 and 1817, has been described above. The series of negotiations of a full settlement with the Fante, commenced in April 1816, appeared moreover to offer prospects of success. A second mission arrived in Kumase on 15 July 1816, and, returning to the coast to obtain a mandate from the Fante chiefs, reappeared in the capital on 26 March 1817 with assurances that the Fante had agreed to pay the *apeato* or war-tax imposed upon them and would henceforth acknowledge the authority of the Asantehenc.[207]

In its relations with the various European mercantile interests on the Gold Coast the Asante government seemed, too, to have achieved its more immediate objectives. On 7 February 1817, a treaty had been signed with the British, declaring 'perpetual peace and harmony between the British subjects in this country, and the subjects of the King of Ashantee'.[208] The longstanding accord between the government and the Dutch authorities in Elmina remained firm. 'With the King of Asante', remarked Daendels, 'we are on the best understanding. He has much respect and friendship for the Dutch.' [209] Indeed, with the reassertion of the Asante hegemony over the southern provinces, Daendels saw the way open for the Asante government to undertake a massive programme of modernization, and submitted proposals to Osei Bonsu:

1st. To make his Kingdom rich by trade, and by the cultivation of Cotton, Sugar, Coffee, Indigo.
2nd. To draw large revenues himself, by making provisions for his treasury, from the Colonial products.
3rd. That the making of roads, and obtaining large revenues, will place him in a position to build great palaces filled with royal furniture and ornaments.
4th. That he shall drive along the new roads he will make in fine coaches, or on horse-back, like the Moors and Arabs.
5th. That the Asante will carry trade into the heart of Africa, over the Kong mountains, and will much enrich his country and treasury.
6th. That he will give his successor such an education that he will follow in his footsteps in order that the Asante Kingdom may remain great and mighty and more and more increase in power.
7th. That his army shall conquer all his enemies and extend his boundaries as far as he shall please, through the improvement of the arts of war which his

---

206 Bowdich, 1819, p. 244.
207 Huydecoper's Journal, entries for 15 July 1816, and 26 March 1817.
208 For text, see Dupuis, 1824, p. cxix.
209 General State Archives, The Hague, KvG 384: Daendels to Department of Trade and Colonies, dd. Elmina, 6 December 1816, Report II.

Generals will obtain by intercourse with the Whites: and that his name after his death, shall be handed down in legend to his descendants as the founder of all arts and sciences, and of the greatness of the Asante Kingdom.[210]

The Danish authorities in Christiansborg, although lacking the enthusiasm of the Dutch for the Asante cause, were nevertheless in no doubt – especially after Osei Kwame's effective interdiction on the Danish trade in 1788–9 [211] – that their extensive commercial interests in the southeastern provinces were best promoted in harmony with the government in Kumase. Indeed, the results of the Børgesen mission to Asante in 1792, when Osei Kwame had readily responded to a Danish request for ten or twelve thousand soldiers to assist them in suppressing disorders east of the Volta, had convinced them of 'the unbelievedly great might' of the Asante.[212]

In the favourable circumstances of the second decade of the nineteenth century, the Asante government seemingly made one important innovation in its system of control over the southern provinces: an assembly of representatives of local chiefs was instituted, as an instrument for relating more closely the central to the local authorities. Whether the assembly met regularly, and perhaps annually like the Asantemanhyiamu, and whether it always met in one place, is not known. But in September 1822 it was in session at Abora-Dunkwa, seat of the central government's administration in southern Fanteland. Its proceedings in the matter of tribute were witnessed by a messenger of the British present at the meeting:

He saw at Abrah representatives from the Elminas, Accras, Wassaws, Assins and some other states tributary to Ashantee. The caboceers of Annamaboe were invited to join them, but they had declined doing so. It was understood that this assembly was convened to receive the commands of the King on various important points. One was said to be a demand of an additional tribute, and an alteration in the mode of payment. The slave trade was at its height when these states were brought under the Ashantee yoke, and the taxes imposed on them were receivable in slaves. The great reduction in the value of human beings and the want of purchasers for them of late years, have determined the King not to take them in payment hereafter. He requires gold or European goods in their stead . . .[213]

210 *Ibid.* KvG 349: Daendels to Osei Bonsu, dd. Elmina, 19 June 1816, and Daendels to Huydecoper, dd. Elmina, 23 June 1816.
211 See Kea, 1970b, *passim.*
212 For the Børgesen mission, see Nørregård, 1966, p. 156; Kea, 1969, pp. 45–6; Fynn, 1971, pp. 132–6.
213 PRO, CO. 267/56: Chisholm to Governor MacCarthy, dd. Cape Coast, 30 September 1822.

The body was forerunner of the Legislative Assembly of Native Chiefs upon the Gold Coast, first convened by the British authorities in April 1852 and interestingly enough immediately used by them as the instrument for the introduction of a new poll tax.[214]

[214] PRO, CO. 96/25: Resolutions of 19 April 1852, and Governor Hill to Packington, dd. 2 August and 20 October 1852.

CHAPTER 5

Kumase and the southern provinces: the politics of retrenchment

The breakdown of relations with the British

In the third decade of the nineteenth century a combination of circumstances induced the Asante government radically to revise its political and military thinking, and to pursue a policy of retrenchment with respect to the southern provinces. Principal among the causes of change was undoubtedly the deterioration, despite the treaty of 1817, of its relations with the British on the Gold Coast.

The evidence leaves no room for doubt about the equivocal nature of the British attitude toward Asante in and after 1817. In the copy of the treaty retained by the Asante government, Article 4 read:

> In order to avert the horrors of war, it is agreed that in any case of aggression on the part of the natives under British protection, the king shall complain thereof to the governor-in-chief, to obtain redress; and that he will in no instance resort to hostilities without endeavouring, as much as possible, to effect an amicable arrangement.[1]

In the copy of the treaty taken by Bowdich to London, however, the wording had become slightly but significantly changed:

> In order to avert the horrors of war, it is agreed, that in any case of aggression on the part of the natives under British protection, the Kings shall complain thereof to the Governor in Chief to obtain redress, and that they will in no instance resort to hostilities, even against the other towns of the Fante territory, without endeavouring as much as possible to effect an amicable arrangement, affording the Governor the opportunity of propitiating it, as far as he may with discretion.[2]

The British Governor, John Hope Smith, had no hesitation in construing the rewritten clause as involving an abrogation by the Asante government of sovereignty over the coastal Fante. When in a letter of 25 October 1817 the Asantehene referred to the Fante as his 'slaves' –

---

1 Dupuis, 1824, p. cxix.
2 Bowdich, 1819, p. 127. The 'Kings' has reference to the Asantehene and Dwabenhene.

that is, presumably *nkoa* or subjects [3] – Smith hastily dispatched a protest to Acting Consul Hutchison in Kumase:

There is a most offensive paragraph in the king's letter . . . You will expressly state to the king, and in the most decided terms, that the Cape Coast people are not his slaves, nor have they ever been acknowledged as such; neither can they nor any of the natives residing under British protection be included in that most degrading title . . . Any interference on the part of the king in matters concerning the people residing under the protection of the forts, cannot possibly be allowed.[4]

Smith demonstrated in practice, moreover, his disregard of both the spirit and the letter of the treaty by the support, and even encouragement, he gave to Fante dissidents at the time of the Gyaman campaign (pp. 148–9). Of his conduct Cruickshank, who was to be closely associated with the subsequent administration of Governor Maclean, remarked:

The supposed disasters of the Gaman war presented a favourable opportunity of throwing off the yoke, and good faith was sacrificed to their [British] views of policy. It is humiliating to be compelled to make this admission, and to confess that a king of Ashantee had greater regard for his written engagements than an English governor. But the policy was as short-sighted as it was perfidious. The king's authority was fully established throughout the country . . .[5]

The matter was one to which the government in Kumase addressed itself with the arrival there of Joseph Dupuis to renegotiate the treaty, when, as the Consul described it, he was enlightened 'regarding the complexion of court policies, as they related to Fantee'.[6] At a meeting of the council on 9 March 1820, with the copy of the treaty of 1817 before him, the Asantehene Osei Bonsu clarified his understanding of the situation:

he never could or would relinquish his right of sovereignty from the conquest of Fantee, over the whole country. Elmina Town, which for wealth and population, greatly exceeded Cape Coast, acknowledged his supremacy; and the Dutch governor compelled the people to obey him, for that reason he was the friend of the Dutch. The natives themselves were his friends, and he never had any palavers there. Danish Accra, English Accra, Tantum and Apollonia never disputed his title; the people never gave him any trouble, and therefore if his power was acknowledged so far to the east as Accra, and so far to

3 PRO, T. 70/41: Osei Bonsu to Smith, dd. Kumase, 25 October 1817.
4 PRO, T. 70/1606: letter from Smith to Hutchison, dd. Cape Coast, 21 November 1817.
5 Cruickshank, 1853, I, 140–1.
6 Dupuis, 1824, p. 128.

the west as Apollonia, he must surely be the master of Cape Coast which lay in the centre.[7]

Dupuis conceded the point: he could scarcely do otherwise in view of the fact that the Fante had themselves acknowledged the Asante overlordship. Hence by the terms of the revised treaty which was agreed upon, the issue of sovereignty was clarified in Article 5:

The King of Ashantee claims the Fantee territory as his dominions, which the consul, on the part of the British Government, accedes to, in consideration and on the express condition that the king agrees to acknowledge the natives, residing under British protection, entitled to the benefits of British laws, and to be amenable to them only in case of any act of aggression on their part.[8]

The distinction – to become of crucial importance later – was thus made between sovereignty over the Fante, which the Asante government was to retain, and administrative and judicial jurisdiction, which the British would assume. The formula seemed capable of reconciling the interests of both parties. Governor Smith, however, hastened to dispatch to the African Company Committee in London his opinion, 'that no individual, however imbecile, who has ever had influence over the affairs of Africa, has by his timidity and malignancy, (an expression as true as it is strong) so much reduced the influence of Europeans as Mr. Dupuis. . .'[9]

In the event, the British government failed to ratify the revised treaty. Thenceforth the Asante and British moved seemingly inexorably toward war. Early in 1821, apparently in an attempt to reduce tension, Asante government officials in the Cape Coast area removed their headquarters to the Dutch lodge at nearby Mouri, where they reconvened their court and continued to exercise jurisdiction. Opentri of Abora Dunkwa was placed on the active list once more, and was posted to Mouri to assist the administrators there. Governor Smith, choosing to categorize as murders the judicial executions carried out at Mouri, ordered his troops to arrest Opentri and his followers – 'Fantees', commented the commander of the force, 'who were assembled to assist the Ashantees in enforcing some very unjust demands made by them on the people of Cape Coast'.[10] In the fighting on 10 February 1821, Opentri was killed. The senior Asante still resident in Cape Coast, the travelling commissioner Owusu Dome, sent Governor Smith an official protest at the act of war, and withdrew his mission

7 *Ibid.* p. 131.
8 *Ibid.* p. cxxi.
9 PRO, T. 70/1606: Smith *et al.* to Committee, dd. Cape Coast, 19 May 1820.
10 Dupuis, 1824, pp. 201–3: letter from Colliver, dd. Cape Coast, 21 April 1821. See also Reindorf, 2nd ed., n.d., pp. 170–1.

to Abora-Dunkwa.[11] The Aborahene Osam Kofi, one of the most important of the southern Fante chiefs, complained formally to the Asantehene, requesting him to demand compensation from the British.[12]

MacCarthy and the revival of resistance

Less than a month after the affray at Mouri, the British government abolished the African Company and so assumed direct responsibility for the forts and settlements on the Gold Coast. Under the regime of Governor Sir Charles MacCarthy of Sierra Leone, the British attitude toward Asante became increasingly bellicose. Writers in the newspapers founded or controlled by MacCarthy, *The Royal Gazette and Sierra Leone Advertiser* and *The Royal Gold Coast Gazette and Commercial Intelligencer,* began to evince a seemingly pathological hatred of all things Asante. Osei Bonsu, for example, became 'the sable monster', 'the tyrant', and 'the great barbarian' whose aim was that 'without reservation or exception all white men or mullatoes should be immolated to the Ashantee Fetish . . . [so that] their skulls and limbs might ornament the banqueting room'.[13] In the pages of the same journals Captain Gordon Laing, to die in the sands north of Timbuktu only three years later, managed to couple in four grossly inelegant lines of verse the current disapproval of the pro-Asante Fante merchant Brew with a chauvinistic resolve to discontinue payment of the tributes ('customs') due to the Asante government:

> Lets drive from this country, the trait'rous Brew,
> And down with the power of O'Saii Tootoo;
> Shou'd he send to demand his customs' arrears,
> He'll get a *discharge* from our brave Volunteers . . .[14]

The MacCarthy script-writers developed the new scenario, in fact, in the immediate aftermath of the second serious military engagement of the period: that of 21–22 February 1823, when troops were sent to arrest the Asante administrative officers at Abora-Dunkwa. Unlike the earlier attack on Mouri, however, that on Abora-Dunkwa failed, and MacCarthy's forces were routed.[15]

Throughout the remainder of 1823 the British devoted their efforts to the total subversion of Osei Bonsu's policies of pacification. By 12 December MacCarthy was able to assure Earl Bathurst that 'the whole

---

11 Dupuis, 1824, pp. 203–8.
12 Reindorf, 2nd ed., n.d., p. 171. Djang, 1936, p. 109.
13 *Royal Gold Coast Gazette,* 18 March 1823.
14 *Ibid.* Reprinted in *The Royal Gazette and Sierra Leone Advertiser,* 12 July 1823.
15 For an account of the episode, see Reindorf, 2nd ed., n.d., pp. 172–3.

of the tribes residing along the shore, from Apollonia to the Volta . . . are all in arms against the common enemy . . . our friends are increasing daily, and the Ashantee tributaries [are] seeking shelter under the British flag'.[16] Fortunately the historian is not dependent solely upon MacCarthy's despatches for an account of the events of 1823. There were, indeed, many groups in the southern provinces who still maintained opposition to incorporation into Greater Asante. In 1820, for example, Fante dissenters complained of Asante 'interference in the Municipal regulations of the Towns'. Moreover, the government's policy of converting tributes in slaves to ones in gold or ivory – the very matter which was to be discussed at the assembly of representatives of southern chiefs in 1822 (p. 164) – fostered discontent, and it was reported that 'a partial change has taken place in Wassa, where the people have deposed the Magistrates appointed by the King and have elected those of their choice'.[17] But the architect of renewed resistance to the government in Kumase was undoubtedly MacCarthy, as Governor Sir Neil Campbell acknowledged in 1825 when he wrote of those who had been 'the constant allies of the Ashantees until they were bribed, cajoled or frightened, by threats of destruction from Sir Charles MacCarthy (and even stronger measures) to join his alliance'.[18]

In 1823 a number of southern chiefs had in fact clearly demonstrated their reluctance to join any rebellion against the government in Kumase. Among the leaders of Fante opposition to MacCarthy's policies was Aduanan Apea, ruler of the Adwumako towns, and responsible to the Asantehene for the collection of Fante tributes which were transmitted to the capital through Esikumahene (see p. 75).[19] In May 1823 a large mission from Kumase, of two hundred men headed by Owusu Dome, had held discussions with Aduanan Apea.[20] As a result, in mid-1823 Captain Laing was ordered to occupy Adwumako and, so it was blandly reported, 'after considerable hesitation he [Aduanan Apea] was prevailed upon to take an active part in the war'.[21] Having thus declared, under duress, his support for the British, Aduanan Apea's defection was reported to the government in Kumase by the Esikumahene Kwasi Amankwa, and some forty Adwumako subjects who were in the capital at the time were arrested and exe-

16 PRO, CO, 267/59: letter from MacCarthy to Bathurst dd. Cape Coast, 12 December 1823.
17 PRO, CO. 2/11: Robertson to Bathurst, dd. Cape Coast, 27 November 1820.
18 PRO, CO. 267/74: Campbell to Bathurst, dd. Cape Coast, 5 November 1826.
19 Djang, 1925, p. 50. Reindorf, 2nd ed., n.d., p. 178.
20 *Royal Gold Coast Gazette*, 7 June 1823.
21 PRO, CO. 267/58: Chisholm to MacCarthy, dd. Cape Coast, 8 August 1823.

cuted.[22] Another Fante Chief, 'Abagay', who had failed to show sufficient enthusiasm for MacCarthy's policies, was seized and imprisoned
in Cape Coast Castle,[23] while the prominent and strongly pro-Asante
Samuel Brew was arrested, sentenced to deportation to Sierra Leone,
and was taken on board H.M.S. *Cyrene* in 16 May 1823. Eight days
later he was found with his throat cut, and there were at least rumours that he had been murdered.[24]

By August 1823, Major Chisholm was able to report to MacCarthy –
with 'particular satisfaction' – that he had succeeded in closing the
great-road between Kumase and Elmina for the last two months, and
that his 'active proceedings' had induced the Wassa to rebel. The
despatch to the borders of the Wassa country of a force of 600 men
of the Cape Coast Militia was no doubt a significant aspect of these
'active proceedings'.[25] MacCarthy's agents succeeded, furthermore, in
persuading the rulers of the inner provinces of Denkyira and Twifo
to take up arms against their government. To Campbell, three years
later, this seemed a particularly inadvisable policy since, as he commented, both were 'brothers and relations of the King of Ashantee,
who were brought up at Coomassie, who can never expect forgive-
ness'.[26] While no such close ties of kinship in fact existed between the
two and the Oyoko royals in Kumase, it is certainly true that the
Denkyirahene Kwadwo Tsibu had been raised in the capital.[27] In or
about 1820, however, he had become involved in a series of court
cases there. Although the Gyakye counselor Kwadwo Adusei Kyakya
had acted as his legal adviser and had ably defended him, on the
death of the Asantehene Osei Bonsu in 1823 Kwadwo Tsibu feared for
his own safety and fled the capital with charges against him still outstanding. In the circumstances he may well have been predisposed to
accept MacCarthy's overtures.[28]

Meanwhile MacCarthy's officers had been not inactive in the south-
eastern provinces. In late 1822 Captain Blenkarne arrested there an
Asante 'captain' named Agyei: he was the senior counselor Asante
Agyei, who held the portfolio for foreign affairs.[29] He was released on

22 Reindorf, 2nd ed., n.d., p. 179.
23 PRO, CO. 267/61: Lt. Col. Grant to Bathurst, dd. Cape Coast, 31 July 1824.
24 See Priestley, 1969, p. 141.
25 PRO, CO. 267/58: Chisholm to MacCarthy, dd. Cape Coast, 8 August 1823.
26 PRO, CO. 267/74: Campbell to Bathurst, dd. Cape Coast, 5 November 1826.
27 Reindorf, 2nd ed., n.d., p. 181.
28 Reindorf, 2nd ed., n.d., pp. 181–5. *Royal Gold Coast Gazette,* 1 November 1823.
29 Reindorf, 2nd ed., n.d., p. 180, described Asante Agyei as 'the renowned linguist
   of Kumase', and as son of the Adumhene Adum Ata. He appears in fact to have
   been born in the southeastern province of Akwamu, to have entered into the
   Asantehene's service in or about 1805, and subsequently to have achieved high

22 November, at the intercession of the Accra chiefs.[30] On his journey back to Kumase he is reported to have met large numbers of Asante traders bound for Accra, and to have advised their return to the capital. Some three hundred, however, continued to Danish Osu, assuming that they would be safe there. They were either murdered or made prisoners, and their goods were confiscated.[31] Later investigations by Treasury officials in London of various discrepancies in MacCarthy's accounts suggested that he had bribed the Osu chief, Dowuona, to commit the outrages.[32] The violence spread to Dutch Accra, where an Asante chief and three followers were slain. Blenkarne reputedly showed his approval by sending the instigators two hundred heads of cowries. Many Accra, by contrast, expressed their regrets and attempted to bury the Asante dead near Osu. 'It was', commented Reindorf, 'a very trying ordeal for the people of Dutch Town to see their old friends so cruelly treated.' [33] From the British point of view, however, the situation had evolved very satisfactorily: Accra support for the MacCarthyite cause was now guaranteed by their fear of Asante retribution. Hence Blenkarne was enabled to proceed with the next stage of the operation.

In the course of the rapidly developing crisis in the southeast, the Asante government had sent messengers to both Dokuwa and Adow Dankwa, rulers of Akyem Abuakwa and Akuapem respectively, to determine their loyalty. Both dispatched messengers back to the capital to reassure the government, and Dokuwa prepared to appear there in person. With promises of support from the British, however, dissident factions became active in both provinces. In Akyem Abuakwa the subordinate chiefs of Apapam, Apedwa and Tete initiated moves to destool Dokuwa, and they killed Tano Asiakwa, possibly the Asante commissioner then stationed there and certainly an adherent of the central government.[34] In Akuapem the chief of Aburi, Kwafum, led the opposition to Adow Dankwa, and ordered a massacre of an Asante trading party on the great-road at Agyankuma just south of Aburi.[35] Blenkarne then sent messengers to both Dokuwa and Adow Dankwa to win them over. According to Reindorf, whose evidence may

office. He was probably adopted into Adum Ata's household since Adum Ata's family was itself of ultimate Akwamu origins. See Asante Collective Biography Project: Asante Agyei.

30 General State Archives, The Hague, KvG 351: letter from the Commandant, Dutch Accra, dd. 26 November 1822, enclosing letters from Blenkarne dd. 22 and 26 November 1822.

31 Reindorf, 2nd ed., n.d., p. 180.

32 E. F. Collins kindly brought this matter to my attention.

33 Reindorf, 2nd ed., n.d., p. 181.

34 Reindorf, 2nd ed., n.d., p. 175.

35 *Ibid.* pp. 176–7.

well derive from those present, Dokuwa asked: 'Suppose the whitemen fail to destroy the power of Asante, what will become of me, my sons, and my subjects? Whither shall we flee? The whitemen could sail away to Europe, the Akras would be safe on the Coast, but upon me and my subjects the Asantes would pour out revenge', to which Blen karne's messenger, an Accra man, replied: 'Suppose the whitemen run away from the Coast, will they not put a stop to the coming in of guns, powder, flint, and knives? . . . The whitemen have brought out corn with them, have determined to conquer Asante and plant the corn in the soil of Kumase and eat some of it before returning to Europe.' Dokuwa reluctantly capitulated, and was summoned to Accra to confirm her new allegiance to the British.[36] Adow Dankwa, by contrast, refused to defect. Blenkarne accordingly raised a force of four thousand men in Accra, and, joining with the Aburihene, trapped Adow Dankwa in his capital, Akuropon. Over a hundred Asante in the town were reported killed or enslaved, and Adow Dankwa was taken under escort to Accra.[37]

While MacCarthy's agents were thus raising rebellion in the southern provinces, the Asante government appears to have vacillated, being understandably reluctant to authorize further military campaigns in the troubled areas. Indeed, since the demobilization of the armies of the south in 1816 and 1817, only one large force appears to have been placed upon a war footing: the body commanded by the Nsutahene Yaw Sekyere which had been sent into the central trans-Volta provinces to punish the Nkonya and Wusuta for their failure to provide contingents for the Gyaman expeditionary force in 1818.[38] But from March 1823 rumours circulated that three Asante armies, of ten thousand men each, were marching on the coast. 'So panic struck were the people', commented Chisholm, 'at the name of the Ashantee army that I really believe they would willingly have embraced an opportunity of submitting to their oppressors had the presence of the European officers amongst them not inspired them with confidence.' [39]

British intelligence reports were probably correct in indicating that the government in Kumase would launch no major military operation

---

36 *Idem.*

37 *Idem.* The extant British reports of these proceedings are, not unexpectedly, incomplete. Reindorf's account, however, is supported in general by reports on the situation made by the Danish Governor Richelieu immediately upon his arrival in Christiansborg at the beginning of January 1824: see National Archives, Copenhagen, Guinea Journal, despatches to Copenhagen of January 1824.

38 Rattray, 1929, p. 261.

39 *Royal Gold Coast Gazette*, 25 March 1823. PRO, CO. 267/58: Chisholm to MacCarthy, dd. Cape Coast, 8 August 1823; CO. 267/59: MacCarthy to Bathurst, dd. Cape Coast, 12 December 1824.

at least until the army commanded by Nsutahene had returned to the capital,[40] and the indications were that it was meeting with strong resistance in the early months of 1823.[41] The continued unrest in Gyaman, moreover, was a source of much anxiety to the government, and many councillors feared that Asante might find itself engaged in simultaneous fighting in both the north and south: a situation specifically forbidden by the laws of Okomfo Anokye.[42] At a time when clear leadership was essential, Osei Bonsu fell ill, afflicted by a leg ulcer and chest ailment. By mid-1823 he was unable to attend to government business, and shortly thereafter retired to a village outside the capital.[43] At the Odwira held in July or August 1823, the Council in Kumase was reported to have been deeply divided upon basic policy. By the very beginning of November 1823 the first reports of the death of Osei Bonsu had reached the Gold Coast.[44]

Only the confidence which the British felt, that in the circumstances the government in Kumase was incapable of mobilizing its military resources, can explain MacCarthy's decision to take the offensive in January 1824. There was, however, an element of miscalculation in the premises on which MacCarthy worked. Although in 1823 the government in Kumase had not fully redefined its policy towards the British, it did view with grave disquiet the defection of the chiefs of Denkyira, Twifo and western Wassa: provinces which, whether under the terms of the treaty of 1817 or the unratified agreement of 1820, could in no way be regarded legitimately as within the sphere of British interest. Orders were issued for the arrest of the three chiefs to stand trial in Kumase. A force of two thousand men which crossed the Pra in May 1823 under the command of Owusu 'Akara' and Kwame Butuakwa, was despatched presumably to effect the arrests.[45] Troops were, moreover, pulled back from the Gyaman front for service in the south,[46] and by late July or early August the army south of the Pra had increased to one of about nine thousand men. But while the government had thus decided to establish a strong military presence in the southern provinces, no authorization had been given for the troops to engage with the British. Confronted by Captain Laing and the Anomabo militia, the Asante commanders therefore withdrew their forces rather than risk hostilities.[47] The belief

40 CO. 267/58: Chisholm to MacCarthy, dd. 8 August 1823.
41 *Royal Gold Coast Gazette,* 21 January, 25 March, 21 May and 22 November 1823. Reindorf, 2nd ed., n.d., p. 303.
42 See, e.g. Kyerematen, 1966, pp. 228 ff.
43 *Royal Gold Coast Gazette,* 16 August and 25 October 1823.
44 *Ibid.* 1, 15 and 22 November 1823.
45 *Ibid.* 7 June 1823.
46 *Idem.*
47 PRO, CO. 267/59: MacCarthy to Bathurst, dd. 12 December 1823.

thus gained currency, that the British had little to fear from the Asante army south of the Pra, and in January 1824 MacCarthy moved his troops northwards into Wassa. On the 21st of that month an Asante force unexpectedly engaged the invaders; MacCarthy and eight European officers were killed, and of the two hundred and fifty enrolled men in his command, only some seventy returned.[48] In an account of the matter subsequently given to Major Ricketts by Kwadwo Akyampon Bakki, the Asante resident commissioner for Elmina, it was made clear that the Asante commanders had no idea that they were fighting a British-led expedition, and had still lacked any authority to do so.[49]

The basis for retrenchment

Since 1807 the broad politico-military strategies of Osei Bonsu's government had been linked to two basic goals: first, the closer incorporation of the provinces into Greater Asante; and second, the attainment of the highest level of accommodation to the interests of the European mercantile powers on the Gold Coast which was compatible with the unification of Greater Asante. It has been seen, however, that the policies of the British (though neither of Dutch nor Danes) on the Gold Coast were, between 1817 and 1823, such as to generate a situation of acute confrontation. In the changed circumstances, Osei Bonsu's policies of accommodation had not so much failed as become irrelevant: the options open to the Asante government seemed to be either war with the British, or retrenchment in the southern provinces. The struggles in the Asante councils between the advocates of one or the other policy – between what will for the present be called the 'war' and 'peace' parties – is analysed more fully below (see Chapter 12). Suffice it to note here that until the very end of his reign Osei Bonsu appears to have resisted the arguments of the war party.[50] 'Certain it is, as the king confessed to me,' remarked Dupuis, 'that neither inclination, policy, nor the desire of getting the good things, possessed by the whites in their castles, could ever induce him to do them any injury.'[51] The moderation which the Asante showed in the face of British provo-

---

48 For an eye-witness account of the engagement, see Ricketts, 1831, chapter III.

49 *Royal Gazette and Sierra Leone Advertiser*, 2 October 1824. Claridge, 1915, I, 364–5.

50 The belief that Osei Bonsu died on the same day as MacCarthy, see, e.g. Fuller, 1921, p. 70, is fallacious. So too is the report by Holman, 1840, p. 213, that Osei Bonsu lived just long enough to learn of MacCarthy's defeat. It is possible, however, in view of Asante practice, that the news of Osei Bonsu's death was not made public until the day of the Asante victory.

51 Dupuis, 1824, pp. 215–16, note.

cation until Osei Bonsu's death leaves little doubt that Dupuis' assessment of his attitude was indeed an accurate one.

In a communication of November 1820, Robertson, then Acting Consul for Asante, made several comments of considerable perspicuity, based partly upon talks with a treasury official from Kumase. 'I am assured beyond a doubt', he wrote,

> that the Ashantee Government are much perplexed and cannot find means even by extortion to sustain their power . . . From what I have drawn from him in our conversation I think that the Ashantee Government would gladly accept any reasonable overture that might be made to them for resigning all claims to this Frontier [i.e. the central maritime provinces].[52]

Crucial to an understanding of why a policy of retrenchment could be regarded by Osei Bonsu and members of the peace party as realistic in the circumstances, is an appreciation of the nature of the reaction of the Asante government to the abolition of the maritime slave trade by the Danes, British and Dutch, all effectively within the first fifteen years of the nineteenth century. Although for a time such coastal merchants as Samuel Brew at Mouri and Ankra at Accra succeeded, with Asante backing, in maintaining sales especially to Spanish and Portuguese ships from the Americas,[53] nevertheless the demand for slaves on the coast dropped to unprecedentedly low levels. The economy of Asante, however, as Osei Bonsu pointed out in 1820, was not one based upon slave-raiding for export purposes: 'I cannot make war to catch slaves in the bush, like a thief. My ancestors never did so. But if I fight a king, and kill him when he is insolent, then certainly I must have his gold, and his slaves, and the people are mine too. Do not the white kings act like this?'[54] Slaves were in fact of crucial importance to the Asante economy not so much for the export trade as for satisfying the labour requirements of agriculture and industry. The use of an unfree labour force on the Asante farms has been referred to above (p. 52).[55] It seems clear, however, that while free Asante commoners were also heavily involved in food production, there were other spheres of enterprise which were abhorrent to them; in which, therefore, dependence upon unfree labour was all but total. Principal

52 PRO, CO. 2/11: Robertson to Bathurst dd. Cape Coast, 27 November 1820.
53 Bowdich, 1819, p. 339, maintained for example that at least one thousand slaves were sent from Asante to two ships sailing under the Spanish flag in the period May–September 1817.
54 Dupuis, 1824, p. 163. Curtin's recent study of the Atlantic slave trade suggests in fact that exports of slaves from the Gold Coast rose to a peak in the decade 1741–51 – that is, in the main period of Asante territorial expansion – and then fell irregularly throughout the remainder of the century, see Curtin, 1969, pp. 224–5.
55 Dupuis, 1824, p. xxxi, refers also to the employment of slave fishermen on Lake Bosumtwe.

of these was gold mining, against which activity strong religious taboos operated. 'The Ashantees', observed James Africanus Horton in 1873, 'do not dig gold themselves, nor will they even pick up dust or coins that fall by accident, believing that such are jealously appropriated by the ground-fetish, but they have no scruple in making slaves work for them.' [56]

In ways outlined above (p. 86), the emergence of a servile caste within Asante society was inhibited. The continuous recruitment of slaves was therefore necessary to maintain the labour force at the required level. The input of slaves into metropolitan Asante society occurred, as Cruickshank noted, in any one of three ways: they were 'either taken in war by the Ashantees, received as tribute from subjugated states, or purchased by them'.[57] But while the numbers of slaves purchased, or taken in tribute by government, could be regulated according to demand, those taken in the course of military operations could not. And therein lay one of the problems created by the abolition of the maritime slave trade: that while, for example, rebel leaders captured in the course of punitive expeditions might be executed, and many of their followers allocated to Asante towns and villages as labourers, surpluses might build up that previously would have been disposed of by sale at the coast. Thus Osei Bonsu outlined to Dupuis the magnitude of the problem which faced him after the Gyaman campaign of 1818–19:

When I fought Gaman, I did not make war for slaves, but because Dinkera (the king) sent me an arrogant message, and killed my people, and refused to pay me gold as his father did. Then my fetische made me strong like my ancestors, and I killed Dinkera, and took his gold, and brought more than 20,000 slaves to Coomassy. Some of these people being bad men, I washed my stool in their blood for the fetische. But then some were good people, and these I sold or gave to my captains: many, moreover, died, because this country does not grow too much corn like Sarem [the savannah], and what can I do? Unless I kill or sell them, they will grow strong and kill my people.[58]

Two related problems arose from the glut of slaves on the market in the 1810–20 period – a glut which, according to Bowdich, brought the price of a slave in Kumase down to 2,000 cowries, or one basket of kola.[59] The first was the difficulty which the government faced in reassessing tributes in order to relate them realistically to the changed market. In some southern provinces which had previously paid in slaves, the tribute was converted to one in gold or ivory; the change,

[56] Boyle, 1874, p. 15.
[57] Cruickshank, 1853, II, 246.
[58] Dupuis, 1824, p. 164.
[59] Bowdich, 1819, p. 333.

however, proved highly unpopular and according to Robertson in 1820, 'the difficulty of paying the annual Tribute in Gold or Ivory is so much greater than when it was paid in Slaves that almost every district is in a state of insurrection'.[60] The second problem was that Asante traders, whether public or private, found that the European merchants in the coastal settlements would deal only in gold or ivory.[61] But ivory was undoubtedly in short supply, and much of it had to be procured from beyond Greater Asante, and especially from Kong with which state Asante enjoyed far from satisfactory relations,[62] while gold, although mined in metropolitan Asante and in many of the provinces, was nevertheless carefully conserved: the wealth of the kingdom, as of the individual citizen, being assessed in terms of ownership of the metal.[63]

The collapse of the Atlantic slave trade, then, while not without economic consequences for Asante, was not as damaging as many writers have supposed.[64] Indeed, none of the several visitors to the capital between 1816 and 1820 gave any indication that the period was one of marked economic recession. On the contrary, the reconstruction of the great-roads (see pp. 33–5) and the programme of urban renewal in Kumase – which included the building of a museum to house the Asantehene's collections – suggested that the economy possessed considerable buoyancy.[65] It has been argued elsewhere that, in the changed commercial situation, the Asante government was able rapidly and efficaciously to achieve a major transference of mercantile capital away from the coastal markets and to the northern ones: the level of kola exports was stepped up to meet the demands of the Hausa caravan traders, and the town of Salaga (Route IV, mile 167) was developed to handle the greatly increased volume of trade.[66] While a certain amount of Asante business continued to be transacted at the coastal markets, from which purchases of guns and gunpowder, and of European iron (considered superior in temper to the northern product) were made, by and large the supremacy of the northern

60 PRO, CO. 2/11: Robertson to Bathurst dd. 27 November 1820.
61 Dupuis, 1824, p. 162. Bowdich, 1819, p. 334.
62 Bowdich, 1819, p. 334. Cruickshank, 1853, II, 280.
63 Bowdich, 1819, pp. 334–5: 'Gold they are all desirous of hoarding.'
64 For a recent restatement of this view, see Fage, 1969, p. 403.
65 For this programme, see Bowdich, 1819, p. 309. The new stone-built museum was first projected by Osei Kwadwo (*idem*), but was not commenced until after the Gyaman war, Dupuis, 1824, pp. 137, 176; Hutton, 1821, p. 275. It was completed early in 1822, see *Royal Gold Coast Gazette*, 7 May 1822. Artisans from the coast were employed in the construction; and the prayers of northern *imāms* solicited for its well-being, see Royal Library, Copenhagen: *Cod. Arab. CCCII*, I, ff. 107, 188; II, f. 1. It was blown up by the British in 1874, after its contents had been looted.
66 Wilks, 1971a, pp. 124–32.

trade was clearly established in the 1810s, and cloth and silk and a wide range of manufactured goods flowed into Asante in return for the kola.[67] Trade on the Gold Coast fell in volume so disastrously for the European merchants that many of the lodges and forts had to be abandoned. When Bowdich arrived in Kumase in 1817, he quite rightly recognized the Muslim merchants from the north as the main competitors for the Asante trade.[68]

The position of Osei Bonsu and the peace party in the Asante councils, then, may be seen as resting upon four principal lines of reasoning: first, that the maintenance of political control over the northern provinces had become of greater strategical importance than over the maritime; second, that in view of the difficulties in achieving the pacification of the southern provinces, and of the problems about the mode of payment of tributes, the costs to the nation in holding them were no longer offset by any proportionate returns; third, that the close relations enjoyed with the Dutch, and the continued loyalty of the Elmina, guaranteed the government one secure maritime market through which vital supplies of war materials might be obtained; and fourth, that the minimization of political conflict with the British consequent upon withdrawal would in any case obligate them to re-open the great-roads to their settlements since they were themselves economically dependent upon the Asante trade. It seems unlikely, however, that the peace party would have contemplated, in Robertson's terms, 'resigning *all* claims to this Frontier'. As it will be seen below, a policy of retrenchment might involve the relinquishment to the British of administrative and judicial control over certain provinces, so that the responsibility for the maintenance of public order, and especially the safeguarding of the southern great-roads, would be delegated to them. But the Asante government, as Osei Bonsu had stressed in 1820, would still regard itself as possessed of ultimate sovereignty over such territories. In the event, however, the death of Osei Bonsu in 1823 brought about an abrupt change in Asante policy toward the southern provinces.

The decision for war

Reindorf reported a tradition that Osei Bonsu 'on his death bed earnestly exhorted Osei Yaw never to take up arms against the whitemen on the Coast'.[69] Asante tradition as recorded by Kyerematen, however, adds that Osei Yaw Akoto, fearing that his rival Kwaku Dua

[67] Bowdich, 1819, p. 334.
[68] *Ibid.* p. 53.
[69] Reindorf, 2nd ed., n.d., p. 193.

– known for his pacific policies – might be chosen to succeed Osei
Bonsu, 'seized the stool and immediately took it to war'.[70] Dupuis
received reports that Osei Bonsu 'departed this life in grief and vexation, bequeathing to his successor the kingdom and the palaver', and
that Osei Yaw

commenced his reign by an *edict* against the British, wherein they were
accused . . . of perfidy, infractions of treaties, violations of public faith,
treachery, cruelty, etc. To revenge which, and to appease the shade of the
departed conqueror, in the region of spirits, the new monarch vowed eternal
war against the British until he had obtained satisfaction; declaring (in the
form of the great oath of his predecessors) that he would not cease from
hostility until he had watered the grave of the departed Sai Quamina [Osei
Bonsu] with the blood of white men, etc.[71]

The events of the years 1824–6 have been recounted in detail elsewhere.[72] Briefly, the Asante troops which had engaged and defeated
MacCarthy's force in January 1824 were reinforced and ordered to
remain in the south. Late in March they were moved up to the Pra
river, and on 25 April marched southwards again to drive the British
out of Efutu, only some 8 miles northwest of Cape Coast. A new
force of 6,000 men, commanded by a 'General Adinking' who has not
been identified, arrived at Elmina late in April to strengthen the
administration in the southwestern provinces.[73] On 28 May the new
Asantehene Osei Yaw entered Efutu in person, with fresh troops, and
in late June detachments were moved into positions on the edge of the
beleaguered town of Cape Coast. British-led forces failed to dislodge
them after heavy fighting on 11 June. However, due in part to the
onset of the rains and to a serious outbreak of smallpox among his
troops, and in part to the concern of the Asantehemaa in Kumase
that both the Gyaman and Akyem might take advantage of the situation to attack Kumase itself, Osei Yaw decided to withdraw his army
from the southern provinces in August.[74] Another smaller army
which had been posted to the border of the Akyem provinces, apparently commanded by the Atwoma-Agogohene Kwaku Bene, was
also pulled back: it had been under heavy attacks organized from
Christiansborg – the Danes at this time having committed themselves
to full support of the British.

Although in virtually every engagement the Asante forces in the

70 Kyerematen, 1966, p. 352.
71 Dupuis, 1824, p. 215.
72 See, e.g. Claridge, 1915, I, chapters XX and XXI, *passim*. Reindorf, 2nd ed. n.d.,
chapters XVI–XVIII, *passim*.
73 General State Archives, The Hague, KvG 352: Elmina Journal, entries for 29
April and 1 May 1824.
74 *Royal Gazette and Sierra Leone Advertiser*, VI, no. 324, 21 August 1824.

south-central provinces had won the day, the British commanders nevertheless proceeded to congratulate themselves on 'the recent successes which have been obtained, with so much bravery, by His Majesty's forces over the Ashantee tribes, and the enemy's consequent retreat to Coomassie'.[75] All indeed was relatively quiet throughout 1825: a matter that should have given little consolation to the British since Osei Yaw was engaged in obtaining support in council for a major offensive to effect full military reoccupation of the southeastern provinces. There was sufficient consensus in council for a senior official, Kra Kosie, to be sent to announce 'the good message' to the provincial chiefs of the southeastern provinces: that the government was committed to the reassertion of its authority there.[76] There was also, however, some conflict in council, the Dwabenhene Kwasi Boaten heading those who remained adherents of the policies of Osei Bonsu's government.[77] The predicting priests of the Tano and Dente shrines also apparently advised against war.[78] After a series of deliberations, in the course of which considerable pressure seems to have been put upon the remaining supporters of peace party policies, Osei Yaw obtained the mandate he had wanted. At the end of a meeting, so one source reports, 'in which the majority, as members at "War Council", pronounced in favour of war, (though not from their own willingness, but there was force behind it), a great amount of ammunitions were distributed to the Ashanti Warriors'.[79] An interesting account of proceedings in this meeting was published in 1925. It appears to be based on a much earlier Twi source,[80] and concerns the argument of one councillor – possibly the Nkonsonhene – that special treatment should be accorded the Akuapem during the projected campaign, since the first Asantehene, Osei Tutu, and his adviser Okomfo Anokye, both had associations with it:

Foreman of Eku: Now turning to the point of squashing Akuapem, I believe all present are conversant of the great prophecies of the sooth-sayer Anotchi, who before his transformation forbade us to raise War against Akwapem, as

[75] PRO, CO. 268/20: Bathurst to Major-General Turner, dd. London, 29 October 1824.
[76] Djang, 1925, p. 59.
[77] Reindorf, 2nd ed., n.d., p. 193.
[78] *Ibid.* pp. 193–4.
[79] Djang, 1926b, p. 69.
[80] Djang, 1925, pp. 58–9. The author inclines to the view that an original Twi text was the work of the Akuapem missionary David Asante, other of whose historical notes are to be found in *Native Reports in Tshi*, first published in the 1860s, and in Struck, 1923 (conjecturally). David Asante's father, Owusu Akyem, was in Kumase at the time of the meeting and may have been present at it (see above, p. 134). After his capture at the battle of Katamanso in 1826, Owusu Akyem returned to live in Akuapem.

a town in it known as Berekusu near Aburi, was the place where our noble and late King Osei Tutu was born [81] and received his early training. To say the most of it Okomfo Anotchi who made this realm to be as great as it now stands was a man from this state (Akwapem) and I am perfectly certain, that should we raise war directly against them, the result, I am afraid to say, would be fatal, for he predicted against it. The only thing we can do therefore is to threaten them with war and surely our threats shall be so fearful and they need not go far from surrendering unto us. (Cheers by drums, hootings and shout.)

They must, of course be subjected to the stern Ashantee rule.

The rest of the nations must be invaded accordingly. Before I resume my seat I will not hesitate to say that His Majesty's suggestion promoted in this matter is valid and must be supported by us all.

The invasion, of course must be indirect where necessary.

(The foreman of Akuosong sat.)

The King then asked how Anotchi who was their greatest Medical man could have been an Akwapem man.[82] He was accordingly answered to his entire satisfaction by one of the old heads when he nodded the Royal head automatically, but then forced the assembly to agree to all his proposals. Amidst the beating of the various drums, the sounding of the violent horns and a great display of the Royal paraphernalia and attendants, His Majesty adjourned the session insisting on the necessity to get to arms and wait for Nkrakosie's return.[83]

Information was shortly to reach the capital, however, that Kra Kosie had been waylaid in the Akyem country, and murdered. The news strengthened further the resolve of the government:

the King, when he heard it, said that it was a very gross offence to slay an Ashantee man without anything wrong done by him. That the custom forbade Ambassadors to be killed when carrying messages from place to place. That the rebels had violently dishonoured the authority of the Ashantee state. He concluded therefore by fixing a very short date for preparation to wage war and he swore to lead the army in person (contrary to custom).[84]

Two small forces were immediately despatched to the southern central provinces, to ensure that no attack on the main army would come from that direction. They met with no opposition from the Fante.[85] In view of the possible threat to Cape Coast, Governor Neil Campbell was instructed to proceed thence from Sierra Leone, and, if the Asante government appeared cooperative, to negotiate 'some defini-

---

81 Compare Reindorf, 2nd ed., n.d., p. 51; Rattray, 1929, p. 272; Fuller, 1921, p. 8.
82 The question of whether Okomfo Anokye was an Akuapem remains to this day capable of generating acute controversy. For a brief review of the issue, see Ward, 1958, p. 115.
83 Djang, 1925, pp. 58–9.
84 *Ibid.* p. 59.
85 Djang, 1926b, p. 66.

tive arrangement of peace with them'.[86] Meanwhile, however, the main Asante army commanded by Osei Yaw in person had marched into the southeastern provinces, and in late July 1826 established camp some 20 miles northeast of Accra, near Dodowa. On 7 August, at Katamanso, the army engaged with that led by Lt Colonel Purdon, Officer Commanding the British forces on the Gold Coast, and suffered a serious defeat. Estimates of the relative size of the two armies are highly discrepant. Djang, for example, assessed the British force at 50,600 men, and in agreement with Reindorf, the Asante at 40,960: 12,000 men forming the Adonten or centre under Bantamahene Awua; 10,000 forming the Nifa or right-wing under Dwabenhene Kwasi Boaten; 8,000 the Benkum or left-wing under the Asumegyahene; 2,000 the Apakanpiafo or bodyguard under Gyaasewahene Opoku Frefre; and 8,690 the Ankobeafo or reserve under the heir apparent Kwaku Dua. Purdon himself reported his army as numbering almost 12,000 men, and the Asante as at least 25,000, while Ricketts thought the Asante had about 10,000 men and the British 11,000.[87] But the British had no clear idea either of the size of the Asante forces or even of their own. It is certainly unlikely that the Asantehene would accompany in person any army as small as 10,000 men, and it may be that the figure of upwards of 40,000 is acceptable on the assumption that included within it were the carriers and camp followers.[88]

It seems clear that the Asante defeat resulted in part from the unfamiliarity of its commanders with the problems of fighting over such open terrain as the plains around Katamanso.[89] Many accounts agree, moreover, that the Asante might well have carried the day had it not been for the use by the Colonial Corps of a weapon unknown to them: the Congreve rocket. But there was also an element of political miscalculation which contributed to the Asante defeat, for the government had failed to allow for the trepidity with which those local chiefs who had succumbed to MacCarthy's 'persuasive' methods in 1823 viewed the prospects of Osei Yaw's reassertion of authority over the southeast. The politicians of the war party, moreover, had failed to anticipate the possibility of defections on the part of provincial rulers considered to be loyal. Yet among the forces which were unexpectedly committed to support of the British were, for example, those of Kwadwo Tsibu Kuma of Assin Attendansu,[90] and of Akoto of the

86 PRO, CO. 268/26: Bathurst to Campbell, dd. London, 20 June 1826.
87 For accounts of the armies from various viewpoints, see PRO, CO. 267/74: Purdon to Bathurst, dd. Accra, 10 August 1826; Ricketts, 1831, p. 124; Reindorf, 2nd ed., n.d., pp. 198–213; Djang, 1926b, pp. 65–79; *Native Reports in Tshi*, 1913, pp. 12–16.
88 See *Royal Gazette and Sierra Leone Advertiser*, 14 October 1826.
89 See, e.g., Reindorf, 2nd ed., n.d., p. 203.
90 *Ibid.* p. 194.

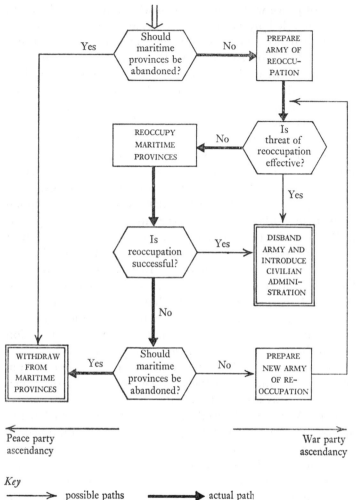

Fig. 4 Osei Yaw Akoto's government. British policy, 1824–6. Decision-logic

powerful trans-Volta province of Akwamu.[91] Although later writers have tended to regard Katamanso as a catastrophic defeat as a result of which the government finally lost control of the southern provinces, in 1826 Governor Campbell himself observed otherwise:

From what I saw of the field of battle, and have ascertained here [Cape Coast] and at Accra, I am certain that the results of the battle have been grossly exaggerated. The Ashantees were not prepared to meet so large a force together, and some circumstance occasioned a panic, after the natives *had been repulsed* by them. It is impossible to say what occasioned it, but it must have

91 PRO, CO. 267/74: Purdon to Bathurst, dd. 10 August 1826.

been only in apprehension, and probably the fire of the rockets and opening of our guns . . .[92]

In a military sense, then, Osei Yaw had lost a battle, but not the war. Politically, however, the magnitude of the defeat at Katamanso was sufficient to discredit his policies, and to restore the ascendancy of the peace party in the Asante government. The basic decision-logic of the situation in which Osei Yaw had found himself in 1824–6 is shown in Figure 4, which illustrates the path by which the goal of withdrawal from the southern provinces was finally attained. By contrast with the government's formulation of its Wassa policy in the previous decade, when all groups within council seemingly shared as a common goal that of the fuller political incorporation of the Wassa into Greater Asante (see Figure 3), the deliberations of 1824–6 revealed an increasing polarization of opinion in council as members became committed to quite incompatible ends.

The search for peace

The reversal of Asante policy after the defeat of Katamanso was not achieved without some convulsion in the political life of the capital. The powerful Gyakye (or Adusei Atwenewa) counselor, Kwadwo Adusei Kyakya, who Dupuis had identified as a leading figure in the peace party of 1820,[93] is said to have initiated proceedings to have Osei Yaw removed from office. The Asantehene reacted by bringing charges against Kwadwo Adusei: that he had been party to the flight of the Denkyirahene Kwadwo Tsibu from Kumase (see p. 171), and that he had advised the government wrongly on both the strategy and tactics to be used in occupation of the southeastern provinces. Kwadwo Adusei was condemned to death and, with other members of his family, was executed in 1829.[94] Yet Osei Yaw had nevertheless accommodated his views to those of the new majority in his councils, and had rejected for the time at least the possibility of further military ventures in the south. Indeed, in January 1827 he had authorized the Adansehene to

[92] PRO, CO. 267/74: Campbell to Bathurst, dd. 12 November 1826.
[93] Dupuis, 1824, pp. 152–3.
[94] National Archives, Copenhagen, Generaltold kammerets Arkiv, 1760–1848, Guineiske Journaler 1834: Jackson to Lind, dd. Cape Coast, 7 December 1829. See also Kyerematen, 1966, pp. 352–3. Institute of African Studies, Ghana, IASAS/127: Jachie Linguist Stool, recorded by J. Agyeman-Duah, May 1964. Reindorf, 2nd ed., n.d., pp. 182–3, 203, 209. NAG, Kumase, D. 538: Kuntanase History, n.d.; according to this source, the death sentence on Kwadwo Adusei Kyakya was confirmed by Kokofuhene, Bekwaehene, Nsutahene, and Dwabenhene, and he was pounded to death in a mortar.

approach the British with the suggestion that peace talks should be held at Assin Nyankomase (Route VI, mile 78).[95]

The new Asante diplomatic offensive did not meet with immediate success. In particular, those who had become known to the British as the 'allied chiefs' – that is, those who had fought under Purdon at Katamanso – were extremely suspicious of the overtures, and it was only after numerous messages had been exchanged that it was finally agreed that negotiations should be opened at Cape Coast.[96] The first part of the Asante embassy arrived there on 18 September, and its twenty members met with the British Governor on 16 October 1827. The remaining envoys arrived on the coast on 23 October, bringing the total size of the mission to one hundred and twenty men.[97] The 'allied chiefs' of Cape Coast, Fante (Mankessim), Anomabo, Adwumako, Esikuma, Denkyira, Twifo and Wassa participated in the negotiations, and those of Akwamu, Accra, Akuapem and Akyem Abuakwa, who failed to arrive in Cape Coast in time, were nevertheless retrospectively regarded as associated in the proceedings. Under the provisions of a treaty which was proposed by the British, the Asantehene was required to deposit with them, as security, 4,000 oz of gold, and two hostages from the royal family. Most significant, however, was Article 3: 'That the king of Ashantee do renounce for himself, his heirs and successors for ever, all and every right to collect tribute (as a token of dependency) from any of the aforesaid nations in alliance with Great Britain, and that he do acknowledge each and all of these states to be free and independent.'[98] In reciprocation, the British by Articles 6 and 7 proposed to bind themselves to restrain the 'allied chiefs' from acts of aggression against Asante, under sanction of expulsion from 'confederacy'. In other words, as Metcalfe has observed, 'what the peace terms of 1827 proposed . . . was not, in reality, the creation of a score or more "sovereign independent states", but the replacement of Ashanti overlordship by British guidance and influence'.[99]

The Asante mission arrived back in the capital on 4 February 1828, and was afforded an official reception at which over two hundred senior chiefs ('230 great umbrellas') were present: the implication is that members of the Asantemanhyiamu had already arrived in the

95 See Ricketts, 1831, pp. 133–44.

96 For a recent useful summary of the negotiations of 1827–8, see Metcalfe, 1962, pp. 46–57. See also Claridge, 1915, I, chapter XXII, *passim*.

97 Holman, 1840, p. 199. Reindorf, 2nd ed., n.d., p. 250, named the head of the Asante mission as 'linguist Okwakwa', who must be presumed to have been the Domakwaihene and Akyeamehene Akuoko Nimpon. See further, Ricketts, 1831, pp. 145–6.

98 For a full text of the draft treaty, see Metcalfe, 1964, pp. 114–15.

99 Metcalfe, 1962, p. 52.

capital to consider ratification of the treaty. There was little doubt that the desire for peace was one which had much popular support: 'since we arrived', reported John Buckman of Cape Coast, who had accompanied the mission back to Kumase, 'the inhabitants has not fail of playing for rejoice for peace'.[100] The government, although expressing reservations about the amount to be deposited as security, apparently found the general terms of the treaty acceptable. On 13 February a letter was sent to Lumley at Cape Coast, to indicate the acceptance in principle of the terms of the treaty,[101] and a further mission – of some forty officials representing members of the Asante-manhyiamu – left the capital for there, instructed to finalize plans for ratification.[102] Before the negotiations were complete, however, a number of the 'allied chiefs' attacked and imposed a blockade upon Elmina. In mid-April Osei Yaw made a formal protest to the British, pointing out that the matter embarrassed him before his people since he had proceeded on the assumption that the Elmina, as his subjects, were automatically covered by the terms of the proposed treaty.[103] He requested the British Governor to ensure that the Fante would not obstruct the movement between Elmina and Kumase of the resident commissioner Kwadwo Akyampon Bakki or members of his staff. When the British failed to respond satisfactorily to the protest,[104] further negotiations towards ratification of the treaty became increasingly futile.

That the Asante government was unable to identify the main direction of British diplomacy on the Gold Coast in the period is scarcely surprising: there was none. Indeed, in a report laid before Parliament in London by Special Commissioner Rowan in mid-1827, attention was drawn to the extraordinary confusion which prevailed in British thinking about Asante:

it seems unfortunate that, while the interests of the Ashantees and the British with reference to trade are the same, the latter should be so much identified with those whose motives and objects are at variance with both. The principal obstacle to an extended trade with the interior is formed by the present allies of the British. Their object is to throw every impediment in the way of direct intercourse, in order that they may become exclusively the factors of each party and impose upon both. Formerly those tribes were disunited and

---

100 Undated letter from John Buckman, 'a lad of colour' educated at Cape Coast, in Ricketts, 1831, pp. 148–9.
101 PRO, CO. 267/95: Osei Yaw to Governor Lumley, dd. Kumase, 13 February 1828.
102 PRO, CO. 267/94: Lumley to Huskisson, dd. Cape Coast, 3 March 1828.
103 PRO, CO. 267/95: Osei Yaw to Governor dd. Kumase, 12 April 1828. See also Ricketts, 1831, pp. 154–5.
104 *Ibid.* Hingston to Osei Yaw, dd. Cape Coast, 1 May 1828. See also Ricketts, 1831, pp. 155–6.

weak, but they have been united by the policy of the British, and in proportion as they feel their strength, will the barrier which they oppose be effectual in restricting the trade. If this be the case, it would follow that the British have now only the choice of withdrawing their support from those with whom they have latterly been united or of relinquishing the hope of extended commerce.[105]

In the circumstances, in view of the continuing low level of trade consequent upon the failure to reach a political settlement with the Asante government, the British Secretary of State for War and the Colonies, William Huskisson, was to advocate a policy parallel to that already accepted in Kumase: withdrawal from the Gold Coast.[106] Under pressure from the merchant lobby, however, the British government finally agreed to accept a much diminished responsibility for the trading posts there: in 1828 their administration was handed over to a Committee of Merchants in London, which was to receive a small annual grant-in-aid of not more than £4,000. The Committee of Merchants in turn was to submit for approval to the Secretary of State the names of five merchants resident upon the Gold Coast, 'who would form themselves into a council of government'.[107]

In the meantime, in Kumase the gravest doubts continued to be entertained about the good faith of the British. On 2 July 1828 a large public meeting was held at Dwaberem, at which the Asantehene addressed the chiefs and people in the presence of the two envoys from the British, Buckman and his Fante colleague John Carr. 'He told us', reported Carr,

our master sent us here for peace, but he find that was false, but that was not because he find all what answer he gets from Cape Coast do not agree with white men's affair; in the first place, there is a demand for four thousand ounces of gold for the security of peace, two hostages royal families, and deliver what prisoners he had . . . He says, in his great doubt, he is the person that conquer all the black on this Gold Coast, when he comes to make peace with them, he impose an heavy sum first, and after they depreciate to him in manner as he did to us, he always reduce the sum to one half or one third, and receive them into friendship, and that is not the case now at present, so that he find that what demand my master made, does not seem he as ever will take him in friendship again.[108]

105 Parliamentary Papers, 352, Accounts and Papers (1826–7), vii, p. 267: Rowan's Report on his Visit to the Gold Coast, June 1827 (reprinted in Metcalfe, 1964, pp. 110–2).
106 PRO, CO. 267/150: Colonial Office memorandum by D. Smith, dd. April 1838.
107 PRO, CO. 268/27: Hay to Committee of Merchants, dd. London, 30 October 1828.
108 Ricketts, 1831, pp. 167–9: Carr to Ricketts, dd. Kumase, 12 July 1828.

On 11 July Osei Yaw summoned Buckman and Carr to the palace, and developed further his view of what constituted a genuine peace settlement:

. . . that king of England he know that he was conqueror of all European kingdoms, and the king of Ashantee was the same before on all blacks, and whenever he fights and conquers, if be that the people give up to serve and make peace with him, he was to bid a great amount that he like; but after having seen that the people truly making good peace through their fidelities, these then he make uses to reduce some off, but they [the British] said that nothing will be reduced off; that shews that it was not a good peace, but still reckon him as an enemy. Even if the amount was ten thousand ounces of gold bidden, and it reduced to eight thousand ounces, he would yield it; but this shews treachery, and not good friendly peace hereafter . . .[109]

The Asantehene's concerns were partly procedural: that until the British went through the motions of reducing the quantity of gold they had demanded after Katamanso, then they had not publicly and overtly evinced their desire for peace. But his concerns were also in part practical ones; most importantly, his administrators in Elmina were still harassed by the Fante and could not travel to Kumase. He would not again fight against the British, Osei Yaw stated, and if they chose to attack him, he 'rather blow up at once', that is, commit suicide in the way considered particularly honourable by the Asante.[110] On 18 July 1828 he summoned Buckman and Carr to his country house at Breman, reiterated his desire for peace, but made clear his view that the next moves could only come from the British side.[111]

The treaties of 1831 and the question of sovereignty

The first President of the newly created Council in Cape Coast, John Jackson, intimated in late 1829 his wish to retire from the post. The resident merchants pressed strongly for the appointment of a non-trader to the position; and on 19 February 1830 Captain George Maclean of the Royal African Colonial Corps became second president. Appreciating the fundamental importance of obtaining peace with Asante, Maclean immediately resumed the negotiations for a treaty which had been broken off in July 1828. Rapidly re-establishing communications with Osei Yaw, and conducting extensive negotiations with Asante envoys in both Cape Coast and Accra, Maclean's efforts came to fruition on 27 April 1831, when a Treaty of Peace and of Free

---

109 *Ibid.* pp. 165–7: Buckman to Ricketts, dd. Kumase, 12 July 1828.
110 *Idem.*
111 Ricketts, 1831, pp. 169–71: Carr and Buckman to Ricketts, dd. Breman, 18 July 1828.

Commerce was signed at Cape Coast.[112] In addition to the two main parties to the treaty, 'allied chiefs' from eight of the Fante towns (Cape Coast, Mankessim, Anomabo, Ekumfi, Abora, Egya, Adwumako and Esikuma) and from Denkyira, Assin, Twifo, Wassa and Amanahia, either witnessed it, or were named in the preamble.[113] To the considerable disquiet of the British, however, who had hoped to associate the Danes of Christiansborg in the same agreement,[114] the latter nevertheless proceeded to enter into a separate treaty on 9 August of the same year. The 'allied chiefs' of such coastal towns as Labadi, Teshi and Ada, and of the trans-Volta region including Akwamu, subscribed to it, as well as the Danish and Asante representatives.[115]

By the terms of the Anglo-Asante treaty of 1831, the Asantehene deposited 600 oz of gold for six years with the British, and delivered into their care the two princes Owusu Ansa and Owusu Nkwantabisa. The important provisions, however, were contained in Article 2. To provide 'for the better protection of the lawful commerce', it was stipulated that, 'The paths shall be perfectly open and free to all persons engaged in lawful traffic, and persons molesting them in any way whatever, or forcing them to purchase at any particular market, or influencing them by any unfair means whatever, shall be declared guilty of infringing this treaty, and be liable to the severest punishment'; while, in line with the general trend of Asante political strategy in the period, it was agreed that,

> as the king of Ashantee has renounced all right or title to any tribute or homage from the kings of Dinkera, Assin, and others formerly his subjects, so, on the other hand, these parties are strictly prohibited from insulting, by improper speaking or in any other way, their former master, such conduct being calculated to produce quarrels and wars.

The Danish-Asante treaty contained essentially similar provisions:

> The Prince of Assianthee renounces for himself and his heirs all right to claim that the Negro Chiefs, allies of His Majesty the King of Denmark, shall owe allegiance to him for taxes or duties or other things whatsoever, which may be taken to imply that they are his subjects . . . In so far as the Assianthees may desire access to the coast, in order to trade in person, there shall be

---

112 For the negotiations, see Metcalfe, 1962, pp. 80–9.
113 For the full text, see Claridge, 1915, I, 409–11.
114 See Metcalfe, 1962, pp. 92–3.
115 An incomplete text is published in *Further Correspondence respecting Anglo-German Claims in the Neighbourhood of the Gold Coast*, PRO, African (West), 384, 1891. For a full text see National Archives, Copenhagen, Guinea Journals, 1831, 311. The failure of the treaties to clarify the position of Akuapem and Akyem, certainly to be counted among the 'allied chiefs', became a source of conflict between Britain and Denmark until 1850, see Nørregård, 1966, chapter 21, *passim*.

accorded to them free and unhindered passage through Akim and Aquapim, or by any other route they may select through the territory of the contracting parties.

The treaties of 1831 were to regulate relations on the Gold Coast between the British and Asante for some thirty years, and between the Danes and Asante until 1850, when the former relinquished all their possessions there.

In a letter of mid-1831 from the Committee of Merchants in London to the Under-Secretary of State for the Colonies, the essential community of interest between the Asante and British governments was emphasized:

You will perceive that by this treaty, the trade with the Ashantees is placed upon a more favourable footing than it has been at any former period, as they have a free communication secured to them with the sea, without interruption by the intermediate tribes who have hitherto required that the trade from the interior should pass through their hands. The establishment of this free intercourse was for above half a century the great object both of the Kings of Ashantee and of the late African Committee, but they were always foiled in it by the neighbouring chiefs.[116]

There seems little doubt, indeed, that the treaty became a reality since in 1831 both governments were in fact committed to policies of retrenchment on the Gold Coast, and because both were dominated by those who regarded the expansion of trade as of greater economic significance than the acquisition or maintenance of territory as such. But the position of the British changed again as Maclean, by stages described in a recent study by Metcalfe,[117] brought together the 'allied chiefs' into what was to become the British Protected Territory (and later Colony) of the Gold Coast. Despite the general excellence of the relations which prevailed between Maclean's administration and the government of Kwaku Dua I, who succeeded Osei Yaw as Asantehene in 1834, it is in Maclean's interpretation of the treaty of 1831 that the roots of renewed Anglo-Asante discord must be sought.

It is arguable that in nineteenth century Asante political thought, notions of sovereignty and of conquest were inextricably linked: that is, that rights of sovereignty were seen as generated principally if not solely by acts of conquests. On the other hand, rights of sovereignty were regarded as distinguishable from the exercise of authority. Thus, for example, it was held 'that by right of conquest Fantee, including Cape Coast and every other town in the neighbourhood, belonged exclusively to the empire of Ashantee, with the reservation of a judicial

116 PRO, CO. 267/112: Committee of Merchants to Hay, dd. London, 25 July 1831.
117 Metcalfe, 1962, especially chapters 8–9 and 11–12.

authority to the African company over such towns as stood in the vicinity of any of the castles'.[118] The distinction between sovereignty ('belonging exclusively') and administrative control ('judicial authority') was one highly relevant to the Asante government's interpretation of the treaty of 1831 with the British. In return, that is, for guarantees of free access to coastal markets, the government regarded itself as having conferred upon the British a right to administer certain of the old southern provinces, but not as having relinquished – since no act of conquest by the British was involved – ultimate rights of sovereignty over those territories. It is a not uncommon arrangement in Asante land law, for the 'land' to belong to one person (in this case the southern provinces to the Asantehene), but for the 'subjects' on it to be placed under a different person (in this case, the Fante and others under the British Governor).

British views of the implications of the 1831 treaty varied. In 1844 Maclean himself subscribed to the distinctly odd thesis, that the Asante government had 'formally ceded to the British Crown' sovereignty over certain of its Gold Coast possessions at a time which he could specify in no other detail than 'either previously to, or during the Ashantee war'; and that while the British government had technically renounced its sovereignty over such possessions in 1828, this was not in practice the case 'simply because such renunciation must have proved ruinous to the settlements and been fraught with misery to the natives themselves'.[119] The more orthodox British view, as stated for example in the report of the Select Committee on West Africa in 1842, rested upon two arguments, first, that of the fact of 'the control over them [the southern chiefs], which by vicinage, we are enabled to exercise', the second, that of the absence of rights of sovereignty over those thus under control: 'Their relations to the English Crown should be, not the allegiance of subjects, to which we have no right to pretend, and which it would entail an inconvenient responsibility to possess, but the deference of weaker powers to a stronger and more enlightened neighbour, whose protection and counsel they seek. . .' [120] The members of the Select Committee were clearly unprepared to allow that sovereignty over the coastal districts remained vested in the Asante government, even while accepting that it had not passed to the British. Those more familiar with the situation, however, saw the matter otherwise. Thus an administrator like Cruickshank, erstwhile Judicial Assessor and Acting Governor, looking back

118 Dupuis, 1824, pp. 262–3.
119 PRO, CO. 96/4: Maclean to Lord Stanley, dd. Cape Coast, 2 February 1844.
120 *Report from the Select Committee on the West Coast of Africa*, C. 551, 1842, The Gold Coast.

in 1853 over the two previous decades, could argue that the treaty of 1831 guaranteed the independence of most of the former southern provinces of Asante, which were

relieved from the yoke of Ashantee, and the king no longer permitted to treat with them in any way, except through the [British] governor, to whom he was to apply for redress in all cases of injury done to himself or people . . . The governor was now enabled to direct his whole attention to the better government of the people whom this treaty placed under his protection, and for whose peaceable conduct *he had become responsible to the King of Ashantee.*[121]

As late as 1865 Special Commissioner Ord, appointed from London to enquire into the condition of the British settlements on the Gold Coast, could quite explicitly endorse Cruickshank's interpretation of the matter. 'On the conclusion of the treaty of 1831', he wrote, 'Governor Maclean directed his attention to the improvement of the natives thus placed under his protection, and for whose peaceable conduct he had become responsible to the King of Ashantee.' [122]

Free trade and mercantilism

Maclean's administration, which extended from 1830 to 1843, was one remarkable for the confidence which the Asante government placed in it. With few lapses, both of the major contracting parties to the treaty scrupulously observed its provisions throughout the thirteen years, and the issue of sovereignty was one which seemed of little practical concern. In the situation of relative tranquillity, a revival of agriculture in the southern territories occurred, and a steady increase in the export of palm-oil resulted.[123] Gold dust, however, continued to be the most important of all exports, and the main supplies of it still came from Asante (as did the little ivory that reached the coast).[124] British takings of gold from the Gold Coast, which had fallen as low as 600 oz in 1823,[125] rose to around 50,000 oz in the middle of the century.[126] This quantity, and that taken by the Dutch, must be presumed nevertheless to have represented a comparatively small proportion of total production. Some consignments of gold dust from

---

121 Cruickshank, 1853, I, 176–8. See also II, 23. Italics not in original.
122 *Report of Colonel Ord, appointed to enquire into the condition of the British Settlements on the Western Coast of Africa*, C. 170, 1865. See also *The Anglo-African*, III, no. 7, 22 July 1865.
123 Cruickshank, 1853, II, 286.
124 *Ibid.* II, 278–80.
125 See Rowan's Report, dd. June 1827, in Metcalfe, 1964, pp. 110–12. 1822: 10,896 oz; 1823: 600 oz; 1824: 2,011 oz; 1825: 17,063 oz; 1826: 7,071 oz.
126 Cruickshank, 1853, II, 279.

Asante probably continued, as in the 1820 period, to go to the northern markets,[127] but much was absorbed either into general circulation there, or was deposited in the government's Great Chest (pp. 418–19). 'The paths and thoroughfares of the country', reported Cruickshank, 'became as safe for the transmission of merchandize, and as free from interruptions of any description, as the best frequented roads of the most highly civilized countries of Europe'.[128] The Asantehene, wrote Alexander, with the reference to 1834,

is so well disposed to us, since the lesson which his people received at the battle of Dodowah in 1826, as to ensure safe conduct from any part of the coast inland, to a distance of five or six hundred miles, in the first instance. The king of Ashantee might then (in the security of *Arab* merchants, who visit and reside at Coomassie,) arrange for the safe conduct of travellers across Africa, – either to the Red Sea or Mediterranean. 'I do not say it unadvisedly,' said Mr. Maclean to me; 'but at this moment the English are held in such estimation on the coast, that I would ensure any traveller's safety to Mecca from Cape Coast, if he conducts himself properly.' [129]

In the aftermath of Katamanso, Asante trade with the coast had taken place mainly at Assini, beyond the British sphere of influence.[130] With the signing of the treaty of 1831, however, important changes in the mode of the trade renewed between Kumase and the Gold Coast occurred. The market was thrown open to private merchants, and the officially sponsored 'passages' of state traders, the *batafo,* were discontinued.[131] The mercantilist system gave way, temporarily, to a free trade one. Kwisa, lying thirty-two miles south of the capital, was designated the main trading station on the great-road to Cape Coast and adjacent ports,[132] and the movement of commodities between the coast and Kwisa was taken over by local Fante, Assin and other carriers, referred to by Cruickshank as the 'thousands eagerly seeking to be employed, and anxious to offer their services at a much more moderate rate'.[133] One of the immediate advantages to the Asante government lay in the saving of the heavy brokerage fees previously paid by its traders at the coast.[134]

As it looked apparent, however, that the new political conditions so favourable to trade were other than transitory, the private carriers

---

127 Dupuis, 1824, pp. lvii–lviii. For the export of Asante gold to Timbuktu, see Clapperton, 1829, p. 202, and for the onward despatch of the metal from Timbuktu to Morocco, see the accounts of al-Ḥājj Ḥāmad al-Wangāri, in Jackson, 1820, pp. 347–8.
128 Cruickshank, 1853, II, 31.
129 Alexander, 1837, I, 154–5.
130 Ricketts, 1831, p. 174.
131 Cruickshank, 1853, II, 32.
132 T. B. Freeman, in *The Western Echo,* I, no. 10, 24 February 1886, p. 8.
133 Cruickshank, 1853, II, 32.
134 *Idem.*

became more enterprising. 'The certainty of protection', noted Cruickshank,

and the profitable nature of mercantile speculation at the time, allured numbers to try their fortune as trading adventurers. Small capitalists invested what gold they had in goods, and either carried them into the interior, or sent them in charge of confidential agents to be sold . . . The prospect of elevating their condition by careful industry, had only yet been opened up to those engaged in trade, who perceived the road to wealth and consequence now plainly exposed to them.[135]

Whereas in the former Asante 'passages' of traders to the coast, unfree labourers were used as porters, in the new situation a wage-earning class arose to perform the role:

The land carriage of all this merchandize, in a country where beasts of burden are not used, gave employment to many thousands in transporting the goods. The porterage, considering the great distance of the journey, and the time occupied in accomplishing it, was exceedingly trifling; but the ignorance of the value of labour properly directed, and their natural distaste for a steady, regular and laborious employment, made them prefer occasional jobs of this description, which gratified also a rambling disposition, to agricultural pursuits, or any other occupation requiring fixed habits of application.[136]

Particularly prominently represented among the new entrepreneurs were the Fante, 'carrying out', so Freeman commented, 'the peculiar habits and characteristic of their subdivision of the Accan race, namely an apparently unconquerable taste for petty trading'. From Kwisa, he added, they extended their activities to Kumase, to the surrounding districts, and even into the northern savannahs, 'until they have occupied all the principal towns and villages as trading posts, and become widely scattered over the kingdom'.[137] Much the same account of the matter was given by Cruickshank. 'All was now cheerful bustle and activity', he observed.

There was not a nook or corner of the land to which the enterprize of some sanguine trader had not led him. Every village had its festoons of Manchester cottons and China silks, hung up upon the walls of the houses, or round the trees in the market-place, to attract the attention and excite the cupidity of the villagers.

In the principal towns on the main line of communication with Ashantee, extensive depots were formed, where every species of goods suited to the traffic might be got in abundance; and in Coomassie, the capital, many agents constantly resided, who received steady supplies of goods by an uninterrupted system of conveyance from the coast.[138]

135 *Ibid.* II, pp. 32, 34.
136 *Ibid.* II, pp. 33–4.
137 *The Western Echo,* I, no. 10, 24 February 1886, p. 8.
138 Cruickshank, 1853, II, 33.

The movement of the southern merchants northwards from Kwisa, into and beyond Kumase, was still a minor one as late as 1839, but must have assumed major proportions shortly after that date.[139]

The rapid growth in private entrepreneurship, although conducive to the general expansion of trade, was predictably viewed with much disfavour by the great mercantile establishments of the country, whether Asante or European. As early as 1834 the Dutch and British authorities on the Gold Coast had entered into an agreement, in which they expressed jointly their hope that the system of free and open trade into the interior might be stopped, since it was 'on all hands allowed to be most pernicious and dangerous'.[140] The Asante government, too, began soon to calculate the political and economic risks in having its trade with the coast controlled by those who were no longer its subjects, and in 1835 sent an official note to the British which argued that the settlement of Fante traders in Asante territory was contrary to the terms of the treaty of 1831.[141] In November of that year Danish, Dutch and British wholesale and retail merchants on the Gold Coast, with the Asante government's note before them, agreed not to engage in the conveyance of goods inland but to welcome Asante traders once more at their forts and lodges.[142]

Though there was thus general agreement within both the Asante and European commercial establishments that a return to a more structured and controlled pattern of trade was desirable, the private entrepreneurs had acquired such momentum that it was not to be until a decade later that their activities were curtailed. On the European side, measures were put into effect drastically to reduce the credit which the coastal merchants had been extending to the independent traders, and many of them were put out of business. 'The carrying system received its death-blow', wrote Cruickshank; and the new policy 'enabled those who preferred a sure store trade to make such a reduction of price, as induced the Ashantees to come to the coast, instead of making their purchases from the petty traffickers, or from the depôts in the interior'.[143] On the Asante side, alarmed by the spread of the private traders into Kumase and northward of it, the government finally halted their activities by legislation: in 1844 a decree was issued in Kumase prohibiting the residence of coastal traders in Asante.[144]

In the 1840s, then, the Asante caravan trade to the Gold Coast re-

139 *The Western Echo,* I, no. 10, 24 February 1886, p. 8.
140 PRO, CO. 267/126: Anglo-Dutch Agreement dd. 28 February 1834.
141 PRO, CO. 98/1(A): Minutes of Council, Cape Coast, entry for 12 October 1835.
142 PRO, CO. 267/144: Committee of Merchants to Earl Grey, dd. 30 November 1835.
143 Cruickshank, 1853, II, 39.
144 General State Archives, The Hague, KvG 365: Elmina Journal, entry for 31 December 1844.

vived, and the Company of State Traders – the Bata *fekuo* – was rapidly expanded to meet the new needs; and for the next two decades of the reign of Kwaku Dua I, the mercantilists dominated the politics of the capital. A graphic description of the relations before 1873 of the *batafo* of Asante, and the powerful coastal merchants, was given by Casely Hayford:

There were merchant princes in those days, when such men as the Hon. Samuel Collins Brew, the Hon. George Blankson, the Hon. James Bannerman, Samuel Ferguson, Esq., the Smiths, the Hansens, and others flourished . . . The King of Ashanti knew most of these merchant princes, and His Majesty, at stated times in the commercial year, sent some of his head tradesmen with gold dust, ivory and other products to the coast to his friends in exchange for Manchester goods and other articles of European manufacture. In one visit the caravan cleared off several hundred bales of cotton goods, which found their way into the uttermost parts of Soudan.

It was part of the State System of Ashanti to encourage trade. The King once in every forty days, at the Adai custom, distributed among a number of chiefs various sums of gold dust with a charge to turn the same to good account. These chiefs then sent down to the coast caravans of tradesmen, some of whom would be their slaves, sometimes some two to three hundred strong, to barter ivory for European goods, or buy such goods with gold dust, which the King obtained from the royal alluvial workings. Down to 1873 a constant stream of Ashanti traders might be seen daily wending their way to the coast and back again, yielding more certain wealth and prosperity to the merchants of the Gold Coast and Great Britain than may be expected for some time yet [that is, from 1903] to come from the mining industry and railway development put together. The trade chiefs would, in due course, render a faithful account to the King's stewards, being allowed to retain a fair portion of the profit. In the King's household, too, he would have special men who directly traded for him. Important Chiefs carried on the same system of trading with the coast as did the King. Thus every member of the State, from the King downwards, took an active interest in the promotion of trade and in the keeping open of the trade routes into the interior.[145]

While Casely Hayford referred to the old staples of gold dust and ivory as principal of the commodities brought to the coast by the Asante traders, it was clearly the case that a lively demand for slaves still persisted in the British Protected Territory. Cruickshank observed that 'some thousands of these are added to the population of the country under our protection every year', an adult male being then valued at between £6 and £8. Most, he commented, were *nnɔnkɔfo* (singular, *ɔdɔnkɔni*), that is, persons from the northern savannahs received in Kumase either as tribute from such provinces as Dagomba and Gonja or purchased at the markets there, or those taken prisoner

145 Casely Hayford, 1903, pp. 95–6.

in the course of military campaigns.[146] It was only following the total breakdown in relations between Asante and Britain in 1873–4 that the Governor of the Gold Coast decided finally to legislate against the importation of unfree labour into the newly created Colony, declaring it illegal 'to bring any person, whether slave or free, into the Protected Territory from Ashantee or elsewhere in order that such person should be dealt with as a slave or pawn'.[147]

The Dutch connection under Kwaku Dua I

The excellence of the relations which the Asante government enjoyed with the British administration on the Gold Coast during the two decades after 1831 in no way prejudiced its continuing association with the Dutch establishment in Elmina. In late 1834 and early 1835 a representative of the Dutch visited Kumase to explore the possibility of opening there a recruiting depot for the army of the Dutch East Indies.[148] The government's response proving favourable, General Verveer visited the capital in early 1837. Prepared to sign a contract for the supply of 2,000 men annually, he returned to Elmina with the Asantehene's agreement to provide half that number. A son of the Huydecoper who had conducted the mission to Kumase in 1816–17 was appointed to represent the Dutch interest there. Fired with considerable enthusiasm for the project, Kwaku Dua commenced building a new 'krom' or village originally named 'Elmina', and within it a barracks – 'a large square building . . . with the name "Dutch Fort" '. He ordered from the Dutch artillery pieces – though the suppliers took the precaution of selecting immobile canon on ship- rather than field-carriages.[149] The new depot may have been the one near the Asantehene's country seat at Eburaso, some 3½ miles from Kumase, of which T. B. Freeman gave some account: 'the royal arsenal of the same name, where all the stores and munitions of war are kept, consisting of powder, lead-bars, etc. No stranger is allowed to visit this place. It is occupied by a strong guard, and is said to cover as large a space of ground as the palace.' [150]

It is an indication of the peaceful condition of the times, that the

146 Cruickshank, 1853, II, 244–7.
147 *Abolition of Slavery within the Protectorate,* C. 1139, 1875, pp. 42–3; Proclamation by Governor Strahan, dd. 17 December 1874.
148 For this topic, see Van Dantzig, 1966, *passim.*
149 General State Archives, The Hague, KvG 421: Governor Tonneboeyer to Minister of Colonies, dd. Elmina, 27 May 1837. At the time of the maritime slave trade the Asante had maintained barracks for the reception of prisoners-of-war, see for example, the 'sort of military depot' at Amoafo (Route VI, mile 18) referred to by Dupuis, 1824, p. 61.
150 *The Western Echo,* I, no. 9, 10 February 1886, p. 2.

government found it difficult to procure sufficient men; by the end of the first year only seventy-five had been enlisted.[151] But the British, fearing the effects of recruitment upon trade and industry – quite unrealistically, as it turned out – made it known that they considered the Dutch activities as tantamount to restoration of the maritime slave trade.[152] The Dutch, in return, protested to Kwaku Dua that too high a proportion of the Asante trade was being directed to the British trading posts,[153] though it was recognized that part of the problem resulted from the fact that the great-road through Wassa to Elmina (Route VII) remained insecure.[154] In 1841, bowing finally to international pressure, the Dutch government ordered the closure of the recruiting agency in Kumase, and stipulated that henceforth only freemen, or freed men of two years' standing, might be taken into service.[155] Between March 1837, and February 1842, only 1,987 soldiers had been enlisted, and by no means all had arrived via the Kumase depot.[156] The project had not, however, been completely abandoned. The Asante government maintained a post of counselor with special responsibility for Dutch affairs. In the 1840s and 1850s it was held by Akyampon – described as 'the Dutch speaker' [157] – who was entrusted with arrangements to revive recruiting in that decade.[158] In 1855 the Asante authorities began enlisting men once again. In 1859 a track was opened from Elmina through Axim and Amanahia into Aowin, where it linked with the great-road VIII to Kumase.[159] Although circuitous, the road was not only much more secure than Route VII, but was also conveniently less open to observation by the British. The recruiting agency in the capital was officially reopened in the same year. The rule, however, that no slaves could be enlisted doomed the enterprise to failure, and in the four and a half years from 1858 to mid-1862 apparently no more than 445 enlisted men sailed from Elmina.[160]

151 General State Archives, The Hague, Archives of the Ministry of Colonies, MvK 4252/441: Verveer to Huydecoper, dd. Elmina, 5 August 1838.
152 See, e.g. PRO, CO. 267/144: Maclean to Committee of Merchants, dd. Cape Coast, 27 November 1837.
153 General State Archives, The Hague, MvK 4252/441: Verveer to Huydecoper, dd. Elmina, 5 August 1838.
154 *Ibid.* KvG 362: Elmina Journal, entry for 19 February 1836.
155 *Ibid.* KvG 421: Royal Decree of 15 September 1841.
156 *Ibid.* KvG 421: Statistics of recruits sent to Java, March 1837 to February 1842.
157 *Ibid.* KvG 394: Governor General to Minister of Colonies, dd. 6 April 1853. This was probably Akyampon Tia, the Nkwantananhene, who was sent to the north later in 1853, or his brother and successor Akyampon Yaw. Pel, n.d., p. 15.
158 Coombs, 1963, p. 3.
159 General State Archives, The Hague, KvG 716: cabinet correspondence, Governor to Ministry of Colonies, dd. Elmina, 28 November 1859.
160 *Ibid.* KvG 716: Governor to Ministry of Colonies, dd. Elmina, 12 July 1859. Coombs, 1963, p. 3.

Symptomatic of the character of the times was the increasingly urbane quality of public life in the capital. Numerous European and other visitors testified to the elegance of the surroundings in which they were wined and dined by the Asantehene,[161] whether at the palace in Kumase or at the country house in Eburaso – 'the Windsor of Ashantee'.[162] With the royal collection of European silver-plate much in evidence, Kwaku Dua was accustomed to dine in European dress (a fashion already set by Osei Bonsu),[163] and the heir apparent Osei Kwadwo might attend in European military uniform. During dinner a band, trained by Dutch musicians in Elmina, clad in blue uniforms trimmed with red, and equipped with flutes, clarinets, French horns and drums, would play.[164] 'I had seen', declared Freeman with some astonishment in 1841, 'the proud sanguinary Monarch of Ashanti, whose smile is life, and whose frown is death, among his people, dressed in European clothes, surrounded by his warlike Chieftains, sitting at a table, and eating in public, with several Englishmen, some of whom were Christian missionaries. . .'[165] Years later Kwaku Dua could be seen driving around Kumase in the horse-drawn carriage presented to him by Freeman on behalf of the Wesleyan Missionary Society in 1841.[166] But most symbolic, perhaps, of the image of Kumase as a national capital was the Aban, the stone-built Palace of Culture in the centre of the city to which most visitors were sooner or later conducted (Plate V).[167] Markedly different in architectural style from that prevalent in the surrounding wards, the Aban had been completed in 1822 (see p. 178n). It was one of the most cherished projects of Osei Bonsu, who had been interested to learn of the functions of its

---

161 See, for example, the dinner party for Freeman, Smith, Brooking, Huydecoper, *et al.*, in 1841, T. B. Freeman, 1843, pp. 138–43; that for Governor Winniet, described in Winniet's Diary, entry for 24 October 1848; and that for the missionary Wharton, in Moister, 1875, pp. 114–15.

162 Freeman, in *The Western Echo*, I, no. 9, 10 February 1886, and II, no. 20, 30 June 1886.

163 See Bowdich, 1819, pp. 114–15 and 122. Compare Huydecoper's Journal, entry for 21 April 1817.

164 Freeman, 1843, pp. 139–40. For the training of the musicians, see General State Archives, The Hague, KvG 365: Elmina Journal, entry for 21 May 1844. The band was also used for general ceremonial purposes, see Journal of the visit of the Rev. W. West and the Rev. John Owusu Ansa to Kumase, in *Wesleyan-Methodist Magazine*, September 1862, p. 861: 'some two or three hundred men, under arms, preceded by a small band of music, the musicians being dressed in the Dutch uniform, had been appointed to receive us; and, as soon as we made our appearance, the drums, and fifes, and clarionet struck up . . .'

165 Freeman, 1843, p. 143.

166 In 1848, see Winniet's Diary, entry for 21 October; and in 1862, see Journal of West and Owusu Ansa, in *Wesleyan-Methodist Magazine*, October 1862, p. 957.

167 See Strömberg, 1890, p. 16. See also *Gã Kanemo-Wolo*, III, Basel, 1895, p. 7.

distinguished and older counterpart, the British Museum.[168] While one part of the building housed the wine store,[169] most was given over to display of the Asantehene's collections of arts and crafts. 'We entered a court yard', reported Freeman of his visit to the Aban in 1841,

ascended a flight of stone steps, and passed through an ante-room into a small hall, in which were tastefully arranged on tables thirty-one gold-handled swords. In the same room were several of the King's calabashes, overlaid with gold, out of which he drinks palm-wine. Passing into another room, we found the King seated in company with Osai Kujoh, and attended by Apoko, and other linguists. On tables in different parts of the room various articles manufactured in glass were arranged, such as candle-shades, beautifully cut glass tumblers, wine-glasses, etc; and almost every piece was decorated with golden ornaments of various descriptions . . .[170]

In 1874, during the brief occupation of the capital by British forces, a number of uninvited guests were able to make their own surveys of the Palace of Culture. 'The rooms upstairs', observed Winwood Reade of the London *Times*, 'reminded me of Wardour Street. Each was a perfect Old Curiosity Shop. Books in many languages, Bohemian glass, clocks, silver plate, old furniture, Persian rugs, Kidderminster carpets, pictures and engravings, numberless chests and coffers . . . With these were many specimens of Moorish and Ashantee handicraft . . .'[171] Boyle, of the *Daily Telegraph,* wrote of 'the museum, for museum it should be called . . . where the art treasures of the monarchy were stored',[172] and before the British seized as booty the more attractive items prior to blowing up the building, Stanley of the *New York Herald* listed some of the pieces: yataghans and scimitars of Arabic make, Damask bed-curtains and counterpanes, English engravings, an oil painting of a gentleman, an old uniform of a West Indian soldier, brass blunderbusses, prints from illustrated newspapers, and, among much else, copies of the London *Times* and *Bristol Courier* for 17 October 1843.[173]

In 1848, on the occasion of his visit to Kumase, Governor Winniet publicly thanked Asantehene Kwaku Dua for the 'kind protection' he had extended to the missionaries of the Wesleyan Society in his capital.[174] They themselves, indeed, in the 1840s felt that the Christian cause was progressing and reported in 1843, for example, that

[168] Bowdich, 1819, p. 147.
[169] Boyle, 1874, p. 354.
[170] T. B. Freeman, 1843, p. 141.
[171] Reade, 1874, pp. 357–8.
[172] Boyle, 1874, pp. 354–5.
[173] Stanley, 1874, pp. 233–4.
[174] Winniet's Diary, entry for 21 October 1848.

The King continues to evince great kindness for the Missionaries; and . . .
he had sent a message to the Mission-House signifying that he proposed to
attend Christian worship there on the following Lord's day . . . He dressed
himself one day in European costume, and proceeded, in the carriage presented to him by the Missionary Committee, to the sacred town of Bantama.
According to custom, a human sacrifice would have been offered on the
occasion; but the King forbad it, saying to the executioners, 'I am going to
travel in the white man's way, and dress in the white man's way, and we
must adopt white man's fashion, and not kill a man today.' [175]

But the missionaries were unduly optimistic, and failed to appreciate
fully the extent of the suspicion with which their activities were still
viewed by the more conservative elements within Asante society. In
particular, their eagerness to establish a school in Kumase along the
lines of those in the British Protected Territory was not only regarded,
as they recognized, 'by some of the Chiefs with jealousy',[176] but also
forced the government to examine the whole issue of its policy towards
education and literacy. At least one closed meeting of the Council
was devoted to this matter in 1844 or 1845.[177]

A personal interest in education had been manifest by a number of
Asante rulers. As early as the mid-1740s, for example, the Asantehene
Opoku Ware had sent to the Dutch in Elmina twelve boys and two
girls with the request that they should be educated in Holland, for
which purpose he handed over ten tusks of ivory. The Dutch, however, found that the payment would cover merely the cost of the
education of the fourteen children at the Rev. Capitein's school in
Elmina, and only the envoy Gyakye, who had brought both the scholars
and tusks to the coast, was allowed to proceed to Europe with the
latter.[178] In 1818 Osei Bonsu had expressed a desire that a number of
princes (that is, his sons or those of his predecessors in office) should
receive an English education. The matter was one of much concern
to the councillors, since many high military and administrative offices
in the capital were held by members of the class. Hutchison, British
consul in Kumase at the time, reported the general reaction:

His Majesty has been anxious all along that some of his family should receive
an English education, that they might maintain their influence in the Empire,

---

[175] *The Friend of the Africans*, no. 2, 1 July 1843, p. 23.
[176] *Idem*. For the Wesleyan schools in the Protectorate, see, e.g. Cruickshank, 1853, II,
263–4.
[177] Letter from Chapman, in *Wesleyan-Methodist Magazine*, July 1846, p. 728,
reporting information given him in Kumase in the 'greatest secrecy'.
[178] General State Archives, The Hague, Archives of the Second West India Company,
WIC 113: De Petersen to the Amsterdam Chamber, dd. Elmina, 1 May 1744. The
account given by Eekhof, 1916, pp. 222–3, and repeated by Bartels, 1959, p. 8,
and Debrunner, 1967, p. 75, is inaccurate in describing Gyakye as one of the
fourteen children.

as, from the order of succession, they must fall into the second rank after his decease. Preparations were accordingly made for some of the Princes to be sent to [British] Head Quarters, when the Aristocracy and great Chiefs repairing in a body, represented to the King their unwillingness that any innovation should take place respecting the established customs of the nation . . . In consequence of this representation the King was reluctantly compelled to give up the point.[179]

The Gyaasewahene Opoku Frefre subsequently explained to the consul, in confidence, that 'their interest obliged them to cheat the King a little, which they could not do if any of his children or followers were educated by Englishmen'.[180] Opposition to education in the period, however, did not extend to that provided by the Muslims: Osei Bonsu was allowed to send children to the school in Kumase founded and presided over by the Imām, Muḥammad al-Ghamba'.[181]

In 1842 Freeman requested permission to open a Wesleyan school in the capital itself. He was informed by the senior counselor, Kwame Poku Agyeman, that 'several of the Chiefs had said, their King could neither read nor write, nor could they, and therefore they thought it would not be proper for their children to be educated'.[182] Kwaku Dua himself, supported by Kwame Poku Agyeman and others, expressed a concern about education: 'the danger of it making the people rebellious'.[183] But although the subject remained one of discussion in council, the Asantehene finally permitted a school to be opened and even sent two boys to it 'for instruction in general knowledge'.[184] The Bantamahene Gyawu also expressed much interest in the mission and the school, and asked to send a number of his children to it.[185] The conservative opposition was sufficiently strong, however, to continue to frustrate the development of any major missionary thrust in the Asante capital. Some further account of the matter is offered in Chapter 14.

Although, then, Christian education was to make little progress in the Asante capital under Kwaku Dua, a number of princes did succeed in obtaining schooling in Europe. Owusu Ansa and Owusu Nkwantabisa, who had been handed into British care in 1831 (see p. 190) had been placed at school at Cape Coast, since the Asantehene Osei Yaw

179 Hutchison to Governor Smith, dd. Kumase, 3 February 1818, cited in Bowdich, 1820.
180 *Idem.* See also Huydecoper's Journal, entry for 3 April 1817: the Elmina envoy in Kumase, Kwadwo Akon, had, so Huydecoper reported, 'often said openly that writing is a dangerous business and must be discouraged'.
181 Dupuis, 1824, p. 107. See further, Wilks, 1966a, pp. 319, 328.
182 T. B. Freeman, 1843, p. 168.
183 *Ibid.* p. 150.
184 *The Friend of the Africans,* no. 25, June 1845, p. 11.
185 Methodist Mission Archives, London: Chapman to Freeman, dd. Kumase, 10 November 1843.

refused permission for them to be sent to England. Kwaku Dua, however, reversed the decision, and in 1836 the two, then in their teens, sailed for Britain. The younger, Owusu Ansa, was a son of Osei Bonsu, and the older, Owusu Nkwantabisa, of Osei Yaw. Enjoying 'all the advantages of a liberal and religious education',[186] they were repatriated in 1841 at the request of Kwaku Dua, and both accompanied Freeman on his second visit to Kumase at the end of that year. Owusu Nkwantabisa died in 1859, but Owusu Ansa had a long and distinguished though chequered career which will be discussed in Chapter 14. Two other princes had been sent in or about 1836 for education in Holland. One, Kwame Poku, was a son of the Atene Akotenhene of Kumase Adusei Kra (died 1836), and a grandson therefore of the Asantehene Opoku Fofie who had reigned for under two years in succession to Osei Kwame. He returned to the Gold Coast from Holland in 1847. Having forgotten his own language, he clearly found difficulty in readjusting to society, and he committed suicide at Elmina in 1850. The other prince, Kwasi Boakye, a child of nine years, was a son of Kwaku Dua himself.[187] After schooling in Amsterdam, he studied mining engineering in Freiberg; went to Surabaja in Java as mountain engineer; became Director of Mines for Java; and by the 1870s had turned to coffee planting.[188]It does not seem likely that Kwasi Boakye ever returned to his homeland.

The problem facing the Asante policy-makers was that of avoiding the subversive effects of education – that is, the alienation of individuals from society through their indoctrination with values incompatible with the prevalent ones – whilst achieving certain desirable ends – most notably, the creation of a literate class increasingly necessary in the interests of efficacious administration. In the early nineteenth century Osei Bonsu had taken the first steps to establish a chancery in Kumase, utilizing the services of Muslims literate in Arabic,[189] and the Gyaasewahene, Head of the Exchequer, employed a Muslim secretary to keep records of political events.[190] Correspondence between Osei Bonsu and the chiefs and imāms of the northern provinces is extant.[191] Although written communications were also

---

186 T. B. Freeman, 1843, p. 143.

187 For Kwame Poku, see General State Archives, The Hague, KvG 366, entry for 28 January 1848, and KvG 367, entry for 22 February 1850. For Kwasi Boakye see *ibid.* MvK 4252: report by Tonneboeyer to Minister of Colonies, dd. Elmina, 31 August 1836.

188 Ramseyer and Kühne, 1875, pp. 316–17. See also Methodist Mission Archives: Dedel, Netherlands Minister, to General Secretaries, dd. The Hague, 23 June 1843, who reported that Kwasi Boakye 'is very bright indeed; he follows the public lectures for civil engineers at the Delft Academy'.

189 See Wilks, 1966a, pp. 328–9.

190 Bowdich, 1819, p. 296.

191 Levtzion, 1965, *passim.*

exchanged with the European establishments on the coast in the period, in the early nineteenth century the government in Kumase had no regular access to secretaries literate in Dutch, English or Danish. The deficiency became increasingly felt after 1831, but by the middle of the century it is clear that the services of such clerks had become a *sine qua non* of effective government. 'Letters are received daily by the governor and magistrates', reported Cruickshank of Cape Coast,

from Ashantee, Akim, Wassaw, Assin, Appollonia, and all the towns of Fantee. Many of the chiefs have a secretary in constant attendance upon them, very frequently their own sons, who have received their education at the schools. The merchants also receive written orders for goods, from trading correspondents in the interior. In short, the people now generally have all the advantages which are to be derived from the written communication of their wants and feelings.[192]

Owusu Ansa did ultimately come to assume an administrative role in Asante in which the benefits of his English education were at a premium (see Chapter 14). But the loss of the skills of others, like Owusu Nkwantabisa through his early death, or Kwasi Boakye by migration to the East Indies, could ill be afforded by the nation. The failure rapidly to build up a cadre of Asantes literate in European languages, which was a result in part at least of the general conservative opposition to education, left the government in the unsatisfactory position of having to recruit foreign clerks into service. In 1836, for example, Maclean sent to Kumase a young man to reside there 'as the king's writer, or secretary'.[193] Another report shows that in 1859 Kwaku Dua procured the services of a young Dutchman, Pieter de Heer, as secretary in charge of the Dutch correspondence.[194] The Wesleyan catechist, J. S. Watts, was detained in Kumase for some nine years after 1862, apparently not unwillingly, and in at least one letter described himself as 'linguist'.[195]

The policy of retrenchment in the southern territories, envisaged by Osei Bonsu and given practical force by Osei Yaw after 1826, appears then to have been vindicated in the general prosperity which came to prevail, both in Asante and in what became the British Protected Territory of the Gold Coast, in the period when Kwaku Dua I presided over the government of the former and George Maclean over that of the latter. In particular, it became apparent that the relinquish-

192 Cruickshank, 1853, ii, 263–4.
193 Wrigley to Wesleyan Committee, dd. 17 October 1836; see Beecham, 1841, p. 311.
194 General State Archives, The Hague, KvG 716: cabinet papers, Governor to Minister of Colonies, dd. Elmina, 10 May 1859.
195 *Correspondence relative to the Cession*, C. 670, 1872, p. 13: Kofi Kakari and Owusu Ansa to Governor, dd. 24 November 1870. Ramseyer and Kühne, 1875, pp. 89, 99, 101.

ment of control over dissident provinces, far from entailing the dissolution of the nation as adherents of the war party would have argued, was consonant with the expansion of trade and conducive to the development of innovative and modernizing policies in the domestic sphere.[196] Predictably, news of Maclean's death in 1847 was received with much regret in Kumase:

the King of the Ashantees and his people equally deplored his loss. The protection which the traders of that country enjoyed in their visits to the coast, through the terror of his name, and the redress which they never failed to receive upon just complaint being made, induced them to look upon him also as their protector. So necessary did the king consider him for the peace of the country, that he was in the habit of making stated prayers and sacrifices to his Fetish, for a continuance of his health and friendship.[197]

196 For a further consideration of literacy, and of innovation in general, in nineteenth century Asante, see McCaskie, 1972, *passim*.
197 Cruickshank, 1853, I, 196.

1 Amoafo, on the Cape Coast great-road

II The Asantehene Agyeman Prempe I, probably with Commissioner Hull, 1891

III The Asantehene Agyeman Prempe I at Elmina, 1896

IV   Owusu Dome, Asante Ambassador at Cape Coast, 1820

v The Aban: the Kumase Palace of Culture

vi The attack on the Asante garrison on Duffo Island, 1870

VII Letter of *ca.* 1808 on the position of Muslim slaves in Asante

VIII   The Qur'ān of Asante Imām 'Uthmān Kamagatay

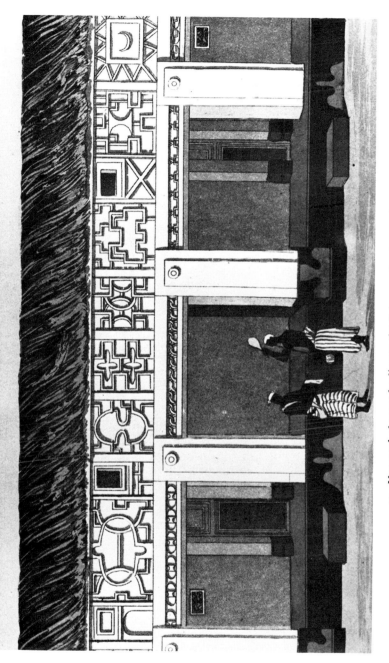

ix   Near end of street leading to the Palace, early nineteenth century

x   Street leading to the Palace, late nineteenth century

xi Kumase: the Great Court *ca.* 1820

XII   Kumase: the Great Court *ca.* 1900

XIII   View of Kumase from the Aban, 1874

XIV   The Exchequer Court, Kumase, 1817

xv   Dampans in Adum Street, Kumase, 1817

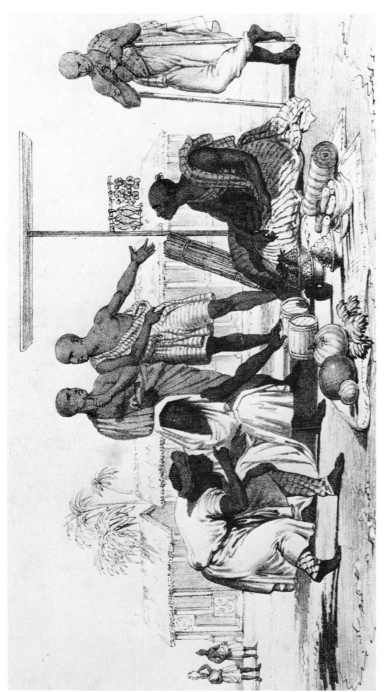

XVI Traders in the Dwaberem, Kumase

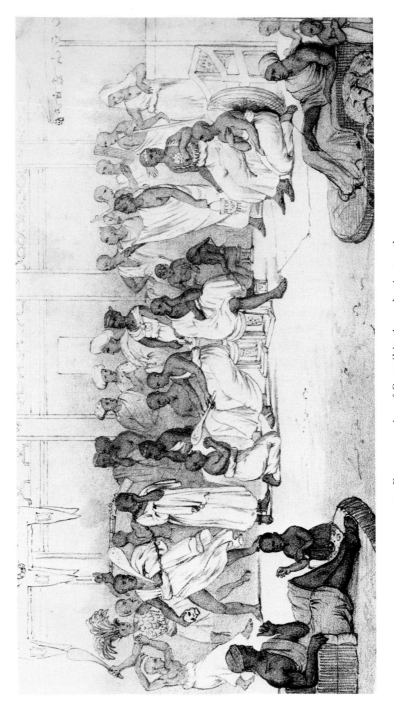

XVII Kumase: session of Council in the early nineteenth century

XVIII   Sen Kwaku, envoy to the British, 1874

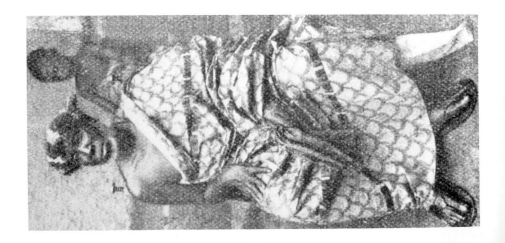

XXI   Owusu Ansa, *ca.* 1840

CHAPTER 6

Asante and the Gold Coast: the politics of indecision

The Protected Territory of the Gold Coast: the problems of the British

In the report of the Select Committee on West Africa, submitted to the British Parliament in 1842, it was found that the earlier British jurisdiction over 'the four ill-provided forts of Dixcove, Cape Coast, Annamaboe, and British Accra, manned by a few ill-paid black soldiers', had been transformed by Maclean, who had come to exercise 'a very wholesome influence over a coast not much less than 150 miles in extent, and to a considerable distance inland, preventing within that range, external slave trade, maintaining peace and security, and exercising a useful though irregular jurisdiction among the neighbouring tribes . . .'[1] In their relations with the local rulers of the former southern provinces of Asante, the officers of Maclean's administration had not in fact found themselves involved in what had been perhaps the principal cause of conflict between those rulers and the central government in Kumase: namely, the payment of tributes or taxes. Maclean had possessed no authority to attempt to levy such. When in 1843 the British government took steps to take over from the Committee of Merchants a direct responsibility for the administration of the settlements on the Gold Coast, the issue of where sovereignty lay then became, for the British, a critical one. James Stephen, Permanent Under-Secretary of State for the Colonies, was among the most vocal of those who doubted whether the British had acquired, in any effective sense, sovereign rights on the Gold Coast. 'A very little skill', he pointed out,

is all that is required to make out the title of any European state to sovereignty over savage tribes – that is, to make it out argumentatively, so far as to reduce to silence any other European state which denies it. Of all nations in the world, England is the most accessible to this sort of *ad homines* argument, because in every part of the globe, we have furnished examples

[1] *Report from the Select Committee on the West Coast of Africa*, C. 551, 1842, The Gold Coast.

which our adversaries would allege against us, in support of the doctrine that the European races are entitled to command and that other races are bound to obey.[2]

By 1849, however, the Whig government in London was suggesting the introduction of some form of direct taxation into the Protectorate,[3] a proposal which if effected, would indeed have conferred upon the British real, as opposed to 'argumentative', claims to sovereignty. Governor Winniet's objection that the imposition of direct taxation would create widespread dissent probably delayed the introduction of such measures until after his death at the end of December 1850.[4] But Winniet's successor, S. J. Hill, who assumed office in October of the following year, proceeded to convene – as the Asante government had done thirty years earlier (see p. 164) – an assembly or 'rude Parliament' of the chiefs of the Protected Territory in order to approve, on 19 April 1852, passage of the Poll Tax Ordinance.

As Winniet had anticipated, the British administrators almost immediately found themselves faced with extensive rebellions, as indeed had their Asante predecessors in similar circumstances. In late 1853 and early 1854 the Gã of Osu and Labadi, and the Teshie, Ada and others of the southeastern Gold Coast, resorted to arms to sustain their refusal to pay the poll-tax, and the more militant of their leaders urged the severance of the British connection. The unrest spread into the Akuapem and Akyem districts, and also flared up on the western coast. Governor Hill felt that only the fear that a return to Asante overrule might prove even less tolerable, deterred the people from 'shaking off their sworn allegiance to the British Government'.[5] Late in 1854 H.M.S. *Scourge* proceeded to avenge 'the insulted honour of the British flag' and bombarded a number of the coastal towns in which the rebels were known to be active: a regrettably effective measure which had not been available to the earlier Asante administrators of the southern provinces.[6]

In 1853 Cruickshank, aware of the strong currents of opposition in the Protectorate to the British administration, endeavoured to present the matter in the best possible light. 'The impartiality of our decisions', he wrote,

---

2 PRO, CO. 96/2: minute by Stephen, dd. 16 November 1843, cited in Metcalfe, 1962, p. 300. In 1847 Stephen maintained the position, that 'we have at the Gold Coast no sovereignty properly so called beyond the precincts of the several forts we occupy there', see CO. 96/9: minute by Stephen, dd. 15 February 1847.

3 PRO, CO. 96/19: Earl Grey to Winniet, dd. Howick, 6 August 1849.

4 *Ibid.* memorandum by Winniet, dd. London, 1 August 1849.

5 PRO, CO. 96/30: Hill to Newcastle, dd. Accra 29 January 1854. For a useful account of the tax revolts, see Reindorf, 2nd ed., n.d., pp. 326–35.

6 PRO, CO. 96/31: Hill to Grey, dd. 1 October 1854.

the equal distribution of justice to rich and to poor, the curb put upon the oppressor, and the general trammels which sought to tame down the restive and almost incorrigible tempers of the chiefs to a proper degree of submissive obedience, made them sigh for a return of former lawlessness, and almost regret that they had thrown off the yoke of the King of Ashantee, who, provided he obtained his revenue, did not care how much his vassal chiefs oppressed their people.[7]

But the truth was that the British administration, hampered by bad roads which it had done little to keep up,[8] unable to afford to maintain large garrisons of troops in the Protectorate, and faced with tax revolts as soon as it attempted to raise new revenues, by the mid-1850s was experiencing many of the same difficulties which earlier had induced the Asante government to hand over to it administrative responsibility for the region. In 1857 Charles Bannerman wrote in *The Accra Herald* of the deterioration in the situation which had occurred since 1850:

Now, we see the British authority hardly acknowledged in Akim, utterly cast off in Aquapim, Crobboe, Crepee and Awoonah [Anlo], and actually laughed at in places nearer to the seat of Government. We see in many places lawlessness predominant, property insecure, panyarring and other hideous practices revived. We see in fact in the Eastern district, (once so orderly and flourishing,) all those symptoms which announce the approach of anarchy and general confusion.[9]

In the same year, 1857, Governor Sir Benjamin Pine, who had succeeded Hill, wrote to the Secretary of State for the Colonies in London and recommended to him much the same solution as the Asante government had found for much the same problem: withdrawal. Maintaining that slavery and pawning could not be suppressed, that the poll tax could not be collected, that suitable administrators could not be attracted to the Gold Coast, and that the commercial value of the settlements had been overstated, Pine observed of 'our protectorate over the countries on the Gold Coast . . . [that] I can have no hesitation in advising that it should at once be withdrawn'.[10]

The Protected Territory and Greater Asante: the Akwamu and Akyem

The unsatisfactory state of affairs in the Protectorate in the middle of the nineteenth century was clearly a matter of grave concern to the

7 Cruickshank, 1853, II, 11.
8 T. B. Freeman reported, for example, that in his travels in Asante, Dahomey and elsewhere, over a period of nineteen years, he had never found roads worse than those in Akyem, see Dickson, 1961, p. 34.
9 *Accra Herald*, no. 3, 5 October 1857.
10 PRO, CO. 96/41: Pine to Labouchere, dd. Sierra Leone, 10 October 1857.

Asante government, and there were members of council who urged the necessity of intervention. Indeed, there were those who, since 1831, had remained committed to the view that the decision to withdraw from the southern provinces had been one inimical to the interests of the nation, and who, over the years, had consistently advocated intervention whenever a conflict of interest between the government and the British administration had become manifest. The fundamental problem, that the treaties of 1831 had failed to define with precision the extent of the territorial jurisdictions conceded to the British and Danes, was complicated further by the fact that local politics in the southern districts continued long after 1831 to be dominated by the old opposition between pro- and anti-Asante factions. In Akuapem, for example, a series of violent upheavals had characterized relations between, on the one hand, the Akuapemhene Adow Dankwa, his nephew Owusu Akyem (see p. 134), and the Kontihene of Akuropon Kofi Kra, all of whom had pro-Asante sympathies, and on the other hand, the later Akuapemhenes Adum and Kwadade who were both of the opposite persuasion. Adow Dankwa was deposed in 1836 and killed in 1839. Owusu Akyem was slain in 1844. Adum, successor of Adow Dankwa, was in turn deposed in 1845, and deported by the Danes to Copenhagen. Finally, Kofi Kra appealed to the Asantehene Kwaku Dua for support in his struggle against Kwadade, and offered to return to Kumase various items of regalia which had fallen into Akuapem hands at the battle of Katamanso twenty years earlier. He was arrested by Kwadade and sentenced to death. The Danes, however, took him into custody in Christiansborg, where he hanged himself.[11]

There is no evidence that even the more hawkish members of the Council in Kumase advocated intervention in Akuapem affairs in the 1840s, though doubtless the troubles there were seen as illustrative of the unfortunate consequences of the central government's policy of withdrawal. There were, however, other matters in which the government might more obviously be expected to pursue an active policy, yet seemed incapable of formulating either its immediate or long-range goals. By far the most politically sensitive of such areas was that of the status of a number of provinces over which the British or Danes claimed jurisdiction, but within which strong movements for a reversion to earlier arrangements existed. Among those who joined the 'allied chiefs' and fought against the Asante armies at Katamanso were, for example, the Akwamu whose capital lay east of the Volta. But the Akwamuhene had earlier exercised jurisdiction on behalf of

11 For some account of these events, see Reindorf, 2nd ed., n.d., pp. 308–17; Nørregård, 1966, chapter 21.

the Asantehene over a number of small Ewe chiefdoms, each of which had sent through him to Kumase two men annually as tribute.[12] After 1826 the Ewe claimed their independence – of Asante and Akwamu alike. In 1829, with the assistance of the 'allied chiefs' of Accra, Akuapem, Akyem and elsewhere, and of the Ewe of Peki who remained attached to Akwamu, the rebellions were suppressed. In 1833, however, further uprisings occurred and the Peki switched sides. Although the Anlo of the eastern seaboard responded to requests for help from Akwamu, their combined forces suffered a major reverse.[13] The Akwamuhene Akoto is said to have retired into Asante – to Adanse.[14] Although the terms of his submission are not known, he succeeded in reconciling himself to the Asantehene Kwaku Dua. Akwamu reverted to its status as a province of Greater Asante. Although presumably enjoying the support of some members of the Council in Kumase, Akoto's request that the government should intervene militarily to restore his standing east of the Volta was turned down: 'probably', commented the Danish Governor Carstensen, 'because of the Asante king's good memory of the battle of Dodowa [Katamanso]'.[15] Encouraged nevertheless, Akoto took the offensive against the Ewe, having informed the Danes that he did not acknowledge their authority over his territory.[16] Although a later Akwamuhene in 1858 was apparently interested in the possibility of accepting British protection,[17] Akwamu in fact retained its association with Asante until 1874, and was only fully incorporated into the Gold Coast Colony by a treaty of 27 July 1886.[18]

The Akwamu problem had resulted from Akoto's *volte-face* in 1826. The issue of the Akyem Kotoku was more complex and had its origins in the 1810–16 period. The loyal Kotokuhene Kwaakye Adeyefe – whose capital at Dampon lay only forty-four miles from Kumase on Route V(a) – had handed over to the Asantehene Osei Bonsu the mother, mother's sister, and sister of Kwadwo Kuma, the Kotoku royal who headed the anti-Asante faction. The three women were executed in what was clearly an attempt totally to eradicate Kwadwo Kuma's branch of the stool family. Kwadwo Kuma, however, was in exile in Akyem Abuakwa and was given assistance in both munitions and men

12 See, e.g. Institute of African Studies, Ghana, EWE/V/3: Botuku Tradition, recorded by E. Y. Aduamah, June 1963, p. 3.
13 For these campaigns, see Reindorf, 2nd ed., n.d., pp. 297–306; Welman, 1969, pp. 10–12.
14 Reindorf, 2nd ed., n.d., p. 306.
15 National Archives, Copenhagen, Guinea Journals: diary of Carstensen, entry dd. Christiansborg, May 1843.
16 *Ibid.* entry dd. Christiansborg, 10 February 1843.
17 See Metcalfe, 1964, p. 276, note 1.
18 Reprinted in Sarbah, 1906, p. 157.

by the Okyenhene Ata Wusu Yiakosan, already himself committed to rebellion. Kwadwo Kuma was thus enabled to occupy Dampon. Kwaakye Adeyefe fled to Kumase, accompanied by his nephew Kofi Agyeman. They took with them the stool of Akyem Kotoku. For a time Kwadwo Kuma equivocated and, seeking recognition from the government, was instructed to proceed to Kumase to take an oath of allegiance. Fearing for his safety, however, he finally and irrevocably adopted the rebel cause when he ordered the massacre of the Kumase residents in Dampon. Marching southwards to link up with the rebel forces of the Okyenhene and Akuapemhene, Kwadwo Kuma assumed command of them on Ata Wusu Yiakosan's death in 1811. By the time of the collapse of the revolts in 1816, and of Kwadwo Kuma's death (see p. 161), Kwaakye Adeyefe had died in Kumase. Kofi Agyeman was considered too young to succeed. One Amoako Panin was therefore placed in charge of Akyem Kotoku affairs; he was apparently not a royal but husband of the queen-mother Boadiwa.

For a few years the situation remained stable until, under strong pressure from the British, Dokuwa of Akyem Abuakwa in or about 1822 attempted to induce Amoako Panin to associate himself with the 'allied chiefs' (see p. 186). When he refused, however, a son of his by Boadiwa was established by Dokuwa on Akyem Abuakwa land at Gyadam, and afforded recognition as Kotokuhene. This was Afrifa Akwada. By an unusual chance, however, the new ruler was shortly after killed by a falling tree, and the Akyem Kotoku of Gyadam selected as his successor, Kofi Agyeman.[19] Aware of his earlier pro-Asante sympathies, Dokuwa opposed the choice and Kofi Agyeman preferred for a time to take refuge with the Danes in Christiansborg.[20] But the treaties of 1831 had left the status of Akyem Kotoku quite unclear, and the British came increasingly to regard at least the parts of it adjoining the Protected Territory – the districts south and east of the Birrim River – as under their jurisdiction. Kofi Agyeman clearly found himself in a dilemma, his northern lands still within Asante and his southern lands claimed as part of the Protectorate. In 1852 he was among those who visted Accra to approve Governor Hill's proposals for the introduction of the poll tax,[21] and as far as is known the Asante government offered no protest. Three years later a dispute arose over the ownership of certain lands near the Pra River, and an Akyem Kotoku chief swore the Great Oath of Asante that the area was under the authority of Kofi Agyeman as evidenced by the fact

[19] This account is based upon Reindorf, 2nd ed., n.d., pp. 153–60 and 192–3; and Kwabena Ameyaw, see Institute of African Studies, Ghana, KAG/7: Akim Oda (Kotoku) Traditions, recorded 18 January 1966.
[20] Nørregård, 1966, p. 206.
[21] Reindorf, 2nd ed., n.d., pp. 324–5; Kimble, 1963, p. 174.

that he sent agents to collect taxes from those mining gold on it. On this occasion the Asante government protested strongly to the British authorities, that if Akyem Kotoku was indeed within the British Protected Territory, then it must be allowed that an offence had been committed by the use of the Asante oath. Caught in something of a legal tangle, the Acting Governor of the Gold Coast is reported to have 'caused the king to be informed that he was aware of the greatness of the crime of swearing the king of Ashantee's oath, and that if the king wished it, he would, although not now acting as judge, hear the case himself . . .' [22]

The Protected Territory and Greater Asante: the Assin crisis

The lack of any decisive policy towards the Akwamu and Akyem Kotoku on the part of the Asante government resulted from the dominant peace party's resolve to avoid any situation of confrontation with the British, but to maintain the treaties of 1831 as the regulatory bases of Asante's relations with the European administrations on the Gold Coast. A similar indecision thus also characterized the government's approach to the especially sensitive matter of the status of the two Assin districts. Incorporated into Greater Asante in the earlier eighteenth century, the Assin appear to have remained consistently loyal throughout the disturbed period of the 1760s and 1770s. [23] It was seemingly in the 1790s, during the troubled later years of the reign of Osei Kwame, that a dispute arose between the Assin Apemanim whose territories lay mainly north of the Pra, and the Assin Attendansu whose territories lay south of the river in the Konkom Forest (whence they claim their ancestors had moved after the Banda campaign in the time of Osei Kwadwo, being tired of 'fighting too much'). [24] In 1820 Osei Bonsu himself dictated an account of the conflict to William Hutton. After fighting had broken out between the two Assin polities, so Osei Bonsu observed, 'the king of Ashantee, as a mediator, sent them a present of gold to settle the palaver, but they would not do so, but still continued to fight. They refused to accept the king's mediation.' [25] The case was still unsettled when Osei Bonsu became Asantehene. He summoned the disputants to Kumase. The Assin Apemanim were represented by Amo, and the Assin Attendansu by the blind Kwadwo Tsibu and his deputy, Apute. Judgement was given in favour

22 PRO, CO. 96/35: memorandum by Sir G. Barrow, dd. Colonial Office, London, 21 December 1855.
23 See, e.g. PRO, T. 70/31: Mill to Committee, dd. Cape Coast, 22 June 1772.
24 Institute of African Studies, Ghana: K. Y. Daaku, Oral Traditions of Assin-Twifo, 1969, pp. 3 ff.
25 Hutton, 1821, p. 337.

of Amo, and Apute was detained in Kumase as hostage. Apute escaped, however, and the Assin Attendansu then repudiated the Asantehene's verdict.

After further attempts by the government to reconcile the parties failed, Osei Bonsu was obliged to despatch a military force into the disturbed provinces. It was commanded by the Anantahene Apea Dankwa and the Gyaasewahene Opoku Frefre. The Fante chief of Abora, Ate, assisted the rebels and was taken captive, tried in Kumase, and committed as prisoner to the care of the Esikumahene. He, too, escaped, and permitted Kwadwo Tsibu and Apute to establish a military base in the southern Fante country. In 1806 the government in Kumase ordered its armies in the south to march to the coast (see p. 145). All resistance was rapidly crushed. In 1807 Kwadwo Tsibu was surrendered to the Asante forces by Torrane, British Governor of Cape Coast Castle, and shortly afterwards Apute's partisans were defeated and dispersed.[26]

In 1826 Kwadwo Tsibu's successor, Kwadwo Tsibu Kuma ('junior') of Assin Attendansu, fought against the Asante at Katamanso,[27] but the Assin Apemanim, then under Ntedwa, remained loyal.[28] In the aftermath of the battle, however, sections of the Assin Apemanim under the Mansohene Gyebi ('Gabri'), crossed the Pra and also settled to its south.[29] Kwadwo Tsibu Kuma and Gyebi were thus numbered among the 'allied chiefs' who attested to the Anglo-Asante treaty of 1831. Yet neither was as firmly committed to the British cause as their overt avowals of it suggested, and shortly after the death of Osei Yaw in 1833, they entered into negotiations with the new Asantehene Kwaku Dua presumably for the reabsorption of their lands and people into Greater Asante. Receiving protests from the Fante chiefs, Maclean agreed that the two Assin rulers should be placed under the superintendence of the Protectorate chief Kwasi Otu, the then Aborahene.[30] Secret discussions with the Asante government were, however, continued,[31] and members of council in Kumase found themselves faced with the issue of whether to repossess the Assin districts and thereby come into conflict with the British administration in Cape Coast.

26 See Meredith, 1812, pp. 132–63. Hutton, 1821, pp. 336–42. Hutton's account was somewhat confused by his inability to distinguish events in the reign of Osei Bonsu from ones in that of Osei Kwame, see p. 338, note 2.
27 PRO, CO. 267/74: Purdon to Bathurst, dd. Accra, 10 August 1826.
28 Reindorf, 2nd ed., n.d., p. 194.
29 *Despatches . . . relating to the warfare,* C. 703, 1853, pp. 21–3: Cruickshank to Newcastle, dd. London, 18 May 1853.
30 See Metcalfe, 1962, p. 142.
31 Among the prisoners in Cape Coast jail in 1841, for example, was a certain Arko, committed for negotiating with the Asante government to 'betray' the Assin into its power, see *Report from the Select Committee on the West Coast of Africa,* C. 551, 1842, the Gold Coast, pp. 162–6.

The issue became a critical one in 1844, by which time H. Worsley Hill had taken over as Governor from Maclean. A situation of crisis developed when an Asante woman, belonging to a party of official traders (*batafo*) returning to Kumase from Cape Coast, was robbed and murdered near Foso in Assin country (Route VI, mile 82). The heads of the trading party identified the culprit and seized him. The Assin chief in the locality maintained that he had insufficient jurisdiction to try the case, and sent the prisoner to Kwadwo Tsibu Kuma of Assin Attendansu. But Kwadwo Tsibu Kuma himself felt unable to hear the case, and in turn handed the prisoner over to Governor Worsley Hill in Cape Coast. The Asante Council, however, received no communication from Worsley Hill on how he proposed to handle the matter: a violation in its view of the spirit if not the letter of the 1831 treaty. In Kumase the war interest used the occasion to urge a more aggressive Assin policy. The issue, commented the missionary Chapman who was in the capital at the time, 'very soon created a strong and very bitter feeling in the minds of both King and Chiefs and of the people generally, and a prompt and bloody chastisement of the Assins was everywhere advocated'.[32] The problem was debated at two sessions of the Council in 1844. The Asantehene Kwaku Dua addressed the members, referred to the excellence of the relations which he had enjoyed with Maclean, and, while acknowledging that difficulty might be experienced in restraining those demanding intervention, made known his personal preference for the peaceable negotiation of a settlement with the British. The Bantamahene Gyawu and Asafohene Akwawua Dente, on the other hand, urged authorization for the immediate despatch of troops into Assin. Finally the advocates of negotiation obtained the decision. Chapman was empowered to travel to Cape Coast and to inform the Governor that the Council demanded the execution of the murderer, before Asante witnesses, at the place where the crime had been committed. At the same time, however, the war party was appeased by Kwaku Dua's announcement that if the proposal was not accepted by the British, then he would take the field in person and if necessary seize Cape Coast Castle. As a mark of the Council's seriousness of purpose, the road to Cape Coast was immediately closed at Kwisa.[33]

In the event, Worsley Hill averted a crisis by accepting the Asantehene's terms. The basic problem of the Assin, however, remained unresolved. In 1848 Winniet, who had succeeded Worsley Hill two years

[32] Methodist Mission Archives, London: Chapman to General Secretaries, dd. Cape Coast, 11 December 1844. C. 893: *Further Correspondence Respecting the Ashantee Invasion,* Part IV, 1874, pp. 61–7: Chapman to Perks, dd. Fort Beaufort, 29 September 1873.
[33] *Idem.*

earlier, met with Kwaku Dua in Kumase and the matter was discussed.[34] The Asantehene subsequently claimed that Winniet had agreed to assist in arranging for the Assin 'to return to Ashantee and live with me',[35] and there seems little doubt that this was the case. But by late 1851 another and more bellicose Governor, S. J. Hill, had taken office, and was quite unprepared to allow the Assin to reassert allegiance to the Asantehene. In 1852 Gyebi was summarily fined 30 oz of gold, but Kwadwo Tsibu Kuma was put on trial, charged with 'receiving a bribe in gold from the King of Ashantee, and endeavouring to induce his captains to accept proportions of the same, in order to bring them under the authority of that monarch; the rule in this country obliging every man taking such a present to serve the donor.'[36] The 'bribe' amounted in fact to 400 oz of gold, presented by Kwaku Dua in token of his sincerity in wishing the Assin to reoccupy their lands north of the Pra and to come once more under his jurisdiction. Governor Hill, however, declared Kwadwo Tsibu Kuma deposed and imprisoned him in Cape Coast Castle. He was released when other Assin and Fante chiefs protested, but Hill insisted that hostages should be handed over for his good conduct; that those Assin who had already crossed the Pra River should return into the Protected Territory; and that Assin and Fante should cooperate in the construction of a military road from Cape Coast to the Pra.[37] News of the strong reaction to his policies in Kumase reached Hill, who, in an oddly contorted piece of reasoning, attempted to justify to London his arrest of Kwadwo Tsibu Kuma:

I was most anxious to prevent this chief's intention of joining the Ashantees, as I had reasons for believing, if such move had occurred, the King of Ashantee, feeling himself compromised by the consequent breach of treaty, might have been induced to listen to the strong war party existing in his dominions, and possibly commit some act of aggression on the nations under our protection, which would lead to a war; as I believe it is only the peacable disposition of the present King that prevents a collision between Ashantee and the Fantee States . . .[38]

Hill's declared policy notwithstanding, both Kwadwo Tsibu Kuma of Assin Attendansu and Gyebi of Assin Apemanim reassured Kwaku

34 Winniet's Diary, entry for 24 October 1848.
35 *Further Papers Relating to the warfare* . . . , C. 456, 1855, pp. 9–10: Kwaku Dua to Cruickshank, dd. Kumase, 28 November 1853.
36 *Despatches . . . relating to the warfare* . . . , C. 703, 1853, pp. 1–2: Hill to Packington, dd. Cape Coast, 23 October 1852. See further, Methodist Mission Archives: Freeman to General Secretaries, dd. Cape Coast, 9 April 1853.
37 *Ibid.* pp. 2–3: Hill to Packington, dd. Cape Coast, 27 October 1852.
38 *Ibid.* pp. 1–2: Hill to Packington, dd. Cape Coast, 23 October 1852.

Dua that their desire for reincorporation into Greater Asante remained unchanged: in which resolve they were undoubtedly much strengthened by Hill's announcement of the new poll tax in the Protectorate.[39] The war party in Kumase was able to provoke the government, finally, to act. A party of some two or three hundred men was instructed to proceed to Jukwa, twelve miles northwest of Cape Coast, ostensively to perform funeral rites for the Denkyirahene Kwadwo Tsibu who had been raised in Kumase (p. 171) and who had died in Jukwa in or about 1850. On its return to Kumase, however, the mission was to escort the two Assin chiefs and their followers out of the British Protected Territory. In charge of this phase of the operation was Akyampon, seemingly the counselor responsible for Dutch affairs (see p. 199) and probably to be identified as Akyampon Tia, brother of Kwaku Dua himself. But the mission was supported, in case of trouble, by a body of 6,000 troops commanded by the heir apparent Osei Kwadwo and the Anantahene of Kumase, Asamoa Nkwanta.[40]

The mission left Kumase on 15 March 1853, and the support troops some six days later. As a result of reports smuggled out of Kumase by the Wesleyan missionary Laing in his messenger's sandals, Hill was forewarned, and despatched a detachment of soldiers under Lt Brownell to intercept the Akyampon mission.[41] According to the official British accounts, Brownell proceeded to Osei Kwadwo's camp, and persuaded the Asante commanders to withdraw their forces.[42] In fact, Brownell appears to have intercepted the mission one day's journey south of the Pra and to have arrested Akyampon. The Asante troops then moved up, took Brownell and thirty soldiers captive, and proceeded to establish camp at Foso. An exchange of prisoners was made, and ultimately both Brownell and Akyampon were released.[43] The Asante commanders awaited further instructions from their government, which again appeared incapable of determining what policies to pursue. Before any decision had been made, Hill ordered the arrest of Kwadwo Tsibu Kuma and Gyebi, and arranged their trial at Dunkwa on 16 April 1853 before a tribunal of 'allied chiefs' and in the presence of the British Judicial Assessor. They were con-

39 General State Archives, The Hague, KvG 394: Governor General to Minister of Colonies, dd. Elmina, 6 April 1853.

40 *Idem.*

41 *Despatches . . . relating to the warfare . . .*, C. 703, 1853, pp. 11–12: Laing to Freeman for onward transmission to Governor Hill, dd. Kumase, 31 March 1853.

42 *Ibid.* pp. 5–8: Hill to Newcastle, dd. Cape Coast, 8 April 1853; and pp. 16–17: Hill to Newcastle, dd. 26 April 1853. NAG, Accra, ADM. 1/2/7: Hill to Newcastle, dd. Cape Coast, 8 April 1854, enclosure, Annual Report for 1853.

43 General State Archives, The Hague, KvG 394: Governor General to Minister of Colonies, dd. Elmina, 6 and 19 April 1853. See also Ghartey, in Boyle, 1874, p. 402.

demned to death and publicly beheaded, with Hill's approval, on 18 April.[44]

The extradition issue and the first reoccupation of the Protectorate

Conscious of the delicate nature of the situation, the British attempted to clarify their jurisdiction vis-à-vis that of the Asante government by drafting a new treaty which specifically named Amanahia, Eastern and Western Wassa, Twifo, Denkyira, Ahanta, Fante, Assin, Akyem, Akwamu, and all the coastal districts between Amanahia and the Volta, as under British authority; full protection was, however, to be guaranteed to all Asante traders and travellers visiting there. A Fante merchant, George Blankson, proceeded to Kumase in September 1853, to negotiate ratification of the treaty, with instructions to inform the government that unless it was approved, all supplies of war materials to Asante would be halted, and an embargo placed upon all trade from Asante to the coast from Grand Bassam to the Volta.[45] Protesting that he had acted peaceably by withdrawing his troops from Foso earlier in the year, and that he had not broken the treaty of 1831 which he regarded as still binding upon all the contracting parties, Kwaku Dua refused to sign the new one.[46] To have done so would in any case have involved him in relinquishing jurisdiction over territories which the government had never regarded as in any sense under British authority. Nevertheless, it was generally assumed that peace had been restored.[47]

The developing conflict between the Asante government and the British administration on the Gold Coast, however, was further exacerbated as arrangements between the two powers for the extradition of criminals, escaped slaves, and the like, began to break down. During the governorship of Maclean few difficulties had in fact arisen; Metcalfe, for example, refers to proceedings for the extradition of Kwawu persons from the Protected Territory to Asante, and of runaway Denkyira slaves from Asante to the Protected Territory.[48] Maclean himself observed that 'practically speaking . . . I have seldom known any but

44 *Despatches . . . relating to the warfare . . .* , C. 703, 1853, pp. 16–17: Hill to Newcastle, dd. Cape Coast, 26 April 1853.

45 *Further Papers relating to the warfare . . .* , C. 456, 1855, pp. 10–11: Acting Governor Cruickshank to Kwaku Dua, dd. Cape Coast, 5 September 1853.

46 *Ibid.* pp. 9–10: Kwaku Dua to Cruickshank, dd. Kumase, 28 November 1853; and p. 7: Cruickshank to Newcastle, dd. Cape Coast, 12 January 1854.

47 See, for example, Methodist Mission Archives, Freeman to General Secretaries, dd. 14 January 1854. But for the view of Acting Governor Fitzpatrick, that the Asante were preparing for a renewed struggle, see NAG, Accra, ADM. 1/2/7: Fitzpatrick to Newcastle, dd. Cape Coast, 3 August 1853.

48 Metcalfe, 1962, p. 134.

criminals to seek the protection of the British flag', and acknowledged that such should be extradited. It was frequently more convenient, on the other hand, simply to pay the value of runaway slaves rather than undertake their return to Asante.[49] At a later date Kwaku Dua was to explain what he understood to be the nature of his arrangement with Maclean:

In poor George Maclean's time, I made agreement with him in certificate, the one in Cape Coast Castle, and another in my hand, therein stated, that any Fantee person run up to me to deliver him and to bring him to Cape Coast. And if any slave of mine also run away to Cape Coast, you are to deliver him back also to me.[50]

In fact, as Metcalfe has shown,[51] extradition procedures began to break down in the middle of the century, when the British convinced themselves that returned slaves would become 'human sacrifices': '. . . in many cases the runaway Ashantee seeks a refuge from the fate which is likely to overtake him at the murderous customs which are often taking place at Coomassie, and a natural repugnance is, of course, felt about surrendering him'.[52] In 1850 Winniet had also hesitated to extradite a runaway slave on the grounds that he had been ill-treated, but overcame his scruples when Kwaku Dua threatened to close the great-road to Cape Coast to traders.[53] When, however, the British adopted the device of having the Asantehene's Great Oath sworn upon Asante messengers who came to collect runaway slaves, that they would not be executed in Kumase, Kwaku Dua became extremely agitated about his reputation. Fearing that they might meet with accidental death in his capital, he was known rather to have freed them and restored them to their homelands.[54]

As a result of dissatisfaction with the state of affairs in the British Protected Territory, and of disagreements with the Administration there about the interpretation of the treaty of 1831 with respect to both territorial jurisdictions and extradition procedures, the war party in Kumase began to gain markedly in strength. The disgrace and death in 1859 of its titular head, the heir apparent Osei Kwadwo, secured for a time the peace party ascendancy (p. 491). In 1862, however, a new issue arose, and those who had long advocated decisive intervention in the affairs of the Protected Territory could no longer be restrained. A wealthy and elderly Asante citizen, Kwasi

49 *Report from the Select Committee on the West Coast of Africa*, C. 551, 1842: the Gold Coast, citing Maclean to Gold Coast Committee, dd. 16 December 1837.
50 PRO, CO. 96/60: Kwaku Dua to Governor Pine, dd. Kumase, 9 February 1863.
51 Metcalfe, 1962, pp. 133–40.
52 Cruickshank, 1853, ii, 236–9.
53 PRO, CO. 96/19: Winniet to Earl Grey, dd. Cape Coast, 4 June 1850.
54 Cruickshank, 1853, ii, 236–9.

Gyani, was accused of hoarding rock gold, thereby breaking the law that all nuggets, as opposed to gold dust, had to be despatched to the Mint in Kumase.[55] He was summoned to appear before court in Kumase, but with a number of followers – eighty according to some accounts, 400–600 according to others – he fled to Denkyira in the British Protected Territory.[56] In December 1862 officers from Kumase arrived at Cape Coast to request his extradition to stand trial. Governor Richard Pine refused the request, accepting Kwasi Gyani's claim that the charges were false.[57] On 9 February 1863, Kwaku Dua sent off a letter of protest to Pine:

> But little time before your coming, about 70 persons of Wassaw, your own subjects, ran away to my country, and the Governor of Cape Coast Castle sent a soldier to me for them, and I tried as much as possible, and got them for the soldier to deliver them to him. These persons I subsisted them 4 oz. 8 acs. gold dust to maintain them in the way, because the Governor being a good friend to foreshown agreement, and also to me. But when you came, any of my slaves run to Cape Coast, you and your subjects take them, and would [not] bring him to me, so you have taken more of my subjects, and even my grandson, and now you are going to take Quashie Gainie also. So you must not blame me for keeping my subjects from coming down to Cape Coast, but when disturbances arise, then all the blame is upon you, because you have broken the rule of agreement.[58]

The letter was carried to Cape Coast by Amankwa Akuma, who arrived there on 17 February. Against the advice of prominent members of his own council, Pine again refused the Asantehene's request, and denied that any extradition agreement existed between his administration and the Asante government.[59] Realizing, however, that war might be imminent, Pine immediately halted the supply of war materials to Asante from British sources. He also requested the Dutch authorities in Elmina to stop supplies through their importing firms, but the Governor there 'expressed his regret that he was unable to do more than remain neutral, as the king of Ashantee was his ally'.[60]

Pine proceeded to place the Protected Territory on a war footing, envisaging the mobilization of 50,000 irregulars to be raised by the Protectorate chiefs, and to be supported by 2,000 regulars, mainly of

55 PRO, CO. 96/58: Pine to Newcastle, dd. Cape Coast, 10 December 1862. Kwasi Gyani is reported to have been a 'captain' of the Bantamahene, see Methodist Mission Archives: West to Boyce, dd. Cape Coast, 11 March 1863.

56 Horton, 1870, p. 53. *The African Times*, II, No. 22, 23 April 1863, p. 113: anon. letter dd. Accra, 11 April 1863.

57 PRO, CO. 96/58: Pine to Newcastle, dd. Cape Coast, 10 December 1862.

58 *Despatches . . . explaining the cause of war*, C. 385, 1864, pp. 6–7: Kwaku Dua to Pine, dd. Kumase, 9 February 1863.

59 *Ibid.* p. 7: Pine to Kwaku Dua, dd. Cape Coast, 21 February 1863.

60 *Ibid.* p. 5: Pine to Newcastle, dd. Accra, 10 March 1863.

the West India Regiments. With such a force, he announced, 'I would undertake (driving the hordes of Ashantee before me) to march to Coomassie'.[61] In the situation of extreme crisis, Kofi Agyeman of Akyem Kotoku contributed to the heightening of general tension by harbouring other refugees wanted for trial in Kumase and by insulting the Asantehene's messengers.[62] In some fear of removal from office following the collapse of his policies of non-intervention, the Asantehene Kwaku Dua finally modified his personal position.[63] 'Nowadays', he is reported as stating in council, 'when the oath of the kingdom is forfeited by any of you, and to escape the punishment you run away to the Protectorate for refuge, if I am to be denied of such one's return, it is for you to decide whether the kingdom will stand.' [64] Although many members of council urged the advisability of waiting a season before taking the field, a majority favoured the immediate invasion of the British Protected Territory. Owusu Koko, son of the Asantehene Osei Bonsu and himself Akyempemhene of Kumase, was appointed commander-in-chief of the operations.[65] One division of 2,000 men was despatched to the southwest, instructed to avoid hostilities if possible but to hold the Wassa and Denkyira in check. A second division of 8,000 men was moved across the Pra with orders to establish advance camps in Assin on the great-road to Cape Coast. The main force, led by Owusu Koko in person and reputedly numbering 20,000 men, overran and burned the Akyem Kotoku towns, established a base camp at Gyadam on the Birrim River, and occupied forward positions at Esikuma in northern Fanteland.[66] By the middle of May 1863 the initial military operations were complete, and in the few engagements that had been fought the strength of the Asante fighting forces had been demonstrated. The ease with which the British Protected Territory could be invaded had been proven, and there was little to suggest that the coastal towns could be readily defended. Many of the

61 *Ibid.* p. 10: Pine to Newcastle, dd. Cape Coast, 12 May 1863.
62 *Ibid.* pp. 10–11: Pine to Newcastle, dd. Adwumako, 10 June 1863. For a fuller account of the complex affairs of Akyem Kotoku in the period, see Ward, 1958, p. 222; Institute of African Studies, Ghana, KAG/7: Akim Oda (Kotoku) Traditions; and Horton, 1868, p. 120.
63 Horton, 1870, p. 56. *The African Times*, II, no. 23, 23 May 1863, p. 127; II, no. 24, 23 June 1863, p. 138.
64 *The African Times*, XIV, no. 159, 30 September 1874, pp. 33–4: Notes for History. – Origin of Ashanti Invasion of 1873–4, by J. Dawson, dd. Kumase, 14 May 1873.
65 *Idem.*
66 Horton, 1870, pp. 57–63, from which source the sizes of the Asante divisions are taken. The Special Correspondent of *The African Times* estimated the number of men mobilized at the higher figure of 60,000, see II, no. 22, 23 April 1863, p. 126. See also Ellis, 1893, pp. 226–9; and PRO, CO. 96/61: Pine to Newcastle, dd. 12 May 1863.

southern chiefs, moreover, displayed little enthusiasm for the British cause, and the government in Kumase had despatched messengers to the Akyem, Akuapem, Accra and others assuring them that it was not waging war against them.[67]

From his base at Gyadam-on-Birrim, in mid-May Owusu Koko opened negotiations with the British and demanded as a condition of peace the extradition of the various refugees in the Protectorate wanted for trial in Kumase, including apparently Kofi Agyeman of Akyem Kotoku and Kwasi Gyani. As reported by Horton,

. . . Prince Osoo Cokkor sent by one of the captives (Fantees) a symbolical message to the Governor, consisting of two sticks, one short and the other long, and requested him to make his choice. If he took the short one, he was to give up the Ashantee runaways, and the war would be at once at an end; but if he retained the long one, he, the Prince, would continue the war for the next three years amidst all the difficulties.[68]

Horton reported that Governor Pine selected the long stick, informing Owusu Koko that he was prepared to fight for seven years if necessary – 'until the kingdom of Ashantee should be prostrated before the English Government'. The Council in Kumase decided nevertheless that the main armies should be withdrawn from the south before the onset of the summer rains. Despite Owusu Koko's reluctance to accept the decision,[69] by the middle of the year only a few detachments of Asante soldiers remained in the Protected Territory. The implication of a letter sent by Kwaku Dua to Pine in August was that the Asantehene was awaiting the meeting of the Asantemanhyiamu at Odwira time before deciding what policy to pursue.[70] In the meantime a court of enquiry, over which Kwaku Dua presided, was set up in Kumase to investigate the conduct of the troops during the campaign, 'to ascertain if the Prince [Owusu Koko] and his subordinate captains had done their duty in the field as became brave and faithful subjects'. As a result at least one senior commander, Akuoko ('Ekkuah Koom'), was placed on trial for dereliction of duty, condemned to death, and executed.[71] There can be little doubt that the Council anticipated that the military commanders would be required to take the field again before long.

The Asante withdrawal notwithstanding, the British continued to

67 *The African Times*, II, no. 24, 23 June 1863, p. 139: anon. letter, dd. Christiansborg, 12 May 1863. See also Dieterle's memoirs, in *Evangelisches Missionsmagazin*, 1900, p. 261.

68 Horton, 1870, p. 65. *Despatches . . . explaining the cause of war*, C. 385, 1864, pp. 10–11: Pine to Newcastle, dd. Adwumako, 10 June 1863.

69 *The African Times*, III, no. 25, 23 July 1863, p. 9: anon. letter dd. Cape Coast, 13 June 1863.

70 *Despatches*, C. 385, 1864, p. 12: Pine to Newcastle, dd. Accra, 26 August 1863.

71 *The African Times*, III, no. 28, 23 October 1863: report from Special Correspondent, dd. Cape Coast, 14 September 1863.

build up their military resources in the Protected Territory and, as reinforcements of the 2nd, 3rd, and 4th West India Regiments arrived on the coast, a forward base was established at the Pra River on Route VI.[72] Before any further encounters between Asante and British forces could occur, however, mortality from sickness at the Pra camp assumed alarming proportions, and in May 1864 orders from London came for the evacuation of the base and the termination of all offensive operations against Asante.[73] In July Pine was obliged to report to London that he had 'not the slightest reliable information to convey with respect to our relations with the King'.[74] It seems clear, however, that Kwaku Dua was once more attempting, with some success, to dissuade his Council from sending more troops into the Protectorate. Certainly when, towards the end of 1865 and through the good offices of George Blankson, the British invited the government to send a mission to Cape Coast, it responded favourably. Four envoys, with their retinues, arrived there to take part in discussions on 19 and 20 December 1865 and 8 January 1866. Both sides to the talks concurred in the desire for peace. But on 16 January the Acting Governor Conran injudiciously issued a proclamation to the effect that the Asantehene had sued for peace, and that this had been granted. Upon news of Conran's action reaching Kumase, the greatest indignation prevailed, and whatever hopes the peace party had of regaining its ascendancy were ended. Kwaku Dua repudiated the announcement, and decreed that no further diplomatic exchanges with the British could occur until Kwasi Gyani had been extradited.[75] 'Even when a woman runs away because she has been ill-treated', he announced, 'she has to be returned; Kwasi Gyani has run away and he must be surrendered otherwise the road will remain closed.' [76] It was the turn of the British to be alarmed. On 11 June 1866, W. C. Fynn arrived in Kumase, empowered by Conran to suggest a compromise: that Kwasi Gyani should be deported to Sierra Leone. At a meeting of the council the following day, the proposal was rejected.[77] Kwasi Gyani was, nevertheless, deported, and Asante envoys witnessed his departure from Cape Coast on 10 July.[78] In Kumase the government stood firm: messengers sent there by Conran arrived back in Cape Coast in early October and re-

[72] Horton, 1870, pp. 69–73.
[73] PRO, CO. 96/64: Cardwell to Chief Justice Hackett, dd. 23 May 1864.
[74] PRO, CO. 96/64: Pine to Cardwell, dd. 13 July 1864.
[75] Horton, 1870, p. 74. Nagtglas to Minister of Colonies, dd. Elmina, 26 February, 1874, in Wolteringen, n.d. pp. 46–7.
[76] General State Archives, The Hague, KvG 776, minutes of negotiations with Negro rulers: minute dd. 2 May 1866.
[77] Instituut voor Taal- Land- en Volkenkunde, Leiden MS H. 509: anon. diary, entries dd. Kumase, 11 and 12 June 1866.
[78] *The African Times*, VI, no. 62, 23 August 1866, p. 15: anon. letter dd. Cape Coast, 11 July 1866.

ported that Kwaku Dua would keep the roads closed, and would reject any settlement that did not include the surrender to him of Kwasi Gyani and Kofi Agyeman.[79]

The outflanking of the Protected Territory

Throughout the second half of 1866 a state of undeclared war existed between the British and Asante. The former took steps to prevent the flow of war materials inland from the coast. 'There are', Administrator Conran reported, 'but two modes through which the Ashantees . . . can receive supplies from the coast during war, the Assinee and Volta'; both, he argued, had to be closed to the Asante trade.[80] In Kumase, however, those who advocated decisive military intervention in the Protected Territory dominated the councils, and were not insensitive to the logistics of the situation. Measures were taken to protect and strengthen both the eastern and western approaches to the Gold Coast.

On the eastern flank of the Protected Territory fighting had broken out in 1865 between the Ada on the west bank of the Volta and within the British ambit, and the Anlo on the east bank who, although the British claimed a jurisdiction over them, had continued to acknowledge an Asante connection. In February 1866 the British moved troops up to the Volta, crossed it in April, and after heavy fighting put the Anlo to flight.[81] The Asante government reacted cautiously, deciding to consolidate its political presence east of the river before establishing a military one there. By November 1866 envoys from Kumase were in negotiation with the Akwamuhene,[82] and in early December they met with Anlo representatives at Dzelukofe on the coast near Keta and offered them 'the alliance, friendship and protection of their King'.[83] Both the Akwamu and Anlo acknowledged the protection of the Asantehene, and the government released to them supplies of war materials.[84] On 1 August 1867 Anlo delegates arrived in Kumase,[85] and

79 *Ibid.* VI, no. 65, 23 November 1866, p. 51: anon. letter dd. Cape Coast, 11 October 1866.
80 PRO, CO. 96/72: Conran to Blackall, dd. Cape Coast, 6 September 1866.
81 For these events, see Horton, 1870, pp. 75–89; Claridge, 1915, I, 548–52.
82 In 1864 the Akwamuhene Dako Yaw Kuma had been killed by his own people, by report because of his attachment to Asante, see Methodist Mission Archives: Solomon to General Secretaries, dd. Domonasi, 12 May 1864; and France to General Secretaries, dd. Prampram, 10 June 1864. His successor, Kwafo Akoto I, seems however to have preserved the Asante connection in the early part of his reign.
83 *The African Times,* VI, no. 69, 23 March 1867.
84 *Ibid.* VI, no. 67, 23 January 1867, p. 81, anon. letter dd. Accra, 7 December 1866, containing news from Odumase Krobo, 29 November 1866; p. 93, anon. letter dd. Cape Coast, 6 January 1867.
85 Leiden MS H. 509, Instituut voor Taal- Land- en Volkenkunde, entry for 1 August 1867.

presumably detailed plans for Asante military intervention east of the Volta were discussed, for the first army took the field shortly afterwards.[86] It was organized by the Gyaasewahene of Kumase, Adu Bofo, who gave command of it to one of his principal officers, Nantwi.[87] Meeting with strong resistance from a coalition of northern Ewe ('Krepi') led by an Akyem Kotoku, Dompre, the government was obliged to increase its military commitment east of the Volta. Late in 1868 the Gyaasewahene in person took command on the eastern front, with a force reputedly of 30,000 men.[88]

The British, meantime, had launched their own diplomatic offensive east of the Volta, and on 28 August and 14 November 1867 had obtained agreements with the Akwamu and Anlo respectively. But as Horton remarked with specific reference to the Anlo agreement,

this treaty was only worth the paper on which it was written, inasmuch as at the very time of signature and subsequently, the Awoonahs [Anlo], with their allies the Aquamboos and Ashantees, were committing the grossest acts of robbery, murder, and pillage in the Protectorate, had entirely stopped the navigation of the Volta and blockaded the roads to Creepee, and had formed an alliance offensive and defensive with the Ashantees, who were in arms against the Protectorate.[89]

Indeed, in March 1869 the British Acting Administrator Simpson arrived in Akwamu to attempt yet again to detach its people from the Asante cause, and was immediately arrested. The Akwamuhene would have sent him prisoner to Kumase had not Adu Bofo ordered his release on the grounds that, unlike the missionaries Ramseyer and Kühne and the trader Bonnat who had been seized and sent to the capital, Simpson enjoyed the protection of his official status.[90] The truth of the matter was that both Akwamu and Anlo were fully committed to support of Adu Bofo, whose troops reoccupied the trans-Volta provinces with comparative ease, from Buem in the north to the southern seaboard.[91] Hostile towns and villages were destroyed with the 'robbery, murder, and pillage' referred to by Horton, but many other localities either had remained loyal to the government or

[86] Horton, 1870, pp. 80–1.
[87] Ramseyer and Kühne, 1875, pp. 57; 136.
[88] *Ibid.* p. 203.
[89] Horton, 1870, pp. 88–9.
[90] PRO, CO. 96/79: Granville to Kennedy, dd. London, 17 May 1869. See Claridge, 1915, I, 578–9.
[91] For a recent account of the reoccupation, see Johnson, 1965, pp. 44–50. A story is told that in the course of the campaigns, Adu Bofo and an Anlo captain named Tamaklo took oaths of friendship by exchanging 'drinking names'. Adu Bofo interpreted *tamaklo* in Twi to mean 'I take the town', while Tamaklo interpreted *adu bofo* in Ewe to mean 'chief of the magic', see Wilks, field-notes, interview with R. Antonio, dd. Kumase, 15 October 1958.

hastened to reaffirm their allegiance to it: Wusuta, Tonkor, Aveme, Tsome, Tafiefi, Buem, Adele and the rest.

At various strategic points in the reoccupied territories the government established small garrisons. When the British brought a gunboat up the Volta in 1870 to attack that on the island of Duffo some fifty miles upstream (Plate VI), they found it held by some thirty men commanded by an Asante captain who, rather than surrender, tied his gold around his neck and committed suicide by drowning.[92] In British official reports the garrison was misrepresented as a 'comparatively small band of these piratical rebels, aided from time to time by the presence of Aquamoos and Ashantees [who] have closed the river . . .'.[93] While the creation of such small garrisons is indicative of the government's desire to maintain a limited military presence in the reoccupied territories, it seems likely that by the time of the return of Adu Bofo's forces to the capital in July and September 1871,[94] a beginning had already been made in revivifying the civilian administration there. That some sort of jurisdictional arrangements were made even for districts the most remote from the capital is shown by the contemporary reference to the assignation of responsibility for Agu ('Aja', see p. 57) to Kwasi Domfe, Nsumankwaahene of Kumase.[95]

Not only on the eastern flank of the British Protected Territory, but on the western also, the government's new policies were executed with vigour. In March 1867 the British and Dutch had agreed to rationalize the pattern of their interests on the Gold Coast. A treaty was ratified between the two on 5 July, and the proposals subscribed to became operative on 1 January 1868.[96] By it the Dutch relinquished to the British all interest in the districts east of the Sweet River (between Cape Coast and Elmina), and the British to the Dutch all interest in the districts west of that river. Specifically, the Dutch posts at Mouri, Kormantin, Apam and Accra were exchanged for the British posts at Beyin, Dixcove, Sekondi and Komenda, while the British also abandoned claims to jurisdiction over Amanahia, Wassa and Denkyira. In view of its old-standing compact with the Dutch, the Asante government presumably regarded the change in the situation in the southwest as greatly to its advantage, and no objection appears to have been registered. Thus while the troops of Nantwi and Adu Bofo were

---

92 *The African Times*, x, no. 110, 23 August 1870, p. 17: letter from E. Bannerman, dd. Duffo, 1 July 1870. See also Reade, 1873, II, 171–4, and Reade, 1874, pp. 129–31 (who referred to the Asante captain as having blown himself up with gunpowder).
93 PRO, CO. 96/85: Ussher to Kennedy, dd. Accra, 8 July 1870. NAG, Accra, ADM. 1/2/16: Kennedy to Kimberley, dd. Sierra Leone, 4 July 1870, 20 September 1870, and 13 October 1871.
94 Ramseyer and Kühne, 1875, pp. 130, 135. Bonnat, in Gros, 1884, pp. 227–9.
95 Ramseyer and Kühne, 1875, p. 163.
96 For the text of the treaty, see Metcalfe, 1964, pp. 320–1.

carrying out the reoccupation of the eastern territories, other forces were deployed in the west to protect the branches of the great-road VIII: the essential supply routes for war materials and other commodities landed on the western coast.[97] By mid-1868 an Asante army was reported to have 'driven in the whole of western Wassaw', and to have occupied the Denkyira and Twifo countries.[98] Yet the Anglo-Dutch treaty of 1867 did in fact create problems which became of grave concern not only to the government in Kumase but also to the British and Dutch administrations in Cape Coast and Elmina respectively.

To the coastal Fante west of the Sweet River, who over several decades had come to regard themselves as under British protection, the treaty of 1867 appeared a gross betrayal of their interests which left them exposed to any punitive measures that the Asante government might choose to take against them. 'They look upon the Dutch', it was explained,

as feudatories to Ashantee; and this opinion is unfortunately strengthened by the fact of the payment to the king at Coomassie, of a yearly tribute by the Dutch for the ground upon which Elmina stands, and also by the uniform deference and friendship exhibited by the Dutch to that great native power, the mortal and traditional enemy of the Fantee race.[99]

Early in 1868 widespread disturbances broke out when a number of chiefs refused to recognize the treaty of 1867 and proceeded to safeguard what they saw as their interests. A Fante army was raised to impose a blockade on Elmina town. Messengers were sent from Kumase offering the Dutch Governor Boers military assistance if he wished it. It was apparently not considered necessary. Indeed, when the British Governor-in-Chief from Sierra Leone met with the Elmina chiefs in October 1868 and intimated to them that the blockade would be lifted if they renounced their allegiance to Asante, rather they strongly reaffirmed it.[100] The Asante government appears in fact to have decided that the situation called for an essentially political rather than military solution.

The task of carrying out the pacification of the southwest was entrusted to Akyampon Yaw, of the Boakye Yam Kuma stool. The post was one which carried special responsibilities for the affairs of Elmina and the districts to its west. Late in 1868 Akyampon Yaw left Kumase with an escort of some two or three hundred armed men.[101] His com-

97 See, e.g. Reade, 1874, pp. 122–3.
98 PRO, CO. 96/77; Ussher to Kennedy, dd. Cape Coast, 7 August 1868.
99 PRO, CO. 96/76: Ussher to Kennedy, dd. Cape Coast, 6 April 1868.
100 For this episode, see Claridge, 1915, I, 568–73.
101 Akyampon Yaw and his predecessor in office, Akyampon Tia, were both sons of the latter's predecessor, Boakye Yam Kuma, see Wilks, fieldnotes, interview

mission was to negotiate settlements with local chiefs, to bring and try
cases against those who had shown themselves enemies of Asante, and
generally to prepare the way for the resumption of civilian administration in the southwestern districts. He proceeded from Kumase by
Route VIII and Route VIII(b) through Aowin to Kwankyeabo, seat
of the Sanwihene Amandufo. Horton reported that he was detained
there for four months: [102] Amandufo was one of the principal buyers
of arms from French traders (and illicitly from British) for the Asante
government.[103] From Kwankyeabo Akyampon Yaw travelled along the
coast through Amanahia, Axim (November 1869), and Sekondi to
arrive in Elmina on 27 December.[104] In each town, courts were set up
in which those identified as leading opponents of the government's
policies were tried, and frequently executed. In Elmina, for example,
a white Jamaican, W. C. Finlason, was brought before Akyampon Yaw
and accused of having written letters to *The African Times* expressing
hostility toward the Elmina, and of having acted as secretary to the
newly formed Fante Confederation at Mankessim, which master-
minded the blockade of Elmina. Condemned to death, it was only the
intervention of the Dutch which saved him from execution.[105] Akyampon Yaw's 'bloody march along the sea-coast' became something of a
cause celèbre.

Although 5,000 Asante troops had been sent into the southwest to
give Akyampon Yaw whatever support was necessary, no use was made
of them: five months after he had entered Elmina they were still in
Assini.[106] Having encountered virtually no opposition in carrying out
his directives, in 1870 Akyampon Yaw appears to have assumed duties
as Provincial Commissioner for the southwest and to have begun the
reorganization of the central government's administrative agencies
there. The situation at Beyin, where Ahuru Kwame was resident
commissioner in 1870, has been referred to above (p. 153). The
success which Akyampon Yaw achieved in restoring the government's
position on the western flank of the British Protected Territory may
be measured by the circumstances there a decade later. In 1881 the

with Nana Boakye Yam, dd. Kumase, 2 August 1965. Among the wives of Boakye
Yam Kuma was the Asantehemaa Ama Sewaa, by whom he fathered the
Asantehene Kwaku Dua I. Hence Akyampon Yaw is referred to as brother of
Kwaku Dua, see Horton, 1870, p. 120, and as uncle of Asantehene Kofi Kakari,
see Ramseyer and Kühne, 1875, p. 207.
102 Horton, 1870, p. 123.
103 For Amandufo's order of 1,000 guns for the Asantehene placed with a French
trader, Chatelain, see Reade, 1873, II, 34–5.
104 Horton, 1870, pp. 120–8. See also Nagtglas to Minister of Colonies, dd. Elmina,
26 February 1871, in Wolteringen, n.d., pp. 46–7.
105 See Horton, 1870, pp. 168–70, evidence of J. A. Fynn, dd. 6 January 1870; and
pp. 125–7, evidence of W. C. Finlason, dd. 26 March 1870.
106 Horton, 1870, p. 132.

British District Commissioner in Axim, Firminger, reported on the continuing extent of Asante influence in the west, and remarked on the arrival of a new Asante resident commissioner, Kete Kwabena, at Beyin less than thirty miles away. 'I find', he wrote,

that the Awooins [Aowin] have long been on the most intimate terms with the Ashantis, and that their disregard for English law is owing to the advice from Coomassie. While at Bayin some days ago, I discovered that Awoosie Ackah, the king, had sent one of his cane bearers on a friendly mission to Coomassie to reside there, and had received Ketey Cobran to stay at Bayin, no doubt to keep the two stools well informed of all that was going on. Should any trouble occur with Ashanti I am assured that all the people from Bayin to the frontier would join them. I am also informed beyond doubt that three-hundred (twenty-five pound) kegs of powder were smuggled across the frontier last month.

The gunpowder was thought to be consigned to Kumase.[107] It may have been conveyed there by the Beyin representative, Kwabena Awuo, whose arrival in Kumase was noted by J. Parker. Kwabena Awuo, he reported,

was sent to take an oath and say that the Chief of Bayin in Appolonia had sent him to the King of Coomassie, with his compliments, and to say that the people of Bayin were in agreement with the King of Coomassie and under his rule, and that whenever anything of importance happened at Bayin he would at once inform the King of Coomassie; and to ask that if there were any news at Coomassie the King would not fail to inform him of it, also to remind the King that Bayin town in Appolonia had supplied the King with plenty of arms and ammunition, he had only to apply at once to the Chief of Bayin, and all would be supplied to him.[108]

By 1870, then, the Asante presence on the western Gold Coast appeared secure. Indeed, in early 1871 a further development occurred which promised to consolidate further their position there: the French made known their intention of abandoning the post at Assini. The Dutch administrators attempted to assess the implications of the proposed measure. It must, they observed,

necessarily be of great influence on the state of affairs on the Coast. As is known, several European nations occupied a closed line of forts on the Coast, controlling the Coast, and the people of the interior, such as Asante, were dependent on them for contact with the sea. This situation will now change. Instead of the French we will now have the Asante as neighbours in

107 *Affairs of the Gold Coast and threatened Ashanti Invasion*, C. 3064, 1881, p. 32: Firminger to Colonial Secretary, dd. Axim, 26 January 1881. See also Ellis, 1883, pp. 223–4.
108 *Affairs* . . . C. 3064, 1881, p. 49: J. Parker to Griffith, dd. Kumase, 24 January 1881.

Apollonia, and they will much increase their power, once established on the sea-shore, and if they will not menace us, they will at least look at us from a quite different, independent point of view. Nor will the English be indifferent to the changed situation. Up to now our possessions have been between those of the English and those of the French, but from now we shall be between the Asante and the English . . .[109]

With the successes achieved through Adu Bofo's campaign in the east thus matched by those achieved through Akyampon Yaw's mission in the west, to the councils in Kumase the situation in 1871 must have appeared such as to vindicate their decision in 1866 to abandon, *vis-à-vis* the Gold Coast, the accommodationist views which had dominated Asante political thinking since 1831. Yet it remained the case that the basic problem of the government's ongoing relationship with the British administration on the Gold Coast had still not been resolved, and the indications are that even many of the more moderate members of the war party still did not favour direct military intervention in those territories unambiguously under British control. Paradoxically, it was political developments in Fanteland in the period which suggested to the government a new – but as it turned out, abortive – approach to the matter.

Asante, British, and Dutch: the Elmina problem

The Anglo-Dutch treaty of 1867 had alienated from their loyalty to the British administration many of the leaders of Fante nationalism, who began to agitate for what was in effect a revival of the old Assembly of the Representatives of the Southern Chiefs of the early 1820s (see p. 164) and of the Legislative Assembly of Native Chiefs of the Gold Coast of 1852 (see p. 208). In January 1868 a new assembly was convened at Mankessim to represent 'the Fanti Nation', and after a number of meetings at which such offices as 'President of the Fanti Confederation', 'Chief Magistrate of the Fanti National Supreme Court', and 'Field Marshal Commanding in Chief of the Fanti Forces' were canvassed, on 18 November 1871 the constitution of the Fante Confederation was formally promulgated and attested to by thirty-one chiefs or their representatives.[110] Strong support for association with the Confederacy came from other parts of the Gold Coast, and most notably Accra. Although the leaders of the Fante Confederation

109 Minute on the Elmina protest against cession to the British, dd. 18 January 1871, in Wolteringen, n.d., pp. 22–3. I have followed a translation by A. Van Dantzig.
110 See Kimble, 1963, chapter VI, *passim*. For the text of the constitution, see Casely Hayford, 1903, pp. 327–40; Sarbah, 1906, pp. 199–209.

hastened to assure the British administration of their loyalty,[111] it is clear that the drive towards self-government enjoyed a wide measure of popular support stemming from the general dissatisfaction with the way in which the affairs of the British Protected Territory were being managed. Not atypical of the sentiments of the time – and restating those of a decade earlier (p. 209) – was the view of an anonymous writer in the *African Times:*

> We are at a loss to imagine what possible object the British Government can have in remaining any longer on this Coast, except to take money from us to put into the pockets of the officials . . . It is a literal fact that the Government on the Gold Coast, at all events by its acts, distinctly proclaims that it is here only to collect taxes to pay the officials. As for protection, they tell us plainly they will give none to any one any where; and as for the mode in which they administer justice, positively it is a disgrace to civilization; it would be a disgrace to the Ashantees.[112]

In such circumstances, in a period when relations with the British authorities had broken down, the Asante government seemed inclined to recognize the Fante Confederation Council as the legitimate administration for the Gold Coast, and sought to observe the usual diplomatic conventions. Thus, for example, the Asantehene Kofi Kakari sent an official to attend the meeting of the Confederation Council at Mankessim on 7 December 1869, to deliver reports on the progress both of Adu Bofo in Akwamu to the east and of Akyampon Yaw ('Ackampon Anantoo') in Aowin to the west, and to assure the Fante that the Asante government intended no hostilities against them.[113] Moreover, an agreement made between the Fante Confederation Council and the Wassa chiefs on 9 November 1871 was attested by one Kwame as the 'Ashantee King's representative'.[114]

Unknown at the time to either the Asante government or the Fante Confederation Council, in 1869 discussions had commenced in Europe on the cession to Britain of all the Dutch settlements on the Gold Coast.[115] When news of the proceedings finally reached Kumase, the Asantehene delivered, by letter dated 24 November 1870, a strong protest against the transfer particularly of Elmina:

> The fort of that place have from time immemorial paid annual tribute to my ancestors to the present time by right of arms, when we conquered Intim

111 PRO, CO. 96/89: Kings President of the Fante Confederation *et al.* to Kennedy, dd. Mankessim, 24 November 1871.
112 The *African Times*, VII, no. 81, 23 March 1868, p. 104: letter dd. Accra, 20 January 1868.
113 *Ibid.* IX, no. 103, 23 February 1870, p. 87.
114 *Ibid.* XI, no. 127, 23 January 1872, p. 77.
115 See Coombs, 1963, Chapter 4, *passim.*

Gackidi [Ntim Gyakari], King of Denkera. Intim Gackidi having purchased goods to the amount of nine thousand pounds (£9,000) from the Dutch, and not paying for them before we conquered Intim Gackidi, the Dutch demanded of my father Osai Tutu I, for the payment, who paid it full the nine thousand pounds (£9,000), and the Dutch delivered the Elmina to him as his own, and from that time tribute has been paid to us to this present time. I hope therefore your Excellency will not include Elmina in the change, for it is mine by right.[116]

The protest was effective in delaying negotiations, and Kimberley, Secretary of State for the Colonies in London, insisted, 'before proceeding further with the Convention, that the Dutch Government should procure, by such means as they think fit, the renunciation of the claim of the king of Ashantee to Elmina, else this Government may find itself involved in a war with the Ashantees'.[117]

The Dutch Governor Nagtglas in Elmina found himself thus faced with two problems to resolve: first, to have removed from there the overt signs of the Asante government's authority, namely Akyampon Yaw and his staff, and secondly, to obtain from the Asantehene some sort of formal withdrawal of his claims to the town. On 14 April 1871 a naval party from the *Het Loo* landed at Elmina and seized the Asante commissioner. He was informed that he would be landed at Assini with some forty or fifty of his retinue, whence he could make his way back to Kumase.[118] When one hundred and fifty Asante tried, albeit unsuccessfully, to force their way into the Dutch fort, the plan to deport him was dropped. On 20 May he was freed following the arrival in Elmina of three Asante envoys, Owusu Ansa, Afrifa and Kotirko.[119] In mid-June, after the departure of Nagtglas from the coast, the acting Governor Hugenholz arrested Akyampon Yaw once more, and did deport him to Assini.[120] He remained there, presumably under orders to reorganize his staff at that place. For a third time, however, he was seized: on this occasion by a British detachment from H.M.S. *Coquette*. Roughly treated by Colonel Foster who was in charge of the operation, he was landed at Cape Coast on 28 October 1872. Within

---

116 *Correspondence relative to the Cession by the Netherlands Government . . . of the Dutch Settlements on the West Coast of Africa*, C. 670, LXX, 1872: Kofi Kakari and Owusu Ansa to Ussher, dd. Kumase, 24 November 1870. The statement of Asante claims to Elmina may be compared with that made by Osei Bonsu in 1817, see p. 167 above. The sum of £9,000 clearly represents 1,000 peredwans.

117 *Ibid.* memorandum, Colonial Office to Foreign Office, dd. London, 3 February 1871.

118 General State Archives, The Hague, archives of the Ministry of Foreign Affairs, B. 79, Afst. iv: Nagtglas to Minister of Colonies, dd. Elmina, 16 April 1871.

119 *Ibid.* Nagtglas to Minister of Colonies, dd. 1 June 1871.

120 *Ibid.* Hugenholz to Minister of Colonies, dd. 21 June 1871.

a few days his possessions were being sold all over the town.[121] From Cape Coast he was sent under escort to the Pra River. He arrived back in the capital, with some three hundred followers, late in December 1872.[122]

Meanwhile, before leaving the coast for Holland, Governor Nagtglas had sent to Kumase a clerk, Henry Plange, to attempt to obtain the government's renunciation of its claims to Elmina. Plange returned to Elmina on 26 October 1871 with a document containing just such: a declaration that the Asantehene received from the Dutch not a tribute but a salary and that he was therefore a friend of, but not a sovereign over, Elmina. The document was supposedly attested by the Asantehene Kofi Kakari and three senior counselors, (Nsuase) Kwaku Poku Agyeman, Boakye Tenten, and Yaw Nantwi.[123] While the document arrived in British hands after the final decision had been taken to assume control of Elmina, it must certainly have strengthened their view of the legality of the action.[124] The Convention between Britain and the Netherlands was ratified on 17 February 1872, and the transfer effected the following April. That the document of 19 August 1871 – known as the Certificate of Apology – was spurious was suggested in the English *Standard* as early as 1874,[125] and in 1893 Ellis published a powerfully argued case for that view [126] Certainly it misrepresented the official position of the government in Kumase. In January 1873 Akyampon Yaw had in fact brought the whole matter before council in Kumase, and a Court of Enquiry was set up. Accusations were brought by Akyampon Yaw against the envoy Afrifa, that while in Elmina he had sworn an oath to the Dutch that Akyampon Yaw was there without the government's authority; that Afrifa had therefore been instrumental in the Dutch decision to arrest and deport him; and that Afrifa had virtually surrendered Elmina to the British. When it was found that Afrifa had returned to Kumase from Elmina with many goods which he had concealed in a village near Kumase, the case seemed proven. Afrifa was flogged and placed in the stocks ('in log'), and his wives and property were seized.[127] The Dutch reports of the relevant period show that there was indeed substance to Akyampon Yaw's charges, and that Kotirko may also have been involved in the

---

121 British Parliamentary Papers, *Gold Coast*, I, C. 266, 1873: Salmon to Hennessy, dd. Cape Coast, 28 October 1872. *The African Times*, XII, no. 140, 28 February 1873, p. 97.
122 Ramseyer and Kühne, 1875, pp. 207–8.
123 See text in Crooks, 1923, p. 400.
124 See Coombs, 1963, chapter 5, *passim*.
125 *Ibid.* p. 102.
126 Ellis, 1893, pp. 270–3.
127 Ramseyer and Kühne, 1875, p. 208.

matter.[128] In a letter of 20 May 1871, Governor Nagtglas informed his British counterpart, Ussher, of the results of meetings on 18 and 19 May with the Asante officials:

As I brought to their knowledge that the king of Ashantee had forwarded a letter to His Excellency the Administrator of his British Majesty's Possessions on the Gold Coast, in which he lays claim to the sovereignty by tribute of the Forts of Elmina, and also of the town by right of conquest and in virtue of certain pecuniary considerations, the messengers appeared to be astonished, and returned an answer as follows:

'The Ashantees have never quarreled with Elmina consequently they could not have conquered Elmina as they never fought with Elmina.'

With regard to the tribute, they said that the king of Ashantee is a servant of the king of Holland so that the latter pays him wages, and not at all a tribute.[129]

Taking together the evidence of the Dutch Governor and the findings of Akyampon Yaw's Court of Enquiry, there seems little doubt that the so-called Certificate of Apology did not represent accurately the views of the central government, and that its fabrication had involved collusion between the Dutch officers, their agent Plange, and at least one Asante official. Plange himself had in fact returned to Kumase in July 1872, sent there by both British and Dutch administrations to notify the government that the British had assumed authority over Elmina.[130] It was only after some weeks that the Council of Kumase agreed to receive Plange, but no answer was given to his message:[131] the matter was tabled for the meeting of the Asantemanhyiamu at the forthcoming Odwira. At its session of 2 September, Plange was asked to attend. The discussion centred, however, on the question of the release of the European captives in Kumase, but a number of the members of the assembly used the occasion to avow their readiness to fight the British.[132] Later in the year, as further information reached the capital about the circumstances of the transfer of Elmina, Plange was placed under arrest.[133] He was summoned to appear before Akyampon Yaw's Court of Enquiry in February 1873, to testify on the part he had played in the negotiations over Elmina,[134]

---

128 Kotirko appears to have left Kumase about this time. He later resided in Adanse, and was a senior councillor to Adansehene in the 1880s, see Asante Collective Biography Project: Kotirko.

129 General State Archives, The Hague, archives of the Ministry of Foreign Affairs, B. 79, Afst. conf. 40: Nagtglas to Ussher, dd. Elmina, 20 May 1871.

130 Ramseyer and Kühne, 1875, p. 172.

131 *Ibid.* pp. 175–6.

132 *Ibid.* pp. 180–1. Plange's Journal, in Brackenbury, 1874, I, 43–8.

133 Ramseyer and Kühne, 1875, pp. 196–7.

134 *Ibid.* pp. 211–12.

but the diplomatic immunity which he enjoyed saved him from the consequences of his actions.

The decision for war

The death of Kwaku Dua I occurred at about midnight on 27 April 1867, and the enstoolment of Kofi Kakari as successor was carried out on 28 May.[135] Between those two dates a fierce struggle occurred as the adherents of the war party ensured that the successful candidate would be one amenable to their goals. No marked changes in policy became apparent, then, when Kofi Kakari assumed office. It had been generally recognized since at least 1862, that the treaty of 1831 had ceased to provide any realistic basis for the reconciliation of Asante and British interests, and a state of war had existed between the two powers since 1866. Nevertheless, until 1872 the more bellicose members of the war party in Asante appear to have been held in check, the new Asantehene undoubtedly exercising a moderating influence. In the early months of that year, however, the news reaching the capital from the south was such as to convince a majority of councillors that the solution to the British problem had to be a military one. Not only was the British assumption of authority over Elmina and the western coast totally incompatible with the fundamental strategical interests of the nation, but the Asante government's attempts to establish novel channels of diplomatic communication with the Gold Coast through its recognition of the Fante Confederation proved abortive when, in December 1871, the British proceeded to arrest the leaders of the Confederation and to preside over its dissolution.[136] At the annual session of the Asantemanhyiamu in September 1872 (which was attended among others by Adansehene, Bekwaehene, Kokofuhene, Dwabenhene, and Mamponhene in person), the government received a clear mandate to pursue more aggressive policies: of the more politically powerful members of that Assembly, only the Mamponhene Kwabena Dwumo seemingly refrained from supporting the general call for war.[137]

It was probably the Asantemanhyiamu that was reconvened on 22 October 1872. Ramseyer and Kühne reported 'that a high council had been held in Bantama, when the chiefs had sworn they would march against the Coast, to which the king replied, "If you go, I shall go

[135] Instituut voor Taal- Land- en Volkenkunde, Leiden MS H. 509, entries dd. Kumase, 27 April and 28 May 1867.
[136] See Kimble, 1963, pp. 249–56.
[137] Ramseyer and Kühne, 1875, pp. 180–1. See also Plange's Journal, in Brackenbury, 1874, I, 43–8.

with you." ' [138] Yet the evidence shows that the objectives of the government remained still limited ones: broadly, to reassert control over the coast from Elmina westwards to Sanwi, to have its title to Elmina unambiguously recognized, and to reincorporate into Greater Asante the 'Akhans', that is, the Twi-speaking Akyem, Assin, Denkyira and Wassa peoples. [139] To the Asante tacticians, the decision may have been seen as one which would not necessarily involve the nation in armed confrontation with the British since, the treaty of 1831 having become inoperative, the government could exercise its legal right to resume residual sovereignty over such of the old southern provinces as it chose. In a letter to the British Administrator Harley dated 20 March 1873, the Asantehene Kofi Kakari stated the position quite explicitly:

His Majesty further states that your Honour's restoring him these tribes – viz., Denkeras, Akims, and Assins – back to their former position as his subjects, and also restoring the Elmina fort and people back in the same manner as they were before, will be the only thing or way to appease him, for he has no quarrel with white men . . .[140]

The Anantahene Asamoa Nkwanta was appointed Chief of Staff, and his pupil, the Bantamahene Amankwatia, was given command of the main force which was to advance along Route VI.[141] Amankwatia left Kumase on 9 December 1872, crossing the Pra River on 22 January 1873. After defeating the forces put into the field by the British in a number of engagements in March and April, he established a forward base at Dunkwa, only some sixteen miles north of Cape Coast. A second army under Nantwi of the Gyaasewa was moved along Route V into the Akyem country to stabilize the situation there, and a third army under Adu Bofo along Route VIII into Wassa.[142] It has been argued that a massive mobilization of men had preceded the invasion, and that the total number of troops put into the field approximated to 80,000.[143] Numerous accounts of the military operations are extant.

138 Ramseyer and Kühne, 1875, p. 187.
139 *Further Correspondence respecting the Ashantee Invasion*, C. 819, 1873: Dawson to Salmon, dd. Kumase, 29 December 1872; Kofi Kakari to Harley, dd. Kumase, 20 March 1873. *Further Correspondence*, C. 892, 1874: Bantamahene Amankwatia to Governor, dd. Mampon (west of Fante Akroful), 20 October 1873.
140 *Further Correspondence*, C. 819: Kofi Kakari to Harley, dd. March 1873. See also Brackenbury, 1874, I, 79–80.
141 *The Times* (London), 29 July 1873, citing information from Owusu Ansa.
142 Useful accounts of the structure of the armies are found in Boyle, 1874, pp. 146–50, from the evidence of a captured officer from Amankwatia's staff; also House of Commons Papers, C. 266–I *Gold Coast*, Pt II, 1873: evidence of Kwadwo Mensa, a Peki slave from Asante, taken by F. Foster, 26 February 1873. See also Fuller, 1921, pp. 114–17.
143 See Miles, n.d., p. 9.

Most, however, were written from a British point of view, and apart from the more obvious biases, lacked any clear appreciation of Asante strategy and tactics.[144] While it is beyond the scope of this study to offer any account of the Asante campaigns, it is apparent that by the middle of 1873 – with his advance troops by then only five miles from Cape Coast – Amankwatia had achieved a reoccupation of the British Protected Territory that was extraordinarily swift and well executed. Meanwhile, in Kumase, following the meeting of Akyampon Yaw's Court of Enquiry on 10 February 1873, Elmina delegates present in the capital had reaffirmed their loyalty to the government, and Akyampon Yaw took an oath to liberate their town. He left for the south almost immediately, authorized to raise forces in Schwi and Sanwi (Kwankye-abo) and to proceed, under the cover provided by the armies of reoccupation, to revive once again the administration for the southwest based upon Elmina.[145] He was reported to have died from wounds received when H.M.S. *Druid* bombarded Beyin on 16 October 1873.[146]

In early September 1873 the main Asante forces were reported to be in almost unassailable positions near Cape Coast, and to have planted old farms and areas of wasteland: 'food is abundant in their camp; of ammunition they have a plentiful supply; they are confident in the superior skill of their generals, their organization, discipline, and numbers'.[147] By the end of the month, however, there were rumours of dissension among the field commanders, when one of the provincial chiefs was reported to have refused to obey Amankwatia and to have decided to return to Kumase.[148] The growth of strong anti-war sentiment in Kumase in the second half of 1873, and the emergence once more of a peace party majority at the Council of 27 October in that year, will be discussed in detail below. By the beginning of November there were reports that morale among the Asante troops had fallen low, rumours of the state of political uncertainty in the capital having reached them. 'Discontent prevails, by all accounts', reported Boyle; 'the fighting men want to get home, to enjoy well-earned repose and the booty of their campaign.' [149] Nevertheless, as Boyle admitted in his despatches of 6 November from the advance British position at Abakrampa, in the engagements of that day

the Ashantees spread slowly but surely across our front and down either flank, until at the moment at which I write three parts of the ellipse round our

144 See, e.g. Brackenbury, 1874, I, chapter II, *passim;* Wood, 1874, pp. 4–13; Maurice, 1874, Chapters III–V, *passim.*
145 Ramseyer and Kühne, 1875, pp. 212–13.
146 See Claridge, 1915, II, 26; 79.
147 *The African Times,* XII, no. 148, 30 October 1873, pp. 190–1: letter dd. Cape Coast, 10 September 1873, from 'One of the Fanti Confederation'.
148 *Ibid.* letter dd. Cape Coast, 21 September 1873, by the same author.
149 Boyle, 1874, p. 64.

position are wrapped in smoke. Numbers even greater than we had thought must they have had to complete such an investment . . . I fear the scheme they have in view is utterly to harass us, to give us no rest day or night until exhaustion opens some gap. Unless help comes they may possibly succeed.[150]

But it was on that very day that messengers arrived at Amankwatia's camp with the orders from government to withdraw his troops. A council of field commanders was held in the evening, and arrangements made to begin falling back the following morning. Understandably perhaps, the Asante commander-in-chief got drunk and had to be carried back to his quarters! [151] While the British correspondents, unaware at the time of the decision of the Council in Kumase, initially described the Asante forces as 'in flight', they subsequently acknowledged that the withdrawal was carried out with the same precision as the reoccupation. 'The army of a civilised nation', conceded the military historian Brackenbury, 'need not have been ashamed of a retreat conducted with such skill and such success.' [152]

Kofi Kakari in 1873–4: the retreat from reality

It was paradoxical that at a time when the peace party had regained its ascendancy in the councils in Kumase, war interests still prevailed in those in London. With £800,000 granted him by Parliament, Major-General Sir Garnet Wolseley was actively putting together a large expeditionary force for an invasion of Asante. It was to include 2,500 soldiers of the Black Watch, Royal Welch Fusiliers, Rifle Brigade and Naval Brigade; 2,000 of the West India Regiments and the Sierra Leone and Nigeria colonial forces; and several thousand auxiliaries mobilized from within the British Protected Territory of the Gold Coast. The first columns left Cape Coast on 27 December 1873 and, marching northwards by Route VI, arrived at the Pra River on 2 January. In the circumstances the government in Kumase found itself beset by the same lack of decision that had characterized its policy towards the British for much of the century. As its requests to Wolseley to halt the offensive operations and negotiate a settlement were one after the other rejected, so the government came to realize that it had totally lost political initiative to the British. The indications are, that in the circumstances of acute crisis the Asantehene Kofi Kakari turned for advice away from both councillors and counselors, and increasingly to the religious authorities – including those natural allies in his struggle against the Europeans, the powerful Muslim notables of the

150 *Ibid.* pp. 80–1.
151 Brackenbury, 1874, I, 268–9.
152 *Ibid,* I, 302.

northern hinterlands. 'The Moorish necromancers and fetish priests', it could be remarked in 1874, 'continue to be the guiding spirits in Ashantee politics.' [153]

As early as February 1873, Kofi Kakari received advice from a Muslim whom he had sent into the interior 'to consult an oracle', that the Asante cause would only prosper if the European prisoners in Kumase were released.[154] That advice was ignored. In August a mission headed by a member of the *nsumankwaafo* or physicians arrived back in the capital from Dagomba ('Angwa'): it had been sent there 'to purchase a very strong medicine (aduru) which would destroy the people at the Coast', but had in obscure circumstances become involved in a fracas with the vendors.[155] The arrival in Salaga of another mission, presumably late in 1873, was reported in an anonymous Hausa manuscript from that town:

One day the king [of Asante] sent for Hausa malams, for ones that had been born in Hausa, not there [in Salaga]. The chief of Kpembe called together his people, and told them. The ward-head Labaran stood up, and asked the malams. They were all afraid, except Malam Ahmad Batunbuce [the Timbuktu], who agreed that he would go . . . They returned and reported to the chief that the Hausa were afraid, except for one malam. The chief said, 'Yes, go and give him a thousand [? head of cowries] . . . The malam prepared, and started off . . .[156]

On his way to Kumase Ahmad Batunbuce met refugees who informed him of Wolseley's attack upon the city, and he returned to Salaga. A later Arabic work, however, reported that at least one Hausa from Salaga did reach Kumase: 'war broke out between Kakari and the Christians. He sent to Salaga to request that a man of learning from among the Hausa should come to help him with prayers. Malam Binafi al-Hawsāwī went and stayed with him and made prayers for him. He died there . . .' [157] Again, early in December when news had reached Kumase of the build-up of British forces on the coast, Kofi Kakari gave to the Muslims in the town the sum of ten peredwans of gold (221/2 oz) 'for using sorcery to hinder the white men from rising',[158] while another sum of 100 oz of gold was expended in obtaining from the north 'a wonderful mohammedan charm, which with a mere shake of the hand was to have the effect of causing the governor [Wolseley] to go back'.[159]

[153] Maurice, 1874, p. 16.
[154] Ramseyer and Kühne, 1875, pp. 210–11.
[155] *Ibid*, pp. 231–2.
[156] 'Gottlob Adolf Krauses Haussa-Handschriften', xxxix, no. 24/35, in *Mitteilungen des Seminars für Orientalische Sprachen*, xxxi, Berlin, 1928.
[157] Al-Hājj 'Umar b. Abī Bakr, cited in Ahmad Bābā al-Wa'iz, 1950, pp. 84–6.
[158] Ramseyer and Kühne, 1875, p. 250.
[159] *Ibid*. p. 271. Steiner, 1896, pp. 90–1.

On 9 January 1874, when news had reached Kumase of Wolseley's arrival at the Pra, the government sent a trusted official, Owusu Koko Kuma, to negotiate the cessation of hostilities with the British commander, and one of the European prisoners, Kühne, was released as a token of goodwill. But also included in Owusu Koko Kuma's party of fifteen were a number of Muslims whose leader carried the 'wonderful mohammedan charm'.[160] In the event, Wolseley refused to meet with Owusu Koko Kuma,[161] who arrived back in the capital some days later. The Muslims, however, appear to have remained – with the charm – at the Kwisa control post on the metropolitan border. Their head was described by Boyle as 'the great prophet of this country . . . Suleiman'.[162] He was almost certainly the Dafin scholar Sulaymān Kunatay who, it is said, was asked 'to do for Kofi Kakari what Okomfo Anokye did for Osei Tutu',[163] and whose father, 'Ali b. Imam Siddīq, had been in the Asantehene's service in 1869 before leaving Kumase for Bonduku to continue his studies there.[164]

The British advance forces, Lord Gifford's scouts, reached the Adanse scarp below Kwisa on 16 January 1874, having met with no opposition to their advance on Kumase. The *nkwansrafo* or patrolmen from the Kwisa post regarded the scouts with some indifference, and explained that they had no authorization from the government to fight the British (see pp. 49–50). The only indication of the Asante attitude to the invasion came in fact from Sulaymān. According to Henty, 'a priest came forward, with five or six supporters, and warned them back, for that five thousand men were there ready to destroy them'.[165] According to Boyle, Sulaymān 'showed himself at top of the Adansi hill when Gifford was laboriously climbing up, and solemnly devoted us all to perdition'.[166] But Boyle also observed that other British troops found on the top of the hill several animal sacrifices and 'on a stick beside them was a *saphi*, or charm in Arabic, invoking the direst curses on the invaders if they should dare to pass the spot'.[167]

160 Ramseyer and Kühne, 1875, pp. 263–7, 271.
161 Brackenbury, 1874, II, 52–4.
162 Boyle, 1874, pp. 293–4.
163 Wilks, field-notes: interview with Imām Sa'īd b. 'Alī b. Sulaymān b. 'Alī Kunatay, dd. Nkenkaasu, 16 September 1968; interviews with al-Ḥājj Muḥammad Sofa dd. Wa, 16–18 April 1964. Institute of African Studies, Ghana, field-notes, J. J. Holden, The Samorian Impact on Buna and Bonduku, p. 48, miscellaneous notes dd. 2 August 1969. Sulaymān's father, 'Alī, was a student of Karamoko Muḥammad b. 'Uthmān of Jenene, whose son was the famous al-Ḥājj Ṣāliḥ who died in 1931, see Wilks, 1968, p. 170, n. 2.
164 See further, *Ta'rīkh al-Muslimīn fī balad Kankaso*, by al-Ḥājj 'Uthmān b. Isḥāq Boyo, privately printed, 1966, *passim*.
165 Henty, 1874, p. 341. Compare Ramseyer and Kühne, 1875, p. 291.
166 Boyle, 1874, pp. 293–4.
167 *Ibid.* p. 286.

The saphi (Twi *safi, sabe,* Dyula *sewe*) was presumably the 'wonderful charm' purchased by Kofi Kakari for 100 oz of gold. The text was translated by one of the Hausa soldiers in Wolseley's force, and proved to be a manifesto, in standard Muslim form, urging upon the British the desire of the Asante for peace:

This is a prayer to God, and a wish that the white men would fight among themselves, and return to their own country. May pestilence and disease seize them! The writer of this is the great High Priest, who invokes God to do these things. Europeans never possessed any land in this country, and all the angels of Heaven are invoked to drive them out. The writer of this paper received much money, and a promise of five slaves; and through the strength of charms his invocations will have effect.[168]

To the British, surprised at meeting with no effective opposition at the Adanse scarp, it appeared that 'the stupid Ashantees have given up without a blow'.[169] And certainly the manifesto did not deter the Major-General, confident in his military, if not moral, superiority. The manifesto, however, was of significance: it signalized the final attempt by Kofi Kakari to avoid violent and direct confrontation with the British. From Kwisa northwards, the expeditionary force was obliged to fight its way through to Kumase against what Brigadier-General Sir Archibald Alison, commander of the white troops, declared to be fiercer fighting than he had ever encountered in India or the Crimea.[170] Finally Wolseley entered and burned an empty capital, blew up the stone built Palace of Culture, and the next day began the long retreat to the coast.

In the aftermath of the campaign the Muslims were accused of having deceived the Asantehene by assuring him that they were allowing Wolseley's expedition to advance upon the capital in order that its provisions and goods should all fall into Asante hands. Owusu Koko Kuma, who had earlier been a trader in Cape Coast and had some insight into European modes of thought, was among the most vociferous of the critics of the Asantehene's Muslim entourage.[171] Yet for Asante the writing had long been on the wall. As early as 1817 the Gyaasewahene Opoku Frefre, himself no mean general, had observed that 'England was too fond of fighting, her soldiers were the same as dropping a stone in a pond, they go farther and farther'.[172] In 1874

[168] Dooner, 1874, p. 45.
[169] Boyle, 1874, p. 285.
[170] *Ibid.* p. 329.
[171] Brackenbury, 1874, II, 336–7. Clearly the reference is not to the exiled Akyempemhene Owusu Koko, but to Owusu Koko Kuma. For Owusu Koko Kuma, see for example, *Gold Coast, Part I*, C. 266, 1873, p. 160: Salmon to Hennessy, dd. Cape Coast, 19 October 1872, in which he is described as 'a relative of the present king'. See also Ramseyer and Kühne, 1875, p. 182. He was a son of the Saamanhene Akyampon Panin.
[172] Hutchison's diary, entry for 26 September 1817, in Bowdich, 1819, p. 381.

they had entered Kumase, the first foreign troops ever to do so. And although in military terms the operation was by no means a decisively successful one, in political terms one clear British objective had been attained: henceforth the Asante government recognized the old southern provinces as irretrievably lost. By a British Order in Council of 6 August 1874, they were constituted the Gold Coast Colony – Her Majesty Queen Victoria to 'hold exercise and enjoy any power or jurisdiction . . . in the same and as ample a manner as if Her Majesty had acquired such power or jurisdiction by the cession or conquest of territory'.[173]

[173] For the full text, see Metcalfe, 1964, pp. 368–9.

CHAPTER 7

Kumase and the northern provinces: an overview

Asante as savannah power

In the earlier nineteenth century among the major northern provinces of Greater Asante were Banda, Bron, Dagomba, Gonja, 'Guasoo', Gyaman, Nkoransa, Nsoko, and Takyiman. For the greater part of the century most were to retain some measure of association with Kumase. Thus, although the capital was within the forest zone, the greater part of the territory which it controlled, more so after the retrenchment in the south, lay in the grasslands. To that extent, there-fore, Asante has to be regarded as being a savannah rather than a forest power. It is the abundance of the evidence for the southern connections, and the comparative paucity of that for the northern, which has generated the stereotype of Asante as 'coastal kingdom' or 'forest state'.[1]

The northern frontiers of Greater Asante in the nineteenth century cannot be determined with precision, since adjunct territories are diffi-cult to distinguish from outer provinces. There can be no doubt, how-ever, that the northern hinterlands over which the government in Kumase exercised some measure of authority equalled or exceeded in area that of the metropolitan region and the southern provinces com-bined. It is virtually impossible to make even the most tentative estimate of the size of the population in the northern provinces in the nineteenth century. In 1819 Bowdich gave figures for the number of troops that could be mobilized from three of the northern inner provinces: Nkoransa, 10,000; Takyiman, 6,000; and Bron, 12,000.[2] The reliability of Bowdich's information is, moreover, in some degree supported by later references to the size of the Nkoransa fighting forces, which Dawson in 1873 reported as 6,000 men,[3] Hay in 1879 as 10,000,

---

1 For an early and inadequate attempt to challenge the stereotype, see Wilks, 1961, *passim*.
2 Bowdich, 1819, p. 317.
3 Brackenbury, 1874, II, 362.

and two sources of 1881 as 5,000 and 4,000.[4] In the campaigns on the Gold Coast in 1873, the Nkoransahene Ata Fa commanded 10,000 men.[5] Comparison with the figures for districts of the metropolitan region (Table 5, p. 87) and for various of the southern provinces (p. 126) suggests that no gross disparity in resources of manpower existed between these districts and at least the inner provinces of the north. The outer provinces of the north, by contrast, undoubtedly had much lower population densities. Indeed, large parts of Gonja were then, as now, almost uninhabited: hence, for example, the frequent allusion of Dupuis' Muslim informants to 'the Desert of Ghofan [Gbuipe]'.[6] Yet a number of urban centres did exist in the north in the nineteenth century. The Dagomba capital of Yendi, for which reliable figures are extant, had a fairly constant population of around 6,000 people,[7] and was thus comparable in size with the towns of the greater *amanhene* in the metropolitan region. The trading town of Salaga in eastern Gonja was much larger. Although its population fluctuated greatly, for part of the nineteenth century it enjoyed the distinction of being the largest town within Greater Asante. As early as 1820 Dupuis heard of it as being twice the size of Kumase – that is, presumably of the order of 40–50,000 people.[8] Before the government imposed an embargo upon kola supplies to the town in 1875, Bonnat had estimated its population as having been over 40,000.[9] Thereafter the town shrank in size, but in 1876 Bonnat considered it still to contain between 12,000 and 15,000 people.[10] In the same year Gouldsbury gave the population as 8,000; [11] in 1877 Opoku as 20,000; [12] and in 1882 Lonsdale as 10,000.[13]

In the eighteenth century the northwestern provinces, linked to Kumase by Routes I and II, possessed for the Asante government a strategic importance seemingly outweighing that of the northeasterly ones. The highly important market centre of Bighu (near Namasa, Route II, mile 117), which had been founded in the fifteenth century near to the still older town of Jorga, was settled by Malian Dyula traders attracted by the gold resources of the area. At the same time

4 *Affairs of the Gold Coast and threatened Ashanti Invasion,* C. 3064, 1881, p. 21.
5 Boyle, 1874, p. 146.
6 Dupuis, 1824, pp. xxxvi, cxxxi.
7 Barth, 1857–9, III, 645: population 5,000. *Further Correspondence,* C. 3386, 1882, p. 90, Lonsdale's itinerary of 1881–2: population 6,000. PRO, CO. 879/38, African (West) 448, p. 77, G. E. Ferguson to Governor, dd. 9 December 1892: population 6,320. For a consideration of this matter, see P. Ferguson, 1973, p. 308.
8 Dupuis, 1824, p. xl.
9 Bonnat, Salaga, in *The Liverpool Mercury,* 12 June 1876.
10 *Idem.*
11 PRO, CO. 96/119: Gouldsbury to Governor, dd. Accra, 27 March 1876.
12 Opoku, 1885, p. 306.
13 *Further Correspondence,* C. 3386, 1882, p. 90: Lonsdale's itinerary of 1881–2.

Malian artisan groups played an important role in the development of the gold mining industry. The region was known to the Dyula as Ton, that is, the country of the Akan.[14] The earliest Asante military activity in the region took place in the early eighteenth century. Osei Tutu's expedition against Ahwene Koko (or Old Wankyi) may be dated to *ca.* 1712,[15] and Opoku Ware's expedition against Takyiman to 1722/3.[16] The evidence suggests that the market of Bighu collapsed in the period, not apparently as a direct result of the Asante invasions but rather in consequence of a breakdown of town life, as conflict between the diverse ethnic groups represented there led to rioting and finally to urban warfare. Many of the Dyula traders re-established their businesses at other centres within the region, such as Banda and Bonduku: they were presumably the 'southern Manding tribes' who, according to Dupuis, had 'submitted to the yoke of vassalage, under the government of Ashantee, and were permitted to enjoy their inheritances peaceably . . .'.[17] It was through such Dyula centres that the great-roads system of Asante became tied into the important network of routes which linked together the many other Dyula towns beyond the frontiers of Greater Asante – Kong, Wa, Bobo-Dioulasso, Safane, and the like. Such trade as did come to Asante from the Central Sudanese towns of Hausaland and Bornu appears in the eighteenth century to have followed a traverse of its northern hinterland (see p. 14) to reach the markets of the northwest. Thus, for example, in the 1770s or early 1780s the Sharīf Imhammad, commercial agent to the ruler of the Fezzan, followed a route through Katsina, Nikki, Zugu, the Kotokoli country and Yendi (Route IV, mile 250) into central Gonja, whence he turned south to follow the great-road III towards Kumase, passing 'Keffee' (Gbuipe, mile 164) and 'Gondufee' (Gbonipe, mile 161) before finally turning back at 'Kalanshee' – probably Nkoransa (mile 68).[18]

The creation of a northern administration

Little is known of the early stages in the development of civilian administration in the northern provinces. In many places, however, the memory survived into this century of a system of resident commissioners apparently similar to that in the southern regions. The Imām Sa'īd b. Mālik Timitay of Bonduku (born *ca.* 1858) noted for example

14 Wilks, 1961, pp. 1–13; 1962, *passim;* 1971b, pp. 354–62.
15 Daaku, 1968, *passim;* Ozanne, 1966, *passim.*
16 See, e.g. *Tadhkira li 'l-Muta'akhirīn,* entry for 1135 A.H.
17 Dupuis, 1824, p. xxxvi.
18 Reported by Lucas, in *Proceedings of the Association for Promoting the Discovery of the Interior Parts of Africa,* 1791, pp. 329–32 and map facing p. 311.

of the Gyaman, that 'ever since their conquest by the Ashantis up to the time of our [the European] occupation they paid tribute in slaves and produce to Coomassie, and representatives of Ashanti, equivalent to our [European] consuls, used to reside in Bontuku and other Jaman centres to enforce Ashanti requests'.[19] There seems little doubt that in the northern as in the southern provinces, the main architect of the policies of pacification and incorporation was the Asantehene Osei Kwadwo. The example of Banda (or Banna, Route II, mile 145) may be taken as illustrative of these policies, and may be compared with the case study of Wassa in the southwest discussed fully above (Chapter 4, pp. 154–61).

Banda was a pluralistic society comprising a chiefly Nafana class and a Muslim Dyula trading class, both immigrant groups probably of the early eighteenth century; and various older 'autochthonous' communities. There are strong traditions that the association of the Banda with Asante dated back to the early eighteenth century.[20] Military occupation of the district, however, seems to have been carried out by the Dadiesoabahene of Kumase only in the reign of Osei Kwadwo, after information had been received of the murder of Asante traders there.[21] By report, the Bannahene blew himself up with gunpowder when it became apparent that the Asante forces could not be stopped. A settlement was concluded at Dadiase (or Banda Ahenkro), and the Muslim Dyula conducted the negotiations. By its terms, the Banda formally acknowledged Asante overlordship and agreed to pay an annual tribute in sheep.[22] To offset the costs of the expedition, many youths were taken captive to Kumase. There they were trained within the newly created Nkonson and Hiawu organizations.[23] Among the captives was a certain Abū Bakr Bamba from the Dyula community. Impressing Osei Kwadwo with his talents and devotion to

19 Fell, cited in Pitt, 1926, p. 74. See also National Archives of Ghana, Kumase, File D. 216: letter from T. E. Fell, dd. 15 July 1913.
20 See, e.g. Dupuis, 1824, p. 230. Institute of African Studies, Ghana, IAS/BA/1: Tradition of Banda, recorded by Kwabena Ameyaw, 20 November 1965, pp. 2–3.
21 IASAS/12: Dadiesoasba Stool History, recorded by J. Agyeman-Duah, 19 January 1963. See also Dupuis, 1824, pp. 240–1. The account of the Banda campaigns given by Bowdich, 1819, pp. 237–8 and 301, appears to be in error in confusing a number of distinct episodes. A short but useful description of the campaign is given in Reindorf, 2nd ed., n.d., pp. 131–2. The expedition is perhaps to be dated to 1765, see General State Archives, The Hague, KvG 126, Elmina Journal, entry for 16 July 1765, reporting that 'Zaay', that is, Osei Kwadwo, had marched three days journey beyond 'Benda'. On the other hand, Asante forces were heavily engaged in the south at that time, for which see Fynn, 1971, pp. 99–101, and the reference may not be to the northern town.
22 Institute of African Studies, Ghana, IAS/BA/1, p. 4.
23 Reindorf, 2nd ed., n.d., p. 131. For the two stools, see IASAS/47 and 97: Nkonson and Hiawu Stool Histories, recorded by J. Agyeman-Duah, 17 March and 10 October 1963.

Asante interests, he was freed and appointed a junior counselor. He was granted land near the capital and assigned duties of a religious nature there. He was also made resident commissioner of Banda, and thereafter travelled regularly between Kumase and the province. Abū Bakr Kyeame – as he became known – was succeeded in office by his son Limām Sa'īd Bamba, who also reputedly held his appointment from Osei Kwadwo; and by his grandson al-Ḥājj Muḥammad Bamba who died at a very advanced age in the reign of Asantehene Mensa Bonsu.[24]

Shortly after his accession Osei Kwadwo was faced also with a refusal by the Gyaman to pay tribute. The claim was made by the rebels that no booty had been received after a campaign in which they had fought during the reign of Kusi Obodom: presumably the expedition of 1759 led by an unidentified 'Ackoddom'.[25] Faced with simultaneous unrest in the southwestern provinces of Denkyira, Wassa and Twifo, Osei Kwadwo was able to reassert his authority in Gyaman only after armies despatched there had twice been repulsed. As in the case of Banda, the younger captives were 'preserved to recruit the losses his armies had sustained', and the adults were either killed or sent to the coast for sale.[26] The rebel Gyaman seem to have received support from the Gonja provinces of Gbuipe and Kong. Other districts, however, which were either contiguous to or part of Gyaman – the 'Shouy', 'Ghombati', and 'Ponin' of Dupuis' account [27] – apparently submitted voluntarily: 'The subjugation of Gaman at this time laid the Sarem [savannah] country prostrate at the feet of the conqueror, who penetrated Shouy, Ghombati, and Ponin, in a sort of *friendly* way to receive the submission of the southern and western tribes, and invite the Caboceers to court.' [28] It seems highly likely that the first resident commissioners in Gyaman, as in Banda, were appointed in this period.

Some account has been given above of the regularization of relations with Dagomba in the reign of Osei Kwadwo, and probably in or shortly after 1772 (see pp. 22–3). One version of Dagomba traditions, much corrupted in the transmission, suggests that negotiation of the settlement took place at Kpembe in eastern Gonja, and that the Ya Na was represented by the Wulana of Yendi (perhaps the Zohe Na, the senior eunuch functionary) and the Asantehene by one Akyampon.[29] While no account of the terms of the settlement is extant, the matter of tribute was presumably arranged (see p. 66). It may have been on

24 Wilks, field-notes: interview with al-Ḥājj Sa'īd b. al-Ḥājj Muḥammad Bamba, dd. Kumase, 22 July 1963.
25 General State Archives, The Hague, KvG 120: Elmina Journal, letter dd. Accra, 22 August 1759.
26 Dupuis, 1824, p. 241.
27 *Ibid.* p. lvi.
28 Dupuis, 1824, p. 242.
29 Fisch, 1913, p. 75.

this occasion, too, that the two parties concluded an agreement whereby the government in Kumase assumed responsibility for the reorganization and re-equipment of the Dagomba fighting forces. Creation of units of gunmen known as the Kambonse, literally 'Asantes', was the joint task of Dagomba bowmen who were sent to Kumase for training in musketry, and of Asante military personnel posted to the province.[30] To this day the Kambonse officers in Dagomba use Twi titles of office (Kyidom, Gyahefo, Asiedu, Tumfuo, etc.); on public occasions wear Asante dress; assume Twi personal day-names, Kofi, Kwadwo, Kwasi and the rest; and use as a mark of office the Asante *asipim* chair.[31]

According to traditions followed by Tamakloe, it was Osei Kwadwo who first stationed Asante officials in the Dagomba capital, Yendi.[32] They came to occupy a part of the town known as Kambonse-yili, 'Asante section'.[33] The earliest resident commissioner of whom record has been found was Akyampon Tia, brother of the Asantehene Kwaku Dua I and later Nkwantananhene of Kumase: occupant, that is, of the Boakye Yam Kuma stool. His posting to Yendi seemingly occurred in 1853.[34] Another officer of the central administration to be sent to Yendi, in the 1860s, was one Asamoa who was described as a son of the Asantehene in a Hausa report of the matter: *Sarki Santi ya aiko dansa sunansa Samuwa,* 'the Asantehene sent his son named Asamoa'.[35] In the last quarter of the nineteenth century the residency was held by Yaw Mensa. A son of Akyampon Tia's brother Akyampon Yaw, in this century Yaw Mensa also succeeded to the Boakye Yam Kuma stool in Kumase. It was probably one of Yaw Mensa's nephews, in turn, to whom the British District Commissioner in Yendi in 1916 made allusion: 'there lives today at Yendi an Ashanti, a visitor to his uncle there, who, before the advent of the Germans, acted as a kind of consul and tax-gatherer.'[36] The Asante residents worked closely with

30 For a useful account of the Kambonse, see National Archives of Ghana, Accra, ADM. 11/824: A. W. Davies, 'History and Organization of the Kambonse in Dagomba', 1948. Davies rightly associated the origins of the Kambonse with the reign of Ya Na 'Abdallāh (Gariba), but wrongly with that of Asantehene Kwaku Dua I.
31 See, e.g. Tait, 1955, pp. 194-5.
32 Tamakloe, 1931, p. 33.
33 Wilks and Ferguson, field-notes: interview with Imām al-Ḥājj 'Abdallāh b. al-Ḥājj al-Ḥasan (born *ca.* 1880), dd. Yendi, 8 September 1968.
34 NAG, Accra, ADM. 1/2/7: Fitzpatrick to Newcastle, dd. Cape Coast, 3 August 1853.
35 Institute of African Studies, Ghana, IASAR/22 (iv), *al-Khabar Zabarima,* compiled by Malam Isḥāq of Wa *ca.* 1923.
36 Wilks and Ferguson, field-notes: interviews with Kwaku Dua, al-Ḥājj Shehu 'Umar b. Haliru, and Opanin Domfe Kyere, dd. Kumase, 31 October and 22 and 23 November 1973. Cardinall, 1920, p. 9.

one of the eunuch officials in Yendi, the Balogo Na, who was responsible *inter alia* for seeing that the tribute was paid.[37] Other Asante officers may have supervised the affairs of the once important market of Gamaji on the outskirts of Yendi, where the long-distance traders conducted their business.[38] Among the Asante resident in Yendi were also members of the Kumase *adumfo* or executioners, for those condemned to death even in the court of the Ya Na had to be handed over to the Asantehene's representatives for the sentence to be carried out.[39] As Ya Na Andani observed in 1892, 'I am not an Ashanti King to rule my people with knife'.[40] The *adumfo* were themselves responsible to a senior functionary who held the title 'Kunkuma'.[41] He was named thus after one of the most important of all Asante *suman* or 'medicines',[42] one which had, so it was reported, a special use in swearing in 'the trusted messenger between chiefs who delivers his messages *oratio recta*, in the identical words in which they are spoken; the penalty for any perversion of the message [being] death by the fetish Kunkuma'.[43] Significantly, the Kunkuma in Yendi was responsible for communications between the central government in Kumase and the local Dagomba authorities. To this day the occupant of the office retains the function of intermediary between Ya Na and Asantehene, and looks after the affairs of Asante residents in, or visitors to, Yendi. The first occupant of the office of Kunkuma was reputedly a Dagomba commoner who was taken captive to Kumase after the expedition of 1772, found favour there with Osei Kwadwo, and served for several years in the administration in the capital before being posted back to Yendi as a representative of the central administration.[44]

The formulation of a northern policy

It is of considerable interest that the Muslim scholars in Kumase in the early nineteenth century looked back upon the policies of Osei

37 NAG, Accra, ADM. 67/1/2: minute re appointment of Balogo Na, 10 August 1925.
38 Phyllis Ferguson, field-notes: interview with Imām al-Ḥājj 'Abdallāh, dd. Yendi, 16 December 1969.
39 Ferguson, field-notes: interview with Malam al-Ḥasan b. Yidan Mole Muḥammad, dd. Yendi, 13 February 1970. Wilks, field-notes: interview with Imām al-Ḥājj 'Abdallāh, dd. Yendi, 8 September 1968.
40 PRO, CO. 879/38, African (West) 448: Ferguson to Governor, dd. 9 December 1892, p. 65.
41 Ferguson, field-notes: interview with Imām al-Ḥājj 'Abdallāh, dd. Yendi, 13 February 1970.
42 See, e.g. Rattray, 1927, pp. 12–14.
43 Davies, 1948, 'History and organization of the Kambonse in Dagomba', p. 5.
44 *Idem.*

Kwadwo in the north as having been too cautious, and regarded the period as one of lost opportunities. The Asante might have achieved domination in the northwest as far as the Bawle country beyond the Komoé River, so they argued, had not 'this scope of ambition exceeded the aim or the judgment of the monarch. . .'.[45] But the armies of Opoku Ware had pushed outwards the frontiers of Greater Asante to what were probably their effective limits granted the existing modes of communication. Osei Kwadwo's achievement lay rather in establishing a political administration in the northern provinces, and in thus creating there as in the south the beginnings of the transition from military to civil rule. Although the sub-imperial roles maintained in the north by at least two of the major *aman* of the metropolitan region, namely Dwaben and Mampon, were later to be seen by central government as dysfunctional with respect to the unity of the nation (see chapter 3, pp. 115–19), there is little to suggest that this was the case during the reign of Osei Kwadwo. Indeed, Osei Kwadwo might be seen as endeavouring to maintain a balance of power between the southern *aman* such as Bekwae and Kokofu, which were growing increasingly powerful with the expansion of the coastal trade, and the northern *aman* such as Mampon and Dwaben which had expanded far into the grasslands and which derived advantage from their access to the savannah markets. It was this balance, if such existed, which was disrupted with the accession to the Golden Stool of Osei Kwame.

Upon the death of Osei Kwadwo in 1777, the Oyoko-Bremanhene of Kumase, Nto Boroko, succeeded in mustering strong support for the enstoolment as Asantehene of the reigning Kokofuhene Kyei Kwame. Mobilizing men from the Bron districts, the Mamponhene Atakora Kwame marched upon the capital. He brought with him the young Osei Kwame, whom he enstooled as Asantehene after putting the Oyoko-Bremanhene to death.[46] Osei Kwame was a son of the former Mamponhene Safo Katanka, whose role in the pacification of eastern Gonja in the mid-eighteenth century has been discussed above (p. 21). Safo Katanka is said to have been much influenced by Islam. He created a special group of Muslims, who were subsequently attached to the Nsumankwaafo or physicians of Kumase, for his son's protection, and earned the epithet *Mampon Safo a wɔ kyere Nkramo amono*, 'Safo of Mampon who takes Muslims alive' (that is, who does

---

45 Dupuis, 1824, pp. 242–3, where Dupuis misinterpreted references to 'Bahooree', that is, to the Bawle, as being to the sea, Arabic *bahr*.

46 J. Agyeman-Duah, field-notes: interview with Afua Sapon, former Mamponhemaa, dd. 29 September 1962. See also Kyerematen, 1966, p. 328.

not kill them).[47] Had Osei Kwame not been so young (see Chapter 9), he might have succeeded in pursuing revolutionary policies which would have left Asante a savannah power with a strong commitment to Islam. But the overthrow of Osei Kwame's sponsor Atakora Kwame occurred shortly after his accession, and greatly weakened the new Asantehene's position. The Asantehemaa Konadu Yaadom – known as a woman of 'violent passions, and great ambition'[48] – emerged as the *éminence grise* of Asante politics in the period. In Mampon, moreover, Owusu Sekyere Panin who had seized power from Atakora Kwame was raising rebellion against Osei Kwame, and had established a distant base in the Nchumuru country (see p. 116).[49] News of an expedition against Owusu Sekyere Panin, which the Ankasehene Yamoa Ponko was appointed to lead, had reached the British on the Gold Coast in somewhat garbled form by 1780. Governor Roberts understandably expressed some doubts about the nature of the situation in Asante:

We can get no perfect Account of the State of the Ashantee Kingdom, the present King being a Minor; as far as we can learn, he is governed entirely by his Mother, which has thrown that once populous and powerful Country into great Disorder, so as to weaken it very much; besides, the Duncoes [in this context, 'northerners'], a powerful People, have revolted and are at War with the Ashantees.[50]

The complex politics of the period will be discussed more fully in Chapter 9. As Osei Kwame matured, however, so he began to move his adherents into positions of power. One of the earliest demonstrations of his growing control over the political machine was his confrontation with the Kumase Adontehene Amankwa Osei, who had apparently controlled fiscal policy during the early part of the reign. Bringing accusations of embezzlement against him, Osei Kwame imposed upon him a heavy fine and took four of his villages – Eseso, Ehwia, Abira and Adugyanma – in settlement of the debt.[51] Subsequently Amankwa Osei was removed from office and his family deprived of all rights to

---

47 Institute of African Studies, Ghana, IASAS/22: Nsumankwa Stool History, recorded by J. Agyeman-Duah, 26 October 1962. Wilks, field-notes: interview dd. Kumase, 26 October 1962. Both accounts were received from the nonagenarian Domfe Kyere of the Nsumankwaa stool.
48 Bowdich, 1819, p. 239.
49 See, e.g. Reindorf, 2nd ed., n.d., p. 134. Rattray, 1929, p. 239.
50 PRO, T. 70/32: Roberts *et al.* to Committee, dd. Cape Coast, 8 October 1780. T. 70/33: Roberts *et al.* to Committee, dd. Cape Coast, 3 February 1781.
51 These villages were later attached to the new Atipin Stool which Osei Kwame created for his eldest son Owusu Ansa, see Institute of African Studies, Ghana, IASAS/9: Atipin Stool History, recorded by J. Agyeman-Duah, 28 October 1962. See further, Kumase Divisional Council Archives, Manhyia: Agyeman Badu v. Kwaku Mensa, case commencing 16 November 1964.

the Adonten stool. It was awarded instead to Kwaaten Pete. A son of the Nsutahene Oduro Panin,[52] Kwaaten Pete had earlier served in Osei Kwadwo's administration as the Adusei Atwenewa counselor, and had been entrusted with the arrest of the Ya Na of Dagomba in 1772 (see p. 22).[53] There are strong indications in the documents that Kwaaten Pete was among those committed to the prosecution of a vigorous northern policy. Certainly the reformed Adonten stool was assigned special responsibilities there: its occupant in the 1810s, Owusu Nkwantabisa, was reported to have been overseer of the affairs of Daboya in central Gonja.[54]

As Osei Kwame thus consolidated his power, so opposition became increasingly violent. Among those to rebel against him was Esom Adu, then in charge of the Exchequer. He was apparently shot, probably in or about 1790, and Opoku Frefre was appointed to take over his functions.[55] In the later 1790s the struggle for power in Kumase assumed major proportions, and the Asantehemaa Konadu Yaadom was reported 'to have mustered a strong party against him [Osei Kwame]'.[56] In 1797 the young Opoku Kwame died. Son of Konadu Yaadom, he had been placed upon the Akyempem stool of Akyeremade as heir apparent by Osei Kwadwo, but, being only about nine years of age in 1777, his candidacy had not been considered by the electors in Kumase.[57] Although Osei Kwame notified both the British and Danish Governors of the loss and received presents and condolences from them,[58] he was accused by Konadu Yaadom of having poisoned Opoku Kwame. The death at about the same time of Poku Amankwa, whose identity has not been satisfactorily established, was also attributed to Osei Kwame.[59] After an attempt was made on her life, Konadu Yaadom fled the capital. She took with her the new heir apparent

52 See, e.g. Rattray, 1929, p. 259. According to Rattray, 1929, Figure 67, Kwaaten Pete had also married the Mamponhemaa Abena Saka after the death of her first husband, the Dwabenhene Osei Hwidie.
53 Kumase Divisional Council Records, Manhyia, Kumase: Court Record Book commencing 4 April 1935, pp. 227 ff., constitutional case, Adonten Stool. Reports that Kwaaten Pete had been already appointed Adontenhene by Osei Kwadwo, and that it was Kwaaten Pete who was disgraced by Osei Kwame (see, e.g. Fuller, 1921, pp. 36–7) seem to be in error.
54 Bowdich, 1819, pp. 235–6.
55 Personal communication from A. C. Dente, October 1973.
56 National Archives, Copenhagen, Guinea Journal, 1798, no. 365: report by Governor Wriesberg, dd. Christiansborg, 6 November 1797.
57 Wilks, field-notes: interview with Asantehene Nana Sir Osei Agyeman Prempeh II, dd. Kumase, 12 November 1962. See also Asante Collective Biography Project: Opoku Kwame.
58 General State Archives, The Hague, KvG 15: Minutes of Council, dd. Elmina, 24 February 1798.
59 National Archives, Copenhagen, report by Governor Wriesberg, dd. 6 November 1797.

Opoku Fofie, the junior full brother of Opoku Kwame.[60] After a coup in Kumase, as a result of which Osei Kwame was placed under house-arrest and a number of his supporters were executed, Konadu Yaadom and Opoku Fofie returned there. They made a bid for popular support by proposing a series of liberal measures which included, apparently, the substitution of transportation for life (by sale at the coast) for the death penalty over a wide range of offences, and the imposition of a number of other curbs upon the Asantehene's powers.[61] In circumstances the details of which are not clear, Osei Kwame left the capital and took refuge in Dwaben. There he is reported to have formed an attachment, incestuous under Asante law, with Agyeiwaa Badu ('Gyawa'), a sister of the later Dwabenhemaa Ama Sewaa.[62] When Osei Kwame failed to reappear in Kumase for the Odwira of 1798, the Anantahene of Kumase Apea Dankwa presided over his removal from office. He was banished to a village with a few wives and slaves, and Konadu Yaadom successfully promoted the candidature of Opoku Fofie for the vacant office.[63] Some of the charges brought against Osei Kwame were documented by Dupuis, who reported that

the origin [of his deposition] was his attachment to the Moslems, and, as it is said, his inclination to establish the Korannic law for the civil code of the empire. Sai Koamina [Osei Kwame], according to the Bashaw [Imám Muḥammad al-Ghamba'], was a believer at heart; but the safety of his throne would not allow him to avow his sentiments. His name is handed to posterity as the most merciful of the race of kings. Towards the close of his reign, he prohibited many festivals at which it was usual to spill the blood of victims devoted to the customs; yet he could not be prevailed upon to relinquish the barbarous practice of watering the graves of his ancestors with human gore. These and other innovations were of a tendency to alarm the great captains; they feared, it is said, that the Moslem religion, which they well know levels all ranks and orders of men, and places them at the arbitrary discretion of the sovereign, might be introduced, whereby they would lose that ascendancy they now enjoy. To anticipate the calamity they dreaded, a conspiracy was entered into, and he was deposed.[64]

60 National Archives, Copenhagen, Guinea Journal, 1799, No. 15: report by Wriesberg, dd. Elmina, 14 December 1798, and despatch of the same date. See also Wriesberg's report of 6 November 1797. For a recent consideration of the destoolment of Osei Kwame, see Fynn, 1971, pp. 137–8.

61 *Idem.*

62 Bowdich, 1819, p. 239. Reindorf, 2nd ed., n.d., p. 134. Rattray, 1929, fig. 31 facing p. 196. According to Bowdich, 1819, p. 281, Osei Kwame took with him to Dwaben the Golden Stool. There are extant traditions, however, which suggest that the Golden Stool may have been buried near Bantama during the troubles of 1798, and that its whereabouts were for a time uncertain.

63 Bowdich, 1819, pp. 238–9.

64 Dupuis, 1824, p. 245.

The belief that one Asantehene had become a Muslim was still current in Kumase around 1870.[65]

That Osei Kwame was strongly inclined towards Islam, and was architect in the tradition of his father of innovative policies towards the northern hinterlands, may explain why his deposition in 1798 was followed by uprisings in the northwest intended to achieve his restoration to power.[66] The lead was taken by the Gyaman,[67] supported by Kong – though whether in this case the Gonja division or Watara state of that name is not clear. The provinces of Banda, Takyiman and Nkoransa remained loyal to the new Asantehene, Opoku Fofie. The rebel forces were allowed to extend themselves over the grasslands north of Sekyedumase (Route III, mile 46), but were thrown back with great slaughter at the battle of 'Barbanou' – presumably Boaben (Route III, mile 78).[68] Among the prisoners were over five thousand Muslims who, although taken in an act of rebellion, were treated charitably: none was executed or sold into slavery, but many either bought their own freedom or were ransomed by their co-religionists. Others were liberated probably in or about 1808 when the government decreed the release and repatriation of all Muslim captives in Asante.[69] It is unclear whether the Gyamanhene Bina Kombi was slain in the campaign, but his nephew and heir apparent took refuge in Gbuipe. Adinkra, from a rival segment of the Gyaman ruling class – and at the time known for his support of Opoku Fofie – was confirmed as Bina Kombi's successor.[70] While thus leaving the central authority in Gyaman intact, a decision which was later regarded as a sign of weakness, the government appointed residents ('magistrates') in a number of the minor towns.[71]

The campaigns had lasted for fifteen months,[72] and Opoku Fofie died shortly afterwards, having reigned for under two years.[73] Rumours were extant that his death had been in some way brought about by

[65] Bonnat, in Gros, 1884, p. 169.

[66] Dupuis, 1824, p. 245.

[67] The Gyaman were apparently in rebellion by 1799, see *Royal Gold Coast Gazette*, 27 May 1823.

[68] Dupuis, 1824, pp. 245–6.

[69] *Ibid*. pp. 246–7. For the decree, see p. 263 below.

[70] Dupuis, 1824, p. 249. See also G. A. Robertson, 1819, p. 177, who described Adinkra as a relative of the Asantehene. It is not impossible that the two houses were linked by marriage.

[71] *Royal Gold Coast Gazette*, 27 May 1823.

[72] Dupuis, 1824, p. 245.

[73] *Ibid*. p. 245 and note. Bowdich, 1819,, p. 240, maintained that Opoku Fofie lived only a few weeks 'after being elevated to the stool'. Bowdich may have been in error, but it seems likely that Opoku Fofie was only formally enstooled on the Golden Stool after the campaigns.

Osei Kwame.[74] Upon the news reaching the north, renewed outbreaks of fighting occurred there. On this occasion the lead was taken by the Gbuipewura, presumably strongly supported by the Gyaman refugees in his town. His forces attacked and occupied Banda, and prepared to move against Nkoransa. The Nkoransahene Guakro Fa, in an attempt to protect his territory, marched out to meet the invaders, and was slain in the fighting.[75] The purpose of the rebels must be presumed again to have been to restore Osei Kwame to office. In fact, however, in 1800 (or perhaps 1801) the electors in Kumase chose as Asantehene another half-brother of Opoku Kwame and Opoku Fofie: Osei Bonsu. He was enstooled as Osei Tutu Kwame.[76]

Osei Bonsu immediately appointed the Bantamahene Amankwatia to command of a new army, and a heavy defeat was inflicted upon the rebel forces at Kaka (Route III, mile 116). The Gbuipewura was taken prisoner, and either died or was executed in the Asante camp.[77] At about the same time the Gyamanhene Adinkra launched an attack upon Buna, whose ruler had supported the Gbuipewura and had slain one of the Gyaman district heads. After an indecisive engagement near Bole, Adinkra defeated the Buna forces at Anwiego some six miles south of that town, and the Bunamansa was slain.[78] It was perhaps while Adinkra's troops were thus occupied that what Dupuis called 'a partial revolt of the people' – the opponents of Adinkra – occurred in Gyaman. 'Availing themselves', he reported,

of an opportunity which they deemed favourable, [they] transferred their allegiance from the reigning prince, a tool of the court of Coomassy, to the nephew of their late monarch, who had sought protection of the sultan of Ghofan [Gbuipe], the prince who lost his life on the desert confines in the prosecution of his plan for subverting the government of Ashantee.[79]

The attempted coup, however, failed, and with it all resistance to the new regime of Osei Bonsu ended. 'These commotions', Dupuis was able to add,

74 Dupuis, 1824, p. 245.
75 *Ibid.* p. 248. See also the evidence of Abū Bakr al-Ṣiddīq, in Wilks, 1967b, pp. 160–1.
76 The accession date given by Dupuis, 1824, p. 247, of 1215 AH, that is, between 25 May 1800 and 13 May 1801, is compatible with all other evidence, and may be accepted.
77 Dupuis, 1824, p. 248.
78 Tauxier, 1921, p. 102. A contemporary account of the campaign is provided by Abū Bakr al-Ṣiddīq of Timbuktu, who was taken prisoner at Buna, see Wilks, 1967b, pp. 160–2. An inferior text suggests that Adinkra was fighting the Nkoransa but this seems clearly in error and is not found in the preferred version. For a discussion of this point, and of the campaigns in general, see Goody, 1965, pp. 29–35, and Wilks, 1961, pp. 22–4.
79 Dupuis, 1824, p. 249.

were . . . quickly suppressed, and the vigour of the Ashantee councils (which, as the king says, never slumber) gained the nation a more exalted character than it, perhaps, ever enjoyed before. A profound peace of five years duration subsequently fixed that character abroad, and created a flattering belief in other powers, that at length the empire was controuled by more moderate principles. What greatly contributed to the national satisfaction was the arrival of ambassadors at Coomassy from Abomey, Salgha, and Yendy, bearing honourable presents, and congratulatory messages to the young Sai . . .[80]

The five years' peace was clearly measured from the time of the battle of Kaka, probably in 1801, to the outbreak of the Assin and Fante troubles in 1806 (see p. 145). It was a period in which the deposed Osei Kwame approached Osei Bonsu privately, suggested 'several schemes of conquest', advised him to distrust the very people who had brought about his own deposition, and requested death. He was executed, with all the ceremony and privileges due to a royal, by strangulation,[81] and envoys arrived in Accra in February 1804 to notify the Dutch of the event and to confirm Osei Bonsu's accession.[82] Paradoxically, once secure in power the new Asantehene pursued with vigour a northern policy directly continuous with that the foundations of which had been laid by Osei Kwadwo, and the fuller development of which had been pursued by Osei Kwame. Thereby Osei Bonsu opened for his successors the option of following, *vis-à-vis* the disturbed southern provinces, a policy of retrenchment. For whatever reasons, moreover, Osei Bonsu felt able in pursuit of his goals in the north, overtly to associate himself with Muslim interests with a degree of freedom that had seemingly been unattainable by his predecessor Osei Kwame.

The Muslims in Kumase under Osei Bonsu

Under Osei Bonsu the Muslims came to exercise – as 'traders and courtiers'[83] – an influence in the cultural and political affairs of the capital quite incommensurate with their numbers.[84] Thus Bowdich wrote of 'the Moorish chiefs and dignitaries by whom the King is surrounded, whose influence is powerful, not only from their rank but

[80] *Idem.*

[81] Bowdich, 1819, pp. 239–40.

[82] General State Archives, The Hague, KvG 192 and Amerikaansche Raad 119: Elmina Journal, letter from Linthorst, Accra, entered under 19 February 1804.

[83] Dupuis, 1824, p. cxxix, note.

[84] In the 1810s the Muslim community in Kumase probably approximated to 1,000 persons, see Wilks, 1966a, pp. 318–19. The suggestion in Wilks, 1961, p. 24, that Osei Bonsu had commenced his reign with a persecution of the Muslims, was in error, and rested upon a misreading of the sources.

their repute';[85] and Dupuis was led to observe that 'the character of true believers . . . stood very high with the king, for he consulted them upon many important occasions, where the interests of the nation were concerned; and moreover, he never engaged in any warlike enterprize without their society'.[86]

Osei Bonsu came to be regarded by the Muslims as 'a friend on whom they could always rely for protection'.[87] In correspondence the Imām Mālik of Gbuipe, for example, addressed the Asantehene as 'the honest king, the Saviour of the Muslims' and as 'sympathizer with the Muslims, fearing no-one but Allāh',[88] while Ṣūma b. Muḥammad Bābā (Bamba) of Kumase described himself as *ḥabīb Saī*, 'friend of Osei'.[89] Proselytization was permitted, and believers gained merit by adopting non-Muslims, including Asante, into their households – each according to his means – and raising them in the faith.[90] While only a limited number of conversions were achieved by such means, in its magico-religious aspects Islam began to make a growing impact upon all levels of Asante society. The market for protective amulets was seemingly an inexhaustible one:

When a charm was applied for, one of the oldest [of the pupils] wrote the body of it, and gave it Baba [Imām Muḥammad al-Ghamba'], who added a sort of cabalistic mark, and gave it a mysterious fold; the credulous native snatched it eagerly as it was held out to him, paid the gold, and hurried away to enclose it in the richest case he could afford.[91]

Such amulets were especially valued for the protection which they afforded the Asante soldier (and indeed, a war-gown adorned with many such amulets, each consisting of several tightly folded layers of paper, a cotton binding, and an envelope of leather or metal, undoubtedly did deflect shot).[92] Torrane noted at the time of Osei Bonsu's appearance on the Gold Coast in 1807, that 'he is attended with many Moors and every Ashantee man has a Gregory, or Fitisch, which is a little square cloth inclosing some little sentences of the Alcoran; some have many'.[93] A six-line amulet might cost almost half an ounce of gold, so that, as Bowdich commented, 'a sheet of paper would support an inferior Moor in Coomassie for a month'.[94] 'A few lines written by

[85] Bowdich, 1819, p. 53.
[86] Dupuis, 1824, p. 98. Compare Hutton, 1821, p. 323.
[87] Dupuis, 1824, pp. 97; 99.
[88] Royal Library, Copenhagen, *Cod. Arab. CCCII*, I, ff. 146; 188.
[89] Dupuis, 1824, p. cxxv.
[90] *Ibid.* pp. 98, 107, and 163.
[91] Bowdich, 1819, p. 90. Compare Dupuis, 1824, p. xi.
[92] See e.g. Kyerematen, 1964, p. 31.
[93] PRO, T. 70/35: Governor Torrane to Committee, dd. Cape Coast, 20 July 1807.
[94] Bowdich, 1819, p. 272.

Baba', Hutton observed, 'is believed to possess the power of turning aside the balls of the enemy in battle, and is purchased at an enormous price; writing paper is consequently very valuable at Ashantee.' [95] For a complete amulet-covered war-gown obtained from Dagomba for the Gyaasewahene Opoku Frefre, Osei Bonsu was reported to have paid thirty slaves, and for one for the Adumhene Adum Ata, twenty.[96] Correspondence is extant between the Kamshe Na, senior Muslim functionary in Dagomba, and Imām Muḥammad al-Ghamba' in Kumase, concerning the supply of such amulets to the Asantehene.[97]

Recognition of the efficacy of Islamic protective medicine – albeit at a socio-psychological level – was complemented by a rising consciousness of the utility of prayer. 'The Ashantees', reported Bowdich, 'believe that the constant prayers of the Moors . . . invigorate themselves, and gradually waste the spirit and strength of their enemies.' [98] The significance of the Qur'ān, if the evidence of Dupuis is to be accepted, also became widely recognized: 'The Ashantees without knowing the content of the Koran, are equally persuaded that it is a volume of divine creation, and consequently that it contains ordinances and prohibitions, which are most congenial to the happiness of mankind in general.' [99] The situation was summed up, curiously yet revealingly, by the Muslims in the capital: 'the king', they maintained, 'and all his idolatrous subjects believed in it [the Qur'ān] too'.[100] And there were, indeed, many indications in Osei Bonsu's overt behaviour of his leanings towards Islam: in, for example, his use on occasion of Arabic salutations,[101] in the Islamic talismans hanging in his bed-chamber,[102] and in his appearance in public from time to time in a cloth 'studded all over with Arabic writing in various coloured inks'.[103] From Sharīf Ibrāhīm al-Barnawī the Ashantehene obtained a particularly fine copy of the Qur'ān, 'that when any trouble came he might hold it up to God, and beg his mercy and pardon'.[104] The Qur'ān, he was reported as saying, 'is strong, and I like it because it is the book of the great God; it does good for me, and therefore I love all the people that read it' (whereupon, so Dupuis observed, 'the Moslems instantly prostrated themselves, and prayed aloud: the king

95 Hutton, 1821, p. 323.
96 Bowdich, 1819, p. 271. Dupuis, 1824, p. 173.
97 *Cod. Arab. CCCII*, I, f. 107.
98 Bowdich, 1819, p. 272.
99 Dupuis, 1824, p. 247, note.
100 *Ibid*, p. 180.
101 *Ibid*. p. 109.
102 Bowdich, 1819, p. 308.
103 Dupuis, 1824, p. 142.
104 Hutchinson's Diary, entry for 20 November 1817, in Bowdich, 1819, p. 398.

too extended his arms, looking upwards as if to receive a blessing').[105] When Sharīf Ibrāhīm left Kumase at the head of a Meccan caravan, he was reportedly 'entrusted with offering to the *manes* of the Prophet special gifts which the king and chiefs had given him'.[106]

Although Osei Bonsu maintained a syncretic position and never relinquished his attachment to the older cults,[107] his attitude was considered by the Kumase Muslims as conferring considerable merit upon him. Since he would 'sometimes give ear to the law, (of Mohammad)' they argued: 'a misguided infidel, he was yet superior by far, to many other sovereigns, and particularly to the king of Dahomy, his eastern neighbour, who was an infidel of infidels (Kaffar ben al Koufar)'.[108] Aware of the doctrinal problems involved in serving a pagan ruler,[109] Muslims in the reign of Osei Bonsu did nevertheless assume positions of importance in the service of the Asante nation. Thus, for example, when Osei Bonsu convened an *ad hoc* council near Anomabo on 25 June 1807 to negotiate with the British Governor Torrane, prominent among those assembled was a Muslim Hausa chief:

The governor was obliged to visit each man of rank, before he could be received by the king . . . Every one of them was seated under a huge umbrella, surrounded by attendants and guards . . . One of these men and his attendants excited some curiosity and attention: his dress and appearance were so different from those of the others, that it evidently proved, he must have come from countries situated a considerable distance inland. He was a tall, athletic, and rather corpulent man, of a complexion resembling an Arab, or an Egyptian . . . He was a follower of the Mohammedan religion, possessed much gravity; but was communicative, condescending, and agreeable. He had about him a great number of sentences from the Alkoran, which were carefully incased in gold and silver, and upon which he set a high value. He was a native of Kassina . . . He said, he had been at Tunis, and at Mecca; had seen many White men and ships; and described the method of travelling over the great desert. This person commanded a body of men, who fought with arrows, as well as muskets . . . He had many persons in his train, who were of the same colour, but varied a little as to dress: they were all habited in the Turkish manner, but did not wear turbans.[110]

Of seventeen leading members of the Kumase Muslim community a decade later, it was noted that many 'enjoyed rank at court, or were

105 Dupuis, 1824, p. 161.
106 Ainé, 1857, p. 27, using an unidentified work of Dupuis. Compare Rattray, 1923, p. 227, note. For a further consideration of the Muslim community in Kumase in the period, see Wilks, 1966a, *passim*, on which this section is based.
107 See e.g. Dupuis, 1824, pp. x–xi. Hutchison's Diary, entries for 2 and 8 November 1817, in Bowdich, 1819, pp. 393–4.
108 Dupuis, 1824, pp. 97–8.
109 Wilks, 1966a, pp. 322–6.
110 Meredith, 1812, pp. 157–8.

invested with administrative powers, entitling them even to a voice in the senate'.[111] Certainly 'Moorish dignitaries' attended the session of the National Assembly on 22 September 1817, at which the new treaty with the British was made law.[112] In the negotiations of the treaty revisions three years later, Imām Muḥammad al-Ghamba' and his associates Muḥammad Kamagatay and Abū Bakr Turay played an important role, working under the direction of the senior counselor Kwadwo Adusei Kyakya.[113] The Imām, Muḥammad Kamagatay and Ṣūma b. Muḥammad Bābā were also among those closely associated with Adusei Kyakya in his defence of the Denkyirahene Kwadwo Tsibu (see p. 171).[114] The Imām described himself as 'a member of the king's council in affairs relating to the believers of Sarem and Dagomba'.[115] He and Abū Bakr appear to have had special responsibility for the affairs of the eastern Gonja districts and perhaps of Dagomba along Route IV, and Muḥammad Kamagatay and Ṣūma for the central and western Gonja districts along Routes II and III.[116] Similarly Jalāl b. Qudsī al-Burumī, 'the Bron', was probably concerned with the districts along Route IV(a).[117] Other important Muslim functionaries involved in the northern administration, however, were resident in the provincial towns. Thus Dupuis reported the arrival at court in 1820 of 'a deputation of the Moslems of Bouromy [Bron] and the Volta, headed by their Caboceer (an Arab by extraction)',[118] and at the town of 'Kherabi' two journeys south of Bonduku on Route I resided another functionary – 'head bashaw of the believers' who, it was reported, 'governs, for the king, the Moslems of the north-west'.[119] Although after 1826 the Asante government was to pursue a policy of retrenchment with respect to its southern dependencies, as late as 1820 Osei Bonsu could still regard the situation there with considerable optimism. 'What have you to fear?' Kwadwo Adusei Kyakya asked him:

The great God of the Moslems, who is the same as the white men worship, is your guardian. He defends your dominions on the land side, where the believers live; and he protects you on the sea coast, for he gives you a great name in the land of white men, and turns their king's heart to do you good. 'Yes,' answered the sovereign, spreading out his hands and looking up towards

111 Dupuis, 1824, p. 95.
112 Bowdich, 1819, p. 146.
113 Dupuis, 1824, pp. 147–8; 152–3.
114 Reindorf, 2nd ed., n.d., p. 182.
115 Dupuis, 1824, p. 97.
116 *Ibid.* p. 170.
117 *Ibid.* pp. 170–1.
118 *Ibid.* p. 95.
119 *Ibid.* p. lviii.

heaven, as the Moslems do in prayer, 'I am a thankful slave of the God of all gods and men – I am not ungrateful, I am not proud and ignorant' . . .[120]

In fact, however, the very option of retrenchment in the south had been created for the Asante government by the success with which its interests in the northern hinterland had been consolidated under Osei Bosu.

The expansion of the northern trade

In the aftermath of the battle of Kaka in 1801, the government took measures to strengthen its control over what the Muslims called the steppes (*saḥrā*),[121] that is, the empty plains of western and central Gonja. 'This defeat', Dupuis reported, 'led to the occupation of a considerable territory, bordering the desert, which, heretofore, belonged by a sort of feudal, yet a limited title, to the Ashantee monarchy; although, in reality, its inhabitants enjoyed a state of comparative independence.' [122] While the nature of the changes effected at this time are not reported, it is clear that such Gonja divisions as Gbuipe, Bole and Daboya retained their outer provincial status. Indeed, it was probably not until in or about 1844 that resident civilian administrators were first stationed in them. The maintenance of control over so sparsely populated a region was not in itself a matter of great consequence, but for the fact that in the eighteenth century the major outlet for the Asante trade northwards – the market of Gbuipe – was located in it; and, as Lonsdale was to comment later: 'the Ashantis must have a market to the north where they could buy sheep, cattle, and cloth, and to which they could bring the kola nut'.[123] The market of Gbuipe was of sufficient importance for the town to be shown on European maps of the first quarter of the eighteenth century,[124] and certainly in a later part of the century traders were visiting it from as far away as the Fezzan (p. 245). It may be supported that the Asante trade was first directed to it after the military occupation of the region in 1732/3. However that may be, all sources indicate that in the early nineteenth century the government took the decision to divert the

---

120 Dupuis, 1824, p. 248.

121 *Ibid.* Arabic route-book, p. cxxxi.

122 *Ibid.* p. 249.

123 *Further Correspondence*, C. 3386, 1882, p. 72: Lonsdale's report on his mission, 1881–2.

124 See Guillaume de l'Isle, *Carte d'Afrique Dressée pour l'usage du Roy*, Paris, 1722, which shows Gonja ('Gonge') and the three Gonja towns of Gbuipe ('Goaffy'), Tuluwe ('Teloué'), and Kafaba ('Caffaba'). The later map by d'Anville shows the same three towns correctly located along the Black Volta river, although this was believed to be a tributary of the Senegal, see Jean Baptiste Bourguignon d'Anville, *Afrique publiée sous les auspices de Monseigneur le Duc d'Orléans Prémier Prince du Sang*, Paris, 1749.

Asante trade away from the Gbuipe market, and to the newer centre of Salaga in the easterly Kpembe division of Gonja.

An account of the development of Salaga, the *Qiṣṣat Salgha* written at the very end of the nineteenth century by Maḥmūd b. 'Abdallāh of that town, recorded that 'an Arab from Hausaland' built the first market there. 'And thereupon', the writer commented, 'the market of Ghūfī [Gbuipe] was removed to Salgha after they had held it in the town of 'Umfaha [Mpaha] for a short time.' [125] The present day Gonja view of the matter is essentially similar. 'The Asante used Gbuipe as a slave market', the Wasipewura of Daboya maintained; 'when the Asante destroyed Gbuipe . . . it was then that Salaga became strong.' [126] Some indication of the date of these events was given by the author of the *Qiṣṣat Salgha*. After the relocation of the market, so he noted, an important *shaykh* from Katsina, one Malam Cediya, arrived in Salaga and built the first mosque there. A flood of immigrants followed, so that Salaga became 'a town with a population of many races (*ajnās*)'.[127] Probably from Malam Cediya's great-grandson, who was resident in Salaga when the *Qiṣṣat* was compiled, its author learned that the *shaykh*'s arrival in Salaga followed *al-ḥarb fī balad Kashina,* 'the war in the country of Katsina'. It seems likely that the reference is to the jiḥad in Katsina which terminated with the fall of the city in 1807, as a result of which many of its prominent citizens fled and settled elsewhere.[128] The evidence, then, indicates that the transference of the Asante trade from Gbuipe to Salaga most likely occurred in the aftermath of Amankwatia's campaign of 1801, and that the rapid development of Salaga was an immediate consequence of the reorganization.

It has been argued elsewhere that the abolition of the maritime slave trade by the Danes in 1803, the English in 1807 and the Dutch in 1814 led the Asante government to commit itself to the more intensive development of its northern trade.[129] The decline in the export trade through the coastal ports, moreover, lent support to the claims of that minority of politicians who were already prepared to argue that withdrawal from the turbulent southern provinces need not prove detrimental to the national interest. But as late as 1820 Osei Bonsu could seemingly still argue for the resumption of the export of slaves.

125 See translation in *Ghana Notes and Queries,* III, 1961, pp. 24–30.
126 Phyllis Ferguson, field-notes: interview with Wasipewura Asafu, dd. Daboya, 23 March 1970. See further, Institute of African Studies, Ghana, Research Project in Oral Tradition, no. 1, Gonja: interview with Malam Baba of Nfabeso, Salaga, dd. 1969, pp. 50–1.
127 *Ghana Notes and Queries,* III, 1961, p. 28.
128 Barth, 1857–9, I, 478. The reference might be, alternatively, to the Amazaa wars with Gobir at the turn of the century. The argument would not be affected.
129 Wilks, 1971a, pp. 130–1.

He claimed that since he did not conduct campaigns to procure slaves, the abolition as such had not 'lessened the number either of domestic or foreign wars'; and he remarked that, deprived of the possibility of transporting overseas the prisoners of war who could not be absorbed into the Asante towns and villages, he was faced with the undesirable alternative of having to put them to death.[130] In his discussions with Consul Dupuis, indeed, Osei Bonsu outlined the advantages of the institution of slavery as he (ignorant of the forms it took in the Americas) conceived them to be:

the white men . . . do not understand my country, or they would not say the slave trade was bad. But if they think it bad now, why did they think it good before. Is not your law an old law, the same as the Crammo [*Kramo*, 'Muslim'] law? Do you not both serve the same God, only you have different fashions and customs? Crammos are strong people in fetische, and they say the law is good, because the great God made the book; so they buy slaves and teach them good things, which they knew not before. This makes every body love the Crammos, and they go every where up and down, and the people give them food when they want it . . .[131]

Yet Osei Bonsu's government had in fact realistically adjusted its policies to the changed circumstances over a decade earlier, and the Asantehene was indulging in a little sophistry at Dupuis' expense.

In so far as any one event may be taken as signalizing Osei Bonsu's final commitment to the pro-Muslim northern policies of Osei Kwame, it was the decision taken in council in or about 1808 to free and repatriate all Muslim slaves: apparently despite opposition from venal Muslim interests. Letters despatched by the Kumase Imām Muḥammad al-Ghamba' to inform his northern counterparts of the decision show that the Asantehemaa Konadu Yaadom ('Qunādua') was present, and imply that one of Osei Kwame's most powerful protégés approved the proceedings – the Adontenhene Kwaaten (or more fully, Koranten) Pete (see p. 252):

Allāh brought trials and misfortunes upon Asante, the country of the pagans. Qarantan, the Sultan, his mother Qunādua, and all the elders met in council. They said that perhaps Allāh had brought all this trouble because the rights of the Muslims had been violated. They decided to set free all the Muslims, men and women, young and old, who had been captured and enslaved, and to send them back to their countries. The Muslims rejoiced because of that decision . . .[132] (Plate VII).

130 Dupuis, 1824, pp. 162–4.
131 *Idem.*
132 Royal Library, Copenhagen, *Cod. Arab. CCCII*, III, f. 5. The provisional translation in Levtzion, 1966, p. 104, has been followed. Imām Muḥammad – also known as Baba – arrived in Kumase in 1807, see Bowdich, 1819, p. 240. Konadu Yaadom died in 1809. The council meeting, then, probably occurred in 1808.

By a fortuitous coincidence, the period following the abrupt decline of the maritime slave trade was one of sharply rising demand for the kola nut – a commodity available in abundance in a number of Asante provinces. One effect of the wave of Islamic reform which swept across the Central Sudan at the beginning of the nineteenth century was to increase the use of kola, as recourse to alcoholic stimulants was progressively abandoned. Traders from Hausaland and Bornu – the powerful *madugai* or caravan-leaders – rapidly established a pattern of regular trading expeditions to the new market at Salaga, thereby eliminating the long journey across the hinterland to Gbuipe. Many of them continued their journeys into the capital itself, so that Bowdich for example could refer to 'the hourly arrival in Coomassie of visitors, merchants, and slaves'.[133] By 1817 the commercial preeminence of the northern markets, and most notably of Salaga, was clearly established. 'The preference of the Ashantees,' remarked Bowdich,

for the Dagwumba and Inta [Gonja] markets, for silk and cloth, results not merely from their having been so long accustomed to them, but because they admit of a barter trade. The Boosee or Gooroo [Hausa *goro*, 'kola'] nut, salt, (which is easily procured, and affords an extravagant profit,) and small quantities of the European commodities, rum and iron, yield them those articles of comfort and luxury, which they can only purchase with gold and ivory from the settlements on the coast.[134]

The revival of the Asante trade with the British settlements on the coast, after ratification of the treaty of 1831, has been described above. It may now be suggested that this revival was in part consequent upon the markets for coastal goods which the Asante traders were able to establish in the northern hinterlands. Thus for example, in 1844 Allen and Thomson met in Accra,

several parties of Ashanti traders, starting off for the interior, with various articles of European produce, but principally salt, which they exchange for gold-dust and ivory. Everything is borne on the heads of slaves, a portion of whom of course belong to the commissariat department, and carry provisions for two or three days. These Ashanti traders communicate with all the nations of the interior adjoining their country, but they do not pass the frontier. Others meet them at appointed and regular markets, to interchange their commodities. It requires twelve days to reach the place called Sari, to meet those of Mallowa . . .[135]

The traders were clearly travelling to Salaga in Sarem (Twi *seremu*, 'the grasslands'), a market frequented by the Hausa (Twi *marwa*,

133 Bowdich, 1821c, p. 2. See Wilks, 1966a, pp. 320–2. Wilks, 1971, pp. 132–4.
134 Bowdich, 1819, p. 334.
135 Allen and Thomson, 1848, II, 183.

Dyula *maraba*). A decade later Barth was able to give an illuminating though brief account of the intricate nature of the business operations then conducted at Salaga, drawing attention for the first time to the important role of the Mossi donkey traders:

As regards Selga, the district to which the Hausa traders go for their supply of this article [kola], three points are considered essential to the business of the kola trade; first, that the people of Mosi bring their asses; secondly, that the Tonawa, or natives of Asanti, bring the nut in sufficient quantities; and thirdly, that the state of the road is such as not to prevent the Hausa people from arriving. If one of these conditions is wanting, the trade is not flourishing. The price of the asses rises with the cheapness of the guro [kola]. The average price of an ass in the market of Selga is 15,000 shells [cowries]; while in Hausa the general price does not exceed 5000. But the fataki, or native traders, take only as many asses with them from Hausa as are necessary for transporting their luggage, as the toll, or fitto, levied upon each ass by the petty chiefs on the road is very considerable.[136]

The relocation of the principal northern market at Salaga brought it within an eastern division of Gonja, Kpembe, which had been virtually independent of the authority of the Yagbumwura in western Gonja since the earlier eighteenth century. It has been seen that an Asante force reoccupied the province in 1751, when civil disturbances occurred there following the death of the Kpembewura Morukpe. The new Kpembewura and two subordinate skin-holders – the Kulupiwura and probably Kanankulaiwura – were arrested, and became parties to the contract by the terms of which the relationship of Kpembe to the central government was defined (see p. 21). It appears that as a result of the contract Kpembe acquired inner provincial status, by contrast with the central and western divisions of Gonja. Certainly, however, with the growth of Salaga in the early nineteenth century, the skin of Kpembe gained greatly in importance and prestige: 'thanks to Salaga', wrote the author of the *Qiṣṣat Salgha*, 'Kpembe became a great and powerful sultanate'.[137] While the enhanced desirability of the skin led to increasing competition for it, the maintenance of political stability in the province at the same time became of much concern to the central government. Thus, for example, a dispute involving the Kpembewura and the Kanankulaiwura was transferred to Kumase in 1817, when both had to appear before Osei Bonsu. The Kanankulaiwura was removed from office.[138] Any disruption of the Salaga market was thus averted. On the other hand, as the government in Kumase prepared for war in 1825 (see p. 181), business in Salaga was severely dislocated:

136 Barth, 1857–9, III, 364.
137 *Ghana Notes and Queries*, IV, 1962, p. 6.
138 Hutchison's Diary, entries for 20, 25 and 28 November 1817, in Bowdich, 1819, pp. 396–7; 401.

because of the mobilization of men into the armies, the kola crop of 1825 was either not harvested or not marketed, and the Hausa caravans were detained in Salaga for a year.[139]

The central government administration in Salaga appears to have developed – as in Yendi – into a large and elaborate one, though details of it are lacking for the earlier nineteenth century. In the 1870s Gouldsbury reported the Asante population of Salaga as to be 'counted by hundreds', and Opoku as numbering 'many hundreds' – comprising 'officials, weavers, and traders'.[140] A Hausa manuscript probably written not long after 1875 recorded that at that time the town was 'full of Asante people – among them buyers and sellers, and influential servants [*bayi*, literally "slaves"] of the king'. Among the latter was a head-weaver (*sarkin saka*) and a town-warden (*mai jirangari*), while the senior Asante resident was one Amakye ('Amaki').[141] Amakye's predecessor in office may have been the functionary who arrived back in Kumase in late March or early April 1871, bringing presents for the Asantehene which included a race-horse. He had, according to Ramseyer and Kühne, 'been sent two years before to Sarem, a tract of country to the north, a tributary of Ashantee'.[142] Certainly an earlier occupant of Amakye's post – referred to as 'Chief of Salagha' – was the Boakye Tenten who was later to have a distinguished career in the capital as occupant of the Boakye Yam Panin senior counselorship.[143] The system of resident administrators in the northeastern provinces extended, moreover, beyond the larger towns such as Salaga and Yendi, and into remote rural areas. Dadiase, for example, lay in the Adele country, some ninety miles east of Salaga which was the nearest point on Route IV, and some thirty-five miles north of the nearest point on Route IV(a) to Kete Krakye. Yet in 1884 it was observed that 'the Governor (*Staathalter*) of Kumase in his time resided in Dadiase', and that 'from the many people he brought with him, and who spread out into the whole district, they [the Adele] learned Twi'.[144] In 1969 the aged Imām of Yendi was able to give some account of the elaborate apparatus of control which extended even northwards of Gamaji, the

139 Clapperton, 1829, p. 68.
140 PRO, CO. 879/9, African, 95: Gouldsbury's report on his journey into the interior, dd. 27 March 1876. Opoku, 1885, p. 271.
141 Krauses Haussa-Handschriften, in *Mitteilungen des Seminars für Orientalische Sprachen*, XXXI, 1928, pt 3, 105 and text 24, xxxix.
142 Ramseyer and Kühne, 1875, p. 120. The reference may be to elsewhere in Gonja, though not to Dagomba, which is Twi *Anwa*.
143 *Further Correspondence*, C. 3386, 1882, p. 64: Lonsdale's report on his mission, 1881–2.
144 Diary of David Asante, 26 February 1884, in Christaller, 1886, p. 32. See Johnson, 1965, p. 34. The existence of a number of important shrines in the region may account for the administrative arrangements there.

trading entrepôt just outside the Dagomba capital. 'There were', he recollected,

Asante who supervised affairs at Gamaji. The Asante carried the kola on their heads to Salaga. The King of Asante controlled the road between Kumase and Salaga, Salaga and Gamaji, and from Gamaji as far as Sansanne Mango. At each place the Asante had camps and trained soldiers, but the local chiefs were responsible for road maintenance.[145]

The nationalization of the kola trade

In the period of the development of the Salaga market, and of the regularization of the kola trade especially with Hausaland, northern merchants were not only permitted, but were encouraged, to visit Kumase. 'I must give them gold and provisions', commented Osei Bonsu in 1820, 'and send them home happy and rich, that it may be known in other countries that I am a great king, and know what is right.' [146] It is clear, however, that later in the century this 'open door' policy was reversed. The author of the *Qiṣṣat Salgha*, for example, remarked that in the period before 1874 the northern merchants were prohibited from following Route IV southwards of Yeji on the Volta River: 'The Hausa used to come to Salaga with their belongings, and trade in kola. They could not cross the Yagi [Yeji] river because the Asante would not let them do so.' [147] A fuller account of the restrictions upon access to the metropolitan region of Asante was given by al-Ḥājj 'Umar b. Abī Bakr (died 1934), himself a member of an old established Hausa trading family:

My knowledge of Asante is not great, but I know it to be true that there was not one Zongo [i.e., stranger Muslim community] in the whole land of Asante until Kumase was conquered at the time of the Sultan of Asante, Karikari [i.e., 1874]. Up to that time the land of Asante was closed. No Hausa entered it, and no-one else except slaves who the Asante bought. The market was at the town of Salaga . . . Hausa, Mossi, Dagomba, Borgu, Nupe and Wangara took their goods to Salaga to sell, and bought kola from the Asante, and returned to their own lands. They did this until the time of the war between Karikari and the Christians.[148]

The account of the Salaga trade given by Barth suggests that the exclusion of stranger Muslims from Kumase had already occurred by the middle of the century, and certainly in 1857 Borgu traders to

145 Ferguson, field-notes: interview with al-Ḥājj 'Abdallāh b. al-Ḥājj al-Ḥāsan, dd. Yendi, 16 December 1969.
146 Dupuis, 1824, p. 167.
147 *Ghana Notes and Queries*, III, 1961, 28–30.
148 Aḥmad Bābā al-Wa'iz, 1950, pp. 84–6.

Salaga commented on the prohibition on their proceeding thence to the capital.[149] It may be that the decision to prohibit their access to the capital was taken by the Asantehene Kwaku Dua I in 1844, when a similar restriction was placed upon coastal traders (see p. 196). It may be that the measure was in part politically motivated, being prompted by apprehensions about the growth of Muslim power in Asante. In 1818 the Imām Muḥammad al-Ghamba' had defied Osei Bonsu and had withdrawn support from the expeditionary force fighting in Gyaman; [150] and in 1839 the then *shaykh* of the Kumase Muslims was under arrest for his part in a conspiracy against Kwaku Dua led by the Gyaasewahene Adu Damte.[151] But in economic terms the effect of the policy of exclusion was essentially to achieve partial nationalization of the kola trade, by establishing full government control over the marketing of the nut up to the time of its sale to the foreign buyer in Salaga. At the same time the trade was also bureaucratized: that is, government operatives took over marketing functions in competition with private entrepreneurs, and special protection was afforded the public or nationalized sector of the industry. 'The Asante Hene', so Rattray's Dwaben informants recounted, 'had the power to close the road until his kola should have reached the early market.' [152]

In the 1920s Rattray was able to obtain a detailed account of the organization of the kola trade in the later nineteenth century, from a trading functionary of Mampon:

Trading for the Stool was conducted by the following *fekuo* (groups), who were generally subjects of the *Gyase* Chief, i.e. the *Akyeremadefo* (drummers), the *Asokwafo* (horn-blowers), the *Asoamfo* (hammock-carriers) and the *Agwarefo* (bathroom attendants). About the month of November in each year, the *Omanhene* sent these subjects, in charge of the *Ankobea Hene,* to Jamasi, Wiamoase, and Asaman to buy *besi* nuts (kola). A man's full load consisted of 2,000 nuts, which was called an *apakan* (load); a lighter load was 1,500 nuts. The price of a full load varied from as much as a *nsoansafa* to a *nsoansa* of gold-dust (i.e. from 5*s* to 10*s*) according to the season's crop. This kola was carried to Salaga and retailed from £1 to £2 a load. A slave in the Salaga market was worth 10,000 to 14,000 nuts. I went once to Salaga with 40 *apakan*. They were carried by free men. It was no disgrace for a free man to carry a load while trading. Each carrier was allowed to carry as many extra nuts as he was able, attached to the Chief's load, and these he could trade on his own account. The extra bundle was known as *nsitiri* (lit. place on top). The *Omanhene* sent his heralds with us, carrying an *afona* (state sword) as

149 Crowther and Taylor, 1859, p. 103.
150 Wilks, 1966a, pp. 335–6.
151 Beecham, 1841, p. 93, citing T. B. Freeman. Methodist Mission Archives, London: Brooking to General Secretaries, dd. Kumase, 14 February 1842. See further Wilks, 1971, *passim,* upon which this section is based.
152 Rattray, 1929, p. 187.

an insignia of office to show we had been sent by the Chief. As soon as we had passed, these heralds closed the path until we had disposed of our kola, i.e. for about twenty days . . . After the road was thrown open, the heralds remained on duty and exacted a toll of twenty-five nuts on each load from all other traders, twenty for the *Omanhene*, five for themselves.[153]

When Lonsdale travelled the road from Kumase to Salaga in 1881, he noted the presence of central government agents at Adwira (mile 59): 'stationed at this town are three of the Coomassie or King's officials'.[154] The Mampon trader remembered the passage of traders being controlled not only at Adwira but also at Atebubu (mile 99), and he showed the nature of the control to have been both fiscal and political:

The King of Ashanti had all the roads guarded, and all traders were detained until inquiries had been made about them, when they were allowed to pass, on payment of 3s to 4s worth of gold-dust. Northern Territory men were not permitted to trade south of Salaga. There was always competition to carry a Chief's kola, because thereby the carriers had access to the early market for any surplus which they chose to carry.[155]

After the deportation by the British of the Asantehene Agyeman Prempe I in 1896, the Mamponhene took over the operation of the Adwira station. This brought him into conflict with the British military administrators, who regarded the central government's revenues as having passed to them by right of conquest. In 1903 Captain Norris of the Gold Coast Regiment noted:

We had a good bit of work to do at Mampon collecting caravan taxes, etc. A good many of the traders complained that they had already paid the tax at Ejura [Adwira], a village about 25 miles north of Mampon. We found that the King of Mampon had sent men up to Ejura and was making the natives pay tax for bringing cattle, etc. through.[156]

A detachment of troops was sent to Adwira to arrest the collectors, and, their having admitted that they were acting for Mamponhene, the case was sent to Kumase for trial. The colonial administration was henceforth to derive the benefits of the structure of tolls developed by its Asante forerunner in the north in the nineteenth century.

The regulative controls which the Asante government had imposed upon the kola trade, probably after 1844, were extended to other commodities in wide demand. Thus, for example, imports of river-bed salt from Daboya into metropolitan Asante were prohibited, apparently in the interest of the producers at the coastal lagoons of Ada and Keta:

153 *Ibid.* pp. 109–10.
154 *Further Correspondence*, C. 3386, 1882, p. 68: Lonsdale's report on his mission, 1881–2.
155 Rattray, 1929, p. 111.
156 Norris, 1928, pp. 213–15.

The whole country [of Gonja] uses Daboya salt. The Grunshi use it too, and people come from a long distance to buy it; from Dagomba, Konkomba, Basari, and as far as Kabre. Only the Asante, when they were powerful, forbade it to come into their country. They gave preference to the salt of Ada (? and Dabūdī), which was being sold at a very high price. And when they saw Daboya salt in the country, even a handful, they taxed it.[157]

Most closely controlled of all commodities in the northern dependencies, however, were undoubtedly munitions of war. As early as the 1770s or 1780s the Fezzan merchant Imhammad, who travelled across the hinterland to Nkoransa, commented on the matter:

Fire Arms are unknown to such of the nations on the South of the Niger as the Shereef has visited; and the reason which he assigns for it is, that the Kings in the neighbourhood of the coast, persuaded that if these powerful instruments of war should reach the possession of the populous inland States, their own independence would be lost, have strictly prohibited, and by the wisdom of their measures, have effectually prevented this dangerous merchandize from passing beyond the limit of their dominions.[158]

The missionary Riis, on the occasion of his visit to Kumase in 1839–40, was able to give some further account of the government's policy:

The Asante, so far as it lies in their power, prevent all traffic between the Africans living on the other side of Asante, and the Coast, partly to rule out any opportunity for those people to purchase guns and gunpowder, with which they would not only achieve a position in which they could throw off Asante rule, but also, since they are said to be a people far more numerous than the Asante themselves, even rapidly to gain an overlordship over them; and also, partly to avoid giving up to others the profit which the lively Asante trade with this African people continually brings to them.[159]

In 1875, when the Asante residents in Salaga were under attack from the Nchumuru, the Kpembewura pointed out to the Asante commissioner there, 'You have restrained me from buying guns and gunpowder, so how now will I obtain war supplies'? [160] Nevertheless, the decision in the later eighteenth century to modernize the Dagomba fighting forces by the training of units of gunmen showed that the government was capable of applying its policy selectively in the wider interests of imperial security (see p. 248). Very limited supplies of munitions may also have found their way into the northern provinces

157 In general the Hausa version of the *Qiṣṣat Salgha*, prepared by Imām al-Ḥāsan of Salaga, for which see Withers Gill, 1924, p. 7, has been preferred at this point to the Arabic text, which seems corrupt, see *Ghana Notes and Queries*, III, 1961, 18–19. 'Dabūdī' may refer to Labadi, near Accra.
158 Reported by Lucas, in *Proceedings*, 1791, p. 267.
159 A. Riis, 1840, p. 229.
160 Krauses Haussa-Handschriften, *Mitteilungen des Seminars für Orientalische Sprachen*, XXXI, 1928, text no. 24, p. xxxix.

– and indeed into central Asante – from the markets of the Middle Niger and ultimately, therefore, from the ports of Sierra Leone and the Senegal region.[161]

The revolt of the Gyamanhene Adinkra

With the development in the northern hinterlands of an apparatus of political control, successive Asante governments clearly achieved a degree of stability which had proven quite unattainable in the southern provinces. In most areas, for much of the century, the tribute structure remained intact; the trade regulations effective; and the relationship between local rulers and the agents of central government one of mutual cooperation. But although the century was thus characterized by a relative absence of conflict, there were nevertheless not a few occasions when the central government was obliged to re-establish a military presence in various provinces and to turn to its resources of coercion to sustain the political order.

One of the most serious rebellions in the north in the nineteenth century was that of the Gyamanhene Adinkra, erstwhile partisan of the Asantehene Opoku Fofie (p. 254). The indications are that the first signs of trouble occurred in or about 1811, when the Gyamanhene had made for himself a Golden Stool, thereby challenging the Asantehene's claims to sovereignty over Gyaman. Adinkra, however, surrendered the stool to Kwame Butuakwa – then an official of the Treasury in Kumase – who was sent to demand it.[162] Subsequently Adinkra came under strong criticism from the more militant of his advisors, and relations with Kumase deteriorated rapidly. The testimony of Osei Bonsu himself, and of Owusu Dome, shows that in or about 1815 Adinkra withheld the Gyaman tributes.[163] The Muslims in Kumase maintained further, that Adinkra 'had cast off his allegiance to the king of Ashantee, and transferred a tribute which he formerly paid him to the Sultan of Kong'[164] – presumably the Watara state of that name. It is possible that the rapid growth of the Salaga market had led to a decline in the Asante trade to Bonduku, the major emporium

---

[161] See Beaton, 1870, pp. 51–2: 'from reliable reports received from travellers and released prisoners . . . the Ashantees are not quite dependent on the supply of ammunition from the coast, but obtain it through Timbuctoo and adjacent places.'

[162] For early accounts of this event, see Bowdich, 1819, pp. 244–5; *West-African Sketches*, 1824, pp. 228–32. For oral accounts, see e.g. Delafosse, 1908, pp. 231–2. Wilks, field-notes: interview with Bafuor Osei Akoto, dd. Kumase, 11 April 1966. For the date of 1811, see Kumase Divisional Council Archives, Manhyia: Civil Record Book 12, Yaw Num v. Kwadwo Appan, case commencing 27 April 1931.

[163] Dupuis, 1824, Introduction, p. xxviii, and pp. 164–5.

[164] *Ibid.* p. 98.

of the Gyaman region, and that it was this which induced Adinkra to attempt to secede from Greater Asante. Certainly the protracted negotiations between the central government in Kumase and the local authorities in Gyaman failed to achieve the reconciliation of their interests. On 6 November 1817 the Council of Kumase agreed on the military reoccupation of Gyaman, and on 23 November the Asantemanhyiamu, in extraordinary session, approved the decision.[165]

Osei Bonsu in person accompanied the expeditionary force which took the field in the dry season of 1817/18. The Asante infantrymen encountered the strongest resistance from the Muslim cavalry of Gyaman, and forces from the western Gonja divisions lent support to the rebels.[166] The campaign was particularly sanguinary, but short: by the end of August 1818, messengers from the Asantehene had arrived in Elmina to notify the Dutch that Gyaman ('the Bontoukor nation') had been defeated, and Adinkra slain.[167] The Asante forces remained in the field, however, throughout the following dry season, presumably because, taking advantage of the disturbed situation in the northwest, a Bambara army sent by Da Kaba of Segu had followed the Black Volta southwards to attack Bole and Buna, whose people sought and found refuge in Asante.[168] It was thus not until the middle of 1819 that Osei Bonsu re-entered Kumase.[169] As a result of the rebellion, changes were made in the status of Gyaman. Dupuis wrote of 'the annexation of that kingdom to Ashantee as a province, in lieu of the tributary rank it enjoyed before'.[170] The implication is, perhaps, that Gyaman was more fully incorporated within Greater Asante as an inner rather than outer province. The Imām of Bonduku was reported to have been taken captive by the Kumase Gyaasewahene Opoku Frefre, but to have been released 'after promising by solemn oath and written treaty that neither he nor his people would ever be hostile to Asante'.[171] A sister of Adinkra, Tamia, and a son, Apaw, were among those taken prisoner to Kumase. Tamia was later repatriated by Kwaku Dua I. Apaw, however, almost immediately escaped, and attempted to raise rebellion once again.[172] Although he was killed,[173]

165 PRO, T. 70/41: Hutchison to Smith, dd. Kumase, 23 November 1817. See also Hutchison's Diary, entry for 23 November 1817, in Bowdich, 1819, p. 399.
166 Dupuis, 1824, pp. 98, xxxvi–xxxvii, cxxx, note.
167 General State Archives, The Hague, KvG 351: Elmina Journal, entries for 28 August and 5 November 1818.
168 *The Royal Gazette and Sierra Leone Advertiser*, VI, no. 333, 16 October 1824, p. 370.
169 General State Archives, The Hague, KvG 351: entry for 31 August 1819.
170 Dupuis, 1824, pp. 263–4.
171 Reindorf, 2nd ed., n.d., p. 165, who refers to the 'Mohammedan priest named Adumamu', cf. the Twi *adimɛm*, from Dyula *limam*, Arabic *al-imām*.
172 *Royal Gold Coast Gazette*, 27 May 1823. Reindorf, 2nd ed., n.d., p. 165.
173 *Ibid.* p. 165.

the situation in Gyaman was to remain disturbed for some years, and the government's attempts in 1823 to obtain a mutually acceptable settlement were rejected.[174]

Osei Yaw, Katamanso, and the northeast

The accession to the throne in 1824 of Osei Yaw, who was committed to the restoration of Asante authority in the southern provinces, led to a temporary relaxation in the government's control of northern affairs. The failure of the Gonja – probably of the Kpembewura – to supply the quota of fighting men during the mobilization for service in the south in 1823–4 went for example unpunished.[175] After the Asante defeat at Katamanso in 1826, however, when the new majority in the councils had taken the decision to disengage in the south, a renewed concern with the situation in the north became immediately apparent. In Kpembe province the Sungbunwura, affirming his loyalty to Osei Yaw, sought assurances of assistance from government for a bid to supplant the incumbent Kpembewura.[176] In the same years, as relations between Osei Yaw and the Dwabenhene Kwasi Boaten worsened, so the decision was taken in Kumase to curtail or abolish the sub-imperial role which Dwaben played in the northeast. The dependencies between Krakye and Nanumba were removed from Boaten's authority, and brought directly under the Asantehene.[177] When resistance to the new arrangements became manifest, Osei Yaw appointed the Ananta-hene of Kumase, Enuben Akyaw, to command of an army, by report initially of 10,000 men.[178] He was instructed to occupy the dissident provinces and to proceed thence to Kpembe to settle affairs there.

Enuben Akyaw moved his forces across the Afram Plains to the Volta, and thence along that river through Akroso and Krakye towards Kpembe. Unexpectedly strong resistance was encountered, however, from the Nchumuru and their allies. The Asante troops were forced not only to retire from their positions at Krupi (or Kulupi), only some twelve miles southeast of Salaga, but in the course of the retreat Enuben Akyaw himself was slain.[179] The Landers received some ac-

174 *Royal Gold Coast Gazette*, 15 November 1823; 21 August 1824; 14 October 1826.
175 Lander and Lander, 1832, II, 191–2.
176 See Johnson, 1966b, p. 32, citing traditions obtained from Krakye by J. E. K. Kumah.
177 Reindorf, 2nd ed., n.d., p. 285.
178 Lander and Lander, 1832, II, 192–3.
179 Reindorf, 2nd ed., n.d., p. 285. See further, Institute of African Studies, Ghana, JEK/7–8: Gyamboae Nkomi Traditions, and History of Kratchis, recorded by J. E. K. Kumah, 15 and 10 September 1964. National Archives of Ghana, Accra, ADM 11/782: History of the Krakye recorded April 1920, from the Krakyewura Kwadwo Dente.

count of what became known in tradition as the 'Krupi and Pawurubi war', from kola merchants returning from Gonja who arrived near Busa on the Niger early in September 1830. 'The people of Gonja'. they reported,

had been by no means inactive, for having heard of the great preparations that were making at Coomassie, and being convinced that those preparations were designed against their own lives and liberties, they formed a plan of attacking their invaders and defeating their project, which succeeded to the utmost of their wishes, and even beyond their expectations. When they had learnt from a swift-footed messenger of the departure of the Ashantee army from Coomassie, and the road which they had taken, they stationed large bodies of stout, well-armed men in ambuscade at various places in the bush, close to the pathway, and awaited the coming of the foe. While the latter was drawing near to Gonja, not suspecting danger of any kind, and straggling about in imagined security, the men in ambush rushed out upon them, made a sudden and desperate attack on their whole force at the same moment, which threw the Ashantees into confusion, and the latter dropping their arms, fled into the woods. The carnage is reported to have been dreadful . . .[180]

According to the Landers' informants, Osei Yaw almost immediately equipped a larger force to take punitive action against the rebellious districts. 'This news', they commented,

spread consternation among all classes of people in Gonja, and alarmed the strangers that had located in the country, insomuch that, on the advance of the second formidable army, they could not command sufficient resolution to go out against it, but deserted their dwellings and dispersed themselves through all parts of the adjacent countries, till such time as their enemies should think proper to return to Coomassie.[181]

Following orders, the Asante soldiers put to fire 'the city of Gonja' – presumably Kpembe rather than Salaga (though by mid-1830 it was already being rebuilt). The final stages of the campaign were directed against the Nchumuru and Krakye, who had apparently received help from the Dwabenhene Kwasi Boaten after his flight into Akyem Abuakwa in 1831 (see p. 119). Reindorf reported that three thousand captives were taken from the two provinces.[182] A Danish report of 1833 referred to the Krakye 'having lately been attacked and driven towards Akwamu by the Asante'.[183]

The situation in the northeastern provinces was to remain relatively tranquil for almost half a century until, with the developing interest

---

[180] Lander and Lander, 1832, II, 192–3.
[181] *Ibid.* pp. 193–4.
[182] Reindorf, 2nd ed., n.d., p. 285.
[183] National Archives, Copenhagen, Generaltold Kammerets Arkiv. Guinea Journals, 1832–3, Lind *et al.* dd. Christiansborg, 27 April 1833. (Communicated by R. Kea.)

of the British in the region, a new factor was introduced into it. The aptitude of the Kumase officials stationed there is suggested by the fact that on those few occasions between 1830 and 1875 when resolution of a local problem proved beyond their capabilities, it was seldom necessary for the central government to do more than authorize the intervention of loyal provincial chiefs. The mid-nineteenth century Atebubuhene Daiwia, for example, acted at least twice in such a capacity. When Kwadwo Gyeyini, priest of the Dente shine at Krakye, incited his followers to rebellion, Daiwia headed a force which restored order and proceeded to the arrest and execution of the ringleader.[184] And again, when disorders occurred in Kpembe province as the skin came once more into dispute between the Kanankulaiwura and Sungbunwura, it was Daiwia who was instructed by the Asantehene Kwaku Dua I to intervene and impose a settlement: the skin, it was ruled, was henceforth to be held, rotationally, by the three eligible subordinates, Sungbunwura, Kanyasewura and Kanankulaiwura.[185]

The Central Gonja campaign of 1841–4

The administrative system in the outer provinces was in the nature of the case far less developed than that in less peripheral districts, and in the late 1830s the situation in the far northwest deteriorated to a point at which massive intervention by the central government became necessary. The origins of the conflict lay in the local politics of the western and central Gonja divisions, and specifically in their struggles for control of the senior skin, that of Yagbum. When the Yagbumwura Danga died – perhaps in the early 1830s – the vacant position was taken by the Bolewura Safo. The Tuluwewura Kali, however, rallied support from other divisions and attempted to displace Safo.[186] Both parties apparently appealed to the ruler of Buna – not itself a part of Gonja – to act as an independent arbitrator. The Bunamansa arranged a meeting of the protagonists, but leaked information to the Tuluwewura which enabled him to massacre many of Safo's leading supporters. Safo committed suicide, but a number of his partisans took refuge in

---

184 *Further Correspondence*, C. 7917, 1896, p. 135: Ferguson, Memorandum, Ashanti and the Brong Tribes, enclosed in Ferguson to Acting Governor, dd. Atebubu, 24 November 1893.

185 *Ibid.* p. 151: Ferguson to Adjutant, Atebubu Expeditionary Force, dd. Atebubu, 20 December 1893. The dates of Daiwia's reign are not known accurately, but he was fourth in office before Gyan Kwaku, Atebubuhene in 1881, see, e.g. Arthur, n.d., p. 103.

186 The origins of the conflict are described in an anonymous Hausa work, probably of nineteenth century date, entitled *Al-khabar Sarki Safu Bulay*, 'History of the Bolewura Safo', see National Archives of Ghana, Accra, MSS in Arabic and Hausa.

Wa to the north. Tuluwewura Kali took the skin of Yagbum but, dying shortly afterwards, was succeeded by the Kongwura Sa'īd Nyantakyi.[187] The new Yagbumwura rapidly consolidated his position by appointing adherents and relatives to village headships throughout the Mankumpua and Kong districts in the west. Demanding from Wa the surrender of the Bole refugees there, and being refused, Nyantakyi invaded that country but was repulsed. The potentiality for conflict increased greatly when a force from Gyaman under Date arrived in Gonja in support of Nyantakyi. The other divisional chiefs in Gonja one by one committed themselves: the Wasipewura Kankaranfu of Daboya for Nyantakyi, for example, and the Gbuipewura Agyei Yafa against. A further engagement between the opposed forces resulted in a victory for the Bole-Gbuipe-Wa alliance, and Date retired to Gyaman while Nyantakyi began creating a new base for his forces at Daboya.

The sources suggest that requests that the Asantehene should settle the dispute were received in Kumase from both Wa and Gbuipe. The government, however, had clearly failed to appreciate the gravity of the situation, for it responded by sending only a small mission to attempt to reconcile the contending parties. By report, its members returned to Kumase after receiving information that the Yagbumwura Nyantakyi would refuse to accept them as arbitrators and had threatened to fight the Asantehene should he insist on intervening.[188] Probably at the same time the Wasipewura refused to send the Daboya tributes to Kumase,[189] and supposedly made for himself a calabash of gold[190] – thereby showing his disregard for the national system of honours and awards (see p. 77).[191] What had commenced as a local conflict had thus developed into rebellion. The reason, according to a contemporary commentator, lay in the long-standing resentment of those in 'Donkor land' to being denied, despite being Asante subjects, free access to the Gold Coast for purposes of trade.[192] However that may be, the government was obliged at last to take remedial action in the disturbed

---

187 This account is synthesized from two principal sources: (i) National Archives of Ghana, Accra, ADM 56/1/201: statement by the Yeri Na, Malam Ishāq, Malam 'Abdallāh, al-Ḥājj Sa'īd, and Malam 'Abd al-Qādir, of Wa, enclosed in Acting Provincial Commissioner, Northern Province, to Chief Commissioner, Northern Territories, dd. 25 July 1930; (ii) Braimah, 1970, pp. 11–33, whose excellent account is marred by an incorrect chronology.

188 Braimah, 1970, p. 20. Institute of African Studies, Ghana, IASAS/22: Nsumankwa Stool History, recorded by J. Agyeman-Duah, 26 October 1962.

189 Wilks, field-notes: interview with Karamoko al-Ḥājj Abū Bakr, dd. Kandinga, 11 September 1968.

190 Wilks, field-notes: interview with al-Ḥājj Ismā'il b. 'Abd al-Mu'min, Asante Nkramo Imām, dd. Kumase, 3 August 1965.

191 For a similar case involving a chief in Sarem, see Ramseyer and Kühne, 1875, p. 183.

192 National Archives, Copenhagen, Generaltold Kammerets Arkiv 1760–1848: Guinea Journals, No. 184, 1843. (Communicated by R. Kea.)

provinces, and the Nsumankwaahene of Kumase, Domfe Ketewa, was appointed to command of an army. It was reputedly the first to have taken the field during Kwaku Dua's reign.[193] Moving his troops into western Gonja probably in 1841, Domfe Ketewa met with opposition greater than anticipated, and reported back to the Council in Kumase his inability to deal with the situation. This time the government appointed one of the senior military functionaries, the Anantahene Asamoa Nkwanta, to command of the whole operation; chose the Nseniehene Kwadwo Apea Agyei as deputy commander; and authorized the mobilization of a new army to move in support of Domfe Ketewa's smaller task force.[194]

Facing massive military intervention in his territory, but hoping to avert disaster, the Wasipewura Kankaranfu obliged Nyantakyi to leave Daboya. He moved, with a rapidly diminishing body of supporters, northwards along Route III. Asamoa Nkwanta nevertheless occupied Daboya and, refusing to believe that the Yagbumwura was not still in the province, insisted that Kankaranfu arrange his surrender.[195] Despairing of being able to obtain a settlement, Kankaranfu invited the Asante captains to a meeting in his palace – and blew up with gunpowder himself and many of the assembled officers.[196] Clearly the plan misfired. Domfe Ketewa may have been killed, but Asamoa Nkwanta and Kwadwo Apea Agyei survived – and were both to die during the fighting in Dwaben in 1875. Notwithstanding whatever losses they had suffered, the Asante troops moved northwards in pursuit of the Yagbumwura Nyantakyi, and finally captured him apparently in the Navrongo district: over 300 miles north of Kumase and well beyond the imperial frontiers.[197] Nyantakyi was executed. The troops reentered Kumase on 3 June 1844, some three years after the start of the campaign. They were reviewed by Kwaku Dua I before crowds estimated in excess of 100,000 persons. One hundred and forty officers had died, either in action or from sickness. Because of the impoverished nature of the country in which the army had been deployed, little booty had been acquired, and many of the captives taken had succumbed to disease.[198] Among those who survived, however, was Kara-

---

193 Institute of African Studies, Ghana, IASAS/22, Nsumankwa Stool History.
194 *Ibid.* Also IASAS/3: Ananta Stool History, recorded by J. Agyeman-Duah, 25 January 1963. A brief notice of the campaign is to be found in Duncan, 1847, I, 37.
195 Braimah, 1970, pp. 24–6.
196 *Ibid.* pp. 26–8. Wilks, field-notes: interview with Karamoko al-Ḥājj Abū Bakr, dd. Kandinga, 11 September 1968.
197 Braimah, 1970, p. 31. National Archives of Ghana, Accra, ADM 56/1/201: statement dd. 25 July 1930.
198 Methodist Mission Archives, London: Chapman to General Secretaries, dd. Kumase, 21 June 1844, and Journals, 1 and 3 June 1844.

moko 'Uthmān Kamagatay, a Gbuipe scholar resident in Daboya and member of the same family as that of Muḥammad Kamagatay who had served Osei Bonsu earlier in the century (see p. 260). Better known in Asante as Kramo Tia, Kwaku Dua was later to appoint him Imām of Asante (*Asante Adimɛm*), a position which his descendants continue to hold to the present time.[199]

In August 1844 Kofi Aban headed a mission from Kumase to the coast to inform the Dutch and British Governors of the successful conclusion of the northern campaign, and to make them gifts of a horse and leopard.[200] The victory, however, had to be measured in political rather than economic terms: the heavy expenditure incurred in provisioning and otherwise maintaining in the field a large army for so long a period and so distant from the metropolitan region, could not have been significantly offset by any returns from booty and must have placed an extraordinary strain upon the Treasury. It is significant that the imperial ideal continued to dominate the thinking about the north of a peace party administration which had earlier presided over the reduction of the Asante commitment in the south. The relatively unproductive outer provinces of central and western Gonja had seemingly to be held secure at whatever cost to the nation. With the termination of military operations, however, steps were taken to create an effective civilian administration within them. Some years earlier a new junior counselorship had been created under the Butuakwa stool. A palace attendant, Kra Boadu, was promoted to become first occupant of the post.[201] In 1839 he took part in a mission to the Dwabenhene in exile, Kwasi Boaten,[202] and having presumably acquitted himself with credit, after 1844 his office was assigned special responsibility for Gonja affairs. Resident commissioners – known in Gonja as *etangpo* (singular, *tangpo*) – were also stationed in all the principal towns,[203] and a war indemnity of one thousand men was imposed upon Nyantakyi's successor on the senior skin of Yagbum, 'Abd al-Mu'min. The debt was apportioned between the various divisional chiefs, and

199 Wilks, field-notes: interviews with Imām al-Ḥājj Ismā'īl b. 'Abd al-Mu'min Kamagatay, dd. Kumase, 3 August 1965; Karamoko "Umar b. Abī Bakr Kamagatay, dd. Kumase, 11 April 1966; Imām 'Abdallāh b. Yaḥya Kunatay, dd. Daboya, 11 September 1968.
200 General State Archives, The Hague, KvG 365: Elmina Journal, entry for 26 August 1844. In 1844 the Asantehene refused John Duncan a permit to travel through Asante, on account of the war; see Duncan, 1847, I, 37; 235. See also Duncan to Librarian, Royal Geographical Society, London, dd. Anomabo, 7 December 1844. (I am grateful to Marion Johnson for calling my attention to this letter.)
201 Institute of African Studies, Ghana, IASAS/59: Boadu Linguist Stool History, recorded by J. Agyeman-Duah, 3 May 1963.
202 Reindorf, 2nd ed., n.d., p. 289.
203 Braimah, 1970, p. 32.

the Bolewura Adama, for example, solicited the support of the Wa in raiding as far north as the Dagarti village of Issa – which had given some support to the partisans of Nyantakyi – in the attempt to fill his quota.[204]

It is interesting that as late as 1937 the Gonja people in Kumase petitioned the Asantehene for permission to appoint a headman, responsible to the Kra Boadu stool. 'In accordance with traditions and facts which are absolutely indisputable', they argued,

. . . originally we owed allegiance to The Otumfuor Asantehene through the Asantehene's Linguist in the person (Okyiame) Buadu (Deceased) who has been in order of succession succeeded by Okyiame Kofi Ewuah which is known to all Ashantis . . . That our Supreme Commander the Yabohene [Yagbumwura] aforesaid with all his Kabonya [Gonja] tribe collected and despatched to the Otumfuor Asantehene 1,000 (One thousand) persons to progress the Administration of the Asantehene to match and advance the Asanteman, the said persons were conveyed to The Asantehene through their Leader Asantehene's Linguist Buadu (Deceased) now succeeded by Okyiame Kofi Ewuah in office; this facts are absolutely undeniable.[205]

The rebellion of the eastern Bron

The campaign of 1841–4 was the last occasion on which the Asante government chose to involve itself in massive military intervention in the affairs of the far northern provinces. Indeed, no serious threat to its hegemony in the whole region seems to have occurred until 1874, when the eastern Bron initiated what was to become a widespread movement of rebellion. The constituency of the dissidents was much the same as that of the rebel leaders in the 'Krupi and Pawurubi war', but the causes of the 1874 risings were quite specific. Before embarking upon the reoccupation of the southern provinces in 1872–3, the Asantehene Kofi Kakari had sought the advice of the priest of the Dente shrine at Krakye, and had been counseled strongly against the projected war. Suspecting the eastern Bron, over whom the influence of Dente was all but total, of a reluctance to fight, Kakari thereupon ordered their mobilization. In the subsequent campaigns, the Bron troops were apparently thrown into the fiercest engagements: at Elmina and Abakrampa in 1873, and at Amoafo and Odaso (in opposition to Wolseley's advance) in 1874.[206] The survivors returned to their home

204 National Archives of Ghana, Accra, ADM 56/1/201, statement dd. 25 July 1930. See also Dougah, 1966, pp. 22, 65.
205 Kumase Divisional Council Archives, Manhyia: petition from eight *malams*, 'people of Kabonya in the Northern Territories of the Gold Coast', dd. 12 June 1937.
206 *Further Correspondence*, C. 3386, 1882, pp. 70, 78: Lonsdale's report on his mission, 1881–2. *Ibid.* pp. 100–1: Concise History of Abruno Rebellion against Ashanti, recorded by C. V. E. Graves, being 'a genuine translation (in their own

towns clearly committed to resist any further demands which the government might make upon them. In circumstances which will be described more fully below, in February 1874 the Dwabenhene Asafo Agyei rescinded his allegiance to Kofi Kakari and, quite apparently with the support of the British Administration on the Gold Coast, encouraged the eastern Bron likewise to declare against the Asantehene. The priest of Dente, so it was reported,

> sent messengers to Ashanti to say that many years before the Brunfo [Bron] had considered Ashantis as the most powerful people they had heard of, but that it was now quite obvious that there was one still more powerful, and that was the 'English white man', so that the Brunfo did not see why they should not prefer the white man to Ashanti.[207]

Despite the successful occupation of Dwaben carried out by central government troops in November 1875, the rebel cause in the northeast gained rapidly in strength as the Nchumuru and Buem, to the north and south of Krakye respectively, and the Atebubu, declared themselves in support. The most serious and immediate aspect of the rebellion lay in the threat it presented to the government's administration in Salaga, where messengers arrived from the chief of Buem (*sarkin Bum*) and the chief of Krupi (*sarkin turu*)[208] to announce that they would 'seize the Asante, execute the important persons, and take as slaves all the lesser men'.[209] On the advice of the Kpembewura, the Asante senior commissioner Amakye left Salaga with a force of gunmen, and fought his way through the Nchumuru lines south of the town. Other Asante who remained there, relying on the protection of the Kpembewura, found themselves helpless when he acknowledged his inability to withstand the rebel forces and threw the town open to them. The Asante were massacred or made prisoner, and all their property appropriated.[210] The graphic account of these events was recorded in Hausa from someone who was clearly witness to them. It is in substantial agreement with the report of Theophil Opoku, who visited Salaga in 1877. Of the Krakye, Nchumuru and other members of the rebel front, Opoku commented,

> all these people formerly served the Kumase king, and on the instigation of the Dwabeng King all banded themselves together against their oppressors,

> version) from two of the natives who had been my travelling companions or guides . . .'

207 *Idem.* For a recent consideration of the rebellion, see Johnson, 1965, pp. 50–4.
208 See *Further Correspondence*, C. 3386, 1882, p. 90: 'Krupi. – Five small villages bearing this name, and under one headman who is a fetish priest called May Turu': Hausa *mai turu* and *sarkin turu* are semantically equivalent.
209 Krauses Haussa-Handschriften, *Mitteilungen des Seminars für Orientalische Sprachen*, XXXIX, 1928, text no. 24, p. xxxix.
210 *Idem.*

and on an appointed day, especially in Salaga, killed many hundreds of Kumase people, who were living among them as officials, weavers and traders. Some of the skulls and bones of the murdered men were still to be seen strewn on the waste land and on the plains, where the corpses had become prey for jackals. It was the Dwabeng king especially, with the priests and elders of Krakye whom he used as his right hand, who instigated those people, Salaga included, to unanimous action.[211]

The British, quick to seize the opportunity of extending their influence into the northern provinces of Asante, and concerned to attract the trade of Salaga away from Kumase and by a direct route down the Volta to the coast at Accra instead, took steps to enter into an agreement with the eastern Bron. On 8 March 1876, before Special Commissioner Gouldsbury, the priest of Dente and the chief of Krakye swore on oath,

that we will oppose no obstacle in the way of free trade between Saharah [Salaga], the interior, and the Coast, and that we will offer no impediment whatever to the passage to and fro through Crackey of lawful and peaceful traders, or to that of the merchandise or produce they may carry with them, or be possessed of. That we will use our zealous efforts to maintain the roads henceforth and for ever in open, free, and safe condition, it being our earnest desire to cultivate friendly relations and intercourse with the subjects and allies of Her Majesty Queen Victoria, and to encourage and foster free trade between the interior and Her Majesty's possessions on the Coast, to which end we will always use our best efforts and influence.[212]

The priest of Dente explained his view of the agreement to Opoku in the following year. The influence which Dente possessed over Queen Victoria, he claimed, had led her to sanction Wolseley's invasion of Asante in 1874. 'The Queen of England had allied herself secretly with Dente', he added, so that 'the Grandfather [Dente] is so closely bound with the Queen of England that a division of the persons is impossible, and only they themselves can say whether the Queen is the Grandfather or Grandfather the Queen.'[213]

It is in fact difficult to assess the precise extent to which the British had been active in inspiring the rebellion in the eastern Bron region. Certainly, however, as early as 1873 Captain Glover had systematically compiled information of relevance to the subversion of Asante authority there. 'If you hold Saraga', claimed one of those interrogated, 'you have destroyed Ashantee, for this reason, that on hearing of your arrival in Saraga all the tribes under Ashantee rule would come over

211 Opoku, 1885. The translation by Johnson, 1965, p. 50, has been followed.
212 *Further Correspondence*, C. 3386, 1882, p. 14: Treaty between Gouldsbury and the chief Kwasi Basammunah, and priest Kwasi Dente, of Krakye, dd. 8 March 1876.
213 Opoku, 1885. See Johnson, 1965, p. 52.

to your side.' [214] 'If the white man reaches Saraga', maintained another, 'Ashantee is destroyed . . . At Cararchee [Krakye] you must consult the fetish, which is powerful, otherwise it will stop your progress. This fetish is always consulted by the Ashantees, and if it is gained over then the Ashantees must be destroyed.' [215] But the most encouraging view of all was expressed by a priestess of the Dente shrine, that 'when you reach Chomorroo [Nchumuru] let it be your headquarters for at least a week or ten days, during which time you will have many tribes flocking to your standard, all burning to wreak vengeance on the Ashantees'.[216] The 'tribes' named by the priestess included not only the Dagomba districts of Yendi ('Yawdey'), Savelugu ('Sarblago') and Karaga ('Garagan'), but also such towns beyond the imperial frontiers as Gambaga ('Gumbarga'), Sansanne Mango ('Samserrymargo'), Wagadugu ('Walkerdokoo') and Kupela ('Kopiahlar'). But in fact the rebellion never did extend into the territories north of Salaga. In or about May 1881, with assurances of British support, the secessionist provinces entered into a formal defensive alliance. The subscribers to it were the Krakye and their neighbours ('the Brunfo generally'), the eastern Gonja, the Buem, a number of dissident Nsuta who had taken refuge in Krakye, and, unexpectedly, the Kwawu.[217]

The decline of Salaga and the rise of Kintampo

The reaction in Kumase to the revolt of the eastern Bron, and to the loss of the Salaga market in 1875, was a surprisingly restrained one. The Asantehene Kofi Kakari had been removed from office on 21 October 1874, and was succeeded by Mensa Bonsu at the head of a peace party government committed to policies of national reconstruction. Rejecting any military solution to the problems facing it in the north, the government sent two missions to Krakye to persuade – so it was reported – 'the Chief Priest of Denty and the Brum and Buem people generally to return to their allegiance'.[218] The members of both missions were massacred after which, as Lonsdale remarked in 1882, 'no Ashanti messengers have been sent to Kratshie'. But the main thrust of the government's policy was directed to the recovery of Salaga. The weapon chosen to effect this end was the imposition of economic sanctions: all movement of kola to the market was stopped.

214 *Further Correspondence Respecting the Ashantee Invasion*, no. 3, 1874, p. 172: evidence of 'Abdallāh, 'a native of Anago country', dd. 2 October 1873.
215 *Idem*, evidence of 'Arjeah, an Anago man', dd. 2 October 1873.
216 *Idem*, evidence of 'Azettu, native of Groomah . . . brought to Cararchee as fetish-woman', dd. 2 October 1873.
217 *Further Correspondence*, C. 3386, 1882, p. 78: Lonsdale's report on his mission of 1881–2. For the Nsuta, *ibid.* p. 63.
218 *Ibid.* p. 78.

Early in 1876 the Kpembewura commented on the impact of the embargo upon the town:

> . . . the caravans have to a great extent ceased to come down to Saharah. At one time, that is, when the Saharah market was well supplied with cola nuts, as many as 10,000 people from the interior often entered Saharah in one day. It was from Ashantee and Juabin that the cola nuts were brought to this country, but as the Ashantees are our enemies and the Juabin country now belongs to Ashantee there is no expectation of getting nuts from these districts.[219]

The government did, however, also promote certain positive measures in order to create a new structure within which revival of the Salaga trade might take place. By a commission dated 31 July 1875, the Twi-speaking Frenchman Marie-Joseph Bonnat was appointed to the Asante administration as co-governor of a district extending on both sides of the Volta southwards from Ycji (Route IV, mile 143). He was empowered to develop trade in the area, and was guaranteed a commercial monopoly for six years.[220]

Bonnat first arrived in Kpembe, for discussions with Kpembewura, on 29 January 1876. By no coincidence, the British Special Commissioner Gouldsbury arrived in Salaga the following day and for the same purpose. Fearing perhaps the reprisals which might follow the reimposition of Asante rule, and swayed by British promises to open the direct route from Salaga to Accra, the Kpembewura expressed a strong attachment to the British interest. 'Rather than have the Ashantees back again in my country to rule it as they did formerly', Gouldsbury reported him as saying, 'I and my people would sooner that Saharah should cease to have any trade at all.' [221] Bonnat, however, maintained that this was mere rhetoric, and that 'the Salagas know that only in submitting to Ashantee will their town recover its former importance'.[222] Notwithstanding his failure to restore the Kumase-Salaga trade, Bonnat's evaluation of the situation in the event proved accurate. Salaga did enjoy some revival of its trade in the later 1870s, but in 1882 its turn-over was estimated at only one-third that of a decade earlier. Before 1875 Salaga had been one of the most important business centres within Asante: all transactions there were monetized,[223] and the level at which commodities changed hands was one of the major determinants of price levels throughout the provinces and

---

219 PRO, CO. 879/9, African, 95: Gouldsbury's report on his journey into the interior, dd. 27 March 1876.
220 See text in *L'Explorateur*, 1876, III, 238. Ermann, 1876, p. 361. For studies of Bonnat's career, see Bevin, 1960; Johnson, 1968; and Johnson, 1971.
221 PRO, CO. 879/9, African, 95: Gouldsbury's report dd. 27 March 1876.
222 Bonnat, 'Salaga', in *The Liverpool Mercury*, 12 June 1876.
223 Rattray, 1929, p. 110.

the metropolitan region. By 1882, as Lonsdale observed, its role had become a much more modest one: 'instead of being the emporium at which the kola nut was the great attraction, the trade became of a more general character; goods, cattle and sheep, ivory, etc. from the interior and articles of European manufacture from the coast changed hands'.[224]

The British attempts to render ineffective the Asante embargo upon the Salaga trade, by developing a direct route between that market and Accra, were in turn severely handicapped by the counter measures taken by the government in Kumase to enforce its sanctions. Detachments of soldiers from the so-called 'Hausa' regiments which had been formed in the capital were posted at strategic points along the Volta to frustrate the activities of the smugglers. Authorized to shoot sanction-breakers, their activities were a source of grave concern to the British, the more so since many of them had deserted British service for that of Asante. Thus, of the districts between Kpong ('Porng') on the lower Volta, and Salaga, Governor Ussher noted in 1880:

This border country is the true destination of the bands of Houssa deserters who were so graphically described by Captain Ellis as having been formed into two regiments by the King of Ashantee. These men hang about, and rob and murder travellers between Salaga and Porng, and lay embargoes, with the aid of native petty chiefs, upon all goods and produce passing to and fro. This is a serious matter . . .[225]

The policing of the Volta was not an innovation (see p. 226), but the employment of the best trained soldiers for the purpose probably was.

By early 1877 it appeared that Mensa Bonsu's policies were proving successful. 'Ambassadors', it was reported, 'from the Kings of Gamin and Salaga are now in Coomassie, negotiating the renewing of permanent friendly relationship with Ashantee and reopening of trade.' [226] But the government's use of sanctions against Salaga did not in the end achieve the anticipated result of forcing Kpembewura to reaffirm allegiance to the Asantehene; the Asante administrators had failed to allow for the extent to which the British were prepared to involve themselves in the northern hinterland in the last quarter of the nineteenth century. The situation in eastern Gonja, however, deterioriated rapidly during the period of its autonomy, and the final collapse of the Salaga market was a direct consequence of the failure of the Kpembe authorities to maintain the framework of law and

224 *Further Correspondence*, C. 3386, 1882, pp. 71–2: Lonsdale's report on his mission of 1881–2.
225 National Archives of Ghana, Accra, ADM/1/470: Ussher to Secretary of State, dd. Accra, 5 April 1880. (Old classification.)
226 *Wesleyan Advertiser*, 7 March 1877: letter from B. Tregaskis, citing communication in the *West African Reporter*, 31 February 1877, from its Cape Coast correspondent.

order without which trade was unable to flourish. The old rivalries for the Kpembe skin, which successive Asante governments had been able to handle if necessary in the court in Kumase, became exacerbated and led, in 1892, to civil war. Salaga was plundered and burned, and the Kpembewura Nakpo died during fighting the following year.[227] Ya Na Andani of Dagomba, who had intervened in the conflict on behalf of the victorious party, addressed letters to the people of Kpembe exhorting them to unity: 'Why does not Salaga act like one country? . . . Salaga is the market of the Emir of Kumase and the country of the Musi [Mossi], and our country, and all the countries . . . I do not want to spoil your country, you spoil one another.' [228] Significantly, it will be seen below that in 1893 the new Kpembewura Yusuf became involved in negotiations for the reabsorption of his country into Greater Asante; but in the following year, seemingly inconsistently, intimated his willingness to serve the British. Fortunately his own appraisal of the matter as he saw it is on record:

There is no doubt that all we Gbanye [Gonja] people here . . . were formerly dependants of the Ashanti, but now there are no Ashanti, therefore our land is without a Lord. Disorder has come upon us, yes we have even had a war, we have destroyed and have not been able to create order again. For this reason I, Jusufu, King of Kpembe . . . declare that I do not wish that it should remain without a Lord.[229]

When the British finally established effective control over Kpembe at the end of the century, they themselves legitimated their position there by reference to 'our succession to the old Ashanti Empire, of which Gonja formed a province'.[230] A most illuminating tribute to the relative success of the earlier Asante administration in the region occurred in a magisterial comment on the situation in Salaga delivered by the Mogho Naba, ruler of the Mossi kingdom of Wagadugu: 'when the Ashanti was in power the Gonjas and Dagombas dared not break the market regulations there, and [he] hoped that the English as successors to Ashanti power in Salaga will regulate Salaga affairs, and foster the existence of commercial relations between them and the Mossi'.[231]

The government's decision in 1875 to enforce an embargo upon the

227 See Braimah and Goody, 1967, pp. 40–7.
228 PRO, CO. 879/52, African (West) 549, pp. 60 and 102: letter from 'the Emir of Yendi, who ordered a Muslim priest to write it', addressed to the people of Salaga and the son of the Kpembewura.
229 Account in Hausa of the meeting between Kpembewura Yūsuf and G. E. Ferguson, 2 September 1894; see Goody, 1966, p. 50.
230 PRO, CO. 879/52, African (West) 562, p. 11: Notes on the Neutral Zone, revised 3 September 1898.
231 PRO, CO. 96/277, African (West) 506: Memorandum of Political Proceedings, Wagadugu, 10 July, 1894, in Ferguson's Final Report on his Second Mission to the Interior, dd. 31 August 1896.

Salaga trade necessitated the designation of an alternative market in the north and, just as Salaga had grown at the expense of Gbuipe in the early part of the century, so Kintampo was developed at the expense of Salaga. By 1882 the transition had been largely effected. The Asante, reported Lonsdale,

> established a market near the north-eastern [*sic*] corner of their kingdom and called it Kuntampoh; the Mahomedans call it Tintinpoh. It is here where the kola trade has its headquarters . . . At the present time the Houssa caravans divide at Yendi, the more important portion going to Kuntampoh, taking with them the better part of their merchandise, the others taking the road to Salagha. These latter buy in Salagha such articles from the coast as they may fancy or which may be of use to them, knives and any implements in the market at the time. A portion of this Salagha party then proceed to Kuntampoh to assist in the general business, and return again to Salagha with any surplus money to buy more coast goods or to pay for those already obtained there. The importance of Kuntampoh is no doubt increasing, and entirely because it commands the kola trade.[232]

A few caravans continued to make the 15 to 20 days' journey between Bonduku and Salaga, and with respect to them Lonsdale remarked, 'the Ashantis are very jealous of the trade which passes between these two places, avoiding their market at Kuntampoh, and they made ineffectual attempts to compel it to go to Kuntampoh'.[233] In fact, three hundred trained troops equipped with Snider rifles were stationed in the northwest under command of Owusu Koko Kuma, deployed there partly to control smuggling in that quarter.[234] That their efforts were not entirely ineffectual is shown by Kirby's report on Kintampo – 'the great market of this part of Africa' – which he visited in 1884. The Asante population of the town he estimated at between 3,000 and 4,000; and the Muslim population at between 30,000 and 40,000, comprising 'Mahomedan traders from Timbuctoo, the country behind Sierra Leone, Gaman, Salagha, and the interior'.[235]

The early growth of the Kintampo market has been studied by Arhin.[236] Originally a halting-place for travellers on Route III, local Hausa traders from Kunso some 20 miles to the northeast were the first to move there after it had been declared the kola mart. Around that nucleus a cosmopolitan merchant community rapidly formed. The local authorities in the town comprised a representative of the

232 *Further Correspondence*, C. 3386, 1882, p. 72: Lonsdale's report on his mission of 1881–2.
233 *Ibid.* p. 73.
234 *Affairs*, C. 3064, 1881, p. 48: Parker to Griffith, dd. Kumase, 24 January 1881.
235 *Further Correspondence*, C. 4477, 1885, p. 85: Kirby to Colonial Secretary, dd. Kyekyewere, Asante, 10 March, 1884. *Ibid.* p. 94: Kirby's report of his Mission to Kumase and the interior provinces of the Asante Kingdom, dd. 16 April 1884.
236 Arhin, 1965, pp. 138–42.

Nkoransahene and a headman elected by the Muslim community, but the central government also had stationed two officials there. The first to hold the posts were Prapraho, about whom little is known,[237] and Kukurantumi, who was from the *nkonnwasoafo* group in Kumase.[238] Their duties were described by Arhin's local informants:

The Asantehene . . . sent two resident officials, Prapraho and Kukurantumi, to supervise the market together with the Nkoranzahene's representative, Kwaku Appea. The supervisors had three duties: to collect tolls in kind which were then divided in three parts for the Asantehene, the Nkoranzahene and the supervisors; to perform rituals of purification, pacification and thanksgiving in connection with the market spirits; and finally to maintain peace and order at market gatherings by means of the oaths of the Nkoranzahene and the Asantehene. Disputes were settled in the first instance by the supervisors, in the second at the Nkoranza's court, and in the third and final instance at the Asantehene's court.[239]

Other functionaries of the central government involved in the organization of the Kintampo trade were resident at such outposts as Dawadawa, twenty-six miles to the north on Route III: in 1892 its chief, so it was remarked, 'levies transit tolls for the king of Asante on the caravans coming from Yendi and Salaga'.[240]

The struggle for power in Gyaman

The Asante government's decision to relocate its principal northern market outlet in the inner province of Nkoransa was clearly based in part upon an acknowledgement of the general excellence of the relations which had long prevailed between the rulers of that province and Kumase. But the decision also involved a delicate political calculation of the reactions of the rulers of the adjacent province of Gyaman: one which had a long history of rebellion. There is in fact some difficulty in determining the course of relations between the Kumase and Gyaman in the post-1874 period, due largely to the unfortunate bias in the evidence of one of the principal witnesses: the testimony of Captain Lonsdale, conductor of the British mission to Bonduku between April and July 1882, has to be carefully checked against that of other observers.[241]

[237] *Further Correspondence*, C. 4477, 1885, p. 94: Kirby's report dd. 16 April 1884: 'a headman called Poporokoo'.
[238] He was killed in 1893, see *Further Correspondence*, C. 7917, 1896, p. 152: Ferguson to Adjutant, Atebubu Expeditionary Force, dd. Atebubu, 20 December 1893.
[239] Arhin, 1965, pp. 141–2.
[240] Kling, 1893, p. 138.
[241] A most useful account of the matter is to be found in Goody, 1965, pp. 38–85. The present account, however, differs in interpretation on a number of points.

Shortly after his accession to office late in 1874, the Asantehene Mensa Bonsu sent messengers to the Gyamanhene Agyeman to remind him that he was still 'the wife of the King of Ashanti'.[242] Accompanying the messengers, apparently with instructions to remain as resident in Bonduku, was one Opoku. He was almost certainly the Kwaku Poku who had served as Domakwaihene and Akyeamehene in Kofi Kakari's administration.[243] The Gyamanhene informed the mission that he was no longer 'wife' of the Asantehene, but had now 'married the British Government'. Taking note of the reply, Mensa Bonsu next sent messengers to the British Governor, to inquire whether Gyaman had indeed been taken into the Protected Territory. He was informed that such was not the case.[244] In mid-1875 Mensa Bonsu decided to appoint Alister Campbell, one of the Europeans recently recruited into his administration, to lead a mission to Gyaman, but for reasons not yet apparent, the plan was not put into operation. In 1876, however, envoys from Gyaman did arrive in Cape Coast to request protection ('a flag') from the British.[245] The event was one which led to a period of intensive diplomatic conflict between the government of Asante and that of the Gold Coast Colony. Both wanted influence in Gyaman. But while the British at the time were in no position to establish a strong presence so far inland, Mensa Bonsu continued to resist those of his councillors who advocated Asante military intervention there.

Early in 1877 envoys from Gyaman arrived in Kumase to hold peace talks, and as a result Mensa Bonsu decided to send a new mission to Gyaman. The task of organizing it was given to Owusu Ansa, the English-educated son of Osei Bonsu. The services of Campbell being no longer available, conduct of it was entrusted to another European, Carl Nielson, who was appointed 'His Majesty's Commissioner and headman for a Mission of Peace to the King of Gaman' (see pp. 622–3).[246] The mission left Cape Coast on 8 April 1878. Nielson, however, died in June near Bonduku,[247] and his second-in-command,

---

242 Compare Rattray, 1929, p. 201: 'The Asante Hene had given the King of Gyaman the title of *me ye* (my wife).'
243 The report by Fuller, 1921, p. 138, that Kwaku Poku was slain at the battle of Odasu in 1874, is seemingly in error.
244 *Further Correspondence*, C. 3687, 1883, p. 112: report by Lonsdale on his mission to Asante and Gyaman, April to June 1882, dd. 14 April 1883.
245 National Archives of Ghana, Accra, ADM/1/467: despatch from Governor to Secretary of State, dd. 26 January 1877.
246 National Archives of Ghana, Accra, ADM 1/2/361: Huydecoper to Smith, dd. Banda, 9 August 1879. *Affairs of the Gold Coast and threatened Ashanti Invasion*, C. 3064, 1881, pp. 52–3: Owusu Ansa to Ussher, dd. Cape Coast, 17 May 1880.
247 A report in *The African Times*, xix, no. 207, 1 November 1878, attributed Nielson's death to the Gyamanhene's neglect of the mission. A report that he was shot in a skirmish was denied by those present, see *Affairs of the Gold*

J. J. C. Huydecoper took over. He was probably a grandson of the W. Huydecoper who had conducted the mission to Kumase for the Dutch in 1816–17. According to the report of one of the hammockmen, Nielson had delivered to the Gyamanhene the message that 'the Queen of England had given the whole country from Kerinkando [*sic:* Kwankyeabo] near Assini to Dahomey to the King of Ashanti'[248] – a somewhat optimistic interpretation of the British denial that they had taken Gyaman under protection. Subsequently Owusu Ansa had no doubt that the mission had been a success, though much of its cost had fallen upon him personally. 'The great chieftains of Gyaman', he wrote, 'have become now friendly to the King of Ashanti.'[249] In April 1879, however, further messengers arrived at Cape Coast from Sehwi as well as Gyaman, to inquire into the status of the Neilson–Huydecoper mission, and to express a continuing antipathy towards serving the Asantehene.[250]

Since the belief was current that the Asante government had paid to the British sums of money – doubtless the 1874 war indemnity – in return for which its continuing sovereignty over Gyaman had not been challenged, the British decided to send their own mission to Sehwi and Gyaman. Its members left Cape Coast on 15 May 1879, under the command of John Smith. His report of the findings of the mission proved far from palatable to the British administrators on the Gold Coast and it was soon, as Ellis commented, 'lost sight of in one of the pigeon-holes in the Private Secretary's office'.[251] It is, however, a document of crucial importance for an understanding of the true state of affairs in Gyaman and the adjacent Sehwi province in the period. On 10 June, in the Sehwi capital of Wiawso, Smith found that its ruler Kwaku Kyei favoured the British interest but, that as a result of the Nielson–Huydecoper mission, most of his principal chiefs wished to retain the old association with Asante.[252] Shortly after, in fact, Kwaku Kyei himself appears formally to have reaffirmed his allegiance to the Asantehene.[253] In Gyaman, too, the situation proved such as to give

Coast, C. 3064, 1881, p. 55: evidence of Owusu Taseamandi, 5 February 1881, contrary to Kwadwo Obimpi, 24 March 1879, and Tamfuben, 25 March 1879.

248 *Ibid.* evidence of Tamfuben, 25 March 1879.
249 *Affairs of the Gold Coast*, C. 3064, 1881, p. 52: John Owusu Ansa to Ussher, dd. 17 May 1880.
250 *Ibid.* pp. 4–5: Brandford Griffith to Kimberley, dd. 5 January 1881. Ellis, 1883, p. 195.
251 Ellis, 1883, pp. 222–3.
252 *Ibid.* pp. 196–7. For the Smith mission, see also PRO, CO. 96/126: Lees to Hicks Beach, and enclosure, dd. 5 May 1879; Ussher to Hicks Beach, dd. 24 July 1879; and CO. 96/128: Ussher to Hicks Beach, dd. 8 November 1879.
253 *Affairs of the Gold Coast*, C. 3064, 1881, p. 41: John Ahinaquah to District Commissioner, Axim, dd. 4 February 1881. When Lonsdale visited Wiawso in

little encouragement to the British. Smith arrived in Bonduku in July 1879, and found that the Gyamanhene Agyeman did indeed head a secessionist faction there. His principal supporters were the Takyimanhene Kwabena Fofie and the Siakwahene Bekwi, both of whom had sought refuge in Gyaman in circumstances which will be outlined below. But Smith also found that there was a strong movement to remove Agyeman, who was from the Yakase branch of the ruling group, from office. It was led by Kokobo, from the same branch: a chief 'strongly in favour of an Ashanti alliance'. The central government's representative, Kwaku Poku, was not only still resident in Bonduku but was, Smith noted, 'living on the most friendly terms with the chiefs of the Kokobo faction, and domineering over King Ajiman himself'.[254] Kokobo himself had apparently formed a government-in-exile in Banda, where he was making preparations to enter Bonduku and seize the Gyaman stool. Huydecoper, Commissioner and Headman of the Mission of Peace in succession to Nielson, had been accredited to Kokobo by instructions from Mensa Bonsu dated 30 September 1878; and he took up residence in Banda in December of that year.[255] Of a final meeting which Smith held with the Gyaman authorities prior to his return to the coast, he commented that 'the chiefs openly declared that King Ajiman was their enemy, and refused to take an oath of allegiance to him'.[256]

It is indicative of the success with which Asante governments in the nineteenth century had established a new political order in the northern territories that, in the critical period following the British sack of Kumase in 1874, it was only in the eastern Bron provinces that the apparatus of control was totally destroyed. Elsewhere the leaders of secessionist movements found themselves, as in Gyaman, unable to obtain a sufficiently strong local constituency to sustain a thrust to independence. The decision by Mensa Bonsu's government to reject policies of military intervention in the northern provinces, but to depend upon the new civil service to sustain a diplomatic initiative, appears to have been based upon a realistic and well informed appraisal of the situation at the time. Early in 1881 the Governor of the Gold Coast Brandford Griffith conceded, albeit reluctantly, the success which had attended the Asante efforts:

I am somewhat suspicious that the Ashantis are working quietly with a view to the reacquisition of their lost territories. There is a wonderful network of

1882, however, Kwaku Kyei seemed once more to favour the British cause, see *Further Correspondence*, C. 3687, 1883, pp. 125–6.
254 Ellis, 1883, p. 198.
255 National Archives of Ghana, Accra, ADM 1/2/361: Huydecoper to Smith, dd. Banda, 9 August 1879.
256 Ellis, 1883, pp. 200–1.

communication between the natives which enables them to pick up informa·
tion and to work quietly towards the attainment of any desired object, and
they practise a diplomacy which, in its way, and after their fashion, they
deserve credit for.[257]

Yet, although the government in Kumase might well have congrat
ulated itself upon the general effectiveness of its policies, nevertheless
evidence of the extent to which its authority had in fact declined existed
in the number of local conflicts which it was unable any longer to
contain within acceptable limits. When for example a dispute occurred
between the Wankyihene (Route II, mile 90) and the Takyimanhene
(Route II, mile 71) in late 1874 or early 1875, Mensa Bonsu instructed
the Gyamasehene of Mampon to arbitrate.[258] The Takyimanhene
Kwabena Fofie, however, refused to observe the truce which the Gyamasehene called for, and the forces of Wankyi and Nkoransa were
therefore authorized by the government to assist the Gyamasehene in
occupying Takyiman town. Kwabena Fofie fled to Gyaman, accepted
the protection of the Gyamanhene Agyeman, and with his assistance
attempted to regain his country.[259] In the course of the fighting the
troops of Agyeman and Kwabena Fofie attacked Berekum (Route I,
mile 96) and Wam and Abesim to its south, burning the towns and
taking many prisoners to Gyaman.[260] Kwabena Fofie himself again retired to Gyaman, to become one of the principal adherents of Agyeman
in his pursuit of independence from Kumase.

Another struggle in the northwest developed between the Badu and
Siakwa: Nkoran groups whose forebears, originally from the Buna
area, had taken an oath of allegiance to Asantehene Opoku Ware in the
1740s and had settled for a time near Kumase before being given grants
of land in the Nsoko region (Route II, mile 110).[261] The Nsokohene and
Bannahene associated themselves with the cause of the Baduhene
Krosuma, while Kyei Kofi of Siakwa appealed to Gyamanhene Agyeman for assistance. The Bannahene and Gyamanhene agreed to arbitrate the dispute, but the latter's representatives were murdered by
the Banda while the Nsoko put Kyei Kofi to death.[262] The Siakwa

257 *Affairs*, C. 3064, 1881, pp. 4–5: Brandford Griffith to Kimberley, dd. 5 January
1881.
258 For the date, see *Further Correspondence*, C. 3687, 1883, p. 118: Lonsdale's
report on his mission of 1882.
259 Institute of African Studies, Ghana, BA/4: Tradition of Wenchi, recorded by
Kwabena Ameyaw, November 1965, p. 9; Wenchi field-notes, by T. A. Mustapha,
1965, p. 35.
260 *Further Correspondence*, C. 3687, 1883, pp. 111–13: Lonsdale's report on his
mission of 1882.
261 Kumase Divisional Council Archives, Manhyia: Ohene Kru Kwame v. Ohene
Kwasi Berkoi, heard before Asantehene Agyeman Prempeh II, 26 June 1933.
262 Institute of African Studies, Ghana, BA/1 and BA/2: Traditions of Banda, and

took refuge in Gyaman, where Kyei Kofi's son Bekwi had taken his place among the supporters of Agyeman by 1879.[263] Probably in that same year Agyeman supplied troops for an attack upon the Badu and Nsoko towns. Their inhabitants were obliged to retire into Banda.[264] The Banda towns were then in turn invaded, and the Bandahene Sakyame with his people, and the Badu and Nsoko refugees, retired to Longero under the protection of the Nkoransahene. Over the next two or three years the situation became, as Lonsdale observed, an extremely confused one. The Kintampo and Salaga roads were closed to all Gyaman traders, and the Banda, Badu and Nsoko made a number of sallies against the troops in occupation of their towns.[265] Lonsdale, nevertheless, regarded the whole matter as 'a purely border quarrel' which did not justify the intervention of the central government in Kumase.[266] Mensa Bonsu appears to have acted on much the same assumption, probably because his information indicated that the Gyamanhene Agyeman's constituency – other than the Takyiman and Siakwa refugee one – had been eroded yet further. 'Native reports concerning Gaman', wrote Ellis, 'asserted that King Ajiman had contrived to retain possession of the throne, but that Prince Korkobo was, in all but name, the actual ruler, and had been nominated Ajiman's successor'.[267] The Asantehene did nevertheless decide to send a peace-keeping force of 3,700 soldiers into the northwest in the dry season of 1880–1, to reinforce Owusu Koko Kuma's small detachment there.[268] At about the same time a new factor in the situation developed: the *cause celèbre* of Owusu Taseamandi.

Among the prisoners brought to Kumase after the Gyaman campaign of 1818–19 was one Tamia, a sister of the rebel Gyamanhene Adinkra. Given in marriage to the Kumase Adumhene Kwadwo Sampane (died 1826),[269] their daughter Apomahwene in or about 1840 in turn married the Asante heir apparent Osei Kwadwo and gave birth to Owusu Taseamandi.[270] Brought up in Kumase, Owusu Taseamandi was re-

of Hani and Nsoko, recorded by Kwabena Ameyaw, 20 November and 15 February 1965.

263 Ellis, 1883, p. 198. *Further Correspondence*, C. 3386, 1882, p. 45: evidence of Gyaman messengers, dd. Accra, 28 October 1881–'Beckui, son of Tchee [Kyei], recently dead.'

264 *Further Correspondence*, C. 3687, 1883, p. 118: Lonsdale's report on his mission of 1882.

265 *Ibid.* pp. 119–20, 127.

266 *Ibid.* p. 119.

267 Ellis, 1883, p. 223.

268 *Affairs*, C. 3064, 1881, pp. 48–50: J. Parker to Lt Col. Griffith, dd. Kumase, 24 January 1881. PRO, CO. 879/18, African (West) 232: enclosure in Griffith to Kimberley, dd. 6 February 1881.

269 Ricketts, 1831, p. 125.

270 Reindorf, 2nd ed., n.d., p. 165. *Affairs*, C. 3064, 1881, pp. 47–8: Mensa Bonsu ('Cobbina Bonso') to Governor, n.d. but received 4 March 1881. *Ibid.* pp. 71–2:

garded as having strong claims to the **Gyaman** stool. Although like Adinkra and the reigning Gyamanhene Agyeman, he belonged to the Yakase segment of the ruling house, Mensa Bonsu apparently had confidence in his loyalty: though a Gyaman, Owusu Taseamandi was also an *oheneba*, a prince of the Golden Stool. Hence, Mensa Bonsu saw it desirable to send him to Gyaman 'because a portion of the Gamans have declared themselves enemies to the Ashantis'.[271] With the loyal Kokobo as head of the faction supporting Owusu Taseamandi, the situation in Gyaman might have looked reasonably stable. Then at the time of the Odwira, on 10 January 1881, when Kumase was crowded with visiting dignitaries, Owusu Taseamandi vanished.[272] The government claimed that he had been abducted, and implied that the British authorities on the Gold Coast were involved. But Owusu Taseamandi appeared in Cape Coast on 18 January and, according to the British, claimed their protection. The Council in Kumase viewed the matter with grave concern and sent messengers to demand his extradition. 'It was necessary', Ellis commented,

in the interests of Prince Korkobo of Gaman, the good friend and ally of Ashanti, that Awoosoo should be detained in Coomassie, and the unexpected escape of a person of such importance in Ashanti politics created the greatest consternation, which feeling, when it became known that the fugitive had claimed British protection, was soon mingled with a longing for revenge.[273]

It seems quite likely that Owusu Taseamandi had fled Kumase simply because he did not wish to return to Gyaman. But when news reached Kumase that Owusu Taseamandi had committed suicide at Elmina in July 1881,[274] the belief that he had not willingly left Kumase was much strengthened. Those in the Asante councils who took the view that Mensa Bonsu's non-interventionist policies had allowed the Gyaman problem to remain too long unsolved were able to obtain a

Memorandum by Edmund Bannerman, dd. 2 February 1881, which was probably in error as naming Tamia's husband as the earlier Adumhene Adum Ata.

271 *Affairs*, C. 3064, 1881, p. 12: statement by Owusu Taseamandi, dd. Elmina, 18 January 1881. An elder brother of Owusu Taseamandi had earlier been permitted to return to Gyaman, where he was believed to have been murdered. He may have accompanied Tamia there, when she was repatriated by Kwaku Dua, see Reindorf, 2nd ed., n.d., p. 165, and *Affairs*, C. 3064, 1881, pp. 47–8: Mensa Bonsu to Governor, Kumase, n.d., but received 4 March 1881.

272 *The African Times*, xxii, no. 238, 1 July 1881: anon. letter dd. Accra, 6 May 1881.

273 Ellis, 1883, p. 237.

274 Ellis, 1883, p. 311, maintained that he jumped to his death from the walls of Elmina castle. Burton and Cameron, 1883, ii, 321, assert that he was found hanging in the bush outside Elmina. Since he had been ordered on board a ship for transportation, he was generally assumed to have committed suicide, but others maintained that he had been kidnapped and murdered on orders from Kumase.

mandate for a more positive approach. In the dry season of 1881–2 the Bantamahene Awua was authorized to establish a base camp near Kintampo, though there is no evidence to suggest that the intention was ever other than to make a token show of force.[275] In the event, however, it was the Gyamanhene Agyeman who commenced hostilities. On 5 February 1882 messengers from the Asantehene arrived in Cape Coast with news that Banda had again been attacked,[276] and a few days later more messengers arrived both there and at Accra to announce that Agyeman had placed himself at the head of a body of soldiers and was determined to wage war against the government's forces.[277] In May the Gyaman overran both Nsoko and Wankyi,[278] but fighting also broke out between the partisans of Agyeman and those of Kokobo.[279]

In the situation of crisis that prevailed, the British decided to send Lonsdale to both Kumase and Gyaman, and commissioned him to attempt to dissuade Mensa Bonsu from ordering a full-scale invasion of the disturbed northwestern provinces. With a staggering disregard for the historical record, Lonsdale outlined his assessment of the existing state of affairs:

the fact of finding King Osu [*sic:* Osei] Mensah so anxious to seize upon a purely border quarrel between his neighbour [Gyaman] and a Chief or Chiefs [Banda, Nsoko, etc.] over whom his claim of service, and therefore of protection, is of the most recent origin, only directs one's attention the more towards the general policy of the country of Ashanti, i.e., the policy of the reconstruction of the kingdom to something of its former size, strength, and importance . . . I have mentioned the policy pursued by the King of Ashanti in the Banda affair as being only a part of his general scheme of reconquest of his neighbours and former vassals. In carrying out this programme, he has attempted to cause disturbances outside even the limits of the country he desired to regain.[280]

In Kumase Lonsdale found the advocates of an invasion of Gyaman strongly represented in council. Yet, with the support of the peace party, he was able to obtain Mensu Bonsu's agreement to refrain from moving his troops until he, Lonsdale, had talked with the Gyamanhene.[281]

275 *Further Correspondence*, C. 3687, 1883, pp. 81; 114; 120: Lonsdale's report on his mission of 1882.
276 *Further Correspondence*, C. 3386, 1882, p. 44: J. Owusu Ansa to Governor, dd. Cape Coast, 8 February 1882.
277 *Idem*, also p. 47: Governor Rowe to Kimberley, dd. Accra, 23 March 1882.
278 *Further Correspondence*, C. 3687, 1883, p. 118: Lonsdale's report on his mission of 1882.
279 Ellis, 1883, p. 203.
280 *Further Correspondence*, C. 3687, 1883, pp. 119–20: Lonsdale's report on his mission of 1882.
281 *Ibid.* pp. 110–13.

In Gyaman, in June 1882, Lonsdale found the situation scarcely in accord with his expectations. 'The principal mover in the ebullition against the Ashantis', as he described it, was not Agyeman but the Kyidomhene Paimpi [282] (who, remarkably, had fought in the Asante armies against MacCarthy's forces in 1824).[283] Agyeman he found to possess little personal influence, and to have 'apparently little hold over some of his powerful Chiefs'.[284] Indeed, in view of the lack of support for his policies the Gyamanhene welcomed the opportunity presented by Lonsdale's visit to retreat from the aggressive position which he had adopted towards Kumase. Overruling Paimpi, he announced that he would recall his troops from the field, and would not fight the Asantehcnc's forces even if attacked! [285] Yet Lonsdale still continued to be to some extent a victim of his own prejudices. Having convinced himself that the government's resident commissioner in Bonduku, Kwaku Poku, was a prisoner there, he made arrangements to take him back to Cape Coast. But Kwaku Poku, who had indeed suffered some loss of property at the hands of Agyeman, politely pointed out that, 'it was impossible to leave the country until Adjiman, who was "wife to the King of Ashanti", had made restitution of the many things which he had taken from him, and moreover he could not think of travelling unless he could do so in the state befitting a man of his position'.[286] He was to remain at his post in Bonduku for many years more. Although the struggle between the opposed factions in Gyaman was to continue,[287] Lonsdale had nevertheless contributed towards the resolution of the conflict with the central government. It was symptomatic of the relaxation of tension that in August 1882 messengers from the Imām of Bonduku arrived at Accra to announce that the Gyaman Muslim traders hoped shortly to visit the coast.[288] By 1887 relations had improved to a point at which the Gyamanhene was prepared once more to permit his subjects to use the Asante great-roads,[289] and in the following year the Muslim Dyula or Wangara of Gyaman ('Gammans (Wongoras)') were moving freely within the metropolitan region.[290]

282 *Ibid.* pp. 118, 121.
283 R. A. Freeman, 1898, p. 204.
284 *Further Correspondence*, C. 3687, 1883, p. 124: Lonsdale's report on his mission of 1882.
285 *Ibid.* p. 121.
286 *Ibid.* p. 122.
287 See, e.g. Binger, 1892, II, 174 ff.
288 *Further Correspondence*, C. 3687, 1883, p. 71: Moloney to Kimberley, dd. Accra, 19 September 1882.
289 *Further Correspondence*, C. 5357, 1888, pp. 62–3: Lonsdale to Administrator, dd. Denkyira, 10 June 1887.
290 *Further Correspondence*, C. 5615, 1888, p. 33: Barnett to Governor, dd. Eduabin, 26 February 1888.

The Nkoransa problem

In the situation of crisis which had prevailed in the northwest in the early 1880s, provincial rulers whose fundamental loyalty was not in question had seen an opportunity to press specific grievances on the attention of the central government. In 1881 or 1882 the Nkoransahene Ata Fa, in whose territory the market of Kintampo lay, closed the great-road to Kumase at Kofiase near Donkoro Nkwanta (Route III, mile 57), thereby registering a protest, first against the many demands made upon him by Mensa Bonsu for the extradition of men wanted for trial in the capital,[291] and secondly against the heavy tolls levied there on his traders.[292] Having stressed, however, his intention 'to again join with the Coomassies' once his complaints were met, he did so when the short-reigned Kwaku Dua II gave him redress in 1884.[293]

Ata Fa died at an advanced age in 1885, and his successor Kofi Abamo held office for only a few months. In the period of intense political activity which preceded the election of Agyeman Prempe as Asantehene in 1888, the next Nkoransahene, Kwasi Poku, played an ambivalent role and refused to commit himself to clear support of either of the principal candidates.[294] On his victory in 1888, Agyeman Prempe therefore required that Kwasi Poku should take an oath of allegiance to him. According to Ferguson's account of the matter, the Nkoransahene

represented that there was no reason to doubt his loyalty, to prove which he swore that he would recover for the King of Ashanti his authority over the Brong tribes which was lost in 1874 when those tribes asserted their independence. The King of Ashanti was very pleased, and presented Opoku with a gold sword and other decorations.[295]

But Agyeman Prempe's councillors may have remained uncertain of Kwasi Poku's loyalty,[296] and their realization of the vulnerability of the Kintampo market should serious disturbances occur in Nkoransa decided them to encourage the development of Wankyi as an alternative trade outlet.

291 *Further Correspondence*, C. 3687, 1883, pp. 95–6: Badger to Private Secretary, dd. Accra, 4 December 1882.
292 *Further Correspondence*, C. 4477, 1885, p. 85: Kirby to Colonial Secretary, dd. Kyekyewere, Asante, 10 March 1884. *Ibid.* pp. 93–4: Kirby's report on his mission to Kumase and the interior provinces of the Asante kingdom, dd. 16 April 1884.
293 *Further Correspondence*, C. 4477, 1885, p. 94: Kirby's report.
294 *Further Correspondence*, C. 7917, 1896, p. 136: Ferguson's Memorandum on the Asante and the Bron Tribes, dd. 24 November 1893.
295 *Idem.*
296 The reign of Kwasi Poku is treated in a paper by W. Owen, 'Nkoranza under Ohene Kwasi Opoku Katakyie I', forthcoming. Owen shows that Kwasi Poku's attitude towards Kumase remained an ambivalent one.

According to an account of the matter received in Wankyi in 1965, the Asantehene requested the Wankyihene 'to find a Mallam who could pray to God and make medicine so that the Wenchi town would become a market town'. It proved possible to obtain the services of Malam Ma'azu, a Hausa from Hadejia who had been trading in Kenedugu (Mali) and had there married a daughter of its ruler Tieba. 'Mallam Ma'azu stayed in Wenchi and prayed to God', it was claimed, 'and a year later traders came to the Wenchi town.' [297] The trading community was much enlarged when the Asantehene sent officials from Kumase to settle there a group of Muslim Bamba from Banda, and to charge the Wankyihene with their protection.[298] One Obosom Boami from the *nkonnwasoafo* group in Kumase was appointed 'consul' for the newly created market, and was responsible *inter alia* for the collection of tolls there for the central government.[299] In deciding to develop the Wankyi market, the authorities in fact displayed considerable foresight. The loyalty of the Nkoransahene Kwasi Poku was indeed demonstrated by his readiness to supply Agyeman Prempe with troops to fight the rebel Mamponhene Owusu Sekyere in September 1888.[300] But Kwasi Poku faced strong opposition from dissident groups within Nkoransa and in that month took his own life to avoid destoolment. His successor, Kofi Fa, was brought to office on a secessionist platform. Required to take an oath of allegiance to Prempe, and to surrender many Asante rebels who had taken refuge in his territory, he refused both demands.[301]

The rebellion of the Nkoransahene Kofi Fa presented a particularly grave threat to the Kumase authorities. On 24 January 1889 the Gyamanhene Agyeman had entered into a Treaty of Protection with the British. The agreement was indeed almost immediately repudiated: the aged Paimpi pointed out that he personally, and the Gyaman in general, would witness with satisfaction the return to the coast of the visiting mission.[302] The episode indicated, nevertheless, that the British were finally prepared to extend their protectorate into the northern territories of Asante. In the following year, on 25 November, the British signed a further Treaty of Protection with the Atebubu, thus reaffirming their support for the rebel eastern Bron coalition. When therefore the Nkoransahene Kofi Fa refused to take an oath of alle-

---

297 Institute of African Studies, Ghana, T. A. Mustapha, field-notes, Wenchi, 1965: interview with the Hausa headman of Wenchi.

298 *Ibid.* interview with Malam Abū Bakr Bamba.

299 *Ibid.* pp. 26, 49, and 64. See also BA/4: Tradition of Wenchi, recorded by Kwabena Ameyaw, November 1965, p. 10.

300 *Further Correspondence*, C. 7917, 1896, p. 136: Ferguson's Memorandum dd. 24 November 1893.

301 *Ibid.* p. 137.

302 R. A. Freeman, 1898, pp. 206–7, 297.

giance to Agyeman Prempe I, the government found itself threatened by the possible emergence of an alliance of dissident provinces extending across the whole of its hinterland from northeast to northwest. The main goal of British policy became quite apparent, moreover, in March 1891 when the Governor of the Gold Coast extended an invitation to the Asantehene to place all of his territories under British protection. The offer was rejected, and the Asantehene appears to have enjoyed full support in council for the immediate despatch of a punitive expedition to Nkoransa. The event marked the final abandonment of the belief of the earlier period, that economic sanctions would be sufficient to the maintenance of political order in the northern territories.

In mid-1892 government troops entered Nkoransa and sacked its towns. In October Kofi Fa sent messengers to the British Governor. He requested British protection, and offered a tribute of £48 in gold dust. 'I will agree with all your laws [which] should be given to me', wrote Kofi Fa, who claimed that the Asante soldiers had massacred two hundred men and taken prisoner two thousand women and children.[303] In the following year, therefore, full military reoccupation of the province was authorized from Kumase. According to Ferguson, who had been sent by the British to the north 'to organize a system of spies on the Ashanti army', the invading force was between 10,000 and 17,000 strong, excluding camp followers, and between 300 and 700 of the troops were equipped with Snider rifles.[304] It was commanded by the Bantamahene Amankwatia Kwame. Strengthened by reinforcements from Gyaman and from the eastern Bron, the Nkoransa succeeded in winning the first engagement, but thereafter the Bantamahene's forces carried all before them.[305] The Nkoransahene himself fled into the eastern Bron country. Asante troops pursued him as far as the Pru River, but then withdrew to their base camp near Kintampo.[306] British intelligence officers believed that the Asante army was being rested preparatory to invading Atebubu and the eastern Bron territories. In response to a request from the Atebubuhene, on 28 September 1893 the British decided to station a small expeditionary force there: it comprised 300 Hausa soldiers with one Maxim gun.[307]

303 *Further Correspondence*, C. 7917, 1896, pp. 79–80: Kofi Fa to Governor, dd. 13 October 1892.
304 *Ibid*. p. 95: Hodgson to Inspector-General, dd. Accra, 29 September 1893. *Ibid*. p. 117: Ferguson to Hodgson, dd. Abetifi, 7 November 1893.
305 *Ibid*. pp. 88–9: Hull to Hodgson, dd. 17 September 1893, reporting the evidence of George Appia, recently returned from Kumase.
306 *Ibid*. p. 117: Ferguson to Hodgson, dd. 7 November 1893.
307 *Ibid*. p. 89: Hodgson to Inspector-General, dd. 29 September 1893. Foreign Office Confidential Print 6364, Papers Relating to West Africa, pp. 189–90: Atebubuhene to Brandford Griffith, dd. Atebubu, 17 May 1892.

Having defeated the Nkoransa, however, the Asante commander despatched a small force to occupy the Mo country north of Kintampo,[308] but otherwise held his army inactive. Indeed, in a letter of 19 October to the British Governor the Asantehene specifically disclaimed any intention of attacking Atebubu.[309]

New initiatives in the north

In the early 1890s the Asante government still continued basically to subscribe to the principle which had dominated political thinking throughout much of the century, and which had been clearly enunciated by Osei Bonsu in 1820: 'never to appeal to the sword while a path lay open for negociation'.[310] In a series of moves on several fronts, in the second half of 1893 the Kumase authorities launched a new diplomatic offensive which was seriously to threaten the whole programme of limited intervention in the north which the British had pursued more or less consistently since 1874. In Nkoransa itself Kwaku Fokuo was groomed to succeed Kofi Fa.[311] Both the head of the Benkum of Nkoransa, and the Akyeamehene, were of that name; it was apparently the former, a strong supporter of Agyeman Prempe, who was chosen.[312] The loyalty of the Banda, moreover, was ensured when they were promised jurisdiction over parts of Nkoransa territory.[313] In the far northwest the Bole of Gonja, who in June 1892 had entered into a Treaty of Trade and Friendship with the British and had agreed 'to desist from entering in any alliance that the King of Kumasi might propose', were nonetheless induced to reaffirm allegiance to the Asantehene and to send men to join the expedition against the Mo.[314] In late September or early October officials from Kumase – the herald Kofi Akwa and the sword-bearer Opoku – transmitted to the

308 *Further Correspondence*, C. 7917, 1896, p. 106: Prempe (Kwaku Dua III) to Acting Governor, dd. Kumase, 19 October 1893.

309 *Ibid.* p. 152: Ferguson to Adjutant, Atebubu Expeditionary Force, dd. 20 December 1893.

310 Dupuis, 1824, pp. 225–6.

311 *Further Correspondence*, C. 7917, 1896, p. 152: Ferguson to Adjutant, Atebubu Expeditionary Force, dd. 20 December 1893.

312 W. Owen, personal communication: Owen's field-work in Nkoransa reveals that another candidate also under consideration for the Nkoransa stool was Kwasi Gyambibi of Antoa – presumably the father of Agyeman Prempe. Kwasi Gyambibi's mother did indeed have some connection with Nkoransa, and the nickname 'Gyambibi' is that of a shrine there, see Wilks, field-notes: interview with Akyempemhene Boakye Dankwa and Hiahene Mensa Bonsu, dd. Kumase, 18 November 1958.

313 *Further Correspondence*, C. 7917, 1896, p. 154: Ferguson to Adjutant, dd. 25 December 1893.

314 *Idem.* For the Bole treaty, see Foreign Office Confidential Print 6733, pp. 1–2: Treaty with Tuluwe and Bole, dd. 1st June 1892.

Atebubuhene a message which, if not conciliatory, at least opened a way for further dialogue:

The King of Ashanti presents his compliments to you all. He has heard that the people of Atabubu and the Brong people are deserting their country. If they like peace he is for peace, if they like war they will have it. He desires that the King of Atabubu and the King of Mampon should return to serve him, that they should eat fetish with him, after which they are to make peace between him and the King of Nkoranza, or else give up the refugee King of Nkoranza. That the King of Atabubu, the King of Nkoranza, and the Brong people should take their oath of allegiance to him; should they not do so they are not for peace with Ashanti. If they are for peace the King of Ashanti is for peace. If the messengers return with unfavourable reply to their King the army then at Abeasi would proceed against Atabubu and the Brong people. Should the invasion of Atabubu and the Brong people as well as the capture of the Nkoranzas not be feasible, then the army would retire to Kuntampo and wait there till they can fight them. Five days were given to consider the demands of the King of Ashanti. The King of Ashanti swears three great oaths of Opoku Wari, Sai Tutu, and Fedu Ajumani [that is, Kwaku Dua I].[315]

The negative response of the Atebubuhene to the message was conditioned no doubt by the presence of the British force – and its Maxim gun – in his town. Undeterred, however, the Kumase negotiators turned their attention to the subordinate chiefs of the Atebubuhene. In December 1893 for example, one of them, the Amantinhene, received a message from Kumase relayed through the Adwirahene:

remember the history of your ancestors, your ancestors served Ashanti and you should do the same, whenever there is a little dispute between Ashanti and Nkoranza, you run away to Atebubu. This time should the white man go back without any harm to Ashanti you will have to square it with Ashanti. They, the white men, always carry ammunition with them, they do not mean anything this time, and you had better return to Ashanti or after they are gone you will have to answer to Ashanti.[316]

By contrast with the somewhat menacing character of the approaches to the Atebubuhene and the Amantinhene, those to the Kpembewura Yūsuf, recently enskinned after the civil war in the division, were by contrast indirect and exploratory. Indeed, Muslims from Bole were asked to act for the Asantehene as negotiators in Salaga: 'a great part of Bole', commented Colonel Scott of the Atebubu Expeditionary Force, 'is Mahommedan and possesses the same sympathies as Salaga'.

315 *Further Correspondence*, C. 7917, 1896, pp. 141–2: report on a meeting at Atebubu, by Ferguson, dd. Atebubu, 20 November 1893. *Ibid.* p. 139: Ferguson's Memorandum, dd. 24 November 1893. The two texts vary slightly.
316 *Ibid.* p. 152: Ferguson to Adjutant, Atebubu Expeditionary Force, dd. 20 December 1893.

Writing from Atebubu, Ferguson expressed his misgivings about the new developments in Gonja: 'The people of Bole are strongly sympathetic with Salaga, they have espoused the Ashanti inceptions of the war [against Nkoransa], and it is the general belief that if the alliance is not checked it will necessitate the Atebubu Expeditionary Force being detained to give confidence to the people here, and to watch operations.' [317] Kpembewura Yūsuf in fact proved not averse to resuming direct trade relations with Kumase by the old great-road through Atebubu, and hoped moreover for Asante support for his projected attack upon Yeji – whose chief was a supporter of the defeated Kpembewura Nakpo.[318] Since Yeji, like Salaga, was within what the British and Germans had chosen to define as a 'Neutral Zone', the former were in some doubt as to what course of action to follow. 'I regret to learn', wrote Acting Governor Hodgson of the Gold Coast,

that Kabachi-wula, the present King of Salaga [Kpembewura Yūsuf], meditates an attack on Yeji in consequence of the support given by the people of that country to the late King, but although any step which brings the Salagas nearer to the Ashantis is much to be deprecated you [Colonel Scott] have acted rightly in taking no action, having regard to the fact that Yeji is within the neutral zone. I have already represented to the Secretary of State the extreme desirability, indeed necessity, of preventing an alliance between the Salagas and Ashantis, and I have now again done so. Were such an alliance effected Kuntempo would cease to exist as a market town, and the greater part of the trade which now finds its way into the Gold Coast would be diverted. The possibility of such an alliance is a very strong argument in favour of a forward policy with regard to Ashanti and its absorption within the Protectorate.[319]

The Asante government's undoubted revival of influence in Salaga in particular, and the north in general, was unquestionably one of the many reasons which convinced the British that their position in the hinterland could be finally secured only by the occupation of Kumase itself.

The Samorian factor in Asante politics

By the beginning of 1894 the British administrators on the Gold Coast had become acutely conscious of the precarious nature of their

317 *Ibid.* p. 153: Scott to Colonial Secretary, dd. Atebubu, 25 December 1893. *Ibid.* p. 154: Ferguson to Adjutant, dd. Atebubu, 25 December 1893. I am indebted to Bruce Haight for pointing out that Nuhu, Imām of Bole at the time, was himself a Salaga man.
318 Braimah and Goody, 1967, p. 38.
319 *Further Correspondence*, C. 7917, 1896, p. 156: Hodgson to Scott, dd. Accra, 10 January 1894. See also NAG, Accra, ADM. 12/3/5: Hodgson to Ripon, dd. Accra, 9 January 1894.

position in the Asante hinterland.[320] The major threat in that quarter, however, was yet to materialize. In 1895 the forces of the Almami Samori – soldiers seasoned by years of guerilla fighting against the French – occupied Bonduku, and from that base thrust eastwards to establish advance positions in such towns within the ambit of Asante as Banda, Gbuipe, Bole and Mengye.[321] The Gyamanhene Agyeman had finally accepted French protection, in preference to that of the Asante or the British, on 12 July 1893. His appeals to the French for assistance against Samori, however, met with no response. He requested support, therefore, from the only two other powers in a position to respond: the British and, ironically enough in view of his earlier stance, the Asante. His request to Governor Maxwell of the Gold Coast was contained in a letter of August 1895, and was duly rejected by virtue of his association with the French.[322] His appeal to the Asantehene was forwarded through the Asante resident commissioner in Bonduku – the Opoku who had been stationed there since 1874 – but apparently failed to arrive in Kumase because the great-road was closed in Nkoransa.[323] Agyeman was driven into exile, and Samori recognized the by then extremely aged Paimpi as effective ruler of Gyaman.[324] But that the Asante government would have intervened in support of Gyamanhene Agyeman was most unlikely: the evidence indicates that in fact close communications existed between the Asantehene and the Almami, and that a programme of cooperation between the two was being discussed.

Shortly after the occupation of Bonduku, Samori despatched messengers to the Asantehene to explain that he had invaded Gyaman because of Agyeman's refusal to allow him to open a trade path through that territory.[325] The messengers also stated that Samori would help defeat any Asante chief who refused to renew allegiance to Agyeman Prempe I.[326] Reports, seemingly unfounded, were current in France that Samori had visited Kumase in person.[327] On the Gold

320 PRO, CO. 879/38, African (West) 448, pp. 30–1: Ferguson to Governor, dd. Bimbila, 29 August 1892. Foreign Office Confidential Print 6364, pp. 209–10.
321 PRO, CO. 96/297: Maxwell to Chamberlain, dd. 16 August 1897.
322 PRO, CO. 96/259: letter from Agyeman, dd. August 1895, in Maxwell to Chamberlain, dd. 19 August 1895.
323 PRO, CO. 879/40, African (West) 465: Nkoranzahene to Ferguson, dd. 19 July 1895.
324 Paimpi was executed by the French in Bonduku, on or about 30 August 1898, see Foreign Office Confidential Print 7674, 1899, West Africa, Part 1, p. 47: Governor of the Gold Coast to Governor of the Ivory Coast, dd. 29 October 1898.
325 PRO, CO. 96/261: Stewart to Governor, dd. 11 October 1895, in Maxwell to Chamberlain, dd. 25 October 1895.
326 *The Times* (London), 4 January 1896: citing report of a trader from Akumadan.
327 *Further Correspondence*, C. 7918, 1896: Chamberlain to Maxwell, dd. 15 November 1895.

Coast the belief was initially widespread that Samori was acting in collusion with the French, whose sympathies towards the Asante cause were well known: 'Being desirous of ensuring as much opposition as possible to the occupation of Kumasi by British troops in the event of a refusal on the part of the King to accept a British Resident, the French had induced Samory, it is thought, to enter Kumasi so as to give assistance to the King'.[328] When it became known, however, that Samori had notified the Governor of the Gold Coast of his desire to establish relations with the British rather than the French,[329] the view of the matter changed:

The tricolour does not wave in Kumasi. To any one who has been studying the interior problems for any length of time, the conclusion that Samory was invited to Ashantee by Prempeh can not be avoided. The report actually reached us a short while ago that an alliance for offensive and defensive purposes had really been effected by Prempeh with Samory, and that the former had made the latter a present of Slaves and Gold dust.[330]

In fact the Asantehene had indeed responded to Samori's message by despatching a mission to Bonduku. Comprising three hundred officials and retainers, and carrying a gift of 100 oz of gold for Samori, it arrived in Bonduku late in October 1895. According to the report of a Hausa who witnessed the proceedings there, the Kumase envoys announced that the Asantehene 'asked Samory to help him recover all the countries from Gaman to the Coast which originally belonged to Ashanti'.[331] In a letter of 6 November addressed to the Governor of the Gold Coast, the Nkoransahene stated that he was anticipating being attacked by Samori's forces – 'at the instigation of Kumasi'.[332] According to another report, however, Samori had requested 1,000 oz of gold to finance such an attack, and this the Asante government had considered too expensive.[333] But certainly the balance of power in the west and northwest was showing signs of changing to the advantage of Asante: late in 1894 the Sehwi appear unambiguously to have reaffirmed their allegiance to the Golden Stool.[334]

328 *Gold Coast Chronicle*, 7 October 1895, p. 2.
329 PRO, CO. 96/260: Samori to Governor, n.d., in Maxwell to Chamberlain, dd. 6 September 1895.
330 *Gold Coast Chronicle*, 27 November 1895, p. 2.
331 *Further Correspondence*, C. 7918, 1896: Maxwell to Chamberlain, n.d. but received 13 December 1895. PRO, CO. 96/263: report by Sowete, in Maxwell to Chamberlain, dd. 10 December 1895.
332 *Further Correspondence*, C. 7918, 1896: Maxwell to Chamberlain, n.d. but received 25 November 1895.
333 PRO, CO. 96/263: report by Sowete.
334 *Further Correspondence*, C. 7917, 1896, pp. 227–9: 'The Ashantis in this Western Protectorate' to Governor, dd. Cape Coast, 1 October 1894. NAG, Accra, ADM 11/1483: telegram, District Commissioner, Cape Coast, to Governor, dd. 22 February 1895.

The course of events was such as to cause alarm to the British authorities not only on the Gold Coast but in London. It was probably the development of cordial relations between the Asantehene Agyeman Prempe I and the Almami Samori, at a time when the British position in the Asante hinterland had been weakened by the Kumase government's diplomatic overtures there, which finally decided the British upon massive military intervention once more. By a telegram of 15 November 1895, Chamberlain instructed Governor Maxwell of the Gold Coast to notify Samori of 'intended action against Kumasi', and to advise him not to interfere.[335] On 20 November Maxwell sent a letter by special messengers to Samori, stating that the British were preparing to wage war against Asante, and requiring that Samori should not allow his troops to enter Asante – prematurely described as 'English territory'.[336] On 17 January 1896, the British expeditionary force commanded by Colonel Scott entered Kumase unopposed. Three days later the Asantehene Agyeman Prempe I made a formal act of submission to Governor Maxwell. With a total disregard for all recognized conventions, Maxwell thereupon ordered the arrest of the Asantehene, the Asantehemaa, and of various officials and functionaries.[337] The prisoners were taken to the coast and held at Elmina, before being transferred to Sierra Leone where they disembarked on 5 January 1897. In view of reports that, by the inland roads, the Asantehene remained in communication with his subjects, and they with Samori, the further decision was taken to transfer the prisoners to Seychelles.[338] The Asantehene left Sierra Leone for exile on 19 August 1900, and was not to be repatriated until 1924. The spectre of an alliance between the forces of Samori and those of Asante did, however, continue to haunt the British to the end. In mid-1896, for example, reports circulated that the Nkoransa had been joined by Samori for an attempt to expel the British from Kumase.[339] And, during the last Anglo-Asante war of 1900, the Asante plan of campaign was deemed 'to be superior to that of mere savages'[!]: among the many rumours current was one that Samori

---

[335] *Further Correspondence*, C. 7918, 1896: Chamberlain to Maxwell, dd. 15 November 1895.

[336] PRO, CO. 96/262: Governor to Samori, dd. 20 November 1895, in Maxwell to Chamberlain, dd. 23 November 1895.

[337] The overview of the matter taken by al-Ḥājj ʿUmar b. Abī Bakr of Salaga and Kete Krakye, in his poem in Hausa, *Waka Nasara*, was that the Asantehene suggested to Samori an alliance to defeat the Christians, but that 'the Christians learned of their intentions, and managed to outwit and capture Prempe' (manuscript in possession of al-Ḥājj Yaʿqūb b. Imām al-Ḥājj al-Ḥasan, of Yendi).

[338] PRO, CO. 96/295: report by Vroom, dd. 19 June 1897, in Maxwell to Chamberlain, dd. 14 July 1896.

[339] *The Times* (London), 14 August 1896.

(although by then himself in fact a prisoner of the French) had joined the forces ranged against the British.[340]

The British as heirs to Asante power in the north

In many of its northern provinces, in the politically confused period between 1874 and 1896, the Asante government had succeeded in retaining a considerable measure of control despite British attempts to subvert its authority there. The relations between the central government and the Ya Nas of Dagomba in the later part of the century exemplify well the resilience of the ties which had been developed with that outer province in the eighteenth and early nineteenth centuries. The tribute which had been imposed upon the Dagomba as part of the political settlement between the Asantehene Osei Kwadwo and the Ya Na 'Abdallah (Gariba) in the early 1770s was suspended at some time during the long reign – from *ca.* 1833 to *ca.* 1864 – of Ya Na Ya'qūb. The implication of the account of the matter given by the court drummer-historians of Dagomba is that the Asante concession was in acknowledgement of the conditions of peace and stability which had prevailed in the province. 'Now that you have finished paying', so the Asantehene is reported to have announced, 'if you do not fight any more the debt is finished but if you should fight again and kill each other the debt remains.' [341] Due to the insanity of Ya Na Ya'qūb in the later years of his reign, however, conflicts developed between the prospective candidates for the skin. On his death, his son 'Abdallāh took power, but three of the deceased ruler's brothers – the Sunson Na Yaḥya, Yo Na Jibrīl, and Mionlana 'Issa – challenged his claim and appealed to the Asantehene Kwaku Dua I for support, offering a tribute of two thousand slaves for his intervention.[342]

Having carried out in 1863 extensive military operations within the British Protected Territory of the Gold Coast, the government in Kumase was seemingly too preoccupied with its affairs in the south at the time to make any positive response to the request from Ya Na Ya'qūb's brothers. 'Abdallāh consolidated his position as Ya Na in succession to his father. On Kwaku Dua's death in 1867, however, the new Asantehene Kofi Kakari required Ya Na 'Abdallāh formally to affirm his allegiance to him and insisted, in view of the disturbances in Dagomba, that a tribute must be restored.[343] In order to meet the Asante demand, Ya Na 'Abdallāh carried out a series of expeditions

340 Biss, 1901, p. 61.
341 Institute of African Studies, Ghana, Tait MSS: MS B, p. 57.
342 *Ibid.* Tait MSS: MS A, p. 21.
343 *Ibid.* Tait MSS: MS B, p. 57. For a recent analysis of these events in Dagomba, see Ferguson, 1973, pp. 254–69.

against both the Bassari to the east and the Grunshi to the northwest.[344]

On the Adae of 10 August 1873, news reached Kumase of an outbreak of violence in Dagomba, when after a fracas presumably in
Yendi between the Muslims and Asante visitors there, the former had
lured a number of the latter into a trap and had had them killed. 'It
was thus evident that the central tribes had thrown off the yoke of
Ashantee', declared the missionaries Ramseyer and Kühne grandiosely.
Quite inconsistently, they added, 'to our surprise, however, a mohammedan hung himself in the town [Kumase], and the affair at Sarem was
represented as a dispute between the Ashantee chiefs'.[345] The nature
of the incident remains obscure, but certainly there is no indication
that either the Ya Na 'Abdallāh, who died in 1876,[346] or his successor
the Ya Na Andani played any part in the rebellion of the eastern
Bron or subsequently displayed any interest in joining the anti-Asante
coalition. Although the great-road from Yendi to Kumase was closed
as a result of the embargo on the Salaga trade, when Lonsdale visited
Yendi in 1882 he nevertheless found the Asante residents there free
and unharmed, and learned from traders that presents still reached the
Ya Na from Kumase. 'The Yendis', so the Asantehene announced,
'must not believe all that they hear of the humiliation of Ashanti by
the British.' [347] Ten years later a large number of Asante not only
remained in Yendi, but also continued to play a part in civic affairs.[348]
In 1968 the nonagenarian Imām of Yendi, al-Ḥājj 'Abdallāh b. al-
Ḥājj al-Ḥasan, gave some account of Asante activity there in the latter
part of the century:

Before the Germans came to Yendi, the Asante had been very powerful.
Asante people used to come to Yendi, to the Ya Na, to collect slaves. Some
of the Asante would just visit the town, and some would stay. They had a
place known as Kambonseyili, 'Asante quarter'. These were not the Kambonse
gunmen, who were mainly Dagomba, but proper Asante who came to collect
the slaves. After the collapse of Asante, some of them stayed. They intermarried. The elder Asante died, and only the women and children remained,
who have now become Dagombas. These Asante were also the executioners.

344 Klose, 1899, pp. 502–3. Von Zech, 1898, p. 132. Tamakloe, 1931, pp. 37–8. See
    also the text in Withers Gill, *A Short History of the Dagomba Tribe*, Accra, n.d.,
    recorded by Imām al-Ḥasan of Salaga from Malam Muḥammad Kundungunda,
    grandson of Ya Na Ya'qūb. See further, Ferguson, 1973, pp. 176–91.
345 Ramseyer and Kühne, 1875, pp. 231–2.
346 PRO, CO. 96/118: District Commissioner, Accra, to Acting Colonial Secretary,
    dd. 28 August 1876.
347 *Further Correspondence*, C. 3386, 1882, p. 76: Lonsdale's report on his mission
    of 1881–2.
348 PRO, CO. 879/38, African (West) 448, p. 65: Ferguson to Governor, dd. 9
    December 1892.

If someone committed a murder, the Ya Na's police would arrest him, and he would be taken to the Asante for execution. The Ya Na would send any Dagomba who was found guilty to the Asante executioners. Similarly, anyone found having sexual intercourse with a wife of the Ya Na would be sent to the Asante. Every year, all through the year, slaves would be collected, and then once a year they would be given to the Asante who would take them to Kumase. There was a fixed quota every year. If the Asante found that it was not correct, then the Ya Na would have to go to his own villages to make the number up. The Kambon Na, the head of the gunmen, would actually get the slaves, but it was the Balogo Na of Yendi who planned the whole operation and told the gunmen what to do.[349]

In 1896, when the British had occupied Kumase and had taken the Asantehene Agyeman Prempe I captive to the coast, the Ya Na finally recognized that the bonds which had linked him, and his predecessors in office, to the government of Asante for over a century and a half, had been broken. In a letter in Arabic to the British, he observed: 'The Germans write twice from Kraki [Krakye]. I refuse their letters. They say you refuse letters, so we come and fight. I want to be English, not German. I belonged to Ashanti. English conquer Ashanti, I now belong to English . . .'[350] Certainly, too, the British military commander in the region regarded Dagomba as having passed from Asante to British over-rule in 1896 precisely in consequence of the occupation of Asante:

The political situation in Dagomba is peculiar and worthy of attention. It must be remembered that in the days of the Ashanti power Yendi was a vassal kingdom, and, moreover, the Ashantis were able to keep their vassal states in very real subjection. Any demand, however exorbitant, was cheerfully complied with, and all sorts of rules restricting those insignia of royalty, which most appeal to the native mind, were devised and strictly enforced, e.g., the number of sacred and war drums were limited, and the kings and chiefmen were not allowed to use palanquins, etc. When the annual tribute or any special fine was to be collected, a commissioner was despatched from Kumasi for this purpose. He was not accompanied by any powerful escort, but his slightest wish was readily obeyed, and opposition of any sort was never dreamt of.

On hearing of the fall of Kumasi and the seizure of Osai Prempeh's person, these vassal states naturally concluded that the obedience and annual tribute

349 Wilks and Ferguson, field-notes: interview with Imām al-Ḥājj 'Abdallāh, dd. Yendi, 8 September 1968.
350 PRO, CO. 879/52, African (West) 549, p. 110: letter from Ya Na Andani, n.d., but received 7 January 1898. Compare National Archives of Ghana, Accra, ADM 11/1622: notes of meeting with chiefs and headchief of Nanumba, 25 February 1918 – 'In former times the Nanumbas and Dagombas were all under the Ashantis . . . After the Ashanti war [1896] we got a message from Ashanti to say we and Dagomba were under the English . . . When the Ashantis were defeated we were under the English, and it is right that both the Dagombas and the Nanumbas should be under the English.'

exacted by the Ashanti would now be promptly enforced by the conquerors of Ashanti . . .[351]

Only the Germans subscribed to a different view of the matter, and proceeded to occupy eastern Dagomba, including the capital town of Yendi, notwithstanding the British view of themselves as heirs to the Asante power.

It was testimony to the success with which Asante governments had created conditions of relative stability in the northern provinces of Greater Asante, that as the new British military administrators moved in to establish their commands, everywhere they became strongly aware of the earlier achievements of their Asante predecessors. As Major H. P. Northcott, first British Commissioner and Commandant in the Northern Territories of the Gold Coast, observed, 'In listening to the native accounts of their tribal traditions, perhaps the most remarkable fact is the constant reference to the far-reaching powers possessed by the kings of Ashanti before they suffered their first reverse at our hand'.[352] Yet, although the Asante and the subsequent British administration in the northern territories maintained there a rule of law which did much to facilitate commercial intercourse, there is little doubt that the importance of the hinterland derived largely from the workers which it supplied to the farms and mines of Asante and of the Gold Coast Colony. The unfree labour – the *nnɔnkɔfo* – recruited by the Asante authorities in the nineteenth century was replaced by the forced labour recruited by the British authorities in the twentieth. It was a consequence of the exploitative nature of the situation, that the paramount powers whether before or after 1896 showed little inclination to foster the material advancement of the north. Thomas has referred to the 'restrictive attitude on the part of the [colonial] administration towards social change which sprang from education or missionary activity'.[353] *Plus ça change ça change rien.* In 1817 Bowdich attempted to convince the Asantehene of the altruistic desire of the British to spread the benefits of civilization to his kingdom. In a bantering reply which expressed his scepticism, Osei Bonsu alluded to the Gonja division of Kong, most distant of all his domains. 'This motive', he commented,

cannot be the real one. I well see that you are much superior to the Asante in industry and the arts; for in the fort of Cape Coast itself, which is only a small establishment, you have many things which we do not know how to make: but there exists here, in the interior, a people, those of Kong, who are

351 *Ibid.* p. 401: Report on the Neutral Zone, by Captain A. H. C. Kenney-Herbert, dd. 24 June 1898.
352 Northcott, 1899, p. 17.
353 Thomas, 1973, p. 79.

as little civilized relative to us as we are relative to you. They do not know how to make ornaments of gold, to build comfortable houses, or to weave garments. However, there is not a single one of my Asantes, not even the poorest, who would leave his home for the sole purpose of going to teach the people of Kong. Now, how do you wish to persuade me that it is only for so flimsy a motive that you have left this fine and prosperous England . . . ? [354]

[354] Anonymous review of Bowdich, 1819, in the *Journal des Savants*, 1819.

CHAPTER 8

Asante and its neighbours: the politics of entente

The Muslim role in foreign affairs

Other than with the British on the Gold Coast, successive Asante governments for the most part maintained good relations with those countries beyond the imperial frontiers with which they had contact. After the middle of the eighteenth century the Asantehenes evinced few signs of interest in extending their hegemony beyond the limits established under Opoku Ware, and in the early nineteenth century, indeed, the decision could be taken to relinquish administrative control over many of the southern possessions. Conversely, it was rarely that foreign powers – with the exception of the British – were prepared to commit their resources in any major military confrontation with the armies of Asante. The avoidance of conflict was facilitated, moreover, by the existence in most quarters of effective neutral zones within which, apparently by tacit agreement, the major continental powers refrained from claiming hegemony. To a considerable extent, the Asante government relied upon the good offices of both Muslim residents and visitors to mediate its relations with its northerly neighbours.

In the period of the rapid expansion of the kola trade in the early nineteenth century, many merchant princes from the towns of Hausaland and Bornu arrived in Kumase. They may be supposed to have been involved in negotiating with the Asante authorities the terms within which trade might proceed. It has been noted that as early as 1807 a Katsina *shaykh* had placed himself and his retinue at the service of the Asantehene during the invasion of the Fante country in 1807 (see p. 259). In 1820 another Katsina notable was reported 'recently arrived at Coomassy on a trading speculation from the former city'.[1] In or about 1815 a Bornuese *sharīf*, al-Ḥājj Ibrāhīm, had arrived in Kumase. Two other *sharīfs* accompanied him, but left for Timbuktu and Mecca in the following year.[2] Other than paying a visit to the Dahomean court at Abomey, al-Ḥājj Ibrāhīm remained

1 Dupuis, 1824, p. cxxxiii.
2 Ainé, 1857, p. 27.

in Kumase with such of his companions as Muḥammad 'Abd al-Salām al-Maruwī, 'the Hausa', until early 1818 when he departed for Cairo.[3] The importance of the class of *sharīfs* – those claiming descent from the Prophet Muḥammad – in both the political and economic spheres was remarked upon by Dupuis:

These descendants of the prophet's family are received at Ashantee with hospitality unlimited in its scope; they become the honoured guests of kings and ministers, while the population in bulk venerate them as demi-gods, and look for an increase of wealth in proportion as they compete in tendering respect and offers of service to their visitors: for no man is ignorant of the pretensions they set up on account of their sanctified genealogy, and their consanguinity to kings and emperors of the past and present day . . . There have been three of these princely visitors at Coomassy during the reign of Sai Quamina [Osei Bonsu], and none ever came so far to the south and west before; a circumstance that induces the present sovereign of Ashantee to arrogate to himself a greater degree of glory than his ancestors ever enjoyed. The last of these princes was the Sheriffe Brahima who . . . after a residence partly at Coomassy and partly at Abomey, the capital of Dahomy, during the space of nearly three years, quitted the former for Nikky, with an ample fortune, and in charge of a large caravan of pilgrims, who had entered into engagements with the Sheriffe for protection to Cairo.[4]

The extent to which the Muslim merchants combined their private business activities with the acceptance of official appointments as trade commissioners and consuls is not clear. Certainly, however, there was a functionary in Kumase in 1816 who was described as 'the ambassador from Malabar', that is, from Hausaland. He had resided in the Asante capital for many months, but had apparently experienced difficulty in obtaining audiences, the Asantehene Osei Bonsu being then preoccupied with the conduct of his armies in the southern provinces.[5] The ambassador was, noted Huydecoper, 'a king': that is, one guesses, a *sharīf*. Although no comprehensive list of such high-ranking visitors to Asante can be compiled, the indications are that they continued to arrive there throughout the century and could obtain exemption from the government's later restrictions upon free access to the capital. One such was Sharīf Aḥmad from Baghdad, who died in 1854. His travels had taken him from Khorasan in the east to Sansanding in the west, and in the course of them he had journeyed

---

3 Dupuis, 1824, p. cxxxiv.
4 *Ibid.* pp. xiv–xv. For Sharīf Ibrāhīm, see also Bowdich, 1819, pp. 92; 205, and Hutchison, in Bowdich, 1819, pp. 397–8, 403, 406, 414–16. See also the two talismanic texts by him, in Royal Library, Copenhagen, *Cod. Arab. CCCII*, II, ff. 26–7; 266–7, referred to in Levtzion, 1966, pp. 113–14.
5 Huydecoper's Journal, entry for 16 June 1816.

from Sofara near Jenne southwards through Wagadugu to Asante.[6]
In 1882 Brun found a Moroccan at Elmina who was prepared to
accompany him to Kumase, and he was joined on the way by a Tuni-
sian marabout who had travelled to Asante via Ghadames, Ain Salah,
Timbuktu and Salaga, and was teaching at Praso on the borders of
Asante and the Gold Coast Colony.[7] There can be little doubt that it
was largely through the services of such peripatetic dignitaries that
the Asante government maintained irregular contact with the more
distant courts, and in 1820 Dupuis received some account of the
privileged position which they enjoyed as commissaries. The Muslims,
he reported,

> may travel secure and unmolested in all known parts of the African continent,
> yet such of them as are subject to the rule of heathen princes, will
> not willingly venture their persons in the territory of a hostile state;
> like the heathens they may not pursue a direct journey to the place of their
> destination, avoiding thereby the capital cities and abodes of princes and
> sovereigns, but must directly shape a course to the metropolis of each king-
> dom, there to participate in the hospitality of the court, to make known their
> intentions, and to claim the protection of the sovereign as far as his influence
> may extend, and all this may be accomplished by the Moslem with or without
> a present, as his property or circumstances suggest themselves to his royal
> host. Nay, on the journey from Coomassy to Haoussa, he seldom disburses a
> mitskal of gold or cowrees (the value of ten shillings) but, on the contrary, is
> frequently a gainer by the generosity of princes, and his daily wants are
> moreover liberally supplied at their expence, and oftentimes with unbounded
> hospitality.[8]

Asante functionaries, including the *batafo* or state traders, might travel
under the protection of such Muslims, and Dupuis referred to them
as occasionally visiting such distant towns as Segu on the Niger to the
northwest, Fada N'Gurma ('Ghoroma') and beyond to the northeast,
and the Borgu towns, from Nikki to Busa on the Niger, in the east.[9]

The design for a continental alliance

Little information is extant on the content of Asante exchanges with
more distant courts. There is evidence to suggest that in the 1820s,
however, the government involved itself in an ambitious scheme to
establish what was in effect an organization of West African states
for mutual security: the growing threat presented by the British on the
Gold Coast was viewed with grave disquiet in Kumase, and con-

6 Barth, 1857, II, 37–8.
7 Gros, n.d., pp. 153, 160.
8 Dupuis, 1824, pp. cix–cx.
9 *Ibid.* pp. cvii–cviii.

sidered a matter of concern to other powers also. Thus sometime before the end of 1823 approaches were made from Kumase to someone described as 'a Mahommedan Priest of Tillibo, a town in the interior'. The source is in fact a Sierra Leonean one, and *telebo* is not a toponym but the Malinke word for 'the East'.[10] 'This man', it was reported,

though not a Prince, has considerable influence over many strong and warlike tribes in the East, both Mahommedans and Pagans; so that he is considered for his wisdom as a sort of oracle: to him it seems the Ashantee King long before the Governor last sailed for Cape Coast [McCarthy returned to Cape Coast on 28 November 1823], applied for his influence to induce those Nations to assist him in the War with the English, which they accordingly did.[11]

In the absence of further evidence, positive identification of the 'Mahommedan Priest' is impossible. The reference, however, is most probably to Shaykh Aḥmadu Lobbo, who had recently established himself as *amīr al-mu'minīn* over the region of Massina on the Middle Niger.[12] Certainly commercial relations between Asante and Massina in the period were important: in 1826 Muḥammad b. Aḥmad of Massina spoke, for example, of the dependence of his country upon Asante for gold supplies.[13]

Following the defeat of Governor MacCarthy's forces on 21 January 1824 (p. 175), messengers were despatched from Kumase to the 'Mahommedan Priest of Tillibo' to give an account of the battle. The information was in turn transmitted by letter to 'the Mandingoes or Morea people', that is, to the Maninka-mori probably of Kankan, whence it became known to the British in Sierra Leone some time before news of the Governor's death was to reach them by ship. In anticipation of renewed hostilities, the Asante government was reported to have requested 'other powerful nations in the interior who were their friends, to come forward in the cause and send down more troops'. The British believed that as a result of these overtures, men loosely described as 'the Bambarians and the mixed tribes around them' had been sent to fight against the British and furthermore, that 'other powerful nations more to the East, either had or would come forward with great force to support the Ashantees'.[14] It seems

10 Compare PRO, CO. 2/5: communication dd. 16 March 1816 – 'Tiliboo or Sun rising, a general name for the East'.
11 *The Royal Gazette and Sierra Leone Advertiser*, VI, no. 319, 10 July 1824, p. 315.
12 Smith, 1961, pp. 179–80. Ba and Daget, 1955, *passim*.
13 Clapperton, 1829, pp. 202, 331–3.
14 *The Royal Gazette and Sierra Leone Advertiser*, VI, no. 319, 10 July 1824, p. 315. Reindorf, 1895, Appendix, lists 'Hausa' among the Asante troops at Katamanso in 1826, but the reference is insufficiently precise to enable their origins to be identified.

difficult to escape the conclusion that the Asante position *vis-à-vis* the British threat evoked a positive and sympathetic response from the Muslim leaders of reform in the Western Sudan. It is perhaps significant in this context, that a quarter of a century later the Asantehene Kwaku Dua I was reported to have said often, 'that Aḥmadu is greatest of all the blacks' – a reference it would seem either to Aḥmadu Lobbo himself or to his son and successor Aḥmadu b. Aḥmadu who presided over Massina affairs from 1844 to 1852.[15]

While Asante overtures to the Muslim reformers appear, then, to have been sympathetically received, those to Da Kaba, ruler of the Bambara kingdom of Segu, met with rejection. According to 'Abd al-Qādir, a *sharīf* in the service of Da Kaba, envoys from Kumase arrived in Segu on or about 1 May 1824:

> messengers arrived from King Assay (O'Saii) to Dakaba, informing him that he was at war with the English; that he had killed the Governor and plenty of white people, and requesting Dakaba to assist him. That Dakaba returned for answer, he was at peace with the English; that he had plenty of trade with them, and that as a great number of his subjects were residing among the English on the coast, he could not help any person to make war on them.[16]

Although it is clear that Da Kaba was indeed particularly concerned to establish close relations with the British,[17] the reason for the Asante government's inability to draw together Massina and Segu into an effective military coalition was quite apparent: Aḥmadu Lobbo had claimed authority as *amīr al-mu'minīn* over those considered their Bambara subjects by the rulers of Segu, and by 1826 the forces of Aḥmadu Lobbo and those of Da Kaba had been fighting intermittently for at least a decade.[18] Nevertheless, the British government saw the situation as one fraught with danger, and its administrators in Sierra Leone suggested that 'two or even three thousand pounds would be well expended in sending a messenger to Sego to secure an alliance with Dakaba, to render security on this point doubly sure . . . '.[19] No comparable threat was to be presented to the British until the end of the century, when the Asantehene Agyeman Prempe I and the Muslim reformer Samori were to begin negotiating a mutual defence pact.

15 Methodist Mission Archives, London: 1852 correspondence box, undated report on Asante by T. Laing.
16 *The Royal Gazette and Sierra Leone Advertiser*, VI, no. 333, 16 October 1824, pp. 369–70.
17 See, e.g. *West-African Sketches*, 1824, Sketch XXIV: open letter from Da Kaba to 'the kings and chiefs of the west'.
18 Clapperton, 1829, p. 331. *The Royal Gazette and Sierra Leone Advertiser*, III, no. 159, 16 June 1821; IV, no. 219, 10 August 1822.
19 *Ibid.* VI, no. 333, 16 October 1824, p. 370.

Buna and the special role of the Dyula

In the conduct of its relations with the Muslim powers of the far north and northwest, the government in Kumase appears to have assigned an important role to the adjunct territory of Buna – separated from the most northwesterly outer provinces of Greater Asante by the Black Volta River. Referred to as Sukalia ('Soke Aila') – the name of one of its principal wards – by Dupuis' informants in 1820, they described Buna as being fourteen journeys from Kumase and six from the Watara capital of Kong. It was, Dupuis reported, the market for 'Enkasy': 'the first Moslem principality in the north-west . . . tributary to Kong'.[20] In fact Buna was the market for a small Kulango state which was, however, quite clearly within the ambit of Asante rather than of Kong throughout the nineteenth century. Thus when the Bambara troops of Da Kaba of Segu invaded the region in 1818–19, it was into Asante that the inhabitants of Buna fled (see p. 272). In 1892 Ferguson unambiguously referred to it as 'an Ashanti country'.[21] At the beginning of the present century Chief Commissioner Fuller of Asante learned that it had been practice for the deaths of Asantehenes to be reported to Buna and vice versa, although, he maintained, 'no other known relations existed between the two Courts'.[22] When in 1882 the Asantehene Mensa Bonsu required the Bunamansa to make a clear expression of support for the government in its conflict with the Gyamanhene Agyeman, the Bunamansa was by report sympathetically disposed toward Agyeman.[23] Yet when in 1924 the Asantehene Prempe I was repatriated to Kumase after his long exile in the Seychelles, the idea became current that not only would he resume authority over western Gonja but would also be 'taking over Buna (French Ivory Coast)'.[24]

From the somewhat conflicting information, two matters emerge. First, ancient and seldom discussed links – about which no more will be said – existed between the ruling dynasties of Asante and Buna.[25] But secondly, the Buna Muslim community played a singularly important role in mediating relations between the Asante government and those powers within whose territory the Dyula traders and *'ulamā*

20 Dupuis, 1824, p. lii.
21 PRO, CO. 879/38, African (West) 448, p. 35: Ferguson to Governor, dd. Christiansborg, 19 November 1892.
22 Fuller, 1921, p. 1.
23 *Further Correspondence*, C. 3687, 1883, p. 120: Lonsdale's report on his mission of April to July 1882.
24 National Archives of Ghana, Tamale, ADM/1/126: informal diaries, Commissioner, Southern Province, entry dd. 23 June 1927.
25 See, e.g. Meyerowitz, 1952, pp. 104–5. A number of informants, who requested anonymity, intimated to the present writer that the ruling Oyoko dynasty of Asante had its origins in Buna.

travelled, did business, and taught. The importance of Buna as a centre of Islamic scholarship has not been fully appreciated. At the turn of the eighteenth and nineteenth centuries 'Abdallāh b. al-Ḥājj Muḥammad al-Watarāwī presided over a community of scholars there drawn from countries as distant as those of the Diawara (present day Mali), Futa Jalon (Guinea), and Futa Toro (Senegal).[26] Half a century later Barth referred to Buna ('Gona', that is, Arabic *Ghuna*) as 'a place of great celebrity for its learning and its schools in the countries of the Mohammedan Mandingoes to the south'.[27] It was with these schools that the Kamagatay Imāms of Asante were closely associated. The Asante Imām (*Asante Adimɛm*) 'Uthmān Kamagatay, who was brought from Daboya to Kumase in 1844 (see p. 278), had probably earlier studied there. Certainly his copy of the Qur'ān – preserved in Kumase and regarded as the Qur'ān for the Asante nation (Plate VIII) – was copied in Buna.[28] Imām 'Uthmān's son, Abū Bakr, was sent by the Asantehene Kwaku Dua I to study in Buna. When Imām 'Uthmān died, at an advanced age and seemingly in the mid-1890s, the Asantehene Agyeman Prempe I sent his official messengers to escort Abū Bakr back to Kumase to assume the imāmate vacated by his father's death. Abū Bakr returned with his son, 'Abd al-Mu'min, who had been born in Buna about 1860, and had been schooled there. 'Abd al-Mu'min in turn succeeded his father in 1919, and held the imāmate until his death in 1964.[29]

Abū Bakr b. 'Uthmān Kamaghatay was associated in Buna with Karamoko 'Alī b. Ṣiddīq Kunatay and his son Sulaymān, both of whom also had major involvements in Asante affairs (see p. 240). In 1964 the aged al-Ḥājj Muḥammad Sofa of Wa remembered meeting the three – 'working for the Asantehene' – in Buna in 1887/8.[30] In 1896 Ferguson referred, significantly if not completely accurately, to the 'head priest' of Buna being also 'chief priest' of Kumase.[31] It would seem that in the schools of Buna a cadre of Muslims existed, trained for service in various capacities to the rulers of Asante. In 1870 a Buna Muslim named Ibrāhīm, who had apparently recently arrived

26 See the testimony of Abū Bakr al-Ṣiddīq of Timbuktu, in Wilks, 1967b, p. 157.
27 Barth, 1859, III, 496.
28 Wilks, field-notes: meeting with Asante Imām 'Abd al-Mu'min b. Abī Bakr Kamagatay, dd. Kumase, 12 February 1963.
29 Wilks, field-notes: interview with Imām al-Ḥājj Ismā'īl b. 'Abd al-Mu'min Kamagatay, dd. Kumase, 3 August 1965; interview with Karamoko 'Umar b. Abī Bakr Kamagatay, dd. Kumase, 11 April 1966. Because of Imām Abū Bakr's advanced age, 'Abd al-Mu'min apparently assumed the duties of the office in 1908.
30 Wilks, field-notes: interviews with al-Ḥājj Muḥammad Sofa, dd. Wa, 16–18 April 1964.
31 PRO, CO. 96/277, African (West) 506, 1896: Ferguson's Final Report on his Second Mission to the Interior, dd. 31 August 1896.

in Kumase from somewhere on the Niger, gave some account of the matter. Kumase, he observed,

contains a large number of Muslims who had come, like me, from the interior. They fill in general the functions of doctors to the king, who holds them in high regard. They give him, as well as the chiefs, all manner of amulets, which have come to have more value than the fetishes. Many times a week, they wash the king with water prepared for this purpose. After having stayed a certain time in Kumase, they return to enjoy in their country the fortune more or less great which they have thus acquired.[32]

But the Muslim consultants of the Asantehene were also involved in matters political. In 1870 they apparently maintained the view, unpalatable to Kofi Kakari, that the loss of Elmina through its transfer to the British would be linked with the fall of Kumase itself. Of this, Reade received some account from Elmina informants:

There was in Coomassie a famous doctor of the Moslems; he wrote certain words upon paper, sewed them up in leather cases, and sold them as charms against wounds in the war. He fumigated the nostrils of the sick with the smoke of mysterious herbs set on fire: he wrote texts of the Koran on a wooden board, washed off the ink into water, and gave it to patients as a draught: he cupped for fever, inoculated for small-pox,[33] applied the hot iron; he also divined future events from a book filled with diagrams, or from figures drawn in the sand. The king called him and said he wished to know the future of Coomassie. The priest made auguries and replied that the fall of Elmina would be also the fall of Coomassie. The king, who did not expect such an answer, went to an old Ashantee sorceress. But she, having consulted the gods of the country, delivered the same oracle. 'The fall of Elmina would be also the fall of Coomassie.' 'Well,' said the king, 'what does it matter? Elmina has been from the creation of the world, and so has Coomassie. It is impossible that either can fall.'[34]

In 1873 the Muslims advised the government to release the European prisoners in Kumase – Bonnat, Kühne and the Ramseyers. 'This war', they maintained, 'will not end to your advantage as long as you keep the white men, who are constantly crying to God, – prisoners; let them go, and you will conquer.'[35] And, as Wolseley's expeditionary force advanced upon Kumase in 1874, the Muslims were reported – probably distortedly – to have claimed 'that they had brought the white men in order that the king might get all their provisions and goods.'[36] The manifesto addressed to the British in 1874 by the 'great

[32] Gros, 1884, p. 168.
[33] In 1817 Hutchison, see Bowdich, 1819, p. 409, noted that smallpox inoculation was practised in Asante by the Muslims.
[34] Reade, 1874, pp. 327–8.
[35] Ramseyer and Kühne, 1875, pp. 210–11.
[36] Brackenbury, 1874, II, 336.

High Priest' – probably either 'Alī or Sulaymān Kunatay (see p. 240) – expressed not only the concern of the Asante in particular about the aspirations of the British on the Gold Coast, but also reflected the more general Muslim discomfiture in the face of Christian European expansion.

The Asante Imām Abū Bakr, who was strongly to support the Asante partisans in their struggles with the British in 1900, studied in Buna under a Sharīf Aḥmad from Futa – presumably an 'Umarian Tijani.[37] 'Alī Kunatay studied under Karamoko Muḥammad b. 'Uthmān Tarawiri, who died in Buna in the earlier 1890s, and who had himself been taught by al-Ḥājj Maḥmūd Karantaw,[38] leader of a *jihād* in the 1860s in the Boromo region almost 500 miles northwest of Kumase by the extension of Route III. A full investigation of the intellectual and ideological background of the Muslims prominent in Kumase affairs is greatly needed. Certainly one observer in the 1870s came to regard, as one of the most significant aspects of Asante foreign policy in that period, the relations which it enjoyed with Muslim powers to the north – and anticipated the sort of alignment which was to emerge, much to the alarm of the British, between Agyeman Prempe I and the Almami Samori at the end of the century:

The fetish priests, meanwhile, are beginning to lose their prestige, due to the spread of Islam, which already counts many adepts in Asante. The Muslims of the banks of the Niger are already, in thousands, crossing the Kong mountains and are spreading across the vast southerly region of Guinea. They conduct at the same time propaganda and commerce . . . These people come from the Niger, from the oases of the Sahara, and even from Morocco and Tripoli. They cross extensive countries, inaccessible to whites, and everywhere enjoy not only great privilege but sure respect. It is readily apparent that they exercise over the blacks a real influence, hostile to that of the Europeans. I say hostile, for when in our walks [in Cape Coast] we happened to pass groups in which there were Muslims, the blacks turned around in order not to greet us, and only their stranger guests fixed us with looks which, without being angry, were totally lacking in goodwill. I have the conviction that Africa will be the scene of the most formidable war which has ever occurred between Islam and Christianity.

At present, the hostility is limited to the local wars between the English and the Asante . . .[39]

Asante, the Mossi of Wagadugu, and the Fon of Dahomey

Asante relations with the savannah powers of the north, conducted through the agency of the Muslim traders and scholars, appear then

37 Wilks, field-notes: interview of 11 April 1966, cited above.
38 For the chain of teachers, see Institute of African Studies, Ghana: IASAR/232; 438. See also Wilks, 1968, *passim*.
39 Hertz, 1885, pp. 135–7.

to have been sustained at an eminently satisfactory level throughout the nineteenth century: certainly there was little reason for the government to anticipate any major military confrontation in that quarter. Although information is lacking, the mediating role which the Kamaghatay and Kunatay played in the northwest was probably paralleled by that of similar groups elsewhere. The Baghayughu *'ulamā* of Yendi, for example, had close historical links with the Mossi kingdom of Wagadugu,[40] while the Muslim Yarse of Wagadugu probably traded regularly to Salaga and the other markets of the Asante hinterland. Between Kumase and Wagadugu, seat of the powerful Mogho Naba, the traveller might follow Route IV via Salaga and Yendi, and the journey – one of over 500 miles – was reckoned to take twenty-five days.[41]

The northernmost outer provinces of Greater Asante and the southernmost provinces of Mossi were separated by a broad belt of rugged country inhabited by stateless peoples: Kusase, Nankanse, Kassena, Talense, Builsa and Sisala for example.[42] At the beginning of the nineteenth century contact between the two countries appears, on the available evidence, to have been minimal: a few Asante traders visited Wagadugu particularly to buy shea butter which was much used for cosmetic purposes,[43] and the presence of Mossi traders in Kumase was not unknown.[44] With the growth of the Salaga market, however, the two powers were brought together for the first time in an ongoing relationship. As Barth pointed out, the regular supply of donkeys from Wagadugu was one of the factors essential to the well-being of the caravan trade at Salaga.[45] But Salaga also became one of the most important outlets for the Mossi trade in general, so that by the end of the century it could be observed, 'that the King of Mosi considers it undesirable to have a market near his capital, as he is desirous to monopolize the Salaga trade by sending as heretofore his four or five great caravans every year and selling the goods he receives to neighbouring tribes'.[46]

In the early 1890s, when the Asante government had not for a decade and a half exercised control over Salaga, it was reported that 'the king of Salagha [presumably the Kpembewura] has an oath of

---

[40] Ferguson, 1973, pp. 55–73.
[41] Dupuis, 1824, p. cvii.
[42] Compare PRO, CO. 879/38, African (West) 448, p. 56: Ferguson to Governor, dd. 9 December 1892 – 'Between Dagomba and Mosi there is a belt of inhospitable barbarous tribes, through which caravans often have to fight their way.'
[43] Dupuis, 1824, p. cvii.
[44] Bowdich, 1821c, p. 2.
[45] The reference in Clapperton, 1829, p. 338, to Wagadugu supplying asses to Gonja 'to carry the drums of the army' rests, presumably, upon a misunderstanding of the Arabic text which he used.
[46] PRO, CO. 879/38, African (West) 448, p. 35: Ferguson to Governor.

friendship and freedom of trade with the Mosi king.' [47] The agreement had clearly superseded an earlier one between the Asantehene and Mogho Naba, on the basis of which excellent relations came to prevail between the two governments. In the middle of the nineteenth century, for example, a former trader described Kupela, the important town where caravans proceeding to Wagadugu from Salaga, and from the Hausa towns, met.[48] 'Kupeala', he commented, 'is four days from Wardyga, the Mossi capital, whither the king of Asante often sent presents; and one month from Salak, an Asante town, where they bring kola nuts.' [49] In 1964 Skinner reported the tradition that the Mogho Naba and Asantehene had customarily exchanged gifts each year.[50]

Problems of a quite different order from those in the north existed in the east, where the expansion of both Asante and the powerful Dahomean state in the eighteenth century had brought the two into a situation of potential conflict. According to Dupuis' Muslim informants, the first Dahomean embassy to Asante had arrived in Kumase in the early eighteenth century while Osei Tutu was still ruling.[51] Whether the report was accurate or not, it is clear that by the time of Asantehene Kusi Obodom relations between the two powers had deteriorated to the point of war. In the early 1760s the government of Dahomey offered assistance to rebel forces in the easterly Asante provinces of Bron ('Bouromy'), Kwawu and Akyem. An Asante army was put into the field and routed the dissidents.[52] Contrary to the advice of many of his leading councillors, Kusi Obodom decided to move his army across the Volta, presumably in pursuit of the rebels but also, as Dupuis reported, 'to revenge the injury he had sustained'. A fierce but inconclusive battle was fought between the Asante and Dahomean forces early in 1764, and Kusi Obodom ordered a withdrawal. The Asante army, however, was attacked again at the crossing of the Volta, and suffered heavy casualties.[53] Among the commanders who were lost were the Adontenhene of Kumase Boakye Dankwa,[54] the Kumawuhene Kwame Basowa,[55] and the Dwabenhene Kofi Akraase.[56] On the return of the armies, Dupuis reported, the capital 'was

---

[47] *Ibid.* p. 31: Ferguson to Governor, dd. 29 August 1892.
[48] Bowdich, 1819, p. 180, mistakenly regarded Kupela as the Mossi capital.
[49] Koelle, 1854, p. 6.
[50] Skinner, 1964, p. 97.
[51] Dupuis, 1824, p. 243, note.
[52] *Ibid.* pp. 237–8.
[53] *Ibid.* pp. 238–9. PRO, T. 70/31: Mutter to Committee, dd. Cape Coast, 27 May 1764.
[54] Mutter, dd. 27 May 1764. Rattray, 1929, p. 221.
[55] Rattray, 1929, p. 221.
[56] In traditions recorded, for example, by Rattray, 1929, pp. 183 and 221, the Dwabenhene who was slain is named as Dankwa. It appears that an earlier Dwabenhene Dankwa Afrapo has been confused with the Kumase Adontenhene

filled with grief and mourning'. The government decided against any renewal of the war, so the Kumase Muslims maintained, lest it gave 'umbrage to the Sultan of Dogho [Oyo], who is the protector of Dahomy, which is a remote appendage of his crown'.[57] Robertson was later to refer to the Asante dislike of the Oyo: they gave them, he said, 'the name of inepa bonee [Twi, "bad people"]' and related 'some of their barbarities on this marauding expeditions with horror'.[58] Nevertheless, despite the Dahomean victory at the Volta, the Alafin of Oyo was by report 'anxious to reconcile the wounded feelings of that court [Kumase], from an apprehension that the government would not neglect the opportunity, at a period of tranquillity, for carrying the war into the Dahoman territory . . .'.[59] Accordingly, the death of the Dahomean ruler Tegbessu and the accession of Kpengla [60] provided the occasion for a gesture of conciliation: an embassy was despatched to Kumase with gifts for the Asantehene. Osei Kwadwo, who had succeeded Kusi Obodom in 1764, accepted the mission, and reciprocated by sending 'a splendid embassy' to the Dahomean capital.[61] Henceforth, despite the high potential for conflict between the two nations, relations were to be conducted by and large according to agreed diplomatic procedures.[62] A Dahomean embassy arrived in Kumase in or about 1777 to congratulate Osei Kwame upon his accession to the throne,[63] and another in or about 1802 to convey similar felicitations to Osei Bonsu.[64]

It was perhaps as a result of the exchange of missions during the reigns of Osei Kwadwo of Asante and Kpengla of Dahomey that the Togo hills came to be recognized as constituting a neutral zone between the two spheres of influence. Nevertheless, as Robertson pointed out, the preoccupation of the Asante government with the campaigns in its southern provinces in the 1810s provided an opportunity for the Dahomey to strengthen their position on the frontier,[65] and the attack upon Atakpame during the reign of Adandoza (conventionally, 1797–1818) probably occurred in this period.[66] Certainly in 1822 Governor

---

Boakye Dankwa. Certainly Kofi Akraase's successor as Dwabenhene, Akuamoa Panin, was already in office by 1767, see above, p. 115, note 200.

[57] Dupuis, 1824, p. 239.

[58] G. A. Robertson, 1819, p. 282.

[59] Dupuis, 1824, p. 243, note.

[60] See Boahen, 1965, p. 2.

[61] Dupuis, 1824, p. 243.

[62] *Ibid.* p. cviii.

[63] *Ibid.* p. 244.

[64] *Ibid.* p. 249.

[65] G. A. Robertson, 1819, pp. 268–9.

[66] Kea, 1969, p. 35, suggests, however, that the attack upon Atakpame may have been occasioned by the aggressive policy pursued by the Asante province of Akwamu.

MacCarthy was in receipt of a message from Dahomey expressing pleasure at the build-up of British forces on the Gold Coast.[67]

No study of Asante-Dahomean relations in the earlier part of the nineteenth century would be complete without reference to the highly interesting though fictionalized account published in 1856 by Greenhalgh – who clearly drew upon factual materials from an unidentified source. Referring to the town of 'Allaroonah' in the Togo hills ('near the point of junction of the kingdoms of Dahomy and Ashantee' [68] and on 'the most direct, and probably the safest route for the commerce of the interior to reach the eastern part of the kingdom of Ashantee'),[69] Greenhalgh described the town's struggles to free itself from Dahomean overlordship recently accepted under duress.[70] After an 'Allaroonah' force inflicted a defeat upon a Dahomean army, wrote Greenhalgh,

a report of the repulse sustained by the Dahomans, and their vast preparations for a renewed attack upon Allaroonah, spread with surprising rapidity far and wide, reaching even the Ashantee court at Coomassie, and filling it with alarm, for the king was then engaged suppressing a revolt in a distant province of his dominions. Supposing that it would be their monarch's wish to cement more fully the peace already existing between Ashantee and Dahomy, the chiefs who remained in the capital at once despatched an ambassador, with a numerous retinue and valuable presents to Abomey.[71]

Subsequently, however, Dahomean forces carried out a number of raids upon villages within the eastern frontiers of Asante. The Asantehene equipped an army to defend his border, and with the support of the 'Allaroonahans' inflicted a defeat upon the Dahomey. By the terms of the peace settlement, according to Greenhalgh's account, 'Allaroona' recovered its independence while the Dahomeans agreed to send hostages to Kumase and to 'swear the king's oath not to make war again on Ashantee'.[72] Whatever the source of the account, it appears to have reference to the Dahomean failure to consolidate its position, after the attack upon Atakpame, in the neutral zone which separated its territories from those of Asante. The naming of the 'Kumase' gate at Abomey, the Dahomean capital, and of the 'Kumase' palace there, may have commemorated the same failure. Burton observed that, 'when Dahomian kings fail to capture an attacked place, they erect at one of the capitals a palace which is dubbed after the

67 *Royal Gazette and Sierra Leone Advertiser*, no. 208, 25 May 1822, citing letter dd. 3 April 1822.
68 Greenhalgh, 1856, p. 9.
69 *Ibid.* p. 17.
70 *Ibid.* pp. 19–27.
71 *Ibid.* p. 112.
72 *Ibid.* pp. 392–3, 416–17, 427.

victor, and this satisfied the vanquished. Hence, because Dahome was defeated by Ashante, the Komasi Palace at Agbome was added to the older establishments.'[73] Although Duncan gave a different account of the matter,[74] both he and Burton were in agreement in attributing the naming of the gate and palace to the ruler Gezo (1818–58).

Whether or not the evidence is to be read as indicating a recurrence of hostilities between Asante and Dahomey perhaps in the 1830s, any major military confrontation was certainly averted. In the next decade relations appeared normal, and the 'constant interchange of people' – including members of official missions – was remarked upon.[75] When, for example, Duncan attended an audience in Abomey on 12 June 1845, he noted the presence of a number of Asante. The leader of the mission was a son of the Asantehene – who Duncan regarded as 'a conceited fop, and on the whole a sharp, shrewd youngman'.[76] Five years later there was still a 'Prince of Ashantee' in Abomey, perhaps the same person. Named as 'Ah-saa-baa', possibly Owusu Ba, he had a staff of some forty retainers including a messenger or ambassador from Kumase, 'Oh-coo-coo'.[77]

With the deterioration in its relations with the British in the second half of the nineteenth century, the Asante government appears (as in the 1820s) to have intensified its efforts to obtain alliances with other continental powers. Prior to the reoccupation of the British Protected Territory in 1873, messengers were sent to the ruler of Dahomey to invite his cooperation, but the reply was received that 'the King of Dahomey had consulted his "great fetish", and that he had been advised not to join the Ashantis, as they would be certain to be beaten by the "white man" '.[78] Messengers were also despatched at the same time to the ruler of Borgu ('the King of the Barubas') whose territory lay to the northeast of Dahomey, with a request – as it was reported – for an ointment capable of deflecting missiles.[79] Both missions took the great-road through Salaga. Again, at the time of the war scare of 1880–1, the Asantehene Mensa Bonsu sent envoys to Dahomey, this time by the southern road through Agu. They asked for Glele's promise of assistance in checking the power of the rebel Bron coalition in the northeastern territories of Asante, should the major Asante

73 Burton, 1864, I, 196, note. See also Boahen, 1965, p. 2.
74 Duncan, 1847, II, 273–4.
75 Methodist Mission Archives, London: 1852 Correspondence Box, Report on Asante by T. Laing, n.d.
76 Duncan, 1847, I, 234–5; 237–8.
77 PRO, FO. 84/816: Beecroft's Journal of a Mission to Dahomey, entries for 1 and 7 June 1850. The name *Oh-coo-coo* is perhaps 'Akuoko'.
78 *Further Correspondence*, C. 3386, 1882, pp. 74–5: Lonsdale's Report on his mission of October 1881 to February 1882.
79 *Idem.*

armies become heavily involved elsewhere.[80] Glele, by this time himself increasingly apprehensive of the threat presented by the European powers, responded more favourably, and apparently urged the Anlo whose territory lay east of the Volta to assist the Asante in any war with the British.[81] That the Asante government was thereby regaining some sort of initiative in its old easternmost provinces was remarked upon by Dahse:

The wild mountain country of Akwamu stretches north of Krobo on both sides of the Volta, but mainly on the eastern bank, and has seemed until now scarcely to belong to the Protectorate of the Gold Coast. It is inhabited by a rough people, not exceeded in frightfulness by the Asante or the Dahomey. The people of Akwamu were always openly or secretly allies of Asante, and through Akwamu and then Angla [Anlo], or as the English say Awoonah, Asante maintains its connection with Dahomey.[82]

The pre-eminence of diplomacy

The Asante penchant for the art of diplomacy was remarked upon by many observers. In the early part of the nineteenth century the counselor for foreign affairs could be described as holding the highest non-hereditary position in the administration,[83] and the maxim was observed, 'never to appeal to the sword while a path lay open for negociation'.[84] The image projected by members of missions proceeding from the capital was a matter of official concern, so that 'when the King sends an ambassador, he enriches the splendour of his suite and attire as much as possible; sometimes provides it entirely; but it is all surrendered on the return . . . and forms a sort of public wardrobe'.[85] Later in the century Reade essayed a comparison between Sir Garnet Wolseley's command of the techniques of negotiation, and that of the Asante functionaries against whom he was pitted. Wolseley, he observed,

had made his reputation as a soldier, and now [1873–4] aspired to be a diplomatist. But he was matched against men compared with whom he was merely a child. It is a mistake to suppose that the Africans are a stupid people because they have no books, and do not wear many clothes. The children do

80 *Ibid.* p. 75.
81 *Affairs of the Gold Coast and threatened Ashanti Invasion,* C. 3064, 1881, p. 89: District Commissioner Parker to Colonial Secretary, dd. Ada, 16 February 1881. *Ibid.* p. 83: Brandford Griffith to Kimberley, dd. Elmina, 27 and 28 February 1881.
82 Dahse, 1882, p. 95. I am indebted to Marion Johnson for supplying this reference.
83 Lee, 1835, p. 168.
84 Dupuis, 1824, p. 226.
85 Bowdich, 1819, p. 294. Bowdich, 1821a, p. 26. The Head of the Wardrobe belonged to the Abanase division of the Asantehene's household.

not go to school, but they sit round the fire at night or beneath the town-tree in the day, and listen to their elders, who discuss politics, and matters relating to law and religion. Every man in a tribe, and every slave belonging to a tribe, has learnt at an early age the constitution by which he is governed, and the policy pursued towards foreign tribes. In such a land as Ashantee the king and chiefs are profoundly skilled in the arts of diplomacy . . .[86]

Reade, indeed, saw the strength of the Asante negotiators as predicated upon their lack of both scruples and illusions. But the professional standards which had become accepted within the Asante diplomatic corps were interestingly exemplified in the mild protest registered by the members of the Asante Embassy to London against their treatment, prior to their embarkation in 1895, by the Governor of the Gold Coast:

We cannnot bring this to a close without mentioning the fact that since our arrival here [Cape Coast] we have been closely studying his Excellency's policy towards us, and have observed how contemptuously he has been treating individual members of the Embassy, and have satisfied ourselves as to the direction in which it tends, and shall lay same before our royal master, who has invariably treated Her Majesty's officers to his court with unvarying respect and esteem.

We would rather leave it with the civilised world to say whether any person or persons who are the bearers of a message from one party to another, professedly friendly, should be treated other than courteously, gentlemanly, and at least for the time being, as un-amenable to the laws of the land to which they are sent.

Our royal master, we may at once assure you, for the information of his Excellency, is so immoveably desirous of maintaining peace and mutual regard between Ashanti and the Government of the United Kingdom, and to cherish a lasting friendship with the good people of your Government, that no petty annoyances would be allowed to defeat his aim and good will.[87]

Despite the view, assiduously fostered by the British, that the survival of the Asante nation in the nineteenth century was predicated upon its constant recourse to arms in the pursuit of political ends, the reverse would seem to have been the case: namely, that the existence of a body of trained and experienced negotiators enabled successive governments to sustain the thrust towards defined political goals despite the military reverses which the nation from time to time suffered. The point was interestingly developed by C. S. Salmon, Colonial Secretary and Acting Administrator of the Gold Coast in the 1870s:

[86] Reade, 1874, p. 288.
[87] *Further Correspondence*, c. 7918, 1896, p. 57: Asante Embassy to Hodgson, dd. Cape Coast, 30 March 1895.

Asante and its neighbours: politics of entente

The Ashantes are a proud people, who think themselves now to be an important nation, and believe that they are ultimately destined to be a great power in Africa. Their ambassadors have always stoutly maintained before the governors of the English possessions and the officials of other nations, that they were the representatives of a people raised up by the hand of God for the greatness of Africa. This can scarcely be called mere braggadocio, for the Ashantes have often been defeated by England, and yet they are still to the front. No mere savages could have recovered so rapidly or so completely, for example, as they have done from the effects of the late war. It is a thing unknown among low-class races to regain power and prestige they have once lost. Only high-class races can do this, who have a policy which lives through defeat, who pursue with perseverance and determination a fixed national idea . . .[88]

[88] Salmon, 1882, pp. 890–1.

CHAPTER 9

The dynastic factor in Asante history: a family reconstruction of the Oyoko royals

The emergence of the Houses of Osei Tutu and Opoku Ware

Central to the structure of the royal Oyoko dynasty of Asante is the line of descent which links Maanu in the seventeenth century with the Asantehemaa Ama Sewaa Nyaako in the twentieth. In 1907 Nana Agyeman Prempe I, then in exile in the Seychelles, compiled in written form an extensive corpus of genealogical material pertinent to the history of the dynasty.[1] The relationships between the Asantehenes and Asantehemaas, following what must be accorded the status of a 'received' version, is shown in Figure 5. The dynasty appears a remarkably compact one, any tendency towards differentiation into distinct segments having seemingly been averted.[2] This observation must, however, be qualified in a number of important respects. First, such a pedigree essentially charters the 'winners' rather than the 'losers'. The succession on the death of Osei Tutu, for example, was contested by Boa Kwatia, and on that of Opoku Ware, by Dako. Both were descended from Birempomaa Piesie through her daughter Otiwaa Kese. Neither gained the Golden Stool, but it was, for example, only after heavy fighting that Kusi Obodom emerged successful in 1750.[3] Dako and many of his supporters were slain, others migrated into the Bawle country (in the present Ivory Coast), and those of his family who remained in Asante seemingly relinquished all further claims to highest office. A more powerful collateral line – since the stool of Kokofu was held within it – was that stemming from another daughter of Birempomaa Piesie, namely Kyerema. Attention will be drawn

---

1 The genealogical material in the chapter, unless otherwise indicated, is derived from the manuscript, 'The History of the Ashanti Kings and the Whole Country Itself', dictated by Nana Prempe I. The work was commenced on 6 August 1907. I am very grateful to the late Nana Sir Osei Agyeman Prempe II, who allowed me access to it from time to time.

2 Until, perhaps, the present: the relatively distant relationship of Nana Opoku Ware II to his predecessor is unparalleled even by that between Kusi Obodom and Opoku Ware I.

3 See Priestley and Wilks, 1960, p. 93, for Dutch reports of the matter. See also Fynn, 1971, p. 88.

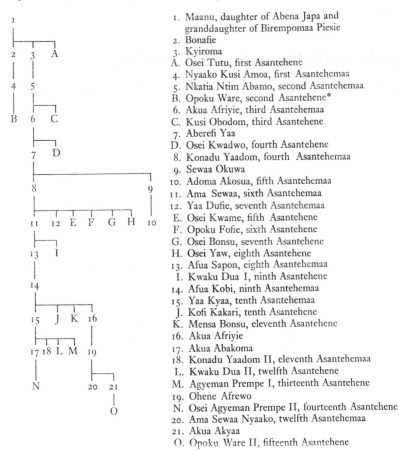

1. Maanu, daughter of Abena Japa and granddaughter of Birempomaa Piesie
2. Bonafie
3. Kyiroma
A. Osei Tutu, first Asantehene
4. Nyaako Kusi Amoa, first Asantehemaa
5. Nkatia Ntim Abamo, second Asantehemaa
B. Opoku Ware, second Asantehene*
6. Akua Afriyie, third Asantehemaa
C. Kusi Obodom, third Asantehene
7. Aberefi Yaa
D. Osei Kwadwo, fourth Asantehene
8. Konadu Yaadom, fourth Asantehemaa
9. Sewaa Okuwa
10. Adoma Akosua, fifth Asantehemaa
11. Ama Sewaa, sixth Asantehemaa
12. Yaa Dufie, seventh Asantehemaa
E. Osei Kwame, fifth Asantehene
F. Opoku Fofie, sixth Asantehene
G. Osei Bonsu, seventh Asantehene
H. Osei Yaw, eighth Asantehene
13. Afua Sapon, eighth Asantehemaa
I. Kwaku Dua I, ninth Asantehene
14. Afua Kobi, ninth Asantehemaa
15. Yaa Kyaa, tenth Asantehemaa
J. Kofi Kakari, tenth Asantehene
K. Mensa Bonsu, eleventh Asantehene
16. Akua Afriyie
17. Akua Abakoma
18. Konadu Yaadom II, eleventh Asantehemaa
L. Kwaku Dua II, twelfth Asantehene
M. Agyeman Prempe I, thirteenth Asantehene
19. Ohene Afrewo
N. Osei Agyeman Prempe II, fourteenth Asantehene
20. Ama Sewaa Nyaako, twelfth Asantehemaa
21. Akua Akyaa
O. Opoku Ware II, fifteenth Asantehene

* For the possibility that there was an Asantehene between Osei Tutu and Opoku Ware, see Priestley and Wilks, 1960, pp. 85–91.

Fig. 5   Pedigrees of the Asantehenes and Asantehemaas, received version [4]

below to the fact that a number of Kokofuhenes made bids for the Golden Stool, including Kyei Kwame in 1777 and Offe Akwasim in 1823. Although none succeeded, the family – unlike that of the descendants of Otiwaa Kese – was long able to preserve from extinction its claims to the kingship. It is important, then, to realise that the genealogical structure of the dynasty as shown in Figure 5 depicts the pattern of success: it identifies, of the collateral lines deriving from Maanu, that particular line which, from the perspectives of the mid-twentieth century, is *the* royal one. There is, however, a more important way in which the pedigree presented in Figure 5 must be seen as

4 Comparison may be made with the material given by Reindorf, 2nd ed., n.d., Appendix D; and Rattray, 1927, p. 327.

simplifying the structure of the dynasty, indeed, almost to the point of falsification. While the pattern of matrifiliation expresses the fundamental unity of the dynasty, it will be shown that it is with reference to the patterns of patrifiliation that *de facto* divisions within it become recognizable. The study of the former pattern is the study of the attributes of royalty; and the study of the latter patterns is that of the politics of kingship.

The importance of the *ntoro*, cultic associations the membership of which is by patrifiliation, has been stressed by a number of writers.[5] The first Asantehene, Osei Tutu, belonged to an Adufude group, a sub-division of the Bosommuru *ntoro* the members of which use the names 'Osei' and 'Owusu' in alternate generations. The fragment of the royal genealogies shown in Figure 6 will serve to illustrate the extraordinary cohesiveness of the Adufude line created through the marriage in alternate generations of *ahenemma* – sons of Asantehenes – to royal women.[6] The line in question represented originally the strongest of all possible lines: the ideal Asantehene was seen as being royal – *adehyeɛ* – by virtue both of his matrilineal descent from Maanu (see Figure 5) and of his patrilineal descent from Osei Tutu (see Figure 6). This line, which may be referred to in English as the House of Osei Tutu,[7] was weakened by the Asantehene Kwaku Dua I, who brought about the downfall of the heir apparent Osei Kwadwo in 1859, and who failed to give any royal woman as wife to the Akyempemhene Owusu Koko or to any of the other sons of Asantehene Osei Bonsu. The politics of the matter will be discussed fully in later chapters, with particular reference to the heir apparent Osei Kwadwo's bid for the Golden Stool before 1859, to Owusu Koko's attempts to assume the role of kingmaker in 1867 and thereafter, and to Owusu Ansa's achievement of a senior advisory position in government in the 1870s.

The House of Osei Tutu, then, had ceased to provide candidates for the Golden Stool in the second half of the nineteenth century, having as it were lost its royal component. But it will also be apparent from Figure 6 that no immediate successor to Osei Tutu could have been found among his grandsons; that is, Osei Kwadwo, the surviving son of Owusu Afriyie by Akua Afriyie, was born some two decades or more after his grandfather's death. Opoku Ware and Boa Kwatia contested

[5] See, for example, Rattray, 1923, chapter II; Meyerowitz, 1951, chapter VII (citing an unpublished work of Dr J. B. Danquah); Kyerematen, 1966, pp. 74 ff.; Fortes, 1969, pp. 198–202; Denteh, 1967, pp. 91–6.

[6] The basic genealogical data is taken from Nana Prempe I, 1907, 'The History of the Ashanti Kings'. The historical data is extracted from the relevant cards, Asante Collective Biography Project.

[7] The writer has heard this concept expressed by elderly Asante as *Osei Tutu Ntom;* presumably from *ntoro-mu,* 'something within the *ntoro*'.

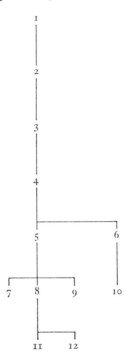

1. Owusu Panin of Nyameani, Aberenkesehene.
2. First Asantehene Osei Tutu, died 1712 or 1717.
3. Owusu Afriyie, appointed Akyempemhene by his father; married the third Asantehemaa Akua Afriyie; died *ca.* 1750.
4. Fourth Asantehene Osei Kwadwo, born *ca.* 1735; died 1777.
5. Owusu Ansa, appointed Asokore-Mamponhene by his father; married fourth Asantehemaa Konadu Yaadom; died *ca.* 1784.
6. Owusu Afriyie, appointed first Nkarawahene by his father; appointed first Apagyahene by Osei Kwame; resident commissioner in Akuapem in the late 1810s; married eighth Asantehemaa Afua Sapon; died 1826.
7. Osei Kofi, heir apparent.
8. Seventh Asantehene Osei Bonsu, born *ca.* 1779; died 1823; enstooled as Osei Tutu Kwame.
9. Osei Badu, heir apparent; died 1807.
10. Heir apparent Osei Kwadwo, born *ca.* 1810; died 1859.
11. Owusu Koko, born *ca.* 1820; appointed first Potrikromhene by his father; appointed Akyempemhene by Kwaku Dua I; banished, 1867; killed, 1884.
12. Owusu Ansa, born *ca.* 1822; educated in England; senior adviser to Mensa Bonsu; died 1884.

Fig. 6 Some descendants of Aberenkesehene Owusu Panin, in the Adufude *ntoro* [8]

the Golden Stool. Opoku Ware was successful, and thereby a second House was to come into existence. By report, Opoku Ware's mother was daughter of one of the sisters of Osei Tutu; and his father was the Amakomhene Adu Mensa, of the Asafode sub-division of the Bosommuru *ntoro* – a group characterized by the alternation of the names Adu and Opoku. It is worthy of note that Opoku Ware's mother is remembered in tradition as having been three years pregnant and fourteen days in labour, and that her son, born with a quavering right hand, grew very tall and very fair in colour.[9] Those who met with Opoku Ware in the 1740s remarked that 'he was taller than anyone else in the kingdom, and red instead of black in colour . . . His body was very thin, rather like a consumptive. His hands and feet were

---

8 Compare NAG, Kumase, D. 94: Akyeamehene Kwasi Nuama, Kyidomhene Kofi Nsenkyere and sub-chiefs to Chief Commissioner, Asante, dd. Kumase, 8 March 1915. '[The Akyempemhene] Prince Osei Tutu is the son of Prince Owusu Ntobi who was the son of King Osei Bonsu I of Ashanti. King Osei Bonsu was the son of Prince Owusu Ansa of Asokori-Mampon who also was the son of King Osei Kwadjo Kŏawia of Ashanti. King Osei Kwadjo Kŏawia was the son of Prince Owusu Afriyie who was the son of King Osei Tutu of Ashanti.'
9 Fuller, 1921, p. 25. Kyerematen, 1966, p. 251.

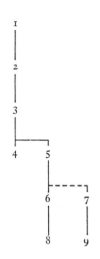

1. Adu Mensa, Amakomhene; married the first Asantehemaa Nyaako Kusi Amoa.

2. Second Asantehene Opoku Ware, enstooled *ca.* 1720; died 1750.

3. Adu Twum, *akyamfohene* of Kumase; appointed first Akankade *okyeame* by Osei Kwame; died *ca.* 1778; married Asantehemaa Konadu Yaadom.

4. Opoku Kwame, born *ca.* 1768; appointed Akyempemhene (as heir apparent) by Osei Kwadwo; died (or killed) 1797.

5. Sixth Asantehene Opoku Fofie, born *ca.* 1775; appointed Akyempemhene (as heir apparent) 1797; enstooled Asantehene 1798; died 1799.

6. Adusei Kra, born *ca.* 1794; appointed Atene Akotenhene; died 1836.

7. Adu, probably son of Opoku Fofie, married Ata Sewaa, daughter of Akua Akrukruwaa and granddaughter of Asantehemaa Konadu Yaadom.*

8. Kwame Poku, born *ca.* 1823; sent to school in Holland, 1835.

9. Opoku Ahoni, born *ca.* 1818; second heir apparent under Kwaku Dua I; killed probably in or about 1848.

* The identity of Adu is unclear; it is not impossible that he and Adusei Kra are one and the same. When fuller information was lacking, Nana Agyeman Prempe used 'Adu' to denote a prince (*oheneba*) of the House of Opoku Ware, and 'Owusu' for one of the House of Osei Tutu, see Nana Prempe I, 1907, *passim*.

Fig. 7   Some descendants of Amakomhene Adu Mensa, in the Asafode *ntoro*

twice as long as they should be in relationship to his body.'[10] It seems indicated that Opoku Ware was born with a tumour affecting both the central nervous system and the pituitary gland, giving rise to gigantism in childhood and acromegaly in adulthood.[11]

The structure of the House of Opoku Ware is shown in Figure 7. Like that of Osei Tutu, it was to lose its royal component in the nineteenth century, a result in part of the early deaths of Opoku Kwame and Opoku Fofie and of the subsequent execution of Opoku Ahoni. From the perspectives of the mid-eighteenth century, however, it appeared that the future rulers of the nation would be chosen from among the descendants of Maanu, but in alternation from the two Houses: a system not without precedent among the Akan.[12] Indeed, sometime before the death of Opoku Ware in 1750 formal recognition of the constitutional arrangement was made, when it was agreed by the National Assembly that the Golden Stool should become regarded

[10] Rømer, 1760, pp. 190–1.
[11] Tallness, and lightness of skin, are associated symptoms of the condition. The epithets *tenten* and *kɔkɔ* were both recorded by his contemporaries, see Rømer, 1760, p. 204.
[12] See, for example, Wilks, 1959, *passim*.

as the common ancestral stool of both Osei Tutu and Opoku Ware
– *Osei ne Opoku Sika Dwa* [13] – so symbolizing the unity of the two
Houses as such.

The new constitutional arrangement notwithstanding, the death of
Opoku Ware was the occasion of acute conflict. The Asantehemaa
Akua Afriyie had only one surviving son, Osei Tutu's grandson Osei
Kwadwo, but he was apparently considered still too young to hold
highest office. Clearly, too, no candidate could be found among the
grandsons of Opoku Ware: none, perhaps, had yet been born. Anticipating conflict, Opoku Ware had indicated his choice of a collateral royal,
Dako, to hold office until such time as Osei Kwadwo might succeed. It
has been suggested above, however, that the struggle which ensued
between Dako and Kusi Obodom probably reflected a deeper conflict
between those who favoured the administrative reforms proposed but
abandoned by Opoku Ware, and those who resisted radical change in
the political establishment (pp. 127–9). The successful contestant, Kusi
Obodom, was uterine brother of Akua Afriyie, but belonged neither
to the House of Osei Tutu nor to that of Opoku Ware. It is noteworthy in this context that, presumably early in his reign, Kusi
Obodom ruled that the Golden Stool could not be considered the stool
of both Osei Tutu and Opoku Ware, and so challenged the hegemony
of the two united Houses.[14] Already elderly in 1750, by 1760 the public
image which Kusi Obodom projected was one of effeminacy and
drunken indolence. The Bantamahene Adu Gyamera assumed command of a movement to remove him from office, but the crisis was
averted when the Asantehene authorized his adversary to pursue more
vigorous policies against the nation's enemies.[15] In 1764, when his
eyesight was beginning to fail, Kusi Obodom took the politically wise
decision to abdicate in favour of Osei Kwadwo. He resided for the
few remaining months of his life in Akyeremade, the Kumase ward
belonging to the Akyempemhene. On his death his body was not placed
in the royal mausoleum at Bantama, nor was his stool kept with those
of his predecessors in office.[16]

Osei Kwadwo was elected Asantehene apparently without opposition. His impeccable ancestry was complemented by his known commitment to furthering the earlier reformist policies of Opoku Ware,
which the nation seemed at last ready to accept. The matter of the
succession appeared, moreover, finally to be capable of clear resolution.

[13] Kyerematen, 1969, pp. 5–6.
[14] Kyerematen, 1969, p. 6.
[15] Priestley and Wilks, 1960, p. 93. Fynn, 1971, pp. 85–6; 93.
[16] Rattray, 1927, p. 144. Kyerematen, 1969, p. 6. Kusi Obodom died very shortly
after his abdication, and certainly in the second half of 1764, see PRO, T. 70/31:
Mutter to Committee, dd. Cape Coast, 21 January 1765.

Since it would be the turn of the House of Opoku Ware to provide an Asantehene upon the death of Osei Kwadwo, the obvious candidate was Opoku Kwame. Born about 1768, Opoku Kwame was grandson of Opoku Ware through the marriage of his son Adu Twum to the Asantehemaa Konadu Yaadom. Establishing a constitutional precedent, Osei Kwadwo made Opoku Kwame the Akyempemhene when that stool became vacant through the death of Adusei Kra. Hitherto reserved for the head of the *ahenemma* or princes, it was thus transformed into the *abakomdwa,* the stool for the heir apparent among the *adehye* or royals.[17] The prospects for an orderly succession, moreover, seemed further enhanced when Konadu Yaadom and Adu Twum produced a second son, Opoku Fofie, in or about 1775. Upon Osei Kwadwo's death in 1777, however, Opoku Kwame was presumably considered too young to succeed. Once again the nation became embroiled, as in 1750, in a struggle between two rival candidates neither members of the House of Osei Tutu nor of that of Opoku Ware. A faction headed by Nto Boroko, Oyoko-Bremanhene of Kumase, moved to elect the Kokofuhene Kyei Kwame as the new Asantehene. The Mamponhene Atakora Kwame entered Kumase with Bron troops, put Nto Boroko to death, and presided over the election of Osei Kwame – a Mampon youth who was little older than Opoku Kwame (see p. 250).[18] The matter of Osei Kwame's succession is one of considerable complexity, and further analysis of the structure of the female royal line is necessary in order to understand it.

The Oyoko Royals of Mampon

The Asantehemaa Akua Afriyie (Figure 5, no. 6) was thrice married. By her first marriage to the Kaasehene Kwasi Ko two children were born; neither apparently survived into the period of concern here. By her second marriage to the Abradehene Opoku Tia one daughter was born, Aberefi Yaa (Figure 5, no. 7). Finally, by her third marriage to the Akyempemhene Owusu Afriyie, all her children died in childhood with the exception of Osei Kwadwo – the later Asantehene. By the normal rule of succession, then, Aberefi Yaa should have become Asantehemaa. Indeed, according to the received version of the royal genealogies, the survival of the dynasty was dependent upon Aberefi Yaa: 'at that time the royal families were nearly finished and the only one royal family left was Abrafie [Aberefi Yaa].'[19] Although Aberefi

[17] See Nana Prempe I, 1907, p. 32.
[18] Kyei Kwame was certainly older. By report, he had been made Kokofuhene in or about 1765, although then only a youth, see Rattray, 1929, p. 200.
[19] See Nana Prempe I, 1907, p. 7.

Yaa did not in fact become Asantehemaa, she became ancestress of all subsequently to succeed to that position. There is, however, reason to believe that some distortion has occurred at this point in the received version of the royal genealogies, which must therefore be subjected to critical scrutiny.

In order to understand the mid-eighteenth century situation, it is important to bear in mind the broad geo-political configuration of the nation to which reference has already been made; to the division, that is, between the northern bloc of *aman,* dominated by Mampon and Dwaben and vitally concerned with control of the savannah hinterland, and the southern bloc, dominated by Kokofu and Bekwae, and having a major involvement in the affairs of the coastal provinces and the European establishments on the seaboard. It is said that prior to the reign of Osei Kwadwo the Asantehemaas resided at Kokofu, where they served also as Kokofuhemaas but travelled to Kumase whenever necessary.[20] Yet the Asantehemaa Akua Afriyie's daughter Aberefi Yaa was sent, probably in her childhood, to the Bretuo royals of Mampon, in the northern bloc, presumably in the interests of maintaining some sort of accommodation between northern and southern interests. According to the received versions of the genealogies, she married three Mamponhenes in succession, namely, Atakora Panin, Asumgyima, and Safo Katanka. Atakora Panin succeeded Akuamoa Panin on the Mampon stool, perhaps in 1742,[21] at an advanced age. Aberefi Yaa must herself then have been very young. Certainly she did not conceive, and the marriage was dissolved. Aberefi Yaa was then remarried to Asumgyima, who became Mamponhene in succession to Atakora Panin probably in the late 1740s. By report, Konadu Yaadom – later to become Asantehemaa – was born of this marriage. And finally, on the death of Asumgyima, Aberefi Yaa is said to have been married to the new Mamponhene Safo Katanka, who held office seemingly from the mid-1750s to the late 1760s. By this marriage Sewaa Okuwa (mother of the Asantehemaa Adoma Akosua) is reported to have been born. The genealogy shown in Figure 8 is based upon the received version of the Asante royal genealogies and upon the best available data for Mampon.[22]

It must be assumed that Aberefi Yaa was never elected Asantehemaa because her domicile was in Mampon and not Kokofu. The problem,

20 Rattray, 1929, p. 201, note. Kyerematen, 1966, p. 325.
21 If Rattray's informants were correct, that Akuamoa Panin fought at Takyiman (1722–3) and in Gyaman (*ca.* 1740), then the Akyem campaign in which he died must have been that of 1742. Rattray, 1929, p. 237.
22 Recorded by Agyeman-Duah, 1960, *passim,* who utilized the testimony of the ex-Mamponhene Kwaku Dua and ex-Mamponhemaa Afua Sapon. The data differ significantly from those recorded by Rattray, 1929, fig. 67. Rattray, however, expressed his misgivings about his own data, see fig. 67 and p. 235, note.

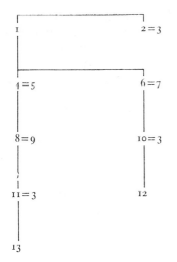

1. Mamponhemaa Adoma
2. Mamponhene Atakora Panin
3. Aberefi Yaa, daughter of Asantehemaa Akua Afriyie
4. Mamponhemaa Akyaama
5. Antoahene of Kumase, Sarkodie Date
6. Mamponhemaa Konadu
7. Oben Amoa
8. Mamponhemaa Abena Saka
9. Dwabenhene Osei Hwidie
10. Mamponhene Asumgyima
11. Mamponhene Safo Katanka
12. Asantehemaa Konadu Yaadom
13. Sewaa Okuwa, mother of Asantehemaa Adoma Akosua

Fig. 8   The three marriages of Aberefi Yaa, received version

moreover, was one which was compounded in that her two recorded daughters by Mampon royals, Konadu Yaadom and Sewaa Okuwa, also had a Mampon domicile and, so it will be shown, both made Mampon marriages. It was not until the reign of the Asantehene Osei Kwadwo that an attempt to resolve the problem was finally made. The stool of the Asantehemaa was removed from Kokofu to Kumase, and a new one created in Kokofu for the Kokofuhemaas who would henceforth be distinct from the Asantehemaas.[23] Since it has been seen that the only surviving female royals were resident in Mampon, it was necessary to draw one of them back to Kumase. Konadu Yaadom was accordingly divorced from her Mampon husband, brought to Kumase, enstooled as Asantehemaa, and married to Adu Twum. It has been shown above that the first son of this marriage, Opoku Kwame – a member of the House of Opoku Ware – was then recognized by Osei Kwadwo as heir apparent. That Osei Kwame and not Opoku Kwame in fact succeeded to the Golden Stool on the death of Osei Kwadwo in 1777 reflects the ongoing concern of the Mampon Bretuo royals to maintain their position *vis-à-vis* the Oyoko dynasty of Asante, and, indeed, effectively to create a third House within it additional to those of Osei Tutu and Opoku Ware. Crucial to the understanding of the intricacies of the matter are the marriages of Konadu Yaadom.

Safo Katanka is known to have been Mamponhene at least as early as 1758.[24] Even had he only recently succeeded Konadu Yaadom's

[23] Kyerematen, 1966, p. 325.
[24] General State Archives, The Hague, WIC 114: Ulsen to Assembly of Ten, dd. Elmina, 20 November 1758. In 1751 Safo Katanka had led an expedition into Gonja, see above p. 21, but he may not yet have been Mamponhene.

father, Asumgyima, her birth must then have occurred before 1758. She died in 1809, and a particularly lavish funeral custom was performed.[25] If, however, she was not less than fifty-one years of age at her death, she could certainly not have been very much older since she is said to have died in childbirth.[26] The evidence suggests that she was in fact in her middle fifties (her death probably resulting from her conception at so late an age). She had been, so Bowdich reported eight years later, 'a second Messalina, and many young captains who refused to intrigue with her, from fear or disgust, have been ultimately the victims of her artifice and venegeance'.[27] However that may be, Konadu Yaadom is certainly remembered as a much married woman. According to the received version of the genealogies – see Table 10 – she had five husbands and bore at least twelve children of whom four reputedly became Asantehenes. Examination of the received version indicates, however, the presence of a serious chronological anomaly.

The marriages of Konadu Yaadom and Akyaama

The last child of Konadu Yaadom was born in 1809. The penultimate child, Osei Yaw, became Asantehene in 1824; one source gives his age on accession as seventeen,[28] but another shows that he must have been

Table 10 *Husbands and children of Konadu Yaadom, received version*

Mother	Husband	Children
	1. Apahene Owusu of Mampon	No children
	2. Mamponhene Safo Katanka	1. Akyaa Kese, died in childhood 2. Ama Sewaa, later Asantehemaa 3. Osei Kwame, later Asantehene
Konadu Yaadom	3. Kumase *okyeame* Adu Twum	4. Opoku Kwame, later heir apparent 5. Yaa Dufie, later Asantehemaa 6. Akua Akrukruwaa 7. Opoku Fofie, later heir apparent and Asantehene
	4. Asokore-Mamponhene Owusu Ansa	8. Osei Kofi, later heir apparent 9. Osei Bonsu, later Asantehene 10. Osei Badu, later heir apparent
	5. Owusu Yaw, of Anowo, Kumase	11. Osei Yaw, later heir apparent and Asantehene 12. Unnamed child, died at birth with mother

25 PRO, T. 70/984: Accra Day Book, entry for 28 June 1809. Bowdich, 1819, p. 289.
26 Nana Prempe I, 1907, p. 9.
27 Bowdich, 1819, pp. 240–1.
28 See Nørregård, 1966, p. 195, who unfortunately does not identify what is presumably a contemporary Danish source.

born some years earlier.[29] The tenth child, following the received version, died during the invasion of the south in 1807, but no evidence of his age has been noted. The ninth child, Osei Bonsu, was, however, Asantehene from 1800 until his death in 1823, and a number of references to his age are extant.[30] His birth can be assigned with some confidence to the period 1779 ± 3, when Konadu Yaadom was therefore in her early to mid-twenties. The eighth child Osei Kofi, who was passed over in favour of Osei Bonsu in 1800, appears to have survived to fight, and die, at Katamanso in 1826,[31] but his date of birth is unknown; it was presumably in the late 1770s. Konadu Yaadom's son Opoku Fofie, her seventh child according to the received version, became Asantehene in 1798 but died within two years. No report of his age has been yet found, but since he fathered several sons – the later Apesemakohene Kwame Akyamfo, for example, and Atene Akotenhene Adusei Kra [32] – his birth may reasonably be assigned to the mid-1770s. It appears, then, that the dates of birth of his two elder sisters Akua Akrukruwaa (who died of smallpox in 1807) and Yaa Dufie, and of his elder brother Opoku Kwame, must be placed in the late 1760s and early 1770s, when Konadu Yaadom was in her teens. There is, then, to this point a remarkable coherence in the data: soon after his accession in 1764 the Asantehene Osei Kwadwo brought Konadu Yaadom from Mampon, enstooled her the first Asantehemaa to hold office in Kumase, and gave her in marriage to Adu Twum, Akyamfohene or head of the shield-bearers in Kumase (later to be promoted to Akankade Counselor by Osei Kwame). The Asantehemaa Konadu Yaadom thus came to play a crucial role in the consolidation of the Houses of Opoku Ware and of Osei Tutu. By her marriage to Adu Twum, son of Asantehene Opoku Ware, she gave birth to members of the former House, and by her next marriage to Owusu Ansa, son of Asantehene Osei Kwadwo, to members of the latter (see Figures 6 and 7). The clear implication of the chronology, however, is that Konadu Yaadom could not previously have given birth to three children by a marriage to Mamponhene Safo Katanka; she could not, in other words, have been the mother of Akyaa Kese, of the Asantehemaa Ama Sewaa, and of the Asantehene Osei Kwame. The received version of the royal genealogies stands in need of reconstruction.

The problem may be summarized thus: while there is no reason to doubt that Akyaa Kese (who will henceforth be ignored since she

---

[29] See Bowdich, 1819, p. 246, who referred to him as heir apparent in 1817 in terms which suggest that he must then have been more than ten years of age.

[30] See, for example, Bowdich, 1819, pp. 38; 240. General State Archives, The Hague, KvG 349: Daendels to Ministry of Colonies, dd. Sierra Leone, 28 December 1815. Hutton, 1821, p. 216.

[31] Kyerematen, 1966, p. 339. Reindorf, 1st ed., 1895, Appendix.

[32] Asante Collective Biography Project: Kwame Akyamfo; Adusei Kra.

died in childhood), Ama Sewaa and Osei Kwame were children of the Mamponhene Safo Katanka, their mother could not have been Konadu Yaadom. Yet in the received version of the matter, Safo Katanka is recorded as having married a daughter of Aberefi Yaa: which, since he is said himself also to have married Aberefi Yaa, indicates a union of dubious status in Asante law.[33] Since the daughter could not have been Konadu Yaadom, as the traditionalists maintain, and since no other daughter of Aberefi Yaa and Asumgyima is reported, the implication is that a royal of importance has been omitted in the received version of the genealogies. It thus becomes of much significance that Dutch documents of the 1750s refer to one 'Akjaanba' in contexts which suggest that she was, if not Asantehemaa, at least the current senior woman of the dynasty – 'the king's aunt'.[34] The assumption is reasonable, then, that she was the wife of Safo Katanka and mother of the later Asantehemaa Ama Sewaa and Asantehene Osei Kwame. The name 'Akjaanba' is clearly Akyaama (Akyaa Ama), that borne for example by Safo Katanka's maternal grandmother, the Mamponhemaa (see Figure 8). The pattern of naming in Asante, moreover, is such as to suggest that the relationship of the Oyoko royal Akyaama to the Mampon Bretuo royal Akyaama should be structurally identical with the known relationship of the Oyoko royal Konadu Yaadom to the Mampon Bretuo royal Konadu. Examination of the relevant evidence suggests that this was indeed so. The reconstruction offered in Figure 9 differs from the received version of the genealogies in three respects. First, that after her divorce from Mamponhene Atakora Panin, Aberefi Yaa was married next to one Akyampon Yaw and later to Mamponhene Asumgyima, but never to Safo Katanka. Secondly, that Akyaama and Sewaa Okuwa were daughters of Aberefi Yaa and Akyampon Yaw; and thirdly, that it was Akyaama and not Konadu Yaadom who was married to Safo Katanka and subsequently gave birth to Ama Sewaa and Osei Kwame.

The Mampon Bretuo factor in the history of the dynasty

Some account may now be offered, with reference to the data in Figure 9, of the development of the Mampon Bretuo factor in the Oyoko dynasty of Asante. One should start, perhaps, with the attack upon Kumase launched by the Sehwi ruler Abirimuru in the aftermath of the Asante defeat on the Pra in 1717.[35] Opoku Ware had led his forces

[33] See Rattray, 1929, p. 29.
[34] General State Archives, The Hague, WIC 114: Ulsen to Assembly of Ten, dd. Elmina, 20 November 1758.
[35] Priestley and Wilks, 1960, pp. 85–91.

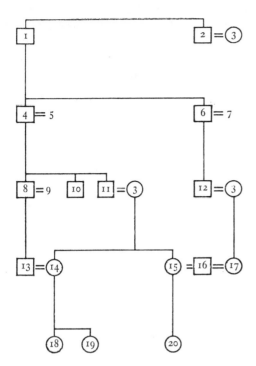

1. Mamponhemaa Adoma
2. Mamponhene Atakora Panin
3. Aberefi Yaa, daughter of Asantehemaa Akua Afriyie
4. Mamponhemaa Akyaama
5. Antoahene of Kumase, Sarkodie Date
6. Mamponhemaa Konadu
7. Oben Amoa
8. Mamponhemaa Abena Saka
9. Dwabenhene Osei Hwidie
10. Ago Mansa
11. Akyampon Yaw, later Asoromasohene of Kumase
12. Mamponhene Asumgyima
13. Mamponhene Safo Katanka
14. Akyaama, Asantehemaa (or *in statu* Asantehemaa)
15. Sewaa Okuwa
16. Apahene Owusu
17. Asantehemaa Konadu Yaadom
18. Asantehemaa Ama Sewaa
19. Asantehene Osei Kwame
20. Asantehemaa Adoma Akosua

Key

⬤ Oyoko royals   ▢ Mampon Bretuo royals

All descent lines shown from female royals

Fig. 9 Reconstruction of the royal genealogies to show marriages between the Oyoko and the Mampon Bretuo

into the field to avenge the defeat, when his capital was sacked.[36] Most accounts are in agreement that Opoku Ware's mother, Nyaako Kusi Amoa, and most of the other royals were either captured or massacred.[37] Two royal women alone survived. One was Nkatia Ntim Abamo, who became Asantehemaa in succession to Nyaako Kusi Amoa,[38] and the other was her daughter Akua Afriyie, who had been taken into captivity into Wassa but who was later returned.[39] The two children of Akua Afriyie's first marriage (see p. 333) were apparently both daughters. Little is known of them since neither seems to have

[36] For a useful account of the event, see Fynn, 1971, p. 61.
[37] Reindorf, 2nd ed., n.d., p. 81. Fuller, 1921, p. 26.
[38] Reindorf, 2nd ed., n.d., p. 82.
[39] Fuller, 1921, p. 27.

had children. Presumably, however, it was anticipated at the time of their births that one or other of them would be enstooled Asantehemaa in Kokofu, and so continue the royal line. It is therefore not especially surprising that Akua Afriyie's third daughter by her second marriage, that is, Aberefi Yaa, should have been sent to the Bretuo royals of Mampon. Born probably in 1725 or soon thereafter, she was married first to the aged Mamponhene Atakora Panin. It may be that the failure of her two elder sisters to bear children became a matter for alarm when she, too, failed to conceive. Atakora Panin and Aberefi Yaa were divorced, and she was remarried – following here the suggested reconstruction of the royal genealogies – to Akyampon Yaw, a son of the former Mamponhemaa Akyaama and brother of the reigning Mamponhemaa Abena Saka who had, therefore, high expectations at that time of himself succeeding to the Mampon stool.[40]

Akyampon Yaw is said to have fought in the Takyiman campaign of 1722–3 and in the Gyaman campaign of *ca.* 1740.[41] Aberefi Yaa's divorce from Mamponhene Atakora Panin, and remarriage to Akyampon Yaw, is probably to be dated to *ca.* 1744: about two years, that is, after Atakora Panin's accession (see p. 334) when she was still only around nineteen years of age. The births of Sewaa Okuwa and Akyaama may accordingly be placed in the mid-1740s. A second divorce occurred soon after, and probably before the birth of any other children. The circumstances of the divorce were connected with the death of the Mamponhemaa Abena Saka. Her sister Ago Mansa was advanced as candidate for the vacant stool. She was opposed by Adowa, who was presumably from a different branch of the Bretuo royals. The dispute was adjudicated by Atakora Panin, who awarded the stool to Adowa. Thereupon Ago Mansa and her brothers, including Akyampon Yaw, quitted Mampon. They established themselves at Wono (12 miles northwest of Kumase), a town belonging to the important Gyamase stool.[42] Subsequently, and not long before his death, Akyampon Yaw accepted from the Asantehene Opoku Ware the position of Asoromasohene under the Dadiesoabahene of Kumase:[43] presumably offered him, as was common, by virtue of his status as father of Oyoko royals. In Mampon, however, Aberefi Yaa was remarried to the new Mamponhene Asumgyima: as an Oyoko royal given to the Mampon Bretuo

[40] The possibility must also be allowed, that Aberefi Yaa married one of Akyampon Yaw's brothers rather than he himself. In genealogical terms the matter is of no consequence. The later appointment of Akyampon Yaw as Asoromasohene of Kumase seems, however, significant in the context.

[41] Institute of African Studies, Ghana, IASAS/155: Asoromaso Stool History, recorded by J. Agyeman-Duah, 15 June 1965.

[42] IASAS/162: Gyamfi Wono Stool History, recorded by J. Agyeman-Duah, 10 January 1966.

[43] IASAS/155: Asoromaso Stool History.

royals, she could not be permitted to leave Mampon and go into exile with Akyampon Yaw. Since Akyampon Yaw never recovered his status within Mampon, he was subsequently seemingly struck out of the Oyoko royal genealogies: the marriage between him and Aberefi Yaa was retrospectively annulled. Since, however, their descendants could not be left genealogically fatherless, in the received version of the matter Safo Katanka was substituted for Akyampon Yaw as father of Sewaa Okuwa: hence Safo Katanka had to be regarded as having been married to Aberefi Yaa. Similarly, Konadu Yaadom was substituted for Akyaama as mother of Ama Sewaa and Osei Kwame: she, too, had therefore to be regarded as also married to Safo Katanka. Hence the anomaly was generated in the received version of the royal genealogies, that Safo Katanka married both Aberefi Yaa and Aberefi Yaa's daughter Konadu Yaadom!

Safo Katanka's accession to power, and Akyaama's attainment of womanhood, were separated in time by no more than a few years. Their marriage probably occurred in or about 1760, when Akyaama was around fifteen years of age. Of the three children of the marriage, the youngest was Osei Kwame. He became Asantehene in 1777. Reindorf recorded that he was aged only twelve on his accession,[44] and despite the *prime facie* implausibility of the report, other sources confirm its accuracy.[45] The three children of Safo Katanka and Akyaama, namely Akyaa Kese, Ama Sewaa, and Osei Kwame, should therefore be seen as being born between 1762 $\pm$ 1 and 1765.[46] They were born, that is, during the last years of the reign of the Asantehene Kusi Obodom and the first year of that of Osei Kwadwo. Certainly Kusi Obodom would not have considered the Mampon-domiciled Oyoko as ever likely to assume major office whether as Asantehemaas or Asantehenes. Having, so it would seem, increased his chances of survival by affording recognition as heir apparent to Osei Kwadwo, of the House of Osei Tutu, thereafter his principal concern was that no harm should come to Osei Kwadwo such as to throw the nation into turmoil. When, for example, Osei Kwadwo had sexual intercourse with no less than four of Kusi Obodom's wives, a capital offence quadrupled, the Asantehene nevertheless spared his life and took vicarious forms of compensation.[47]

---

44 Reindorf, 2nd ed., n.d., p. 133.
45 According to Bowdich, 1819, p. 237, Osei Kwame succeeded at a 'very early age'. In an English source of 1778 he is described as 'a minor', see PRO, T. 70/32: Miles *et al.* to Committee, dd. Cape Coast, 25 June 1778. In a still later report of 1780 he is again referred to as 'a minor', Asante being 'governed entirely by his mother', PRO, T. 70/32: Roberts *et al.* to Committee, dd. Cape Coast, 8 October 1780.
46 That Safo Katanka was still alive in this period is confirmed by references to him in Dutch sources, see, e.g. KvG 301: list of presents sent to Asante, 1767.
47 Reindorf, 2nd ed., n.d., pp. 130–1. When one of Kusi Obodom's sons, Adabo,

It was, then, Osei Kwadwo who on accession had to face what was, from the standpoint of the Houses of Osei Tutu and Opoku Ware, the potential challenge of the Oyoko royals of Mampon.

The received version of the royal genealogies is probably correct in reporting that Konadu Yaadom had first been given by her father Asumgyima in marriage to the Apahene Owusu, a Mampon Bretuo royal of the Babiru branch [48] (see Figure 9). When, therefore, Asantehene Osei Kwadwo decided to remove Konadu Yaadom to Kumase and enstool her as Asantehemaa, Apahene Owusu was deprived of a wife. In fact, an exchange had to be made. According to the received version of the matter, Apahene Owusu was compensated for his loss of Aberefi Yaa's daughter, Konadu Yaadom, by the award in marriage of Aberefi Yaa's other daughter Sewaa Okuwa (see, again, Figure 9). It is noteworthy in this context that Adoma Akosua, daughter of Apahene Owusu and Sewaa Okuwa, was Asantehemaa from 1809 to 1819, and in that capacity purchased from Mampon, for 100 peredwans, her father's town, Apa (see p. 108). It remained under the immediate jurisdiction of Kumase until it was restored to Mampon by the British colonial administration in this century.

It may be assumed that Osei Kwadwo's decision to remove the Asantehemaa stool from Kokofu to Kumase was not one welcomed by the Kokofu. It may be assumed further, that his decision to transfer Konadu Yaadom from Mampon to Kumase was not one pleasing to the Mampon. Yet with his subsequent recognition of Opoku Kwame, of the House of Opoku Ware, as heir apparent, it might have seemed that the Oyoko royals of both Mampon and Kokofu had in effect been eliminated from the succession. Certainly contemporary observers anticipated an orderly transition when news of Osei Kwadwo's death in 1777 reached them. 'I am far from thinking', noted Richard Miles in Cape Coast, 'this Event will cause any very great revolution either in the Trade or Politicks of the Country'.[49] Yet, unexpectedly, the claims of Opoku Kwame were totally ignored in what developed as a power struggle between northern and southern interests. It has been remarked above, that the enstoolment of the Kokofuhene Kyei Kwame as Asantehene was prevented only by the intervention of Mamponhene Atakora Kwame and his Bron auxiliaries, who by a display of superior force procured the enstoolment of Osei Kwame. In chapter 7 the suggestion was made that the reign of Osei Kwame was a period in which Asante politics were dominated by those who saw the future of the nation as essentially that of a savannah power, looking towards the

committed a like offence, he was however castrated. See also Kyerematen, 1966, p. 283.

[48] Nana Prempe I, 1907, p. 7.

[49] PRO, T. 70/32: Miles to Committee, dd. Cape Coast, 19 January 1778.

vast northern hinterlands and the Western Sudan rather than towards the coast and the maritime connections with Europe and the Americas. Certainly Osei Kwame's attachment to Islam was among the factors which led to his destoolment in 1798 (see pp. 253–4).

When the heir apparent Opoku Kwame died in 1797, Konadu Yaadom had accused Osci Kwame of having him poisoned (see p. 252). Opoku Kwame's full brother, Opoku Fofie, nevertheless did survive. He was made heir apparent in succession to Opoku Kwame, and was elected Asantehene upon the destoolment of Osei Kwame in 1798. The House of Opoku Ware finally held the Golden Stool once more. It was rumoured that the death of Opoku Fofie in 1799 was again the result of the machinations of the ex-Asantehene Osei Kwame.[50] The succession, however, proceeded regularly. It was the turn of the House of Osei Tutu and three candidates were available: Osei Kofi, Osei Bonsu, and Osei Badu. Osei Bonsu was chosen in preference to his older brother, and enstooled with the official name of Osei Tutu Kwame. In 1804 he agreed to the execution of Osei Kwame (see p. 256). From the standpoint of the early nineteenth century some sort of order appeared at last to have emerged in the affairs of the Oyoko dynasty. It may have been at this time, that is, during the later Asantehemaaship of Konadu Yaadom, that the court historians revised the royal genealogies so as totally to suppress all reference to Akyaama.[51] Thus it might appear that in the aftermath of the struggle between Konadu Yaadom and Akyaama's son Osei Kwame, from which Konadu Yaadom emerged successful, the principle of dynastic unity (see p. 329) was reasserted by the assignation of 'classificatory' mother status to Konadu Yaadom *vis-à-vis* the deceased Osei Kwame and his surviving sister Ama Sewaa. Be that as it may, Table 11 shows the pattern of evolution of the dynasty as it would have appeared to the early nineteenth century observer: two Houses defined with reference to patrifilial ties, and providing Asantehenes in alternation, had emerged, and the only two Asantehenes who had come from neither House had in fact both re-

[50] Dupuis, 1824, p. 245.
[51] Attention is here drawn to the fact that during the enstoolment of an Asantehene an interesting role is played by the female occupant of the Akyaama stool. The Gyaasewahene, Akyeamehene and Nseniehene of Kumase approach her to ask for her 'son' to be made Asantehene. Thrice she refuses, and then finally hands over the Asantehene-elect. She is given a fee as *aseda*, and the proceedings can then continue. See, for example, *Souvenir Programme: Enstoolment of Otumfuo Opoku Ware II Asantehene*, Kumase, 1970, p. 6. The occupant of the Akyaama stool is the *obaa-panin* of the old Oyoko Pampasu ward of Kumase, and controlled the *atinafo*, that is, those who were responsible for the well-being of the young royals and princes, see Wilks, field-notes: interview with Nana Afua Kobi, dd. Kumase, 9 December 1973. There appears at least a possibility that the Akyaama stool was created for the eighteenth century royal of that name after her exclusion from the dynasty.

linquished power in their lifetimes to members of one or other of the two.

Table 11 *The Oyoko Dynasty of Asante, from an early nineteenth century perspective* [52]

House of Osei Tutu (see Figure 5)	House of Opoku Ware (see Figure 6)	Others
Osei Tutu, late seventeenth to early eighteenth centuries	—	—
—	Opoku Ware, *ca.* 1720–50	—
—	—	Kusi Obodom, 1750–64; abdicated
Osei Kwadwo, 1764–77	—	—
—	—	Osei Kwame, 1777–98; destooled
—	Opoku Fofie, 1798–9	—
Osei Bonsu, 1800–23	—	—

The early nineteenth century dynastic annals

It is a significant fact that it was precisely in the period of the early nineteenth century that the Asantehene Osei Bonsu decided upon the desirability of establishing in literary form not only a chronology for his predecessors, but also annals of their separate reigns. The matter is of sufficient interest and importance to merit treatment at some length. The origins of a chancery, within the Gyaasewa or Exchequer, are probably to be sought in the eighteenth century. It has been noted that treaties were apparently being drawn up in Arabic as early as the middle of that century (see p. 21). Certainly by the beginning of the nineteenth century Arabic was being used for a variety of purposes. Among the many Muslims who attended Osei Bonsu during the invasion of the south in 1807, some belonged to what Robertson described as 'an Arab medical staff': among their other duties was that of recording the casualties.[53] Although no transcripts of court proceedings have survived, they were reported to have been kept: thus of the trial of Apea Nyanyo on 8 July 1817 it was remarked, 'the Moorish secretaries were there to take notes of the transactions of the day'.[54] Because of Asante's trade with both north and south, it was necessary to maintain some sort of concordance between the Muslim, Christian and Asante calendars. A number of manuscripts survive from the early

[52] The dates given for the reigns are the writer's.

[53] PRO, T. 70/35: Torrane to Committee, dd. Cape Coast, 20 July 1807. G. A. Robertson, 1819, p. 151.

[54] Lee, 1835, p. 164. Lee (the former Mrs Bowdich) used her late husband's notes, though took certain liberties with them. For the trial, see Bowdich, 1819, p. 129.

nineteenth century which show that the Muslims in Kumase were engaged in this exercise. The Gyaasewahene, who was responsible for the overall direction of the economy, was therefore vitally concerned with the scheduling of trade and the like; and calendrical matters were assigned to his staff.[55] Certainly the Gyaasewahene Opoku Frefre had a Muslim secretary in his employment (a resident earlier, it would seem, in Oyo, capital of the Alafins of the Yoruba), who is was said, 'records the greater political events'.[56] Official communications, too, were conducted in Arabic. Had not the British government found itself virtually without the services of qualified Arabic translators at the time,[57] diplomatic correspondence between the two powers might have done much to assuage their worsening relations.[58] As it was, contact between the court in Kumase and the rulers and imāms of the northern provinces was maintained through this medium, and a number of letters dating from the first two decades of the nineteenth century are still extant [59] (see Plate VII). There was, then, no technical obstacle to the compilation, in Arabic, of annals of the dynasty.

It is reasonably sure that the Arabic annals of the Oyoko dynasty do not survive.[60] It is possible that they were destroyed or lost at the time of the sack of Kumase in 1874, when the Aban – the Palace of Culture – was blown up. R. Austin Freeman, who visited Kumase in late 1888, was led to doubt their very existence, and referred to 'certain mysterious "Moslem records" . . . which I am disposed to regard with extreme suspicion'.[61] There can be no doubt, however, that they were known to Bowdich in 1817 and to Dupuis in 1820. Bowdich referred to 'the anxiety of the Ashantee government for daily records, immediately upon the establishment of the Moors, who were only visitors until the present reign'.[62] The event which Bowdich appears to have had in mind was the settlement in Kumase of Shāykh Muḥammad al-Ghamba' in 1807.[63] Using Bowdich's notes, his widow certainly saw the matter that way, for in 1835 she wrote: 'it is only about twenty-

55 See Levtzion, 1966, p. 115. Rattray, 1929, pp. 109–10, note.
56 Bowdich, 1819, p. 296.
57 Jackson, 1820, pp. 406–7.
58 The British did, however, finally get round to sending Arabic translations of the Bible to Kumase, see Ricketts, 1831, p. 142.
59 See Levtzion, 1966, *passim*.
60 Attention is drawn to the Arabic collection in the Institute of African Studies, Ghana. The manuscript IASAR/40, an Asante regnal list (with dates) written by the Gonja Qāḍī 'Abdallāh in the early part of this century, is based upon a European source ultimately derivative from Dupuis. IASAR/148 is a work of unknown authorship entitled *The Names of the Kings of Asante as kept by the shāykhs*. It appears not to be in the tradition of the lost annals.
61 R. A. Freeman, 1898, p. 438.
62 Bowdich, 1819, p. 232.
63 *Ibid.* p. 240. See also Wilks, 1966a, pp. 319–20.

seven years back, that any written records of the kingdom have been preserved, and these are kept in Arabic; the Ashantee not being a written language'.[64] If the compilation of the annals was indeed commenced in 1807, then it is one of those strange coincidences of history that exactly one hundred years later Nana Agyeman Prempe I, in exile in Seychelles, commenced the compilation of a new set of dynastic annals, 'The History of the Ashanti Kings and the Whole Country Itself' (see p. 327, n. 1).

Bowdich was aware of the revolutionary character of the decision to produce written annals of Asante history, and of the momentous break with tradition which it represented. He was cognizant of the law of Okomfo Anokye forbidding direct reference to the deaths of rulers, and wrote: 'To speak of the death of a former king, the Ashantees imagine to affect the life of the present equally with enquiring who would be his successor; and superstition and policy strengthening this impression, it is made capital by law, to converse either of the one or the other.' [65] Noting that orally transmitted traditions lacked absolute dates ('the inability of the natives to compute time'),[66] Bowdich recognized that 'the chronology can only be founded on that of the Moors'.[67] Since, however, the Arabic annals were of recent compilation, Bowdich saw this as exposing 'the perplexities and deficiencies of their early history too candidly, to leave any encouragement to the researches of strangers'.[68] But Bowdich was in any case disadvantaged in the situation; neither he nor any member of his party had a knowledge of Arabic. In the circumstances Bowdich could do no more than glean what information he could from those with access to the annals, and this he incorporated into his chapter on 'History'.[69] Three years later Dupuis was also made aware of the distinction between the status of the orally transmitted traditions and that of the written annals. 'The unlettered heathen', he commented, mistaking the restrictions upon the recounting of tradition for lack of knowledge, 'is so decidedly ignorant and disinterested about researches into past ages.' He was, however, referred to the *'ulamā*. 'Enquire of the Moslems', he was told, 'who pray to the great God, and hold strong fetish; they know these things, and more: they can tell you'.[70] It is fortunate that, unlike Bowdich, Dupuis had a knowledge of Arabic. But it is unfortunate that, while Dupuis reproduced intact a number of route

64 Lee, 1835, p. 174, note.
65 Bowdich, 1819, p. 228.
66 *Idem.*
67 *Ibid.* p. 232.
68 *Idem.*
69 *Ibid.* chapter II.
70 Dupuis, 1824, p. lxxxiii.

books which he obtained from Kumase,[71] he chose to incorporate the material from the annals into his chapter, 'Historical Memoirs of Ashantee', where it is intermingled with his own observations and with additional data from various sources.

The tradition of maintaining annals was an old established one in the Western Sudan. The best known early examples, of the sixteenth and seventeenth centuries, are the several works on the rulers of Bornu written by its Imām, Aḥmad b. Fartuwa, and the Timbuktu annals of the Songhai rulers, the *Ta'rīkh al-Sūdān* of 'Abd al-Raḥmān al-Sa'dī and the *Ta'rīkh al-fattāsh* of Ibn al-Mukhtār. By the early eighteenth century the tradition had spread as far south as Gonja, when a number of short works were written there treating the origins of the Gonja dynasty, and the conversion of its members to Islam.[72] Parts of these works, together with a chronicle of Gonja affairs in the first half of the eighteenth century, were compiled in the middle of the century into the *Tadhkira li 'l-Muta'akhirīn* (see p. 18, n. 99). Its redactors are named as al-Ḥājj Muḥammad b. al-Muṣṭafā and Imām 'Umar Kunandi b. 'Umar. That the Gonja annals were the model for the later Asante annals would seem, *prima facie,* likely. In point of fact, it is known that a short work on the conversion of the early Gonja rulers with their reign lengths, which forms the basis of the first parts of the *Tadhkira li 'l-Muta'akhirīn,* was extant in Kumase in the early nineteenth century, for a copy of it from there has been preserved.[73]

Among the Muslims whose acquaintance Dupuis made in Kumase in 1820 was the one known as Kantoma to the Asante. The name is a shortened form of 'Karamo Toghma', that it, Toghma the scholar.[74] Karamo Toghma described himself in a route-book which he had written as 'Muḥammad Kama'atay, called Kantūmā'.[75] 'Kama'atay', that is, Kamagatay, is the well known Dyula family name borne, for example, by many members of the *'ulamā* class in Gonja. It is clear, in fact, that Kantoma had been born into precisely that class. He is referred to in one letter addressed by the Imām of Gbuipe to the Asantehene Osei Bonsu as *Muḥammad b. al-Muṣṭafā Imām Ghunja.*[76] Since 'Toghma' is a Malinke nickname used in Gonja for a person having the

---

71 *Ibid.* pp. cxxiv–cxxxiv.
72 See Wilks, 1966c, pp. 26–8. The writer has subsequently located a comparatively uncorrupted text of the work on the coming of the Nbanya to Gonja, see Wilks, field-notes, interview with al-Ḥājj Muḥammad b. Limam Khālid, dd. Yendi, 14 August 1968, supplement.
73 Royal Library, Copenhagen, *Cod. Arab. CCCII,* iii, ff. 236–7. See further Levtzion, 1966, p. 112.
74 *Cod. Arab. CCCII,* ii, f. 27.
75 Dupuis, 1824, p. cxxviii. See also *Cod. Arab. CCCII,* iii, f. 6.
76 *Cod. Arab. CCCII,* i, f. 188.

same birth-name as his father, Kantoma's father may then be identified as the Imām of Gonja, Muḥammad al-Muṣṭafā. He appears to have held the imāmate until his death in the early nineteenth century, when his junior brother Mālik, then Imām of Gbuipe, succeeded him.[77] When Dupuis was in Kumase, Kantoma was one of the small clique of Muslims who were in constant attendance upon the Asantehene:[78] he is known to have conducted some of Osei Bonsu's correspondence with the northern provinces.[79] Awaiting the government's permission to undertake the pilgrimage to Mecca,[80] Kantoma was described by Dupuis as 'moderately well skilled in the Arabic language, which he said he had studied in Haoussa.'[81] *Prima facie*, then, Muḥammad b. Imām Muḥammad al-Muṣṭafā – Kantoma – would seem to be the obvious person to have compiled the annals of the Asante dynasty based upon the model of the earlier annals of Gonja provenance. The identification is much strengthened by the fact that Kantoma was grandson of 'Umar Kunandi, one of the two redactors of the *Tadhkira li 'l-Muta'akhirīn:* thus Kantoma's paternal uncle, the Imām of Gbuipe Mālik, is described as son of 'Umar Kunandi b. 'Umar al-Amīn.[82]

Dupuis indicated that information from the Asante annals was narrated to him by several of the leading scholars of the Kumase Muslim community, including its head, Muḥammad al-Ghamba' (the 'Bashaw'); his trading agent Abū Bakr Turay – exceptionally gifted in Arabic [83]; and Kantoma. 'This sketch of history,' he wrote, 'relating to a period when Ashantee was scarcely known to us, even as an inland nation, was related by the Bashaw, Aboubecr, Kantoma and some others. Its interest may be trifling with the public, for it is confessedly a plain narrative, designed to show the progressive aggrandizement of the empire, and its influence over the Moslem powers.'[84] It is regrettable that little of its content can be recovered from Dupuis' writings, and still less from those of Bowdich. The annals appear to have been commenced from the opening year of the second millennium after the *hijra,* that is, from 1000 AH (AD 1591/2): clearly no more than a convenient literary device. Dupuis' rendering of the opening section probably took considerable liberties with the original: 'As early as the

[77] *Ibid.* III, f. 5; II, f. 1.
[78] Dupuis, 1824, pp. 109; 158; 160; 176. Compare Reindorf, 2nd ed., n.d., p. 182.
[79] *Cod. Arab. CCCII,* II, f. 1.
[80] Dupuis, 1824, p. cxxix.
[81] *Ibid.* p. 104. He had also apparently visited Dahomey and Benin, *ibid.* p. cxxvii, and it is possible that it was Kantoma who had recruited, in Oyo, Opoku Frefre's Muslim secretary.
[82] *Cod. Arab. CCCII,* II, f. 204. For a further discussion of this matter, see Levtzion, 1966, pp. 111–12.
[83] Dupuis, 1824, pp. 96–7.
[84] *Ibid.* p. 250. Dupuis, p. 229, also noted that he had suppressed material relating to the pre-Osei Tutu period, as of no interest to his readers.

hejyran year 1000, and from that to 1050 (AD 1640,) Ashantee occasionally ruled, by its influence, over part of Akim, Assin, Quahou, and
Akeyah: it was then esteemed a powerful little monarchy . . .' [85]
Neither Bowdich nor Dupuis give any indication of what was contained in the presumed second section of the annals, that is, that
covering the period 1050–1100 AH (AD 1640/1–1688/9), though Bowdich does present material on the founding of Kumase by Osei Tutu
and of Dwaben by 'Boitinnë, that is, Boama Koko Boate.[86] Bowdich
also noted 'the report of the Moors, that the kingdom had been
founded about 110 years'.[87] It is curious, that if the annals are considered to have been written in 1807, that is, in 1221 or 1222 AH, then
the creation of the kingdom may have been assigned to 1111 or 1112
AH – between AD 1699 and 1701; this is the correct date for the wars
against Denkyira as a result of which Asante has always been regarded
as having established its political independence. It should also be
noted that, of what he thought to be the same war, Dupuis wrote: 'This
Dinkira war, according to the Moslem records, commenced in their
year, 1132 (AD 1719) . . . This, they say, was the first great war in
which the believers were compelled to unite their arms with the
heathens of Ashantee, Banna, Juabin, and other tributary states in
the North, led on to battle by Sai Tooto . . .' [88] Dupuis had clearly
made what was, despite Austin Freeman's comment to the contrary,[89]
a simple mistake. The war referred to was not that against *Denkyira*,
but that against the Gyamanhene *Adinkra* in which the Muslims of
Kumase were indeed required to fight despite their manifest reluctance.[90] The Asante forces were mobilized for the campaign not in
1132 but in 1232 AH, that is, in 1817.

From the material recorded by Dupuis in particular, it would seem
that the annals consisted basically of a series of entries for each
Asantehene, giving a date for his accession and listing the wars which
he fought. It may be, too, that some sort of evaluation – presumably
panegyrical – was included for each reign. Certainly that given by
Dupuis, 'on the wisdom as well as valour of Sai Tooto', reads like a
fairly literal translation from the Arabic: 'he was, as they say, the
great, and the good; for, in his reign, justice was ever on the alert, and
the claims of his subjects were listened to without distinction of rank

85 *Ibid.* p. 225.
86 Bowdich, 1819, p. 232. For Boama Koko Boate, see Rattray, 1929, p. 169.
87 Bowdich, 1819, p. 232.
88 Dupuis, 1824, p. 229.
89 R. A. Freeman, 1898, p. 438, note.
90 Dupuis, 1824, p. 98 and note. Hutton, 1821, pp. 323–4. A letter of the period
   from the Imām of Gbuipe to Osei Bonsu predicted that the Asantehene would
   overthrow 'Dinkira', that is, Adinkra, see *Cod. Arab. CCCII*, I, f. 146; Levtzion,
   1966, pp. 110–11.

or title',[91] and so too, perhaps, does that on Osei Kwame: 'his name is handed to posterity as the most merciful of the race of kings. Towards the close of his reign, he prohibited many festivals at which it was usual to spill the blood of victims . . .'[92] The sequence of wars, as recorded by Bowdich and Dupuis – despite certain obvious errors arising from misunderstandings – was a reasonably accurate one, and the general pattern of Asante expansion indicated by it remains broadly acceptable. The chronology of the reigns, by contrast, is erroneous: it has been, however, almost universally accepted by later writers, including Nana Agyeman Prempe himself in 1907,[93] and was seriously called into question only in 1960.[94] The chronological material recorded in Kumase by Bowdich and Dupuis is summarized in Table 12.

Table 12 *Early nineteenth century chronology of the Asantehenes*

Asantehene: Arabic form from Dupuis	Dates from Dupuis		Dates from Bowdich	Corrected dates: Priestley/Wilks
	Muslim year	Conversion		
Sai Abūku:				
accession	1144	1731/2	1720	ca. 1720
death	1156	1743/4	—	1750
Sai Akūsī:				
accession	—	—	1741	1750
Sai Kudjūḥ:				
accession	1166	1752/3	1753	1764
Sai Kwāmīn:				
accession	1196	1781/2	1785	1777
destoolment	—	—	1798	1798
Sai Abūku:				
accession	1212	1797/8	—	1798
death	—	—	1799	1799
Sai Tūtu Kwāmīn:				
accession	1215	1800/1	—	1800

With the exception of that for the accession of Opoku Ware, the dates given by Bowdich and by Dupuis are in fairly close agreement; the discrepancies are ones of no more than three years at any point, and may be accounted for by errors in conversion to the Christian calendar on Bowdich's part. Both sets of dates, however, are seriously inaccurate. It is clear that the compiler, though having access to an-

[91] Dupuis, 1824, p. 229. Compare the panegyric in the *Tadhkira li 'l-Muta'akhirīn* for the Gonja ruler 'Abbās (died 1709): 'he was a powerful king; he subdued people by force and acted equitably in authority . . . he had the greatest number of subjects, the most numerous army and the widest country; he was richest in fortune and most impressive in dignity . . .'
[92] Dupuis, 1824, p. 245.
[93] Nana Prempe I, 1907, p. 31.
[94] Priestley and Wilks, 1960, *passim*.

nals of the *early* Gonja rulers (*Cod. Arab. CCCII*, III, ff. 236–7), had no copy of the fuller *Tadhkira li 'l-Muta'akhirīn* before him. Had this been available, a more accurate chronology could have been devised since, for example, an obituary notice for Opoku Ware is entered under the year 1163 AH (AD 1749/50). Reference to the data shows that the errors in the chronology assume serious proportions with the reign of Osei Kwadwo. According to the account given Dupuis, Osei Kwadwo withdrew from public affairs in old age, rumours of his death circulated, and Burum Akombra and Ofusu headed a rebellion in the southern provinces which was only suppressed by Osei Kwame.[95] Although Osei Kwadwo was only in his forties at the time of his death, it appears that the report of his retirement led the annalist to assign him a reign of thirty – instead of thirteen – years. *Prima facie,* it might seem that the computations of reign-lengths were made from estimates based upon the testimony of living informants. Yet it may be more than a coincidence, that if the veridical reign-lengths, and those given by Bowdich, are arranged in descending order of magnitude, two virtually identical series are obtained: respectively, 30/21/14/13/1, total 79, and 32/21/13/12/1, total 79. Meyerowitz has reported on a method of recording reign-lengths used in Takyiman: a small piece of gold was deposited annually in a special receptacle.[96] P. Ferguson has likewise shown that the length of the reign of a Ya Na of Dagomba could be computed from the cows' tails which were put aside annually at the Damba festival.[97] There is at least a possibility that some such practice had been followed in Asante, and that the annalist had access to such material. Indeed, when Dupuis noted of one ruler, that he reigned 'twelve lunar years, short of some months', the implication is that the Odwira marked the end of the twelfth year, but that Dupuis himself added the rider since he knew that the festival always fell a few months short of the end of the Christian year.[98] There is, then, the possibility that the annalist had accurate information on the reign-lengths of the eighteenth century rulers of Asante, *but did not know which reign-length should be assigned to which Asantehene and dis-*

[95] Dupuis, 1824, p. 244, who misinterpreted the name 'Burum Akombra' as implying that the leader was a Bron. For the rebellion, see also Reindorf, 2nd ed., n.d., p. 134; Bowdich, 1819, p. 237; IASAR/148, *The Names of the Kings*, the 'Ankara and Fasu war'. There is a monumental confusion in Asante tradition between this rebellion and the sack of Kumase by Abirimuru of Sehwi prior to the reign of Opoku Ware, see for example, Reindorf, 2nd ed., n.d., pp. 80–1; Rattray, 1929, pp. 201; 220. There is also confusion with the Mansrahene Brumu Ankoma, of the Nsoko region, who was executed by Opoku Ware in the early 1740s, see IAS/BA/3: Nwase-Branam Tradition, recorded by Kwabena Ameyaw, 16 February 1965.

[96] Meyerowitz, 1952, pp. 29–30. See also Flight, 1970, *passim.*

[97] Ferguson, 1973, p. 11.

[98] Dupuis, 1824, p. 235.

tributed them wrongly.[99] Unless a text of the annals is found, however, further investigation of this matter seems fruitless.

Osei Bonsu's interest in the uses of literacy was clearly innovatory. He was allowed to send a number of children to the Muslim school in Kumase,[100] but his councillors prevented him from sending others to the English school in Cape Coast: it was against 'the established customs of the nation'.[101] The production of written annals of the Oyoko dynasty, however, represented a major break with tradition, and was almost certainly politically motivated. Examination of the materials recorded by Bowdich and Dupuis reveals a number of interesting points. First, the unity of the Houses of Osei Tutu and Opoku Ware, expressed in the conceptualization of the Golden Stool as that of both Osei Tutu and Opoku Ware, was reasserted in the annals by the fiction that the two Asantehenes were brothers.[102] Secondly, Kusi Obodom who belonged to neither house was conveniently treated as a third brother.[103] Thirdly, Osei Kwadwo was correctly located in the descendent generation ('nephew') from Kusi Obodom, and in the ascendent generation once removed ('grandfather') from Osei Kwame, Opoku Fofie and Osei Bonsu.[104] And finally, the breach between the descendants of Akyaama and those of Konadu Yaadom appears already to have been glossed over by the treatment of Osei Kwame, Opoku Fofie and Osei Bonsu as brothers.[105] It is significant that the annals apparently made no reference whatsoever to any succession being contested: there is, for example, not the slightest suggestion in the writings of Bowdich and Dupuis that Osei Kwame had virtually usurped the stool, and both accounts of his reign commence with the suppression of the rebellion in the southern provinces.[106] While the annalist had, then, to ignore succession disputes, he was clearly at liberty to refer not only to defeats which the Asante armies suffered in the course of the wars of expansion, but he was also able to treat seriously the nature of the political opposition which each ruler faced. There is no concern to suppress the fact that attempts were made to overthrow Opoku Ware and so abort the reforms which he proposed; nor is the fact of Osei Kwame's destoolment glossed over. The annalist, while strongly committed to expressing the principle of dynastic unity, was nevertheless enabled to treat each ruler as a historical

99 The different dates given by Bowdich and Dupuis for the accession of Opoku Ware remain, on any hypothesis, a difficult problem.
100 Dupuis, 1824, p. 107.
101 Hutchison to Smith, dd. Kumase, 3 February 1818, in Bowdich, 1820.
102 Bowdich, 1819, p. 234. Dupuis, 1824, p. 233.
103 Bowdich, 1819, p. 236.
104 *Ibid.* p. 237.
105 Dupuis, 1824, pp. 245; 247.
106 Bowdich, 1819, p. 237; Dupuis, 1824, p. 244.

personage whose successes had to be matched against his failures.[107]
The annals are to be seen as exemplifying yet one more aspect of the
major social transformations which were occurring within the nation:
in particular, the increasing concern with achievement was such that
even the Asantehenes who had long joined their ancestors had lost
their immunity from secular criticism.

Osei Bonsu and the problem of the succession

In contrast to the situation which prevailed in the earlier part of the
eighteenth century, by the beginning of the nineteenth century the
survival of the Oyoko dynasty was no longer threatened by any shortage of female royals. Disregarding the more distant collateral branches
of the family, such as that of Kokofu, there were five closely related
senior women whose children had claims to the throne. All were descendants of Aberefi Yaa, and their relationship is shown in Figure 10.

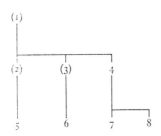

(1) Aberefi Yaa
(2) Sewaa Okuwa
(3) Akyaama
4 Konadu Yaadom, born *ca.* 1752
5 Adoma Akosua, born *ca.* 1765
6 Ama Sewaa, born *ca.* 1763
7 Yaa Dufie, born *ca.* 1770
8 Akua Akrukruwaa, born *ca.* 1772

Fig. 10 Senior female Oyoko royals, early nineteenth century (brackets indicate
those dead, or presumed dead)

In accordance with the constitutional procedures which seemed to
have gained acceptance, Osei Bonsu should have afforded recognition,
as heir apparent, to a member of the House of Opoku Ware. Akua
Akrukruwaa, daughter of Konadu Yaadom and Adu Twum of the
House of Opoku Ware, had married but appears to have given birth
to only one child, a daughter Ata Sewaa. It was, however, probably
not until about 1818 that Ata Sewaa herself was old enough to be
married. Her husband, Adu, was almost certainly a son of the Asantehene Opoku Fofie (see Figure 7, p. 331), and their first born son,
Opoku Ahoni, was the first candidate for the Golden Stool to become
available from the House of Opoku Ware since Opoku Fofie. It will
be obvious, then, that earlier in the century Osei Bonsu had been
unable to name as heir apparent anyone from the House of Opoku

107 Compare also Hutton, 1821, p. 262, who reported on Osei Bonsu's desire to
  have accounts of the Fante, Assin and Gyaman campaigns written in English.

Ware: no candidate was available. But upon Osei Bonsu's death in 1823 Opoku Ahoni was still too young to be among those considered for the succession: a consequence of the unexpectedly early death of Opoku Fofie.[108]

Although no direct report on the matter has been found, it appears that in the circumstances the representatives of the House of Opoku Ware followed the logical course: having no one available for the heir apparency, they agreed that the House of Osei Tutu should take their turn and provide a candidate. Osei Bonsu's senior brother Osei Kofi was ineligible, having been rejected by the electors in 1800. The choice therefore fell upon Osei Bonsu's junior brother, Osei Badu (see Figure 6, p. 330). He was enstooled as heir apparent though not upon the Akyempem stool. The misfortunes which had befallen both Opoku Kwame and Opoku Fofie were attributed partly to the fact that custom had been violated when the Akyempem stool had been transferred from the head of the princes to the heir apparent (see p. 333), and a new stool was accordingly created for Osei Badu in the Adum and not the Akyeremade ward.[109] Osei Badu, however, held the position for only a few years: it has been noted above that he died in the course of the invasion of the south in 1807. A new election had therefore to be held. The House of Opoku Ware still lacked any candidate, and reference to Figure 6 will show that the genealogically 'ideal' candidate from the House of Osei Tutu – Osei Kwadwo, son of Owusu Afriyie and Afua Sapon – had not yet been born. There were, however, two others available: Osei Yaw who was a son of Konadu Yaadom herself, and Kwaku Pimpim who was a son of Konadu Yaadom's daughter Yaa Dufie. While neither belonged to the major line within the House of Osei Tutu, that is, to that shown in Figure 6, both nevertheless were among the descendants of Osei Tutu. Reference to Figure 11 will show the nature of the relationship.

It must have been one of the last political victories of the Asante-hemaa Konadu Yaadom, not long before her death in 1809, to achieve the recognition of her youngest son Osei Yaw as heir apparent. In 1817 Bowdich remarked of him that he appeared 'very inferior in ability; but the Ashantees say otherwise'.[110] Kwaku Pimpim is known to have fought in the Gyaman campaign of 1818–19; and, with little expectation of ever succeeding as Asantehene, he was subsequently given the new position of Mamesenehene within the Ankobea group

---

108 See Bowdich, 1819, p. 295.
109 See Kyerematen, 1966, pp. 291–3. Nana Prempe I, 1907, pp. 33–4. The Adum-hene, head of the Adum ward of Kumase and in charge of the executioners and police, was thus made responsible for the care of the heir apparent.
110 Bowdich, 1819, p. 246.

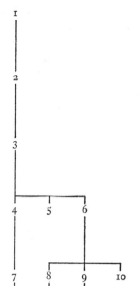

1. Owusu Panin, Aberenkesehene (see Figure 6 p. 330)
2. Asantehene Osei Tutu.
3. Akyempemhene Owusu Afriyie.
4. Asantehene Osei Kwadwo, by Owusu Afriyie's marriage to the Asantehemaa Akua Afriyie.
5. Osei Tiri, by Owusu Afriyie's marriage to an unrecorded non-royal woman. Created first Nkonsonhene by Osei Kwadwo. Fought at Banda *ca.* 1765.*
6. Osei Yaw, by Owusu Afriyie's marriage to an unrecorded non-royal woman. Second Nkonsonhene.
7. Apagyahene Owusu Afriyie; married Asantehemaa Afua Sapon; died 1826.
8. Owusu Yaw of Anowo ward, Kumase. Married Asantehemaa Konadu Yaadom (see Table 10, p. 336).
9. Owusu Penemo (alias Abu), third Nkonsonhene, married later Asantehemaa Yaa Dufie; fought at Katamanso, 1826†
10. Owusu Ansa Titrawa, Nkonsonhene under Kwaku Dua I.‡
11. Heir apparent Osei Kwadwo, b. *ca.* 1810.
12. Asantehene Osei Yaw, born *ca.* 1800.
13. Kwaku Pimpim, created Mamesenehene of Kumase; born *ca.* 1790.

* Institute of African Studies, Ghana, IASAS/47: Nkonson Stool History recorded by J. Agyeman-Duah, 17 March 1963.

† Reindorf, 1st ed., 1895, Appendix.

‡ Reindorf, 2nd ed., n.d., p. 112.

Fig. 11   Reconstruction of the relationship of Asantehene Osei Yaw and Mamesenehene Kwaku Pimpim to the House of Osei Tutu

in Kumase.[111] At the time of Konadu Yaadom's death, then, the situation with respect to the succession to the Golden Stool seemed a reasonably assured one. That to the position of Asantehemaa also presented no problem. Adoma Akosua was senior of the royal women in the next generation (Figure 10, p. 353), and she was enstooled accordingly. She held office as Asantehemaa until 1819 when, so it will be seen (p. 485), she was destooled and executed following her attempt to overthrow Osei Bonsu. Dupuis, who was in Kumase the following year, learned only that she had 'formed a connexion with a chief of Bouromy [Bron], whose ambition suggested a plan to seat himself upon the throne'.[112] In the absence of further indication of motive, it is impossible to suggest the nature of the abortive coup. Herself by

[111] Institute of African Studies, IASAS/172: Mamesene Stool History, recorded by J. Agyeman-Duah, 22 April 1966.

[112] Dupuis, 1824, p. 115.

background one of the Oyoko royals of Mampon, it may be that she had secured the support of Bron troops from there in order to gain the stool for one or other of her own sons Osei Kwasi or Osei Kwadwo Kuma [113] (both of whom appear to have been virtually ignored in the deliberations on the heir apparency). However that may be, the office of Asantehemaa passed in 1819 to the next senior royal, Ama Sewaa,[114] and with her accession a new factor was to be introduced into the history of the dynasty.

The origins of the House of Kwaku Dua

It has been shown that Ama Sewaa was a full sister of the Asantehene Osei Kwame, both being children of the Mamponhene Safo Katanka by his marriage to Akyaama (Figure 9, p. 339). Under the dispensation whereby the Asantehene Osei Kwadwo had brought Konadu Yaadom from Mampon to Kumase, had made her Asantehemaa, and had given her in marriage to Adu Twum (of the House of Opoku Ware), and in view of her subsequent marriages to Asokore-Mamponhene Owusu Ansa and to Owusu Yaw of Anowo (both of the House of Osei Tutu), it seemed that any descendants of Ama Sewaa had been effectively eliminated from the succession to the Golden Stool. Ama Sewaa made, in fact, three 'morganatic' marriages, seemingly recognizing the fact that her sons would make no claims to highest office. Data on the three marriages are summarized in Table 13. Her first husband, the Gyakyehene Apaw Panin, was a son of the Asantehene Kusi Obodom. The six children were all probably born in the 1780–90 decade, and the marriage ended with the death of Apaw Panin.[115] Her second marriage, to Boakye Yam Kuma, was regarded as far less conventional. As Rattray remarked, 'the sixth Queen mother, Ama Sewa, contracted a *mésalliance* and married Boakye Yam, of the Bosompra *ntoro*, thereby introducing new names into the royal line, "spoiling the *ntoro*".' [116] Boakye Yam Kuma, nevertheless, had a distinguished ancestry. His paternal grandfather, Boakye Yam, had been a senior *obirempon* of Denkyira who, together with his followers, had transferred allegiance to Osei Tutu. He was made Nkwantakesehene of Kumase and fought

---

113 Both are referred to in Nana Prempe I, 1907, p. 9, but their father is identified only as Owusu.

114 According to Dupuis, 1824, p. 116, Ama Sewaa was younger sister of Adoma Akosua, an accurate enough description in terms of Asante kinship terminology.

115 Apaw Panin's successor as Gyakyehene was Yaw Pense, who was referred to by Bowdich in 1817 (1819, p. 203), and who fought at Katamanso in 1826, see Reindorf, 2nd ed., n.d., p. 203.

116 Rattray, 1927, p. 325.

Table 13 *The Marriages of Ama Sewaa*

Mother	Husband	Children
Ama Sewaa	1. Gyakyehene Apaw Panin	1. Kyenkyenhene
		2. Kwame Kusi
		3. Died in childhood
		4. Died in childhood
		5. Died in childhood
		6. Afua Sapon, later Asantehemaa
	2. Boakye Yam Kuma, of Heman and Nkwantanan, Kumase	7. Oti Akenten
		8. Akyampon Kwasi
		9. Kwaku Dua
	3. Okyere Kotoku, of Dwaben	10. Died in childhood
		11. Kwame Boaten

in most of the wars of the early eighteenth century.[117] His status was such that he was given as wife Ago, the *obaa-panin* of the Anyinase stool and herself a member of a collateral branch of the Oyoko royals. Akyampon Kwasi, son of Boakye Yam and Ago, later succeeded as Anyinasehene: he is said to have taken part in many campaigns, the latest being that against Banda in *ca.* 1765.[118] Akyampon Kwasi was the father of Boakye Yam Kuma.[119] By matrifiliation, Boakye Yam Kuma belonged to the Nkwantanan stool of Kumase: a position created for the Akwamu chief Duku Abadi who had been among the troops placed at Osei Tutu's disposal on his return from Akwamu to Asante.[120] Boakye Yam Kuma himself succeeded to the Nkwantanan stool probably under Osei Kwadwo. He continued in office under Osei Kwame and must have been among the group of officials who strove to consolidate that Asantehene in power: such, certainly, is the implication of the fact that upon Apaw Panin's death, the widowed Ama Sewaa – sister of Osei Kwame – was given him in marriage.

Of the three sons of Boakye Yam Kuma and Ama Sewaa, the date of birth of the youngest can be established with some confidence. A number of references to Kwaku Dua's age indicate 1792 and 1803 as outside limits for his birth; [121] but the general trend of the evidence is such as to suggest that it may be narrowed to 1797±2. There seems little doubt that Boakye Yam Kuma perished in the course of the

---

117 Institute of African Studies, Ghana, IASAS/136: Nkwanta-kessie Stool History, recorded by J. Agyeman-Duah, 7 October 1964.

118 IASAS/78: Anyinase Stool History, recorded by J. Agyeman-Duah, 16 September 1963.

119 Wilks, field-notes, interview with Nana Boakye Yam, dd. Kumase, 2–3 August 1965.

120 IASAS/23: Boakye Yam Stool History, recorded by J. Agyeman-Duah, 3 March 1963.

121 T. B. Freeman, 1843, p. 59: 'about 36' in 1839. National Archives of Ghana, Accra, ADM 1/2/4, Winniet's Diary, entry for 9 October 1848: 'about 52 to 56'.

struggle between the forces loyal to Osei Kwame, and those support-
ing Konadu Yaadom, in 1797–8 (see pp. 252–3). Osei Kwame himself
escaped to Dwaben, where he was given sanctuary.[122] His sister, Ama
Sewaa, accompanied him. There she entered into her third marriage,
that to Okyere Kotoku who was a son of the Dwabenhene Akuamoa
Panin. It would seem that Ama Sewaa took with her at least her son
Kwaku Dua, for he is still remembered as having been raised in the
Dwabenhene's palace.[123]

It is not clear when, and in what circumstances, Kwaku Dua began
to be considered a possible candidate for the Golden Stool. His elder
brothers Kyenkyenhene, Kwame Kusi and Oti Akenten may not have
survived the troubles of 1797–8: certainly data on their subsequent
careers are as yet lacking. Akyampon Kwasi, by contrast, did survive,
but appears to have relinquished all claims to royal status and to have
associated himself with his father's stool. He can be identified with
some confidence with the Akyampon Tia who served in the provincial
administration in Dagomba, and was subsequently appointed a junior
okyeame – his father's stool (that of Nkwantananhene) being transferred to the Gyaasewa and redesignated a counselor's position. Akyampon Tia probably died in or about 1870.[124] Kwaku Dua, however, was apparently already recognized as having claims on the succession by 1818: he and Kwaku Pimpim are remembered as the only
two royals – other than Osei Bonsu himself – who distinguished themselves by assuming active service during the Gyaman campaign.[125]
The election of his mother, Ama Sewaa, as Asantehemaa in 1819 enhanced his position further. Upon the death of Osei Bonsu in 1823 it
appears that the candidacy of Kwaku Dua was advanced against that
of the heir apparent, Osei Yaw.[126] The aspirations of the Kokofuhene
Offei Akwasim to highest office were also known.[127] Osei Yaw is said
to have seized the Golden Stool and, disregarding the due constitutional processes, to have taken the field against the British immediately
(pp. 179–80). There is at least a strong possibility that an agreement
was made between Osei Yaw and Kwaku Dua, that Kwaku Dua would
drop his opposition to Osei Yaw in return for recognition as heir apparent. Though member neither of the House of Osei Tutu nor that

Methodist Mission Archives, London, West to General Secretaries, dd. Kumase,
9 June 1862: 'somewhat more than 60'.
122 Bowdich, 1819, pp. 238–9.
123 IASAS/204: Nkontonko Stool History, recorded by J. Agyeman-Duah, 31 July
1967.
124 Wilks, field-notes, interview with Nana Boakye Yam, dd. Kumase, 2–3 August
1965. See further, Asante Collective Biography Project: Akyampon Tia.
125 IASAS/172: Mamesene Stool History.
126 Kyerematen, 1966, p. 352.
127 Rattray, 1929, p. 202.

of Opoku Ware, Kwaku Dua was thus given the *abakomdwa* – the heir apparent's stool – in Adum.[128] It must also be kept in mind, that, although from the House of Osei Tutu, Osei Yaw was still regarded as the candidate for the House of Opoku Ware. It appears that in consequence, his blackened stool is classed as an Asafode one, together with those of Opoku Ware and Opoku Fofie, although Osei Yaw himself was of the Adufude *ntoro* (see p. 355, Fig. 11).[129]

Over the next few years Kwaku Dua extended his constituency within the nation, becoming identified with peace party politics while nevertheless maintaining with the army his reputation as a soldier. At the battle of Katamanso he commanded the eight or nine thousand men of the Ankobea division.[130] It is said that he, with the Dwabenhene Kwasi Boaten and Kuntanasehene Barima Antwi, saved the Golden Stool after Osei Yaw had ordered a retreat.[131] In the confused period which followed the Asante defeat in 1826, Kwaku Dua seems not to have associated himself with any movement to remove Osei Yaw from office, thus honouring their putative earlier agreement. He became Asantehene in 1834, following the death of Osei Yaw, apparently without opposition.

Kwaku Dua recognized Osei Kwadwo of the House of Osei Tutu (see Figure 6, p. 330) as heir apparent, and took the seemingly unprecedented step of acknowledging, as second heir apparent, Opoku Ahoni of the House of Opoku Ware (see Figure 7, p. 331).[132] In principle, therefore, he appeared to accept the ongoing rights of the two houses to the Golden Stool. In point of fact, however, he undoubtedly sought to preside over the extinction of those rights. Again, the evidence is regrettably complex, and can be understood only with reference to the marriage patterns of the Oyoko royal women of the period.

Ama Sewaa was succeeded as Asantehemaa by Yaa Dufie, at some time during the reign of Osei Yaw. Yaa Dufie died, probably early in the reign of Kwaku Dua. Akua Akrukruwaa having succumbed to smallpox in 1807, reference to Figure 10 (p. 353) will show that there was no other surviving senior royal in the generation of the granddaughters of Aberefi Yaa. Afua Sapon from the descendent generation was accordingly made Asantehemaa. She was the only surviving daugh-

---

128 Nana Prempe I, 1907, p. 34.
129 See Kyerematen, 1969, p. 2. Compare Rattray, 1927, p. 327.
130 Djang, 1926b, p. 70.
131 Kyerematen, 1966, p. 352. For the incident see also Reindorf, 2nd ed., n.d., p. 207; Rattray, 1929, p. 172.
132 Methodist Mission Archives: T. B. Freeman's Journal, entry for 25 December 1841. Throughout this journal the heir apparent is referred to as 'Osei Adum Kwadwo'. See also letter from Brooking, dd. Kumase, 19 July 1842, in *The Western Echo*, I, no. 18, 13 May 1886, p. 8: 'Apoko Ahoni, the third King, as he is called (i.e. next to the heir apparent in claim to the throne)'.

ter of Ama Sewaa, and the only sister, therefore, of Kwaku Dua.[133] She had also been married, not long before 1810, to the Apagyahene Owusu Afriyie (see Figure 6). Their oldest child, the heir apparent Osei Kwadwo, had been born in or about 1810.[134] Of their other eight children, six survived into adulthood. All were daughters, and the last must have been born at about the time of their father's death at Katamanso in 1826.[135] The six daughters, their husbands, and their

Table 14   *Marriages of the daughters of Asantehemaa Afua Sapon*

Daughters of Asantehemaa Afua Sapon	Husband	Children
Afua Kobi, born *ca.* 1815,[136] died 1900	1. Kofi Nti	1. Kwabena Anin, later heir apparent 2. Kofi Kakari, later Asantehene 3. Mensa Bonsu, later Asantehene 4. Yaa Kyaa, later Asantehemaa 5. Akua Afriyie
	2. Boakye Tenten	No children
Yaa Afere, born *ca.* 1817, died 1882 [137]	1. Kamkam	1. Abena 2. Konadu 3. Akua De 4. Nantwi
	2. Boadi	5. Akosua Berenya
	3. Asabi Boakye	6. Yaw Twereboanna 7. Kwame Boaten 8. Adwowa 9. Kwaku Nkruma 10. Infant, died at birth
Akua Afriyie, born *ca.* 1819	Boakye Dankwa	1. Infant, died at birth 2. Infant, died at birth 3. Kofi Mensa, later second heir apparent 4. Several infants, died at birth
Odae, born *ca.* 1822	1. Apaw	No children
	2. Name uncertain	1. Kwasi Agyeim (Kwasi Kyisi?) 2. Infant, died young
Afua Sewaa, born *ca.* 1824	Adonten Boaten	No children
Aberefi, born *ca.* 1826	Unmarried	—

133 See T. B. Freeman, 1843, p. 125.
134 Methodist Mission Archives: Hart to General Secretaries, dd. Kumase, 13 May 1850.
135 Ricketts, 1831, pp. 124–5, where he is referred to under his personal name, (Owusu) Gyamadua. See also Asante Collective Biography Project: Apagyahene Owusu Afriyie.
136 It was remarked of her that, around 1873, 'she is about fifty-five years of age, but looks younger', see Brackenbury, 1874, II, 331.
137 *Further Correspondence,* C. 3386, 1882, pp. 36, 39, 42, 61.

children by each marriage, are shown in Table 14, which includes, therefore, many of the principals in the affairs of the dynasty in the second half of the nineteenth century.

The politics of the dynasty under Kwaku Dua I

Close examination of Table 14 reveals a number of highly significant aspects of dynastic politics during the reign of Kwaku Dua I. Most obviously, the principle was adhered to that senior women of the dynasty should not be given in marriage to princes of either the House of Osei Tutu or of Opoku Ware. Thus Afua Kobi's first marriage, which probably took place about the time of Kwaku Dua's accession, was to Kofi Nti, who was shortly to be made counselor of the Boakye Yam Panin stool. His only claim to special status seems to have been that his mother, Yaa Kyaa of Akorase, was herself a daughter of the Asantehene Osei Kwadwo.[138] The five children of the marriage were born between about 1835 [139] and 1850.[140] Kofi Nti may not have died until the late 1860s,[141] and Afua Kobi bore no further children to her second husband, Boakye Tenten, who succeeded Kofi Nti in the counselorship. The first marriage of Yaa Afere was likewise to a commoner, the Aberenkesehene Kamkam, and none of their children seems ever to have been considered for high office – as Asantehene or Asantehemaa. Again, Odae was married to one Apaw of Gyakye, but bore no children to him, and by a second husband had only one surviving child; Afua Sewaa was married to the Adontehene Boaten, but bore no children; and Aberefi remained unmarried at the time of her early death.[142] It is difficult to resist the suggestion of the evidence, that not only were marriages to princes of the Houses of Osei Tutu and Opoku Ware disallowed, but that the husbands of the younger sisters were discouraged from having children by them: it is said, for example, that

138 Wilks, field-notes, interview with Nana Yaa Kyaa, dd. Akorase, 5 August 1965.
139 The second son, Kofi Kakari, was said by Owusu Ansa to be aged 36 in 1873, see *The Times*, 29 July 1873. Compatible information is given by Boyle, 1874, p. 274; Stanley, 1874, pp. 56 and 144 (reporting Kühne). Horton, 1870, p. 84, suggests that he was somewhat older – thirty-five on his accession; and Bonnat, see Gros, 1884, p. 218, that he was somewhat younger – 'over twenty-five' on his accession.
140 The fourth child, Yaa Kyaa, was estimated to be about 40 in 1891, see *Further Correspondence*, C. 7917, 1896, p. 73: Hull to Governor, dd. Accra, 27 May 1891. Since, however, her first son was born in or about 1860, she must clearly have been older. Her younger sister Akua Afriyie, moreover, gave birth to a child on 10 January 1867, see Instituut voor Taal- Land- en Volkenkunde, Leiden MS H. 509: entry for that date. Even was this her first child, Akua Afriyie could scarcely have been born later than about 1850.
141 In September 1870 Kofi Kakari made a 'yearly festival' for his father, see Ramseyer and Kühne, 1875, p. 85.
142 One of the three, Odae, Afua Sewaa or Aberefi, died in 1847, see Methodist Mission Archives: Wharton to Freeman, dd. Kumase, 16 November 1847.

Afua Sewaa 'died leaving no child because her husband did not care much for her . . .' [143] The matter becomes clearer with reference to the marriages of Yaa Afere to Asabi Boakye, and of Akua Afriyie to Boakye Dankwa, for both husbands were sons of Kwaku Dua himself.

Afua Kobi had been married early to an important member of Kwaku Dua's administration, and there was little action the Asantehene could take. At the end of his life, however, he made clear his opposition to any of the sons of the marriage being considered as candidates for the Golden Stool: 'the old King', it was reported, 'remarked that it was no use for the sons of Afuah Cobree to have the "stool", because neither of them would be able to "keep his house in order" '.[144] Yaa Afere herself, however, helped foster Kwaku Dua's design when she formed an illicit union with a minor functionary, Boadi of the *nseniefo*. Boadi was presumably executed, and Yaa Afere was fined 12 oz of gold ($£48$) and was divorced from her husband, the Aberenkesehene Kamkam.[145] Kwaku Dua thus could control the marriages of two of the daughters of the Asantehemaa Afua Sapon: the as yet unmarried Akua Afriyie and the divorced Yaa Afere. Akua Afriyie was married to Kwaku Dua's eldest son, Boakye Dankwa, and Yaa Afere to a younger son, Asabi Boakye. The two marriages occurred at much the same time. Kofi Mensa, third son of Boakye Dankwa and Akua Afriyie, was born in 1857,[146] and Yaw Twereboanna, first son of Asabi Boakye and Yaa Afere, in or about 1860. In or before 1848, the second heir apparent Opoku Ahoni (of the House of Opoku Ware) had been executed. It will be seen later that *ca.* 1857 Kwaku Dua had removed the Asantehemaa Afua Sapon and her son the heir apparent Osei Kwadwo (of the House of Osei Tutu) from their respective positions, and in 1859 carried out a major purge of his political opponents. The evidence, then, suggests strongly that in the late 1850s Kwaku Dua adopted an aggressive policy designed to strengthen his personal position *vis-à-vis* members of the two old Houses within the dynasty, and that the marriages of his sons Boakye Dankwa and Asabi Boakye to senior royals must be seen as an integral part of that policy. That Kwaku Dua was in fact intent upon establishing a new house – the House of Kwaku Dua – is clear; for in the same period he was also creating further marriage alliances between others of his sons and members of the younger generation of royals, the granddaughters of Afua Sapon.

143 Nana Prempe I, 1907, p. 13. Ramseyer and Kühne, 1875, p. 147, reported that a brother of Owusu Ansa had been executed for forming an attachment to an unnamed royal woman.
144 *Further Correspondence*, C. 4052, 1884, p. 57: Barrow to Governor, dd. Accra, 5 July 1883, reporting 'the Elders and Chiefs of Coomassie'.
145 Nana Prempe I, 1907, pp. 11–12.
146 Ramseyer and Kühne, 1875, p. 234.

Reference to Table 14 (p. 360) will show that, with Yaa Afere and Akua Afriyie in the senior generation married to sons of Kwaku Dua, the two most important women in the junior one were Yaa Kyaa and Akua Afriyie. Their status, as the first and second born of the women in the generation, was further enhanced by the fact that their mother Afua Kobi, as eldest daughter of the sisterless Afua Sapon, had succeeded her as Asantehemaa. Yaa Kyaa was married to Kwasi Abayie, son of Kwaku Dua by his wife Takyiaw – herself a daughter of the Asantehene Osei Bonsu.[147] The first child of Yaa Kyaa, Kwaku Dua Kuma, was born in or about 1860, presumably shortly after the marriage was contracted. Akua Afriyie was married to Kwaku Dua's son, Krapa, at what must have been much the same time, since when Krapa was killed in 1873 [148] she had given birth to two sets of twins and five other children. Kwasi Abayie was alive in 1866,[149] but died very shortly thereafter.[150] Yaa Kyaa was remarried immediately to Kwasi Gyambibi, another son of Kwaku Dua by his wife Konadu Sompremo, also a daughter of Osei Bonsu.[151] Their fourth child Agyeman Prempe (alias Kwaku Dua), was born probably in 1873.[152] Similarly, after the death of Krapa, Akua Afriyie was remarried to yet another son of Kwaku Dua, Asafo Boakye.[153] For convenience, the marriages of Yaa Kyaa and Akua Afriyie are summarized in Table 15.

Six of the sons of the Asantehene Kwaku Dua, then, were linked by marriage to the most senior Oyoko royals, that is, to those within the class of the daughters and granddaughters of Afua Sapon. It appears, indeed, to have been one of the distinctive characteristics of the new style of government introduced by Kwaku Dua, that the *ahenemma* or

[147] *Further Correspondence*, C. 4052, 1884, p. 55: Barrow to Governor, dd. Accra, 5 July 1883.

[148] Ramseyer and Kühne, 1875, p. 256.

[149] Instituut voor Taal- Land- en Volkenkunde, Leiden MS H. 509: entry for 3 September 1866.

[150] 'Kwasi Abayie' was a nickname, all the sons of Kwaku Dua being correctly named, according to the system within the *ntoro*, Boakye.

[151] Rattray, 1927, p. 333.

[152] See, for example, *Further Correspondence*, C. 7917, 1896, p. 10: Hodgson to Knutsford, dd. Accra, 9 December 1889. It is difficult to see that he could have been born as early as 1870, as other sources suggest, for example, *The Gold Coast Independent*, 29 November 1924. For a discussion of the matter, see Tordoff, 1960, pp. 34 and 56, note 8, who cites an informed Asante view that he was born one month before the beginning of the 1873–4 war.

[153] In the received genealogies, Kwasi Gyambibi is also recorded as having married a royal of a collateral branch: Yaa Ntiaa, daughter of Pokuwaa, granddaughter of Adwowa Sewaa, and great-granddaughter of the Asantehemaa Yaa Dufie. Brackenbury, 1874, II, 331–2, states that one of Kofi Kakari's sisters was married to Kwasi Gyambibi, and the other to 'Barempa', a son of Osei Bonsu; and p. 322, that 'Barempa' was married to 'the queen's sister'. The two statements are incompatible. Presumably Barempa had been confused with Asafo Boakye – 'a general of the royal blood' – also mentioned on p. 332.

Table 15 *Marriages of Yaa Kyaa and Akua Afriyie, senior daughters of Asantehemaa Afua Kobi*

Mother	Husband	Children
Yaa Kyaa, died 1917	1. Kwasi Abayie, died *ca*. 1867	1. Kwaku Dua Kuma, later Asantehene 2. Akua Fokuo 3. Kwabena Kyeretwie 4. Akua Abakoma (see Figure 5) 5. Akua Afriyie
	2. Kwasi Gyambibi, died 1903	6. Ama Mansa 7. Yaa Kyaa 8. Boayae 9. Agyeman Prempe, later Asantehene 10. Agyeman Badu, later heir apparent 11. Konadu 12. Adwowa Santuo 13. Ama Adusa, later Asantehemaa Konadu Yaadom II (see Figure 5)
Akua Afriyie, died 1921	1. Krapa, died 1873	1. Twins, died young 2. Ohene Afrewo (see Figure 5) 3. Kwasi Berkon 4. Akosua Nsia 5. Twins, died young 6. Akosua Manhyia 7. Akua Badu
	2. Asafo Boakye, died 1925	8. Ama Kom 9. Twins, died young 10. Ama Agyeman 11. Twins, died young 12. Yaa Baa 13. Kwaku Dua 14. Fredua Agyeman 15. Infant, died at birth

princes should be assigned a more active role in political affairs than they had hitherto played. It is possible to identify a number of stages in the process. Kwaku Dua's eldest son, Boakye Dankwa, was offspring of a marriage probably made before Kwaku Dua became Asantehene: that to Konadu of the family of the Adwomfohene (or head of the guild of goldsmiths). Boakye Dankwa (husband of the senior Akua Afriyie) thus became in time himself Adwomfohene.[154] Three other sons, Kwasi Abayie (husband of Yaa Kyaa), Kwasi Gyambibi (second husband of Yaa Kyaa), and Kwame Serebo, were presented before the Kumase council and given positions within the new Manwere group. Kwasi Gyambibi and Kwasi Abayie, both of whose mothers were daughters of Osei Bonsu, assumed the titles of Ayebiakyerehene and

154 IASAS/13: Stool History of the Asantehene's Adwomfohene, recorded by J. Agyeman-Duah, 29 December 1962.

Somihene respectively.[155] Kwame Serebo may have been given the new Asabi stool, to become known as Asabi Boakye (third husband, that is, of Yaa Afere).[156] It should be stressed again that all the sons of Kwaku Dua assumed the *ntoro* name Boakye, and had to be distinguished by nicknames. Indeed, Kwasi Gyambibi, Kwasi Abayie and others bore precisely the same name as Kwaku Dua's first son Boakye Dankwa (who alone needed no nickname).[157]

Two stages thus seem distinguishable in the acquisition of office by the *ahenemma*. The first is exemplified in the case of Boakye Dankwa, who took an existing office by right of matrifiliation; and the second in the cases of Kwasi Gyambibi, Kwasi Abayie and Kwame Serebo, in which new offices were created for them. A third stage was that in which sons of Kwaku Dua were moved into important existing offices over which he exercised rights of appointment. Thus the son nicknamed Krapa (first husband of the junior Akua Afriyie) became Kyidomhene; and another son (second husband of Akua Afriyie) was given the Asafo stool – that of the Akwamuhene of Kumase – and became known as Asafo Boakye. Among others of the sons of Kwaku Dua to be awarded high positions, though not necessarily within the lifetime of their father, were Antoa Mensa (alias Boakye Dankwa), Antoahene; Bempe, Akorasehene; Boakye Bobi, Kaasehene; Boakye Adade, Hiahene; Boakye Atansa, Akomfodehene; Kofi Adwene, Kyidomhene; Kwame Boakye Dontwo, Atene Akotenhene; Kwame Kyerematen, Somihene; Yaw Boakye, Nkwantakesehene; and Yaw Ntem, Atene Akotenhene. Curiously, the position of Akyempemhene – Head of the Princes – was held until the end of Kwaku Dua's reign by Owusu Koko, son of Osei Bonsu and leading representative of the House of Osei Tutu (see Figure 6, p. 330). Although denied by Kwaku Dua the royal wife he might have expected in order to preserve the viability of his House, Owusu Koko nevertheless became one of the most active supporters of the new House of Kwaku Dua, and his career will be followed in some detail in later chapters. He was succeeded in office, expectedly enough, by another son of Kwaku Dua I, Kofi Boakye alias Kofi Subiri.

The ascendancy of the House of Kwaku Dua

The structure of the House of Kwaku Dua is shown in Figure 12. The males all belong to the Aboade branch of the Bosompra *ntoro* (in

155 IASAS/83 and 84: Somi and Ayebiakyere Stool Histories, recorded by J. Agyeman-Duah, 27 August and 13 September 1963.
156 Reindorf, 2nd ed., n.d., p. 112.
157 Wilks, field-notes, interview with Akyempemhene Boakye Dankwa and Hiahene Mensa Bonsu, dd. Kumase, 18 November 1958.

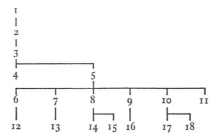

1. Boakye Yam, born in Denkyra;
   became Nkwantakesehene of
   Kumase; died *ca.* 1720 (?).
2. Akyampon Kwasi, Anyinasehene;
   died *ca.* 1765 (?).
3. Boakye Yam Kuma, Nkwantananhene;
   married the sixth Asantehemaa
   Ama Sewaa; died 1797/8.
4. Akyampon Kwasi, born *ca.* 1795;
   became Boakye Yam Kuma *okyeame*;
   died *ca.* 1870 (?).
5. Kwaku Dua, born *ca.* 1797;
   became heir apparent, and
   Asantehene in 1834; died 1867.
6. Boakye Dankwa, born *ca.* 1820;*
   married Akua Afriyie, daughter
   of Asantehemaa Afua Sapon.
7. Asabi Boakye; married Yaa Afere,
   daughter of Asantehemaa Afua Sapon.
8. Kwasi Abayie; married Yaa Kyaa,
   daughter of Asantehemaa Afua
   Kobi; died *ca.* 1867.
9. Krapa; married Akua Afriyie,
   daughter of Asantehemaa Afua
   Kobi; died 1873.
10. Kwasi Gyambibi; married Yaa
    Kyaa, daughter of Asantehemaa
    Afua Kobi; died 1903.
11. Asafo Boakye, born *ca.* 1830;
    married Akua Afriyie, daughter
    of Asantehemaa Afua Kobi; died 1925.
12. Kofi Mensa, born 1857; second heir
    apparent; died 1873.
13. Yaw Twereboanna, born *ca.* 1860;
    candidate for Golden Stool, 1886; died 1908.
14. Kwaku Dua Kuma, born *ca.* 1860;
    Asantehene 1884; died 1884.
15. Akua Abakoma, mother of
    Asantehene Osei Agyeman Prempe
    II (Edward Prempe Owusu).
16. Ohene Afrewo, grandmother of Asantehene
    Opoku Ware II (Kwaku Adusei).
17. Agyeman Prempe, born 1873; Asantehene
    1888; died 1931.
18. Agyeman Badu, born *ca.* 1875; heir
    apparent; died 1917.

* The date rests on the assumption that Kwaku Dua first married soon after his
return from the Gyaman campaign in 1818.

Fig. 12   Some descendants of Nkwantakesehene Boakye Yam, in the Aboade *ntoro*

which, among others, the names Akyampon and Boakye alternate).
After the death in 1859 of the heir apparent Osei Kwadwo (of the
House of Osei Tutu), the matter of the succession presented Kwaku
Dua with certain problems – since all the children yet born to the
royals married to his sons were infants too young to be considered. By
default, the heir apparency was given to Kwabena Anin, the eldest
son of Afua Kobi by her marriage to the counselor Kofi Nti (see Table
14, p. 360). Shortly before his death in 1867, however, Kwaku Dua
indicated to the Akyempemhene Owusu Koko that he wished Kwaku
Dua Kuma (Agyeman Kofi), the son of Yaa Kyaa and Kwasi Abayie,

to succeed him.[158] Precisely why Kwaku Dua's choice fell upon Kwaku Dua Kuma rather than any other of his grandchildren is unclear; since, however, Kwaku Dua was relying upon Owusu Koko to effect his wishes, it is perhaps significant to note that Kwaku Dua Kuma's paternal grandmother Takyiaw was the full sister of Owusu Koko – both being children of Osei Bonsu by his marriage to one Asantewaa.[159] In the event, Kwaku Dua Kuma was not accepted; to a council demanding aggressive leadership against the British, the election of a seven years old boy to the Golden Stool was not feasible. Owusu Koko attempted to carry out what was virtually a coup, failed, and went into exile (see Chapter 13). Instead, Kofi Kakari was chosen; the younger full brother of Kwabena Anin. With no claims to membership of the Houses of Osei Tutu, Opoku Ware or Kwaku Dua, Kofi Kakari was said sometimes to have remarked, 'that his ascendancy to the throne of Ashantee was like a dream to him'.[160] He appointed his younger full brother, Mensa Bonsu, as heir apparent,[161] and recognized as second heir apparent the young Kofi Mensa – thereby following a constitutional procedure introduced by Kwaku Dua himself.[162]

Kofi Kakari was removed from office in 1874. Kofi Mensa having died the previous year, the candidacy of Kwaku Dua was seemingly advanced once more. He was again rejected, and the heir apparent Mensa Bonsu became Asantehene. Although, then, in both 1867 and 1874 the wishes of Kwaku Dua with respect to the succession seemed to have been ignored, there is in fact evidence to show that both Kofi Kakari and Mensa Bonsu were regarded as essentially managers – *ahwɛfoɔ* – of the affairs of the nation on behalf of Kwaku Dua Kuma, and that Kofi Mensa was technically second in line to him rather than to Mensa Bonsu. Some account of the matter was obtained by Barrow in the course of his visit to Kumase in 1883. 'A nominal subsidy of 24 ounces of gold,' he wrote,

was paid by Kalkali to young Quacoe Duah as an acknowledgment that the 'stool' was only assumed and occupied at pleasure. The operation was repeated when Mensah assumed the 'stool' in 1874 by his paying young Quacoe Duah a subsidy of 20 ounces of gold. These payments, I am told, were made in order to establish that the sons of Afuah Cobree were holders of the

158 *Further Correspondence*, C. 4052, 1884, pp. 56–7: Barrow to Governor, dd. Accra, 5 July 1883.
159 *Ibid.* p. 60.
160 Ramseyer and Kühne, 1875, p. 309.
161 Nana Prempe I, 1907, p. 34. Known as Kwame Mensa, see Ramseyer and Kühne, 1875, p. 309, he assumed the name Bonsu upon his accession, see *Further Correspondence*, C. 4052, 1884, p. 57.
162 Ramseyer and Kühne, 1875, p. 234.

'stool' only at the will of the young Quacoe Duah who would assume oc-cupancy when old enough.[163]

Mensa Bonsu was in turn removed from office in 1883. In the view of the sons of Kwaku Dua, who held so many positions of power within the administration, both Kofi Kakari and Mensa Bonsu were surrogates of the House of Kwaku Dua. Nevertheless, both created for them-selves much broader political constituencies, and in 1883 Kofi Kakari made a bid for reinstatement as Asantehene. The struggle between his supporters and those of Kwaku Dua Kuma is described in Chapter 13; it ended only with the decisive armed intervention of the old Akyem-pemhene Owusu Koko. Kwaku Dua Kuma was enstooled, as Kwaku Dua II, in 1884. He died forty-four days later. In the period of an-archy which ensued, the struggle for the Golden Stool finally resolved itself into one between two members of the House of Kwaku Dua: the son of Asabi Boakye and Yaa Afere, Yaw Twereboanna (see Table 14, p. 360), and the son of Kwasi Gyambibi and Yaa Kyaa, Agyeman Prempe (Table 15, p. 364). From it, Agyeman Prempe emerged suc-cessful in 1888; but whichever candidate had been chosen, the sur-vival of the House of Kwaku Dua as such appeared assured. It is, however, instructive to observe the means by which the new Asante-hene sought to consolidate his position within the House by the elimination of certain sources of potential danger to him. Reference to Table 14 will show that of the six daughters of the Asantehemaa Afua Sapon, by 1888 not one (or at most one) child of the last four sur-vived. Akua Afriyie's son Kofi Mensa was dead, and Kwasi Agyeim is almost certainly to be identified with the Kwasi Kyisi, son of Odae, whose possible candidacy for the Golden Stool was mooted in 1884 – after which no more was heard of him.[164] Only Afua Kobi and Yaa Afere (who had herself died in 1882)[165] had families. Agyeman Prempe, as Asantehene, took immediate steps to curtail the growth of Yaa Afere's family. An edict was issued, making it a capital offence to have sexual connection with any of her daughters, that is, with any of Yaw Twereboanna's sisters. When the Asoamfohene Kwasi Agyei ignored the ruling in 1895, by forming a liason with Akosua Berenya, he was publicly executed.[166]

163 *Further Correspondence*, C. 4052, 1884, p. 57.
164 *Further Correspondence*, C. 4906, 1886, p. 6: report of messengers from Kumase, dd. 16 October 1884.
165 *Further Correspondence*, C. 3386, 1882, p. 39: Watt to Acting Colonial Secretary, dd. Cape Coast, 2 February 1882.
166 Musgrave, 1896, p. 170. *Gold Coast Chronicle*, 14 September 1895, p. 2. It was also claimed that the husbands of four of Yaw Twereboanna's sisters were executed, 'with the object . . . of leaving their widows childless', see NAG, Accra, ADM 12/3/6: Maxwell to Ripon, dd. Accra, 14 May 1895. By 1908 the

For over a century, from 1824 when Kwaku Dua was recognized as heir apparent, to 1931 when Agyeman Prempe died, the Oyoko dynasty of Asante was dominated by the House of Kwaku Dua – a house which, so it has been shown, derived matrilineally from the Oyoko royals of Mampon. Indeed, viewed thus, Kwaku Dua I has to be seen as more closely identifiable with Osei Kwame than with any of the rulers from the Houses of Osei Tutu and Opoku Ware. The hegemony of the House of Kwaku Dua was seldom challenged in the nineteenth century. Since Yaw Twereboanna was a member of it, and Kofi Kakari and Mensa Bonsu were its surrogates, the struggles in which they were involved must be seen as essentially internecine. The intervention of the Kokufuhene Offe Akwasim as candidate in the election of 1823–4 appears to have been no more than a token measure to keep Kokufu's claims to royalty before the electorate. When the Kokofuhene Kwame Apeagyei, nephew of Offe Akwasim, made a bid to supplant Kwaku Dua I in 1845, the threat was seemingly easily averted: Kwame Apeagyei was shot.[167] It has been shown, too, that Kwaku Dua I accomplished the elimination from the succession of the second heir apparent Opoku Ahoni in or about 1848, and of the first heir apparent Osei Kwadwo a decade later; neither was from his House. The only other challenge to the Aboade rulers of Asante seems to have come from the descendants of Adoma Akosua, the Asantehemaa who was executed in 1819. Adoma Akosua's only daughter was Akua Sewaa, whose eldest daughter Pokuwaa is probably to be identified with the Ama Pokuwaa who died in Kumase of smallpox in 1883.[168] Among Pokuwaa's sons was Osei Kwaku Goroso; the identity of his father has not been established but the use of the name 'Osei' for Pokuwaa's sons suggests that he may have been from the House of Osei Tutu. However that may be, Osei Kwaku Goroso would appear to have been involved in the attempt to overthrow Mensa Bonsu in 1880, but to have been considered at best a marginally possible candidate for the Golden Stool in 1887. Subsequently he threw his support

number of royal women had dropped dangerously low, nine seniors having died in rapid succession. Curiously, it was believed that the cause lay in the neglect of the soul-cult of Bediako, a brother of Kusi Obodom, see National Archives of Ghana, Kumase, D. 725: Akua Afriyie to Chief Commissioner, dd. Kumase, 14 May 1908.

167 Methodist Mission Archives: Wharton to General Secretaries, dd. Kumase, 31 May 1846, enclosing extract from diary dd. Kokofu, 27 April 1846. According to Rattray, 1929, p. 202, Kwame Apeagyei was first banished to Offinso.

168 *Further Correspondence*, C. 4052, 1884, p. 60: Barrow to Governor, dd. Accra, 5 July 1883. Barrow described Ama Pokuwaa as a daughter of Afua Sapon, which is correct in classificatory kinship terms. Pokuwaa's mother, Akua Sewaa, and Afua Sapon would have been described as 'sisters' in that their grandmothers – Sewaa Okuwa and Akyaama – were full sisters, see the reconstructed genealogy, Figure 9.

behind Yaw Twereboanna, and his role in organizing the opposition to Agyeman Prempe will be referred to in a later chapter.

It remains only to note that in the present century it would seem that a conscious effort has been made to return to the constitutional arrangements of the eighteenth century, whereby the Golden Stool alternated between members of the Adufude *ntoro* (the House of Osei Tutu) and of the Asafode *ntoro* (the House of Opoku Ware). The contest of 1931 resulted in the election to the Golden Stool – as Osei Agyeman Prempeh II – of Edward Prempeh Owusu, whose matrifilial links with Oyoko dynasty are shown in Figure 12 (p. 366). His father was the Bosommuru Faben *okyeame* Kwaku Owusu (also known as Owusu Nkwantabisa), a member of the Adufude group. The principal opposition to the election of Edward Prempeh Owusu came from Osei Kwadwo, of the same group,[169] who was matrilineally descended from the Asantehemaa Yaa Dufie, through his mother Badu, his grandmother Pokuwaa, and his great-grandmother Adwowa Sewaa, Yaa Dufie's daughter. His father was the Otikromhene Yaw Afriyie, a son of the Asantehene Osei Yaw,[170] and reference to Figure 11 (p. 355) will therefore clarify the nature of his relationship to the House of Osei Tutu. The next election, that of 1970, resulted in the accession of Barima Kwaku Adusei (J. Matthew Poku) to the Golden Stool. He is descended from the Asantehemaa Afua Kobi through his great-grandmother Akua Afriyie, his grandmother Ohene Afrewo, and his mother Akua Akyaa. Through his father he is a descendant of the Asantehene Opoku Ware.[171] Upon the enstoolment of Edward Prempeh Owusu in 1931, it was the wish of the Asantehemaa and others that he should assume the official designation of Osei Tutu II. Troubled by the emotive significance of the name, the colonial administrators discouraged the proposal. He became known instead Osei Agyeman Prempeh II,[172] thereby emphasizing his uterine kinship with Agyeman Prempe I. In 1970, by contrast, there was no opposition when Barima Kwaku Adusei took the official stool name of Opoku Ware II.

169 NAG, Kumase, D. 2984: Osei Kwadwo to Chief Commissioner, dd. 20 May 1931. See also D. 324, *passim*, and D. 1638, *passim*.
170 IASAS/163: Oti Kurom Stool History, recorded by J. Agyeman-Duah, 17 February 1966. The first Otikromhene Oti Awere was son of the Asantehene Osei Tutu. See further, Kumase Divisional Council Archives, Manhyia, Civil Record Book 12: Yaw Kyiri v. Kwadwo Abuagyie, case commencing 30 July 1931.
171 Nana Opoku Ware II is son of the Abontendomhene of Gyakye Kwabena Poku, son of Kwame Adusei of Gyakye, son of Bepoahene Amankwa Boko, son of Okyeame Kwadwo Adusei, son of Dwuansahene Opoku Tano, son of Akyempemhene Adusei Kra, son of Opoku Ware I: information from Nana Opoku Ware II, dd. Kumase, 3 November 1973.
172 NAG, Kumase, D. 2984: Konadu Yaadom *et al.* to District Commissioner, Kumase, dd. 10 June 1931.

The Oyoko dynasty: unity in diversity

It has been pointed out to the writer on many occasions that 'in Asante we attach more importance to marriage than to descent'.[173] In this essay in family reconstruction it has been accepted that all those to hold office as Asantehene have indeed been closely related to each other by matrifiliation. Yet the class of *de jure* royal women, defined as those descended from Maanu, clearly includes, but is far more extensive than, the sub-class of *de facto* royal women, defined as those whose sons retain serious claims to highest office. Membership of the former class is determined by descent, but of the sub-class – so it has been argued – by marriage. The particular configuration of the descent line linking Maanu, in the seventeenth century, with living *de facto* royals is, in other words, correlate with the pattern of marriages over time. In ontological terms, it is descent which is important to the structure of the Oyoko dynasty; but in phenomenological terms, it is marriage. It would be a misinterpretation of the evidence to suppose that a double descent system existed. The thesis argued in this chapter may rather be stated thus: that in structural terms, analysis of the basic genealogical matrix and the superimposed pattern of marriages shows that a highly compact dynasty – defined by matrifiliation – was created, within which three strongly individuated Houses – specified by patrifiliation – nevertheless emerged. The distribution of Asantehenes by matrifiliation, shown in Figure 5 (p. 328), may be compared with that by patrifiliation, shown in Table 16.[174]

The sphere of dynastic politics may be identified as that within which members of the Houses and royals outside them, and their respective constituents, sought to maximize their advantages whether through conflict or accommodation. It will be observed, however, that no Asantehene not a member of one of the three Houses ever died in office. It is arguable that whereas in the eighteenth century national politics were largely a matter of dynastic politics, by the later nineteenth century the reverse was true: dynastic politics had become an extension of national politics. In the major upheavals which brought

---

173 See, for example, Wilks, field-notes, interview with C. E. Osei and Akua Afriyie, dd. Kumase, 5 August 1965.
174 The matter of the Houses is not one which is freely discussed in Asante. The writer can only record his impressions, that the House of Osei Tutu is that sometimes referred to as the 'red' Oyoko, and the House of Opoku Ware, as the 'black' Oyoko. Since the first occupant of the Golden Stool belonged to the 'red' House, to refer to a royal as a member of the 'black' House has something of a pejorative connotation. The division appears in some way to be linked with the figures of Twum and Antwi, traditionally remembered as non-Oyoko rulers in the Kwaman area which was later to become the heartland of the Asante kingdom. Twum was 'black' and Antwi 'red'. The writer offers these observations with the greatest reservation.

371

Table 16 **The Oyoko rulers of Asante, distributed by Houses**

Dates	House of Osei Tutu	House of Opoku Ware	House of Kwaku Dua	Others
?	Osei Tutu I			
ca. 1720–50		Opoku Ware I		
1750–64				Kusi Obodom, abdicated
1764–77	Osei Kwadwo			
1777–98				Osei Kwame, destooled
1798–9		Opoku Fofie		
1800–23	Osei Bonsu			
1824–33	Osei Yaw ————→			
1834–67			Kwaku Dua I	
1867–74				←——— Kofi Kakari, abdicated
1874–83				←——— Mensa Bonsu, destooled
1884			Kwaku Dua II	
1888–1931			Agyeman Prempe I	
1931–70	Osei Agyeman Prempe II			
1970–date		Opoku Ware II		

the nation to civil war in the mid-1880s, Yaw Twereboanna was chosen as figurehead by one party, Agyeman Prempe by the other; the former was in his mid-twenties, the latter in his teens, and both were members of the House of Kwaku Dua. It is arguable, too, that fundamental changes occurred over time in the relationship of the Asantehene to his subjects. The major phases can be – tentatively – identified. Osei Tutu and Opoku Ware were essentially leaders of the nation, and possessed at least some of the attributes of the divine king; they conducted the wars which established Asante as an imperial power. Osei Kwadwo, Osei Kwame, and Osei Bonsu were, by contrast, essentially constitutional monarchs who pressed through the reforms which transformed Asante from a predominantly military power into a civil polity. The production in the early nineteenth century of written annals of the dynasty was, it might seem, in some way expressive of this change. With Kwaku Dua I a new style of government was introduced; a modernizing autocrat, he broke the power of the chiefly classes and ruled by mandate of the people. He moved Asante rapidly in the direction of nation-statehood. Kofi Kakari, Mensa Bonsu and Agyeman Prempe assumed many of the characteristics of the presidential monarch; they reigned rather than ruled, overseeing the affairs of a nation in a state of convulsive change, in which political power had become relatively widely diffused within a populace increasingly divided by the emergence of class interests. It may be thought that it was precisely the existence of a dynasty which so well exemplified the principle of unity in diversity which enabled the nation to achieve such a series of transformations; that it was through the counterpoise of House to House that political opposition could manifest itself, and policy changes could be achieved, for the most part within the framework of established constitutional procedures. Certainly such an assumption will inform the following chapters of this study, in which the attempt is made to identify the major trends of political change in nineteenth century Asante, and to analyse the nature of the transformations which resulted.

CHAPTER 10

Kumase as the seat of government: the structure of decision-making

The city of Kumase

In the earlier part of the nineteenth century, so it has been shown, Kumase was a city with a population of between 15,000 and 25,000 people. As the seat of government, it attracted those from throughout the imperial territories and even beyond whose ambitions led them to seek a career in the administration. It was a phenomenon to which Bonnat drew attention later in the century:

The tremendous importance of the king of Achanty draws to Coumassie a large number of young men, belonging to the best families of the kingdom. They come under the aegis of the throne not only, as they say, to serve the king, but they are drawn above all by the hope of coming to the particular attention of the king, and they neglect no opportunity of pleasing him . . . One sees them continually following in his footsteps, soliciting his favours and his smiles.[1]

During the long reign of Kwaku Dua I, a period of relative prosperity and tranquillity, the city undoubtedly grew in size. By the 1860s its population may have risen to as high as 40,000.[2] It was apparently decreed during the early part of Kwaku Dua's reign, that provincial rulers and other prominent citizens should erect for themselves buildings in the capital, where they might reside during the annual Odwira or when otherwise summoned there.[3] In 1817 the city was reckoned to have twenty-seven streets;[4] yet an observer in the mid-1880s, when it was in a state of decay, could even then trace some fifty streets.[5]

As premier town within the metropolitan region, and first city of Greater Asante, the growth and development of Kumase had been a

1 Gros, 1884, p. 194.
2 *The Times*, 29 July 1873, reporting Owusu Ansa.
3 *Magazin für die neueste Geschichte der evangelischen Missions und Bibelgesell-schaften*, 1840, III, 275: letter from Riis dd. Kumase, 31 December 1839. Methodist Mission Archives, MS of 1860 based upon Freeman's diaries, ch. V.
4 Bowdich, 1819, pp. 322–3.
5 *The African Times*, XXVII, no. 292, 1 January 1886, p. 11.

matter of especial concern to Osei Bonsu. His most cherished project, the construction of the Palace of Culture, had not been carried through to the exclusion of a more general concern with the appearance of the city. In 1817 Bowdich had commented upon the Asantehene's interest in English architecture, and noted that 'he meditated great improvements and embellishments in his capital, on his return from the [Gyaman] war, when it was intended that every captain should be presented with an extraordinary sum out of the public treasury, for adorning or enlarging his house'.[6] Already a new town plan had been partly worked out. The houses along the main road which linked the two suburbs of Bantama and Asafo, to the north and south of the city respectively, were to be rebuilt, and labourers were already engaged in constructing a wide and straight street from the city to the village of Breman on the Mampon road, where Osei Bonsu had a country seat: the intention was to destroy a number of villages in the neighbourhood and to rehouse the people along the new street.[7]

Kumase was built upon the eastern slopes of a rocky ridge rising, on the south, east and west, from the marshes of the Nsuben rivers.[8] It had been possible in 1764 to refer disparagingly to Kumase, as 'the King of Ashantee's Town (or Capital, if a great number of Hutts deserve that name)'.[9] Certainly those who were to visit the city in the nineteenth century were to gain a very different impression. In 1816 Huydecoper noted that 'the streets are very clean and straight, and the houses excellently built, the latter being fairly tall but for the most part of only one storey'.[10] In the following year Bowdich described the central city – Kumase, that is, excluding such suburbs as Bantama and Asafo – as oblong in shape and about four miles in circumference.[11] 'Four of the principal streets', he wrote,

6 Bowdich, 1819, p. 309.
7 *Idem.* For a detailed account of the construction of the road and the cottages, see Kumase Divisional Archives, Manhyia: Asantehene's Divisional Court B, Civil Record Book 32, Apagyahene Owusu Afriyie II *v.* Tafohene Yaw Dabanka, hearing of 11 September 1944.
8 Baden-Powell, 1896, plate facing p. 110, essayed a 'bird's-eye view' of the town as seen from the southeast. Although Kumase was by then much diminished in size as a result of the troubles of the 1880s, its population having shrunk to less than one-tenth of the earlier level, the sketch nevertheless gives a useful impression of its physical setting.
9 PRO, T. 70/31: Mutter to Committee, dd. Cape Coast, 20 July 1764.
10 Huydecoper's Journal, entry for 26 May 1816.
11 The estimate of its size may be somewhat exaggerated. In the early nineteenth century the central city was probably only about one-half a square mile in extent. It clearly had a high density of population even though perhaps no more than half the townsfolk lived within it. But the City of London in the same period had a population density of the order of five times as high: area, approximately one square mile, and population, over 125,000. The figures reflect the fact that in Kumase no one lived above ground level.

Ichnographical Sketch of COOMASSIE, *with the principal Streets and the Situations of remarkable Houses.*

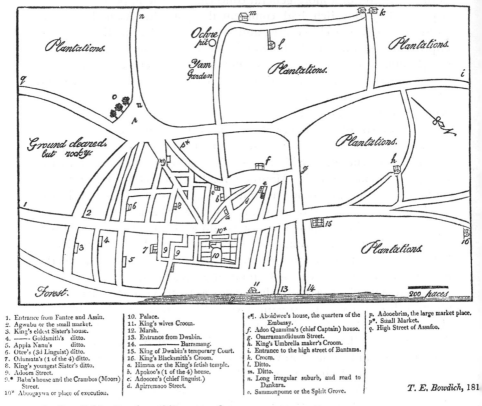

1. Entrance from Fantee and Assin.
2. Agwabu or the small market.
3. King's eldest Sister's house.
4. ——— Goldsmith's ditto.
5. Appia Nanu's ditto.
6. Otee's (3d Linguist) ditto.
7. Odunnata's (1 of the 4) ditto.
8. King's youngest Sister's ditto.
9. Adoom Street.
9.* Baba's house and the Crambos (Moors) Street.
10* Aboogaywa or place of execution.

10. Palace.
11. King's wives Croom.
12. Marsh.
13. Entrance from Dwabin.
14. ——— Barramang.
15. King of Dwabin's temporary Court.
16. King's Blacksmith's Croom.
a. Himma or the King's fetish temple.
b. Apokoo's (1 of the 4) house.
c. Adoocee's (chief linguist.)
d. Apirremsoo Street.

e¶. Aboidwee's house, the quarters of the Embassy.
f. Adoo Quamina's (chief Captain) house.
g. Osarramandiduum Street.
h. King's Umbrella maker's Croom.
i. Entrance to the high street of Bantama.
k. Croom.
l. Ditto.
m. Ditto.
n. Long irregular suburb, and road to Dankara.
o. Sammonpome or the Spirit Grove.

p. Adooebrim, the large market place.
p. Small Market.
q. High Street of Assafoo.

T. E. Bowdich, 181

vi Bowdich's city plan of Kumase, 1817

are half a mile long, and from 50 to 100 yards wide. I observed them building one, and a line was stretched on each side to make it regular. The streets were all named, and a superior captain in charge of each; ours for instance, was Aperremsoo, big gun or cannon street, because those taken when Dankara [Denkyira] was conquered, were placed on a mound at the top of it, near to Adoo Quamina's house . . . The street above where we lived was called Osamarandiduüm, meaning literally, 'with 1000 muskets you could not fight those who live there'.[12]

Bowdich's excellent town plan of Kumase is reproduced above (Map vi).

As seat of the central government, life in the town was dominated by the affairs of the palace. Situated in the eastern quarter of the central city, the palace complex covered some five acres. On the

12 Bowdich, 1819, p. 322.

376

northern side stood the Aban, the only structure of stone. The remainder of the buildings were in the traditional style and consisted, as Winniet observed,

of a number of square court yards connected with each other by doors at the corners, and having, on 1, 2, 3, or all sides a room entirely open on the side looking into the yard raised from 1 to 4 feet above the level of the yard, and communicating with it by steps made with clay . . . the Royal apartments are of much larger dimensions than those of the people, and are kept exquisitely clean.[13]

Entrance to the palace was along an impressive passageway lined by the offices and living rooms of functionaries – *abotenafo* – who worked for the Asantehene. Bowdich referred to it as the 'piazza, which lines the interior of the wall secluding the palace from the street', and offered a brief description of it:

the piazza is 200 yards long, and inhabited by captains and other attendants on the King; above is a small gallery. Piles of skulls, and drums ornamented with them, are frequent in this piazza . . . The upper end of the piazza . . . is more ornamented, and appropriated to the superior captains, who have each a suite of rooms, marked by the small doors under the piazza.[14]

Bowdich's drawing of the passageway in 1817 may be compared with the photograph of it taken after the British occupation of the city in 1896, when signs of decay were all too apparent (Plates IX, X).[15]

The long passageway led into a large yard on to which a number of spacious rooms abutted. This was the Pramaso, or better, Pramakeseso,[16] the Great Court, where the Council of Kumase was regularly convened. 'The meetings of the supreme court of justice and legislation', wrote Bonnat with reference to the early 1870s, 'takes place every day in the great court of the royal palace called Apramosso. This court measured 30 to 35 metres long by 14 to 15 metres wide; all around ran a gallery which was supported by square columns resting on bases ornamented with bas-relief in red earth, polished and shining, truly magnificent'.[17] Dupuis' drawing of the Pramakeseso in 1820 shows that the galleries had not then been constructed (Plate XI).[18] They are visible in the photograph of the buildings taken at the end of the

13 Winniet's Diary, entry for 19 October 1848. The plan of the palace of the Kumawuhene – one of the last in the traditional style to survive in this century – was probably not unlike that of the old palace in Kumase, see Rattray, 1929, p. 56.
14 Bowdich, 1819, p. 308.
15 Steiner, 1900, p. 23.
16 Twi *pramaso*, 'courtyard, square, plaza, etc.', and hence *pramakeseso*, 'great courtyard, etc'.
17 Gros, 1884, p. 189.
18 Dupuis, 1824, frontispiece.

century, after the Asantehene had been deported and they had fallen into disuse (Plate XII).[19] Beyond the Pramakeseso, within the inner recesses of the palace, were housed a number of administrative departments, the most important of which were the various sections of the Treasury (Foto). Beyond those again were the Asantehene's personal rooms, including the kitchens (Sodo), bathrooms (Adware), and the harem (Mmaam) in the charge of the eunuchs. Behind the palace, on the edge of the marshes, was the settlement where the Asantehene's wives resided when not summoned to the palace; the whole area was prohibited to the citizenry.[20]

Around the palace to all but the east clustered many of the seventy-seven wards into which Kumase was divided: Adum, Apremoso, Asikasu, Bampanase, Bogyawe, Nsuase and the rest. An artist's sketch of part of the city in 1874, as seen from the roof of the Aban, gives a useful impression of its layout (Plate XIII).[21] The view appears to be that to the northeast, over the wards in which lived many of the *asomfo* including the heralds or *nseniefo* and the sword-bearers or *afenasoafo* – those who might be seen 'pelting along the street, brandishing their gold handled sword, the insignia of their office, at the rate of eight or nine miles an hour [for] the king's business demands haste'.[22] They maintained constant communications between the Asantehene and those officials who worked within the palace on the one hand, and the many functionaries who had their offices in the city on the other. Principal among these latter was the Gyaasewahene, who lived in the ward called Asikasu lying only two or three hundred yards west of the palace entrance. His house contained another court which was second in importance only to the Pramakeseso in the palace; this was the *pato* to the right of the open yard shown in Plate XIV.[23] It was there that the Gyaasewahene presided most days over the Exchequer Court;[24] and it was there that an appeal against a decision of the Asantehene's court – Pramakeseso – might be heard, when the case would be conducted by the counselors of the *amanhene* led by the Senior Counselor or Akyeamehene of Mampon.[25] Immediately to the south of the palace was the Adum ward the head of which, the Adumhene, could be regarded as High Sheriff.[26] He was responsible

---

19 Hodgson, 1901, plate facing p. 295. It appears that the Great Court was destroyed by the British in 1874, but was rebuilt without substantial change, see Gros, 1884, p. 189, note.

20 Bowdich, 1819, pp. 289–90. T. B. Freeman, 1843, pp. 146–50.

21 Grant, n.d., III, 324.

22 *The Gold Coast News*, I, No. 15, 27 June 1885, p. 4 (from T. B. Freeman's lost journals).

23 Bowdich, 1819, Plate 6 facing p. 307.

24 *Ibid.* p. 296.

25 Rattray, 1929, p. 105, note.

26 *Papers relating to Her Majesty's Possessions in West Africa*, C. 1402, 1876, p. 87: Mensa Bonsu to Governor, dd. Kumase, 2 September 1875.

both for the *adumfo* or executioners and *abrafo* or police: 'there is a very rigid police discipline in Coomassie', so Ramseyer reported, 'after nightfall no one is allowed to leave the town, the police, whom we ourselves saw, distinguished by their long hair, going about the streets armed'.[27] The Gyaasewahene and Adumhene thus both resided very close to the palace. Most of the senior officers of the government likewise had their houses in what may be termed the inner wards; that of the Gyakye *okyeame,* for example, adjoined the residence of the Gyaasewahene. Two of the most senior councillors lived, however, outside the central city: the Kontihene or Bantamahene at Bantama to the north, and the Akwamuhene or Asafohene at Asafo to the south.[28] The suburb of Bantama enjoyed a special distinction since the royal mausoleum was located there; [29] it was customary for the Asantehene to visit it in person every Adae.

Map vii identifies a number of the wards and streets of the central city, shown in its relationship to the principal suburbs and to the exits on to the great-roads. Although the central city grew in size over the first three quarters of the nineteenth century, there is no reason to believe that its morphology changed radically in that period or indeed until after 1896.[30] The structure of the city, indeed, was determined by the one principal function which it had throughout that century: the provision of government. Thus in 1839 Freeman remarked of the central city, that 'the houses are all erected on the same plan, from that of the King, down to the lowest rank of Captains; and these are, with a few exceptions, the only persons who are allowed to build in any public situation'.[31] Half a century later Ramseyer and Kühne made the converse point, that 'most of the free in Coomassie are so connected with the palace, that they bear the title of chiefs, and fulfill a particular office'.[32] In 1839 Freeman gave some account of the central city. 'The streets are large', he wrote,

and more clean and uniform than I have seen in any other native town since my arrival in Africa. The breadth of some of them is at least thirty yards, and the average length from three hundred to six hundred yards . . . A row of splendid Banyan-trees, planted at a considerable distance from each other, occupies some of the large streets, affording a delightful shade from the burning rays of the sun. The streets differ also in appearance from those of

27 Brackenbury, 1874, II, 339 (reporting Ramseyer). See also Reade, 1874, p. 286 (reporting Kühne).
28 Bowdich, 1819, p. 289; T. B. Freeman, 1843, p. 57; Gros, 1884, pp. 214–16.
29 Rattray, 1927, frontispiece.
30 The map is based principally upon Bowdich's town plan of 1817; Kirby's map of 1883, see *Further Correspondence,* C. 4052, 1884; Armitage and Montanaro, 1901, endpiece; Biss, 1901, facing p. 194; and upon the writer's observations in Kumase.
31 T. B. Freeman, 1843, p. 55.
32 Ramseyer and Kühne, 1875, p. 105.

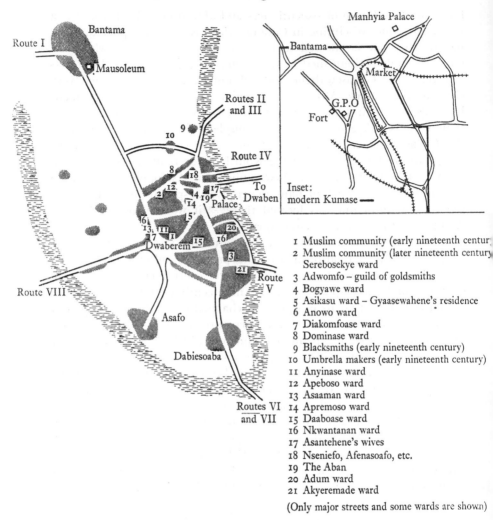

1 Muslim community (early nineteenth century)
2 Muslim community (later nineteenth century)
  Serebosekye ward
3 Adwomfo – guild of goldsmiths
4 Bogyawe ward
5 Asikasu ward – Gyaasewahene's residence
6 Anowo ward
7 Diakomfoase ward
8 Dominase ward
9 Blacksmiths (early nineteenth century)
10 Umbrella makers (early nineteenth century)
11 Anyinase ward
12 Apeboso ward
13 Asaaman ward
14 Apremoso ward
15 Daaboase ward
16 Nkwantanan ward
17 Asantehene's wives
18 Nseniefo, Afenasoafo, etc.
19 The Aban
20 Adum ward
21 Akyeremade ward

(Only major streets and some wards are shown)

vii Morphology of the old city of Kumase

other towns which I have seen in the interior, by the houses on each side having open fronts, the floor being raised from two to three feet above the level of the ground. The space between the ground and the level of the floor, and in some houses a foot or two even above that level, presents a front of carved work, beautifully polished with red ochre. In several, the carved work is continued up to the roof; and where that is the case, it is covered with white clay, which has the appearance of a lime white-wash. The roofs are made chiefly with bamboo-poles, or sticks, with the bark stripped off, and thatched with palm-leaves.[33]

[33] T. B. Freeman, 1843, pp. 54–5.

Freeman's observations were fully endorsed – plagiarized even – by Governor Winniet of the Gold Coast, who visited Kwaku Dua in 1848. Kumase, he wrote,

is very different in its appearance from any other native town that I have seen in this part of Africa. The streets are generally very broad and clean, and ornamented with many beautiful banyan trees, affording a grateful shade from the powerful rays of the sun. The houses looking into the streets are all public rooms on the ground floor, varying in dimensions from about 24 feet by 12 to 15 feet by 9. They are entirely open to the street in front; but raised above its level from one to six feet, by an elevated floor consisting of clay polished with red ochre. They are entered from the street by steps made of clay, and polished like the floor. The walls consist of wattle work plastered with clay and washed with white clay. The houses are all thatched with palm leaves, and as the leaves of the roofs extend far over the walls, the front basement of the raised walls which is generally covered with rude carvings of various forms, have their beautiful polish preserved from the effects of both sun and rain. This mode of building gives the streets a peculiar aspect of cheerfulness.

The loggias which opened on to the streets and were so conspicuous a feature of the central city, were known as *adampan* (singular, *ɔdampan*, here Anglicized dampan), meaning literally, 'empty rooms.' No one in fact lived or slept in them for they were, as Winniet remarked, 'public rooms'. It was behind them, invisible from the main streets, that the rooms lay where the citizenry lived. Approached by a small door beside the dampan, as many as thirty or forty rooms might be arranged within an open yard; and a household would comprise from 50 to 250 occupants according to the status of its senior members.[34]

The possession of a dampan, opening on to a thoroughfare, was the prerogative of the various officials of the government. Thus Bowdich referred to the 'open front, (which none but captains are allowed to have to their houses)'.[35] In 1824 Dupuis in fact made clear the purpose of the dampans, in describing them as 'designed for the dispatch of public business'.[36] They were the offices – the bureaus – wherein the functionaries transacted their daily business.[37] The connection be-

---

[34] Winniet's Diary, entry for 9 October 1848. T. B. Freeman, 1843, p. 55. It must be assumed that most households were, by size, in the lower rather than upper brackets. For a traditional ground plan of a Kumase house, that of the Asantehemaa, see Meyerowitz, 1951, pp. 195–6. For a more elaborate plan, that of the palace of the Kumawuhene, see Rattray, 1929, p. 56.

[35] Bowdich, 1819, p. 305.

[36] Dupuis, 1824, p. 83.

[37] In an unpublished paper, 'Asante Security in the Northwest' (1973), Dr Kwame Arhin refers to the fact that a village might be known as *adampan* when a superior chief had given the village head permission to open an office or 'hall' there – 'which was equivalent to granting it "municipal" status'.

tween office and offices is interestingly illustrated from the reign of Kofi Kakari. In mid-1872, at the beginning of his sixth year as Asantehene, Kofi Kakari finally obtained possession of his predecessor's fortune.[38] In July so many new dampans were in course of construction that building materials were in short supply throughout the city.[39] Later in the month the reason became apparent: the Asantehene was elevating to public office new men in whom he had confidence, 'men who till now', so it was reported, 'had only been his chamberlains, and whose office it was to carry his sedan chair and large umbrella'. On 5 August those who had been promoted publicly thanked the Asantehene at an assembly in the town [40] – when, it may be supposed, the new dampans were opened for business. The relationship between having official standing, and owning a dampan, continues to be acknowledged in Asante. Thus when in 1942 the Aboasohene claimed to hold the traditional post of Akyamfohene, or head of the shield-bearers, his inability to prove that his predecessors in office had owned a dampan in the capital weighed heavily against him. 'If you are the head of the Akyemfuo, according to you', the Court remarked, 'and you have no Adanpan in Kumasi neither can you prove by any act that you are the head of them, how can your case be believed?' [41]

It is indicative of the essential nature of Kumase as a centre of government and administration, that it was on the appearance of the dampans that so much care and attention was lavished. Before the annual Odwira each received a new colour wash to impress the visiting dignitaries, and the Asantehene personally inspected the results.[42] The immaculately ochred floors and elaborate bas-reliefs were the equivalent of the present day executive's carefully tended carpets and murals. But it was also clearly the case that in times of war, when many officials were on active service, the unused dampans were neglected and even allowed to fall. When Dupuis visited Kumase in 1820, in the aftermath of the Gyaman campaign, it obviously bore a different aspect from that which had so impressed Bowdich only three years earlier.[43] In the troubled years of the mid-1880s the number of dampans in the city dwindled to twenty; [44] and even of Bantama it was reported, 'the once noble Dampan or Portico in which its chief

---

38 Ramseyer and Kühne, 1875, p. 171.
39 *Ibid.* p. 172.
40 *Ibid.* p. 177.
41 Kumase Divisional Council Archives, Manhyia: Gyaase Native Authority Record Book 13: Gyaasewahene *v.* Aboasohene, case commencing 27 January 1942. For a similar issue, see Asantehene's Divisional Court B, Civil Record Book 4: Osei Kofi *v.* Yaw Dwuma, commencing 24 March 1936.
42 Ramseyer and Kühne, 1875, p. 147.
43 Dupuis, 1824, pp. 70, 83.
44 *The African Times*, XXVII, no. 292, 1 January 1886, p. 11.

reposed, is rapidly falling into decay as also the buildings of his residence behind it'.[45] Of the central city itself Coppin gave a graphic account of the decline it had undergone in less than two years. 'We went off', he wrote,

to see the town or what was the town. Street after street has disappeared. Some of them just traceable, others quite obliterated by the high grass that grows upon them. A path for the most part not wider than a sheep walk is all that is left of the most spacious and frequented streets of the city . . . Except in the king's quarter, where the greatest number of houses are clustered together, there are no lines or groups of houses of considerable extent. Here and there cut off from each other and surrounded by the high grass are a few compounds. So many houses have fallen into ruins, through their tenants removing to other towns and villages being unable to subsist here. Not being rebuilt, they fall utterly to the ground, the grass grows high above them until such gaps are made between those houses that remain that the stranger is tempted to think that no city was ever here . . .[46]

The central role of Kumase as seat of the imperial administration was again the subject of a comment by Governor Maxwell, some months after its occupation by the British in 1896. 'A great many houses,' he remarked, 'are still in ruins. The fact is that Kumasi has no special importance as a town in the absence of a Native King and his Court and the people who at one time kept up house there to which to resort on special occasions now live entirely in bush villages.' [47] Bowdich's drawing of a group of dampans in Adum Street, just south of the palace, conveys an excellent impression of their appearance at their best (Plate XV).[48] 'Each open front', he remarked, 'denotes the residence of a captain, being used for talking palavers, receiving strangers, observing or superintending customs, and evening recreation.' [49] In the period of its prosperity before 1883, there were reported to be one hundred and fifty such dampans in Kumase,[50] and the majority of them were presumably located in the inner wards where their occupants could be in close communication with the palace.

Much of the life of Kumase revolved around the two large assembly grounds, Dwaberem – 'The Great Market' – and Apremoso – 'The Place of the Cannons' – at which Asantehene, officials, and people came together regularly on formal and sometimes informal occasions. In 1873 Owusu Ansa gave some account of the matter: 'The two chief

45 Methodist Mission Archives: Coppin's journal of his visit to Asante, 1885, Book VII, p. 5.
46 *Ibid.* pp. 2–3.
47 NAG, Accra, ADM 12/3/6: Maxwell to Chamberlain, dd. Accra, 19 November 1896.
48 Bowdich, 1819, Plate 9 facing p. 308: 'Part of Adoom Street'.
49 *Ibid.* p. 308.
50 *The African Times*, XXVII, no. 292, 1 January 1886, p. 11.

streets, or squares as they are called, are Market-square and Cannon-square, the latter taking its name from a trophy of European cannon in it. They were taken from the Dutch many years ago. In it the King sits in State, and gives public audiences to his subjects.' [51] Dwaberem was in fact the major retail market in Kumase. It was also used, for example, for military reviews [52] and for the reception of distinguished visitors.[53] It is indicative of the nature of the priorities which prevailed in the city, that because of its use for government purposes no permanent market stalls could be erected there. The wealthier traders were obliged to mark their premises with a wooden contraption which could be easily removed [54] (Plate XVI), while their less prosperous colleagues simply seated themselves wherever there was space. By a strange and seemingly inappropriate contiguity, immediately to the south of Dwaberem was the Asamanpomu, 'The Bush of the Ghosts', where the bodies of those executed were consigned; it marked the end of the town in that quarter.[55]

Immediately to the north of Dwaberem, on the road leading to Bantama, stood one of the raised mounds, *sumpene,* which played so important a part in city life. Another stood on the eastern side of Apremoso, at its junction with Bogyawe.[56] The earliest description of a *sumpene* seems to be that by Bowdich, who observed, 'small circular elevations of two steps, the lower about 20 feet in circumference, like the bases of the old market crosses in England, were raised in the middle of several streets, on which the King's chair was placed when he went to drink palm wine there, his attendants encircling him'.[57] Freeman gave a more detailed account of the *sumpene,* describing them as made of clay hardened in the sun, as polished with red ochre, and as being between six and eight feet in height and about ten feet in diameter at the top. 'They are ascended', he added, 'by pyramidal ledges, or steps running all round, and rising one above another, about a foot in depth, and 18 inches in width. Around these ledges the officers of the Household, with attendant domestics take their seats, and thus a group is formed of from fifty to a hundred persons, all distinctly seen. . .' [58]

It was customary at the time of the Great Adae for the Asantehene

51 *The Times,* 29 July 1873.
52 Ramseyer and Kühne, 1875, p. 135.
53 See, for example, Bowdich, 1819, p. 34; Dupuis, 1824, p. 70; T. B. Freeman, 1843, p. 46.
54 Lee, 1835, plate facing p. 127, and see also p. 364.
55 Bowdich, 1819, p. 323. T. B. Freeman, 1843, p. 56.
56 Gros, 1884, p. 187.
57 Bowdich, 1819, p. 323.
58 *The Gold Coast News,* I, no. 15, 27 June 1885, p. 4.

to hold a series of public parties. A description of one such, held by Kwaku Dua in March 1862, is extant:

On the day of the great Adai, he goes in procession to some open part of the town, and takes his seat on one of the numerous red-ochre platforms, which may be seen in all directions, and which have been raised for his accommodation when he is pleased to drink palm-wine in public. When he has taken his seat, all the chiefs, and the strangers that may happen to be in town, are expected to present themselves to pay their respects; after which, presents are distributed, the king returns to his palace, and the crowds disperse. On the following morning he goes to visit the tombs of his ancestors, at the sacred village of Bantama; and in the evening drinks palm-wine in public, surrounded by his chiefs and their people.[59]

Such parties were held, however, on innumerable other occasions. Between 22 July and 1 August 1867, for example, Kofi Kakari gave three parties at Dwaberem and one at Bogyawe in order to collect donations for the funeral customs for Kwaku Dua I; and one at Dwaberem in honour of messengers from Anlo who had arrived in the capital. In the same period a party was also given at Dwaberem for Kofi Kakari: 'July 28. On Monday morning at 9 o'clock all the Asante people made a party at the (Edwiabieriem) in order to give thanks to H. M. the King of Ashantijn, who came there (Edwiabieriem), until 12 o'clock and then the King of Ashantijn got up to go home.' [60]

The Dwaberem *sumpene* was, in fact, the more generally used for festive occasions. Indeed, Bowdich suggests that under Osei Bonsu 'state' tippling was an almost daily occurrence there: much palm wine, he wrote, 'is expended in the almost daily ceremony of drinking it in state in the market place'.[61] Hutchison reported one such party of 19 October 1817 which was a somewhat mixed success; 'About 7 o'clock A.M. the King's drums announced his going to the market-place, where all the chiefs went and were drenched with wet till 2 o'clock P.M. when the King sent for rum and palm wine and dismissed them drunk and dirty.' [62] No doubt the sessions at Dwaberem did much to oil the wheels of government. The Bogyawe *sumpene*, by contrast, stood near the spot at which public executions were carried out, and was in general associated with the more sombre occasions.[63] Dur-

59 *Wesleyan-Methodist Magazine*, October 1862, p. 954: visit of West and Owusu Ansa to Kumase.
60 Instituut voor Taal- Land- en Volkenkunde, Leiden MS H. 509: entries for 22, 23, 24, 26 and 28 July, and 1 August 1867.
61 Bowdich, 1819, p. 293.
62 Hutchison, in Bowdich, 1819, p. 392.
63 It is unclear how many *sumpene* had been built in the city. It is clear, however, that those at Dwaberem and Bogyawe were the most used. Two *sumpene* have been constructed just outside the present palace at Manhyia, rather less than

ing the slow death of one condemned man Kwaku Dua was reported to have harangued the populace – 'telling them that, if any of them committed murder, he would have them tortured in the same way'.[64] It was thus to Dwaberem rather than to Bogyawe that the Asantehene's hornblowers went every midnight, to play, as Bowdich reported, 'a very peculiar strain, which was rendered to me, "King Sai thanks all his captains and all his people for to-day" '.[65]

Although as the seat of government, Kumase was centrally concerned in the financing and planning of trade, it never functioned as a commercial entrepôt until after 1896. Salaga (and later Kintampo) in the north, and Adubease (and later Ankase) in the south,[66] were designated the markets for Kumase and developed as the major distributive points in the import and export trade. The city thus remained functionally one. When Reade visited it in 1874, it was the dampans or public offices which most impressed him. 'The first thing I noticed in Coomassie', he wrote, 'was the number of houses so built. This town was the Court, and the residence of the nobles, each of whom had a vast crowd of clients and slaves.' [67] Many functionaries, the *asomfo,* were concerned solely with departmental matters, and worked within either the palace or the Gyaasewahene's residence. Others, the 'nobles' of Reade, were assigned governmental responsibilities, but were also answerable for the affairs of their wards and of the villages or towns which were attached to them. Thus, for example, the counselor or *okyeame* who held the Boakye Yam Panin stool would be almost daily in attendance at the Great Court – Pramakeseso – at the palace. But he managed also the affairs of twelve villages, from which however he was able to recruit personnel to assist him whether in his administrative work or in the running of his household. From the villages, too, the counselor could request wives (*ayite* wives). Some account of the system was given by Okyeame Boakye Tenten II in 1965:

The Boakye Yam Panin stool has twelve villages under *adekurofo.* The *adekurofo* have no function in the Court. But in the old days each village sent

---

a mile northwest of the old one. The *sumpenekese,* or big *sumpene,* is still called Dwaberem, and the *sumpenekuma,* or little *sumpene,* Bogyawe, see Wilks, fieldnotes, meeting with Nana Sir Osei Agyeman Prempeh II, dd. Kumase, 14 April 1966. See also Kyerematen, n.d., p. 1, who observes that the present *sumpenekese* (Dwaberem) is used 'for festal occasions' and the *sumpenekuma* (Bogyawe) for 'funerals and other serious or mournful occasions'.

64 *Wesleyan-Methodist Magazine,* October 1862, p. 955: visit of West and Owusu Ansa to Kumase.

65 Bowdich, 1819, p. 300.

66 *Further Correspondence,* C. 3386, 1882, p. 58: Lonsdale's report on his mission of 1881–2.

67 Reade, 1874, p. 363.

representatives to the Kumase house as 'domestics'. They were not *fie-nipa* [household slaves] but subjects of the Boakye Yam Panin stool. In the old days they would help the *okyeame* as messengers and the like. Many of them would have minor stools – sometimes they had actual miniature stools and sometimes not. Such officials would be responsible for the *okyeame's* sandals, his keys, and so forth. In the old days we also had many servants; we had for example twelve cooks. The villages would also send in women as *ayite* and the *okyeame* could choose wives from them. They lived in the Kumase house . . . The sons of an *okyeame* by his *ayite* wives might in time go back to their mothers' villages to become *adekurofo*. But it would be possible for such a son later to come back to Kumase to succeed to the Boakye Yam Panin stool.[68]

According to the nature of the duties of the official under whose management they were, so other villages might supply soldiers, carriers, policemen, road labourers, messengers, and the like.

The highly complex apparatus of government which was based upon Kumase differed not only in degree but in kind from the older Akan system of *ɔmansohwɛ*, 'management of the *ɔman*'. To those who were, in whatever sense, subjects of the Asantehene, Kumase was the *abankɛsemu*: best literally translated as 'big government', the term was used to distinguish central government as such from other modes of the exercise of power and authority. It is to the further elucidation of this notion that the remainder of this chapter, and Chapter 11, are devoted.

The Asantemanhyiamu: National Assembly

Major discrepancies seemingly exist between the various accounts of the distribution of power and authority within the Asante political system in the nineteenth century. The Europeans who spent over four years in captivity in Kumase between 1869 and 1874 each, for example, gave a different account of the matter. Kühne expressed an ambivalence:

it has sometimes appeared to him as if the King was quite absolute – he could kill whom he liked, fine whom he liked, and order what he liked. At other times the chiefs seemed to have immense power, and even at times the general feeling of the pure Ashantee people had influence; and he speaks as if this made the problem very confused.[69]

In contrast, Bonnat maintained that, 'the Asante state is under a despotic government. Every inhabitant, from the greatest chief to the

68 Wilks, field-notes, interview with Nana Boakye Tenten II, dd. Kumase, 3 August 1965.
69 Maurice, 1874, p. 267.

lowest slave, belongs body and possessions to the king, and is at the mercy of his wishes and caprices. He alone, following his whims, elevates or demotes the low and the high.' [70] Again, Ramseyer commented, 'that the reins of the Ashantee government are not exclusively in the hands of the king, nor does he possess unlimited power, but shares it with a council . . .' [71] It may be that the contradictions between the various accounts are more apparent than real: that Bonnat was describing the Asantehene in his capacity as head of the executive agencies of the state, while Ramseyer and Kühne were concerned with his role in the decision-making process. And certainly no observer, Bonnat included, denied the existence in Asante of a conciliar system. There are, indeed, numerous references in the literature to such: to institutions variously described as 'privy council',[72] 'cabinet',[73] 'council of state',[74] 'Council of Kumase',[75] 'House of Commons',[76] 'high council',[77] 'senate',[78] 'Grand Assembly',[79] 'Kotoko council',[80] 'Supreme Council of the Empire',[81] and the like.

The highest conciliar body in Asante was the Asantemanhyiamu, 'the Assembly of the Asante Nation',[82] the origins of which may be assumed to date from the very beginnings of the kingdom. In the early nineteenth century Robertson observed of its functions:

A senate of the Chiefs regulates the affairs of Government, and decides all disputes as a supreme tribunal. Even claims on the crown are determined by their opinion; and where individuals have been treated either with injustice or severity, redress is given agreeably to the determination of a majority of votes . . . The King, with the consent of the Senate, collects and disposes of the national wealth; hence he raises armies, and prompts all other public measures.[83]

Membership of the Asantemanhyiamu was on a territorial basis. All the *amanhene* and certain senior Kumase chiefs were entitled to a

[70] See *L'Explorateur*, 1875–6, II, 621 ff.
[71] Ramseyer and Kühne, 1875, p. 305.
[72] Bowdich, 1819, pp. 46, 105.
[73] Dupuis, 1824, pp. 120, 127, 153.
[74] See *L'Explorateur*, 1875–6, II, pp. 622.
[75] *Further Correspondence*, C. 4906, 1886, p. 4: Coppin to Griffith, dd. 18 May 1885.
[76] *Further Correspondence*, C. 3687, 1883, p. 160: Barrow to Rowe, dd. Kumase, 27 April 1883. *Further Correspondence*, C. 5615, 1888, p. 39: Barnett to Governor, dd. Kumase, 20 March 1888.
[77] Ramseyer and Kühne, 1875, p. 180.
[78] Dupuis, 1824, p. 95. G. A. Robertson, 1819, p. 199.
[79] Ramseyer and Kühne, 1875, p. 93.
[80] *Ibid.* p. 305.
[81] *Further Correspondence*, C. 4052, 1884, p. 73: Owusu Ansa to Governor, dd. Accra, 27 August 1883; p. 82: Barrow to Colonial Office, dd. Sussex, 16 October 1883.
[82] See, e.g. Christaller, 1881: ɔmanhyiam, parliament, or literally, 'the assembling of the nation'.
[83] G. A. Robertson, 1819, pp. 198–9.

seat, and provincial rulers were also represented: thus, for example, a number of Dagomba dignitaries were present at a meeting of 22 September 1817, at which the Anglo-Asante treaty was ratified.[84]

It was a consequence of the relative slowness of communications that the full Asantemanhyiamu met routinely only once a year – at the time of the Odwira when subordinate rulers were in any case required to visit the capital to reaffirm their allegiance to the Asantehene (pp. 75–6). In the first six decades of the nineteenth century, the Odwira fell within the period August to early October on the Gregorian calendar: the annual session of the Asantemanhyiamu took place, therefore, during the second rainy season.[85] The Asantehene Kofi Kakari, however, moved the Odwira back to the November to January period, the dry season,[86] thereby facilitating the journey to the capital of those involved.[87] The political significance of the Odwira was well summarized by Freeman, who observed,

it is a kind of annual parliament wherein, towards the latter end of the festival, all matters of political and judicial administration are discussed by the King and Chiefs in Council, and where the latter answer all questions relating to their respective provinces, and are subjected to the consequences of appeals, from their local Judicial Courts, to the Supreme Court of the King in Council.[88]

Thus at the Odwira of 1870 reference was made to 'the meeting of the grand assembly, which took place on November 3rd, when the high dignitaries of the kingdom, the princes of Mampong, Dwaben, etc., came together to talk over everything of importance which had occurred in their respective districts since the last feast of yams'.[90]

Extraordinary sessions of the Asantemanhyiamu might also be called in situations of crisis, or when guidance was required on major innovations of policy – 'on state emergencies' – as Bowdich observed, 'or unprecedented occasions, such as the Treaty with the British Government'.[90] It will be obvious, however, that the responsibilities of the *amanhene* and provincial rulers toward their own territories were incompatible with their regular or frequent participation in the affairs of central government. The seats of even the senior *amanhene* all lay journeys of two or three days from Kumase. Typically, then, a delay of at least four to six days would occur between the issue of

---

84 Bowdich, 1819, p. 146.
85 Mean monthly rainfall, Kumase: August, 2.92 inches; September, 6.95 inches; October, 7.94 inches.
86 Mean monthly rainfall, Kumase: November, 3.86 inches; December, 1.21 inches; January, 0.67 inches.
87 Ellis, 1887, p. 260. Rattray, 1929, p. 109, note.
88 T. B. Freeman, in *The Western Echo*, I, no. 13, 24 March 1886, p. 8.
89 Ramseyer and Kühne, 1875, p. 93.
90 Bowdich, 1819, p. 253.

a summons to such an *omanhene* to attend council in Kumase, and his actual arrival there: [91] thus slowing down the decision-making process at the centre while leaving the local *oman* temporarily acephalous. Indeed, the ambivalent attitude of the *amanhene* towards visiting the capital for any purpose became institutionalized in the custom of 'troubling' the Asantehene, which served – as reported at the time of Agyeman Prempe I (alias Kwaku Dua III) – to pass on to the Asantehene a part of the expenses of travelling into Kumase:

> for example, in the case of the Kings of Bekwai and Mampon, when the former was summoned to Kumasi, he stated that he had no carriers and Kwaku Dua was compelled to send some to him; when Bekwai arrived outside the town he sent to say that he had no cloth and the King was obliged to give him one. In the same way, it was necessary for Kwaku Dua to send a litter for him; before the King of Mampon would come. The reason for this is that these people consider it beneath their dignity to come when they are summoned, and it is only after their superior has made them some concession to satisfy their pride that they will obey the summons . . .[92]

Many outlying chiefs were nevertheless unable or unwilling to meet the expenditure in time and money incurred in attending frequent meetings in the capital, and might send representatives in their stead. Thus a meeting of the Asantemanhyiamu on 17 February 1872 was attended by Mamponhene and Adansehene in person, but only by representatives of Dwabenhene, Bekwaehene and Nsutahene (though the meeting held on 2 September in the same year, at Odwira time, was attended by all the senior *amanhene*).[93] Again, at a session of the Asantemanhyiamu convened in late August 1875 to deliberate an important matter – the military occupation of Dwaben – only representatives of Bekwaehene, Mamponhene, Kokofuhene, Agonahene and Nkoransahene were present.[94] But there were also times when the Asantemanhyiamu was required to be in almost continuous session: for example, during the situation of crisis that prevailed in 1872–3 as the Asante armies carried out a reoccupation of the British-protected southern provinces, and the mandate of the Council was necessary for decisions which would involve *amanhene* and provincial rulers alike in considerable outlays of both men and money. It was in

---

[91] Ramseyer and Kühne, 1875, p. 135, suggest that Mamponhene may on occasion have travelled to the capital on horseback. Unless, however, his retinue had been similarly mounted, this could not appreciably have affected travelling time.
[92] *Further Correspondence*, C. 7917, 1896, p. 67: Hull to Governor, dd. Kumase, 22 April 1891, reporting Thomas Odonkor. Compare the account of the entry of Dwabenhene into Kumase, Rattray, 1929, p. 187, note.
[93] Ramseyer and Kühne, 1875, pp. 157–9, 180–1.
[94] *Papers relating to Her Majesty's Possessions in West Africa*, C. 1402, 1876, p. 87: Mensa Bonsu to Governor, dd. Kumase, 2 September 1875.

fact in the context of the 1872–3 meetings that Ramseyer and Kühne made their observation, that Asante was governed by

a council which includes, besides his majesty, his mother, the three first chiefs of the kingdom [Dwabenhene, Bekwaehene, and Mamponhene], and a few nobles of Kumasi (Coomassie). This council is called 'Asante Kotoko,' or the Ashantee porcupine, which means that like the animal of that name, nobody dare touch them . . . It is this Kotoko council which rules the entire kingdom, and deals with the people, who must obey, whatever their own wishes or inclinations may be, in the most despotic way. In case of war the people have no voice, and to enforce obedience they must be ever under the consciousness that the king and his council are the arbitrators of their life and death. In important matters all the other chiefs of the kingdom are called together to discuss the case, but they are sure to vote in accordance with the view of the council, for who would dare to oppose the Kotoko? [95]

The 'Kotoko council', however, was not a different body from the Asantemanhyiamu: *kɔtɔkɔ* was an epithet for the Asante in general,[96] and the terms 'Kotoko council' and 'Asantemanhyiamu' are thus identical in connotation. But the account which Ramseyer and Kühne gave of its composition shows that when the Council was in constant session, many of its members in fact chose not to exercise their right to attend other than the obligatory annual meeting – and thus virtually abrogated responsibility to the members from Kumase and those few of the *amanhene* who considered national politics to take precedence over their local *oman* affairs.

It is noteworthy that despite the improvements in transportation in the twentieth century, members of council from even nearby towns still found, as I. K. Agyeman attested, much inconvenience in visiting the capital:

the people in Kumase were accessible day and night for sometimes meetings lasted till 12 o'clock p.m. and one could not expect say a man from Mampong to be able to endure this. And those were hard days when new problems arose almost everyday which needed immediate settlements, especially in September 1921 when the Golden Stool was desecrated, we sat sometimes from six o'clock in the morning till six o'clock the next day, for many days. Such schedules were very much to the inconvenience of members who came from outside Kumase. And this was why people from Kumase were always required to be members of the Council . . . It was also a question of expenditure for each one of those chiefs to come with a retinue and have to lodge in Kumase for some time.[97]

[95] Ramseyer and Kühne, 1875, pp. 305, 308.
[96] See, e.g. Christaller, 1881, p. 253.
[97] Triulzi, 1969, p. 66: interview with Mr I. K. Agyeman, member of the Ashanti Confederacy Council, 1935–58.

The structure of decision-making

Although, then, in the nineteenth century a few committed members of the Asantemanhyiamu might endeavour to attend its extraordinary meetings however frequently scheduled, it is clear that the volume of general legislative work had expanded far beyond the capacities of that body to handle it. Many observers testified to the sheer amount of business which had to be dealt with in the capital. In August 1817, for example, Bowdich complained that he was able to obtain audiences with the Asantehene Osei Bonsu only when despatches arrived from the coast, since 'the King and his Council labour under so much anxiety and business at the present moment'.[98] Freeman had much the same experience some two decades later, being unable to gain interviews with Kwaku Dua I 'on account of the pressure of business he had in hand'.[99] The Asantehene, Freeman remarked, 'is remarkable for his laborious efforts in the discharge of his duties as the supreme judicial authority of the kingdom. Day after day consecutively, with the exception of birthdays, fetish-days and periods of customs, he sits in the palace for many hours, hearing and deciding cases'.[100] And Bonnat, in the early 1870s, noted how the Asantehene Kofi Kakari

knows daily what is happening in the most humble villages of his empire; from all parts he receives reports and minute details . . . Conversely, day and night, the orders of the king are sent out in all directions . . . The king of Achanty is one of the busiest men that one could see; he must attend to all the petty affairs of his kingdom, and, furthermore, to war, to religion, to commerce, to agriculture, to weights and measures, to prices and tariffs of all kinds, and finally . . . to the exercise of justice which is not the least of his responsibilities.[101]

Several writers made reference to deliberations continuing far into the night, in the torch-lit courts of the palace.

The origins of the Council of Kumase

It is reasonable to suppose that the volume of government business had begun to increase considerably in the latter part of the eighteenth century, as a result of the extensive reforms initiated by Osei Kwadwo in the aftermath of the wars of expansion. It may be supposed, therefore, that corresponding changes in the conciliar structure were made necessary by the inability of the Asantemanhyiamu to deal promptly

98 Bowdich, 1819, p. 95.
99 T. B. Freeman, in *The Western Echo*, I, no. 17, 21 May 1886, p. 8.
100 *Ibid.* I, no. 8, 30 January 1886, p. 2.
101 *L'Explorateur*, 1875–6, II, 622. Compare also Brun, in Gros, n.d., p. 169, describing Mensa Bonsu as 'l'homme le plus occupé de tous ses états'.

and efficiently with the increasing amount of legislation which had to be passed, and general policy which had to be determined. The mode of decision-making exemplified by the Asantemanhyiamu is that known in Asante as *asetenakɛse*, literally 'the great sitting down together' – the Great Sessions. A quite different mode is that expressed in the term *agyina*, denoting a small deliberative body or 'inner' council. The evidence suggests that such a body began, in the late eighteenth century, to take over in an *ad hoc* fashion certain decision-making functions from the Asantemanhyiamu. It is, however, only from the second decade of the nineteenth century that any account of it is extant.

In 1817 Bowdich, whose knowledge of Asante government was based in part upon conversations with the Gyaasewahene Opoku Frefre,[102] referred to 'the three estates of the Ashantee government'. He identified the first as the Asantehene; the second as the Asantemanhyiamu, that is, 'the General Assembly of Caboceers and Captains' or 'the Assembly of Captains'; and the third as 'the Privy Council, or Aristocracy'.[103] Bowdich used the term 'Aristocracy' in its older sense of 'oligarchy', and considered the third estate to be dominated by four functionaries. Thus he wrote of 'the four captains composing the Privy Council, or Aristocracy, which checks the King';[104] of 'the aristocracy or four captains controuling the King';[105] and of 'the aristocracy or council of four'.[106] In 1817 the four functionaries in question were the Bantamahene Amankwatia, the Asafohene Kwaakye Kofi, the Gyaasewahene Opoku Frefre, and the Adumhene Adum Ata (none of whom, it may be noted, were hereditary title-holders). An examination of those actually attending 'Privy' or Inner Council meetings in the period confirms the important role of the four, but shows that in addition to the Asantehene a number of the senior counselors were always present. Thus the four councillors and three counselors were in attendance at the late evening meeting on 23 May 1816, to receive a confidential report from the Dutch emissary Huydecoper.[107] But for the unexplained absence of the Bantamahene, the same officers constituted the Council which assembled on 19 June 1816 to consider the current unrest in Wassa in relationship to the plan to reconstruct the great-road to Elmina.[108] Again, a Council of 22 May 1817, convened to consider whether

102 Bowdich, 1819, p. 92.
103 *Ibid.* pp. 105, 124, 128, 146, and 252–3.
104 *Ibid.* p. 105.
105 *Ibid.* p. 85.
106 Bowdich, 1821a, p. 22.
107 Huydecoper's Journal, entry for 23 May 1816.
108 *Ibid.* entry for 19 June 1816.

negotiations towards a treaty of trade and friendship with the British should be entered into, was attended by the same four councillors, by several counselors, and on this occasion by a number of the Asantehene's Muslim advisers: 'Moors of authority'.[109]

The Inner Council functioned, like the Asantemanhyiamu itself, both as a court of justice and as a decision-making body. Bowdich noted, for example, how its members having at one session tried and condemned to death for cowardice a military officer, then proceeded immediately to a consideration of the Fante tributes.[110] Dupuis reported, similarly, how the hearing of a case of assault, brought by a Nkoransa Muslim against a non-Muslim, was interrupted to permit a discussion of (again) Fante affairs.[111] A most interesting graphic representation of the Inner Council in session in the early nineteenth century was given by Mrs R. Lee – the former Mrs Sarah Bowdich (Plate XVII). It was clearly drawn from Bowdich's own notes and sketches. 'This plate', wrote Lee,

presents a model of the council, held in one of the courts of the palace at Coomassie. The king is seated on a stool before the royal chair, a sort of humility practised by him on his birth-day; [112] he rests his elbow on the head of a favourite slave. Behind the king stands his sister [that is, the Asantehemaa], the only woman admitted to the councils. The cause of this council is the punishment of a rebellious Caboceer (or Governor of a town), who is led, chained, into the court, by the captain who has conquered him, and who carries the skull of an enemy in his hand; his followers are dancing and flourishing behind him. In the centre of the plate is one of the ministers, or linguists, making a messenger swear to be true to his duty, before he starts, which oath he enforces by biting a sword. Behind these stand the Moorish secretaries of the kingdom; next to the messenger's group sits Agay [Asante Agyei], the foreign minister, listening to the palaver, or discussion, surrounded by the king's deformed criers, and a fetish woman mixing poison for the captive, – doom [*odom*],[113] as it is called, and which, if it chokes him, will prove his guilt. Behind the king stands the prime minister,[114] who is conducting the affair. At the corners are two of the four members of the Aristocracy; he who has the scales is Apokoo [Opoku Frefre], the treasurer of the kingdom, weighing the gold designed for the victorious chieftain; the other is Odumata [Adum Ata], who has one of the sheep by his side, with which the king rewards those who particularly please him in the conduct of state affairs.[115]

109 Bowdich, 1819, pp. 46–51.
110 *Ibid.* p. 58.
111 Dupuis, 1824, pp. 117 and 124, note.
112 That is, in this context, the day of the week on which the Asantehene was born.
113 For the ordeal by *odom*, see for example Rattray, 1927, p. 31.
114 The reference is to the senior counselor, the Gyakye *okyeame* Kwadwo Adusei Kyakya.
115 Lee, 1835, p. 365.

Implicit in Lee's description is the recognition that the function of the counselors within the Inner Council differed from that of the councillors; in terming the former 'ministers' she intended presumably to emphasize their executive roles. The matter, however, is one of considerable complexity. In his *Essay* of 1821 Bowdich attempted to explain the role within the Inner Council of the four councillors who he regarded as dominating its proceedings. It is they, he wrote,

whom the king always consults on the creation or repeal of a law; whose interference in foreign politics or in questions of war or tribute amount to a veto on the king's decision; whose chief, Amanquatea, like the ancient Mayors of the Palace, can alone sanction the accession even of the legitimate heir to the throne (who must await his presence however procrastinated), and whose power as an estate of the government always keeps alive the jealousy of the General Assembly [the Asantemanhyiamu].[116]

But Bowdich also acknowledged that the prerogatives of the four differed markedly in the various fields into which the Inner Council was extending its authority. In the sphere of foreign policy, including matters of war and tribute, he remarked that the Asantehene gave 'his vote individually in common with the other members of the council': that is, the majority view prevailed.[117] On such issues the four councillors might make 'bold declarations . . . which amount to injunction',[118] an arrangement justified on the grounds that 'the interference of the Aristocracy in all foreign politics, makes the nation more formidable to its enemies, who feel they cannot provoke with impunity, where there are so many guardians of the military glory; who, by insisting on a war, become responsible in a great degree for the issue . . .'[119] In the sphere of domestic administration, by contrast, Bowdich maintained that the four councillors 'watch rather than share . . . generally influencing it by their opinion, but never appearing to control it from authority'.[120] This situation, he added, was advocated on two grounds, first, 'that an almost independent administration of the King, was better calculated for the domestic government, because the decrees of a monarch have naturally more force with the people, (over whom his power is unlimited)', and second, 'that a civil power in the Aristocracy could not be reconciled to the Assembly of Captains',[121] that is, to the Asantemanhyiamu. In other spheres, too, the power of the four appears to have been much restricted. 'In exercising his judicial authority', Bowdich wrote, 'the King always

116 Bowdich, 1821a, p. 22.
117 *Ibid.* p. 21.
118 Bowdich, 1819, p. 252.
119 *Idem.*
120 *Idem.*
121 *Ibid.* p. 253.

retired in private with the Aristocracy to hear their opinions, to encourage their candor without diminishing his majesty in the eyes of the people',[122] while in the field of legislation, Bowdich added, the Asantehene 'was said always to give them a private opportunity of defending the old law, rather than of objecting to the new; though, from the same state policy, the latter was announced to the Aristocracy as well as to the Assembly of Captains, before the people, as the sudden and arbitrary pleasure of the King'.[123]

It would seem then that the powers of the Inner Council, dominated as it was by four functionaries, were by no means clearly delimited in the 1810s, and that at least the fiction was maintained, that on all but foreign policy issues the four councillors always deferred to the Asantehene. Yet the extent to which decision-making functions had devolved, *de facto* if not *de jure,* upon those resident in Kumase by the early nineteenth century should not be understated. Indeed, one of the four councillors, the Gyaasewahene or Head of the Exchequer, presided over a court held in his own house in the Asikasu ward of which Bowdich – who was able to attend a few of its sessions – has left some account:

Apokoo [Opoku Frefre] holds a sort of exchequer court at his own house daily, (when he is attended by two of the King's linguists, and various state insignia,) to decide all cases affecting tribute or revenue, and the appeal to the King [that is, to the Pramakeseso] is seldom resorted to . . . He was always much gratified when I attended, and rose to seat me beside him. I observed that all calculations were made, explained, and recorded, by cowries. In one instance, after being convinced by a variety of evidence that a public debtor was unable to pay gold, he commuted sixteen ounces of gold, for twenty man slaves. Several captains, who were his followers, attended this court daily with large suites, and it was not only a crowded, but frequently a splendid scene.[124]

It seems clear, too, that at least some of the senior counselors presided over courts which, although limited in powers, nevertheless carried some of the work of government. One such court was held by the Gyakye counselor, Kwadwo Adusei Kyakya, of whom it was remarked on an occasion when he had himself been fined 20 ounces of gold for accepting a bribe, that 'Adoosee's friends alleged that he ought not to pay anything, because when any palaver comes he settles it at once; but if he is not there, they have to go to council'.[125] Such courts were perhaps of similar standing to those which counselors were sometimes authorized to set up in disaffected provinces: accompanying

122 *Idem.*
123 *Idem.*
124 *Ibid.* p. 296.
125 Hutchison, in Bowdich, 1819, p. 393.

in their political capacity the army, the counselors were empowered to use the field courts to negotiate treaties, fix indemnities, and try rebels.[126] In 1820 Hutton was much impressed by the importance of the counselors ('linguists'). The Gyaasewahene and Bantamahene, he argued, 'may have more power than Adoosey [Adusei Kyakya], but I incline to think, from the situation he holds as head linguist, as well as from his great abilities, both as an orator and a statesman, that they have not more influence'.[127] But whatever the relative authority of councillors and counselors, there is no doubt that members of the Asantemanhyiamu in the period viewed with considerable misgivings the extent to which other bodies in the capital were assuming decision-making functions. Indeed, in 1817 Bowdich specifically remarked how, to 'the Assembly of Captains', the Inner or Privy Council was by 1817 regarded as 'already sufficiently invidious for the health of the constitution'.[128]

No clear evidence survives of the stages by which the Inner Council did in fact become transformed into the powerful Council of Kumase, which was in time to take over many of the functions of the Asantemanhyiamu. Yet already by 1820 there were indications that the Inner Council was in process of change; that it was becoming a more broadly based body as those with particular forms of expertise were co-opted on to it seemingly to control the quality of the decisions taken. A council, for example, met on 23 March 1820 in order to consider the articles of the second Anglo-Asante treaty prior to ratification. Analysis of its composition shows that it included seven regular members, namely, the Asantehene; the four councillors, the Bantamahene Amankwatia, Asafohene Kwaakye Kofi, Gyaasewahene Opoku Frefre, and Adumhene Adum Ata; and two counselors, the Gyakye *okyeame* Kwadwo Adusei Kyakya and the Akankade *okyeame* Kwasi Kankam. But it also included five other members co-opted for their close involvement in the matter under discussion. Kofi Ado Koko and Soaben were respectively the Amoafohene and Dompoase-hene: that is, chiefs of metropolitan Asante towns lying on the great-road linking the capital with British headquarters at Cape Coast.[129] Asamoa Kwadwo was the Kumase functionary responsible for the administration of the Assin and northern Fante districts through which the great-road also passed.[130] Adu Brade, son of a former

126 Bowdich, 1819, p. 298. Bowdich, 1821a, p. 19.
127 Hutton, 1821, p. 273.
128 Bowdich, 1819, p. 253.
129 For Kofi Ado Koko ('Adukon', 'Ado Koum'), see Dupuis, 1824, pp. 166, 182. For Soaben, see Dupuis, 1824, pp. 54, 166; and Hutton, 1821, p. 192.
130 Dupuis, 1824, p. 166. Asamoa Kwame either was, or was later to become, the Anantahene of Kumase.

Asantehene, had lived for a time in Cape Coast as ward of the British Governor Torrane (1805–7), and by virtue of the experience thus gained had subsequently become one of the government's principal negotiators with the British.[131] And finally, the Saamanhene Akyampon, head of the traditional Gyaase, was the functionary generally responsible for protocol.[132]

The same principle of co-option was also alluded to by the Imām Muḥammad al-Ghamba' of Kumase in 1820, when he informed Dupuis that he was 'a member of the King's council in affairs relating to the believers of Sarem and Dagomba'.[133] It was a principle which was to be cited in this century, to justify the inclusion of five extraordinary members – the so-called 'educated commoners' – in the revived Asanteman Council. 'Co-option was a practice that was already there, not just hereditary right', commented Dr I. B. Asafu-Adjaye in 1969: 'the vernacular phrase is that "When you know how to wash your hands well, you are invited to eat from the same bowl as your elders".' [134]

The decision-making process in the early nineteenth century

In 1963 the late Asantehene Nana Sir Osei Agyeman Prempeh II described what he considered the major variables in the Asante legislative process. These were, first, the *amansεm* and *asenni*, the debate leading to the decision; secondly, the *mmara*, that is, the law or decree with penalties attached for non-observance; and thirdly, underpinning all, the *ahenni*, the exercise of royal power and authority. Of the two components of the debate, *amansεm* represented the votes given by the *bedwafo* or councillors in the mode *atirimusεm*, 'closed debate': that is, their votes and their votes only affected the decision.[135] By

131 For Adu Brade, see Bowdich, 1819, pp. 87–8, 111–12, 119, 121, 135. Hutchison, in Bowdich, 1819, p. 418. Dupuis, 1824, pp. 158; 166. Lee, 1835, pp. 177–8. Ricketts, 1831, p. 124, reported his death at Katamanso in 1826, but Reindorf, 2nd ed., n.d., referred to his presence in the expedition against Dwaben in 1831. Bowdich was perhaps in error in describing him as son of Osei Kwame; the name 'Adu' is characteristic of the Asafode *ntoro* and Opoku Fofie may therefore have been his father.
132 Dupuis, 1824, p. 100: 'Agampong, the captain of the palace, or of audiences'. Akyampon had probably come to office as a young man in or about 1820, and may be the same person as the 'Akjampong . . . chief over the [Asantehene's] household', referred to by Ramseyer and Kühne, 1875, p. 308. It must remain an open question whether he is to be identified with the Saamanhene Akyampon Panin who was executed in 1887.
133 Dupuis, 1824, p. 97.
134 Triulzi, 1969, p. 18: interview dd. 9 August 1969. For the maxim, see also Rattray, 1916, p. 103.
135 Compare the comment on membership of the Council of Kumase in 1905: 'perhaps the predominant sentiment actuating . . . pride of office is one of

contrast, *asenni* represented management by the *asennifo*, that is, the counselors and advisers who had no vote but who organized and conducted the proceedings, and whose influence was therefore also a major determinant of the decision. It was, furthermore, central to the legislative process that the Nseniehene and his subordinate the Dawurufohene (the heads of the heralds and the gong-beaters) efficaciously publicized the decision throughout Asante; and that the *abrafo* and the *adumfo*, police and executioners, effectively enforced the *mmara* or law.[136]

The nature of the debate, or more broadly, of politics (*amanyɔ*), will be discussed in subsequent chapters with reference to the ideological factors. The complexity of the decision-making process as such, however, will be illustrated here by reference to the series of legislative and executive transactions which culminated in the acceptance by the Asante of the treaty with the British in 1817. The British mission, initially led by James with Bowdich as second in command, was received in the capital on 19 May 1817, when some thirty thousand people gathered to witness its entry.[137] On the following day members of the mission were required to announce its objects at Dwaberem 'that all the people might hear it'; [138] and in the evening to hand over the gifts brought for the Asantehene in the palace, privately: 'a policy, to prevent any favourable bias of the body of caboceers and people anticipating the King's and his councils satisfaction of our motives and professions', so Bowdich observed.[139] On 22 May members of the mission were called before the 'Privy' or Inner Council, when a number of councillors expressed their distrust of British aims.[140] The following day the party was required to appear before a gathering of Muslims – 'of the Moorish caboceers and dignitaries' – and each of its members to take oath upon the Qur'ān that he had no evil intentions towards Asante.[141] On 24 May the British negotiators were summoned to an audience at which were assembled 'two long files of counsellors, caboceers, and captains' – lesser functionaries being in attendance in addition to their senior colleagues. The matter of the treaty was vigorously debated. It was the practice at such gatherings, so Bowdich

vanity; for the sittings of the Council are held with closed doors, and matters are discussed with the secrecy so dear to the heart of the Ashanti', Colonial Reports – Annual, no. 523, Ashanti, Report for 1906, p. 8
136 Wilks, field-notes, meeting with Nana Agyeman Prempeh II, dd. Kumase, 5 November 1963.
137 Bowdich, 1819, pp. 31–41. For a valuable examination of the conduct of the mission, see Collins, 1962, *passim*.
138 Bowdich, 1819, p. 43.
139 *Ibid*. p. 44.
140 *Ibid*. pp. 46–51.
141 *Ibid*. p. 56.

noted, that 'after the audience was gone through, the King retired to council' – and returned later to announce the decision.[142] On this occasion the decision was to despatch messengers to Cape Coast to obtain certain assurances from Hope Smith, the British Governor, of the seriousness of his purpose.[143] The Council was reconvened on 26 May when the messengers were brought before it, and for two hours briefed by one of the counselors: a measure which Bowdich understood as intended to 'conciliate the Captains', that is, to satisfy those present that the decision of 24 May was in fact being executed.[144]

Until the return of the messengers from Cape Coast, some five weeks later on 5 July, all negotiations on the treaty were suspended. On 7, 9 and 12 July the Council debated the replies,[145] and again decided that further information on the attitude of the British authorities in Cape Coast was essential to the determination of the matter. Adu Brade was commissioned to proceed there. While news was awaited from him, however, the articles of the proposed treaty were debated by the 'Privy' Council on 11 and 12 August, and on 22 August were brought before a larger gathering to which were co-opted 'deputies from the Fantee towns in the interior' – though whether Asante administrators or local chiefs is not clear.[146] On 27 August the expected messengers arrived back from Cape Coast, and the despatches they carried were discussed in council two days later. It was resolved, on the basis of the new information, that all outsanding disputes with the British should be regarded as settled, and the 'Preliminaries of a General Treaty' were signed by the Asantehene and witnessed by the Gyaasewahene Opoku Frefre ('Keeper of the Treasury') and the Gyakye Counselor Kwadwo Adusei Kyakya ('Chief Linguist').[147] It was announced by the Asantehene that the treaty itself would be formally executed at 'the annual assembly of Kings, caboceers and captains . . . when all his tributaries will be present for the yam custom',[148] that is, at the annual meeting of the Asantemanhyiamu.

On 6 September, at Odwira, the terms of the treaty were debated by 'the whole of the caboceers, captains, and tributaries', and its acceptance was approved.[149] It was signed the following day by the Asantehene and by four others 'deputed from the General Assembly of caboceers and captains', two of whom were the Gyaasewahene

142 *Ibid.* p. 119.
143 *Ibid.* pp. 57–64.
144 *Ibid.* p. 66.
145 *Ibid.* pp. 82–9.
146 *Ibid.* pp. 105–8.
147 *Ibid.* p. 113.
148 *Ibid.* pp. 105, 120.
149 *Ibid.* p. 124.

Opoku Frefre and the Adumhene Adum Ata.[150] But the treaty still had to be announced as law, *mmara*. The procedure was, first, for the counselors displaying badges of office to promulgate it, detailing the nature of the penalties for transgressions, before both the 'Privy' Council and the Asantemanhyiamu.[151] Thus on 22 September, four months after the commencement of the negotiations and over two weeks after the arrival in Kumase of those attending Odwira, this was done:

On the Monday there was a general assembly of caboceers and captains, the King of Dwabin being present, with his linguists, also several Dagwumba caboceers, and the Moorish dignitaries. The King announced the execution of the Treaty by himself and the deputies, and impressed, in a long speech through his linguists, that he would visit the least offence against it with the greatest severity.[152]

The new law, as the treaty had become, had next to be publicized among the people. This was the responsibility of the Nseniehene, the head of the criers.[153] Members of the *nsenie* group would be despatched to the towns and villages of Asante, to summon, 'by the sound of horns or gong-gongs, all the people, who are obliged to assemble at this signal: the order or the law is announced and all who hear must reply to it by a special cry according to the special circumstances'.[154] Because of the importance of the new treaty in the view of the Asante government, however, additional measures were taken to make known its contents. On 23 September the Asantehene had a letter despatched to the British Governor to require the coastal chiefs of the southern provinces to send representatives to Kumase to assent to it:

The King of Ashantee desires me to request you will write to all the Governors of the English Forts on the African Coast, to order the Caboceers of each Town, to send a proper person to Cape Coast, and that you will add one Messenger yourself, that they may all proceed to Cummazie, to take the King's Fetish in his presence, that none may plead ignorance of the Treaty concluded between His Majesty and the British.[155]

---

150 *Ibid.* p. 128. The other two were 'the two oldest captains . . . Nabbra and Ashantee'. The first was probably the Kronkohene Daabra Kwadwo. The second may have been the person of that name, from the *atumtufo* or royal guard, who fought at Katamanso, see Reindorf, 1st ed., 1895, Appendix. The signatures of the Dwabenhene and his counselors, which also appeared on the copy of the treaty transmitted to London, were added later, for which see Dupuis, 1824, pp. 138–9 and cxix–cxx.
151 Bowdich, 1819, p. 256.
152 *Ibid.* pp. 146–7.
153 *Idem.*
154 Bonnat, in *L'Explorateur*, 1875–6, II, 622.
155 PRO, T. 70/41: Hutchison to Hope Smith, dd. Kumase, 23 September 1817. See also Bowdich, 1819, pp. 146–7.

The structure of decision-making

The councils that had debated the Anglo-Asante treaty had been simultaneously occupied with the serious crisis that had arisen in the province of Gyaman, whose ruler, Adinkra, had withheld the annual tributes.[156] Early in 1817 it was made known to Adinkra that if no settlement was reached within a year, military occupation of his country would be ordered. Two missions from Gyaman arrived in Kumase between May and September 1817, but no settlement acceptable to central government was reached.[157] On 6 November the Council in Kumase apparently decided that the expedition should take the field in two (Asante) months' time, that is, in the dry season in late January 1818. Since, however, troops from the *amanhene* and provincial rulers would be required, messengers were despatched to summon them to the capital once more for an extraordinary session of the Asantemanhyiamu – most members having returned to their towns after the successful completion of the deliberations on the Anglo-Asante treaty. On 8 November Hutchison witnessed 'the entrance of the chiefs, caboceers, etc into the town, to meet in council, and determine on the method of conducting the war'.[158] After debate, the decisions of the Asantemanhyiamu were given the force of law (*mmara*) on 23 November: the Asantehene made a formal public announcement of the impending operation, and signalized his intention of accompanying the armies in person.[159] In 1817, then, in the matters both of the Anglo-Asante treaty and the Gyaman rebellion, similar patterns of decision-making were followed: the initial debates were conducted by the Inner Council, sometimes in the presence of co-opted members, and were then discussed further in the higher council – the Asantemanhyiamu. The decisions were finally given legislative status by being formally and publicly promulgated by the Asantehene and his counselors, and publicized by the *nseniefo:* after which the executive agencies, whether bureaucratic or military, put into force the new legislation.

Interestingly, the difference between Asante and British political practice became clearly exemplified in this very context. In 1819 charges were brought against Governor Hope Smith that he had failed to suppress treasonable activities in Cape Coast at the time when the Asantehene and his armies were in the field in Gyaman. Demanding payment of a penalty of 1,600 oz of gold from the British, and the same sum from the townsfolk of Cape Coast, for their infringement of the

156 See, e.g. Bowdich, 1819, pp. 94–5.
157 *Ibid.* p. 245.
158 Hutchison, in Bowdich, 1819, p. 394. PRO, T. 70/41: Hutchison to Hope Smith, dd. Kumase, 16 and 23 November 1817.
159 Hutchison, in Bowdich, 1819, p. 399.

treaty,[160] Osei Bonsu argued that in the course of the negotiations with the British mission in 1817, 'they told me if I broke the law [i.e. the treaty], I was to pay gold; and if the governor broke it, he must pay it. Now all the people know it was the governor who broke it; for when Cape Coast was insolent, he would not hear my palaver: but told them to give the gold to him, and fight the king'.[161] Producing the treaty for the inspection of the British Consul Dupuis in Kumase in March 1820, the Asantehene insisted that the penalties for its infringement would be found written into it, and his view was endorsed not only by his councillors but also by a Fante – an independent witness – who had accompanied the 1817 mission to the capital. But there were no such clauses, and the Asante councillors had been duped through their inability to examine the English text. Dupuis explained to the Asantehene, that when the king of England 'was forced into palavers, nothing but war could settle the dispute'. Then it is true, commented Osei Bonsu, that 'the other white men cheated me'.[162] And the sorry fact was, that while the Asante had regarded the treaty as having been given the force of law, the British had never considered it as other than a matter of political expediency in the pursuit of certain immediate advantages.

The Council of Kumase in the later nineteenth century

In the early 1870s Bonnat was able to follow in Kumase the activities of what he called the *conseil d'état*. Like the French council of that name, it functioned as a court both of justice and of legislation, and it is quite apparent that it had evolved out of the earlier Inner Council – the Privy Council of Bowdich. It met daily, other than on those inauspicious times in the calendar when no work was undertaken,[163] from 7 a.m. to 2 or 3 p.m., and was sometimes reconvened in the evenings. Its sessions were held in the Great Court of the palace, the Pramakeseso. The Asantehene, Bonnat reported, was assisted by

five linguists or interpreters who are at the same time his counselors. They are called *quamis* [i.e. *akyeame*]; each holds one of the great Secretariats [164]

---

160 Dupuis, 1824, Introduction, *passim,* and especially p. xxxi.
161 *Ibid.* pp. 133–4.
162 *Idem.*
163 See, e.g. Dupuis, 1824, p. 126: 8 March 1820, 'a day dedicated to superstitious rites . . . no access could be gained either to the palace or the houses of the great officers, all public business was at a stand'. See also *ibid.* p. 137: 10 March 1820, 'the king secluded himself within the palace, and declined transacting public business; the day was considered of an ominous cast'.
164 Bonnat uses the term 'commandements', by analogy with the four Secretaries of State, or *commandements,* of the old French monarchy.

of the capital. In this type of Conseil d'État sit, also, as councillors all the princes of blood and all the chiefs of Kumase. The meeting of this court of justice and of legislation takes place every day in the great plaza of the palace called Apromosso . . . Throughout the whole of the sessions the picture presented by this court is very imposing. The king is seated under the far gallery, raised about two metres above the ground to which one climbs by several stages. Around him is a score of his officers; in front of him, in two rows, are twelve *affana assuafo [afenasoafo]*, armed with swords with golden hilts; to right and to left are displayed fetishes of all sorts. Further back, in the court, are the executioners drawn up in many rows five to six metres long, and the court criers, a kind of usher responsible for keeping silence. It is these who, at intervals, utter the cry *tie! tie! tie!*, which is to say: Listen! listen! listen! Between them, in front of the king, a passage of about three metres is kept open, which serves for the accusers and accused to come to present and defend their case. The five *quamis*, seated under their umbrella, surrounded by their people, are situated to the right of the king; slaves hold before them the long and short staffs decorated with gold and silver. The one represents rapid discussions and easy cases; the other bad cases and long debates. To the left, on the same line, are the principal officers of the king, covered also by large umbrellas. At the end of the court, facing the monarch, are seated, under a large low umbrella, the two principal chiefs of Kumase, the prince Boykey [Asafo Boakye], general-in-chief of the army, and Amanqua [Amankwatia], who, from the lowest ranks of the people, knew how to raise himself to one of the highest positions of the State, because he had control of munitions and arms.[165]

In 1874 Kühne listed the principal members of what he chose to call 'the king's general council'. Four counselors held seats: Boakye Tenten, Nsuase Kwaku Poku, Yaw Nantwi and Kwasi Apea, respectively of the Boakye Yam Panin, Domakwai, Akankade and Butuakwa stools. Next, on Kühne's ranking, came the two senior military commanders, the Bantamahene and Kontihene Amankwatia and the Asafohene and Akwamuhene Asafo Boakye. The princes were represented by Owusu Barempa, a son of Osei Bonsu and surrogate for his brother, the banished Akyempemhene Owusu Koko. The Akuroponhene Kwame Agyepon, an officer within the Kyidom, was a member, as was the Anantahene Asamoa Nkwanta, most respected of all the military commanders. Seats were also held by Kwasi Domfe, Nsumankwaahene or Head of the Physicians; by Akyampon Panin, the Saamanhene; by Agyei Kese, the Adumhene; and by Kofi Nkwantabisa, Asomfohene or Head of the Swordbearers. Finally, among 'sundry others', were two of the Asantehene's personal 'chamberlains', namely, Bosommuru Tia and Bosommuru Dwira.[166]

---

165 *L'Explorateur*, 1875–6, II, p. 622.
166 Brackenbury, 1874, II, 332. The absence of the Gyaasewahene Adu Bofo from

Clearly members of the Council of Kumase in the 1870s were widely recruited from the military and administrative élites of the capital. Clearly, too, membership was to some extent a matter of achievement and patronage, as the case of the Akuroponhene Kwame Agyepon shows. 'He was appointed to the Stool', so it is remembered, 'by the King's own prerogative right. Nana Kwame Adjeipong it is said was a stool dependent at the King's Court and was appointed to the stool [of Akuropon] as a result of the faithful service rendered to the King.' [167] His successors as Akuroponhene were not members of later councils. It is regrettable, however, that no detailed information survives on the mode of election, or selection, of councillors. Another list of the membership of the Council of Kumase – then described as the 'House of Commons' – is extant for 1888.[168] Since the period was one of conflict and interregnum, comparisons with the earlier list must be made with care. The Council was apparently presided over by the Asantehemaa Yaa Kyaa, acting as Asantehene, and by her sister Akua Afriyie, acting as Asantehemaa, and comprised seventeen official members (excluding the counselors) though others might be in attendance. Only the Asafohene Asafo Boakye and the Nsumankwaahene Kwasi Domfe had retained their seats since 1870, having survived the wars of 1873–4 and the internecine struggles of 1883–8. What does seem clear is that the size of the Council had become fixed at about eighteen; that is, in normal times, the Asantehene and some seventeen councillors (again, excluding the counselors from consideration). Indeed, when the British reconstituted the Council in August 1905 – the 'Coomassie Council of Chiefs' – they also set its membership at eighteen, 'all chiefs who, according to tradition, would have formed the Advisory Board of the late dynasty'.[169]

In 1905 the colonial administrators in Asante acknowledged that membership of the Council of Kumase 'implies a recognised status of which the fortunate few are proud, and the many, envious'.[170] Yet, assuming that the Council had been one of fixed membership, Chief Commissioner Fuller could express his confusion on the issue: 'I had not been in Ashanti many months before I realised the difficulty Coomassie matters presented . . . I could not get a grip over Coomassie matters. They eluded me. Each Chief came and told me the story

the list reflects the fact that he held a field command for most of the period during which Kühne was in Kumase.
167 IASAS/199: Akropong Stool History, recorded by J. Agyeman-Duah, 13 March 1967.
168 *Further Correspondence*, C. 5615, 1888, p. 39: Barnett to Governor, dd. Kumase, 20 March 1888.
169 Colonial Office, Annual, no. 523, Ashanti, Report for 1906, p. 8.
170 *Idem.*

he wished me to believe and I had to draw conclusions as I could'.[171]
Table 17 shows the actual composition of the Council of Kumase in or

Table 17 *Distribution of seats on the Council of Kumase (excluding counselors)*

Kumase stool	Membership of Council of Kumase		
	1870	1888	1905
Bantama	Amankwatia	Awua	Osei Bonsu
Asafo	Asafo Boakye	Asafo Boakye	Kwaakye Kofi
Adum	Agyei Kese	Asamoa Kwame	Asamoa Toto
Gyaasewa	Adu Bofo	Opoku Mensa	Kwame Tua
Akyempem	Barempa (acting)	Kofi Boakye *	Kwasi Adabo
Ananta	Asamoa Nkwanta	Yaw Adu Kofi	Kwabena Safo
Nsumankwaa	Kwasi Domfe	Kwasi Domfe	—
Saaman	Akyampon	—	Kwabena Kokofu
Akuropon	Kwame Agyepon	—	—
Asomfo	Kofi Nkwantabisa	—	—
'Chamberlains'	Bosommuru Tia	—	—
	Bosommuru Dwira	—	—
Nkwantakese		Kwaku Kan	—
Hiawu		Hiawu Boaten	—
Kronko		Kwadwo Apan	—
Asoromaso		Kwaku Yeboa	—
Aboaso		Kwasi Kobia	—
Deboso		Ata Famfam	—
Boakye Yam Kuma		Asase Asa	—
(unidentified)		Ano Ata	—
(unidentified)		Yaw Bodi	
Heir-apparent		Agyeman Prempe	—
Adonten		—	Kwame Frimpon
Antoa		—	Kwaku Ware
Oyoko		—	Kwame Dapaa
Atutue		—	Kwasi Bosompra
Domakwai		—	Kwasi Nuama †
Kyidom		—	Kofi Nsenkyere
Dadiesoaba		—	Kwabena Sekyere
Ankobea		—	Kwame Kusi

* Kofi Boakye was son of Kwaku Dua, and *odikuro* of Adwuamen-Akorase, see Wilks, field-notes, interview with Nana Yaa Kyaa, dd. Akorase, 5 August 1965. More commonly known as Kofi Subiri, he became Akyempemhene in succession to Owusu Koko, and died in the Seychelles in 1901. Owusu Barempa, a son of Osei Bonsu, had acted as Akyempemhene during the exile of Owusu Koko.
† Kwasi Nuama appears on this list as a councillor, that is, as Domakwaihene, and not as counselor, a role he also filled as Akyeamehene.

about 1870 (incomplete list), in 1888, and in 1905. Comparison of the three columns will suggest that while those acquiring the more senior positions in Kumase were virtually assured of a seat in council, lesser office holders might or might not succeed in attaining such an honour. Comparison of the columns will show, too, that in the nineteenth

171 National Archives of Ghana, Kumase, File D. 102: Memorandum by F. C. Fuller, dd. 28 August 1916.

century a number of heads of service agencies within the public and palace administrations were represented on the Council. Thus the Asomfohene was, for example, head of the sword-bearers – those employed as members of embassies, official trade delegations, and the like whose badge of office was a decorative sword; and the Debosohene was head of the Abanase, one of the departments concerned with the organization of palace affairs. The members of the Council of 1905 were chosen by Chief Commissioner Fuller, who described the procedure which he had followed: 'I convened the Chiefs, explained to them my object and asked the principal men to nominate all those who had formerly ranked as Councillors of the King. After days of discussion [a number of] Chiefs were recognized by me as the best candidates for the new Council . . .' [172] But by 1905 many of the older administrative agencies had been virtually closed down or rendered ineffective, and the seats which their heads had held in the Council were accordingly reallocated. They were filled principally by Kumase ward heads, such as the Atutuehene who presided over the affairs of Adenkyemenaso, or the Dadiesoabahene who looked after the suburb of that name.

Council of Kumase and Asantemanhyiamu

However much members of the Asantemanhyiamu might have regarded with suspicion the increasing assumption of legislative functions by Kumase officials in the early nineteenth century, certainly such important decisions as that to enter into treaty relations with the British, or to carry out the invasion of Gyaman, were not taken before the issues had been debated by the higher body. Although it is not yet possible to identify with any confidence the stages by which the early Council of Kumase, the 'Privy Council', evolved into the more widely based later Council, a number of hypotheses may tentatively be advanced. From what is known of the general character of the reign of Kwaku Dua I, it would seem that the power of the *amanhene* was drastically curtailed, and that the Asantemanhyiamu was seldom convened other than at the time of the annual Odwira. The campaigns in the north in the early 1840s appear to have been conducted with Kumase troops alone; the nation engaged in few other wars in the period, thus lessening the Asantehene's dependence upon the manpower resources of the *amanhene*. Kwaku Dua ruled, moreover, basically through executive government: through *asenni* (the counselors and advisors) rather than through *amansεm* (the councillors). But

172 National Archives of Ghana, Kumase, File D. 102: Memorandum by F. C. Fuller, dd. 28 August 1916.

while Kwaku Dua had curtailed the power of the *amanhene* by seldom convening the Asantemanhyiamu, the power of the Kumase functionaries who dominated the Inner Council – the embryonic Council of Kumase – was also reduced, paradoxically, by his increasing the membership of that Council and by his giving the incoming members equal voting status with the older incumbents.

A report on a meeting of the Council convened by Kwaku Dua in 1844 is indicative of the nature of the transformations which had occurred. It was held in the palace, and was attended 'by all the principal chiefs resident in the town, with their chief men, amounting to over 2,000 persons . . . something very serious was occupying the minds of all present'. The issue before the Council was in fact one on which relations with the British hinged: an Asante official trading party had suffered injury in the British Protected Territory (see p. 215). According to an eye-witness account, after the facts of the case had been brought before the councillors the Bantamahene Adu Gyawu and Asafohene Akwawua Dente addressed the meeting:

under the impulse of very strong feelings, the two principal Chiefs, Gawu and Ankowa (the first having 5,000, and the second 4,000 armed retainers) arose, and in the silence which instantly followed, each raising the right arm and addressing the King, requested him to allow them to take the great oath of the nation, binding themselves by its dreadful penalties at once to call together their followers, and to go without loss of time to the country where this crime has been committed, and avenge the King and country for the insult which had been offered to them . . . Their proposal was received with immense satisfaction by Chiefs and people.

Yet 'happily', so it was reported, 'the King was not carried away with the tide of feeling'. He thanked the Bantamahene and Asafohene for their assurances of support, but informed the Council that he had already made arrangements with the Wesleyan missionary, Chapman, to proceed to Cape Coast and arbitrate the issue with the British authorities there.[173] The prior decision of the executive branch of government was not, apparently, challenged by the Council. The extent to which Kwaku Dua used the instrument of the political purge to institute executive government – to foster general administrative competence on the part of his officers while discounting charisma and leadership other than his own – will be alluded to further in Chapter 12. Nevertheless, it would seem that in extending the base of the Council of Kumase, Kwaku Dua created an institution potentially of considerable power, which under the surrogate rulers who followed him in office – Kofi Kakari and Mensa Bonsu – was enabled to extend its functions and to

173 *Further Correspondence Respecting the Ashantee Invasion*, C. 893, no. IV, 1874, pp. 61–7: Chapman to Perks, dd. Fort Beaufort, 29 September 1873.

make claims to being the effective central government of the nation.

The Asantehene Kofi Kakari came to office with the support of politicians, dominant in both the Asantemanhyiamu and the Council of Kumase, who were committed to war with the British if no satisfactory resolution of the conflict between the two powers was rapidly available. Requiring therefore a continuing mandate from both Councils for this policy – one which was to require in time the total mobilization of the nation's resources for war – Kofi Kakari relinquished any attempt to maintain his predecessor's mode of executive government, and in fact made extensive use of the services of both upper and lower Councils. Mensa Bonsu was by contrast almost totally concerned with national reconstruction after the debacle – for both the Asante and the British – of 1874: when, that is, it became clear to both powers that the politics of accommodation rather than confrontation must prevail at least *pro tem*. It was not until the reign of Mensa Bonsu that for the first time the two Asante Councils were to come finally into conflict.

By the early 1880s it was possible for Lonsdale to report from Kumase, that

the government of the [Asante] kingdom lies entirely in the hands of the Coomassie Chiefs. The King's counsellors cannot be called a representative body. The Provincial Kings, and with only very few exceptions, the important Chiefs, have not a word to say in the Government of their country, and, I should say, only ask to be let alone and at peace.[174]

The burden of Lonsdale's comment appears to have been, that it was in consequence of the concern of the *amanhene* and provincial rulers to regulate their own affairs at the local level, that they were prepared to accept a minimal role in the routine transactions of government in the capital. But the fact of the matter was, that the Council of Kumase appears to have become established and recognized as a second house by prescriptive right rather than through any process of constitutional revision which only the Asantemanhyiamu might have validated. The *de facto* position was not, therefore, one which could be formally defined. Thus in 1883 Owusu Ansa argued the case for a strict construction of the Asante constitution, and maintained that whatever the *de facto* position, the exercise of national decision-making functions by the Kumase councillors had no clear basis in law:

Coomassie has been from the commencement of the Ashanti confederacy the capital of that kingdom and the seat of the general Government, and it is there that the King has always resided, and there also has the great stool always been deposited. On this account the people of Coomassie have always

174 *Further Correspondence,* C. 3386, 1882, p. 66: Lonsdale's report on his mission to Kumase, Salaga and Yendi, 1881–2.

arrogated to themselves rank and prestige superior to that of the other provinces forming the empire, and they have from time immemorial considered themselves as representatives of the whole Ashanti nation, and have invariably assumed towards their neighbours of the other provinces a bearing which the latter, although they submitted to it, never liked.[175]

It was a corollary of the view, that Owusu Ansa went further to assert the sovereignty of the Asantemanhyiamu. 'At this time', he observed of the Odwira, 'the chiefs who come to Kumase meet in an assembly where all projects concerning the provinces are discussed and decided. They profit from considering all the nation's affairs. Nothing can be done without the approval of this assembly. . .'[176] But Owusu Ansa nevertheless conceded that the decline in the power of the Asantemanhyiamu ('the Supreme Council of the empire') *vis-à-vis* that of the Council of Kumase – a change which he saw as culminating with the lower body's assumption of the right to remove an Asantehene from office – had resulted from the readiness of *amanhene* and other provincial rulers to divest themselves of general responsibility for the direction of national affairs:

The people of the other provinces having thus in a manner surrendered in ordinary matters the executive power, as it were, to Coomassie, the Chiefs of the latter began to assume powers which by the constitution they were not entitled to exercise, and this finally led to their deposing the King, Kari-kari [Kofi Kakari], without the consent and approval of the Supreme Council of the empire.[177]

The development of the conflict between upper and lower Councils will be considered below. The matter was one, however, which was to continue to engage the attention of British colonial administrators in the twentieth century. 'The Kumasi Chiefs', observed the Acting Colonial Secretary of the Gold Coast in 1916,

who, His Excellency [the Governor] understands, are the survivors of the War Chiefs and chosen Councillors, whom the Ashanti King was accustomed to gather around him, – constitute in themselves something resembling an extra-constitutional body; and the Governor is doubtful how far it is advisable to continue to place over much authority, power or influence in their hands.

The Governor accordingly requested 'a Memorandum explaining in detail the precise position filled, and the part taken by the Kumasie Council in the Administration of Ashanti, both in the past, under

---

175 *Further Correspondence*, C. 4052, 1884, pp. 72–3: Owusu Ansa to Governor, dd. Accra, 27 August 1883.
176 Cited in Gros, 1884, p. 170.
177 *Further Correspondence*, C. 4052, 1884, pp. 72–3: Owusu Ansa to Governor, dd. 27 August 1883.

native rule and at the present time; and especially with regard to the position which its members occupy *vis-à-vis* the various Amahin [*amanhene*] in the Dependency'.[178]

The fullest information was offered by Crowther, Secretary for Native Affairs, who based his observations upon interviews with Asante political prisoners – a number of whom had themselves been members of the Council of Kumase before 1900. At the end of the nineteenth century, Crowther learned, 'the old Coomassie council' included six senior title-holders from the capital, the Kontihene, Akwamuhene, Adontenhene, Oyokohene, Kyidomhene and Gyaasewahene, together with 'all the supporting *safohenes* or subchiefs, of these various dignitaries'. In terms of what Crowther described as 'a very complicated and not very rigid constitution', he acknowledged that the relationship between the Council of Kumase and the Asantemanhyiamu was virtually impossible to define. 'The paramount stool of Coomassie', he wrote,

. . . controlled a group of states e.g. Juabeng, Mampong, Kumawu etc. . . . But Coomassie is not in itself one of these states . . . and though it may be said that the life of the Oman of Ashanti is imperfect without all the component parts, nevertheless it has . . . its own council of central Government which in minor matters directs the action of the Oman as a whole. When large issues were involved this central council would unquestionably be augmented by the presence of the great divisional chiefs or their representatives.[179]

In the nineteenth century, while the Asantemanhyiamu remained under the constitution the supreme council of the nation, its powers had in fact become greatly eroded as the Council of Kumase had increasingly assumed the functions of central government. In the period of colonial overrule in the earlier twentieth century, the British administration recognized in 1905 the existence of the 'Kumasi Council of Chiefs', and in 1935, that of the 'Ashanti Confederacy Council'. But the Council of Chiefs was in fact reconstituted by Chief Commissioner Fuller of Asante in pursuance of Sir Donald Stewart's policy of 'restricting the power of the Coomassie Chiefs to purely Coomassie matters'. This interpretation of the Asante constitution was bitterly opposed by the Kumase establishment but nevertheless was firmly enforced.[180] The Kumasi Council of Chiefs was, there-

178 National Archives of Ghana, Kumase, D. 102: letter from C. H. Harper, dd. Accra, 22 June 1916.
179 File D. 102: Memorandum on Succession to Kumase Stools, by the Secretary for Native Affairs, enclosed in Colonial Secretary to Chief Commissioner for Asante, dd. Accra, 20 October 1916.
180 National Archives of Ghana, Kumase, File D. 102: Memorandum on the Kumase Council of Chiefs, by F. C. Fuller, dd. 28 August 1916.

fore, structurally but not functionally continuous with the Council of Kumase of the preceding century. The Confederacy Council, by contrast, although created as an instrument of Indirect Rule, was fashioned on the basis of the traditional conservative and constitutionalist view (restated and redefined in 1929 by Rattray),[181] that nineteenth century Asante had enjoyed a confederate structure and that the *amanhene* had possessed autonomous jurisdictions except in so far as they had voluntarily relinquished powers to the central government. A contrary view was cogently argued by Wallace-Johnson, in his *Report on the Restoration of the Ashanti Confederacy* which was submitted to the Asantehene in 1935. 'There has never been', so Wallace-Johnson maintained,

any Confederacy in Ashanti and . . . the term Confederacy now applied is wrong. For, according to the national customs of the Ashanti, no Stool ever claimed equality to the Golden Stool. No chief ever sat in parallel line with the Ashantihene. Many chiefs, so far, including the Mamponghene, through family allegiance, willingly submitted themselves to the supreme power of the Ashantihene. Others were subdued by conquest. Thus, Ashanti was no less than a Monarchy or a Kingdom with the Ashantihene as the King.[182]

At the first session of the Confederacy Council in June 1935, the Mampon representatives expressed their rejection of the construction of the Asante constitution that had by then become current. 'They were not', they stated,

in agreement with the provision made by [the colonial] Government to the effect that the Asantehene should not interfere or have voice in the Stool Affairs of the various Divisions or States comprising the Ashanti Nation. They added that the Asantehene was the overlord of all the Stools in Ashanti and as such it was unconstitutional for him to be told not to have a voice in matters affecting Stools.[183]

It was not until 1946, however, that the members of the Confederacy Council, concerned to legitimate the authority of that body, began to argue explicitly for its institutional continuity with the Asanteman-hyiamu of the nineteenth century:

Before the disintegration of Ashanti following the unfortunate incidents of 1896, the original Council of Ashanti was not a Confederacy but a National Council . . . Be it resolved . . . that inasmuch as the term 'Ashanti National Council' (i.e. Asanteman Nhiamu) is more in keeping with the traditional facts existing in Ashanti prior to its disintegration by the British Government, the government may be respectfully requested to delete the words

181 Rattray, 1929, especially chapters x–xv.
182 Archives of the Asanteman Council, Manhyia, Kumase: report dd. 6 February 1935.
183 *Ibid.* Minutes of the Ashanti Confederacy Council, 6 to 17 June 1935, p. 24.

'Ashanti Confederacy Council' and to substitute the words 'Ashanti National Council' . . .[184]

Eight years later the search for continuity was to be pressed – unsuccessfully as it turned out – one stage further. 'A special correspondent', claimed the *Ghana Nationalist*,

quoting sources close to the central committee of the Convention People's Party, reports to this agency that after secret meetings held last week by high CPP officials with Mr. K. A. Gbedemah, Minister of Finance and Director of operations of the Party, it was decided to send a delegation to Otumfuo the Asantehene, Nana Sir Osei Agyeman Prempch, requesting him to accept their suggestion to be made the Monarch of the Gold Coast. This means that if the Otumfuo accepts the request, a Monarchial State will be established like Britain and some other Empires. But a Cabinet system of Government will still exist with a Prime Minister at the head.[185]

The conflict between the two Councils, Asantemanhyiamu and Council of Kumase, was never fully resolved. It will be suggested in a later chapter, however, that by the end of the nineteenth century the constitutional issue had become singularly irrelevant to a nation by then divided by ideological and class differences of a far more fundamental nature.

184 *Ibid.* Minutes of an emergency session of the Ashanti Confederacy Council, June 1946. See further, Triulzi, 1972, pp. 106–7.
185 *Ghana Nationalist* (Accra), no. 177, 20 October 1954.

CHAPTER 11

Kumase as the seat of government: the structure of the executive

The development of the Exchequer

In the early eighteenth century supervision of Asante financial affairs appears to have been the responsibility of Adunnya Safe, a Denkyira who had been among the early adherents of Osei Tutu and who had subsequently been appointed both Domakwaihene and Akyeamehene – head, that is, of the *akyeame* or counselors.[1] Adunnya Safe enjoyed a long period in office, taking part in the Takyiman campaign of 1722–3, and the Gyaman campaign of *ca.* 1740, under Opoku Ware. He is probably to be identified with the 'great or first servant of the Assiante King Poku (named Soffie)' who led a force of 5,000 men into Akwamu in 1742.[2] Resident in the Nsuase ward of Kumase, it is said that the Treasury was physically located there and that all transactions were conducted under control of the Nyante shrine. It was to Nsuase, therefore, that the Asantehene's personal treasurer, the Sanaahene, had to go in order to draw from the Akyeamehene the palace's share of the revenues.[3] A strong tradition exists, however, that it was as a result of the conquest of Takyiman that Opoku Ware, on the advice of the captive Takyimanhene Ameyaw Kwaakye, was enabled to make major changes in the Asante revenue system. As Reindorf reported the matter,

the whole treasure of the [Takyiman] kingdom was taken by the Asantes, whose power was greatly increased by this victory. Several improvements were, by Amo Yaw's advice, made in the government and social conditions of Asante. He taught Opoku to make gold and silver weights, to claim the estate of a deceased chief or general, also to enact laws fining offenders in order to add to his power and reduce that of his subjects.[4]

1 Institute of African Studies, Ghana, IASAS/43: Safie and Amoanim Stool History, recorded by J. Agyeman-Duah, 28 March 1963. See also Reindorf, 2nd ed., n.d., pp. 54–9.
2 General State Archives, The Hague, WIC 113: despatch to the Assembly of Ten, dd. Elmina, 9 April 1742.
3 Institute of African Studies, Ghana, IASAS/43.
4 Reindorf, 2nd ed., n.d., p. 72. Compare Fuller, 1921, p. 28; Meyerowitz, 1951, pp.

Whatever the accuracy of the tradition, it was immediately after the Takyiman campaign that Opoku Ware created a new post in his administration, that of the Fotosanfohene. The Fotosanfohene was made responsible for the Foto, the leather satchel in which standard weights of the kingdom were kept; he was, in other words, head of the cashiers, or more correctly, weighers, who handled payments in and out of the Treasury. The new office was given to one Esom Anin, a palace servant; it has remained ever since an appointive position.[5]

In a later period in his reign, when it is known that Opoku Ware had committed himself to a comprehensive programme of administrative reform (see pp. 127–9), it would seem that he addressed himself principally to matters of finance. The foundations were laid of a new department of government, the Gyaasewa Fekuo: a term which can be translated with reasonable felicity as the Exchequer.[6] In order, presumably, to establish the independence of the new department from the hereditary title-holders, Opoku Ware utilized the services of the *ahenemma* or princes in its development. Thus he appointed as first Gyaasewahene, or Head of the Exchequer, one of his own sons, Adusei Atwenewa. Too young, however, to assume his responsibilities immediately, Adusei Atwenewa's maternal uncle Ntim Panin was made acting head of the group.[7] Another son of Opoku Ware, Frimpon, was assigned to the new post of Ahwerewamuhene.[8] He became responsible for the custody of the Sika Mmra or Golden Elephant's Tail, which was the formal symbol of the nation's wealth just as the Sika Dwa or Golden Stool was that of its political sovereignty.[9] At the same time a new *okyeame*'s position was created: that of Counselor to the Exchequer. Known as the Adusei Atwenewa *okyeame* stool, Opoku Ware appointed Oduro Panin to it; he was later to become

203–4. For a summary of the early role of Takyiman in the gold industry, see Wilks, 1971b, pp. 354–60.

5 IASAS/157: Nnibi Stool History, recorded by J. Agyeman-Duah, 27 August 1965.

6 *Gyaasewa* means 'little Gyaase'. It is said that the stool here referred to was originally called *Gyaase,* but that this title was later usurped by the Saamanhene, so necessitating the coining of the new title *Gyaasewa,* see Kumase Divisional Council Archives, Manhyia: file KTCS/0130, Statement by the Asantehene, dd. 24 March 1947. To avoid confusion, however, throughout this work the title of Gyaasehene is used only to refer to the Saamanhene (who remains constitutional head of the whole Gyaase group) and the title of Gyaasewahene is used always to refer to the stool originally created by Opoku Ware for his son Adusei Atwenewa.

7 Wilks, field-notes, personal communication from A. C. Denteh, dd. 7 July 1965. Wilks, field-notes, interview with Opanin Kwadwo Poku, dd. Kumase, 23 December 1958. See further Kumase Divisional Council Archives, Manhyia: J. K. Edubofuor versus C. E. Osei, case commencing 21 December 1939.

8 IASAS/140: Ahwerewamu Stool History, recorded by J. Agyeman-Duah, 13 November 1964.

9 For the Sika Mmra, see Wilks, 'The Golden Stool and the Elephant's Tail: the Rise of the Asante Middle Class', forthcoming.

Nsutahene and to be succeeded in Kumase by his son Kwaaten Pete.[10] Finally, the older offices of Sanaahene and Fotosanfohene were placed in the Gyaasewa.

What Dupuis described as Opoku Ware's 'new code of laws, adapted for the government of the various departments of the state'[11] were, not unexpectedly, violently resisted by the political establishment, and the Asantehene was obliged to abandon his aspirations to radical reform. Under his successor, Kusi Obodom, the Gyaasewa Fekuo appears to have remained otiose. It is significant that the one new administrative agency created during his reign, that of the *akwanmofo* or inspectors of roads (see pp. 35–6), was apparently placed under the Kontihene of Kumase rather than under the Gyaasewahene, within whose jurisdiction it more rationally belonged (and to which it was later transferred). Under Kusi Obodom, moreover, the old Akyeamehene Adunnya Safe still retained his control over finance: he is the 'Saffe, Treasurer of the King' who was in receipt of a present from the Dutch in 1755 or 1756.[12] It was, then, probably only with the election of Osei Kwadwo as Asantehene in 1764, on a platform of reform, that responsibility for financial affairs was finally transferred from the Akyeamehene to the Gyaasewahene. Yet there are indications in the evidence that the development of the new department was initially hampered by staffing problems: that the ideal of a new style of administration would remain unattainable until professional administrators of a new kind could be found to run it. Thus it appears to be widely believed that Ntim Panin's stewardship of the Gyaasewa ended disastrously: that he was accused of converting Gyaasewa property to his own use, and committed suicide before trial.[13] Osei Kwadwo confirmed in office Opoku Ware's son, Adusei Atwenewa, by then old enough to assume the responsibilities of the post.[14] It appears, however, that the position was regarded during his incumbency as a sinecure, and that the control of finance was in the hands of the Adontenhene Amankwa Osei until he, too, was disgraced (see p. 251).

[10] Wilks, field-notes, interview with Opanin Kwadwo Poku, dd. Kumase, 23 December 1958. Oduro Panin is said to have fought in the Akyem campaign of 1717 and the Takyiman campaign of 1722–3, see Rattray, 1929, p. 258. This can only have been in his youth. He was succeeded as Nsutahene by Oduro Kuma, who reigned for one year only and was succeeded in turn by Amankwa, see Rattray, 1929, p. 259. Amankwa was Nsutahene in 1766, see General State Archives, The Hague, WIC 506: Huydecoper to Minister of Colonies, dd. Elmina, 22 December 1766.

[11] Dupuis, 1824, p. 235.

[12] General State Archives, The Hague, WIC 114: minute by Ulsen, dd. 20 November 1758.

[13] Kumase Divisional Council archives, Manhyia, Edubofuor *v.* Osei, evidence of J. K. Edubofuor, 17 January 1940.

[14] Wilks, field-notes, personal communication from A. C. Denteh, dd. 7 July 1965.

Nevertheless, within the lower echelons of the department a programme of training had been undertaken, and the personnel were becoming available who would take over its operations.

Under Osei Kwadwo the position of Fotosanfohene was held by Esom Adu, probably successor once removed of the first occupant Esom Anin.[15] After the Adontenhene's disgrace, it appears that Esom Adu effectively ran the Gyaasewa and indeed he is sometimes regarded as having held the post of Gyaasewahene. It was during this period that the Kumase Oyokohene Buapon is said often to have attended court with a retinue which included a young servant of his – one Opoku who had been born, in or around 1760, at Anyatiase near Lake Bosumtwe. Osei Kwadwo was much impressed by Opoku's talents, and nicknamed him Frefre (Twi *frɛde-frɛde*, 'nimble'). When the Oyokohene died, Osei Kwadwo instructed Esom Adu to take Opoku Frefre as part of the death duties, and to place him in the Treasury for training.[16] When Esom Adu was killed in rebellion during the reign of Osei Kwame, probably *ca.* 1790, Opoku Frefre assumed his duties,[17] and – Adusei Atwenewa having presumably died earlier – was soon confirmed in office as Gyaasewahene. He was to head the Exchequer until his death in 1826, and over a period of a quarter of a century was to build it into an organization capable of handling with comparative efficiency the complex fiscal affairs of imperial Asante. In this task he enjoyed the close collaboration of Kwadwo Adusei Kyakya ('the hunchback'), a grandson of the Akyempemhene Adusei Kra and greatgrandson, therefore, of Asantehene Opoku Ware.[18] Details of the early career of Kwadwo Adusei are lacking, but it would seem that he was appointed to the Adusei Atwenewa *okyeame* stool when Osei Kwame promoted its incumbent, Kwaaten Pete, to the position of Kumase Adontenhene upon the disgrace of Amankwa Osei. As counselor to

[15] IASAS/157, Nnibi Stool History, 27 August 1965, omits Esom Adu from the list, which mentions Esom Anin; Yaw Afirimu; and Kwaakye Abamu who served under Osei Bonsu and Osei Yaw. Accurate office lists for stools not vested in any family are frequently not available.

[16] Details of the career of Opoku Frefre are extracted from the Asante Collective Biography Project: pre-code sheet, Opoku Frefre. Among the major sources for his career are Kumase Divisional Council archives, Manhiyia, Edubofuor *v.* Osei; Wilks, field-notes, meeting with Nana Sir Osei Agyeman Prempeh II, dd. Kumase, 19 December 1958; and personal communication from A. C. Denteh, dd. 7 July 1965. He was, of course, well known to the early nineteenth century visitors to Kumase.

[17] Bowdich, 1819, p. 238.

[18] Wilks and Ferguson, field-notes: information from the Asantehene Nana Opoku Ware II, dd. Kumase, 3 November 1973. Reindorf, 2nd ed., n.d., p. 182, refers to Kwado Adusei Kyakya as Denkyira by origin; if this was so, it can only have reference to his maternal ancestry. See further IASAS/126 and 127: Jachie Stool History and Jachie Linguist Stool History, recorded by J. Agyeman-Duah, May 1964.

the Gyaasewa, Kwadwo Adusei perhaps lost favour with Osei Kwame at the time of the rebellion of his superior, Esom Adu; certainly Osei Kwame's failure to appreciate the services of Kwadwo Adusei is remembered to have brought that Asantehene into conflict with his councillors.[19] The Adusei Atwenewa *okyeame* stool may have been placed in abeyance.[20] It was not until 1807 that Kwadwo Adusei was fully restored to favour. In that year one Agyin, *okyeame* to the Gyakyehene Yaw Pense, was convicted of cowardice during the invasion of Fante. Removing him from his post, Osei Bonsu decided at the same time to transfer the office from Gyakye to Kumase. He appointed Kwadwo Adusei to it, and re-confirmed him as counselor to the Gyaasewahene.[21]

Opoku Frefre and Kwadwo Adusei occupied adjacent residences in the Asikasu ward of Kumase. Both moreover presided over subordinate courts which relieved the Asantehene's councils of much business (p. 396). Those who visited the capital during the reign of Osei Bonsu attested to the highly important role which the two played in the political life of the capital. Indeed, in the 1810s Opoku Frefre was generally regarded as the most powerful of the councillors, and Kwadwo Adusei as most influential of the counselors. When Osei Bonsu left the city for a few days in August 1817, to attend to business at his country home in Breman, it was Opoku Frefre and Kwadwo Adusei who assumed charge of affairs.[22] And when at the end of that month the Preliminaries of a General Treaty with the British were drawn up, the two to give assent to them on behalf of the Asantehene were 'Adoocee, Chief Linguist' and 'Apokoo, Keeper of the Treasury'.[23] The careers of the two, neither members of the old aristocratic families of Asante, exemplify the opportunities for advancement which had become possible for men of talent and ability within the new administration.

The Treasury in the nineteenth century

Throughout Greater Asante, other than in the far northern provinces where cowries circulated, by the nineteenth-century gold dust (*sika-futuro*) had long been the established currency, and all payments into and out of the Treasury had to be made in it. The principal repository of the gold dust was the Adaka Kese or Great Chest. It was

19 Kyerematen, 1966, p. 335.
20 For such a procedure in the present century, see Kumase Divisional Council archives, Manhyia, statements on the Butuakwa *okyeame* stool by Nana Sir Osei Agyeman Prempeh II, dd. 12 January 1961 and 28 November 1966.
21 See IASAS/126 and 127, Jachie Stool History and Jachie Linguist Stool History.
22 Bowdich, 1819, pp. 110–12.
23 *Ibid.* p. 113.

a large wooden coffer fashioned out of the buttresses of the silk cotton tree, and ornamented with metalwork. Said to have measured about seven by three by two feet, the finances of the nation were regarded as in an eminently satisfactory state when the Great Chest was full: as it had been under Kwaku Dua I.[24] A crude calculation will show that the value of the Great Chest when full is likely to have been upwards of 400,000 oz, or to the value of at least £11½ million sterling at the current nineteenth century equivalent of £3 12s the ounce.[25]

Before deposit in the Great Chest all gold dust was weighed, and tied in cloth into bundles of not less than one peredwan and usually not more than ten (that is, from 2¼ to 22½ oz). The Great Chest was housed in the palace in a room called the Damponkese, literally 'the great big-room'. The Gyaasewahene had the keys to it, and he also provided watchmen to guard it.[26] Such was the situation under the Asantehene Agyeman Prempe I in the late nineteenth century,[27] and so it had been at the beginning of the century under Osei Bonsu: Opoku Frefre, as Bowdich remarked, 'is the keeper of the royal treasury [kept] in a large apartment of the palace, of which he only has the key'.[28] But it seems to have been the case that upon the death of an Asantehene the decision might be taken to remove the Great Chest to the residence of the Asantehemaa until such time as it was considered prudent to return it to the Damponkese. The operation was the task of the Asoamfohene, head of the official carriers and hammock-men – the *asoamfo*. This was done upon the death of Kwaku Dua I, and it was not until the beginning of the sixth year of his reign in mid-1872 that the surrogate ruler Kofi Kakari was given possession of it. The occasion was one of the rare times at which the whole contents of the Great Chest were weighed. This was done 'in a large scale held by four strong slaves'.[29] But as Ramseyer and Kühne, who were in Kumase

24 Wilks, field-notes: interviews with Opanin Kwaku Owusu, dd. Kumase, 13 and 14 April 1966. Kwaku Owusu is a brother of the late Sanaahene Kwadwo Nyantakyi I, and had worked in the Treasury as a 'weigher' under Agyeman Prempe I. Then young, he held too junior a position to have a knowledge of the higher budgetary operations. For Kwaku Dua's Treasury, see also Ramseyer and Kühne, 1875, p. 171: 'he had collected more money than any of his predecessors'.

25 The volume of the Great Chest may be computed as somewhat over 1 million c.cs. It is assumed that perhaps 25% of its capacity was accounted for by the wrappings of the gold dust, and that the density of the gold dust approximated to 15 gms. per c.c.

26 It is possible that the watchmen were supplied by the Nkarawahene, head of a corps of armed guards created for the Gyaasewa by Osei Kwadwo, see IASAS/108: Nkarawa Stool History, recorded by J. Agyeman-Duah, 19 November 1963.

27 Interview with Kwaku Owusu, dd. Kumase, 13 April 1966.

28 Bowdich, 1819, p. 296.

29 Ramseyer and Kühne, 1875, p. 171. The large scale of the type described, said only to have been possessed by the Asantehene, was known in Asante as *akontuma*, being clearly used like a yoke.

at the time, emphasized, 'Kwakoo Dooah's treasure was regarded as crown property, that might be used for national but not for personal expenses'.[30]

The Great Chest was not opened regularly. The working capital of the Treasury was kept in a series of other receptacles each holding 1,000 peredwans (or 2,250 oz) of gold dust. These receptacles were of two sorts, the *apem nnaka* (singular, *apem adaka*), 'the boxes of one thousand [peredwans]', and the *apem brɔntoa* (singular, *apem brɔtoa*), 'the bottles of one thousand [peredwans]'. The *apem adaka* was a small box made of wood bound with metal bands. Each peredwan within it was separately wrapped in a piece of cloth and could thus readily be withdrawn without further weighing.[31] The *apem brɔtoa*, by contrast, was an imported vessel, hence its name 'the bottle from Europe'. It was in fact the wine flagon holding one gallon,[32] and was used for the storage of gold dust which had not been weighed out into packets. Under interrogation, a captured staff officer of the Bantama-hene told the British in 1873 that the Asantehene had much gold 'in a thousand jars one upon the other':[33] clearly *apem brɔntoa* had been mistranslated. It was, then, through the *apem nnaka* that the flow of money, whether into or out of the Treasury, took place. The Gyaasewahene controlled the overall budgetary aspects of finance within the framework of general policy as laid down by the Councils, and it was he who had to authorize all payments. The actual banking operations, however, were conducted within two sub-departments of the Exchequer, namely the Mint and the Treasury proper.

A major source of revenue for the Treasury was the death duties, and a considerable part of the gold received was in ingot form: wealthy individuals, that is, would usually have their gold dust melted down and cast into highly decorative forms, a protection against theft as well as an outlet for their aesthetic sensibilities.[34] By law, also, all

30 *Ibid.* p. 184.

31 In 1881 Huppenbauer saw five *apem nnaka* in Kumase. He gave the weight of each as about 140 pfund and the value as approximately 200,000 francs, see Huppenbauer, 1914, p. 46. 140 pfund is equivalent to 7 kilos, that is, exactly the weight of 1,000 peredwans. 200,000 francs was equivalent to £8,000 sterling, and the value of 1,000 peredwans was in fact £8,200 computed at £3 12s the ounce. Kyerematen, 1964, p. 45, is thus in error in stating that the *apem adaka* was so named because it contained gold dust to the value of £1,000. T. F. Garrard, in a personal communication, suggests that the *apem adaka* was a direct copy of the small European money chests of the fifteenth and sixteenth centuries.

32 For a photograph of *brɔntoa* in the Mampon stool property, see Kyerematen, 1964, p. 88. The Queen Anne gallon was abandoned for the imperial gallon in England in 1824. The density of pure gold is 19.3 grams per c.c. The Queen Anne gallon would thus hold 1,000 peredwans if the gold dust was packed to a density of about 18 grams per c.c., and the imperial gallon if packed to about 15 grams per c.c.

33 Boyle, 1874, p. 146.

34 It is interesting to note, however, that in the early nineteenth century a tax of

gold nuggets found in mining operations throughout Asante had to be surrendered to the Treasury,[35] which then made repayment in gold dust of a considerable part of the value of the nugget – the sum to be divided between the finder and the chief of the district in which the mining operations had taken place.[36] Over one hundred workers were employed in the Mint in reducing the ingots and nuggets to gold dust. They were known as the *buramfo* (*ebura*, 'a forge'), belonged to the Eburaase ward of Kumase adjoining Akyeremade, and their head was the Adwomfohene who presided over the guild of goldsmiths. An interesting account of their operations in the early 1870s is extant:

. . . as anywhere else, in Achanty gold is found as natural nuggets and as ingots. M. Bonnat reported a good number of these pieces of a respectable size, and if the gold arrives in Europe as dust it is because it is in this form that it constitutes the existing currency of the country, and that ingots and nuggets are smelted and reduced to dust to facilitate trade. In Coumassie alone, there are more than a hundred workers exclusively involved in this work, and with great interest [Bonnat] watched them accomplishing this.

The ingots or the nuggets which it is wished to convert to gold dust are placed in a small crucible of terracotta, which is put in the fire of an African furnace. In this crucible the smiths add a certain quantity of red earth, well dried and crushed. When the gold has melted, the crucible is drawn from the fire and vigorously shaken in order to mix the gold and the sand. This work demands skill and great dexterity. The contents of the crucible are then thrown into a large wooden vat filled with water, into which a little red earth has already been mixed. This water is agitated, poured out, and renewed until the gold dust, well washed, can be put on one side.[37]

The *buramfo* of the Mint worked in one of the yards adjacent to the Damponkese.[38]

The Treasury proper was the responsibility of the Fotosanfohene, head of the *fotosanfo* or weighers. A *foto* was a leather bag used to hold all the accoutrements for weighing gold dust: scales (*nsania*), scoops (*mfamfa*), spoons (*nsaawa*), weights (*mmrammo*), a variety of

20% had apparently to be paid on the value of all gold dust thus melted down, see Bowdich, 1819, p. 320.

35 Horton, 1870, p. 53. Ellis, 1887, p. 277.

36 Rattray, 1929, p. 163, suggests that nuggets were treated under the law of treasure-trove, and that the Asantehene would customarily return in gold dust two-thirds of their value. A case is on record of a woman, Adwowa Bua, who found a nugget of 135 oz on land belonging to the Akrokyerehene Abu. She surrendered it to him, and he sent it to the Asantehene Kwaku Dua I. On this occasion Kwaku Dua is said to have retained a mere £16 – two peredwans – and to have returned the value of the remainder in gold dust to Abu to share with the finder, see National Archives of Ghana, Kumase, D. 301: letter from Akrokyerehene *et al.* to Chief Commissioner, dd. 3 June 1910.

37 Bonnat, in *L'Explorateur*, 1876, III, 2; Gros, 1884, p. 197.

38 Interview with Kwaku Owusu, dd. Kumase, 14 April 1966.

small storage boxes, and sometimes nest weights of European manufacture. The Fotosanfohene had custody of *the* Foto, in which the standard weights of the Treasury were kept. It was presumably the one which Bowdich saw in use in the Exchequer Court, of which he remarked, 'Before the footoorh or treasury bag is unlocked by the weigher, though it be by the King's order, Apokoo [that is, the Gyaasewahene Opoku Frefre] must strike it with his hand in sanction'.[39] But each of the *fotosanfo* (literally, those who open the *foto*) had his own *foto*, the weights within it having been carefully checked against the standard ones. A senior weigher, who might be involved in the movement of large sums of money into or out of the Great Chest, would have a *foto* containing weights up to the highest value in regular use, the *peredwan-du* or ten peredwans.[40] The junior *fotosanfo* were, by contrast, almost entirely concerned with operations of one peredwan or below; that is, with weighing out into smaller denominations single peredwans drawn from an *apem adaka,* or with receiving small sums and making them up into peredwans for deposit.[41]

The weighers were responsible for recording all transactions in which they were involved. Bowdich remarked that although the Gyaasewahene had a secretary literate in Arabic, he was not concerned with the Treasury accounts which, rather, were kept by 'a local association which is said to be infallible'; that is, 'all calculations were made, explained, and recorded, by cowries'.[42] A weigher's *foto* would thus contain a box of shells for this purpose. The system was basically a simple one. Every peredwan removed from the Great Chest or from an *apem adaka* was replaced by a cowrie, and a cowrie was removed each time a peredwan was paid in.[43] Accounts were balanced at the end of each day, so that any error could be detected and the *fotosanfo* who had been involved immediately questioned.[44] Major audits

39 Bowdich, 1819, p. 297.
40 The view seems to be in error, that no *foto* could contain a weight higher than one peredwan, for which see, for example, Kyerematen, 1964, p. 43. The late Sanaahene Kwadwo Nyantakyi I certainly denied that this was so, see IASAS/41, Sana Stool History, recorded by J. Agyeman-Duah, 3 February 1963.
41 In 1966 Kwaku Owusu showed the writer his *foto*, which he had not used since the Treasury ceased to function at the time of the British military occupation of Kumase in 1896. The *foto* was carefully wrapped in five layers of cloth, and Kwaku Owusu's attitude towards it was one of both pride and reverence. It was common in the past for charms of one kind or another to be kept in the *foto*, to make the owner's transactions successful ones. Kwaku Owusu's *foto* contained twenty-seven weights ranging in values from one peredwan to one pesa, the latter valued at about 1d in the nineteenth century. See interview with Kwaku Owusu, dd. Kumase, 13 April 1966.
42 Bowdich, 1819, p. 296. Hutton, 1821, p. 267.
43 Interviews with Kwaku Owusu, dd. Kumase, 13 and 14 April 1966. Compare Rattray, 1929, p. 117.
44 *Ibid.* p. 118.

were carried out once in each Asante month, at the end of the Great Adae (Akwasidae),[45] for it was at that time that the greatest volume of Treasury business was transacted.[46] Maladministration within the Treasury, especially when peculation was suspected, could carry the death sentence.[47]

In addition to the Treasury proper (Damponkese) and the Mint (Ebura), a third major sub-department within the Exchequer was that concerned with revenue collection, the Atogye. It was run by the *togyefo* (singular *ɔtogyeni*, literally 'those who receive the taxes'), who travelled to the villages and towns of Greater Asante to collect the tributes, taxes, tolls levied on travellers, and the like. Those to be appointed to such positions had in most cases probably received their early training within the Treasury, as *fotosanfo*. Each had his own *foto* which he carried with him on his journeys. For this purpose the *foto* was placed within a special shoulder-bag, which served also as a receptacle for the gold dust which was collected. The satchel was known as *kotokuo*,[48] and those who were entitled to carry one could also be referred to as the *kotokuosoafo*. Their head, who was normally in attendance at the Damponkese, was the Kotokuokurahene, 'chief of the satchel-carriers'. Like all officials who worked in the treasury division of the Gyaasewa, the *togyefo* or *kotokuosoafo* had as their insignia of office a bunch of keys, which were always displayed whenever they were travelling or otherwise acting in their official capacity. Responsible for maintaining the flow of taxes into the Treasury from all parts of the imperial territories, the revenue collectors enjoyed a particularly high status among the *asomfo* or public servants. In the 1810s, for example, one Kwadwo Abrantia was well known on the Gold Coast as 'collector of the King of Asante's tributes'. He worked on the Accra circuit.[49] In May 1817, however, he was posted temporarily to Elmina, as acting resident commissioner there. The Dutch agent in Kumase, Huydecoper, hastened to write to the Director-General in Elmina, to inform him that 'Cudjo Abrantaa . . . when he arrives at Accra fort to collect tribute (*kostgelden*), is used to receiving a salute of 7 guns,

45 Interview with Kwaku Owusu, dd. Kumase, 14 April 1966. Compare Rattray, 1927, p. 116, note, who implies that audits were also made at the Little Adae (Awukudae).

46 See, for example, *The Gold Coast Aborigines*, XVI, no. 115, 30 June 1900, p. 3. Casely Hayford, 1903, pp. 95–6.

47 Interview with Kwaku Owusu, dd. Kumase, 14 April 1966. Rattray, 1927, p. 116, note. Compare Hutchison, in Bowdich, 1819, p. 416.

48 Compare Asante *kotokuo* with Malinke *kotoku*, 'satchel, money-bag'. For a photograph of two *kotokuosoafo*, see Kyerematen, 1964, p. 42.

49 See for example, General State Archives, The Hague, KvG 501: Roelesson to Director-General, dd. Accra, 22 October and 17 December 1816. Huydecoper's Journal, entry for 3 April 1817.

and accordingly he expects to be given the same honour when he arrives at Elmina.' [50] Whether or not the Director-General came up to expectations in this regard is not recorded, but the Dutch Great Council there did vote to pay him living expenses as long as he was in the town at the rate of one ounce of gold per month.[51] Kwadwo Abrantia is probably the 'Obrantu' who is remembered as having been instrumental in saving the life of Kwaku Dua at Katamanso in 1826. When Kwaku Dua became Asantehene eight years later, he is said to have acknowledged his indebtedness to the revenue collector by promoting him to high office within the Treasury.[52]

The *togyefo* or revenue collectors worked in close association with the members of another sub-department of the Treasury, namely, the *batafo* of the Bata or Company of State Traders. The roles of the *togyefo* and *batafo* were, however, clearly differentiated. Whether the *batafo* were made payments from the Treasury in order to purchase goods, such as guns and gunpowder, which were required by the government, or whether they carried commodities such as kola and ivory for sale at markets in or beyond the frontiers of Asante, their business was essentially transactional and they were expected to generate profits from it. The functions of the Bata are described in some detail in Chapter 15. The head of the organization was the Batahene, a position customarily held by the Asokwahene of Kumase who was directly responsible to the Gyaasewahene.[53] Like the *togyefo*, the public traders had to be skilled in the use of the *foto* and had usually served as weighers in the Treasury. The early stages in the career of Kwame Butuakwa were perhaps not atypical. His mother was a daughter of the Asantehene Opoku Ware and a royal of the Heman stool; and his father was probably from the family of the Fotosanfohene Kwaakye Abamu who held office under Osei Bonsu and Osei Yaw. Trained in the Treasury under his father, Kwame Butuakwa was soon transferred into the Bata. He was trading in the Anomabo district before 1807. Clearly a man of considerable administrative abilities, he was not however to make his future career in the Treasury. Moving into the provincial service, he held the post of resident commissioner for Abora-Dunkwa from about 1816 to 1823, and a new counselor's post was

50 Huydecoper's Journal, entry for 7 May 1817.
51 KvG 350: minutes of the Great Council, Elmina, 19 June 1817.
52 National Archives of Ghana, Kumase, D. 538: History of Ahuren, recorded 1929. According to this source 'Obrantu' was appointed either Fotosanfohene or Sanaahene, but he is not recorded in the office lists of these stools (see, however, p. 417, note 15 above).
53 Wilks, field-notes, interview with the Asokwahene Kofi Poku, dd. Kumase, 3 August 1965. IASAS/1: Asokwahene-Batahene Stool History, recorded by J. Agyeman-Duah, 3 February 1963.

created for him: the Butuakwa *okyeame* stool.[54] While the *fotosanfo* who worked in the Damponkese did so under constant supervision, those who went on to receive appointments as revenue collectors and public traders had obviously to be carefully chosen for their integrity. Cases of peculation by such functionaries appear to have been comparatively rare. One occurred in 1817, when a collector returned from Danish Christiansborg and was suspected of having embezzled 23 oz out of the 62 oz which had been given him as the rent of the establishment.[55] The matter resolved itself into one of whether the Danes had paid the rent up to the end of June, soon after which the revenue collector was there, or in advance up to the end of the year. The case came before court on 24 November 1817. Opoku Frefre, it was reported, 'who is his chief, was loudest against him, he said he had used him disrespectfully . . . and at the same time he had cheated the King; he therefore left him to the mercy of his Majesty'.[56] Osei Bonsu took a most serious view of the matter: 'by degrees', so it appeared, 'the King worked himself to such a height of passion, that throwing his cloth around him, and hastily rising, he ordered the captain's arrest'. Obtaining, however, the intercession at some considerable expense of the Bantamahene and Asafohene, the revenue collector was able to convince Osei Bonsu of his innocence of the charge. By 5 December he was back in his office, and had been authorized to proceed once more to the coast.[57]

The operations of the various sub-departments of the Exchequer concerned with finance were closely and intricately linked with those of the Asantehene's household treasury which contained the Sanaa. The Sanaa was essentially a *foto,* but was distinctive in that the bag was made out of an elephant's ear, a prerogative of royalty.[58] It was also distinctive in that the weights within it were said to be of gold and to differ from the standard.[59] 'It is to be observed', remarked Bowdich,

---

54 Asante Collective Biography Project: Kwame Butuakwa. See also, for example, Bowdich, 1819, pp. 79, 83, 89, 112, 116, 138, 157, 244–5. IASAS/170: Hemang Stool History, recorded by J. Agyeman-Duah, 24 January 1966. Wilks, field-notes, interviews with Okyeame Bafuor Osei Akoto, dd. Kumase, 11 April 1966; 31 October and 2 November 1973. Kumase Divisional Council Archives, Manhyia: Kumasihene's Tribunal, Civil Record Book 12, Yaw Num *v.* Kwadwo Appan, commencing 27 April 1931. There is some doubt about the name of Kwame Butuakwa's father; Okyeame Yaw Num gave it as Kofi Agyepon, and Okyeame Bafuor Osei Akoto as Twumase. There is general agreement, however, that he served as *fotosanni.*
55 Bowdich, 1819, p. 134.
56 Hutchison, in Bowdich, 1819, p. 400.
57 *Ibid.* pp. 404–5.
58 Kyerematen, 1964, p. 43.
59 Hutton, 1821, pp. 218–19 and 256.

that the King's weights are one third heavier than the current weights of the country; and all the gold expended in provision being weighed out in the former, and laid out in the latter, the difference enriches the chamberlain, cook, and chief domestic officers of the palace, as it is thought derogatory to a King avowedly to pay his subjects for their services.[60]

The Sanaa was not kept with the Great Chest in the Damponkese, but in a different part of the palace known as the Abanase. The head of the Abanase was the Debosohene, the Asantehene's barber and manicurist, whose office dated from the beginnings of the kingdom. The office of Abobotrafohene, Master of the Bedchamber, was also created by Osei Tutu, but was redesignated Abanasehene, Master of the Wardrobe, by Osei Bonsu when its incumbent became responsible for the Asantehene's clothes. Again dating from the reign of Osei Tutu, the office of Sanaahene was that of the custodian of the Sanaa. Three further positions were created in the early nineteenth century by Osei Bonsu to strengthen the Sanaahene's administration. The first of these was the Anonomsahene, who also was given charge of the Asantehene's drinks. The second was the Nnibihene: the title was created for Kwaakye Abamu who had earlier seemingly been Fotosanfohene in the Damponkese, but who had relinquished that post on being brought into the Household as a member of the *akrafieso* – the Asantehene's 'soul washers' or *akradwarefo*. And the third, the position of Apentenhene, was created to assist Anonomsahene and Nnibihene; Osei Bonsu appointed to it one of his own sons, Owusu Afriyie.[61]

The Sanaahene and his assistants were, then, officers of the Abanase, one of the major divisions of the Household. The Sanaahene, like the Fotosanfohene, employed his own trained weighers, but the *fotosanfo* of the Sanaahene were a quite distinct group from those who worked in the Damponkese. It was of the former group that Rattray was given a short but interesting description:

The king's treasurers, known as *afotosanfo* . . . were also custodians of the keys of the king's boxes and servants of the bed-chamber. They kept the king's household accounts, balancing accounts every twenty days, and keeping an accurate tally by the use of cowrie-shells. Any serious errors in accounts

---

60 Bowdich, 1819, p. 293. It is argued by T. F. Garrard, in his forthcoming *A History of Akan Goldweights*, that the actual weights used by the Asantehene were not in fact physically heavier than the regular ones, but that a second weight – *kyekyerekon* – would be added to produce the differential referred to by Bowdich.

61 Wilks, field-notes, interview with Opanin Kwaku Owusu and Sanaahene Kwadwo Nyantakyi II, dd. Kumase, 4 August 1965. See further IASAS/41, 51, 65, 96 and 157: Sanaa, Anonomsa, Debooso, Abenase and Nnibi Stool Histories, recorded by J. Agyeman-Duah, 3 February, 14 March, 23 April, 11 October 1963, and 27 August 1965. NAG, Kumase, D. 295: Apentehene Kwaku Dua *et al.* to Chief Commissioner, Asante, dd. 16 July 1914.

were punished by decapitation. The King of Ashanti was bathed every morning to the accompaniments of the rattling of the treasury keys. The *afotosanfo* were also the royal barbers and manicurists.[62]

Rattray added that the keys to the Sanaa were kept by the Asantehene, the Sanaahene, and the Debosohene (Deberehene).[63] The relationship between the Exchequer and the Sanaa is one peculiarly difficult to establish, since while the latter survives as a functioning institution, the operations of the former were taken over by the British colonial administration after 1896. It would seem that certain forms of revenue accrued to the Sanaa directly, most notably perhaps the fees paid in court for the use of the Asantehene's oaths. The major source of income to the Sanaa, however, was undoubtedly from the Damponkese: 'it is from the Foto that the Sanaa is taken'.[64] The position of the Sanaahene was indeed somewhat anomalous. He took the oath of allegiance directly to the Asantehene, and was responsible to him and not to the Gyaasewahene for the management of the Sanaa. On the other hand, he was politically a subordinate of the Gyaasewahene, and to that extent was within the Exchequer group.[65] The anomaly is exemplified in the established procedures for distributing that part of war booty set aside for personal remuneration, when the whole of the Abanase received through the Gyaasewahene a portion equal to his own:

If the Asantehene is sharing booty with the Gyaasewa, he will give a portion to Buabasa Gyaasewahene. Buabasa will then divide his portion into two. He will give the one portion to Sanaahene. The Sanaahene will then take his portion home, and divide it into two. He will give one portion to Debosohene. The Sanaahene will then divide his own portion into two. He will keep one portion, and will share the other portion between Anonomsa, Nnibi and Apenten.[66]

The financial operations of the various sub-departments of the Exchequer were supported by one other: that concerned with legal affairs. The senior member of it was the occupant of the Adusei Atwenewa (or later, Gyakye) counselor's stool. Overall administrative supervision of the group, however, was probably among the responsibilities of the Nkonsonhene, a post first created by the Asantehene Osei Kwadwo for his paternal half-brother Osei Tiri but not itself a coun-

[62] Rattray, 1927, p. 116, note.
[63] Rattray, 1929, p. 117.
[64] IASAS/41: Sanaa Stool History, 3 February 1963.
[65] Wilks, field-notes, interview with Kwaku Owusu and Kwadwo Nyantakyi II, dd. Kumase, 4 August 1965.
[66] *Ibid.* 'Buabasa' was a praise-name given to Opoku Frefre, but subsequently used by later Gyaasewahenes.

selorship.[67] Two further counselor's posts were established by Osei Kwame, and added to the group: the Akankade *okyeame* stool to which a son of Opoku Ware, Adu Twum, was appointed; [68] and the Boakye Yam Panin *okyeame* stool, which was given to Boakye Yam, a minor functionary who had acquired great wealth under Osei Kwadwo.[69] A fourth post was added to the group by Kwaku Dua I, who transferred the Boakye Yam Kuma stool from the Kyidom into the Gyaasewa and appointed his paternal half-brother Akyampon Tia – a son of Boakye Yam Kuma – to it as a junior counselor.[70] The Adusei Atwenewa or Gyakye counselor appears to have maintained a general brief for the legal affairs of the Exchequer and for matters of tribute, debt and the like which came before the Exchequer Court; the closeness of the relationship between the counselor Kwadwo Adusei Kyakya and his superior, the Gyaasewahene Opoku Frefre, has been alluded to above. The Boakye Yam Panin counselor, by contrast, was assigned more specific duties, and was responsible for the legal affairs of the Bata or State Traders.[71] The Akankade counselor appears to have been involved with the work of the Exchequer outside the financial sphere. And finally, the evidence suggests that the Boakye Yam Kuma counselor was concerned with the affairs of the Sanaa. A report is extant that the second counselor to hold the position, Akyampon Yaw, had been 'Chief Barber' to Kwaku Dua I; if this is not read to imply that he had been Debosohene, then at least it indicates his close association with the Abanase group of the Household.[72] Certainly the intimate nature of his connection with the Sanaa is not in doubt: in 1866 his son Kofi Boakye, no more than a youth, was found guilty of having slept with a wife of the Sanaahene Sanaa Poku, and Akyampon Yaw was obliged to pay 24 oz of gold in compensa-

67 IASAS/47: Nkonson Stool History, recorded by J. Agyeman-Duah, 17 March 1963.
68 Adu Twum had previously been Akyamfohene, head of the shield-bearers, see Kyerematen, 1966, pp. 328 ff.
69 IASAS/73: Boakye Yam Linguist Stool History, recorded by J. Agyeman-Duah, 6 June 1963. According to Bowdich, 1819, p. 319, at his death Boakye Yam left upwards of twenty gallons of gold dust, or, presumably, twenty flasks of about 1,000 peredwans each. If the figure is accurate, then his estate would have been valued at the contemporary rate of exchange at around £150,000 sterling. See also Bowdich, 1819, p. 254.
70 Wilks, field-notes, interviews with Nana Boakye Yam, dd. Kumase, 2–3 August 1965. See also IASAS/23: Boakye Yam Stool History, recorded by J. Agyeman-Duah, 3 March 1963.
71 Wilks, field-notes, interview with Asokwahene Kofi Poku, dd. Kumase, 3 August 1965; interview with Nana Boakye Tenten II, dd. Kumase, 3 August 1965.
72 *The African Times*, XII, no. 140, 23 February 1873, p. 97. The report refers to the 'Chief Barber' as 'the highest position any one can aspire to in Ashanti'. It has been seen that the Debosohene was the ranking official in the Abanase and, indeed, in the Household.

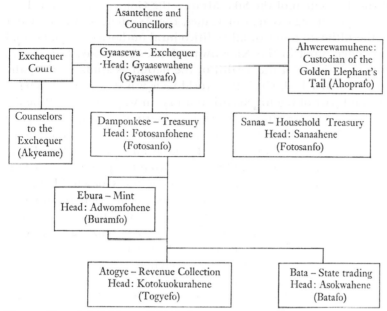

Fig. 13 Financial divisions of the Exchequer

tion.[73] Such trangressions of good form were no doubt unavoidable, and were dealt with summarily; breaches of professional ethics were a different matter. In 1817 no less a personage than Kwadwo Adusei Kyakya was accused of having accepted a bribe to misrepresent a case to be heard before the Asantehene. 'This coming to the King's ear', it was reported, 'he sent in a fury to Adoosee, who, on being charged with it, thought his life would be the forfeit, and sent an express to Apokoo [Opoku Frefre] to come and intercede for him; Apokoo being at his croom, it has been several times talked before the King, but no settlement, has taken place.' Opoku Frefre's hasty return to the capital saved his leading counselor from anything worse than a fine of 20 oz of gold and six or eight sheep. But 'notwithstanding his abilities', it was noted of the counselor, 'and that he takes his seat as usual, the King looks at him with a gloomy eye'.[74]

The basic structure of the financial divisions of the Exchequer is shown in Figure 13. The complexity of the organization must, however, be emphasized: its many ramifications require a full study in their own right. It must finally be noted, however, that underpinning the whole structure at a level of ritual and doctrine was the Ahwere-

---

[73] Instituut vorr Taal- Land- en Volkenkunde, Leiden MS H. 509, entry for 3 May 1866.
[74] Hutchison, in Bowdich, 1819, p. 393.

wamuhene, Custodian of the Sika Mmra – the Golden Elephant's Tail. Within the traditional system of values, the Asantehene was seen not only as the ultimate fount of all politico-jural authority as symbolized by the Golden Stool in the Nkonnwasoafohene's custody, but also as the ultimate assignee of the wealth of the nation as symbolized by the Golden Elephant's Tail. Until this world view was seriously challenged in the second part of the nineteenth century, in ways which will be described in Chapter 15, it was seen as a 'natural' feature of society that politico-jural authority flowed downwards from the Asantehene to the people under the Golden Stool, and as an equally 'natural' feature of society that wealth flowed upwards from the people (by various forms of taxation) to the Asantehene, under the Golden Elephant's Tail. One model of the good citizen was the *sikani,* that person who had accumulated wealth through his or her own efforts whether privately or in public service, but from which the state (especially through death duties) was ultimately to be the beneficiary. Those formally recognized by the Asantehene as *asikafo* (singular, *sikani*) were awarded the right to have a (real) elephant's tail carried before them as the mark of their achieved status, and these were borne by the *ahoprafo* – whose head was the Ahwerewamuhene and who were themselves children of men of rank and distinction.[75]

By the early nineteenth century the office of Gyaasewahene was clearly the most important within the central administration, for upon the efficient operation especially of the financial divisions of the Exchequer was predicated the very possibility of adequate government within the sprawling territories of Greater Asante. Opoku Frefre was seen by contemporary observers as 'the King's treasurer or gold keeper', 'Keeper of the Treasury', 'Overseer of the king's trade', and the like.[76] But the peculiar importance which came to be attached to the position stemmed from the fact that the Gyaasewahene was not only the ranking official within the central administration but was also one of the senior councillors of the Asantehene; he was member, that is, of both the legislative and executive branches of government. It followed, moreover, that as a councillor, in times of war he might assume high military command. Thus to others of his contemporaries, Opoku Frefre was known as 'the king's captain-general' and as 'the chief general of the army'.[77] Half a century later the situation looked remark-

75 The concept of the Sika Mmra, and the development of a nobility of wealth, are topics more fully explored in Wilks, 'The Golden Stool and the Elephant's Tail: the Emergence of the Asante Middle Class', forthcoming.

76 General State Archives, The Hague, KvG 350: Elmina Journal, Huydecoper to Daendels, dd. Kumase, 9 January 1817. Bowdich, 1819, pp. 113, 296.

77 Meredith, 1812, p. 167. Dupuis, 1824, p. 90. Compare Huydecoper's bewildered and somewhat confused remark, 'General Pokoe (that is, former General, for he is now the First Linguist'), see Huydecoper's Journal, entry for 22 May 1816.

ably similar, when the Gyaasewahene Adu Bofo, son of Opoku Frefre, could be described as 'keeper of the keys, treasurer, eventual commander of the army'.[78] It is some measure of the reliability of the many hundreds of *asomfo* who were skilled in the various operations of the financial divisions of the central administration, that the Gyaasewahene was able to undertake so wide a range of duties necessitating his frequent absence from the Exchequer, as councillor, and even for long periods of time from the capital, as field commander.

The Exchequer and the budgetary process

While the main sources of revenue to the Treasury in the nineteenth century can be identified with some confidence, it is not yet possible to rank these in order of magnitude nor indeed to quantify the available data in any satisfactory manner. Undoubtedly, however, one of the most important sources of revenue in the early nineteenth century were the tributes, and it will be seen that as these diminished when political control over some of the southern provinces was relinquished in 1831, so adherents of the war party argued that the loss of income must prove disastrous to the finances of the nation. Any attempt to make even a gross computation of the value of the tributes in the nineteenth century must inevitably fail since many assessments were under continuous review in the light of general budgetary requirements, and appeals could be made to the Exchequer Court and adjustments obtained (see p. 396). From many areas, moreover, tributes were levied in goods, and there is obviously considerable difficulty in computing the real value to the Treasury of a tax of, for example, two hundred head of cattle or three hundred bags of snails. Three known figures for the late 1810s, which were apparently not subject to constant fluctuation, may be recapitulated. The small outer province of Bonzina paid 100 oz of gold annually, the larger inner province of Sehwi, 450 oz, and the British African Company, 72 oz:[79] a total of 622 oz from the three sources alone.

At the risk of grave inaccuracy, an attempt may be made to compute the annual value of the tributes from the two large northern provinces of Gonja and Dagomba. Bowdich is quite specific, that their capitals and each of their large towns were required to pay 500 slaves, 200 cows, 400 sheep, and a quantity of cloth annually.[80] From what has been described of the situation later in the century (Chapter 2, pp. 64–71), it is reasonable to suppose that such tributes from Dagomba were

[78] Ramseyer and Kühne, 1875, p. 308.
[79] Bowdich, 1819, p. 321. Hutton, 1821, p. 235.
[80] Bowdich, 1819, pp. 320–1.

431

paid at least by Yendi and the three major divisional towns of Savelugu, Mion, and Karaga, and from Gonja by at least Yagbum and the
five major divisional towns of Bole, Daboya, Kong, Kpembe and
Tuluwe. Ignoring the tribute in cloth, the magnitude of the total
revenues from the two provinces in question was of the order of
5,000 slaves, 2,000 cows, and 4,000 sheep annually. The current price
set by the Exchequer Court in the period upon the value of man slaves
was twenty for 16 oz of gold.[81] A fat bullock, sold by Treasury agents
on the Kumase market, would realize 1½ oz of gold, and sheep fetched
about 1 oz for five.[82] On the basis of such highly imperfect figures, an
annual value of the order of 7,800 oz would seem indicated. Even,
however, if such a figure is considerably reduced to a more conservative one, the importance of the northern provinces in fiscal terms is
apparent. Certainly some explanation suggests itself of why Kwaku
Dua I was prepared to keep an army in the field for three years, from
1841 to 1844 – an extremely costly operation since it had presumably
for the most part to be provisioned from Kumase [83] – in order to restore political order in the western and central Gonja divisions (see
Chapter 7).

Bowdich reported that the Gyaasewahene 'has care of all the tributes,
which are deposited, separately . . .' [84] The implications of his observation are unclear, but it is possible that at least part of the tribute
from each province was deposited in a distinct *apem adaka* and that
the level of tribute required from a particular province could thus
always be adjusted to the expenditure on it. The costs of suppressing
rebellion, for example, might thus be made to fall upon the province or provinces involved, and not upon general revenue. If such was
the case, then the method of depositing tributes in the Damponkese
was the financial component of the ɔhwɛso system. It has been seen
that resident commissioners, the *amradofo,* were stationed in the
major towns of Greater Asante as representatives of government. They
were directly responsible to the central administration. It was the
practice, however, also to assign to various stools in Kumase a special
relationship with particular provinces or districts. The official in the
capital became ɔhwɛfo (plural, *ahwɛfo*) or overseer of the province. In
the early nineteenth century, for example, the Gyaasewahene was
overseer of Akwamu, the Asafohene of Denkyira, and the Adontenhene
of Daboya.[85] In the first half of the eighteenth century the *ahwɛfo* had

81 *Ibid.* p. 296.
82 *Ibid.* p. 324. Bowdich made conversions at £4 to the ounce of gold.
83 Methodist Mission Archives, London: Chapman to General Secretaries, dd.
 Kumase, 21 June 1844.
84 Bowdich, 1819, p. 296.
85 Bowdich, 1819, p. 235.

apparently been fully responsible for the affairs of the provinces, but under Osei Kwadwo and his successors much of their work was taken over by the new administrators, the *amradofo,* the *togyefo,* and so forth. In the nineteenth century the overseers continued to serve as *adamfo* or patrons to the local provincial rulers: when they attended the annual Odwira, or were otherwise summoned to Kumase, the *ɔhwɛfo* would act as host to the visitor and generally superintend his business there. More importantly, however, it was apparently the case that the tribute collected from a given province by the *togyefo* was first received by the appropriate overseer in Kumase before being paid into the Treasury.[86] But if the tribute failed to arrive and the province was found to be in a state of rebellion, then it was the duty of the relevant overseer to arrange the necessary military operations. He was responsible for financing the expedition, for which purpose he would hope to be able to draw sufficient funds from the tribute boxes but might have to make loans from the Kumase financiers.[87] But in any case, a counselor would accompany the expedition and, after order had been restored, would proceed to fix the indemnity to be paid by the rebels, from which the expenses of the campaign would be recouped. 'One of the king's linguists', Bowdich noted, 'always accompanies an army of any consequence, to whom all the politics of war are entrusted, and whose talent and intelligence in negotiating, are expected to mature the fruits of the military genius of the generals, and to reimburse the expense of the war by heavy fines and contributions.' [88]

While, then, it appears likely that the tributes were handled as a separate account for budgetary purposes, it is not yet possible to arrive at any figure for annual revenue under this particular head. The same is unfortunately true of the income derived from the poll taxes levied within the metropolitan area, since for the greater part of the nineteenth century these were imposed according to the exigencies of the general financial situation. It has been suggested above, however, that towards the end of the century the various taxes may have been consolidated into one annual head-tax payable before Odwira (see p. 70). An approximate computation of the yield can be made. The tax was fixed at $\frac{1}{10}$ oz of gold per married man. The category is one broadly congruent with that of men able to bear arms, and reference

---

[86] *Idem.*

[87] See the case of Yaw Sekyere, reported in *Royal Gold Coast Gazette,* 21 January, 25 March, 21 May, 21 June, and 22 November 1823.

[88] Bowdich, 1819, p. 33. Compare Bowdich, 1821a, p. 19: 'no Ashantee army ever proceeds on a campaign without one of them [the counselors] being attached to it, and if the king is present, three or four, to settle the tributes, to make "the great laws" (treaties), and to try and condemn enemies or rebels at the moment of their falling into their power'.

to chapter 3, pages 87–91, will suggest 120,000 as a relevant figure for the number of persons within the category. On such a basis, then, the Odwira tax would have yielded 12,000 oz. Of that sum, however, only three-sevenths – or somewhat over 5,100 oz – accrued to the Treasury in Kumase.[89]

It is clear that duty was levied on the commodities carried by private traders at the various *nkwansrafo* posts through which they passed. Bowdich referred specifically, for example, to the 'customs paid in gold by all traders returning from the coast, levied near Ansa in Assin'.[90] According to one of Rattray's elderly informants, who had been a trader in the late nineteenth century, the duty on the load, on the routes to the coast, was then fixed at '3s to 4s worth of gold-dust'[91] – presumably the much used weight known as *domafa*. The same informant asserted that kola traders on the northern roads were taxed twenty-five nuts on the load of about two thousand, the value of the load then varying between 5s and 10s according to the season.[92] Clearly no estimate of the total revenues from duties can be offered. It is perhaps appropriate at this point to allude again to the revenue derived from the fines (*nsumen*) collected from those causing nuisances on the roads, that is, failing to keep the ways cleared. Though the source of his information is unknown, Reindorf indicated that the revenue from the source might approximate to 3,000 peredwans annually, one-third of which (or 2,250 oz) accrued to the central government.[93] Since the penalty for a nuisance was set at one *domafa,* the implication is that granting the reliability of the figure, of the order of 140,000 such fines were imposed in the year! Of the various other forms of personal taxation which were permitted under Asante law, death duties (*awunyadie*) were by far the most important and 'gave to the monarchy', as Bonnat remarked, 'immense strength and immeasurable riches'.[94] The taxation of estates upon death will be discussed in Chapter 15.

Not all Treasury income was derived from taxes and tributes, for

89 A brief description of the method of collecting taxes in the metropolitan region in the early part of the reign of Kwaku Dua I was given in Beecham, 1841, pp. 115–16, with reference to Adanse. 'Every captain or subordinate chief', he wrote, 'gives up, in the form of a tax, a certain portion of his income to his superior; and he, again, pays a tax to the king. While Mr. [T. B.] Freeman was detained at Fomunah, he frequently saw the captains of Korinchi [Adansehene Kwantwi] bring their respective quotas, amounting from one toku, value five-pence, to four tokus; but by what rules these payments were regulated, he did not ascertain.' It seems clear that the taxes were paid to the Adansehene twice in each Asante month at the two Adaes.
90 Bowdich, 1819, p. 320.
91 Rattray, 1929, p. 111.
92 *Ibid.* pp. 109–10.
93 Reindorf, 2nd ed., n.d., p. 131.
94 Gros, 1884, p. 194. Compare Bowdich, 1819, pp. 254 and 319.

the state was a major participant in the organization of production and trade for revenue purposes. Little is known of the ivory industry, which was not of major importance in Asante. Bowdich noted that a tax was imposed upon private elephant hunters,[95] but Dupuis' passing reference to 'hunters of elephants in the king's name, and on his account'[96] may indicate that there was a level of state involvement in the enterprise. It was, however, in the gold industry that the participation of the state was the most apparent. Among the principal sources of Treasury revenues Bowdich included 'the daily washings throughout Dankara, and the hills dividing Akim and Assin; very rich in gold'.[97] Recent investigations in the former area have revealed the presence of numerous shafts sunk into the gravels of the Jimi River. From them, dredging operations produced many objects from *foto* bags: scales, scoops and weights. That not only digging and washing, but also weighing, operations were carried out at the river suggests at least the possibility that Treasury officials visited the workings in person, to take possession of the yields.[98] Bowdich referred also to a second major area of production for the Treasury: 'the small pits in Soko, which with the washings were reported to yield, sometimes 2,000 ounces per month, at others not more than 700'.[99] The allusion is to Nsoko (Route II, mile 110), and to the rich auriferous region drained by the Tain River and its tributaries between Routes I and II. Each of the small chiefdoms in the district was closely administered from Kumase. The overseer or ɔhwɛfo of Nsoko itself, for example, was the Kumase Adumhene, who was also responsible for Hani to the west; of Namasa near Hani, the Akyɛmpɛmhene of Kumase; and of Branam, northeast of Nsoko, the Dadiesoabahene.[100] Although in view of its proximity to Bonduku, Dupuis wrongly assumed the region to be part of Gyaman, he also learned of the intense activity there. 'During the season of the rain', he reported, 'my informants relate, there is occupation for eight or ten thousand slaves for two months; and the metal they collect, added to the produce of the pits . . . now finds its way to Ashantee'.[101] It is possible to make a tentative estimate of pro-

95 Bowdich, 1819, p. 320.
96 Dupuis, 1824, pp. cviii–cix.
97 Bowdich, 1819, p. 320.
98 I am indebted to Dr James O. Bellis for his description of the Jimi River sites.
99 Bowdich, 1819, p. 320.
100 The first resident commissioner at Branam is remembered as having been Tano Agyei of Dadiesoaba, Kumase, who established his headquarters at the new town of Nwase some time in the second part of the eighteenth century. He was succeeded in turn by Kwasi Dagyaw. See Institute of African Studies, Ghana, IAS/BA/3: Nwase-Branam Tradition, recorded by Kwabena Ameyaw, 16 February 1965.
101 Dupuis, 1824, p. lvii. Dupuis named the stream on which the miners worked as the Barra, but, wrongly identifying the Tain with the Tano, assumed it to be a tributary of the latter.

duction. In the nineteenth century a slave washing for gold, presumably on a rewarding stretch of river, might be expected to win to the value of not less than 1s 6d a day, rising to 3s or even 5s.[102] Taking then the most conservative figures, valuing gold at £3 12s the ounce and placing output at 1s 6d *per diem,* a labour force of 8,000 might be expected to wash 5,000 oz per month during the season. While a basis for the comparison of Bowdich's and Dupuis' sets of data does not exist, it will be apparent that they are not necessarily discrepant. The great importance of these goldfields to the central government is reflected in the fact that the whole area remained, in this century, a part of the Kumase division as such although incorporated by the British into the Wankyi District for purely administrative purposes.[103]

There were, however, other and ancient workings much nearer Kumase. In the Oweri Valley in Asante Akyem for example, open-cut mining on the reefs, with banking and benching to a depth of some 200 feet, was practised at least from the early eighteenth century onwards, and a number of the mines came to be controlled directly by the Exchequer; a study of the Oweri Valley industry is in course of preparation by the writer. Late in the nineteenth century, moreover, the dependence upon alluvial mining probably lessened further as improvements occurred in mining technology. Perhaps under Mensa Bonsu, but certainly under Agyeman Prempe I, new mines were opened southwest of the capital. Most famous of these was the 'King Prempe's Mine' – *Nana Prempɛ Nkoron.* When after 1896, and with some difficulty, the British finally located it, to their surprise they found it to have been worked on advanced principles: the reef had been followed into the hillside for 250 to 300 feet, and the galleries (timbered throughout their length) measured 7 feet by 9 feet.[104] The mine subsequently became part of the Nkwanta Concession granted by the Gold Coast government to Claude's Ashanti Goldfields Ltd. Situated between Manso Nkwanta and Essuowin, the first European company to operate it did so under the name 'King Prempeh's Treasure Mine, Ltd'.[105]

One final source of revenue which was of major importance to the central Treasury were the profits made by its own commercial agents. While the ultimate origin of the public traders is doubtless to be found

---

102 Bowler, 1911, pp. 101–2. Another report states that slaves washing the rivers would produce between $\frac{1}{2}$ and 1 pennyweight a day, that is, between about 1s 9d and 3s 6d, see *The African Times,* xxxvii, no. 421, 1 October 1896, but having reference to *ca.* 1881.

103 See, for example, *The Gold Coast Chiefs List,* 1941.

104 Armitage and Montanaro, 1901, p. 239.

105 Junner, 1935, p. 36. For traditional mining in the Manso Nkwanta district, see Arhin, 1970c, *passim.* For the antiquity of the industry there, see p. 20.

in the eighteenth century, it appears to have been in the reign of Osei Bonsu that an organization began to develop capable in time of challenging the dominant position which the private traders had hitherto enjoyed. It was indicative of the change which was occurring, that in the mid-1810s Osei Bonsu was engaged in negotiating preferential terms for the *batafo* with the European merchant establishments on the Gold Coast.[106] The central government had acquired no legal powers to interfere in the marketing operations of the private traders,[107] but by 1820 the prestige of the latter was clearly on the wane. After the Asantemanhyiamu, on 6 November 1817, had taken the decision to invade Gyaman in two months' time, the state traders were directed to the Gold Coast to procure supplies. The stock of rum, gunpowder and cloth which the British held in Cape Coast, so it was reported, 'was metamorphosed into gold dust in the lapse of a few days only'. Dupuis drew the distinction between these transactions and those of the private traders. 'These', he wrote, 'were benefits conferred by the court alone. In regard to the inferior classes of traders, they, not being bound by the royal restrictions, speculated freely and sought their own markets, either with the officers of [Cape Coast] castle, or among the free merchants in the town'.[108] The massive expansion of the Company of State Traders, the Bata Fekuo, under Kwaku Dua I is discussed in Chapter 15. It was customary for payments from the Treasury to public traders to be made monthly, at the Great Adae. It is some indication of the expansion which occurred in the course of the nineteenth century, that in 1817 Bowdich reported that about 40 peredwans of gold was disbursed each Adae; [109] but by the end of the century the many 'Mercantile Agents of the King' *each* received between 500 and 1,000 peredwans annually.[110] While no estimate of the profits derived by the Treasury from the activities of the public traders can be made, these were clearly very substantial even after the costs of transportation had been met. According to Hutton, the profits made by goods purchased on the Gold Coast by Asante traders, and retailed in Kumase, ranged from 100% to 400%.[111]

The major sources of revenue may thus be identified, but their magnitudes cannot satisfactorily be quantified. On the basis of the few figures which have been presented, the writer might speculate that the annual revenue of the central government for much of the nineteenth century was not less than 20,000 peredwans and probably not

---

106 Huydecoper's Journal, entry for 9 January 1817.
107 Bowdich, 1819, p. 257.
108 Dupuis, 1824, Introduction, pp. ix–x.
109 Bowdich, 1819, p. 282.
110 *The Gold Coast Aborigines*, XVI, no. 115, 30 June 1900, p. 3.
111 Hutton, 1821, pp. 332–3.

more than 50,000: that is, perhaps between £160,000 and £400,000 on
the nineteenth century rate of conversion. Despite the size of the
bracket, however, any such estimate must remain both highly impres-
sionistic and highly tentative. Yet the question of revenues must remain one of critical importance for the analysis of the major differences of policy which were to develop between the imperialists and
mercantilists in the course of the nineteenth century, since the latter
maintained that any loss of revenue on the tribute account resulting
from the relinquishment of control over certain of the southern provinces would be more than offset by the increase of revenues on the
trade account.

The difficulties which present themselves when any attempt is made
to analyse the structure of government income become even more apparent in the investigation of expenditure. It is likely that defence,
including internal security, constituted one of the major charges upon
the Treasury though payments under this head must have varied
greatly from year to year.[112] Some data on the costs of maintaining in
the field a national army are extant. On 22 October 1872 members of
the Asantemanhyiamu took the decision to carry out a reoccupation
of the British Protected Territory of the Gold Coast. The force which
took the field early in December was one probably of over 60,000 men
(see p. 82). A year later, on 27 October 1873, the Council met in
Kumase to debate the future of the operations, and the Asantehene
announced that the costs of the campaign to date were estimated at
6,000 peredwans, or about £48,000 at the then current rate of exchange.[113] No breakdown of the expenditure is available, but it is
assumed that the sum was paid from the Damponkese and not the
Sanaa since the latter was seemingly much run down at the time.[114]
Comparable figures for other campaigns have not been found, and it
has been noted above that many of the lesser campaigns in suppression
of rebellion and dissent were financed within the framework of
the ɔhwɛso system. Such campaigns, in theory at least, would constitute no charge upon general revenues (though it is difficult to
believe that the costs of the northern campaigns of 1841–4, which
escalated far beyond initial expectations, had not to be underwritten from the general fund). One other set of figures does exist,
however, the precise relevance of which must remain undecided. A national army, which was accompanied by the Asantehene Osei Yaw in
person, occupied the southeastern provinces in 1826. It comprised

112 See Ramseyer and Kühne, 1875, p. 171, who commented (not entirely accurately)
 that Kwaku Dua I had only undertaken one war during his long reign and 'had
 therefore collected more money than any of his predecessors'.
113 *Ibid.* p. 243.
114 *Ibid.* p. 184. See also Boyle, 1874, pp. 275–6.

probably upwards of 40,000 men in all (see p. 183), and carried a very substantial amount of gold. After its defeat at Katamanso, the British made an immediate estimate of the value of the booty taken from the Asante as £½ million.[115] The presumption is that the figure was greatly exaggerated, but remarkable confirmation of it comes from Djang. Writing of the spoils collected by the rebel troops from the baggage so precipitously abandoned by the Asante, he reported:

These were great and valuable, and consisted of the Royal chest of Osei with gold nugget weighing over 20,000 oz, including several pots of gold dust also weighing nearly 30,000 oz. of gold; in addition to which were the treasures of the captains chiefs and sub-chiefs, the values of booties left in the field of Akantamansu by the Ashantis was over 90,000 oz of gold estimated approximately at £450,000.[116]

The implications of the account seem clear, that the campaign of 1826 was underwritten by the Treasury to the extent of at least 13,000 peredwans (29,250 oz) of gold dust – taking no account of what might already have been spent – and of nugget gold to the value of 9,000 peredwans (20,250 oz) which could be sold on the coast if needed. Had these sums been totally expended, as indeed in a sense they were, then the cost of the campaign was approximately equivalent to the figure tentatively suggested above for minimum gross annual income. The disastrous losses at Katamanso were to provide the spokesmen for the peace interest in the capital with an especially persuasive argument against further ventures of a similar nature.

Another major charge upon the Treasury were the costs of the central administration itself. It should be emphasized that the executive branch of the government was the largest employer within the nation. The Exchequer alone gave work (though not necessarily on a full-time basis) to several thousands of people, ranging from the senior officials within the highest echelons of the organization to, for example, the porters of the Bata within the lowest. But other of the administrative agencies also employed many men, for example, the *dawurufo* or gong-beaters who publicized governmental decrees throughout the towns and villages of Asante; [117] the *afenasoafo* or swordbearers who constantly

115 *Royal Gazette and Sierra Leone Advertiser*, Extraordinary Issue, 9 October 1826, reporting despatches of 7 August.
116 Djang, 1926, pp. 78–9. The source of Djang's very detailed information on Katamanso has not been identified, but may have been a nineteenth century Twi one. Compare also Reindorf, 2nd ed., n.d., p. 276, who referred to the loss of 'the public treasury chest' at Katamanso.
117 The Dawurufohene was a subordinate of the Nseniehene, who also presided over the *nseniefo* or heralds. The Nseniehene is said to have had one thousand functionaries in his charge, see IASAS/81: Nsenie Stool History, recorded by J. Agyeman-Duah, 4 July 1963.

travelled the roads maintaining communication between the central authorities and the outlying districts and provinces; and the *nkwansrafo* who maintained control over the movement of travellers along the roads and the *akwanmofo* who had to keep those roads passable. The composition of a mission sent to Cape Coast early in 1820 is instructive. Entrusted with delicate negotiations with the British, it was reported to have 'entered the place with a degree of military splendour unknown there since the conquest of Fantee by the king'. Its leader was a son of the Asantehene Osei Kwame, Owusu Dome of the Kumase torchbearers or Atene, who 'had been dignified by his sovereign, with a commision that qualified him to decide for peace or war upon the spot, and to act accordingly'.[118] Owusu Dome was attended in his suite by several subordinate officers including the counselor Ano Panin [119] and two Muslim scribes, and by 1,200 retainers, 500 of whom were soldiers and the remainder bearers and servants of one sort or another.[120] Large as it was, the size of the mission was by no means exceptional under a government which placed great reliance upon the negotiation of disputes.[121]

No adequate data have yet been compiled on the financing of the complex and varied operations of the administration. Basically, however, it appears that the procedure followed was to provide officials with working capital from the Treasury appropriate to their needs.[122] Upon completion of a commission, the capital sum was repaid to the Treasury presumably after deduction of expenses, and at the same time any profits made, or revenues collected, were surrendered after the functionary had taken his own fees in accordance with fixed scales of remuneration. Certainly the public traders in the later part of the nineteenth century worked within just such a system,[123] and that it was already operative in the earlier part of the century is perhaps implied by Bowdich's interesting description of the concession made to newly appointed office holders, of being lent gold repayable only after several years:

It is a frequent practice of the King's, to consign sums of gold to the care of rising captains, without requiring them from them for two or three years, at the end of which time he expects the captain not only to restore the principal,

118 Dupuis, 1824, Introduction, pp. xxiv–xxv and xxviii.
119 Ano Panin ('Endo') was an Adanse who had settled in Kumase, had served in the *adumfo* or executioners, and had taken part in a mission to Gyaman prior to the 1818 invasion. Osei Bonsu subsequently created for him a new counselor's post, that of *okyeame* to the Ananta. See IASAS/142: Ano Panin Linguist Stool History, recorded by J. Agyeman-Duah, 23 November 1964.
120 Dupuis, 1824, Introduction, p. xxviii. Hutton, 1821, pp. 128–9, 324.
121 Dupuis, 1824, pp. 225–6.
122 See, e.g. Hutchison, in Bowdich, 1819, p. 404.
123 Casely Hayford, 1903, p. 96.

but to prove that he has acquired sufficient of his own, from the use of it, to support the greater dignity the King would confer on him. If he has not, his talent is thought too mean for further elevation.[124]

Bowdich reported that revenue collectors, the *togyefo*, were entitled to a fee of at least 15 oz of gold for every 100 oz collected.[125] Elsewhere he asserted that the collectors received two peredwans out of every ten collected.[126] The former figure is equivalent to a commission of approximately 13%, and the latter to one of 20%. In the late nineteenth century the collectors were reported to have been awarded one-seventh of the revenue, or just over 14%.[127] The precise percentage was probably related to the rank of the functionary in charge of the task, and perhaps to its intrinsic formidability. Two cases from 1817 appear to bear this out. When Adu Brade, son of an Asantehene, was appointed to collect a fine from the Komenda, he received 30 oz out of the 150 oz, a commission of 20%.[128] By contrast, the more junior collectors who received a fine of 250 oz of gold from Aggrey of Cape Coast received 40 oz, that is, 16%.[129] According to Reindorf, the *akwanmofo* – whose onerous work necessitated constant travelling – were entitled to the still higher figure of 33⅓% of the fines which they made.[130] One final detail may be mentioned. In the early nineteenth century the Nseniehene Kwadwo Ampan was said to have been entitled to a fee from the Asantehene of 10 ackies, or five-eighths of an ounce of gold, for publicizing a government decree in the capital, and to have received also 20 ackies 'from the people'.[131] Presumably the *dawurufo* who performed the same function in the outlying towns and villages were remunerated in a similar manner though on a lower scale.

The economic life of the Asante capital and its surrounding district showed certain marked characteristics to which allusion should be made. First, prices of virtually all commodities were extraordinarily high. Reference has been made to the fact that goods bought on the Gold Coast were retailed in Kumase at from 100% to 400% above the purchase price.[132] Detailed analysis of actual prices will show that in fact the range of profit margins was rather more flexible than those

---

124 Bowdich, 1819, p. 295.
125 Bowdich, 1821a, p. 27.
126 Bowdich, 1819, p. 255.
127 Kumase Divisional Council archives, Manhyia: Agyeman Prempe I to District Commissioner, Kumase, dd. 26 October 1927.
128 Bowdich, 1819, pp. 87–8, 101, 113, 121.
129 PRO, T. 70/41: Osei Bonsu to Governor, Cape Coast, dd. Kumase, 1 October 1817.
130 Reindorf, 2nd ed., n.d., p. 131.
131 Bowdich, 1819, p. 256.
132 Hutton, 1821, pp. 332–3.

Table 18 *Comparative prices in Cape Coast and Kumase, 1817*

Commodity	Measure	Cape Coast prices			Kumase prices			Profits
		£	s	d	£	s	d	%
India silk	Piece	4	0	0	11	0	0	175
Sarstracunda	Piece	1	10	0	7	10	0	400
Glasgow dane	Piece	1	10	0	2	12	6	75
Romal	Piece	1	0	0	1	5	0	25
Guinea stuff	Piece		10	0		15	0	50
Silesia cloth	Piece		10	0		15	0	50
Rum	Gallon		10	0	2	10	0	400
Portuguese tobacco	Roll	6	0	0	10	0	0	66⅔
Gunpowder	¼-barrel	4	0	0	20	0	0	400
Iron	Bar	1	0	0	1	15	0	75
Lead	Bar		10	0		17	6	75
Flints	Hundred		5	0	1	15	0	600

figures suggest (though the average price differential between the
coast and Kumase was indeed about 200% over a wide range of commodities). Reference to Table 18, which is based upon data given
by Bowdich,[133] will show that profit margins were highest on goods
for which no local substitutes existed, such as Indian silk, Sarstracunda,
rum, gunpowder and flints, and lowest on inferior cloth, iron, and
lead. The situation with respect to importations from the northern
markets was very similar. Table 19 is also based upon Bowdich,[134] and
shows that profits were high upon livestock and foodstuffs, and especially on beef and yam, but lower upon cloth and other manufactured
goods. There can, then, be no doubt that the cost of living in central
Asante was very high compared with that both on the coast to the
south and in the savannahs to the north.[135]

Those working within the higher echelons of the administration
were clearly well remunerated. They, together with the successful private businessmen – traders, moneylenders, and the like – formed a
wealthy class, the *asikafo,* the most prominent members of which were
those awarded the distinction of having an elephant's tail carried before them. Yet Bowdich remarked upon the extraordinary cheapness
of labour. 'So disproportionate was the price of labour to that of

133 Bowdich, 1819, p. 331. Certain re-calculations have been made in the interests of
increased comparability, and in some cases of accuracy. The coast prices may be
compared with those given by Hutton, 1821, pp. 465–70. The prices are here
calculated at £4 the ounce of gold.
134 Bowdich, 1819, pp. 324, 331.
135 Indeed, comparison of the price data from Kumase with those from other large
centres such as Kano or Timbuktu suggests that Kumase probably had one
of the highest costs of living in West Africa, at least in the early nineteenth
century.

Table 19 *Comparative prices in Salaga and Yendi, and Kumase, 1817*

Commodity	Measure	Salaga/ Yendi prices			Kumase prices			Profits
		£	s	d	£	s	d	%
Fezzan silk	Piece	1	0	0	2	0	0	100
Dagomba cotton cloth	Sq. yard		2	6		5	0	100
Gonja tobacco	Pound		1	0		2	6	150
Sandals	Pair		5	0		10	0	100
Cushions	Each		10	0	1	0	0	100
Hausa locks	Each		2	6		5	0	100
Fat bullock	Each	1	0	0	6	0	0	500
Sheep	Each		4	0		15	0	275
Fowl	Each			5		1	8	200
Horse	Each	8	0	0	24	0	0	200
Yams	Ten			8		3	4	400

provision', he wrote, 'that I gave but two tokoos [about 1s.] for a slab of cotton wood, five feet by three.' [136] The distinction between rich and poor, between *asikafo* and *ahiafo,* was in fact one all too apparent to those who visited the capital. While, for example, polygamy was the rule among the former, the freemen among the *ahiafo* seldom had more than one wife and the slaves remained for the most part unmarried.[137] While the 'higher orders' enjoyed a diet of dried fish, fowls, beef and mutton, the 'poorer classes' lived on stews made from dried deer, monkey, and animal pelts.[138] Unlike their superiors who were 'nice and clean', the 'poorer sort of Ashantees and slaves' were neglectful of personal hygiene.[139] Every town house, it was said, 'had its cloacae, besides the common ones for the lower orders without the town'.[140] The political consequences of the uneven distribution of wealth will be discussed in Chapter 15; clearly, however, retail prices were such that many of the goods which found their way on to the Kumase market were beyond the reach of numerous citizens.

Bowdich apparently regarded the Asante economy as an inflationary one in the early nineteenth century. 'The surprising exorbitance', he remarked with reference to Kumase prices, 'is to be accounted for by the abundance of gold, yet labour and manufacture was moderately purchased.' [141] He appears, in other words, to have accepted the classical quantity theory of money, that its purchasing power is directly related to the amount of money in the economy; and accordingly to

136 Bowdich, 1819, p. 306.
137 *Ibid.* p. 317.
138 *Ibid.* p. 319.
139 *Ibid.* pp. 318, 376.
140 *Ibid.* p. 306.
141 *Ibid.* p. 324.

have identified the continuous expansion of money (gold dust) in Asante as the cause of the high prices there. While adequate data are lacking, it may be that prices had moved sharply upwards in the early part of the nineteenth century, as the state traders came increasingly to dominate the commercial sector of the economy. But there is no evidence to support the view that the economy was in fact an inflationary one. The level of prices in Kumase presumably resulted from determinate policies evolved within the Exchequer in accordance with general policy, first, to work towards the goal of creating a near monopoly of trade for the state, and second, thereby to stimulate the flow of money from the private purchaser to the Treasury by price fixing. At the same time it appears also to have been policy to restrict the availability of private loan capital: in 1817 the interest rate was set at 33⅓% per month of forty-two days.[142] Not surprisingly, the merchants on the Gold Coast, who knew perfectly well the prices which goods were fetching in Kumase, had been able to appraise the situation accurately and attempted to turn it to their own advantage by increasing the cost of goods to public as opposed to private traders. Suspecting what was happening, Osei Bonsu sent public traders to Cape Coast incognito: without, that is, their insignia of office. He was incensed by what he learned. 'Is it thus', he asked,

the governor shews his friendship for me, charging me an ounce of gold for an anker of rum, or a keg of powder; six ackies for a romal, an ounce for a piece of taffety silk, and all the other goods at the same high prices? . . . God made white and black men: he loves all men; he does not say they must not be friends because they differ in colour. White men read books, and know the great God, therefore the blacks say, these are strong people; their fetische is good. This is true, but then they must not do evil. Now when I send gold to Cape Coast to buy goods, and the governor does not know it, so I buy powder at two and three kegs to the ounce, and three ankers of rum to the ounce, and seven ackies for the best guns, and I get one hundred bars of lead for two ounces . . . I think a white man cannot do this; therefore I say to my captains, See what the Fantees do; they cheat me, and dishonour the English governor. Then my captains take up the sword, and swear they must march to the water side, and live in the towns. But I do not want to kill old men and women and children for their gold, as my soldiers do, I prefer friendship.[143]

The traditional Asante view of wealth, it has been suggested, was one of its natural flow upwards in society, from the producer to the Sika Dwa or Golden Stool. The Sika Mmra, or Golden Elephant's Tail, was ritual token of this view. In this light, the development of mercan-

142 *Ibid.* p. 257.
143 Dupuis, 1824, pp. 123–5.

tilism in nineteenth century Asante may be seen as involving the creation of new instruments for the fuller achievement of that state of society. Money – gold dust – was equated with wealth (to the exclusion of, for example, agricultural production). Wealth was equated with power. The greatness of the Asante nation was therefore to be measured in terms of its wealth: by the size of its Great Chest. Exchequer policy, consequently, was to be directed towards the maintenance and stimulation of the flows of money upwards within society, from the people to the Great Chest whether by taxation or through the control of production and commerce. But with a full Treasury the government would, in turn, be able to pursue without impediment those policies determined to be the most conducive to the well-being of its citizenry.

The politics of mercantilism will be discussed more fully in Chapter 15. It is perhaps some measure of the relevance of the system to the Asante circumstances, that in the period in which it was temporarily abandoned (see pp. 193–8), the economy showed distinct signs of stress: shortages became endemic, and inflation (this time with little doubt) rampant. In April 1842, for example, food was reported in very short supply in Kumase, and even locally grown plantains were almost unobtainable. Foodstuffs which did find their way on to the market were 'vastly overpriced'.[144] Even after the government had taken the decision in 1844 to revitalize the Bata and to afford it full protection against the coastal traders, the economy remained for a time stricken. In 1845 so acute were the shortages of the essentials of life that most of the townsfolk of Kumase had left it for the countryside.[145]

The central administration: patterns of recruitment and promotion

Bowdich reported that the Asantehene Osei Bonsu 'is considered to take better care of the treasury than any of his predecessors', and specifically attributed the improvement to the Asantehene's policy towards recruitment and promotion: 'he cautiously extends his prerogative, and takes every opportunity of increasing the number of secondary captains, by dignifying the young men brought up about his person, and still retaining them in his immediate service'.[146] In fact, as in so many other respects, Osei Bonsu appears to have been pursuing a policy initiated by Osei Kwadwo, of whose reign Bowdich himself

144 Methodist Mission Archives: Brooking to Freeman, dd. Kumase, 29 April 1842. But compare Pel, n.d., p. 22.
145 Methodist Mission Archives: Chapman to General Secretaries, dd. Kumase, 31 March 1845.
146 Bowdich, 1819, p. 246.

noted: 'the Aristocracy was retrenched and conciliated by this monarch, who raised his favourite captains to the vacant stools, uniting three or four in one . . .' [147] Elsewhere Bowdich made reference to 'the aristocracy in Ashantee; who, until Sai Cudjo's time, always acquired this dignity by inheritance only'.[148] The view of Osei Kwadwo, as the first ruler to emphasize as credentials for office qualifications other than descent, was one which was to persist. Referring to 'the system first adopted over a hundred years ago, by Sai Cudjo', an anonymous writer in the 1880s pointed out that, 'the Ashantees acknowledge the advantage of encouraging every virtue, the direction of which is to advance the interest of the country, by enlisting among the nobility any person who distinguishes himself in the patriotic display of every such virtue'.[149]

The change which was taking place was clearly one which greatly augmented the power of the Asantehene, who acquired the right to appoint persons to an increasing number of offices, or at the very least to exercise a right of veto over those chosen and presented to him by stool electors. Thus as an Asante informant explained to Robertson, 'the King, with the consent of the Senate, collects and disposes of the national wealth; hence he raises armies, and prompts all other public measures; appointments to public offices are also in his gift'.[150] The way in which successive rulers chose to exercise their right of appointment would largely determine the quality of the administration with which they had to work. Osei Bonsu, as Bowdich remarked, used his prerogative 'cautiously'. Kofi Kakari, by contrast, patently used his powers of appointment for his personal ends. 'He seemed to wish to raise his position', it was said, 'by elevating that of his friends'.[151] Although Kühne pointed out that a knowledge of the Inner Court had been denied him during his long stay in Kumase, he believed that the hereditary title-holders in the capital had totally lost 'their privileges and immunities'. The Asantehene, he maintained,

is now a despot, restrained only by his natural fear of a turbulent and warlike people. He raises and degrades from the highest to the lowest rank, at pleasure. Amanquattiah himself [the Bantamahene] is a mere creature of the king, whose ancestry no one knows, or, at least, troubles about. Koffee Kal-

147 Bowdich, 1819, p. 236 and see also p. 252, note. The sense of the remark is obscure. In the French edition of the work (*Voyage dans le Pays D'Aschantie,* Paris, 1819, p. 333), the passage reads: Osei Kwadwo 'started by diminishing the number of members of the aristocratic council, not naming to the places they vacated except in the proportion of one in four. He gave them to his favourite captains . . .'
148 Bowdich, 1821a, p. 54.
149 *The African Times,* XXIV, no. 266, 1 November 1883, p. 122.
150 G. A. Robertson, 1819, p. 199.
151 Ramseyer and Kühne, 1875, pp. 176–7.

calli, in fact, has a habit of appointing children to vacant 'stools,' and the proportion of caboceers under manhood is extraordinarily large.[152]

Kofi Kakari's idiosyncrasies apart, however, the conventional Kumase view of the matter was probably that outlined in 1916 by Kwame Kyem, later to become Bantamahene. In an effort to disabuse the British colonial administrators in Asante of the notion that 'no person outside the family of an occupant of a stool was allowed to succeed him', he observed:

As the Chiefs were raised to their respective offices by the King at his pleasure so he destooled or killed them as he liked when they misconducted them- selves . . . *The Principle underlying the formation of the several Clans with their stools by the King was to set a goal before all thrifty, patriotic and honourable citizens of Coomassie.* The King made the respective stools and gave them to people as promotion for their help, and it was by means of such promotions that he got round him true and trusty friends, and any ordinary thrifty young man serving the King and his country, with distinc- tion, expected to be honoured in due course with such promotion in the same way that an English patriot would expect to be knighted by the King. As the rank and dignity of a knight is not transmissible, so the rank of a chief was not transmissible from uncle to nephew. To be promoted by the King then and by the Government now was and is the ambition of all thrifty, patriotic, honourable and hard-working young men in Coomassie.[153]

In Asante the concept of service is expressed as ɛsom (or ɔsom); ad- ministrative roles are therefore described by the term ɛsomdwuma, 'work in service'. Those employed in such roles are known as *asomfo*. They are also referred to as *nhenkwaa* (singular, *ahenkwaa*), 'the king's servants' – a term which may be treated for most practical purposes as synonymous with '*asomfo*'.[154] The broad category of the *asomfo* or the *nhenkwaa* included servants of the Household, such as the cooks (*sodofo*) and provisioners (*patomfo*); the public servants such as the revenue collectors (*togyefo*) and traders (*batafo*); and those who had duties in both spheres, such as the physicians (*nsumankwaa*),[155] the soul-washers (*akradwarefo*), and stool-carriers (*nkonnwasoafo*). The ranking position within the *asomfo* was that of the head of the mes- sengers or sword-bearers, who carried the title Asomfohene; he could

152 Boyle, 1874, pp. 276–7, citing Kühne.
153 National Archives of Ghana, Kumase, File D. 102: Kwame Kyem to Acting Chief Commissioner, dd. Kumase, 19 June 1916.
154 This section is partly based upon Wilks, 1966b, p. 219 ff., though a number of important corrections have been made.
155 National Archives of Ghana, Kumase, unaccessioned file: Edward Prempeh (Agyeman Prempe I) to District Commissioner, dd. Kumase, 14 April 1928, refer- ring to the Nsumanfieso or 'Pharmacy' within the palace 'where we had well trained and qualified Physicians in charge, whose duty it was to attend the sick and the injured'.

not, however, interfere in the affairs of departments other than his own.

To acquire a position in service was the aspiration of many youths throughout Asante, who chose to leave the relative security of life within the framework of village and matrilineage for the highly competitive environment of the capital. Bonnat, it has been seen, wrote of the large number of young men who arrived in Kumase seeking to enter into service and hopefully to secure advance by winning the attention of the Asantehene (see p. 374). The fortunate ones, Bonnat added,

are used by the king to spread his laws and his decrees in all the provinces; he uses them also for a large number of ordinary petty services; it is one of them who he chooses to remind him of an event or an idea at a specific time; he sends them to collect tributes and taxes, and even empowers them to judge cases in his name which the pagnifos [*mpaninfo*] could not settle but which did not seem to him of sufficient importance to necessitate his intervention.

These missions of trust give to these young men called oïnqua [*nhenkwaa*] great privileges. Armed with royal authority, they seize on the way everything which pleases them; drinks and victuals especially are frequently the objects of their requisitions.[156]

A quarter of a century later G. E. Ferguson made a similar observation (though by then revenue collection had become 'extortion' and the whole system 'barbarous'). 'For full three hundred years', he wrote, with some exaggeration, 'persons were collected from all parts of its vast dominions, and who, having been instructed in the barbarous customs and manners practised at Kumasi, including extortion and execution, were distributed as residents, royal executioners, tax collectors and other official agents in every part of his dominion'.[157] Certainly, however, the *nhenkwaa* of Asante were no exception to the generalization, that the class of petty bureaucrats is seldom a popular one. The Basel missionary Perregaux, whose knowledge of Asante dated from the end of the nineteenth century, made the point in a somewhat curious fashion:

There were servants of the king (ohenkwa, pl. ahenkwa, literally slaves or servants of the king) who were in charge and who were on their part just as bad as the policemen of the English government today. They were more dreaded than the thiefs themselves. Arriving, for example, on a mission in a village, they seized without ceremony chickens and whatever food they wanted, which is just like the present policemen. Thus the townsfolk, notified

---

156 *L'Explorateur*, 1875–6, II, 623; Gros, 1884, pp. 194–5.
157 PRO, CO. 879/45, African (West) 506, 1896, p. 253: Ferguson's Final Report on his Second Mission to the Interior, dd. 31 August 1896.

in advance of their arrival, hastened to secure as quickly as possible all the chickens, sheep and goats . . . These are . . . in brief, important people but in general those not having a very good reputation; they are usually chosen from among young men with 'eyes of fire' (won ani yehyen), that is to say, the audacious who believe that everything is possible.[158]

It is only fair to add, however, the observations of both Ferguson and Perregaux related to a period when many of the established norms of public behaviour had broken down under the stresses to which the central government had been subjected. There was in fact legislation against the very abuses to which Perregaux referred, which dated back to the early part of the century. In 1817 Osei Bonsu had enacted, that

all persons sent on the King's business shall no longer seize provisions in any country, whether tributary or otherwise, in his name; but requiring food, shall offer a fair price for the first they meet with, if this is refused, they shall then demand one meal, and one meal only, in the King's name, and proceed. This extends to all messengers sent by the head captains, whose servants, as well as the King's, have been long in the habit of extorting goods from traders, and tobacco and provisions in the market place, in the names of their masters, which they shall do no longer without incurring the same penalty which is attached to the former part of this law, 110 periguins.[159]

In the nature of the case, it is no longer possible to follow the careers of those many individuals who were fortunate enough to enter into service, but who failed to achieve promotion into the higher echelons of the administration. That of Asante Agyei, however, exemplifies well the success which might be, though seldom was, attained. Born probably in the late 1780s in the southeastern province of Akwamu, of commoner status, as a youth he became a salt carrier on the Volta between Akwamu and Krakye. Coming to the attention of the Akwamuhene Akoto, he was taken into his service as a member of the palace guard. In or about 1805 charges were brought against Akoto which necessitated his travelling to Kumase to answer them. Agyei was among the retainers who accompanied him. In the course of Akoto's trial before Osei Bonsu and the council, Agyei intervened to speak for three hours in his defence. Highly impressed by the young man's debating abilities, the Asantehene retained him in his service. For a time, however, the new *ahenkwaa* enjoyed no especial favour, but, after carrying out a particularly delicate commission in a situation in which the Asantehene was in conflict with the majority of his councillors, Asante Agyei (as he became known) finally achieved advance-

158 Perregaux, 1906, pp. 168–9.
159 Bowdich, 1819, pp. 255–6.

ment. He was given a junior counselorship, and a grant of a house, wives, slaves and gold dust to support the dignity of his new office. Further promotion followed rapidly. Having delivered before council a classical statement on the place of wealth within society (see below, p. 699), he was advanced to second ranking counselor and awarded a further grant of property. In or about 1815 he was appointed counselor to the army about to take the field against the Akyem rebels. The Asante commander, Amankwa Abinowa, protested about Asante Agyei's youth, requesting instead the services of either Kwadwo Adusei Kyakya or Oti Panin. Osei Bonsu nevertheless confirmed the appointment, insisting that Asante Agyei 'has the best head for hard palavers'.[160] Acquitting himself with distinction, Asante Agyei henceforth enjoyed the major responsibility for diplomatic affairs. He had, so it was observed, 'continued to advance by his splendid talents, and his firmness in the cause of truth, till he was raised to be the linguist for all foreign palavers, the highest office he could hold which was not hereditary'.[161] Thereafter he travelled almost constantly. In 1817 he was in Assin; in 1820 perhaps in Gyaman; and in 1822 in Accra. His death occurred probably in 1823.[162]

Bowdich remarked that in a society such as Asante, the achievement of high office through talent rather than birth was not so unusual as was commonly supposed: 'the histories of Agay [Asante Agyei] and some others of the Ashantee chiefs and ministers', he added, 'supporting my impression. The barbarian must be original; if he becomes eminent, it is by the force of his own genius.'[163] Although not foreigners, Opoku Frefre and Kwadwo Adusei Kyakya were both, like Asante Agyei, self-made men; their careers which have been outlined briefly above (pp. 417–18) attest to the important role which they played in the evolution of the Exchequer. But while outstanding talent could unquestionably find its reward, it must at the same time be stressed that the efficacious performance of most administrative tasks required a mastery of relevant skills and knowledge. The *togyefo* and *batafo*, for example, had to possess an understanding not only of the intricate Asante system of weights, but also of the various currencies and measures of the European merchants on the coast and of the Muslim merchants of the northern hinterland; the *afenasoafo* had to be adept in the accurate oral transmission of messages, and the *nseniefo* in the accurate oral publication of decrees; the counselor had to combine

160 Bowdich, 1819, p. 249.
161 Lee, 1835, p. 168.
162 See Asante Collective Biography Project: Asante Agyei. Among the principal sources for the career of Asante Agyei are Bowdich, 1819, pp. 248–9; Hutchison, in Bowdich, 1819, pp. 392–3; Lee, 1835, pp. 152–79; Reindorf, 2nd ed., n.d., p. 180.
163 Bowdich, 1821c, p. 77.

forensic capabilities with an intimate knowledge of legal precedents and of constitutional procedures; and the resident commissioners had to match a keen appreciation of central government policy with equally keen insights into the nature of local politics. It was in Kumase that the appropriate training facilities could be provided, since it was there that the accumulation of the relevant expertise was to be found in the bureaus – dampans – of the inner city and the palace complex. It was, in other words, among the more important functions of a senior administrator that he should supervise the training of those who were to work within his department. Conversely, for the career oriented commoner arriving in the capital it was essential initially to secure an attachment to the establishment of such a functionary in however menial a role and for however minimal a return: carrying water and washing clothes, for example, in return for food, but hoping always ultimately to be permitted to train for a more prestigious and lucrative occupation. To leave the rooms which lay hidden from public view and to take a place in the dampan which was open to the street was in a real sense the beginnings of a career in the administration.

Strangers, then, formed one component in the establishments of functionaries within the administration, and so might themselves in time gain *asomfo* status. After his arrival in Kumase Asante Agyei thus appears to have been attached to the household of the Adumhene Adum Ata,[164] and, but for his outstanding abilities which he clearly lost no opportunity of displaying and which kept him before the attention of the Asantehene, he might well in time have become one either of the *adumfo* or of the *abrafo*, executioner or policeman. According to Rattray, another important intake into the lower ranks of the administration was that of slaves,[165] and Warrington maintained that in the past the *asomfo* had been principally recruited from the male descendants of unfree females, and had the status of *fie nipa*, 'people of the house'.[166] It was undoubtedly the case that in a situation in which a department was seriously short of personnel, then unfree trainees could be brought into it.[167] There were indeed certain accepted constitutional procedures which could be used virtually to draft individuals into the adminstration. Thus the Asantehene had the right to take any male hunchback born in the kingdom for training in the *nseniefo*[168] (which is presumably how the career of Kwadwo Adusei

---

164 Reindorf, 2nd ed., n.d., p. 180.
165 Rattray, 1929, p. 92.
166 See Matson, 1951, pp. 75–6.
167 Thus in the period of administrative expansion still continuing under Osei Bonsu, reference may be found to 'foreign slaves . . . who from talent, devotedness, or policy have become confidential favourites of the Kings and Chiefs', see Bowdich, 1821b, pp. 18–19.
168 Rattray, 1927, p. 279.

Kyakya commenced). Again, the Asantehene could take as death duties already trained personnel in lieu of gold dust: he is said, for example, customarily to have taken *inter alia* one weigher and one sword-bearer upon the death of a Bekwaehene.[169] There is, however, no justification for the sweeping statements of both Rattray and Warrington, who appear to have argued from the correct observation, that many *asomfo* belonged to no matrilineage, to the erroneous conclusion, that they were therefore of slave origins.

In the nature of the case a functionary of the administration most usually obtained trainees, those to acquire the specific skills of his bureau, by retaining in his house his own or his brothers' sons (and in the third generation, their sons), rather than seeing them transfer at some stage to the houses of their respective mother's brothers. It was indeed a generally accepted rule, that members of the *asomfo* or *nhenkwaa* class had claims upon the services of their sons which took precedence in law over those of the sons' mothers' kin. 'As long as I am alive', asserted the Asokwahene, head of the Bata, in 1965, 'I can keep my sons with me if I can support and maintain them. If the *wofa* [mother's brother] tried to take them, I would sue him. Only when I die can the *wofa* take them. But when I die my brother may take my wife, and in that way my brother may keep the sons, and not the *wofa*'.[170] The class of sons, and grandsons, belonging in this way to an office within the administration are known as the *mmamma* of the stool. Sons and grandsons thus grew up in an environment in which they would naturally become familiar with the particular skills of the group. They became virtually apprentices of their fathers: *wudi wo agya akyire a, wusua ne nante*, 'when you follow your father, you learn to walk as he does'. As such, the *mmamma* of the junior generation within the group usually had their own organization; that is, their interests were represented by a *mmammahene* who was, as it were, the senior apprentice. The situation with respect to the Gyaasewa stool itself was explained as follows:

The Gyaasewahene has a *mmammahene*, who will usually succeed him to become Gyaasewahene. The Gyaasewahene chooses his *mmammahene* and trains him. He might choose one of his younger brothers, or he might choose

169 Rattray, 1929, p. 162.
170 Wilks, field-notes, interview with Nana Kofi Poku, Asokwahene, dd. Kumase, 3 August 1965. See also Rattray, 1929, p. 132, for the assertion of the Asumegya, that 'as a reward for our services in the battle of Feyiase, the Asante Hene promised never to claim the children of Asumegya women, by the Kumasi *ahenkwa*, as Kumasi subjects, or to make the sons of such persons follow their father's profession'. For an interesting case turning on the issue of the sons of *nhenkwaa*, see Kumase Divisional Council Archives, Manhyia: Asantehene's Divisional Council B, Civil Record Book 34, J. W. Quashie v. J. B. Amankwa, commencing 24 May 1945.

one of his sons. He will choose one of his sons especially when his senior sons are older than his junior brothers. The *mmammadwa* are service stools. *Mmamma* means 'children-children.' So the *mmammadwa* is a stool for the sons. But if it is the case that there are not enough sons, or good ones, then they may take the father's sister's sons. But what they cannot do is to take the father's wife's brother's sons. But a sister herself will not usually want her children to go to her brother. She will prefer them to go to her husband. So it is usually the sons who follow and succeed . . . What I am saying is that the *mmamma* are usually the father's sons. But sometimes they may be the father's sister's sons who more usually would go to the husband. A service stool is what we call *esomdwa*, a stool for someone in the service of the Asantehene, or of one of his officers. Those who occupy *esomdwa* form the administration of the state, and we call the administration *amammu* or *amammua*.[171]

It appears in fact not to have been uncommon, if the size of the *mmamma* fell unduly low, for a functionary to request that his sister allow some of her sons to join it, and permission was likely to be forthcoming particularly when the office was a wealthy one. Although technically the sister's sons were not *mmamma*, their status was unimpaired. They enjoyed the same rights as the *mmamma* and might even in time succeed to the highest offices within the group.

It will be apparent that when the electors for a vacancy in the administration came to survey the possible candidates, those with the requisite expertise were most likely to be found among the *mmamma* of the stool in question; and that although the Asantehene had the ultimate right of appointment, that right would usually but not always be exercised in favour of one of them. Reference to Plate IV and Plate XVII will suggest at how early an age children might begin to participate in public life. 'Whenever I go to court', explained the Boakye Yam Kuma *okyeame,*

one of my sons always follows me. He carries my stick. It is possible that this son will succeed me, but it will depend upon the kingmakers [stool electors]. But the Asantehene if he wishes, can appoint someone to the stool. He can put anyone who he wants on it . . . But as I said, my son always goes to court with me and carries my staff, and if the kingmakers like him they will put him forward to succeed me. Recently I took my son to Bekwae when the Asantehene sent me there. If you are a bad administrator, the Asantehene may decide to appoint an outsider to the stool because he will have no confidence in the way you have trained people. But the Asantehene has never had to do this with the Boakye Yam Kuma stool.[172]

171 Wilks, field-notes, interview with Mr C. E. Osei and Nana Akua Afriyie, *obaa-panin* of the Pinanko stool, dd. Kumase, 5 August 1965.
172 Wilks, field-notes, interview with Nana Boakye Yam, dd. Kumase, 2–3 August 1965.

A similar position was outlined by the Boakye Yam Panin *okyeame:*

> In the old days sons did not roam about, but always followed the chief and learned from him. But the kingmakers will choose who they want to occupy a vacant post. I myself have a younger brother who I am training in the duties of an *okyeame,* and I send him with messages. He may succeed me. I also have a *mmammahene* who is the son of one of my daughters. It will be for the kingmakers to decide whether they want the *mmammahene* or my younger brother to succeed me . . . The *mmammahene* is the head of the sons. My *mmammahene* only goes to court on big occasions. But I often consult with my *mmammahene* who is an adult and knows about things.[173]

What has been referred to above as a 'department' is termed in Asante, a *fekuo.* Thus one may speak of the Bata Fekuo or the Sanaa Fekuo, both of which were part of the wider Gyaasewa Fekuo. The heads of such *fekuo* were known as *asomfo kese,* 'senior servants'. They held stools at some time formally created by an Asantehene, and each was entitled to maintain a dampan in the city whether within or without the palace complex. The manpower requirements of a *fekuo* would vary according to the functions assigned to it. The Asoamfohene, head of the hammock-men in the capital, is said to have had no more than one hundred men in the group.[174] It has been noted that, by contrast, the Nseniehene presided over a *fekuo* of one thousand criers and gong-beaters (see p. 439, note 117). Such a *fekuo* as the Bata must, at least under Kwaku Dua I, have been larger still. It follows from what has been said, that the key group within any *fekuo* comprised, in structural terms, a set of brothers, their sons and grandsons, and sometimes their sisters' sons – the *mmamma* of the stool. Especially in the larger departments, however, the *mmamma* would quite clearly not be sufficiently numerous to carry out all the duties assigned to them. It was therefore in these particularly, that strangers arriving in the capital might hope to find a position. It was also to them that unfree persons might necessarily have to be drafted. But it also follows from what has been said, that office within the *fekuo* would not be as readily accessible to the strangers and unfree members as to the *mmamma.* Thus the head of a *fekuo* would most commonly be a son of a previous head. It was the prerogative of the departmental head, moreover, to create such subordinate posts as he considered essential to the effective discharge of his responsibilities. Such lesser posts would tend also to be distributed among the *mmamma.* Their occupants might have actual miniature stools as the symbol of their office (see above, p. 387).[175]

173 Wilks, field-notes, interview with Nana Boakye Tenten II, dd. Kumase, 3 August 1965.
174 Rattray, 1927, p. 134, note.
175 The Asantehene might, however, choose to elevate the status of such a minor post. See, for example, the case of the 'miniature' stool held by Kwaku Fi and

A clear description of the type of office under consideration in this section was given by the Asantehemaa Konadu Yaadom II in 1932. 'There exist', she wrote,

two sections of Chiefs' stools in Ashanti namely, (1) Mmamadwa i.e. sons' stools which is only inherited by sons of its former occupants, and (2) Abusua Dwa i.e. family Stool which can only be inherited matrilineally. In the event of the former Stool falling vacant, the Asantehene in his own discretion, can appoint any of the sons of its former occupants, whom he finds has rendered royal and faithful services to him and the country at large, to be installed thereon.[176]

The central administration: the case of the Bata fekuo

In so large and complex an administration, no one *fekuo* can be assumed to be typical. The Bata, however, will be examined in some detail since in both evolutionary and structural terms it exemplifies a number of the more interesting characteristics of an *ɛsomdwa* or service stool. The position of the Batahene, as it has been noted above, was held by the Asokwahene of Kumase. The Asokwa group comprised principally the *asokwafo* proper, the hornblowers, and the *akyeremadefo*, the drummers, and has long been regarded as a general service organization of *asomfo*. 'In the old days', remarked the Boakye Yam Panin *okyeame*, 'the Asokwafo did any jobs which the Asantehene required.'[177] Thus, apart from their titular roles as hornblowers and drummers, they served also as sextons to the royal family, maintained the palace area, and repaired the building within it.[178] The evidence suggests that their services were also used for purposes of trade from an early period. In 1714 for example, an Asante military officer 'Anti Benine' (possibly the Amanse Abodomhene Nti Panin) arrived on the Gold Coast from Twifo, and was accompanied by Kyerema, 'the King of Ashantee's Drummer', who was to make purchases of arms there.[179]

Kwame Nsia in the late nineteenth and early twentieth century, which was reclassified after 1924 by Agyeman Prempe I, who named it the Omanti Stool and gave it two villages and 'sixty strong people of Kumasi soil', IASAS/71: Omanti Stool History, recorded by J. Agyeman-Duah, 31 May 1963.

176 NAG, Kumase, D. 525: Kumasihema Kwaaduwa Yiadom to Prempeh II, dd. Kumase, 27 February 1932. For an informative case between the *mmamma* and the putative royals of the Asafo (Akwamu) stool, see Kumase Divisional Council Archives, Manhyia, Akwamu Tribunal Record Book: Kwame Awua *v.* Kofi Amoaten, case commenced 16 July 1933.

177 Wilks, field-notes, interview with Nana Boakye Tenten II, 3 August 1965.

178 IASAS/1: Asokwahene-Batahene, recorded by J. Agyeman-Duah, 3 February 1963. Wilks, field-notes, interview with Asokwahene Kofi Poku, dd. Kumase, 3 August 1965. Rattray, 1927, pp. 114–15.

179 PRO, T. 70/1464: Komenda Journal, entry by Baillie, dd. 8 December 1714. General State Archives, The Hague, KvG 82: Elmina Journal, entry for 28 March 1715.

According to the generally accepted account of the matter, the first and second Asokwahenes, Nuamoa and his full brother Akwadan, were among the many Denkyira who voluntarily transferred their allegiance to Osei Tutu in the late seventeenth century. Having thus severed their links with their matri-kin, on Akwadan's death his son Asokwa Kese was appointed by Opoku Ware to succeed him. Asokwa Kese, in turn, was followed by two other sons of Akwadan, Akosa and then Kwadwo Anto.[180]

Kwadwo Anto held office under the Asantehene Osei Kwadwo. He fought in the Kumase forces in the campaign against the Banda early in that reign, but was subsequently unable to pay the *apeato* or war-tax of 30 peredwans which fell upon the Asokwa people. The debt was settled on his behalf by his nephew Boakye Yam, a wealthy *ahenkwaa*.[181] The action may have saved Kwadwo Anto from dismissal, but clearly the affairs of the *asokwafo* were in a sorry state. When Kwadwo Anto died, Osei Kwadwo appointed one of his own sons, Kwasi Ampon, to the vacant position.[182] It was probably from this time onwards that the general service organization became transformed into the Bata, and the Asokwahene became responsible for the operations of what was essentially the commissariat of the Company of State Traders (the financing of its work being the direct responsibility of the Gyaasewahene and the officers of the Treasury as such). The reformed organization was further strengthened in the next reign, that of Osei Kwame. The services of Boakye Yam to the *asokwafo* were recognized when he was promoted to a new counselor's post – the Boakye Yam Panin *okyeame*[183] – and assigned special responsibility for the affairs of the Bata. Under Kwasi Ampon and Boakye Yam the Bata appears to have been generally renovated and converted into an efficient department able not only to assume the more exacting commercial role required of it under Osei Bonsu, but also to supply personnel for a number of other administrative tasks. Thus Kwame Dendo, a 'senior horn-blower', accompanied Kwadwo Abrantia on his mission to Elmina in 1817 (see pp. 151–2), and was charged *inter alia* with reporting back to the

180 IASAS/1: Asokwahene-Batahene. Wilks, field-notes, interview with Kofi Poku. An account of the origins of the Asokwa group was also recorded in 1907 by Nana Agyeman Prempe I, p. 70 (for which see above, p. 327, n. 1): 'Akodan and Nuamoah the chief of the musicians also came to assist the Ashantis with 1000 men. The trumpet which Akodan carried himself was made of gold.' Rattray, 1927, p. 114, note, referred to one Adu Bankoto as first head of the *asokwafo* under Osei Tutu.
181 IASAS/73: Boakye Yam Linguist Stool, recorded by J. Agyeman-Duah, 6 June 1963.
182 IASAS/1: Asokwahene-Batahene.
183 IASAS/73: Boakye Yam Linguist Stool, recorded by J. Agyeman-Duah, 6 June 1963.

government on the state of work on the reconstructed great-road.[184] Amon Bata, 'the trader', was appointed a resident commissioner, and was stationed in Abora-Dunkwa in 1822.[185] In 1815 a party of some two hundred men arrived in Accra to collect revenues and to 'open the road for trade and for peaceful meetings in the future'. Head of the whole party was Amankwa Boahen.[186] He is very probably the same official as the Asokwa Amankwa, 'the king's gold hornblower', who two years later was one of the resident commissioners for Accra.[187]

Kwasi Ampon continued to hold the position of Asokwahene or Batahene under Osei Bonsu, and was apparently still alive in 1817.[188] The counselor Boakye Yam, however, died in Akuapem in 1814, having accompanied an Asante army there 'in his political capacity'.[189] The Asokwa stool was next awarded to Ata Kwadwo, son of Kwasi Ampon and grandson therefore of Osei Kwadwo.[190] There is some difficulty, however, in establishing a satisfactory list of the incumbents of the office over the remainder of the nineteenth century. The reconstruction in Table 20 (p. 458) is highly tentative, and it is unclear whether the third unit – Yaw Sapon and his descendants – was in any way genealogically attached to either the first or second. It may have been in consequence of the large and amorphous nature of the Bata organization, that the *mmamma* remained weak. There was, indeed, no *mmammahene*. The observations of the Asokwahene in 1965 summarize his perceptions of the principal characteristics of the office:

The Asokwa stool is *ɛsomdwa*. The Asokwa people are servants of the Asantehene. The kingmakers and the stool elders choose a candidate when the office is vacant, and they present him to the Asantehene. The Asantehene can object to the choice of the kingmakers, and ask them to put someone else forward . . . The Asokwa stool is not *mmammadwa*. Any *ahenkwaa* at the palace who is from Asokwa can be chosen by the Asantehene to occupy the stool. The *asokwafo* must undergo training in horn-blowing. Every night they meet together, in Asokwa, for training. There is no *mmammahene* for the Asokwa stool. But there is a *mogyamogyahene*. He is an elder from the family who deputizes for the Asokwahene, and is eligible for the Asokwa stool. Boakye Yam is my nephew, appointed by the Asantehene to be my

184 Huydecoper's Journal, entry for 26 April 1817.
185 Reindorf, 2nd ed., n.d., p. 172.
186 National Archives, Copenhagen, miscellaneous archives from Guinea 1703–1815, Christiansborg Council proceedings, minute by Schiønning, dd. 31 July 1815.
187 Bowdich, 1819, p. 83. PRO, T. 70/41: Bowdich to Governor, dd. Kumase, 9 July 1817.
188 Kwasi Ampon is probably the 'Umpon' referred to by Bowdich, T. 70/41: Bowdich to Governor, dd. Kumase, 18 June 1817.
189 Bowdich, 1819, p. 289.
190 IASAS/1: Asokwahene-Batahene, Ata Kwadwo may be the 'Ata Kwado' or 'Ata Krobi' referred to in Methodist Mission Archives, Wharton to General Secretaries, dd. Kumase, 31 May 1846.

Table 20 *The Asokwahenes of Kumase*

Unit I	Unit II	Unit III	Title holders
			1. Asokwahene Nuamoa, temp. Osei Tutu
			2. Asokwahene Akwadan, temp. Osei Tutu and Opoku Ware
			3. Asokwahene Asokwa Kese, temp. Opoku Ware
			4. Asokwahene Akosa, temp. Opoku Ware and Kusi Obodom
			5. Asokwahene Kwadwo Anto, temp. Kusi Obodom and Osei Kwadwo
			6. Asokwahene Kwasi Ampon, son of Asantehene Osei Kwadwo, temp. Osei Kwadwo to Osei Bonsu
			7. Asokwahene Ata Kwadwo, temp. Osei Yaw and Kwaku Dua I
			8. Asokwahene Yaw Sapon, temp. Kwaku Dua I. Destooled
			9. Asokwahene Kwasi Gyetoa,* also know as Kwasi Ampon; held office for thirty or forty years before *ca.* 1910
			x. Akua Sae, sister of Kwasi Gyetoa
			10. Asokwahene Ata Kwadwo, in office in the 1920s
			11. Asokwahene Kofi Poku, enstooled 1930; still in office 1970

* Bowdich, 1819, p. 362, refers to an earlier hornblower chief of this same unusual name.

okyeame. If there is any trouble, I inform Boakye Yam Panin before contacting the palace . . . We cannot send people from the Asokwa stool to the Boakye Yam Panin stool: we are not inheritors . . . The Asantehene used to send the *asokwafo* to the coast to make purchases of salt, tobacco, etc. Hence I am also known as the Batahene. In the old days all the *asokwafo* would be *nhenkwaa* in the palace. When the Asokwahene was in Kumase, the *mogyamogyahene* would be responsible for looking after affairs in the village, Asokwa. In the old days everyone, whether sons or nephews, would be required to serve the Asantehene as *nhenkwaa*. Some would be hornblowers, some would be messengers, some would weed the royal gardens, and so forth.[191]

After the death of the counselor Boakye Yam in 1814, Oti Panin was appointed to the vacancy. The present *okyeame* gave some account of what he perceived to be the nature of the stool. It is, he asserted, 'for the sons . . . But the stool can go to nephews as well as sons, and to anyone of the family wherever he lives. It is *mmammadwa*, but if the sons cannot administer the affairs of the stool, then the nephews may be brought in if the Asantehene agrees. But the Asantehene can also appoint outsiders to it'.[192] Oti Panin was in fact son of Boakye Yam.[193]

191 Wilks, field-notes, interview with Kofi Poku.
192 Wilks, field-notes, interview with Boakye Tenten II.
193 *Ibid*. Compare Bowdich, 1819, p. 289.

Known to Bowdich in 1817, he was then regarded as most junior of the four ranking counselors in the capital.[194] He was wounded at Katamanso in 1826, and taken prisoner. After interrogation by the British he was handed over to the Osu, who in turn sold him to the Akwamuhene Akoto. Oti Panin having once prosecuted a case against Akoto in Kumase, the Akwamuhene had him murdered.[195] He was followed in office by Kofi Boakye, probably one of his sons. He was subsequently destooled,[196] and it seems likely that this was in 1839 when his superior officer, the Gyaasewahene Adu Damte, was involved in rebellion against Kwaku Dua I (see below, p. 488). Kofi Boakye survived, however, for another ten years.[197] In the meantime Kwaku Dua had chosen to appoint to the counselorship someone from outside the *mmamma*. This was Kofi Nti, a son of Yaa Kyaa of Akorase who was herself a daughter of Asantehene Osei Kwadwo.[198] Kofi Nti was married to a royal of the Golden Stool, the later Asantehemaa Afua Kobi, and was to father two Asantehenes, Kofi Kakari and Mensa Bonsu (see Chapter 9). His appointment to the Boakye Yam Panin stool looks, then, to have been one of political expediency. Certainly his career as an administrator gives no evidence of distinction but only of length: he appears not to have died until the late 1860s.[199] The office reverted to the *mmamma*. It was awarded to Boakye Tenten, a son of Oti Panin, who had risen in the provincial administration to one of its most senior posts, that of Resident Commissioner for Salaga.[200] He also married his predecessor's wife, Afua Kobi, but no children were born of the marriage. Boakye Tenten's distinguished career as counselor will be referred to below. He was killed in the course of the internecine struggles of 1884. 'Regarding his public career', one obituary read, '. . . he proved one of the truest friends of Ashantee'.[201]

Boakye Tenten may perhaps have had only adopted children. Certainly no son of his succeeded him. A younger brother survived, another son of Oti Panin, but he was clearly regarded as too old for the position at a time when vigorous leadership was at a premium. Kwaku Fokuo was appointed to the vacancy. An Akyem Kotoku by birth, he was presumably among those strangers who arrived at the

---

194 Bowdich, 1819, pp. 106, 289. Hutton, 1821, p. 275.
195 Ricketts, 1831, p. 125. PRO, CO. 267/93: Report of Commissioners into the State of the Colony of Sierra Leone, Appendix, Hansen to Commissioner, dd. Accra, 17 September 1826. Reindorf, 2nd ed., n.d., p. 211.
196 IASAS/73: Boakye Yam Linguist Stool, 6 June 1963.
197 Methodist Mission Archives: Hillard to Beecham, dd. Kumase, 16 January 1849.
198 Wilks, field-notes, interview with Nana Yaa Kyaa, dd. Akroase, 5 August 1965.
199 See, for example, Ramseyer and Kühne, 1875, p. 85.
200 *Further Correspondence*, C. 3386, 1882, pp. 63–4: Lonsdale's report on his mission, 1881–2.
201 *The Gold Coast Times*, IV, no. 154, 12 February 1885, p. 3.

capital seeking advancement. He was one of the successful ones. In circumstances which are not known, he was adopted into the household of Boakye Tenten and was, indeed, often referred to as his son.[202] He was active in his government's attempts to restore political order in the northern hinterlands in the early 1890s, and was a member of the embassy to London in 1895. He accompanied the Asantehene Agyeman Prempe I into exile in 1896, and died in Seychelles on 17 September 1900. A tribute was paid to him in 1896 by Major Barter of the British expeditionary force:

> The right-hand man of the King, the Chief Linguist, as he was called, was a chief by name of Kokofuku, and a very fine fellow he was, six feet three inches in height, all muscle and bone, and with a fine deep voice. He had visited England, and was one of those who had recognised the uselessness of resistance. One of our officers having asked him in a quiet moment why the Ashantis had not fought, he candidly replied that our arms were better than theirs, or they would not have allowed us to enter Kumassi.

In the highest panegyrical tradition of his class, Barter added: 'I think Kokofuku must be a sportsman at heart'.[203] Nevertheless, in 1900 the British confirmed as successor to Kwaku Fokuo the aged surviving son of Oti Panin. He was enstooled as Oti II, but by 1907 the position was vacant once again. A sister's son of Boakye Tenten and Oti II, Yaw Barima, was chosen for office and enstooled as Oti III. He served with the Gold Coast Regiment in East Africa in the First World War, subsequently taking an active role in the agitation for the restoration of Agyeman Prempe I. He abdicated only in 1959, blind and in ill health. He was succeeded by his sister's son, the present incumbent Boakye Tenten II.[204] The pattern of succession to the Boakye Yam Panin stool is summarized in Table 21.

It will be seen that the *mmamma* proper of the Boakye Yam Panin stool provided its occupants throughout the nineteenth century with the exception of two, Kofi Nti and Kwaku Fokuo. A number of stools which were not matrilineally inherited had existed in Kumase from the time of Osei Tutu.[205] In the general Asante context they were clearly anomalous, and were recognized as such within the framework of the

202 See, for example, *Further Correspondence*, C. 5615, 1888, p. 40: Nominal Role of Principal Persons and Chiefs, Kumase, 15 March 1888. *Further Correspondence*, C. 7918, 1896, p. 60: Brew to Knutsford, dd. London, 22 May 1895. NAG, Accra, ADM. 11/1372: evidence of Kwaku Fokuo, dd. 11 May 1896, in Regina v. John and Albert Owusu Ansa.

203 Barter, 1896, p. 451.

204 IASAS/73: Boakye Yam Linguist Stool. Wilks, field-notes, interview with Boakye Tenten II.

205 See Hagan, 1971, Figure 3. It must be remembered, however, that a number of stools were originally vested in matrilineages and only later were the lineage members deprived of their proprietary rights in them.

Table 21 *The Boakye Yam Panin counselors*

Unit I	Unit II	Unit III	Title-holders
(genealogical diagram: 1–2, branching to 3 5 7 x, then y 8, then 9)	4	6	1. Boakye Yam, temp. Osei Kwame to 1814 2. Oti Panin, 1814–26 3. Kofi Boakye, 1826–(?)1839; destooled; died 1849 4. Kofi Nti, (?)1839–*ca.* 1869; grandson of Asante-hene Osei Kwadwo; husband of the Asantehemaa Afua Kobi 5. Boakye Tenten, *ca.* 1869–84 6. Kwaku Fokuo, 1884–96; exiled; died 1900 7. Oti II, 1900–7 x. Daughter of Oti Panin 8. Yaw Barima alias Oti III, 1907–59; abdicated y. Sister of Yaw Barima 9. Boakye Tenten II, 1959 to date

constitution. They appear not to have presented any special problems in law. Legal issues did arise, however, in the late eighteenth century, not so much as a result simply of the creation of many new service stools, *εsomdwa,* but rather in consequence of the access to wealth which was enjoyed by the new functionaries: revenue collectors, state traders, resident commissioners, and the like. The matter was fundamentally a clear one: the *mmamma* of such stools were carrying the main burden of work within the reformed administration, and were accumulating the funds of skills and expertise upon which government was becoming increasingly dependent, yet at the same time as a class they lacked any definable status within Asante law. Appropriately enough, it was the Gyaasewahene Opoku Frefre – under whose office so many of the new functionaries served – who brought the case before the Asantehene. Because of the importance which the event has in the development of Asante constitutional law, it is well remembered to the present time.

In 1958 the Asantehene Nana Sir Osei Agyeman Prempeh II gave a summary of the case:

Opoku Frefre had no family. He was a slave. But Opoku Frefre became very rich and he did many services for the Asantehene and the Gyaasewa prospered. So Opoku Frefre asked Nana Osei Bonsu how he could be rewarded for all the good he had done, because he had no family. Nana Osei Bonsu told Opoku Frefre not to worry. He said he would allow the Gyaasewa stool to pass to Opoku Frefre's sons. So the Gyaasewa stool can pass in the male line, and many of the descendants of Opoku Frefre have held it . . . Even the present Gyaasewahene is a descendant of Opoku Frefre.[206]

The episode took place on the occasion chosen by Opoku Frefre to display his wealth publicly, before the Asantehene and his peers, in

[206] Wilks, field-notes, meeting with Nana Sir Osei Agyeman Prempeh II, dd. Kumase, 19 December 1958.

the week beginning 10 November 1817.[207] The drama of the incident is recapitulated in the orally transmitted accounts of it. 'My Nana Poku Frefreh', C. E. Osei stated before the Kumase Divisional Council in 1940,

displayed his wealth before the Asantehene and his councillors and as custom prescribes the Asantehene sent his 'Kotoko' scale to him to fill it and he did fill it with an amount of about £240. The Asantehene then sat in state and my Nana Poku Frefreh displayed his wealth before him, and was declared or acknowledged a wealthy man. While greeting the assembled Chiefs and on nearing the Asantehene, tears streamed down his cheeks. Upon enquiry by the Asantehene through his Linguists, my Nana Poku Frefreh explained that though he had been permitted to expose his wealth before the Otumfuo [Asantehene] and his Chiefs, that he had improved the status of the stool he was occupying yet he felt sorry that after his death his name might go into oblivion, in that he was the stool subject and had no surviving relatives who would succeed him after his death and as man was born to make a name he was sorry and that was why he was shedding tears. The statement deeply touched the heart of the Asantehene who then decreed that he would permit his sons also to succeed to the stool after his death so as to immortalize his name. My Nana Poku Frefreh passed to the unknown in the reign of the Asantehene Nana Osei Yaw.[208]

What had become the *de facto* situation was thus given legal recognition. Opoku Frefre had voiced the anxieties of the many *asomfo* who, having left their villages and lineages to pursue a career in the new central administration, found themselves – and therefore their sons who would succeed them – without adequate legal status.

The pattern of succession to the Gyaasewa stool after Osei Bonsu's decree is shown in Table 22. It exemplifies *par excellence* the strength which the *mmamma* might acquire under the new regulation. Despite the fact that singularly few of the Gyaasewahenes died naturally in office – the majority being either destooled or killed in one circumstance or another – the claims of the descendants of Opoku Frefre on the post were such as to prevail over those of any other aspirants. Although the descent of Adu Nantwiri II from Opoku Frefre was somewhat indirect, the only real exception to the generalization is that of Kwame Tua in the early twentieth century, whose career will be referred to further in Chapter 15. He was a member of the Kumase *asokwafo,* and brother of Kwasi Gyetoa (see Table 20, p. 458), and was appointed to the position of Gyaasewahene by the British in token of his services to them. Since the Asantehene had never relinquished his right of appointment to the Gyaasewa stool, and since the colonial administration had assumed by conquest the prerogatives of the

207 Hutchison, in Bowdich, 1819, pp. 395–6.
208 Kumase Divisional Council archives, Manhyia: J. K. Edubofuor versus C. E. Osei, 1939–40.

Table 22 *The Gyaasewahenes of Kumase* *

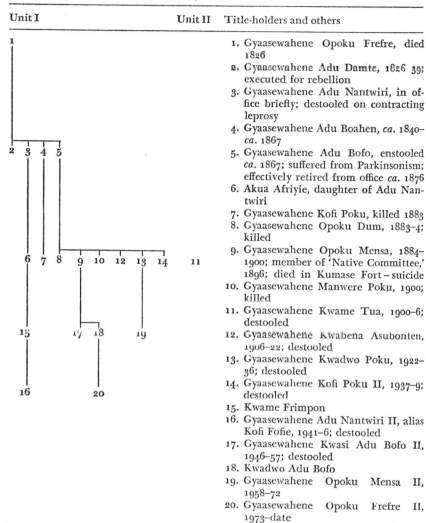

Unit I	Unit II	Title-holders and others

1. Gyaasewahene Opoku Frefre, died 1826
2. Gyaasewahene Adu Damte, 1826–39; executed for rebellion
3. Gyaasewahene Adu Nantwiri, in office briefly; destooled on contracting leprosy
4. Gyaasewahene Adu Boahen, *ca.* 1840–*ca.* 1867
5. Gyaasewahene Adu Bofo, enstooled *ca.* 1867; suffered from Parkinsonism; effectively retired from office *ca.* 1876
6. Akua Afriyie, daughter of Adu Nantwiri
7. Gyaasewahene Kofi Poku, killed 1883
8. Gyaasewahene Opoku Dum, 1883–4; killed
9. Gyaasewahene Opoku Mensa, 1884–1900; member of 'Native Committee,' 1896; died in Kumase Fort – suicide
10. Gyaasewahene Manwere Poku, 1900; killed
11. Gyaasewahene Kwame Tua, 1900–6; destooled
12. Gyaasewahene Kwabena Asubonten, 1906–22; destooled
13. Gyaasewahene Kwadwo Poku, 1922–36; destooled
14. Gyaasewahene Kofi Poku II, 1937–9; destooled
15. Kwame Frimpon
16. Gyaasewahene Adu Nantwiri II, alias Kofi Fofie, 1941–6; destooled
17. Gyaasewahene Kwasi Adu Bofo II, 1946–57; destooled
18. Kwadwo Adu Bofo
19. Gyaasewahene Opoku Mensa II, 1958–72
20. Gyaasewahene Opoku Frefre II, 1973–date

* This Table was compiled from material in the Asante Collective Biography Project, extracted from a wide range of oral and written sources which cannot be fully listed here. A reasonably high degree of accuracy is claimed for the reconstruction, although it has been necessary at several points to reconcile conflicting views held by members of the Gyaasewa.

Asantehene, the appointment of Kwame Tua was quite constitutional; [209] no Asantehene, on the other hand, was ever likely to have made it.

The Gyaasewa stool came to provide a model which the *mmamma*

[209] Wilks, field-notes, interview with C. E. Osei and Akua Afriyie, dd. Kumase, 5 August 1965.

of other service stools, *ɛsomdwa,* strove to emulate. Reference to Tables 20 and 21 will show that they did so with varying degrees of success. In the perfect pattern of *mmamma* succession, to which the Gyaasewa of all service stools the most nearly approximated, it will be seen that the implicit system was one in which high office was monopolized in each generation by a set of brothers.[210] Clearly within the Gyaasewa itself, the rule was observed that no 'sons' should succeed until the 'brothers' had been exhausted, and no 'grandsons' until the 'sons' had been exhausted [211] or, in other words, that no apprentice should take an office for which one of his masters was candidate. The trend, then, was towards the emergence of highly structured guilds, the preferred mode of entry to which was by patrifiliation. The service stools were clearly not matrilineally inherited. But neither were they patrilineally inherited even though sons might regularly succeed: the composition of the category of those having the requisite skills for a specific office was heavily weighted, statistically, in favour of the *mmamma.*

Reference to Tables 20 and 21 (pp. 458, 461) will suggest that there was a tendency in the twentieth century for sister's sons rather than sons increasingly to attain office: thus the counselors Yaw Barima and Boakye Tenten II both succeeded their mothers' brothers on the Boakye Yam Panin stool. The trend was already discernible by 1916, when Kwame Kyem advanced the thesis that the principle of matri-lineality was becoming asserted anew and applied for the first time to the service stools:

The Coomassie Chiefs are now trying to form royal family for their stools. They have advised the Government to make a rule that in future candidates for vacant stools shall be elected from the royal families of the said stools. They are doing so in order to perpetuate the office in their families, but such thing never existed . . . The several chiefs of Coomassie were made by the King when necessity called for them . . .[212]

But while Kwame Kyem described what was occurring accurately enough, he offered no explanation of the phenomenon. The service stools were ones which, in the nineteenth century, provided their members with lucrative positions: commissions and fees were sizeable and

---

210 The extraordinary success of the sons of Adu Bofo in the attainment of office is made all the more impressive in that yet another of them, Sanaa Poku, be-came Sanaahene, see Wilks, 1966b, p. 222. He was killed in the fighting in the aftermath of the coup of 1883.

211 The term *fekuo* appears to be from *afe,* 'a person of equal age or status', and *ekuo* 'group'. The writer was thus led to suggest the use of the term 'fraternity' to draw attention to important structural characteristics of the administrative departments, see Wilks, 1966b, p. 220.

212 National Archives of Ghana, Kumase, File D. 102: Kwame Kyem to Acting Chief Commissioner, dd. Kumase, 19 June 1916.

often impressively so. The loss of Asante independence in 1896 changed the situation drastically; the work of many of the service stools was taken over by the new colonial administration. Fuller investigation of the matter will almost certainly show that members of the privileged class in the Asante administration – the *mmamma*, the sons and grandsons as such – moved as rapidly as possible into the new sector of government, becoming messengers, office cleaners, policemen, and the like. More importantly, they sent their sons to school, and they in turn became clerks, schoolteachers, works foremen, sanitary inspectors and so on. In the vestigial older administration, no longer a highly competitive sphere, the way was open for the sisters' sons increasingly to take over office and to attempt to establish, as Kwame Kyem remarked, 'royal families' in offices in which talent and training were no longer at a premium.

The bureaucratic process in Kumase

'The two or three last kings of Ashantee', Bowdich remarked in 1821, 'have artfully enlarged the royal prerogatives, at the expence of the original constitution.'[213] The writer has argued elsewhere that the major transformations which occurred in the character of the Asante administrative structures appear in so many cases to have begun in the reign of Osei Kwadwo that one may usefully speak of a 'Kwadwoan revolution in government'.[214] In a recent paper Hagan has rightly pointed out that many of the offices which were to become of importance within the new central administration were ones which had been created by Opoku Ware,[215] and indeed, there is no doubt that it was Opoku Ware who first recognized the necessity of reform and took the early steps towards it. The 'Owarean revolution', however, was abortive, arrested in its initial stages by the strength of the conservative opposition. It was under Osei Kwadwo that the theme of reform was once again advanced, and the first measures taken to transform the executive branch of government into what was, by the standards of the time, an efficient and professionalized instrument of national policy. Few new stools of senior rank were created by Osei Kwadwo,[216] though the administrative responsibilities of a number of existing ones were redefined and rearranged. Weber's generalization appears borne out in the case of Asante, that 'bureaucratization is occasioned more by intensive and qualitative enlargement and internal

213 Bowdich, 1821a, p. 21.
214 Wilks, 1966b, pp. 216–7. Wilks, 1967a, p. 212.
215 Hagan, 1971, *passim*.
216 *Ibid.* fig. 3.

deployment of administrative tasks than by their extensive and quantitative increase'.[217] Thus it has been seen that the Bata which came increasingly to operate the commercial sector of the economy in the nineteenth century, was not a newly created department but had been formed out of much older service groups, most notably the hornblowers and the drummers. Similarly the basic organization of the new diplomatic service was provided by two older groups, the swordbearers and the court criers; no ambassador would proceed on a mission without being accompanied by members of each.[218] The one class of functionaries which clearly did not correspond to any earlier group was that of the resident commissioners, and it is significant that a word was borrowed into Twi to describe them – *amradofo*. They appear to have been recruited from all other sections of the administration: Kwame Butuakwa, for example, from the *fotosanfo*, Asokwa Amankwa from the *asokwafo*, Dongwa from the *afenasoafo*, and so forth.

It has been shown how the possession of a bureau – *dampan* – in the city was one of the marks of the senior official. The large decorative umbrella under which he appeared in public was another. The class of such officials was a precisely delimited one. Each titled position within it was one approved and formally recognized by the Asantehene. Each new incumbent had to swear an oath of allegiance to the Asantehene upon one of the Swords of State according to rank, and to pay the appropriate allegiance fee. It is very commonly said that 'in the old days' the titled chiefly establishment of Kumase comprised about two hundred and fifty persons. The figure is a least compatible with that for the number of dampans in the city in the third quarter of the nineteenth century, that is, one hundred and fifty excluding, presumably, the many offices within the palace complex (see p. 383). When the James mission was received in Kumase in 1817, Bowdich noted the presence of 'at least a hundred large umbrellas, or canopies'.[219] At the reception of the Dupuis mission three years later about the same number were in evidence, though a few belonged to provincial rulers.[220] On T. B. Freeman's entry into Kumase in 1839 he counted seventy umbrellas,[221]

217 *Wirtschaft und Gesellschaft*, 1922, III, ch. 6, and see Gerth and Mills, 1948, p. 212.
218 See West, 1857, plate facing p. 188. The plate was lithographed from a 'photograph' of an Asante embassy at Cape Coast, 23 November 1856, which comprised the head of the mission (centre), two swordbearers (left), and two criers (right). Three of the members are named as Anantuo, Asabre, and Mensa in Methodist Mission Archives, Miscellaneous Letter Book, abstracts, January 1857. The plate is reproduced on the jacket of this book.
219 Bowdich, 1819, p. 34.
220 Hutton, 1821, p. 212.
221 T. B. Freeman, 1834, p. 48.

but on his return there in 1841 he remarked that the number was larger: there were 'a hundred and twenty-five large Kaborsir's umbrellas, of various colours, some of which were very handsome'.[222] Twenty years later, at the reception for West and Owusu Ansa, two hundred and six large umbrellas were counted.[223] The series of figures clearly reflects growth in the size of the chiefly establishment in Kumase over the half century, but probably not at the indicated rate of a 100% increase in that period.[224] Reference, however, to the curves of growth for the Kumase establishment given by Wilks and Hagan, the former based upon a sample of one hundred and forty-six stools and the latter upon one of one hundred and ninety-four, will show that rate of proliferation of office in the first part of the nineteenth century – while exponentially continuous with that of the preceding and following periods – was certainly running as high as 5% per decade.[225] It must be emphasized that such figures relate only to growth in the chiefly establishment as such. They take no account of the many lesser functionaries who the heads of *fekuo* could, within their terms of reference, appoint to ensure the effective discharge of their departmental duties. It has been noted above that such lesser functionaries might sometimes have miniature stools as token of their position. They might also have miniature umbrellas. Of their reception in the capital on 17 March 1862, West and Owusu Ansa wrote: 'we counted as many as two hundred and six large umbrellas, while the small English umbrellas that were held over the heads of petty officials greatly exceeded in number the large ones'.[226]

The administrative class in Kumase was a wider one than the class of senior officers of the central administration. The two hundred and fifty or so members of the chiefly establishment included, for example, ward heads and military commanders who did not in many cases belong to the executive branch of government, but may have been participants in the decision-making process by virtue of having attained seats in the Council of Kumase. Many of them still held stools vested in lineages, the succession to which was usually by matrifiliation. By contrast, it was the *asomfo*, the public and Household servants, who constituted the central administration: the personnel of the *batafo, fotosanfo, nseniefo, dawurufo, sanaafo, afenasoafo, nkwansrafo, amra-*

---

222 *Ibid.* p. 124.
223 *Wesleyan-Methodist Magazine*, September 1862, p. 862.
224 Hutton, 1821, p. 213, remarked that he was told in 1820 that 'only some of the king's captains' were present at the reception. The reference may have been, however, to the absence of most of the chiefs from outside Kumase. In February 1828, when the Asantemanhyiamu was in session, there were '230 great umbrellas in Kumase', see p. 186 above.
225 Wilks, 1966b, p. 230. Hagan, 1971, p. 54.
226 *Wesleyan-Methodist Magazine*, September 1862, p. 862.

dofo, akwanmofo, and so forth. A number of features in combination served to distinguish the *asomfo* from other categories of officials. First, they held office by appointment from the Asantehene. Secondly, they were assigned to a specific *fekuo* or department, usually acquired the necessary skills by training within it, and were normally expected to make their careers there. Thirdly, they might expect to hold administrative positions for life, and to achieve progressively higher rank within the department and perhaps promotion to titled positions; there were, however, bars to advancement for incompetency and inefficiency, and for such failings, as also for peculation, the functionary might lose not only his job but even his property and perhaps life. Fourthly, the *asomfo* were remunerated for their services in a number of ways, but most frequently with reference to a fixed scale of fees and commissions. And finally, the *asomfo* were permitted to establish personal fortunes, and indeed accumulated wealth was one mark of their success, but precisely because such wealth was personal and not lineage property, it was upon their estates at death that the Treasury's rights to death duties fell the most heavily. In consequence, deprived of sizeable inheritances, the sons of *asomfo* – the *mmamma* – had to remain as achievement oriented as their fathers had been. The distinctive features of the *asomfo* of Asante are so significantly alike to those identified by Weber in his general model of a bureaucracy that there can be little hesitation in characterizing the 'Kwadwoan revolution in government' as a bureaucratic one.[227]

There are two indications that the nature of the Asante bureaucracy as it was conceived in the later eighteenth century – the idea of the *asomfo* as 'pure' servants of the state – was one which was inevitably to be subject to pressures for modification in certain predictable directions. First, the effect of the decree which the Gyaasewahene Opoku Frefre obtained from Osei Bonsu in 1817 was such as to initiate a trend towards the development of a patrimonial bureaucracy. The *mmamma* were acknowledged as a corporate entity in law, and their claims on specific offices within the central administration thus acquired a legitimacy which might generate conflict with the principle of merit in matters of promotion and advancement in general. Secondly, the failure of Osei Kwadwo and his successors to create a wage structure for the new administrators, but to rely upon a system of fees and commissions in an economy which was probably sufficiently highly monetized to make the first alternative possible, opened the way for the emergence of what Weber called 'entrepreneurial tax-farming'. In fact, as the Company of State Traders grew in the nineteenth cen-

227 *Wirtschaft und Gesellschaft,* 1922, III, ch. 6, and see Gerth and Mills, 1948, pp. 196–204.

tury into what was the most complex and powerful organization within the state, so the nature of its intricate financial operations approximated more and more closely to the capitalist model. The Mercantile Agents in effect borrowed money from the state to finance business operations which would yield them substantial profits after the loan capital had been repaid at interest. It will be shown in Chapter 15 that the leadership of the movement which developed in the late nineteenth century for the conversion to a free enterprise economy arose precisely within the higher echelons of the state trading organization. It will be shown, too, that the Asantehene Mensa Bonsu endeavoured to create a new style civil service within which the primacy of the merit principle would be reasserted and the paramountcy of the interests of the state re-established – even though in order to do so it proved necessary to recruit personnel from outside Asante.

In view of the far-reaching nature of the changes in government set in motion by Osei Kwadwo, it is surprising that he was not to meet with concerted resistance of the sort that had brought the nation to the point of civil war in the reign of Opoku Ware. It has been pointed out elsewhere, however, that Osei Kwadwo and his immediate successors underwrote political by military reform. A new internal security organization was created, the Ankobea, which was in effect both a militarized arm of the bureaucracy and a bureaucratized arm of the military. Of the six senior positions within it, that of Ankobeahene was created by Osei Kwadwo, those of Atipinhene and Apagyahene by Osei Kwame, and those of Anaminakohene, Atene Akuaponhene, and Atene Akotenhene by Osei Bonsu.[228] There is, however, no evidence that the Ankobea had ever to be used in any major way in defence of the revolution. To some extent its very existence was perhaps sufficient for the achievement of its purpose. But there are also indications that the bureaucratic revolution was carried out with considerable finesse. Certainly a number of older stools, such as that of the Adontenhene, were totally changed in character by edicts depriving the lineages in which they were vested of any ongoing rights to the office (see pp. 251–2). The case of the Gyaasehene, nonetheless, seems to have been more typical. In constitutional law the Gyaasehene was, and remained, the ranking officer within the groups from which the new bureaucracy was developed, swordbearers, criers, hornblowers, drummers, and the like. He was 'the captain of the palace' [229] or 'chief over the household'.[230] As the Gyaasewahene, 'the little Gyaasehene', came to assume

228 Wilks, 1966b, p. 225. Wilks, 1967a, p. 213. Hagan, 1971, pp. 56–8, and see also p. 51 for an account of an earlier force of similar nature, the Ananta.
229 Dupuis, 1824, p. 100.
230 Ramseyer and Kühne, 1875, p. 308.

the leading position within the central administration, however, the Gyaasehene increasingly associated himself not with the affairs of the capital but with those of the principal town which belonged to him, Sawua. By the latter part of the nineteenth century he was better known as the Saamanhene, outranking the Sawuahene and effectively exercising his functions and prerogatives. It will be seen below that in the 1880s the Saamanhene Akyampon Panin came to play an important role in Kumase politics. His constituency, however, was not an urban one but a rural one based upon Sawua; and he represented not the administrative class of the capital but rather the rubber tappers and traders of the surrounding countryside. The stool has remained one vested in the matrilineal descendants of Ama Birago, ancestress of the Gyaasehenes.[231]

Despite the upheavals which followed Opoku Ware's attempts at reform, the final emergence of a bureaucratic class under Osei Kwadwo and his successors occurred with a remarkable absence of conflict. The existence of the Ankobea notwithstanding, the phenomenon must be related to the fact that the new administration was fashioned to a considerable extent out of older Household groups the status of which had been recognized within the original constitution of the kingdom. Indeed, it is an important feature of Asante constitutional development in the late eighteenth and early nineteenth centuries, that conflict between the functionaries of the new central administration and those of the Asantehene's Household seems to have been minimal. More specifically, in the critical area of finance which is potentially the most generative of conflict, none seems to have occurred: it has been seen that the Asantehene's personal treasurer, the Sanaahene, was able to function as an officer both of the Household – the Abanase – and of the public Exchequer. Indeed, even within the reign of the first Asantehene Osei Tutu the principle appears to have been accepted, that state revenues were not at the exclusive disposal of the Asantehene: at that time the Akyeamehene and chief of Domakwai controlled the Treasury (see p. 414). An interesting tradition is on record which alludes to the origins of the limitations on the Asantehene's control of revenues.

The first *okyeame* of the Asantehene Osei Tutu was Boansi Kofu ('who called the Asantehene *wofa*, uncle'). There came a time, it is

231 National Archives of Ghana, Kumase, File 2984: correspondence on the election of Saamanhene Akyampon II, 27 June 1932, containing a genealogy (unfortunately incomplete) of the stool family. By a decree of 24 March 1947 the Asantehene Sir Osei Agyeman Prempeh II deprived the Saamanhene of the right to use the title *Gyaasehene*, though confirmed his position as head of the Gyaase group. From that date the Gyaasewahene accordingly became known as the Gyaasehene, see Kumase Divisional Council Archives, Manhyia: file KTCS/0130, Statement by the Asantehene, dd. 24 March 1947.

said, when Okomfo Anokye addressed the Council and stated that 'a great taboo' had fallen on the nation in that there was dissatisfaction among the chiefs; that Boansi Kofu was spokesman for the malcontents; and that the complaint was that the Asantehene retained for his own exclusive use revenues derived from constitutional cases coming before his court. Boansi Kofu is said openly to have agreed that the facts were correct, and to have stated that as Akyeamehene of Asante 'he usually sat in the sun with his stick to conduct cases but when money was collected the King took all without giving him a farthing'. His declaration was supported by the other councillors. Osei Tutu responded, so the tradition has it, first by removing Boansi Kofu from the position of Akyeamehene and creating him first Atutuehene, 'so that he should have to sit in the sun no longer'; secondly by awarding him a pension of one peredwan a week 'for his boldness in revealing such a secret which might have led to a national crisis'; thirdly, by appointing a Denkyira, Adunnya Safe, as new Akyeamehene; and fourthly, by decreeing that henceforth revenues should be shared between the Asantehene and his councillors and counselors, and that the new Akyeamehene would be responsible for carrying out that duty on the eves of the Great and Little Adae.[232] The tradition is probably to be taken as veridical. Certainly the development of the powerful Exchequer division under the Gyaasewahene in the late eighteenth and early nineteenth centuries was not the occasion of any conflict between the Asantehene and the other estates of government.

It has been shown that the broad class of the *asomfo* was one which was vertically structured: that is, each member of it belonged to a specific department or *fekuo*, was trained in the skills relevant to the work of that department, and would usually expect to make his career within it.[233] There were, however, certain groups of officials who, although closely associated with specific departments, nevertheless possessed common professional capabilities on the basis of which an identity of interest was established which cut across departmental affiliations. One of the principal of these groups was that which comprised the counselors or *akyeame*, whose preoccupation with legal work served to distinguish them from other members of the bureaucracy. In 1873 Owusu Ansa gave some account of their duties in court: 'the King administers justice in person, and is assisted by judicial assessors, or, as they are called in the country, Linguists. The litigants state their cases and call their witnesses. They are then examined by the assessors or Linguists, and, after a consultation, the Linguists advise the King as

232 IASAS/32: Atutue Stool History, recorded by J. Agyeman-Duah, 12 October 1962.
233 'Mohr und Ramseyer's Reise nach Kumase (1881)', in *Geographische Gesellschaft zu Jena*, 1882, I, 19.

to his decision, which is final'.[234] Much of the work of the counselors was, however, carried out in settings other than the courtroom. It has been seen, for example, that they were attached to armies and empowered, after the military had discharged their responsibilities, with trying and sentencing offenders and with drawing up agreements on the basis of which political order was restored. Their services were frequently utilized in ambassadorial roles; thus the Boakye Yam Panin counselor, Kwaku Fokuo, was one of the traditional members of the embassy to London in 1895 (which also included senior personnel of the new civil service). Again, in the capital itself the counselors might hold supernumerary courts of their own to relieve the pressure of work upon the regular ones. The counselors were also commonly used as political trouble shooters, to such an extent indeed that they appear frequently to have fixed in advance the course that debates in council would take. In 1927 Rattray gave an interesting summary of the major role which the *okyeame* played in the administration:

He is the prime minister and chief adviser to the king. His power and position are well exemplified in this well-known proverb: '*Kuro ebo a, efiri kyeame, kuru gyina a, efiri kyeame*' ('If a town becomes broken, it is the fault of the *okyeame*, if a town stands [firm] it is due to the *okyeame*') . . . One or more of the king's *akyeame* went on circuit for their royal master when important cases arose elsewhere. They were also sent, in times of peace, as envoys and ambassadors.[235]

Rattray's seemingly facile comparison of the role of the senior counselor with that of prime minister is one which should not be treated too lightly. The counselors undoubtedly occupied a quite unique position within the central administration. Although their functions were entirely executive ones, they had constant access not only to the Asantehene but also to the decision-making bodies: although having no votes in council, no meetings could be held in their absence. With complete access to information from the legislative branch of government, they dominated the executive branch. As early as 1820 Hutton, with considerable insight, was led to essay a comparison of the position within the administration of the Gyakye counselor Kwadwo Adusei Kyakya with that of the four so-called Privy Councillors – his own departmental head, the Gyaasewahene Opoku Frefre; the Bantamahene Amankwatia; the Asafohene Kwaakye Kofi; and the Adumhene Adum Ata. 'Apokoo and the other three', wrote Hutton, 'who form the aristocracy, may have more power than Adoosey, but I incline to think, from the situation he holds as head

234 *The Times,* 29 July 1873.
235 Rattray, 1927, pp. 277–8.

linguist, as well as from his great abilities, both as an orator and a statesman, that they have not more influence.' [236]

There is no evidence to show whether, in the early nineteenth century, the counselors met regularly together to discuss policy; whether, that is, there was any tendency towards the emergence of a 'cabinet' within the executive branch. What is highly significant in this context, however, is the fact that European observers in the period commonly equated the role of the counselor with that of the minister in the systems of government with which they were more familiar. Thus the Gyakye counselor Kwadwo Adusei Kyakya was 'a confidential minister' or 'the minister premier'.[237] The Akankade counselor Kwasi Kankam was 'another minister'.[238] Oti Panin, the Boakye Yam Panin counselor, was 'the Minister of the King of Ashantee',[239] and Asante Agyei was 'the foreign minister'.[240] It is unfortunate that so much of the work of the counselors was not such as to be visible to the stranger in the capital, and there is little information available on their activities – other than their public appearances – for most of the nineteenth century. It is, however, quite apparent from the letters and journals of the missionaries who visited the capital at the time of Kwaku Dua I, that for at least the first part of his reign the main burden of the day to day administration of affairs was carried by the Akyeamhene Kwame Poku Agyeman. He was, Freeman remarked in 1839, 'the only person who is allowed to visit the King at *any* time he wishes . . . and seems to have great influence with him'.[241] Significantly, the three Europeans who spent the longest amount of time in Kumase in the nineteenth century, Ramseyer, Kühne, and Bonnat, appear all to have been aware of the distinction between the familiar role of the counselors as advocates in court – as so-called 'linguists' or 'spokesmen' – and their less familiar but more important role as the senior officers of the executive branch. Thus Ramseyer and Kühne referred to the Akyeamehene Kwaku Poku as 'head of the linguists, minister of foreign affairs'.[242] The most revealing comment, however, came from Bonnat and has been referred to above (p. 403). The Asantehene, he remarked, had persons to assist him in the administration of justice, namely, 'cinq linguistes ou interprètes qui sont en même temps ses conseillers. On les appelle *quamis* [akyeame]; ils occupent tous un des grands commandments de la capitale.'

236 Hutton, 1821, pp. 272–3.
237 Dupuis, 1824, pp. 90, 152. Hutton, 1821, p. 315.
238 Dupuis, 1824, p. 90.
239 PRO, CO. 267/93, Appendix: Hansen to Commissioners, dd. Accra, 17 September 1826.
240 Lee, 1835, p. 365.
241 T. B. Freeman, 1843, p. 61.
242 Ramseyer and Kühne, 1875, p. 308.

The matter of the ministerial roles of the counselors in the nineteenth century is one greatly in need of further investigation. There can be little doubt, however, that a number of the counselors came to be the effective and indeed recognized heads of the departments to which they were initially attached. It has been seen that the Boakye Yam Panin *okyeame* was closely associated with the affairs of the Bata. At some point in time which has not been determined, the Asokwahene, titular head of the Bata whose stool had been created by Osei Tutu, was made subordinate to the Boakye Yam Panin counselor, whose stool had been created some three quarters of a century later by Osei Kwame. 'The Boakye Yam Panin stool', Nana Boakye Tenten II observed in 1965,

is *mmammadwa* . . . All the Asokwa people, the hornblowers, come under me. The Batahene serves me. The Batahene stool is *mmammadwa*. I have married from there, and I have some of my children there. So one of my sons could contest for the Asokwa stool, and if the kingmakers liked him, be made chief. If the Asokwahene was one of my sons, then he could contest for the Boakye Yam Panin stool. But he probably would not.[243]

It was clearly a mark of the importance which the counselorship acquired, that the two husbands of the Asantehemaa Afua Kobi both held it and that in other circumstances both Kofi Kakari and Mensa Bonsu would have been members of its *mmamma*.

Other than the counselors, there was certainly at least one further set of persons within the ranks of the bureaucracy whose common interests transcended departmental affiliations. These were the *ahenemma*, the princes, who in effect constituted the *mmamma* of the Golden Stool though they had no claims to it. Not all princes pursued their early careers within the bureaucracy, but a significant number did. Reference has been made, for example, to the two sons of Asantehene Osei Kwadwo who became resident commissioners, Owusu Gyamadua in Akuapem and Owusu Bannahene in Accra; the former had apparently served earlier as a revenue collector and the latter as a trader (see pp. 136 and 139). Owusu Dome was a son of Osei Kwame, and a member of the torchbearers group in Kumase; he had a distinguished career in the diplomatic service (p. 149 and n.). Again, Adu Brade was a son probably of Opoku Fofie, and became the government's principal negotiator with the British (p. 398 and n.). Owusu Ba, most likely a son of Osei Bonsu, was perhaps permanent ambassador to the court of Abomey in Dahomey (p. 323). Unlike the more typical members of the administrative class, the prince who displayed energy and talent might expect rapidly to acquire a titled position of

243 Wilks, field-notes, interview with Nana Boakye Tenten II, dd. Kumase, 3 August 1965.

importance (as opposed to the sinecures which they often obtained as children). Thus both Owusu Bannahene and Owusu Dome rose to become Kyidomhene, technically a military position but in fact one involving the management of the many towns and villages which belonged to the stool. Others might acquire senior positions within the Ankobea, the internal security forces. Owusu Gyamadua, for example, became Apagyahene, and that stool together with the Atipin, Atene Akoten and Anaminako were usually occupied by princes. Yet again, others might use their wealth and prestige to advance their candidacy to stools controlled by their matrikin. The case may be cited of a grandson of the Golden Stool, Osei Bonsu, becoming Mamponhene; his father was Owusu Kwabena, son of the Asantehene Osei Bonsu and a member of the *asoamfo* or hammock-men of Kumase, and his mother was Akosua Atiaa, a Mampon royal.[244]

The prince's prospects for advancement were undoubtedly better than those of other *asomfo*. Nevertheless, there were always far more princes in Kumase than there were titled positions open to them. Many lesser functionaries are referred to in the sources who, from their names, may well have belonged to the princely class. Yet little more is known of them precisely because they failed to attain high office and remained among the unknown multitude upon whose services good government was ultimately predicated. It has been shown in Chapter 9 that in the second half of the nineteenth century an extraordinary number of positions within the chiefly establishment in Kumase had been acquired in one way or another by the sons of Kwaku Dua I. Yet it also appears to have been felt that to some extent that the Asantehene had acted without adequate reason in creating, within the new Manwere *fekuo,* stood for others of his sons which were little more than sinecures: the Ayebiakyere, Somi and Asabi offices.[245] Certainly among the programmes of modernization to which Mensa Bonsu subscribed, was one which had probably been formulated by Owusu Ansa: that the class of princes, membership of which was ascribed by birth, should be transformed into an open order to which those not among the *mmamma* of the Golden Stool, and indeed not necessarily citizens of Asante, might be admitted in recognition of their services to the nation. Thus in 1879 a Sierra Leonean, Dr Africanus Horton, was en-

---

244 Rattray, 1929, genealogy facing p. 254, refers to Owusu Kwabena as a son of Osei Yaw. Owusu Ansa, however, specifically wrote of Owusu Kwabena (who died about 1877) as 'his own brother', see Basel Mission Archives, Ramseyer's personal file, Owusu Ansa to Ramseyer, dd. 7 July 1877. See also Ramseyer and Kühne, 1875, p. 308.

245 For the principle of 'not creating unnecessarily a new position', as stated by Nana Osei Agyeman Prempeh II, see National Archives of Ghana, Kumase, D. 1491, District Commissioner, Kumase, to Chief Commissioner, 15 December 1938.

abled to become a 'Prince of Asante' (see p. 78). The concept of the new Order of Princes represented, perhaps, the ultimate application of the bureaucratic principle in the Asante context. Only the idea of monarchy remained unassailed.

In the course of the bureaucratic revolution the *asomfo* as a class had been allocated new sets of duties and new sets of rights, and had acquired a status which distinguished them from all other groups within society. Service, *εsom,* had become almost the reverse of servitude, *nkoasom.* The most junior functionary travelling on official business was respected and even feared: he was the representative of the *abankesemu,* the central authority, and he came from Kumase, the imperial city. Some impression of the connotation of the name was conveyed to Mohr in 1881 on the occasion of his having travelled from Kumase to Begoro – an Akyem Abuakwa town which had not been under the rule of Asante for fifty years.

'Have you seen Kumase?' That is very like asking us, 'Have you seen Europe?', said the people of Begoro, plaguing me to tell them about that city after my happy return from it. Implicit in the mere name of Kumase, for our people, is the essence of everything powerful, grand, and terrifying. There was a time which has not yet been forgotten, when the 'tumfoo' [Asantehene] in Kumase was the master over life and death for the Akems.[246]

In the very same year the British Special Commissioner Lonsdale alluded to the same intangible quality which Asante seemed to possess:

I left [Fomena] on the 2nd of November, and at 11:30 a.m. crossed from Adansi into Ashanti . . . No sooner has one entered Ashanti and passed through one or two of the numerous small villages which dot the road than one is aware of having reached a new country. A system of some kind impresses itself upon the senses.[247]

It has been the purpose of this chapter to attempt to indicate something of the nature of that 'system'. Yet it is a fact, that the perceptions of the Begoro people as of Lonsdale in 1881 were those of outsiders. The system which appeared so monolithic from without was in reality a product of a society which was both highly politicized and politically strongly polarized. It is to this matter that the next chapter is addressed.

246 'Mohr und Ramseyer's Reise nach Kumase (1881)', in *Geographische Gesellschaft zu Jena,* 1882, I, 19.
247 *Further Correspondence,* C. 3386, 1882, p. 59: Lonsdale's report on his mission of 1881–2.

CHAPTER 12

Political polarization in nineteenth century Asante [1]

The Asantehenes as 'hawks' and 'doves'

The view that an Asantehene should be above politics was not one, apparently, that enjoyed currency in nineteenth century Asante. Throughout the century observers commented upon the extent of the ruler's involvement not only in government but in politics. 'The king', reported those familiar with Kofi Kakari's administration, 'takes great interest in politics and the affairs of the nation.' [2] Twenty years earlier the missionary Hart had remarked upon Kwaku Dua's insistence upon thoroughly understanding an issue before allowing it to come up for public debate. 'There is wisdom in so doing', he observed, 'as he dare not act without his Chiefs': [3] that is, the Asantehene needed to be able to argue convincingly before his councillors. One of the more fundamental issues upon which opinion was deeply divided in the nineteenth century was that of policy towards the British, and it was a significant indicator of the polarization in political life, that each Asantehene was identified in terms of a primary commitment to either a 'hawkish' or a 'dovish' approach. Osei Bonsu, despite the many wars he fought, was placed in the second category. It was, Dupuis observed of him, 'a maxim associated with the religion he professed, never to appeal to the sword while a path lay open for negociation. He maintained that he would defy even his enemies to prove that his assertion deviated from the truth.' [4] Much the same tribute was paid to him by Bowdich: 'however assured the king of Ashantee may be of the flagitious actions or expressions of any tributary or chief, it is always the form to affect a disbelief of the report, and to send two or three state officers to see if the offender persists or recants'.[5] By contrast, Osei

---

1 This chapter is based upon the Ninth Melville J. Herskovits Memorial Lecture, delivered at the University of Edinburgh, 1 December 1970, see Wilks, 1970.
2 Brackenbury, 1874, II, 330.
3 *Wesleyan-Methodist Magazine*, October 1850, p. 1108: F. Hart to General Secretaries, dd. Cape Coast, 29 June 1850.
4 Dupuis, 1824, pp. 225–6.
5 Bowdich, 1821a, p. 28.

Bonsu's successor, Osei Yaw, was considered 'hawkish' and commenced his reign, it was reported, 'by an *edict* against the British, wherein they were accused . . . of perfidy, infractions of treaties, violations of public faith, treachery, cruelty, etc. To revenge which . . . the new monarch vowed eternal war against the British until he had obtained satisfaction.' [6]

The next ruler, Kwaku Dua I, is remembered still in Asante as 'the most peaceable of the dynasty'. The missionary Freeman remarked, that 'his habits are distinguished for sobriety, and his disposition is mild and placable'.[7] In 1863 a writer on the Gold Coast commented, 'We have, I believe, to thank the peaceable mind of the King, Quacoe Duah, that we have lived in peace so many years',[8] and Ellis reiterated the general view, 'that Osai Kwaku Dua was the most pacific ruler that had ever sat on the stool of Ashanti'.[9] But Kofi Kakari, who succeeded Kwaku Dua in 1867, was a man of different disposition. He accepted office, according to one report, after having taken oaths to reverse his predecessor's policies. 'Swear to us once more', his officers were said to have insisted, 'that you wish to wage war. Your uncle Kwaku Dua never waged war. But our kingdom was founded and grew large through war.' [10] According to Reindorf's report, Kofi Kakari ordered 'one of his executioners to extol him thus: *Kakari gyambi, Ayeboafo a ode ntutea beko aperem ano,* "Kakari the hero, the champion who will fight at the cannon's mouth with his narrow guns" '.[11] Yet another account stated that on his accession Kofi Kakari swore, 'Mein handel soll der Krieg sein' – my trade shall be war [12] – apparently a scornful allusion to the emphasis placed upon the promotion of commerce by those of opposite persuasion. But Kofi Kakari's successor, Mensa Bonsu, opened his reign with assurances that he intended to emulate the policies of Kwaku Dua I and that he stood for the maintenance of 'peace, trade and open roads'.[13] Finally, the short-reigned Kwaku Dua II (1884) was, like Mensa Bonsu, associated with 'dovish' policies and came to office on a programme of peace.[14] The rulers of Asante

6 Dupuis, 1824, p. 215.
7 T. B. Freeman, in *The Western Echo*, I, no. 8, 30 January 1886, p. 2.
8 *The African Times*, II, no. 24, 23 June, 1863: anon. letter dd. Christiansborg, 12 May 1863.
9 Ellis, 1893, p. 226. See further, Ramseyer and Kühne, 1875, p. 171.
10 See the biographical material on 'Misidateri' recorded by W. Rottmann, Mose der Koransier, in *Die Evangelische Heidenbote der Basler Mission*, 1892. I am indebted to Mr T. McCaskie for this reference.
11 Reindorf, 2nd ed., n.d., p. 114.
12 Steiner, 1900, p. 7. Cf. Ramseyer and Kühne, 1875, p. 202.
13 *Papers relating to Her Majesty's Possessions in West Africa*, C. 1343, 1876: Strahan to Carnarvon, dd. Cape Coast, 8 January 1875, reporting the arrival of messengers from Mensa Bonsu.
14 *Further Correspondence*, C. 3687, 1883, p. 158: Barrow to Rowe, dd. Kumase, 27 April 1883.

from the beginning of the century until 1884 were, then, quite clearly identified by their contemporaries as, in sequence, dovish, hawkish, dovish, hawkish, dovish and dovish.

The peace and war parties

Many nineteenth century observers recognized that the differences in attitude manifest by the rulers of Asante reflected an underlying polarization in political outlook which affected all participants in the decision-making process. In 1820, in the course of his negotiations in Kumase, the British consul Dupuis for example acknowledged the opposition which existed between what he referred to as the army interest, resisting acceptance of the second Anglo-Asante treaty, and the peace interest, advocating it. Urged to provide gold to win over the adherents of the former, Dupuis was advised: 'Do this, and you will immediately have a party that shall carry all before them in the cabinet; for the king is disposed to do all he can for you, but he must not oppose his great captains . . .'[15] The strong influence of the army interest in the Council, surely enough, rapidly declined to a point at which Dupuis could refer to the 'few ambitious chiefs of the opposing faction, who were hardy enough to persist in demanding war . . . a faction that had secret interests in keeping alive the embers of discord'.[16] From about the middle of the century onwards, commentators began to refer with increasing regularity to the existence in Asante of what they chose to call the peace and war parties. In 1852, for example, the British Governor Hill expressed his fears that Kwaku Dua might be 'induced to listen to the strong war party existing in his dominions, and possibly commit some act of aggression on the nations under our protection'.[17] In the following year the Governor observed further, that especially in matters of foreign affairs the war party might easily overrule the pacific Asantehene.[18] 'There is', commented an anonymous writer in 1867, 'always a powerful war party in Ashantee.'[19] 'Two parties [*partis*] exist', noted the Frenchman Bonnat, 'that of peace . . . and that of war.'[20]

In the 1870s and 1880s, through their intelligence network, the British began to amass a substantial body of data on the processes of government in Asante, and commentators like Maurice, Ellis and

[15] Dupuis, 1824, pp. 152–3.
[16] *Ibid.* pp. 156 and 159.
[17] *Despatches . . . relating to the warfare*, C. 703, 1853, p. 2: Hill to Packington, dd. Cape Coast, 23 October 1852.
[18] *Ibid.* p. 13: Hill to Newcastle, dd. Cape Coast, 13 April 1853.
[19] *The African Times*, VII, no. 77, p. 55.
[20] Bonnat, in Gros, 1884, p. 229, with especial reference to the Council of 22 July 1871.

Lonsdale presented more detailed analyses of politics in terms of the opposition between peace and war parties. In 1874, for example, Maurice – who drew heavily upon information supplied by the missionary Kühne [21] – in an account headed 'Rival Parties in Coomassie' offered some remarks on the composition of the opposed forces in Kofi Kakari's councils at the time of the debates of late 1873:

His mother [the Asantehemaa] has from the first detested the war, and used her utmost influence, which is very considerable, over her son to prevent its occurrence; to cause the recall of the army; and now to induce him to accept our [the British] terms. On the same side the chiefs who have been fighting against us range themselves without exception. The King, moreover, is seriously alarmed himself.

On the other hand, there are, as might be expected, a certain number of Marathanomakoi, who have known only war with the interior, or the wars with us in 1864 or in older times, when they have almost invariably been able to boast of success, and who, now being too old to fight, banter the younger men on their degeneracy; a certain number of chiefs who were not engaged this time against us, through various causes; a set of men who have all their lives hung round the King, flattering him to the top of his bent as invincible, 'the white man slayer,' etc. Then, too, there are a not inconsiderable number of men who have been resident in and about Coomassie all their lives, and look upon it as the centre of the universe.[22]

Maurice also essayed a brief but more general description of the relationship between the army interest as such, and the war party in the Councils of 1872, prior to the invasion of the British Protected Territory. 'War is the thing', he observed of Kofi Kakari,

which he has sworn at the time of his coronation to prepare for his country. It is a continued condition of peace for which some apology is needed. The opportunity is the only excuse that is needed for war . . . To this it must be added that the desire for war was, in all probability, not so strong even in his mind as in that of some of the war leaders . . . It would almost seem as if there was a War cabinet or court which surrounded the King, the members of which, though very influential over a young monarch, have no assigned position and authority during peace, but who become supreme in the field the moment war breaks out . . . The old King [Kwaku Dua] had curbed in the war spirit to an extent that was certain to make it break out more powerfully when the reins of government fell into the hands of a young man.[23]

---

21 Maurice, 1874, pp. 266–7. Maurice, then Special Correspondent for the *Daily News* of London, noted that Kühne, who had spent four years in Asante, was better at reporting discrete facts than in answering questions about 'the relative power of the King, the chiefs, the fetish priests, and the Ashantee people'!

22 Maurice, 1874, p. 268.

23 *Ibid.* pp. 16–19.

Similarly, in his analyses of Asante politics in the reign of Mensa Bonsu, Ellis saw the nature of the decisions taken as reflecting the relative strength of peace and war parties – the former of which he frequently termed the 'court' party since the Asantehene was aligned with it. Thus, of the situation in 1880, Ellis commented: 'the war party in Coomassie were desirous of invading Adansi, and were quite willing to take the risk of another war with England. Opposed to the war party were the king, the queen-mother, and the court party . . .'[24] When Lonsdale visited Kumase in 1882, he found the peace party in power, but the war party sufficiently strong for Mensa Bonsu to be anxious to appease its leaders. He was cordially received, so he reported, 'by those Chiefs who . . . are in opposition to the extreme [i.e. war] party, either through personal jealousy, personal hostility, or want of coincidence with them in the general policy'.[25] But it was Lonsdale's view that the Asantehene was fully responsible to the Council of Kumase, and, so he maintained, 'the party in his councils which adheres to its programme with the greatest pertinacity and boldness would, I think, always direct him'.[26]

It is not being argued here, of course, that the parties of nineteenth century Asante were similar to those of mid-twentieth century Ghana – or, for that matter, of Europe. But it *is* being suggested that the parties of nineteenth century Asante bore sufficient resemblance to those of nineteenth century Europe for nineteenth century European commentators to be prepared to write of both in the same terms. It may be noted that it was by no means apparent to political observers in the late eighteenth century, that parties had any permanent place in the English political scene; and in 1784 it could be argued that

by the frequent coalitions between *whig* and *tory* leaders, even that party distinction, the most famous in the English history, has now become useless: the meaning of the words has thereby been rendered so perplexed that nobody can any longer give a tolerable definition of them; and those persons who now and then aim at gaining popularity by claiming the merit of belonging to either party, are scarcely understood.[27]

The consolidation of a bi-party system in England in the course of the nineteenth century was paralleled in significant respects, so the evidence indicates, by developments in Asante.

To judge from the ease with which the opponents of the second Anglo-Asante treaty were won over in 1820, the degree of polarization in political attitudes was probably still low in the reign of Osei Bonsu.

24 Ellis, 1883, pp. 203–4.
25 *Further Correspondence*, C. 3687, 1883, pp. 110–12: Lonsdale's report on his mission to Asante and Gyaman, April to June 1882.
26 *Ibid.* p. 117.
27 De Lolme, 1822, pp. xviii–xix.

On the other hand, it may have been precisely with reference to the issue of the southern provinces in the decade 1816–26, when British policy had become unquestionably aggressive and unaccommodating, that the Asante government found itself confronted with problems of novel starkness: in the resolution of which conflict within the Councils materialized at an hitherto unknown level, and resulted in the co-alescence of the factions within it into party-like structures. Indeed, the sort of change that was occurring may be illustrated by reference to the two examples of decision-making already considered in detail. In the case of the decision-logic underlying the government's determination of its Wassa policy in 1816–17 (see p. 160), it will be observed that the goal was an agreed one, namely the fuller incorporation of the Wassa into Greater Asante, and that conflict arose only from disagreement about the optimal route to the agreed goal. But in the case of the determination of the government's policy *vis-à-vis* the southern provinces in 1824–6 (see p. 184), conflicting and incompatible goals by contrast existed: namely, whether or not abandonment of control over them was in the national interest. The indications are that for much of the remainder of the century it was on the question of the southern provinces (and therefore on that of confrontation with, or accommodation to, the British interest on the Gold Coast) that Asante politicians were the most fundamentally and irreconcilably divided. To that extent, therefore, the characterization of the bi-polarity that emerged in terms of 'peace' and 'war' parties was appropriate. It will be shown in a later chapter, however, that the issues of peace and war were each linked with other variables, and that a more adequate and embracing description of the political divisions within Asante society was between those subscribing to mercantilist policies and regarding the state as essentially organized for the promotion of trade – the adherents of the 'peace' party – and those subscribing to imperialist policies and regarding the state as essentially organized for the control of territory and the exaction of tribute – the adherents of the 'war' party.

It is arguable that the development of the bi-party system in Asante received a major set-back in 1884, when the figureheads of both parties – Kwaku Dua Kuma and Kofi Kakari – died or were killed within two weeks of each other, at a time moreover when a third political force had been making its influence felt in national affairs. The situation of turmoil which followed, in which central government was rendered ineffectual as rival factions made recourse to arms, was ended only with the recognition of Agyeman Prempe (Kwaku Dua III) as Asantehene-elect by the Council of Kumase in March 1888.[28] Curiously, in 1892 a

---

28 *Further Correspondence*, C. 5615, 1888, pp. 37–40: Barnett to Governor, dd. 20 March 1888, reporting Prempe's installation on the Adum, or Asantehene-elect, stool.

not entirely dissimilar disruption was to occur in English political life. 'The sudden interjection of the question of the Home Rule into English politics', wrote one contemporary observer,

caused a new party division on fresh lines, which necessarily broke up the traditional associations of public life, and threw both parties into a state of confusion that has not yet [1896] disappeared . . . In short, the introduction of a new issue shattered the old basis of cleavage, and it is not surprising that new, solidified parties were not formed in an instant.[29]

In Asante, having in 1891 firmly rejected an offer of British protection, Agyeman Prempe nonetheless proceeded to emphasize the continuity of his policies specifically with those of the peace party administration of Kwaku Dua I at the time of Governor Maclean. 'I wish', he informed an emissary of the British in 1893,

to remain always on good terms with the Governor as my grand uncle Adjuman [Fredua Agyeman, i.e., Kwaku Dua I] did with Governor Maclean. I want to encourage trade as Adjuman my grand uncle did in the time of Governor Maclean . . . Adjuman is my grand uncle, I wish for peace and quietness as Adjuman did in the time of Maclean.[30]

The Asante nation, acutely aware of the effects of factional discord, responded clearly to Prempe's advocacy of the goals of the old peace party – of 'peace, trade and open roads'. In June 1894, the Asantemanhyiamu met in Kumase, debated and approved Prempe's policies, and proceeded to afford him formal and full recognition as Asantehene.[31]

The growth of the war interest under Osei Bonsu

For the period between 1820 (to take the negotiation of the second Anglo-Asante treaty as an arbitrary base line) and 1884, the sources are sufficiently full not only for periods of war party or peace party supremacy to be recognized, but also for those points in time at which the preponderance of one party gave way to that of the other to be identified. It will become apparent that any analysis of Asante politics in the nineteenth century must take account of a distinction between *reigns* and *governments*. For while it has been seen that each Asantehene was identifiable as essentially 'dovish' or 'hawkish', or as associated with the policies of either peace or war party, nevertheless the times at which peace party governments gave way to war party

29 Lowell, 1896, I, 71–2.
30 *Further Correspondence*, C. 7917, 1896, pp. 106–7: message from Agyeman Prempe I to Acting Governor, transmitted through District Commissioner H. Vroom, dd. Kumase, 19 October 1893.
31 *Ibid.* pp. 201–2: Agyeman Prempe I to Governor, dd. Kumase, 28 June 1894. *Gold Coast Methodist Times,* 31 August 1894.

ones, and vice versa, did not correspond necessarily with the ends and beginnings of reigns. Thus periods occurred in which a hawkish ruler might have to accommodate his policies to those of a peace party majority in his Councils, and a dovish ruler to those of a war party majority. In such a situation an Asantehene might attempt to change the political complexion of his Council by purging or otherwise removing from office a number of his opponents: but, in thus refusing to accommodate to the will of the majority, he incurred the risk of himself being removed from office. Among the seventy-seven laws regarded, traditionally, as given by Okomfo Anokye at the inception of the nation, was one that the Asantehene should be the last to express his views in Council, but that his decision should never be challenged under penalty of death.[32] Even in the late nineteenth century the Asantehene's constitutional right to veto a decision of the majority of his councillors was still recognized.[33] But it is indicative of the degree to which the kingship, though not the Golden Stool, had become both secularized and politicized from the later eighteenth century onwards, that this right could not, with impunity, regularly be exercised.

In the later part of the reign of Osei Bonsu, dissatisfaction with his policies was becoming increasingly manifest in council. In 1816 and 1817, for example, the confidence which Osei Bonsu reposed in the Dutch Director General Daendels in Elmina (see pp. 155–61) was by no means accepted by the councillors. 'All the King's officers', reported Huydecoper, Daendel's representative in Kumase,

> are persuaded that the General is an enemy of Asante. Because of my protests the King is to some extent on our side, but his subordinates are by no means of a like mind . . . One of his secretaries, who is also his uncle and is named Aquassie Kankema [Akankade *okyeame* Kankan], has always been most loyal to the General. He is a very wise old man . . . He was never able to convince the majority, it is true, but I cannot fail to praise him for the good opinion he has of our government and for the way in which he has defended us.[34]

Although Osei Bonsu refused to abandon his Dutch policy, in May or June 1817 he did make a major concession to the more militant councillors when he agreed to reject an offer of 800 oz of gold made by envoys from Gyaman as atonement for the recent acts of rebellion in their country (see p. 271). He thereby virtually committed himself to military operations against the province. 'The aristocracy', reported Bowdich, 'were obstinate, and urged the King, that his other tribu-

32 Kyerematen, 1966, pp. 236–7.
33 *Further Correspondence*, C. 7917, 1896, p. 181: Vroom to Governor, dd. Christiansborg, 24 April 1894.
34 Huydecoper's Journal, entries for 6 and 7 April 1817.

taries would laugh at him, if he did not get the King of Gaman's head.' [35] Osei Bonsu himself took the field, and left civil affairs in the hands of the Asantehemaa Adoma Akosua. That all opposition to Osei Bonsu had not collapsed, however, became rapidly apparent. In collaboration with an unidentified Bron chief, Adoma Akosua and a number of the royal wives and princes began to plan the seizure of power from Osei Bonsu. Few details of the episode are extant. The Asantehene, learning of it, hastily despatched back to the capital a force under Owusu Kwadwo (whose identity has not been established). The movement was easily crushed. Subsequently, upon Osei Bonsu's return to Kumase in 1819, the ringleaders were placed on trial. Adoma Akosua was executed by strangulation, a number of the royal wives by decapitation, and the Bron chief and his supporters suffered even less pleasant ends. All in all, some seven hundred of the dissidents were reported slain.[36]

The success of the Gyaman campaigns of 1818–19, and the considerable amount of booty which was distributed among the participants,[37] did much to restore Osei Bonsu's prestige. In 1820 he was able with comparative ease to obtain a majority in favour of the revised Anglo-Asante treaty. Although he insisted, so Dupuis reported of the debates, 'upon an unconditional submission to his plan of negotiation', he nevertheless recognized the virtue of winning over, rather than overruling, the opposition. 'I must do what the old men say', he told the Consul in explanation of his inability simply to ignore those of differing opinion.[38] The subsequent failure of the British government to ratify the treaty, however, and the refusal to provide passages for members of the Asante embassy to London,[39] in the view of most of the councillors clearly and conclusively demonstrated the unreal nature of Osei Bonsu's peace policy. By 1822 the war party probably commanded a majority in council, and was exercising effective power. When on 1 February 1823 the Asante resident commissioner at Abora Dunkwa, Kwame Butuakwa, executed the death sentence on a sergeant of the Royal African Corps found guilty of insulting the Asantehene, it was clear that he was acting on the orders not of Osei Bonsu but of the war party government:

the Sergeant, after his capture, was sent, under escort, to the king, who personally desirous of living in peace with the British Government, raised objections to the sergeant's being brought to Kumase, and released him . . . The chiefs and captains of Asante then took the responsibility upon them-

[35] Bowdich, 1819, p. 245.
[36] Dupuis, 1824, pp. 115–16.
[37] *Ibid.* pp. 80–1.
[38] *Ibid.* pp. 140–8.
[39] *Ibid.* pp. 168–9 and 188–90.

selves, and authorized Butuakwa to kill the Sergeant in spite of the king's objections. Before carrying out the order, Butuakwa was reported to have said: 'How often I have tried to keep together the powerful kingdom of Asante by my eloquence, but they will not have it'.[40]

Recognizing finally that peace with the British was not attainable on any terms compatible with the national interest, Osei Bonsu probably concurred in his government's decision, in 1823, to reoccupy the southern provinces. The Councils were, however, bitterly divided ones (see p. 174). It was reported that throughout the whole of the Odwira of 1823, which took place in late July or August, 'great dissentions existed among the Chiefs, and some of them had the confidence to tell the King, *"they would have nothing to do with the war"* '.[41] Not least of the problems was that while many councillors were pressing for war against the British, and earlier in the year two thousand or more troops had been pulled back from the northwest for service in the southern provinces,[42] nevertheless the situation in Gyaman remained serious (see p. 273): and it was among the laws of Okomfo Anokye, that the Asante should never conduct two or more wars simultaneously. By October there was something of a crisis of confidence, and the government offered liberal terms to the Gyaman to end resistance – only to learn that its messengers had been executed there.[43] Probably in October 1823, Osei Bonsu died (see p. 174). 'The distressed Sai Quamina', Dupuis wrote of him, 'was no more, having as it would appear, departed this life in grief and vexation, bequeathing to his successor the kingdom and palaver together.' [44]

The consolidation of the peace interest after 1826

Upon Osei Bonsu's death, Osei Yaw Akoto by report seized the Golden Stool and immediately 'took it to war', thereby avoiding contest with the young candidate of the peace interest, Kwaku Dua.[45] Although the British had believed Osei Yaw to be aligned with the peace interest, information nevertheless reached them that he had declared that he would have the blood of white men to 'water' the grave of Osei Bonsu.[46] The Councils were still believed to be divided, and it was reported that 'the leading men of the oligarchy are divided as to the best means to be adopted to bring about a peace, and some of them

40 Reindorf, 2nd ed., n.d., p. 172. See also *Royal Gold Coast Gazette,* 11 March 1823.
41 *Ibid.* 7 September 1823 (italics original).
42 *Ibid.* 7 June 1823.
43 *Ibid.* 15 November 1823.
44 Dupuis, 1824, p. 215.
45 Kyerematen, 1966, p. 352.
46 *Royal Gold Coast Gazette,* 1, 15 and 22 November 1823.

have gone so far as to declare publicly their disapprobation of the contention with Europeans, especially the English, who have made them great by their trade'.[47] Gaining in stature, however, from the defeat of the British forces at Asamankow in 1824, Osei Yaw enjoyed the support of a war party government for a further two years, in which time a number of his opponents, such as the 'vaandrig' Kwame Boampon, sought refuge in rebel southern provinces.[48] With the defeat of Osei Yaw's armies at Katamanso in 1826, however, the peace party came to power once again. The Gyakye counselor Kwadwo Adusei Kyakya, a leader of the peace party in the latter part of Osei Bonsu's reign,[49] attempted to have the Asantehene removed from office.[50] Osei Yaw, in turn, brought charges against the counselor (see p. 185) and sentenced him to be stoned to death.[51] Kwadwo Adusei and many members of his family were executed in 1829, a measure which apparently commanded much popular support.[52] Osei Yaw, nevertheless, adjusted his views to those of the peace party government and accepted, however reluctantly, its programme of handing over to the local European establishments on the Gold Coast effective administrative control over the southern provinces. With the ratification of the treaties of 1831 by British and Danes, the programme became finally realized, and Osei Yaw remained in office until his death in 1833.[53]

As a result of the excellence of the relations which were maintained between the government and the British administration of Maclean, the peace party majority in the Asante Councils became a strongly entrenched one. The pacific Kwaku Dua I, who was elected to office upon the death of Osei Yaw, was to reign for thirty-four years and for most of them to enjoy the support of that party. A series of crises, however, disturbed the tranquillity of the period: as political attitudes hardened, so recourse to political violence became increasingly common. Although Kwaku Dua's election had apparently not been vigorously contested, opposition to his policies became rapidly manifest. In particular, his conciliatory overtures to the exiled Dwabenhene

47 *Ibid.* 22 November 1823.
48 General State Archives, The Hague, KvG 352: Elmina Journal, entry for 26 August 1825.
49 Dupuis, 1824, p. 153.
50 Kyerematen, 1966, p. 352.
51 Reindorf, 2nd ed., n.d., p. 209. Kyerematen, 1966, pp. 352–3. Institute of African Studies, Ghana, IASAS/127: Jachie Linguist Stool, recorded by J. Agyeman-Duah, May 1964.
52 National Archives, Copenhagen, Generaltold kammerets Arkiv, 1760–1848, Guineiske Journaler, 1834: Jackson to Lind, dd. Cape Coast, 7 December 1829.
53 The exact date of Osei Yaw's death has not been ascertained, but news had already reached the Gold Coast of the accession of Kwaku Dua ('Kwasy Duah') by 10 January 1834, see National Archives, Copenhagen, Generaltold kammerets Arkiv, 1760–1848, Guineiske Journaler, 1834: entry dd. 10 January.

Kwasi Boaten, in whose household he had grown up, proved a source of discord. By the terms of the peace settlement of 1835, Kwasi Boaten was granted amnesty, and subsequently he was paid grants-in-aid from the Asante Treasury to enable him to resettle his people in their home towns (see p. 119). Disquiet was seemingly expressed by the Kumase functionaries who had carried out the occupation of Dwaben in 1831, including the Bantamahene Apraku (alias Awua Yam), the Asafohene Asafo Agyei, the Gyaasewahene Adu Damte, the Dadiesoabahene Yaw Da, the Akuroponhene Ansere Tepa and the Amoakohene Oten Kwasi. The exiled Dwabenhene accordingly announced it as a condition of his return, that those who had led the military operations against him in 1831 should be executed.[54] That Kwaku Dua seriously entertained Kwasi Boaten's demand reflected his willingness to preside over the liquidation of his principal political opponents: for the list consisted largely of veterans of Osei Yaw's campaigns on the Gold Coast of 1823–6[55] who constituted perhaps an 'old guard' still basically attached to the imperial values of that period. First to fall was the Bantamahene Apraku. Charging that he had recently released, without formal authorization, a Wassa chief who had long been in his custody, Kwaku Dua placed him on trial. Found guilty, he was condemned to death and executed.[56] The Gyaasewahene, the wealthy and powerful Adu Damte, made plans to seize control of Kumase and remove Kwaku Dua from office. The plot was discovered, and Adu Damte was also executed.[57] The *shaykh* of the Kumase Muslims was found to be implicated, and was under house arrest when Freeman visited the capital in 1839.[58] In the extensive purge which followed, the Dwabenhene's demand was satisfied as the remaining opposition leaders were killed.[59] The execution of many lesser officers implicated in the abortive coup continued throughout 1840,[60] and by report some sixty members of the *mmamma* of the Gyaasewa group alone fell.[61]

[54] Reindorf, 2nd ed., n.d., p. 293; Rattray, 1929, p. 173.

[55] See Reindorf, 1st ed., 1895, Appendix: list of Asante commanders at Katamanso, 1826.

[56] Beecham, 1841, p. 92, citing the evidence of the Wesleyan missionaries.

[57] *Ibid.* p. 93. Compare Kumase Divisional Council Archives, Manhyia, Kumase: Gyaasewa stool succession, J. K. Edubofuor v. C. E. Osei, evidence of C. E. Osei dd. 31 January 1940, and of Kronkohene Kwaku Duah, dd. 9 April 1940. Ricketts, 1831, p. 125, described Damte ('Damachies') as son of Opoku Frefre, attributed the capture of MacCarthy in 1824 to him, but wrongly reported his death in 1826.

[58] Beecham, 1841, p. 93. Methodist Mission Archives, London: Brooking to General Secretaries, dd. Kumase, 14 February 1842.

[59] Reindorf, 2nd ed., n.d., p. 293.

[60] Methodist Mission Archives, London: Mycock to General Secretaries, dd. Cape Coast, 6 November 1840.

[61] Kumase Divisional Council Archives, Manhyia, Kumase: Edubofuor *v.* Osei, evidence of Kronkohene Kwaku Duah, dd. 9 April 1940, who maintained that

The positions which had become vacant as a result of the purge were filled by Kwaku Dua with candidates of his own choice. The Bantama stool was given to Gyawu, possibly the Anantahene of that name, and the Asafo stool to Akwawua Dente. The two, with the Domakwai-hene Ọpoku (Kwame Poku Agyeman) – Osei Yaw's senior counselor who had not been implicated in the attempted coup – were to become the pillars of Kwaku Dua's ongoing administration. At the meetings of the Asantemanhyiamu in 1844, when the Assin murder case was debated, Gyawu and Akwawua Dente were among those urging the despatch of troops there: a stance befitting those holding any senior military appointments in the capital (see p. 408). Their advocacy of military intervention seems, however, to have been token, as was the Asantehene's announcement that he would lead any army in person. It had already been decided that a small mission would follow the Wesleyan missionary Chapman to the coast, to insist that the British Governor should bring the murderer to justice in accordance with the prevailing construction of the terms of the 1831 treaty.[62]

Despite the purge of his political opponents, Kwaku Dua's policies continued to come under heavy criticism from elements within his councils. 'Often in meetings of the Chiefs over which he presided when the question of peace or war with the Protectorate was under discussion', commented T. B. Freeman, Kwaku Dua was 'publicly accused of the want of energy and courage'.[63] Although Freeman surmised that the Asantehene 'seldom resented these public sallies', in fact the war party opposition had rapidly closed its ranks after the purge and had regrouped around the figure of the heir apparent, Osei Kwadwo, son of the Asantehemaa Afua Sapon (see p. 330, Figure 6). The position adopted by Osei Kwadwo towards the Gyaasewahene Adu Damte's abortive coup is unclear, though certainly by that time he had already made public his dissatisfaction with Kwaku Dua's southern policies. In 1839 he appears to have played no prominent part in civic life,[64] but by 1842 he enjoyed the Asantehene's confidence and was to be seen with him on various public occasions.[65] In that year, to Freeman, 'he expressed his satisfaction at the good understanding which now

Adu Damte was son of Esom Adu, and that Kwaku Dua put to death 'all the sixty save three of the children of Poku Frefreh who helped Damte'. But see p. 463, Table 22 above.

[62] *Further Correspondence*, C. 893, Pt IV of 1874, pp. 61–7: Chapman to General Secretaries, Wesleyan Missionary Society, dd. Fort Beaufort, 29 September 1873.

[63] *The Western Echo*, I, no. 12, 17 March 1886, p. 8.

[64] Certainly Freeman's account of his visit to Kumase in 1839 made no mention of him, see T. B. Freeman, 1843, pp. 11–96, nor did that of Riis in 1839–40, see Riis, 1840.

[65] See, e.g. Freeman, 1843, pp. 139–41, 152.

exists between Ashanti and England, and his wishes that it might always continue,' [66] and the missionary subsequently commented

that the once fierce and impetuous Osai Kujoh, the heir-apparent to the crown, who has so often threatened that when he should come to power he would visit the Fantis with all the miseries of war, now takes the Missionary by the hand, declaring that he loves him, and talks with satisfaction and delight about peace and all the various blessings following in its train.[67]

It may be supposed that the rapprochement between the Asantehene and the heir apparent reflected the need to project an image of unity at a time when an Asante army – that of the Anantahene Asamoa Nkwanta – had taken the field in the northern provinces. It may also be suggested, that in the 1840s the proponents of both mercantilist and imperial ideologies found common ground in their support of Kwaku Dua's centralist, integrationist policies toward the *amanhene* of the metropolitan region. In general, then, the decade following the purge seems one in which the advocates of an aggressive southern policy avoided confrontation with the peace party majority in Kwaku Dua's government, but slowly recovered their strength as dissatisfaction with British non-observance of the spirit (if not of the letter) of the 1831 treaty grew. Relations between Osei Kwadwo and the Asantehene seemingly continued to be good until the end of the decade.[68]

The rise and fall of the opposition in the 1850s

In 1852–53, when two Assin chiefs opted to serve Asante rather than the British administration of the Gold Coast (see pp. 214–18), a situation of crisis developed in which the war party in the capital picked up sufficient support to force through Council the decision to place an army on a war footing. The assessment of the situation made by the British Governor Rowe, that Kwaku Dua would be strong enough to restrain the war party, was thus proven wrong.[69] Asamoa Nkwanta, veteran of the northern campaigns, was chosen to lead the expeditionary force, but Osei Kwadwo, significantly, was given joint command. The troops occupied Foso (Route VI, mile 82). When, however, the British executed the two Assin chiefs on 18 April 1853, the Asante government's immediate purpose – to enable them freely to reaffirm their allegiance to the Asantehene – was thwarted. Kwaku Dua ordered the

66 *Ibid.* p. 177.
67 *Wesleyan-Methodist Magazine*, December 1844, p. 1042: statement by T. B. Freeman.
68 See, e.g. Winniet's Diary, entries for 24 and 26 October 1848. Methodist Mission Archives, London: Hart to General Secretaries, dd. Kumase, 13 May 1850.
69 *Despatches . . . relating to the warfare*, C. 703, 1853, pp. 1–2: Hill to Packington, dd. Cape Coast, 23 October 1852.

recall of the army,[70] an act which, as Freeman commented, 'will doubt-less be considered in Kumasi as anything but honourable to the power of Ashanti'. Whether in fact there was a change in government after 1853 is not clear, but, to cite Freeman again, there was cause to believe that 'an attempt will be made to wipe out this disgrace'.[71] Kwaku Dua appears increasingly to have lost the confidence of his councillors and, as it was later reported, ill-feeling 'sprung up between him [Kwaku Dua] and the family of his sister [Afua Sapon], which increased during the latter years of his reign, and at length ripened into hatred'.[72] In or about 1857 Kwaku Dua removed from office his sister, the Asante-hemaa Afua Sapon, on the grounds that she was plotting to supplant him by her son Osei Kwadwo.[73] According to the account of the matter given by Ramseyer and Kühne, 'in a moment of excitement, Kwakoo Dooah once sent to his sister a silken band, with a message to the ef-fect, that the best thing she could do was to hang herself. She accepted the brotherly suggestion, and committed suicide.' [74] Osei Kwadwo was removed from the heir apparency. His death – after being 'for some time in disgrace' – occurred on 19 June 1859.[75] Then about fifty years of age, it is unclear whether or not he was executed. Ramseyer and Kühne reported that a son of Afua Sapon was 'accused of aspiring to the throne, and was sacrificed, with the honour due to his rank, viz., by having his neck broken with an elephant's tusk'.[76] But the mission-aries named the victim as Opoku — perhaps by confusion with Opoku Ahoni who had been next in line of succession to Osei Kwadwo, and whose execution had occurred in 1848 in circumstances which will be discussed in Chapter 14.

In 1860 Owusu Ansa noted, that 'many of the Royal family have met an unhappy end, brought on through opposition to the present King's government'.[77] When he visited Kumase two years later, he remarked upon the number of new office holders he met – 'the old ones I knew having fallen by the King's knife, on account of their taking part of the rebellion which the heir apparent to the throne was trying to raise against his uncle, the present King . . .' [78] Kwaku Dua's second purge

70 The brief account in Ramseyer and Kühne, 1875, p. 310, is in error in claiming that the two Assin chiefs were killed by the Asante.
71 Methodist Mission Archives, London: Freeman to General Secretaries, dd. Cape Coast, 3 May 1853.
72 Ramseyer and Kühne, 1875, p. 309.
73 Fuller, 1921, p. 87.
74 Ramseyer and Kühne, 1875, p. 309.
75 General State Archives, The Hague, KvG 716: minute dd. 12 July 1859.
76 Ramseyer and Kühne, 1875, p. 309.
77 Methodist Mission Archives: Owusu Ansa to General Secretaries, dd. Cape Coast, 11 April 1860.
78 Methodist Mission Archives: Owusu Ansa to General Secretaries, dd. Cape Coast, 13 June 1862.

of his political opponents seemed indeed to have reached its climax in 1859. Between mid-April and mid-June of that year Kwasi Myzang of Elmina was in the capital, and he estimated that in the two months over one thousand people were killed.[79] Among those to fall was the Akwaboahene Adu Tutu, who had apparently attempted to seize the Bantama stool and displace from it Kwaku Dua's appointee, Gyawu. With him, by report, seventy-four other officers – presumably of the Konti division – were executed on conspiracy charges.[80] In the aftermath of the purge the Asantehene once again filled the vacant offices with those adjudged to be in sympathy with his goals. Afua Kobi, daughter of Afua Sapon, was made Asantehemaa: she was to become one of the strongest supporters in Council of peace party policies. Her son, Kwabena Anin, was made heir apparent: significantly, he was described upon his accession to that office as of 'peaceable character'.[81] The effect of the purge was to secure majority support of the Asantehene's southern policies for a further four years.

The war party ascendancy and the accession of Kofi Kakari

By 1863 relations between the government and the British administration on the Gold Coast had deteriorated gravely. The question of jurisdiction over Akyem Kotoku had for some time proven a source of conflict between the two powers (see pp. 212–13). It was, however, the refusal of Governor Pine to extradite to Kumase, to stand trial for fraud, the Asante refugee Kwasi Gyani (see pp. 219–20), which seems finally to have decided the majority of Kwaku Dua's councillors that confrontation with the British could no longer be avoided. 'It was well known on the Gold Coast', observed Ellis,

that the result of this refusal would be war. It is true that Osai Kwaku Dua was the most pacific ruler that had ever sat on the stool of Ashanti, but even if he were disposed to overlook what must have appeared to him to be a breach of contract, the chiefs of Ashanti would not have suffered him to do so. In fact, if he did not declare war his throne would be endangered. Consequently, at a grand palaver held at Kumassi, the King asked the assembled chiefs if it was to be submitted to, that a subject, having violated the laws of his country, should find protection in a neighbouring state, and the King have no power to demand his surrender; and in a scene of the greatest excitement it was universally agreed that such an insult could only be avenged by war. The King, however, had not then a sufficient stock of gunpowder for such a struggle, so to gain time he sent a second message to Governor Pine

79 General State Archives, The Hague, KvG 716: minute dd. 12 July 1859.
80 See Institute of African Studies, Ghana, IASAS/17 and 39: Akwaboa and Bantama Stool Histories, recorded by J. Agyeman-Duah, 7 March 1963 and November 1962.
81 General State Archives, The Hague, KvG 716: minute dd. 12 July 1859.

complaining strongly of his action, and immediately began purchasing large quantities of arms and ammunition at Elmina.[82]

That Kwaku Dua's failure to have endorsed the policies of the war party in 1863 might well have led to his removal from office was also the view of Horton: 'the very throne on which he sat was in danger. If he had not acted promptly in this affair, his people would have branded him as a coward, and consequently unworthy to occupy the stool of the long-famed and brave kings of Ashantee'.[83] It was thus the war party majority in the Council of Kumase which presided over the military operations in the British Protected Territory in the first half of 1863. Its actions, however, were apparently endorsed by the Asantemanhyiamu at the Odwira later in the year, before which assembly Kwaku Dua swore that no foreigners should enter his capital other than as prisoners-of-war.[84] Yet the elderly Asantehene – by this time nearing seventy years of age – remained a master of political strategy. He appointed to command of the force which took the field (see pp. 221–2) one who was widely recognized as 'of great talent and generalship', who was apparently married to one of his daughters,[85] and who had emerged to a position of leadership within the peace party government. This was Owusu Koko, a son of the Asantehene Osei Bonsu. His early career cannot be traced in detail, but his father is known to have created him Potrikromhene when he was still a child, in or about 1819, and to have assigned to the office military functions within the Ankobea group.[86] It may have been in the northern campaigns of the early 1840s that Owusu Koko obtained his first field command, for by 1863 he was regarded as an 'experienced general'.[87] At a date which has not been determined, he succeeded Owusu Ansa as Akyempemhene.[88] His rise to power probably followed this promotion. In late 1861 or early 1862 he had made a public display before the Asantehene of his wealth, which he had apparently invested in the purchase of guns. 'He had', so it was reported, 'exhibited his muskets before the king. Three thousand were displayed on the occasion each carried by one of his own people.'[89] It is significant, therefore, that

82 Ellis, 1893, pp. 226–7.

83 Horton, 1870, p. 56. See also *The African Times,* II, no. 24, 23 June 1863, p. 138.

84 *Ibid.* III, no. 31, 23 January 1864, p. 80: anon. letter dd. Cape Coast, 14 December 1863.

85 *The African Times,* II, no. 24, 23 June 1863, p. 137: Special Correspondent, dd. Cape Coast, 13 April 1863.

86 Institute of African Studies, Ghana, IASAS/202: Potrikrom Stool History, recorded by J. Agyeman-Duah, 16 August 1967.

87 Horton, 1870, p. 5.

88 Wilks, field-notes: interview with Akyempemhene Boakye Dankwa, dd. Kumase, 18 November 1958.

89 *Wesleyan-Methodist Magazine,* October 1862, p. 954: visit of West and Owusu Ansa to Kumase, journal entry for 26 March 1862.

Ramseyer and Kühne considered Owusu Koko in 1863 to have been 'the second man in the kingdom'.[90] In 1883 – when he was a senior statesman some seventy years in age – it was possible for people to remember him 'as having practically managed Ashanti affairs during the reign of the former Quacoe Duah'.[91]

It was, then, to Owusu Koko that Kwaku Dua entrusted the operations within the British Protected Territory. They were executed with much skill, the Akyem Kotoku towns being rapidly occupied and forward positions established at Esikuma in northern Fanteland. The politics of the campaign, however, proved more complex than its military aspects: Owusu Koko faced a crisis as a struggle between peace and war party adherents became manifest among the staff officers at his field headquarters. An army mutiny seemed at least possible. Owusu Koko himself held to the compromise measures which had been authorized by Kwaku Dua, which were to limit operations in such a way as to avoid direct military confrontation with the British forces. Thus after inflicting a defeat upon the Fante at Bobikuma, he withdrew his troops to Swedru before the British could involve themselves.[92] He also despatched a messenger to Governor Pine, to assure him that he, 'the Ashanti General does not desire to molest either Europeans or Fantees . . .'[93] From Kumase, on the one hand, orders came for the return of the armies, Kwaku Dua supposedly claiming that too many men were being lost.[94] Owusu Koko's subordinate commanders – many of whom like him belonged to the princely class – on the other hand strongly urged him to follow up his victories with a decisive thrust to the coast.[95] While the Akyempemhene withstood the pressures from below, he is also reported thrice to have refused the orders from above.[96] Finally, however, in June 1863 Owusu Koko terminated the campaign. 'The Ashantee general-in-chief', Horton reported, 'knowing from experience how disastrous it is to keep a large army in the field during the rainy season, principally from climatic affections, quietly withdrew into his own territory; and, after disbanding most of his men, he quartered a few in the principal high roads to the kingdom.'[97]

90 Ramseyer and Kühne, 1875, p. 202.
91 *Further Correspondence*, C. 4052, 1884, p. 74: Rowe to Derby, dd. Accra, 1 September 1883.
92 Ellis, 1893, p. 229. Horton, 1870, pp. 62–4.
93 *Further Correspondence*, C. 891 Pt II of 1874, p. 189: Pine to Owusu Ansa, dd. Cape Coast, 22 May 1863.
94 *The African Times*, XIV, no. 159, 30 September, 1874, pp. 33–4: Origin of the Asante Invasion, by J. Dawson, dd. Kumase, 14 May 1873.
95 Horton, 1870, p. 63.
96 *The African Times*, III, no. 25, 23 July 1863, p. 9: letter dd. Cape Coast, 13 June 1863.
97 Horton, 1870, p. 65.

Considerable confusion characterized the political and military thinking of both Asante and British decision-makers in the four years from 1863 to 1867. In Kumase, the opponents of Kwaku Dua's policies – undoubtedly feeling outmanoeuvred in the conduct of the 1863 campaign – dominated the Councils, while Kwaku Dua himself assumed an increasingly bellicose position as it became clear that no new formula for peace with honour could be devised. A curious yet revealing comment on the attitudes of the Asantehene in the last few years of his reign was provided by the Fante, Joseph Dawson, who visited Kumase as emissary of the British: 'During the interval of this [1863] and the death of Kueku Duah, who in vain sought the opening of the path for free trade, and did it in such cunning way as not to expose the Ashanti full dependence on the Coast, there was no free trade, only petty trade on the frontier; and he died'.[98]

The Asantehene Kwaku Dua I died at about midnight on 27 April 1867.[99] Kwabena Anin, who had been appointed heir apparent after the purge of 1859, was clearly not acceptable as successor to the current government, and his candidature does not seem to have been sponsored by any group. Indeed, before his death Kwaku Dua had suggested to Owusu Koko the extraordinary idea of electing as Asantehene the seven years old son of Yaa Kyaa, one of his own grandchildren (see pp. 366–7).[100] The child was named Agyeman Kofi, but became better known as Kwaku Dua Kuma, Kwaku Dua 'junior'. A report of the matter was communicated to Barrow in Kumase in 1883:

during the illness of the old King Quacoe Duah which ended in his death, he sent for Prince Owusu Kokor believing he was about to die, and enjoined him to see that the 'stool' was retained for his grandson the young man of that name who now [1883] aspires to occupy it. The old King remarked that it was no use for the sons of Afuah Cobree [Kobi] to have the 'stool', because neither of them would be able to 'keep his house in order.' There was some little difficulty in arranging at the time for the occupation of the vacant 'stool'.[101]

98 *The African Times,* XIV, no. 159, 30 September 1874, pp. 33–4: J. Dawson, dd. Kumase, 14 May 1873.
99 Instituut voor Taal- Land- en Volkenkunde, Leiden MS. H. 509: anon. diary, entry dd. Kumase, 27 April 1867.
100 *Further Correspondence,* C. 4052, 1884, p. 31. According to an earlier source, he was even younger, being between 8 and 10 years of age in 1874, see *Correspondence relating to the Affairs of the Gold Coast,* C. 1140, 1875, p. 84: Strahan to Carnarvon, dd. Cape Coast, 4 September 1874. It is still customary for the Akyempemhene to be summoned to attend a dying Asantehene, see Kyerematen, n.d., p. 6. An injunction given by the dying man is regarded as binding and is known as *saman-seɛ.*
101 *Further Correspondence,* C. 4052, 1884, pp. 56–7: Barrow to Governor, dd. Accra, 5 July 1883.

The 'little difficulty' resulted from the fact that the war party had itself decided to advance the candidacy of a son of Afua Kobi: namely, Kwabena Anin's younger brother Kofi Kakari.

In 1867 Kofi Kakari was about thirty years of age.[102] He appears personally to have had no aspirations to highest office,[103] and had not been a prominent advocate of war with the British. He seems nevertheless to have responded with alacrity to the suggestion of the war party leaders that he should run for office. In April 1867, therefore, it was Kofi Kakari who appeared to Owusu Koko to constitute the major obstacle to his assumption, in the name of the young Kwaku Dua Kuma, of leadership of a new peace administration. On the death of Kwaku Dua I, Owusu Koko accordingly arrested the Asantehemaa Afua Kobi and her two sons Kofi Kakari and (presumably) Mensa Bonsu. They were released only after Kofi Kakari had taken an oath never to accept the throne, and after all had sworn not to take reprisals against the Akyempemhene.[104] The reaction of members of the Council of Kumase to Owusu Koko's arbitrary intervention in the electoral process was adverse. Upon the completion of the funeral customs for Kwaku Dua, the Council met in the palace and Kofi Kakari was released from his oath not to take the throne on the grounds that it had been sworn under duress. At the same time Kofi Kakari testified against Owusu Koko and a number of his subordinates, who were charged with what was in effect kidnapping. Owusu Koko was sent into exile, and seven of his gun-chiefs, his stool carrier, and several *nhenkwaa* were condemned to death and executed.[105] The proceedings probably occurred around 28 May, on which date the choice of Kofi Kakari as Asantehene was announced:

Monday in the afternoon at 3 on the 28 May the Asante people made the appointment of a new King named Koffee Karkarie and He sat with the Court and was carried by two slaves on their heads, and with all the gold emblems surrounding him . . . and all the Captains of Asante in two parties, before him and behind him, went with him, walking around all the streets, and playing, to give thanks to all the people.[106]

---

102 See, e.g. Owusu Ansa, The King of Ashantee, in *The Times* (London), 29 July 1873.

103 Ramseyer and Kühne, 1875, p. 309.

104 See *Der Evangelische Heidenbote*, 1892, pp. 76–8: 'Mose der Koransier', communication from W. Rottmann concerning the career of an Nkoransa servant of an Asante functionary 'Ntonikra' (that is, Bosommuru Ntorekra) who was in Kumase in 1867. I am grateful to T. McCaskie for first drawing my attention to this source.

105 *Idem*. See also Basel Mission Archives: Ramseyer to Basel, dd. 18 August 1883.

106 Instituut voor Taal- Land- en Volkenkunde, Leiden MS H. 509, entry for 28 May 1867. I am grateful to Dr R. Baesjou for kindly placing his translation of this diary at my disposal.

Kofi Kakari publicly affirmed his intention to lead the nation to war (see p. 478). And it was probably on this occasion that two towns belonging to the Akyempemhene, Nyinahin and Nkawie-Panin, were transferred to the Bantamahene's jurisdiction.[107] The rupture of relations between Owusu Koko and Kofi Kakari seems to be one of the incidents obliquely alluded to in Asante tradition as *sraman gyedua,* literally, 'lightning (spares) the tree', that is, 'the Asantehene's escape'.[108]

The politics of the war years, 1869–73

The sequence of Asante military and diplomatic operations in the early years of Kofi Kakari's reign has been discussed above (pp. 235–8). Despite the relative success of Adu Bofo's campaigns in the east, and of Akyampon Yaw's mission to the southwest, Kofi Kakari appeared nevertheless reluctant to sanction the full-scale invasion and reoccupation of the British Protected Territory. The fact of the matter was, that although he had been brought to power by a war party majority, his position *vis-à-vis* the politicians remained – and was to remain throughout his reign – ambiguous. The problems he faced in establishing a *modus vivendi* with his councillors were compounded by the residual effects of another incident which had convulsed Kumase in 1867, following the death of Kwaku Dua I. The three major accounts of the incident vary considerably in detail.[109] It appears that in the days immediately after the death, the princes – as was something of a tradition – ran amuck and slaughtered a number of citizens. Among the slain was one variously described as nephew, favourite, and 'principal lieutenant' of the Anantahene Asamoa Nkwanta. Rejecting arguments that such actions, on the death of an Asantehene, were sanctioned by custom, Asamoa Nkwanta demanded retribution. When this was not forthcoming, he mobilized his followers and threatened to burn Kumase. The case was mediated by the Asantehemaa Afua Kobi on one account; by the two princes Owusu Sekyere and Owusu Ntobi on another. Owusu Ntobi was a son of Osei Bonsu,[110] and Owusu Sekyere was probably the Kyidomhene of that name, a son of Osei Kwame. According, however, to an Nkoransa slave who was in Kumase at the time, it was Owusu Sekyere who was the culprit, and his

107 Institute of African Studies, Ghana, IASAS/107: Nyinahin Stool History, recorded by J. Agyeman-Duah, 6 January 1964.
108 See Ramseyer and Kühne, 1875, p. 238, for Kofi Kakari's own observation.
109 *Ibid.* p. 310. Bonnat, in Gros, 1884, p. 217 (who is followed by Perregaux, 1906, p. 132). The third version is that recorded from the Nkoransa slave, in *Der Evangelische Heidenbote,* 1892. Some differing details are given in Fuller, 1921, p. 100.
110 NAG, Kumase, D. 94: Kwasi Nuama *et al.* to Chief Commissioner, dd. Kumase, 8 March 1915.

mother and uncle were slain in retribution. Fuller identified the uncle as Kwame Nimako. He was probably the head of the prince's household ('intendant') who, according to Bonnat's version, was surrendered to Asamoa Nkwanta with all of his family – 'those persons who were the most valuable to him [the offending prince]'. On the other hand, Ramseyer and Kühne named the offender as Boakye 'Aso' and reported that he and two of his sisters were executed, and his mother's life spared only on the payment of 80 oz of gold. It would seem that the former account is to be preferred; Oheneba Boakye Asoa was still living at the time of Mensa Bonsu when he held the position of Asramponhene in Kumase.[111] Whatever the case, clearly Asamoa Nkwanta was finally pacified by the execution of a number of the transgressor's people. And there, supposed Bonnat, the matter rested. It is significant, however, that Asamoa Nkwanta was reported subsequently to have 'kept aloof from the palace'.[112] Although he was the most experienced and talented of the field commanders, 'the Ashantee Von Moltke' according to Owusu Ansa,[113] apparently he declined to serve on the active list during the mobilization of 1867–8.[114] Ellis maintained that as a result of the disaffection of Asamoa Nkwanta, the growth of the war party was for some time inhibited.[115]

It was probably the case that Asante society had never been politically so deeply divided as it was to become during the period when Kofi Kakari presided over the affairs of the nation. As a pseudonymous writer in *The African Times* had argued in 1863, Kwaku Dua I had pursued policies of peace and coexistence with the British, but had acted in the domestic sphere with the ruthlessness of 'an absolute and despotic monarch in the broadest sense of those terms'.[116] Kofi Kakari, by contrast, displayed no marked enthusiasm for the liquidation of his political opponents, and despite the oaths he took on accession, appears to have sought to hold a middle course between an increasingly

111 Kumase Divisional Council Archives, Manhyia, Court B Record Book 9: Yaw Duku v. Yaw Amu, commencing 11 June 1937.

112 Ramseyer and Kühne, 1875, p. 310.

113 *The Times* (London), 29 July 1873. Compare Ramseyer and Kühne, 1875, p. 310: Asamoa Nkwanta, 'the old "ruler of the battles" '.

114 Ramseyer and Kühne, 1875, p. 310.

115 Ellis, 1893, p. 252. Another similar incident is also reported. It is said that on Kwaku Dua's death, Owusu Koko himself had proposed slaying Apea Kyeame, nephew of Kwame Butuakwa and the then incumbent of the Butuakwa stool. See Wilks and Ferguson, field-notes: interview with Bafuor Osei Akoto, dd. Kumase, 31 October 1973. Apea Kyeame replied that, since Owusu Koko was a son of the Golden Stool, it was his privilege to be despatched first. Both called together their followers and only the intervention of the Asantehemaa prevented a clash.

116 *The African Times*, III, no. 29, 23 November 1863, p. 60: letter from Tom Coffee, dd. Cape Coast, 14 October 1863.

militaristic war interest and an increasingly radical peace one. By the very nature of the times, however, no such position was tenable, and by early 1871 reports were reaching the Gold Coast that a number of the Asantehene's principal chiefs (though of what political persuasion is unclear) had become 'very rebellious, refusing to pay the accustomed tax and to obey the orders to repair to the capital'.[117]

Leadership of the war party in the early part of Kofi Kakari's reign was assumed by the Bantamahene Amankwatia. Born about 1833 probably at Akrofuom (Route VI, mile 42), he was appointed Bantamahene by Kofi Kakari to replace the elderly Gyawu who was too closely identified with the policies of Kwaku Dua. Amankwatia, it has been noted, was described as 'a mere creature of the king, whose ancestry no one knows, or, at least, troubles about'.[118] The new officer had nevertheless the distinction of having been instructed in military science by the famous Asamoa Nkwanta, and had acquired a reputation as a field commander of merit.[119] He was, so Kühne observed, 'a restless and ambitious chief . . . and, possessing great wealth and rank, raised and headed a strong war party'.[120] He was strongly supported by Owusu Barempa, another son of Osei Bonsu who had come to act as Akyempemhene after the exile of his brother Owusu Koko.[121] During the week commencing 2 September 1871, the Gyaasewahene Adu Bofo's troops were received and reviewed in the capital. The armies' losses exceeded one thousand men, and one hundred and thirty six chiefs had died including six from Kumase.[122] Although the casualties had thus been by no means light, the campaigns were regarded as highly successful ones and Adu Bofo – as Fuller later reported it – 'was now a large slave-owner and had acquired great wealth'.[123] Certainly the Gyaasewahene's triumph encouraged others of the aspiring field commanders to associate themselves the more unambiguously with the war party. Adu Bofo himself, however, for a time held to a moderate line: a result, it was then assumed, of the fact that in July 1869 he had voluntarily entrusted to the British – as personal guarantee of the safety of the European captives – his late brother Adu Nantwiri's

117 *Ibid.* x, no. 118, April 1871, pp. 11–12: report on peace negotiations, Cape Coast Castle, 14 March 1871.
118 Boyle, 1874, pp. 276–7.
119 Reade, 1874, p. 100. Owusu Ansa, in *The Times* (London), 29 July 1873. Ramseyer and Kühne, 1875, p. 292.
120 Reade, 1874, p. 100.
121 Fuller, 1921, p. 114. Brackenbury, 1874, II, 331–2. Ramseyer and Kühne, 1875, p. 308.
122 Ramseyer and Kühne, 1875, pp. 135–7, 158. An extraordinary session of the Asantemanhyiamu was called on Adu Bofo's return, to receive a report on the state of the nation, see *Correspondence relative to the Cession*, C. 670, 1872, p. 26: Crawford to Salmon, dd. Praso, 14 October 1871.
123 Fuller, 1921, p. 114.

son, Kwame Poku.[124] In fact, however, as news of the negotiations between Dutch and British for the transfer of Elmina to the latter reached Kumase in late 1870 (see pp. 231–2), Adu Bofo appears to have committed himself fully to the policies of the war party even though Kwame Poku was not to be released by the British until mid-1872.[125]

The differences in policy between the more moderate and more extreme sections of the dominant war party, which had not been resolved in debate in the Council of Kumase, were brought for discussion before an extraordinary meeting of the Asantemanhyiamu in February 1872. It met on the 17th, the very day on which the governments of Britain and the Netherlands ratified the convention on Elmina. The Asantehene opened the substantive proceedings by announcing that he saw no reason why the European prisoners in Kumase should not be freed as requested by the Governor of the Gold Coast. Thereupon, as reported by observers present at the meeting,

Adu Bofo simulated surprise, and pretended to confer for some moments with his friends. Very soon however he began to explain that Asen, Akem, Akra, and Akuapem, which all formerly belonged to Ashantee, had been drawn over to serve the white men, who on their part had subsequently broken their treaty of peace with Ashantee by refusing to give up a runaway chief.

Upon the Asantehene observing that such issues were by then dead ones, Adu Bofo vehemently disagreed:

At all events the right thing would be to regain our authority over these tribes. I have been to war. I have gained victories, used much powder, and lost more than a thousand men, and now am I to give up all that has been gained? No! never, never will I let these prisoners go free! never, I say! [126]

The Asantehene, reported Kühne, 'took the votes of the chiefs, and Adoo Buffoo had the majority'.[127] Most of the Kumase members, including the Domakwai and Akankade counselors Nsuase Kwaku Poku and Yaw Nantwi, supported the Gyaasewahene's position, as did the representatives of Dwaben, Nsuta and Bekwae. Having carried the majority with him, Adu Bofo announced that he was prepared to ransom the prisoners for a sum of 800 peredwans (or £6,480). One Kumase member, supported by Mamponhene Kwabena Dwumo and Adansehene Oben, argued that the nation was moving towards involvement in an unwanted war.[128] On 20 February, however, the Asantehene met

124 Ramseyer and Kühne, 1875, p. 174.
125 *Gold Coast, Part I*, C. 266 of 30 June 1873, p. 92: Pope Hennessy to Asantehene, dd. Cape Coast, 4 June 1872.
126 Ramseyer and Kühne, 1875, p. 158. See also the report on the 'great solemn Assembly' of 17 February by Ramseyer and Kühne in *Der Evangelische Heidenbote*, 1872, p. 83.
127 Reade, 1874, p. 99.
128 Ramseyer and Kühne, 1875, p. 159.

with his counselors, and the decision was executed: a message was despatched to the Governor of the Gold Coast containing a demand for the payment of the ransom of 800 peredwans.[129]

The opposition to the dominant majority in the Councils made a bid to overthrow Adu Bofo, and fighting broke out in March. When Owusu Ansa left Kumase towards the end of the month the situation appeared an acutely dangerous one. His account of it was summarized in a letter to Basel from Widmann, dated 18 April 1872:

The Peace Party, who would free our prisoners without ransom and roused their voice against the preponderant majority at the above mentioned proceedings [of 17 February], have begun a war against Adubofo and it seems that he must be defeated. The people themselves are also very dissatisfied, since there is dreadful suffering as long as there is not peace with the English Government and the Coast. This struggle between the Peace and War Parties in Kumase is an unexpected change in affairs, the issue of which cannot be seen.[130]

The fighting must in fact have ended as abruptly as it had flared up, for by the end of March Kofi Kakari felt the situation sufficiently under control to take a few days' vacation at his country house at Manhyia, outside the city.[131] He did, however, make the decision to advance the Odwira in order to take advantage of an early meeting of the Asantemanhyiamu.[102] The change in the calendar was made known immediately by his bringing forward the next Great Adae from 7 April to 31 March.[133]

The regular annual meeting of the Asantemanhyiamu commenced, then, on 2 September 1872. 'In the king's palace', noted Plange, who had been sent from Elmina with official notification of the British usurpation of authority over Elmina, 'were assembled, viz., the great chiefs from various great towns surrounding Coomassie, also King of Beckwhy, Duabbin, Mampon, Cokofoe, and Fommanah, etc., also the chiefs, linguists, and principalities, inhabitants of Coomassie, etc.' [134] Himself seriously ill, Adu Bofo was represented by his son and a subordinate officer, Nantwi.[135] The proceedings were opened by the Asantehene reporting on the exchange of correspondence with the

129 *Der Evangelische Heidenbote*, 1872, p. 82.
130 *Ibid.* p. 83, summarizing Widmann's letter of 18 April 1872.
131 Ramseyer and Kühne, 1875, p. 165.
132 *Ibid.* p. 180.
133 *Ibid.* p. 165: Kofi Kakari 'surprised the capital by a sudden resolution to hold the Bantama feast on the 1st April'.
134 Plange's Journal, in Brackenbury, 1874, I, 43.
135 Ramseyer and Kühne, 1875, p. 180. Nantwi, often known as Gyakye Nantwi, was active in Gyaasewa affairs until his death on a mission to Accra in 1880. Although sometimes referred to as a 'linguist', he appears not to have held the senior Gyakye counselorship, see Asante Collective Biography Project: Nantwi.

Governor of the Gold Coast, announcing the British claim to jurisdiction over Elmina, and bringing to the attention of the Assembly the British request that the ransom for the prisoners should be lowered to £1000 or less. The debate then opened with Afrifa, one of the government's negotiators who had recently returned from the Gold Coast, testifying to the British attitude:

Affilfa. – I was told by the Governor to come and beg his majesty, that his Excellency desires to have peace with the king, but if these white men still in captives the peace cannot be established, so therefore his Excellency begs the king to let his Excellency pay amount of £1000, for the redeeming of the white men.

King. – I beg the linguists present here to inform this matters to the representatives of Adu Boffoe, what the Governor requested him.

Bwaachi-tintsin, step-father of the king. – I beg the son of Adu Boffoe to bring his opinion in this matter.

Adu Boffoe's Son. – This is only play of the Governor with us; we have asked £8000 as ransom of the captives white men, and if the Governor likes to buy them, and not able to pay such sum, he should begs to reduce them to be £6000; but all at once his Excellency cast £7000 in his pocket; no! my father cannot accept this, as he had much trouble of the white men to brought them here.

King. – I beg you will go to counsel first before you should tell something about this matters.

Adu Boffoe's families from counselling. – Our opinions are about these matters, we will accept no less or no more that 600 prayquen [peredwans], equal to 1350 oz. or 21,600 dols. as the head money of the white men.

After allowing Plange to present the British case to the Assembly, the Asantehene again intervened in the debate:

King. – I have heard the goodness of the Governor towards me and the Ashantees, therefore I beg Adu Boffoe's families to reduce the said 600 praquen to enable me to answer the Governor.

Adu Boffoe's families. – He ask Affilfa again, can't Governor not to pay any money more than the £1000, he said or what?

Affilfa. – So far as I know Governor begs the king as a good friend to let him pay only £1000 as recompensation of Adu Boffu.

Members of the Assembly then voiced their opinions individually:

Achampon, King's Steward. – This £1000, only we cannot understand why king asked £6480, and now Governor promised to pay £1000, keeping rest in his pocket: Governor thought that we are fool!

King of Beckwy. – If we do not accept the £1000, and not agree to let these white men free to go to the coast, what will come? . . .

King of Dwabin. – Then war will come, but remember that from time memorial or from ancient time you never heard that the Fantees declared war against Ashantees, but always Ashantees against the Fantees: and how is it? These white men we sell them for gold: if Governor agrees the price, he can buy them; if not, we will keep them for curiosity. Another thing, if the Governor has not money to pay the amount we ask, let him give the Assins, Ackims, and Dencirras, in the place of these white men, and we will give them up to him (Governor), but not any less money . . .

King of Fommanah. – Governor has only pinching us with the £1000 to hear some word from us, and that is all. Governor will hear is a war; and seeing I am the King of Fommanah, even I am the smallest king, I know that the Governor will not be able to come to me.

King's Mother. – You think also that I am woman; it is so, but my right arm is strong enough to meet unnumbered Fantees, whoever likes to declare war against the Ashantees.

Ammanquateah. – If lice or louse are too much in the hair and troubles you, should better to shave the hair and get rest.[136]

But as Reade remarked, following Kühne's account of the matter, the Asantehene 'was a young man, and had only been four years on the throne; he could not resist the united will of so many powerful chiefs.'[137] Accepting the majority view, he finally requested approval for a reduction of the fluctuating sum to a compromise of £2000:

. . . I am willing to let these white men go to their country free, without ask any cent, but the chiefs stick upon the said money, and I beg the chiefs are here present, that as I wish to have peace with the coast, the amount of £4000 you said to be reduced as to come to the amount of £2000.[138]

By September 1872, political power had then passed to the militaristic wing of the war party: that is, to those who saw in the reoccupation of the British Protected Territory the only solution to the southern problem. Among those prominent councillors who continued to advocate a more moderate position, perhaps broadly in line with that of Kofi Kakari himself, were the Mamponhene Kwabena Dwumo, the Asafohene of Kumase, Asafo Boakye, and the aged and much respected Asamoa Nkwanta. The 'high council' – presumably the Asantemanhyiamu – met yet again on 22 October, and members took oaths to march to the Coast.[139] The main army left Kumase on 9 December 1872, and some brief account of the campaigns has been offered above (pp. 236–8). In late December Akyampon Yaw arrived back in the capital in possession of a detailed knowledge of the chicanery which had attended the British seizure of Elmina, of the ominous buildup of their naval power along the western Gold Coast, and of their aggression committed against his own person. His case against the

136 Plange's Journal, in Brackenbury, 1874, I, 43–8.
137 Reade, 1874, pp. 100–1.
138 Plange's Journal, in Brackenbury, 1874, I, 48.
139 Ramseyer and Kühne, 1875, p. 187.

British was well summarized by Thomas Gibson Bowles, protagonist in London of the Asante cause:

When therefore, this great personage arrived in Coomassie in the last days of December, and related how he had been inveigled by the English with 'friendly greeting' to a palaver or conference as a 'good and trusty ally,' how he had there been seized by an armed force, bound, robbed and dragged off a prisoner; when he pointed to this as a proof that these same English intended, whatever they might say, to oust the Ashantees altogether from their footing in Elmina, to keep them altogether from the sea, and to deliver their commerce over to the black mail of the Fantees; and when he declared besides, which was true, as is attested at this moment by bombarded villages, that not only the Elminas but many other of the neighbouring tribes sympathised with their Ashantee brethren; when he, as doubtless he did, said all this . . . ,[140]

then there could be little doubt that support for the war in Kumase became so much the stronger among even the moderate elements in the Councils.

The growth of popular anti-war sentiment

Throughout the deliberations of the early 1870s Kofi Kakari had allowed the conciliar process to operate freely, utilizing both the upper and lower Councils to establish the widest possible consensus within the nation on the issue of war or peace with the British. Only once in the period is there a report of political executions. In October 1871, a counselor and another officer were executed in Kumase, but the charges were that they had themselves attempted to subvert the recognized decision-making procedures. 'The king', it was reported,

rose in anger from his council, and withdrew raging to his room . . . The councillors were beside themselves with excitement, and the people on the market place gathered up their wares, and fled trembling into their houses; nothing but absolute necessity made any of them leave their homes that night . . . We heard soon after, that the cause of the king's anger had been some tricks which his chiefs had played him, in regard to the succession to the chieftainship of Nouta [*sic:* Nsuta].[141]

The personal popularity which Kofi Kakari undoubtedly enjoyed stemmed in part from his ready assumption of the role of presidential monarch, which was in marked contrast to the autocratic disposition of his predecessor. His public image was undoubtedly further enhanced by the liberality with which he distributed favours, both of office and money.

140 Bowles, 1874, p. 132.
141 Ramseyer and Kühne, 1875, pp. 141–2.

Kofi Kakari's cautious and indeed conservative approach to politics in 1871 and 1872 appears to have maintained to a quite remarkable degree a working understanding between the major interests represented in the Councils, such that the minority were usually prepared to concur in the decisions of the majority. Yet radical opposition to the government's policies had by no means been eliminated. The peace party was indeed in disarray, with one of its effective leaders, Owusu Koko, in exile, and one of its royal figureheads, Kwabena Anin, seemingly rendered politically innocuous. Its constituency among the commoner masses of Asante, however, was an expanding one. In September 1870 the rising tide of popular agitation had been remarked upon, on the occasion of the Asantehene's public appearance to celebrate funeral rites for his father:

the king arrived at last, looking sullen and tired as he lay in his sedan chair, giving one the impression that he felt compelled to endure these noisy exhibitions, to conciliate the people whose chiefs had placed him on the vacant throne. It is only by slow degrees that the strongest sovereign can act independently of them.[142]

By early 1871 it had become clear that anti-war sentiment was growing rapidly, and a writer on the Gold Coast could allude to the 'general cry for peace among his [Kofi Kakari's] population, which must be heard'.[143] The origins of the anti-war movement will be discussed more fully below. By the time of the massive mobilization in December 1872, conducted on the basis of the Council's decision of 22 October, unrest among the conscriptees was marked. The Asantehene's people, reported Dawson, 'who are going to war – I mean the commons, not the captains – are all murmuring very much. They do not have enough muskets . . .'[144] Although by an appeal to motives which ranged from the noble to the ignoble – from the defence of the nation to the anticipation of booty – the government succeeded in instilling in the conscriptees some measure of enthusiasm for the impending operations, this did not long survive the hazards of the campaigns.[145] Troops returning to the capital in late 1873 were clearly appalled by the extent of the casualties and had had confirmed their fears about the current inadequacy of their weaponry. 'Soldiers', reported the captive missionaries, 'came continually into the town, some of whom said plainly, "Even if the king send us forward again, we will not go unless he ac-

142 *Ibid.* p. 87.
143 *The African Times*, x, no. 118, April 1871, pp. 11–12: report on peace negotiations, Cape Coast Castle, 14 March 1871.
144 *Further Correspondence*, C. 819, 1873, pp. 4–7: Dawson to Harley, dd. Kumase, 19 December 1872.
145 Kühne, in Maurice, 1874, pp. 267–8. Ramseyer and Kühne, 1875, p. 205.

company; we are sick of it. The white men have guns which hit five Ashantees at once. Many great men and princes have fallen" ' [146]

Attention has been drawn above to the revival of anti-war feeling among the troops in the field (pp. 237). But although such senior commanders as Adu Bofo continually requested the government for more troops and money with which to prosecute the war,[147] many of the junior officers appear to have become radicalized by their experiences. It was presumably from them that the petition which reached Kumase in September or October 1873 originated, asking the government to recall the armies.[148] Kofi Kakari took an unexpectedly unsympathetic view of the matter, responding:

> You wished for war and you have it. You swore you would not return till you could bring me the walls of Cape Coast, and now you want we to recall you because many chiefs have fallen, and you are suffering. When I danced on the market-place in times past, you said, 'he wishes for war.' It was not I, it was you who wished it . . . In due time I will send you an answer.[149]

Anti-war sentiment, however, was also rapidly growing in the capital as the effects of the campaigns became felt there. Shortages of essential commodities such as salt gave way to general shortages of foodstuffs as the need to provision the armies drained the villages of produce. Food prices became so high that many were obliged to sell their household effects in order to raise the requisite cash.[150] Rumours, often exaggerated, of losses in the field kept the populace in a state of continuous agitation, and Muslims and shrine priests made prayers constantly for an Asante victory.[151] The behaviour of the Asantehene became noticeably erratic and unpredictable,[152] and the death of his sixteen years old brother on 2 September 1873 was followed by a wave of executions over the next eight days. That a number of princes and members of the royal house fell, suggested that perhaps for the first time in his reign Kofi Kakari was carrying out a purge of his opponents. 'It was really a reign of terror', it was remarked, 'and none could understand whether it was an outburst of ungoverned passion, or an intimation of absolute power'.[153]

Whatever purpose was served by the resort to terror in early September, the normal processes of law were soon restored, and on 27 October the war issue was brought before Council for debate. The

[146] Ramseyer and Kühne, 1875, p. 252.
[147] *Ibid.* p. 239.
[148] *Idem.* See also Kühne, in Maurice, 1874, pp. 267–8.
[149] Ramseyer and Kühne, 1875, p. 239.
[150] *Ibid.* pp. 220, 229.
[151] *Ibid.* pp. 208–11, 220–2.
[152] *Ibid.* pp. 220, 222–3, 230.
[153] *Ibid.* p. 236.

majority of the members had clearly abandoned their earlier position, and now argued for the recall of the armies. Kofi Kakari stated that this was possible only if the members of council were prepared to re-imburse to the Treasury the costs of the campaigns, which were esti-mated at 6,000 peredwans, or in the sterling equivalent of the time, £48,000.[154] The councillors' acceptance of the condition must be taken as signalling the return to power of a peace party government. It was, however, only in a series of council meetings commencing on 20 No-vember that the policy reversal was confirmed. The Asantehene, now associated with the minority party, opened the proceedings by stating that since Kumase had been built it had never been invaded. The councillors, including those who had been involved in the cam-paigns,[155] responded that 'ancient times were not now', that is, that the balance in military technology had changed to the disadvantage of the Asante fighting forces.[156] But it was the intervention in the debate of the Asantehemaa Afua Kobi which seems to have been quite de-cisive. 'I am old now', she announced,

I lived before Kwakoo Dooah, and I have now placed my son on the Ashan-tee throne . . . What is to be done? I do not wish for our successors to say my son was the cause of the disturbance of the sixty *nkurow*. From olden times it has been seen that God fights for Ashantee if the war is a just one. This one is unjust. The Europeans begged for the imprisoned white men. They were told to wait until Adu Bofo came back; then they said they wanted money. The money was offered, and even weighed. How then can this war be justified? . . . Taking all into consideration, I strongly advise that the white men should be sent back at once, and God can help us.[157]

Envoys were despatched from the capital to recall the armies. As their return was awaited, Kofi Kakari evinced his concern with the many wild and often grossly inaccurate rumours which were circulating about the campaigns. He had, it was recorded, 'sworn the great oath before his chiefs, that whoever dared to make game of a soldier, or even to hint that the army had achieved nothing, should be put to death'.[158] On 12 December he despatched messengers to outlying vil-lages to announce the victory.[159] Perhaps the Asantehene sought thus to re-establish his popularity with the veterans and so secure for him-self a new constituency. But the enthusiasm which the entry of the main army into the capital on 22 December generated rapidly dis-appeared as the full extent of the casualties became apparent (see

154 *Ibid.* p. 243.
155 Maurice, 1874, p. 268, citing Kühne.
156 Reade, 1874, p. 285, citing Kühne.
157 Ramseyer and Kühne, 1875, p. 247. Reade, 1874, p. 285.
158 Ramseyer and Kühne, 1875, p. 250.
159 *Ibid.* p. 251.

pp. 82–3). Kofi Kakari's popularity, moreover, dropped still further as he put into effect the decision on the reimbursement of the costs of the campaigns, which had been taken by the Council on 27 October. 'The chiefs', it was reported,

were now ordered to repay to the king the cost of the campaign, and to re-place the ammunition which had been used in vain. Of some was demanded sixty, of others forty or fifty peredwanes. They were terribly excited, and appealed to the council at the palace for a mitigation of these enormous de-mands, with little success. Similar sums were demanded from some of the chief people, one of whom had to sell not only his slaves, but his wife, to furnish the five peredwanes; he sold his son too for nine dollars, and the poor boy cried bitterly. There were many upright, quiet men who had wished for peace and free trade, who lost half their families by the war, and were afterwards obliged to sell the other half to pay for it.[160]

At the beginning of January 1874, it was observed: 'in Coomassie the Queen Mother is at the head of the peace party, and, it is said, threatens to destroy herself if war is persisted in'.[161] But the decision on war or peace was one which no longer rested with the government in Kumase, and the advance into Asante of the British Expeditionary Force under Wolseley continued. On 9 January six of the senior coun-selors sent on behalf of the Asantehene a despatch to Wolseley, re-questing him to suspend military operations while terms for peace were discussed.[162] On the same day the missionary Kühne was released without ransom, as a gesture of goodwill from the new government. Wolseley's reply was scarcely encouraging. 'I am glad to find from your letter', he wrote,

that your Majesty has resolved upon peace; but before I can enter into any negotiations whatever with your Majesty, it is essential that you should con-vince me of the sincerity of your intentions by at once sending in to me the other prisoners now held by you . . . Her Most Gracious Majesty Queen Victoria is as anxious as your Majesty can be for the establishment of a last-ing peace between England and Ashanti. But in order that peace may be last-ing, it is essential that your Majesty and your people should learn that you can no more prevent an army of white men marching into your territory, whenever your Majesty's hostile proceedings make such a step necessary on our part, than you can stop the sun from rising every morning.[163]

Kofi Kakari, it has been pointed out, turned in the situation of crisis increasingly to his Muslim advisers (pp. 238–42), hoping that

---

160 *Ibid.* p. 260.
161 *The African Times*, XIII, no. 152, 26 February 1874, p. 17: letter from the *Standard* correspondent, dd. Fomena, 26 January 1874.
162 Brackenbury, 1874, II, 52–3. Maurice, 1874, pp. 262–3.
163 Brackenbury, 1874, II, 54–5. Maurice, 1874, pp. 263–5.

through their good offices the invading force might still be held back from the capital. But the new government had also taken the precautionary step of ordering remobilization of the recently disbanded troops, and messengers had been despatched in all directions from Kumase on 9 January.[164] By the 10th the preparations for a renewed struggle were visibly under way: people were to be seen in the capital making bullets of lead and iron, and drying and packing corn and cassava as provisions for the troops.[165] The policy of remobilization was a highly unpopular one: 'the people are thoroughly sick of the contest for the time', it was reported, 'and as the chiefs wish for peace, too, the passive resistance is enormous'.[166] It proved extremely difficult for those responsible for the mobilization to collect their fighting men.[167] That the government was in fact able to put forces back into the field was a result in no small measure of its political wisdom in entrusting the operations to two commanders who had been identified not with the war party but with the more moderate element in council. The Mamponhene Kwabena Dwumo was appointed supreme commander of the army,[168] and the Anantahene Asamoa Nkwanta assumed leadership of the advance forces in the field.[169] Asamoa Nkwanta, in particular, was immensely respected and liked by the Asante troops,[170] and was popularly known as Srafokra, with the sense of, 'the soldiers' guardian spirit'.[171] In consequence of their confidence in those conducting operations, the forces that had been mobilized offered fierce opposition to the British Expeditionary Force throughout the last five days of its advance upon Kumase, and Wolseley, having entered the capital on the evening of 4 February, was obliged to commence the withdrawal to the coast on the morning of the 6th. 'It was out of the question', reported Wolseley's Assistant Military Secretary, 'to undertake any operation which might involve another battle; because any increment to our list of sick and wounded would have placed it beyond his power to remove them back . . .' [172]

The Dwaben secession and the abdication of Kofi Kakari

Although Wolseley's forces had by no means achieved the victory for which they had hoped, the sack of Kumase was seen by the Asante

164 Reade, 1874, p. 285, citing Kühne.
165 Ramseyer and Kühne, 1875, p. 267.
166 Maurice, 1874, p. 273, citing Kühne.
167 Brackenbury, 1874, II, 138–9.
168 Boyle, 1874, p. 304.
169 *Ibid.* pp. 319, 326.
170 Owusu Ansa, in *The Times*, 29 July 1873.
171 Fuller, 1921, p. 129.
172 Brackenbury, 1874, II, 239.

councillors as the ultimate demonstration of the failure of war party policies. Moving cautiously, the government sent an envoy – a merchant of Dwaben and Kumase – to overtake the retiring army and express to Wolseley the Asantehene's desire for peace.[173] He met with Wolseley on 9 February, and succeeded in persuading him to await the arrival of Asante negotiators at Fomena. The mission arrived there on the 13th. It was led by Asabi Antwi, one of the government's senior diplomats, who brought a gift of 1,000 oz of gold as token of goodwill.[174] Wolseley produced, and explained, a draft of his proposed peace settlement. By its terms, the Asante government was required to pay a war indemnity of 50,000 oz of gold, and to renounce all claims to sovereignty over the Denkyira, Assin, Akyem, Adanse, Elmina and peoples of the western Gold Coast. In return, freedom of trade was guaranteed between Asante and the British Protected Territory. The envoys queried the size of the indemnity, and objected to the inclusion of the reference to Adanse – which Wolseley had added since the Adansehene Oben had apparently vaguely intimated his intention of resettling his people in Wassa country.[175] No report of the subsequent debate on the proposed treaty by the councils in Kumase has been found, but, surprisingly perhaps, its terms were accepted. On 14 March 1874 it was ratified at Cape Coast by an Asante mission headed by Kwame Antwi – seemingly the Asabi Antwi who had treated with Wolseley at Fomena. Its members included seven other Kumase administrative officials and representatives from Dwaben, Bekwae, Kokofu, Nsuta, Mampon and a number of the Kumase rural towns: [176] the mission was acting, quite clearly, on behalf of the Asantemanhyiamu. Also included in the party was Kofi Nti, sixteen years old son of Kofi Kakari, whom the Kumase Council requested should be sent to England for education. He attended the Surrey County School and accepted an appointment in Trinidad before returning to the Gold Coast to play an important role in Asante politics in the mid-1880s.[177]

Although the Asantemanhyiamu was thus still functioning in March 1874, it was among certain of its more prominent members that the earliest indications appeared that dissatisfaction with the regime of Kofi Kakari might manifest itself in the adoption of secessionist goals.

173 *Ibid.* p. 249.
174 *Ibid.* p. 266. See also, Kumase Divisional Council Archives, Manhyia: Kumasihene's Tribunal, Civil Record Book 5, Kwaku Dua v. Kwasi Mensa, commencing 22 November 1928. Asabi Antwi became the Asabihene under Mensa Bonsu.
175 Wolseley to Kimberley, two despatches dd. Fomena, 13 February 1874, in Stanley, 1874, pp. 239–42.
176 *Further Correspondence*, C. 1006, Pt IX of 1874, pp. 10–11.
177 Fuller, 1921, pp. 143–4.

The Adansehene Oben and Dwabenhene Asafo Agyei had both come to power in their respective localities as a result of the powerful support they had enjoyed from the Asantehene Kwaku Dua: neither had any clear constitutional claims to the offices, Oben being strictly Fomenahene and directly responsible to the Domakwaihene of Kumase,[178] and Asafo Agyei – a son of the Dwabenhene Kwasi Boaten who had died in exile in 1839 – being Kontihene of Dwaben and *omanhene* only by appointment from the capital.[179] On 12 February 1874 Oben had expressed to Wolseley his view that 'his people were looked upon more as enemies than as friends by the King of Coomassie . . . and that he was kept altogether in the dark as to the King of Ashanti's movements, except in so far as they related to his own immediate tribe'. He expressed his desire to come under British protection.[180] The immediate cause of Asafo Agyei's revolt against Kofi Kakari was reported as 'a matter of the strategic defence of his kingdom': that is, both Asafo Agyei and Bantamahene Amankwatia had urged upon the Asantehene the necessity of utilizing all available troops to halt Wolseley's march toward Kumase, but both had been overruled and the Dwabenhene instructed to deploy his forces to oppose Glover's advance from the southeast.[181] Learning, however, of Wolseley's entry into Kumase, Asafo Agyei abandoned his defensive positions along the Anum river and on 10 February made his own submission to Glover.[182] From that date onwards Asafo Agyei refused to acknowledge the authority of the Asantehene. As the situation of crisis developed, the government in Kumase had little difficulty in inducing the Adansehene Oben to reconsider his position, and by April the threat of war had persuaded him to relinquish his idea of migrating into the Protectorate.[183] But with the Dwabenhene, the situation was more complex. Asafo Agyei had long cultivated an alliance with the Akyem Abuakwa in the Protected Territory,[184] and his influence with the eastern Bron of the Krakye region and with the Kwawu was such that the revolt spread rapidly into those provinces (see pp. 144, 279–82). On 15 February the Asantehene sent 14 oz of gold and a gold dish to

178 Ayase Sub-State Council Office: petition to the Minister of Local Government from Nana Bosompem Buobai *et al.*, dd. Ayase, 8 February 1960.

179 See, e.g. Rattray, 1929, p. 174.

180 Brackenbury, 1874, II, 270–2.

181 *Further Correspondence*, C. 4052, 1884, p. 83: Barrow to Colonial Office, dd. Sussex, 16 October 1883.

182 Glover to Wolseley, dd. Essiemampon, 10 February 1874, in Stanley, 1874, p. 251. Brackenbury, 1874, II, 264.

183 *Correspondence*, C. 1140, 1875, p. 14: Lees to Carnarvon, dd. Cape Coast, 4 May 1874. *The Gold Coast Times*, I, no. 7, 29 April 1874.

184 Adu Boahen, 'Juaben and Kumasi Relations in the Nineteenth Century', unpublished paper, Institute of African Studies, Ghana, 1965.

Glover, with a request that he should discourage the Akyem Abuakwa from interference in Dwaben affairs.[185] Large sums of money were also sent to Asafo Agyei in an attempt to reconcile him to the Asantehene.[186] But with the ambition to establish Dwaben in the leadership of a large eastern confederacy extending to the Volta, Asafo Agyei proceeded systematically to dismantle the whole political infrastructure linking his country with Kumase.

By July 1874 Kofi Kakari's continuing position as Asantehene was threatened. 'The King', reported Lees of his meeting with him, 'appeared to me to feel that the state of affairs was critical, and to appreciate fully the gravity of the situation, but while admitting that there was a desire to dethrone him and that the tributary tribes had deserted him he said that the Chiefs of Coomassie had sworn to fight to maintain him on the throne.' [187] On 12 August the Council of Kumase met to debate the Dwaben problem, when it seems that the peace party made clear its position, that whatever its attitude on the question of relations with the British, it did not intend to preside over the disintegration of the nation. On the following day, nevertheless, Kofi Kakari swore before Lees – representing Governor Strahan of the Gold Coast – that he would renounce all authority over Dwaben.[188] From that time onwards whatever support he had continued to enjoy within the Council of Kumase diminished rapidly. The Asantehemaa Afua Kobi and the new Bantamahene Awua initiated moves to remove him from office.[189] In October the Kokofuhene Yaw Berko – a Kwaku Dua appointee [190] – called a meeting of the Asantemanhyiamu in Kumase, and on the 21st Kofi Kakari was summoned to it and informed of his deposition.[191] Among the formal charges brought against him were first, 'that he never listens to counsel, and that since he ascended the throne, the kingdom of Ashanti has known no peace, but continued wars',[192] and secondly, that he had desecrated the coffins of the Asantehene Osei Yaw and Asantehemaa Afua Sapon by removing from them for his own use gold ornaments and other valuables.[193] Kofi Kakari maintained before the Assembly that the charges against

185 Brackenbury, 1874, II, 275.
186 *The Gold Coast Times*, I, no. 7, 29 April 1874.
187 *Correspondence*, C. 1140, 1875, pp. 82–3: Lees to Strahan, dd. Cape Coast, 31 August 1874.
188 *Idem.*
189 *The African Times*, XXIII, no. 253, 2 October 1882: letter dd. Cape Coast, 3 August 1882.
190 Methodist Mission Archives, London: Wharton to General Secretaries, dd. Kumase, 31 May 1846.
191 *The African Times*, XV, no. 162, 31 December 1874 and 1 January 1875, p. 2.
192 *Idem.*
193 *Further Correspondence*, C. 4052, 1884, p. 56: Barrow's report on his visit to Kumase, dd. Accra, 5 July 1883, citing 'the Elders and Chiefs of Coomassie'.

him were spurious: that when his military commanders had fought successful campaigns east of the Volta his people were satisfied, but that he was now being blamed for the unsuccessful outcome of the invasion of the Protectorate.[194] Returning to the palace, Kofi Kakari threatened to destroy himself and the Golden Stool should any attempt be made to displace him from it. After five days a compromise was reached: Kofi Kakari should be allowed to go into exile with sixty wives, five hundred retainers and a quantity of gold provided that he surrender the Golden Stool and agree to abdicate.[195] He departed from Kumase in state, accompanied by three senior functionaries who chose to give up office in order to remain with him, and by his five hundred retainers 'many of whom', so it was reported, 'were chiefs of importance, promoted during his reign'.[196] He took up residence in Kwawma, near Eduabin.

The accession of Mensa Bonsu, and the occupation of Dwaben

The Kokofuhene despatched messengers to the Governor of the Gold Coast without delay to inform him of Kofi Kakari's abdication.[197] Details of the subsequent proceedings to elect a successor are at present lacking. 'They have', observed the leader-writer for *The African Times* in December, 'deposed the King, Koffee Kalkalli, who has submitted to a decree he had not the power to resist. They are now endeavouring to form combinations for a new general organization; but any such organization in native Africa, that has no power to surround itself with the prestige of great military success, is but a rope of sand.'[198] Certainly such adherents of the war party as remained in positions of power made no attempt to put forward a candidate, and the writer for *The African Times* had failed to appreciate the extent to which the traditional oligarchies of the peace and war parties were in process of disintegration as the anti-war movement of the earlier 1870s was becoming transformed into a broad front for major social and political change. In October 1874, when rumours of Kofi Kakari's impending departure from office had first become current, a leader-writer for *The Gold Coast Times* had advanced another view. 'The dethronement of Kofi Kulcarry', he had written,

194 *The African Times*, xv, no. 162, p. 2.
195 *Idem.* See also Fuller, 1921, pp. 145–6. Burton and Cameron, 1883, II, 315, referred to Kofi Kakari's 'compulsory abdication', and Steiner, 1900, p. 10, to his having been 'forced to abdicate'.
196 *The African Times*, xv, no. 162, p. 2.
197 *Correspondence relating to the Queen's Jurisdiction on the Gold Coast*, C. 1139, 1875: minutes of meeting, Cape Coast Castle, 7 November 1874.
198 *The African Times*, xv, no. 162, p. 6.

was a foregone conclusion; no autocrat could go to the lengths he had gone without meeting at the hands of his enraged and outraged subjects the just punishment his acts merited, and raising an ebullition of popular feeling which he in vain might strive to suppress. It is not always nor at all times that despots can tamper with the feelings of their subjects; neither can they outrage decency nor set at defiance public opinion, without suffering from the storm they by their acts have raised . . .[199]

The matter was expressed more articulately by Bonnat, soon himself to join the Kumase administration, who for the first time drew attention to the appeal which aspects of the government of the Protectorate of the Gold Coast had for the more radical Asante politicians:

being already initiated as regards the language of the country, and in continual contact with all classes of society, from the slave to the prince, from the page and buffoon to the King's councillors – I was enabled really to study Ashanti as I had wished to do. I had gained their sympathies, and they replied with all frankness to my questions. I became convinced of the progress, slow but sure, of the new ideas that had found an entry into Ashanti, and which were mining and penetrating it throughout. Liberty, the security of property as well as of person, which existed under the Protectorate, made the Ashantees feel the burthen of the despotism which weighed upon them, and of the expeditions which impoverished them. The people longed for a change in the condition of public affairs.[200]

It may be that in 1874 the exiled Akyempemhene Owusu Koko made a brief re-entry into Kumase politics to sponsor once again the candidacy for the Golden Stool of Yaa Kyaa's son Kwaku Dua Kuma, still in that year only some fourteen years of age.[201] The other candidate to be put forward was Mensa Bonsu, son of Afua Kobi and younger brother of Kofi Kakari, who was about thirty-five years old. The contest was not a protracted one. Messengers from the capital arrived at Cape Coast on 8 January 1875 to inform the Governor that Mensa Bonsu had been elected Asantehene and to express his commitment to peace party policies: 'the messengers went on to say that the King of Coomassie desires to be on the same friendly terms with the Governor as those which existed between the old King (meaning Quacoe Duah) and Governor Maclean, and that his wish is for peace, trade, and open roads'.[202] It may be supposed that the immediate necessity for strong leadership, as indicated by the Dwaben crisis, had led to Mensa Bonsu's candidature being preferred to that of Kwaku Dua Kuma. Although Owusu Koko subsequently declined to reassume office under

199 *The Gold Coast Times*, I, no. 13, 20 October 1874, p. 51.
200 *The African Times*, XIV, no. 160, 30 October 1874, p. 40.
201 *Correspondence*, C. 1139, 1875: minutes of meeting, Cape Coast Castle, 7 November 1874.
202 *Papers relating to Her Majesty's Possessions in West Africa*, C. 1343, 1876, p. 60: Strahan to Carnarvon, dd. Cape Coast, 8 January 1875.

Mensa Bonsu, the election may probably have involved some sort of agreement between the two sides. It has been shown in Chapter 9 that both Kofi Kakari and Mensa Bonsu were in a sense surrogate rulers for Kwaku Dua Kuma whose genealogical claims to the Golden Stool were so much stronger than theirs.

In 1874 there had been persistent rumours that other of the greater *amanhene* – those of Bekwae, Kokofu and Nsuta – were not insensitive to the attractions of the secessionist position which the Dwabenhene had espoused.[203] Mensa Bonsu put the issue to the test soon after his election. An extraordinary session of the Asantemanhyiamu was convened for late August 1875. Other than the Kumase members, it was attended by representatives of the *aman* including Mampon, Kokofu, Bekwae, Asumegya, Agona and Nkoransa. It was argued that any agreement Kofi Kakari had made with Dwabenhene Asafo Agyei was nullified by the latter's subsequent conduct in disrupting trade, in failing to maintain a rule of law, and in arresting and executing agents of the central government. The vote in the Asantemanhyiamu was unanimous: Asafo Agyei should be deposed or war declared against him.[204] Since however Asafo Agyei's deposition could not be brought about without the use of force, Mensa Bonsu immediately placed an army upon a war footing. It was commanded by the Bantamahene Awua, and of the *amanhene* at least those of Kokofu and Asumegya were able to supply troops at such short notice.[205]

The first attacks upon Dwaben towns were launched on 12 September 1875,[206] but the major invasion occurred between 31 October and 3 November. At one stage in the fighting three of the Kumase field commanders blew themselves up with gunpowder to avoid capture: the Adumhene Agyei Kese and the two veterans of the northern campaigns of thirty years earlier, the Anantahene Asamoa Nkwanta and the Nseniehene Kwadwo Apea Agyei.[207] Nevertheless by 3 November the Dwaben supporters of Asafo Agyei had run out of gunpowder, and had to abandon their towns. They fled southwards to take refuge within Akyem Abuakwa, under British protection.[208] On 8 November Mensa Bonsu despatched a letter to Governor Strahan:

203 See, e.g. *Correspondence*, C. 1140, 1875, p. 82: Lees to Strahan, dd. Cape Coast, 31 August 1874.
204 *Papers*, C. 1402, 1876, p. 87: Mensa Bonsu to Governor, dd. Kumase, 2 September 1875.
205 Rattray, 1929, pp. 176; 203.
206 *Papers*, C. 1402, 1876, pp. 87–8: (Kofi) Asafo Agyei to Strahan, dd. Juaben, 12 September 1875.
207 Rattray, 1929, p. 176. The Nseniehene is still commemorated in the epithet, *kyere adanka*, 'he seized the powder keg', see IASAS/22: Nsumankwa Stool History recorded by J. Agyeman-Duah, 26 October 1962.
208 *Papers*, C. 1402, 1876, pp. 105–6: Gouldsbury to Strahan, dd. Dwaben Forest, 6 November 1875; pp. 110–11: Gouldsbury to Strahan, dd. Wankyi, Asante Akyem, 8 November 1875.

An official messenger from my General (Awuah) has reached me, and informed me that the Ashantees and the Djabins fought on the 3rd instant, and that Awuah (my General) had gained a decided victory, and taken the town of Djabin, and that murderer, Asafu Agai, has run away and concealed himself in the forest.

At last Asafu Agai, the great disturber of this country, is fallen; and I hope and trust we shall soon have peace and trade flourish in the country, and the good understanding between us continue for the prosperity of the countries which we govern.

A report says that Asafu Agai is on his way to Akim. If it be true, I earnestly beg you Excellency not to allow him to be detained in the Protectorate, but deliver him up to me, for he is a great and notorious murderer . . .[209]

The request was turned down, and Carnarvon, Secretary of State for the Colonies in London, hastened to express his misgivings about the outcome of the central government's victory: 'It is with regret that I have received the information of these renewed disturbances of the peace, and of the success of the king of Coomassie, which, as you [Strahan] observe, will probably tend to revive the power and prestige of the Ashanti kingdom, a result which can scarcely be regarded without anxiety'.[210] Carnarvon's misgivings seemed confirmed when Captain Baker, sent with a small force to Kumase to collect the third instalment of the war indemnity, was informed that it was not ready, and although it was subsequently paid – the last that was – he was hooted in the streets of the capital.[211] Thus, remarked Ellis, 'in less than two years from the burning of Coomassie the Ashanti diplomacy had met with such success that Mensah had recovered the whole of the Djuabin territory, repudiated the payment of the war indemnity, re-established the prestige and power of the Ashanti name, and outwitted the Colonial Government upon every point'.[212]

The new administration of Mensa Bonsu

In the early years of his reign Mensa Bonsu clearly enjoyed the support of a very wide constituency. The decisiveness of his handling of the Dwaben problem won him the backing of the surviving adherents of the old war party ideologies, while his ready assumption of the role of presidential monarch – comparable with Kofi Kakari in the first part of his reign – reassured the radical politicians that the prospects

209 *Ibid.* p. 114: Mensa Bonsu to Governor, dd. Kumase, 8 November 1875.
210 PRO, CO. 96/115: Carnarvon to Strahan, dd. 29 December 1875. For recent accounts of the diplomatic intricacies surrounding the re-absorption of Dwaben, see Johnson, 1971, and Lewin, 1974, pp. 104–20.
211 Ellis, 1883, pp. 39–40.
212 *Ibid.* p. 187.

for reform were real ones. The decision of the government, moreover, to eschew the use of its military resources in the solution of the problems posed by continuing rebellion in the northeastern provinces and by the struggle between secessionists and centralists in Gyaman (see pp. 287–95), left Mensa Bonsu free to focus his attention on the task of national reconstruction. In essaying new approaches to the theme of politics, the Asantehene was aided by the fact that his government – the Council of Kumase – was to a significant extent dominated by new personalities. Of the prominent councillors who had served Kofi Kakari and earlier, in some cases, Kwaku Dua I, relatively few survived to play active roles in the work of reconstruction. Thus the Kyidomhene Krapa, who had been killed in the campaign in the south in 1873,[213] had been succeeded by Kwadwo Finam; the Boakye Yam Kuma counselor Akyampon Yaw, who died near Beyin in the same year, had been succeeded by Asase Asa; the Butuakwa counselor Apea Kyeame, slain at Amoafo in January 1874,[214] by Kwame Dwuben; the Bantamahene Amankwatia, killed in the same battle,[215] by Awua; and the Adumhene Agyei Kese, Anantahene Asamoa Nkwanta and Nseniehene Kwadwo Apea Agyei, all of whom had died in the Dwaben campaign in November 1875, by Kyereme Dense, Sie and Yaw Akroko respectively. The Akuropohene Kwame Agyepon, who had remained among the supporters of Kofi Kakari in 1874, had been replaced by Safo Anwona and, similarly in the reshuffle of office in 1874, the Domakwaihene and chief counselor Kwaku Poku (Nsuase Poku) had apparently been posted to Bonduku, and replaced in Kumase by Amankwa Nyame (see p. 288). The Akyempemhene Owusu Koko continued in retirement from active politics. Finally, the Gyaasewahene Adu Bofo – already seriously ill in 1871 [216] – played little part in the affairs of state under Mensa Bonsu, and, although still alive in 1883, had effectively relinquished office to Kofi Poku by about 1876. Many of those whose services had been lost had been men of great experience; some, like Asamoa Nkwanta, Kwadwo Apea Agyei and Apea Kyeame, had been officers of the Council of Kumase for between thirty and forty years. The men who replaced them were by and large unknown and unproven and – with a few exceptions such as Bantamahene Awua – were never to achieve the stature of their predecessors in office.

[213] Ramseyer and Kühne, 1875, p. 256.
[214] Boyle, 1874, p. 332.
[215] *Ibid.* p. 331.
[216] Ramseyer and Kühne, 1875, p. 138. Adu Bofo was already in the early stage of Parkinsonism by 1871, and was paralysed in his later years, see Asante Collective Biography Project: Adu Bofo. See also Wilks, field-notes: Interview with Gyaasehene Opoku Frefre II, dd. Kumase, 5 December 1973.

In the first year of his reign Mensa Bonsu presided over the beginnings of what was to prove a programme of extensive administrative reform. The creation of the new model civil service, in which Osei Bonsu's son Owusu Ansa played so important a role, will be discussed in detail in Chapter 14. At the same time the first steps were also taken towards army reform, and the formation of the new regiments of professional soldiers will also be considered in that chapter. The second measure presumably proved popular with the radicals, since it indicated the way in which the much-disliked system of military conscription might ultimately be abolished without prejudice to national defence interests. By 1876, however, despite the success which seemed to be promised by his innovatory policies, the broad consensus of opinion on which Mensa Bonsu had depended was already becoming eroded. The particular issue which proved initially divisive was that of the government's decision to allow the Wesleyan missionaries to re-establish a station in Kumase. The matter became a pressing one with the arrival in the capital of the Rev. Thomas Picot on 10 April 1876. Perhaps because one of Kofi Kakari's last acts had been to express his desire that missionaries should return to Kumase 'for the education of the young',[217] the government's action in permitting Picot to visit the town was apparently regarded in some quarters as a politically provocative one. The ailing Adu Bofo, although formerly one of Kofi Kakari's principal supporters, was induced to emerge briefly from his retirement to oppose the measure – and thereby to stimulate the beginnings of a revival of the old war party. The question of the missionaries was brought for debate before the Council of Kumase on 21 April 1876. Mensa Bonsu argued that the missionaries were welcome if they played the sort of role that Freeman had during the reign of Kwaku Dua I: that was, 'to help the peace of the nation and the prosperity of trade'. But, aware of the strength of feeling on the matter, the Asantehene equivocated, pointing out also that children had work to do and could not be spared for schooling; that his subjects had to obey the laws of the nation and could not be permitted freedom of conscience; and that the customs of Asante were not compatible with Christianity which made people proud and, as in Fanteland, led to the breakdown of accepted social conventions. The Bantamahene Awua took a still firmer line: that polygamy and slavery could not and should not be abolished in Asante; that Christianity was not wanted there; and that all that was required of the Europeans on the coast was trade. Adu Bofo spoke last. The Asante, he declared, will never accept Christianity but will remain true to the ways of their

217 *Correspondence*, C. 1140, 1875, p. 57: Strahan to Carnarvon dd. Cape Coast, 30 June 1874.

forefathers. As had happened so often in the past, Adu Bofo's intervention in council proved decisive: Picot departed for the coast the same day.[218]

The outcome of the debate of 21 April was clearly a triumph for the conservatives. Late in the year, however, the progressives achieved something of a victory in obtaining a majority decision in council for radical reform of the penal code. The matter – referred to by outside observers as the 'abolition of human sacrifice' – will be discussed fully in Chapter 14. The trend of events was such as to induce the more militant of Mensa Bonsu's opponents to attempt to overthrow him by force and to reinstate Kofi Kakari in office. Kofi Kakari, it was reported, 'made an attempt to go to Coomassie to stir up his party to *Revolution*'.[219] Details of the attempted *coup* are lacking. Fighting, however, seems to have occurred in the capital, and the insurgents shot dead one of Mensa Bonsu's senior counselors, Okyeame Yaw Nantwi, and severely wounded another, Boakye Tenten, before order was restored. The extent of Kofi Kakari's involvement may have been unclear. Certainly Mensa Bonsu dissuaded his chiefs from injuring him. Kofi Kakari was nevertheless removed from Kwawma where he had been living in some luxury, was deprived of much of his property, and was banished to the town of Akuropon some eleven miles northwest of the capital.[220] While the precise date of the abortive *coup* has not been ascertained, it clearly occurred in the first half of 1877: news of it was sent by Owusu Ansa in Cape Coast to Ramseyer in Switzerland on 7 July.

Domankama and the revival of the war party

Throughout the remainder of 1877 and until 1879, the government's programme of reconstruction appears to have proceeded unimpeded. The tranquillity of the times, however, was abruptly shattered in 1879. 'In the latter part of the year 1879 and in 1880', reported Ellis, 'Ashanti was convulsed by internal dissensions.'[221] A movement arose known as Domankama, the 'Creator' cult. Its leader appears to have been one Okomfo Kwaku (or Okomfoku) of Adwumakase, who presided over the Abonsam-komfo or 'priests of (Sasa-) Bonsam': sorcerers organized into local cells upon a political model, that is, each cell having its own *ohene* and *ohemaa,* male and female

---

218 *The African Times,* XVII, no. 180, 1 August 1876, pp. 21–2, and no. 181, 1 September 1876, pp. 33–4: report on Picot's visit to Kumase. Methodist Mission Archives, London: Picot to Boyce, dd. Cape Coast, 3 May 1876.
219 Basel Mission Archives: Owusu Ansa to Ramseyer, dd. 7 July 1877.
220 *Idem.* See also Fuller, 1921, p. 146.
221 Ellis, 1883, p. 202.

chiefs, its own *akyeame* or counselors, its own *nseniefo* or criers, and its own *adumfo* or executioners. It is said that Okomfo Kwaku possessed the means of inducing people to follow him even against their will – that is, of 'bewitching them'.[222] The Domankama movement grew into one with over a thousand adherents.[223] Although deeply rooted in traditional witchcraft practices, it assumed a highly political character. Its emergence to strength in 1879 is probably to be seen as a reaction against the modernizing policies of Mensa Bonsu's government, which violated the spirit of the 'timeless' laws given by Okomfo Anokye at the inception of the nation. Indeed, the founder of the movement himself claimed to be a reincarnation of the much revered Okomfo Anokye, while his deputies took the names of the early Asantehenes. But the Abonsam-komfo, while highly conservative in outlook, were also nationalistic in aim, rebelling against Mensa Bonsu's failure to restore to Asante its former pre-eminence through the reconquest of the Bron, Kwawu, Gonja and other lost provinces. Thus in late 1879 two emissaries of Domankama had visited Kwawu to announce that Okomfo Anokye had returned to lead the nation, and that it was his intention shortly to visit the province. The Kwawu chiefs viewed the visitation as an attempt to coerce them into renewing their political allegiance to the Golden Stool of Asante.[224]

Probably early in 1880 armed members of the movement entered Kumase and gave a display of musketry at Dwaberem, the Great Market, apparently to demonstrate their strength and militancy.[225] Shortly afterwards, a group re-entered the capital and, firing guns, forced their way into the palace. Taking 'all sorts of liberties', one of their number tried to shoot Mensa Bonsu.[226] Following the abortive assassination attempt, the Asantehene ordered a purge of the movement. As late as the 1920s Rattray met with one Yaw Adawua who claimed to be a survivor to the 'two hundred Bonsam 'Komfo who

---

222 Wilks and Ferguson, field-notes, interview with Opanin Domfe Kyere, dd. Kumase, 23 November 1973. A centenarian, Domfe Kyere has first-hand knowledge of the movement. See further, Kumase Divisional Council Archives, Manhyia, Kumasihene's Tribunal Record Book 10: Kwame Kusi v. Akwasi Kobi, 23 June 1930; and Record Books 10 and 12: Yaw Num v. Kwadwo Appan, case commencing 5 June 1930. In the course of enquiries made in Asante-Akyem in 1959, the writer was able to obtain some account of the organization of the cult, but informants still evinced much reluctance in speaking of it, and wished to remain anonymous.

223 Interview with Domfe Kyere. Basel Mission Archives: Ramseyer to Basel, dd. 19 June 1880, citing information from Asabi Antwi and Bosommuru Dwira as transmitted through Owusu Ansa.

224 Ramseyer to Basel, dd. 19 June 1880.

225 Kumase Divisional Council Archives, Manhyia, Kumasihene's Tribunal Record Book 10: Kwame Kusi v. Akwasi Kobi.

226 Ramseyer to Basel, dd. 19 June 1880. Interview with Domfe Kyere, dd. Kumase, 23 November 1973. See further Lewin, 1974, p. 89.

had been killed in the reign, and by the order of, King Mensa Bonsu'.[227] There can be little doubt that the Abonsam-komfo enjoyed the active support of Mensa Bonsu's political opponents and particularly of those who sought the restoration of Kofi Kakari. Among those executed for their participation in the movement was, for example, one Kwaku Ntwia. A son of Pampasuhene Yaw Kyira of Kumase, Kwaku Ntwia had fought in the campaigns of Kofi Kakari and had been personally honoured by that Asantehene.[228] Another to die was Odami, who owed his appointment to the Bomfa stool to Kofi Kakari's Gyaasewahene, Adu Bofo.[229] Again, another to be found guilty of association with Domankama was Yaa Bobu, daughter of Kwame Butuakwa and wife of his two successors in the counsclorship, Apea Kyeame and Kwame Dwuben. At the intercession of the Asantehemaa Afua Kobi, Mensa Bonsu spared the life of Yaa Bobu. The heavy fines imposed upon her, however, virtually ruined her current husband Kwame Dwuben – who is known to have become a strong supporter of Kofi Kakari's restoration.[230] And finally, among the many other followers of Domankama was at least one royal with aspirations to the Golden Stool: Osei Kwaku Goroso. He was arrested and detained, but was saved from execution by his status. He was later to move into the Gold Coast Colony, and his subsequent career will be referred to below.[231] In this general context it is significant that it was in 1880 that the old war party finally re-emerged as a strong force within the Council of Kumase. At the very least it would seem arguable that the growth of Domankama, and the recovery of the war party, were distinct but related manifestations of a conservative reaction against the departure, by Mensa Bonsu's government, from the traditionally accepted canons and prescriptions of political behaviour.

The issue on which the war party was able to re-activate its constituency was that of the Adanse secession. The government's policy towards Adanse since 1874 has been examined in a recent study by Agbodeka.[232] Kumase negotiators had been at work in Adanse almost continually since the Adansehene Oben had first contemplated secession in 1874. As a result a movement for the restoration of normal

227 Rattray, 1927, p. 29.
228 Kumase Divisional Council Archives, Manhyia, Kumasihene's Tribunal Record Book 4: Osei Yaw v. Yaw Bredwa, commencing 5 July 1928.
229 *Ibid.* Record Book 7: Kwadwo Poku *v.* Kwame Adu, commencing 22 August 1929.
230 *Ibid.* Record Books 10 and 12: Yaw Num *v.* Kwadwo Appan, commencing 5 June 1930.
231 Interview with Domfe Kyere, dd. Kumase, 23 November 1973. Another follower of Okomfo Kwaku was Bako Kyere of the Kumase Nsumankwaa. He was spared since he was considered to have been bewitched against his will, but to have done no wrong.
232 Agbodeka, 1971, pp. 91–3.

relations with Kumase had been built up in Adanse, headed by the Adubeashene, Dompoasehene and Twumasehene. Early in 1879 the Adansehene Nkansa – who had succeeded Oben three years earlier – declared destooled the three chiefs and replaced them by his own nominees. The government entrusted the handling of the situation to one of its experienced negotiators, Yaw Agyei, but somewhat unexpectedly the government of the Gold Coast also sent Captain Hay, Acting Colonial Secretary, to Adanse in March to represent its interests there. Hay expressed his support for the secessionist cause, arrested at least one of its opponents, ordered the Kumase negotiators to leave Adanse territory, and intimated that the British were prepared to resort to force in support of Adanse independence.[233] But the inclusion of the Adanse among those over whom the Asante government by the Treaty of Fomena had relinquished authority had in fact occurred as a result of the Adansehene's avowed intention of migrating into British protected territory. In the view of the government, since the Adanse had been persuaded instead to remain within Asante, the British lacked any mandate for intervention in their affairs. The demand for an immediate invasion of Adanse was one, therefore, on which the war party in Kumase could reasonably hope to rebuild its constituency.

In the aftermath of the assassination attempt of 1880, the Bantamahene Awua and Bekwaehene Yaw Poku emerged as leaders of the resurgent war interest. By late 1880 there was, so Ellis reported, 'an influential war party in Kumassi, which included, among other powerful chiefs, Opoku, chief of Bekweh, and the Ashanti General, Awua, chief of Bantama, who were desirous of removing the last important trace of the national defeat [of 1874] by annexing Adansi'.[234] In December 1880 the two leaders both took oaths in public, that they would force the Adansehene to return allegiance to the government.[235] What was, however, presumably of the gravest concern to Mensa Bonsu was that at least some of the more militant supporters of the reviving party were beginning again to agitate for the restoration of Kofi Kakari. 'The war party in Coomassie', Ellis maintained,

had fast been gaining the upper hand. The bellicose chiefs spoke of Quoffi Calcalli as a man who, whatever might have been his other shortcomings, was, at all events, not afraid of the white men, and recommenced their intrigues with that individual . . . Confusion began to reign in Coomassie,

233 Details of the diplomatic contest are to be found in PRO, CO. 96/126, no. 32: Lees to Hicks Beech, dd. 25 February 1879; no. 83: Lees to Hicks Beach, dd. 14 April 1879.
234 Ellis, 1893, p. 363.
235 Ellis, 1883, pp. 205; 238. *Affairs of the Gold Coast*, C. 3064, 1881, p. 4: Griffith to Kimberley, dd. 5 January 1881.

and the struggle for supremacy between the court and the war party was fast approaching a crisis . . .[236]

Ellis, whose excellent information was derived from the various intelligence agents despatched by the British into Asante in the period,[237] reported that the ex-Asantehene was not averse to the approaches made to him:

People began to talk of the good old times when Quoffi Calcalli was king, and that wily ex-monarch, who had outlived the contempt with which he had at first been regarded for outraging Ashanti prejudices by continuing to live when disgraced, commenced to intrigue with the people of Kokofuah, the most thickly populated district in Ashanti, and the one which supplies the largest contingent for the army.[238]

The war scare of 1881 and the Boakye Tenten mission

In January 1881, the war party was enabled to make further political capital out of the case of Owusu Taseamandi, whose disappearance and perhaps abduction from Kumase on the 10th of that month was believed to have taken place with the complicity of the British authorities on the Gold Coast (see pp. 292–3). To make matters more difficult for the government, in the same period the situation in the north-western provinces assumed crisis proportions as the Gyamanhene Agyeman began to place the troops loyal to him on a war footing (p. 294). Extending their platform further, the war party councillors claimed that the ex-Dwabenhene Asafo Agyei, in complicity with the Gã Mantse Taki, had been permitted by the British whose protection he enjoyed to plan the launching of an invasion of Asante from the eastern districts of the Colony.[239] In early 1881, Ellis reported,

affairs were in rather a critical condition in Coomassi owing to the struggle for supremacy between the war and court parties . . . Numerous influential chiefs, who had hitherto belonged to the court party or had equally held aloof from both sections, now joined the war party, which carried everything before it, and at the 'palaver' which was held Mensah could do nothing but acquiesce in their proposals; in fact any attempt on his part to stem the popular current would only have resulted in his downfall.[240]

236 Ellis, 1883, pp. 205–6.
237 See, e.g. *Affairs*, C. 3064, 1881, p. 8: Griffith to Joseph Parker dd. Elmina, 5 January 1881, instructing him to proceed to Kumase and report on the military situation, on the new model army, on the position of Bekwaehene on the Adanse issue, and so forth.
238 Ellis, 1883, p. 202.
239 Ellis, 1893, p. 363.
240 Ellis, 1883, p. 237.

The 'palaver' in question was almost certainly the annual meeting of the Asantemanhyiamu – the Odwira having fallen in early January. Mensa Bonsu was instructed to send messengers immediately to the British Governor, among other things to demand – with the threat of force if necessary – the surrender of Owusu Taseamandi. He was reported to have sworn before the messengers, that 'all black men are subject to me and I will have my revenge for all this'.[241] The mission arrived in Cape Coast on 19 January, and command was taken of it by the experienced diplomat Asabi Antwi who had already been on the coast for some months. There can be little doubt that he was reflecting the prevailing mood of the councillors in Kumase when he announced in Cape Coast that Asante troops would enter the Colony through Assin unless Owusu Taseamandi was handed over immediately.[242]

The British commenced to place the Colony on a war-footing. Available troops were moved up to the Pra river, reinforcements of the West India regiments were sent for, and naval forces off the coast were alerted.[243] In Asante, too, the Bantamahene Awua and Bekwaehene Yaw Poku began to mobilize the men of their districts.[244] But by sending the mission to Cape Coast, Mensa Bonsu had in fact skilfully played for time. 'So far', observed Ellis, 'but no further, was Mensah influenced by the powerful war party.'[245] The Asantehene argued that mobilization was premature until a reply had been received from the government of the Gold Coast, and carried the majority of councillors with him at the expense of being 'regarded with a feeling of contempt by the leaders of the war party'.[246] Working systematically 'to gather round him all his adherents and strengthen his position', a number of the more recent converts to the war party cause changed sides once again. In the fierce struggle for control of the government which developed in late January, each side endeavoured, as Ellis reported it, 'by eloquence, taunts, threats, and promises, to win over wavering opponents to its side'.[247] The Kokofuhemaa, interestingly, interceded with the Asantehemaa Afua Kobi in the interests of peace,[248] and it was the influence of the women's lobby that was to prove decisive. At a meet-

---

241 *Ibid.* p. 238.
242 *Affairs*, C. 3064, 1881, p. 17: Executive Council meeting, Cape Coast Castle, 22 January 1881.
243 *Ibid.* see e.g. pp. 50–1: Griffith to Kimberley, dd. Cape Coast, 6 February 1881; p. 84: Captain Hope to Griffith, dd. *H. M. S. Champion*, Elmina, 28 February 1881.
244 Ellis, 1883, p. 238.
245 *Idem.*
246 *Ibid.* pp. 205–6, 238–9.
247 *Ibid.* pp. 239–41.
248 *Affairs*, C. 3064, 1881, p. 49: Parker to Griffith, dd. Kumase, 24 January 1881.

ing of council in the last few days of January, the Asantehemaa intervened in the debate in a manner reminiscent of the session in November 1873 described above:

The queen-mother, who possessed enormous influence, threatened to commit
suicide 'on the heads' of the principal chiefs of the war party if they per-
severed in their intentions, and this threat sealed the fate of their party. Most
of the bellicose chiefs returned to their own towns to sulk in dignified silence,
and Mensah had things entirely his own way.[249]

'It is said', Mensa Bonsu announced to the Council, 'that white men
are coming across the Pra. We have done nothing, we have no quarrel
with them. Let us sit still; and, if they wish to fight, let them fire the
first shot.' [250] A new mission was immediately despatched to the Gold
Coast, and on 17–18 February delivered to the British an assurance of
peace and a disavowal of Asabi Antwi's earlier threat of invasion.
Significantly, the mission was headed by the Ankobea counselor Kofi
Bene. 'He reiterated several times', it was reported, 'that he was the
late King Quako Dua's man, who was celebrated for his peaceful
disposition, and the friendly terms he was on with Governor Maclean
and the English Government, and that the present desire of the King
of Ashanti was that all things should go on peaceably as before'.[251]
Clearly, as Burton and Cameron remarked, 'the peace-party had
utterly overthrown the war-party'.[252]

Certain signs of the general relief at the elimination of the threat to
the government from the war party opposition became rapidly visible.
With the possibility of war now a remote one, something of a boom in
building swept the nation. By February 1881 the Asantehene had set
the fashion by ordering the rebuilding of the villages on Route VI
between Amoafo and the capital.[253] Later in the year Lonsdale commented on the many new houses being built in the villages along
Route IV.[254] 'His young men', commented Mensa Bonsu, 'were always
trading to the coast with the object of gaining wealth, so that they
might build for themselves good houses . . . and so make Coomassie

249 *Ibid.* p. 80: Griffith to Kimberley, dd. Cape Coast, 27 and 28 February 1881.
Ellis, 1883, p. 242.
250 Ellis, 1883, p. 242.
251 *Affairs,* C. 3064, 1881, p. 69: Dudley to Colonial Secretary, dd. Cape Coast, 17
February 1881, p. 86: report of a meeting between Griffith and the Asante
messengers, Elmina, 18 February 1881. For Kofi Bene, see Kumase Divisional
Council Archives, Manhyia, Kumasihene's Tribunal, Civil Record Book 14,
Kwasi Wuabu *v.* Kwame Kusi, commencing 29 February 1832.
252 Burton and Cameron, 1883, II, 319.
253 *Affairs,* C. 3064, 1881, p. 85: Buck and Huppenbauer to Jackson, dd. Dweraso, 18
February 1881.
254 *Further Correspondence,* C. 3386, 1882, p. 67: Lonsdale's report on his mission
of 1881–2.

the fine town it formerly was'.[255] In 1881, moreover, the Asantemanhyiamu decided to send a further mission of peace to the Gold Coast, hoping to remove all remaining causes of misunderstanding between the two governments. Numbering, with retainers, over four hundred men, it included delegates from the Bantamahene and Asafohene of Kumase and from Bekwaehene, Mamponhene, Kokofuhene, Nsutahene, Asumegyahene and Amoafohene, together with two sons of Asantehene Kwaku Dua I representing the princes, and a bevy of administrative officers of the central government.[256] Chosen to head it was the Boakye Yam Panin counselor, Boakye Tenten – husband of the Asantehemaa and himself for a time a supporter of the war party.[257] The mission left Kumase on 3 April; met with Governor Rowe at Praso on the 16th and 17th of the month for discussions; [258] and proceeded thence to Elmina where talks were held with various Colony chiefs on 28 May and with Governor Rowe again two days later.[259] With a working understanding with the British authorities on the Gold Coast in hand, the main task of the mission had been accomplished. But whether on his own initiative or on that of the government in Kumase, Boakye Tenten retained his staff in Elmina for over three months while plans were made for his extended tour of many of the major towns of the Colony. The mission finally left Elmina on 13 September. Arriving in Anomabo on the 15th, it was accorded a fine reception by 'the king and his chiefs' and was donated over £22 in cash, and sheep, fowls and yam, by the citizens of the town.[260] At Apam all preparations 'to insure an impressive reception' had been made by Sub-Collector Hagan, and at Winneba 'Mr. Bartells and King Ghartey', so it was reported, 'had organized such a reception as could not fail to give the most punctilious native Prince gratification'.[261] The mission finally left Accra for Kumase on 15 October.[262] As an exercise in public relations, it had proved a major triumph. 'The reception of Prince Buaki and his chiefs', reported Lonsdale, 'was, throughout the journey, enthusiastic.' [263] The view seemed sustained

255 *Ibid.* p. 64.
256 *Affairs,* C. 3064, 1881, pp. 135–6: 'List of Chiefs in the Suite of Prince Buaki'.
257 Ellis, 1883, p. 294.
258 *Affairs,* C. 3064, 1881, pp. 134–5: Rowe to Kimberley, dd. Praso, 19 April 1881; pp. 139–41: notes of a meeting at Praso, 17 April 1881.
259 Ellis, 1883, pp. 306–11. The British had an Arabic transcript of the proceedings of 30 May prepared and sent to Kumase, see Balme Library, University of Ghana, *Al-risālah bi 'l-malak yasamma Būakī.*
260 *The Gold Coast Times,* I, no. 10, 24 September 1881: letter dd. Anomabo, 18 September, 1881.
261 *Further Correspondence,* C. 3386, 1882, p. 4: Lonsdale to Governor, dd. Accra, 25 September 1881.
262 *Ibid.* pp. 5–6: Rowe to Kimberley, dd. Accra, 16 October 1881.
263 *Ibid.* p. 4: Lonsdale to Governor, dd. Accra, 25 September 1881. There was nevertheless an attempt, as Boakye Tenten observed, 'to frustrate his mission

of those in both Asante and the Gold Coast who had long argued that it was the presence of the British which had intensified conflict between the inland power and the coastal peoples. It was doubtless a result of the goodwill engendered by the Boakye Tenten mission that contributors to *The Gold Coast Times* in the following year forcefully maintained the position that the Gold Coast and Asante were truly one nation united by common languages and common origins, and that it had been the 'wicked design' of the European to divide them in order to rule.[264] The debate could not have failed to influence in turn the Gold Coast intellectuals who, within a few years, were to argue passionately for a 'federal Gold Coast and Ashanti', remarking on the 'obtuseness' of the British colonial administration since the time of Governor Maclean [265] and articulating the belief that 'the Gold Coast and Ashanti will lead the way in what will prove the grandest conception of the twentieth century . . . to work out for themselves a civilisation whose fruits shall abide and influence sister communities, because they will be the fruits of peace and good-will among men'.[266]

The collapse of the presidential monarchy

By the end of 1881 the government in Kumase appeared to have eliminated the challenge from the war party, to have restored public confidence in its administration, and to have laid the foundations for the development of closer ties with the Gold Coast. Yet all was still not well with the state of the nation. To the dismay of those who had steadfastly supported Mensa Bonsu in his struggle with the resurgent war party, the Asantehene's conduct became increasingly erratic as he sought to secure his personal position against any future challenge. On 22 June 1879 Mensa Bonsu had inaugurated a new Palace Guard. Its personnel were equipped with the most up-to-date weaponry available, and were placed under the command of one Frimpon – newly designated as Tuotuohene, 'chief of the rifles'.[267] The Guard had probably saved the Asantehene's life in 1880. Later in that year, fearing further attempts on his person, the Asantehene had augmented the Guard by transferring to it, among others, professional soldiers from

. . . from the enemies of the Ashantis', see *Further Correspondence*, C. 3386, 1882, p. 32: Owusu Ansa to Sherwin, dd. Cape Coast, 21 January 1882. Reports were circulated that Mensa Bonsu had 'sacrificed' two hundred virgins! 'I never heard such a thing yet', remarked Owusu Ansa, 'and no person would credit such nonsense . . .'

264 *The Gold Coast Times*, I, especially no. 44, 20 May 1882; no. 46, 3 June 1882; no. 51, 8 July 1882; and no. 52, 15 July 1882.
265 See e.g. Casely Hayford, 1903, p. 131. *Ibid.* p. 243.
266 *Ibid.* pp. 246-8.
267 *Affairs*, C. 3064, 1881, p. 54: Owusu Ansa to Governor, dd. Cape Coast, 17 May 1880.

the regular army. Ellis reported that 'he turned his Houssa corps into a body-guard, and ensured its fidelity by gifts and promises of future favour; he gathered round him his ocrahs and retainers, and with this force, armed principally with breech-loading rifles, he easily managed to stifle disaffection and maintain his position'.[268] A report of early 1881 indicated that the Asantehene's Palace Guard numbered six hundred riflemen.[269] But the creation of a specially privileged *corps d'élite* under the Asantehene's direct control became a matter of grave concern to the councillors when they realized that he intended to use it not only to ensure his personal safety but also as an instrument of political repression. In January 1882 the execution of Kwabena Sapon, head-drummer and probably Atumpanhene, and of Kwabena Pepon of the Papafoafo or fan-bearers, gave some indication that the trend towards liberalization characteristic of the earlier part of Mensa Bonsu's reign had now been reversed.[270]

On 2 May 1882 Lonsdale entered Kumase on his second visit there, and found the situation tense. The Council of Kumase was much concerned with the Gyaman problem, and the Englishman was led to believe that another revival of the war party was imminent. Adherents of what he called the 'extreme party' received him with a 'sullenness of demeanour' even though their leader, the Bantamahene Awua – a soldier rather than a politician – was personally friendly. On the other hand, Lonsdale added, 'by those Chiefs who . . . are in opposition to the extreme party, either through personal jealousy, personal hostility, or want of coincidence with them in the general policy, I was received with cordiality'.[271] In Lonsdale's estimation Mensa Bonsu was not a very decisive legislator; he was inclined towards 'the counsels of peaceful and prudent advisers' and was anxious to carry out reforms, but he was 'wanting in sufficient self-assertion to overrule the suggestions of influential counsellors, to whose good opinion he defers to much'.[272] Lonsdale's assessment of the situation was, however, partial and was far from being supported by the facts. At a meeting of the Council of Kumase on 27 May the Bantamahene argued persuasively and excitedly for the immediate invasion of Gyaman, and appeared to carry many

268 Ellis, 1883, p. 202. One is reminded not only of Osei Bonsu's policy in the earlier nineteenth century, of 'attaching a foreign force to repress the discontents of the lower orders', Bowdich, 1821a, p. 28, but also, irresistibly, of Nkrumah's policy in the mid-twentieth for which see for example Ocran, 1968, chapter III.

269 *Affairs*, C. 3064, 1881, p. 48: Parker to Griffith, dd. Kumase, 24 January 1881.

270 *Further Correspondence*, C. 3386, 1882, p. 42: D.C., Cape Coast, to Colonial Secretary dd. 14 February 1882.

271 *Further Correspondence*, C. 3687, 1883, p. 110: Lonsdale's report of his mission of 1882.

272 *Ibid.* p. 117.

of his colleagues with him. After a short consultation between a number of the peace party members and the Asantehene, the decision to arbitrate further was announced and the Bantamahene's protests were denied further hearing.[273] Within two or three weeks Awua was accused by the Asantehene of plotting his overthrow. He was arrested, beaten and imprisoned, and his younger brother (and presumed successor) and two of his *akyeame* were executed.[274] One of the *nseniefo,* Sen Kwaku, who had conducted embassies to the British as long ago as 1874 (Plate XVIII),[275] protested at the treatment of Awua, and was immediately himself executed.[276] The Nseniehene Yaw Akroko ('Yaw Krow') in turn denounced the execution of one of his more experienced negotiators – and suffered a like fate.[277] Among the next to fall was Boampon of Abankro – a subordinate of the Gyaasewahene Kofi Poku who probably held the post of Abontendomhene.[278] In no case, apparently, was any attempt made to follow the due processes of law.

In 1882, then, Mensa Bonsu made recourse to the instrument of terror in an attempt to avert not only further attempts on his life but also, seemingly, further challenges to his political prerogatives as he now widely construed them. Symptomatic of the transformation of his role from that of presidential monarch to that of autocrat was his introduction, in the same period, of new and widely resented taxation policies. From the beginning of Mensa Bonsu's reign the government had pursued austere fiscal policies in the attempt to finance an extensive programme of national reconstruction from a Treasury gravely depleted as a result of the campaigns of 1869–74. In 1882, however, Mensa Bonsu introduced new measures designed to raise the level of taxation throughout the metropolitan region. It was probably in that year that a 50% tax was imposed upon the gold-mining industry.[279] Bekwae informants in this century still remembered that it was Mensa Bonsu who 'demanded more than his ordinary tribute of gold from the mines of Manso Nkwanta and the neighbouring villages'.[280] But Mensa Bonsu's demands were felt by a much wider section of the populace than that engaged in the mining industry. 'The sorest point of all with his subjects', observed Ellis, 'was that he despoiled them

[273] *Ibid.* p. 112.
[274] *Ibid.* p. 65: Sago and Annaman to Lonsdale, dd. Cape Coast, 29 July 1882; p. 159: Palaver at Kumase, 28 April 1883. *The African Times,* xxiii, no. 253, 2 October 1882: letter dd. Cape Coast, 3 August 1882.
[275] Brackenbury, 1874, ii, 38; 41; 45. Henty, 1874, p. 320. Stanley, 1874, plate facing p. 126.
[276] *Further Correspondence,* C. 3687, 1883, p. 96: Badger to Private Secretary, dd. Accra, 4 December 1882.
[277] *Ibid.* p. 160: Palaver in Kumase, 28 April 1883.
[278] *Idem.*
[279] Maxwell, 1896, p. 52.
[280] Rattray, 1929, p. 151.

of their gold on the shallowest pretexts, and imposed exorbitant fines for the most trivial offences.' [281] Typical of the many cases which were protested, was that of a chief in Manso Nkwanta, a town under the jurisdiction of the Asafohene Asafo Boakye of Kumase:

> One by name Quashie Cassa, a headman in the town of Inquanta went against the King's oath, so the King (Mensah) sent to Inquanta for him; the King's servants who went fined him 11 ounces instead of the usual fine of 36 dollars [or about 2¼ oz], of which (36 dollars), 18 would go to the King, 9 to Asafu Buaki, and 9 to elders and King's servants. This custom, rate of fine, and disposition of it has obtained for years.[282]

The Asantehene, too, was believed to be acting in collusion with certain of the *amanhene* systematically to despoil the *asikafo,* the men of wealth within the community. Thus it was reported by the Dadiase-hene Amofa, that

> his immediate King, Osai Yaow, King of Kokofu, was in the habit from time to time of disclosing to King Mensah of Ashantee the names of people in Kokofu Province who had made money ('riches'), that then King Mensah would devise some pretext to find fault with them as a justification from his point of view for the imposition of a fine upon them, and that when the fine thus inflicted was paid, Mensah returned one half thereof to Osai Yaow, retaining the other half himself.[283]

Amofa maintained that his own son Kofi Kra had been fined 1,800 dollars, or some 112 oz of gold, on such a spurious charge.[284] As if to demonstrate that his position was beyond the law, Mensa Bonsu began apparently to indulge his sexual proclivities by taking the wives of his commoner subjects: 'the "young men" ', it was reported, 'and all the servants of Coomassie complained that Mensah used to take their wives from them, and then those who complained the husbands were killed.' [285]

The reign of terror, 1882, and the spread of resistance

The extraordinary failures of judgement of Mensa Bonsu in 1882, and his apparent personality disintegration, must presumably be seen as related not only to his obvious fears of further attempts upon his life, but also to the political isolation in which he personally existed after

281 Ellis, 1883, p. 202.
282 *Further Correspondence,* C. 3687, 1883, p. 159: Palaver at Kumase, 28 April 1883.
283 *Further Correspondence,* C. 4052, 1884, p. 36: Barrow to Governor, dd. 5 July 1883.
284 *Idem.*
285 *Further Correspondence,* C. 3687, 1883, p. 160: Palaver at Kumase, 28 April 1883.

1881.[286] The widely based and popular support which he had enjoyed in the early part of his reign had been all but totally dissipated. In 1881 Mensa Bonsu had indeed managed, with considerable skill, the defeat of the recrudescent war interest, but the indications are that he was at the same time under growing pressure from radical politicians whose constituency, inadequately represented in the councils, nevertheless extended into many sections of the wider Asante community. It was certainly the view of Owusu Ansa that had Mensa Bonsu acceded to the demands of the war party in 1881, by authorizing a mobilization, then 'there would probably be a revolution, and he would lose his throne'.[287] The missionaries Buck and Huppenbauer thought that if attacked by the British, the Asante might defend themselves; but added that 'they are also quite displeased with their government, and some speak of running away'.[288]

The war party resurgence in 1880–1 appears to have stimulated a revival of the movement of popular agitation for reforms of a kind by then certainly no longer acceptable to the Asantehene. 'Throughout the masses of Ashanti', observed Lonsdale in 1882,

it has become a well based fact that there are other means and methods of government than those in practise in Kumasi, and they regard with much aversion being compelled to go into camp, thinking, without daring openly to express their thoughts, that the white man on the coast has a much fairer and happier manner of dealing with the natives of his Protectorate than that in practise in Ashanti under their Kings and Chiefs.

The comparison has caused dissatisfaction with their lot, and has given an undoubted lean towards disloyalty to their recognised rulers . . .[289]

A number of confidential interviews which Lonsdale was enabled to conduct in towns and villages along Route I to Bonduku, designed 'to test the feelings of the people of Ashanti', revealed not only the continuing importance of the anti-conscription issue but also the rising tide of agitation about the Asantehene's recourse to terroristic methods:

Not only did they murmur against the hardness of having to fight in a cause in which they took no interest, and in the meantime, having to give up their ordinary pursuits of husbandry and trade, but they moaned that they were powerless to help themselves against the murderous customs still retained by the King, notwithstanding his promises . . . No man, as they have often declared, can be certain that he may not be summoned to appear

286 I have had the advantage of a number of valuable discussions on this theme with Thomas Lewin, whose appreciation of its importance preceded mine.
287 *Affairs*, C. 3064, 1881, p. 80: Griffith to Kimberley, dd. 27 and 28 February 1881.
288 *Ibid*. p. 85: Buck and Huppenbauer to Jackson, dd. Dweraso, 18 February 1881.
289 *Further Correspondence*, C. 3687, 1883, p. 115: Lonsdale's report on his mission of 1882.

before the King at any moment, fined for some imaginary offence, a sum he cannot pay, and in the end lose his head.[290]

By September 1882 the purge of his opponents which Mensa Bonsu had initiated in June appears to have reached a new pitch, and few days passed without executions occurring in the capital. One Kwabena Fua, who was himself arrested but released after payment of almost 30 oz of gold, thereby survived to give some account of the matter. 'Under the impression that a gigantic plot existed to destroy the Ashanti power,' he reported in October, 'the King ordered the arrest of all of his councillors and linguists, about 70 of whom have already been massacred.' [291] It was a measure of the Asantehene's command of the resources of coercion, that he was able to extend the purge into one of the leading towns of the metropolitan region, Mampon. Relations between the central government and successive Mamponhenes since 1874 had been in some respects innovatory. After the invasion of Dwaben in 1875, the Mamponhene Kwabena Dwumo – who had served under both Kwaku Dua I and Kofi Kakari – was apparently required to live in Kumase while the affairs of his district were administered by a comparatively minor officer there, the Siwutiriasehene.[292] On Dwumo's death probably in 1881, the electors of Mampon placed Atakora Kwaku II upon the stool but he was to hold office for only about one year.[293] He was suspected of disloyalty to the government, and when he died suddenly in May 1882, rumours became current that he had been poisoned.[294] The electors next chose as Mamponhene the younger half-brother of Atakora Kwaku, Osei Bonsu. Not surprisingly, in view of the dangerous state of affairs in Kumase, Osei Bonsu failed to appear there to take the oath of allegiance to Mensa Bonsu. According-ing to Kwabena Fua, the Asantehene arrested and imprisoned Osei Bonsu, his mother the Mamponhemaa, and some forty members of the stool family.[295] Osei Bonsu was removed from office, but escaped execution: indeed, he lived to become Bantamahene of Kumase from 1900 to 1916, and Mamponhene once more from 1916 until his death in 1930 (see p. 475).

By late 1882 reaction against Mensa Bonsu's excesses was gathering momentum. 'The Ashanti people', stated Kwabena Fua, 'are ripe for

---

290 *Idem.*
291 *Further Correspondence,* C. 3687, 1883, p. 81: District Commissioner, Cape Coast, to Private Secretary, dd. 26 October 1882, citing Kwabena Fua 'just arrived from Coomassie'. Ellis, 1893, p. 373.
292 Rattray, 1929, p. 241, but also see pp. 249–50.
293 *Idem.*
294 *Further Correspondence,* C. 3687, 1883, p. 116: Lonsdale's report on his mission of 1882.
295 *Ibid.* p. 81: D.C., Cape Coast, to Private Secretary, dd. 26 October 1882.

rebellion, as they have all turned against the King in consequence of his late cruelties'.[296] The massacre, observed Ellis, 'which took place in September 1882 terrorised for a time the malcontents, though it added to the general discontent, and nothing but a leader was required to produce an insurrection'.[297] The new organized movements of re-sistance to Mensa Bonsu sprang up in the southern districts of the metropolitan region. The danger was one which the central govern-ment had recognized earlier in the year, and had tried to avert:

> The general feeling of the people as regards dislike to the present system of government is appreciated by the King and his Kumasi Chiefs, and this mani-fests itself to the well-informed and close observer by some instances in their (the King and Kumasi Chiefs) behaviour towards certain provincial Kings and Chiefs, almost amounting to leniency. The reason for such leniency being a doubt as to strict loyalty in case of oppressive carrying out of the King's numerous petty orders and ceremonies. Those to whom this relaxation is more particularly extended are they who reside on the borders of the kingdom, for instance, the Bekwaifo and the Amafuli [Amoafo].[298]

Early in 1883, nevertheless, revolts occurred in rapid succession in Manso Nkwanta, Bekwae, Dadiase and Denyase. In February messen-gers were sent to the Gold Coast from Manso Nkwanta to announce that the chiefs of twenty-nine towns and villages there – able to raise, it was claimed, 6,000 fighting men – had thrown off their allegiance to Mensa Bonsu.[299] It was probably in February also that a plan to free the Bantamahene Awua, who had remained imprisoned in Kumase for eight months, succeeded. He was enabled to escape to the relative se-curity of Manso Nkwanta.[300] In the same month three representatives of the commoners ('young men') of Bekwae also left for the coast, and informed the British that although the Bekwaehene remained still loyal to Mensa Bonsu, one thousand of their number had assembled at Yawkwakukrom and would no longer serve the Asantehene.[301] Later in February the Bekwaehene Osei Yaw sent a message to the Adansehene Nkansa, intimating that he too might refuse any longer to recognize Mensa Bonsu; and Amofa of Dadiase did likewise.[302]

In the organization of resistance in the southern towns of Asante an important and catalytic role appears to have been played by the nu-

296 *Ibid.* p. 81.
297 Ellis, 1893, p. 374.
298 *Further Correspondence*, C. 3687, 1883, p. 116: Lonsdale's report on his mission of 1882.
299 *Ibid.* pp. 130–1: Rowe's interviews with the Manso messengers, dd. Cape Coast, 3 March, and Elmina, 4 March 1883.
300 *Ibid.* p. 160: Palaver at Kumase, 28 April 1883.
301 *Ibid.* p. 132: interview between Rowe and the Bekwae messengers, dd. Elmina, 4 March 1883.
302 *Ibid.* p. 146: Palaver at Fomena, 19 April 1883.

merous citizens of the Gold Coast Colony who had been attracted into the area by the mining industry and expanding rubber trade. These were the 'young men' or 'scholars' who the British described as 'possessing a little education, absentees from our towns on the coast line, who had settled themselves in the villages round about . . . Thus these villagers were often led astray and often into rebellion and hostility with their lawful or properly constituted King and Chiefs.' In the Asante country, it was remarked, 'there are many of this sect of people scattered over its provincial towns and villages doing a vast amount of harm to the extension of trade. . .'[303] The movement in Manso Nkwanta was described, for example, as having been 'greatly led and advised by numerous Cape Coast educated natives, who are working at the gold mines in Inquanta'.[304] Similarly, the Bekwaehene claimed that unrest in his district had been fermented by 'the action of a "young man", a scholar from Anamaboe, who was hanging about some of his villages encouraging rebellion'. He was identified as one Siroh, 'either a Houssa trader or a Houssa slave purchased by some one on the coast'.[305] The radicalism of the political activists from the south endeared them neither to the authorities in Asante nor to those in the Gold Coast Colony, but clearly held an appeal for the discontented masses of their host country. In 1883 Barrow was led to essay a comparison with the situation in India, where 'many half-educated people of this class have from time to time given the Indian Government much trouble by going among the peasantry in remote districts . . . preaching discord and dissension, just as these "scholars" do here'.[306]

The radical upsurge and the overthrow of Mensa Bonsu

The leaders of resistance to Mensa Bonsu in the outlying districts of the metropolitan region were, from the inception of the movements, deeply divided in terms of the ultimate goals they sought to attain. A small extreme minority wished to establish the total independence of their districts and to obtain guarantees of non-intervention from the governments of both Asante and the Gold Coast Colony. A large and articulate minority argued for obtaining British protection and so becoming integrated with the Colony. But – as time was to show – the majority desired reintegration into Asante once reforms of the system of government had been achieved. The development of these move-

303 *Further Correspondence,* C. 4052, 1884, p. 53: Barrow's report dd. Accra, 5 July 1883.
304 *Further Correspondence,* C. 4477, 1885, p. 79: Kirby to Colonial Secretary, dd. Kumase, 5 February 1884.
305 *Further Correspondence,* C. 4052, 1884, p. 36: Barrow's report dd. 5 July 1883.
306 *Idem.*

ments will be considered further below. It was, however, from within Kumase and its villages that the combination emerged which was finally to topple the regime of Mensa Bonsu. Probably late in 1882 Owusu Koko, the aged Akyempemhene and former councillor of Kwaku Dua I, came out of his long retirement to lend at least his moral authority to those planning the Asantehene's overthrow. He was to find that the growth of revolutionary sentiment in the capital had, for the time being, made largely irrelevant his old-style brand of peace party politics.

The *coup* which broke the power of Mensa Bonsu was carried out by those described as 'young men of the town', that is, by the *nkwank-waa*.[307] The broad class of *nkwankwaa*, literally 'youngmen', comprised most importantly those who belonged to old and well-established families but whose personal expectations of succeeding to office or even of acquiring wealth were low. Supporters of government in periods of tranquillity, in times of stress and conflict the *nkwankwaa* were a potentially turbulent element in society, since lacking in any strong commitment to the maintenance of the *status quo*. In such times, moreover, they found a natural constituency for their revolt against the established political order among the underprivileged, the *ahiafo*. The leaders of the *nkwankwaa* in the early 1880s, as is appropriate to a movement which although popular and mass-based had necessarily to be organized in secrecy, are not identified in contemporary reports. It is likely, however, that prominent roles were assumed by those who had become radicalized at the time of the campaigns of 1869–74, and who had gained their first experience of political action in the anti-war and anti-conscription movements of that disturbed and violent period. In February 1883 the *nkwankwaa* organizations took over control of the capital. As far as is known no serious opposition was encountered other than from the palace complex within which Mensa Bonsu, with whatever troops of the special Guard he could still command, had established a strongpoint. The first reports to reach the Gold Coast suggested that it was on the issue of an end to terror ('human sacrifice') that the insurgents had won the overwhelming support of the people in and around Kumase.[308] But at least elements within the movement saw the abolition of the Asante monarchy as a necessary precondition of the more major reforms which they advocated. On 24 February the 'Latest News from Ashantee' to have reached the coast was that, 'what was

---

307 For a general comment on the political role of the *nkwankwaa* within Asante society, see Busia, 1951, pp. 10–11. The *nkwankwaa* organizations were abolished by the Ashanti Confederacy Council in 1936 – 'in view of the fact that they are the cause of political troubles throughout Ashanti', see *Minutes of the Second Session*, decision of 23 January 1936.
308 *The Gold Coast Times*, II, no. 84, 24 February 1883, p. 2.

expected some time ago has taken place; King Mensah no longer wields his sceptre; his people have dethroned him; and they have also risen up as one man against him. The natives seem now to be opposed to any system of government, bearing the aspect of a monarch.' [309] The report of the Asantehene's removal from office was premature. The implication of the news item, however, is that the lesson of the reigns of both Kofi Kakari and Mensa Bonsu had been seen by the radical politicians to be, that attempts to establish a presidential monarchy in Asante and to make the incumbent of the Golden Stool increasingly responsive to the needs and aspirations of the wider community, were necessarily always frustrated by the lack of adequate constitutional restraints on the Asantehenes' personal command of the instruments of terror and coercion.

By 3 March it was reported on the Gold Coast that 'the king is surrounded by his people at Coomassie, but as all communication with that place is cut it is not known whether he is dead or alive'.[310] In fact the Asantehene was alive, having had numerous kegs of gunpowder placed around the upper storey of that part of the palace which included the harem, and having threatened to blow up himself, the Golden Stool, the palace – and whatever parts of the city fell within the blast area – should any attempt be made to dislodge him.[311] The members of the Council of Kumase were in much doubt as to how to proceed in so unprecedented a situation, and were unsure, presumably, of their own standing *vis-à-vis* the insurgents. Within a few days of the *coup,* however, with the backing of the Domakwaihene Amankwa Nyame and others, Owusu Koko took an initiative in restoring normalcy by seeking a successor to Mensa Bonsu. Having returned so recently from exile, the Akyempemhene apparently felt the lack of an organized constituency on the basis of which he could manage for a third time the candidacy of Yaa Kyaa's son Kwaku Dua Kuma. As a *pro tem* measure, therefore, it was planned to bring the aging ex-Asantehene Kofi Kakari back into office.

'The people are clamouring to get the ex-king Calcalli on the stool', reported *The Gold Coast Times* on 3 March; 'they are not after all so much opposed to a monarch.' [312] But the report misrepresented the state of affairs in the capital. Owusu Koko sent messages to Kofi Kakari in Akuropon 'to inform me', as the ex-Asantehene himself described it, 'that he wished that I should come on the "stool" instead of Mensah, and also that I should come to Coomassie to drink fetisch with the Chiefs'. A later report suggested that Kofi Kakari sought to enlist the

309 *Idem.*
310 *Ibid.* II, no. 85, 3 March 1883, p. 2.
311 *Further Correspondence,* C. 3687, 1883, p. 160: Palaver at Kumase, 28 April 1883.
312 *The Gold Coast Times,* II, no. 85, 3 March 1883, p. 2.

aid of the Nsutahene Yaw Akoma in arresting leading members of the Council of Kumase known to be strongly opposed to him, including the counselor Boakye Tenten; the retired Adu Bofo and two of his sons, the acting Gyaasewahene Kofi Poku ('Ba Poku') and Sanaahene Sanaa Poku; the Hiawuhene Boakye; and the Pekyihene Yaw Kra. Kofi Kakari would at the same time enter into an agreement with the *nkwankwaa* party ('der ganzen jungen Mannschaft') to return to Kumase.[313] One Osei Kofi was sent from Akuropon to the capital to negotiate the agreement – but, as Kofi Kakari wryly commented, they 'sent him back to me to say that the "young men" of the town say they do not want me to be King over them'.[314]

On 8 March [315] Mensa Bonsu invited members of the Council of Kumase to the palace to discuss a message which had been received concerning the return to Kumase of the Bantamahene Awua.[316] The councillors were apprehensive, rumours having been circulating in the town that Mensa Bonsu intended having them shot.[317] Much on their guard, they nevertheless attended the meeting and were greatly perturbed when, in the midst of the deliberations, a member of the *sodofo* or cooks with rifle and cartridge-belt emerged from within the harem. Somewhat lamely, Mensa Bonsu observed that the cook was a madman. The councillors immediately disarmed him. 'It was intended', they claimed, 'that the man who came out of the women's yard should shoot a Chief, and then explode the kegs of powder.' [318] But there can be little doubt that the councillors had in fact gone to the palace with a plan of action carefully worked out in collaboration with the insurgent leaders who controlled the town. While Mensa Bonsu was surrounded by his councillors, the *nkwankwaa* swiftly occupied the palace and removed everything of value. 'While I was holding the palaver with the Chiefs about Awooa,' Mensa Bonsu later complained, 'the people broke into my palace, and stole all my wives, gold, and everything I possessed.' [319] The Asantehene thus reduced to impotency, Owusu Koko and Asafo Boakye entered the *nkonnwafieso* or stool-room within the palace, and took possession of all the royal stools there – including the Golden Stool itself.[320] On the evening of the same day

[313] Basel Mission Archives: Dilger to Basel, dd. Bompata, 12 August 1883.

[314] *Further Correspondence*, C. 3687, 1883, p. 157: Asanti's statement to Barrow, 3 May 1883.

[315] *Further Correspondence*, C. 4052, 1884, p. 50: Barrow's report dd. 5 July 1883.

[316] *Ibid.* p. 10: Mensa Bonsu's statement to Kirby, Abrade, 12 May 1883.

[317] *Further Correspondence*, C. 3687, 1883, p. 160: Palaver at Kumase, 28 April 1883.

[318] *Idem.*

[319] *Further Correspondence*, C. 4052, 1884, p. 10: statement to Kirby, 12 May 1883.

[320] *Ibid.* p. 73: Owusu Ansa to Governor, dd. Accra, 27 August 1883. *Further Correspondence*, C. 3687, 1883, p. 160: Palaver at Kumase, 28 April 1883.

Mensa Bonsu was informed by the councillors that he must leave Kumase. He was instructed to stay in Sawua, a town some eight miles southeast of the capital and seat of the Saamanhene (or Gyaasehene) Akyampon Panin. Two days later, however, he was removed from Sawua to Abrade, ten miles to the northeast of Kumase.[321] The discovery had been made, so it would seem, that Mensa Bonsu had in some way succeeded in smuggling out of Kumase 3,200 oz of gold dust, and that he had handed this sum over to Akyampon Panin for safe keeping.[322]

Mensa Bonsu made one attempt, in March or April 1883, to reestablish his authority. He convened an extraordinary meeting of the Asantemanhyiamu at Abrade, 'to talk over the insurrection'. But the members, including Bekwaehene, Mamponhene, Kokofuhene and Manso Nkwantahene, to all of whom messengers were certainly sent, refused to obey the summons.[323] Thereafter Mensa Bonsu appears to have accepted his loss of power and to have withdrawn from active political life. His mother, the Asantehemaa Afua Kobi, who was to be deposed in 1884, may have joined him in exile. Later in the century they returned to Kumase where they lived in very modest circumstances (Plates XIX and XX).[324] Following the British occupation of Asante in 1896, harassed by the new administrators who suspected him of knowing the whereabouts of a hidden part of the Treasury of Kwaku Dua I, Mensa Bonsu was arrested and sent under escort to Praso.[325] There, on 21 April 1896, he died. The official British view was that his death resulted from dysentery.[326] Rumours circulated, however, that he had died from starvation while undergoing punishment,[327] or that he had poisoned himself.[328] Afua Kobi died soon after, in 1900;[329] she was about eighty-five years of age.

321 *Further Correspondence*, C. 4052, 1884, p. 10: Mensa Bonsu's statement to Kirby dd. 12 May 1883.
322 *Further Correspondence*, C. 5357, 1888, p. 35: Kwadwo Yinna *et al.* to Lonsdale, dd. Cape Coast, 17 January 1887. *Further Correspondence*, C. 5615, 1888, p. 122: Barnett's report on the state of affairs in Asante, n.d. but received in Accra 10 May 1888. See also Lewin, 1974, p. 199, note 3.
323 *Further Correspondence*, C. 4052, 1884, p. 10: Mensa Bonsu's statement, 12 May 1883.
324 Steiner, 1900, p. 24. Huppenbauer, 1914, p. 55.
325 PRO, CO. 96/271: Maxwell to Chamberlain, dd. 9 March 1896.
326 PRO, CO. 96/273: Hodgson to Chamberlain, dd. 8 May 1896, enclosing deposition from the inquest. NAG, Accra, ADM 12/3/6: Maxwell to Chamberlain, dd. Accra, 9 March 1896, and Hodgson to Chamberlain, dd. Accra, 8 May 1896.
327 *The Gold Coast Independent*, II, no. 77, 25 July 1896, p. 3.
328 Lewin, 1974, p. 101. Steiner, 1901, p. 52, note.
329 *Idem.*

The beginnings of the constitutional crisis

The formal charges which were regarded as constituting the legal basis for the removal of Mensu Bonsu from office in 1883 were summarized by Barrow after his discussions with the councillors in April:

1. The cruel tyrannical acts of Mensah towards all his people.
2. His profligacy, with the heavy fines and barbarous cruelties inflicted by him on the husbands and relations of the women he degraded.
3. His ordering and enforcing decapitation without the knowledge and consent of his Chiefs.
4. The enormity and injustice of the fines imposed by him upon his subjects, especially on those living in the provinces.

In addition, Barrow listed the broad directions in which reform was sought:

5. A feeling of general mistrust on the part of his people towards their superior Chiefs and authorities associated with and serving under such a diabolical form of government as Mensah's.
6. A desire on the part of the population in general for more freedom, and a better form of government, which would free them from the trade exactions and exclusions many were groaning under.
7. A desire to be more like their neighbours on our [the British] side of the Prah, so as to develop commerce and civilization.[330]

After the departure from the capital of Mensa Bonsu, however, the political situation there remained still a confused and tense one. 'The feeling', remarked Barrow, 'was one of general uneasiness, nobody being sure of what was going to happen. It seemed to me to be general distrust, perhaps jealousy, amongst the people, rather than amongst the elders and Chiefs, who may have shared the feeling themselves, but concealed it better.'[331] The senior councillors were prepared to accept the short-term goals of the *nkwankwaa,* but continued to approach more fundamental political issues in terms of the restatement of the classical peace party position. 'We want no more cruelties, or taking off of heads, or taking of other men's wives', maintained Boakye Tenten: 'we want a good King, peace, open roads, and trade.'[332] But the *nkwankwaa,* whose aims remained more radical, were still in control of the town and showed no eagerness to surrender their newly acquired power to the Council of Kumase.

Captain Barrow arrived in the capital on 26 April 1883, on a fact-finding mission for the government of the Gold Coast. He reported

---

330 *Further Correspondence,* C. 4052, 1884, pp. 58–9: Barrow's report dd. 5 July 1883.
331 *Further Correspondence,* C. 3687, 1883, p. 158: Palaver at Kumase, 27 April 1883.
332 *Idem.*

that 'in the present state of general feeling inside Coomassie, I could not have had a private meeting with the elders and Chiefs'.[333] The substance of a private conversation which he held with Boakye Tenten, so he found, became almost immediately known to the 'young men'.[334] The suggestion that Mensa Bonsu should be invited into the town to meet with Barrow was one that originated from the councillors, who added the caveat 'that they were afraid that if they did so the young men of the town might flog the King'.[335] When Barrow was invited to address the Council of Kumase on 27 April, some forty members – officials and functionaries – were present, but the proceedings were protracted ones 'owing chiefly to the interruptions made by the 300 or 400 "young men" of the town who were in the court yard intently listening to every word the interpreter uttered'.[336] When Barrow complained to Boakye Tenten of 'the noisy behaviour of the young men' the secretary observed: 'it has hurt us more than it has you; but we are in difficulties just now in having nobody on the stool, and so we have to put up with a good deal'.[337] What had in fact happened was that the mode of decision-making had been changed under the insurgent regime from *atirimusεm* to *kwasafosεm*, that is, from closed to open debate.

By April the established councillors had reached near unanimity on tactics: since the *nkwankwaa* had refused to accept the reinstatement of the ex-Asantehene Kofi Kakari in office, the candidacy of the young Kwaku Dua Kuma should be canvassed. The *nkwankwaa*, on the other hand, remained unconvinced of the virtues of a monarchical system, and for a brief period of time Kumase existed under a republican form of government: *kwasafoman*. Indicative of the claims of the *kwasafohyiamu*, or Council of commoners and chiefs, to legitimacy was the display of the Golden Stool in its customary place during the reception of Barrow on 26 April.[338] Indicative, too, of the support which the new regime enjoyed was the arrival in Kumase on 5 May of the heads of some twenty villages who had rebelled against Mensu Bonsu and now came to reaffirm their allegiance to the government. Reports, moreover, were reaching the capital that representatives of Mampon, Nsuta, Nkoransa and Manso Nkwanta would also shortly arrive there.[339] The situation in Kumase had, however, already begun to change with Kofi Kakari's re-entry into politics at the beginning of May. For some time rumours had circulated in Kumase that notwith-

333 *Idem.*
334 *Ibid.* p. 159: Palaver at Kumase, 28 April 1883.
335 *Ibid.* pp. 149–50: Barrow to Rowe, dd. Kaase, 25 April 1883.
336 *Ibid.* p. 158: Palaver at Kumase, 27 April 1883.
337 *Idem.*
338 *Ibid.* p. 152: Barrow to Governor, dd. Kumase, 29 April 1883.
339 *Ibid.* p. 154: Barrow to Governor, dd. Kumase, 5 May 1883.

standing the rejection of his candidacy for office by the *nkwankwaa*, he might nevertheless attempt to seize the Golden Stool by force. Alone among the councillors, Owusu Koko discounted the reports. On 2 May, however, a small force led by one of Kofi Kakari's captains, Kwasi Adabo, was found to be advancing on Bantama through Owhim. Owusu Koko hastily called the townsfolk of Kumase to arms to 'resist this unprovoked assault upon their town, their laws and customs'.[340] A number of skirmishes occurred between the two groups before Kwasi Adabo finally retired to Akuropon.[341] The fracas seemed of no great significance and a few days later it was reported that Kofi Kakari enjoyed the support only of the Akuroponhene Safo Anwona and some two hundred men from his town and villages.[342] In other parts of metropolitan Asante, however, the point had been taken: Kofi Kakari was available for re-election if wanted.

In March 1883 the Bekwaehene Osei Yaw, under strong pressure from his own commoners, had finally committed himself to the secessionist position and had sent messengers to the Governor of the Gold Coast to solicit British protection;[343] he was in favour, so it was reported, 'of an adoption of the more civilised and just laws of the constitution which he had heard the people enjoyed who lived on the other side of the Prah under British rule'.[344] By early April Amofa of the Kokofu town of Dadiase and Owusu of the Kumase town of Denyase had both unequivocally declared for independence.[345] To the other members of the Asantemanhyiamu, it seemed that only by convening that body in order to elect a new Asantehene could the political crisis be ended. Most, however, had become reluctant after the fighting of 2 May to assemble in Kumase under the aegis of the regime of the *nkwankwaa*. Thus on 10 May messengers from Nsuta arrived in the capital to say that,

The King of Nsuta would come to Coomassie and assist to put matters straight by putting a King on the 'stool' if the other Kings and Chiefs would do the same, viz., Kokofu, Becqui, Marmpon, Inquanta, etc., so that all may be of one mind, but as he hears they will not come to Coomassie he will not do so himself.[346]

340 *Idem.* Kwasi Adabo, descendant in the male line of the Akyempemhene Adusei Kra, was himself to be appointed to that office in 1900.
341 *Ibid.* pp. 155–6: Asanti's statement to Barrow, dd. 3 May 1883.
342 *Further Correspondence*, C. 4052, 1884, p. 5: Kirby to Barrow, dd. Kumase, 7 May 1883.
343 *Further Correspondence*, C. 3687, 1883, p. 134: interview of the Bekwae messengers with Rowe, Christiansborg, 3 April 1883.
344 *Further Correspondence*, C. 4052, 1884, p. 36: Barrow's report of 5 July 1883.
345 *Further Correspondence*, C. 3687, 1883, p. 146: Palaver at Fomena, 19 April 1883.
346 *Further Correspondence*, C. 4052, 1884, p. 7: Barrow to Governor, dd. Kumase, 10 May 1883.

The following day the Edwesohene returned a similar message.[347] Five days later the Mamponhene and other *ahene* of that district announced that they would not visit Kumase until certain fines imposed upon them by Mensa Bonsu had been returned.[348] It is possible that the Asantemanhyiamu assembled at some other location. Certainly by the end of May a number of its members – among others the Mamponhene Kwame Adwetewa, Nsutahene Yaw Akoma, Kokofuhene Osei Yaw and Agonahene Kwasi Atuahene – had evolved a common policy. Surprisingly, they had agreed to support the candidature of Kofi Kakari and to mobilize their men if necessary to recover the Golden Stool by force of arms. 'If the Chiefs who are on my side come and ask me to go to Coomassie,' announced Kofi Kakari, 'I will go there.' [349]

Throughout the remainder of May and June Kofi Kakari's constituency grew rapidly. Making Breman, only some three miles north of Kumase, the centre of operations, by the middle of the year the roll of those committed to Kofi Kakari included Mamponhene, Nsutahene, Kokofuhene, Kokofuhemaa, Kumawuhene, Agonahene, Asokorehene, Beposohene, Sekyerehene, Asamanhene and Konahene. Claiming to exercise the authority of the Asantemanhyiamu, in June or early July they met at Breman and formally elected Kofi Kakari as Asantehene. On 30 July 1883, representatives of the assembly arrived in Cape Coast to inform the District Commissioner there of the election, and on 6 August they met with Governor Rowe in Accra. They urged him to use his influence in persuading the Kumase councillors to surrender the Golden Stool to Kofi Kakari.[350] In Kumase, however, matters had also taken a new turn. Brought together by a mutual determination not to recognize Kofi Kakari as Asantehene, the popular leaders and the councillors finally succeeded in arriving at a common programme. Having found themselves for some months in a situation 'of such an unusual character that no precedent existed for directing the "people of Coomassie" as to the procedures to be adopted in order to meet the circumstances which surrounded them',[351] the councillors acknowledged the necessity 'for the introduction and tuition amongst them of a better code of government'.[352] The *nkwankwaa* joined with them

347 *Idem.*
348 *Ibid.* p. 11: Barrow to Governor, dd. Kumase, 16 May 1883.
349 *Ibid.* pp. 53–4: Barrow's report dd. 5 July 1883. See also Basel Mission Archives: Ramseyer to Basel, dd. 18 August 1883.
350 *Further Correspondence*, C. 4052, 1884, p. 17: Rowe to Derby, dd. 7 August, and enclosure dd. 6 August 1883. *Ibid.* p. 18: District Commissioner, Cape Coast, to Assistant Colonial Secretary, dd. Cape Coast, 30 July 1883. Basel Mission Archives: Ramseyer to Basel, dd. 28 August 1883.
351 *Further Correspondence*, C. 4052, 1884, p. 82: Barrow to Colonial Office, dd. Sussex, 16 October 1883.
352 *Ibid.* p. 11: Barrow to Governor, dd. Kumase, 16 May 1883.

in sponsoring the candidacy of Kwaku Dua Kuma for Asantehene. Still only in his early twenties, it was reasoned that he "may be bent to listen to wise councils and accept the introduction of schools, etc. into Ashantee'.[353] He was considered, moreover, to be 'quiet and intelligent, but not aggressive or demonstrative'.[354]

By the middle of 1883 there were, then, two Asantehenes-elect, the one chosen by the Asantemanhyiamu with his seat in Breman, and the other chosen by the Council of Kumase with his seat in the city. The nation thus found itself involved in a constitutional crisis of a novel kind: no major trial of strength between the older and newer Councils had occurred before. Owusu Ansa, who had become one of the principal campaign managers for Kofi Kakari, stated the nature of the problem. Mensa Bonsu, he observed, was deposed by 'the rebel Chiefs of Coomassie', and,

> having done so they now desire to place Quacoe Duah on the stool without even consulting the other provinces. Those provinces object to Quacoe Duah being made King whilst Kari-kari and Mensah are alive, as they know that the more pretenders there are to the stool the more troubles must arise, and therefore the majority of the provinces espouse the cause of Kari-kari, believing him to be most entitled to the stool, and his restoration bring about that peace and union which is so much desired.[355]

Political bipolarity and the Asante constitution

With the stabilizing role of the old peace and war parties no longer operative in the conflict in late 1883, factions began to emerge with widely divergent ideological commitments – to the restoration of strong central government; to reform under a republican system; to the creation of a federal structure with increased and guaranteed powers to the localities; and to union with the Gold Coast Colony. Lacking precedents in constitutional law to which reference could be made, Asante was to move towards civil war. As all attempts at the political resolution of the issues failed, its leaders turned increasingly to the use of violence in the attainment of their goals. The change in the dominant mode of political action, from the conciliar to the convulsive, will be examined in the next chapter. Further analysis of the content of the ideological clusters which have been provisionally labelled – in conformity with nineteenth century practice – the 'peace' and 'war' parties, will be attempted in Chapters 14 and 15.

---

[353] *Ibid.* p. 82: Barrow to Colonial Office, dd. 16 October 1883, citing Owusu Ansa to Barrow, dd. Cape Coast, 25 April 1883.
[354] *Ibid.* p. 31: précis of Barrow's Asante report, dd. 20 August 1883.
[355] *Ibid.* p. 73: Owusu Ansa to Governor, dd. Accra, 27 August 1883.

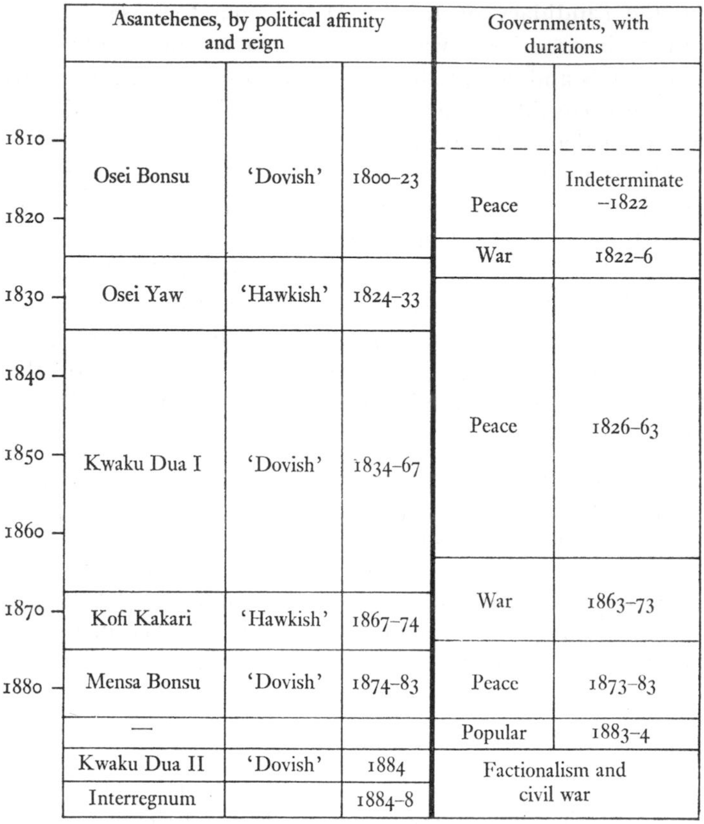

Asantehenes, by political affinity and reign			Governments, with durations	
Osei Bonsu	'Dovish'	1800–23	Peace	Indeterminate –1822
			War	1822–6
Osei Yaw	'Hawkish'	1824–33	Peace	1826–63
Kwaku Dua I	'Dovish'	1834–67		
Kofi Kakari	'Hawkish'	1867–74	War	1863–73
Mensa Bonsu	'Dovish'	1874–83	Peace	1873–83
—			Popular	1883–4
Kwaku Dua II	'Dovish'	1884	Factionalism and civil war	
Interregnum		1884–8		

(left margin year axis: 1810, 1820, 1830, 1840, 1850, 1860, 1870, 1880)

Fig. 14 Nineteenth century Asante – reigns and governments. (Possible short-term changes of government in, for example, 1853 and 1881, are not shown)

The data presented in this chapter are summarized in Figure 14. It has been argued that political attitudes in nineteenth century Asante, before 1883, had become progressively polarized in terms of approaches to the issue of British encroachment upon the southern provinces: that is, that an individual's stance on the matter of peace or war with the British was for much of the century diagnostic (though not infallibly so) of his position on the broader spectrum of political commitments. The emergence of recognizable parties in council was a result of this polarization. That a rudimental two-party system developed was a reflection of the starkness of the alternatives which confronted successive governments in their handling of the southern problem. It is arguable, furthermore, that the relatively high degree of political stability which Asante enjoyed before 1883 was to a considerable extent a consequence of the consolidation of the peace and war party oligarchies, and of the subsumption of factional issues to the overriding concerns of national politics.

It will be apparent from Figure 14 that 'dovish' rulers were brought to office when the peace party controlled the Councils, and 'hawkish' rulers when the war party did. That this was so resulted from the elaborate constitutional procedures which governed the election to office of an Asantehene.[356] If the stool became vacant by the death of the previous occupant, the electoral contest began on the eighth day after the burial. The Asantehemaa had the privilege of making the first nominations. The sponsors of various candidates would therefore attempt to convince her of the virtues of their man and of the strength of his support. In her deliberations the Asantehemaa would consult with, among others, the Kokofuhemaa and the Gyaase, Ankobea and later Manwere groups of Kumase: the major εsomdwa. The Bantama-hene would next ask the Gyaasewahene for the name of the Asante-hemaa's choice, for consideration by the Council of Kumase. The Council had the right to reject the nominee, in which case the Asante-hemaa might present two further names – presumably usually of those ranked second and third on her list. If these two were rejected, the Council could then proceed to make its own nominations. When, as usually was the case, the electoral process became resolved into a contest between two candidates, the Mamponhene might be summoned to the capital to oversee the contest since the Bantamahene, presiding over the Council of Kumase, was likely at that stage to have become a partisan of one candidate or the other. Ideally, the Asantehene-elect should have been chosen by the fortieth day from the death of his predecessor in order that he could preside over the funeral customs held at that time. He assumed temporarily the title of Nkwankwaahene, 'head of the young men', – signifying that he had won the support not only of the chiefs but of the people. Messengers were then despatched to the *amanhene* and other provincial rulers – and sometimes to those of neighbouring powers including in the nineteenth century the British and Dutch governors on the Gold Coast – to inform them of the choice and to invite them to send representatives to the forthcoming enstoolment proceedings.

The procedures for the election of an Asantehene were, therefore, such as to allow a high degree of politicization of the electoral process without violation of the accepted constitutional forms. It has been seen that, in the nineteenth century, interregna (whether following the

356 Kumase Divisional Council Archives, Manhyia: Notes of Asante Customs prepared by Captain Warrington and reviewed by a Committee of the Ashanti Confederacy Council, 24 July 1942, pp. 12–13. Busia, 1951, p. 97. Agyeman-Duah, 1965, *passim*. Kyerematen, n.d., pp. 12 ff.

death or the removal from office of the incumbent ruler) were in fact periods when the opposed parties might put their relative strengths to the test by the promotion of rival candidates. But while interregna were thus potentially periods of heightened political activity, they were not necessarily so: that is, the intensity of the political struggle would tend to be maximal when the disbalance in the strengths of the opposed parties was least, and *vice versa*. When the power of the war party was particularly diminished in 1874, for example, Mensa Bonsu was brought to office with little opposition.

In the nature of the case, then, an Asantehene would always commence his reign with the support of a majority in the Council of Kumase. Inevitably, however, in a system so responsive to changes in the state of the nation, the political composition of the Council would at some stage begin to shift and the indications appear that a change of government was possible. In such circumstances the opposition faced the risk that, with the concurrence of the majority, the Asantehene might set aside normal constitutional observances and resort to the instrument of terror to preserve the *status quo*. Kwaku Dua I, for example, held back the emergence of a war party government for four years by the purge of his opponents in 1859; Kofi Kakari conducted an ineffectual purge in September 1873, the precise object of which was never clear; and Mensa Bonsu utilized the same device in 1882 in an attempt to safeguard his own position. The use of such tactics of terror seems, however, in the long term to have been counter-productive and to have had the effect of stimulating rather than suppressing opposition. Governments could change, and when they did the incumbent Asantehene found himself obliged either to accommodate his policies to those of the new majority, or to face the possibility of removal from office. Within the space of nine years both Kofi Kakari and Mensa Bonsu had been forced out of office.

Reference to Chapter 9 (see especially Table 16, p. 372) will also show that it was rulers not belonging to one of the established Houses within the dynasty who were the most liable to removal from office. But it will also be apparent that it was precisely in such reigns, when the constitutional restraints upon challenging the royal authority were weakened, that political activity became not only the more intense but also the more diverse. It has been shown that fundamental issues about the nature of an Asantehene's powers were of concern during the last years of Osei Kwame's reign (see p. 253) as during those of Kofi Kakari and Mensa Bonsu. By contrast, the conflict between Osei Bonsu and his councillors in 1822–3, or that between Kwaku Dua I and the heir apparent Osei Kwadwo in the 1850s, were generated by issues – however basic these may have been – concerning governmental policies, but did not involve questions of the constitutional powers of the monarchy.

A number of Asante maxims explicitly acknowledge that responsibility for the conduct of the affairs of state rested not solely upon the ruler but upon his councillors and administrators: for example, *ɔhene nya ahotrafo pa a, na ne bere so dwo*,[357] 'when a king has good councillors then his reign is untroubled', and *ɔhem-mone nni babi, na ɔbɔfo-bone na ɔwɔ babi*,[358] 'there is nowhere a bad king, but there are bad ambassadors'. In 1882 Lonsdale alluded to the same matter:

It is, of course, the King or the head of the country to whom is given the credit, or who bears the opprobrium, of all that transpires either in the kingdom or in the outside policy of Ashanti. But the correctness of supposing every good or bad action or every outcome of the politics of Ashanti to emanate from the King uncounselled, would be wide of the mark.[359]

It would seem that, in the nineteenth century and with respect to the sphere of decision-making, the ideal which was widely subscribed to was that of the Asantehene as presidential monarch: that is, presiding over, and being bound by the deliberations of, both Asantemanhyiamu and Council of Kumase. In point of fact that ideal was the most nearly attained in those early years of an Asantehene's reign when he still enjoyed the support of the majority in council which had been responsible for his election to office. Conversely, rejection of that ideal was implicit whenever organized terror was used to influence the course of government. The principle, within Akan society in general, of the ruler's responsibility to his council was one that was to be forcefully restated by the Gold Coast lawyers at the turn of the century. 'The King', observed Casely Hayford,

is the Chief Executive Officer of the State, but not the Executive Council of the State. Such a council exists, and any acts done by the King without its concurrence are liable to be set aside . . . The King is the President of the Legislative Board, but he seldom, if ever, initiates any legislative act. It is the province of the people, through their representatives, the Councillors, to introduce legislation, and say what law shall direct their conduct.[360]

In like vein, Mensah Sarbah commented:

The Council of the people is the only effective instrument or body which tempers the will or power of the ruler. For no discreet or wise ruler would undertake any matter of importance affecting his people, until it has been discussed at length in council . . . The Public Council occupies the most

---

357 Christaller, 1879, maxim 1310; Rattray, 1916, maxim 416.

358 H. N. Riis, 1854, p. 129. Compare Christaller, 1879, maxim 1300; Rattray, 1916, maxim 408.

359 *Further Correspondence*, C. 3687, 1883, p. 117: Lonsdale's report on his mission of 1882.

360 Casely Hayford, 1903, pp. 41–3.

prominent position in the constitution of the body politic; to suppress it is to destroy the best, safest, and surest means for ascertaining the views of the public, as well as for influencing and instructing them in matters relating to their welfare and good government. Its existence opens a field for many to interest themselves in public affairs; it is an incentive to municipal enterprise; promoter of the patriotism that toils for the public good, that strives to effect reform, whose watchword is progress.[361]

Speculating on the arrest and exile of Asantehene Agyeman Prempe I and many of his leading councillors by the British in 1896, Mensah Sarbah thought that had the colonial authorities appreciated 'that an African king or other ruler is not ordinarily a despot or other irresponsible person, but is, as a matter of fact, the first among his equals, and controlled by them in the Council which represents the whole people and expresses their will, possibly the deportation of African rulers would not have been a common occurrence'.[362] The insistence of the lawyers on the representative and dynamic qualities of the Akan council is related, it is suggested, to the basic argument of this chapter, that no analysis of the *modus operandi* of the councils of nineteenth century Asante is possible without major reference to the underlying system of political beliefs which conditioned the deliberations of Asantehene and councillors alike and determined the policies which, collectively, they evolved.

[361] Sarbah, 1096, pp. 11–12.
[362] *Ibid.* p. 235.

CHAPTER 13

Disorder in politics:
from constitutional crisis to civil war

The Owusu Koko coup

Throughout the middle part of 1883 the partisans of Kwaku Dua Kuma and of Kofi Kakari sought systematically to enlarge their respective constituencies. No major attempt was made to resolve the constitutional crisis in which the nation found itself. Indeed, no such attempt seemed possible since consensus on the basic rules and values which guaranteed the maintenance of the political system as a whole was clearly no longer present. The validity of the monarchical system had been challenged from within the capital itself, while a number of the outlying district heads had ceased to acknowledge the continuing right of the Oyoko dynasty to superintend their affairs. Interestingly, the political analysts on whom the government of the Gold Coast Colony relied failed initially to appreciate the significance of the novel trend of events, and persisted for a time in viewing the situation in terms of the old dichotomy of peace and war parties. Assured by the authorities in Kumase that Kofi Kakari, if elected, 'would endeavour to recover back by intrigue or by force of arms if necessary the countries he had renounced all right and title to under the Fommenah Treaty',[1] Barrow proceeded to inform the Colonial Office in London that:

it is the war party who clamour for Kalkalli's election, and by that term 'war party' I mean to indicate a small hidden section of the population of the Ashantee kingdom capable by Kalkalli's restoration of such expansion into larger numbers as would aim at the recovery of the lost countries of Ashantee . . . I feel assured that Kalkalli's restoration would mean war with us within five years from the present time.[2]

The view was one shared by the editors of *The Gold Coast Times*, who argued that, 'Calcalli might immediately he gets to the throne manifest the desire to maintain peaceful relations with the colony like many of his predecessors. But there would soon be a time when a sinister change

1 *Further Correspondence*, C. 4052, 1884, p. 56: Barrow's report dd. 5 July 1883.
2 *Ibid*. p. 83: Barrow to Colonial Office, dd. Sussex, 16 October 1883.

would be perceived. We know Calcalli very well.'[3] In late May Barrow had threatened Kofi Kakari that if he seized the Golden Stool by force, then the British would feel disposed to demand the balance of 49,000 oz of gold still owing them under the terms of the treaty of 1874.[4] The message, so it was reported, left Kofi Kakari dumbfounded – as well it might since considerably more than 1,000 oz of the war indemnity had already been paid.[5] Barrow's clumsy attempt to influence the course of events seems to have achieved nothing in averting the conflict which was imminent.

Probably late in July 1883, Kofi Kakari sent an armed party to Kwapra just north of Breman, where the chief Kwasi Tabiri was arrested, and to Nkwantakese (Route II, mile 12) where two other prisoners were taken: Yaw Mpre, described as 'Inspector of Roads' and presumably an officer of the central administration (see p. 35), and the Nkwantakesehene, Nkwanta Owusu, a veteran of the war with the British in 1874 and of the campaign against Dwaben in 1875.[6] The three were taken to Kofi Kakari's capital of Breman and there, for reasons unknown, executed.[7] That Kofi Kakari should not only claim to be Asantehene but should begin to exercise the prerogatives of that office was a matter which the authorities in Kumase were disinclined to ignore. On 3 August reprisals were taken: a raiding party attacked Breman, killed seven persons, and retired to Kumase. The counselor Boakye Tenten, who had chosen to accompany the party, was captured. As husband of the Asantehemaa Afua Kobi and step-father of Kofi Kakari, his life was spared.[8] On the following day fighting occurred in the capital itself. Reports, which may have been exaggerated, stated that seventeen chiefs were slain, and three thousand people died in all.[9]

The attack upon Breman had the effect of mobilizing Kofi Kakari's supporters into action. The Kokofuhene Osei Yaw sent a contingent of thirty men under one Apea to assist in its defence.[10] Both the Nsuta-

---

3 *The Gold Coast Times,* II, no. 85, 3 March 1883, p. 2.
4 *Further Correspondence,* C. 4052, 1884, pp. 53–4: Barrow's report dd. 5 July 1883.
5 The matter of the indemnity remained a perplexing one. Boakye Tenten believed that in 1881 it had been re-computed at 18,000 oz, of which 16,000 were paid soon after, see Brun's report, in Gros, n.d., p. 145.
6 Institute of African Studies, Ghana, IASAS/136: Nkwanta-Kese Stool History, recorded by J. Agyeman-Duah, 7 October 1964.
7 *Further Correspondence,* C. 4052, 1884, p. 28: statement of the messenger Kwaku Dua from Kumase, dd. Christiansborg, 16 August 1883; p. 29: List of Chiefs and Headmen killed.
8 *Ibid.* p. 27: Daniel to Assistant Colonial Secretary, dd. Cape Coast, 11 August 1883, citing messengers from Kokofuhene.
9 Basel Mission Archives: Ramseyer to Basel, dd. 18 August 1883.
10 *Further Correspondence,* C. 4052, 1884, p. 27: Daniel to Assistant Colonial Secretary, dd. 11 August 1883.

henc Yaw Akoma and Agonahene Kwasi Atuahene moved their troops southwards to place themselves at the disposal of Kofi Kakari. Alarmed, in turn, by the rapid build-up of the forces around Breman, the Nkonnwasoafohene – head of the stool-carriers of Kumase – sent a message to Kofi Kakari to announce that should any attempt be made to seize the Golden Stool by force, the Akyempemhene Owusu Koko was prepared to destroy it.[11] At much the same time, about the end of the first week in August, the councillors in Kumase sent a delegation to Tafo to ask the Kumase Benkumhene, whose town it was, to declare his support for Kwaku Dua Kuma. At Oduro village, on the way to Tafo, the Nsutahene and Agonahene intercepted the party, and massacred its members. Among the eight prominent functionaries reported to have been slain were the Gyaasewahene Kofi Poku and the Sanaahene Sanaa Poku. Fighting flared up immediately. The Kumase forces engaged Kofi Kakari's soldiers only a mile or two outside the city, and drove them back to Breman. They followed up their victory by attacking Tafo. Kofi Kakari's supporters fell back upon Kenyase, some five miles northeast of Kumase on Route IV, and gave battle. The Kumase forces again proved superior and, to avoid capture, both Nsutahene and Agonahene committed suicide. The Mamponhene Kwame Adwetewa was taken prisoner by the victors,[12] who also secured the release of Boakye Tenten. Reports gave Kwaku Dua's casualties as sixty killed and fifty wounded, and those of Kofi Kakari as eighty killed and sixty wounded.[13] Kofi Kakari himself narrowly avoided capture. Abandoning his capital at Breman, he sought refuge at Fufuo (Route I, mile 17) under the protection of his old protégé, the Akuroponhene Safo Anwona.[14] A Kumase force was sent to apprehend him. The Akuroponhene and a number of his followers were slain at Fufuo,[15] but Kofi Kakari again escaped.

According to one report the major fighting occurred on 10 August; it must in fact have taken place several days earlier.[16] By the middle of the month it appeared that although no decisive military victory had been achieved, both sides sought to avoid further escalation of the conflict. Owusu Koko took the initiative in sending proposals to Kofi Kakari for a conference 'of all the chiefs and headmen living in

11 *Idem.*
12 *Ibid.* p. 28: statement by Kwaku Dua, dd. 16 August 1883; p. 29: List of Chiefs and Headman killed; p. 72: Brennan to Inspector-General, dd. 21 August 1883. Compare Rattray, 1929, p. 262.
13 *Further Correspondence,* C. 4052, 1884, p. 72: Brennan to Inspector-General, dd. 21 August 1883.
14 *Ibid.* p. 74: Owusu Ansa to Governor, dd. Accra, 27 August 1883.
15 *Ibid.* p. 29: List of Persons killed by the Kumase party.
16 *Ibid.* p. 72: Brennan to Inspector-General, dd. 21 August 1883. Basel Mission Archives: Dilger to Basel, dd. Bompata, 12 August 1883.

Coomassie and its neighbourhood', at which a formula for peace should be worked out. An account of the ensuing proceedings had reached the Gold Coast by 4 September, and merits extensive quotation. Kofi Kakari, it was reported, agreed to the proposal,

ignorantly thinking that perhaps as the influential men of the nation were to meet and consult together their sympathies would be more towards himself than towards the young prince, his greater age and experience he thought, being strong arguments in his favour. General Owosucorcor had no delay to make, and immediately on receiving the ex-king's reply to his message he urged that the place of meeting should be appointed and then took care at the same time to make the necessary arrangements as to the hour. This done, he left his-would-be Majesty Calcalli in contemplation of the probable consequences of the intended interview and the possibility of being able once more, to sway the sceptre. But as the hour draws nigh imagine the scene in the two camps. In Quacoe Duah's, there is nothing save bustle and activity; swords glistening in the mid-day sun; here and there groups assembling, armed with sniders; – there in the midst stands the renowned but cunning warrior Owosucorcor. He is giving orders to his troops to prepare for a general massacre; and at a given signal, in a manner unobserved, to surround the place of meeting and to open fire upon the ex-king and his people, their mortal enemies. In Calcalli's there is the ex-king himself surrounded by a brilliant retinue with all the pomp and pageantry peculiar to Western monarchs and a host of 6000 men; satisfaction – unsimulated satisfaction – beams on the faces of all his followers; they are in eager expectation of the coming but delusive prospect of a glorious triumph; there is no thought of the evil of a dreadful massacre! The hour however for the holding of the grand palaver at length arrived; and evidently Calcalli and his adherents were the first to reach the place appointed. For sometime they strained their eyes in vain for their opponents; but could only perceive of all the princes of the other side (at a distance of some three or four hundred yards away) the figure of prince Buaki and his followers approaching them, but no sign of Quacoe Duah or Owosucorcor; and they were beginning to think that perhaps they would not be coming or had lingered back, when lo – as if by magic – a tremendous fussilade was opened up and a succession of hot and murderous volleys was poured upon them to which being unprepared, they could not reply, notwithstanding that the 6000 men included the flower of the ex-king's army. Heaps upon heaps of dead and dying marked the destructive work of the cruel snider. A panic then ensued and flight was resorted to, which Calcalli and his terror stricken host then skilfully effected but not until he had left 1500 of his devoted followers, dead on the fatal spot, lying weltering in their blood . . . General Owosucorcor's sniders unmistakeably did the mischief. He had only a small body and if his men had not made such dangerous use of this weapon, the massacre would in all likelihood not have proved so successful.[17]

[17] *The Gold Coast Times,* III, no. 111, 7 September 1883, pp. 3–4.

Later reports placed the number slain as high as 2,000 – 'the sniders of the prince having been more destructive in their work than originally believed, some bullets penetrated three or four men at a time'.[18] Among the dead was the Mamponhene Kwame Adwetewa, who had been released to attend the conference! Kofi Kakari himself escaped the slaughter, and sought refuge in Bekyem on the Gyaman road (Route I, mile 44), hoping ultimately to reach Nkoransa and raise new support there. At the end of August, suffering from exhaustion and hunger, he was surrendered to Kumase troops sent out to find him. He was carried into the capital on the shoulders of a slave, and placed under strong guard.[19] As a result of his brilliantly executed though far from bloodless coup, Owusu Koko had emerged as the strong man of Asante politics.

The reorganization of the opposition

In Kumase, in mid-September, Kwaku Dua was formally confirmed as Asantehene-elect, and assumed many of the functions of Asantehene while preparations were made for his full enstoolment on the Golden Stool.[20] Reports reached the Gold Coast of the immediate satisfaction which was felt in the capital:

With his accession to power certainly must begin a new era for the country. He is much liked by his people, the majority of whom are natives of Coomassie, the belief therefore may be expressed that he will endeavour to bring about a thorough change in their favour . . . But much will depend on the counsel that will be tendered for his acceptance by those whom he may seek as advisors. Owosucorcor will in all probability be the only reliable prop of the young king's authority and being a man of considerable skill and tact will take care that his master shall have the best use of his services. In a word he will see that no undue advantage is taken of him and will fairly study his interests.[21]

Satisfaction, however, turned rapidly to dismay as Owusu Koko proceeded to consolidate the power of the new government by an immediate recourse to terroristic methods. From Accra, Owusu Ansa – former head of Mensa Bonsu's civil service and brother of Owusu Koko – took the step of writing directly to Lord Derby at the Colonial Office in London on what he described as a subject 'of the utmost importance to

18 *Ibid.* III, no. 112, 14 September 1883, p.3.
19 *Idem.* Basel Mission Archives: Owusu Ansa to Ramseyer, dd. 21 September 1883. See also Ellis, 1893, p. 376. *Further Correspondence*, C. 4052, 1884: Rowe to Derby, dd. Christiansborg, 7 September 1883.
20 *Further Correspondence*, C. 4477, 1885: Rowe to Derby, dd. Christiansborg, 12 January 1884. *The Gold Coast Times*, III, no. 113, 21 September 1883, p. 2.
21 *Ibid.* 21 September 1883, p. 2.

the most vital interests of the Gold Coast Colony as well as those of my own mother country Ashantee'. He gave an account of the situation in Asante, and requested the 'prompt attention of Her Majesty's Government being given to this question, with a view to the staying of the horrible and extensive shedding of blood that is being carried on by Prince Owusoo Korkor at present'.[22] Reports indicated, in fact, that by late September 1883 over a thousand people believed to have been sympathetic towards Kofi Kakari had been executed on the orders of Owusu Koko.[23]

The recourse to such draconian measures by the new regime of the Akyempemhene had the effect of alienating from it immediately one of its major constituencies: that of the radical reformers. Seeing the pressure of international opinion as the one remaining deterrent to the excesses of their governments, they pressed for the opening of a British consulate in Kumase. 'Public opinion in Ashantee', it was reported,

has taken a new departure. The people say that it would be almost impossible for them to tolerate a monarchy without the co-existence of a British consul in Coomassie, as they perceive that the presence of such an individual would be the only sure means of keeping the kings in order, and circumscribing that prerogative which they still enjoy of demanding ad libitum the execution of their subjects. So it is not impossible that Quacoe Duah will be in equal danger of deposition as those who preceded him. The truth is this they (the people) do not know what steps to adopt to maintain peace, and are just as fast for a policy as they were before the coronation of Quacoe Duah. They manifested a predilection for Quacoe Duah but now when they have got him on the stool, they are ignorant of what is the best thing to do with him.[24]

Owusu Koko responded to the mounting agitation by imposing a new scale of fines on those 'offending the king'. 'The people', it was remarked, 'have numerous objections against a monarchy it would seem although the majority of them were in favour of Quacoe Duah and succeeded in getting him on the throne'.[25]

The new government thus began rapidly to lose its constituency in Kumase. The situation in other parts of central Asante, moreover, remained confused. That many of the leading partisans of Kofi Kakari had perished in the fighting of early August or in the massacre which followed, and that he himself had been captured, did nothing to resolve the underlying constitutional crisis. Indeed, it seems likely that the conference called by Owusu Koko in mid-August had been regarded

22 *Further Correspondence*, C. 4052, 1884, pp. 92–3: Owusu Ansa to Derby, dd. Accra, 18 October 1883.
23 *The Gold Coast Times*, III, no. 114, 28 September 1883, p. 2.
24 *Idem*.
25 *Ibid*. III, no. 115, 5 October 1883, p. 3.

as having the status of an extraordinary session of the Asanteman-hyiamu. Owusu Koko's violation of all the principles upon which that Assembly's very existence depended must, therefore, have underscored the extent of the conflict of interest between it and the Council of Kumase.

One consequence of the new government's intolerance of opposition was that, unable to work without danger in Asante, a group of Kofi Kakari's supporters laid the foundations of an organization in the Gold Coast Colony for the continuing management of his candidacy and the movement to restore constitutional rule in Kumase. The strategy of the Cape Coast caucus was first, to seek to persuade the government of the Colony to permit Kofi Kakari to move there; [26] secondly, to lobby for that government's support of his cause; [27] thirdly, to rebuild the network of Kakari partisans within Asante itself; and fourthly, to involve chiefs within the Colony in its aims. The caucus was to become a powerful factor in Asante politics over the next few years. It was headed, until his death on 13 November 1884, by the experienced Owusu Ansa himself: 'director of the Karikari cause in the Protectorate'.[28] Its early membership included Kofi Tando, head of the Asante residents in Cape Coast and 'a staunch adherent of Coffee Kalikali'.[29] It was soon joined by Yaw Awua as 'employé of Prince Ansah'.[30] A former member of the *asokwafo* of Kumase, Yaw Awua's career within the caucus will be discussed at greater length in Chapter 15.

The work of the Cape Coast caucus was hampered for a time by the activities of those seeking to use it for personal advantage.[31] Its operations, nonetheless, were soon such as to draw protests from the Council of Kumase, that the authorities in the Colony were allowing their territory to be used as a base for rebellion against Kwaku Dua Kuma. Trouble, commented Kirby after his visit to Kumase in February 1884, 'has been fanned greatly by paid agents on the coast, and very serious charges are brought against Prince Oosoo Ansah by the Coomassies of being one of the ringleaders in this movement'.[32] Certainly by late 1883 the caucus was receiving messages of support from a number

26 *Idem.*

27 See, e.g. *Further Correspondence*, C. 4052, 1884, pp. 72–4: Owusu Ansa to Governor, dd. Accra, 27 August 1883. *Ibid.* pp. 92–3: Owusu Ansa to Lord Derby, dd. Accra, 18 October 1883.

28 *Further Correspondence*, C. 4477, 1885, p. 95: report by Kirby, dd. Accra, 15 April 1884.

29 *Ibid:* Torry to Governor, dd. Accra, 28 December 1883.

30 *Ibid.* p. 146: Young to Derby, dd. Accra, 30 December 1884.

31 *Further Correspondence*, C. 4052, 1884, p. 75: Rowe to Derby, dd. Accra, 5 September 1883.

32 *Further Correspondence*, C. 4477, 1885, p. 95: Kirby's report, dd. Accra, 15 April 1884.

of towns in Asante. A servant of Kofi Kakari, who had escaped his captors in Kumase, arrived in Cape Coast to say that Yaw Pompeni, a senior officer of Mamponhene, had raised four hundred men for the imprisoned Kofi Kakari, and that more fighting had been in progress at the very beginning of November.[33] By December further declarations of support had come from Mampon, and from the Kuntanasehene Owusu Yaw and Amoafohene Osei Kwadwo.[34] Within the Colony itself, the Akyem Kotokuhene Ata Fua and the Akyem Bosumehene Kofi Ahinkora were both thought to 'have strong party feelings in that country [Asante]'; the former had expressed support for Kwaku Dua Kuma and the latter, considered at the time the more powerful and influential, for Kofi Kakari.[35] But by far the most important accession of strength to the cause of Kofi Kakari in late 1883 was that of the Saamanhene Akyampon Panin, the traditional Gyaasehene of Kumase and chief of Sawua, whose position within the administration in the capital had been largely taken over by the Gyaasewahenes but who retained an important rural constituency (see p. 470). His continuing custody of the money given him by Mensa Bonsu (see p. 538) made his support so much the more welcome.[36] Despite, however, the successes which had attended the efforts of the caucus in reorganizing the opposition to Kwaku Dua Kuma after the events of mid-1883, the councillors in Kumase had been able to make substantial gains in many of the districts which had formerly been in favour of Kofi Kakari.

The enstoolment of Kwaku Dua Kuma as Asantehene

From Nsuta, in early 1884, Yaw Akoma's successor Kwaku Dente visited Kumase. He had come, it was reported, 'accompanied by his principal Chiefs, to make the best terms for his country on their again giving their allegiance to Coomassie'.[37] In Agona Kwame Nimako had been elected to the stool made vacant by the death of Kwasi Atuahene, and had declared himself 'a staunch adherent of the Coomassies'.[38] The young Dwabenhene Yaw Sapon, who had lived in Kumase since 1875,

33 *The Gold Coast Times*, III, no. 121, 16 November 1883, p. 3. For Yaw Pompeni, see also *Further Correspondence*, C. 5615, 1888, p. 129: Barnett to Commissioner, Native Affairs, dd. Eduabin, 4 November 1887.
34 *Further Correspondence*, C. 4477, 1885: Torry to Governor, dd. Accra, 28 December 1883.
35 *Further Correspondence*, C. 4052, 1884, p. 88: Kirby to Colonial Secretary, dd. Akyem Swedru, 25 September 1883. *Further Correspondence*, C. 4906, 1886, p. 38: Firminger to Governor, dd. Praso, 19 April 1886.
36 *Further Correspondence*, C. 4477, 1885: Torry to Governor, dd. Accra, 28 December 1883.
37 *Ibid.* p. 79: Kirby to Colonial Secretary, dd. Kumase, 5 February 1884. *Ibid.* p. 93: Kirby's report, dd. 15 April 1884.
38 *Idem.*

had shown no inclination towards the Kakari cause,[39] and the Nkoransahene Ata Fa, after remaining neutral throughout the dispute, in
February 1884 finally expressed the readiness to recognize once more
the authority of the central government in Kumase – 'provided that
neither Mensah or Karikari are again placed on the stool, and also
that fines on all goods passing through Coomassie are greatly reduced'.[40] Progress had been made, moreover, in districts previously
under the control of secessionist leaders. In Bekwae Osei Yaw was deposed in February 1884, charged with having spent excessively in his
pursuit of his interests in the Colony. 'The wish of the Becques', Kirby
reported, 'is for again joining Coomassie.' [41] By February 1884 the
Manso Nkwanta – among the first to rebel a year before – had become
divided. While one faction remained uncompromisingly hostile to the
central government, another was 'for returning to the new Coomassie
rule under Quacoe Duah'. It was led by the Bantamahene Awua, still
in exile there, whose offer to support Kwaku Dua Kuma was conditional upon his reinstatement to office in Kumase and the restitution
of part of the property which Mensa Bonsu had seized from him.[42] The
fact was that people in many of the districts which had seceded, having
'been of the opinion that directly they renounced the rule and authority of Coomassie all taxes, fines, etc. would cease', had become rapidly
disillusioned with the realities of independence, and finding that
little assistance could be expected from the government of the Gold
Coast Colony, had begun to negotiate terms for reunification.[43] The
secessionist leader of Denyase, Owusu, had indeed committed suicide
rather than struggle further with the wearisome problems of his independent administration.[44]

Of the more important towns of the metropolitan region, only two
had continued to give the Council of Kumase cause for concern. The
Kokofuhene Osei Yaw had remained strongly in support of Kofi Kakari
throughout 1883. Widespread discontent grew up in his district, however, particularly as a result of the heavy taxes he had imposed to help
finance the Kakari campaign. In January 1884 Amofa of Dadiase – who
had been Nifahene of Kokofu before his own rebellion – assumed
leadership of the other Kokofu divisional heads. He arrested and
imprisoned Osei Yaw. Assuming many of the functions of Kokofuhene,
Amofa remained personally inclined towards secession but found him-

39 *Further Correspondence*, C. 4052, 1884, p. 57: Barrow's report, dd. 5 July 1883.
40 *Further Correspondence*, C. 4477, 1885, p. 94: Kirby's report, dd. 15 April 1884.
41 *Ibid.* p. 91: Kirby's report.
42 *Ibid.* p. 79: Kirby to Colonial Secretary, dd. Kumase, 5 February 1884. *Ibid.* p. 92:
Kirby's report.
43 *Ibid.* p. 82: Kirby to Governor, dd. Kumase, 4 February 1884. *Ibid.* p. 91: Kirby's
report.
44 *Ibid.* pp. 91–2: Kirby's report.

self at the head of a coalition many of the members of which were in favour of reunification with Kumase.[45] In Mampon the situation was in some respects similar. Yaw Boakye had been elected to succeed Kwame Adwetewa, and in early 1884 he headed a small group which remained still loyal to Kofi Kakari. The majority of the people of the district, however, seem to have wished for reconciliation with the Council of Kumase, and the Gyamasehene Brobe was thought likely to take over control of Mampon affairs. He was said to be able to call upon more men than the Mamponhene, and was known to be 'strongly in favour of again joining Coomassie'.[46]

In the early months of 1884, then, despite the activities of the Cape Coast caucus, the campaign for Kwaku Dua Kuma's recognition as Asantehene was carrying district after district. The old Kakari strongholds had been abandoned by a citizenry in fear of reprisals. Amidst the ruins of Kokofu town only some fifty people maintained a bare existence,[47] and the condition of Mampon and Nsuta towns was little better. 'This seems to be general', noted Kirby, 'with all the towns who espoused the Karikari cause.'[48] Kumase, by contrast, was rapidly being rebuilt, its roads cleared and new ones constructed. Many who had left the town for their villages were returning, and laying out new farms around it.[49] 'The lesson to the Coomassie Chiefs by the rebellion is such that their new rule will be much better', so Kirby then thought: 'the people seem exceedingly well satisfied with their choice of Quacoe Duah as their future King, and the Chiefs informed me that they have no anxiety for the future welfare of their country.'[50] Confident that all serious opposition was at an end, the Council of Kumase announced that Kwaku Dua Kuma would be enstooled as Asantehene on the Golden Stool on 17 March. In accordance with customary procedures, the *amanhene* and other provincial and district heads were invited to the capital to participate in the ceremonies. A week or so in advance, the capital was beginning to fill up with visiting dignitaries and their followers.[51] It seemed that a session of the Asantemanhyiamu might be held for the first time since 1881 and that, moreover, representatives would be present from most if not all parts of the metropolitan region.

In the last few days before the enstoolment, alarming reports reached the Council of Kumase. One after the other, the visitors were being molested on their way into the capital, some seized, some robbed. First,

45 *Ibid.* pp. 90–1: Kirby's report.
46 *Ibid.* p. 93: Kirby's report.
47 *Ibid.* p. 91: Kirby's report.
48 *Ibid.* p. 93: Kirby's report.
49 *Ibid.* p. 82: Kirby to Governor, dd. Kumase, 4 February 1884. *Ibid.* p. 92: Kirby's report.
50 *Idem.*
51 *Ibid.* p. 95: Kirby's report.

the Nkawiekumahene Antwi Agyei, then the Besiasehene Kukoro, the Mpatasehene Adu Kwaku, the Atwomahene Antwi Agyei (alias Antwi Tia), and finally the Edwesohene Kwame Wuo: each was harassed and dissuaded from entering Kumase. It soon became clear that Kwasi Kasa, most militant of the Manso Nkwanta rebels and shortly to become head of the Manso Nkwanta towns, had organized a series of tactical strikes to disrupt the proceedings in Kumase.[52] Subsequent events left little doubt that those of the Nkwanta not won over by the exiled Bantamahene Awua had been induced, by the Cape Coast caucus through the agency of Saamanhene Akyampon Panin, to make common cause for a time with the opponents of Kwaku Dua Kuma. The activity of Kwasi Kasa's columns marked the beginning of a new phase in the conflict: the struggle for control of the towns and villages of the Atwoma country west and southwest of Kumase. A district upon which the capital was largely dependent for food supplies, the Atwoma chiefs had been regarded as politically responsive to the edicts of the Council of Kumase, but by early 1884 the indications were that the Atwoma might be induced to revolt against the domination of an essentially urban leadership. Seemingly without any appreciation of the gravity of the situation or of the potential strength of the coalition which was emerging in the rural areas, the councillors in Kumase put back the enstoolment proceedings for one (Asante) month, and on 28 April 1884 made Kwaku Dua Kuma – Kwaku Dua II – Asantehene [53] (even though, as the councillors complained, 'the remaining Chiefs would not go to Coomassie for fear of Quasic Quassah').[54]

The Akyampon Panin coup

After sponsoring the candidacy of Kwaku Dua Kuma in 1867 and perhaps 1874, Owusu Koko had finally succeeded in bringing his ward to office. Yet the ruthlessness which the Akyempemhene had shown in pursuit of that goal, and the belief that the new Asantehene would in fact be used as a tool for his sponsor's own purposes,[55] had left Kwaku Dua II with an extremely fragile constituency. Rather than attempt to placate the opposition and appeal for national unity, however, Owusu Koko carried out still another purge directed to the total annihilation

52 *Further Correspondence*, C. 4906, 1886, p. 6: statement of messengers from Kumase, 16 October 1884.
53 *Further Correspondence*, C. 4477, 1885: Young to Derby, dd. Christiansborg, 15 May 1884.
54 *Further Correspondence*, C. 4906, 1886, p. 6: statement by messengers from Kumase, 16 October 1884.
55 *Further Correspondence*, C. 4052, 1884, p. 73: Owusu Ansa to Governor, dd. Accra, 27 August 1883. Steiner, 1896, p. 106.

of Kofi Kakari's kinsfolk. 'Owusucorcor suggested to Quacoe Duah', it was reported,

> the necessity of putting to death as many of Calcalli's relatives as they could collect. So Quacoe Duah it seems, acting on this advice, ordered the sudden massacre of some three hundred people or thereabouts who were either near or distant relatives. The scenes in the streets were literally heart rending. Children were torn away from their mothers and dashed against trees. Mothers were butchered here and there in cold blood; fathers were no better treated; as many as could manage to do so had to fly for their lives.[56]

Then, on 10 or 11 June 1884, only forty-four days after his enstoolment, Kwaku Dua II died. Most contemporary reports were in agreement that he had fallen victim to the smallpox epidemic then raging,[57] but Owusu Koko accused Kofi Kakari of complicity in the death.[58] 'Nothing save anarchy and general lawlessness prevailed', commented *The Gold Coast Times,* and reports were received of renewed fighting on 7 July in the course of which Kofi Kakari had supposedly been killed.[59] In fact, Kofi Kakari had died two weeks earlier, on 24 June. Owusu Koko and Boakye Tenten sent a messenger with news of the death to the Governor of the Gold Coast, and attributed it to dysentery.[60] But it soon became common knowledge that Kofi Kakari had been slain on the orders of Owusu Koko. Some reports affirmed that the former Asantehene had been executed in a manner customary for royals – having had his neck broken with an elephant's tusk.[61] According to a tradition that survived, however, Kofi Kakari had been choked with his own chewing stick, a feat accomplished by one Asamoa Kyekye of the Kumase *adumfo* or executioners.[62]

There can be little doubt that had Kofi Kakari been spared, the pressure for his restoration would have become irresistible: he alone possessed on the one hand the requisite political experience and stature to lead the nation, and on the other, a surviving constituency on the basis of which a new administration could be put together. In July 1884

---

56 *The Gold Coast Times,* IV, no. 144, 23 July 1884, p. 3.
57 *Idem. Further Correspondence,* C. 4477, 1885: Young to Derby, dd. Christiansborg, 11 July 1884. Steiner, 1896, p. 106.
58 Steiner, 1896, p. 106. See also *Further Correspondence,* C. 7917, 1896, p. 136: memorandum by Ferguson, dd. 9 November 1893. For a recent discussion of the view that Kwaku Dua II was poisoned, see Lewin, 1974, p. 183.
59 *The Gold Coast Times,* IV, no. 144, 25 July 1884, p. 3.
60 *Further Correspondence,* C. 4477, 1885: Young to Derby, dd. Christiansborg, 11 July 1884.
61 Steiner, 1896, p. 106; 1900, p. 10; 1919, p. 44, following Ramseyer.
62 Rattray, 1929, p. 209 and note. Asamoa Kyekye may be the same person as the Kyekye remembered as a leader of the Kumase *nkwankwaa* in the same period, see Lewin, 1968: interview with al-Ḥājj Sulaymān dd. 14 August 1968.

at least one observer thought it 'more than likely that Owosukorkor the king maker will now ascend the throne himself'.[63] The Asante-hemaa Afua Kobi attempted to sponsor the candidacy of Kwasi Kyisi (see p. 368, son of her sister Odae, and called a meeting of the Asante-manhyiamu to consider her selection. Not unexpectedly, the heads of the districts and provinces ignored her summons and made clear their unwillingness to enter Kumase unless a neutral observer from the Gold Coast Colony – 'an officer of high rank' – was present.[64] The Kokofu-hene, Bekwaehene, Kuntanasehene and Berekumhene (of Berekum town, Route I, mile 96), sent requests to the Colony soliciting assis-tance.[65] At the same time the Atwoma were induced by the Manso Nkwantahene Yaw Amponsa to withhold foodstuffs from Kumase: a hold-up which held an obvious appeal to farmers accustomed to having to market their produce in the capital at the artificially low prices fixed by the government there. In a situation which indicated the necessity for the utmost caution, Owusu Koko once again showed a lack of any realistic appreciation of the nature of the problem. Mobilizing the available fighting men from the capital, Owusu Koko directed attacks upon the Atwoma towns of Twedie and Trebuom (Route VIII, miles 8 and 13). The towns were not defended and the Kumase force com-menced looting them and their villages. At Ofuase, mid-way between Twedie and Trebuom, they were however attacked unexpectedly by Manso Nkwanta troops which, after heavy fighting, won the day. Reports that eleven senior Kumase functionaries had been killed in the engagement turned out to be exaggerated, though certainly the list of dead included the Anantahene Sie and the Gyaasewahene Opoku Dum. More importantly, among those taken prisoner to Manso Nkwanta were Owusu Koko and Boakye Tenten.[66] Both were exe-cuted, and the skull and jaw bones of the latter were sent to Cape Coast as token of the Nkwanta victory.[67]

In authorizing the disastrous action against the Atwoma towns, Owusu Koko had badly miscalculated both the military and political odds. With the assistance of members of the Cape Coast caucus, the Saamanhene had used part of the treasury money in his custody to purchase Snider rifles and ammunition, and to buy support for a

63 *The Gold Coast Times*, IV, no. 144, 23 July 1884, p. 3.
64 *Further Correspondence*, C. 4906, 1886, p. 6: statement by messengers from Kumase, 16 October 1884.
65 *The Gold Coast Times*, IV, no. 144, 23 July 1884, p. 3.
66 *Further Correspondence*, C. 4477, 1885, p. 147: Yaw Awua to Colonial Secretary, dd. Cape Coast, 8 December 1884; and pp. 147–8: Carr to District Commissioner, Cape Coast, dd. Praso, 12 December 1884.
67 *The Gold Coast Times*, IV, no. 154, 12 February 1885, p. 3. *The Gold Coast News*, I, no. 1, 21 March 1885. National Archives of Ghana, Accra, ADM 11/1482: Carr to District Commissioner, Cape Coast, dd. Praso, 27 December 1884.

personal bid for power.[68] There seems little doubt that he had been involved in the organization of the hold-up of foodstuffs, and had a clear understanding with the Manso Nkwanta leaders. As the Kumase forces had moved into Atwoma, so Akyampon Panin had brought up his troops to establish a camp near Kaase, only some three miles south of the capital. From there he sent messengers into the town to announce that he was preparing to enter it.[69] When reports of the defeat in Atwoma and of the death or capture of many of the senior councillors reached Kumase, Yaa Kyaa (mother of the late Kwaku Dua II) hastened to Akyampon Panin's camp and surrendered the town to him.[70] She 'begged the King of Sawiah [Sawua]', so it was reported, 'that he might go and arrange everything right at Coomasie and other villages . . . So King of Sawiah went and arrange everything alright'.[71]

Akyampon Panin entered Kumase probably late in November 1884. Like the organizers of many successful coups, he appears to have had no immediate and clearly defined political aims capable of appealing to a wide constituency. It may be presumed that his first act was to name the members of a reconstituted Council of Kumase. Since there was no Asantehene, Akyampon Panin took over Owusu Koko's role as effective president of the Council – or 'Head of Parliament' as he was described in Kokofu sources.[72] The Asantehemaa Afua Kobi, mother of Kofi Kakari and Mensa Bonsu, was declared deposed, and joined her son Mensa Bonsu in exile. Yaa Kyaa, who seemed disposed to cooperate with the new regime, succeeded her.[73] The most senior of all the councillors still in Kumase was the Asafohene Asafo Boakye, son of Kwaku Dua I, whose highly developed instinct for survival had brought him safely through the reigns of Kofi Kakari and Mensa Bonsu and through the succession of regimes which followed (and was indeed to carry him through the civil war, the reign of Agyeman Prempe I, and an exile of over a quarter of a century in the Seychelles). His readiness to accommodate his views to those of Akyampon Panin

---

68 *Further Correspondence*, C. 5615, 1888, p. 122: Barnett's report on Asante, received Accra, 10 May 1888.
69 Methodist Mission Archives, London: Journal of Coppin's visit to Asante, 1885, Book VI, p. 44, and VII, p. 11.
70 *Idem.*
71 *Further Correspondence*, C. 4477, 1885, p. 147: Yaw Awua to Colonial Secretary, dd. Cape Coast, 8 December 1884.
72 *Further Correspondence*, C. 5357, 1886: District Commissioner, Cape Coast, to Colonial Secretary, dd. 25 March 1887. NAG, Accra, ADM 11/1482: statement of messenger from 'King of Korkorfoon', n.d.
73 *Further Correspondence*, C. 5357, 1886, p. 8: Badger to Governor, dd. Christiansborg, 20 October 1886, enclosing list of principal authorities in Kumase. There is some doubt about the precise date of Afua Kobi's retirement from office. Her daughter Yaa Kyaa was certainly Asantehemaa by April 1885, see Methodist Mission Archives, London: Coppin's Journal, Book VI, p. 49.

secured his continuing membership of council. Among the few others nominated to the Council who represented continuity with the past was Bosommuru Dwira, a son of the Asantehene Osei Yaw.[74] As a 'young and hot headed' man, he had been one of Kofi Kakari's personal chamberlains in the early 1870s,[75] but under Mensa Bonsu had pursued a career in the diplomatic service and joined, for example, Boakye Tenten's important mission of 1881 (see pp. 526–7). Among supporters of the regime seemingly destined for positions of power was Akyampon Panin's own son, Owusu Koko Kuma, who had started his career as a member of the *batafo* or state traders; who had subsequently become one of Kofi Kakari's confidential messengers to the Gold Coast; and who, under Mensa Bonsu, had been much involved in the development of the new model army (see Chapter 14). The Akankade counselor Kwaku Nantwi Kaakyera, who had been appointed to that position after Yaw Nantwi's death in 1876, may not have been in the capital at the time of its surrender to Akyampon Panin; but if not, he certainly returned soon after to join the new administration.[76]

Yet, having named a new Council of Kumase, there seemed no immediate way in which Akyampon Panin could make its authority effective much beyond the urban area: no way, in other words, in which the Council could begin once again to exercise the functions of a central government. When for example the missionary Coppin visited Amoafo, Bekwae, Dadiase and Denyase in April and May 1885, he was led to comment:

I need scarcely say that these places are the names of provinces as well as of towns. Each has its certain number of small towns and villages within its prescribed territory. Formerly each of these places was tributary to Kumasi. They have now thrown off the yoke. Each maintains its own authority, and administers absolutely to its own affairs. I had eyewitness of this.[77]

The situation in the northern provinces was no more encouraging, all having ceased to send tribute to a government without effective authority. 'The Council of Kumase', added Coppin, 'informed me that the towns in the northern part of the kingdom which were once tributary to it have also thrown off the yoke . . . From all I can learn, *not one* of all the vassal states now pays tribute or in any way submits or refers any of its affairs to the capital.'[78] The loss of revenues, and

74 Wilks and Ferguson, field-notes, interviews with Okyeame Bafuor Osei Akoto, dd. Kumase, 31 October and 2 November 1973.
75 Brackenbury, 1874, II, 331.
76 Methodist Mission Archives, London: Coppin's Journal, Book VII, p. 1.
77 *Further Correspondence*, C. 4906, 1886, p. 4: Coppin to Governor, dd. Cape Coast, 18 May 1885.
78 *Idem.*

(with the collapse of administration) the lack of employment opportunities, was reflected in the decayed state of the capital:

> The greater number of the distinguished nobles have either died, been
> killed in battle, or made away with. Only two or three important personages
> are left.
>
> The city is being gradually forsaken by its inhabitants, because there is
> nothing to sustain them. This explains the disappearance of rows of houses
> which once lined the streets, the dilapidated state of most that remain, the
> thoroughfares overgrown with grass in most places from 12 to 15 feet high,
> the encroachments of the bush on all sides, and the general ruinous appear-
> ance which the place presents.
>
> Gold digging and earth washing, once so strictly forbidden in the capital,
> is now extensively carried on. The poverty of the people forces them to this.
> All that Kumasi now possesses and can control is a few villages. These are
> insufficient to furnish subsistence to all its inhabitants.[79]

Clearly the programmes of urban renewal which a year earlier had
been restoring to Kumase something of its earlier splendour had all
been abandoned after the death of Kwaku Dua II. In the circumstances
Akyampon Panin himself chose to leave responsibility for the city in
the capable hands of Asafo Boakye, and to make his headquarters at
rural Sawua – eight miles to the southeast.

The movement for confederation

In the latter part of 1884 the most important matter that Akyampon
Panin and his councillors had to decide was that of establishing a
timetable for the restoration of normal rule: that is, for the election
and enstoolment of a new Asantehene. The question was one of much
complexity. The only surviving royal with any claims to experience in
leadership was Mensa Bonsu. That no faction sponsored his candidacy
doubtless reflected his continuing unpopularity. No other candidate
could be found who possessed any established reputation or who could
command any appreciable constituency. It might therefore have
seemed that as a matter of political strategy, the work of national reconstruction should precede the search for an Asantehene. But it was
also arguable that the very possibility of reconstruction was predicated
upon the recognition by all factions of a new Head of State. Many
leading Asante politicians clearly felt in the circumstances, that the
only way out of the dilemma was to invite the government of the Gold
Coast to make available its good offices in the resolution of the conflict.
Certainly Akyampon Panin, convinced that no attempt to sponsor a
candidate for the Golden Stool could immediately succeed, chose in-

[79] *Ibid.* pp. 4–5. Compare Coppin's Journal, Book VII, pp. 2–5.

stead to cultivate relations with the British administration in an attempt to revive the authority of the Council of Kumase. The almost total lack of revenues of that Council meant that money could not be used to purchase political support. Instead Akyampon Panin appears to have relied upon the two major political assets which he enjoyed: first, the continuing support of the Cape Coast caucus, and second, his position as natural heir to that organization which had been built up within Asante in 1883 and 1884 to work for Kofi Kakari's restoration.

The challenge to Akyampon Panin's bid for leadership in Asante affairs emerged from just those southerly districts of the metropolitan region where support for the idea of secession had been the strongest in 1883: Bekwae and Dadiase. Both were towns which, by reason of their withdrawal from the affairs of the central government, had escaped the worst consequences of the internecine struggles which had followed the deposition of Mensa Bonsu. In February 1884 Osei Yaw, the secessionist Bekwaehene, was destooled without undue disorder and his successor Kakari was elected with a clear mandate to work for reunification.[80] Following the death of Kwaku Dua II in June, Bekwaehene Kakari was among those who supported the Asantehemaa Afua Kobi in her move to convene the Asantemanhyiamu and proceed forthwith to the election of a successor.[81] He was also among those willing to have the authorities on the Gold Coast involved in the proceedings as mediators. By the beginning of 1885 Bekwae, in marked contrast to Kumase, was flourishing. Some five or six thousand people lived in the town, which boasted a newly opened Wesleyan school. From the town and the villages Kakari was believed able to raise 10,000 fighting men. His court of justice, moreover, was the most senior one surviving in the area, and even Kumase people were availing themselves of it.[82] In early 1885, too, Dadiase continued to thrive. But the secessionist leader there, Amofa, remained in power and was generally thought of as 'head chief of Kokofu'.[83] Kokofu town itself had not been rebuilt, and there were some who considered its traditional dynasty extinct – all those who had claims upon the stool having been 'helped off'.[84]

In 1885, when it became clear that it was not the policy of the Gold Coast government to give support to individual separatist leaders

---

80 *Further Correspondence,* C. 4906, 1886, p. 31: Firminger to Governor, dd. Fomena, 8 April 1886.

81 *Ibid.* p. 41: Firminger to Governor, dd. Praso, 17 April 1886.

82 Methodist Mission Archives: Coppin's Journal, Book VI, pp. 33–5. Coppin reported a case about the ownership of a slave which the Bekwaehene heard on 22 April 1885. It was between two Kumase royals and a former member of the Kumase *adumfo* or executioners.

83 *Ibid.* Book VII, pp. 12–14.

84 *Ibid.* Book VII, p. 13.

within Asante, a new political ideology – that of *apam* or confederation – began to gain currency among many hitherto of quite different persuasions. The practical origins of the new doctrine were to be found quite simply in the necessity of organizing joint programmes of action against local chiefs whose policies threatened the common good of the wider region. In late 1885 for example, the Asumegyahene Kwadwo Agyeman was regularly seizing and robbing traders on the road to the coast. 'Numbers of Ashantis', so it was reported in *The Western Echo,*

are disposed to come down to trade; but how can they do so when their property, their liberty, and their lives are at the mercy of every Chief or King who commands the trade routes? This Ajeman commands one of the main roads leading to Coomassi, and as there is no recognised central authority he does what he pleases, and others in their different quarters act in the same manner.[85]

The efforts of the leaders of the new movement were devoted initially to setting up a council to which each participating member would delegate certain powers, principally in the field of offensive and defensive warfare, while otherwise retaining a high degree of local autonomy. To some extent the theoreticians of the movement were in the tradition of the older conservative thinkers whose spokesman, at the end of his life, Owusu Ansa had become (pp. 409–10): that is, of those who chose to see the nation as having originated in some confederative system, and who therefore displayed a strong concern with the maintenance of the rights of the component states and saw the Asantemanhyiamu, by its very composition, as the body the most able to safeguard such rights (see pp. 114–15). On the other hand, the advocates of confederation in 1885 seemingly envisaged a degree of autonomy being reserved to the member communities which would have been quite alien to the thinking of the older generation, but which was likely to gain the support of the separatists. Certainly the aims of the new movement were quite incompatible with those of Akyampon Panin, who continued to represent the centralist tradition which had dominated Asante political thinking – whether within the 'peace' or 'war' party councils – for the greater part of the nineteenth century. In the scenario of those advocating the idea of confederation there was no place for the Council of Kumase – to the restoration of the power of which Akyampon Panin was committed. Already by May 1885 it was clear to one of the earliest observers of the confederation as a political reality, that its success was predicated upon the continuing impotence of the Council of Kumase. 'Affairs in Ashanti', wrote Coppin,

85 *The Western Echo,* I, no. 2, 28 November 1885, p. 5.

are in a transition stage. The once tributary provinces south of the capital, Amoaful, Bekwai, etc., have drunk fetish together. This ceremony of confederation, for such it is, bids fair, in time, to bring about peace and order and prosperity, provided Kumasi continues to become what Kukofu is already, a desolation. Any action that in the least contributes to bring back its former prestige and power will produce corresponding restlessness and variance among the various peoples in Ashanti.[86]

The emergence of the Bekwae Confederacy

In late 1885 and early 1886 the Bekwaehene Kakari and Dadiasehene Amofa were involved in fierce rivalry for leadership in the southern metropolitan region. The former was committed to ultimate reunification with Kumase, and the latter to separation, but both saw in the realization of the ideal of confederation the only possible means of stabilizing the political situation. In the struggle between the two, Adanse was to become the pawn. Probably late in 1885 the Bekwaehene demanded that the Adansehene Nkansa surrender to him the town of Odumase and the villages of Kyeaboso and Akotakyi (which had apparently been transferred from Bekwae to Adanse in or about 1831 by the Asantehene Kwaku Dua I), and in addition pay him 30 peredwans, or 67½ oz of gold, as compensation.[87] It was thought that even had the Adanse met these demands, the matter would only have been settled with the political submission of the Adanse to Bekwae, and 'probably their consent to join the new Becquai Federation'.[88] At much the same time Bekwaehene Kakari first suggested that members of the confederacy might think of electing an Asantehene – 'of placing a King on the gold stool of Coomassie'.[89] The proposal had the immediate effect of stimulating separatist sentiment once again: Dadiasehene Amofa, Denyasehene Dome, the new Manso Nkwantahene Kwasi Mensa, and, unexpectedly, Amoafohene Osei Kwadwo, all expressed their support for the Adansehene in his struggle against Bekwae.[90]

In a series of moves in November 1885, the Dadiasehene proceeded to display the strength of his own 'confederate forces' by again laying Kokofu waste, and by seizing and executing a number of town heads who were in some way seen as a threat to his position. The Kuntanasehene Owusu Yaw and Fumesuahene Adu Ayin, both of whom served

86 *Further Correspondence*, C. 4906, 1886, p. 5: Coppin to Governor, dd. Cape Coast, 18 May 1885.
87 *Ibid.* p. 31: Firminger to Governor, dd. Fomena, 8 April 1886. *Ibid.* p. 39: Firminger to Governor, dd. Praso, 17 April 1886.
88 *Ibid.* p. 42: Firminger to Governor, dd. Praso, 17 April 1886.
89 *Further Correspondence*, C. 5357, 1888, p. 12: Bekwaehene Yaw Gyamfi to Colonial Secretary, dd. Bekwae, 24 November 1886, enclosing memorandum.
90 *Idem.*

Kumase, were among those killed, as was the Ahuren chief whose town lay less than two miles from Dadiase.[91] According to a somewhat garbled account of the subsequent proceedings which reached the Gold Coast in January 1886, Amofa then himself proposed that a meeting of all provincial and district authorities in Asante – in effect, of the Asantemanhyiamu – should be held to decide how best to restore order to the country. According to the report, many declined to attend for fear that once in Dadiase they would be forced to declare Amofa 'King of Ashanti'. It seems most unlikely, however, that his ambitions in fact extended beyond being recognized as head of a new southern Confederacy Council.[92]

In the meantime the Adansehene Nkansa and Bekwaehene Kakari had begun to prepare for a trial of strength. Up to the time of his death on 1 February 1886, Kakari had expended £4,400 on the mobilization and equipment of an invasion force. He had also greatly strengthened his position *vis-à-vis* that of the Dadiasehene Amofa by putting a further £540 to use in securing the support of Saamanhene Akyampon Panin. Kakari's successor, the young Yaw Gyamfi, was appointed immediately,[93] and pressed forward the plans for the invasion. He contributed a further £7,740 to the general fund, and made a second payment to Akyampon Panin of £324.[94] Throughout March Bekwae columns carried out a number of raids into Adanse territory, reaching no further south than Akrokyere.[95] On 8 April the Adanse council met to consider the situation. Although there was strong support for war, it was finally decided that the dispute should be arbitrated.[96] The truth of the matter was that the Adanse had been able to mobilize only some 2,500 men. 'The armed combination assembled in Becquai', by contrast, numbered about 10,000 men,[97] and included troops from Kumase armed with Snider rifles: described as 'formerly attached to the stool of Coomassie', they had probably been part of Mensa Bonsu's special forces.[98] For the Adanse, the only possibility of restoring any sort of balance in strength lay in obtaining

91 *The Western Echo*, I, no. 3, 9 December 1885, p. 4. For the death of the Kuntanasehene see also Institute of African Studies, Ghana, IASAS/157: Kuntanase Stool History recorded by J. Agyeman-Duah, 21 February 1965.

92 *The Western Echo*, I, no. 7, 20 January 1886, p. 4.

93 *Further Correspondence*, C. 4906, 1886, p. 41: Firminger to Governor, dd. Praso, 17 April 1886.

94 *Further Correspondence*, C. 5357, 1888, p. 12: Yaw Gyamfi to Colonial Secretary, dd. Bekwae, 24 November 1886.

95 *Further Correspondence*, C. 4906, 1886, p. 31: Firminger to Governor, dd. Fomena, 8 April 1886. *Ibid.* p. 41: Firminger to Governor, dd. Praso, 17 April 1886.

96 *Ibid.* pp. 30–1: Firminger to Governor, dd. Fomena, 8 April 1886.

97 *Ibid.* p. 34: Griffith to Granville, dd. Accra, 22 April 1886.

98 *Ibid.* p. 39: Firminger to Governor, dd. Praso, 17 April 1886.

the assistance of the Dadiasehene, who not only had 5,000 men under arms but also enjoyed the support of Kofi Ahinkora of Akyem Bosume, the former adherent of Kofi Kakari.[99] Amofa, however, for the time refused to commit himself to anything more than moral support for the Adanse.

On 10 April 1886 the Bekwae Confederacy Council met. Not only were the Bekwae, Sawua, and at least a section of the Manso Nkwanta represented, but so also were Mampon, Agona and Nsuta. The meeting was a considerable triumph in organization: no more widely representative an assembly had been convened since the last meeting of the Asantemanhyiamu in 1883. By convention, the Bekwaehene stated the case for a peaceful settlement of the dispute with Adanse, and was then firmly overruled by the other participants. Inspector Firminger of the Gold Coast Constabulary, who was present, reported disparagingly of the assembly. 'This federation', he wrote, '. . . consists of the Becquais and the warlike or discontented *young* men of several of the large states of Ashanti, under the command of Chiefs of little note.'[100] His appraisal of the situation was rapidly to be shown wrong. On 23 April 1886 the Adanse forces took the initiative and marched against the confederacy's base at Begroase, some seven miles southwest of Bekwae town. The Dadiasehene, expected to support the Adanse, held his forces immobile. According to an account of the subsequent engagements given by the Bekwaehene Yaw Gyamfi, seven battles were fought between late April and early June.[101] Although the Adanse suffered severe losses, particularly among their field commanders, it is not at all clear that the forces of the Confederacy were able to achieve any decisive victory.[102] On 10 June, however, Adanse hopes of being able to maintain their independent position finally collapsed with the arrival of messengers from the Dadiasehene Amofa who stated:

King Amuofa of Dadiassie sends messengers to tell King Inkansah [of Adanse] that all the Ashantis have joined the Becquais, and had made one mind to go to Coomassie and set a King on the Stool there, which he Amuofa himself had joined them, and wishes Inkansah also to go and swear an oath that he will make peace with the Bequais and cease of fighting.[103]

Rather than join the Confederacy, Nkansa chose the option already considered by his predecessor Oben in 1874 (see p. 510): that of resettling within the Gold Coast Colony. According to the enumeration

[99] *Ibid.* p. 38: Firminger to Governor, dd. Praso, 19 April 1886.
[100] *Ibid.* pp. 38–42: Firminger to Governor, dd. Praso, 17 April 1886.
[101] *Further Correspondence*, C. 5357, 1888, p. 12: memorandum from Yaw Gyamfi, dd. Bekwae, 24 November 1886.
[102] See, e.g. *The Western Echo*, I, no. 18, 31 May 1886; II, no. 20, 30 June 1886.
[103] *Further Correspondence*, C. 4906, 1886, p. 64: Carr to Colonial Secretary, dd. Praso, 13 June 1886.

accepted by the British, 12,411 Adanse crossed into the Colony between 13 and 15 June 1886.[104] The Akrofuomhene Afarkwa led 7,000 of the refugees into the Akyem country, and most of the remainder followed Nkansa into Assin. Six hundred, however, moved into Denkyira under Nkansa's senior adviser and counselor Kotirko (who in 1871 had been one of Kofi Kakari's senior negotiators with the Dutch, but who, after the trial and disgrace of his colleague Afrifa, had left the capital to make a new career for himself in Adanse service).[105]

Although, then, by mid-1886 the members of the Bekwae Confederacy Council had apparently agreed in effect to reconstitute that body as the Asantemanhyiamu, and to proceed to the election of a new Asantehene, in fact the degree of unity which had been achieved for military purposes rapidly vanished as political issues once more came to the forefront. Predictably, the split was to occur between the Bekwaehene and Saamanhene, representing the confederative and centralist positions respectively. In the immediate aftermath of the collapse of Adanse resistance, Yaw Gyamfi occupied Fomena while Akyampon Panin remained near Dadiase lest Amofa should renegue the agreement. When after a few days it became clear that all opposition was ended, Yaw Gyamfi sent messengers to ask Akyampon Panin to indicate his choice of candidate for the Golden Stool. The Saamanhene replied that the Atwoma – that is, his constituents from the Atwoma towns and villages and from Kumase itself – should be involved in the decision, and they were accordingly invited to a meeting to be held in Bekwae.[106] The negotiators were in session in the second week of September 1886. The Kumase (or Atwoma) delegation was headed by Akyampon Panin, and included among others his son Owusu Koko Kuma and the Kra Boadu and Kyerema Kobia counselors, Yaw Boaten and Kofi Kato.[107] The situation, however, was to prove much more complex than it might have appeared to the casual observer of the Bekwae meeting.

The elimination of Akyampon Panin and the transition to civil war

In the initial canvass of possible candidates for Asantehene, two candidates had emerged: Agyeman Prempe and Yaw Twereboanna. Reference to Chapter 9 will show that the former was a son of the Asante-

---

104 *Ibid.* p. 63: Griffith to Granville, dd. Accra, 21 June 1886.
105 Kotirko was an Akyem by origin. For his own account of his career, see National Archives of Ghana, Accra, ADM 11/1482: Kotirko to Colonial Secretary, dd. Christiansborg, 23 May 1887.
106 *Further Correspondence*, C. 5357, 1888, p. 12: memorandum by Yaw Gyamfi, dd. 24 November 1886.
107 *Ibid.* pp. 6–7: Badger to Governor, dd. Christiansborg, 20 October 1886.

hemaa Yaa Kyaa by her marriage to a son of Kwaku Dua I, and the latter a son of Yaa Afere by her marriage to another son of Kwaku Dua I.

In 1886 Agyeman Prempe was about thirteen years of age, and Yaw Twereboanna about twenty-six. In dynastic terms, both were members of the House of Kwaku Dua.[108] Agyeman Prempe was sponsored by the Asantehemaa Yaa Kyaa, who seems rapidly to have won the support of the majority of the members of the Council of Kumase. Yaw Twereboanna, by contrast, was sponsored by the powerful Cape Coast caucus, which hoped to transfer to him the support which had previously been mobilized for Kofi Kakari.

After Owusu Ansa's death in 1884 management of caucus affairs had been taken over by Yaw Awua, but from mid-1886 onwards Kofi Kakari's son Kofi Nti began to play an increasingly important role in it, having returned from the West Indies to a post in the customs service in Cape Coast (see p. 510).[109] In an exchange of messages with Akyampon Panin, Yaw Awua assured him that the government of the Gold Coast was in favour of Yaw Twereboanna rather than of Agyeman Prempe.[110] When Yaa Kyaa pressed Akyampon Panin for the return to the Treasury of the gold which was still in his custody, and when Yaw Twereboanna's mother Yaa Afere offered to allow him to retain it should her son's candidacy succeed, the Saamanhene's opposition to Agyeman Prempe was assured.[111] At a time, then, when some measure of political unity had seemed likely to emerge following the defeat of the Adanse, the Council of Kumase became divided in its aims once again. The Asantehemaa was now in opposition to the leader of the coup which had in fact brought her to office.

The Council of Kumase had agreed upon one convention for the electoral contest: that the Bekwaehene should preside over it.[112] It is almost certain that the delegation which Akyampon Panin led to Bekwae in September 1886 was a partisan one, presenting the case for Yaw Twereboanna. The Cape Coast caucus also proposed to the Bekwaehene that Kofi Nti should proceed to Bekwae as its representative. The request was opposed by the supporters of Agyeman Prempe within the Council of Kumase.[113] The position taken by Akyampon Panin's delegation at the Bekwae assembly was that no decision on the candidates should be taken until other *ahene* had been polled:

108 See above, p. 366, Fig. 12.

109 *Further Correspondence*, C. 5357, 1888, p. 7: Badger to Governor, dd. Christiansborg, 20 October 1886. *The Western Echo*, II, no. 22, 29 July 1886, p. 2.

110 *Ibid.* II, no. 28, 23 October 1886.

111 *Further Correspondence*, C. 5357, 1888, p. 35: Kwadwo Yinna *et al.* to Lonsdale, dd. Cape Coast, 17 January 1887.

112 *Ibid.* p. 7: Badger to Governor, dd. Christiansborg, 20 October 1886.

113 *Idem. Ibid.* p. 6: Griffith to Stanhope, dd. Christiansborg, 30 October 1886.

among those named were the Dwabenhene, Nsutahene, Agonahene, Offinsohene, Kumawuhene, and Nkoransahene. The Bekwaehene had little choice but to concur, and messengers were despatched to the various towns.[114] But essentially, Akyampon Panin was playing for time while the Cape Coast caucus – with its close links with the merchants and junior officials of the Colony[115] – was arranging further purchases of Snider rifles and ammunition. By the end of the Bekwae assembly relations between Akyampon Panin and Bekwaehene Yaw Gyamfi had deteriorated to the point at which an outbreak of fighting in the town was only narrowly averted.[116] Akyampon Panin moved into Kokofu country.

The two leaders were able to agree that oaths should be taken on 25 November to confirm a general amnesty for all those who in the struggles 'had committed unlawfully against the Crown'. Yaw Gyamfi, however complained bitterly of Akyampon Panin 'injuring me at Daddeassee'.[117] In fact in September and October the Saamanhene had devoted himself to the rehabilitation of the Kokofu towns, and had succeeded in obtaining the recognition of Osei Asibe as Kokofuhene after an interregnum of almost three years.[118] Osei Asibe was in time to become the leading protagonist of the Twereboanna cause.

In the last quarter of 1886 the Bekwaehene was much concerned with local affairs: with the threat presented to his traders by the Adanse refugees in the Colony, and with the raids against his territory being organized by both the Adanse and the Manso Nkwanta.[119] At the level of national politics, however, he recognized that his attempt to arbitrate the election had failed. Accordingly, he announced his support for the candidacy of Agyeman Prempe, and assumed leadership of the campaign. Although a report reached the Gold Coast early in November that Akyampon Panin was wavering in his adherence to Yaw Twereboanna, it was probably in error.[120] By December the Mamponhene and Nsutahene were both attempting to dissuade Akyampon Panin and Yaw Gyamfi from having recourse to arms in the resolution of the struggle between them.[121] Although the Kokofu-

---

114 *Ibid.* p. 7: Badger to Governor, dd. 20 October 1886. *Ibid.* p. 12: memorandum by Yaw Gyamfi, dd. 24 November 1886.

115 See, e.g. *Further Correspondence*, C. 5615, 1888, p. 28: Barnett to Governor, dd. Eduabin, 15 February 1888.

116 *Further Correspondence*, C. 5357, 1888, p. 12: memorandum by Yaw Gyamfi, dd. 24 November 1886.

117 *Ibid.* p. 13.

118 Rattray, 1929, p. 203.

119 *Further Correspondence*, C. 5357, 1888, p. 11: Yaw Gyamfi to Colonial Secretary, dd. Bekwae, 24 November 1886. *Ibid.* pp. 49–51: Lonsdale to Governor, dd. Sehwi Wiawso, 19 February 1887.

120 *The Western Echo*, II, no. 29, 9 November 1886, p. 4.

121 *Ibid.* II, nos. 34/35, 16–23 December 1886, p. 4.

hene had committed himself to Yaw Twereboanna's candidacy, and Bekwaehene and Dwabenhene to Agyeman Prempe's, at the end of 1886 the majority of the leading chiefs in the metropolitan region, including those of Mampon and Nsuta, still held back from identifying themselves with one side or the other.[122] In the middle of January 1887 one further attempt was made to resolve the dispute by political means: the Bekwae conference of the previous September was reconvened. Akyampon Panin once again headed a delegation from Kumase, which included his son Owusu Koko Kuma, Kofi Kakari's former chamberlain Bosommuru Dwira, the Ankobeahene Ata Gyamfi, the Sawuahene Kwabena Anane; and the Butuakwa counselor Kwame Dwuben. The negotiators reached apparent agreement on procedural matters, and the Bekwaehene suggested that a further session should be held – seemingly this time at Sawua – to take the next steps in the election.[123] But, doubtless with the precedents of the last few years in mind (of the Akyempemhene Owusu Koko's coup of August 1883 and that of Saamanhene Akyampon Panin in November 1884) the Bekwaehene had carefully arranged the scenario. As Akyampon Panin and the members of his delegation were on their way back to Sawua the new Edwesohene Kwasi Afrane Kese – a strong supporter of Agyeman Prempe – surrounded and arrested them at Aboasu two miles north of Kokofu town. Akyampon Panin attempted, but failed, to commit suicide. He was imprisoned, but promised that his life would be spared if by a 14 February deadline he had surrendered the treasury money in his possession.[124] Although granted a short stay of execution, he failed to meet the condition and was put to death later in the month.[125] The Edwesohene carried out the sentence, but, as the ranking chief in the Prempe camp, the Dwabenhene Yaw Sapon authorized it and was awarded the Saamanhene's skull.[126] By order of the Asantehemaa Yaa Kyaa, other members of the delegation were also slain, though not apparently without some respect for due process of law. Thus Kwame Dwuben was first tried on the charge of the culpable manslaughter of his own son, and only then sentenced to death.[127]

122 *Further Correspondence*, C. 5357, 1888, p. 7: Badger to Governor, dd. 20 October 1886. *Ibid.* p. 35: Kwadwo Yinna *et al.* to Lonsdale, dd. Cape Coast, 17 January 1887.
123 *Ibid.* p. 61: statement of the Kokofuhene's messenger, in District Commissioner, Cape Coast, to Colonial Secretary, dd. 25 March 1887.
124 *The Western Echo*, II, nos. 37/38, 10–27 January 1887, p. 4. NAG, Accra, ADM 11/1482: Stewart to Colonial Secretary, dd. Praso, 27 February 1887.
125 *The Western Echo*, II, nos. 39/40, 14–28 February 1887, p. 5; and nos. 41/42, 16–31 March 1887, p. 4.
126 Rattray, 1929, p. 177.
127 Wilks, field-notes: interview with Bafuor Akoto, dd. Kumase, 11 April 1966. Institute of African Studies, Legon, IASAS/170: Hemang Stool History, recorded

The seizure of Akyampon Panin and the other delegates was synchronized with two other developments. In Kumase the supporters of Agyeman Prempe carried out the arrest of Yaw Twereboanna himself, and of his known sympathizers; and in the south, the Bekwaehene attacked and burned Kokofu town.[128] By the end of February 1887, the correspondent of *The Western Echo* had no doubt that the opposition to the election of Agyeman Prempe as Asantehene had completely collapsed.[129] Yet it was to be demonstrated once again, that the political consensus essential to the national recovery could be achieved through the instrumentality neither of the coup nor the purge. The Kokofuhene Osei Asibe established a new and heavily guarded campaign headquarters at Tetrefu near Sawua, and proceeded – despite the unavailability of the candidate – to rebuild the Twereboanna cause. Of the greater *amanhene* only Kwasi Poku of Nkoransa any longer refused openly to declare his position. Among those who assured Osei Asibe of their support were the heads of the three northerly metropolitan districts, Mampon, Nsuta and Agona, who thus maintained that coalition of interests which had brought their predecessors in office together in support of Kofi Kakari in 1883. The Cape Coast caucus continued to organize the supply of rifles and ammunition for Osei Asibe, obtaining them through certain merchants at Cape Coast who were, according to Barnett of the Gold Coast Constabulary,

among the loudest to call out on the Government [of the Gold Coast] to bring about peace in Ashanti; but at the same time, for a temporary stroke of business, are not above putting such weapons into the hands of an Ashanti as to lead him to believe that he is invincible against his fellow armed with a flintlock.[130]

In April Osei Asibe took the offensive. The first major battle of the civil war of 1887–8 was fought on 26 April at Ahuren, some six miles east of Bekwae. The Kokofuhene's forces were repulsed.[131] Eighteen days later, on 14 May, Osei Asibe launched a second attack. The result was communicated by messengers to the Administrator of the Gold Coast at the end of May:

by J. Agyeman-Duah, 24 January 1966. Fuller, 1921, p. 162. According to Nana Prempe I, 1907, p. 15, the son was Kwasi, by Kwame Dwuben's marriage to Akua Fokuo, daughter of the Asantehemaa Yaa Kyaa.
128 *Further Correspondence*, C. 5357, 1888, p. 61: statement of the Kokofuhene's messenger, in D.C., Cape Coast, to Colonial Secretary, dd. 25 March 1887.
129 *The Western Echo*, ii, nos. 39/40, 14–28 February 1887, p. 5.
130 *Further Correspondence*, C. 5615, 1888, p. 121: Barnett to Governor, n.d., but received 29 March 1888. *The Gold Coast Echo*, i, no. 7, 25 September 1888, p. 3.
131 *Further Correspondence*, C. 5357, 1888: White to Holland, dd. Cape Coast, 9 June 1887. See also, NAG, Accra, ADM 11/1482: Hayford to Colonial Secretary, dd. Praso, 4 May 1887.

We are messengers from Ossey Asibey, King of the Korkorfoes, and are sent to report, for the information of his Excellency the Governor, that about three weeks ago the King of Beckwa challenged the King of Korkorfoe, through which a dreadful battle took place. The Beckwas were defeated by the Korkorfoes. The King entered into the village of the Beckwas and destroyed it; their Chiefs and captains have been captured and put in irons by Ossey Asibey's orders, but the King of Beckwa is not found. The King of Korkorfoe is now in the land of the Beckwas. The main road leading to Coomassie is now opened for the traders to the interior.[132]

The strengthening of the Twereboanna cause

In the aftermath of the battle of 14 May 1887, the Bekwaehene Yaw Gyamfi took refuge in Kumase, where he died shortly afterwards from exhaustion. The Kokofuhene Osei Asibe had an ultimatum served on the authorities in Kumase, that he would occupy and sack the town unless certain conditions were met: first, the Asantehemaa Yaa Kyaa and her sons were to be placed in his custody; secondly, the Dwabenhene Yaw Sapon was to be surrendered to him for the part he had played in the execution of Akyampon Panin; and thirdly, certain persons who had been active in the deposition of both Kofi Kakari and Mensa Bonsu should be handed over.[133] The evidence suggests that there was much demoralization within the Prempe camp. The Bekwae in particular, having borne the main losses in the struggle with the Adanse, seemed averse to further fighting.[134] It was at this juncture too, that Yaw Awua of the Cape Coast caucus succeeded in inducing other of Prempe's supporters to defect. He was involved, moreover, in organizing political action in the mode *ahupoosɛm*. A term which is not readily translatable into English, in certain respects *ahupoosɛm* was opposite in conception from *kwasafosɛm* (p. 540), government by popular participation. The *ahupoofo*, those involved in *ahupoosɛm*, in essence exercised functions of government on the basis of claims to legitimate authority which they did not in fact possess.[135] A number of Kumase functionaries who had become opposed to the candidature of Agyeman Prempe stationed themselves at various points on the great-roads to Cape Coast and Accra, within the area of jurisdiction of the Gold Coast administration. With their armed followers, they proceeded to confiscate from traders certain goods destined for the

---

132 *Further Correspondence*, C. 5357, 1888, p. 55: statement of Kokofu messengers, in White to Lonsdale, dd. Cape Coast, 1 June 1887.
133 *The Western Echo*, II, nos. 45/46, 16–31 May; 47/48, 15–30 June; and 49/50, 16–30 July 1887.
134 *Further Correspondence*, C. 5357, 1888, p. 62: Lonsdale to Administrator, dd. Akwabosu, 10 June 1887.
135 Hence the modern Twi usage, *ohupooni*, 'a bully'.

supporters of Agyeman Prempe, and to levy taxes on all other commodities whether passing northwards or southwards.[136]

Nominal head of the new movement in the Colony was the elderly Osei Kwaku Goroso, who established himself in Assin, at Kwataa (Route VI, mile 88).[137] He was the great-grandson of the Asantehemaa Adoma Akosua who had been executed for treason in 1819 (see p. 485). According to Lewin, Osei Kwaku Goroso had made an unsuccessful bid to be recognized as heir apparent during the reign of Kofi Kakari, and had been involved in an attempt to usurp the Golden Stool from Mensa Bonsu.[138] Certainly he had been active in the Domankama movement in 1880.[139] Not a serious candidate for highest office in 1887, Osei Kwaku Goroso clearly hoped to obtain recognition within a Twereboanna administration. He was supported by an unidentified Darkwa, who was stationed at Foso (Route VI, mile 82); by Kwabena Asarno, the Kumase Asomfohene or head of the messenger corps, at Kwadoja (Route VI, mile 109); and by the Kumase Ntaherahene Yaw Pepera, at Akyem Dumase (location uncertain, but probably near Route V).[140] Among others to become associated with the movement were Kwasi Apea Nuama of the Kumase *akyeremadefo* (drummers) and his brother Kwame Tua of the *asokwafo* (horn-blowers); Osei Kufuo, either Agyarko Kwadaso Baamuhene or Ampabamehene of Kumase;[141] and Manwere Poku, son of the former Gyaasewahene Adu Bofo (and himself to become Gyaasewahene briefly in 1900), who was arrested carrying munitions into the Protectorate but escaped to establish himself at Engwa some nine miles west of Kwataa.[142]

At a time when the Prempe cause seemed in danger of collapse, and when for a second time the surrender of the capital appeared imminent, the former Bantamahene Awua who had been destooled by Mensa Bonsu in 1882 at last made his re-entry into national politics. Intent on taking over leadership of the Prempe candidacy, he was too experienced a strategist to attempt to do so without first having re-established a personal constituency. In May and early June he had

136 *The Gold Coast Echo*, I, no. 9, 22 October 1888, p. 3.
137 *Idem.*
138 Lewin, 1974, pp. 90 and 259. Lewin, field-notes, interview with Kwadwo Afodwo, dd. Kumase, 27 August 1970.
139 Wilks and Ferguson, field-notes, interview with Opanin Domfe Kyere, dd. Kumase, 23 November 1973. Domfe Kyere maintained that Osei Kwaku Goroso himself was not considered a candidate for the Golden Stool in 1884 because 'a person who has been bewitched cannot become Asantehene'.
140 *The Gold Coast Echo*, I, no. 9, 22 October 1888, p. 3.
141 The second alternative may be indicated, in that the father of Osei Kwaku Goroso is sometimes said to have been Kwaku Frimpon, Ampabamehene at the time of Kwaku Dua I.
142 *The Gold Coast Echo*, I, no. 7, 25 September 1888, p. 3.

systematically mobilized support from a number of towns to the south of Kumase, lying between Routes VI and VIII and including Adankranya near Bekwae, Pekyi East and West, Trede, Mpatase and Nkawie.[143] By July many more of the Kumase towns to the southeast had pledged him their support: Kwaso, Kuntanase, Gyakye, Asiempon, Onwi, Abanase, Apramase, Edweso, and others.[144] Awua became generally accepted as manager of the Prempe campaign.

Awua's intervention markedly changed the situation in both its military and political aspects. The Kokofuhene Osei Asibe found himself increasingly isolated from his principal supporters north of the capital: Mamponhene, Nsutahene and Agonahene. As a result perhaps, in July 1887 he sent messages to Awua and to the councillors in Kumase with proposals to end all fighting. In token of his goodwill, he released the Kumase prisoners in his hands. Osei Asibe's initiative was seemingly welcomed, and at a meeting at Odaso, some seven miles south of the capital, representatives from Mampon, Nsuta, Agona and Nkoransa met with Awua. Oaths were taken that the contest should be pursued without further recourse to arms.[145] The Bekwaehene Kwaku Abrebrese, who had succeeded Yaw Gyamfi, was not represented at the conference, but did join in the subsequent working sessions to attempt – yet again – to establish agreed procedures for the election.[146] The negotiators had access to the policy statement by Administrator White of the Gold Coast: that 'upon the subject of the state of affairs in Ashanti, I have decided that an effort should be made at once by this Government to effect a cessation of hostilities and the establishment, by consent of the parties concerned, of a central government in that country'.[147] The Asante leaders apparently reached agreement upon the desirability of obtaining the service of an officer of the Gold Coast government to act as arbitrator: 'to help them in putting a King on the stool'.[148] Yet further skirmishing between the two sides was reported early in August,[149] and later in the month the Bekwaehene and Awua were said to be insisting that further progress towards the election could be made only if Osei Asibe was removed from the Kokofu stool. Travelling Commissioner Lonsdale became

---

143 *Further Correspondence*, C. 5357, 1888, p. 62: Lonsdale to Administrator, dd. 10 June 1887.
144 *Ibid*. p. 73: statement by Kokofu messengers, to Governor, dd. Accra, 29 July 1887.
145 *Idem*.
146 *Further Correspondence*, C. 5615, 1888, p. 11: Lonsdale to White, dd. 8 August 1887, in Griffith to Knutsford, dd. Christiansborg, 13 April 1888.
147 *Ibid*. p. 10: White to Lonsdale, dd. 22 June 1887.
148 *Ibid*. p. 11: Lonsdale to White, dd. 8 August 1887 .
149 *Further Correspondence*, C. 5357, 1888, p. 75: Lonsdale to Administrator, dd. Eduabin, 22 August 1887.

convinced that the Odaso convention had been 'only a farce',[150] but his judgement was perhaps unduly cynical. Certainly on 26 September he was able to report that the Asante negotiators were well advanced in their work, and that Bekwaehene and Kokofuhene had agreed jointly to administer the government until such time as a new Asantehene had been installed.[151]

It has been shown in Chapter 9 that even in the nineteenth century the Oyoko royals of Kokofu had kept alive claims of their right to the Golden Stool. In the latter part of 1887 the belief gained currency that Osei Asibe aspired himself to the Golden Stool.[152] His co-administrator the Bekwaehene evidently took the matter seriously. In December Osei Asibe publicly denied the report: '. . . the Bekwai King said, I am going to be put on the "stool", but it isn't so, I am only going to put a person on the "stool" '.[153] The Kokofuhene, nevertheless, did appear to be achieving considerable successes in consolidating his personal position. As early as July 1887 he had appointed Yaw Awua of the Cape Coast caucus as his consul on the Gold Coast: 'as the person whom the King desired that all communications between his Excellency [the Governor of the Gold Coast] and the King of Kokofu should pass through'.[154] With emergence of the *ahupoosɛm* movement, exercising control over the flow of commodities between Asante and the Gold Coast, Osei Asibe's administration began to look more like a national than a local one. The change in status was accentuated by his designation of Akyampon Panin's people, the Sawua, as his treasurers.[155] In November or December, moreover, the escape of Yaw Twereboanna from Kumase occurred. He made his way to Osei Asibe's camp.[156] While his presence there may have been something of an embarrassment to the Kokofuhene personally, it seems nevertheless to have led many uncommitted towns and villages finally to declare against Agyeman Prempe. The Kwabre towns to the northeast of Kumase, including Mamponten and Nyameani, assured Osei Asibe of their support, and in their enthusiasm the latter attacked five Kuntanase villages late in December.[157] At the same time reports of nego-

---

150 *Ibid.* p. 76: Lonsdale to Administrator, dd. Asante, 27 August 1887.
151 *Further Correspondence,* C. 5615, 1888, p. 13: Lonsdale to Administrator, dd. Cape Coast, 3 October 1887.
152 Methodist Mission Archives, London: extracts from Wharton's journal, in Wharton to General Secretaries, dd. Kumase, 31 May 1846.
153 *Further Correspondence,* C. 5615, 1888, p. 21: statement of Kofi Mensa, in Barnett to Colonial Secretary, dd. Eduabin, 14 January 1888.
154 *Further Correspondence,* C. 5357, 1888, p. 73: messengers from Kokofu to Governor, dd. Accra, 29 July 1887.
155 *Further Correspondence,* C. 5615, 1888, p. 17: Barnett to Colonial Secretary, dd. Eduabin, 31 December 1887.
156 *Idem. Ibid.* p. 34: Barnett to Governor, dd. Eduabin, 10 March 1888.
157 *Ibid.* p. 17: Barnett to Colonial Secretary, dd. Eduabin, 31 December 1887. *Ibid.*

tiations between Osei Asibe and the Manso Nkwanta refugees in Denkyira indicated that they too had taken oaths to support Osei Asibe and Yaw Twereboanna.[158] Finally a number of the Ahafo towns in the west sent in to Kokofuhene to affirm their readiness to fight for him; the leader of the anti-Prempe forces there was the Kukuomhene, who served the Akuroponhene and had thus been a strong supporter of Kofi Kakari's restoration. He was joined by such towns as Dadiesoaba and Etweneto which had also served the Akuroponhene, and Datano which had served the Saamanhene.[159] In January 1888, Osei Asibe had a least 6,000 to 7,000 men under arms.[160]

The establishment of the Prempe regime

Early in 1888 relations between the two administrators of the government, Bekwaehene and Kokofuhene, began to show signs of strain. The agreement between them made the previous September had apparently to be ratified by an exchange of state drums. Kokofuhene sent two drums to Bekwaehene, but the latter failed to reciprocate. Osei Asibe demanded the return of his drums, but learned that they had been sent to the Edwesohene who had in turn handed them over to Dwabenhene. Osei Asibe issued an ultimatum: either they were returned to him by 25 January or he would march on Bekwae town.[161] What in fact was happening was that neither Kokofuhene nor Bekwaehene were able any longer to hold together the loose coalitions over which they had been attempting to preside. Neither was able to articulate long-range national goals in terms of a political ideology for which any sort of significant mandate existed, and the government which they jointly administered was one which had not been in any way legitimated and which, therefore, lacked authority.

At the beginning of February 1888 the Mamponhene Owusu Sekyere II demanded, and received, 10 peredwans of gold from Osei Asibe in order to retain his support, but then immediately proceeded to take over management of the Twereboanna campaign. Opening a new series of negotiations with Awua of Bantama rather than Bekwaehene

p. 20: Barnett to Colonial Secretary, dd. Eduabin, 14 January 1888. See further, Kumase Divisional Council Archives, Manhyia: Kumasihene's Tribunal, Civil Record Book 3, Kwadwo Nketia v. Kwabena Dumfe, commencing 14 June 1928.

158 *Further Correspondence*, C. 5615, 1888, p. 21: statement by Kofi Mensa in Barnett to Colonial Secretary, dd. Eduabin, 14 January 1888.

159 *Ibid.* pp. 24–5: Barnett to Governor, dd. Eduabin, 31 January 1888. NAG, Accra, ADM 11/1/1137: Notes on Ahafo, dd. 10 July 1899. ADM 11/1/1482: notes of an interview by Hodgson, dd. Victoriaborg, 29 January 1890.

160 *Further Correspondence*, C. 5615, pp. 24–5: Barnett to Governor, dd. Eduabin, 31 January 1888.

161 *Idem.*

as his opposite number, the two agreed to convene a meeting of the Asantemanhyiamu in Kumase. 'The King of Mampon', reported Barnett, '(who is the leading man of the Kokofu faction), with Bantama Awuah (the leading Chief of the opposing side), have sent to inform me that they have agreed to despatch their messengers in concert to all the Kings and Chiefs of Ashanti, requesting them to meet at Kumasi for the purpose of electing a King.' [162] The ten-day period commencing 5 March (a *nkyidwo* Monday) was chosen for the assembly, the time being particularly propitious by the Asante calendar.[163] 'The Kings and Chiefs', Barnett wrote on 24 February,

after infinite trouble and worry, seem now to have come to an unanimous wish that a King should be elected, the King of Kokofu himself sending to me only two days ago, he having, up to then, been the one exception. The two principal claimants for the stool are Prempeh, the son of Yah Kiah, and Achiriboanda, the son of Yah Tra. The former's sponsors are Kumasi, Bekwabin [Bekwae], and Djwabin; the latter, Mompon, Insuta, and Kokofu; it remains to be seen who will give way. Ashanti now is as peaceful as it can be till a King is on the stool. Traders are gradually regaining confidence and realising the fact the roads are open, of course it will take some time before trade is thoroughly developed.[164]

Though by 5 March few members of the Asantemanhyiamu had yet arrived in the capital, the electors there proceeded to confirm Agyeman Prempe as 'Adumhene' or heir apparent. Barnett, as representative of the Gold Coast administration, entered Kumase on 15 March, and was received by over fifty officers and functionaries before a crowd of some 3,000 to 4,000 people. Representatives of both Kokofu and Mampon were present.[165] The installation of a new Asantehene was scheduled for 26 March (*monodwo* Monday), and further messengers were sent to announce the date in all the districts. The outlying *ahene*, however, clearly feared a repetition of the massacre staged by the Akyempemhene Owusu Koko in 1883, and none arrived in the capital.[166] On the morning of the 26th Osei Asibe sent messengers to the city authorities to say that he was not prepared to attend the Assembly unless a general amnesty was approved, covering not only rebellion but all capital offences. The Asantehemaa Yaa Kyaa, the reinstated Bantamahene Awua, and the Asafohene Asafo Boakye offered to meet Kokofuhene outside the town 'and there drink fetish, to wipe out and forget the past conduct of anyone in his camp'. In the early afternoon, however, both Kokofuhene and Mamponhene sent further

162 *Ibid.* pp. 27–8: Barnett to Governor, dd. Eduabin, 15 February 1888.
163 *Ibid.* p. 30: Barnett to Governor, dd. Eduabin, 24 February 1888.
164 *Idem*, p. 31
165 *Ibid.* p. 38: Barnett to Governor, dd. Kumase, 20 March 1888.
166 *Ibid.* pp. 41–2: Barnett to Governor, dd. Kumase, 24 March 1888.

messages to the capital to say that they were not ready for the election and that the installation should be postponed until Monday, 30 April. After much deliberation the electors in Kumase decided to keep to schedule, and just before midnight Agyeman Prempe was recognized as Asantehene. He was given charge of, though not enstooled on, the Golden Stool. Representatives of both Mampon and Kokofu were present and expressed the optimistic belief that Owusu Sekyere II and Osei Asibe would both acknowledge the validity of the election.[167]

Seeking to avoid the excesses of earlier regimes, the new one made reconciliation the keystone of its policy. On 30 March 1888, emissaries from Prempe delivered a message to Osei Asibe: 'The King of Ashanti sends his compliments and best wishes to the King of Kokofu and wishes to inform him that he has been elected to the golden stool, and that he hopes that the King of Kokofu will come and drink fetish with him, that all the past should be forgiven and forgotten'.[168] On the following day messages were also delivered to the Mamponhene:

We were sent by the King with his compliments, and to inform you that he is put on the stool of his grandfather . . . We were sent by the big Chiefs of Ashanti and the mother Princess to inform you that whatever misunderstanding that has taken place is to be thrown aside, and that fetish be taken between you and them, that things may get on in a peaceful manner, and that they are sorry they had in any way offend the King of Mampon.[169]

But the Mamponhene and Kokofuhene still retained intact much of their support, and both withheld recognition from Agyeman Prempe. The role which the Gold Coast government had played in the election was considered to have been – contrary to the understanding – a highly partisan one. Osei Asibe's traders had been particularly effected when, in mid-1887, Lonsdale had closed the Kokofu-Akyem Kotoku road and, for a time, the Praso ferry.[170] The subsequent arrest and imprisonment of Yaw Awua of the Cape Coast caucus much weakened Osei Asibe's links with the coastal merchants. It was believed in the Kokofu camp that both Lonsdale and Barnett, although representatives of the Colony administration, had received from Bantamahene Awua a bribe of 2,250 oz of gold to dispose them towards the Prempe cause.[171] In the circumstances the Kokofuhene began to press for his own recognition as Asantehene, and turned once again to the use of force in pursuit of his goals.[172]

167 *Ibid.* pp. 42–3: Barnett to Governor, dd. Kumase, 29 March 1888.
168 *Ibid.* p. 127: Badger to Barnett, dd. Kumase, 2 April 1888.
169 *Ibid.* p. 125: Halm to Barnett, dd. Kumase, 3 April 1888.
170 *Ibid.* p. 12: Griffith to Knutsford, dd. Christiansborg, 13 April 1888.
171 *Ibid.* p. 125: Halm to Barnett, dd. Kumase, 3 April 1888.
172 *Ibid.* p. 159: District Commissioner, Cape Coast, to Colonial Secretary, dd. 9 August 1888, reporting information from ambassadors from Prempe.

In May both Kokofuhene and Mamponhene launched unsuccessful attacks upon Edweso. Shortly afterwards, acting in concert with the Amoafo and with Dadiase and Adanse refugees from the Colony whose support he had won by his policies for their resettlement in Asante, Osei Asibe attacked and defeated the Bekwae.[173] The Bantamahene Awua moved his troops southwards to assist the Bekwaehene, but arrived only in time to engage one part of the victorious army. Fearing that Osei Asibe would next march on Kumase, Awua established his field headquarters at Kaase three miles to its south. In what must have been a most skilfully planned and executed night raid, the men of the nearby Kwawma villages – adherents of Kokofuhene – seized and escaped with Awua. Osei Asibe put him to death.[174] The indications are that by the execution of so senior an officer, the Kokofuhene alienated a number of his more moderate supporters. 'The several chiefs', so it was reported in the *Gold Coast Echo,* 'who have hitherto taken part in the conflict for the stool, met together, and decided that the policy of Essibey, King of the Kokofoos was calculated to upset the Ashantee kingdom. Having come to this decision, they then allied themselves together and, with their joint forces attacked the Kokofoos, the allied forces gaining the day . . .' [175] In fact, the coalition which defeated the Kokofu army on 26 to 27 June 1888 was built around the forces of Bekwae and Edweso.[176] Osei Asibe and Yaw Twereboanna crossed the Pra and took refuge in Akyem Kotoku.[177] One of the more conservative estimates of the number of Kokofu refugees in the Colony was 17,000, and of the Dadiase, some 4,000 (see p. 92).[178]

The return to legitimate government

On 12 July Governor Sir W. Brandford Griffith of the Gold Coast wrote to the Secretary of State for the Colonies in London acknowledging the extent of the British contribution to the candidacy of Agyeman Prempe:

Now that the Kokofus, together with their King, who stood in the way of every attempt to restore peace in Ashanti, have been driven out of that country, I entertain the hope that King Quacco Duah [that is, Prempe] will be able to consolidate the various sections in Ashanti, maintain his

---

173 *Ibid.* pp. 147–8: Carr to Colonial Secretary, dd. Praso, 3 July 1888.
174 *Ibid.* p. 159: D.C., Cape Coast, to Colonial Secretary, dd. 9 August 1888. For a recent discussion of the episode, see Lewin, 1974, pp. 266–8.
175 *The Gold Coast Echo,* I, no. 3, 26 July 1888, p. 3.
176 *Further Correspondence,* C. 5615, 1888, pp. 147–8: Carr to Colonial Secretary. dd. Praso, 3 July 1888.
177 *Ibid.* p. 147: Carr to District Commissioner, Cape Coast, dd. Praso, 1 July 1888.
178 *Ibid.* p. 158: Griffith to Knutsford, dd. Christiansborg, 20 August 1888.

position, and keep his country in order, so as to bring about a settled state of affairs, and give the country the opportunity of making efforts to regain some of its former prosperity. The newly elected King has had the moral, indeed, I may say the material, support of this Government, by its action in regard to the imprisonment of You Awuah, the Kokofu Agent at Cape Coast, the dismissal of the unworthy Government Interpreter Davies, the stoppage of the Prah road, which prevented the Kokofus resorting to the coast for arms and ammunition, and the prohibition of the sale of these which appears to have led to the recent Kokofu defeat, owing to the exhaustion of their supply of gunpowder.[179]

Yet even with the impressive military successes of the new regime, and its recognition as Government of Asante by the Government of the Gold Coast, conflict was by no means at an end. Not only Osei Asibe, but Yaw Twereboanna and a number of his followers including Osei Kwaku Goroso and his fellow *ahupoofo* remained active in British protected territory. Hoping to retain there a strong base for the continuance of the struggle, Osei Asibe maintained communications with the Mamponhene Owusu Sekyere. The two planned a concerted attack upon Kumase from both south and north.[180] Prempe accordingly petitioned the Gold Coast government to restrain, and if necessary deport, Osei Asibe, and to secure the arrest of the *ahupoofo* – the 'would-be banditti chiefs, as they are likely to block up the trade routes'.[181] Acting on the complaint, the concentrations of Kokofu near the borders of the Colony and Asante were broken up, and the refugees were forced to resettle in the more southerly and easterly towns of Akyem Kotoku. The British response freed the government in Kumase to take the offensive against the Mampon and Nsuta north of the capital. The Edwesohene and Offinsohene were authorized to prepare an invasion force. It took the field in September 1888.[182] The Nsutahene Kwaku Dente retired to Atebubu within the independent eastern Bron confederation. He was accompanied by some five hundred of his subjects. The majority of the Nsuta capitulated to the invading forces and asked for clemency. The army then prepared to attack Mampon, having been reinforced by Asafo Boakye and his troops. The Mamponhene Owusu Sekyere fell back to the north but was defeated. He too took refuge in Atebubu, accompanied by some two or three hundred of his people.[183] In October he clashed with Nkoransa troops and was again defeated. Left virtually without support, he was declared de-

179 *Ibid.* p. 144: Griffith to Knutsford, dd. Christiansborg, 12 July 1888.
180 *Ibid:* Griffith to Knutsford, dd. 4 September 1884.
181 *Ibid.* p. 158: Griffith to Knutsford, dd. 20 August 1888. *The Gold Coast Echo*, I, no. 7, 25 September 1888, p. 3.
182 *The Gold Coast Echo*, I, no. 9, 22 October 1888, p. 3.
183 *Ibid.* I, No. 10, 5 November 1888, p. 3. *Further Correspondence*, C. 7917, 1896, p. 9: Hodgson to Knutsford, dd. Accra, 9 December 1889.

posed in Mampon, and Kwame Apea Osokye – a supporter of Agyeman Prempe – was elected new Mamponhene.[184] Nsutahene Kwaku Dente was to die near Atebubu,[185] but Owusu Sekyere lived to be reinstated in office after the 1896 campaign. Only in Ahafo did the group of towns led by Kukuomhene remain committed to Osei Asibe and the Twereboanna cause. Indeed, it was there that Agyeman Prempe's supporters suffered their only serious set-back. The Asabihene of Kumase Asabi Antwi, whose career in the diplomatic service under Kofi Kakari and Mensa Bonsu has been referred to above, led the Ahafo forces loyal to Agyeman Prempe in an attack upon the Kukuom. Asabi Antwi was slain and his troops defeated.[186] In this way the 'Ahafo problem' was generated, which has continued to be a major issue in Asante politics in the twentieth century and which is currently (1973–4) under review by the Coussey Commission.[187]

The extent of the problems facing the new regime in Kumase in consequence of the all but total breakdown of central government, was outlined accurately enough by Governor Griffith, who in a letter to Agyeman Prempe referred to:

the defection of some of the Ashanti tribes, the uncertain political relationship to you of others whose loyalty you have possibly hitherto counted upon, and the consequent falling back of Ashanti; the spoiling of those large portions of the country which have been deserted by the inhabitants; the consequent gradual decline in the farming, trading, and other business of the country and concurrently, the diminution of the taxes, tolls, and fees collected, the full supply of which are necessary to the proper maintenance, state, and dignity of yourself and your Kings, Chiefs, and principal men, while the happiness, comfort, and faith of the people are unsettled in consequence of the disordered and uncertain state of the whole country.[188]

The policies of the regime were predicated upon two fundamental assumptions, first, that the independence of the Asante nation could and should be preserved, and second, that those who – for whatever reasons – had been opposed to the election of Agyeman Prempe could

---

184 *Ibid.* p. 136: memorandum by Ferguson, dd. 9 November 1893, in Ferguson to Hodgson, dd. Atebubu, 24 November 1893.
185 Rattray, 1929, p. 263. Foreign Office, London, Confidential Prints, C. 6364, Papers relating to West African Negotiations, 1889–92, p. 190: Atebubuhene to Governor, dd. Atebubu, 17 May 1892.
186 NAG, Accra, ADM 11/1/1482: notes of an interview by Hodgson, dd. Victoriaborg, 29 January 1890. PRO, CO. 96/237: Hodgson to Ripon, dd. Accra, 12 October 1893, enclosing Lamb to Colonial Secretary, dd. Las Palmas, 28 January 1893.
187 By explicitly ignoring the historical record, Robertson's recent paper on the Ahafo issue, 1973, *passim*, leaves the reader with a most distorted impression of the development of the dispute.
188 *Further Correspondence*, C. 7917, 1896, p. 48: Griffith to Prempe, dd. Christiansborg, 11 March 1891.

and should be reconciled to him.[189] Upon receipt in 1891 of the offer of British protection, a firm statement was issued in the Asantehene's name: 'my Kingdom of Ashanti will never commit itself to any such policy; Ashanti must remain independent as of old,' he announced; 'there is no reason for any Ashantiman to feel alarm at the prospects, or to believe for a single instant that our cause has been driving back by the events of the past hostilities' (see pp. 120–1).

In the quest for a popular mandate for the policies of reconstruction, the new regime appears to have represented itself as standing in the tradition of the great peace party governments of the middle of the nineteenth century, and the image of Agyeman Prempe as the political successor to Kwaku Dua I was carefully fostered. 'He is the grandson of Agyiman [Kwaku Dua]', messengers informed Governor Hodgson, 'and he only likes peace and trade.' [190] The Prempe regime thus made a broad appeal to the nation on the basis of patriotism, and of subscription to the historic peace party position of 'peace, trade and open roads'. Yet the regime was not insensitive to the necessity for ongoing reform and modernization to bring Asante into a viable relationship with the technologically advanced countries of Europe. It will be shown in the next chapter that in certain important respects the policies pursued by Prempe's administration were continuous with those of the unpopular Mensa Bonsu rather than with those of the much revered Kwaku Dua I. Indeed, while the regime was not prepared to accept the concept of the nation as a confederacy, it was seemingly prepared to abandon the unequivocally centralist position to which the administrations of Kwaku Dua I had been so firmly committed. Under Agyeman Prempe I, the Asantemanhyiamu was consulted as far as was practicable in all major policy decisions, and individual district heads, for a time at least, were permitted a high degree of independence of action even in the field of foreign relations.

By 1890, the Asantemanhyiamu was functioning regularly once more. In that year an embassy to Elmina included representatives of, among others, Dwaben, Bekwae, Mampon, Kumawu, Asumegya, Edweso, Offinso and Gyamase,[191] and in the following year members of the Assembly were summoned to Kumase to debate the British offer of protection.[192] Yet as late as 1893 the Dwabenhene and Bekwaehene

[189] Thus, for example, the decision was taken not to confiscate the lands of those who had fought against Agyeman Prempe – Mamponhene, Kokofuhene, Saamanhene, Nsutahene, the Kwabre chiefs and so forth. See Kumase Divisional Council Archives, Manhyia: Kumasihene's Tribunal, Civil Record Book 3, Kwadwo Nketia *v.* Kwabena Dumfe, commencing 14 June 1928.
[190] *Further Correspondence,* C. 7917, 1896, p. 109: Hodgson's interview with Yaw Nkruma, dd. Accra, 9 October 1893.
[191] *Ibid.* p. 23: report of proceedings at Elmina, dd. 8 July 1890.
[192] *Ibid.* p. 65: Hull to Governor, dd. Kumase, 6 April 1891.

were, for example, still conducting private negotiations with the Gold Coast government.[193] It was in consequence of its concern with conciliation and consensus, that the regime was able to obtain the support of the Asantemanhyiamu for its two immediate short-term goals: first, the re-establishment of Asante authority in the northern provinces, and second, the return and resettlement of the Asante refugees from the Gold Coast Colony.

Prempe, reported Ferguson in 1892, 'is bent on reconquering the tribes who have receded from him'.[194] He is, commented Vroom in the following year, 'straining every nerve to recover his lost prestige amongst the revolted countries'.[195] In pursuit of this end, the regime was able to mobilize considerable support. As early as 1888 the Nkoransahene Kwasi Poku had promised his assistance in ending the long-standing rebellion of the eastern Bron. When it became necessary in 1892, after Kwasi Poku's death, to despatch an army to occupy Nkoransa itself, the troops commanded by the Bantamahene Amankwatia Kwame included contingents from Dwaben, Mampon, Nsuta, Kumawu, Offinso, Edweso and elsewhere.[196] The refugee ex-Mamponhene Owusu Sekyere, moreover, 'becoming very anxious to secure the pardon of Prempe', offered not only to assist in the struggle with Nkoransa but also to 'work out from Atabubu the re-annexation by Ashantee of the Brong people'.[197] The considerable success which attended the regime's northern policies has been discussed above (see pp. 299–301). Its attitude towards Dwaben, Adanse, Manso Nkwanta, Kokofu and Dadiase refugees in the Colony to the south was one which was clearly explained by the delegation to Elmina in July 1890:

the King asked the Governor to give him back all the Ashanties who have sought refuge in this Colony. He (King) would receive them all back kindly and regard them as his loyal subjects. When this is done, he had hopes that the trade would be in a flourishing state and all the trade roads would be kept open and clean and peace would then be maintained for ever.[198]

The refugee leaders, for their part, clearly felt some confidence in the assurances that they would be well received. Unlike preceding regimes, that of Agyeman Prempe had made no use of the instrument of terror

---

193 *Ibid.* p. 108: Bekwaehene to Acting Governor, 22 October 1893. *Ibid.* pp. 111–12: Dwabenhene to Scott, 30 October 1893.

194 Foreign Office, London, Confidential Prints, C. 6364, 1889–92, p. 210: Ferguson to Governor, dd. Bimbila, 29 August 1892.

195 *Further Correspondence*, C. 7917, 1896, p. 106: Vroom to Colonial Secretary, dd. Elmina, 2 November 1893.

196 *Ibid.* p. 138: Memorandum by Ferguson, dd. 9 November 1893.

197 *Ibid.* p. 137.

198 *Ibid.* p. 24: Holmes to Governor, dd. Cape Coast, 9 July 1890; and see also pp. 34–5: Prempe to Governor, dd. Kumase, 22 August 1890.

since coming to power. By mid-1890 the Manso Nkwanta had expressed their desire to return to their home towns,[199] and by the end of the same year the Kokofuhene Osei Asibe and many of the Kokofu and Dadiase refugees had reached the same decision.[200] It was not until September 1893, however, that Osei Asibe finally made preparations to move. Yaw Twereboanna agreed to accompany him.[201] But despite repeated assurances from the Gold Coast administration that the refugees would be allowed to return, the departure of both Osei Asibe and Yaw Twereboanna were in the end prevented by the British.[202]

By 1894 the Prempe regime had succeeded, by the skilful and conciliatory conduct of its affairs, in winning nationwide support: for the first time since 1883 Asante possessed a central authority both with claims to legitimacy and with a clear mandate to govern. Funeral customs for the late Asantehene Kwaku Dua II fell due on Monday, 2 May 1894, and the enstoolment of Agyeman Prempe upon the Golden Stool was scheduled for one (Asante) month later.[203] The Asantemanhyiamu was convened and met in session on 4 June. After due debate, Agyeman Prempe was formally enstooled on Monday, 11 June by, as he himself wrote, 'all my loyal district Kings, Chiefs, and principal men of Ashanti'.[204] The Asantemanhyiamu remained in session until 24 June, during which period the state of the nation was exhaustively reviewed. 'The Chiefs and King with his councillors', it was reported, 'are said to have devoted full two weeks to deliberations as to how order and peace could be restored in the Kingdom, and Ashanti regain its past glory and renown.'[205] Among the more important decisions taken was that to levy a special tax of 10s per head of house, to be applied to the expenses of repatriating Kokofuhene Osei Asibe and his subjects. Subsequently the principle was extended to include the Adansehene Nkansa within the scheme, and each district in the metropolitan region was required to raise 40 peredwans, or £320. Of the fund, 1,000 peredwans were offered to the government of the Gold Coast for its assistance in the matter.[206]

By mid-1894 then, the Prempe regime had become the recognized government of Asante, and the long period of turmoil – of political

199 *Ibid.* p. 35: Prempe to Governor, dd. Kumase, 22 August 1890.
200 *Ibid.* p. 47: Griffith to Prempe, dd. Christiansborg, 11 March 1891.
201 PRO, CO. 96/236: Hodgson to Ripon, dd. Christiansborg, 23 September 1893.
202 See NAG, Accra, ADM 12/3/5: Hodgson to Ripon, dd. Accra, 23 September and 11 October 1893. *Further Correspondence*, C. 7917, 1896, pp. 25–8: Griffith to Prempe, dd. Christiansborg, 16 July 1890.
203 *Ibid.* p. 181: Vroom to Governor, dd. Christiansborg, 24 April 1894.
204 *Ibid.* p. 201: Prempe to Governor, dd. Kumase, 28 June 1894.
205 *The Gold Coast Methodist Times*, 31 August 1894.
206 *Idem. Further Correspondence*, C. 7917, 1896, p. 203: Griffith to Ripon, dd. Christiansborg, 10 August 1894. *Ibid.* p. 227: the Asante in the Western Protectorate *et al.* to Griffith, dd. Cape Coast, 1 October 1894.

purges, coups, and civil war – was ended. On 28 June, four days after
the Asantemanhyiamu went into recess, Agyeman Prempe (or Kwaku
Dua III as he was officially known) addressed a letter to Governor
Griffith in which he set out in magniloquent terms the goals to which
he and his councillors aspired:

I pray and beseech my elders, as well as my gods, and the spirits of my
ancestors, to assist me, to give me true wisdom and love, to rule and govern
my nation, and I beseech you, my good friend, to pray and ask blessings
from your God to give me long life and prosperous and peaceful reign, and
that my friendship with Her Majesty's Government may be more firm and
more closer than hitherto had been done, that bye-gones will be bye-gones,
that Ashanti nation will awake herself as out of sleep, that the hostilities will
go away from her, that the evils which the constant wars has brought upon
her, like destroying our jewels, may die everlastingly from her, and that I
shall endeavour to promote peace and tranquillity and good order in my
Kingdom, and to restore its trade, and the happiness and safety of my people
generally, by making it to the advantage of the refugees to return, inhabit,
and cultivate their respective countries, and thus raise my Kingdom of
Ashanti to a prosperous, substantial, and steady position as a great farming
and trading community such as it has never occupied hitherto, and that the
trade between your Protectorate and my Kingdom of Ashanti may increase
daily to the benefit of all interested in it.[207]

The tragedy was that unknown to the Asante statesmen, the imperial
government in London had already decided that the continued independence of Asante presented an unacceptable threat to its own designs
for empire.

[207] *Ibid.* p. 201: Prempe to Governor, dd. Kumase, 28 June 1894.

CHAPTER 14

Modernization, reform, and the role of the Owusu Ansas in politics

The missionaries as factors of change

Attention has been drawn to the fact that in the early nineteenth century, before any Christian missionary society had begun seriously to consider Asante as a field for proselytization, Osei Bonsu's desire that a number of *ahenemma*, princes, should be sent for education to the Gold Coast, or even to Europe, evoked a hostile reaction from conservative councillors (see pp. 202–3). The visits to Kumase in 1839 of T. B. Freeman of the Wesleyan Missionary Society and of A. Riis of the Basel Mission obliged politicians to articulate their attitude towards the whole problem of cultural innovation. The debate was one which was to continue, intermittently, for the remainder of the century. It was to become inextricably linked with the issue of capital punishment, public execution and what was misleadingly referred to as 'human sacrifice'. It was also to become linked with the matter of the role of the *ahenemma* in government, for it was members of this class – excluded by the constitution from the highest office – who were to play a prominent part in the emergence of the new politics whether in the tradition of Owusu Koko whose penchant for autocracy has been described in the last chapter, or in the tradition of his brother Owusu Ansa whose constructive policies for reform will be treated in this.

An account of Asante attitudes to cultural change, with reference principally to the first half of the nineteenth century, has recently been essayed by McCaskie.[1] The Christian missionaries who visited Asante were by no means insensitive to the fact that they had been chosen to labour in a country which already possessed a highly developed awareness of national identity. The view expressed by Hillard in 1849 was not unrepresentative of the sentiments of his colleagues:

there is a great degree of energy in the Ashanti nation; and were their energies properly directed and governed, they would soon exalt themselves in national importance. I am inclined to think that the time is not far distant

[1] McCaskie, 1972, *passim*.

when this will take place; and also, that God has great ends in view in raising up such a powerful nation in the interior of Africa.[2]

The missionaries saw their task as that of inducing the Asante to abandon the elaborate system of ritual observances associated with the cult of the ancestors. They identified, as pivotal to that system, the custom of killing persons in order that they should become available as servants to those in the *Asaman:* the spirit world where the ancestors dwell. In the 1840s the missionaries found in Kumase considerable interest in the idea of change. Chapman, who was in the capital in 1843–4, reported on the many private conversations he had with Kwaku Dua I, who showed much interest in exotic institutions. 'Many and very interesting were the hours thus spent', Chapman wrote,

when with three or four confidential counsellors, and sometimes one or two of his wives, he would make inquiries respecting the subjects of my teaching and as to who the true God was, and the one Saviour of whom we spoke, and from these themes would go on to questions of municipal and social government, and to the dignity of the Queen of England and the Government of the country, and to its greatness and such like.[3]

If Chapman's reports are to be accepted, in the Kumase of the 1840s there was moreover a widespread belief in the inevitability of change, as apparently indicated by an old prediction:

a strong conviction prevails, that Christianity is to supersede their present system of religion, and that their ancient customs are about to be abolished. I was told on one occasion, by a person who wished me to observe the greatest secrecy, (and I did observe it there,) that, in a private conference between the King and his Counsellors, they came to the conclusion, that the introduction of Christianity about this time being in unison with some ancient tradition, it was in all probability the system by which their own is to be superseded, and by which their nation is to be benefited. A general opinion prevailes, that about this time the national usages of the country will undergo a complete change, that the nation will retain its independent form of government to a certain extent, but that its religion, its rites and ceremonies, are to be altogether changed . . .[4]

Yet while there was thus clearly a strong concern with the idea of change, there was equally clearly a marked reluctance to translate this into any practical programme. Of the situation in the late 1840s it was remarked:

2 *Wesleyan-Methodist Magazine,* May 1849, p. 550: Hillard to General Secretaries, dd. Kumase, 16 January 1849.
3 *Further Correspondence,* C. 893, Pt IV of 1874, p. 61: Chapman to General Secretary, dd. Fort Beaufort, 29 September 1873.
4 *Wesleyan-Methodist Magazine,* July 1846, p. 728: report by Chapman.

a mutual fear existed between the King and the great Chiefs as to the policy of allowing the introduction and spread of Christianity in the country. The monarch was evidently afraid lest his chiefs, in that wild independence which is so strangely mixed up, with the despotism by his government, should accuse him of allowing the innovations of this new European influence to extend in the country; and they, the chiefs, on the other hand, feared to take any steps favorable to the growth of Christianity unless the King clearly took the initiative. – Thus the Queen of Inabin [Dwaben], while extremely favorable to the admission of Christianity into her little provincial kingdom, feared to proceed in the accomplishment of the object she desired, lest she should thereby incur the displeasure of her despotic suzerain.[5]

In March 1844, Kwaku Dua met with his councillors at Bantama to debate the matter of the missionaries. After much discussion it was agreed that the policy of encouraging them to visit Kumase should be continued, their presence being deemed in the national interest.[6] At just about the same time, however, an event occurred which did much to stimulate conservative opposition to the government's policy. Two young members of the royal family, Opoku Awusi and Opoku Ahoni, had both come strongly under Christian influence. Opoku Ahoni, who was next in line in the succession after the heir apparent Osei Kwadwo, pursued the path of learning and was soon able to read and write.[7] Opoku Awusi by contrast displayed the qualities of zealotry when, as Chapman reported it, he publicly burned

that fetish in which he from his childhood had trusted. This was done under circumstances of some interest. The companions of the youth, hearing what was about to take place, assembled to witness the destruction of the first fetish destroyed in Kumasi from conscientious motives. Every thing being in readiness, two or three large drums were brought out; and as the god hung suspended over the waiting flames, one of the party, in imitation of the signal given by the King's death-drum, struck his drum to the well-known sound, 'Cut him down! cut him down! cut him down'! The flames instantly received the long-adored image; while, at the moment of its fall, another drum answered the first, and loudly responded, 'Down'![8]

The event, especially in its derisory imitation of the procedure followed at official executions, was clearly such as to create a scandal. Although thereafter the Asantehene, the heir apparent, and a number

---

5 Methodist Mission Archives, London: MS of 1860, based upon Freeman's diaries, chapter xiii. See also *The Western Echo*, I, no. 16, 1886, p. 8.

6 *Wesleyan-Methodist Magazine*, September 1844, p. 778: Chapman to General Secretaries, dd. Kumase, 24 March 1844.

7 *The Western Echo*, I, no. 18, 31 May 1886, p. 8: letters from R. Brooking, dd. Kumase, 28 June and 19 July 1842.

8 *Wesleyan-Methodist Magazine*, September 1844, p. 777: Chapman to General Secretaries, dd. Kumase, 24 March 1844. *Ibid.* December 1844, p. 1042: report by T. B. Freeman.

of officers including the Bantamahene Gyawu continued to display personal friendship towards the missionaries, the climate of opinion in the capital began rapidly to change. Probably early in 1848 both Opoku Ahoni and Opoku Awusi were executed in the course of what Freeman referred to as 'politico-domestic excitements of the palace'; they perished, he added, 'not without strong suspicions that their attachment to Christianity had been a means, though not ostensibly shown, of shortening their earthly existence'.[9] By this time, however, the debate had become centred upon the issue of what the missionaries called 'human sacrifice' – an issue which they saw as essentially one of the eradication of a highly undesirable and unfortunate religious practice. But to the Asante councillors the matter was rather a very fundamental political one: that of the maintenance of law and order.

The issue of capital punishment

In Asante constitutional law, strict restraints existed upon the exercise of the power of life and death.[10] Technically, only those designated his agents by the Asantehene had the right to execute the death sentence. Those agents were the *adumfo* who, with the *abrafo* or constables, constituted the law enforcement agency under the Adumhene's official superintendence. Although the Asantehene might station *adumfo* in the most distant provinces, such as Dagomba (see p. 249), in general those condemned to death had to be despatched to Kumase for execution; [11] there a final appeal for clemency might be made, or in the case of a man of substance, the commutation of the sentence to a fine in gold might be negotiated (*atitodie*).[12] Held at a place called Akyere-kuro, 'the village of the condemned',[13] the prisoners were brought into the town to be executed at the times of the festivals – the Adaes or the Odwira; of the funerals of prominent citizens; of the entry of em-

---

9 Methodist Mission Archives: MS of 1860 based on Freeman's diaries, chapter XIII.
10 Kyerematen, 1966, p. 228, refers to the law of Okomfo Anokye, that only the Asantehene had the power of life and death, and that its exercise by others was an infringement of his sovereignty. For restrictions upon the powers of the *amanhene* in this context, see Rattray, 1927, pp. 91–2; Rattray, 1929, pp. 104, 139, 141, 161, 163, 184, 187, 210, 212, 227–8 and 231; Busia, 1951, p. 17.
11 See, for example, the case reported in Bowdich, 1819, pp. 27–8, of an elderly citizen of Fomena petitioning the Asantehene to be allowed to be executed there and so 'spared the fatigue of a journey to the capital'.
12 Gros, 1884, p. 190. It was possible for the fine of the condemned to be paid by someone else, to whom the former would then be enslaved. Some recruits for the Dutch East Indian Army were to be obtained in this way, see General State Archives, The Hague, KvG 716: proposals for establishing a recruiting depot at Kumase, 12 July 1859.
13 Rattray, 1927, p. 106, note.

bassies to the capital; and the like.[14] There appears to be little doubt that those thus executed were regarded as being despatched to the *Asaman,* where they constituted a servile class.[15] Similarly, upon the death of a public figure, a number of his close servants and wives would not only expect to be killed, but might insist upon it in order to maintain the relationship which they had enjoyed with him during his lifetime.[16] Basically, however, the mass execution of the condemned in public, on precisely those occasions when crowds were assembled in the capital, was seen as exerting a maximized deterrent effect upon the citizenry: making highly visible for a time the resources of coercion which the Asantehene controlled, and revealing briefly something of that reserve of legal terror and violence upon which the maintenance of the established order was ultimately predicated. In a most perspicuous comment on the matter, Casely Hayford wrote:

> Kumasi being the capital of the premier State of the Union, it formed the central convict establishment. Thither, month by month, were brought from the tributary towns persons who had been convicted of different offences and were sentenced to be executed. There was a chief of the executioners, and it was his duty to act as head-goaler. But the criminals were not executed as soon as they were brought to Kumasi. Some were never killed at all, and, in course of time, were reprieved. On state occasions, when all the people from the tributary provinces would flock to Kumasi, it was usual to execute a large number of those who had been condemned to die. Such public executions would, of course, have a deterrent effect upon the people of the State in general. And when we consider that not only murder but offences like stealing from a farm, rape, swearing an oath upon the King's life, selling a real-born Ashanti, kidnapping, immorality of a certain kind, were all punished with death, it is conceivable the large number of criminals that would be in a convict settlement at a given time. Let the enlightened reader, before moralising on the depravity of the Ashanti, recall to mind the fact that persons were hanged in England for sheep stealing, and witches burnt at Smithfield, not so very long ago.[17]

Seventy years earlier Dupuis, while making lurid reference to 'victims for the altars', nevertheless acknowledged that all those executed had

14 See, e.g. Gros, 1884, p. 190.
15 See *Further Correspondence,* C. 3386, 1882, p. 40: Watt to Acting Colonial Secretary, dd. Cape Coast, 2 February 1882. 'The Rev. Mr. Hayfron . . . does not think that King Mensah is a man of low murderous instincts, killing for the mere sake of killing; but that like all his family – indeed like all Ashantis – he honestly believes in a future state, a world of spirits, where the same social scale as that which exists here will be strictly observed; that there, as here, royalty and headmen and chiefs and generals must have stool-bearers and slaves, and that to let them depart from this earth unattended would be to inflict on them public and unending disgrace in the Ashanti world beyond the grave.'
16 See the interesting case of the Akropon woman reported in Reade, 1874, pp. 361–2.
17 Casely Hayford, 1903, pp. 29–30.

been found guilty of crimes – and most notably, it would seem, of treasonable conduct. They were not, he wrote,

indiscriminately chosen; they pass, indeed, under the name of delinquents, and are so far deserving that anathema, as having been convicted of speaking disrespectfully of the king, or of his government; of having harboured secret intentions inimical to the prosperity of the state; of having violated the civil laws; or of having invoked the wrath of their gods upon the heads of their oppressors; – a crime which, of course, passes for witchcraft and sorcery among the Ashantees . . .[18]

Collins has drawn attention to the way in which, in the early nineteenth century, European observers chose to misrepresent judicial executions as 'human sacrifices'.[19] On the occasion of the visit to Kumase of Governor Winniet of the Gold Coast in 1848, the official interest of the British Government in the matter was made clear. 'I embraced the favourable opportunity thus offered for speaking to him [the Asantehene] on the subject of human sacrifices', wrote Winniet. 'I told him of the anxious desire on the part of Her Majesty that these sanguinary rites should be abolished and begged his serious attention to a question so important to the cause of humanity.'[20] Two days later Kwaku Dua remarked, so Winniet reported, that

the number of human sacrifices made in Kumasi had been greatly exaggerated and that attempts had thus been made to spoil his name. He wished me to understand that human sacrifices were not so numerous in Kumasi as they had been represented and expressed a hope that reports relative to such a subject flying about the country would not be listened to and he then observed, 'I remember that when I was a little boy, I heard that the English came to the coast of Africa with their ships for cargoes of slaves for the purpose of taking them to their own country and eating them; but I have long since known that the report was false, and so it will be proved, in reference to many reports which have gone forth against me'.[21]

When in fact the Europeans visitors to the Asante capital spoke out against what they called 'human sacrifice', the residents could only construe this as an attack upon the penal system as such and as a threat, therefore, to the whole apparatus for the maintenance of public order. 'If I were to abolish human sacrifices', commented Kwaku Dua in 1842, 'I should deprive myself of one of the most effectual means of keeping the people in subjection.'[22] Seven years later he remarked to the missionary Hillard, that 'White people think that I

18 Dupuis, 1824, p. 240.
19 Collins, 1962, pp. 121–2.
20 Winniet's Diary, entry for 24 October 1848.
21 *Ibid.* entry for 26 October 1848.
22 T.B. Freeman, 1843, pp. 164–5.

594

kill my people for nothing; but I do not: if I were not to kill them when they commit theft and other bad things, they would come to the Mission-house, and steal everything you have, and would even take the clothes from your back.' Hillard was impressed by the reasoning, and observed: 'This is to a great extent true; and therefore we cannot urge the immediate abolition of stringent laws, which are doubtless necessary in the present condition of the Ashanti nation: especially when we remember what a short time it is ago when sheep-stealing, etc., were punished as capital crimes even in enlightened England.' [23]

The interference of the missionaries in the internal affairs of the nation, in so sensitive an area, could not fail to elicit a reaction from the conservative politicians. By 1849 it was already apparent to Hillard that although many councillors, and the Asantehene himself, were not opposed in principle to changes in the penal code, they were unlikely actively to press for reform. 'I have never heard any one advocate the cruel customs practised here', he reported, 'but rather the contrary, as they freely confess that they are bad; and as an excuse or palliation of the case, they invariably say that it is the custom of their country, that their ancestors did so, and they must do as they did . . .' [24] Four years later, in 1853, the Rev. T. Laing reported that the prospects for the future of the mission in Kumase appeared dismal in view of Kwaku Dua's own continuing adherence to the traditional values of society.

The state of the work of God in Asante is rather discouraging at present, from the circumstance of the people being afraid to expose themselves to the ire of the king, whose frown means death for people becoming Christians . . . They always do what the king sanctions, whether good or bad, so that as the king is a pagan, they must all remain pagans too.[25]

That Laing, in that very year, involved himself in secretly passing vital political and military intelligence on Asante affairs to the British administration on the Gold Coast (see p. 217), probably became known to Kwaku Dua's efficient espionage service. Although for the remainder of Kwaku Dua's reign missionaries continued to be allowed into the capital, their activities were carefully supervised: the government utilized their services as intermediaries with the British while at the same time minimizing the impact they might have had upon metropolitan society.

23 *Wesleyan-Methodist Magazine*, May 1849, pp. 550–1: Hillard to General Secretaries, dd. Kumase, 16 January 1849.
24 *Idem*.
25 Reindorf, 2nd ed., n.d., p. 235.

The role of the Owusu Ansas in politics

Owusu Ansa as catechist and missionary

The career of Owusu Ansa, son of Osei Bonsu, exemplifies well the nature of the conflict which developed between conservative and progressive politicians, for he more than anyone appeared ideally qualified for leadership of the latter. Owusu Ansa and Owusu Nkwantabisa, son of Osei Yaw, had been delivered into the care of the British in 1831 (p. 190). Owusu Ansa was then only some nine years of age.[26] Both were schooled first in Cape Coast, and then, from 1836, in England (p. 204). Owusu Ansa was baptized into the Anglican Church as John, and Owusu Nkwantabisa as William. Following a request from the Asantehene Kwaku Dua I, both were repatriated to the Gold Coast in 1841, both became members of the Wesleyan Methodist community, and both accompanied T. B. Freeman to Kumase at the end of that year. The Asantehene was much affected at seeing the two again, after their ten years' absence.[27] The British government granted each a pension of £100 a year. They were required by Governor Maclean to reside in Kumase; to pay the greatest deference to the Asantehene while displaying by the example of their lives the virtues of Christianity; and to report twice a year to Cape Coast in order to collect their pensions and generally maintain contact with the British authorities there. In Kumase, however, the paths of the two *ahenemma* or 'princes' diverged radically. In 1842 Owusu Nkwantabisa was charged with adultery with a wife of the senior counselor Kwame Poku Agyeman. The woman was executed, and Owusu Nkwantabisa was reprieved only – as it is said – 'because of his education'. Kwaku Dua suggested that Governor Maclean should likewise take a clement view of the matter; but Owusu Nkwantabisa's pension was stopped.[28] He remained nevertheless in Kumase, and in the late 1840s was among those who conducted the government's correspondence with the British.[29] In 1846–7 he held the position of British Resident in the Asante capital, but Governor Winniet regarded him as unsuited to the office and believed him not to enjoy the full confidence of Kwaku Dua and his people.[30] Owusu Nkwantabisa died in 1859.

Owusu Ansa, by contrast, had left Kumase in 1844. It is likely that he was much affected by the opposition of the many in positions of authority, and notably the senior counselor Kwame Poku Agyeman,

---

26 *Ibid.* p. 251.
27 T. B. Freeman, 1843, p. 124.
28 PRO, CO. 267/179: Maclean to Stanley, dd. Cape Coast, 31 December 1842. State Archives, The Hague, KvG 365: Elmina Journal, entry dd. 30 October 1842.
29 See, for example, PRO, CO. 96/11: Kwaku Dua to Maclean, dd. Kumase, 17 April 1847.
30 *Ibid.* Winniet to Grey, dd. Cape Coast, 10 May 1847. CO. 96/12: Proposition for improving the Government . . . on the Gold Coast, filed 8 February 1847.

who believed that education would encourage rebelliousness in the people.[31] In 1844 the situation worsened as a result of the *cause célèbre* of Opoku Awusi. Kwame Poku Agyeman appears to have been further confirmed in his opposition to the opening of a school in the capital, and his attitude towards both Owusu Ansa and Owusu Nkwantabisa became markedly more hostile.[32] In the circumstances Owusu Ansa decided to seek closer involvement in the affairs of the Wesleyan-Methodist Missionary Society, and left Kumase for Cape Coast. There, it was reported,

he became a regular attendant at our mission-chapel, and an earnest seeker of the salvation which the gospel offers. Having at length experienced the saving power of Christianity, the public profession of which he had previously assumed, he became an agent of this society; and in the offices of interpreter, class-leader, and local preacher, has continued to give such proof of sincere piety and devotedness to the work of the mission, that he has been sent, by the unanimous voice of the missionaries in the district, as a catechist to Kumasi.[33]

Owusu Ansa in fact arrived back in Kumase, as catechist in charge of the station there, on 21 May 1850.[34] At the end of that year he reported the enthusiasm with which he had been received in Dwaben, but remarked that fear still prevented the citizens of Kumase from associating themselves with the activities of the mission.[35] Transferred to Abakrampa and replaced in Kumase by T. Laing, Owusu Ansa nevertheless obtained leave of absence, and proceeded to Kumase probably late in 1852, as relations between the governments of Asante and the Protectorate became acutely strained (see pp. 215–18).[36] On 16 March 1853, he wrote on behalf of Kwaku Dua to Governor Hill to notify him of the visit of Akyampon Tia – of the Boakye Yam Kuma stool – to Jukwa.[37] It would seem clear that Owusu Ansa was not privy to the messages which Laing smuggled out of Kumase, through T. B. Freeman to Governor Hill, and which contained information on Asante's military preparedness.[38] Kwaku Dua appointed Owusu Ansa an emissary to the British authorities, in which capacity he returned to Cape

31 T. B. Freeman, 1843, pp. 150, 168.
32 Methodist Mission Archives, London: Chapman to Freeman, dd. Kumase, 7 October 1844.
33 Fox, 1851, p. 604.
34 *Wesleyan-Methodist Magazine*, October 1850, p. 1108: Hart to WMMS, dd. Cape Coast, 29 June 1850.
35 *Ibid*. January 1852, pp. 96–7: Owusu Ansa to Freeman, dd. Kumase, 27 December 1850. Compare Fox, 1851, p. 604.
36 Methodist Mission Archives, London: Wharton to Osborn, dd. Accra, 4 April 1853.
37 *Despatches . . . relating to the warfare*, C. 703, 1853, p. 8: Owusu Ansa to Hill, dd. Kumase, 16 March 1853.
38 *Ibid*. pp. 15–6: Laing to Freeman, dd. Kumase, 31 March 1853.

Coast.[39] At the beginning of August he was instructed by the Mission Society to return to Kumase and take charge of the station there once again. He begged, however, to be allowed to remain in Cape Coast for a period, referring to the harassing nature of his experiences in Kumase.[40] It seems likely that on the coast Owusu Ansa had learned of Laing's undercover role as agent of the Gold Coast government, and had undergone a crisis of conscience. The Society agreed to revoke his posting to Kumase, and Freeman wrote: 'he (Ossu Ansah) would be best away lest from his national connexions on the one hand, and his English connexions on the other hand, we should place him in a difficult position and produce embarrassment.' [41] Owusu Ansa withdrew from active missionary work, and took a position as master at the Cape Coast Boys' School.[42] There he remained for some years.

In Kumase the purge of Kwaku Dua's political opponents reached its climax in 1859, and the peace party retained a temporary ascendancy (see pp. 491–2). It was probably no coincidence that almost immediately, word reached Owusu Ansa of the Asantehene's desire that he should visit Kumase. In 1860 he informed the Mission Society of this, and at the same time pointed out that his presence there might help in lessening the risk of conflict between the governments of Asante and the Protectorate arising from the recent disturbances in Akyem Kotoku. By this period he clearly aspired to enter into Asante politics, and saw himself as potentially, 'the instrument of his country's salvation'.[43] The Mission Society refused to consider his transfer back to Kumase. In March 1862, however, he was chosen to accompany the Rev. W. West there. Kwaku Dua I issued orders to the *nkwansrafo* to expedite the journey of his 'son'. The party entered the capital on the 15th, and departed for the coast five weeks later.[44] While no account is known to survive of Owusu Ansa's personal meetings with the Asantehene, within a few months of his return to Cape Coast he had submitted his resignation to the Mission Society.[45]

In 1863 Kwaku Dua, under strong pressure from the war interest,

---

39 *Idem*. See also Methodist Mission Archives, London: Freeman to Osborn, dd. Cape Coast, 22 August 1854.
40 *Ibid:* Freeman to General Secretaries, dd. Cape Coast, 3 August 1853; Freeman to Osborn, dd. Cape Coast, 22 August 1854.
41 *Idem*.
42 *Ibid*. Wharton to Osborn, dd. Cape Coast, 13 July 1861.
43 *Ibid*. Owusu Ansa to General Secretaries, dd. Cape Coast, 11 April 1860.
44 *Wesleyan-Methodist Magazine,* September 1862, pp. 858–62, and October 1862, pp. 954–9: visit of the Rev. W. West and the Rev. Owusu Ansa to Kumase.
45 Methodist Mission Archives, London: West to Osborn, dd. Cape Coast, 12 February 1863. The immediate cause of the resignation was said to be marital problems.

finally authorized the despatch of an army into the Protectorate. Its commander, Owusu Koko, was aligned politically with the peace party, and was instructed to limit the military operations in such a way as to avoid direct confrontation with the British (see pp. 221–2; 493–4). In the circumstances, Owusu Ansa is probably to be seen as acting on the basis of an understanding with Kwaku Dua and the peace interest. In April 1863 Governor Pine accepted his offer to serve as intermediary between himself and the Asantehene. Owusu Ansa, however, found the road to Kumase closed and was unable to carry out the task.[46] On 22 May he received a new commission from Pine: to negotiate with Owusu Koko, his brother, whose forces then lay in Akyem Kotoku. According to Owusu Ansa, his intervention was decisive in persuading Owusu Koko to withdraw the army from the Protectorate,[47] thus overruling the views of a number of the more militant subordinate commanders. Owusu Koko, however, insisted on Owusu Ansa's returning with him to Kumase.[48] Back again in Cape Coast by the middle of 1863, Owusu Ansa requested from Pine a new appointment to enable him to return to Asante and negotiate a full peace settlement.[49] But in fact both the Asante and Protectorate governments were by then dominated by those committed to a trial of strength, and Owusu Ansa's offer was not taken up. He was given instead temporary employment in the Customs Department.[50]

Owusu Ansa in the service of Kofi Kakari

On news reaching the coast of Kwaku Dua's death on 27 April 1867, Owusu Ansa proceeded immediately to Kumase. He remained there for some three months, and witnessed the failure of Owusu Koko's attempt to exclude Kofi Kakari from the succession in favour of the young son of Yaa Kyaa, Kwaku Dua Kuma. Although Kofi Kakari was brought to office on a war party platform, he was known to be very attached to Owusu Ansa [51] and offered him a position in his admini-

---

46 *Despatches . . . explaining the cause of war . . .* , C. 385, 1864, p. 8: Pine to Newcastle, dd. Cape Coast, 15 April 1863.

47 *Ibid.* pp. 10–11: Pine to Newcastle, dd. Cape Coast, 10 June 1863; p. 12: Owusu Ansa to Pine, dd. Gyadam-on-Birrim, 1 June 1863. For the commission, see *Further Correspondence*, C. 891, Pt II of 1874, p. 189: Pine to Owusu Ansa, dd. Cape Coast, 22 May 1863.

48 *Ibid.* pp. 188–9: Owusu Ansa to Kimberley, dd. Freetown, Sierra Leone, 22 August 1873. Methodist Mission Archives, London: Tregaskis to Owusu Ansa, dd. 22 August 1877.

49 *The African Times*, III, no. 29, 23 November 1863, p. 52: Owusu Ansa to Pine, dd. Cape Coast, 16 September 1863.

50 *Further Correspondence*, C. 891, Pt II of 1874, pp. 160–1: Harley to Kimberley, dd. Cape Coast, 12 August 1873.

51 *The African Times*, VII, no. 77, 23 November 1867, p. 54: letter dd. Cape Coast, 4 October 1867. See also Leiden MS H.509, entry dd. 2 July 1867: Kofi Kakari

stration. Owusu Ansa returned to Cape Coast at the end of September 1867, but apparently only to put his affairs there in order. He departed again for Kumase on 10 October. Described as one of the 'royal secretaries',[52] he was assigned important responsibilities in the field of foreign affairs. Numerous outgoing letters from Kumase over the next three years were clearly drafted by Owusu Ansa, and frequently signed by him on behalf of the Asantehene.[53] He was assisted by the Wesleyan catechist J. S. Watts, who had been detained in Kumase since 1862 and who had apparently come to be regarded more or less as a public servant.[54] Although Owusu Ansa's return to Asante in 1867 had been approved by Governor Ussher of the Gold Coast, he was not offered any official position.[55] In Kumase, therefore, Owusu Ansa was fully subject to the administrative regulations in force there, and was not permitted to conduct other than official correspondence with foreign agencies.[56] It is apparent, however, that while highly regarded by the Asantehene as an administrator, his political position was such as to isolate him from the dominant majority in the councils; and attempts were made to discredit him.[57]

Owusu Ansa's solicitude for the interests of the Europeans who had been taken prisoner by Adu Bofo in 1869 – for Ramseyer, Kühne and Bonnat – was constant. His frequent intervention with Kofi Kakari on their behalf, 'against the claims of some of the Warrior Chiefs',[58] was believed to have saved their lives. Ramseyer and Kühne themselves referred to Owusu Ansa as 'a man to whom we owe the deepest gratitude, and who seemed to have been expressly sent to Coomassie, to prove a messenger of grace for us during our long trial'.[59] The matter of ransom for the prisoners was the subject of many debates in Council (see pp. 502–3). Of that on 22 July 1871 Bonnat noted: 'The session lasted from morning until 3 p.m. There are, it appears, two parties present, that of peace which wishes to set us free, and that of war which

presented 'the gentleman Owoesoe Ansanh' with 4 oz 8 ackies of gold as a present.
52 *Der Evangelische Heidenbote,* October 1870, p. 113.
53 Methodist Mission Archives, London: Tregaskis to Owusu Ansa, dd. 22 August 1877, p. 7. For examples of such correspondence see *Der Evangelische Heidenbote,* October 1870, p. 113. *Correspondence relative to the Cession,* C. 670, 1872, p. 11: Owusu Ansa to Governor, dd. Kumase, 2 and 4 November 1870; pp. 13: Kofi Kakari and Owusu Ansa to Governor, dd. 24 November 1870.
54 *Idem.* One letter is witnessed by 'J. S. Watts, Linguist'. See also Ramseyer and Kühne, 1875, pp. 89, 99, 101.
55 *Further Correspondence,* C. 891, Pt II of 1874, p. 161: Owusu Ansa to Governor, petition enclosed in Harley to Kimberley, dd. 12 August 1873.
56 *Correspondence,* C. 670, 1872, pp. 10–11: Kühne and Ramseyer to Governor, dd. Kumase, October 1870. Compare Ramseyer and Kühne, 1875, p. 91.
57 Methodist Mission Archives, London: Tregaskis to Owusu Ansa, dd. 22 August 1877, p. 7.
58 *Ibid.* p. 6.
59 Ramseyer and Kühne, 1875, p. 75, note.

opposes our release. This latter, which has at its head the victorious general [Adu Bofo], seems to overrule the other.' [60] Throughout, Owusu Ansa consistently advised the Asantehene to release the captives without ransom. Thereby he incurred the hostility of the supporters of Adu Bofo.[61] It was, however, in his handling of Dutch affairs that Owusu Ansa was to encounter his gravest problems.

In September 1870 it was reported that Owusu Ansa had, 'through the influence of the Dutch, become an object of suspicion to the king', but that he was by then largely restored to favour.[62] Details of the episode are lacking, but the issue presumably revolved around the circumstances of Akyampon Yaw's mission to the southwestern Gold Coast in 1868–9 (see pp. 227–30). On 24 November 1870 Owusu Ansa drafted Kofi Kakari's protest to Governor Ussher on the cession of Elmina to the British, pointing out that Elmina belonged to Asante by 'right of arms' (see text, p. 231). The subsequent correspondence between the British and Dutch resulted in the arrest, on 14 April 1871, of Akyampon Yaw, then Asante Resident at Elmina. Meanwhile, on 2 February 1871 Owusu Ansa had left Kumase to organize an exchange of Fante and Asante prisoners with the British.[63] The transfer was effected at the Pra river on 2 March.[64] He proceeded thence to Cape Coast to act as manager for the Asante embassy headed by Afrifa and Kotirko which had been sent from Kumase to negotiate with the British a settlement of outstanding disputes. The party arrived at Cape Coast on 13 March, and talks commenced the next day.[65] It was presumably upon learning of the arrest of Akyampon Yaw in Elmina that Owusu Ansa and the ambassadors visited that town. On 18 and 19 May 1871, negotiations with the Dutch Commissioner Nagtglas took place. A plea was made for the release of Akyampon Yaw, on which issue Owusu Ansa swore the Great Oath. The talks then took an unexpected course. Afrifa accused Owusu Ansa publicly, of having written the letter of 24 November 1870 without authority. He stated that Elmina did not belong to Asante by 'right of arms'; and asserted that the Asantehene could not have been present when the letter was written since he was forbidden by law to see writing paper! [66] Akyampon Yaw seemingly associated himself with the accusation.[67] In

[60] Gros, 1884, p. 229.
[61] See, e.g. Ramseyer and Kühne, 1875, p. 157.
[62] *Ibid.* p. 89.
[63] *Ibid.* p. 115.
[64] Methodist Mission Archives, London: Tregaskis to Owusu Ansa, dd. 22 August 1877, p. 7.
[65] *Idem. Correspondence*, C. 670, 1872, p. 18: Ussher to Kennedy, dd. Cape Coast, 21 March 1871.
[66] General State Archives, The Hague, Ministry of Foreign Affairs, B. 79, Afst. iv: Nagtglas to Minister of Colonies, dd. Elmina, 20 May 1871. *Correspondence*, C. 670, 1872, pp. 19–20: Nagtglas to Ussher, dd. Elmina, 20 May 1871.
[67] Ramseyer and Kühne, 1875, p. 313.

January 1873, however, he was to bring Afrifa to account on the matter and to have him removed from office and disgraced (see pp. 232–3).

Akyampon Yaw, half-brother of Kwaku Dua I and a leading figure in the war party, represented the 'old guard' in Asante politics and presumably regarded the progressive tendencies of Owusu Ansa with much antipathy. In much distress, on 30 May 1871 Owusu Ansa wrote to the European captives in Kumase informing them of his position: 'A very serious accusation has been brought against me respecting the letter which I wrote to the administrator by the king's order, with regard to the right of the king to the town and fort of Elmina . . . Now, if the king deny having authorized me to write that letter, I shall hardly come up (to Coomassie).' [68] In a letter of 21 June he remarked further:

Now I expect to prove how far the king and his council are conscientious, by their owning or denying that I was fully authorised by them to write that letter. The governor of Elmina has decided not to deliver the usual yearly payment unless he apologises with regard to it. I am waiting to see whether the king really will beg pardon in order to receive that payment (four hundred dollars a year) and my dear brothers, my sense seems to dictate to me that it is best that I should stay here and await the end of all this before I take any further steps. I know my countrymen well enough to be sure that it is advisable for me to be careful. I assure you that if they withdraw themselves from me in this affair, it will be all the worse for them.[69]

The Asantehene apparently did disown the vexatious letter of 24 November 1870, by the so-called 'Certificate of Apology' of 19 August 1871. But the authenticity of that document is itself in question (see p. 233). All that is quite clear is that the rising tide of popular discontent in Asante was such as to persuade the Asantehene of the desirability of Owusu Ansa's return. In October or November, so it was reported, 'the king summoned prince Ansa, whose advice he greatly needed'.[70]

The risk which Owusu Ansa took in returning to Kumase in December 1871 was a calculated one. The British gave him recognition once again, as intermediary between the Gold Coast government and the Asantehene on the matter of the ransom of the European captives.[71] Styling himself 'His Excellency's messenger to the Court of Coomassie', his status in the matter was clearly much enhanced.[72]

68 *Ibid.* p. 312.
69 *Ibid.* pp. 313–14. For a differing account of Owusu Ansa's position, see Coombs, 1963, chapter 5.
70 Ramseyer and Kühne, 1875, p. 141.
71 *Correspondence*, C. 670, 1872, p. 36: Salmon to Fergusson, dd. Cape Coast, 7 December 1871.
72 *Papers relating to the Ashantee Invasion,* C. 266, 1873, p. 86: Kofi Kakari to Salmon, dd. Kumase, 20 February 1872.

Indeed, on his journey back from Cape Coast, with the concurrence of Kotirko and Afrifa he ordered the *nkwansrafo* to close the great-road behind them – in which decision he clearly greatly exceeded his authority. Dressed in British-style military uniform, he was received by Kofi Kakari on 31 December.[73] Privately the Asantehene informed Owusu Ansa of his own increasing sympathies with the peace party and of his desire for 'peace, and a flourishing trade with the Coast'.[74] On 29 January 1872 both Owusu Ansa and Kotirko addressed the Council, reporting that a peace settlement with the British was predicated upon the return of the European captives. Under attack from another of his brothers, the acting Akyempemhene and war party leader Barempa, Owusu Ansa was obliged to defend his actions in closing the Cape Coast road. He had considered it inadvisable, he argued, to allow Asante traders to visit that town until either the disputes with the British had been settled, or a representative of the Asante government returned there.[75] The Council appears to have expressed its confidence in Owusu Ansa's conduct, and to have authorized his continuing employment as general manager of Asante embassies to the Gold Coast. Leaving his plantation outside Kumase in charge of Bonnat, Owusu Ansa arrived back in Cape Coast on 25 April 1872.[76] The prospects for peace appeared good. On 31 May Owusu Ansa wrote to Governor Pope Hennessy to express the pleasure of newly-arrived diplomats from Kumase at the welcome they had received. He reiterated the point that Kofi Kakari himself would release the European captives without ransom but was restrained from doing so by his councillors.[77] The Governor confirmed that up to £1,000 would be paid not as ransom, but to reimburse Adu Bofo his 'expenses'. 'Prince Ansah', reported the Governor, 'who is in constant communication with the Ambassadors, tells me that all difficulties are now removed. He is confident that the King will order the speedy release of the captives.'[78] In Kumase, however, at the meetings of the Asantemanhyiamu commencing 2 September and 22 October, it has been seen that the decision for war was taken. The main army crossed the Pra River into the Protectorate on 22 January 1873. Although Owusu Ansa did not draw back from making known in Kumase his opposition to the war party government,[79] the British authorities nevertheless suspected him

[73] Ramseyer and Kühne, 1875, p. 153.
[74] *Ibid.* p. 155.
[75] *Ibid.* pp. 156–7.
[76] *Ibid.* pp. 153; 155. Methodist Mission Archives, London: Tregaskis to Owusu Ansa, dd. 22 August 1877, p. 9.
[77] *Papers*, C. 266, 1873, p. 88: Owusu Ansa to Governor, dd. Cape Coast, 31 May 1872.
[78] *Ibid.* pp. 89–90: Hennessy to Kimberley, dd. Cape Coast, 8 June 1872.
[79] Ramseyer and Kühne, 1875, p. 215.

of having had advance knowledge of the invasion.[80] The citizens of Cape Coast believed him to be sending military intelligence to Kumase, and to be procuring munitions for the Asante forces. On 13 April 1873 a mob attacked his house and seven of his servants were murdered. Owusu Ansa himself was saved by the intervention of the militia, and was confined in Cape Coast Castle. From there he was deported to Sierra Leone.[81]

Unshaken in the belief in his ability – indeed, mission – to bring about a lasting peace between his country and Britain, Owusu Ansa adressed a letter to the Secretary of State for the Colonies in London, Lord Kimberley. 'My present object', he observed,

in writing to your Lordship is to say, that I think that from my position as a member of the Royal family of Ashantee, which gives me a certain standing in the country, and uncle to the King with whom I have been on terms of intimate friendship, and for my close acquaintance with all the Ashantee nobles and generals, I think if I were put in a position to communicate authoritatively with the King of Ashantee as an Envoy from the Queen I might be able to terminate the present unhappy war on term honourable and advantageous to both sides. I think, to give me weight with the King of Ashantee I ought to have with me some credentials to show I was an authorized messenger from the Queen. It would largely assist me if there were sent with me some Europeans . . . I believe, with proper credentials, I could bring about a lasting peace now.[82]

Unknown to Owusu Ansa, however, in London plans for the invasion of Asante were already being prepared, and on 13 August Wolseley had accepted command of the expeditionary force.[83] Exiled, and his efforts in the cause of peace seemingly ineffective, Owusu Ansa received unexpected support from the Wesleyan Mission Society in London. Benjamin Tregaskis was probably responsible for arranging for Owusu Ansa to be brought from Sierra Leone to England and for preparing, in 1874, what was described as his 'vindication'.[84] 'I think it is evident', Tregaskis later wrote to Owusu Ansa, 'that you were the only person who did, or could, through long years, and down to almost the latest period before the War, influence them [the Asante councillors] at all,

---

80 *Further Correspondence,* C. 891, Pt II of 1874, pp. 160–1: Harley to Kimberley, dd. Cape Coast, 12 August 1873.
81 For Owusu Ansa's own account of the episode, see Hertz, 1885, Chapter XXIV. See also Ellis, 1881, pp. 15–18.
82 *Further Correspondence,* C. 891, Pt II of 1874, p. 188: Owusu Ansa to Kimberley, dd. Freetown, Sierra Leone, 22 August 1873.
83 Wolseley, 1903, II, 267. PRO, CO. 96/101: Kimberley to Wolseley, dd. 10 September 1873.
84 Methodist Mission Archives, London: Tregaskis to Owusu Ansa, dd. 22 August 1877, p. 12.

beneficially.'[85] But in Liverpool, too, Owusu Ansa enjoyed the friendship of Radcliffe, senior partner in the firm of Radcliffe and Durant.[86] A link was thereby forged which was subsequently to become of considerable importance to the Asante government.

Owusu Ansa and Mensa Bonsu's new civil service

Under Kofi Kakari, Owusu Ansa had pointed the way towards important administrative reforms: for he himself was first of a new class of managerial and advisory bureaucrats whose service to the state was based upon what Weber called 'free contract' and whose status was therefore quite distinct from that of the members of the administrative or *asomfo* class which had emerged as a result of the reforms initiated by Osei Kwadwo a century earlier. The distinction was one that was quite apparent to the British officers of the Gold Coast government who, with reference to the arrival on the coast of emissaries from Kumase, observed: 'Mr. Ansah always accompanied the envoys, and seemed to act as their chief adviser.'[87] The emissaries – *asomfo* dependent upon a government which had total control over their persons, property and indeed lives – were instructed in detail on the terms which they had to negotiate; Owusu Ansa's role, by contrast, was to develop initiatives in such a way as to ensure the success of those negotiations.

Owusu Ansa was repatriated in 1874. He appears to have revisited Kumase in that year, probably after the removal from office of Kofi Kakari in October. A quarter of a century earlier Owusu Ansa had shared the view of many of the Wesleyan missionaries, that the politically inarticulate masses of Asante were nevertheless receptive to the idea of change. 'The people of Kumasi', he wrote, 'are in a state of slavery under their masters; they, indeed, listen to the preaching of the Gospel with attentive ear, and they know the freeness and happiness of those who embrace it; yet they so dread their masters that they will not come forward.'[88] By 1874, however, the situation had changed. Out of the anti-war agitation of the early 1870s a movement had emerged with a growing commitment to a more radical programme of social, political and economic reform. Owusu Ansa arrived back in Kumase to find that he enjoyed, for the first time in his career, a vocal political constituency. 'As Providence would have it', he remarked, 'the people

85 *Ibid.* p. 10.
86 *The Times* (London), 18 April 1895, p. 8.
87 *Papers*, C. 266, 1873, p. 161: Salmon to Hennessy, dd. Cape Coast, 19 October 1872.
88 *Wesleyan-Methodist Magazine*, January 1852, pp. 96–7: Owusu Ansa to Freeman, dd. Kumase, 27 December 1850.

acknowledged before me that if they had listened to my advice before the War, they would not now have brought upon themselves the ruin of their Country.' [89] It is clear that Owusu Ansa held talks with the new Asantehene Mensa Bonsu – who had immediately announced his desire for 'peace, trade, and open roads' – and was able to obtain a mandate to design a programme of modernization and reform.[90] 'I am', so he informed Freeman in 1875, 'now working or acting as principal adviser to my nephew Ossai Mensah the King.' [91] Priority was given to the development of the new civil service, and Owusu Ansa was authorized to recruit non-Asante personnel on contract to it. He returned to Cape Coast.

On 18 April 1875, Marie-Joseph Bonnat returned from Europe to the Gold Coast. Having been closely associated with Owusu Ansa during the period of his captivity in Kumase, the Frenchman was on record as sharing the prince's belief in the 'progress, slow but sure, of the new ideas that had found an entry into Ashanti'.[92] Lodging in Owusu Ansa's house in Cape Coast, Bonnat was readily persuaded into entering the service of the Asante government. So, too, was Alister H. Campbell, a prospector of whose earlier career little is as yet known.[93] Owusu Ansa, Bonnat and Campbell left Cape Coast on 28 May 1875, and arrived in Kumase on 7 June. They were received with much ceremony.[94] 'Several days after his arrival', reported the biographer of Bonnat, 'he became the confidential adviser (*conseiller intime*) of the king and one of the most important persons in the State.' [95]

The government was at the time, much preoccupied with the rebellion of the Dwabenhene Asafo Agyei (see pp. 511–12), and there were those within it who urged the immediate recourse to arms. Already Mensa Bonsu had utilized the services of an American gold-miner, Dane McEacheren, by sending him to visit one of the villages attacked by the Dwaben and asking him to publicize the matter once he returned to the Gold Coast. In the tense situation which prevailed in

89 Methodist Mission Archives, London: Owusu Ansa to Buxton, cited in Tregaskis to Owusu Ansa, dd. 22 August 1877, p. 12.
90 *Ibid.* p. 23. It may have been at this time that he was given a grant of land for farming purposes on the West Nsuben River less than half a mile from central Kumase, see PRO, CO. 96/344: Hodgson to Chamberlain, dd. 22 September 1899. On the other hand, he had acquired some land under Kofi Kakari, see Ramseyer and Kühne, 1875, p. 164.
91 *Ibid:* Owusu Ansa to Freeman, dd. Kumase, 10 November 1875.
92 *The African Times*, XIV, no. 160, 30 October 1874, p. 40.
93 According to *The Gold Coast Times*, II, no. 1, 22 May 1875, p. 3, Campbell had recently arrived from England 'for the purpose of obtaining specimens of the feathered tribes of the country, of studying its geology, and obtaining specimens of its auriferous quarts [*sic*]'.
94 Gros, 1884, p. 254. Ermann, 1876, p. 359.
95 Gros, 1884, p. 254.

Kumase, it was arranged that Owusu Ansa should address members of the Council there on 14 June. 'No doubt his exertions will have a great influence upon them', wrote Bonnat, 'for they regret very much to have not listened to the advices he gave them before.' [96] Owusu Ansa was able to persuade the Council into authorizing the two Europeans, Bonnat and Campbell, to negotiate a peace settlement with the Dwabenhene. 'King Mensah', recorded Gros, 'instructed his new adviser [Bonnat] to go and see the rebel monarch and, if he could, restore the revolted people to submission to, and respect for, their sovereign.' [97] But Dwaben envoys who had been in Cape Coast at the time of Bonnat's return from Europe had remarked of him: 'this gentleman says he is going to Coomassie with Ossoo Ansah, who is a Coomassie man, and will teach him Coomassie tricks before he reaches Coomassie'.[98] When Governor Strahan's sympathy towards the Dwaben cause became known there, the failure of the Bonnat–Campbell mission was predictable. Asafo Agyei accused the two Europeans of visiting Dwaben to collect military intelligence, and refused to make any concessions whatsoever in the interests of peace. Bonnat and Campbell returned to the capital on 7 July, after a week's absence.[99]

It was immediately decided to employ the two Europeans on further missions: Bonnat to negotiate an agreement with the Kpembewura of eastern Gonja, upon whose attitude depended the revival of the Salaga trade (see p. 283), and Campbell was to treat with the Gyamanhene whose loyalty was in doubt (see p. 288). In view of Asafo Agyei's declared intention of closing the great-roads across the northern hinterland, Mensa Bonsu strongly affirmed his policy in a letter of 16 July addressed to the Governor of the Gold Coast and witnessed by Bonnat, Campbell and Owusu Ansa:

I, lawful King of Ashantee and its dependencies, do energetically protest against that presumption and usurpation of Asafu Agai, Chief of Djuabin; and in the name of the Treaty [of Fomena] signed by my brother and predecessor with the English Government, and that Treaty which is my duty to see observed. I shall give an escort to Messrs. Bonnat and Campbell to go wherever they please in the interior, and if Asafu Agai's people put

96 *Papers relating to Her Majesty's Possessions in West Africa*, C. 1402, 1876, pp. 80–1: Bonnat to Strahan, dd. Kumase, 11 June 1875; p. 81: Mensa Bonsu to Governor, dd. Kumase, 11 June 1875. D. McEacheren, with Bonnat, Owusu Ansa, and Kofi Nkan, were signatories to this last letter; it is unclear whether he had any official standing in the Asante administration.
97 Gros, 1884, p. 254. *Papers*, C. 1402, 1876, pp. 71–2: Mensa Bonsu to Lyall *et al.*, dd. Kumase, 19 July 1875.
98 *Ibid.* pp. 76–7: Strahan to Carnarvon, dd. Cape Coast, 14 August 1875.
99 *Ibid.* pp. 81–2: Bonnat to Strahan, dd. Kumase, 7 July 1875; pp. 82–3: Mensa Bonsu to Strahan, dd. Kumase, 16 July 1875; pp. 90–5: Bonnat to Strahan, dd. Cape Coast, 30 September 1875.

themselves in the way to the interior, to put their master's threatenings into execution, I shall then be under the necessity of declaring war against the rebellious Chief, and chastise him as he deserves; and I believe, in doing so, I am not trespassing upon the Treaty, but simply making it to be respected and observed strictly.[100]

In August Campbell was back on the Gold Coast, making preparations for the Gyaman mission.[101] By the end of the month he had returned to Kumase,[102] but for reasons which are not clear, the proposed journey was cancelled. Campbell was still in metropolitan Asante in November 1875, and was apparently engaged in trading. Both he and Owusu Ansa were involved in the confrontation between Mensa Bonsu and the British Commissioner Gouldsbury on the 19th of that month, but the latter's account of the matter is so obviously distorted that the nature of the issues are totally obscured.[103] Campbell's subsequent movements have not been traced. Certainly, however, when the mission to Gyaman was finally dispatched from Kumase in 1878, another European had been appointed to lead it.

Bonnat and the scheme to revive the Salaga trade

Campbell's letter of appointment as conductor of the Gyaman mission has not been found. Bonnat's commission is, fortunately, preserved. The failure of the Dwaben negotiations had led a number of councillors – presumably the more traditionally inclined ones – to question the wisdom of employing Europeans in government service. Their doubts increased when a message – of unknown origin – reached the Asantehene to warn him that Bonnat's real purpose 'was to look at the interior, and hand it over to the English Government'.[104] The accusation was not entirely without substance. In 1874 Bonnat had interested a number of *concessionnaires* in Liverpool in a scheme which is best described in his own words:

To penetrate into 'Salaga,' create a trade there at two hundred miles of the nearest sea-shore, far from all European protection, rendered almost impossible by the numerous difficulties which one meets on the navigation of the Volta – in a country of which from centuries the Ashantee Government has kept jealously the entire monopoly of the trade – and thereby open one of the richest parts of central Africa to commerce and civilization . . .[105]

100 *Ibid.* pp. 82–3: Mensa Bonsu to Strahan, dd. Kumase, 16 July 1875.
101 *Ibid.* p. 84: Strahan to Carnarvon, dd. Cape Coast, 6 September 1875.
102 *Ibid.* p. 86: Mensa Bonsu to Governor, dd. Kumase, 26 August 1875.
103 *Ibid.* pp. 116–17: Gouldsbury to Strahan, dd. Bomfa, Dwaben, 30 November 1875.
104 *Ibid.* p. 92: Bonnat to Strahan, dd. Cape Coast, 30 September 1875.
105 *Ibid.* p. 90.

In particular, he secured the cooperation of M. de Cardi, who he had met on the Oil Rivers in 1866,[106] and who agreed to capitalize the venture.[107] It was presumably news of this arrangement which reached the Asante government in mid-1875. In a number of private interviews with Mensa Bonsu and various of the councillors, however, Bonnat was able to convince them of the compatibility and indeed desirability of his assuming a dual role as agent of government and manager of a concession. Details of an agreement of far-reaching consequences were worked out, by the terms of which Bonnat was appointed co-governor of the Voltaic province lying south of Salaga, was awarded a monopoly of trade in the province until 1881, and was assured of an ongoing right to trade there until the expiry of the concession in 1895 when all buildings reverted to the Asante government. The matter was placed before the Council of Kumase on 31 June 1875. Bonnat was required to take an oath of allegiance to the Asantehene, after which no further opposition was offered to the appointment.[108] According to Campbell who was present, 'the ceremony of the signing of the document was conducted with considerable solemnity'.[109] The commission bore the authority of the Asantehene Mensa Bonsu, Bantamahene Awua, Asafohene Asafo Boakye, acting Akyempemhene Barempa, Akyeamehene Amankwa Nyame, Gyaasewahene Adu Bofo, and Adumhene Agyei Kese, and was witnessed by Owusu Ansa – who presumably drafted it – and Akyampon Daban of the *afenasoafo:*

We, Assai Mensah, King of Achanty, in our name and in the name of our chiefs, having received the oath of M. M-J. Bonnat, attaching him to us and wishing to extend our relations, establish the said M. Bonnat as our governor in our name, conjointly with another chief, to be named by us.

The jurisdiction conferred upon him extends from 40 miles above Accrono to Yegui, on both banks of the Volta. The chief duty of M. Bonnat will be to develop and to extend as far as possible our commerce with the interior of Africa, and to establish the bases of a financial system regarding importation and exportation.

To do this and facilitate his duty, we, King and Chiefs of Achanty, give to the said M. Bonnat, agent of M. de Cardi, for six years the entire monopoly of commerce and the right of navigation on the river Volta through the regions under his jurisdiction, that is to say from 10 miles south of Accrono to Jegui, near Salaza.

M. Bonnat has to pay 3% on all kinds of goods imported, and will levy

106 Gros, 1884, p. 33.
107 *Ibid.* p. 248. *Papers,* C. 1343, 1876, p. 59: Bonnat to Colonial Office, dd. Liverpool, 6 March 1875.
108 *Papers,* C. 1402, 1876, p. 92: Bonnat to Strahan, dd. Cape Coast, 30 September 1875.
109 *Ibid.* pp. 84–5: Strahan to Governor, dd. Cape Coast, 6 September 1875.

for us and in our name 5% on all merchandise of exchange and native produce.

At the expiration of the six years, the monopoly will cease and the country will be open to all Europeans desiring to trade in this part of our territory, provided they submit to the laws and customs then established.

We further guarantee to M. Bonnat, as to our Governor, the right of possession for 20 years of all sites necessary for the construction of their establishments, whether on the banks of the river or on the islands of the said river. After the expiration of twenty years, these establishments will become our property and that of our successors.

Given under our name, mark and public seal, Coumassie, 31 July 1875 . . .[110]

No record survives of who was appointed co-governor with Bonnat. It may, however, have been the talented Boakye Tenten, who certainly held the residency of Salaga sometime before 1881.[111]

Bonnat left Kumase en route for Salaga on 5 August 1875, the day appointed by the Council of Kumase. He met with a friendly reception from the Mamponhene Kwabena Dwumo on the 10th, and proceeded to Atebubu which he reached on the 15th. There, despite the remonstrances of the Atebubuhene Gyan Kwaku, he and his escorts were arrested by troops sent from Dwaben. Bonnat was taken under guard to Dwaben town, and brought before Asafo Agyei. After his case had been debated by the Dwaben councillors, he was released on 9 September but obliged to travel back to the coast by the hazardous Akyem route. He arrived in Cape Coast on 28 September.[112] Clearly, not only had the authority of the governor-designate been grossly flouted, but so had that also of the Asante government. Upon news reaching Kumase of the arrest of Bonnat, Mensa Bonsu called an extraordinary meeting of the Asantemanhyiamu. On 2 September the findings of the Assembly were announced: 'it was decided that as Asafu Agai has forfeited his independency by his conduct and breach of the oath or Treaty, he should be deposed or war declared against him'.[113] By 3 November Dwaben had been occupied, Asafo Agyei was a refugee, and the way was clear for Bonnat to return to the north (see pp. 283–4).

On his second attempt to reach Salaga, Bonnat decided to use the Volta route. He equipped a flotilla of five canoes manned by twenty-

---

[110] Published in French translation in *L'Explorateur*, 1876, III, 238. The translation in the pioneering study of Bonnat by Marion Johnson (1971, p. 27) has been basically followed. The 'Accrono' of the text is presumably an error for 'Akroso' – a town on the Volta river some 35 miles below Kete Krakye.

[111] *Further Correspondence*, C. 3386, 1882, p. 64: Lonsdale's report on his mission to Kumase, Salaga and Yendi, October 1881 to February 1882.

[112] *Papers*, C. 1402, 1876, pp. 92–5: Bonnat to Strahan, dd. Cape Coast, 30 September 1875.

[113] *Ibid.* p. 87: Mensa Bonsu to Governor, dd. Kumase, 2 September 1875.

seven men for the purpose, and embarked at Akwamu on 7 December 1875. Halting for some days at Nkami, where he intended to establish a trading post, Bonnat toured a number of the Ewe towns and made himself known to the local chiefs. Although not within the province over which he had jurisdiction, Bonnat had no hesitation in exercising his authority. At a village just south of Kpandu he ordered the release of a man imprisoned for debt. At Anfoega, further south, he exhorted the chief and his elders to keep the peace and maintain their roads for travellers. 'Listen to me carefully', he told them,

and heed my advice. Three months ago I was in Dwaben, and I gave the same advice to Asafo Agyei. Instead of listening to me, he arrested me. God has since punished him for his wickedness, for where is he now? You all know that he is a fugitive in a foreign land, and that his towns and villages have been destroyed.[114]

Kete Krakye was reached on 20 January, 1876, whence Bonnat proceeded by land through Bagyemso and Krupi to Kpembe. He met with the Kpembewura Doshi on the 30th, and entered Salaga the same afternoon. The British Special Commissioner Gouldsbury arrived there a few hours later, having made forced marches in the hope of entering the town before Bonnat. On the 31st the two officers, the one of the Asante government and the other of the Gold Coast government, debated their positions. Gouldsbury, so Bonnat reported,

informs me that his government intends to prevent the Asante from coming to Salaga. I oppose this opinion. Before the war against Asante, Salaga must in fact have had 40–45,000 inhabitants, with a huge floating population. Today more than three-quarters of its houses are empty and falling into ruins, while the population has fallen from 45,000 to 15–18,000. This is why I made the Commandant [Gouldsbury] acknowledge that without the Asante, Salaga would completely lose its commercial importance. But it is clear that the English Governor has learned of my monopoly, and of the attachment which I have to the Asante and which is reciprocated, and that he fears it. He informs me that the monopoly cannot be supported, that Lord Carnarvon hopes to see trade coming down the Volta to the coast, and that as for Gouldsbury, his aim is to open a land route along the left bank of the Volta and to take with him many caravans to the coast.[115]

On 17 January 1876 Owusu Ansa had written from Kumase to 'His Excellency M-J. Bonnat' informing him that Gouldsbury had left the capital for the interior without notifying the Asantehene of his destination; giving him news that the new Dwabenhene Yaw Sapon and the

114 For Bonnat's journey, see Johnson, 1968, *passim*. Extracts from, and abstracts of, Bonnat's diary for the period, and a number of his letters, are published in *L'Explorateur*, 1876, III, 53, 409, 587, 663–8, and IV, 3–5, 36–7, 66–7, 87–8.
115 *L'Explorateur*, 1876, IV, p. 37

Dwabenhemaa had taken the oath of allegiance to Mensa Bonsu; and saying that the Asantehene required his presence in Kumase. Between 5 and 15 February, however, Bonnat had been exploring the Volta between Yeji and Kete Krakye. Whether or not he received the letter from Owusu Ansa on his return to Salaga is unknown, but certainly he had already decided to return to the Gold Coast by the Volta route again. Leaving his agents in charge of affairs at Yeji and Salaga, Bonnat travelled back in March. Near Kpong, on the Lower Volta, he learned that de Cardi was withdrawing support from him: the Liverpool financier suspected Bonnat of collusion in the negotiation of a new concession between Mensa Bonsu and the French firm of Camus.[116] Bonnat decided to return to Europe, both to find new sponsors and to recruit assistants. Learning that Owusu Ansa was on a visit to Cape Coast, Bonnat was able to meet with him there.

In England, Bonnat gravitated to Liverpool once more. In *The Liverpool Mercury* of 12 June 1876 he published – for promotional reasons – an account of Salaga. 'Now that the rebellion in Ashantee has been crushed', he argued,

> by the total defeat of Assafoadjie, who was the leader and most powerful of the rebels, several of whom have since then tendered their submission, there is no doubt that the Ashantees will endeavour to recover Salaga, which will be easy to them, for the Salagas know that only in submitting to Ashantee will their town recover its former importance . . . I repeat again, my conviction is that Salaga is called to be the great emporium of trade of the western part of Soudan, and it will become the Timbuctoo of the west.

At the same time Bonnat had it announced in France, through the pages of *L'Explorateur*, that he intended to establish a workshop on the Lower Volta 'at the eastern frontier of Achanty', to manufacture articles in demand in the interior; and a trading depot in the Mossi ('Mazé') country two hundred miles north of Salaga – 'a place much frequented by Arab merchants who come from North Africa'. He advertised for the services of two young Frenchmen, carpenters, joiners, or the like, who would also be able to make a modest capital investment in the project.[117] Bonnat's plans engaged the attention of the wealthy Liverpool entrepreneur Radcliffe, who offered him hospitality and the benefits of his contacts and experience.[118] The link, first established by Owusu Ansa with the firm of Radcliffe and Durant

---

116 *The African Times,* XVII, no. 182, 2 October 1876, p. 40: Owusu Ansa to Bonnat, dd. Kumase, 17 February 1876. The letter is almost certainly wrongly dated to February rather than January. *L'Explorateur,* 1876, IV, 66–7. See Johnson, 1968, p. 15.
117 *L'Explorateur,* 1876, IV, 587.
118 Gros, 1884, p. 264. Bonnat also used as his English address that of 'Messrs. Radcliffe and Durand, Inner Temple, at Liverpool'.

when he visited Liverpool in 1874, was thus renewed and strengthened.

Late in 1876 Bonnat appears to have abandoned the whole project which he had so enthusiastically promoted, associating himself instead with the newly formed Société des Mines d'Or de l'Afrique Occidentale.[119] No account of the reasons for Bonnat's abrupt change of plan has been found. It would seem likely, however, that Owusu Ansa had written to inform him of the decision of the Asante government to place an embargo on the Salaga trade and to develop Kintampo as an alternative entrepôt (see pp. 286–7). The subsequent history of Bonnat's associates in the Salaga scheme has been briefly reviewed by Johnson: [120] with the rapid rise of the new Kintampo mart, however, interest in the earlier project appears rapidly to have diminished.

Brun and the promotion of the French connection

Originally Owusu Ansa had recruited both Bonnat and Campbell into Asante service within the diplomatic corps, as conductors of missions. It is some measure not only of the personal vision of Bonnat, but also of the receptivity to ideas of change of many of the councillors of the dominant mercantile party in the period, that the possibility of developing trade and industry in Asante through the participation of European entrepreneurs became a recognized one. Bonnat himself returned to the Gold Coast in April 1877, as a director of the Société des Mines d'Or. Reorganized in 1878 as the Compagnie Minière de la Côte d'Or d'Afrique, or the African Gold Coast Company,[121] Bonnat remained as a director and was joined, among others, by Radcliffe of Liverpool. Until his death on 8 July 1881,[122] Bonnat was active in promoting the mining interest in the southwestern Gold Coast,[123] and his association with the Asante government appears to have been terminated. In 1877, however, Bonnat had also entered into a commercial partnership with another Frenchman, Arthur Brun.[124] Although the agreement between the two soon broke down as Bonnat's preoccupation with mining became increasingly obsessive,[125] Brun appears rapidly to have established himself independently, opening houses at Assini and Grand Bassam for the sale of cloth and armaments.[126] It seems highly probable that he was among those who were

[119] Gros, 1884, pp. 264–5.
[120] Johnson, 1968, pp. 16–17.
[121] Burton and Cameron, 1883, II, 271, 297–9.
[122] The date in Gros, 1884, p. 269, is in error. See *The Gold Coast Times*, I, no. 2, 30 July 1881. Burton and Cameron, 1883, II, 299.
[123] See Bevin, 1960, pp. 5–12.
[124] Gros, 1884, p. 265.
[125] Hertz, 1885, pp. 189, 204.
[126] Gros, n.d., p. 140.

organizing the supply through Assini of breech-loading rifles to the government in Kumase – an operation largely master-minded by Owusu Ansa [127] with whom it is known that Brun was already well acquainted in 1877.[128] Brun's links with Kumase were shortly thereafter strengthened by his marriage to a niece of the Asantehene Mensa Bonsu.[129] On 10 April 1880 Brun was appointed consular agent at Elmina for the Netherlands, and a few months later assumed the position also as French consul there. In May 1881 Boakye Tenten, then leading the important government mission to the Gold Coast (see pp. 526–7), visited Brun in Elmina. The talks between the two focused upon the possibility of developing a route from Assini via the Lower Tano river to Kumase, and thereby decreasing Asante dependence upon the English trade for its major imports.[130] It may have been on the same occasion that Brun obtained approval for another project. He had been promised, so he claimed, 'a grant of a concession from the king, of land on the banks of the Pra, facing Praso, to construct there a large factory which he would place under the direct protection of the black king, and for the defence of which the latter would give him, if it was necessary, a chief and soldiers of his army'.[131]

Late in 1881 Brun made known his wish to visit Kumase, to conduct talks on trade. Mensa Bonsu sent carriers to Elmina for him, and he left there on 12 April 1882. He was accompanied by Father Moreau of the Society of African Missions, who intended to study the possibilities of opening a Roman Catholic mission in the capital.[132] The British authorities in Cape Coast were greatly perturbed by the development.[133] Entering Kumase on 22 April, Brun and Moreau were given accommodation in Boakye Tenten's house. The powerful counselor, husband of the Asantehemaa and a known Anglophobe,[134] obtained for Brun many meetings with Mensa Bonsu. Complete agreement was reached upon the desirability of developing the Assini trade. Brun himself was authorized by the government to negotiate on its behalf a peace settlement with the Sehwi, who had rebelled supposedly at the instigation of the British, and were preventing the movement of traders between Assini and the capital (see p. 289 and n. 253).[135] But the talks seem to have covered matters of even more moment. On 9 March 1883

---

127 Ellis, 1883, p. 187.
128 Hertz, 1885, p. 94.
129 Gros, n.d., p. 152 and plate, p. 163.
130 *Ibid.* pp. 144–5.
131 *Ibid.* p. 162.
132 *Ibid.* p. 153.
133 *The Gold Coast Times*, I, no. 39, 15 April 1882, p. 2.
134 Gros, n.d., p. 145.
135 *Ibid.* p. 176.

the Minister of Marine in Paris was informed of a report from Brun, that

the king [of Asante] and his ministers would be disposed to place themselves under a French protectorate if France would support the sovereign and if France would open the route between the capital Coumassie and Assinie, a distance of ten days' march from that residence. Communications had been stopped by a people who say that they are under an English protectorate. Mr. Brun supported the proposition because of its value for French commerce . . . He added that the route from the Soudan by Coumassie is much more direct than that by Senegal.[136]

The Minister was opposed at that time to direct French intervention in Asante affairs, but presumably approved of Brun's commercial project. On 28 April 1883, however, Brun died, and the government in Kumase lost yet another of its European associates.[137] Despite, nevertheless, the failure of the schemes of both Bonnat and Brun, there seems little doubt that it was during the reign of Mensa Bonsu that the doctrine gained acceptance by at least some of the members of the mercantilist majority which then dominated the Councils, that the economic development of Asante should involve the input of both European capital and expertise. It will be seen below that the doctrine was later to become of cardinal importance in the government's attempt to preserve its political independence.

Under Kofi Kakari, then, Owusu Ansa had presided over the first stages in the modernization of the administrative machinery in Kumase, and upon the accession of Mensa Bonsu in 1874 had begun to build up the new civil service by the recruitment of personnel on free contracts. He was present in the capital from May 1875 to March 1876, when he returned to Cape Coast. A letter written by him from that town on 7 July 1877 shows that he had remained in the service of the Asantehene. 'Since my return to this place', he observed, 'I have not ceased in sending Messengers to the King of Ashantee and his Chieftains to tell them what is the proper way to direct their Government; and the King also never ceased in sending to me for advice.' [138]

---

136 Ministry of Foreign Affairs, Paris, Consular Commercial Correspondence, Afrique 86, pp. 35–6: draft letter to Minister of Marine, dd. Paris, 9 March 1883.

137 *The Gold Coast Times*, II, no. 99, 9 June 1883. Brun's widow was named as Adriana Runckle. Since she was a niece of Mensa Bonsu the implication is perhaps that one of Mensa Bonsu's brothers had taken a wife from a burgher family of Dutch Elmina, and that Adriana Runckle was their daughter. For a hostile account of Brun's attempt to open the Kumase–Assini road in the months before his death, in which he enlisted the good offices of the Sanwihene Amandufo as instructed by Mensa Bonsu (Gros, n.d., p. 176), see Brétignère, 1931, pp. 58 ff.

138 Methodist Mission Archives, London: Owusu Ansa to Buxton, dd. Cape Coast, 7 July 1877, cited in Tregaskis to Owusu Ansa, dd. 22 August 1877, p. 23.

Owusu Ansa did not resume residence in Kumase until April 1878. The evidence suggests strongly that during his stay of just over two years in Cape Coast, Owusu Ansa was active in a new project: that of the reorganization and modernization of the Asante fighting forces. That the scheme had top secret classification [139] makes recovery of the details particularly difficult. Broadly, the government in Kumase saw in the creation of new regiments of professional soldiers a way not only of narrowing the gap in military proficiency between the Asante forces and those which the British had shown themselves capable of putting into the field, but also of meeting (other than in times of grave emergency) the popular demand for the abolition of universal military conscription. The tradition was already an old one, of incorporating into the army units of those loosely described as 'Hausa': that is, of those of foreign origins who tended to use the Hausa language as a *lingua franca*. Reindorf reported a tradition that the armies of Opoku Ware which invaded the Akyem country in 1742 included Hausa mercenaries.[140] In 1817 Osei Bonsu possessed 'a guard of foreigners (natives of Coranza)',[141] who were probably the *Hausafo* who fought at Katamanso nine years later.[142] There was also a Hausa component in the Asante army in 1874.[143] The decision of Mensa Bonsu's government to recruit principally foreigners to the new regiments was therefore not without precedents, though Owusu Ansa was prominent among those advocating continuation of the principle. 'Prince Ansah', it was reported, 'is said to have had a large share in suggesting the formation of a Houssa Corps in Ashantee.' [144]

A precondition of the success of the programme of military modernization was the purchase of breech-loading rifles, Sniders and Martini-Henrys, to replace the obsolete flintlocks which had remained the principal weapon of the Asante forces in 1874. 'Ever since the last war', it was commented in 1881, 'large amounts of money have been expended by them in the purchase of modern weapons.' [145] In 1874 a French company had corresponded with Asante envoys in Cape Coast, offering Sniders for sale. Owusu Ansa later claimed that he only learned of the transaction after his return from England in that year,[146]

139 *The Lagos Times and Gold Coast Colony Advertiser*, I, no. 9, 9 March 1881, p. 2.
140 Reindorf, 2nd ed., n.d., p. 80.
141 Bowdich, 1821a, p. 52.
142 Reindorf, 1895, Appendix.
143 Christaller, 1875, p. xv.
144 PRO, CO. 96/126: Dudley to Hay, dd. Elmina, 25 March 1879.
145 *The Lagos Times and Gold Coast Colony Advertiser*, I, No. 8, 23 February 1881, p. 2.
146 *Affairs*, C. 3064, 1881, p. 53: Owusu Ansa to Ussher, dd. Cape Coast, 17 May 1880.

but his disavowal of involvement was made at a time when he was anxious to restore his *bona fides* with the Gold Coast administration. However that may be, certainly the first steps in reorganization had been taken by late 1875: of the army which re-entered Kumase on 5 December after the occupation of Dwaben, it was remarked that one company was equipped with Sniders.[147] Subsequently, Owusu Ansa was able to import some rifles through Cape Coast itself. A consignment of three hundred Sniders ordered by him from England arrived there at the end of December 1878, and after some difficulty reached him in Kumase on 15 January 1879. The rifles were immediately sent to the arsenal some few miles outside the capital (see p. 198).[148]

While British military intelligence was able to keep record of the number of weapons imported through Cape Coast and other of the towns under the jurisdiction of the Gold Coast government, little information was available on those smuggled through the Keta Lagoons in the east or those purchased from the French traders at Assini and other towns to the west.[149] Reports were current that in 1878 or 1879 Owusu Ansa had placed orders for a further 5,000 rifles,[150] and there is no reason why such a purchase should not have made through the agency of Arthur Brun and his associates at Assini and Grand Bassam. When Parker visited Kumase in January 1881, he was led to believe that the total number of men equipped with Sniders was only 1,000, and that a detachment of three hundred of these had already been posted to outstations on the Gyaman road.[151] When Buck and Huppenbauer of the Basel Mission Society watched a review of 5,000 troops in the capital on 5 February 1881, they reported that 1,000 of them had Sniders.[152] Another report of the same period estimated the number of modern rifles in the government's hands at between three and five thousand.[153] On 30 January Owusu Ansa himself had returned to Cape Coast from a visit to Axim, and the next day had met with Governor Brandford Griffith to express his regrets at the

147 *Correspondence Respecting the Affairs of the Gambia*, C. 1409, 1876: Gouldsbury to Strahan, dd. Kumase, 6 December 1875.

148 *Affairs*, C. 3064, 1881, pp. 53–4: Owusu Ansa to Ussher, dd. Cape Coast, 17 May 1880. Ellis, 1883, p. 188.

149 Ellis, 1883, p. 187. See also Ellis, 1881, p. 186.

150 *Affairs*, C. 3064, 1881, p. 53: Owusu Ansa to Ussher, dd. Cape Coast, 17 May 1880.

151 *Ibid.* p. 48: Parker to Griffith, dd. Kumase, 24 January 1881.

152 *Ibid.* p. 85: Buck and Huppenbauer to Jackson, dd. Dweraso, 18 February 1881.

153 *The Lagos Times and Gold Coast Colony Advertiser*, I, no. 9, 9 March 1881, p. 2. In November 1881, Lonsdale reported that he saw 350 men in the capital armed with Sniders, and was told that there were 600 in all, see *Further Correspondence*, C. 3386, 1882, p. 61. It seems unlikely, however, that accurate data would have been released to Lonsdale, whose hostility towards Asante aspirations was readily apparent.

deterioration in relations between the Gold Coast and Asante govern-
ments at the time.[154] British reports suggested, however, that Owusu
Ansa had superintended the despatch of three tons of gunpowder to
Kumase, smuggled through the western ports.[155]

The induction of men into the new regiments was an operation of
considerable complexity, all the more so because of the conditions of
secrecy under which it was originally carried out. It was, however, an
operation for the execution of which a certain expertise was available:
that of those who, under Kwaku Dua I, had been involved in raising
men for the army of the Dutch East Indies (see pp. 198–9). Many of
the recruits to the Hausa regiments were unfree subjects of northern
origins, belonging to Asante chiefs who reluctantly surrendered them
to the central authority for enlistment.[156] They were, it was reported,
'slaves of Houssa, Moshie, Dagomba and Grunshi nationalities requisi-
tioned by the King from his chiefs'.[157] A recruiting drive was also
launched in such northern towns as Salaga, though the quality of
many of the men obtained as a result was not as high as was desired.
The agency in the north was given to Carl Nielson, who is variously
described as Danish, Swedish, or German. He had apparently arrived
on the Gold Coast as a prospector,[158] and the circumstances in which
he entered Asante service are as yet unknown. Ellis referred to him
as 'the German who had rendered himself useful in the formation of
the Ashanti corps of Houssas',[159] and again, as 'a German, who had
been wandering about the interior for some time, made himself useful
in the formation of this *corps d'élite,* and brought down Houssas from
Salagha for the King'.[160]

There is no doubt that the Hausa regiments in Asante were seen
as functionally equivalent to the Gold Coast Armed Police Force
which had been formed in the Colony in 1872, officially approved in
1873, and which was also largely recruited from 'Hausa'. Both forces
were expected to assume the task of maintaining the peace in their
respective territories, to be reinforced only in times of crisis. With
both forces, too, it was intended that at any one time the majority of
the troops would be on detachment duties, the main depots – at
Elmina and Kumase respectively – serving principally as recruiting and

154 *Affairs,* C. 3064, 1881, p. 50: Griffith to Kimberley, dd. Cape Coast, 6 February
1881.
155 Ellis, 1883, p. 216.
156 Compare the comment on the *nnɔnkɔfo* in Cruickshank, 1853, II, 245, that
'among this servile race we find also a good many mongrel Moors little superior
to the others'.
157 PRO, CO. 96/126: Dudley to Hay, dd. Elmina, 25 March 1879.
158 PRO, CO. 96/124: Lees to Hicks-Beach, dd. 15 August 1878.
159 Ellis, 1883, p. 191.
160 *Ibid.* p. 189.

training centres.[161] The Hausa force of the Gold Coast was originally planned as one of 350 men, armed and trained as light infantry, and this level was reached by the end of 1874.[162] In 1875 it was decided to increase the force to 600 men,[163] and thereafter it was expanded further towards a ceiling of around 1,000.[164] The Hausa force of Asante numbered between 300 and 400 men by early 1879,[165] and the evidence of the missionaries Buck and Huppenbauer cited above suggests that it had been brought up to a level of about 1,000 men by 1881.

Just as the senior posts in the Gold Coast Armed Police Force were held by officers of the British administration of the Gold Coast, so those in the Asante Hausa force were given to officers of the Asante government. Of the latter force it was reported that 'Hausa' were deliberately excluded from positions of command lest they might become too powerful and identify themselves with the cause of the Muslims of Salaga in the rebel Kpembe province.[166] Owusu Ansa himself served as Inspector General of the force. With the aid of a British drill-book which he had acquired, he evolved a basic training programme, and secured the services as drill-instructors of a West Indian and a Fante soldier: the former had apparently escaped from prison, and the latter had deserted from Accra.[167] The quality of the training was such that the Bekwaehene Yaw Poku equipped sixty of his personal troops with Sniders, and sent them to Owusu Ansa in Kumase for instruction.[168] Serving under Owusu Ansa, and also concerned with basic training, was Owusu Koko Kuma, the son of the Saamanhene Akyampon Panin, and an unidentifiable Kuma, described as 'captain'.[169] Paymaster to the force was Yaw Damte: [170] he was probably the son of the Sanaahene Sanaa Poku and later himself succeeded to that office with the stool-name Yaw Dadie. Despite reports to the contrary,[171] armourers were employed in the arsenal to maintain the rifles in good condition. Early in 1881 Ellis interviewed Amu Kwaku, a Gã who had been recruited to the force in that capacity:

161 For an account of the history of the Gold Coast Armed Police Force, see Gillespie, 1955, pp. 10–26.
162 *Ibid.* pp. 10; 14.
163 *Ibid.* p. 15.
164 *Ibid.* p. 17.
165 PRO, CO. 96/126: Dudley to Hay, dd. 25 March 1879.
166 *Idem.*
167 *Idem.* See also PRO, CO. 96/126: report by Brew enclosed in Lees to Hicks-Beach, dd. Cape Coast, 14 April 1879.
168 *Affairs*, C. 3064, 1881, pp. 13–14: statement by Owusu Taseamandi, dd. Elmina, 20 January 1881.
169 PRO, CO. 96/126: report by Osei Yaw, enclosed in Lees to Hicks-Beach, dd. 14 April 1879.
170 PRO, CO. 96/126: report by Brew.
171 *Affairs*, C. 3064, 1881, p. 15: statement by Kwabena Anwoa, dd. Elmina, 21 January 1881.

a man named Amoo Quacoo, a blacksmith and a native of Accra, was brought to me, and in the course of conversation stated that he had lately returned from Coomassie, where he had been employed by the king in looking after three hundred Snider rifles stored in the king's house. He said that the rifles were all in good condition, that the Ashantis took great care of them, cleaning and oiling them daily; and that there were about four boxes of ammunition to each rifle.[172]

The training of the recruits to the Hausa regiments not in basic drill, but in weaponry, was a matter handled by procuring the services of instructors from the Gold Coast Armed Police Force. With the approval of Mensa Bonsu, Yaw Damte authorized double rates of pay and free rations for those leaving the one force for the other.[173] Ellis gave some account of the invitation:

To induce trained men of this ['Hausa'] race to desert from the Gold Coast Constabulary, Mensah offered pay at double the rate paid by the Colonial Government, free rations, and some local privileges. The percentage of desertions from the Constabulary, always alarmingly high, at once increased: and these deserters assumed the new role of musketry instructors to the Ashanti army.[174]

In this manner the Asante government acquired the services of some thirty weapon-instructors.[175] Although the Gold Coast government put the best face on the matter, maintaining that Mensa Bonsu was nevertheless 'fully aware of his complete powerlessness against the British Government',[176] the deserters did represent almost 5% of the total Gold Coast Hausa force. Those who thus transferred themselves, moreover, at the same time 'carried away the Queen's rifles and accoutrements'.[177] Rates of pay in the Gold Coast service were 1s a day for a private, 1s 3d for a corporal, and 1s 6d for a sergeant.[178] The evidence suggests that new, and raw, recruits to the Asante Hausa force were paid twice monthly, at the rate of either 18s or 9s for the month of forty-two days: [179] which rate he enjoyed depended presumably on whether he was on free contract, recruited from towns like Salaga, or whether he was of unfree status, supplied to the force by a chief.

---

172 Ellis, 1883, p. 215, who points out that the Gold Coast government concluded that these were all the rifles which the Asante possessed, an illusion soon dispelled by the testimony of Buck and Huppenbauer.
173 PRO, CO. 96/126: report by Brew.
174 Ellis, 1883, pp. 188–9.
175 *The Lagos Times and Gold Coast Colony Advertiser*, I, no. 9, 9 March 1881, p. 2.
176 PRO, CO. 96/126: Ussher to Hicks-Beach, dd. Cape Coast, 24 July 1879.
177 *The Gold Coast News*, I, no. 1, 21 March 1885, p. 3.
178 Gillespie, 1955, pp. 11; 17.
179 PRO, CO. 96/126: report by Osei Yaw.

Trained men went on to a scale of from 12 to 16 dollars a month,[180] which, assuming the month to be the Asante one and valuing the dollar at about 4s, was a marginally better one than that paid on the Gold Coast. And finally, the weapon-instructors were on a scale twice as high. The uniforms of both forces were similar. The Hausa in Asante service wore blue baft tunics, and a red fez with blue tassel.[181] Somewhat incongruously, Owusu Ansa himself appears to have favoured British naval-style dress. 'Mr. Ansah', reported Gouldsbury, 'was arrayed in a uniform, which simulated that of a British officer – the uniform was of no severely determinate style, but had a sort of florid resemblance to that of a naval officer of considerable rank.' [182]

The initial stages in the planning of the Hausa regiments must have been carried out while Owusu Ansa was in Kumase from May 1875 to March 1876. Thereafter, Owusu Ansa applied himself to the purchase of modern weapons on the coast, while Nielson was engaged in obtaining recruits in the northern hinterland. On his return to Kumase in April 1878, Owusu Ansa clearly devoted much of his time and energies to bringing the Hausa regiments to readiness for active service. Ellis considered that this had been accomplished by the spring of 1879.[183] Soon after, members of the force were sent on detachment to out-stations on the Volta, to police the river and curtail the activities of smugglers defying the government's embargo on the Salaga trade (see p. 284). In 1880 some other detachments, of three hundred men in all under command of Owusu Koko Kuma, were established on the Gyaman road (p. 286). Certainly by early 1881 few members of the Hausa force were to be seen in the capital itself,[184] though a number had by then been assigned to special duties within the palace (pp. 527–8).

The Gyaman mission of 1878–9

Although the programme of military reorganization occupied much of Owusu Ansa's attention from 1876–9, his involvement in the development of the new civil service nevertheless continued. In late 1877 or early 1878 the government decided to send a new mission to Gyaman in anticipation of being able to restore tranquillity in that politically disturbed province. The job of organizing the mission was given to

180 *Ibid.* report by Brew.
181 PRO, CO. 96/126: Dudley to Hay, dd. 25 March 1879. Compare Gillespie, 1955, pp. 11, 14.
182 *Papers*, C. 1402, 1876, p. 117: Gouldsbury to Strahan, dd. Bomfa, 30 November 1875.
183 Ellis, 1883, p. 190.
184 *Affairs*, C. 3064, 1881, p. 49: Parker to Griffith, dd. Kumase, 24 January 1881.

Owusu Ansa, who was then in Cape Coast, and 80 oz of gold were sent to him for advance expenditure. Carl Nielson, having completed his assignment recruiting for the Hausa regiments, was chosen to conduct the mission and was appointed 'His Majesty's Commissioner and headman for a Mission of peace to the King of Gaman'.[185] J. J. C. Huydecoper, who had been educated at the Methodist school in Cape Coast (perhaps when Owusu Ansa was master there), was selected as clerk, interpreter and second-in-command to Nielson.[186] Sixty hammockmen, carriers and servants were also hired in Cape Coast – presumably since, as subjects of the Colony, the Gyamanhene would be unlikely to injure them. The mission left Cape Coast on 8 April 1878. In Kumase it was joined by an Asante officer, 'Old' Osei, and by a cane-bearer, Kofi Mpra. Owusu Ansa informed the Asantehene that he estimated the total costs of the mission at about 150 peredwans, or £1,200. The remuneration of Nielson was fixed at £200, and that of Huydecoper – although he demanded more – at £100,[187] while the pay of the hammockmen and others was set at 1s 6d a day.[188]

The Nielson mission proved an ill-fated one. Shortly after its arrival in Bonduku, in June 1878, Nielson himself died apparently having met with the Gyamanhene Agyeman on one occasion only.[189] Leaving the other members of the mission in Bonduku, Huydecoper returned to Kumase for instructions. At a meeting of the Council of Kumase in July he was appointed to succeed Nielson as head of the mission, and was paid a further 40 oz of gold, or £144. He, and the members of council, were instructed to keep secret the matter of Nielson's death.[190] A copy of Huydecoper's commission, drawn up by Owusu Ansa, survives.[191] As an example of the chancery styles of the new civil service, it should be compared with the commission issued to Bonnat in 1875 (pp. 609–10) and with the invitation extended to Dr Horton in 1879 to join the Order of Princes of Asante (p. 78):

KNOW ALL MEN by these present I, Ossai Mensah, King of Ashantee and its dependencies in my name and in the name of our Chiefs do hereby nominate, constitute, and appoint J. J. C. Huydecoper as our Commissioner and headman of our Mission of Peace to the King of Gaman, in the room or place of

185 National Archives of Ghana, Accra, ADM 1/2/361: Huydecoper to Smith, dd. Banda, 9 August 1879.
186 *Affairs*, C. 3064, 1881, p. 52: Owusu Ansa to Ussher, dd. Cape Coast, 17 May 1880. Ellis, 1883, p. 190.
187 *Affairs*, C. 3064, 1881, p. 52.
188 *Ibid.* p. 55: evidence of the hammockman Kwadwo Obimpi, dd. 24 March 1879.
189 The accounts are conflicting on this point, see *ibid.* p. 55: evidence of the hammockmen Kwadwo Obimpi and Tamfuben, dd. 24 and 25 March 1879.
190 *Ibid.* p. 55: evidence of Owusu Taseamandi, dd. 5 February 1881.
191 National Archives of Ghana, Accra, ADM 1/2/361: enclosure in Huydecoper to Smith, dd. Banda, 9 August 1879.

the late C. Nielson our late Commissioner and headman of our Mission of Peace to the King of Gaman, who died on Thursday 13th June 1878, to act for us and settle all matters between Ashantee and Gaman according to the *objects* of our Mission under his charge.

> As witness my name and hand mark and seal. Coomassee Twenty nine day of July one thousand eight hundred and seventy Eight and His Majesty Ossai Mensah's Reign the fifth

Witness of
J. Ossoo Ansah
Prince of Ashantee

Ossai Mensah
King of Ashantee.

Ackampon
State Sword bearer

Adoo
State Sword bearer.

Upon his return to duty in Bonduku in August, Huydecoper found that his hammockmen and carriers had deserted and had travelled back to the Gold Coast through Sehwi.[192] A Fante named Asadu, who described himself as an agent of the Gold Coast administration, and who acted in collusion with the Gyamanhene Agyeman, was found to be responsible for thus sabotaging the work of the mission.[193] At the same time the Gyamanhene had seized the mission's purse: the sum, variously given as 80 oz. or 135 oz of gold, had been advanced personally by Owusu Ansa.[194] Huydecoper's report to Kumase, on the problems he faced in Bonduku, brought him a reposting: by a letter of 30 September 1878 he was instructed to remove to Banda, where the pro-Asante Ankobeahene of Gyaman, Kofi Kokobo, was then residing. Huydecoper remained as Commissioner for Peace in Banda in August 1879, when in a letter to Bonduku he restated his government's position – that Owusu Ansa's gold be returned; that the Gyamanhene reimburse the expenses of the mission; that the Takyimanhene Kwabena Fofie, the Fante Asadu, and other refugees be surrendered; and that the Gyaman open the roads for trade. 'To live in peace and friendship together', he wrote,

that is what His Majesty requires and I think it advisable for the Gamans to agree to this proposal of His Majesty, as these are the only pacific measures that will do good to their country and her people and not otherwise as all my

---

192 *Affairs*, C. 3064, 1881: evidence of Kwadwo Obimpi, dd. 24 March 1879.
193 National Archives of Ghana, Accra, ADM 1/2/361: Huydecoper to Smith, dd. 9 August 1879.
194 *Further Correspondence*, C. 3687, 1883, p. 71: Moloney to Kimberley, dd. Accra, 19 September 1882. *Ibid.* pp. 109 and 122: Lonsdale's report on his mission to Asante and Gyaman, April to July 1882.

ways here are ways of pleasantness and all my paths are peace in the name of His Majesty the King of Ashantee and its dependencies.[195]

Owusu Ansa travelled from Kumase to Cape Coast in August 1879, and found himself immediately involved in a series of legal wrangles. The hammockmen and carriers who had deserted from the Gyaman mission maintained that Huydecoper had failed to pay them, and made claims against Owusu Ansa for £537 4s 8d. When Huydecoper returned to Cape Coast some months later he asserted that he had not received his back pay from the Asantehene, and threatened to sue Owusu Ansa for £1,004 8s 10½d – a sum perhaps computed at £50 or thereabouts per month.[196] In much distress, Owusu Ansa wrote to the British Governor Ussher, accusing Mensa Bonsu of breaking faith and soliciting 'your Excellency's moral influence . . . to cause the King of Ashanti to do me justice and give me satisfaction'.[197] The reasons for the contretemps are unclear. Certainly, however, Owusu Ansa continued to manage Asante affairs on the Gold Coast. Asante envoys who met with Governor Rowe in March 1881, shortly after his arrival from England, insisted on conducting their business through him.[198] Likewise, he played an important role later in the year in facilitating the work of the major mission to the Gold Coast headed by Boakye Tenten, and was deterred from accompanying its members back to Kumase only by Governor Rowe's promise of pecuniary recompense for his services.[199] In danger of having his house in Cape Coast distrained for debt in 1882, Owusu Ansa was sent 120 oz of gold by Mensa Bonsu, who at the same time expressed the wish that he should return to Kumase as adviser.[200]

During the reign of Kwaku Dua I, Owusu Ansa had played a comparatively inconspicuous role in Asante political life. Although limited use of his services as intermediary with the British had been made by the peace party governments which held power until 1863, the views which he must be presumed already to have held, on the necessity of change and the directions which it should take, were not such as to gain him significant support from even the more liberal members of council. Although appointed by Kofi Kakari to a position

195 National Archives of Ghana, Accra, ADM 1/2/361: Huydecoper to Smith, dd. 9 August 1879.
196 *Affairs*, C. 3064, 1881, p. 53: Owusu Ansa to Ussher, dd. Cape Coast, 17 May 1880.
197 *Ibid*. p. 54.
198 *Further Correspondence*, C. 3386, 1882, pp. 106–9: Rowe to Kimberley, dd. Elmina, 11 March 1881.
199 *Ibid*. pp. 8–9: Owusu Ansa to Rowe, dd. Accra, 11 October 1881. *Ibid*. p. 9: Rowe to Owusu Ansa, dd. Accra, 13 October 1881.
200 *Further Correspondence*, C. 3687, 1883, p. 96: Badger to Private Secretary, dd. Accra, 4 December 1882.

of some eminence in the sphere of foreign affairs, Owusu Ansa became increasingly alienated from, and distrusted by, the more extreme elements in the war party who took over direction of national affairs. It was, then, not until Mensa Bonsu was elected Asantehene that Owusu Ansa at last found himself in the position of enjoying support for a programme of national reconstruction based upon the overhaul and renovation of the agencies of government. It has been shown that he played a leading part in pushing through those administrative and military reforms which gave the reign of Mensa Bonsu so distinctive a character. It has been noted, too, that Owusu Ansa was among the earliest advocates of the new economic doctrine, that the development of Asante trade and industry should involve participation of European entrepreneurs on terms to be approved by the government. Owusu Ansa himself in 1881 held a position with the African Gold Coast Company operating in the Colony,[201] and in 1882 was among those concerned with the creation there of the Gold Coast Native Concessions Purchasing Company: founded to act as intermediary between landowning chiefs on the one hand and European companies on the other.[202]

Throughout his career Owusu Ansa had remained a staunch advocate of the view that the interests of the Gold Coast Colony and of Asante were complementary, and that peace between the two was a *sine qua non* of the development of each. It was the view which was to be forcefully restated by the intellectuals of the Gold Coast at the end of the century (see p. 527). In 1880 Owusu Ansa had expressed clearly his own attitudes in a letter to Governor Ussher:

although I feel great obligation to England, yet my walks in the affairs of your Government and my country must be upon true faithfulness and justice, and I am sure if I were to walk otherwise you would be the first of persons to charge me with want of patriotism and faithfulness to my country . . . as I see her prosperity lies in friendly relationship with England I wish her peace with England, and to secure this peace it is my duty, whenever I visit Coomassie, to offer faithful suggestions to the King's council, of which I am a member by birth, which may bring some good to subsist the good understanding between the King of Ashanti and your Excellency's Government, and even to offer faithful suggestions to your Excellency too; and if ever my

---

[201] *Further Correspondence*, C. 3386, 1882, pp. 8–9: Owusu Ansa to Governor, dd. Accra, 11 October 1881. *Further Correspondence*, C. 3064, 1881, p. 89: Owusu Ansa to Griffith, dd. Cape Coast, 19 February 1881.

[202] *The Gold Coast Times*, I, no. 40, 22 April 1882; no. 63, 30 September 1882. It is unclear whether it was this Company which was subsequently reconstituted in or about 1890 as The African Concessions Trust Ltd and The Ashanti Exploration Company, see NAG, Accra, ADM 1/2/45: Griffith to Knutsford, dd. Accra, 8 May 1891; and ADM 1/2/49: Maxwell to Chamberlain, dd. Accra, 22 October 1895.

suggestions were not heeded on both sides I shall have the satisfaction in my mind that I have done my duty.

Hence it is owned by many observing people that whenever I visit Coomassie there was always good trade from many Ashanti traders flocking to the coast, and many people from the protectorate flocking to Coomassie and other Ashanti markets; thus confidence and good feelings between the two nations are manifested by their mingling together.

So my visits to Coomassie have never been attended with evil to both countries, but peace, concord, and friendship.[203]

It was, however a measure of the quality of the man, that while acquiring considerable power under Mensa Bonsu, he retained his commitment to the cause of general reform, and continued to press for revision of the penal code and for the establishment of schools in Asante.

Owusu Ansa and the movement for reform

In 1875 and 1876 Owusu Ansa had been offering encouragement to both the Wesleyan and Basel missionaries to visit Kumase with a view to establishing new stations there. The Rev. Thomas Picot arrived in the capital on 10 April 1876, and stayed in Owusu Ansa's house. It has already been seen that at the debate which took place in the Council of Kumase on 21 April, the Gyaasewahene Adu Bofo and Bantamahene Awua strongly reasserted the conservative position, that traditional institutions must be preserved against the attacks of the reformers, and that Christian missionaries should not be permitted to open schools and stations in Asante (see pp. 518–19). Discouraged, Picot returned immediately to the Gold Coast. Although, however, the old guard war party leaders were thus still able to sway the Council in its deliberations, the proponents of reform enjoyed a strong popular constituency and were working upon a new and detailed specification of their goals. Concerned with fundamental issues of constitutional rights, the legal code of the Gold Coast Colony continued to interest them as a possible model for change. Since the government was still firmly committed to a policy of peaceful coexistence with the British, and since the first steps were being taken towards the creation of the new professional army, the issue of military conscription was not the burning one in 1876 that it had been a few years earlier. Attention was focused rather upon the problem of penal reform: of the use of the instrument of terror by the state through the periodic public and

203 *Affairs*, C. 3064, 1881, p. 54: Owusu Ansa to Ussher, dd. Cape Coast, 17 May 1880. See also *ibid.* p. 89: Owusu Ansa to Griffith, dd. Cape Coast, 19 February 1881, offering his services as Asante ambassador resident in Cape Coast, his salary to be paid from the Treasury in Kumase but to be administered by the Government in Cape Coast.

mass executions of those condemned to death for a wide range of offences.

Asante thinking upon the matter of penal reform had been seemingly much affected by an event which had occurred when Wolseley's forces occupied Kumase. Early on the morning of 5 February 1874 the British Military Commandant Colonel M'Leod ordered the execution of a Fante policeman – a youth of seventeen or eighteen years – who had been caught looting. He was hanged from a tree 'in the most clumsy and barbarous manner', and died slowly.[204] The matter did not go unnoticed by the Asante, that the British too practised 'human sacrifice'. Kofi Kakari was reported to have said subsequently,

that he did not slaughter innocent persons, but only those who had had sentence of death passed on them after a fair trial, these he reserved for such occasions as on which he had to make custom, or on which it was necessary to sacrifice to his fetish, when their sentences were executed, just in the same manner as Sir Garnet Wolseley had caused to be hanged at Coomassie this policeman for the crime he had committed.[205]

With the accession of Mensa Bonsu, however, it was possible to reopen the issue. Among the prime movers was Owusu Ansa, who continually pressed upon the Asantehene the desirability, on humanitarian grounds, of reform.[206] In a letter to Ramseyer, advertising to the topic of the abolition of 'human sacrifice', Owusu Ansa wrote,

it may sound incredible and not to believe this; but if you were to see the present state of Ashantee as I have seen since the war you will not think it is impossible. The present state of the Ashantee people requires, and compells the King and his Chieftains to know, that they must abandon, that wicked custom otherwise, they will lose all their people very soon, however time will prove whether the King is earnest and sincere or not.[207]

The issue was brought for debate before the Council of Kumase probably late in September 1876. Word that the mood of the councillors was favourable to reform was sent to Owusu Ansa who was then in Cape Coast. 'I have been informed officially', he wrote, 'that King Mensah has assembled his Chieftains and they are at Council, and about to send Messengers to the Governor respecting especially the abolition of human sacrifice.' [208] The anticipated messengers did not, however, arrive immediately. The issue appears in fact to have been

204 Stanley, 1874, pp. 227–8.
205 *The Gold Coast Times*, I, no. 19, 29 April 1874.
206 Methodist Mission Archives, London: Tregaskis to Owusu Ansa, dd. 22 August 1877, pp. 17–18, 22–3.
207 Basel Mission Archives: Owusu Ansa to Ramseyer, dd. 7 July 1877.
208 Methodist Mission Archives, London: Owusu Ansa to Tregaskis, dd. 11 October 1876, cited in Tregaskis to Owusu Ansa, dd. 22 August 1877.

tabled for full debate by the Asantemanhyiamu at its annual meeting at the Odwira – which fell in November 1876. While no record of the deliberations has yet come to light, the decisions taken were clearly not only in favour of change in the penal code but were also such as to provide Mensa Bonsu with a national mandate for the general programme of reform. The Asantemanhyiamu authorized the despatch immediately of a mission to the Governor of the Gold Coast to inform him that henceforth only those found guilty of murder would be executed and that the government in Kumase would welcome suggestions about further reforms.[209] The mission was entrusted to Gyakye Nantwi, who had served as Adu Bofo's senior aide in the campaigns east of the Volta in 1868–9, and had survived to become one of the government's principal negotiators with the British.[210] He arrived in Cape Coast on 15 December 1876, and announced that he represented the Asantehene, Mamponhene, Bekwaehene, Kokofuhene and Nkoransahene.[211] The text of his message reveals the nature of the enthusiastic endorsement which the Asantemanhyiamu had given to the policy of rapprochement and collaboration with the Gold Coast Colony:

The King and people send greetings to the Queen and the Governor. They have found some of their old ways not right, and they wish now to learn what is right. The King and people of Ashantee desire to keep good friends with the Governor (Government) that they may learn the wisdom of his Country, for when a man joins himself to a wise man, he gets some of his wisdom, and a nations join themselves to a wise nation they get some of their wisdom. The Governor's nation is a wise nation, the King will join himself to the Governor . . . The King and people know very well that human sacrifice is distressing to the feelings of the Whitemen, and their friendship will not go well while they keep up that custom, they determined to abolish it . . .[212]

The progressive cause in Asante seems to have received something of a set-back from the poor reception which the Gyakye Nantwi mission was afforded on the Gold Coast. 'The only thing I am afraid of', wrote Owusu Ansa,

is, the suspicions of so many, even the chief who brought this message from the King was not well received here, but was suspected, and he returned to Ashantee with disappointments, and I am in fears that through these suspicions Ashantee may be discouraged and drawn back to the old practices –

209 *The African Times*, XVIII, no. 186, 1 February 1877, p. 14: letter dd. 15 December 1876. *Ibid.* no. 187, 1 March 1877, p. 27: letter dd. 26 December 1876.
210 Ramseyer and Kühne, 1875, p. 57. Nantwi made other official visits to the Gold Coast in 1878 and 1880, in the course of the latter dying at Accra in July, see *The African Times*, XXII, no. 238, 1 July 1881, pp. 75–6: letter dd. Accra, 6 May 1881.
211 *The African Times*, XVIII, no. 186, 1 February 1877, p. 14.
212 Methodist Mission Archives, London: Owusu Ansa to Tregaskis, dd. 24 December 1876, in Tregaskis to Owusu Ansa, dd. 22 August 1877, pp. 21–2.

But I have not ceased in sending by messengers, to impress upon the King to stick firmly to his word, and determination, for surely he will see the good from it if he keeps his word.[213]

Nevertheless, in mid-1877 Owusu Ansa maintained that no executions had occurred, at festivals, funerals or the like, since the decree had come into force.[214] The abortive coup of 1877 must surely be viewed as a manifestation of opposition to the radical changes which were being effected by Mensa Bonsu's government, and it is significant perhaps that among those who the insurgents attempted to kill was Boakye Tenten – one of the political leaders seemingly the most committed to practical reform. In 1879 Mensa Bonsu began the creation of the special palace guard and, probably after the attempt on his life at the beginning of 1880, strengthened the force by transferring to it men from the Hausa regiments (see pp. 527–8). Although the Asantehene's personal behaviour thereafter became increasingly erratic, the commanding position of the peace party in the government was confirmed when the threat from the opposition was fought off in late January 1881. Significantly, a small mission was sent to Cape Coast a month later specifically to request the return of the Wesleyans to Kumase. 'The King', so the Rev. J. Fletcher was informed, 'was anxious at this time that the schools and missions should be re-established at Coomassie.'[215] In the course of his talks with Governor Rowe in April and May 1881, Boakye Tenten confirmed the government's policy, and in consequence Ramseyer paid a visit to Kumase in September of that year. He was much encouraged to find the people 'longing for peace' and to learn that no 'human sacrifices' had taken place for many months.[216] Yet, although the decision to liberalize the penal code had been taken by the Asantemanhyiamu as far back as November 1876, there was apparently still much uncertainty about the precise nature of the changes called for.

In April or May 1881, Boakye Tenten had discussed the problem of 'human sacrifice' with Governor Rowe in an attempt fully to appreciate the British position. It was his understanding of the matter, that while Rowe regarded the death penalty as an appropriate punishment for various transgressions of the law, he objected to the sentences being executed at funerals and other customs.[217] Such, certainly,

213 Basel Mission Archives: Owusu Ansa to Ramseyer, dd. 7 July 1877.

214 *Idem*. Methodist Mission Archives, London: Owusu Ansa to Tregaskis, dd. 16 June 1877, in Tregaskis to Owusu Ansa, dd. 22 August 1877, p. 23.

215 *Affairs*, C. 3064, 1881, p. 115: Fletcher's memorandum on the interview with the Asante messengers, Cape Coast, 18 March 1881.

216 *Further Correspondence*, C. 3386, 1882, pp. 21–2: Ramseyer to Governor, dd. Abetifi, 1 October 1881.

217 *Further Correspondence*, C. 4052, 1884, p. 82: Barrow to Colonial Office, dd. Sussex, 16 October 1883

was the account of the matter that Boakye Tenten laid before the Council on his return to the capital. 'I was not to kill any one for dead persons' burial', Mensa Bonsu himself later asserted, but 'that if any one touch any of my wives I was to kill him, that if anyone break any of my laws I was to kill him. If any one would not pay the King's fine kill him. If any one commit murder kill him'.[218] The issue was debated again, probably by the Asantemanhyiamu, at the end of 1881, and after discussions which extended over three days the decision to abolish all public executions at 'customs' was reaffirmed. Hundreds of those condemned to death and awaiting execution were released to mark the occasion and the event, so it was observed, 'caused great joy in Coomassie'.[219] Although the belief was long to persist, that sacrificial killings still occurred in the Asante villages, it was nevertheless generally acknowledged that public executions were no longer carried out in the capital.[220]

Owusu Ansa continued to enjoy the confidence of Mensa Bonsu until the Asantehene was removed from office in March 1883, after the *nkwankwaa* had seized control of the capital. That the situation had become a revolutionary one exemplified interestingly the observation of de Tocqueville, that revolution often occurs not in states which are politically decadent, but in those engaged in major attempts at reform.[221] Owusu Ansa recognized clearly that Mensa Bonsu's increasing resort to coercion and terror in the last three years of his reign had effectively curtailed the normal process of political protest and had thus created the conditions within which the revolutionary *nkwankwaa* movement had emerged. Mensa Bonsu, he wrote, 'began to exercise the grossest tyranny over his subjects and to kill and to fine them on the slightest or no pretence at all. The people of Coomassie becoming tired of his conduct resolved to depose him and they did so'.[222] No sympathizer himself with the *nkwankwaa*, Owusu Ansa's political instincts inclined him to work immediately for a return to legitimate government by what seemed the most obvious route: the restoration of Kofi Kakari as Asantehene. In April 1883 one of Kofi Kakari's *akyeame* or counselors arrived in Cape Coast, and stayed there to co-operate with Owusu Ansa.[223] The growth of the powerful Cape Coast

218 *Ibid*. p. 50: statement by Mensa Bonsu to Kirby, 12 May 1883.
219 *The Gold Coast Times*, I, no. 23, 24 December 1881, p. 2. See also *The Lagos Times*, II, no. 30, 25 January 1882, p. 2.
220 *Further Correspondence*, C. 3386, 1882, p. 39: Justice Watt to Acting Colonial Secretary, dd. Cape Coast, 2 February 1882. *Ibid*. p. 41: District Commissioner, Cape Coast, to Colonial Secretary, dd. 11 February 1882.
221 For a recent discussion of this point, see Welch and Taintor, 1972, pp. 9 ff.
222 *Further Correspondence*, C. 4052, 1884, p. 73: Owusu Ansa to Governor, dd. Accra, 27 August 1883.
223 *Ibid*. p. 23: District Commissioner, Cape Coast, to Assistant Colonial Secretary, dd. Cape Coast, 8 August 1883.

caucus around Owusu Ansa, as 'director of the Karikari cause in the Protectorate', has been discussed above (pp. 555–6). In terms of the constitutional position, Owusu Ansa argued that the Council of Kumase had usurped powers which rightfully belonged to the Asantemanhyiamu, and that the sponsorship of the candidacy of Kwaku Dua Kuma by the former body lacked legal validity.[224] When his brother Owusu Koko came to power by the coup of August 1883, Owusu Ansa was soon to condemn the new regime for its 'horrible and extensive shedding of blood'.[225] He reiterated his belief that Kofi Kakari, having learned from past experience, would 'rule his subjects more in accordance with the ideas of civilized nations' and that his policy would be 'to ensure permanent peace, the opening up of roads, and the development of the vast resources of the interior'.[226]

As the Gold Coast administration came increasingly to regard with favour the Council of Kumase's choice of Kwaku Dua Kuma for Asantehene, so Owusu Ansa's position in Cape Coast, as head of the opposed cause there, became correspondingly insecure. By April 1884 Governor Young, who had replaced Rowe, was already planning the deportation of Owusu Ansa and of his associate, Yaw Awua.[227] The prince's health, however, was deteriorating rapidly and on 13 November he died at Cape Coast.[228] He had lived to hear of the deaths of Kofi Kakari and of the short-reigned Kwaku Dua II, but not to learn of the demise of his brother Owusu Koko, and of his old associate Boakye Tenten, in the *coup* which brought Akyampon Panin to power. In the long struggle which followed, until the Prempe regime finally won an ascendancy in 1888, it is difficult to know where Owusu Ansa's sympathies would have lain. Certainly his vision of the Asante future – of the modernization of its administrative, military and legal institutions, of the development of its economy with the participation of European capital and skills, and of its peaceful coexistence with the Gold Coast Colony – could have seemed of little relevance in a period of turmoil when the nation lacked not only stable government but fundamental agreement upon procedures for moving towards it. Yet the constituency which Owusu Ansa had enjoyed was one which did in fact survive the troubled years, and two of his sons were to play major roles in the reformulation of national goals by the Prempe regime from 1888 to 1894 and by the Prempe government from 1894

224 *Ibid.* pp. 72–4: Owusu Ansa to Governor, dd. Accra, 27 August 1883.
225 *Ibid.* pp. 92–3: Owusu Ansa to Derby, dd. Accra, 18 October 1883.
226 *Idem.*
227 *Further Correspondence*, C. 4477, 1885, p. 89: Young to Derby, dd. Accra, 21 April 1884. NAG, Accra, ADM 12/1/4: Derby to Young, dd. Downing St, 31 October 1884. Derby rejected Young's suggestion that Owusu Ansa should be sent to St Helena, and favoured the Gambia instead.
228 Ellis, 1893, p. 377.

to 1896. Owusu Ansa is perhaps to be seen as one of the earliest Asante patriots – in the nineteenth century sense of that word. 'If it is a sin', he wrote to the Earl of Derby not long before his death, 'to have at heart the true interests of one's country, and to advise one's countrymen what their real interests are then I must confess my Lord that I have sinned grievously, and must have erred greatly in my long career with the English Government, and my Country. . .' [229]

John Owusu Ansa in the Service of Agyeman Prempe I

Both John and Albert Arthur were sons of Owusu Ansa by his marriage to Sarah Boxell of Cape Coast.[230] John Owusu Ansa was born in Kumase in 1851, when his father was catechist there, and Albert Arthur Owusu Ansa in Cape Coast some years later.[231] Both were educated in Cape Coast, though in 1874 Owusu Ansa had thought of sending Albert to complete his studies in Liverpool.[232] In 1873, as a young man, John Owusu Ansa enlisted in the Gold Coast Rifle Corps raised by Captain John Sarbah. He acquired the rank of Sergeant-major, and was recipient from the British of the 'Ashanti War Medal'.[233] The campaigns ended, he remained in Cape Coast when his father returned to Kumase and entered into Mensa Bonsu's administration. He taught at the Cape Coast Government School, and resigned to become clerk in the Audit Department there. The programme of *Un Grand Concert Orchestral et Choral* held in that town at Christmas 1877 announced that the piano was to be played by 'John Ansah, esquire'.[234] In 1880 he left the Gold Coast and for seven years pursued a career presumably in trade on the Lower Niger.[235] In the first thirty or so years of his life there was little to suggest that John Owusu Ansu in any serious way felt or acknowledged the responsibilities of being a grandson of the Asantehene Osei Bonsu. The early career of his younger brother Albert followed, moreover, a some-

229 NAG, Accra, ADM 1/2/373: Owusu Ansa to Derby, dd. Accra, 18 February 1884.
230 In 1877–8 John and Albert Owusu Ansa were both resident with their father in Cape Coast, though Sarah Boxell was dead. There were three apparently senior brothers. Two lived in Asante, and were probably sons of an earlier marriage to an Asante woman. A third was employed by a French firm in Gabon. See Hertz, 1885, p. 106.
231 *Further Correspondence,* C. 7917, 1896, p. 227: the Asante in the Western Protectorate to Governor, dd. Cape Coast, 1 October 1894. *Further Correspondence,* C. 7918, 1896, p. 5: Griffith to Ripon, dd. Cape Coast, 26 December 1894.
232 Methodist Mission Archives, London: Tregaskis to Owusu Ansa, dd. 18 September 1877, pp. 5–6.
233 *The Gold Coast Chronicle,* 31 March 1894.
234 Hertz, 1885, pp. 147, 166.
235 *Further Correspondence,* C. 7917, 1896, p. 216: Memorandum of Interview with John Owusu Ansa, by Griffith, Accra, 13 June 1889.

what similar pattern. In 1881 he had obtained a supernumerary position as clerk on the staff of Governor Rowe, and as such had been present at the meeting of Rowe and Boakye Tenten at the Pra river in April of that year. In March 1883 he was appointed Telegraph Clerk, but in the following year Governor Young dismissed him for insubordination. Reinstated on the intercession of his friends, he chose then to submit his resignation. Turning to commerce, he established a small business in Cape Coast and then moved to Axim to become partner in the firm of Johnson and Ansa.[236]

John Owusu Ansa returned from the Niger in 1886. As far as is known, neither he nor his brother became involved in the support which the Cape Coast caucus gave to Yaw Twereboanna in his bid for the Golden Stool. Indeed, soon after the Prempe regime had come to power, John Owusu Ansa visited Kumase (perhaps for the first time since he had been taken there by his father in 1862, when Kwaku Dua I had presented him with a small boy as servant).[237] His short stay of three weeks, in April 1889, coincided with R. Austin Freeman's second visit there, and the two met by chance in the street. 'I received a surprise', wrote Freeman,

that made me for the moment think that I was the victim of a hallucination, for out of a narrow turning there emerged a gentleman arrayed in the costume of Piccadilly . . . He wore a shapely 'bowler', and a well-fitting, fashionably cut suit of clothes; his cuffs, shirt-front and high collar were faultlessly got up; his patent leather boots were a miracle of polish, and in one of his kid-gloved hands he carried a modish walking cane. But the most astonishing thing was that he wore his clothes and carried his cane with the unmistakable air of a man who was accustomed to them, and not with the embarrassed manner of an occasionally dressed native. Presently the mysterious stranger observed me and approached, and then when he politely introduced himself to me as Prince Ansah, the mystery was solved. We walked about the town for some time and Prince Ansah took me to the house where he was staying, and exhibited with great pride a remarkable assortment of firearms, including an 8-bore elephant gun . . .[238]

John Owusu Ansa's presence in Kumase, however, had a purpose more serious than that of sartorial display. On 26 December 1888 Inspector Lethbridge of the Gold Coast Constabulary had met with the Asantehene to present to him a proposal from the Gold Coast government: that the Asantehene should sign an agreement 'not to enter into any treaty with a foreign Power to take Ashanti under its protection unless with the consent of this Government [that is, of the Gold

[236] Claridge, 1915, II, 385–6.
[237] *Wesleyan-Methodist Magazine*, October 1862, p. 958: visit of West and Owusu Ansa to Kumase.
[238] R. A. Freeman, 1898, pp. 368–9.

Coast], which would have a say in the matter'.[239] Agyeman Prempe intimated his willingness to have the matter debated, but refused a sum of 80 oz of gold offered him by Lethbridge as an inducement.[240] It appears that immediately after this meeting Agyeman Prempe sought John Owusu Ansa's advice, and invited him to Kumase. Certainly the matter was discussed in April 1889, and John Owusu Ansa counselled the Asante government to accept the proposed arrangement. Agyeman Prempe consented to have the relevant document drawn up. John Owusu Ansa's suggestion that he should be appointed Asante representative to the Gold Coast government was also approved.[241] John Owusu Ansa returned to the Gold Coast with Asante messengers deputed to announce the decisions. Governor Griffith met with him in June, firmly refused to recognize him as representative of the Asante government, and expressed surprise that another envoy from Kumase, Kwame Boaten, was unaware of the decisions that had been taken there – although Kwame Boaten pointed out that he had left the capital earlier on quite other business.[242] The outcome of the matter was that no agreement was signed; but the Asante government had experienced, for the first time, the pragmatic and unprincipled quality of the new-style diplomacy of the imperial era.

John Owusu Ansa returned to Kumase. He had previously obtained from the Akuroponhene a concession to mine gold at Asakraka (some 16 miles west of the capital). After some trouble, he succeeded in having the grant confirmed by the Asantehene and council.[243] He commenced mining operations in the second half of 1889, with a labour force which included eight Kru workers. In 1891, however, the enterprise faltered when they left his employment.[244] It is uncertain whether the mine was subsequently reopened. John Owusu Ansa himself claimed that the problem in 1891 had arisen from the fact that the calls upon his time made by public affairs left him inadequate opportunities to supervise the mining operations.[245]

239 *Further Correspondence*, C. 7917, 1896, p. 217: memorandum of an interview with John Owusu Ansa, by Griffith, Accra, 13 June 1889.
240 *Idem*. The British claim, that Prempe had previously asked the Gold Coast government for a loan of 80 oz of gold, was probably a fabricated one. The Asantehene himself repudiated all knowledge of the request, see R. A. Freeman, 1898, p. 129.
241 *Further Correspondence*, C. 7917, 1896, pp. 216–17: memorandum of an interview with Ansa.
242 *Idem. Further Correspondence*, C. 7918, 1896, p. 7: notes of an interview with Asante ambassadors, by Griffith, dd. Cape Coast, 13 December 1894.
243 *Further Correspondence*, C. 7917, 1896, p. 187: Ansa to Governor, dd. Kumase, 5 April 1894. See further, PRO, CO. 96/344: Hodgson to Chamberlain, dd. 22 September 1899.
244 *Further Correspondence*, C. 7917, 1896, p. 67: Hull to Governor, dd. Kumase, 22 April 1891.
245 *Ibid*. p. 187: Ansa to Governor, dd. Kumase, 5 April 1894.

By late 1889 John Owusu Ansa had already assumed responsibility for drafting correspondence with the Gold Coast government, though there was some doubt in the minds of the recipients about the extent of his influence in political matters: the Asafohene Asafo Boakye, son of Kwaku Dua I and the only functionary of importance to have survived in office from the pre-1874 period, was regarded as the dominant figure in the Council of Kumase.[246] There may, indeed, have been some degree of conflict between the older councillors and John Owusu Ansa, as there had been between them and his father. 'The Ashantis had their suspicions of him', commented Governor Griffith in 1889.[247] But if this was so, it did little to inhibit his rise to a position of authority. On 28 April 1891 the British Travelling Commissioner Hull was permitted to address the Asantemanhyiamu. He used the occasion to attempt to discredit John Owusu Ansa. 'I told the King', Hull reported,

who is only a boy of 18 or 19, having, I understand, been born very shortly before the English entered Kumasi in 1874, that he had listened to very bad advice, coming from persons who were afraid to speak the truth, and flattered him, and I warned him of the folly of taking such a course. I also said that I had reason to believe that Prince Ansah, who was not a true Ashanti, was his political adviser in many things . . .[248]

John Owusu Ansa forced a vote of confidence in his capabilities, intimating that he would leave Kumase and return to the Gold Coast since Hull had so misrepresented him. He was thereupon invited to answer the charges before the Asantemanhyiamu, and Hull was obligated to apologize to him before the members.[249] The occasion appears to have been that on which John Owusu Ansa was formally invited to take charge of the foreign affairs bureau. 'His Majesty the King, Kings, Chiefs, and principal men of Ashanti', he wrote, 'solicited me earnestly to assist them to look into the Ashanti affairs with the British Government . . . His Majesty the King, Kings, Chiefs and principal men of Ashanti, having found that without my assistance they could do no better than to leave all the business to my hands with the British Government.'[250] The primary object of Hull's mission had been to induce the Asante government to accept an offer of full British protection – a far more consequential measure than that requested by Lethbridge in 1888. John Owusu Ansa's first task in office, then, was probably to draft the letter of 7 May 1891 (the text of which has been given above, p. 120), in which the British offer was firmly but

246 *Ibid.* pp. 14–15: Hodgson to Knutsford, dd. Accra, 11 January 1890.
247 *Ibid.* p. 217: memorandum of interview with Ansa, dd. Accra, 13 June 1889.
248 *Ibid.* p. 72: Hull to Governor, dd. Accra, 27 May 1891.
249 *Ibid.* pp. 187–8: Ansa to Governor, dd. Kumase, 5 April 1894.
250 *Idem.*

graciously rejected. 'Mr. Hull's mission to Ashanti', he subsequently commented perhaps not without malice, 'might have proved success-ful, or somewhat satisfactorily to both parties, had he not tried to put me away'.²⁵¹ Throughout the remainder of 1891 and in 1892 John Owusu Ansa must have been much concerned with the discus-sions preliminary to the setting up of the 'Ashanti and Prah Mining and Trading Company'.²⁵²

In its conception, the Trading Company represented a return to the position developed by the senior Owusu Ansa during the administra-tion of Mensa Bonsu, that the economic development of Asante would proceed the more rapidly with the participation of European capital and skills. On 26 April 1892 the Asantehene entered into an agreement with Dr J. W. Herivel to create the Company which, with the backing of the Asante government, would subsequently apply to the British Crown for a charter. Herivel himself – born in Alderney and a grad-uate of the University of Paris – had worked as a Wesleyan missionary in France from 1873 until his retirement in 1891.²⁵³ There can be little doubt that his first association with Asante must have been made through French connections. The Company was to finance and manage the construction of railroads and the development of industry – par-ticularly gold-mining and timber – with the co-operation of the Asante authorities, and was to assume responsibility for overseas marketing arrangements. The Asantehene was immediately to supply four hundred labourers to work on laying the railroad tracks. The amount of the royalties to be paid to the Asantehene, and of salaries to his functionaries in so far as they acted as agents of the Company, was to be fixed at a meeting of Herivel with the Council in Kumase.²⁵⁴ Gov-ernor Griffith of the Gold Coast viewed the project with considerable alarm, and deemed it expedient to deter Herivel from pressing forward with a scheme which might greatly have strengthened the Asante econ-omy. In 1893 the actual agreement between the Asantehene and Herivel was impounded by the High Court of the Gold Coast, and Herivel was harassed by the Customs Department until finally in 1894 he was obliged to abandon the scheme.²⁵⁵ Nevertheless, the con-

251 *Idem.* It is significant that in this period John Owusu Ansa lived in the house of the Asomfohene Kwaku Wo, who as head of the sword-bearers was much concerned in the conduct of embassies, see PRO, CO. 96/344: Hodgson to Chamberlain, dd. 22 September 1899.
252 NAG, Accra, ADM 12/3/5: Griffith to Ripon, dd. Aburi, 31 May 1893 –'I think that [Herivel] is probably mixed up with the son of Osoo Ansah who is Secretary to the king of Ashanti.'
253 NAG, Accra, ADM 12/1/2: Hall to Griffith, dd. Cape Coast, 8 May 1893.
254 *Ibid:* Herivel to Ripon, dd. Balham, Easter Monday 1893. PRO, CO. 96/244: enclosures in Griffith to Ripon, dd. 6 April 1894. See also Agbodeka, 1971, p. 161, n. 3.
255 NAG, Accra, ADM 1/9/4: Griffith to Herivel, dd. Accra, 7 May 1894.

ception behind the agreement was one to which the government in Kumase was to remain committed.

The issue of British protection

In 1892 Governor Griffith considered the Asantehene to be a puppet in the hands of his mother the Asantehemaa Yaa Kyaa, and of 'a Mr. John Osoo Ansah'.[256] Two years later the Governor described Ansa as 'the principal adviser of the King in everything', and as 'the Prime Minister of the King of Kumasi' – a title by which Albert Owusu Ansa had also referred to his elder brother.[257] At one of the meetings of the Asantemanhyiamu which was in session from 11 to 24 June 1894, John Owusu Ansa appears to have received a further vote of confidence from that Assembly. 'From what I have gathered from [*sic*: of] him', reported the Asantehene,

as well as my district Kings, Chiefs, and principal men of Ashanti, that he is a very good assistant and a very good adviser, that if he could, and if it is in his power, he would bring up his grandfather's nation to a great and dignified state. If my grandson Prince Ansah is with us here, he is here for the future happiness of his nation . . .[258]

John Owusu Ansa's political position was clearly predicated upon the same fundamental beliefs as those which his father had espoused: that the modernization ('civilisation') of the nation could proceed only on the basis of close association with the Gold Coast Colony. In a letter to Governor Griffith in 1894, he outlined his ideology of change while acknowledging the strength of the conservative opposition:

I have being always trying to bring my country (Ashanti) into the light of civilisation; although my people do not seem to know the good fruits which civilisation bears, and which is being enjoyed by the other civilised world, yet it is my earnest and constant prayer that the light of civilisation should smile upon this benighted land . . . The Ashantees think that in days gone by, were days of prosperity; I repudiated the idea with them and argued that if Ashanti were to take my simple advice, and be one with the British Government they would soon see it clearly that those days that had gone by, for which they call it days of prosperity, were only days of torment, although they had not seen it to be so, but for the one which I proposes will be surely days of continual peace and happiness.[259]

256 PRO, Foreign Office Confidential Print 6364, Papers relating to West African Negotiations: Griffith to Ripon, dd. Accra, 20 September 1892.
257 *Further Correspondence*, C. 7918, 1896, pp. 10–13: notes of an interview with Asante ambassadors, by Griffith, Cape Coast, 13 December 1894.
258 *Further Correspondence*, C. 7917, 1896, pp. 201–2: Prempe to Governor, dd. Kumase, 28 June 1894.
259 *Ibid.* pp. 187–8: Ansa to Governor, dd. Kumase, 5 April 1894.

Like his father, John Owusu Ansa took an active interest in military affairs and appears to have been committed to similar ideas of reform. Holding a rank described as 'Field Marshal', he accompanied the army which occupied Nkoransa in 1892,[260] and claimed subsequently that he had been instrumental in preventing the victorious Asante forces from pursuing the Nkoransahene to Atebubu and thereby risking conflict with the British force there (see pp. 298–9).[261] He was also concerned in planning the organization of military supplies from French commercial agencies. A report that he visited Europe in 1893 to obtain Maxim guns and quick-firing rifles was probably inaccurate,[262] but there is no doubt that he was closely in touch with merchants at Assini and Grand Bassam and that considerable quantities of modern arms and ammunition were imported through those towns.[263] John Owusu Ansa was reported also to have obtained the services of Europeans in the training of the Asante fighting forces,[264] and two Frenchmen who had landed at Grand Bassam were known to have been in Kumase in 1894.[265] Indeed, in 1894 there were strong rumours that John Owusu Ansa had visited the French Protectorate on the Ivory Coast and had opened negotiations with the Chargé d'Affaires at Kwankyeabo for a Franco-Asante treaty. Governor Griffith thought it the case that the French would have no hesitation in disregarding their treaty relations with Britain once they could obtain a firm agreement with the Asantehene.[266] It is highly likely that with an established business at Axim, Albert Owusu Ansa actively assisted his brother in the revival of the French connection which had been built up by their father and Albert Brun some twenty years earlier. Certainly it was about this time that Albert Owusu Ansa began to act as publicist for the Asante cause. Reports, for example, that four hundred persons had been sacrificed in June 1894, when Agyeman Prempe was finally enstooled upon the Golden Stool, led him to despatch vigorous protests to the Governor of the Gold Coast and to various local and British newspapers. 'As a Prince of that country', he wrote in the *Gold Coast Methodist Times,*

260 PRO, Foreign Office Confidential Print 6364: Griffith to Ripon, dd. Accra, 20 September 1892.
261 *Further Correspondence*, C. 7918, 1896, p. 8: notes of an interview with Asante ambassadors, 13 December 1894.
262 *The African Times*, xxxv, no. 338, 1 January 1894.
263 *Idem.* PRO, CO. 879/38, African (West) 448: Ferguson to Governor dd. Bimbilla, 29 August 1892. See also Agbodeka, 1971, p. 151.
264 *The African Times*, xxxv, no. 338, 1 January 1894.
265 *The Times* (London), 12 January 1895, p. 3. One Lieutenant in the French army is reported to have written to offer his services to the Asantehene, see *The Gold Coast Express*, ii, no. 68, 7 May 1900, p. 3.
266 NAG, Accra, ADM 12/3/6: Griffith to Ripon, dd. Accra, 26 June and 10 August 1894; and Griffith to Ripon, dd. Cape Coast, 11 December 1894, citing telegram from Ripon.

I cannot allow such a fabrication, since that there is not a particle of truth in it, to pass uncontradicted. I consider it a pure bogus trumped-up business to get the Christian world against our nationality . . . Happily the sacrifices of days gone by have long been done away with, and for the present only persons who are tried and found to be murderers and conspirators suffer the capital punishment. The administration of justice is impartially administered . . .[267]

On 23 February 1894 the Acting Governor of the Gold Coast, Hodgson, on instructions from London, submitted a new set of proposals to the Asante government. A British Resident was to be stationed in Kumase who would be consulted in such matters as those relating to peace and war, and the Asantehene, Asantehemaa and senior *amanhene* were to receive annual stipends from the British government.[268] The proposals were laid before the Council of Kumase on 19 March, and it was decided that an extraordinary session of the Asantemanhyiamu should be convened to consider them. The Assembly met on 28 March and took note of the business before it. At a second meeting on 5 April, John Owusu Ansa argued for the despatch of an embassy to the Gold Coast, to discuss modifications of the proposals with the Governor. At a third meeting on 7 April the British emissary Vroom informed the Assembly that it was intended to fix the stipend of the Asantehene at £600 per year, of the Asantehemaa at £80, and of the senior *amanhene* at £200. The councillors representing the *amanhene* decided, however, that the matter should be held over until the next session of the Asantemanhyiamu in June, when Agyeman Prempe was to be formally recognized as Asantehene and the *amanhene* might take their seats in person. A letter to that effect was despatched the same day to Governor Griffith. On 9 April Vroom protested the decision to the Council of Kumase without observing due protocol. He was reprimanded by the Asantehene, the Bantamahene Amankwatia and the Asafohene Asafo Boakye. A protest against his conduct was sent to the Governor two days later.[269]

The British authorities in Accra were convinced that it was John Owusu Ansa who was principally responsible for obstructing their proposals. On 1 March 1894 Ferguson had already written to the Governor, that 'while that man Ansa is in Kumasi, we will always have trouble with Ashanti, and the combination of Ashanti trickery with his, so to speak, educated roguery requires to be dealt with firmly'.[270] Reports were current that Griffith, insisting that John Owusu Ansa was

267 *Gold Coast Methodist Times*, 29 September 1894.
268 NAG, Accra, ADM 11/1483: Hodgson to Vroom, dd. Accra, 23 February 1894.
269 *Further Correspondence*, C. 7917, 1896, pp. 179–82: Vroom to Governor, dd. Accra, 24 April 1894. *Ibid.* pp. 183–5: Prempe to Governor, dd. Kumase, 11 April 1894.
270 *Ibid.* p. 221: Ferguson to Governor, dd. Bamboi, 1 March 1894.

a British subject, contemplated his deportation to St Helena – a similar measure to that planned for his father ten years earlier.[271] It was left to Albert Owusu Ansa to point out that he and his brother 'never naturalised ourselves as British subjects nor considered ourselves as such at any time'.[272] The fact of the matter was, that after the formal enstoolment proceedings which were scheduled for 11 June, members of the Asantemanhyiamu were to proceed to a full debate on the state of the nation, when John Owusu Ansa was expected to present a new set of policy guidelines for the approval of the councillors. In-formation that had reached the Gold Coast administration was such as to suggest that John Owusu Ansa's proposals might prove highly embarrassing to the British government.

Between 11 and 24 June 1894, the matter of the nation's future was debated by the Asantemanhyiamu (see p. 587). Hodgson's set of pro-posals of 23 February was agreed to be raising a question 'grave and sweeping, touching as it does the constitution and construction of His Majesty's Independent Kingdom'.[273] The councillors reaffirmed the decision of 1891 to reject the British offer of protectorate status, and appear to have agreed that British aspirations should be satisfied by a treaty of the sort proposed in 1888 – guaranteeing that Asante would not accept the protection of any other foreign power. It is probable that the attention of the councillors was drawn to the nature of the agreement concluded in 1881 between the British and the Amir of Afghanistan. Certainly in a letter to Governor Griffith of 5 October 1894, Albert Owusu Ansa alluded to precisely that matter:

As my countrymen are desirous of continuing their independence, I beg here to strongly suggest to your Excellency that it is essential that the [British] Government ought now to formally acknowledge Ashanti as an in-dependent native empire, or in other words engagements entered into with her similar to the understanding now existing between Her Majesty's Government and the Ameer of Afghanistan by which annexation by any Power is ren-dered impossible.[274]

Although no full report on the debates appears to survive, sub-sequent developments suggest strongly that at its meetings in June the Asantemanhyiamu again discussed the issue of the participation of European enterprise in the development of Asante, and affirmed a

271 *The Gold Coast Chronicle*, 31 March 1894. Compare NAG, Accra, ADM 12/3/6: Griffith to Ripon, dd. Accra, 8 November 1894.
272 *Further Correspondence*, C. 7918, 1896, p. 11: notes of an interview with Asante ambassadors, 13 December 1894.
273 *Ibid.* p. 40: John Owusu Ansa *et al.* to Governor, dd. Cape Coast, 3 January 1895.
274 *Further Correspondence*, C. 7917, 1896, pp. 211–12: Albert Owusu Ansa to Governor, dd. 5 October 1894.

continuing commitment to such a course. John Owusu Ansa suggested to the Assembly that an embassy should be sent to London to negotiate directly with the British government, and cited as precedent 'that the King of Dahomey had sent Ambassadors to England before'.[275] Recognizing that negotiations with the Governor of the Gold Coast had proved singularly unproductive, the Asantemanhyiamu approved the proposal and selected John Owusu Ansa to manage it. Six other members of the mission were named, and it is significant that at least three of them had served in the diplomatic corps in Mensa Bonsu's administration: Kwame Boaten, newly promoted to Kyidomhene; Kwaku Nkruma, described as a chamberlain; and Akyampon Daban of the *afenasoafo*. Of the other three, Kwaku Fokuo was Boakye Yam Panin counselor and adopted son of the renowned Boakye Tenten; Kwabena Bonna held the post of Sepe Nkyetiahene within the *nseniefo;* and Kwadwo Tufuo, referred to as 'armour bearer', was one of the *ankobeafo* of Kumase. On 28 June 1894, after the Asantemanhyiamu had completed its business, a letter was despatched to Governor Griffith notifying him of the names of the members of the embassy which would arrive in the Gold Coast – but withholding information that it would be the intent of the ambassadors to proceed to London.[276]

The embassy to London and the Cade affair

The Asante government made immediate arrangements to finance the embassy by a special tax levy. On 8 September 1894 John Owusu Ansa's credential was drawn up, by the terms of which he was authorized to enter into agreements on behalf of his government: [277]

To the Most Gracious and Illustrious Sovereign, Victoria, Queen of Great Britain and Ireland.
Kwaku Dua III., King of Ashanti, wisheth health and prosperity.
We pray Your Most Gracious Majesty to know that we have appointed our trusty and well-beloved grandson, Prince John Ossoo Ansah, son of the late Prince Ansah, of Ashanti, on our behalf to lay before your Majesty divers matters affecting the good estate of our kingdom and the well-being of our subjects with full power for the said Prince Ansah as our ambassador extraordinary and minister plenipotentiary to negotiate and conclude all such treaties relating to the furtherance of trade and all matters therewith connected as your Majesty shall be pleased to entertain.

275 PRO, CO. 96/270: notes of a palaver, 20 January 1896. The allusion to Dahomey is an obscure one, though the ruler Glele had intimated his interest in sending an embassy to London in 1862: see Burton, 1864, II, 389.
276 *Further Correspondence*, C. 7918, 1896, p. 12: notes of an interview with Asante ambassadors, 13 December 1894.
277 *Ibid.* pp. 122–3.

We therefore pray that your Majesty will be pleased to receive the said Prince Ansah on our behalf and to accord to him your Majesty's most royal favour.

Given at our Court at Kumasi this 8th day of September 1894.

Kwaku Dua III.,

my X mark.

King of Ashanti.

In November Albert Owusu Ansa was appointed to join the embassy, and was apparently authorized to notify Governor Griffith of its ultimate objective. A telegram was despatched by him from Axim:

Prince Albert Arthur Ossoo Ansah having been commissioned by His Majesty King Quacoe Duah the Third of Ashanti to act as one of the special Ambassadors to the Court of St. James, London, left this day by the steamship 'Ambriz' for Cape Coast Castle to await the arrival of the rest of the envoys; it is stated that his elder brother Prince John, who has been acting as Prime Minister to his royal relation for the past four years, is head of the mission; the Embassy hopes to winter in England, and after completing their diplomatic mission to the British Court they will probably visit other European capitals, notably Paris and the Hague . . .[278]

The ambassadorial party, accompanied by over three hundred retainers, made its way slowly to the coast, halting at all the towns and villages to exchange compliments with the local chiefs. The Pra was crossed on 1 December, and Cape Coast was entered nine days later.[279] A series of meetings was held with Governor Griffith on the 12th, 13th, and 15th of that month. His highly objectionable treatment of the mission, and scurrilous attempts to discredit the Owusu Ansas, are a matter of record.[280] Griffith informed the ambassadors that the British government had already notified him that 'in no case would her Majesty receive a mission from a ruler who is accused on apparently good grounds of allowing human sacrifices'; [281] that he, Griffith, did not recognize Agyeman Prempe as Asantehene but only as 'King of Kumasi'; [282] and that in the sight of 'Her Majesty the great Queen

---

278 *Further Correspondence*, C. 7918, 1896, p. 13: notes of an interview, 13 December 1894. *Ibid.* p. 3: notes of an interview, 12 December 1894. *The Gold Coast Chronicle*, 19 November 1894.

279 NAG, Accra, ADM. 11/1483: Vroom to Governor, dd. Praso, 1 December 1894; Vroom to Governor, dd. Dumase, 5 December 1894.

280 *Further Correspondence*, C. 7918, 1896, pp. 3–4: interview of 12 December; pp. 6–14: interview of 13 December; pp. 26–33: interview of 15 December 1894.

281 *Ibid.* p. 14.

282 *Ibid.* p. 28. Compare NAG, Accra, ADM 1/9/4: Griffith to 'King Boateng of Akwawu' dd. Accra, 3 September 1888 – 'The selection of the King now called Kwaku Dua the IV [*sic*], he was properly placed upon the Stool, I regard him as the King of Ashanti, and I shall not treat with any other person or persons connected with Ashanti, except through him . . .'

of England and Empress of India . . . you and your King are as nothing'.[283] Finally, on 21 December, Griffith formally forbade the ambassadors from proceeding to England.[284]

In such decidedly inauspicious circumstances, Griffith decided to send his own emissaries to Kumase to demand that the Asante government give a direct reply to Hodgson's proposals for the appointment of a British Resident in Kumase, as communicated on 23 February 1894. Stewart and Vroom left for the capital, where they held a number of meetings with the Council of Kumase. Until 19 January 1895 it appeared that the councillors were divided on how best to proceed, some urging acceptance of Hodgson's proposals. On that or the following day, however, messages reached the capital from the ambassadors in Cape Coast. Whatever their content, the effect was immediate. On 21 January Stewart and Vroom were abruptly dismissed from Kumase after having been informed that John Owusu Ansa's mission was fully authorized to resolve all outstanding issues in England.[285]

In the meantime, John Owusu Ansa had not been inactive. He had written to England to obtain clarification on three matters: whether the embassy could be refused permission to leave the Gold Coast, whether it could be refused permission to land in England, and whether its members could be arrested, killed or otherwise molested while there. It was indicative of the planning which the embassy had kept a closely guarded secret from the colonial authorities, that John Owusu Ansa's queries were addressed to the Liverpool firm of Radcliffe and Durant – whose association with Asante had now entered its third decade (see pp. 605; 612).[286] The Liverpool company communicated with the Colonial Office in London, and were able to assure the ambassadors, by cable, that they could not properly be prevented from visiting England even though official recognition might not be afforded them. Upon receipt of the information, John Owusu Ansa consigned to Radcliffe and Durant a part of the embassy's purse:

---

283 *Further Correspondence,* C. 7918, 1896, p. 29.

284 *Ibid.* p. 15: Griffith to Ansa *et al.,* dd. Cape Coast, 21 December 1894. NAG, Accra, ADM 11/1483: Vroom to Governor, dd. Accra, 22 December 1894.

285 *Ibid.* pp. 37–8: Stewart and Vroom to Governor, dd. Accra, 5 February 1895.

286 In 1898 the firm of Radcliffe, Son and Durant was listed among 'old established and well-tried firms . . . whose names in West African commercial life are as familiar as household words and are a guarantee of commercial safety and security', see *The Gold Coast Independent,* IV, no. 1, 19 February 1898, p. 2. A Jonathen Ratcliffe of Liverpool had been a member of the Company of Merchants Trading to Africa in 1750, see *Liverpool and Slavery,* by A Genuine 'Dicky Sam', Liverpool, 1884. The Liverpool firm of Messrs. Radcliffe and Co. was active in the West African slave trade in the late 18th century, see Williams, 1897, pp. 234–5, 668. Felix Durand was among French prisoners in Liverpool in 1799; subsequently he married a Liverpool woman, *ibid.* p. 427.

gold dust to the value of about £1,900 by the S.S. *Volta* on 14 January.[287]

The members of the embassy embarked at Cape Coast on the steamship *Accra* on 3 April 1895, and landed at Liverpool on the 24th. They were met there by Kofi Asaam (Frank S. Essien), a former Cape Coast barrister whose services they had procured and who preceded them to England to make advance arrangements,[288] and by James Hutton Brew ('Prince Brew of Dunquah'), another Fante barrister who had settled in London in 1888 [289] and who had agreed to manage the legal affairs of the embassy.[290] The ambassadors spent some days in Liverpool where they may be presumed to have held preliminary talks with representatives of the firm of Radcliffe and Durant. On 5 May they communicated to a London journalist a detailed statement which, since it set out the Asante position with such clarity, is worth quoting at some length:

The destruction of the Ashanti power by the expedition of Sir Garnet Wolseley in 1873 [*sic*] removed the central authority which had previously kept the surrounding countries and tribes in subjection and order. With the success of British arms there devolved upon the destroyer of the Ashanti central power the responsibility for peace and order. The refusal of that responsibility by Her Majesty's Government has been the chief cause, in the eyes of the Ashantis, of the protracted period of civil war and anarchy with its attendant results in the diminution of trade and prosperity. These disasters the Ashantis have fought against, alone and unaided. Their efforts have been crowned with conspicuous success. As far back as 1888 their aim to secure unity and peace had resulted in the election as King of Ashanti of a sovereign whose rule has been characterised by firmness, tact, and wisdom. Since the achievement of this important step in the direction of progress they have succeeded in still further consolidating the peace and prosperity of the country. Refractory tributaries have been taught obedience, roads have been opened, trade has been extended, and the horrible custom of human sacrifice has been long ago finally put an end to by the people's wish and the King's authority. Now that so much has been accomplished by their own unaided efforts, it is felt that native opinion should properly be consulted in settling the terms under which the appointment of a British Resident may be made

287 *The Times*, 18 April 1895, p. 8. NAG, Accra, ADM 11/1482: Stewart to Governor, dd. Accra, 3 March 1895. A further consignment was forwarded on 25 May, by S. S. *Bakama*, to the value of £630 2s, see NAG, Accra, ADM 11/1483: District Commissioner, Cape Coast, to Private Secretary, dd. Accra, 4 November 1895.

288 Kofi Asaam had been, like John Owusu Ansa, a volunteer member of the Gold Coast Rifle Corps in 1873-4, see Kimble, 1963, pp. 85, n. 1, and 90, n. 5.

289 See Priestley, 1969, chapter IV, and especially p. 169, n. 4. Brew claimed to be related to the Owusu Ansas, presumably through their mother, see PRO, CO. 96/267: Brew to Ripon, dd. 9 February 1895.

290 *The Times*, 25 April 1895, p. 10. *The Gold Coast Times*, 21 May 1895, p. 3.

for the protection of British interests. It is understood that unless the terms of the appointment be carefully defined, the appearance of a Resident in Coomassie is likely to be followed at an early date by the definite conversion of the country into a British Protectorate. No secret is made of the dislike with which the chiefs and rulers of Ashanti contemplate the possibility of their receiving under a Protectorate similar treatment to that which has been accorded to the natives resident within the Gold Coast Colony. To them the matter is of momentous importance. With Sir Brandford Griffith, the Governor of the Gold Coast, they could not treat with sufficient confidence. And to the Queen and to her responsible Ministers in London must, the King's Council decided, the final appeal be made for a hearing of the Ashanti cause.[291]

There is little in the statement to justify Governor Griffith's assertion made a few months earlier, that 'the Authorities of Kumasi are pursuing a vacillating, if not a Fabian policy. . .' [292]

On 6 May, from the embassy's new address at 13 Lennox Gardens, Brew officially notified the Colonial Office of their arrival in London.[293] The long, and unsuccessful, struggle to obtain diplomatic recognition had begun. On 22 May Brew despatched to the Secretary of State for Foreign Affairs a closely reasoned and well documented presentation of the embassy's case.[294] The letter was passed to the Colonial Office, and sent on to Governor Griffith for comment. In his reply, which was not received until 3 July, Griffith reiterated his view that the embassy could not claim to represent the Asante nation since Agyeman Prempe was not Asantehene and was known to condone the practice of human sacrifice! [295]

The ambassadors, meanwhile, had been pursuing another objective: the negotiation with Radcliffe and Durant of a concession for the development of the resources of Asante. Detailed reconstruction of the sequence of the negotiations is difficult since they were conducted in conditions of much secrecy. Events in Asante, moreover, were of considerable significance to the course of the talks. On 3 March 1890 a group of Fante concessionaires associated with 'The Ashanti Exploration Company' had obtained from the Bekwaehene a lease over one hundred square miles of land in the Obuase district. Mining operations were commenced there immediately.[296] Among various problems

[291] NAG, Accra, ADM 12/3/6: Maxwell to Ripon, dd. Accra, 13 June 1895, quoting from *The Graphic*, 4 May 1895.
[292] NAG, Accra, ADM 12/3/6: Griffith to Ripon, dd. Cape Coast, 28 September 1894.
[293] *Further Correspondence*, C. 7918, 1896, p. 54: Brew to Colonial Office, dd. London, 6 May 1895.
[294] *Ibid.* pp. 59–61: Brew to Foreign Office, dd. London, 22 May 1895.
[295] *Ibid.* pp. 81–3: Griffith to Colonial Office, dd. Ealing, 1 July 1895.
[296] *Government of the Gold Coast: Report on the Mines Department for the Year 1903–4*, London, 1904, p. 22. PRO, CO. 879/46, African (West) 513, Correspon-

which hampered the work of the company was, however, a political one: that the Obuase district had indeed been administered by the Bekwaehene since the defeat of the Adanse in 1886, but the Adansehene (still a refugee in the Gold Coast Colony) remained technically the owner of the land. The central government in Kumase, moreover, was concerned to establish its own paramount interest in mineral rights throughout Asante. It has been seen that Mensa Bonsu, probably in 1882, enacted legislation giving the central government what was effectively a half interest in the gold mining industry (p. 529), and also that by 1892 the new government was already thinking in terms of the full nationalization of production: of the achievement of an economic take-off involving European investment and management within the framework of a national economic development plan. The status of the Obuase concession was, then, of obvious concern to the Asante government, and it is probable that this topic was among those discussed by the Asante ambassadors with Messrs Radcliffe and Durant of Liverpool in late April and early May.

By July 1895 Edwin A. Cade and an associate had arrived in the Gold Coast from England to study the possibilities for investment.[297] Cade's business affiliations were complex. Himself a partner in the firm of Smith and Cade, West African merchants in London, he had launched the Côte d'Or Mining Company there in 1895 prior to his departure for the Gold Coast. But Cade was also associated with the firm of Radcliffe and Durant, and was probably authorized to hold talks with the Asantehene on their behalf. Certainly Governor Maxwell appears to have viewed Cade's arrival with some alarm, and to have cabled the Colonial Office in London for guidance.[298] Although Maxwell had no legal powers to prevent Cade from securing concessions in Asante, he warned him nevertheless against proceeding to Kumase. On 1 August 1895, however, Cade purchased the lease of the Obuase concession from its Fante owners, J.P. Brown, J.E. Ellis, and J.E. Biney.[299] He then travelled to Bekwae in August, where he secured the approval of the Bekwaehene Yaw Boakye to the new arrangement. Then, on his way to the coast, he obtained the agreement of the Adansehene Kwaku Nkansa.[300] Although Cade did not meet with the

dence Relating to Land Grants and Concessions in the Gold Coast Protectorate, 1897, No. 34, enclosure. The lease was recorded as no. 230 in the Register of Conveyances and Leases at Cape Coast, vol. II, see Turner, n.d., p. 2.

297 *The Gold Coast Chronicle*, 21 August 1895, p. 3.

298 PRO, CO. 96/258: telegrams, Maxwell to Ripon, dd. 18 and 20 June 1895; and CO. 96/267: Maxwell to Ripon, 21 June 1895.

299 *West African Lands Committee: Minutes of Evidence, etc.*, Colonial Office, London, 1916: Question 4972.

300 Turner, n.d., pp. 3–4. Junner, 1935, p. 29. See also PRO, CO. 96/260: Maxwell to Chamberlain, dd. Accra, 5 September 1895, and enclosures.

646

Asantehene, he claimed that the concession was 'later on accepted or agreed to by oath of the King of Kumasi', and doubtless he expected this aspect of the matter to be covered more fully by the Asante ambassadors in England in their negotiations with Messrs Radcliffe and Durant. But Cade also foresaw another alternative should the Asante government revoke the agreement. 'In the event of a purchase not being at present possible', he wrote, 'the position may still be a desirable one in the event of annexation (by Her Majesty's Government) taking place!' [301]

Cade's appreciation of the situation was remarkably accurate. The ambassadors in London regarded him as having acted with impropriety in negotiating the concession with the Bekwaehene. On 27 September they addressed a letter to the Asantehene and the senior members of the Asantemanhyiamu. In it they drew attention to the inadvisability of concessions being granted other than with the central government's approval. Only thus could the uncontrolled exploitation of the nation's mineral wealth be avoided. The Bekwaehene, they urged, should be required immediately to stop any mining operations in his territory.[302] The authorities in Kumase had, however, already in fact brought charges against the Bekwaehene for having confirmed the concession without reference to them, and on or about 20 September Yaw Boakye had acknowledged his offence – had 'drunk a fresh fetish with the King of Kumasi, on account of some trouble between the two places owing to Mr. Cade's visit to Bekwai'.[303] Relations between the local government in Bekwae and the central government in Kumase remained, however, strained, though reports that fighting subsequently broke out between the two (in which the Kumase forces were assisted by troops provided by Samori!) turned out to be false.[304]

The award of the Reckless Concession

In London the Asante ambassadors were working against time, reports having reached them by the beginning of September that a military expedition against Kumase was being planned.[305] The British govern-

[301] NAG, Accra, ADM 1/1/109: Cade to Selborne, dd. London, 22 October 1895, in Chamberlain to Maxwell, dd. 1 November 1895. Turner, n.d., p. 3.
[302] PRO, CO. 96/270: John and Albert Owusu Ansa and the other ambassadors to Mamponhene, Nsutahene, Offinsuhene, Edwesohene, Asumegyahene; and Bantamahene, Asafohene, Adontenhene, Gyaasehene, Kyidomhene, and Oyokohene of Kumase, dd. London, 27 September 1895.
[303] *Further Correspondence*, C. 7918, 1896, p. 124: Stewart to Governor, dd. Kyeaboso, 11 October 1895. NAG, Accra, ADM 1/2/49: Maxwell to Chamberlain, dd. Accra, 22 October 1895.
[304] *The Times*, 18 December 1895, p. 5; 19 December 1895, p. 5; 27 December 1895, p. 3.
[305] PRO, CO. 96/267: John Owusu Ansa to Colonial Office, dd. 5 September 1895.

ment, on the other hand, appears to have been content that the ambassadors should remain in London in the anticipation of ultimately winning diplomatic recognition, since the danger was present that they might otherwise move to Paris or Berlin and there enter into negotiations with the French or German governments.[306] Indeed, the Colonial Office later managed to secure the draft of a letter addressed by Albert Owusu Ansa to the French Foreign Secretary which alluded to the 'friendly communications' between the governments of France and Asante at the time of Arthur Brun, and which stated that 'as our country is an Independent State – with the powers we are armed – I am prepared to advise my colleagues here with me to come to some diplomatic arrangement with your Government'.[307]

The matter of the French connection was explored further in the pages of *The Gold Coast Chronicle:*

it is not at all improbable that the French will do everything they can to get them to visit Paris, and once on French soil the death knell of British prestige in the interior would soon be heard. No one who has been watching the course of events out here, during the past five or six years particularly, will venture to deny that the French would do anything to get the flag of their Republic hoisted now in Ashantee and the presence of the Ambassadors would be regarded in Parisian circles as a very favourable opportunity to get the people of Kumasi on the side of the tricolour. The French, at all events, will not allow the grass to grow underneath their feet; so we had better be careful.[308]

On 6 September, however, the Colonial Secretary, Chamberlain, had instructed Governor Maxwell to issue an ultimatum to the Asantehene.[309] The ultimatum was drawn up by Maxwell under date 23 September 1895, and required that the Asante government should accept a British Resident and that the war indemnity of 50,000 oz of gold, stipulated for in the Treaty of Fomena in 1874, should be paid in full. The ultimatum was taken to Kumase by Stewart and Vroom, who presented it to the Council of Kumase on 10 October. Refusing to wait until other councillors had been summoned to the capital, the two envoys arrived back in Accra on the 25th. When the ultimatum expired at the end of October, no answer had been received from Kumase.[310]

306 NAG, Accra, ADM 12/3/6: Maxwell to Ripon, dd. Accra, 13 June 1895. ADM 12/5/110: telegram, Ripon to Governor, dd. London, 15 October 1895.
307 PRO, CO. 96/270: draft letter, n.d. filed under Gold Coast, Confidential, 25 February 1896. See also NAG, Accra, ADM 12/5/110: cipher telegram, Secretary of State for the Colonies to Governor, Gold Coast, dd. London, 15 October 1895.
308 *The Gold Coast Chronicle,* 19 June 1895, p. 2. For the official view of the matter, see PRO, CO. 96/271: Maxwell to Chamberlain, dd. 19 March 1896 and enclosures.
309 PRO, CO. 96/258: Chamberlain to Maxwell, dd. 6 September 1895.
310 *The African Times,* XXXVII, no. 411, 2 December 1895, p. 182. *Further Corres-*

The fact of the matter seems to have been, that the determination of the British government not to recognize the Asante embassy was matched by the determination of the Asante government not to negotiate through the Governor of the Gold Coast Colony. The British thought it possible that John Owusu Ansa had been in telegraphic communication with his government. They knew, moreover, that the authorities in Kumase were fully apprised of the situation in London before the expiry of the ultimatum, for Akyampon Daban and Kwadwo Tufuo had left England in September, and had arrived in Kumase on 14 October. One report, indeed, suggests that they had returned to England possibly at the beginning of November carrying with them a further 500 oz of gold for the expenses of the embassy.[311] When two junior functionaries, Kwaku Abora of the *afenasoafo* and Kofi Akwa of the *nseniefo,* did arrive in Accra from Kumase on 12 November, they merely informed the British administrators that the ambassadors in London had their government's proposals and were empowered to deal with matters.[312]

In the fall of 1895, then, the ambassadors in England clearly believed that their work was progressing. Their public relations were being handled by sympathetic writers, including Arthur B. Chamberlain of the London *Graphic,* and Kendall Robinson – who proposed visiting Kumase and for a fee of £750 and expenses would 'secure a fair and just presentation of your [the Asante] views and your grievances to the British Public'.[313] The ambassadors had secured the services, too, as Solicitor to the Embassy, of Jonathan E. Harris of 95 Leadenhall-street, London, who had commenced publicizing his clients' case. In a letter to *The Times* of 2 October he had called for their recognition. The Asantehene, he stressed, 'is prepared to open his country to British skill, and does not seek to hamper trade. . .'[314] On 17 October, however, news was officially released in London that Scott had been appointed to command an expedition against Asante. Interviewed the next day, John Owusu Ansa showed considerable surprise and emotion.[315] When the news reached Kumase, preparations

pondence, C. 7918, 1896, pp. 129–30: Stewart and Vroom to Governor, dd. Accra, 26 October 1895. See further, Lewin, 1974, pp. 367–8.

311 *Ibid.* p. 129: Maxwell to Chamberlain, dd. Accra, 28 October 1895. *Ibid.* p. 141: Maxwell to Chamberlain, dd. Accra, 13 November 1895.

312 *Ibid.* p. 116: Maxwell to Chamberlain, telegraph received 12 November 1895. *Ibid.* pp. 141–2: memorandum of proceedings in the reception of messengers from Kumase, dd. Accra, 12 November 1895.

313 PRO, CO. 96/270: enclosure in no. 5921, Arthur Chamberlain to John Owusu Ansa, dd. 30 April 1895; and in no. 5920, Robinson to John Owusu Ansa, dd. London, 13 September 1895.

314 *The Times,* 3 October 1895, p. 12.

315 *Ibid.* 18 October 1895.

against attack were immediately started: the coffins of the deceased Asantehenes, and the Golden Stool itself, were removed from the city to nearby villages for safety.[316]

In London John Owusu Ansa advanced the schedule of the mission's work. On 21 October the six members of the embassy then there concluded an agreement with George Reckless of 11 Kensington Gardens, who was backed by Messrs Radcliffe and Durant. On 24 October the Colonial Office received a letter from the solicitors of Reckless – Messrs Grundy, Kershaw, Saxon, Samson, and Co. of 4 New Court, Lincoln's Inn – stating that their client 'holds a concession from the Ministers and Chief of Ashanti for the formation of a British Chartered Company, for the purpose of opening up and developing the country. . .'[317] On the same day Harris, in the company of Ernest Spencer, M.P., presented himself at the Colonial Office, but was refused an interview. In a letter of 26 October, however, he suggested that the justification for military operations against Asante no longer existed since 'the King, by his representatives here, has agreed to grant to a British company a Charter for the opening up of Ashantee to British enterprise and skill'.[318]

It will be seen from the text given below that the British concessionaires saw in the British South Africa Company a model for what they hoped to create in Asante. It will be readily apparent that the situation in Matabeleland and that in Asante were, in certain respects, structurally similar. But in February 1888 the Ndebele ruler Lobengula had entered into an agreement abrogating his right to negotiate treaties with foreign powers other than with British consent, and it was only nine months later, in October, that he awarded Rudd the concession which was to form the basis of the charter of the British South Africa Company. In contrast, the Asante government appears to have decided to avoid entering into any formal agreement with the British government in any way restricting its sovereignty until a concession for the development of Asante had *first* been negotiated. In 1895, therefore, the Asante ambassadors in London were in no way legally excluded from entering into agreements with French interests should the terms they wanted be unavailable in England. The difference between the Reckless Concession of 1895 and the Rudd Concession of 1888 was, however, a still more fundamental one: for over two decades Asante governments had debated and formulated policy on the issue of European participation in national development, and with the

---

316 *The Gold Coast Chronicle*, 15 November 1895, p. 3.
317 *Further Correspondence*, C. 7918, 1896, p. 107: Grundy, Kershaw, Saxon, Samson, and Co. to Colonial Office, dd. 23 October 1895.
318 *Ibid.* p. 108: Harris to Selborne, dd. 26 October 1895.

Herivel Concession of 1892 the government had reaffirmed its commitment to programmes of modernization first formulated in the reign of Asantehene Mensa Bonsu. As early as 1874 the senior Owusu Ansa had held talks with the firm of Radcliffe and Durant, and these had been resumed by Bonnat in 1876. Thus the concession which had been granted in 1875 to Bonnat, as co-governor of the Voltaic province south of Salaga and as agent of the Liverpool firm of de Cardi, must be seen as establishing the precedent for the more extensive ones awarded to first Herivel and then Reckless, in the 1890s: [319]

To GEORGE RECKLESS, Esquire, and to all to whom these presents shall come: –

Whereas we the undersigned being Princes and Chiefs respectively of Ashanti and John Ossoo Ansah being Ambassador Extraordinary and Minister Plenipotentiary to the King of Ashanti who is possessed of all power and authority from our King, did on the twentieth day of September last agree that in the interests of the Ashanti nation it would be meet that a British Company shall be incorporated for the purposes of acquiring all rights now possessed by the King of Ashanti in the dominions over which he rules.

Now we the undersigned agree when called upon to execute in our names and in the name of the King of Ashanti and for and on his behalf an effectual charter for the purposes of giving mining and other rights to the said Company, for the purposes also of railway construction and other public works, to employ skilled and other labour, to build manufactories, lay out townships, construct waterworks, and waterways, to appoint and maintain a resident agent or agents; to organise a constabulary, to erect a mint and issue coinage, establish factories for trading and other purposes, to establish banks, to grant licenses for trading, mining, and other purposes, to impose such duties as may be deemed expedient on goods imported into the country, to lay out and cultivate plantations for all kinds of vegetable and other products, to establish schools for elementary, technical, and scientific education, to publish newspapers, to aid in the organisation of the military forces of the Kingdom, to assist the King in his Government, including the administration of justice and the codification of laws, the King to undertake to protect life and property and the rights and privileges accorded to the Chartered Company as herein-before mentioned, the King to receive an annual grant from the Company of one-fourth of the nett profits, The Company undertaking to commence to carry out the foregoing operations within one year from the date of the granting of the Charter. British labour and industry is to be fully encouraged and recognised. The said Company to be at liberty to do any matter, act, or thing which in its opinion shall be deemed necessary or expedient; the agent to be at liberty to settle the boundaries of Ashanti with the officials of the English Government. And I, the said John Ossoo

[319] *Ibid.* pp. 108–9: Grundy, Kershaw, Saxon, Samson, and Co., to Colonial Office, dd. 30 October 1895, enclosing copy of the concession.

Ansah, either with or without the consent of the undersigned Chiefs agree if and when called upon to execute any further deed, document, or charter for more effectually vesting in the Company the aforesaid right. It being intended that the said Company shall have the same extensive rights as at present enjoyed by the British South Africa Company whose objects have been fully explained to us and each of us.

In witness whereof we the undersigned have hereunto set our hands, names, signs, and seals in the presence of each other this twenty-first day of October one thousand eight hundred and ninety-five.

JOHN OSSO ANSAH, of Ashanti,	X (L.S.)
KWAMIN BOATIN, Chief of Ashanti,	X (L.S.)
KWAKU FOKOO, Linguist of Ashanti,	X (L.S.)
KWAKU INKRUMAH, Capn. of Chamberlain	X (L.S.)
ALBT. A. OSSOO ANSAH, C. of Ashanti,	X (L.S.)
KWABINA BONDA, Court Crier,	X (L.S.)

Signed, sealed, and delivered as indicated hereon by the said Chiefs, Princes, and Ambassador Extraordinary and Minister Plenipotentiary to the King of Ashanti in the presence of

J. E. HARRIS,
    95, Leadenhall Street, E.C.,
        Solicitor.

BREW OF DUNQUAH,
    5, Park Crescent, W.

Chamberlain's reaction was to refuse to accept the validity of the concession on the frequently reiterated grounds, that Agyeman Prempe was not Asantehene and that the ambassadors therefore lacked standing. The solicitors to both parties to the concession were informed accordingly on 11 November.[320] John Owusu Ansa took the step, therefore, of engaging the services of a barrister, Thomas Sutherst of 34 Grosvenor Square. At the same time he authorized Sutherst to communicate to the Colonial Office the embassy's willingness now to accept a British Resident in Asante on the terms laid down in Hodgson's letter of 23 February 1894 and Maxwell's ultimatum of 23 September 1895.[321] The position of the Colonial Office had become a difficult one. *Prima facie,* it lacked jurisdiction in the matter of an agreement negotiated between a British concessionaire and the representatives of an independent kingdom. Sutherst, moreover, pointed out that he had examined the credentials of John Owusu Ansa, and was satisfied of their authenticity.[322] In a systematic manner, too, he dealt with the extraordinarily naive charges brought against John Owusu Ansa. When

---

[320] *Ibid.* p. 115: Colonial Office to Harris, dd. 11 November 1895. *Ibid.* p. 116: Colonial Office to Grundy, Kershaw, Saxon, Samson, and Co., dd. 11 November 1895.
[321] *Ibid.* pp. 117–18: Colonial Office to Sutherst, dd. 14 November 1895.
[322] *The Times*, 21 November 1895, p. 6.

it was argued, for example, that he claimed to be grandson of a man who was only some twenty-two years of age, Sutherst pointed out that he was of course 'grandson' to the Golden Stool – that is, *ohenenana* – and not to the Asantehene himself.[323]

As a result of Sutherst's intervention in the matter, Chamberlain agreed to accept the embassy's submissions on behalf of the Asante government, provided that they cabled notification of the proceedings for onward transmission to the Asantehene, and provided they returned immediately to the Gold Coast where officers of the Gold Coast government would be prepared to accompany them to Kumase.[324] On 16 November the six members of the mission attested to a document which they firmly believed would avert another war:

Acting on behalf of Kwaku Dua III., King of Ashantee . . . We agree to accept a British Resident at Kumasi, and to conform to all the terms of the Queen's ultimatum, believing that all the promises made on behalf of the Queen, by Her representatives, will be faithfully carried out. The King and Chiefs desire the alliance and friendship of the Queen, and they desire, through the British Government, to open up their territory to trade and commerce. The King and people have long abandoned the practices of human sacrifice. They are anxious to remove all hinderances to trade and the development of the resources of their country . . .[325]

On the same day they cabled to the Gold Coast notification of their acceptance of a Resident.[326] They remained for a time in London while Sutherst continued to harass the Colonial Office by pointing out that the expenses of the proposed military expedition against Asante were being incurred simply because of that body's myopic refusal to afford recognition to the embassy. [327] Finally the embassy cabled again to inform the Asantehene that they were about to return to Kumase, and requesting him to summon a meeting of the Asantemanhyiamu in time for their arrival.[328] Sutherst saw the party off from Euston Station on the night of 26 November, in order to embark on the steamer *Roquelle* at Liverpool the following day. They reiterated to Sutherst that

they were most desirous that the resources of their country should be opened up, describing it as rich in gold and semi-tropical products, such as coffee, cocoa, and india-rubber. They were anxious to see a railway constructed

323 *Further Correspondence,* C. 7918, 1896, p. 120: Colonial Office to Sutherst, dd. 15 November 1895. *Ibid.* pp. 121–2: Sutherst to Colonial Office, dd. 16 November 1895.
324 *Ibid.* pp. 117–18: Colonial Office to Sutherst, dd. 14 November 1895.
325 *Ibid.* p. 122: enclosure in Sutherst to Colonial Office, dd. 16 November 1895.
326 PRO, CO. 96/262: Maxwell to Chamberlain, dd. 23 November 1895.
327 *The Times,* 25 November 1895, p. 7.
328 *Idem.*

across Ashanti, to welcome British trade and commerce, and to cultivate the most friendly relations with Great Britain . . . In the interior on the high land they maintained that the climate was quite healthy, and they affirmed that there would be no danger or difficulty in Europeans working minerals, constructing railways, and generally bringing about the development of the resources of Ashanti.[329]

In fact only some of the ambassadors embarked on the *Roquelle;* Kwame Boaten, Kwaku Fokuo, Kwaku Nkruma and Kwabena Bonna arrived at Cape Coast on 16 December,[330] and on the following day met with Governor Maxwell, confirmed their approval of the agreement of 16 November, and proceeded to Kumase much dismayed by Maxwell's manifest hostility.[331] John and Albert Owusu Ansa remained in Liverpool for ten days, presumably to hold final consultations with Messrs Radcliffe and Durant. They embarked on the steamer *Bokhara* on 7 December, and arrived at Cape Coast on the 27th.[332] Ironically, the *Bokhara* carried 100 tons of supplies and ammunition for the Scott expedition.

1895–1900: the years of derangement

There can be little doubt that the Ansas felt that they had achieved the main purpose of the embassy. In the concession which, with the precedent of the unsuccessful Herivel agreement of 1892 in mind, they had negotiated with Reckless and his sponsors, they had established a blueprint for the development of Asante. Through the partnership of the government and British capital the rapid modernization of the nation would be achieved; and the gap in technological achievement between Asante and the European countries, which had widened so alarmingly in the nineteenth century, reduced. They had, not without wisdom, assumed that a political settlement between the Asante and British governments might easily be negotiable once an arrangement had been made with British capitalists of mutual advantage to both nations. The tragedy in the situation is that they could have been right. They had failed, however, to allow for the 'panic element' which had for so long confused and confounded relations between Britain and Asante.[333] The anxiety in the Colonial Office that the Asante government might seek to strengthen its ties with France gave way to a new fear in October and November 1895, as reports became frequent

329 *Ibid.* 27 November 1895, p. 10.
330 Essien accompanied them, *ibid.* 28 November 1895, p. 6. Musgrave, 1896, p. 67.
331 *Ibid.* pp. 67–9. PRO, CO. 96/263: Maxwell to Chamberlain, dd. 23 December 1895.
332 *The African Times,* XXXVII, no. 412, 1 January 1896, p. 4. Musgrave, 1896, p. 94
333 See Collins, 1962, *passim.*

that Agyeman Prempe was negotiating an alliance with the Almami Samori, who had so long opposed French penetration of the Western Sudan. The British government decided that the solution to the Asante problem had to be a military rather than a political one. Indeed, on 21 November, before John and Albert Owusu Ansa had left London, Chamberlain had cabled Governor Maxwell to inform him, 'expedition must go Kumasi at all events'.[334]

Once the ambassadors had left England for the Gold Coast, Chamberlain sought new grounds on which to impugn their standing. Governor Maxwell obligingly supplied them. He interviewed John and Albert Owusu Ansa on their arrival at Cape Coast on 27 December, and immediately cabled Chamberlain to say that the former had admitted that his credential of 8 September 1894 had not been prepared in Kumase but in Cape Coast at a later date, the seal having been affixed in England.[335] The information was immediately released to *The Times* in London.[336] Chamberlain hoped not only thus to confuse critics of his decision to invade Asante, but also at the same time to put beyond doubt the invalidity of the Reckless Concession. 'The Secretary of State for the Colonies', it was announced, 'desires to warn the public that concessions purporting to be obtained from the King of Coomassie will not be recognised by Her Majesty's Government.' [337] Harris, who had been retained as solicitor in London, attempted to correct the record. The credential had been prepared in Kumase, he pointed out, but three copies of it had been made on parchment in Cape Coast. The Asantehene had instructed a seal to be affixed in London. While the copies had been presented in London, it was always made clear that the original could be produced whenever desired.[338] The Colonial Office refused, however, to take note of the correction, and Harris was later to complain of 'the tyrannical conduct on the part of officialdom, and of which any nation save our own should be ashamed'.[339] Meanwhile in London the police seized letters which had passed between John Owusu Ansa and Clara Abbott of 42 Britannia Road, Fulham, the laundress to the Asante embassy. Suspecting – wrongly – that the two might have married, Maxwell and Chamberlain savoured the possibility of bringing charges of bigamy against the ambassador.[340]

334 *Further Correspondence*, C. 7918, 1896, p. 150: Maxwell to Chamberlain, received 27 December 1895.
335 *Ibid.* p. 150: Maxwell to Chamberlain, received 27 December 1895.
336 *The Times*, 31 December 1895, p. 3.
337 *The African Times*, xxxvii, no. 412, 1 January 1896, p. 4.
338 *Idem.*
339 *Ibid.* no. 417, 1 June 1896, p. 86.
340 PRO, CO. 96/270: Maxwell to Chamberlain, dd. 25 February 1896, enclosing proof of John Owusu Ansa's marriage to Emma Hutchison of Elmina in

At a meeting with Governor Maxwell on 28 December, John Owusu Ansa was informed that Scott's expeditionary force had definite orders to occupy Kumase. He reiterated his belief that a peaceful settlement of all problems was still possible.[341] Leaving Cape Coast with his brother Albert, the two passed through Praso, the British camp, on 1 January 1896. 'They both seemed weighed down with anxiety', commented Musgrave.[342] They finally reached Kumase on 4 January, and became immediately involved in the debate on the invasion.[343] Although there was clearly a sharp division in the Councils, it was generally accepted at the time that John and Albert Owusu Ansa were mainly instrumental in dissuading the government from offering resistance to the advancing British force.[344] As Musgrave noted, undoubtedly the Ansas drew the attention of the councillors to the strength of the invading column.[345] Basically, however, the brothers adhered to the belief that a political settlement was possible since they had accepted the British terms on behalf of the Asantehene by the agreement of 16 November 1895. All that remained, therefore, was for the Asantehene and his Councils to ratify that agreement. Rightly, the Ansas had foreseen that the one issue on which Government Maxwell might assume an uncompromising line was that of the payment of the indemnity of 50,000 oz. They were, however, able to reassure the councillors on this point: as a result presumably of their last discussions with Messrs Radcliffe and Durant in Liverpool, the ambassadors had received from them – 'from an English house' – a cablegram guaranteeing payment up to £200,000.[346] Both the Asante government, and the sponsors of George Reckless, were clearly still anticipating that once a political settlement was obtained, the creation of the Chartered Company for the development of Asante resources would finally take place.

Scott's expeditionary force entered Kumase on 17 January, having encountered no opposition. Sitting in state, the Asantehene watched

October 1884, and letters between him and Clara Abbott. NAG, Accra, ADM 11/1372: Papers Regarding the Committal of the Ansahs for Trial, 1896.
341 PRO, CO. 96/263: Maxwell to Chamberlain, dd. 28 December 1895.
342 Musgrave, 1896, pp. 94–8.
343 *The Times*, 6 January 1896, p. 6.
344 Musgrave, 1896, p. 165. *The African Times*, xxxvii, no. 422, 2 November 1896, p. 162. *Gold Coast Methodist Times*, ii, November–December 1897, p. 4: Brew to Chamberlain, dd. 23 October 1897.
345 Scott's force consisted of some 670 British infantrymen and 250 men of the Royal Artillery, Royal Engineers, and the Army Service and Medical Corps; 400 soldiers of the West India Regiment; about 1,000 Hausa troops; 800 levies from the Gold Coast Colony; and something of the order of 10,000 carriers.
346 *The African Times*, xxxvii, no. 422, 2 November 1896, p. 162. PRO, CO. 96/270: Maxwell to Chamberlain, notes of a palaver in Kumase, 20 January 1896. The offer was transmitted through a Mr Tipping at Cape Coast.

his capital being occupied and in the early evening was persuaded by John and Albert Owusu Ansa to greet the British commander.[347] Governor Maxwell arrived the following day, and it was announced that he would meet with the Asante Council on the 20th. On the 18th, however, John and Albert Owusu Ansa, with Kwaku Fokuo, made official representations to the British Resident-designate, Captain Donald Stewart. The Asantehene confirmed acceptance of the British terms, expressed his willingness to make a private submission to Maxwell, and intimated – obviously with reference to the note guaranteeing payment of the indemnity – that while it would be impossible immediately to settle the matter by a cash transaction, an 'arrangement' had been made.[348] The Asante councillors met in session throughout most of the night of the 19th. That all was not well, however, became soon apparent: returning to their houses in the early hours of the morning, a number of them including John Owusu Ansa were quietly arrested.[349] On the morning of the 20th, with all the British troops drawn up in readiness for trouble, the Asantehene and Asantehemaa were required to make a public submission by embracing Maxwell's feet. After a whispered consultation with Albert Owusu Ansa, who was acting as spokesman, they did so. 'Mother and Son', wrote Musgrave, 'were thus forced to humble themselves in sight of the assembled thousand.'[350] Maxwell then demanded the indemnity, and Agyeman Prempe announced that he could pay immediately in gold the sum of 680 oz, or about £2,500. Maxwell thereupon ordered the arrest and deportation to the Gold Coast of the Asantehene and the Asantehemaa Yaa Kyaa, and a number of senior officials: Agyeman Prempe's father, the Ayebiakyerehene Kwasi Gyambibi, and brother, Agyeman Badu; the Bantamahene, Asafohene, Akomfodehene, Akyempemhene, and Oyokohene of Kumase, respectively Amankwatia Kwame, Asafo Boakye, Boakye Atansa, Kofi Subiri, and Agyekum Panin; the Akyeamehene Kwasi Akoko and Bosommuru Fabem counselor Kwaku Owusu; and the Mamponhene Kwame Apea Osokye, the Edwesohene Kwasi Afrane Kuma, and the Offinsohene Kwadwo Apea.[351] It is revealing of the opposition which had existed in the Asante Councils to the forward policies of the Ansas and their supporters, that Asafo Boakye immediately suspected the Ansas of treachery and publicly accused them of responsibility for the deba-

---

347 Musgrave, 1896, pp. 152–63.
348 PRO, CO. 96/270: Maxwell to Chamberlain, dd. Kumase, 20 January 1896.
349 Musgrave, 1896, pp. 173–4. Baden-Powell, 1896, pp. 119–22.
350 Musgrave, 1896, p. 177.
351 PRO, CO. 96/270: Maxwell to Chamberlain, notes of a palaver, dd. Kumase, 20 January 1896. See further, Lewin, 1974, pp. 372–80, for eye-witness accounts of the events.

cle.[352] Maxwell, however, proceeded forthwith to the arrest of both John and Albert Owusu Ansa, and announced that they would stand trial for forging the documents of the 1895 embassy and for embezzling its purse.

The trial of John and Albert Owusu Ansa commenced in the Supreme Court of the Gold Coast on 12 February 1896. Bail was refused them.[353] On 19 May both were acquitted on all six counts of forgery. A fresh trial was ordered on the indictment for embezzlement, but on the following day all charges were dropped and a *nolle prosequi* was entered by the Attorney General.[354] There was a widespread recognition that the trials had been politically motivated. 'The arraignment of persons before a British Court of Law', it was observed in *The Gold Coast Chronicle,* 'for alleged offenses committed under circumstances and in a country where the Court had no jurisdiction, is a monstrous piece of high handed despotism for which there is no excuse.' [355] In London Jonathan Harris, still an 'unswerving advocate' of the Ansas' cause, maintained that the prosecution had been malicious in intent, and the charges frivolous.[356] In Parliament, Chamberlain was obliged to defend the part played by the Colonial Office in the affair and to justify his decision not to make reparations to the Ansas.[357] But the fact was, that in making *sub judice* the matter of the validity of the Asante embassy's credentials, the Colonial Office had been able to avoid facing the embarrassing questions of the propriety of the invasion and of the legality of the Reckless Concession until such time as the British occupation of Asante was a *fait accompli.* By then, such questions had become academic.

Although the attitude of the Colonial Office was considered to be antipathetic towards the private mining interests,[358] clearly Cade was able to arrive at some sort of understanding about the lease he had obtained on the Obuase land from the Bekwaehene and Adansehene. On 27 April 1896 Chamberlain informed the Directors of the Côte d'Or Mining Company that the concession would be recognized as valid, and on 3 June 1897 it was confirmed for a period of ninety years.

352 *Ibid.* Musgrave, 1896, p. 181. *The Times,* 29 February 1896, p. 15: report from a correspondent, dd. Manso, 30 January 1896. *The African Times,* xxxvii, no. 418, 1 July 1896, p. 107.

353 *The Times,* 13 February 1896, p. 5.

354 *Ibid.* 20 May 1896, p. 7; 21 May 1896, p. 7. See also Fuller, 1921, 'Author's Note' – an apology to the Ansas. For the depositions in the trial, see NAG, Accra, ADM 11/1372: Papers Regarding the Committal of the Ansah's for Trial, 1896.

355 *The Gold Coast Chronicle,* 30 June 1896, p. 3.

356 *The African Times,* xxxvii, no. 417, 1 June 1896, p. 86: letter from Harris, dd. 22 May 1896.

357 *Parliamentary Debates,* House of Commons, 19 June 1896.

358 *The Gold Coast Express,* iii, no. 134, 20 July 1897, p. 2.

The Côte d'Or Mining Company was liquidated, and absorbed into the new 'Ashanti Goldfields Corporation, Ltd', which was floated with a nominal capital of £250,000.[359] The first shipment of gold was made by the new Corporation in July 1898 – from 'one of the largest gold bonanzas in the world'[360] – and by September 1946, 5,751,008 oz of gold had been produced.[361] The history of the Reckless Concession was to be quite different. In 1899 Cade attempted to resuscitate the ideas behind it, and proposed to Chamberlain that the Ashanti Gold-fields Corporation should assume general responsibility for the development of the mineral, timber, water and rubber resources of Asante, and that it should spend £½m. on the construction of a railway. Chamberlain refused to countenance the proposal.[362] On 1 January 1900, on Chamberlain's instructions, a Gold Coast Concessions Ordinance was enacted. No single mining concession was to exceed five square miles, and no person or corporation was to hold such leases totalling more than twenty square miles. Significantly, leases signed before 10 October 1895 were declared exempt from such restrictions: thus validating the Cade Concession of 1 August 1895 while invalidating the Reckless Concession of 21 October.[363]

After their acquittal, John and Albert Owusu Ansa had returned to England, arriving in Liverpool on 12 October 1896. Forbidden to live in Asante, they settled in London, re-establishing business contacts and seeking redress for their wrongful imprisonment.[364] In Kumase, the new Resident created a 'Native Committee of Administration' to take over the functions of the Council of Kumase. In theory its jurisdiction was confined to the capital and its villages, but in practice it maintained some of the attributes of a central government.[365] Three men, all functionaries of considerable experience, were appointed to it: Opoku Mensa, son of Adu Bofo, and Gyaasewahene since 1884; Kwaku Nantwi Kaakyera, signatory of the Treaty of Fomena, and Akankade counselor since about 1877; and the Kumase rural member Antwi Agyei – who, dying in the year of his appointment, was replaced by the Toasehene Kwame Afrifa. Opoku Mensa, senior of the triumvirate, rapidly made clear his commitment to working for Agyeman Prempe's

359 Turner, n.d., p. 6. By a cipher telegram of 18 April 1896, see NAG, Accra, ADM 1/2/49, Hodgson to Chamberlain dd. Accra, 20 April 1896, Chamberlain had proposed a 5% royalty payable by the Company, commuted for the first five years to an annual sum of £500.
360 Junner, 1935, p. 29.
361 Turner, n.d., p. 19.
362 PRO, CO. 96/352: Cade to Chamberlain, dd. 25 March 1899, and Minute by Chamberlain, dd. 13 April 1899.
363 PRO, CO. 96/346: Chamberlain to Hodgson, dd. 22 December 1899.
364 *The African Times*, XXXVII, no. 420, 1 September 1896, p. 133; no. 422, 2 November 1896, p. 162.
365 Tordoff, 1965, pp. 88–90.

return from Sierra Leone to Asante.[366] In London the Ansas began to organize a lobby working to the same end. In late 1897 Brew wrote to Chamberlain advocating the advantages to be gained from the restoration of Agyeman Prempe and the reinstatement of John and Albert Owusu Ansa in positions of influence. 'With the counsel he [Agyeman Prempe] would receive from the Princes Ansah, whose advice he followed in making such submission', commented Brew, 'the prestige of the British Government would be raised to a pitch which you can hardly conceive among the tribes and countries in the hinterland of Ashanti.'[367] But the Secretary of State for the Colonies had no doubt that the repatriation of the Asantehene was incompatible with British interests in Asante: that the presence of the Ansas there would only stimulate discontent, but that the puppet regime established in Kumase – the triumvirate of three senior title holders – might be relied upon to carry out British policy as interpreted to them by the Resident. Opoku Mensa and his two colleagues were thus enabled slowly and stealthily to extend the basis of support for a concerted drive to expel the occupation forces from Asante.[368]

Throughout 1897 rumours had continued to circulate that the Almami Samori remained predisposed to intervene in the affairs of Asante.[369] Indeed, in October of that year John and Albert Owusu Ansa wrote to Chamberlain suggesting that if Agyeman Prempe was restored as Asantehene, he would assist the British in expelling the Samorian forces from his territories.[370] As Samori's power declined, however, so new reports gained currency that the French were supplying the Asante with modern weapons – Chassepots, Militrailleuses, and Maxim Nordenfeldts – and were offering the services of military advisers.[371] But whatever the truth in the accounts of Asante preparations for war in the period, certainly many districts, towns, and villages mobilized with remarkable rapidity after Governor Hodgson addressed a gathering of chiefs and people in Kumase on 28 March 1900 and announced that Agyeman Prempe would never be allowed to return to rule Asante; that Yaw Twereboanna could not be enstooled in his place since 'the paramount authority of Ashanti is now the great

366 PRO, CO. 96/298: memorandum of an interview in Kumase, by Maxwell, 16 August 1897.
367 *Gold Coast Methodist Times*, II, November–December 1897, p. 4: Brew to Chamberlain, dd. London, 23 October 1897.
368 Hodgson, 1901, pp. 88–9. Fuller, 1921, p. 189. Hall, 1939, chapter 2.
369 See, for example, *The Gold Coast Express*, IV, no. 162, 23 August 1897; no. 166, 27 August 1897; no. 175, 7 September 1897; no. 196, 1 October 1897.
370 PRO, CO. 96/333: John and Albert Owusu Ansa to Chamberlain, dd. London, 25 October 1897 and 17 February 1898.
371 *The Gold Coast Express*, II, no. 61, 9 April 1900; no. 68, 7 May 1900; no. 72, 21 May 1900; no. 74, 28 May 1900.

Queen of England'; that 2,000 peredwans must be paid annually as interest on the indemnity for both the 1874 and 1896 expeditions; and that the Golden Stool should be surrendered to the British.[372] The war which had been averted in 1896 largely through the instrumentality of the Ansas thus came to be fought four years later. The costs to the British of the hard-fought campaigns – estimated at over £400,000 – were charged against the revenues of the Gold Coast Colony. Its development, so it has recently been suggested, was thereby retarded for some two decades.[373] Such was the final, and ironical, result of the refusal of the Colonial Office in London to negotiate with the respresentatives of the Asante government in 1895 and to entertain their proposals for the development of the resources of Asante with the participation of European capital.

The decision of Agyeman Prempe's government in 1896, not to offer resistance to the British expeditionary force, had been in certain respects itself a finely calculated act of resistance in view of the gross disparity in the military resources of the two powers. As a result of the decision the British found themselves, although in military occupation of Asante, nonetheless without adequate legal standing there: having claims to legitimacy neither by treaty with the lawful government nor by right of conquest. The various agreements which the British signed with individual *amanhene* – often their own nominees (p. 122) – were of dubious legal validity, and one of the reasons for the decision to arrest and deport the Asantehene and many of his senior officers was undoubtedly the fact that no restraint existed in international law upon their entering still into treaty relations with Britain's colonial rivals, France or Germany. Indeed, it was precisely with the intention of strengthening British claims to authority in Asante that Governor Hodgson had demanded surrender of the Golden Stool. As Chamberlain explained in Parliament, 'in the opinion of the tribe, and according to the custom of the tribe, the possession of the Stool gives supremacy . . . Therefore it was of the greatest importance to get hold of this symbol of sovereignty, if we could possibly do it'.[374] It is paradoxical that it was the war of 1900 which finally gave the British title to Asante – by 'right of conquest' – which they had lacked since 1896. By an Order in Council of 26 September 1901 it was enacted that

the territories in West Africa situate within the limits of this Order, heretofore known as Ashanti, have been conquered by His Majesty's forces, and it

372 PRO, CO. 96/359: notes taken at a Public Palaver of Native Kings and Chiefs, by Hodgson, 28 March 1900, in Hodgson to Chamberlain, dd. 7 April 1900.
373 Haydon, 1970, pp. 116–17.
374 *Parliamentary Debates,* House of Commons, Committee of Supply, 18 March 1901.

has seemed expedient to His Majesty that the said territories should be annexed to and should henceforth form part of His Majesty's dominions, and that provision should be made for the peace, order, and good government of the said territories.

From continuity in change to change without continuity

In the early Asante kingdom, within which most offices were chiefly in style and hereditary in mode, those who attained positions of authority and power constituted a comparatively homogeneous socio-cultural group. Only the traditional courtly education was regarded as appropriate to those entitled by birth to high office. It was based upon knowledge of the ethical and legal code laid down by Okomfo Anokye; upon reverence for the ancestors and for the social order which they in life had established; and upon the inculcation of the military virtues.[375] As a result, however, of the administrative reforms of the late eighteenth and early nineteenth centuries, a new style of education began to develop which differed greatly in character from that in the classical tradition. Less 'humanistic' or value-oriented, it stressed, so it has been shown, practical training for specific careers, and was organized around what was essentially an apprenticeship system. The search for European knowledge and learning was a later outgrowth of this new professionalism in government, and reflected the growing involvement of Asante with both Britain and the Netherlands from the early nineteenth century onwards. Osei Bonsu entertained the idea of selecting *ahenemma,* princes, for European education; and thus of creating from within that class a cadre of advisers and administrators who would have assumed responsibilities most especially in the field of external relations with the European powers. Although the councillors were able to prevent Osei Bonsu from pursuing what they considered a dangerous innovation, nevertheless in the early part of the reign of Kwaku Dua I the objections of the traditionalists were overruled to the extent that four princes, Owusu Ansa, Owusu Nkwantabisa, Kwame Poku and Kwasi Boakye, were permitted to proceed to Europe for schooling. Of the four, only Owusu Ansa was to make a major contribution in Asante affairs. The case of Kwasi Boakye, a man seemingly of immense talents and energy who chose to follow a career as mining engineer and planter in the East Indies, illustrated one of the problems inherent in the programme: that of the loss to the nation of those who through the very fact of their education found themselves with new and attractive options outside Asante.

[375] See, e.g. Bowdich, 1821a, p. 55: 'the young unarmed Soldier, who in his first campaign does not gain his weapon from the enemy, is dismissed to the plantations as unworthy of his former class'.

The alternative to sending young men abroad or to the Gold Coast for training, was to permit the establishment of educational institutions with European curricula in Kumase itself. The Wesleyan and Basel missionary societies were both anxious to associate themselves with the government in developing a programme for educational development. Yet from the Asante point of view both were overly concerned with the propagation of new and alien cultural values to the neglect of the teaching of practical skills, technological and other. While the experiments made by Kwaku Dua I and the Wesleyan missionaries in the field of education were opposed by a number of officials on the grounds that any tutoring in other than the traditional courtly manner was undesirable, others probably remained unenthusiastic about the programme precisely because of its inability to produce the new sort of man for whom there was by then a role in Asante society.

The British invasion of Asante in 1874 had revealed not only the Asante inferiority in weapon technology, which no one had doubted, but also much more generally, the inadequacies of the government's decision-making procedures *vis-à-vis* those of the British. As Kofi Kakari relied increasingly upon the Muslim savants to gain him an advantage over the British, so the bankruptcy of the government's policies in the situation became the more clearly demonstrated. It had lacked adequate insight into the nature of British policy; had employed familiar diplomatic strategies which were no longer effective; and had failed to maintain an appropriate level of informational inputs on the constantly changing political and military situation. The government in Kumase was thus forced to recognize the absolute necessity of adjustment to the new configuration of external relations through the acquisition of a store of relevant knowledge of the European genre. While the matter of mission schools was one which continued to be debated in council, Mensa Bonsu took the immediate steps of bringing Owusu Ansa into a leading advisory position in government, and of opening recruitment to both the administration and the army to non-citizens possessed of the requisite expertise and skills. The administration was thus strengthened by the recruitment into government service of such personnel as M.-J. Bonnat, C. Nielson, J. J. C. Huydecoper and Amu Kwaku at their various levels, or at another, the trained men from the Gold Coast Armed Police Force. Yet, while the modernization of government might thereby be stimulated, the dependence upon the recruitment of foreign personnel was too random and undirected a procedure to be acceptable in the long term. The need remained for the creation of a new institution, within Asante itself, for the regulated and systematic training of future public servants with a requisite degree of European learning. In their meet-

663

ings with Picot in 1876, Mensa Bonsu and his councillors reiterated
the view that the type of school envisaged by the Wesleyan Mission
Society was not that needed in Asante. But whatever plans the government
might have had for developing an alternative system had not
been made public when, in 1883, Mensa Bonsu was removed from
office.

As *coup* followed *coup* and the nation moved towards civil war, so
the Cape Coast caucus was formed in an effort to persuade the Gold
Coast Colony government to intervene in support of Kofi Kakari's candidacy.
Headed first by Owusu Ansa and later by Kofi Nti – both
ahenemma educated in England – one of the main platforms of the
caucus politicians was that of modernization. 'The restoration of
Kari-Kari under the auspices of the British Government', wrote
Owusu Ansa,

> would of course be attended with conditions which would be calculated to
> ensure permanent peace, the opening up of roads, and the development of
> the vast resources of the interior, and therefore the renewal and increase of
> that commerce which has now, by reason of these disturbances almost virtually
> ceased to exist – to the ruin of the mercantile interests of the Colony.[376]

Since the number of Asante who had received a European education,
whether in Europe, in the Gold Coast Colony, or in mission schools in
Asante, remained still small, those who were able to articulate a
policy of modernization were correspondingly few. Nevertheless, it
would be a mistake to underestimate the extent of the constituency
for change which existed in Asante. Awareness of European achievement
in the field of technology had become widely diffused throughout
society as a result of the continuous contact which traders and envoys
had with the towns of the Gold Coast: steamships, for example, had
been regularly plying the coast since 1853; the first traction engine
was landed at Cape Coast in 1873; a field telegraph had been set up in
1874; and the submarine cable linking Accra with London had been
laid in 1886. The number of Asante to visit Europe itself continued,
moreover, to grow. Nine persons from Kumase and five from Kokofu,
for example, represented Asante at the 14th Ethnographic Exhibition
in Paris in 1887,[377] and ten years later there was a troupe of Asante
performers in Prague.[378] A concept of modernity was, in other words,
available to many Asantes whose mode of life continued nevertheless
to be organized on traditional or 'pre-modern' lines.

From 1888 to 1896 the major issue in Asante politics was, quite

376 *Further Correspondence*, C. 4052, 1884, pp. 92–3: Owusu Ansa to Derby, dd.
Accra, 18 October 1883.
377 Fulbert-Demonteil, 1887, *passim*.
378 *The Standard* (London), 11 August 1897.

unambiguously, that of its external relations with the British. The evidence shows that the government of the period adopted the view that the only way to retain the political independence of Asante was to push through a programme of rapid modernization involving the development of the nation's resources with the utilization of European capital and skills. Yet the councils of the nation were still dominated by those who lacked that level of European knowledge and learning which would facilitate their making collective decisions appropriate to the new directions of policy. In the circumstances Agyeman Prempe had brought John Owusu Ansa into government as principal adviser ('Prime Minister'), as Mensa Bonsu had the senior Owusu Ansa twelve years before. Those members of the Council, like Asafo Boakye, who disliked such appointments seem nevertheless to have reconciled themselves to evaluating them on their effectiveness. When however British demands became more insistent, that Asante compromise its sovereignty by the acceptance of a Resident, the Asantehene adopted a further measure unprecedented in Asante constitutional procedures: in 1894 he conferred sweeping powers upon John Owusu Ansa, as Ambassador Extraordinary and Minister Plenipotentiary, to enable him to enter into agreements with European governments and concessionaires on whatever terms he adjudged conducive to the national interest. The signing of the Reckless Concession by John Owusu Ansa and his colleagues in London in the following year constituted a realistic acknowledgment that rapid modernization would require not only the technical services of foreign capitalists but also their participation in the decision-making process. But significantly, the concessionaires were obligated 'to establish schools for elementary, technical, and scientific education'. It has been seen that by 1895 the Colonial Office in London had decided that the continued existence of Asante as a sovereign power was incompatible with the imperial design. The military occupation of Asante in 1896, and the destruction of its institutions of central government, ensured that henceforth the paramount interest in the development of its rich resources would be that of London and not Kumase.

CHAPTER 15

Politics and policies in nineteenth century Asante: the ideological variables

The pre-eminence of tradition

By far the greater part of the Asante population was at all times engaged in agriculture, and the principal sphere of Asante entrepreneurship was neither that of warfare nor of commerce, but that of the exploitation of the land for purposes of food production. For the most part, land belonged to matrilineages or *mmusua* (singular, *abusua*), each under its own head known as the *abusua-panin* who exercised his functions with the assistance of a committee, the *badwa*, composed of the lineage elders or *mpaninfo*. The corporate nature of an *abusua* owning a determinate parcel of land was symbolized by its stool, the *abusua-dwa*, which was usually that of the ancestor first to assume possession of the land in question. The land may have been acquired in historic times by, for example, gift or grant in reciprocation for services usually of a military kind. In many cases, however, the ancestor of the *abusua* is regarded as having been the first person to have occupied the land in remote antiquity (*firi tete*), and the stool belonged therefore to the category of *gu-dwa:* those which have existed from time immemorial and are inalienably vested in specific lineages.[1] A number of such parcels of land, and the *mmusua* to which they belonged, constituted a village over which an *odekuro* presided. Usually himself head of one of the constituent *mmusua*, the *odekuro* and the other lineage heads formed a council for the management of the lands of the village, and saw themselves as responsible, above all, to the ancestors or *asamanfo* for the conservation and improvement of the lands in such a way as to ensure a livelihood for the generations yet unborn. The *odekuro* and the lineage heads were thus *nhwɛsofo* or 'caretakers' of the land for the ancestors and on behalf of the unborn.[2] But the *odekuro* also had another role, since he was considered the local repre-

---

1 The *gu-dwa* are contrasted, for example, with the *po-dwa:* stools created on specified and remembered occasions by a ruler who retained, therefore, residual rights over their disposition.
2 For a recent discussion of the complex matter of Asante land tenure, see Allott, 1966, *passim*.

sentative of government responsible ultimately to the Asantehene through intermediate *ahene* and *abirempon* (see pp. 102–3). Bonnat, in 1875, who had himself farmed Asante land, was one of the earliest writers to give some account of the role of the *odekuro* in local government:

> The kingdom is divided into districts each of which has a capital and a great chief or viceroy, who possesses a court modelled on that of the sovereign. Each village, of greater or lesser importance, which is a component part of a province, has a chief, a sort of mayor, who is so designated by the king . . . The chief of a village, in the same way as the chief of a province, is responsible before the king for his administration. They have particular administrative responsibilities and exercise justice in a manner analogous to that of the power of our justices of the peace.
>
> It is to the exercise of justice, in the small villages, that the first hours of the day are devoted. In the early morning the *odekuro* (magistrate) and the *mpaninfo* (elders), accompanied by those in the village who are not working, go and sit under the most shady tree, the slaves following their master and carrying the chair on which he is to sit. The company, which always includes a large part of the inhabitants, goes to listen to the debate and takes the part of one of the litigants. On most occasions the matter is arranged amicably, the guilty person paying the costs; this consists usually of palm wine which is distributed to those present. If the matter is serious, the penalty consists of a sheep and also of a specified quantity of gold dust which is distributed between the *odekuro* and the elders who comprise the tribunal. It happens sometimes that the accused refuses to submit to the judgement made against him; he may appeal to the viceroy of the province and sometimes even to the king. Certain criminal matters fall outside the jurisdiction of the *odekuro* of a village and even of a viceroy of a province . . .[3]

In fact the *odekuro* was responsible to government not only for the administration of justice at the village level, though this was certainly the most continuous of his functions, but also for the collection of taxes, and for the mobilization of men for war and such public works as road construction and maintenance.[4] In general, however, the village community was largely self-regulating at the local level: subject to such demands on its manpower and other resources as the government might make, but otherwise concerned to manage its lands as autonomously as possible through the traditional and 'timeless' institution of the *abusua*. Essentially, for those making their living from the soil the good life involved maintaining the condition and way of life of the ancestors who had in previous generations farmed the same

---

3 *L'Explorateur*, 1875–6, II, 621–2. Gros, 1884, pp. 188–9.
4 For the acquisition of a dampan or bureau by an *odekuro*, see above, p. 381, n. 37.

land. It was to the ancestors that the new agricultural year was announced with gifts of food and drink:

> Grandfather So-and-so, you (once) came and hoed here and then you left (it) to me. You also Earth, Ya, on whose soil I am going to hoe, the yearly cycle has come round and I am going to cultivate; when I work let a fruitful year come upon me, do not let the knife cut me, do not let a tree break and fall upon me, do not let a snake bite me.[5]

By contrast with such other spheres of entrepreneurship as mining, trading and, in favourable circumstances warfare, over all of which a high degree of administrative control was exercised by government, food production appears not to have been a highly profitable activity. Surpluses were indeed marketed locally, and were especially needed to meet the high level of demand from Kumase itself, but there is little in the evidence to suggest that the proceeds were converted into other than a limited supply of luxury goods – cloths, metal basins, gunpowder (for funerals), and the like – such as to alleviate somewhat the austerity of rural life. There was, then, no wealthy landowning class in Asante, and the agrarian interest as such was not strongly represented in national politics. The notion of good government, *amammupa*, was one basic to all Asante political thinking, and every Asantehene upon election was enjoined to provide it.[6] For the *abusuampaninfo* of rural Asante, the heads and elders of the many landholding lineages, *amammupa* was conceived negatively: while the central government was expected to maintain conditions of law and order within Asante and to guarantee its people freedom of attack from outside, the facility for carrying out these functions so as to impinge only minimally on the affairs of the farming communities was considered the measure of good administration. The arrival in a village of government messengers was an event usually bringing in its wake some sort of dislocation of the rhythm of rural life. Beating 'gong-gong' to summon the villagers, the *dawurufo* might announce the imposition of a new tax, or require the provision of so many men for the army, and would in any case be entitled to payment for their unwelcome services, and food, before proceeding on their way.

There is a strong strain in Asante thought which is profoundly ahistorical. The account of the origins of the nation in the conquests of Osei Tutu, as first chronicled by the Muslims in the early nineteenth century, is regarded not so much as inaccurate, but as irrelevant to the understanding and analysis of the origins of the political order. The alternative approach, to which for example Casely Hayford subscribed in 1903, was to see the nation as essentially the village writ large, and

[5] Rattray, 1923, p. 215.
[6] See, e.g. Kyerematen, n.d., p. 27.

the Asantehene as essentially the *abusua-panin* of the nation.[7] The view was adopted by Rattray, who argued:

it is in the social organization of a people in which lie the germs of the legal system which they are later to develop. If this hypothesis be correct, then it will be well to begin our investigation with an examination of the centre of that social system. This, in Ashanti, is not the King, or Chief, or Clan, or Tribe, or even the individual; it is *the family*. I think that it will be possible to prove that from such a unit may be traced most of the later ramifications and existing practices in the Ashanti Law and Constitution. It is hardly possible for any one to investigate the status and *potestas* of an Ashanti *fie-wura* (house-master) and the position of the other inmates of his *ménage*, without observing how the present-day position and power of sub-Chief, Chief, Head-Chief, and finally of the Asante Hene (King of Ashanti) himself, *vis-à-vis* his subjects, have been modelled upon this simple pattern and developed from this humble beginning.[8]

In 1942 the 'Ashanti Confederacy Council' officially indicated its acceptance of the view, that 'The constitution of any administrative unit in Ashanti is based upon the Abusua system; the same principles govern the constitution of the village Council and the Head Chief's Council . . . The modern Division or independent state may be assumed to have developed by slow and natural stages from a primitive family settlement.' [9]

It was certainly the case that throughout the nineteenth century many of the values of the Asante court remained congruent with those of the village communities and of the dispersed *mmusua*. Indeed, one of the most noteworthy features of Asante culture even at the present time is the importance attached to the preservation and transmission of materials pertinent to the origins of the socio-political order. Accounts of the circumstances of the creation of every office, major or minor, are narrated usually in considerable detail, and referred to the reigns of specific Asantehenes. The corpus of such myths – whether or not the individual items are historically veridical – presents a view of society as essentially timeless and unchanging: that is, the exploits of the first occupant of an office are recounted by an incumbent to legitimize the contemporary status of that particular office, but the cumulative effect of the body of such accounts is to express the constitutional arrangements which order the polity. In the early nineteenth century highly effective control was still maintained over the dissemination of information about the past. The indoctrination of an

7 Casely Hayford, 1903, p. 22.
8 Rattray, 1929, p. 2.
9 Asanteman Council Archives, Manhyia, Kumase: Notes on Ashanti Customs prepared by late Captain Warrington and reviewed by a Committee appointed by Ashanti Confederacy Council, 24 July 1942.

Asantehene with the appropriate mythical values was a matter of cardinal importance. 'During the minority, or the earlier part of the reign of a monarch', Bowdich observed, 'the linguists and oldest counsellors visit him betimes every morning, and repeat, in turn, all the great deeds of his ancestors'.[10] The transmission of sanctioned materials was the responsibility of such trained professional groups as the state drummers, hornblowers and *kwadwom* singers – 'those wonderful minstrels who, on state occasions, drone like a hive of bees, into the king's ear, the names and deeds of dead kings and queens, as far back as their traditional history has any record'.[11] Strong deterrents existed, on the other hand, against the unauthorized transmission of such materials: 'To speak of the death of a former king, the Ashantees imagine to affect the life of the present equally with enquiring who would be his successor; and superstition and policy strengthening this impression, it is made capital by the law, to converse either of the one or the other'.[12] In 1817 Bowdich remarked that traditions about the beginnings of the nation were 'very cautiously adverted to, the government politically undermining every monument which perpetuates their [the Asante] intrusion, or records the distinct origins of their subjects'.[13] Three years later Dupuis observed that the 'unlettered' Asante was 'decidedly ignorant and disinterested about researches into past ages'.[14] The matter, however, was not one of lack of interest but, as Bowdich realized, of the imposition of controls. The case of the Bannahene's skull illustrates well the nature of the mechanisms involved. In 1817 Bowdich was given some account of the campaign which the Asantehene Osei Kwadwo conducted against the Banda of the northwest, and he was informed that the skull of the defeated Bannahene adorned one of the state drums in Kumase.[15] In 1818–19 the incumbent Bannahene rendered great assistance to the central government in the course of the invasion of Gyaman, and in the following year he was present in Kumase for the division of the war booty.[16] But the censors had been active: there had been no war against Banda, so Dupuis was informed on his visit to the capital, and that a Bannahene's skull had been 'placed on the king of Ashantee's great drum, has no foundation whatsoever'.[17] What was in fact historically

10 Bowdich, 1819, p. 296.
11 Rattray, 1923, p. 103. See further, Institute of African Studies, Ghana, IAS/01/A.2, 1962: *Kwadwom,* by J. H. Kwabena Nketia.
12 Bowdich, 1819, p. 228.
13 *Ibid.* pp. 228–9.
14 Dupuis, 1824, p. lxxxiii.
15 Bowdich, 1819, pp. 237–8. See also p. 41. The campaign was presumably that fought against Bannahene Worosa in the reign not of Osei Kwame but of his predecessor Osei Kwadwo.
16 Dupuis, 1824, pp. 79–81.
17 *Ibid.* p. 244.

accurate had become, nonetheless, actionable gossip – *kunorokosɛm*.

By the political manipulation of the past, then, a body of officially sanctioned myth was sustained, in terms of which the political order was described and legitimated. Fundamental to the whole system of myth was the account of the origin of the Golden Stool, the *Sika Dwa* itself, by reference to which the Oyoko dynasty asserted its right to rule.[18] Unlike any other office in Asante, the Golden Stool was subordinate to none and superordinate to all. Conversely, the status of every other office was defined in terms of its formal relationship to the Golden Stool, and each was identified with reference to the nature of that relationship as belonging to one or more of a number of categories which were not necessarily mutually exclusive ones: *Abusua Dwa, Po Dwa, Aban Dwa, Esom Dwa, Kofo Dwa,* and so forth. Fundamental to the whole system, too, were the seventy-seven laws purportedly given by Okomfo Anokye at the time of the kingdom's foundation: that, for example, there should be only one Golden Stool and that no other stool may be decorated with gold; that only the Asantehene had the power of life and death; that the Asantehene must be impartial in dealing with his subjects; that the penalty for treason is death; that Thursday is a day of rest on which no one should farm, embark on war, and the like; that two or more wars should never be conducted simultaneously; that the property of anyone committing suicide while a case against him is pending is subject to seizure; that sexual intercourse during menstruation is forbidden; that false prophecy is punishable by death but that if commuted to a fine, the priest must refrain from further practice; that a child born of a pre-pubescent girl may be claimed by the *nsumankwaafo* or court physicians; and that an albino may be claimed by the *nkonnwasoafo* or stool-carriers.[19]

The emergence of ideology

The strong constitutionalist tradition in Asante was predicated upon a view that change in the political order was aberrant rather than normative, and that the system of authority relationships expressed in the myths could be validated independently of the configuration of power empirically demonstrable at any specific time. Nevertheless, even in the eighteenth century the strength of the constitutionalist position was being eroded as a result of the emergence of political ideology as distinct from, and opposed to, political myth. The notion that the political order was timeless and unchanging was being challenged by

18 See, e.g. Rattray, 1923, pp. 288–90.
19 For a treatment of the laws of Okomfo Anokye, see Kyerematen, 1966, pp. 228 ff.; Kyerematen, 1969, pp. 4–5. See also Rattray, 1929, p. 280; Ramseyer and Kühne, 1875, p. 106.

groups within the nation the interests of which could only be promoted through change – and sometimes radical change. As the apparatus of government became increasingly bureaucratic in character, and as growing numbers of officials attained positions within both the administrative and military branches by appointment on merit rather than by hereditary qualification, so the traditional value-system became progressively outmoded: new national goals were identified and new directions of policy formulated.

One aspect of the transition which occurred has been alluded to: the 'secularization' of the monarchy.[20] It was a corollary of the changing status of the Asantehene, that the mode of decision-making also slowly altered. It has been pointed out above that the *amansɛm*, the debate leading to the decision, is considered in Asante a necessary (though not sufficient) condition of any matter becoming law; and the lengthy process which resulted finally in the passage into law of the Anglo-Asante treaty of 1817 has been described in some detail in Chapter 10. Although an Asantehene might, in times of crisis, take decisions without full debate, this was not an accepted procedural norm in the nineteenth century. In a comment on the reign of Kwaku Dua I, most autocratic of all the rulers in that century, T. B. Freeman wrote:

in all ordinary transactions the business of the state is discussed in open council between the Sovereign, the Great Officers of the Royal Household and the Great Chiefs of provinces; and in these public assemblies, a very large amount of freedom of speech is understood and permitted by law. The present king of Ashantee, for example, has often in meetings over which he has presided since I have known him, when the question of peace or war with the British Protectorate has been the subject of discussion, been publicly accused of want of energy and courage for embarking in war. The monarch seldom resents these petulant sallies, but is rather, proud of them as indicating the high metal of his chieftains.[21]

The evidence suggests that participants in Council debates in the nineteenth century might still continue to appeal to the body of political myths in support of their positions. In the debate which preceded the invasion of the southeastern Gold Coast in 1826, for example, the argument was apparently advanced that hostile acts should not be committed against the Akuapem since Okomfo Anokye (considerably over a century earlier!) had specifically forbidden such (see p. 181). In general, however, debates were well-informed, and alternative policies were proposed and evaluated with reference not primarily

---

20 See particularly above, pp. 344–53.
21 Methodist Mission Archives, London: 1860 MS, based on T. B. Freeman's diaries, chapter v. See also *The Western Echo*, I, no. 12, 17 March 1886, p. 8.

to myth, but to rationally formulated ideological positions: that is, to sets of beliefs based upon an awareness of the processes of historical change, and expressed in terms of realistic political programmes for the achievement of a certain desired future state of society whether through change ('the progressives') or through maintenance of the *status quo* ('the conservatives').

The trend towards the 'secularization' of politics – towards the emergence of ideology in the place of myth – became apparent in the use of the legislative instrument of the Asantehene in Council to enact a series of laws frequently both of an enlighted character and of far-reaching effects upon the existing social and economic orders. Thus, for example, in the sphere of the liberties of the individual, under Osei Kwame it was made illegal to sell out of Asante those who were Asante citizens; [22] under Osei Bonsu all Muslim slaves were freed (see p. 263); and under Kwaku Dua I the seizure (*adwo*) of persons for the debts of another was forbidden.[23] In the field of familial law, Kwaku Dua I legislated to prohibit marriage between grandparent and grandchild,[24] and in that of penal law, Osei Yaw reversed the earlier ruling that madness constituted a defence in homicide cases.[25] In 1876 penal reform became a major topic of debate, and it has been shown how, after debate in both the Council of Kumase and the Asantemanhyiamu, the decision was taken to cease carrying out mass executions on public occasions. The Asantehene and the people, wrote Owusu Ansa, 'have found some of their old ways were not right'. The policy was reaffirmed by the government late in 1881.

At a level of broad generality, all politically responsible Asante were seemingly in agreement in regarding good government as involving, centrally, the generation of wealth. The Asante view of the position of the individual within society, as trustee of the legacy of the ancestors on behalf of the generations yet unborn, carried the implication that the good citizen was the one who worked to bequeath more to his successors than he had acquired from his predecessors. *Sika sene, biribiara nsen bio,* runs a familiar maxim: 'there is nothing as important as wealth'. At a lower level of generality, however, disagreement became manifest on the issue of how wealth was best to be generated. In Chapter 12 the phenomenon of political polarization in nineteenth century Asante was described, and it was suggested that

[22] Reindorf, 2nd ed., n.d., p. 135. For this law see further, *Report from the Select Committee,* C. 551–II, 1842, p. 489: Freeman's Journal, entry dd. 23 December 1842, citing Kwaku Dua I – 'he said he allowed none of his people to sell natives of Ashanti into foreign slavery'.
[23] Rattray, 1923, p. 234. Rattray, 1929, p. 370.
[24] Rattray, 1927, p. 329.
[25] Rattray, 1929, p. 303.

politically conscious citizens tended to identify themselves either with an ideology of mercantilism, conceiving of the state as an instrument for the generation of wealth through the control and promotion of trade (loosely, the 'peace' party), or with an ideology of imperialism, conceiving of it as an instrument for the generation of wealth through the control and exploitation of dependent territories (loosely, the 'war' party). It was argued further, however, that after 1867 the views of those who challenged the validity of the dichotomy between mercantilism and imperialism – the oligarchy of 'peace' and 'war' parties – became increasingly heard. And finally, at a still lower level of generality, ideological differences were apparent in the conflicting views held, as to what ends the surpluses of wealth within society should be applied: or in other words, as to the desirability – and directions – of change. In speaking of the emergence of political *parties* in nineteenth century Asante, the implication is that, however narrowly rather than broadly based these were, the views on ideology and policies of the individuals associated with them formed reasonably coherent and consistently held sets of beliefs; and that if an individual held a specific view, then a strong probability existed that he also held a number of other specifiable ones.

The imperialist ideology of the war party, and the war machine

On his accession as Asantehene in 1867, so Kofi Kakari himself maintained, the legislators expressed criticism of his predecessor Kwaku Dua I for having been so reluctant to make war, and, in a succinct statement of the 'war' party position, argued that it was *'by fighting the Ashantees had multiplied and [become] prosperous'*.[26] It was clearly true that the expansion of Asante had been accomplished principally by force of arms. It has been shown above, moreover, that the resettlement within the metropolitan region of prisoners-of-war, and sometimes of whole civilian communities, was of great importance in maintaining within that region a favourable density of population *vis-à-vis* that of the other parts of Greater Asante (pp. 83–7). This aim was further promoted by the exaction of tributes in slaves especially from the more northerly provinces. As late as the 1870 period, so Ramseyer reported, 'not only was a great part of the population [of Kumase] in a state of slavery, over which the great men of the kingdom maintained a despotic government – but numerous caravans of half-starved and enfeebled slaves were delivered every year in this way to Kumase from distant provinces and tributary states, as

26 *Further Correspondence*, C. 4052, 1884, p. 47: Asanti's statement to Barrow, dd. 3 May 1883.

war booty or tribute'.[27] Kühne, too, spoke of slaves being 'constantly recruited by all sorts of devices from surrounding tribes', and estimated – presumably of the Kumase area – that 'the population appears to consist in about equal parts of Ashantees and slaves, with a few freedmen, whose condition does not differ much from that of the slaves'.[28] The importance of the continuous input of manpower to the Asante economy was considerable: unfree labour was used extensively in agriculture – not least, as Bowdich remarked, 'to create plantations in the more remote and stubborn tracts';[29] in the extractive industry – that is, in gold-mining;[30] and in manufacturing – in, for example, the production of bullets.[31] Furthermore, surplus labour found a ready market in the British Protected Territory, and in the mid-nineteenth century Cruickshank estimated that 'some thousands' of slaves were sold annually into the Protectorate – those originally 'either taken in war by the Ashantees, received as tribute from subjugated states, or purchased by them'.[32]

It seems clear that the Asante councils never authorized military operations which had no object other than the acquisition of captives. 'The Ashantee wars', remarked Cruickshank, 'are never undertaken expressly to supply this demand.'[33] Indeed, in 1820 Osei Bonsu carefully exonerated himself and his predecessors in office from any such charge. 'I cannot make war to catch slaves in the bush, like a thief', he insisted; 'my ancestors never did so.'[34] Nevertheless, it remained the case that a successful campaign much enriched the participants, and most notably those who were in a position to obtain field commands. It was remarked of the Gyaasewahene Adu Bofo, for example, on his return to Kumase in September 1871 after heading military operations east of the Volta, that 'he seemed to have attained the height of his ambition, [and] spoke of his slaves, umbrellas and gold, though he wanted more of that, and hoped to get it'.[35] Five years later, at the Council of 17 February 1872, Adu Bofo strongly urged the military reoccupation of the old southern provinces: 'Asen, Akem, Akra and Akuapem, which all formerly belonged to Ashantee, had been drawn

[27] Steiner, 1900, pp. 17–18.
[28] See Maurice, 1874, p. 271. The estimate of the ratio of free to slave population, which was based upon the observations of Kühne, may be compared with that of Horton, 1868, p. 108, for the British Protected Territory: 'three-fourths are slaves or descendants of slaves'.
[29] Bowdich, 1821b, p. 18.
[30] See, e.g. Boyle, 1874, p. 15.
[31] Reade, 1874, p. 299.
[32] Cruickshank, 1853, II, 246.
[33] *Idem.*
[34] Dupuis, 1824, p. 163.
[35] Ramseyer and Kühne, 1875, p. 138.

over to serve the white men, who on their part had subsequently broken their treaty of peace with Ashantee by refusing to give up a runaway chief . . . the right thing would be to regain our authority over these tribes.' [36] Another of the foremost field commanders of the period, the Bantamahene Amankwatia, maintained the same position in a letter to Wolseley of 20 October 1873.[37] Although the decision to restore Asante influence in the south had been approved by Kofi Kakari himself (p. 235), he maintained subsequently that the commander of the expeditionary force in 1872–3, Amankwatia, had chosen to exceed the objectives of the campaign as determined in council and had thereby caused the Anglo-Asante war:

the road to Wassaw had been stopped by Enemil, King of Wassaw, so Aman Quatia, the Commander-in-Chief of the Ashantee army, was appointed to go and open the road to Wassaw for trade. I ordered him not to touch any white man, because my late uncle Quacoe Duah told me that I must never fight with white man, but when Aman Quatia started he took the main road to Cape Coast, so I sent Chief Sabee Entchwie to tell Aman Quatia not to go to Cape Coast, but to go to Wassaw as I told him, but before Sabee Entchwie got up to him Aman Quatia had already fought some Fantees and white men, so by this way the war came between the Ashantees and the white men.[38]

Leadership of the war party in the 1860s and 1870s was, clearly, in the hands of a number of the senior field commanders, and the implication of the evidence is that they formed a sufficiently powerful and united group not only to dominate the Council, but also to ignore whatever limitations the Asantehene may have attempted to impose upon their aims. It is, so it was remarked in 1874, 'to the interests of these war leaders, Adoo Boofoo, Amanquoitia, Atchampon, etc., to be constantly leading expeditions'.[39]

The structure of the Asante military machine – on the maintenance of which the viability of the imperial ideology was predicated – was one of considerable complexity. At the centre of the organization was the standing army, based upon the capital and, as Beecham for example remarked, largely recruited from the unfree population.[40] An excellent description of the process by which the standing army was built up, through the appointment of captains (*asafohene*, occupying *kofo dwa*, 'war stools') over new recruits, was given by Reindorf:

36 *Ibid.* p. 158.
37 Letter dd. Mampon (Elmina), 20 October 1873, reprinted in facsimile in Brackenbury, 1874, I, frontispiece.
38 *Further Correspondence*, C. 4052, 1884, p. 47: testimony of Kofi Kakari, in Asanti's statement to Captain Barrow, dd. 3 May 1883.
39 Maurice, 1874, pp. 18–19.
40 Beecham, 1841, p. 129.

The kings of Asante do not only appoint the captains over the army, but, in addition, they organise it, and also increase it as occasion arises. Before a captain is appointed, the king collects recruits in readiness for him to drill. They may be either captives made in a recent war, or his own subjects whom he bought as slaves when they failed to pay a certain fine imposed on them as punishment for an oath they had sworn, or they had been bequeathed to him by a deceased chief or captain. Over a number from 500 to 1,000 men thus obtained, the king appoints a captain, and then a grand public meeting was held, and the body of recruits were presented to the newly appointed officer as his soldiers and slaves. The subjects bought have to remain in their own town, but the captives have to stay permanently in the town of the captain, and he himself stays at the capital.

Other presents are made by the king to the captain, a name is given to the band [or] 'asafo', and the men and officer are at the disposal of any of the generals over the five main divisions who require their services.[41]

In 1882 Lonsdale wrote of the 'Chiefs [who] command men supplied them by the King', who 'take the place of a standing army, though they are seldom called together except for war . . .' It was his opinion, he added,

that 2,500 men is the limit any Kumasi Chief could bring together. These would all be armed with flint-lock guns, as would all others, except the King's body guard, who have, to my knowledge, 360 Sniders, and who are reported to have 600. I do not know how many rounds of Snider ammunition they are possessed of. These men I compare to a regular army, though not paid, are regarded as soldiers and accept the position.[42]

It will be apparent from the preceding pages, that many Kumase functionaries in fact held dual appointments, accepting administrative responsibilities in civil government while continuing to hold their military commissions.

The size of the 'trained bands' was not inconsiderable. In the 1840s for example, the captains of the Bantamahene Gyawu commanded 5,000 'armed retainers', and those of the Asafohene Akwawua Dente, 4,000.[43] In 1862 the Akyempemhene Owusu Koko alone commanded 3,000 gunmen.[44] The government could, however, always order a general mobilization of the civilian population. 'When it is required that they [the soldiers of the standing army] be augmented by the forces of the Kingdom', Lonsdale wrote, 'many an unwilling provincial has

41 Reindorf, 2nd ed., n.d., p. 111.
42 *Further Correspondence*, C. 3687, 1883, p. 115: Lonsdale's report on his mission to Asante and Gyaman, April to July 1882.
43 *Further Correspondence*, C. 893, Pt IV of 1874, p. 63: Chapman to General Secretaries, Wesleyan Missionary Society, dd. Fort Beaufort, 29 September 1873.
44 *Wesleyan-Methodist Magazine*, October 1862, p. 955: visit of West and Owusu Ansa to Kumase.

no choice left but to repair to the camp with as good a grace as possible.' [45] The first stage in such a mobilization was to appoint the field commanders – the 'fighting generals' as Owusu Ansa described them. These were to be distinguished from those who, although not responsible for the actual conduct of the operations, nevertheless held high military rank by virtue of the number of men that they were able to mobilize. Although officially designated Commander-in-Chief of the national army, the Mamponhene for example only assumed an active field command if he was otherwise considered skilled in the arts of war.[46] Lonsdale's account of the mobilization procedures shows how the conscription of fighting men was accomplished:

The system of mobilization is to appoint a Chief of high position and ability (whom I will call general) to the command of an army, the rank and file for which is to come from the districts of such and such subordinate Chiefs (or captains). The captains are called upon by the general to bring out their men. The number that each Chief produces varies greatly. These captains who hold rank as Chiefs generally of importance, and frequently of influence, and who are heads of districts, call upon the subordinate Chiefs and headmen of their villages to produce the rank and file. In this manner an army is collected at some place, where a camp is then made. If, before giving any order to mobilise, the general finds the whole army will not be required, he contents himself by telling one of his principal captains to see to it, and remains at home. Then possibly the captain designated may find that half his force only is required, and he acts accordingly. By this system, with requisite knowledge of the standing of the country Chiefs, the importance of any military movement is appreciated, on hearing which Chief or Chiefs have been appointed, or how many captains and headmen are in camp; but this does not necessarily give an idea even of the numerical strength of the army.

It does not, however, follow, as might appear from this, that the district from which the army is drawn is denuded of its fighting population, for according to the emergency, so is the demand, and it may happen that perhaps only one petty Chief or headmen from a particular district is called upon; he again need not take more than a certain proportion from the population of his villages, reserving the remainder for times of greater pressure. In his selection he would be guided by the number of guns possessed by his men, retaining some arms until the last push.

The ammunition is usually supplied by the King for national war; by Chiefs for particular or personal enterprises . . .

The provincial Kings, such as the Kings of Bekwai, Kokofu, and Mampon, of Ashanti Proper, and the outlying Chiefs of the Protectorate of Ashanti in the districts to the N.W., N., and N.E., would be called upon to furnish to

45 *Further Correspondence*, C. 3687, 1883, p. 115: Lonsdale's report.
46 *The Times* (London), 29 July 1873: particulars furnished to a correspondent by Prince Owusu Ansa.

the general strength, according to their supposed population, and under the same rules as I have mentioned as regulating the mobilization.[47]

With so powerful a war machine at their disposal, those who believed warfare and the maintenance of empire to be the *sine qua non* of national growth, and who saw themselves as in the tradition of the great commanders of the era of expansion in the eighteenth century, constituted potentially one of the most cogent interest groups represented in the councils. Yet increasingly throughout the nineteenth century the adherents of the imperial tradition found themselves not only in a minority in council, but also lacking any immediate prospects of coming to power.

The changing economics of warfare

In 1816 the Dutch Governor-General in Elmina, Daendels, presented to the Department of Trade and Colonies in the Netherlands a perspicacious report on the effects upon the local economy of the traffic in slaves. 'The slave trade', he argued,

has caused the trafficking of goods for gold and ivory to be very greatly diminished. It has extinguished industry, and not only caused a reduction in the number of gold-diggers, but also the regular work in the mines to cease in the dry season: so that now digging for gold is practically only done by the slaves of Kings and Caboceers, who win a very small amount compared with former times. It has also much lessened the desire for agriculture, so that one finds periodical famines in many places where former abundance prevailed, the supply of one year then being first consumed during the following year . . .[48]

Four years later the Asantehene Osei Bonsu discussed the problems which faced the nation not as a result of the trade in slaves, but rather of the decline in the maritime markets for them. In doing so, he showed clearly the intimate nature of the relationship between warfare, the imperial ideology, and the slave trade:

If I fight a king, and kill him when he is insolent, then certainly I must have his gold, and his slaves, and the people are mine too. Do not the white kings act like this? Because I hear the old men say, that before I conquered Fantee and killed the Braffoes and the kings, that white men came in great ships, and fought and killed many people; and then they took the gold and slaves to the white country: and sometimes they fought together. That is all the same as these black countries. The great God and the fetische made war

[47] *Further Correspondence*, C. 3687, 1883, pp. 114–15: Lonsdale's report.
[48] State Archives, The Hague, KvG 384: Daendels to Department of Trade and Colonies, dd. Elmina, 6 December 1816.

for strong men every where, because then they can pay plenty of gold and proper sacrifice. When I fought Gaman [1818–19], I did not make war for slaves, but because Dinkera (the king) sent me an arrogant message and killed my people, and refused to pay me gold as his father did. Then my fetische made me strong like my ancestors, and I killed Dinkera, and took his gold, and brought more than 20,000 slaves to Coomassy. Some of these people being bad men, I washed my stool in their blood for the fetische. But then some were good people, and these I sold or gave to my captains: many, moreover, died, because this country does not grow too much corn like Sarem, and what can I do? Unless I kill or sell them, they will grow strong and kill my people. Now you must tell my master [that is, George III of England] that these slaves can work for him, and if he wants 10,000 he can have them. And if he wants fine handsome girls and women to give his captains, I can send him great numbers.[49]

There can be little doubt that it was the sharp decline of the maritime markets for slaves at the beginning of the nineteenth century that was one of the principal reasons for the failure of the imperial or war party to maintain control over the Asante councils other than for short periods in the remainder of the century. Already, by the end of the campaigns in the southern provinces in the 1810s, a marked lack of enthusiasm for the war was becoming apparent among some of the senior field commanders. In 1815 or 1816 the Anantahene Apea Dankwa, who headed one of the armies of the south, died. He was succeeded by his brother, Apea Nyanyo. A breakdown in army morale occurred, and became particularly manifest in the hostile relations between the troops of Apea Nyanyo and those of Bariki ('Bakee', 'Barriekie'), second in command of the army and a son apparently of the Asantehene Opoku Ware.[50] Finally Apea Nyanyo withdrew his army to Kumase without obtaining prior government approval.[51] The two field commanders were placed on trial. That of Bariki opened on 1 September 1816. He was accused of having asserted 'that he could not be expected to forgo the enjoyment of the riches and luxuries of his home, until every revolter was killed'. Found guilty, he was sentenced to be deprived of his office and property, and was subsequently appointed to a junior post as 'overseer of a small river'.[52] The trial of Apea Nyanyo took place on 8 July 1817, and charges of 'cowardice' and 'indolence' were brought against him. He, too, was sentenced to deprivation of his office and property, and was banished.[53] Both officers chose soon after trial to commit suicide rather than suffer the disgrace.

49 Dupuis, 1824, pp. 163–4.
50 Huydecoper's Journal, entries for 29 and 30 April 1816. Bowdich, 1819, p. 232.
51 Bowdich, 1819, pp. 243–4.
52 *Ibid.* p. 73. Huydecoper's Journal, 1 and 2 September, and 28 October 1816.
53 Bowdich, 1819, pp. 129, 243–4.

The decline in the maritime markets for slaves, then, had the effect of making warfare less profitable and therefore less popular, and the dominant position which the peace interest enjoyed in council between 1826 and 1863 was undoubtedly predicated in some measure upon this fact. While the attempt to compute a balance sheet for any of the campaigns of the nineteenth century has not been made, data exist which indicate the order of the costs which might fall upon the treasuries. Thus the Asantehene Kofi Kakari estimated that he had expended 6,000 peredwans, or 13,500 oz of gold, on the invasion of the British Protected Territory in 1872–3 (see p. 438).[54] The sixteen engagements which the Bekwae had fought in the cause of national unity between 1886 and 1888 (see p. 568) were then estimated by Bekwaehene Kwaku Sei to have cost the Bekwae treasury some 3,500 peredwans, or 7,875 oz of gold.[55] To the heavy charges upon public funds must be added the loss to the nation in terms of the heavy casualties which might be expected in any campaign. The deleterious effects of the prolonged campaigns in the southern provinces, which terminated with the defeat at Katamanso in 1826, were still apparent not only in those provinces but in the metropolitan region some thirteen years later, when T. B. Freeman first visited Kumase.

Nor were the towns and villages over the [Adanse] hills, in Ashantee proper, without sad traces of the desolating hand of war. It is true no enemy had swept over them with fire and sword as in the regions nearer to the coast, but many of their former inhabitants had marched to the field of conflict and there bit the dust, and their dwellings standing desolate had fallen to decay declaring a decimated population, so true is it that war is a sore evil to all therein engaged.

In every part of Ashantee through which we passed, the same sad traces were visible, even the Metropolis could not conceal the injury it had thus sustained. There was, indeed, the frontage of each establishment kept up, looking into the streets to secure order, uniformity and even beauty, but the mud and wattle huts behind, often swelling into the size of a small village connected with one street frontage, were, in many instances, nearly desolate . . .

It is evident, therefore, that all needed repose, and the present sovereign [Kwaku Dua I], adverse to war, and wise and prudent in counsel has fulfilled an important providential vocation for which he deserves great credit.[56]

The growth in the early 1870s of popular agitation against the war in the south has been discussed above (pp. 504–9). In a lucid com-

54 Ramseyer and Kühne, 1875, p. 243.
55 *Further Correspondence*, C. 7917, 1896, p. 62: Hull to Governor, dd. Kumase, 6 April 1891.
56 Methodist Mission Archives, London: MS of 1860, based upon Freeman's diaries, chapter v.

ment, Reade acknowledged the inverse relationship which existed between anti-war sentiment and the profitability of the campaigns: 'the Ashantees, though a brave people, are not like European soldiers; they do not love fighting for fighting's sake. They receive no pay, and fight in the hope of plunder.' [57] While, then, a number of the field commanders in the period headed the war interest in the councils, others had been won over to the view that war, although sometimes unavoidable, was in general an economically inefficient and thus undesirable instrument of public policy. Prominent among those associated with the latter position was the Anantahene Asamoa Nkwanta, 'ruler of the battles',[58] who had served as commander of the campaigns in the northern provinces in the early 1840s (p. 277) and of the operations against the British in 1853 (p. 217). Regarded as the 'preceptor' of all the Asante field commanders [59] (the Bantamahene Amankwatia being by report one of his favourite pupils), Asamoa Nkwanta was also credited with the introduction into the Asante fighting forces of the system of platoons each of twenty men, and of techniques of loading and reloading such that even with antiquated guns 'an astonishing fusillade is sustained'.[60] In 1872–3, as senior of the general staff officers, Asamoa Nkwanta had the opportunity of assessing the potentialities of the new breech-loading Snider with which the British had equipped their troops. He joined those who were 'the loudest advocates for peace'.[61]

An interesting account of the composition of the imperial party in the period was given by Kühne, who identified as among its principal constituents the retired or inactive military commanders who were not *au fait* with recent developments in the science of war; the sycophants who surrounded the Asantehene; and a group of traditionalists unable to appreciate the complexities of realistic foreign policy decision-making:

there are, as might be expected, a certain number of Marathanomakoi, who have known only war with the interior, or the wars with us [the British] in 1864 or in older times, when they have almost invariably been able to boast of success, and who, now being too old to fight, banter the young men on their degeneracy; a certain number of chiefs who were not engaged this time [1872–3] against us, through various causes; a set of men who have all their lives hung round the King, flattering him to the top of his bent as invincible, 'the white man slayer,' etc. Then, too, there are a not incon-

57 Reade, 1874, p. 372.
58 Ramseyer and Kühne, 1875, pp. 267–8, 310, 311.
59 Boyle, 1874, p. 146.
60 *Ibid.* p. 149.
61 Maurice, 1874, p. 268.

siderable number of men who have been resident in or about Coomassie all their lives, and look upon it as the centre of the universe.[62]

The change of government which occurred late in 1873, however, marked the effective extinction of the imperial ideology as a viable political choice. Although the campaigns of 1872–3 had been by no means unsuccessful in purely military terms, their high costs in monetary outlay and casualties, and their low returns in booty (*asadeε*), revealed very clearly the transformations which had occurred in the economics of warfare.[63] The anti-war movement of the early 1870s became increasingly concerned in the later part of that decade with the abolition of the whole system of military conscription, and it was under Mensa Bonsu that the government authorized the creation of the new model army: that is, of the force of paid professional soldiers which would ultimately, so it was envisaged, take over the main burden of national defence. When in 1896 Asante faced another invasion, majority opinion was firmly opposed to war with Britain. But while the imperial ideology was moribund, nevertheless advocates of a military response to the threat to the national security were not wanting:

the nation's power had greatly suffered both in actual strength and in prestige by its defeats in the campaign of 1874. There were plenty of fighting men, no doubt, and there existed in favour of war a very strong party, which included the fetich priests and some of the greater chiefs; but many of the older people still lived to remember the disastrous past and offer wise counsels of peace. Two or three Ashantis had, further, visited England, and the tales of their travels must have convinced the king and his advisers that resistance would in the end be hopeless.[64]

In the event, as it has been shown, no opposition was offered to the British expeditionary force which entered Kumase in 1896. The policy for which John Owusu Ansa was principal advocate was adhered to, and it was only after the cumulative experience of the first four years of foreign domination that the Asante leaders finally had recourse to arms once again.

The mercantilist ideology of the peace party, and the apparatus of trade

In 1882 C. S. Salmon, former Acting Administrator of the Gold Coast Colony, suggested that British policy there had been largely determined by the mistaken belief that Asante decision-making was predicated

62 *Ibid.* p. 268.
63 *Ibid.* p. 267.
64 Barter, 1896, p. 444.

upon a view of warfare as being one of the most efficacious instruments of public policy. Yet, he argued, an understanding of the value system of the Asante would have made possible a rapprochement between, on the one hand, the British, and on the other,

those powerful agents which are never absent from the councils of just and peaceful men, whether they be assembled in the old palaces of Europe or in the recesses of an African jungle – that is, the influences which gather around the industrial and commercial pursuits of the people; and although, at bottom, these may rest merely on the wish for material welfare, combined with security, they are, nevertheless, the most powerful of social levers, and impel equally the savage who seeks a bauble for ornament, and the citizen of a civilized State. These influences, moreover, under whatever form they show themselves, are the most legitimate that can be invoked, for they can always be ranged on the side of peace and goodwill. Everywhere men have families and family ties, household interests, home feelings, and national hopes . . .[65]

The interlocking nature of the peace interest and the commercial interest was a feature to which allusion was frequently made. Trade, observed Osei Bonsu in 1820, 'is what I want. I don't want war, that is only the talk of bad men,'[66] Ramseyer and Kühne wrote of the many Asante who, in the militaristic climate of opinion in the early 1870s, stood nevertheless for 'peace and free trade'.[67] In 1875 messengers arrived at Cape Coast to announce that the newly enstooled Mensa Bonsu desired 'peace, trade and open roads';[68] and in 1883 the managers of Kwaku Dua's candidacy for the Golden Stool announced their aims: 'we want a good King, peace, open roads, and trade'.[69]

In 1875 Mensa Bonsu had circulated a letter to the European merchants at Cape Coast, in which he had explained his policy of reconstruction necessitated by his predecessor's expensive campaigns: 'all my people turned their attention and energy to trade, which is the only means to alleviate, if not to repair, the losses sustained in a long period of war . . . all roads might be opened and trade take its free course'.[70] The view of trade which prevailed in Asante throughout most of the nineteenth century was, however, what may appropriately be described as a mercantilist one: *inter alia,* the state was seen as the major participant in the commercial sector of the economy, and its agents were afforded protection – through exemption from taxation and other such

65 Salmon, 1882, pp. 892–3.
66 Dupuis, 1824, p. 130.
67 Ramseyer and Kühne, 1875, p. 260.
68 *Papers relating to Her Majesty's Possessions in West Africa*, C. 1343, 1876: Strahan to Carnarvon, dd. Cape Coast, 8 January 1875.
69 *Further Correspondence*, C. 3687, 1883, p. 158: Barrow to Rowe, memorandum of palavers held in Kumase, dd. 27 April 1883.
70 *Papers relating to Her Majesty's Possessions in West Africa*, C. 1402, 1876, p. 71: Mensa Bonsu to G. J. H. Lyall *et al.*, dd. Kumase, 19 July 1875.

devices – from the competition offered by private entrepreneurs. There were, indeed, periods when the state came to exercise a virtual monopoly of commerce, and independent traders ceased operating other than at the local retail market level. In 1820 Dupuis urged upon the Asantehene Osei Bonsu the desirability of allowing unrestricted and free competition between all merchants, while imposing a tax on all transactions based upon prevailing commodity values. In a brief statement of his position, Osei Bonsu in reply argued that it was trade in itself which generated wealth, and that direct taxation could only inhibit its growth:

the Ashantee fashion is different. None but kings and great men trade here, the same as myself. Sometimes I lend them gold, if they are good people; and then I cannot say, give me the gold back. If they come from another country to trade in Coomassy, they make friends, and give me a present; then, to be sure, I cannot tell them to give me gold, when they buy and sell the goods. Besides, some traders are king's sons and brothers, and great captains: I must not say to them, give me gold, but I must give them gold and provisions, and send them home happy and rich, that it may be known in other countries that I am a great king and know what is right. Thus I please my Gods, and they make me strong.[71]

Osei Bonsu's advisers, however, also offered other than economic objections to the development of independent trading. In 1817 Bowdich reported the opinions of those who believed that the class of private entrepreneurs must incline to attach more weight to the profit motive than to considerations of national security, and that an uncontrolled merchant class would in time present a revolutionary threat to the chiefly establishment:

their government would repress rather than countenance the inclination [to trade], (believing that no state can be aggrandized but by conquest,) lest their genius for war might be enervated by it, and lest, either from the merchants increasing to a body too formidable for their wishes to be resisted, or too artful from their experience to be detected, they might sacrifice the national honour and ambition to their avarice, and furnishing Inta [Gonja], Dagwumba, or any of their more powerful neighbours (who have yielded to circumstances rather than force) with guns and powder (which are never allowed to be exported from Ashantee,) break the spell of their conquests, and undermine their power . . . Were they to encourage commerce, pomp, the idol of which they [the established chiefs] are most jealous, would soon cease to be their prerogative, because it would be attainable by others; the traders, growing wealthy, would vie with them; and for their own security, stimulated by reflections they have now too little at risk to originate, they would unite to repress the arbitrary power of the Aristocracy; and even if

71 Dupuis, 1824, p. 167.

they did not, inevitably (as the chiefs conceive) divert the people's genius for war.[72]

Such, indeed, was the strength of the imperial ideology still, that Osei Bonsu's government was prepared to see trade dominated by Muslim entrepreneurs – whether strangers or provincials – rather than allow the growth of an indigenous Asante bourgeoisie.[73] 'Ashantee was a nation of warriors', remarked the Asantehene in 1820, in justification of the policy; 'the people did not understand these things [trade] like the inhabitants who lived nigher the great water (Niger).' [74] Nevertheless, at the administrative level changes had already been initiated which were to result in the ultimate dominance of the Company of State Traders within the political realm. The Company was in time to become to the mercantile party what the army was to the imperial party.

Titular head of the Company of State Traders as of the army, was the Asantehene. 'The king', it was aptly remarked in 1874, 'is the chief trader in the kingdom.' [75] Effective direction of company policy was in the hands of the Gyaasewahene, in his capacity as Head of the Exchequer: 'the King's treasurer or gold-keeper', it was noted of Opoku Frefre in 1817, 'is also overseer of the King's trade and can send it wherever he wishes'.[76] A functionary of the central administration, the Batahene or Trade Chief, was responsible to the Gyaasewahene for organizing the necessary logistical support for the company operations and some account of the origins and structure of the Bata has been given in Chapter 11. The Batahene, however, had no role in the financing of the business operations: trade capital was paid out of Treasury funds to mercantile agents specially designated as such by the Asantehene and Gyaasewahene.

'Kumasi', wrote Casely Hayford, 'was the centre of a state system which directly fostered the trade of the coast and connected it with the trade of the hinterland'.[77] His general description of the operations of the Company of State Traders – of the 'constant stream of Ashanti traders . . . daily wending their way to the coast and back' – has been cited above (p. 197), and a number of accounts of the way in which the Company's activities were financed are extant. In 1817 Bowdich remarked that monthly, at the Adae, the Asantehene disbursed some 40

72 Bowdich, 1819, pp. 335–6.
73 Wilks, 1971a, pp. 132–4.
74 Dupuis, 1824, p. 167.
75 Reade, 1874, p. 416.
76 State Archives, The Hague, KvG 350: Huydecoper to Daendels, dd. Kumase, 9 January 1817.
77 Casely Hayford, 1903, pp. 28–9.

peredwans, or 90 oz of gold, to various functionaries present.[78] The better part of a century later Casely Hayford referred to the same practice, and offered a fuller explanation of it:

Every fortieth day the *Adayi* custom fell. It was a time of national festival and general rejoicing. The King on this occasion distributed among his several chiefs, according to their rank, large sums of money. They were not supposed to use the money for their own self-indulgence, but they were expected, like the stewards in the parable, to trade with the money of their master, so that he who had received seven peregwans might add seven peregwans thereto, and render a due account when called upon to do so; though, as a matter of fact, it was seldom that an account was called for. In this way the State naturally encouraged thrift, and in olden days it was quite common to see thousands of Ashantis coming down regularly to the coast and buying goods for their masters, which in turn found their way into the very heart of Africa.[79]

However, the mercantile agents or 'stewards' to whom public monies were entrusted were not themselves among those who travelled whether to the coastal or interior markets. They were essentially involved in market manipulation, and upon their success measured in terms of profits would depend their future eligibility for additional capitalization. The goods which they chose to market were carried in caravans often of two or three hundred persons.[80] Although a mercantile agent might decide to send a number of his own slaves with the caravan, its organization and basic staffing was the responsibility of the Asokwahene. In a manner reminiscent in some respects of mobilization for war, the Asokwahene would appoint the trade chiefs who were to conduct the caravan to its destination. These would be lesser functionaries of the Asokwahene. The trade chiefs thus appointed would then recruit the necessary personnel – including unfree labourers and women as carriers – from the many Asokwa villages surrounding the capital.[81] A brief report of such caravans leaving Accra was made in 1841:

We met several parties of Ashanti traders, starting off for the interior, with various articles of European produce, but principally salt, which they exchange for gold-dust and ivory. Everything is borne on the heads of slaves, a portion of whom of course belong to the commissariat department, and carry provisions for two or three days. These Ashanti traders communicate with all the nations of the interior adjoining their country, but they do not pass the frontier.[82]

[78] Bowdich, 1819, p. 282.
[79] Casely Hayford, 1903, p. 28.
[80] *Ibid.* p. 96.
[81] Wilks, field-notes, interviews with Asokwahene Kofi Poku, dd. Kumase, 3 and 5 August 1965.
[82] Allen and Thomson, 1848, II, 183.

The trade chiefs were generally responsible for the safety of their charges. Indeed, when a woman member of a caravan was robbed and murdered in Assin in 1843, the 'captain of the trading party' investigated the crime, apprehended the murderer, and handed him over to the local Assin authorities who in turn sent him to the British in Cape Coast Castle (pp. 215–16). The 'captain' was obliged to present a full report on the matter to the Council in Kumase on his return, and 'the conduct of the Heads of the trading party was highly approved'.[83] As a matter of routine, on their return to Kumase the heads of caravans would report to the mercantile agents, and their commissions would be calculated: 'the trade Chiefs would . . . render a faithful account to the King's stewards, being allowed to retain a fair portion of the profit'.[84] Members of the Asokwafo enjoyed exemption from military service,[85] although in times of war the commissariat was used to supply the armies with both ammunition and foodstuffs.[86]

The era of the mercantilists

For a brief period in the early 1830s the operations of the Company of State Traders were suspended on the southern routes, and private entrepreneurs were allowed unrestricted access to the markets of Asante (pp. 193–8). By 1835, however, the mercantilist interest – British and Dutch as well as Asante – were of one voice that the situation which had developed was 'most pernicious and dangerous'. From the subsequent debates on the matter the Company re-emerged seemingly with greatly increased powers. The revival of the Asante caravan trade with the Gold Coast in the 1840s had, according to Cruickshank, two immediate effects upon the economy of the British Protected Territory. First, the many Fante and other coastal labourers who had started carrying goods into the interior were thrown out of work and had to move into agriculture, thus stimulating the production of palm oil. And secondly, money (in the form of gold dust earned in Asante) became scare in the Protectorate, and the British were obliged to import greatly increased quantities of cowries as a 'circulating medium'.[87] The Asante

---

83 *Further Correspondence*, C. 893, Pt IV of 1874, pp. 62–3: Chapman to Wesleyan Missionary Society, dd. Fort Beaufort, 29 September 1873.
84 Casely Hayford, 1903, p. 96.
85 IASAS/1: Asokwahene-Batahene Stool History, recorded by J. Agyeman-Duah, 3 February 1963.
86 See, for example, *Further Correspondence*, C. 7917, 1896, p. 88: Hull to Acting Governor, dd. Nsuaem, 17 September 1893. Ramseyer and Kühne, 1875, p. 267. Rattray, 1929, p. 124.
87 According to Cruickshank, 1853, II, 37–40 and 45, in the mid-nineteenth century imports of cowries ran at about 150 tons annually, or some 130 million shells. Bowdich, 1819, p. 330, maintained that cowries at that time circulated in the

government in turn had to maintain – 'under very severe penalties' – its ban on the use of cowries in the metropolitan region lest production of gold dust should begin to fall.[88]

The great age of mercantilism in Asante extended from the late 1830s through to the early 1880s. During that period the Company of State Traders enjoyed all but total protection from any form of competition. In 1816 and 1817 Osei Bonsu had involved himself in inducing the European merchants' houses on the Gold Coast to give preferential terms to the *batafo* or official traders, thereby eliminating the private entrepreneur as an effective competitor. In December 1816 there arrived at Elmina one 'Adoe Djewoe trader, eldest son of the Marshall Amanquatia': [89] that is, the future Bantamahene Gyawu, son of Bantamahene Amankwatia. The willingness of the Dutch Director-General to afford him special terms produced an outcry from the independent traders who, so it was reported, 'praise the General's trading methods very highly but complain about the preference given to the son of Amanquatia'.[90] Osei Bonsu, on the other hand, was encouraged to try further to formalize the arrangement with the Dutch:

> The cashier or treasurer of General Poikoe [Opoku Frefre] has been ordered by the King to send about 25 oz. of gold to Elmina with which to purchase gunpowder. The King wants to see whether the General will meet him in the matter of price, or whether he will treat him as on a level with his subjects. For this reason I [Huydecoper] have thought it necessary to write a letter . . . to the General, asking him to make a distinction between the King's trade and that of all other persons, and to treat the representatives of the King as he did the son of Amanquatia.[91]

A similar approach was probably made to the British at Cape Coast, to whom Osei Bonsu expressed misgivings that many Asante were introducing themselves to the authorities there as 'attached to him in various capacities', and asked that henceforth only those should be regarded as accredited who were either introduced by letter or carried his cane.[92] Some account of the attempt by the British to turn the growth of mercantilism in Asante to their own advantage has been given above (p. 444).

northern provinces of Dagomba, Gonja and Gyaman, but not in Asante proper. Dupuis, 1824, p. cxi, stated that neither Asante proper, nor the province of Gyaman, were in the cowrie currency area, though other of the dependencies may have been. For the cowrie currencies of West Africa in general, see Johnson, 1970a and 1970b, *passim*.

88 Cruickshank, 1853, II, 244–7.

89 State Archives, The Hague, KvG 349: Elmina Journal, entry for 16 December 1816, citing Huydecoper to Factors, dd. Kumase, 26 November 1816.

90 Huydecoper's Journal, entry for 9 January 1817.

91 *Idem.*

92 Bowdich, 1819, pp. 94; 132.

The protection afforded the *batafo* engaged in the kola trade north-wards has already been referred to: the Asantehene could, among other things, close the roads early in the season until the official traders had taken advantage of the prevailing high prices in the northern markets.[93] The government, moreover, maintained a tight control over smuggling operations by means of its agents, the *nkwansrafo* who were stationed along the great-roads and whose duty it was to examine the credentials of all travellers. All wholesale transactions were forbidden at other than the officially recognized markets. For the last sixty years, wrote Salmon in 1882, the Asante 'have wholly or partially closed their frontiers. They will not allow the inland people to proceed to the coast to trade, for they fear they will be there supplied with fire-arms and gunpowder to be used against themselves. All commodities must be taken to Kumassi, or to localities specially designated by the council of chiefs.'[94] In the late 1870s, for example, in view of the uneasy relations which prevailed between the government in Kumase and the Adanse chiefs, the market of Adubease in Adanse was transferred to Ankase, a town within the immediate ambit of Kumase. In 1881 Lonsdale gave some account of the structure of the new market:

Akankowasi [Ankase] is a small village in which a market is held every Friday, at which a very large number of people assemble. It is here that goods from the coast change hands to a considerable extent. Many traders, not residents of Coomassie, preferring to sell what they have carried up at this place to going on to Coomassie and running the risk of detention there. Most merchandise purchased here increases very much in value on arrival in Coomassie (from 25 to 50 per cent.), which is at most only one and a half day's journey, spirits in particular.

People from all the surrounding towns and villages congregate here on the market day. A Chief has charge of the town, but there are several court officials permanently stationed there to decide petty cases, and report all they think of sufficient importance to Coomassie.[95]

The relocation of the principal market for the northern trade, from Gbuipe to Salaga and subsequently from Salaga to Kintampo, has been discussed above. An excellent although unsympathetic account of the operation of the mercantile system at the time of the Asantehene Kofi Kakari was given by Boyle under the rubric, 'Secrets of Cape Coast Trade':

The only middle man in the commerce of this coast is King Koffee himself, and he does the agency with a vengeance. The whole interior trade from the

93 Rattray, 1929, p. 187.
94 Salmon, 1882, p. 890.
95 *Further Correspondence*, C. 3386, 1882, pp. 58–9: Lonsdale's report on his mission of 1881–2.

outer confines of his dominion, as far as that unknown point where the absorbing capacity of the East Coast merchants begins to be felt, passes through his hands. The *modus operandi* is this: The arrival of an inland trader is signalled from the first village where he touches Ashantee ground; straightway messengers are sent from Coomassie to escort the stranger, and to see that he does no business on the way; he reaches the king with bales unpacked; the king receives the whole, gives the trader a receipt, and sends half-a-dozen servants, trained to the business, into Cape Coast, with the inventory of the goods detained. They go to work singly, entering every store, and ascertaining the current price both of the ivory they have to sell and the merchandise the king proposes giving them in return. Having gathered all the necessary information they hasten back to Coomassie, and confidentially instruct the king, who promptly values the ivory and cloths of his 'guest' at 50 per cent. of the current price just reported to him. He also informs that wretched man what goods he proposes to give him in return, valuing each article at twice the price of Cape Coast Castle. The trader has no choice but to accept. The messengers come down again, as ragged as before, but heavy with gold dust. They fulfil the king's order, doing a small cheat on their own account if possible. The trader is sent away mulcted just 75 per cent. of his legitimate profit. Perhaps at this price he makes a good thing of it, but beyond doubt King Koffee clears 75 per cent.[96]

In 1903 Casely Hayford maintained that until 1873 the Asante trade had yielded 'more certain wealth and prosperity to the merchants of the Gold Coast and Great Britain than may be expected for some time yet to come from the mining industry and railway development put together'. He advocated restoration of the mercantilist system destroyed by the British after 1896.[97] Whatever its advantages to foreign merchants, however, there can be little doubt that throughout much of the nineteenth century a very considerable part of the Asante gross national product was derived from the operations of the Company of State Traders. Its activities, moreover, were a source of income to the many citizens associated with it at whatever level: to the carriers who were permitted to trade on their own account, and on the same advantageous terms, whatever they could carry over the regulation load; to the trade chiefs who conducted the caravans and received commissions on the transactions; and to the mercantile agents who, after repaying with interest the loans from public funds, were left nevertheless with substantial profits. Not only capital, but life and limb, were much less at risk in participation in the commercial rather than the military enterprises of the nation.

The growth of popular opposition to military conscription from the 1870s onwards was to some extent paralleled by the growth of popular

96 Boyle, 1874, pp. 109–10.
97 Casely Hayford, 1903, pp. 95–100.

opposition in the 1880s to the continuation of government restrictions on independent trading. The ideology of mercantilism as well as of imperialism was to come increasingly under attack from radical thinkers. In 1900, nevertheless, after four years of British occupation, the state of the nation under the strong mercantilist governments of the nineteenth century could be compared most favourably with that under the colonial administration:

The spirit of discontent had been brewing since the occupation of Kumasi. It has been said over and over again that since the English took the country, the Kings and Chiefs have become poorer and poorer and that their ultimate ruin in purse was inevitable owing to the heavy exactions to which they were subjected. Mentioning this complaint once to a European friend he said 'Ah, but the Kings of Ashanti fined them heavily.' But he received the rejoinder 'Ah, but the Ashanti Kings paid them well.' He took money from the people, but he gave back money to the people; so that money circulated from the people to the King and from the King to the people. Every forty days the King held what the natives call Adai at which it is estimated he spent about £1000 making presents to all classes of people in sums ranging from 3 tokoos 1/- to 2 and even 3 pereguins £24 6s. The Chiefs and Captains received each from half Perguin £4 1s. to 2 or 3 pereguins according to rank; and the lower subjects in proportion.

Hence it will be seen that the resources of the Chiefs were never exhausted. Besides the Chiefs of Kumasi acted as Mercantile Agents for the King, each receiving from 500 to 1000 pereguines yearly which they in turn distributed to their Subchiefs or Captains and other subjects, who took it to the coast for goods which they took into the interior; and made thereby fabulous profits: they rendered account to the King at the end of each year. With these resources, there is no wonder that they were immensely rich and could afford to meet the exactions of the King who well knew their various wealth.[98]

The incomparability of wealth

It is clear that within Asante it was not only possible for the individual to acquire wealth but for him to do so was universally commended. In 1817 Bowdich observed how members of the chiefly class in Kumase were able not only conspicuously to consume, but also to save: 'the chiefs are fed bountifully by the labours of their slaves, and sharing large sums of the revenue, (the fines their oppression has imposed on other governments,) with incalculable fees for corruption or interference, refine upon the splendor of equipage even to satiety, and still possess a large surplus of income daily accumulating.' [99] While quantifiable data are in the nature of the case exceptional, there are a few

98 *The Gold Coast Aborigines*, XVI, no. 115, 30 June 1900, p. 3.
99 Bowdich, 1819, pp. 335–6.

indications of the impressive extent of the fortunes which functionaries might amass. The career of Boakye Yam, nephew of the Asokwahene Kwadwo Anto and *ahenkwaa* in the administration of Osei Kwadwo, has briefly been referred to above (p. 456). Promoted counselor by Osei Kwame, he lived to serve in Osei Bonsu's administration until his death, at the end of a long career, in or about 1814. Although he was said to have made large gifts of gold during his lifetime to his son and successor in the counselorship, Oti Panin,[100] his estate at death in gold dust was nonetheless computed at 'five jars (said to hold about four gallons each) and two flasks'.[101] Each gallon may be assumed to have approximated to, but not reached, 1000 peredwans (see p. 420), and his fortune may therefore be computed – assuming the accuracy of Bowdich's testimony – at somewhat below 45,000 oz of gold (or £162,000 at the then current equivalence of £3 12s the ounce).[102] Again, upon the disgrace in 1817 of Apea Nyanyo of the Ananta, the government was reported to have seized his estate of three jars of gold dust, representing by the same accounting a fortune somewhat under 27,000 oz.[103]

Such individuals constituted within society a well defined class, the *asikafo* (singular *sikani*, from Twi *sika*, 'gold'), though not all members of the class commanded fortunes of the size of those of Boakye Yam or Apea Nyanyo. A useful definition of the concept of *asikafo* was offered by Oheneba Sakyi Djang in 1936:

By this is meant rich men who own large estates, and are capable of granting large loans; in ancient times they owned many slaves. All Sikafo are highly respected, so long as it is known in the community that they obtained their riches by honest means and hard work. They are well-to-do people, on whom the state relies for pecuniary assistance, especially in granting loans.[104]

A slight but significant shift in emphasis may be detected in the Asante saying, *okaniba na ode ka*, 'the good citizen is he who assumes debts'.[105] The ideal is exemplified in the career of Yamoa Ponko, the details of

---

[100] *Ibid.* p. 254.
[101] *Ibid.* p. 319.
[102] I am grateful to a number of chemists who suggested that the purity of alluvial gold is likely to be between 85% and 95%, and that the lower limit for the density of gold dust (which assumes that the grains are roughly shaped but about the same size) would be approximately 14 grams per c.c. It is assumed that the gallon in question was the Queen Anne wine gallon, equal to 231 c. in. and not the imperial gallon which was introduced only in 1824. A computation of the value without reference to the cultural factor (that 1000 peredwans was a recognized storage unit) would suggest that the estate was one of about 36,000 oz, or of the order of £130,000.
[103] Bowdich, 1819, p. 319.
[104] Djang, 1936, p. 114.
[105] See Kyerematen, 1966, p. 90.

which are still recounted. Yamoa Ponko had become wealthy by trading in the north at Daboya,[106] and was chosen by the Asantehene Osei Kwadwo to occupy the Ankase stool.[107] The future Asantehene Osei Kwame, as a child, was entrusted to his care at Ankase for some three years.[108] When Osei Kwadwo imposed a general war tax upon all chiefs, in order to replenish the Treasury, the Hiahene Kofi Maafo – then senior office-holder within the Kyidom division – was unable to pay the 30 peredwans required of him. Yamoa Ponko assumed the debt, and as a result he rather than Kofi Maafo became recognized as Kyidomhene.[109] In that capacity he lived to serve his former protégé Osei Kwame, and was appointed by him to command of the army despatched against the rebel Mamponhene Owusu Sekyere Panin probably in 1778 or 1779 (see p. 251). Before his death Yamoa Ponko agreed to hand over all of his property to Osei Kwame on the condition that the latter should attend his funeral in person. His only remaining estate at the actual time of his death appears to have been the one hundred retainers who were in the northern hinterlands trading under two younger sons of Yamoa Ponko, Gyasi Kwame and Kyei Kuma. All were taken as death duty, and were incorporated into the Asantehene's new Atipin group.[110] Yamoa Ponko was, it is said, 'a man of opulence and a person of property qualification, and did enhance and enrich the Kyidom stool with all available jewellery'.[111] Among the class of the *asikafo,* too, were numbered women entrepreneurs whose wealth was likewise conspicuously made manifest. Kanin Abena Toprefo, for example, had been involved in the northern trade like Yamoa Ponko, whose relative she may have been. Purchasing land, she founded the new village of Wioso and established a market nearby with the permission of Osei Kwame. When the Asantehene honoured her by visiting the market in person, she is said to have presented him

106 Institute of African Studies, Ghana, IASAS/154: Hia Stool History, recorded by J. Agyeman-Duah, 2 February 1965. In this tradition an accurate chronological framework is lacking, Yamoa Ponko being variously associated with Asantehenes from Osei Tutu to Osei Yaw. However, the successor of Yamoa Ponko, the Kyidomhene Anti Kusi, held office for one month only (see IASAS/158), and his successor, Kyidomhene Gyasi Tenten, was the incumbent under Osei Bonsu, see e.g. Bowdich, 1819, pp. 75, 283.
107 IASAS/158: Kyidom Stool History, recorded by J. Agyeman-Duah, 16 February 1966.
108 *Idem.*
109 Kyerematen, 1966. Essentially the same account occurs in IASAS/154, Hia Stool History, but is wrongly associated with the reign of Osei Yaw.
110 Kumase Divisional Council Archives, Manhyia: Civil Record Book 9, Kumase-hene's Tribunal, Kwaku Dua v. Kwasi Kyi, commenced 1 May 1930.
111 IASAS/158, Kyidom Stool History, recorded by J. Agyeman-Duah 16 February 1966.

with 125 peredwans of gold dust, and the councillors who accompanied him with 30 peredwans.[112]

It was not unknown for individuals to make false claims to wealth for the prestige thereby gained. The successful deception practised by the Akuroponhene Gyamfi Kwadwo during the reign of Osei Yaw is still well remembered. Having supposedly amassed a fortune, he willed his total estate to the Asantehene conditional upon his attending the funeral. Upon Gyamfi Kwadwo's death, however, it was found that his gold pots were in fact filled mainly with brass filings or *dutu* (the circulation of which was specifically forbidden by one of the laws of Okomfo Anokye). The corpse was tried and beheaded.[113] But there was nevertheless some check upon such deceptions, for one of the greatest marks of distinction to which a citizen might aspire was that of making a public display of the wealth which he had accumulated. 'This is generally done once in a life', observed Hutchison, 'by those who are in favour with the King, and think themselves free from palavers.' [114] Thenceforth the citizen was entitled to have an elephant's tail – the symbol of wealth – carried before him by *ahoprafo*, elephant's tail-bearers. The respect which the *asikafo* were afforded is indicated by the high status of these youthful petty functionaries.

These troops of boys who carry the elephants tails, are the sons of men of rank and confidence; for whenever the King dignifies a deserving subject, with what may be termed nobility, he exchanges some of his own sons or nephews, (from eight to fourteen years of age,) for those of the individual, who maintains them, and for whom they perform the same offices, as his own and others do for the King.[115]

A number of persons publicly displayed their wealth in the week beginning 9 November 1817. Among them was the Gyaasewahene Opoku Frefre, who invited Hutchison to both his village and town houses to inspect his gold.[116] Unexpectedly, Opoku Frefre used the occasion to obtain from the Asantehene recognition of the legal status of the *mmamma* (see pp. 460–2). Another account of the display of wealth (by a functionary whose name is regrettably not recorded) is

112 Kumase Divisional Council Archives, Manhyia: Civil Record Book 3, Kumasehene's Tribunal, Kofi Anane *v.* Kwadwo Fodwo, commenced 20 September 1927.
113 According to Kyerematen, 1966, this occurred in the reign of Osei Kwadwo. But see IASAS/199, Akropong Stool History, recorded by J. Agyeman-Duah, 13 March 1967, in which Gyamfi Kwadwo is associated with the reign of Osei Yaw. The latter account must be correct, for the successor of Gyamfi Kwadwo, the Akuroponhene Ansere Tepa, was among those executed in the purge of 1839, see above, p. 488, and Reindorf, 2nd ed., n.d., p. 293.
114 Hutchison, in Bowdich, 1819, p. 395.
115 Bowdich, 1819, p. 295.
116 Hutchison, in Bowdich, 1819, pp. 387–9 and 395–6.

of especial interest for its detail on the place of the elephant's tail in the ceremony. On 29 March 1862 it was reported:

several chiefs arrived [in Kumase], in order to take part in the ceremony, which was that of the display of wealth, by an old chief, in order to be entitled to the honour of having the elephant's tail carried before him; an honour to which only the wealthy can aspire . . . A very ludicrous part of the anticipated ceremony came off in the afternoon [of 30 March] . . . A slave had been selected to enact the part of elephant. Besmeared all over with chalk, holding in his hand a small tusk, which he occasionally applied to his mouth, and having an elephant's tail attached by a piece of string behind, he was started off; while some forty or fifty men, armed with muskets, and supplied with blank cartridges, followed in pursuit, keeping up an almost constant fire. His elephantship, as we were informed, made his way, according to usage, to a small kroom not far from Kumasi, where he fell down as if shot, and lay there until the chief himself appeared to cut off the tail; who, having thus hunted the elephant, and possessed himself of its caudal appendage, was considered, as I suppose, entitled to have it borne in triumph before him. The subsequent part of the ceremony, that of the display of wealth, occupied a considerable part of three days.[117]

Award of the privilege of having an elephant's tail carried before one by *ahoprafo* [118] was clearly part of that system of honours to which reference has been made above (pp. 77–9): of what was described in 1883 as the 'Ashanti peerage system . . . which shows that the power of that kingdom is not based entirely upon a blind reverence for bodily strength and martial prowess'.[119] As fount of all honours and by consent the most wealthy individual in the kingdom, the Asantehene possessed his own elephant's tail – the Sika Mmra. The Ahwerewamuhene is custodian of the Sika Mmra or Golden Elephant's Tail,[120] in just the way that the Nkonnwasoafohene is custodian of the Sika Dwa or Golden Stool. The Sika Mmra symbolizes wealth and the Sika Dwa, authority.

117 *Wesleyan-Methodist Magazine*, October 1862, pp. 955–6 and 958: visit of West and Owusu Ansa to Kumase. A fuller account of the ceremony was given by the Akyeamehene Apea Nuama in 1925, see NAG, Accra, ADM 11/1338: Notes of Enquiry into the Constitution and Organization of the Kumasi Adonten Stool, pp. 77–8.
118 The term is difficult to render in English, but see the Twi *ɔho-nya*, 'wealth', and *pra*, 'to sweep up, gather up'; hence, perhaps, 'those who gather up wealth'.
119 *The African Times*, xxiv, no. 266, 1 November 1883, p. 122.
120 IASAS/140: Ahwerewamu Stool History, recorded by J. Agyeman-Duah, 30 November 1964. The relationship is unclear between this stool and that of the Ahoprafohene, see IASAS/143: Ahoprafo Stool History, recorded by J. Agyeman-Duah, 30 November 1964. The latter position appears to have been in abeyance for the greater part of the eighteenth and nineteenth centuries. It is noteworthy that among the presents which Osei Bonsu chose to despatch to George III of England in 1820 was 'a gold elephant's tail, composed of a thick bunch of wire: a sort of fan or fly flap, used by the king, or rather to him alone', see Dupuis, 1824, p. 174.

The wealth with reference to which an individual might be recognized as *sikani* had in the nature of the case to be self-acquired and not inherited, and it was therefore at the unrestricted disposal of the owner during his lifetime. It follows then, that the award to an individual of an elephant's tail was in recognition of his having amassed a new fortune. The point is made in the Asante maxim ɔdehye *nhyehye, na sika na ehyehye:* 'one becomes famous not by being noble born but by being wealthy'.[121] Clearly, then, those who attained the status of *asikafo* did so outside the structure of activities of the *abusua* or matrilineage. Many, in fact, had pursued successful careers in the new administration, a matter which was commented on in 1823 with reference to the appointment of resident commissioners in the provinces. 'The system of placing a caboceer or a chief in every conquered town of consequence', it was observed, 'has tended much to enrich the superior classes of society generally . . . the measure enables them to maintain a numerous retinue.'[122] Yet although there was a recognizable class of *asikafo* in Asante, there were nevertheless strong restraints upon the emergence of a distinctly *asikafo* class consciousness and class interest: upon, that is, the growth of a bourgeoisie (*amamma*) of the sort that Osei Bonsu had envisaged and feared. Among the various instruments of government which inhibited any such development was that of the *awunyadie* or death duties, a tax system which was apparently first introduced by the Asantehene Opoku Ware following the existing practice in Takyiman.[123] *Sika yɛ fɛ na ɔpɛgyafo yɛ na*, it is said: 'gold is fine, but the heir is lacking'.[124] In theory, as Bowdich remarked, 'the King is heir to the gold of every subject, from the highest to the lowest'.[125] In practice it would seem that a small estate, of the ordinary farmer for example, was left intact, to be apportioned by the family of the deceased. Conversely, the estates of *asomfo* or *nhenkwaa*, the functionaries of the bureaucracy, were wholly at the disposal of the government.[126] In other cases the estate was carefully appraised by agents of the Treasury, after which its distribution was decided upon. The system without doubt was operated the more or less stringently according to the current state of the nation's finances. Thus of the reign of Osei Bonsu, it was reported that the heir was customarily allowed only 10 peredwans, or 22½ oz, of gold dust, and then only if the estate was a large one. The Asantehene, however, would contribute towards the funeral expenses and, if the heir was a man of influence

---

121 See, for example, Rattray, 1916, p. 118.
122 *Royal Gold Coast Gazette*, 7 June 1823.
123 Reindorf, 2nd ed., n.d., p. 72.
124 H. N. Riis, 1854. Rattray, 1916, p. 163.
125 Bowdich, 1819, p. 254. Hutton, 1821, p. 318. Ellis, 1887, p. 277.
126 Ellis, 1887, p. 277.

and especially if he could show that the deceased had left large debts, a further sum might be restored to him.[127] Of the operation of the system during the reign of Kofi Kakari, Bonnat remarked,

The sovereign authority and absolute power of the king are not irrelevant to the might of the State. The notables, whose fortune and life depend upon the royal pleasure, are in consequence completely docile. When a chief dies, all his goods without exception become the property of the king. He names the successor of the deceased, who he selects ordinarily from the family, though he could just as easily choose from among strangers and even from outside the nobility. According to the position which the one elected is called upon to take, the king adds to his inheritance a certain quantity of gold and slaves. This gives the monarchy immense strength and riches.[128]

Under Agyeman Prempe I the system appears, for obvious reasons, to have been modified, and it became usual for the Treasury to take about one-half of an estate as *awunyadie*. In the case of important office holders, however, the successor might have to pay upon enstoolment a further tax, known as *ayibuadie* or *amuhuma*, assessed according to the size of his inheritance. Certain stools had, in various circumstances, won the privilege of not having *awunyadie* levied upon their occupants; such were the Adonten, Benkum, and Nifa of Kumase. The *ayibuadie*, nevertheless, would then tend to be assessed at a correspondingly higher rate.[129] Clothing and household effects were not usually regarded as taxable, and were taken by the heirs.[130] Certain items of gold ornaments and jewellery might also sometimes be awarded to the heirs; [131] perhaps because anyone converting gold dust currency into non-circulating objects had already had to pay a 20% tax upon the sum thus converted.[132] Immovable property such as houses and land were not normally regarded as part of the taxable estate. *Awunyadie* was therefore levied principally upon the gold dust comprised in the estate of the deceased, and upon the unfree and even sometimes free subjects belonging to it when it was the estate of a servant of government.[133]

[127] Bowdich, 1819, p. 254. Beecham, 1841, pp. 98–9.
[128] Gros, 1884, p. 194.
[129] NAG, Accra, ADM 11/1338: Notes of an Enquiry into the Constitution and Organization of the Kumasi Adonten Stool, n.d. but 1925, pp. 61 and 79, evidence of Adontenhene Kwame Frimpon and Akyeamehene Apea Nuama.
[130] Ellis, 1887, p. 277. Bowdich, 1819, p. 254.
[131] Bowdich, 1819, p. 254: 'fetish gold'. Bowdich, 1821a, p. 25. Beecham, 1841, pp. 98–9. Ellis, 1887, p. 277.
[132] Bowdich, 1819, p. 320. Opoku Frefre was reported to have paid 20 peredwans to the Asantehene on melting down 100 peredwans of gold dust.
[133] See for example, Kumase Divisional Council Archives, Manhyia, Tribunal of the Akyempemhene, Civil Record Book, Osei Denkyenfere *v.* Kwabena Konadu, commenced 17 June 1925; Kumasihene's Tribunal, Civil Record Book 9, Kwaku Dua *v.* Kwasi Kyi, commenced 1 May 1930.

The impossibility of fortunes being transmitted intact from generation to generation did much, then, to prevent the consolidation of a
bourgeois interest. The government, moreover, seems also to have
introduced measures to increase its supervision over those men of wealth
who were domiciled outside the capital. 'The King', reported Riis in
1839, 'decrees that every prosperous man in his whole land must also
have a home for himself and his people [in Kumase], where he must
appear every year in order to celebrate the [Odwira] festivities.' [134] A
speech of the counselor Asante Agyei, reported by Bowdich, expressed
with clarity the 'correct' attitude towards the *asikafo:* that the existence
of the class visibly enhanced the nation's image, and that members of
it should therefore have an unqualified right to their wealth for the
duration of their lives.

The King confessing a prejudice against a wealthy captain, his linguists,
always inclined to support him, said, 'If you wish to take his stool from
him, we will make the palaver;' but Agay sprung up, exclaiming, 'No, King!
that is not good; that man never did you any wrong, you know all the gold
of your subjects is your's at their death, but if you get all now, strangers will
go away and say, only the King has gold, and that will not be good, but let
them say the King has gold, all his captains have gold, and all his people
have gold, then your country will look handsome, and the bush people fear
you'.[135]

The development of the middle class interest

During the reign of Osei Bonsu the strength of the imperial ideology
remained such that the *asikafo,* however their wealth had been gained,
still regarded the financing of the army as the most profitable outlet
for their capital. As in the cases of Yamoa Ponko and Boakye Yam
already cited, they would cover the expenses of war by loans and
grants. 'Gold', remarked Bowdich, 'they are all desirous of hoarding;
even those less covetous than is generally their nature, that they may
be prepared for the purchase of guns and gunpowder to a large extent,
on any sudden war, and thus ingratiate themselves with the king and
the government.' [136] Although there were those who might, like Gyamfi
Kwadwo referred to above, make the grand gesture of voluntarily
willing their estates to the nation, or of making an endowment to an
office,[137] the philanthropic content of such acts must be adjudged

[134] A. Riis, 1840, pp. 221–35: letter dd. Kumase, 31 December 1839.
[135] Bowdich, 1819, p. 249.
[136] *Ibid.* pp. 334–5.
[137] For a typical benefaction by a present day *sikani*, see *Daily Graphic* (of Ghana),
8 April 1959: 'Opanin Yaw Dwumoh, 65, farmer of Kwamang in the Kwabre
No. 2 local council area, has donated £1,500 to the Kwamang Town Development

against the prevailing level of death duties. Certainly the *asikafo* were strongly motivated by a concern to make profits, seemingly sometimes to the extent (which Osei Bonsu had anticipated) of their placing personal before national interests. In 1822–3, for example, the Nsutahene Yaw Sekyere was given authority to head a punitive expedition against the Nkonya and Wusuta east of the Volta (see p. 173). Meeting with strong resistance, Yaw Sekyere was granted permission to return to Kumase, but elected to remain in the field in the hope of recouping his heavy losses. By mid-1823 he was reported to have been in dire straits: his creditors in Asante were expected to seize his property to pay for the loans he had raised with which to finance the campaign.[138]

With the sharp decrease in the profitability of warfare, which it has been argued followed the decline of the maritime slave trade, it became necessary for the *asikafo* to find other outlets for their activities. It was within the mercantilist system, which dominated the national economy from the early 1840s onwards, that the *asikafo* found those outlets. Under Osei Bonsu the structure of the Company of State Traders had been a comparatively simple one: the *batafo* purchased at the coast, hopefully on advantageous terms, goods the cost of which had been covered by the Gyaasewahene through withdrawals from the Treasury. Later in the century, however, the structure of the Company became much more complex. The mercantile agents emerged as a class of financiers, utilizing loan capital provided by the Treasury but also their own resources, to generate profits both for the government and for themselves. Although business transactions were conducted within the framework of general fiscal policy as determined by the Exchequer division, and although the Bata continued to function as the commissariat of the Company, nevertheless the general operations of the Company became increasingly capitalist in mode. Personal fortunes could be made, and were made, by those who were agents of the Company. Perhaps precisely because this was so, the successful businessmen and financiers were to become progressively alienated from the very system within which they worked. They were frustrated by the restrictions which prevented them from operating, if they so wished, in any sort of fair competition with the Company; and they were frustrated by their inability to transmit their estates even relatively intact to their heirs. Yet the very existence of the mercantile system was predicated upon the maintenance of devices, of which death

Committee for the reconstruction of the town's football park. Opanin Dwumoh has also contributed £300 towards the construction of a feeder road from Kwamang to Duaponko'.

138 *Royal Gold Coast Gazette*, 21 January, 25 March, 21 May, 21 June and 22 November 1823.

duties were one of the most important, designed precisely to locate the sphere of capital accumulation at the level of the Exchequer and not of the individual entrepreneur.

The opposition of the *asikafo* to mercantilism became manifest, at a pre-political level of behaviour, in the diverse stratagems to defeat the system of death duties. As early as 1817 the practice of transferring property to the heirs before death had been remarked upon.[139] The concealment of gold usually by burying it and making its whereabouts known only to an heir or heirs, was also common. A widely practised variation of the dodge was for the heirs to bury part of the gold of the deceased with him, before the arrival on the scene of the Treasury officials. In view of the prevalence of the custom,[140] and the religious objections to opening a grave, the government appears to have tolerated the practice. Any such gold subsequently to be dug up, however, was *ahumtu*, treasure trove: the find had to be reported to Kumase and the Asantehene would decide on its disposition.[141] A practice treated more seriously by government was that of the transfer of gold into external accounts, since its recovery was difficult if not impossible. A case was reported in 1881, of an Asante trader who sought to deposit 170 oz of gold, to the value of about £600, with a firm of Cape Coast merchants. When the facts became known in Kumase, the trader was placed on trial, condemned to death, and executed.[142]

The attempts on the part of the *asikafo* to defeat governmental restrictions on the creation of transmissible private estates appear increasingly to have taken on a political form. In the troubled times which preceded the extensive political purge of 1859 (pp. 491–2), one of the principal causes of unrest was identified as 'the appropriation of inheritance'.[143] That the continuation of the restrictive measures remained a cardinal feature of the policies of the great mercantilist administration of Kwaku Dua I was shown, however, by its apparent overreaction in the case of Kwasi Gyani in 1862. Originally accused of secreting gold nuggets which should have been surrendered to the Treasury, Kwasi Gyani with a number of his followers sought refuge in the Gold Coast Protectorate (see pp. 222–4; 492). His position was made clear to the British authorities: 'he is a man of property

---

139 Bowdich, 1819, p. 254.
140 See, e.g. *The African Times*, xxxvii, no. 422, 2 November 1896, p. 164: 'every man of any importance is buried with from £1000 to £5000 of gold with him'. Following the British seizure of power in 1896, so it was reported, many Asante were digging up such gold.
141 See, e.g. Rattray, 1929, pp. 140, 162, Busia, 1951, p. 57.
142 *Further Correspondence*, C. 3386, 1882, p. 40: Watt to Acting Colonial Secretary, dd. Cape Coast, 2 February 1882.
143 State Archives, The Hague, KvG 395: Schomerus to Ministry of Colonies, dd. 28 June 1856.

[i.e. *sikani*], and declares that the King desires only to entrap him, take his head, and afterwards possession of his property'.[144] To the Asante government, however, the matter of his extradition from the Protectorate was of such importance that, in case of British refusal, war was seen as a reasonable alternative.

With the replacement of the peace party government by a war party one in 1863, and with the death of Kwaku Dua I and the accession to office of Kofi Kakari in 1867, the *asikafo* were able more freely to articulate their opposition to the policies adopted towards them by the previous administration. To judge from a short account given by Reade in 1874, and based upon the observations of Kühne in Kumase, the *asikafo* argued that the expansion of trade and production was being inhibited by the mercantile system in general, and by the exactions of government officials in particular; and that the introduction of *laissez faire* principles would greatly stimulate the economy.

The despotism of Ashantee is injurious to trade, for the king is the chief trader in the kingdom; the gold-mines of the country are neglected; in Coomassie the inhabitants do not care to raise live stock (as Mr. Kühne informed me) lest their property should be seized by the people of the king, who have license to rob as much as they please. It would have been preferable for ourselves [the Gold Coast administration], for the neighbouring tribes, and for the Ashantees themselves, that the monarchy should have been destroyed, or reduced to a nominal chiefdom. In that case the Ashantees would have been able to work their gold-mines without paying all the nuggets they found to the king; and their country would have become a thoroughfare . . .[145]

There are indications that the *asikafo* found their interests not incompatible with those of the new government, and that Kofi Kakari was far more sympathetic towards their aspirations than Kwaku Dua I had been. There are certain aspects of the reign of Kofi Kakari which require detailed investigation in this context. Still commemorated with the sobriquet 'the benefactor' (*akyempoɔ*, literally, 'the giver of bullion'), he is widely remembered as having disbursed to individuals a large part of the gold which he inherited from his predecessor.[146] He is also reported as having appointed children to many vacant posts, and as having awarded others to his personal servants.[147] It may be that Kofi Kakari attempted, as a matter of policy, to lower the level of government, reducing the size of the powerful bureaucratic apparatus and encouraging private entrepreneurs by transferring public funds

144 *Despatches . . . explaining the cause of war*, C. 385, 1864, p. 3: Pine to Newcastle, dd. Cape Coast, 10 December 1862.
145 Reade, 1874, pp. 415–16.
146 See Lewin, 1974, pp. 47–9.
147 Boyle, 1874, p. 277. Ramseyer and Kühne, 1875, p. 177.

to them in the form of grants-in-aid. His unpopular decision to make the costs of the campaigns of 1872–3 a charge upon the participants rather than upon the public treasury (p. 508) may be seen as a corollary of the same policy. It is particularly difficult, however, to identify with any confidence the main directions of Kofi Kakari's domestic policies: the major issues which dominated council debates for the greater part of his reign were ones of external affairs. What is clear is that with his deposition, and the accession of Mensa Bonsu, the mercantilist ideology became once more the dominant one.

In commencing the creation of the new model army and civil service, Mensa Bonsu significantly strengthened the bureaucratic character of the government. It has been shown that the costs of the reforms fell heavily upon the *asikafo* (pp. 529–30), who responded to what they saw as the systematic plundering of their resources of capital by moving to a new and more radical level of political activity. It is highly likely, though not yet demonstrable, that the abortive coup of 1877, intended to restore Kofi Kakari to office, was organized by them. The attempted assassination of Mensa Bonsu by members of the Domankama movement in 1880 probably enjoyed their support. Certainly they were involved in the revolts which spread almost simultaneously throughout the southern districts of the metropolitan region early in 1883. Indeed, Mensa Bonsu himself clearly identified his attempts to increase revenues, by higher taxes and fines, as among the principal causes of these revolts: the Manso Nkwanta, he observed, sent him a message 'to say that they intended going to live under the British, for they had to pay too many taxes and fines under Mensah'. Similarly, so he acknowledged, the Dadiase 'sent to Coomassie, and said they intended joining the British before on account of the fines the King of Kokofu imposed on them; now they intended joining the British on account of the fines King Mensah imposed'.[148] The full extent of the alienation of the *asikafo* from Mensa Bonsu's government, however, must be understood with reference to two more fundamental factors.

It was in the early 1880s that the *asikafo* pioneered the development of a new industry. This was the collection of rubber, the rising overseas demand for which was reflected in soaring prices. Just when the first consignments of rubber were sent from Asante to the coast has not been established. At the beginning of 1884, however, with particular reference to parts of Kokofu, Kirby remarked on 'the india-rubber trade, quite a new industry in this part of the country, being carried on apparently with great success'.[149] It was, then, a matter of much

---

148 *Further Correspondence*, C. 4052, 1884, pp. 9–10: statement by Mensa Bonsu to Kirby, dd. Abrade, 12 May 1883.
149 *Further Correspondence*, C. 4477, 1885, pp. 91, 95: Kirby's report on his mission to Kumase, dd. 15 April 1884. For two recent studies of the Asante rubber

concern to the *asikafo* that the government should not impose restrictive controls upon their enterprise, yet the probability of the new industry being allowed to develop free from public control was low so long as the mercantilists dominated the Council of Kumase. The *asikafo*, moreover, were already aware of the fact that while the old mercantile system which had developed in the 1830s and 1840s was no longer adequate to the circumstances of the 1870s and 1880s, the government was responding not by any moves towards a *laissez faire* economy but rather towards neo-mercantilism: that is, towards the granting of monopolies to foreign firms to develop and exploit the resources of Asante in partnership with the Asante authorities.

That official policy might be to allow foreign entrepreneurs to operate in Asante while the growth of an indigenous capitalist class was inhibited, was an issue which undoubtedly underlay the growing radicalism of the *asikafo* during the reign of Mensa Bonsu. Indeed, it would seem that the period was one in which a populist type movement was slowly gaining strength, based upon a coalition of the interests of the *asikafo* and those of a much broader sector of the populace in general mistrustful of the modernizing policies of Mensa Bonsu's government. 'The people', it was observed in 1883, 'are undoubtedly anxious for a change in the form of government of the country such as they think would bring them an existence of more independence of their King, Chiefs, and masters, and yield them trade, by which means they say and think they can become rich.' [150] The same writer also drew attention to the fact that the Gold Coast Colony was seen as a possible model for change. Remarking on 'the trade exactions and exclusions many were groaning under', he referred to their 'desire to be more like their neighbours on our [that is, the Gold Coast] side of the Prah, so as to develop commerce and civilization'.[151] The interest which the example of the Gold Coast Colony held for the Asante *asikafo* certainly could not have stemmed from any great admiration for the achievements of its government. 'The condition of the Gold Coast Colony and Protectorate', remarked a leader writer in 1883,

at the present moment is one requiring the most serious attention and careful examination. Discontent is rife among all classes . . . The public works of the colony are chiefly conspicuous by their absence and in the few and rare instances where improvements are commenced want of determination or

trade, see Dumett, 1971; Arhin, 1972. Dumett, p. 93, appears in error in suggesting that the rubber trade originated significantly later in Asante than in the Gold Coast Colony. Its development in Asante was, however, retarded by the political unrest in the period 1883–8.

[150] *Further Correspondence*, C. 4052, 1884, p. 12: Barrow to Governor, dd. Kumase, 19 May 1883.

[151] *Ibid.* pp. 58–9: Barrow's report on his mission to Asante, dd. Accra, 5 July 1883.

fixity of purpose at headquarters causes them to be abandoned almost as soon as begun and public money is wasted in a most reckless and insensate manner.[152]

Rather it was, as the Bekwaehene acknowledged (see p. 541), 'the just laws of the constitution' which appealed to the *asikafo:* that is, the absence of direct taxation, of death duties, of restraints upon individual capital accumulation, and the like. Reference has been made above to the important role, in the fermentation of the new ideas, played by the many citizens of the Colony who found employment in the early 1880s in the southern districts of metropolitan Asante.

By the 1880s, then, the level of consciousness of the *asikafo* was such that they should probably be regarded as constituting a small but growing bourgeois middle class with distinct interests and aspirations transcending loyalties and allegiances of a traditional kind. While their long range goals were perhaps unattainable under either the mercantile or imperial party oligarchies – the capitalist ethic being incompatible with the ideologies of each – yet in the short term it was to the subversion of the mercantilist and neo-mercantilist systems that their political energies were directed. They were an important element in the coalition of interests which brought about the downfall of Mensa Bonsu.

The emergence of a lower class identity

At another level within Asante society a growing class consciousness may perhaps be recognized: that is, among the *ahiafo* or underprivileged, a group including elements from both the free and unfree population. When Bowdich visited Kumase in 1817 he became rapidly aware of the social gap which separated the *ahiafo* from the higher status groups, the 'superior' and 'middling orders' (see p. 443). Indeed, as Bowdich saw it, the very survival of the higher status groups in the town itself was predicated upon the labours of the *ahiafo* on the surrounding farms:

the higher class could not support their numerous followers, or the lower their large families, in the city, and therefore employed them in plantations, (in which small crooms were situated,) generally within two or three miles of the capital, where their labours not only feed themselves, but supply the wants of the chief, his family, and more immediate suite. The middling orders station their slaves for the same purpose, and also to collect fruits and vegetables for sale, and when their children become numerous, a part are generally sent to be supported by these slaves in the bush.[153]

152 *The Gold Coast Times,* III, no. 113, p. 2.
153 Bowdich, 1819, pp. 323–4.

Unfree rather than free immigration continued to be the principal source of augmentation of the *ahiafo* throughout the nineteenth century. The newcomers were mainly *nnɔnkɔfo* ('donkors') of northern origins; some were purchased in the markets of the hinterland, some received as tribute from the northerly provinces, and some taken prisoner in the course of the occasional military operations there. The *ahiafo,* then, largely of non-Asante stock, were clearly regarded with considerable distaste by officialdom. In 1817 Osei Bonsu alluded to 'the insolent disposition of the lower orders of Ashantees', and thought them 'the worst people existing, except the Fantees. . .'.[154] In 1841 Kwaku Dua I expressed sentiments even less agreeable: 'The small tribes of the interior fight with each other, take prisoners and sell them for slaves; and, as I know nothing about them, I allow my people to buy and sell them as they please. They are of no use for anything else but slaves; they are stupid, they are little better than beasts.' [155] Yet it was the extent of the cultural gap between the immigrants and their hosts, rather than a racist ideology as such, which found expression in such observations. In 1853 Cruickshank pointed out how *nnɔnkɔfo* in the British Protected Territory might successfully adapt to local mores and so achieve a new identity:

if they arrive in the country at an early age, they are by no means slow in acquiring knowledge, and become very useful to their masters, and sometimes obtain a consideration equal to the native of the country, intermarrying with the Fantees, and becoming members of their families. But if the Donko be grown up before his arrival upon the coast, he generally remains a dull, stolid beast of burden all the days of his life.[156]

Upward mobility was likewise well known in Asante. 'An Ashanti slave,' wrote Rattray, 'in nine cases out of ten, possibly became an adopted member of the family, and in time his descendants so merged and intermarried with the owner's kinsmen that only a few would know their origin.' [157] There was, then, a continuous process by which slaves became absorbed into the general rural population by attaining affiliation with an *abusua* and so acquiring rights of a member: economic status was thereby enhanced even though jural status may have remained restricted in certain ways.[158] But there was also a continuing process by which places within the proletariat – in the sense of the class of those having no *abusua* – were filled by new unfree

154 *Ibid.* pp. 120–1, 250.
155 *Report from the Select Committee on the West Coast of Africa,* Part II, C. 551–II, 5 August 1842, p. 489: Freeman's journal, entry dd. Kumase, 23 December 1841.
156 Cruickshank, 1853, II, 245.
157 Rattray, 1929, chapter v. See also Poku, 1969, *passim.*
158 See Fortes, 1969, p. 263.

immigrants: 'they are', observed Kühne, 'constantly recruited by all sorts of devices from surrounding tribes'.[159] It must be remembered, however, that the ranks of the *ahiafo* were also being supplemented by those Asante whose positions were declining ones: for example, the *awowa* or 'pawn' surrendered as security for a debt, or the government official stripped of all property for peculation or the like.

It is clear from Bowdich's reports that the *ahiafo* constituted a restless and unruly element in the Asante population in the second decade of the nineteenth century. His awareness of them was heightened when he and his colleagues were stoned in the streets of Kumase, having failed totally, as he remarked, 'to conciliate them by the exhibition of the telescope and other novelties!' They were, he felt, beyond the government's control other than when drafted into the armies and placed under military discipline.[160] Unfortunately without giving detail, Bowdich made reference to the 'policy of attaching a foreign force to repress the discontents of the lower orders of their own country'.[161] He also pointed out that a number of unfree subjects did in fact rise to high positions within the administration, where they both represented the interests of the slaves and, conversely, of the government: 'The foreign slaves will naturally find advocates in those of their brethren, which are not few, who from talent, devotedness, or policy have become confidential favorites of the Kings and Chiefs, who reckon on them as a protection against any sudden gust of sedition amongst their impatient subjects.' [162] In exemplification of his argument, Bowdich cited precautionary measures, taken by the government during the mobilization of the Gyaman expeditionary force in 1817, of 'dictating some popular acts, ameliorating the condition of the lower orders of his subjects'.[163] One such enactment was that limiting the quantity of provisions which government officials on duty might demand in the villages through which they passed.[164] 'This law', commented Bowdich,

was particularly consolatory and beneficial to those slaves, who, to prevent famine and insurrection, had been selected (from that fettered multitude which could no longer be driven off to the coast directly they arrived at the capital), to create plantations in the more remote and stubborn tracts; from which their labour was first to produce a proportionate supply to the household of their Chief, and afterwards an existence for themselves: of the greater part of the necessaries for the latter, they had been pilfered in

159 Maurice, 1874, p. 271.
160 Bowdich, 1819, p. 120.
161 Bowdich, 1821a, p. 28.
162 Bowdich, 1821b, pp. 18–19.
163 Bowdich, 1819, p. 95.
164 For the enactment, see *ibid.* pp. 255–6.

common with the poorer class of Ashantees, (nominally but not virtually free), under various pretences, either in their distant plantation or on the arrival at the markets, by the public servants of the King and the Chiefs.[165]

In 1817 Opoku Frefre held that 'there were too many slaves in the country', and that they constituted a threat to the maintenance of public order.[166] The coastal market for slaves had indeed slumped, though opportunities for their export into the British Protected Territory, where the shortage of unskilled manpower was seemingly chronic, continued to exist.[167] Nevertheless, Opoku Frefre was presumably correct in associating the social unrest of the 1810–20 decade with the growth in the class of *ahiafo* which resulted from the abolition of the maritime slave trade by Danes, Dutch and English. Referring to the 'surplus of foreign slaves the abolition had created', Bowdich maintained that the government necessarily had to attempt to incorporate them the more rapidly into Asante society. The abolition, he remarked, must lead to,

the identifying of those diminished importations of slaves (which will remain on hand in the interior kingdoms) with the lowest class of the free population, in the rights of protection: and this will, I am sure, be gradually done, in proportion as the number increases, and invites or rather *demands* the more serious consideration of their apprehensive rulers.[168]

Investigation of the position of the underprivileged strata of Asante society during the reigns of Osei Yaw and Kwaku Dua I is as yet in its initial stages. The long period of mercantilist domination in politics was one in which no sharp economic recession is known to have occurred: the impression is rather that a steady but probably slow rate of growth was maintained, to be disturbed from time to time by strong forward surges. Because of the opportunities for upward mobility within society, the *ahiafo* were not unaffected by the general rise in the level of prosperity, and the indications are that they were relatively quiescent, politically, in the period. Indeed, once the surpluses of slaves which existed in the 1810–20 decade had been dispersed, by distribution locally throughout the Asante villages and towns, the *ahiafo* were unlikely to survive as a group conscious element within society. The well-being of a slave was bound up with that of his master, whose prosperity in turn depended upon that of the

---

165 Bowdich, 1821b, p. 18.
166 Hutchison, in Bowdich, 1819, p. 381.
167 See Cruickshank, 1853, II, 244–7. Cruickshank reported that 'some thousands' of *nnɔnkɔfo* were added to the population of the Protectorate annually: 'the Fantees eagerly purchase them from the Ashantees. They vary in price from £6 to £8, girls and boys being sold at a considerable reduction.'
168 Bowdich, 1821b, pp. 16–17.

abusua, of the village, of the province and of the nation. The aspirations of *ahiafo,* in other words, were bound up with becoming participants in *abusua* affairs, and not in making common cause with those of similar standing in other localities. It was this situation which was to change with the return of an imperial or war party government in 1863, and with the mobilization of a number of armies over the next decade.

It was a consequence of the system of military conscription, that whenever a village head was required to provide a quota of fighting men it was the *ahiafo* who were first chosen. Indeed, at other than high levels of mobilization, *ahiafo* were probably the only persons to be drafted. Hence, as various writers remarked, the rank and file of an Asante army was largely composed of those of slave or otherwise low status.[169] Significantly the military commanders were referred to as *dompiafo,* 'those who pushed forward the army'. Some account of the high level of casualties which an army might expect to suffer as much from disease as from battle, and of the method of 'recruiting the losses', has been offered above (pp. 83–7). It will follow, then, that it was precisely in such a period of constant mobilizations for war, that the *ahiafo* were brought together in such a way and in such circumstances that consciousness of their commonalty might emerge and be articulated. There are indications that the anti-war movement which was emerging to strength in 1871 had, as one of its constituencies, the *ahiafo* one. It is reasonable to assume, moreover, that for the *ahiafo* as for the *asikafo,* the Gold Coast Colony in certain respects appeared to provide a possible model for change. The abolition of slavery in the Gold Coast Colony, by proclamation of 17 December 1874, in particular could not have failed to engage the attention of the Asante *nnɔnkɔfo* and those whose status was, like that of the *awowa* or pawns, also restricted in law.[170] The fuller politicization of what had begun as a movement against conscription began to take place. There were those who, as it could be reported by 1883, agitated for 'the introduction and tuition amongst them of a better code of government, one more in unison with the advance of the lean civilization in their country, or, as they put it, "more like the white man's law" '.[171]

It may be that the 'mongrel Moors',[172] that is, the Muslim converts who formed a small but important component within the *nnɔnkɔfo,*

---

169 See, e.g. Bowdich, 1819, p. 317: slaves form 'the greater proportion of the military force'. Compare Reindorf, 2nd ed., n.d., p. 111; Rattray, 1929, p. 122.

170 *Correspondence relating to the Queen's Jurisdiction on the Gold Coast, and the Abolition of Slavery within the Protectorate,* C. 1139, 1875.

171 *Further Correspondence,* C. 4052, 1884, p. 11: Barrow to Governor, dd. Kumase, 16 May 1883.

172 Cruickshank, 1853, II, 245.

constituted one of the politically more aware elements in the (lower) commoner movement – as their co-religionists were among the activists of the Gold Coast Colony (see, for example, p. 534). It is significant that it was precisely from this group, the so-called 'Houssas', that Mensa Bonsu's government recruited men for the new and prestigious standing army. But it is significant also that the decision was taken to exclude them from positions of higher command 'as there is a jealous fear that they might, in time, get too much the upper hand (like the Pretorian guard of Rome). . .' [173]

The discontent of the *ahiafo* had, then, seemingly grown out of their opposition to the system of military conscription, and may be assumed to have been directed particularly against the revival of the imperial or war party. The discontent of the *asikafo,* by contrast, had developed from their opposition to the state trading system, and was directed principally against the mercantile or peace party. Both signalled the appearance of new levels of social consciousness, incompatible with traditional perceptions of the place of the individual in society as being within a system of 'vertical' or 'pyramidal' allegiances rather than within one of 'horizontal' class interests. But the level of class consciousness among the *ahiafo* remained low, a reflection of the fact that it was only in the wartime context that sustained contact between those from different towns and villages could occur. The *asikafo,* on the other hand, in the nature of the case were in constant and continuous communication with each other, and the level at which consciousness of their class interests developed was correspondingly high. But it is significant that the coalition of interests in the early 1880s, the 'popular front' which brought about the overthrow of Mensa Bonsu, arose around the *nkwankwaa* leaders: commoners of relatively high status within society, but whose opportunities for advancement were curtailed (see p. 535). If the *asikafo* are now to be seen as the rising bourgeoisie of Asante, then the *nkwankwaa* are perhaps to be regarded as the rising petit bourgeoisie. The broad coalition was able successfully to challenge the monopoly of political power previously exercised by the oligarchy of the imperial and mercantile parties, but the divergence between the long-range interests and goals of the *asikafo, nkwankwaa,* and *ahiafo* was such as to prevent their combining to create a third and new party. Therein, it may be argued, is to be found the principal cause of the turmoil which was to characterize Asante politics for the half decade following the successful overthrow of Mensa Bonsu in 1883.

173 PRO, CO. 96/126: Dudley to Hay, dd. Elmina, 25 March 1879.

The entry of the Batafo into middle class politics

The period of disorder in politics, which followed the coup carried out in the capital by the *nkwankwaa* in February 1883, has been described in Chapter 13. Only at the risk of grave over-simplification is it possible to attempt to identify the main principles which guided the actors in the series of counter-coups, political assassinations and purges, and internal wars which followed. The coalition of the wealthy and the exploited which overthrew Mensa Bonsu was one intent upon evolving a new political order based upon the creation of incremental channels of access to political and economic power. The upsurge of revolutionary activity, in part a negative reaction against the increasing harshness of Mensa Bonsu's rule, was also a positive response to the reforming and modernizing aspects of his policies. It is clear, however, that the commoner leaders, having enjoyed a brief period of power in the capital, lacked the ideological commitment, the political expertise and the financial base necessary to sustain their position. By the middle of 1883 they had seemingly agreed to support the Kumase councillors in their bid to place Kwaku Dua II upon the Golden Stool, and thereby to prevent the restoration of Kofi Kakari whose powerful sponsors had already recognized him as Asantehene.

Although Owusu Koko's decisive intervention in the scene in August 1883 was nominally supportive of the candidature of Kwaku Dua II, there is little doubt that the former Akyempemhene was essentially his own man. Certainly his brother, Owusu Ansa, regarded him as sponsoring the young contender 'in order that he, Ossoo Korkor, may make a tool of him'.[174] Son of the Asantehene Osei Bonsu, it has been seen that Owusu Koko had risen to become one of the most powerful figures in the administration of Kwaku Dua I. Politically committed to the policy of rapprochement with the British,[175] he was at the same time a military commander of proven ability. Making what was essentially a bid for personal power on the death of Kwaku Dua I in 1867, Owusu Koko overplayed his hand and was sent into exile. There was no place for him in the administrations of either Kofi Kakari or Mensa Bonsu; the old-style politics in which he had been schooled had become irrelevant in a period in which the trend was towards making government more responsive to public pressures. Following Owusu Koko's seizure of power by coup in 1883, however, the

[174] *Further Correspondence*, C. 4052, 1884, p. 74: Rowe to Derby, dd. Accra, 1 September 1883.

[175] See NAG, Accra, ADM 12/1/4: Barrow to Colonial Office, dd. Sussex, 16 October 1883 – 'Owusu Kokor might be made very useful to us in Councilling and guiding a new King of Ashantee in the Policy of ruling his country in the way we should like to see it ruled for he is a man of experience and moreover respects us and our power.'

ruthlessness with which the opposition was suppressed and Kofi Kakari's kin executed bore the unmistakable imprint of the earlier period; Owusu Koko sought, in other words, to arrest the decay in political life by a return to the model of strong government characteristic of the era of Kwaku Dua I.

Although Owusu Koko enjoyed initially the support of a number of Mensa Bonsu's leading councillors, such as Boakye Tenten, there is little indication that they were inspired by any strong sense of personal loyalty towards him: the toll of lives in the war years had left Owusu Koko one of the few survivors of a generation of politicians whose experience was of very limited relevance to the problems of the post-1874 period. He survived in power for little over a year, when he was overthrown by Akyampon Panin. *Prima facie,* it might seem strange that Akyampon Panin, who was aged, ideologically uncommitted, and politically vacillating, should have succeeded in carrying through the new coup.[176] In fact, however, the overthrow of Owusu Koko was accomplished with the strong support of the *asikafo* who, perhaps of all sections of the community, had most to lose by any return to the political norms of the Kwaku Dua I period. Having earlier worked for the restoration of Kofi Kakari, in late 1884 the *asikafo* needed as nominal head of state just such a figure as Akyampon Panin. Within so fragile a regime it was anticipated that a new strategy could be designed for finding a legitimate candidate for the Golden Stool whose policies would be those endorsed by the *asikafo*.

A study of the role of the *asikafo* during the interregnum is much needed. It is clear that they achieved a new level of political mobilization which was made possible, perhaps, only by the collapse that was occurring in central government. Nothing symbolized more the character of the Akyampon Panin regime than the fact that gold washing was allowed in Kumase itself, an enterprise which contravened the laws of Okomfo Anokye.[177] In April 1885 Coppin observed there women carrying baskets of earth to the Nsuben river, to wash for gold. It was, he commented, 'a remarkable proof that a revolution had indeed taken place within the last few years'.[178] Among the most important of

176 See the comment of Assistant Inspector Stewart of the Gold Coast Police, NAG, Accra, ADM 11/1482: Stewart to Colonial Secretary, dd. Praso, 27 February 1887. 'Ackempon was a man (so I am told) of low origins, a sort of treasurer to the late Kings, and being in possession of a large amount of ready gold dust, he succeeded in bribing the King of Kokofu to support a candidate selected by himself, with the view of securing to himself the peculiar favour of that candidate, should he rise to the occupancy of the great stool'.

177 See, e.g. Bowdich, 1819, pp. 257, 320.

178 Methodist Mission Archives, London: journal of Coppin's visit, 1885, Book VI, pp. 43–4. Burleigh, 1896, p. 508, referred to the existence of gold pits in the capital, which probably dated from the mid-1880s. In 1960 the present writer

the groups backing Akyampon Panin, as Lewin has recently pointed out, was that of the new rubber entrepreneurs. Significantly, Sawua, rural seat of Akyampon Panin, was one of their principal early centres. Significantly, too, one of the more prominent of the first Asante middlemen in the trade to establish himself on the coast was Kwadwo Bi: he is also remembered as one of the members of the Domankama movement to escape from Kumase after the attempt upon Mensa Bonsu's life in 1880.[179] Again, among those to emerge to positions of leadership in the period, as spokesmen for the *asikafo* interest, were a number of members of the *asokwafo* who turned their backs upon their careers within the Company of State Traders. One of the principal of these was Yaw Awua, whose career can be followed in some detail. A son of a senior *asokwa* official ('the royal hornblower of Kumase'),[180] Yaw Awua held minor administrative positions under Mensa Bonsu. In March 1881, for example, he was attached, as 'Speaker and Interpreter from Ashanti into Fanti', to a delegation which visited Cape Coast; [181] later in that year he served on Boakye Tenten's staff as 'Petty Chief Attendant'; [182] and in December was among those chosen to accompany Lonsdale on his journey to the north.[183] He possessed a modest knowledge of the English language. He was almost certainly among those actively involved in the overthrow of Mensa Bonsu, and is reported to have been given custody of five hundred of the rifles belonging to the deposed Asantehene's special guard (p. 527). A supporter of Kofi Kakari's restoration, it was presumably when Owusu Koko consolidated his power in Kumase in 1883 that Yaw Awua sold the Sniders to the Kokofuhene Osei Yaw,[184] and fled Asante. Taking with him gold insignia belonging to the *asokwafo*, Yaw Awua melted these down and with the proceeds established himself as a private businessman ('gold-taker') on the Gold Coast.[185] It was as a result of British antipathy towards the Kakarian cause at the time, that Yaw Awua was arrested by them and imprisoned in Christiansborg Castle.

was able to study a series of extensive underground workings which were revealed in central Kumase near Dwaberem, the old central market. They may have been dug originally to procure red ochre, for which see Bowdich, 1819, plan facing p. 323, but they also showed signs of having been worked for ore.

179 Lewin, field-notes: interview with Adu Gyamera, dd. Kwadaso, 27 August 1970. See Lewin, 1974, pp. 198–200.

180 *The Gold Coast Echo*, I, no. 7, 25 September 1888, p. 3.

181 *Affairs of the Gold Coast*, C. 3064, 1881, p. 113: message from Asante, dd. 16 March 1881.

182 *Further Correspondence*, C. 3386, 1882, p. 3: Rowe to Kimberley, dd. Accra, 14 September 1881, enclosure.

183 *Ibid.* p. 68: message from Lonsdale, dd. 11 December 1881.

184 Hamilton, field-notes, interview with Nana Owusu Ansa, dd. Kumase, 13 August 1968.

185 *The Gold Coast Echo*, I, no. 7, 25 September 1888, p. 3.

Probably in mid-1884, however, he was released.[186] He settled in Cape Coast, working with Owusu Ansa and assuming a position of leadership in the Cape Coast caucus upon the prince's death in November 1884.[187]

In a position to organize the supply of arms and ammunition to Asante, Yaw Awua emerged as one of the most powerful supporters of Akyampon Panin. In 1886 he was instrumental in persuading the regime to support the candidacy of Yaw Twereboanna rather than Agyeman Prempe.[188] In July 1887 the Kokofuhene Osei Asibe, then leading protagonist of Yaw Twereboanna in Asante, informed the Governor of the Gold Coast that henceforth he wished all communications between them to be routed through Yaw Awua.[189] Continuing to muster support in Asante for Yaw Twereboanna, he incurred the displeasure of the British again by his repeated announcements that the Gold Coast administration was opposed to Agyeman Prempe's election. He was rearrested in early 1888 and detained as a political prisoner, this time in Elmina Castle. With the collapse of the Yaw Twereboanna cause and the election of Agyeman Prempe as Asantehene in March 1888, the new government requested the British to surrender to it all of Yaw Awua's property in Cape Coast, since his fortune had been founded upon the illicit sale of *asokwafo* property. The British obliged.[190] Yaw Awua's career had, however, by no means run its erratic course. As a result of the deterioration in relations between the Gold Coast and Asante governments, he was freed in 1893. With the occupation of Kumase in 1896 he was enabled to return there and, enjoying then the patronage of the British, was reported as 'living in some state'.[191] In the war of 1900 he actively collaborated with the British [192] and on 14 March 1901 was rewarded by being made Edwesohene [193] – a stool to which he had no constitutional claims.

The evidence shows that Yaw Awua was one among many members of the state trading organization – of the hornblowers, drummers and

186 *Further Correspondence,* C. 4477, 1885, p. 147: Yaw Awua to Hughes, dd. Cape Coast, 8 December 1884.
187 *Ibid.* p. 146: Young to Derby, dd. Accra, 30 December 1884. For his own account of his early career, see NAG, Accra, ADM 11/1482: statement by Yaw Awua, and notes on an interrogation of Yaw Awua, both undated but probably early 1884.
188 *Further Correspondence,* C. 5357, 1888, p. 35: Kwadwo Yinna *et al.* to Lonsdale, dd. Cape Coast, 17 January 1887. *The Western Echo,* II, no. 28, 23 October 1886.
189 *Further Correspondence,* C. 5357, 1888, pp. 73–4: Kokofuhene to Governor, dd. 29 July 1887.
190 *The Gold Coast Echo,* I, no. 5, 23 August 1888, p. 3; *ibid.* I, no. 7, 25 September 1888, p. 3.
191 *Correspondence relating to the Ashanti War 1900,* C. 501, 1901, p. 30: Hodgson to Chamberlain, dd. Kumase, 16 April 1900.
192 *Idem.* Armitage and Montanaro, 1901, p. 27.
193 *Further Correspondence relating to Ashanti,* C. 933, 1902, p. 32: meeting at Kumase, 14 March 1901.

others of the Bata – to reject the mercantilist idea in the period, and to associate themselves with the political programme of the *asikafo*. Probably of significance in this context was the execution in 1882 of Kwabena Sapon, the 'King's head drummer' and a senior official therefore within the Bata.[194] His successor was presumably the Apea, 'drummer of the King's gold drum', who was persuaded by Yaw Awua in 1887 to join the operations – *ahupoosɛm* of Osei Kwaku Goroso in the British protected territory.[195] He may be identified as Kwasi Apea Nuama, described as son (perhaps in a classificatory sense) of the Asokwahene Kwasi Ampon II; like Yaw Awua, he was later to collaborate with the British and in recognition of his services to be awarded the posts of Akyeamehene and Domakwaihene of Kumase.[196] His career was closely paralleled by that of his brother Kwame Tua, a close associate of Yaw Awua in the *asokwafo*. The British were to confer no less an office than that of Gyaasewahene of Kumase upon him for his 'loyalty'.[197] And finally, among the other recruits from the *asokwafo* to the ranks of the *ahupoofo* in the late 1880s was the Ntaherahene of Kumase Yaw Pepera, chief of the long horns.[198] There are indications, moreover, that Kumase functionaries from departments other than the Bata were actively associated with the *asikafo* movement. Manwere Poku, for example, a son of Adu Bofo, held administrative office within the Gyaasewa. In 1887 he was among those recruited by Yaw Awua into the *ahupoosɛm* movement. Establishing himself first at Engwa, near the headquarters of Osei Kwaku Goroso (p. 576), he subsequently redirected his activities into the Asante Akyem area. He was arrested by a British column and in May 1892 was sentenced to seven years' penal servitude.[199] Not unexpectedly, in 1900 he fought against his former captors. He assumed the Gyaasewa stool upon the death of Opoku Mensa in Kumase on 21 May 1900,[200] but was killed by sniper fire at Gyakye a few weeks later, on 24 August.[201]

Kwasi Adabo, to take one further example, was a descendant of the Akyempemhene Adusei Kra and son of Kusi Abanba.[202] Like his father, he belonged to the *akwanmofo*, those responsible for the up-

194 *Further Correspondence*, C. 3386, 1882, p. 42: District Commissioner, Cape Coast, to Colonial Secretary, dd. 14 February 1882.
195 *The Gold Coast Echo*, I, no. 7, 25 September 1888, p. 3.
196 Asante Collective Biography Project: Apea Nuama. See also Rattray, 1929, p. 178.
197 *Further Correspondence*, C. 933, 1902, p. 2: Stewart to Governor, dd. Kumase, 14 January 1901.
198 *The Gold Coast Echo*, I, No. 9, 22 October 1888, p. 3.
199 NAG, Accra, ADM 12/3/5: Hodgson to Ripon, dd. Accra, 23 September 1893.
200 Hodgson, 1901, p. 174. *Correspondence*, C. 501, 1901, p. 52: Hodgson to Chamberlain, dd. Accra, 14 July 1900.
201 *Ibid.* p. 103: Willcocks to Chamberlain, dd. Cape Coast, 25 December 1900.
202 NAG, Kumase, D. 102: Kwame Kyem to Acting Chief Commissioner, dd. Kumase, 19 June 1916.

keep of the roads (see pp. 35–6). Numbered among those opposed to the policies of Mensa Bonsu, upon his overthrow he was one of the first to organize support for the restoration of Kofi Kakari.[203] Associated later with Akyampon Panin, and then with the Twereboanna cause, like so many of his colleagues he assumed residence in the Gold Coast Colony and became active as a middleman there,[204] co-operating with the British and being rewarded in 1901 with the Kumase stool which Adusei Kra had held.[205] There can be little doubt that it was the increasingly capitalist mode of operations of the Company of State Traders which provided so many of the officers of the central administration with insights into the nature of the economic process such as to induce them to join the general movement of the *asikafo* (to which amorphous class they themselves in many cases belonged) for the abolition of death duties, for the overall relaxation of state controls upon the activities of individual citizens, and for the introduction of a *laissez-faire* capitalist system.

One final career history will be outlined as illustrative of the intimate connection between politics and money in the second half of the nineteenth century. Kwame Poku Sawariso was a *sikani* from Anowo in the Offinso district, and a subject of the Kumase Debosohene. He belonged, indeed, to that élite the members of which had publicly displayed their wealth before the Asantehene – in this case Kwaku Dua I. By one of his wives Kwame Poku had a son Kwaku Kasiyi, who grew up with his father and held a position as stool carrier to the Kofi Kofeni stool of Anowo. During the reign of Mensa Bonsu, Kwasi Kasiyi became involved in opposition politics and fell foul of the Kumase authorities. Two charges were brought against him, first, that he was smuggling gunpowder to the opponents of Mensa Bonsu, and second, that he had had intercourse with the wife of a royal of the Golden Stool, Kwabena Kyeretwie the son of Yaa Kyaa. Yaa Kyaa instructed her agents to assassinate Kwaku Kasiyi. The order was leaked, however, and came to the knowledge of Kwame Poku Sawariso. He enabled his son to escape from Anowo, and took him to Tafo, the town of Kwaku Kasiyi's mother's people. An apology was tendered to the Asantehene through the Kumase Nkonnwasoafohene Kwadwo Amo (himself a Tafo man). Kwaku Kasiyi's life was spared, but a fine of twelve peredwans was imposed on him. This was paid by Kwame Poku Sawariso, by Kwame Bannahene who occupied the Kofi Kofeni stool, and by the Debosohene Ata Famfam. Kwame Poku Sawariso then

203 *Further Correspondence*, C. 3687, 1883, pp. 155–7: Asanti's statement to Barrow, dd. 3 May 1883.
204 Lewin, 1974, p. 152.
205 *Further Correspondence*, C. 933, 1902, p. 32: meeting at Kumase, 14 March 1901.

gave his son a large sum of money and seven servants, ostensibly for him to collect snails in Ahafo in order to repay the fine. In fact, however, Kwaku Kasiyi left Kumase for Ahafo, but immediately fled into the Gold Coast Colony, commenced trading there, and clearly became associated with the exiled Asante politicians. His father was regarded as culpable in the matter, and died in poverty at Anowo. Kwaku Kasiyi himself was obliged to remain in the Colony until the exile of Agyeman Prempe in 1896. On his return to Asante, he found that all of his father's property had been seized. In the Anglo-Asante war of 1900 he took the pro-British position, and from 1906 until his death in 1928 he served as Nkwankwaahene – leader of the 'young-men' – to Tafohene. His estate at death was valued at £2,567.[206] The case of Kwaku Kasiyi is presumably not atypical, of the sons of *asikafo* moving into dissident politics in the last quarter of the nineteenth century, – of those whose fathers had made money in the middle part of that century but who had never themselves seriously questioned the paramount interest which the state claimed to have over the ultimate disposition of all such self-acquired property.

The new faces of mercantilism: socialism or state capitalism

It will be apparent, then, that support first for the restoration of Kofi Kakari, then for the Akyampon Panin regime, and finally for the candidacy of Yaw Twereboanna, manifested itself at two different levels. At that of the traditional-style politics, a number of the *amanhene* of the metropolitan region – of whom the Kokofuhene Osei Asibe and the Mamponhene Owusu Sekyere were to emerge as the most powerful – continued to resist the re-emergence of strong central government. Regarding with anathema any return to the political arrangements of the era of Kwaku Dua I, when power became concentrated to a quite unprecedented extent in the hands of the Asantehene and the Kumase administration, they sought instead a form of looser federation in which the *amanhene* would enjoy a high measure of local autonomy – of states' rights. At the level of the new-style politics, however, the support for Kofi Kakari, Akyampon Panin and Yaw Twereboanna came from the *asikafo* interest: from a broad spectrum of the rising middle class which included most notably the entrepreneurs in the developing rubber industry and the frustrated government functionaries particularly from the state trading organization. To them must be attributed the creation of the Cape Coast caucus as a potential government-in-exile, and of what was in effect its embryonic

206 Kumase Divisional Council Archives, Manhyia: Kumasihene's Tribunal, Civil Record Book 11, Kwaku Afriyie *v.* Yaw Dabanka, commenced 3 November 1930.

administration, the *ahupoosɛm* movement. The intense bitterness of the adherents of Yaw Twereboanna, upon the final enstoolment of Agyeman Prempe as Asantehene, was reflected in a letter which they addressed to the Governor of the Gold Coast in 1894:

We, the Ashantis who have ran to this Gold Coast Protectorate and met safety under your protection, beg most respectfully to bring to your Excellency's notice, through some educated class in this town [Cape Coast], certain facts which have recently taken place in Ashanti.

It is rumoured here amongst us from Ashantee that King Prempe will shortly send his Captain Quacoo Fokoo with 1,000 perigwans of gold, peregwan is equal to £8 2s. sterling cash, to your Excellency, so that your Excellency may send away all Ashantis in the Gold Coast under your Excellency's protection to him, Prempe, thief King of Ashanti. If this rumour be true, we will all kill ourselves rather than to be delivered up into the hands of that tyrant, murderer, cruel, and thief King. All we pray for is that your Excellency may naturalise us as belonging to the Colony and the good Queen your Excellency represent. We beg to bring to your Excellency's notice that about month August this year thief King Prempe was installed at Bantama in Coomassie, the capital of Ashanti, where the late thief Kings are buried, and within the two months 400 human beings were killed, including men, women, boys, and girls. He swore his great oath that if he gets us by cunning and stratagem he will kill all of us without mercy, because we rebelled against the thief King of Ashanti . . . We pray your Excellency may take our petition into serious deep consideration and deliver the country from the hands of those useless, numberless, murderous, thieves, devils, heathens, and self-made Kings, who do not at all allow the progress of the Gospel of our Lord to have its free course and evangelise and civilise the native population.

Of particular concern to the Asante exiles in Cape Coast was the reappearance there of *batafo* from the reorganized central administration in Kumase. They attempted to discredit them:

Nearly two years ago, Prempe, thief King of Ashanti, now poor rat, sent his executioners and gold manufacturers to Cape Coast, the name of whom is Ossay Quacoe; they brought brass and copper rods, and with mixture of one ounce good gold they manufactured into four ounces, and with that nearly ruined the firm of Messrs. F. and A. Swanzy, of London, whom Honourable C. W. Burnett was their agent. That Ossay Quacoe is still living at Cape Coast in a house surrounded by thick bush at the foot of Fort Victoria. Prempe is an inveterate enemy to Her Majesty Queen Victoria. Ossay Quacoe, his executioner and his manufacturer of bad gold, was sent by Prempe to spy Cape Coast and sent him reports every day. So drive away this murderer Ossay Quacoe and his accomplices from Cape Coast so that the town may free from bad gold.

Significantly, the writers directed a specific complaint against the chief architect of Agyeman Prempe's policies, John Owusu Ansa:

Ansah, son of the late Prince John Owoosoo Ansah, a native of Cape Coast, whose mother's maiden name is Sarah Boxell, who gives him [Prempe] all advices touching the English Government and the Gold Coast and his chief counsellor in all his atrocities, because his father's house was sold to Catholics for his debt, and he is rebelled against the English Government. The King of Ashanti is nothing at all now, he is but a mere name, is not more than any of the Gold Coast Chiefs, but, being six days' journey from Cape Coast, he thinks himself secured and boasted himself.[207]

It has been argued above, that the opposition of the *asikafo* to the mercantilist policies of Mensa Bonsu's government was greatly heightened as the trend towards neo-mercantilism became manifest: that is, to the association of European capitalists in the exploitation of the resources of Asante and to the continuing exclusion of the private indigenous entrepreneur. In the aftermath of the overthrow of Mensa Bonsu, the *asikafo* became involved first in preventing the consolidation of the Owusu Koko regime, which represented a return to an older tradition of autocratic government associated particularly with Kwaku Dua I, and then in attempting to deny power to the sponsors of Agyeman Prempe – who were seen as committed essentially to the revival of the programmes of Mensa Bonsu. In the event, their fears in that direction were shown to be well founded. In the brief period of Agyeman Prempe's reign, neo-mercantilism was embraced as a cardinal political principle, and it was only as a result of British pressure upon European concessionaires that the full-scale reorganization and development of the Asante economy was not undertaken by them in collaboration with the Asante government. To the radical *asikafo* politicians Agyeman Prempe was revealed as the '*thief* King': he who sought to deny to them their legitimate fields of profitable activity.

In this chapter it has been argued that in the nineteenth century political tension was being generated within Asante society as a result of the development of what has been called 'horizontal' consciousness. It emerged the more strongly within the indigenous *asikafo* and *nkwankwaa* classes and the less strongly within the *ahiafo* – many of the members of the latter class being in some sense strangers with restricted jural status ('second class citizens'). Political tension resulted, however, not from the emergence of class conflict as such. Indeed, the aspirations of even the *asikafo* and *ahiafo* in the period were in some respects complementary rather than antithetical: both classes shared a common interest in establishing certain basic individual liberties, for example, the freedom from restrictions upon capital accumulation or

---

207 *Further Correspondence*, C. 7917, 1896, pp. 227–8: 'The Ashantis in the Western Protectorate' to Governor, dd. Cape Coast, 1 October 1894. For a more detailed treatment of the Asante dissidents in Cape Coast, see Wilks, 1974, *passim*.

the freedom from military conscription. Both classes were capable, therefore, of common political action to erode the peremptory powers which the government had come to exercise over the lives of its citizenry. Political tension resulted, then, rather from incompatibilities between the emergent horizontal or class consciousness and the older vertical consciousness – that is, the view of the citizen's place within society as fixed within a pyramidically structured system of established (ascribed or achieved) allegiances culminating in the Golden Stool. It is arguable, moreover, that it was precisely in those spheres of national life where interaction between class and establishment interests the most regularly occurred, that conflict the most strongly materialized. Thus many positions of leadership in the *asikafo* movement against mercantilism in the 1880s were assumed by officials of the Company of State Traders.

It has been further suggested that mercantilism and neo-mercantilism became the dominant ideologies within the Asante establishment after the eclipse of the imperial party in 1874. While *asikafo* and *nkwankwaa* interests generated a popular movement of opposition to the government of Mensa Bonsu, they were unable to coalesce into a new party not least because of the Asantehene's increasing resort to terror in the suppression of dissent. The challenge offered by the *asikafo* and *nkwankwaa* to the establishment therefore necessarily took a revolutionary form. But while the overthrow of Mensa Bonsu was accomplished with comparative facility, the putting together of a new stable government presented in the circumstances all but insuperable problems. The continued existence of Asante appeared for a time in doubt. Finally, out of the disorder, emerged a new mercantilist administration. Its general acceptance as the national government in 1894 undoubtedly reflected the growing realization on the part of the majority of the politically sensitive Asante, that the magnitude of the threat presented by the British to the continuing independence of Asante could only be compensated for by the rapid development of the nation's resources in order to narrow the gap between the broad economic capabilities of the two countries. Few appear to have thought the development of a national bourgeoisie to be, in the circumstances, the appropriate instrument for that purpose.

It will be readily apparent that the problems facing Asante politicians in the nineteenth century are structurally continuous in many important respects with those that have beset Ghanaian decision-makers since the nation recovered its independence in 1957. Brief reference to the policies and doctrines of Dr Kwame Nkrumah will adequately suggest the nature of such continuities. Nkrumah developed the thesis, in *Consciencism* and elsewhere, that an indigenous capitalist system had not developed, and should not be allowed to develop, such strength in Ghana (and Africa) as to necessitate revolutionary action to overthrow it.[208] His economic adviser, E. Ayeh-Kumi, was to testify to Nkrumah's belief, 'that if he permitted African business to grow, it will grow to the extent of becoming a rival power to his and the party's prestige and he would do everything to stop it'.[209] The position is virtually identical with that articulated by the Asantehene Osei Bonsu in 1820 (see pp. 685–6), in one of the classic statements of the foundations of Asante mercantilism. In practical terms, just as the emergence of an entrepreneurial middle class was inhibited in nineteenth century Asante by governmental restrictions upon the accumulation of capital and upon free enterprise, so Ayeh-Kumi reported of the policies of Nkrumah, that

it was not possible to enact a law against private Ghanaian businessmen; what was done was to place a squeeze on them and their operations. The banks were not allowed to offer them credit and if they had to, it should be up to a certain limit only. They were not to be issued with enough licenses for importation, they should buy through large firms or Government agencies.[210]

Although Nkrumah attributed the absence of significant capital accumulation in private Ghanaian hands to the effects of colonialism [211] – clearly too narrow an historical perspective – he recognized the corollary, that government was thereby enabled to determine and control the directions of economic development:

colonial rule precluded that accumulation of capital among our citizens which would have assisted thorough-going private investment in industrial construction. It has, therefore, been left to government, as the holder of the means, to play the role of main entrepreneur in laying the basis of the national economic and social advancement. If we turned over to private interests the going concerns capitalized out of national funds and national effort, as some of our critics would like to see us do, we should be betraying the trust of the great masses of our people for the greedy interests of a small coterie of individuals, probably in alliance with foreign capitalists. Production for private profit deprives a large section of the people of the goods and services produced.[212]

208 Nkrumah, 1964, pp. 74–7.
209 *The Rebirth of Ghana,* Ministry of Information, Ghana, 1966, p. 42.
210 *Ibid.* p. 43. Loan capital was restricted in Asante apparently by control of the interest rate. In the early nineteenth century this was reported to have been set at the extraordinary high figure of $33\frac{1}{3}\%$ per month (of forty-two days), see Bowdich, 1819, p. 257; Hutton, 1821, p. 318.
211 Nkrumah, 1970b, p. 14.
212 Nkrumah, 1970a, p. 119.

Whether one was to regard this twentieth century equivalent of the mercantilist ideology of the nineteenth century as 'socialism', as Nkrumah did, or as 'state capitalism', was open to debate.[213] The fundamental principle was in any case clear: 'the government has to take the place of the adventurous entrepreneurs who created the capital basis of industrialization in the advanced countries'.[214] Nkrumah, moreover, fully accepted – as Mensa Bonsu and Agyeman Prempe I had done – the necessity of associating foreign capital and skills in national economic development. Indeed, the Volta River Project evinced, in it conception, that same grandiose vision of progress which also distinguished the concession which Prempe's administration offered to Reckless and his sponsors in 1895. It was only the failure of the Asante scheme to materialize, due to the interference of the Colonial Office, that saved Agyeman Prempe the necessity of facing the problem which so troubled Nkrumah: of how to enjoy the benefits of foreign investment while averting the threat of foreign economic domination.

It has been recently remarked by Bretton, that

African entrepreneurs, businessmen, small industrialists, investors, traders, and middlemen bear the scars of colonial neglect . . . colonial rule was rigged in favor of foreign enterprise. If any economic opportunities remained for Africans, it was for one of two reasons: either the Europeans did not care to enter the particular sector, most likely because it was not profitable, or Europeans simply were not available in sufficient numbers to launch a project and see it through the difficult initial phases.[215]

In fact the *asikafo* of Asante and of much of southern Ghana found in the colonial period an outlet for their skills in the development, in place of rubber, of the cocoa industry. It was an enterprise in which the large European companies attempted, but failed, to compete with the indigenous private entrepreneurs. In the first half of the twentieth century, as a result, the *asikafo* class had not only greatly expanded in size, but had succeeded – despite rather than because of colonial administration – in accumulating considerable capital in its hands. But the British had served the emergent middle class well in one way: the system of death duties had not been retained after the central administration of Agyeman Prempe had been dismantled. Interestingly enough, after Agyeman Prempe had been repatriated and given recognition as 'Kumasehene', many of the prosperous commoners feared that the system of death duties must necessarily be restored. In 1930 they petitioned the Chief Commissioner for Asante, stating that

213 Ikoku, 1971, pp. 52–3.
214 Nkrumah, 1970a, p. 110.
215 Bretton, 1973, pp. 215–16.

722

it was the law of death duties which had in the past held back the progress of the nation, which had created political unrest, and which had brought about the overthrow of Mensa Bonsu. The leader of the Kumase 'young men' was the elderly Kofi Sraha, a rubber trader who had been involved in the opposition to Agyeman Prempe's election and had taken political sanctuary in the Gold Coast Colony.[216]

Unsympathetic to Nkrumah's ideology of socialism (or state capitalism), the rural capitalist class especially in Asante formed the strongest component in the opposition to his policies, and in 1954 had largely underwritten the creation of the National Liberation Movement which was for a time successfully to impede the consolidation of power in the hands of the Convention People's Party. Yet Nkrumah was fortunate to find already at hand an instrument which could be effectively directed against the *asikafo* interest. In 1948 the British had established the Cocoa Marketing Board to purchase all cocoa at levels fixed well below the selling price on world markets – thereby building up Gold Coast government funds at the expense of the private farmer. In 1952 Nkrumah strengthened the government's position further by creating, as a subsidiary of the Cocoa Marketing Board, the Cocoa Purchasing Company: its purpose was to take over from the richer cocoa entrepreneurs the whole process of loan-financing in the industry, thereby at the same time establishing the dependence of a significant section of the population upon the political machine which he controlled. The two immensely powerful bodies came to play a role in Ghana in many respects comparable with that of the similarly powerful Company of State Traders in nineteenth century Asante.

It is unnecessary to press the analogies further. It will be only too apparent that the sequence of events which led to the overthrow of Nkrumah in 1966 can bear detailed comparison with those which resulted in the destoolment of Mensa Bonsu in 1883: attempted coups and assassinations were matched by increasingly repressive enactments aimed at the suppression of opposition. Ghana, too, after 1966 found itself engaged, like Asante after 1883, in a long and painful quest for stable government. History does not, of course, repeat itself; but the courses which events take occur on trend lines which the social scientist is all too prone to investigate in quite inadequate time perspectives. In particular, the tendency is still all too strong to attempt to find in the brief period of colonial overrule the *fons et origo* of situations the true antecedents of which are to be sought in a more remote past. It is not unfitting that Kwame Nkrumah should be honoured with the last words:

[216] National Archives of Ghana, Kumase, D.3, 113/1908: petition against death duties, Kofi Sraha *et al.* to Chief Commissioner, dd. Kumase, 11 October 1930.

In the new African renaissance, we place great emphasis on the presentation of history. Our history needs to be written as the history of our society, not as the story of European adventures. African society must be treated as enjoying its own integrity; its history must be a mirror of that society, and the European contact must find its place in this history only as an African experience, even if as a crucial one. That is to say, the European contact needs to be assessed and judged from the point of view of the harmony and progress of this society.

When history is presented in this way, it can become . . . a map of the growing tragedy and the final triumph of our society. In this way, African history can come to guide and direct African action. African history can thus become a pointer at the ideology which should guide and direct African reconstruction.[217]

[217] Nkrumah, 1964, p. 63.

Glossary of principal Asante terms

In using this glossary the initial vowel or initial nasal 'm' and 'n' should be ignored. Thus both *ahenkwaa* and *nhenkwaa* will be found under 'h'; *ɔman* and *aman* under 'm'; *nsumankwaa* under 's', and so forth. For practical reasons it has not been possible in the text consistently to use the currently accepted Twi orthography, especially in the case of personal and place names. In general, simpler forms have been preferred. Words of the form *-foɔ*, '-people', have been rendered in the text as *-fo* rather than *-fuo*, for example; and of the form *kɛseɛ*, 'big', as *kese* rather than *kesie*. In the glossary, however, the attempt has been made to give the preferred orthography. It must be pointed out that many Asante words can only be defined in context, and that no exact English equivalent exists. The meanings of the words listed below are those in which they are used in the text. For the wider sense which many words have, the reader is referred to J. G. Christaller, *A Dictionary of the Asante and Fante Language called Tshi*, Basel, 1881 (second revised edition, Basel, 1933).

B

ɔbaa-panin	The senior female royal of a family; the occupant of a female stool.
abakomdwa	The stool for an heir apparent.
aban	A building of stone. Hence *abankɛseɛ*, 'castle, citadel'. By extension, *aban*, 'government', and sometimes *abankɛseɛmu*, 'central government.'
batani, pl. *batafoɔ*	A trader, from *ɔbata,* 'to trade'. Used especially to refer to the public or official traders. Hence Batahene, the official responsible for the organization of the trading parties.
benkum	'Left hand', used to refer to the left wing of an army. Hence Benkumhene, commander of the left wing.
birɛmpɔn, pl. *abirɛmpɔn*	Literally 'big man'. An hereditary title held by the heads of territorial chiefdoms, but also attainable by achievement by the very wealthy.
ɔbrafoɔ, pl. *abrafoɔ*	In Kumase, a member of the constabulary responsible for law enforcement. Sometimes loosely used to mean 'executioner', see *adumfoɔ*.
ebura	Literally 'forge', used to refer to the Mint in Kumase. Hence *buramfoɔ*, 'those who worked in the Mint'.

abusua, pl. *mmusua*	Matriclan or matrilineage; kinship reckoned by matri-filiation. Hence *abusua-panin*, pl. *abusua-mpaninfoɔ*, the senior member or members of such a lineage.

D

Adae	A festival at which offerings may be made to the ances-tors, occurring twice in every Asante month of forty-two days. Hence the Akwasidae always held on a Sunday, and the Awukudae on a Wednesday.
Adaka Kɛseɛ	Literally, 'the Great Chest'. Used for the main repository of gold dust in the Treasury.
ɔdampan, pl. *adampan*	An office opening on to the street; the bureau of a gov-ernment functionary, ward head, village head, etc.
Damponkɛseɛ	Literally, 'the great big-room', used for the room in the Asantehene's palace which contained the Great Chest. Hence, 'Treasury'.
dawurufoɔ	'The gong-beaters'; those responsible for publicizing laws in the capital and outlying towns and villages.
ɔdehyeɛ, pl. *adehyeɛ*	Usually used to refer to the royals of a stool, that is, to those having hereditary claims to the succession. Hence the *adehyeɛ* of the Golden Stool, males having rights to the office of Asantehene and females having rights to that of Asantehemaa.
odekuro, pl. *adekurofoɔ*	The head of a village, responsible to the government for the management of its affairs.
ɔdɔnkɔ, pl. *nnɔnkɔfoɔ*	Used to refer to the 'stateless' peoples of the northern hinterlands, such as the Grunshi and Konkomba, who formed a large part of the unfree labour force in Asante.
Adɔnten	The main body of an army; hence Adɔntenhene, the commander of the centre division.
adumfoɔ	'Executioner'; those under the Adumhene of Kumase who were responsible for carrying out the death sen-tence.
dwa	'A stool', the symbol of office. Hence, for example, *abusua dwa*, a family stool; *po dwa*, a stool created by an Asantehene; *aban dwa* or *ɛsom dwa*, a functionary's stool; *kofo dwa*, a military stool; Sika Dwa, the Golden Stool.
Odwira	The major annual festival, of religious and political sig-nificance, at which attendance was obligatory; from *dwira*, 'to purify'.

F

fekuo	Literally, 'a group of persons'. Used to refer to the various specialized agencies or departments of govern-ment, for example, Sanaa Fekuo, 'the Household Treas-ury'.

afenasoafoɔ	'The swordbearers'; the official messengers whose badge of office was the decorative sword. Hence Afenasoafoɔhene, the head of the swordbearers also known as Asomfoɔhene.
foto	The leather bag containing weights, and thus by extension, Foto, 'the Treasury'.
fotosanfoɔ	Those who worked in the Treasury, the weighers and accountants.

G

Gyaase	Literally, 'the hearth', used here to describe the personnel of the Royal Household. Hence Gyaasehene, 'head of the palace personnel'.
Gyaasewa	Literally, 'the little Gyaase', used here to describe the Exchequer organization. Hence Gyaasewahene, 'head of the Exchequer personnel'. (For the problem in the use of the terms Gyaase and Gyaasewa, see pp. 469–70.)

H

ɔhene, pl. *ahene*	A term of wide connotation, 'king', 'ruler', 'head', etc. Hence Asantehene, 'king of Asante'; Mamponhene, 'ruler of Mampon'; Afenasoafoɔhene, 'head of the swordbearers'.
ɔheneba, pl. *ahenemma*	Son of an *ɔhene*. Used here in the sense of a son of an Asantehene, i.e. *ɔheneba* of the Golden Stool. In Asante English, 'a prince' as opposed to an *ɔdehyeɛ*, 'a royal'.
ɔhenenana, pl. *ahenenana*	A grandson of the Golden Stool; strictly, that is, the son of an *ɔheneba* or prince.
ahenkwaa, pl. *nhenkwaa*	Literally, 'the servant of an *ɔhene*'. Used to describe the functionaries of government (including the Royal Household) who almost always held appointive and not hereditary posts. More or less synonymous with *asomfoɔ* (q.v.).
ahiafoɔ	From *ohia*, 'poverty'; hence the impoverished and underprivileged within society.
ahoprafoɔ	Those who carry the elephant tails – symbol of wealth in Asante – before those honoured for acquiring great riches.
ahupooni, pl. *ahupoofoɔ*	Literally, 'an arrogant person'; hence used to describe those exercising authority extra-legally. Similarly *ahupoosɛm*, the exercise of such authority.
ɔhwɛfoɔ, pl. *ahwɛfoɔ*	A manager, overseer, or caretaker of lands, office, etc. Also synonymously, *ɔhwɛsofoɔ*, pl. *nhwɛsofoɔ*. Used here particularly to describe the system whereby Kumase officials exercised an absentee caretakership over distant towns and villages.

K

akoa, pl. *nkoa*	'Subject', a term of wide connotation. Thus a slave is an *akoa* of his master, but all Asantes were *nkoa* of the Asantehene.
nkonnwasoafoɔ	The stool-carriers, hence Nkonnwasoafoɔhene, head of the carriers of the Golden Stool.
Kontihene	Otherwise Krontihene. A military title, nominal commander-in-chief of an army. In Kumase the title was always held by the Bantamahene.
akrafieso	The part of the palace in which were kept the Swords of State, upon which oaths of allegiance were taken.
Kramo, pl. Nkramo	'A Muslim', from Malinke *karamoko*, 'one who can read' (cf. Arabic *qara'a,* 'to read').
akuraa, pl. *nkuraa*	A village.
kuro, pl. *nkuro*	A smaller town.
Akwamuhene	(1) The nominal second-in-command of an army, a title held in Kumase by the Asafohene. (2) The ruler of Akwamu, a district on the Lower Volta.
nkwankwaa	Literally, 'youngmen' and sometimes translated 'commoner'. The men of well established families who did not have high expectations of attaining to office or wealth. Hence Nkwankwaahene, the leader of the 'youngmen' in a town.
akwanmofoɔ	Those responsible for inspecting the roads, and for ensuring that they were kept cleared.
nkwansrafoɔ	Also *nkwansifoɔ*, those who guarded the roads and manned the control points; highway police. Confusion with *nkwansrafoɔ*, 'army scouts', is to be avoided.
Akwasidae	See Adae.
ɔkyeame, pl. *akyeame*	Often translated 'linguist' or 'spokesman', and sometimes in older sources 'secretary', the *akyeame* were responsible for counselling the Asantehene and also served as counsel in all legal proceedings. Here translated as 'counselors', in contradistinction to the 'councillors', that is, the voting members of the Asantehene's councils.
akyeremadefoɔ	Traditionally, the court drummers, but employed in a number of other roles including official trading.

M

mmamma	Strictly, the sons and grandsons within those offices to which succession is by other than matrifiliation. Hence *mmammadwa*, a stool not vested in a matrilineage, an appointive office; and Mmammahene, the head of the *mmamma* of such a stool.
ɔman, pl. *aman*	'Nation', 'state', 'polity', etc. A term not capable of pre-

cise definition. Thus the Asanteman, 'the Asante Nation', but Bekwaeman, 'the Bekwae state (within the Asanteman)'.

ɔmanhene,
pl. *amanhene*

The ruler of an *ɔman*, usually with reference to the larger districts and especially the *amantoɔ* (q.v.).

amansɛm

Debating policy, as opposed to *asenni* (q.v.).

amantoɔ

The larger and older *aman* within Asante, and especially the *akan aman nnum*, 'the five *aman* of first rank' (usually named as Bekwae, Dwaben, Kokofu, Mampon and Nsuta).

amrado,
pl. *amradofoɔ*

'Governor', a loan-word from Arabic *via* Portuguese, apparently applied originally in Asante to the resident commissioners in the provinces.

mmusua

See *abusua*.

N

nifa

'Right hand', the right wing of an army. Hence Nifahene, commander of the right wing.

P

ɔpanin,
pl. *mpaninfoɔ*

Literally 'an old person', 'elder', and used as a term of respect for any senior person (in contrast with *nkwankwaa*, (q.v.). *Mpaninfoɔ* is often used to mean 'councillors', though some members of council will be entitled to higher rank, cf. *abirɛmpɔn*.

apeatoɔ

A special purpose tax, levied to cover the costs of military operations.

apem adaka,
pl. *apem nnaka*

Literally, 'box of one thousand'. A coffer holding 1,000 peredwans of gold dust.

peredwan,
pl. *mperedwan*

An Asante gold weight equivalent to $2\frac{1}{4}$ troy ounces, and conventionally valued at £8 sterling in the nineteenth century.

S

asafo

A company organized for war, or other communal purposes. Hence *asafohene,* a captain, military officer, etc.

sanaa

A bag made of an elephant's ear, used for holding weights. Hence the Sanaa, the Asantehene's Household Treasury, and Sanaahene, the head of the Sanaa.

Asantehemaa

The Queen-mother of Asante, chosen from among the women of the royal Oyoko dynasty.

Asantehene

The King of Asante, chosen from among the men of the royal Oyoko dynasty.

Asantemanhyiamu

Literally, 'the Assembly of the Asante Nation'; the highest legislative council and court.

ɛsɛn,

The court criers and heralds, often employed as mem-

pl. *nsɛniefoɔ* or *nsɛneafoɔ*	bers of diplomatic missions. Hence Nsɛniehene, the head of the criers and heralds.
asenni	Political counselling, as opposed to *amansɛm* (q.v.).
sika	'Gold', 'money'.
Sika Dwa	The Golden Stool.
sikani, pl. *asikafoɔ*	'The man of wealth', 'rich man'.
asoamfoɔ	The hammock-carriers, hence *Soamfoɔhene,* head of the hammock-carriers of the Golden Stool.
asokwafoɔ	Traditionally, the court hornblowers. Among their many duties, the *asokwafoɔ* were royal sextons and official traders. The Asokwahene, or Batahene, was head of the group.
asomfoɔ	From *ɛsom,* 'service'. Administrative officials or functionaries holding appointive rather than hereditary positions, cf. *ahenkwaa.*
nsumankwaafoɔ	The Asantehene's physicians, from *suman,* 'protective medicine'.
sumpene	Raised platforms in the streets, from which public business was on occasion transacted.

T

ɔtogyeni, pl. *togyefoɔ*	The revenue collectors, belonging to the Exchequer.
ntoro	Cultic organizations concerned with the purification ('washing') of the *kra* or soul, membership of which is determined by patrifiliation.
atumtufoɔ	The Asantehene's bodyguards, organized under the Ankobeahene of Kumase.

W

Awukudae	See Adae.
awunyadie	A tax on the estate of a dead person, sometimes loosely referred to as *ayibuadie* (q.v.).

Y

ayibuadie	A tax imposed upon an inheritance, but often used synonymously with *awunyadie* (q.v.).

Guide to sources consulted

PRINTED WORKS, THESES, DISSERTATIONS, ETC.

Agbodeka, F. (1971) *African Politics and British Policy in the Gold Coast 1868–1900*, London.

Agyeman-Duah, J. (1960) 'Mampong, Ashanti: A Traditional History to the Reign of Nana Safo Kantanka', *Transactions of the Historical Society of Ghana*, IV, 2, 21–5.

(1965) 'The Ceremony of Enstoolment of the Asantehene', *Ghana Notes and Queries*, 7, 8–11.

Aḥmad Bābā al-Waʿiz (1950) *Al-Kanz al-Mufīd li 'l-Murīd al-Ṣadīq*, Cairo.

Ainé, P. (1857) *Côte Occidentale D'Afrique, Côte-D'Or*, Paris.

Alexander, J. E. (1837) *Narrative of a Voyage of Observation among the Colonies of Western Africa in the Flagship Thalia*, 2 vols., London.

Allen, M. (1874) *The Gold Coast*, London.

Allen, W. and Thomson, T.R.M. (1848) *A Narrative of the Expedition sent by Her Majesty's Government to the River Niger in 1841 under the Command of Captain H. D. Trotter, R.N.*, 2 vols., London.

Allott, A. N. (1966) 'The Ashanti Law of Property', *Zeitschrift für Vergleichende Rechtswissenschaft*, LXVIII, 2, 129–215.

Anon. (1850) *De Kust van Guinea*, Rotterdam.

Arhin, K. (1965) 'Market Settlements in Northwestern Ashanti: Kintampo', *University of Ghana Institute of African Studies Research Review*, Supplement: *Ashanti and the North-west*, 1, 135–55.

(1967a) 'The Structure of Greater Ashanti (1700–1824)', *The Journal of African History*, VIII, 1, 65–85.

(1967b) 'The Financing of the Ashanti Expansion (1700–1820)', *Africa*, XXXVII, 3, 283–91.

(1968) 'The Missionary Role on the Gold Coast and in Ashanti: Reverend F. A. Ramseyer and the British Take-over of Ashanti 1869–1894', *University of Ghana Institute of African Studies Research Review*, IV, 2, 1–15.

(1970a) 'Ashanti and the Northeast', *University of Ghana Institute of African Studies Research Review*, Supplement: *Ashanti and the North-east*, 2, 1–14.

(1970b) 'Aspects of the Ashanti Northern Trade in the Nineteenth Century', *Africa*, XL, 4, 363–73.

(1970c) 'Succession and Gold Mining at Manso-Nkwanta', *University of Ghana Institute of African Studies Research Review*, VI, 3, 101–9.

(1972) 'The Ashanti Rubber Trade with the Gold Coast in the Eighteen-Nineties', *Africa*, XLII, 1, 32–43.

Armitage, C. H. and Montanaro, A. F. (1901) *The Ashanti Campaign of 1900*, London.

Arthur, J. (n.d.) *Brong Ahafo Handbook*, 1st ed., Accra.

Ba, A. H. and Daget, J. (1955) *L'Empire Peul Du Macina, (1818–1853)*, I, The Hague (2nd ed., 1962).

Baden-Powell, R. S. S. (1896) *The Downfall of Prempeh: A Diary of Life with the Native Levy in Ashanti 1895–96*, London.

Barbot, J. (1746) *A Description of the Coasts of North and South Guinea*, vol. V of

Guide to sources consulted

Churchill's *Collection of Voyages and Travels,* London (1st ed., Paris, 1732).

Bartels, F. L. (1959) 'Jacobus Eliza Johannes Capitein, 1717–47', *Transactions of the Historical Society of Ghana,* IV, 1, 3–13.

Barter, C. (1896) 'Notes on Ashanti', *The Scottish Geographical Magazine,* XII, 441–58.

Barth, H. (1857–9) *Travels and Discoveries in North and Central Africa,* 3 vols., New York.

Beaton, A. C. (1870) *The Ashantees: Their Country, History, Wars, Government, etc.,* London.

Beck, G. (1880–1) 'Eine neue Route nach den Obern Niger und dem Soudan', *Jahresbericht der Geographischen Gesellschaft,* III, supplement, 6, 35–53.

Beckmann, M. (1967) 'Principles of Optimum Location for Transportation Networks', *Quantitative Geography,* eds. W. L. Garrison and D. F. Marble, Part I: 'Economic and Cultural Topics', Evanston, 95–119.

Beecham, J. (1841) *Ashantee and the Gold Coast,* London.

Bevin, H. J. (1960) 'M. J. Bonnat: Trader and Mining Promoter', *The Economic Bulletin of Ghana,* IV, 7, 1–12.

Binger, L.-G. (1892) *Du Niger au Golfe de Guinée par le Pays de Kong et le Mossi,* 2 vols., Paris.

Biørn, A. R. (1788) 'Biørn's Beretning 1788 om de Danske Forter og Negerier', *Nogle Bidrag til Kundskab om den Danske Straekning paa Guinea Kysten* (Thaarups Archiv for Politik, Statistik og Huusholdingsvideskaber 1797–8, III), Copenhagen, 193–230.

Biss, H. C. J. (1901) *The Relief of Kumasi,* London.

Blair, H. A. and Duncan-Johnstone, A. (1932) *Enquiry into the Constitution and Organization of the Dagbon Kingdom,* Accra.

Boahen, A. (1965) 'Asante-Dahomey Contacts in the 19th Century', *Ghana Notes and Queries,* 7, 1–3.

Bowdich, T. E. (1819) *Mission from Cape Coast Castle to Ashantee,* London.

(1820) *A Reply to the Quarterly Review,* Paris.

(1821a) *An Essay on the Superstitions, Customs, and Arts, common to the Ancient Egyptians, Abyssinians, and Ashantees,* Paris.

(1821b) *The British and French Expeditions to Teembo,* Paris.

(1821c) *An Essay on the Geography of North-western Africa,* Paris.

Bowler, L. P. (1911) *Gold Coast Palaver,* London.

Bowles, T. G. (1874) 'The Ashantee War Unnecessary and Unjust', *Fraser's Magazine,* IX, 49, 124–34.

Boyle, F. (1874) *Through Fanteeland to Coomassie: A Diary of the Ashantee Expedition,* London.

Brackenbury, H. (1874) *The Ashanti War,* 2 vols., Edinburgh and London.

Braimah, J. A. (1970) *The Ashanti and the Gonja at War,* Accra.

Braimah, J. A. and Goody, J. R. (1967) *Salaga: The Struggle for Power,* London.

Brásio, A. (1952–6) *Monumenta Missionária Africana: Africa Ocidental,* 7 vols., Lisbon.

Bravmann, R. A. (1972) 'The Diffusion of Ashanti Political Art', *African Art and Leadership,* eds. D. Fraser and H. M. Cole, Madison, 153–71.

Brétignère, M. A. (1931) *Aux Temps Héroiques de la Côte d'Ivoire,* Paris.

Bretton, H. L. (1973) *Power and Politics in Africa,* Chicago.

Burleigh, B. (1896) *Two Campaigns: Madagascar and Ashantee,* London.

Burton, R. F. (1864) *A Mission to Gelele King of Dahome,* 2nd ed., 2 vols., London.

Burton, R. F. and Cameron, V. L. (1883) *To the Gold Coast for Gold,* 2 vols., London.

Busia, K. A. (1951) *The Position of the Chief in the Modern Political System of Ashanti,* London.

Cardinall, A. W. (1920) *The Natives of the Northern Territories of the Gold Coast,* London.

Carson, P. (1962) *Materials for West African History in the archives of Belgium and Holland*, London.

(1968) *Materials for West African History in French archives*, London.

Casely Hayford, J. E. (1903) *Gold Coast Native Institutions*, London.

Christaller, J. G. (1875) *A Grammar of the Asante and Fante Language*, Basel.

(1879) *A Collection of three thousand and six hundred Tshi Proverbs*, Basel.

(1881) *A Dictionary of the Asante and Fante Language Called Tschi*, Basel.

(1886) 'Eine Reise nach Salaga und Obooso', *Geographische Gesellschaft zu Jena*, IV, 15 40.

Clapperton, H. (1829) *Journal of a Second Expedition into the Interior of Africa*, London.

Claridge, W. W. (1915) *A History of the Gold Coast and Ashanti*, 2 vols., London.

Cofie, J. (1963) ' "The Desert of Gofan". Was It Ever Densely Inhabited?', *Ghana Notes and Queries*, 5, 10–14.

Collins, E. (1962) 'The Panic Element in Nineteenth-Century British Relations with Ashanti', *Transactions of the Historical Society of Ghana*, v, 2, 79 144.

Coombs, D. (1963) *The Gold Coast, Britain and the Netherlands 1850–1874*, London.

Cornevin, R. (1952) 'Le Canton de l'Akébou', *Études Dahoméens*, VII, 81–132.

Crooks, J. J. (1923) *Records Relating to the Gold Coast Settlements from 1750–1874*, Dublin.

Crowther, S. A. and Taylor, J. C. (1859) *The Gospel on the Banks of the Niger, Journals of the Niger Expeditions of 1857 and Missionary Notices*, London.

Cruickshank, B. (1853) *Eighteen Years on the Gold Coast of Africa*, 2 vols., London.

Curtin, P. D. (1969) *The Atlantic Slave Trade, A Census*, Madison.

Daaku, K. Y. (1966) 'Pre-Ashanti States', *Ghana Notes and Queries*, 9, 10–13.

(1968) 'A Note on the Fall of Ahwene Koko and Its Significance in Asante History', *Ghana Notes and Queries*, 10, 40–4.

(1970) *Trade and Politics on the Gold Coast 1600–1720*, London.

Daendels, H W (1964) *Journal and Correspondence of H W Daendels, Pt 1*, November 1815 to January 1817, translations edited by E. Collins, Institute of African Studies, Legon.

Dahse, P. (1882) 'Die Goldküste', *Deutsche Geographische Blatter*, 2, 81–111.

Debrunner, H. W. (1965) *A Church between Colonial Powers*, London.

(1967) *A History of Christianity in Ghana*, Accra.

De Graft-Johnson, J. C. (1969) 'The Population of Ghana 1846–1967', *Transactions of the Historical Society of Ghana*, x, 1–12.

Delafosse, M. (1908) *Les Frontières de la Côte d'Ivoire, de la Côte d'Or, et du Sudan*, Paris.

De Lolme, J. L. (1822) *The Constitution of England*, London.

Denteh, A. C. (1967) 'Ntorɔ and Ntɔn', *University of Ghana Institute of African Studies Research Review*, III, 3, 91–6.

Dickson, K. B. (1961) 'The Development of Road Transport in Southern Ghana and Ashanti since about 1850', *Transactions of the Historical Society of Ghana*, v, 1, 33–42.

(1969) *A Historical Geography of Ghana*, Cambridge.

Djang, S. S. (1925) 'Okomfo Anotchi', *The Sunlight Magazine*, II (March and June Quarters), Aburi, 23–5.

(1926a) 'Discussing the Akantamosu Problem,' *The Sunlight Magazine of History and Progress*, II, 2, Aburi, 58–60.

(1926b) 'Full Description on Akantamansu Battle', *The Sunlight Magazine of History and Progress*, III, 1, Aburi, 65–80.

(1936) *The 'Sunlight' Reference Almanac*, Aburi.

Dooner, W. T. (1874) *Jottings en route to Coomassie*, London (published anonymously).

Dougah, J. C. (1966) *Wa and Its People*, Institute of African Studies, Local Studies Series No. 1, Legon.

Guide to sources consulted

Dumett, R. (1971) 'The Rubber Trade of the Gold Coast and Asante in the Nineteenth Century: African Innovation and Market Responsiveness', *The Journal of African History*, XII, 1, 79–101.

Duncan, J. (1847) *Travels in Western Africa in 1845 and 1846*, 2 vols., London.

Dupuis, J. (1824) *Journal of a Residence in Ashantee*, London.

Dyer, H. McN. (1876) *The West Coast of Africa as Seen from a Man o'War*, London.

Eekhof, A. (1916) 'De Neger Predikant Jacobus Eliza Joannes Capitein, 1717–1747', *Nederlandsch Archief voor Kerkgeschiedenis*, The Hague, 138–74 and 200–76.

Ellis, A. B. (1881) *West African Sketches*, London.

(1883) *The Land of Fetish*, London.

(1887) *The Tshi-speaking Peoples of the Gold Coast of West Africa*, London.

(1893) *A History of the Gold Coast of West Africa*, London.

Ermann, L. W. (1876) 'Der Volta-Fluss nach M. J. Bonnat's Forschungen und nach älteren Berichten', *Globus*, XXX, 23, 359–62, and 24, 375–8.

Fage, J. D. (1969) 'Slavery and the Slave Trade in the Context of West African History', *The Journal of African History*, X, 3, 393–404.

Ferguson, P. (1973) 'Islamization in Dagbon: a Study of the Alfanema of Yendi', Ph.D. dissertation, Cambridge.

Ferguson, P. and Wilks, I. (1970) 'Chiefs, Constitutions and the British in Northern Ghana', *West African Chiefs*, eds. M. Crowder and O. Ikime, Ife, 326–69.

Fisch, R. (1913) *Dagbane-Sprachproben*, Hamburg.

Flight, C. (1970) 'The Chronology of the Kings and Queenmothers of Bono-Manso: a Revaluation of the Evidence', *The Journal of African History*, XI, 2, 259–68.

Forlacroix, C. (1969) 'La Pénétration Française dans l'Indénié (1887–1901)', *Annales de l'Université d'Abidjan*, F, I, 1, 91–136.

Fortes, M. (1947) 'Ashanti Survey, 1945–46: An Experiment in Social Research', *Geographical Journal*, CX, 4/6, 149–79.

(1969) *Kinship and the Social Order*, Chicago.

Fox, W. (1851) *A Brief History of the Wesleyan Missions on the Western Coast of Africa*, London.

Freeman, R. A. (1892) 'A Journey to Bontuku in the Interior of West Africa', *Royal Geographical Society*, Supplementary Papers, III, 2, 119–46.

(1898) *Travels and Life in Ashanti and Jaman*, London.

Freeman, T. B. (1843) *Journal of Two Visits to the Kingdom of Ashanti*, London.

Fulbert-Dumonteil (1887) *Les Achantis de l'Afrique Equatoriale*, Paris.

Fuller, F. C. (1921) *A Vanished Dynasty: Ashanti*, London.

Fynn, J. K. (1965) 'The Reign and Times of Kusi Obodum, 1750–64', *Transactions of the Historical Society of Ghana*, VIII, 24–32.

(1966) 'The Rise of Ashanti', *Ghana Notes and Queries*, 9, 24–30.

(1971) *Asante and Its Neighbours 1700–1807*, London.

Gerth, H. H. and Mills, C. W. (1948) *From Max Weber: Essays in Sociology*, London.

Gillespie, W. H. (1955) *The Gold Coast Police 1844–1938*, Accra.

Glover, J. (1874) 'Notes on the Country between the Volta and the Niger', *Proceedings of the Royal Geographical Society*, 286–301.

Goody, J. (1964) 'The Mande and the Akan Hinterland', *The Historian in Tropical Africa*, eds. J. Vansina, R. Mauny and L. V. Thomas, London, 190–218.

(1965) 'Introduction to Ashanti and the North-west', *University of Ghana Institute of African Studies Research Review*, Supplement: *Ashanti and the North-west*, 1, 1–110.

(1966) 'Salaga in 1892', *University of Ghana Institute of African Studies Research Review*, II, 3, 41–53.

Gould, P. R. (1960) *The Development of the Transportation Pattern in Ghana*, Evanston.

Grant, J. (n.d.) *British Battles on Land and Sea*, 3 vols., London.

Greenhalgh, T. (1856) *Kennee-Voo or, The Sacking of Allaroonah*, London.

Gros, J. (1884) *Voyages, Aventures et Captivité de J. Bonnat Chez les Achantis*, Paris.

(n.d.) *Nos Explorateurs en Afrique*, Paris.

Hagan, G. P. (1968) 'The Golden Stool and the Oaths to the King of Ashanti', *University of Ghana Institute of African Studies Research Review*, IV, 3, 1–33.

(1971) 'Ashanti Bureaucracy: A Study of the Growth of Centralized Administration in Ashanti from the Time of Osei Tutu to the Time of Osei Tutu Kwamina Esibe Bonsu', *Transactions of the Historical Society of Ghana*, XII, 43–62.

Haggett, P. and Chorley, R. J. (1969) *Network Analysis in Geography*, London.

Hall, W. M. (1939) *The Great Drama of Kumasi*, London.

Hamilton, R. (1968) *The English Involvement in Ashanti around 1900*, Field Notes: Kumasi Project, 1, Institute of African Studies, Legon, and Program of African Studies, Northwestern University.

Haydon, A. P. (1970) 'The Good Public Servant of the State – Sir Matthew Nathan as Governor of the Gold Coast 1900–1904', *Transactions of the Historical Society of Ghana*, XI, 105–21.

Henty, G. A. (n.d.) *By Sheer Pluck: A Tale of the Ashanti War*, London.

(1874) *The March to Coomassie*, London.

Herskovits, M. J. (1938) *Dahomey: an Ancient West African Kingdom*, 2 vols., Evanston (reprinted 1967).

Hertz, C. (1885) *Sur les Côtes de Guinée*, Paris.

Hilton, T. E. (1960) *Ghana Population Atlas*, Achimota.

Hippisley, J. (1764) Essays: 1 'Populousness of Africa'; II 'Trade at the Forts on the Gold Coast'; III 'Necessity of Erecting a Fort at Cape Appolonia', London.

Hodgson, Lady (1901) *The Siege of Kumassi*, London.

Holden, J. J. (1965) 'The Zabarima Conquest of North-west Ghana', Pt 1, *Transactions of the Historical Society of Ghana*, VIII, 60–86.

Hollingsworth, T. H. (1969) *Historical Demography*, Ithaca.

Holman, J. (1840) *Travels in Madeira, Sierra Leone, Teneriffe, St. Jago, Cape Coast, Fernando Po, Princes Island, etc., etc.*, 2nd ed., London.

Horton, J. A. B. (1868) *West African Countries and Peoples*, London.

(1870) *Letters on the Political Condition of the Gold Coast*, London.

Huppenbauer, D. (1914) *Von Kyebi nach Kumase. Eine Reise ins Hinterland der Goldküste*, Basel.

Hutton, W. (1821) *A Voyage to Africa*, London.

Huydecoper, W. (1816–17) *Huydecoper's Diary, Journey from Elmina to Kumasi 28th April 1816 – 18th May 1817*, translated by G. Irwin, 1962, Legon. (Original journal in General State Archives, The Hague, KvG 349.)

Ikoku, S. G. (1971) *Le Ghana de Nkrumah: Autopsie de la Ire République (1957–1966)*, Paris.

Isert, P. E. (1788) *Reise nach Guinea und den Caribäischen Inseln in Columbien in Briefen an seine Freunde beschrieben*, Copenhagen.

(1793) *Voyages en Guinée et dans les Îles Caraïbes en Amérique*, Paris.

Jackson, J. G. (1820) *An Account of Timbuctoo and Housa, Territories in the Interior of Africa, by El Hage Abd Salam Shabeeny*, London.

Johnson, M. (1965) 'Ashanti East of the Volta', *Transactions of the Historical Society of Ghana*, VIII, 33–59.

(1966a) *Salaga Papers*, 2 vols., Institute of African Studies, Legon.

(1966b) 'The Wider Background of the Salaga Civil War', *University of Ghana Institute of African Studies Research Review*, II, 2, 31–9.

(1968) 'M. Bonnat on the Volta', *Ghana Notes and Queries*, 10, 4–17.

(1970a) 'The Cowrie Currencies of West Africa', *The Journal of African History*, XI, 1, 17–49.

(1970b) 'The Cowrie Currencies of West Africa', Pt II, *The Journal of African History*, XI, 3, 331–53.

(1971) 'Ashanti, Juaben and M. Bonnat', *Transactions of the Historical Society of Ghana*, XII, 17–41.

735

Junner, N. R. (1935) *Gold in the Gold Coast,* Gold Coast Geological Survey Memoir No. 4, Colchester.

Kea, R. A. (1969) 'Akwamu-Anlo Relations, c. 1750–1813', *Transactions of the Historical Society of Ghana,* x, 29–63.

(1970a) 'Four Asante Officials in the South-east Gold Coast (1808)', *Ghana Notes and Queries,* 11, 42–7.

(1970b) 'Osei Kwame's Interdiction on Danish Trade 1788–89', *Ghana Notes and Queries,* 11, 36–41.

Kimble, D. (1963) *A Political History of Ghana: The Rise of Gold Coast Nationalism, 1850–1928,* Oxford.

Klein, A. N. (1969) 'West African Unfree Labour before and after the Rise of the Atlantic Slave Trade', *Slavery in the New World,* eds. L. Foner and E. D. Genovese, Englewood-Cliffs, 87–95.

Kling, E. (1893) 'Auszug aus den Tagebuchern des Hauptmanns Kling 1891 bis 1892', *Mittheilungen von Forschungsreisenden und Gelehrten aus den Deutschen Schutzgebieten,* VI, 105–254.

Klose, H. (1899) *Togo unter Deutscher Flagge: Reisebilder und Betrachtungen,* Berlin.

Koelle, S. W. (1854) *Polyglotta Africana,* London.

Kwamena-Poh, M. A. (1973) *Government and Politics in the Akuapem State 1730–1850,* London.

Kyerematen, A. A. Y. (1964) *Panoply of Ghana,* London.

(1966) 'Ashanti Royal Regalia: Their History and Functions', D.Phil. dissertation, Oxford.

(1969) 'The Royal Stools of Ashanti', *Africa,* XXXIX, 1, 1–10.

(n.d.) *Kingship and Ceremony in Ashanti,* University of Science and Technology, Kumasi.

Lander, R. and Lander, J. (1832) *Journal of an Expedition to Explore the Course and Termination of the Niger,* 2 vols., London.

Lee, Mrs R. (1835) *Stories of Strange Lands, and Fragments from the Notes of a Traveller,* London.

Levtzion, N. (1965) 'Early Nineteenth Century Arabic Manuscripts from Kumase', *Transactions of the Historical Society of Ghana,* VIII, 99–119.

Lewin, T. (1968) *The English Involvement in Ashanti around 1900,* Field Notes: Kumasi Project, 2, Institute of African Studies, Legon, and Program of African Studies, Northwestern University.

(1974) 'The Structure of Political Conflict in Asante, 1875–1900', Ph. D. dissertation, Northwestern University, Evanston.

Lijphart, A. (1968) *The Politics of Accommodation: Pluralism and Democracy in the Netherlands,* Berkeley.

Lowell, A. L. (1896) *Governments and Parties in Continental Europe,* 2 vols., London.

McCaskie, T. C. (1972) 'Innovational Eclecticism: the Asante Empire and Europe in the Nineteenth Century', *Comparative Studies in Society and History,* XIV, 1, 30–45.

(1974) 'The Paramountcy of the Asantehene Kwaku Dua 1834–1867: A Study in Asante Political Culture', Ph. D. dissertation, Cambridge.

Matson, J. N. (1951) *A Digest of the Minutes of the Ashanti Confederacy Council, 1935–49, and a Revised Edition of Warrington's Notes on Ashanti Custom,* Prepared for the Use of District Commissioners, Cape Coast.

Maurice, J. F. (1874) *The Ashantee War,* London (published anonymously).

Maxwell, W. (1896) 'The Results of the Ashanti Expedition, 1895–96', *The Journal of the Manchester Geographical Society,* XII, 1–3, 37–54.

Meredith, H. (1812) *An Account of the Gold Coast of Africa: with a Brief History of the African Company,* London.

Metcalfe, G. E. (1962) *Maclean of the Gold Coast,* London.

(1964) *Great Britain and Ghana: Documents of Ghana History 1807–1957,* Legon.

Meyerowitz, E. L. R. (1951) *The Sacred State of the Akan,* London.

(1952) *Akan Traditions of Origin,* London.

Miles, J. (n.d.) 'Ashanti Military Organization and Techniques: The War of 1873–4', Long Essay Requirement, M.A., SOAS, London.

M'Leod, J. (1820) *A Voyage to Africa, with Some Account of Manners and Customs of the Dahomian People,* London.

Moister, W. (1875) *Henry Wharton, the Story of His Life and Missionary Labours,* London.

Musgrave, G. C. (1896) *To Kumassi with Scott,* London.

Native Reports in Tshi (1913), Akropong. (The first edition of this work was published as *Papers in Tshi* in the 1860s, and was based upon original reports by D. Asante, P. Keteku, I. Ado *et al.* in the Basel Mission Archives.)

Nkrumah, K. (1964) *Consciencism,* London.

(1970a) *Africa Must Unite,* New York.

(1970b) *Class Struggle in Africa,* New York.

Nørregård, G. (1966) *Danish Settlements in West Africa 1658–1850,* translated by S. Mammen, Boston.

Norris, A. W. (1928) 'Three Tours on the West Coast of Africa (1901 to 1906)', *The Gold Coast Review,* IV, 1, 124–53 and 2, 204–31.

Northcott, H. P. (1899) *Report on the Northern Territories of the Gold Coast,* London.

Ocran, A. K. (1968) *A Myth Is Broken: An Account of the Ghana Coup d'État of 24 February 1966,* Accra.

Opoku, T. (1885) 'Eines Neger-Pastors Predigtreise durch die Länder am Volta-strom', *Evangelisches Missions-Magazin,* XXIX, 257–72; 305–26; 353–64.

Ozanne, P. (1966) 'Ahwene Koko: Seventeenth-Century Wenchi', *Ghana Notes and Queries,* 8, 18.

Pel, H. S. (n.d.) *Aanteekeningen gehouden op Eene Reis van St. Geo. Delmina naar Coomassie, Hoofdstaad van het Aschantijnsche Rijk, en gedurende Een Kort Verblijf Aldaar,* Leiden.

Perregaux, E. (1903) 'A Few Notes on Kwahu', *Journal of the African Society,* II, 8, 444–50.

(1906) 'Chez les Achanti', *Bulletin de la société neuchâteloise de Géographie,* XVII, 7–312.

Perrot, C.-H. (1970) 'L'Histoire dans les Royaumes Agni de l'Est de la Côte d'Ivoire', *Annales: Économies, Sociétés, Civilisations,* 6, 1672–3.

Pitt, W. J. (1926) 'The Mfantra', *The Gold Coast Review,* II, 1, 71–7.

Poku, K. (1969) 'Traditional Roles and People of Slave Origin in Modern Ashanti – a Few Impressions', *Ghana Journal of Sociology,* V, 1, 34–8.

Powell, E. A. (1912) *The Last Frontier,* New York.

Priestley, M. (1961) 'The Ashanti Question and the British: Eighteenth-Century Origins', *The Journal of African History,* II, 1, 35–59.

(1969) *West African Trade and Coast Society: A Family Study,* London.

Priestley, M. and Wilks, I. (1960) 'The Ashanti Kings in the Eighteenth Century: A Revised Chronology', *The Journal of African History,* I, 1, 83–96.

Proceedings of the Association for Promoting the Discovery of the Interior Parts of Africa (1791), London.

Ramseyer, F. A. and Kühne, J. (1875) *Four Years in Ashantee,* New York.

Rattray, R. S. (1916) *Ashanti Proverbs,* Oxford.

(1923) *Ashanti,* Oxford.

(1927) *Religion and Art in Ashanti,* Oxford.

(1929) *Ashanti Law and Constitution,* Oxford.

Reade, W. (1873) *The African Sketch-Book,* 2 vols., London.

(1874) *The Story of the Ashantee Campaign,* London.

Reindorf, C. C. (1895) *History of the Gold Coast,* Basel.

(n.d.) *The History of the Gold Coast and Asante,* 2nd ed., Basel.

Renouard, G. C. (1836) 'Routes in North Africa, by Abú Bekr eṣ ṣiddík', *Journal of the Royal Geographical Society,* VI, 100–13.

737

Ricketts, H. J. (1831) *Narrative of the Ashantee War*, London.

Riis, A. (1840) 'The Journey of Riis to Kumasi 1839–40', *Magazin für die Neueste Geschichte der Evangelischen Missions- und Bibel-Gesellschaften*, Pt III, 92ff. and 216–35.

Riis, H. N. (1854) *Grammatical Outline and Vocabulary of the Oji-Language*, Basel.

Robertson, A. F. (1973) 'Histories and Political Opposition in Ahafo, Ghana', *Africa*, XLIII, 1, 41–58.

Robertson, G. A. (1819) *Notes on Africa*, London.

Rømer, L. F. (1760) *Tilforladelig Efterretning om Kysten Guinea*, Copenhagen.

Salmon, C. S. (1882) 'British Policy in West Africa', *The Contemporary Review*, XLII, 878–93.

Samson, E. (1908) *A Short History of Akuapem and Akropong*, Accra. (Work based upon *Akuapem Amansεm*, MS in the Basel Mission Archives, dd. 1880.)

Sarbah, J. Mensah (1906) *Fanti National Constitution*, London.

Skinner, E. P. (1964) *The Mossi of the Upper Volta*, Stanford.

Smith, H. F. C. (1961) 'The Islamic Revolutions of the 19th Century', *Journal of the Historical Society of Nigeria*, II, 1, 169–85.

Stanley, H. M. (1874) *Coomassie and Magdala: The Story of Two British Campaigns in Africa*, New York.

Steiner, P. (1896) *Four Years Captivity in Ashanti*, London.

(1900) *Schreckenstage in Kumase*, Basel.

(1901) *Dark and Stormy Days at Kumassi, 1900; or, Missionary Experience in Ashanti According to the Diary of Rev. Fritz Ramseyer*, London.

(1913) *An der Grenze von Asante*, Basel.

(1919) *Ein Kampf um Asante*, Basel.

Strömberg, C. (1890) *Minnen och Bilder från Guldkusten*, Lund.

Struck, B. (1923) 'Geschichtliches über die Östlichen Tschi-Länder (Goldküste)', *Anthropos*, XVIII, 465–83.

Swithenbank, M. (1969) *Ashanti Fetish Houses*, Accra.

Szereszewski, R. (1965) *Structural Changes in the Economy of Ghana 1891–1911*, London.

Tadhkira li 'l-Muta'akhirīn (text, translation and notes on a mid-eighteenth century Gonja chronicle, in course of preparation by I. Wilks and N. Levtzion).

Tait, D. (1955) 'History and Social Organisation', *Transactions of the Gold Coast and Togoland Historical Society*, I, 5, 193–210.

Tamakloe, E. F. (1931) *A Brief History of the Dagbamba People*, Accra.

Tauxier, L. (1921) *Le Noir de Bondoukou*, Paris.

Tenkorang, S. (1968) 'The Importance of Firearms in the Struggle between Ashanti and the Coastal States, 1708–1807', *Transactions of the Historical Society of Ghana*, IX, 1–16.

Thomas, R. G. (1973) 'Forced Labour in British West Africa: The Case of the Northern Territories of the Gold Coast 1906–1927', in *Journal of African History*, XIV, 1, 79–103.

Tordoff, W. (1959) 'The Brong-Ahafo Region', *The Economic Bulletin of Ghana*, III, 5, 2–18.

(1960) 'The Exile and Repatriation of Nana Prempeh I of Ashanti (1896–1924)', *Transactions of the Historical Society of Ghana*, IV, 2, 33–58.

(1962) 'Brandford Griffith's Offer of British Protection to Ashanti (1891)', *Transactions of the Historical Society of Ghana*, VI, 31–49.

(1965) *Ashanti under the Prempehs 1888–1935*, London.

Triulzi, A. (1969) 'The Ashanti Confederacy (Asanteman) Council, 1935–1957', Field Notes: Adansi-Kumasi Project, Institute of African Studies, Legon, and Program of African Studies, Northwestern University.

(1972) 'The Asantehene-in-Council: Ashanti Politics under Colonial Rule, 1935–50', *Africa*, XLII, 2, 98–111.

Trotter, H. D. and Allen, W. (1848) *A Narrative of the Expedition to the River Niger in 1841*, 2 vols., London.

Turner, G. W. E. (n.d.) *A Short History: Ashanti Goldfields Corporation Ltd., 1897–1947.*

Van Dantzig, A. (1966) 'The Dutch Military Recruitment Agency in Kumasi', *Ghana Notes and Queries*, 8, 21–4.

Von Zech, G. (1898) 'Vermischte Notizen über Togo und das Togo Hinterland', *Mittheilungen von Forschungsreisenden und Gelehrten aus den Deutschen Schutzgebieten*, XI, 89–147.

Wakkad, M. El- (1961) 'Qissatu Salga Tarīkhu Gonja: The Story of Salaga and the History of Gonja', *Ghana Notes and Queries*, 3, 8–31.

  (1962) 'Qissatu Salga Tarīkhu Gonja: The Story of Salaga and the History of Gonja', *Ghana Notes and Queries*, 4, 6–25.

Walckenaer, C. A. (1821) *Recherches Géographiques sur l'Intérieur de l'Afrique Septentrionale*, Paris.

Wallace-Johnson, I. T. A. (1935) *Restoration of the Ashanti Confederacy*, Accra.

Wallis, J. R. (1953) 'The Kwahus – Their Connection with the Afram Plain', *Transactions of the Gold Coast and Togoland Historical Society*, 1, 3, 10–26.

Ward, W. E. F. (1958) *A History of Ghana* (revised second edition), London.

Wartemberg, J. S. (1951) *Sao Jorge d'El Mina, Premier West African Settlement: Its Traditions and Customs*, Ilfracombe.

Watherston, A. E. C. (1908) 'The Northern Territories of the Gold Coast', *Journal of the African Society*, VII, 28, 344–73.

Welch, C. E. and Taintor, M. B., eds. (1972) *Revolution and Political Change*, Massachusetts and California.

Welman, C. W. (1969) *The Native States of the Gold Coast, History and Constitution*, Pt I, *Peki*, London (first ed. London, 1925).

West, T. (1857) *The Life and Journals of the Rev. Daniel West, Wesleyan Minister, and Deputation to the Wesleyan Mission Stations on the Gold Coast, Western Africa*, London.

West-African Sketches (1824), compiled from the Reports of Sir G. R. Collier, Sir Charles MacCarthy and Other Official Sources (mimeographed ed., 1963, Institute of African Studies, Legon.)

Wilks, I. (1957) 'The Rise of the Akwamu Empire, 1650–1710', *Transactions of the Historical Society of Ghana*, III, 2, 99–136.

  (1958a) 'Akwamu 1650–1750: A Study of the Rise and Fall of a West African Empire', M.A. thesis, University of Wales.

  (1958b) 'A Note on Twifo and Akwamu', *Transactions of the Historical Society of Ghana*, III, 3, 215–17.

  (1959) 'Akwamu and Otublohum: an Eighteenth-Century Akan Marriage Arrangement', *Africa*, XXIX, 4, 391–404.

  (1960) 'A Note on the Traditional History of Mampong', *Transactions of the Historical Society of Ghana*, IV, 2, 26–9.

  (1961) *The Northern Factor in Ashanti History*, University College of Ghana.

  (1962) 'A Medieval Trade-route from the Niger to the Gulf of Guinea', *The Journal of African History*, III, 2, 337–41.

  (1966a) 'The Position of Muslims in Metropolitan Ashanti in the Early Nineteenth Century', *Islam in Tropical Africa*, ed. I. Lewis, London, 318–41.

  (1966b) 'Aspects of Bureaucratization in Ashanti in the Nineteenth Century', *The Journal of African History*, VII, 2, 215–32.

  (1966c) 'A Note on the Chronology, and Origins, of the Gonja Kings', *Ghana Notes and Queries*, 8, 26–8.

  (1967a) 'Ashanti Government', *West African Kingdoms in the Nineteenth Century*, eds. D. Forde and P. Kaberry, London, 206–38.

  (1967b) 'Ṣāliḥ Bilāli of Massina, Abū Bakr al-Ṣiddīq of Timbuktu, Wargee of Astrakhan', *Africa Remembered*, ed. P. Curtin, Madison, 143–89.

  (1968) 'The Transmission of Islamic Learning in the Western Sudan', *Literacy in Traditional Societies*, ed. J. Goody, Cambridge, 161–97.

  (1970) *Political Bi-Polarity in Nineteenth Century Asante*, Ninth Melville J. Herskovits Memorial Lecture, Edinburgh University, Edinburgh.

(1971a) 'Asante Policy towards the Hausa Trade in the 19th Century', *The Development of Indigenous Trade and Markets in West Africa,* ed. C. Meillassoux, London, 124–41.

(1971b) 'The Mossi and Akan States, 1500–1800', *History of West Africa,* eds. M. Crowder and J. Ajayi, London, I, 344–86.

(1974) 'Dissidence in Asante Politics: Two Tracts from the Late Nineteenth Century', *African Themes: Northwestern University Studies In Honor of Gwendolen M. Carter,* Evanston (in press).

'The Golden Stool and the Elephant's Tail: the Rise of the Asante Middle Class' (forthcoming).

Williams, G. (1897) *History of the Liverpool Privateers and Letters of Marque with an Account of the Liverpool Slave-Trade,* London.

Wilson, J. L. (1856) *Western Africa. Its History, Condition, and Prospects,* New York.

Withers Gill, J. (n.d.) *A Short History of the Dagomba Tribe,* Accra.

(1924) *A Short History of Salaga,* Accra.

Wolseley, G. (1903) *The Story of a Soldier's Life,* 2 vols., London.

Wolteringen, J. (n.d.) *Bescheiden betreffende de Buitenlandse Politiek Van Nederland,* 2nd period, vol. I, The Hague.

Wood, E. (1874) *The Ashanti Expedition of 1873–4,* Royal United Service Institution Lecture, London.

BRITISH PARLIAMENTARY PAPERS

1842: C. 551-II *Report from the Select Committee on the West Coast of Africa,* Part II, Appendix and Index (Accounts and Papers, XII).

1853: C. 703 *Despatches from Major Hill, the Governor of the Gold Coast, relating to the warfare between the Fantis and the Ashantis* (Accounts and Papers, LXV).

1855: C. 456 *Further Papers relating to the warfare between the Fantis and the Ashantis* (Accounts and Papers, XXXVI).

1864: C. 385 *Despatches from the Governor of the Gold Coast, explaining the cause of war with the King of Ashanti* (Accounts and Papers, XLI).

1865: C. 170 *Report of Colonel Ord, appointed to enquire into the condition of the British Settlements on the Western Coast of Africa* (Accounts and Papers, XXXVII).

1872: C. 670 *Correspondence relative to the Cession by the Netherlands Government to the British Government of the Dutch Settlements on the West Coast of Africa* (Accounts and Papers, LXX).

1873: C. 266-I *Gold Coast: Part II Despatches from Mr. Pope Hennessy respecting the Transfer of the Dutch Possessions on the Gold Coast, etc.* (Accounts and Papers, XLIX).

1873: C. 819 *Further Correspondence respecting the Ashanti Invasion* (Accounts and Papers, XLIX).

1874: C. 890 Part I: *Further papers relating to the Ashantee Invasion.*
  C. 891 Part II: *Further Correspondence respecting the Ashantee Invasion.*
  C. 892 Part III: *Further Correspondence Respecting the Ashantee Invasion.*
  C. 893 Part IV: *Further Correspondence Respecting the Ashantee Invasion.*
  C. 1006 Part IX: *Further Correspondence respecting the Ashantee Invasion* (Accounts and Papers XLVI).

1875: C. 1139 *Correspondence relating to the Queen's Jurisdiction on the Gold Coast, and the Abolition of Slavery within the Protectorate* (Accounts and Papers, LII).

1875: C. 1140 *Correspondence relating to the Affairs of the Gold Coast* (Accounts and Papers, LII).

1876: C. 1343 *Papers relating to Her Majesty's Possessions in West Africa* (Accounts and Papers, LII).

1876: C. 1402 *Papers relating to Her Majesty's Possessions in West Africa* (Accounts and Papers, LII).

1876: C. 1409 *Correspondence Respecting the Affairs of the Gambia and the Proposed Exchange with France of Possessions on the West Coast of Africa* (Accounts and Papers, LII).

1881: C. 3064 *Affairs of the Gold Coast and threatened Ashanti Invasion* (Accounts and Papers, LXV).

1882: C. 3386 *Further Correspondence regarding Affairs of the Gold Coast* (Accounts and Papers, XLVI).

1883: C. 3687 *Further Correspondence regarding the Affairs of the Gold Coast* (Accounts and Papers, XLVIII).

1884: C. 4052 *Further Correspondence regarding the Affairs of the Gold Coast* (Accounts and Papers, LVI).

1885: C. 4477 *Further Correspondence respecting the Affairs of the Gold Coast* (Accounts and Papers, LV).

1886: C. 4906 *Further Correspondence respecting the Affairs of the Gold Coast* (Accounts and Papers, XLVII).

1888: C. 5357 *Further Correspondence respecting the Affairs of the Gold Coast* (Accounts and Papers, LXXV).

1888: C. 5615 *Further Correspondence respecting the Affairs of the Gold Coast* (Accounts and Papers, LXXV).

1896: C. 7917 *Further Correspondence relating to Affairs in Ashanti* (Accounts and Papers, LVIII).

1896: C. 7918 *Further Correspondence relative to Affairs in Ashanti* (Accounts and Papers, LVIII).

1901: C. 501 *Correspondence relating to the Ashanti War 1900* (Accounts and Papers, XLVIII).

1902: C. 933 *Further Correspondence relating to Ashanti.*

ARCHIVES, FIELD MATERIALS, NEWSPAPERS ETC.

All sources under this rubric have been fully identified in the footnotes. However, a number of abbreviations have been used. The major classes of materials are recapitulated below, and abbreviations listed.

United Kingdom

PRO: Public Record Office, London.
   T.70 – Treasury Papers.
   CO – Colonial Office Papers.
   FO – Foreign Office Papers.
   All citations are otherwise given in full in the footnotes.
   (For material from the CO. 879 series see further, *List of Colonial Office Confidential Print to 1916*, HMSO, 1965.)
Methodist Mission Archives, London.
   Correspondence: West Africa.
   T. B. Freeman: Journals and Correspondence.

Holland

General State Archives, The Hague.
   WIC – Archives of the Second West India Company.
   KvG – Archives of the Dutch Settlements on the Coast of Guinea.
   MvK – Archives of the Ministry of Colonies.
   Archives of the Dutch Consulate at Elmina, 1872 – 80.
   All citations are otherwise given in full in the footnotes.
   (For material from the Archives of the Dutch Settlements on the Coast of Guinea

see, 'Het Archief van de Nederlandsche Bezittingen ter Kuste van Guinea', in *Verslagen omtrent s'Rijks oude archieven,* volume XLIV, Part I, Supplement XI, 337–82. See also in general, P. Carson, *Materials for West African History in the archives of Belgium and Holland,* London, 1962.)
Instituut voor Taal- Land- en Volkenkunde, Leiden.
 H. 509 – Anonymous Diary, Kumase, 1866–67.

Denmark

National Archives, Copenhagen.
 All references are cited in full in the footnotes.
Royal Library, Copenhagen.
 References are to the uncatalogued collection, *Codex Arabicus CCCII,* 'Manuscripts from Guinea', three bundles.

Switzerland

Basel Mission Archives, Basel.
 All references are cited in full in the footnotes. Extensive use has been made of the abstracts of materials relating to Ghana prepared by Paul Jenkins.

Ghana

NAG: National Archives of Ghana; Kumase, Accra and Tamale. All references are cited in full in the footnotes.
IAS: Institute of African Studies, University of Ghana, Legon.
 IASAS/ – Asante Stool Histories, recorded by J. Agyeman-Duah.
 IASAR/ – Arabic Manuscript Collection, established principally by al-Ḥājj 'Uthmān b. Isḥāq Boyo and the author.
 IASAM/ – Traditions from the Afram Plains, recorded by K. Ameyaw.
 IASBA/ – Traditions from Brong-Ahafo, recorded by K. Ameyaw.
 IASKAG/ – Miscellaneous Stool Histories, recorded by K. Ameyaw.
 IASJEK/ – Traditions from Krakye, recorded by J. Kumah.
 IASEWE/ – Traditions from the Volta Basin, recorded by E. Y. Aduamah.
Balme Library, University of Ghana, Legon.
 The Furley Collection of translations, transcriptions and abstracts from Dutch and Danish Archival sources has been extensively consulted, but reference has been made to copies of the original documents in most cases.
Kumase Divisional Council Archives, Manhyia, Kumase.
 Record books of cases heard by various Kumase Tribunals and Courts, 1907 to date. All cases are cited in full.

Field materials, etc.

The field notes of the author (1956–date) will be on deposit in the Herskovits Memorial Library, Northwestern University, Evanston. The field notes of P. Ferguson (1968–date) are on deposit in the African Oral Data Archives, University of Indiana, Bloomington.
The Asante Collective Biography Project: the author, T. C. McCaskie and P. Ferguson, ongoing project, Program of African Studies, Northwestern University, Evanston.
Tait MSS A and B: Dagomba Lunse Texts, recorded by the late D. Tait, on deposit in the Institute of African Studies, Ghana.

Newspapers

The Accra Herald (Accra)
The African Times (London)
The Anglo-African (Lagos)
The Daily Graphic (Accra)
The Friend of the Africans (London)
The Gold Coast Aborigines (Cape Coast)
The Gold Coast Chronicle (Accra)
The Gold Coast Echo (Cape Coast)
The Gold Coast Independent (Accra)
The Gold Coast Methodist Times (Cape Coast)
The Gold Coast News (Cape Coast)
The Gold Coast Times (Cape Coast)
The Lagos Times and Gold Coast Colony Advertiser (Lagos)
The Liverpool Mercury (Liverpool)
The Royal Gold Coast Gazette (Cape Coast)
Royal Gazette and Sierra Leone Advertiser (Freetown)
The Standard (London)
The Times (London)
The Wesleyan-Methodist Magazine (London)

Index

The organization of this work is thematic rather than chronological or geographic. In consequence, the attempt has been made to arrange this index synthetically in such a way as to provide the reader with the maximum possible assistance in locating events and persons in time and space. A broad chronological sweep of Asante history may thus be obtained by use of the entries for individual rulers, all of whom have been arranged consecutively under the heading 'Asantehene'. Similarly, a broad overview of the geo-political system may be obtained by use of the entry 'Asante, Greater'. Otherwise, places within Ghana are identified, whenever possible, by the locality code as established in the *1960 Population Census of Ghana*, Volume I, 'The Gazetteer' (Census Office, Accra, 1962). Places lying on or near the old great-roads are also identified by reference to the route number (for which easy reference may be made to map i, page 11), and to their approximate distance from Kumase: the notation IV/109, for example, signifies a location approximately 109 miles from Kumase on Route IV. Persons are identified, whenever appropriate, by reference to the highest office attained, and key dates are supplied when known with reasonable certainty.

Index

Index

Index

Gbedemah, K. A. 413

Gbonipe (III/161), 245

Gbuipe (Gonja division and town 8000502, III/164), market of 261-2, 264, 286, 690; *see also under* Gonja, western and central

George III (of England), 680, 696

Germany 308, 648, 661

Gezo (Dahomey ruler 1818-58), 323

Ghadames (Libya), 312

Ghartey, R. J. (Ghartey IV of Winneba), 9, 526

Ghombaty (unidentified), 247

Gifford, Lord, E. F. 49-50, 240

Glele (Dahomey ruler 1858-89), 323-4, 641

Glover, Captain J. H. 281, 511-2

Gobir (Nigeria), 262n

Gold Coast

–, African Company establishments on (to 1821): jurisdiction of 192; aims of 191; mission to Kumase (1817) *see under* Bowdich; abolition of Company (1821) 169

–, establishments under Crown Rule (1821-8) 169: and *The Royal Gold Coast Gazette and Commercial Intelligencer* 169; confusion in British aims 187-8; beginnings of Protectorate (1827) 186

–, British Protected Territory of (under Committee of Merchants 1828-43): creation of Committee 188-9; aims of 191; growth of Protectorate 191, 207, and indeterminate status of 192-3; proposal for British withdrawal 188

–, British Protected Territory of (under Crown Rule 1843-74): assumption of authority from Merchants 207; status of 192-3, 207-8; area claimed (1846) 126; purchase of Danish establishments (1850) 126; Legislative Assembly of Native Chiefs of the Gold Coast 165, 208, 230; Poll Tax Ordinance (1852) 208, 217; proposal for British withdrawal (1857) 209; weakness of authority in (1857) 209, and administrative mismanagement (1868) 231; exchange of territories with Dutch (1868) 226-7; Elmina cession (1872) 13, 231-4, 317, 500-4, 601-2

–, British Crown Colony: creation of (1874) 126, 242; area of (1883) 126; state of (1883) 704-5; census of (1891) 127

–,–, unity of interests with Asante 526-7, 543; Owusu Ansa on (1880) 625-6; Salmon on (1882) 683-4; John Owusu Ansa on (1894) 637

–,–, as model for reform in Asante 514, 531, 541, 626, 628, 704-5, 709; and Asante rejection of similar constitutional status 645

–,–, use of as base, by Asante refugees 91-2, 119, 569-70, 582, 586-7, and by the *ahupoofo* 575-6, 578, 715, 717-8, 727

–, *also esp.* Chapters 4-6, 13-4

Gold Coast Armed Police Force, 618-9

gold (*sika*), as capital 178, 418, 445; Great Chest as repository 418-9, 439; disposition of nuggets 220, 420-1, 702, and minting of gold dust from 421; personal estates in, *see under* wealth; burial of 701 and n

–, trade in, *see under* trade

–, mining industry: early development of 244-5; state controls over 197, 435-6; unfree labour in 177, 308, 435-6, 675; revenues from 435-6; taxation of 529, 646; technological improvements in 436; adverse affects upon, of slave trade 679, and of mercantile system 702

–,–, European participation in, *see under* economy, infrastructural reorganization

–,–, operations at, Asakraka 634; in Denkyira, Assin, Akyem 435; in Gyaman 65; in Kumase 564, 712 and n; at Manso Nkwanta 20, 436, 529, 534; at Nsoko 435-6; at Obuase 645; in Oweri Valley 436

–,–, *also* 29, 613

Golden Elephant's Tail, *see under* wealth; Ahwerewamu stool

Golden Stool (Sika Dwa)

–, as symbol of political sovereignty 112, 271, 415, 430, 661, 671, 696; as 'black' stool of Osei Tutu and Opoku Ware 331-2; and ownership of land 109-10

–, events affecting: burial of (ca. 1798) 253n; taken to war (1824) 359, (1826) 118, 359; threats to destroy (1874) 513, (1883) 536, 551; desecration of (1921) 391

–, royal dynasty of: early links with Buna 315; creation of Asante 110; 'red' and 'black' moieties 371n; Houses of Osei Tutu and Opoku

774

Index

Index

Muslims (*continued*)
–, views on Asante government 108-9
–, enslaved Muslims, treatment as prisoners of war 254; emancipation of (1808) 254, 263, 673; recruitment into 'Hausa' regiments 618
–, doubts about loyalty of (1818) 268, (1839) 268, 488, (1879) 619, 710; and opposition to 241
–, *see also* Islam; literacy, Arabic

Nafana (of Banda), 77
Nagtglas, C. J. M. (Dutch Governor), 232-4, 601
Nakpo (Kpembewura, mid 18th c.), 21, 67
Nakpo (late 19th c.), 285, 301
Namasa (7307701, IIa/117), 5, 435
Nankanse (northern peoples), 319
Nantan (6801917, IV/16), 107
Nantwi (officer of the Gyaasewa, d. 1880), 225, 226, 236-8, 501 and n, 628 and n
Nantwi (Oyoko royal), 360 Table 14
Nanumba (capital Bimbilla 8262000), 115, 273, 307n
Nassian (I/197), 4
Native Committee of Administration (1896-1900), membership 122, 659; and planning of war (1900) 123, 660
Navrongo (northern district), 277
Nchumuru (principal town Bagyemso), *see under* Bron
Ndenye (district east of Komoé), 56
New Dwaben, 91, 515, *and see under* Dwaben
Nielson, C. (civil servant, d. 1878), 288, 290, 618, 621-2, 663
Nienseli (8103104, IV/213), 6, 55, 60
Nifahene of Kumase (Asokore–Mamponhene), 698
Nikki (Dahomey), 7, 245, 311, 312
Ningo (2064000), *see under* Adangme
Nintin (6705101, IV/27), 97, 103
Nkami (4204601), 611
Nkansa (resident commissioner), 132, 136-7
Nkansa (negotiator), 136-7
Nkansa (Adansehene), 522, 533, 567-70, 587, 646
Nkarawa stool, 136, 419n
Nkatia Ntim Abamo (Asantehemaa, early 18th c.), 328 Fig 5, 339
Nkawie (Panin 6302901, and Kuma 6361000), 497, 577
Nkenkaso (6882000, II/48), 4
nkonnwasoafo, *see under* Stool Carriers

Nkonson stool, 246, 355 Fig 11, 427, *also* 181
Nkonya, *see under* Ewe
Nkoran (Kulango), 74; *see also* Badu, Buna, Siakwa
Nkoransa (state and town 7350000, III/68), on great-road 5, 11, 14, 245, 270, 296, 302
–, provincial status 48, 50-1, 54, 69, 243, 291, or metropolitan status 47, 51, 95, 113-4; exemption from tribute 69; levy of troops from 73, 82, 243-4
–, and rebellions in northwest (ca. 1800) 254-5; service at Katamanso (1826) 73, 616; service during invasion of south (1872-3) 82, 244, and Nkoransahene Ata Fa honoured by Asantehene 77; service during campaign against Mampon (1888) 297, and Nkoransahene Kwasi Poku honoured by Asantehene 77, 296-7
–, growth of Kintampo market 286-7, 291, and *see further under* Kintampo
–, conflicting politics (late 19th c.), opposition to Mensa Bonsu (1881-2) 296; alignment with Kwaku Dua Kuma (1884) 296, and opposition to restoration of Mensa Bonsu or Kofi Kakari 557; equivocating policies towards candidature of Agyeman Prempe (1885-8) 296-7, 572, 574, 577, 583, 586; Kumase invasion of (1892-3) 298-300, 586, 638; fear of Kumase–Samorian alliance (1895) 303; rumoured Nkoransa–Samorian alliance against British (1896) 304
–, *also* 91, 254-5, 515, 540
Nkrumah, Kwame, *see* Kwame Nkrumah
nkwankwaa ('youngmen'), definition of 535, 728, and as 'middling orders' 705, petit bourgeoisie 710, 719
–, leaders of coup against Mensa Bonsu (1883) 530, 535-7, 630, 710, 711, 720; revolt of Bekwae *nkwankwaa* 533, 541; cooperation with activists from Gold Coast 534; rejection of Kofi Kakari candidacy 537; interim exercise of power (1883) 539-40, 541-3; role in confederacy movement (1886) 569; abolition of organizations of (1936) 535n
–, *also* 545, 560n
nkwansrafo, see great-roads, police for
Nkwanta (6708511, IV/39), 97, 103
Nkwantakese (6867000, II/12), 356, 550; incumbents of stool, *see* Boakye Yam, Nkwanta Owusu, Yaw Boakye

786